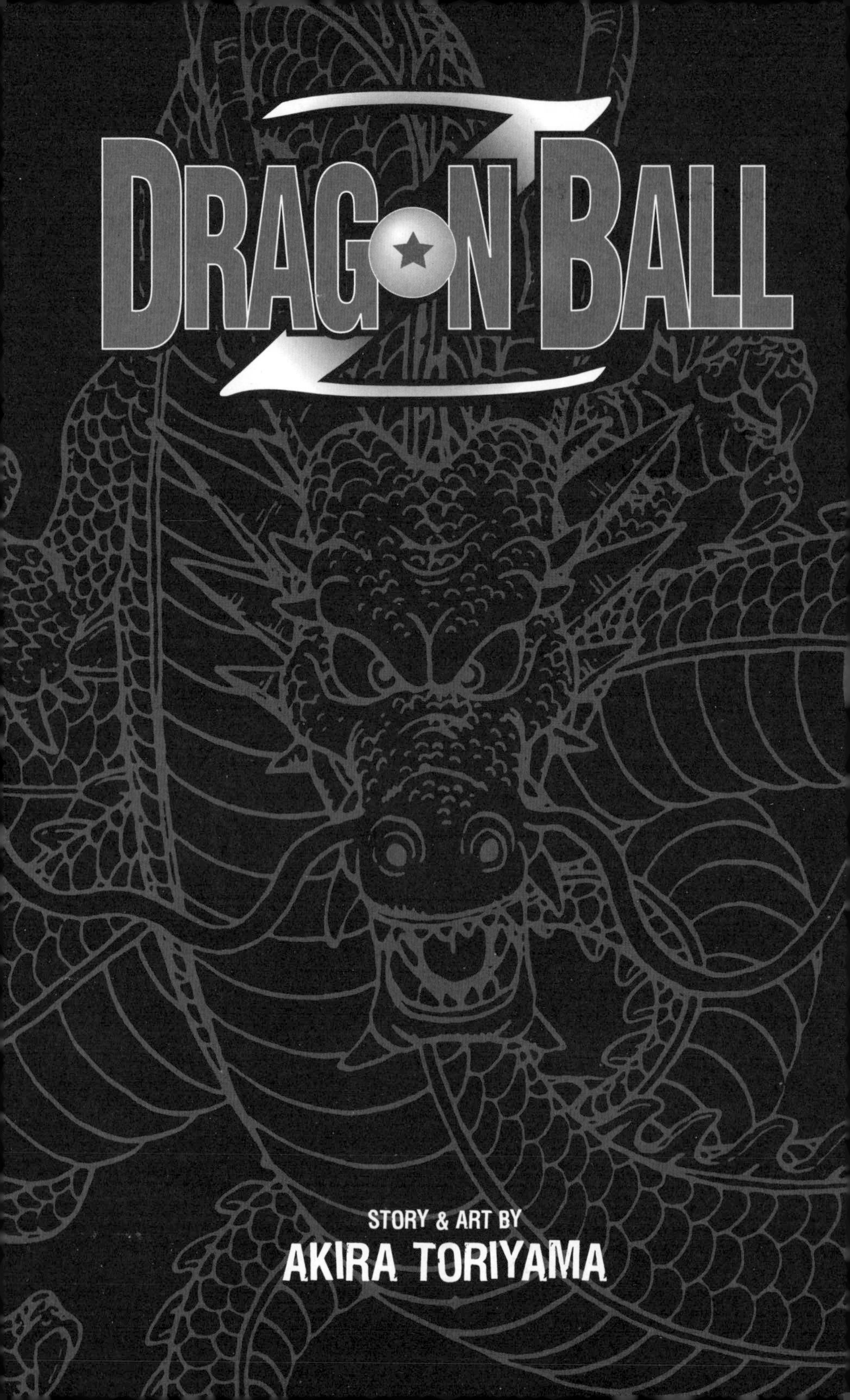
DRAGON BALL Z
STORY & ART BY
AKIRA TORIYAMA

# Dragon Ball Z
## Volume 2
### VIZBIG Edition

**STORY AND ART BY**
## AKIRA TORIYAMA

English Adaptation **Gerard Jones**
Translation **Lillian Olsen**
Touch-up Art & Lettering **Wayne Truman & HudsonYards**
Shonen Jump Series Design **Sean Lee**
VIZBIG Edition Design **Courtney Utt**
Shonen Jump Series Editor **Jason Thompson**
VIZBIG Edition Editor **Amy Yu**

DRAGON BALL © 1984 by BIRD STUDIO. All rights reserved. First published in Japan in 1984 by SHUEISHA Inc., Tokyo. English translation rights arranged by SHUEISHA Inc.

The stories, characters and incidents mentioned in this publication are entirely fictional.

Printed in China

Published by VIZ Media, LLC
P.O. Box 77010
San Francisco, CA 94107

10
First printing, August 2008
Tenth printing, August 2022

www.viz.com

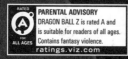

**PARENTAL ADVISORY**
RATED A FOR ALL AGES
DRAGON BALL Z is rated A and is suitable for readers of all ages. Contains fantasy violence.
ratings.viz.com

# DRAGON BALL Z

VOLUME 4
## GOKU VS. VEGETA

VOLUME 5
## DRAGON BALL
## IN SPACE

VOLUME 6
## BATTLEFIELD NAMEK

STORY & ART BY
## AKIRA TORIYAMA

SHONEN JUMP MANGA . VIZBIG EDITION

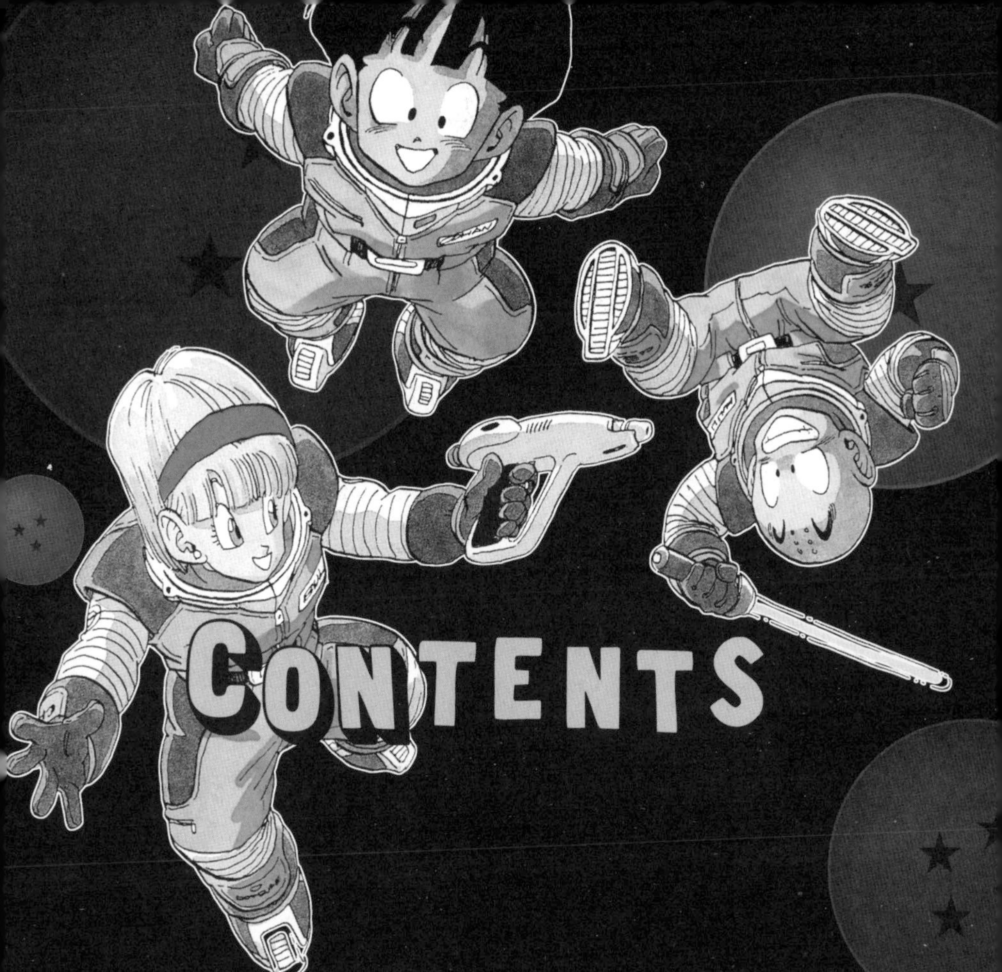

# CONTENTS

## VOLUME 5
## DRAGON BALL IN SPACE



## VOLUME 6
## BATTLEFIELD NAMEK

# CAST OF CHARACTERS

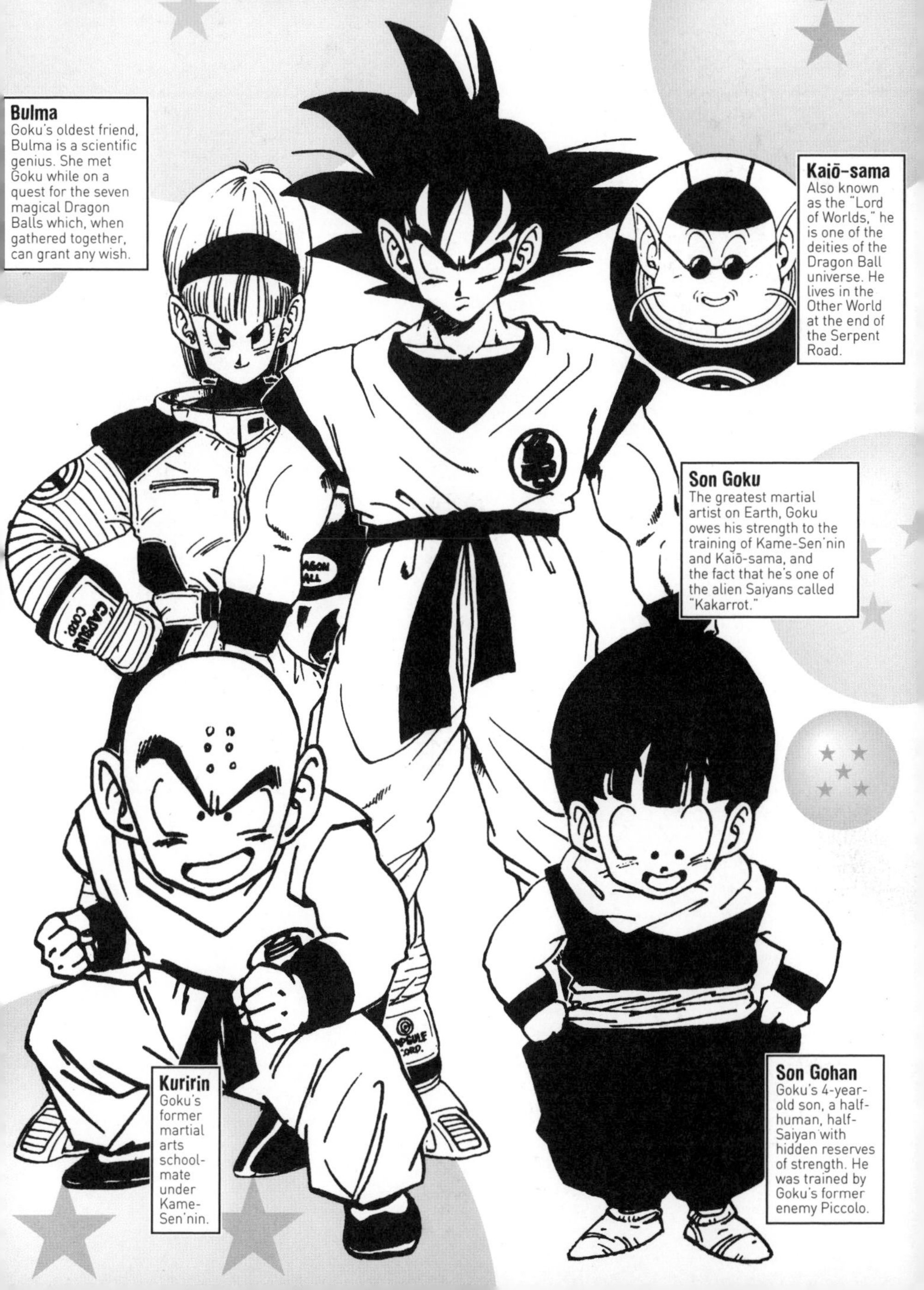
CAPSULE CORP.
CAPSULE CORP.

**Bulma**
Goku's oldest friend, Bulma is a scientific genius. She met Goku while on a quest for the seven magical Dragon Balls which, when gathered together, can grant any wish.

**Kaiō-sama**
Also known as the "Lord of Worlds," he is one of the deities of the Dragon Ball universe. He lives in the Other World at the end of the Serpent Road.

**Son Goku**
The greatest martial artist on Earth, Goku owes his strength to the training of Kame-Sen'nin and Kaiō-sama, and the fact that he's one of the alien Saiyans called "Kakarrot."

**Kuririn**
Goku's former martial arts school-mate under Kame-Sen'nin.

**Son Gohan**
Goku's 4-year-old son, a half-human, half-Saiyan with hidden reserves of strength. He was trained by Goku's former enemy Piccolo.

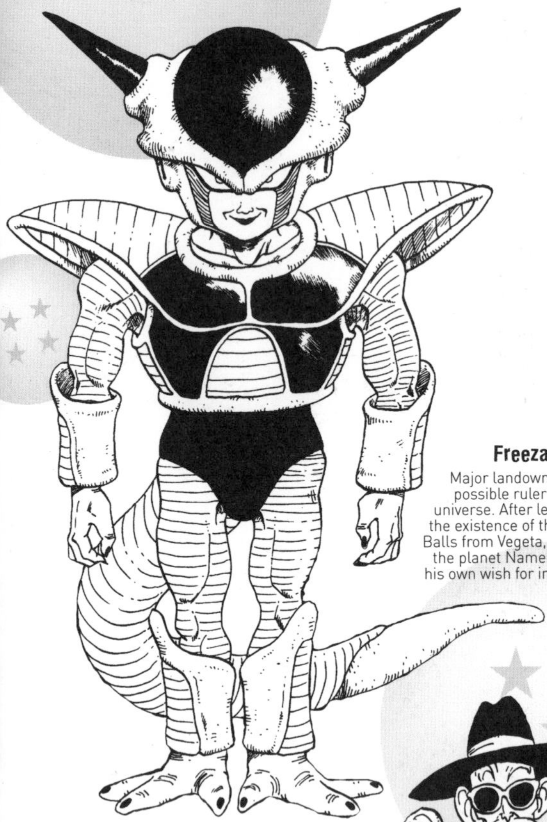

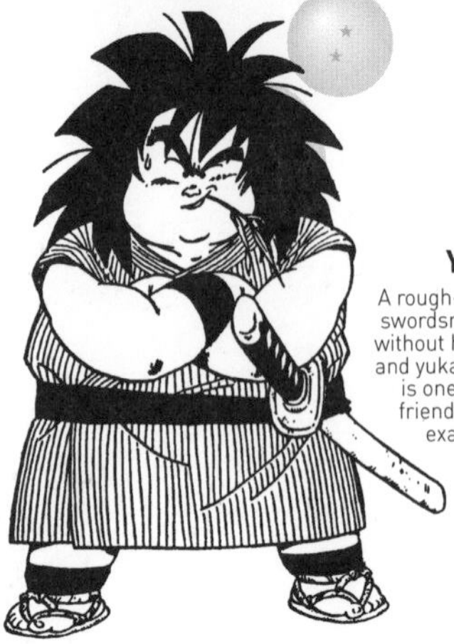

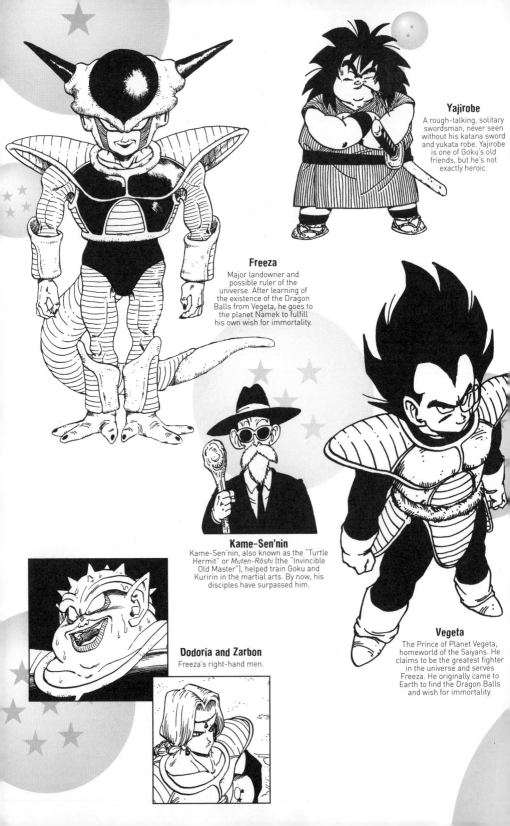

**Yajirobe**

A rough-talking, solitary swordsman, never seen without his katana sword and yukata robe. Yajirobe is one of Goku's old friends, but he's not exactly heroic.

**Freeza**

Major landowner and possible ruler of the universe. After learning of the existence of the Dragon Balls from Vegeta, he goes to the planet Namek to fulfill his own wish for immortality.

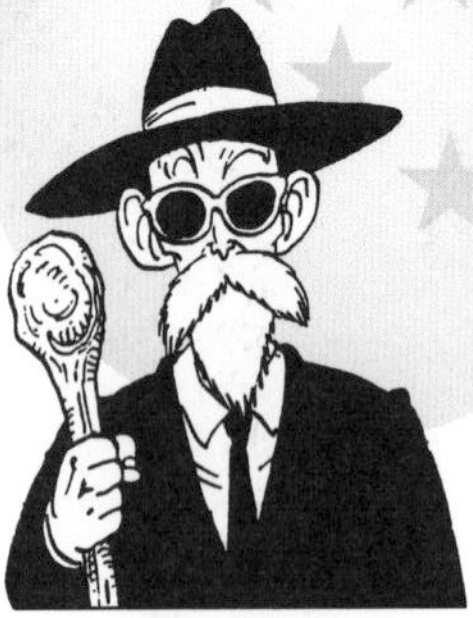

**Kame-Sen'nin**

Kame-Sen'nin, also known as the "Turtle Hermit" or *Muten-Rōshi* (the "Invincible Old Master"), helped train Goku and Kuririn in the martial arts. By now, his disciples have surpassed him.

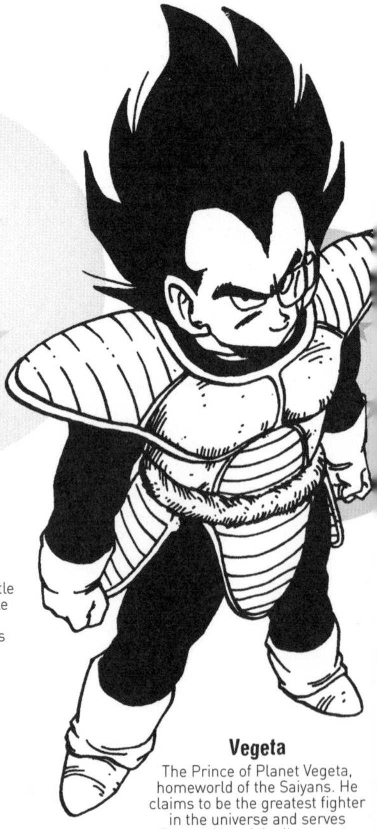

**Vegeta**

The Prince of Planet Vegeta, homeworld of the Saiyans. He claims to be the greatest fighter in the universe and serves Freeza. He originally came to Earth to find the Dragon Balls and wish for immortality.

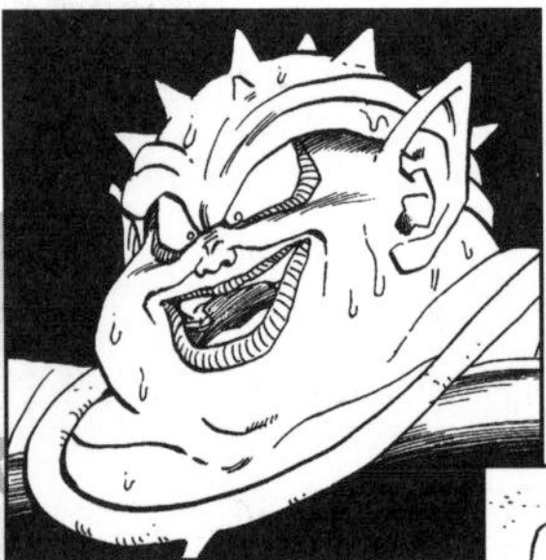

**Dodoria and Zarbon**

Freeza's right-hand men.

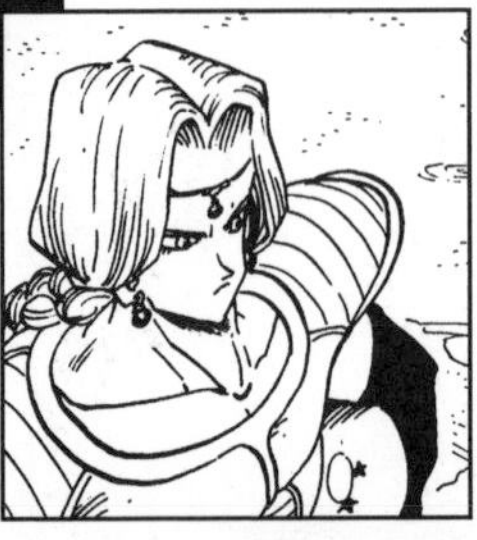

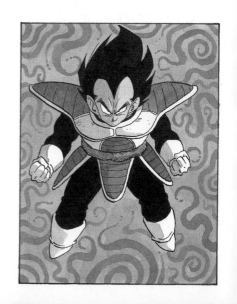

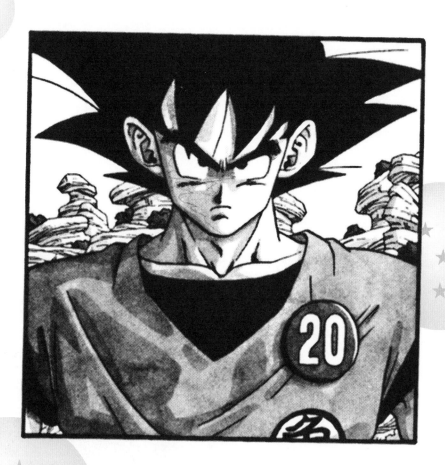

# DragonBallZ

**VOLUME 4**

## GOKU VS. VEGETA

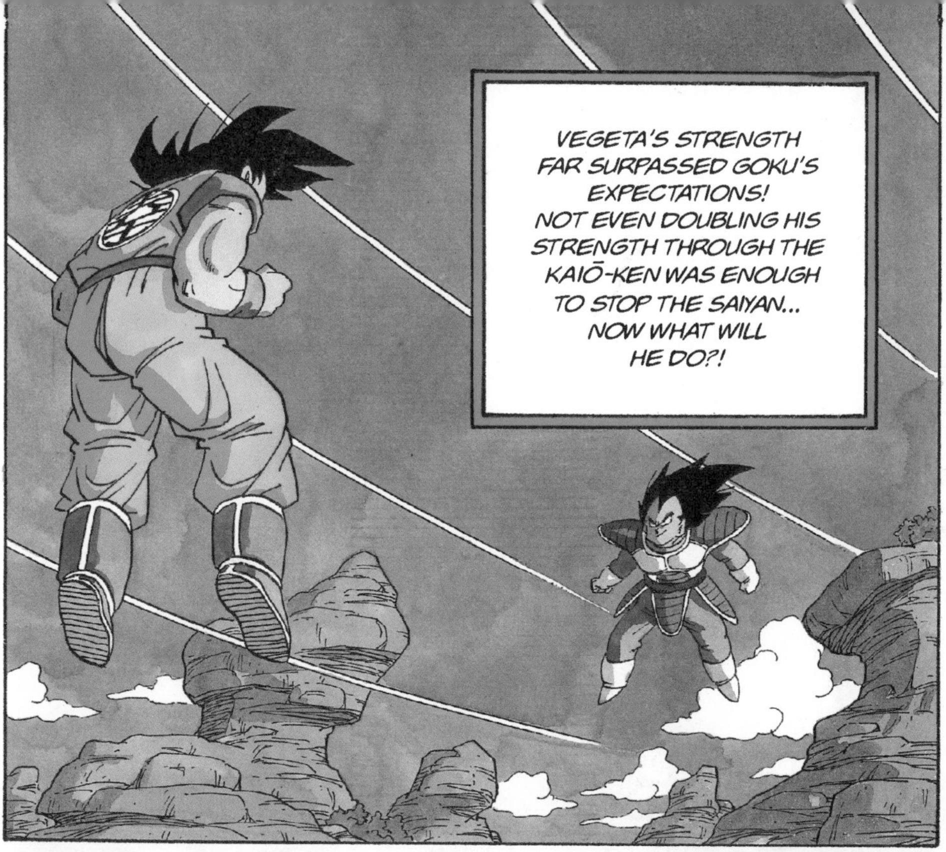
VEGETA'S STRENGTH FAR SURPASSED GOKU'S EXPECTATIONS! NOT EVEN DOUBLING HIS STRENGTH THROUGH THE KAIŌ-KEN WAS ENOUGH TO STOP THE SAIYAN... NOW WHAT WILL HE DO?!

# DBZ:35 • The Decisive Battle at Last!

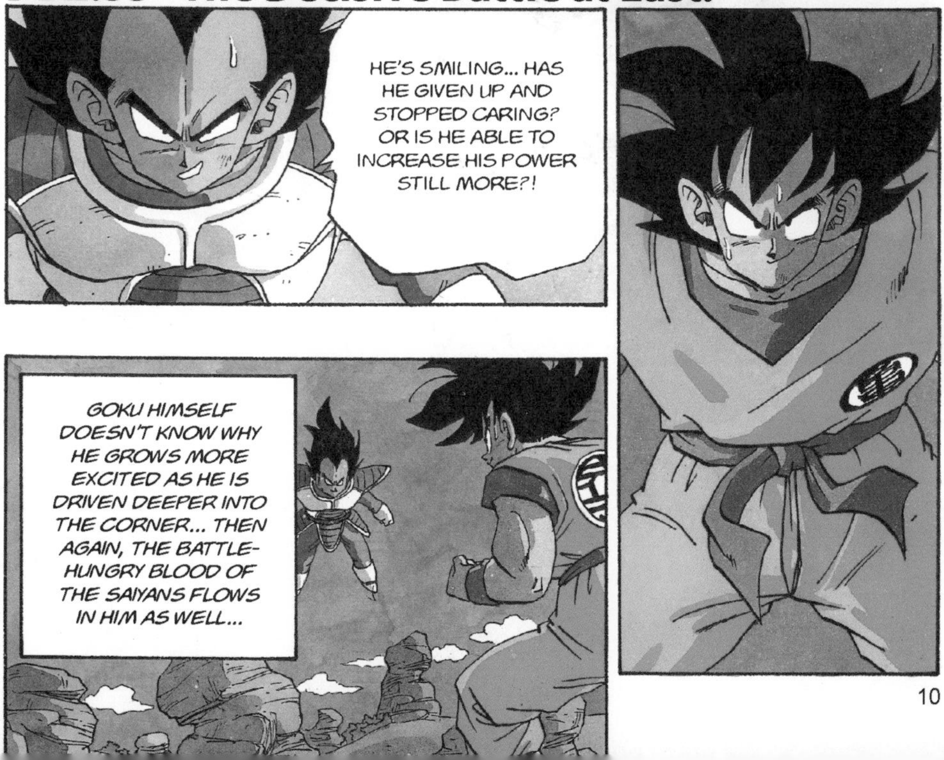
HE'S SMILING... HAS HE GIVEN UP AND STOPPED CARING? OR IS HE ABLE TO INCREASE HIS POWER STILL MORE?!
GOKU HIMSELF DOESN'T KNOW WHY HE GROWS MORE EXCITED AS HE IS DRIVEN DEEPER INTO THE CORNER... THEN AGAIN, THE BATTLE-HUNGRY BLOOD OF THE SAIYANS FLOWS IN HIM AS WELL...

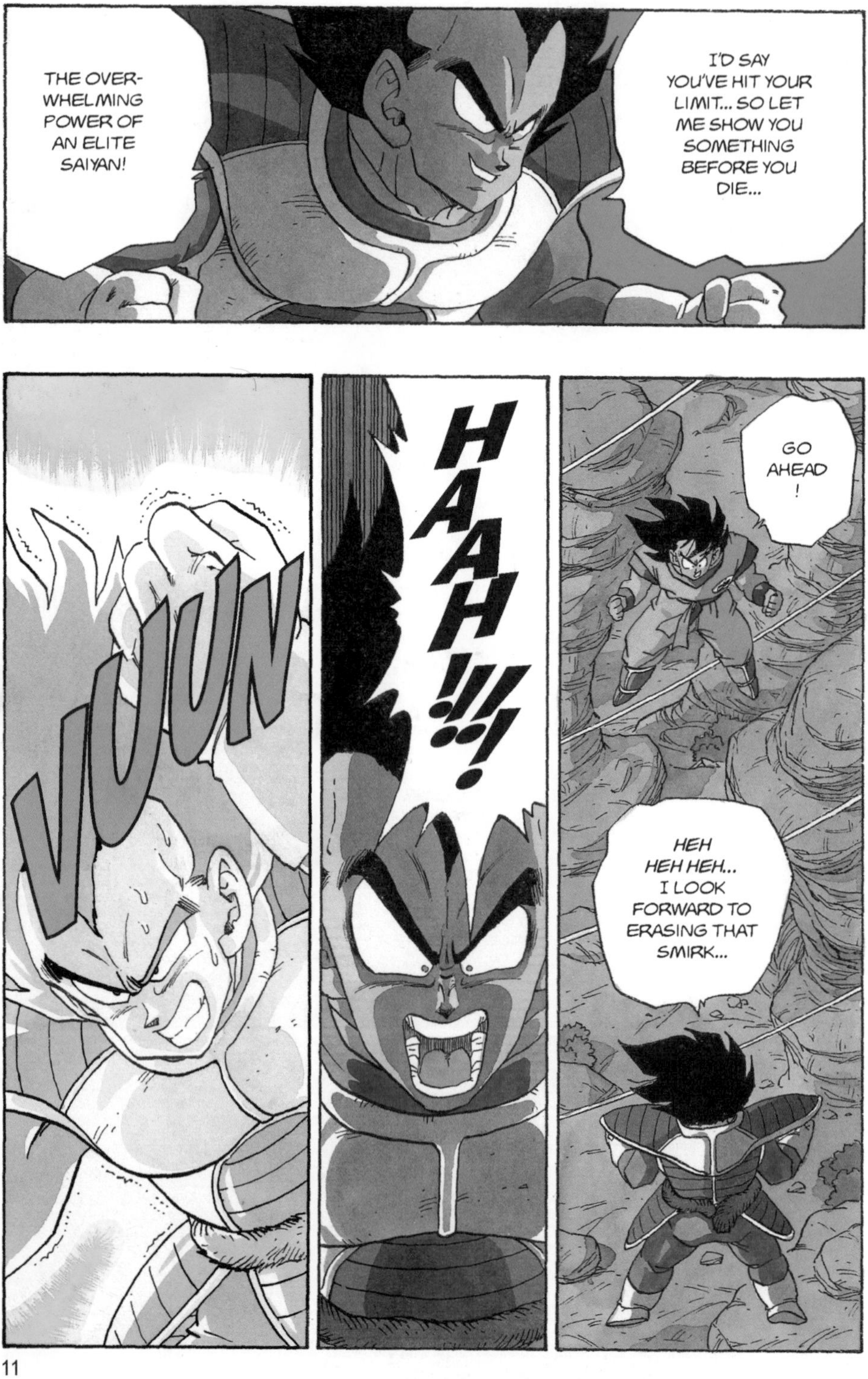
I'D SAY YOU'VE HIT YOUR LIMIT... SO LET ME SHOW YOU SOMETHING BEFORE YOU DIE...
THE OVER-WHELMING POWER OF AN ELITE SAIYAN!
GO AHEAD!
HEH HEH HEH... I LOOK FORWARD TO ERASING THAT SMIRK...
HAAAH!!!!!
VUUUN

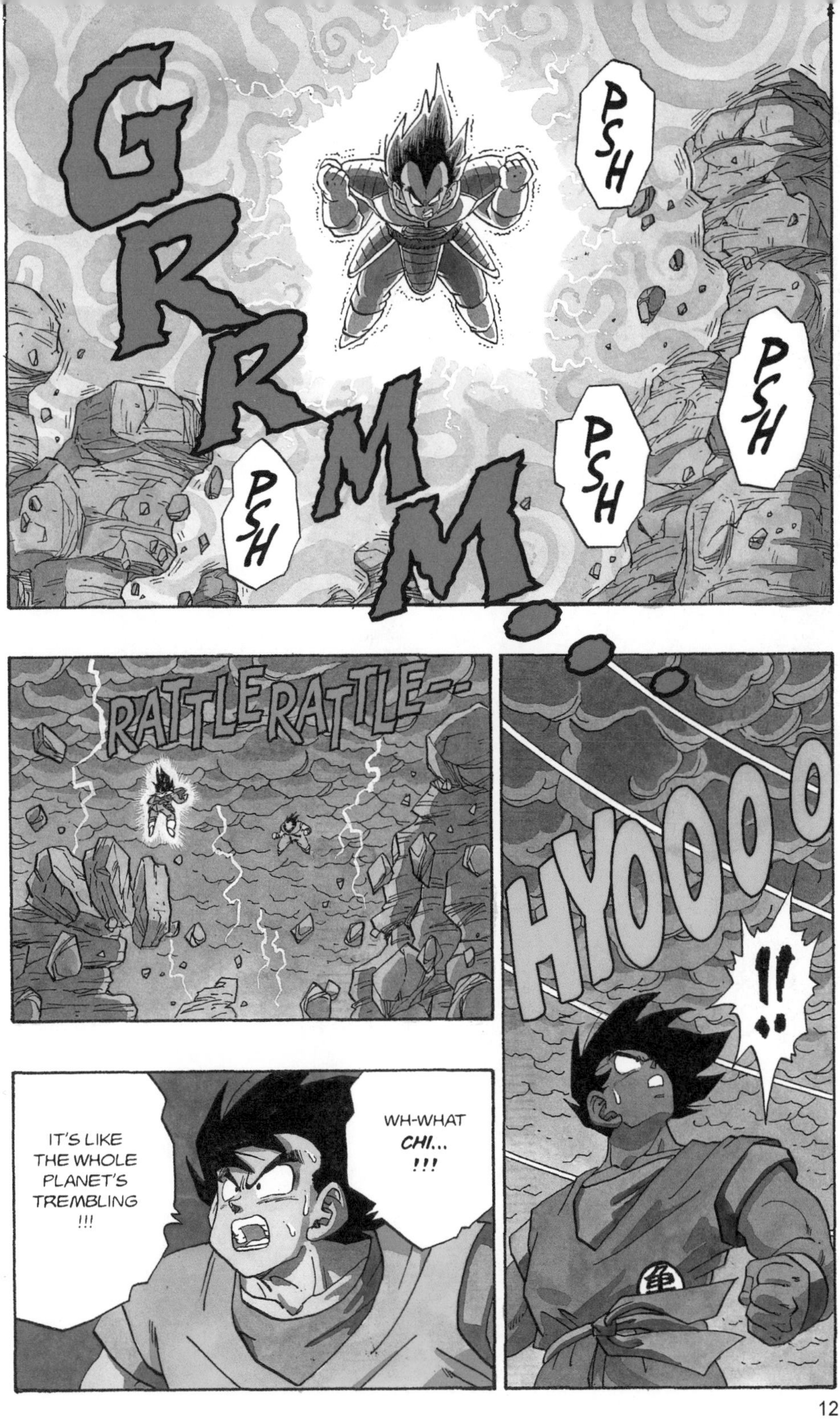
PSH
PSH
PSH
GRRMM...
PSH
HYOOOO
!!
RATTLE RATTLE--
WH-WHAT CHI... !!!
IT'S LIKE THE WHOLE PLANET'S TREMBLING !!!

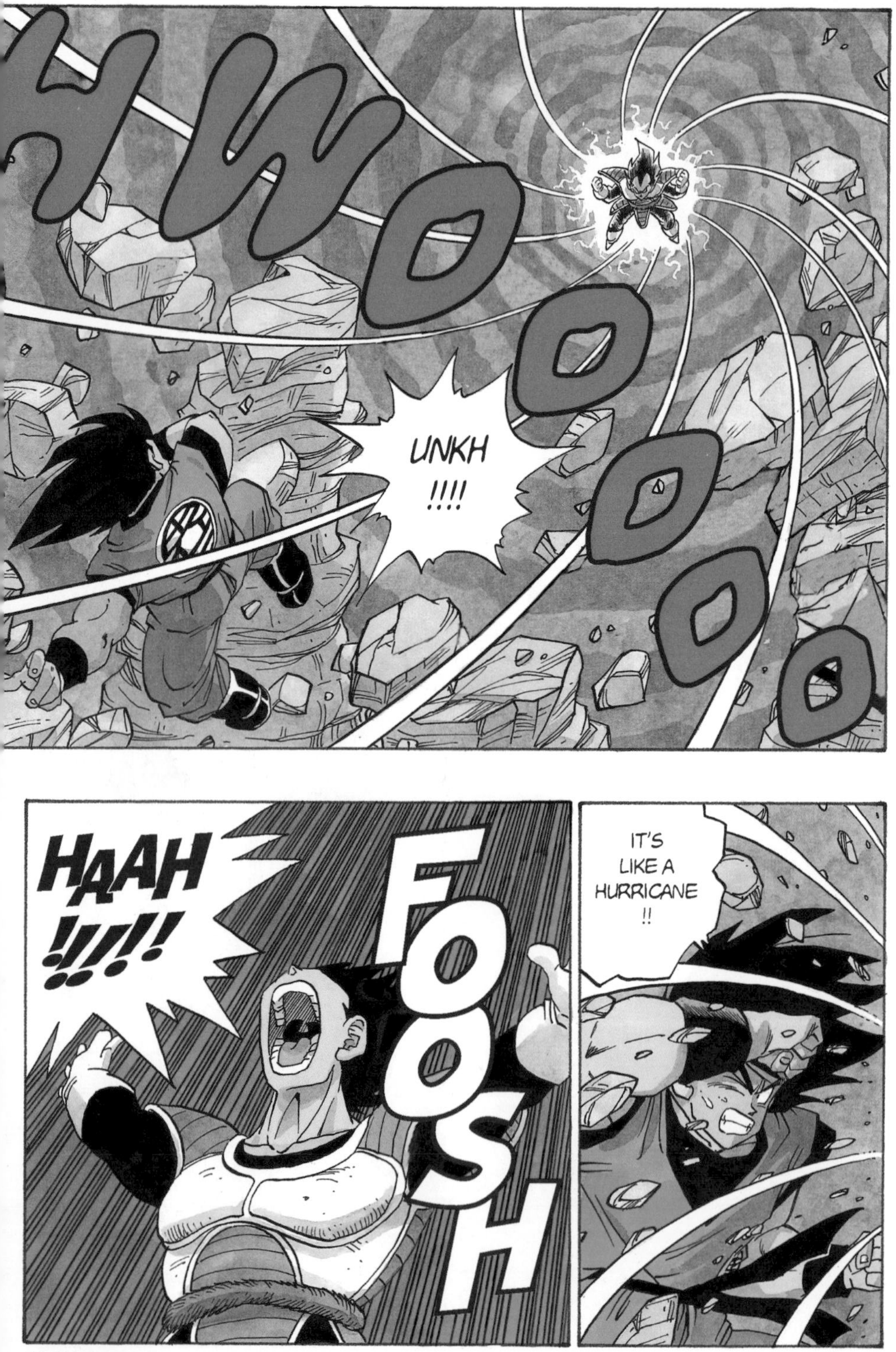
HWOOOOOO
UNKH !!!!
IT'S LIKE A HURRICANE !!
HAAH !!!!!
FOOSH

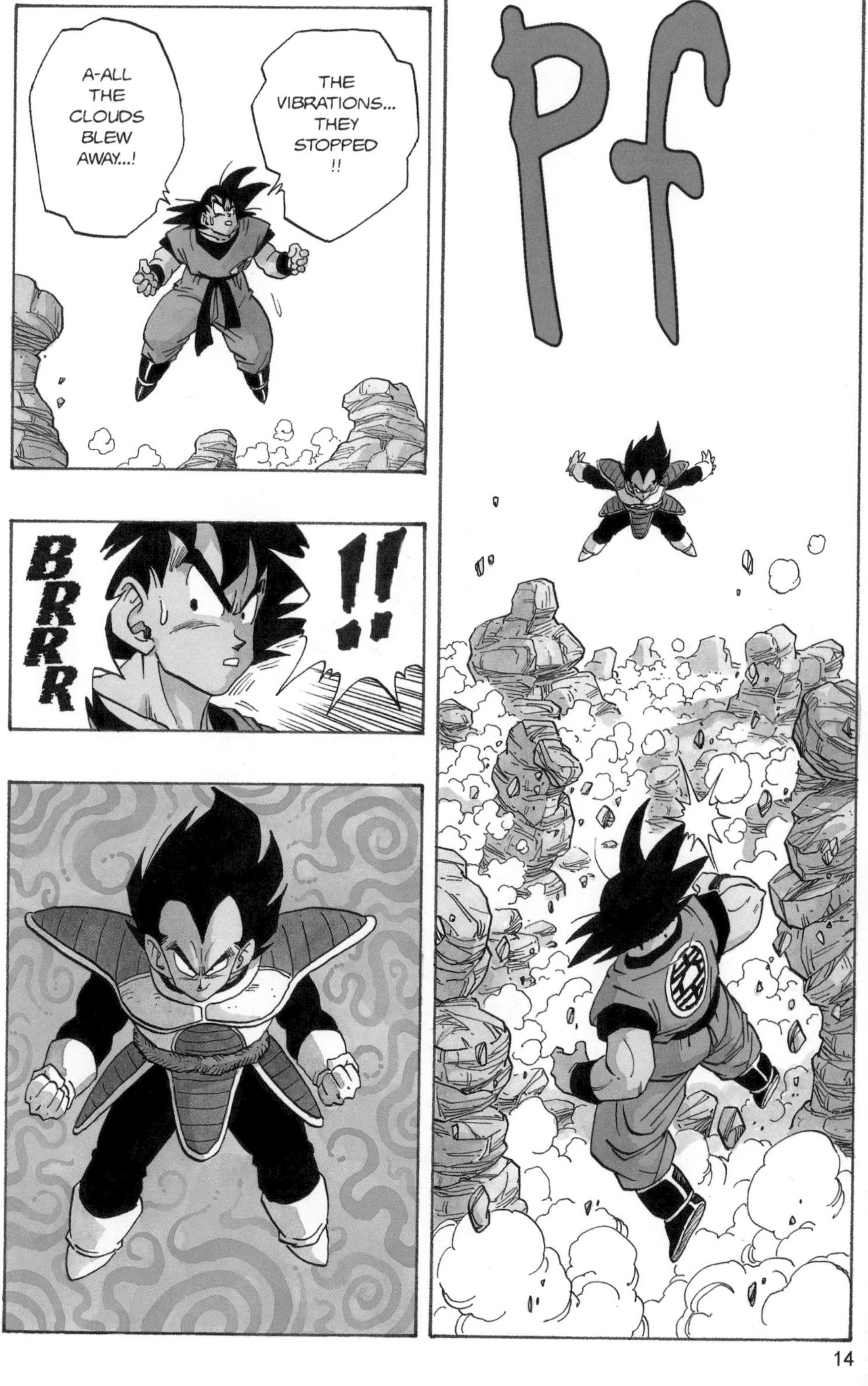
Pf
THE VIBRATIONS... THEY STOPPED !!
A-ALL THE CLOUDS BLEW AWAY...!
!!
BRRRR

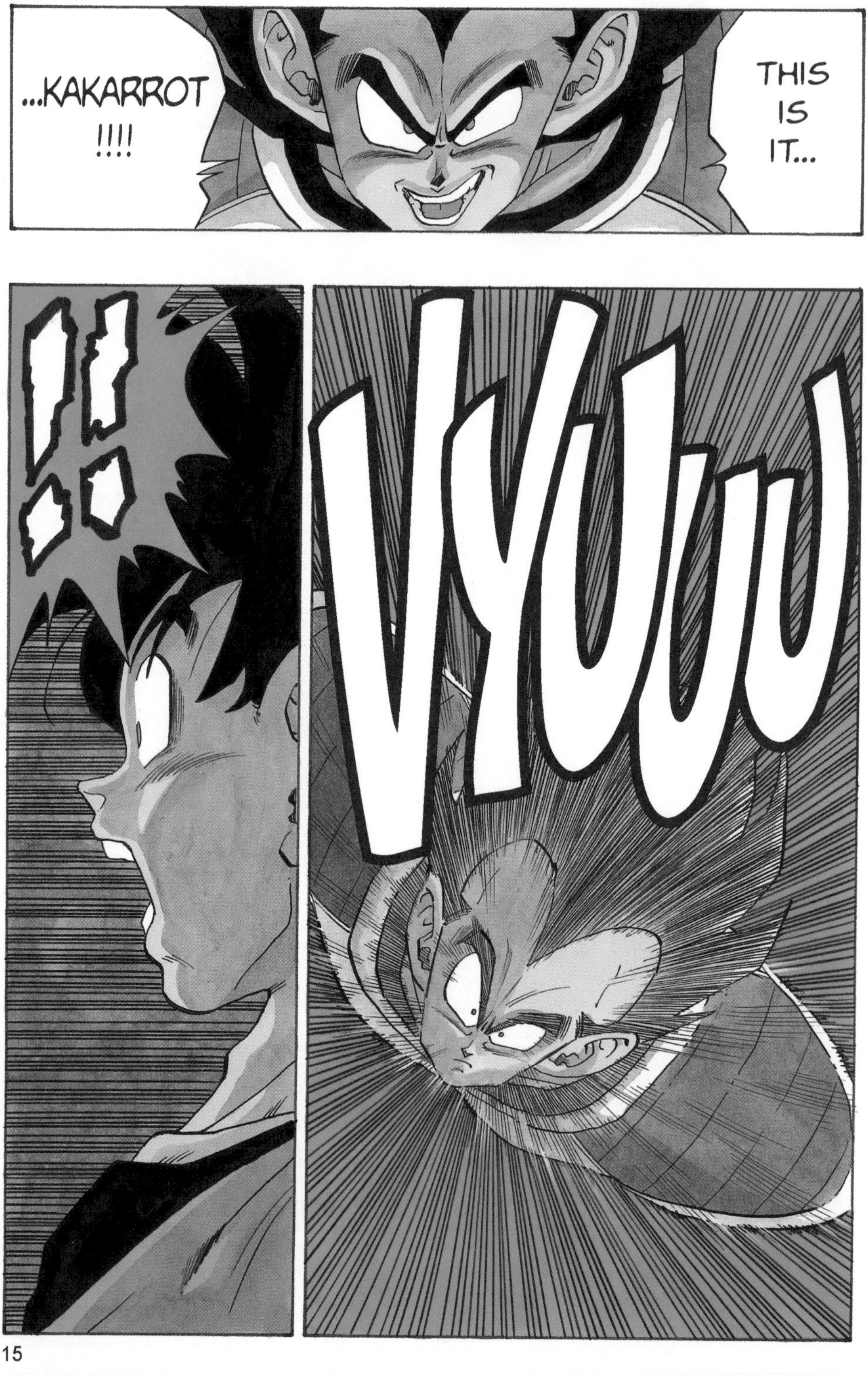
THIS IS IT...
...KAKARROT !!!!
VYUUUU
!!

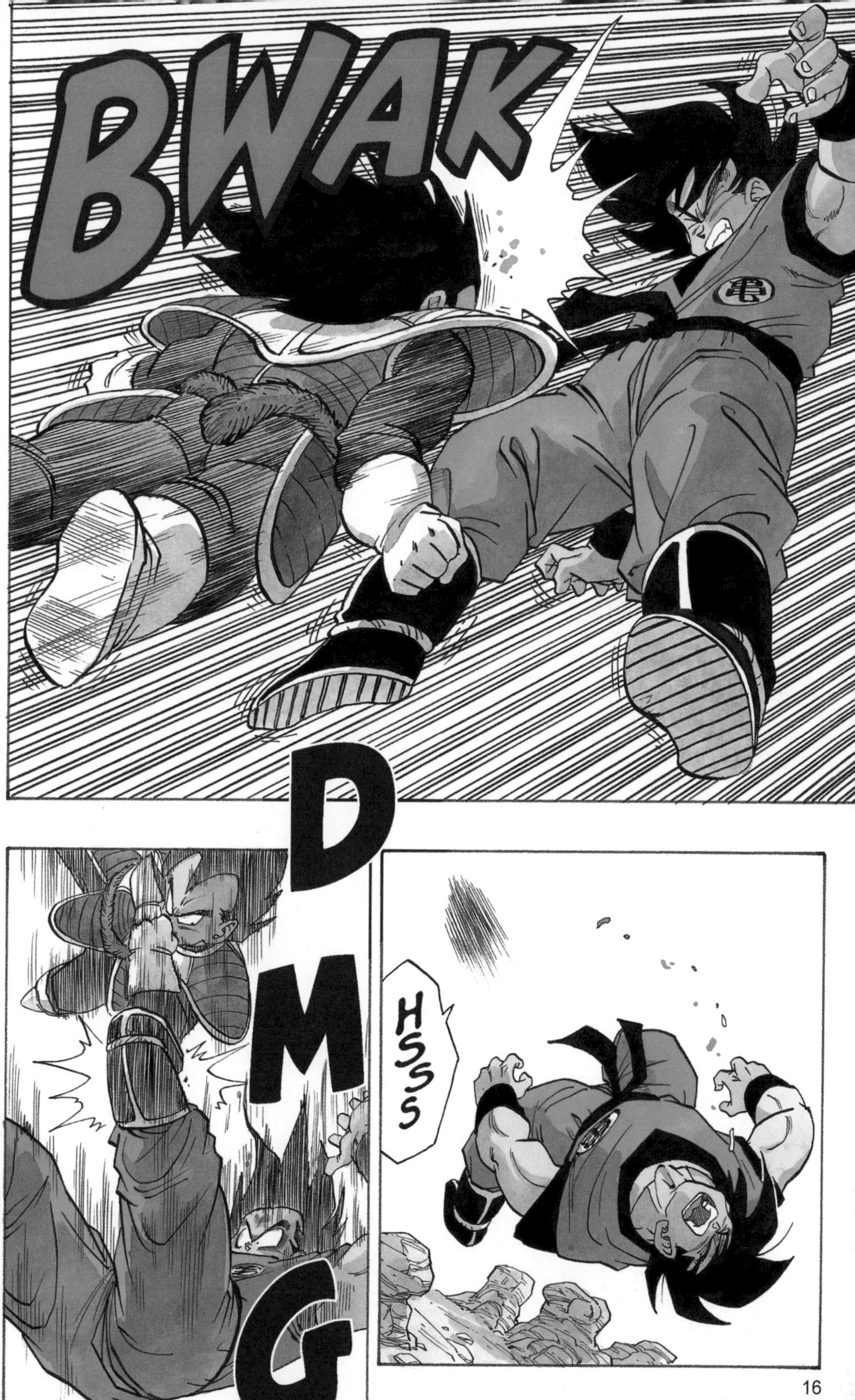
BWAK
HSSS
DMG

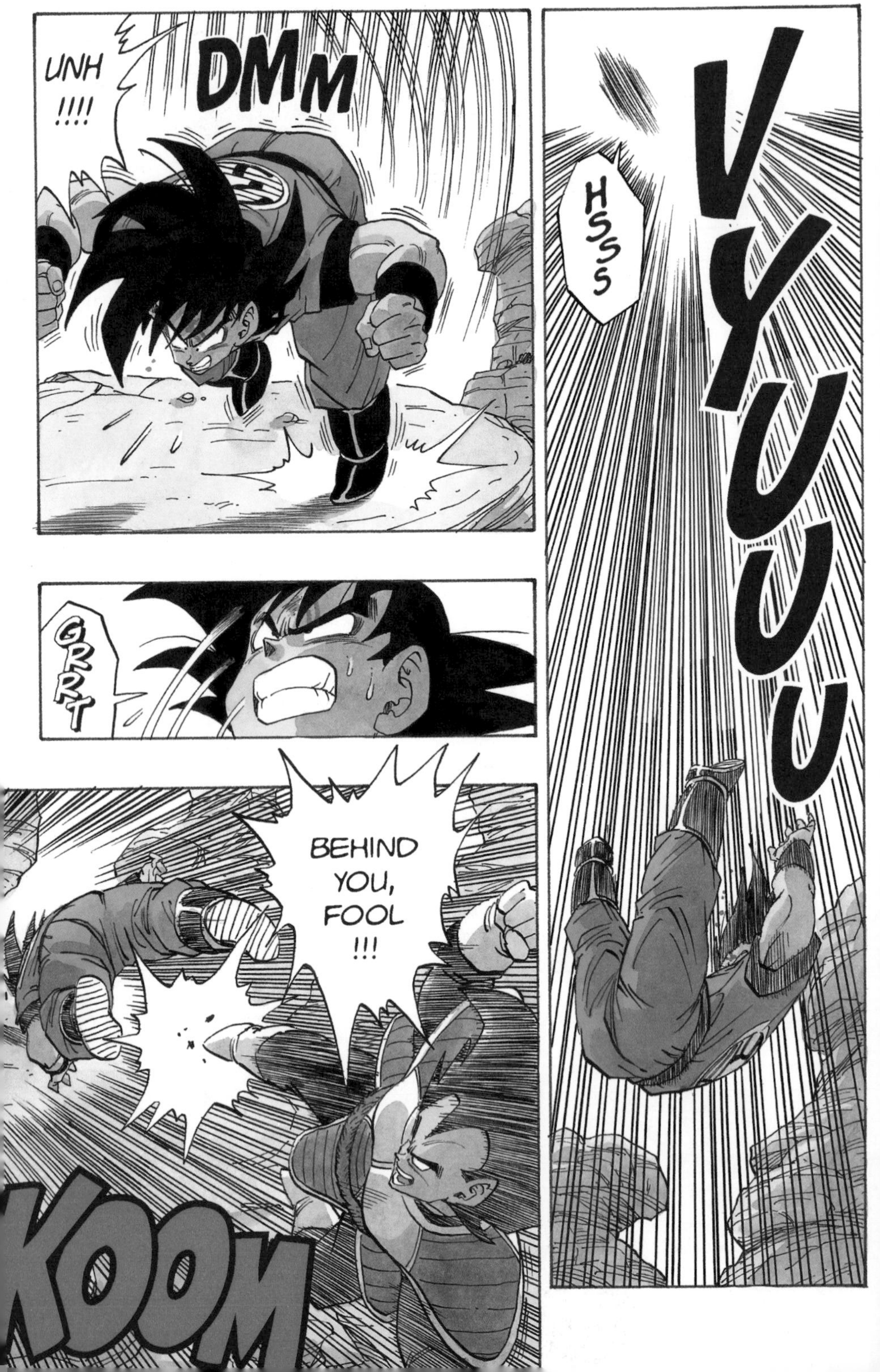
VYUUUU
HSSS
DMM
UNH !!!!
GRRT
BEHIND YOU, FOOL !!!
KOOM

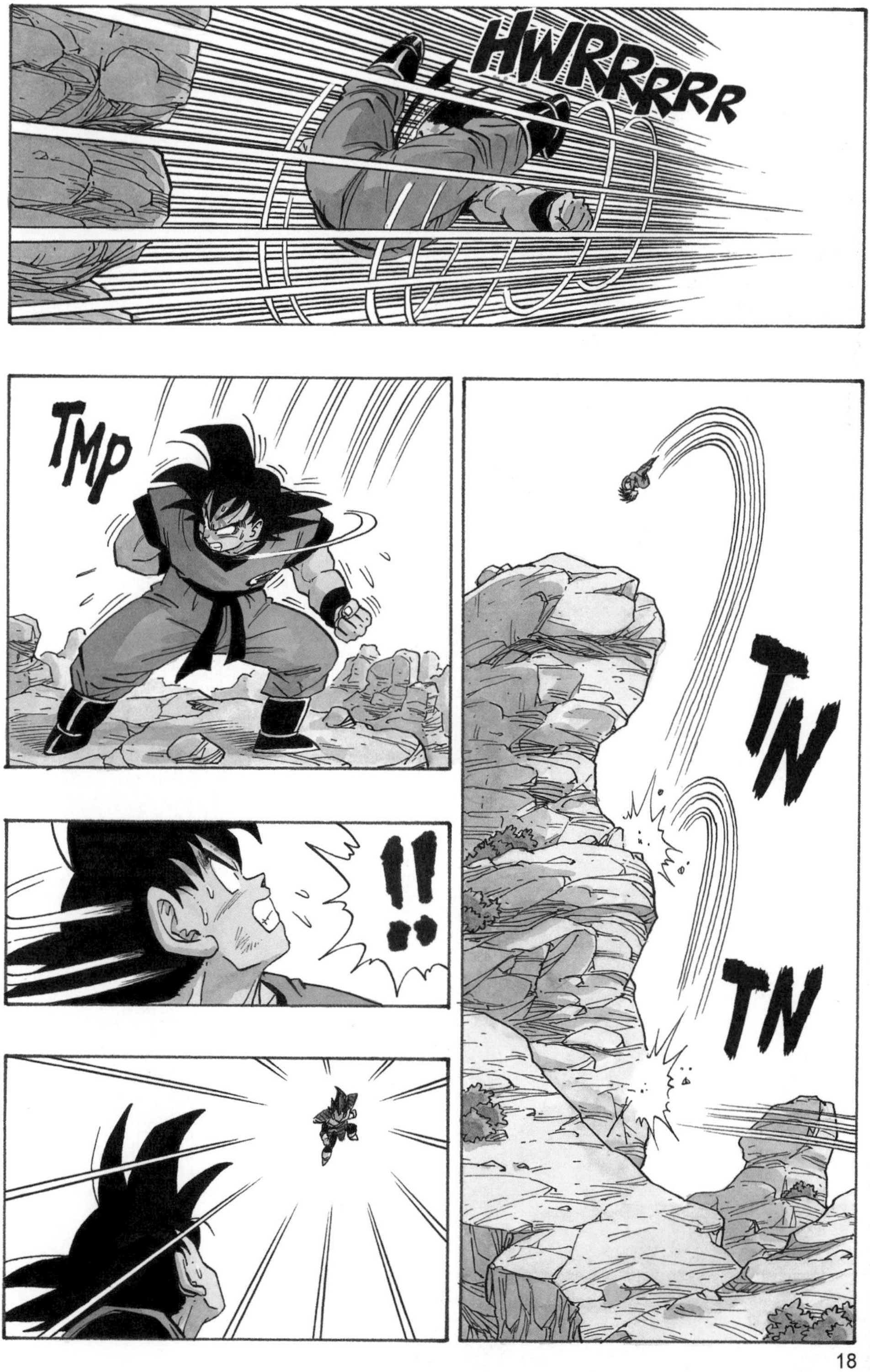
HWRRRRRR
TN
TN
TMP
!!

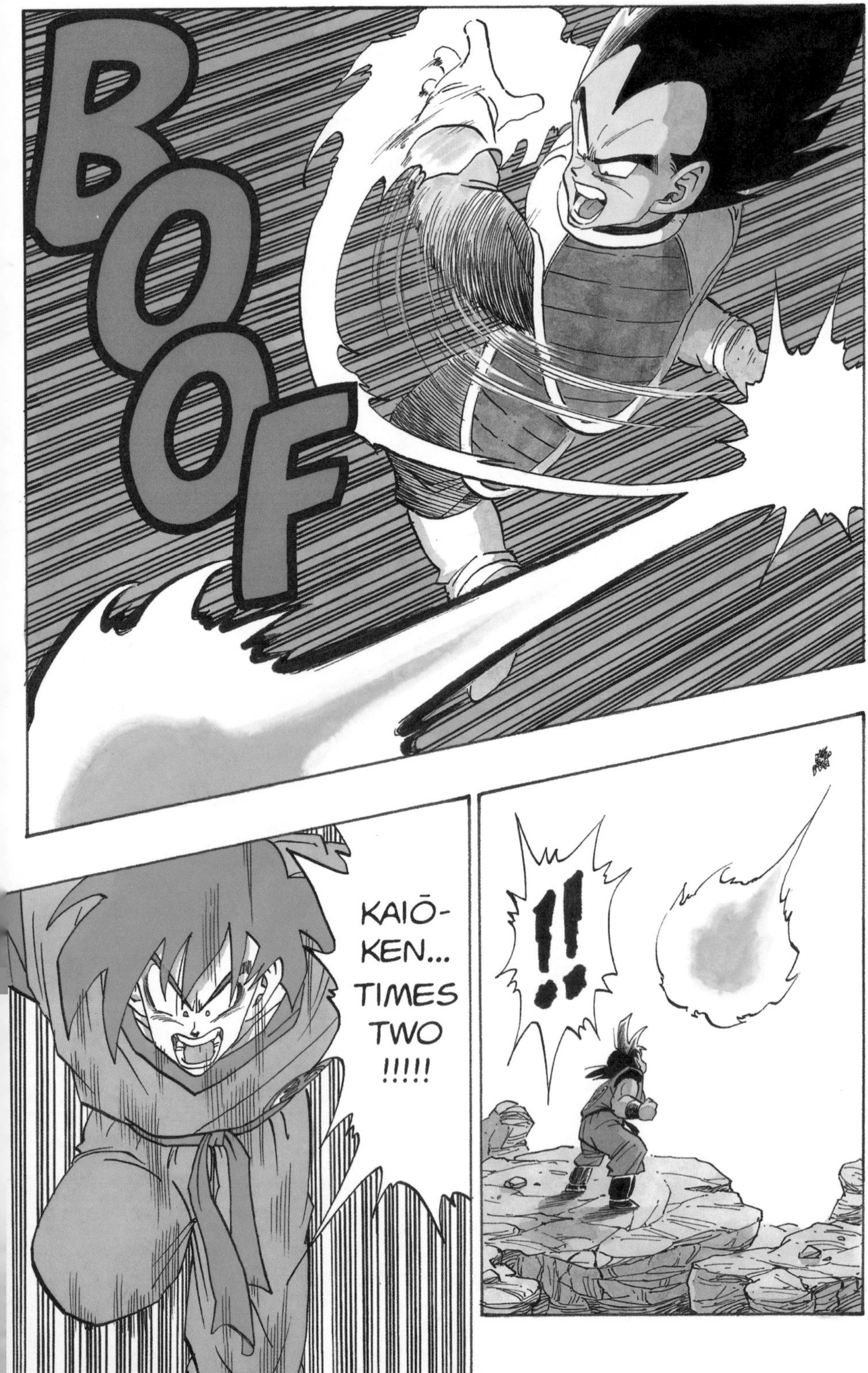
BOOOF
!!
KAIŌ-KEN... TIMES TWO !!!!!

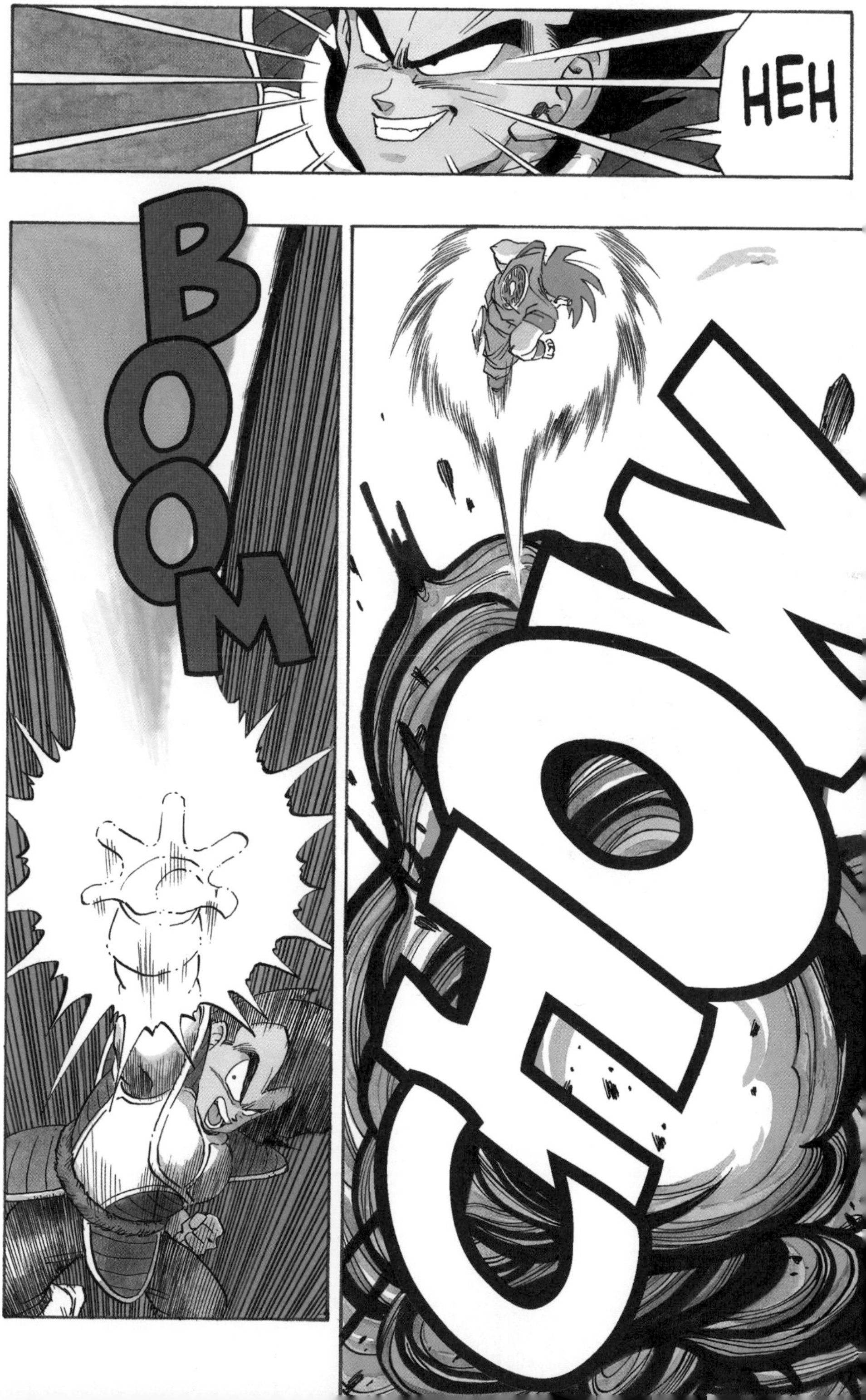
HEH
BOOM

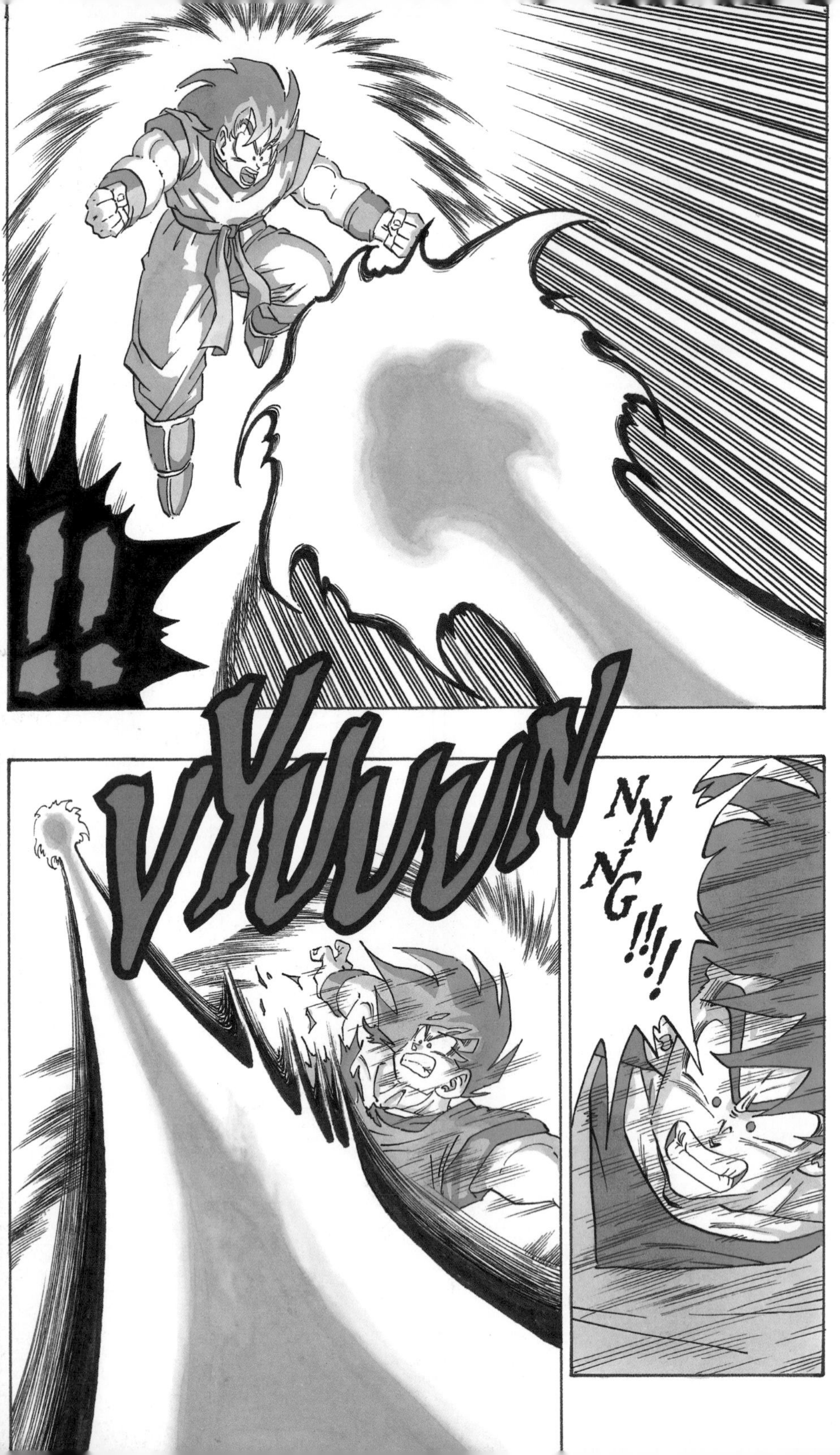
!!
NNNG!!!!
VYUUUN

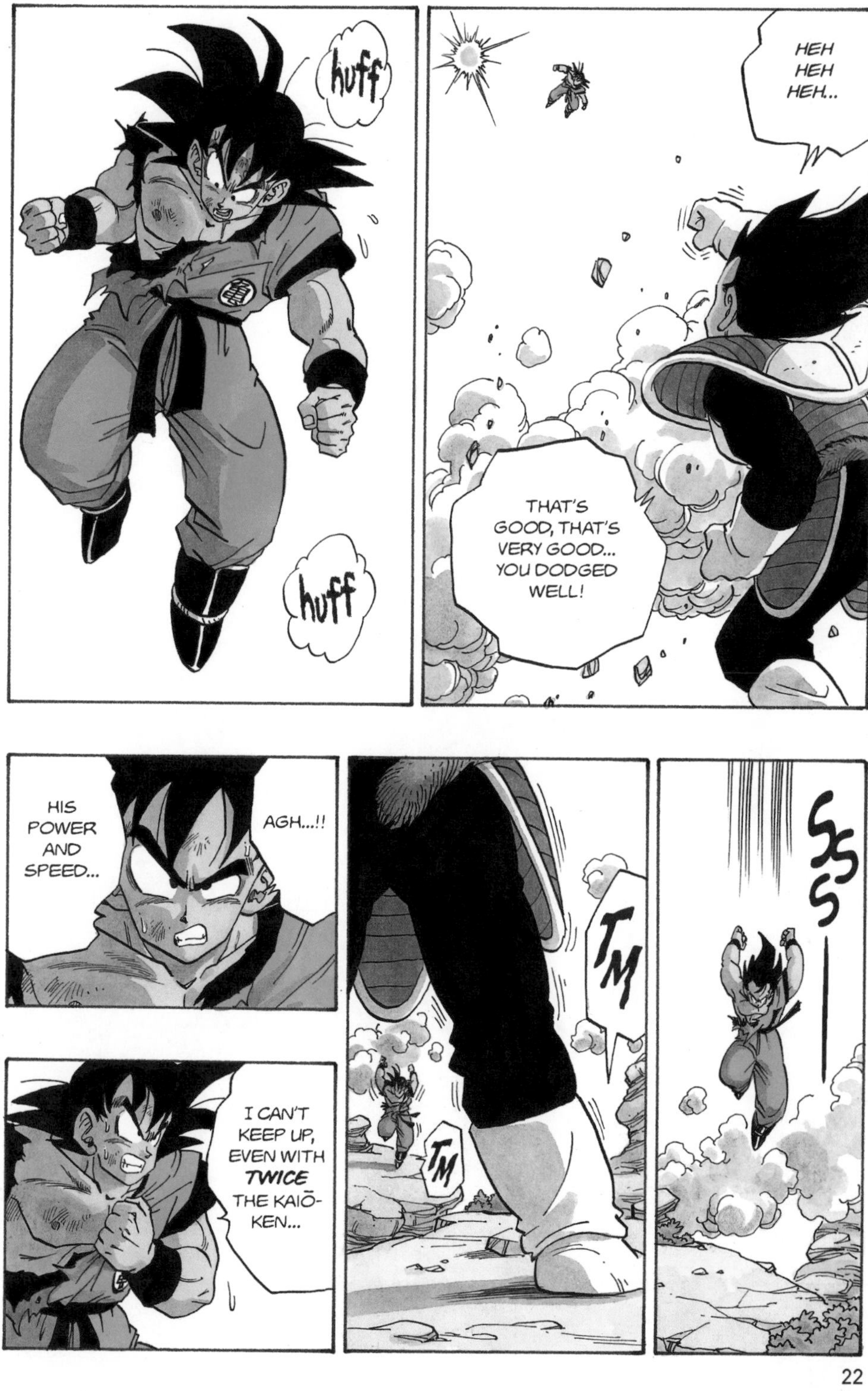
HEH HEH HEH...
THAT'S GOOD, THAT'S VERY GOOD... YOU DODGED WELL!
huff
huff
SSS—
TM
TM
AGH...!!
HIS POWER AND SPEED...
I CAN'T KEEP UP, EVEN WITH **TWICE** THE KAIŌ-KEN...

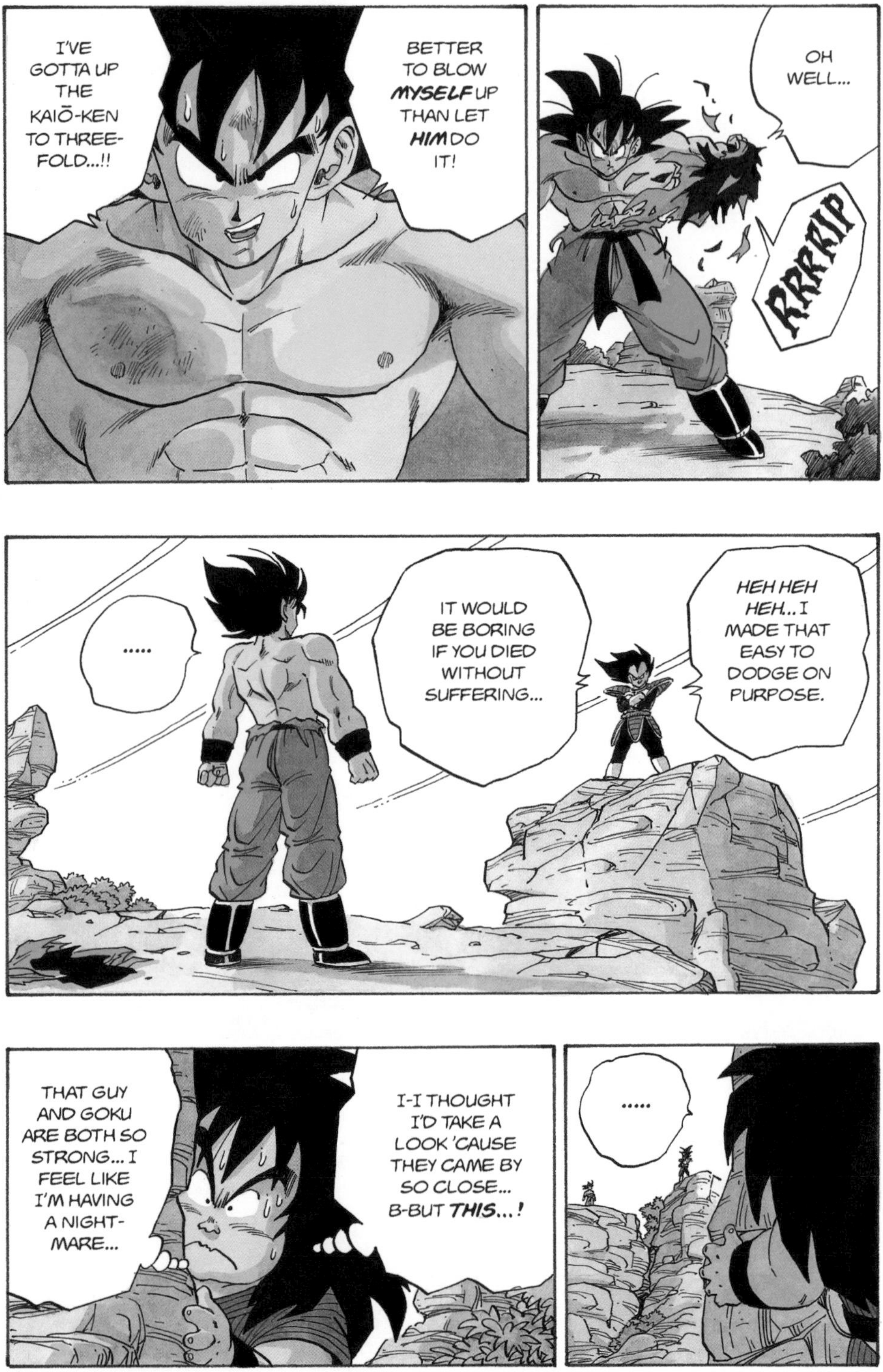
OH WELL...
RRRRIP
BETTER TO BLOW MYSELF UP THAN LET HIM DO IT!
I'VE GOTTA UP THE KAIŌ-KEN TO THREE-FOLD...!!
HEH HEH HEH... I MADE THAT EASY TO DODGE ON PURPOSE.
IT WOULD BE BORING IF YOU DIED WITHOUT SUFFERING...
.....
.....
I-I THOUGHT I'D TAKE A LOOK 'CAUSE THEY CAME BY SO CLOSE... B-BUT THIS...!
THAT GUY AND GOKU ARE BOTH SO STRONG... I FEEL LIKE I'M HAVING A NIGHT-MARE...

# DBZ:36 • Too Much Power?

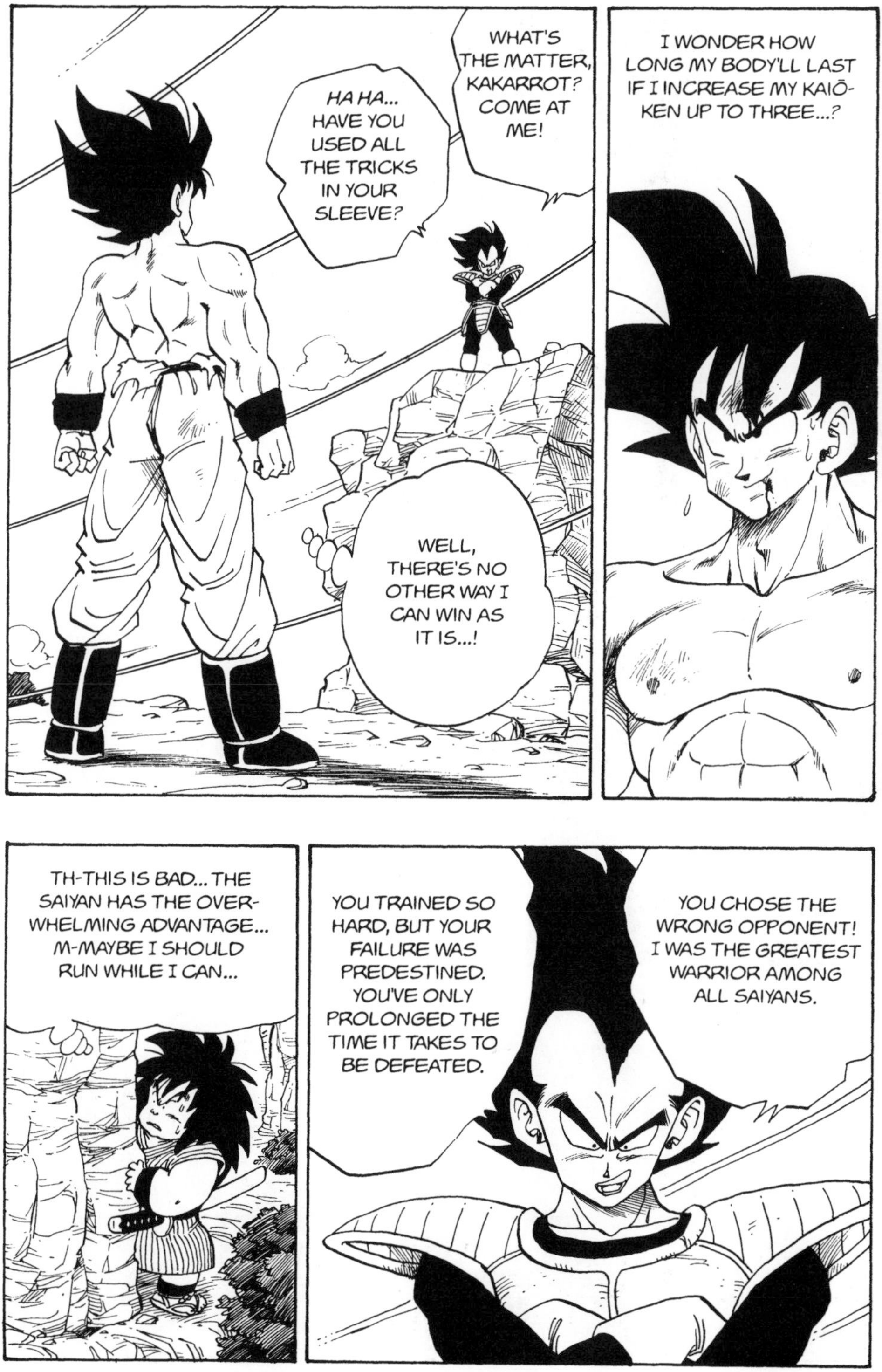
I WONDER HOW LONG MY BODY'LL LAST IF I INCREASE MY KAIŌ-KEN UP TO THREE...?
WHAT'S THE MATTER, KAKARROT? COME AT ME!
HA HA... HAVE YOU USED ALL THE TRICKS IN YOUR SLEEVE?
WELL, THERE'S NO OTHER WAY I CAN WIN AS IT IS...!
YOU CHOSE THE WRONG OPPONENT! I WAS THE GREATEST WARRIOR AMONG ALL SAIYANS.
YOU TRAINED SO HARD, BUT YOUR FAILURE WAS PREDESTINED. YOU'VE ONLY PROLONGED THE TIME IT TAKES TO BE DEFEATED.
TH-THIS IS BAD... THE SAIYAN HAS THE OVER-WHELMING ADVANTAGE... M-MAYBE I SHOULD RUN WHILE I CAN...

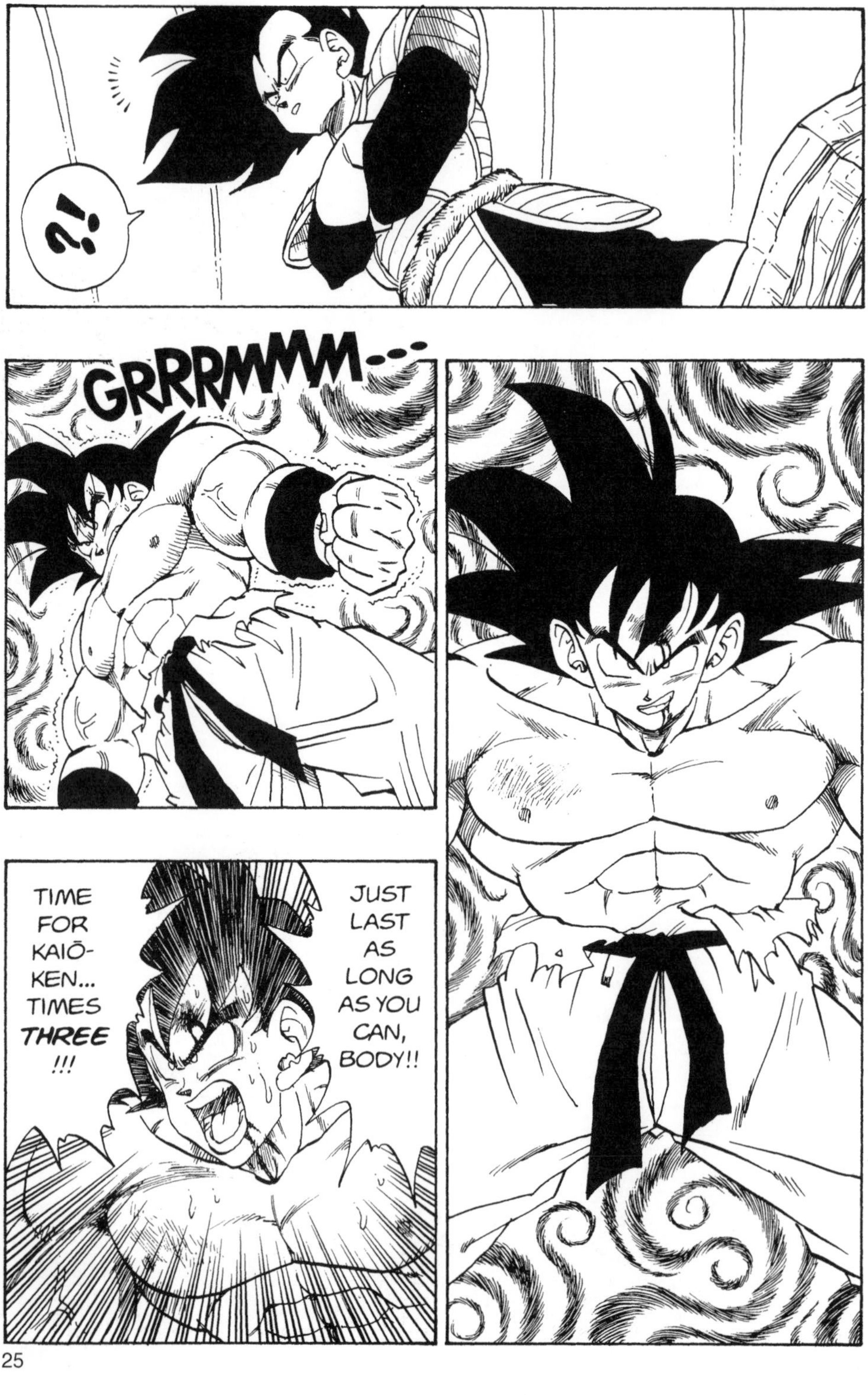
?!
GRRRMMM...
JUST LAST AS LONG AS YOU CAN, BODY!!
TIME FOR KAIŌ-KEN... TIMES *THREE* !!!

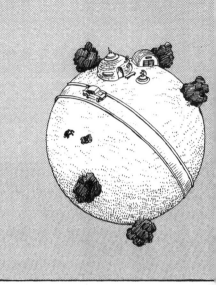

YOU SHOULD NEVER GO BEYOND TWO-FOLD, SON GOKU...!!

N-NO...!!

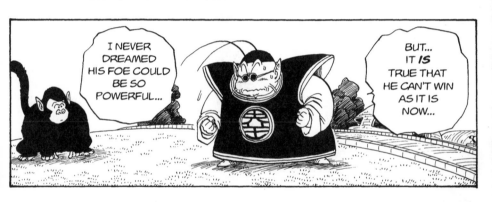

I NEVER DREAMED HIS FOE COULD BE SO POWERFUL...

BUT... IT *IS* TRUE THAT HE CAN'T WIN AS IT IS NOW...

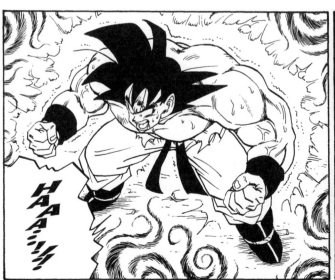

HAAA...!!!

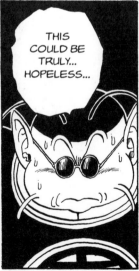

THIS COULD BE TRULY... HOPELESS...

26

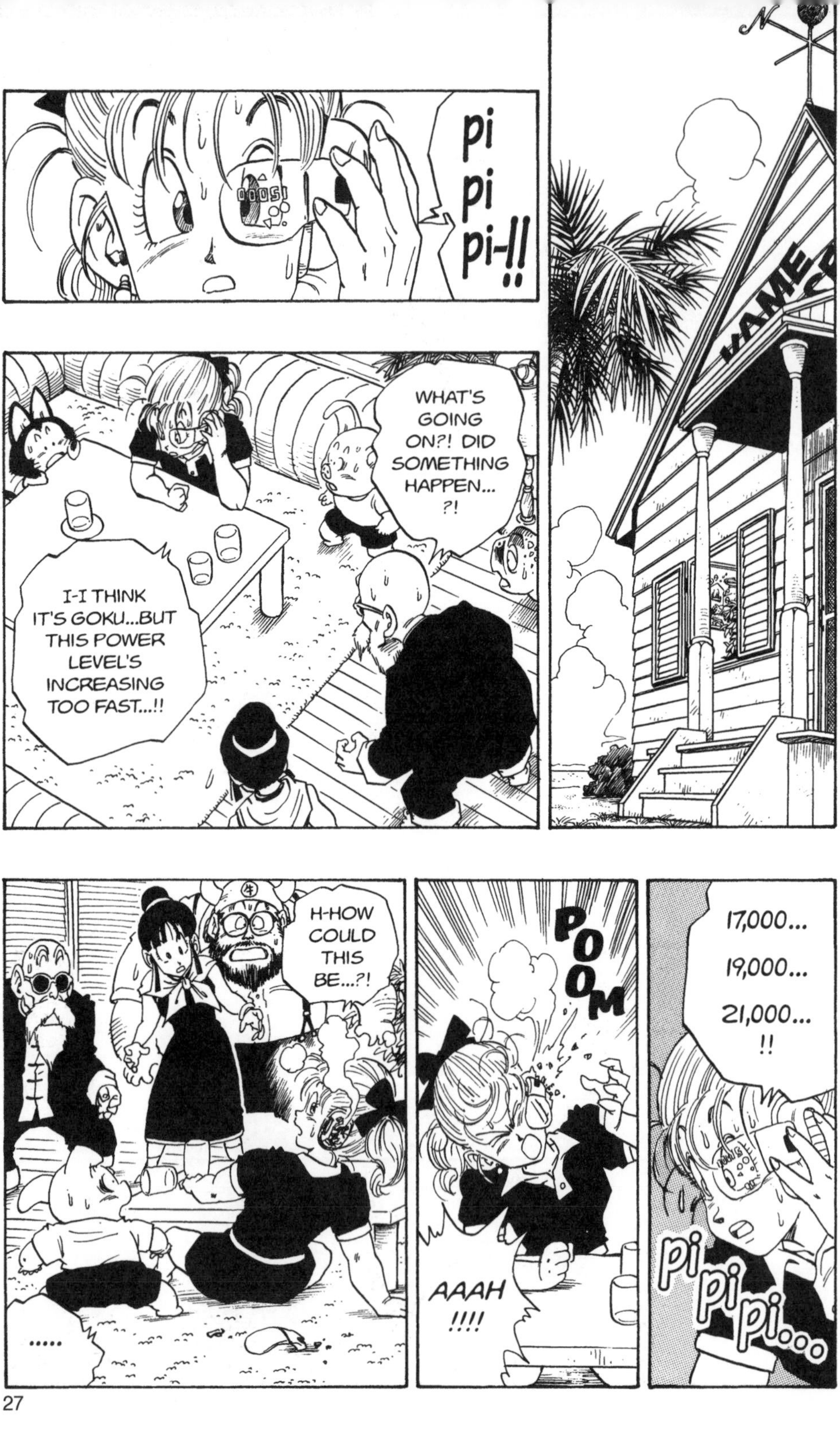
KAME
pi pi pi-!!
WHAT'S GOING ON?! DID SOMETHING HAPPEN...?!
I-I THINK IT'S GOKU...BUT THIS POWER LEVEL'S INCREASING TOO FAST...!!
17,000... 19,000... 21,000...!!
pi pi pi...
POOM
AAAH!!!!
H-HOW COULD THIS BE...?!
.....

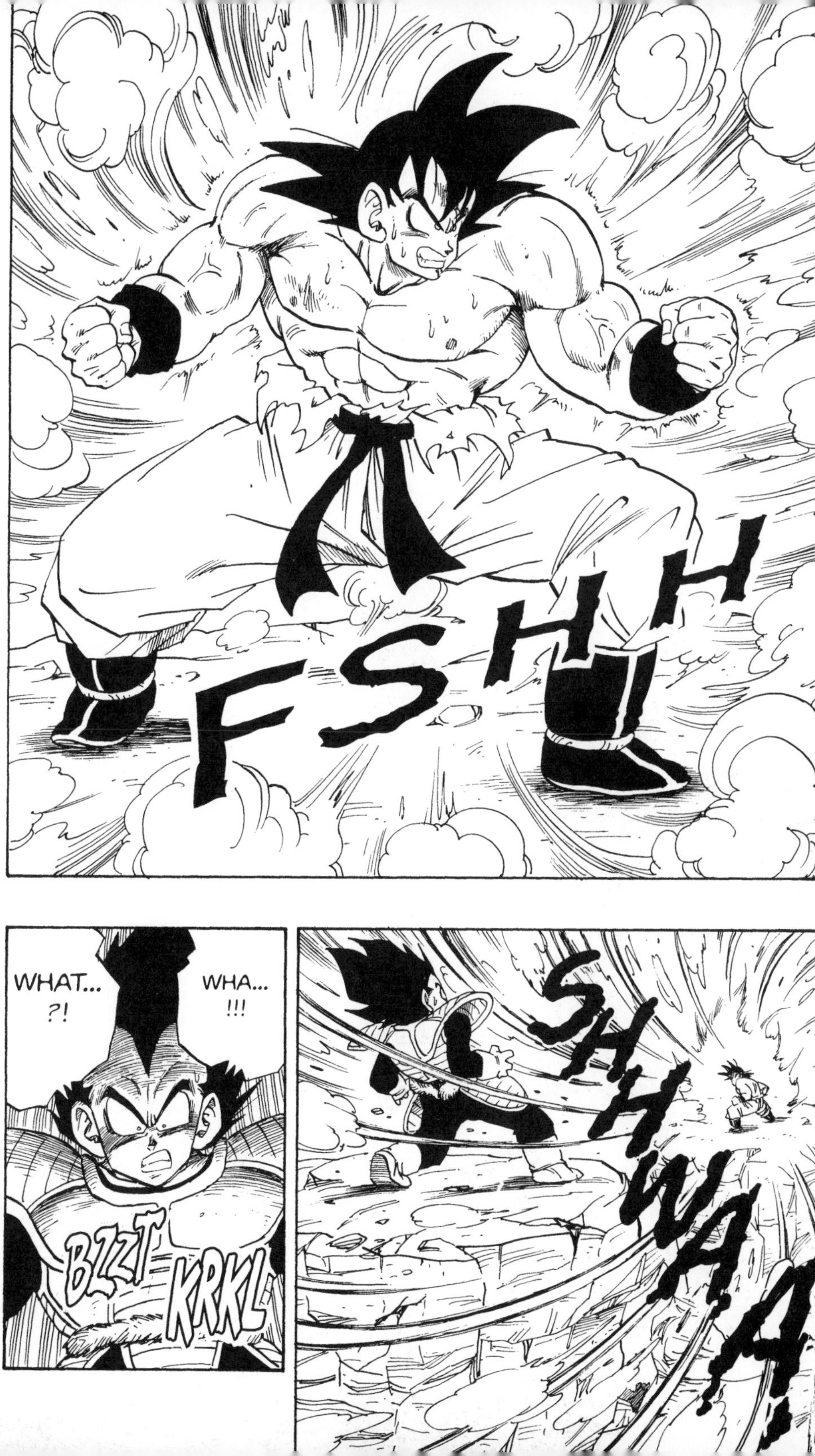
FSHHH
SHHWAA
WHA... !!!
WHAT... ?!
BZZT
KRKL

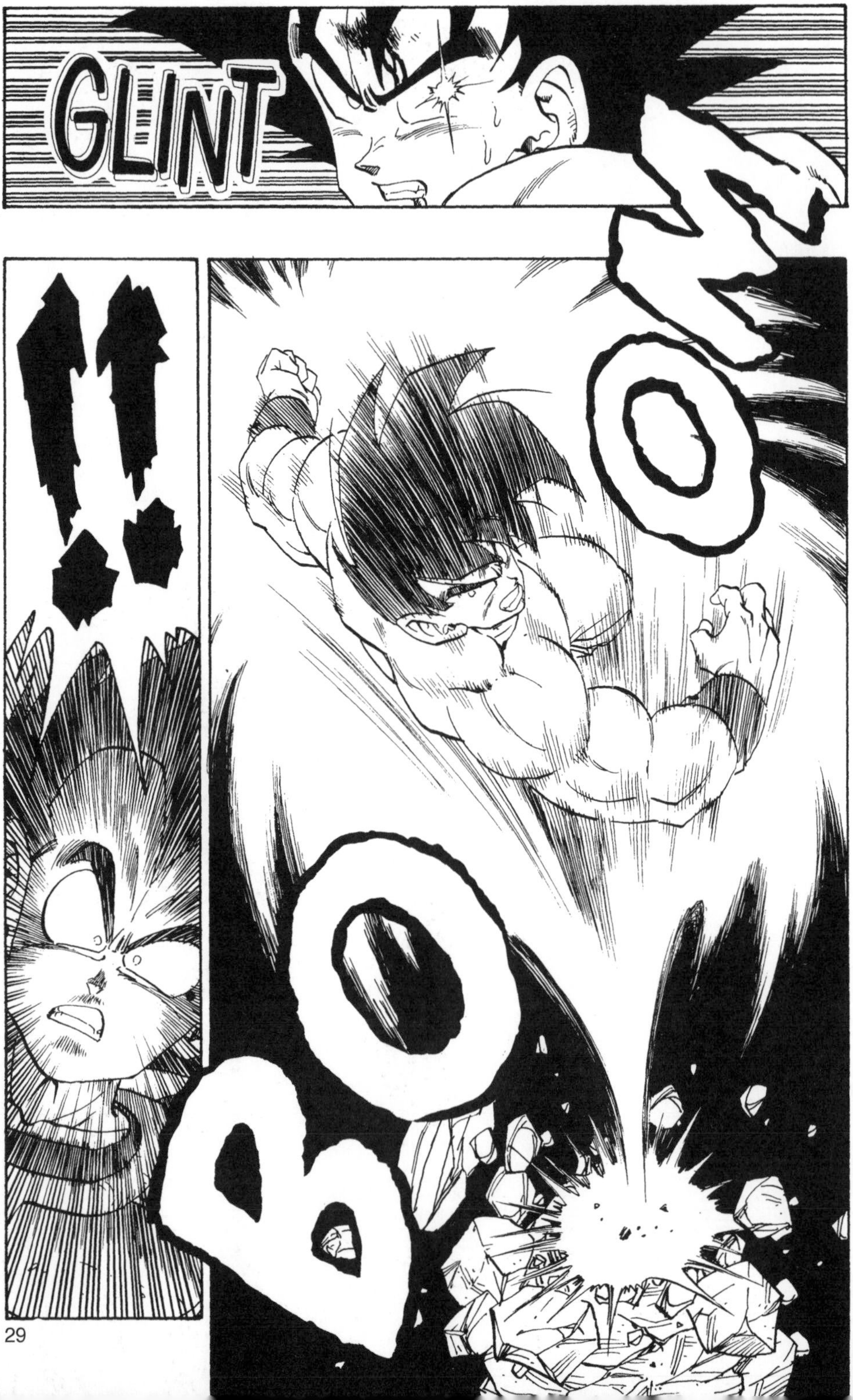
GLINT
BOOM
!!

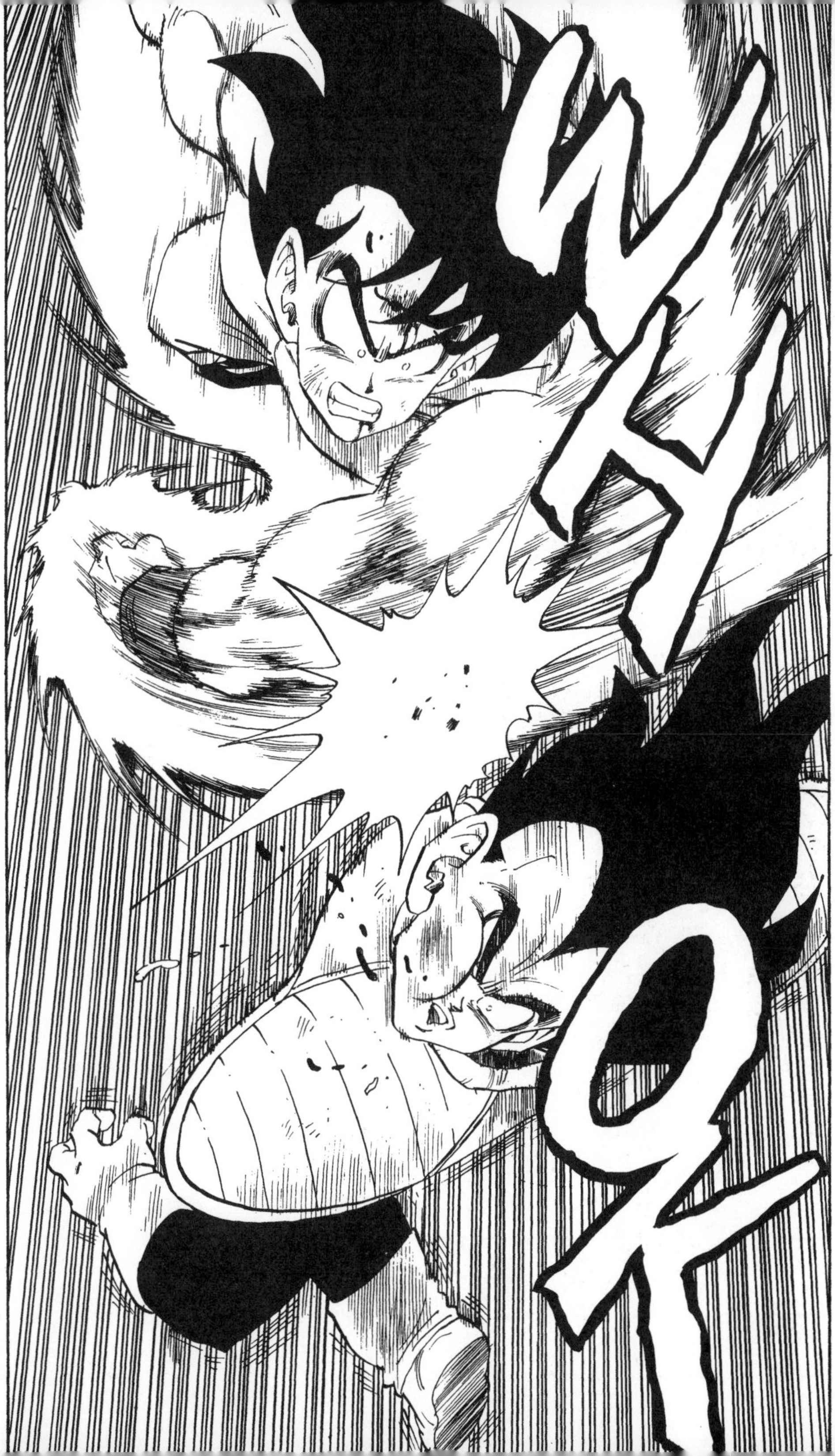

BOOM
FOOSH
DOOM

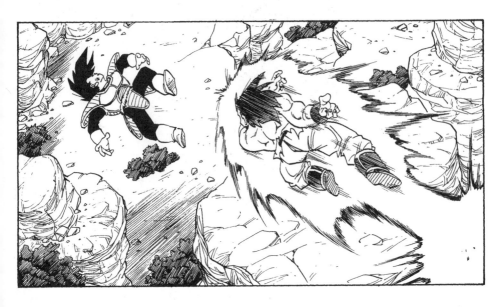

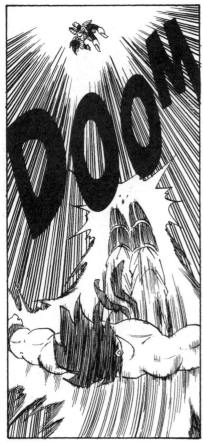

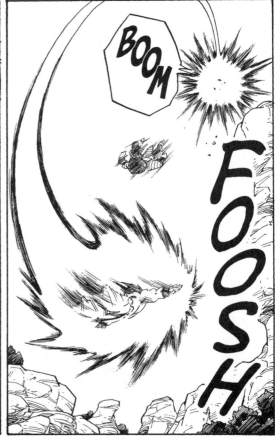

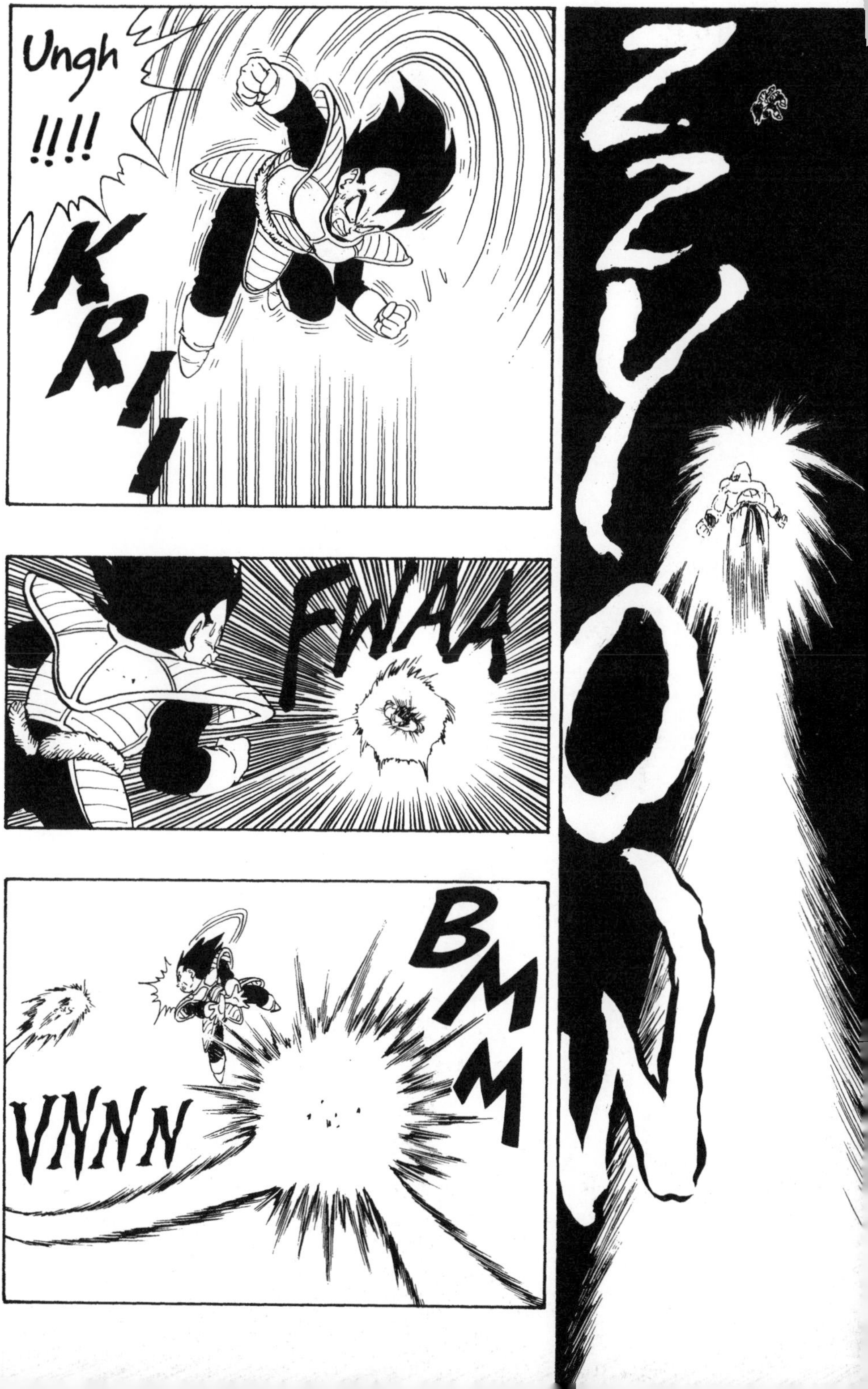
ZZUON
Ungh !!!!
KRII
FWAA
BMMM
VNNN

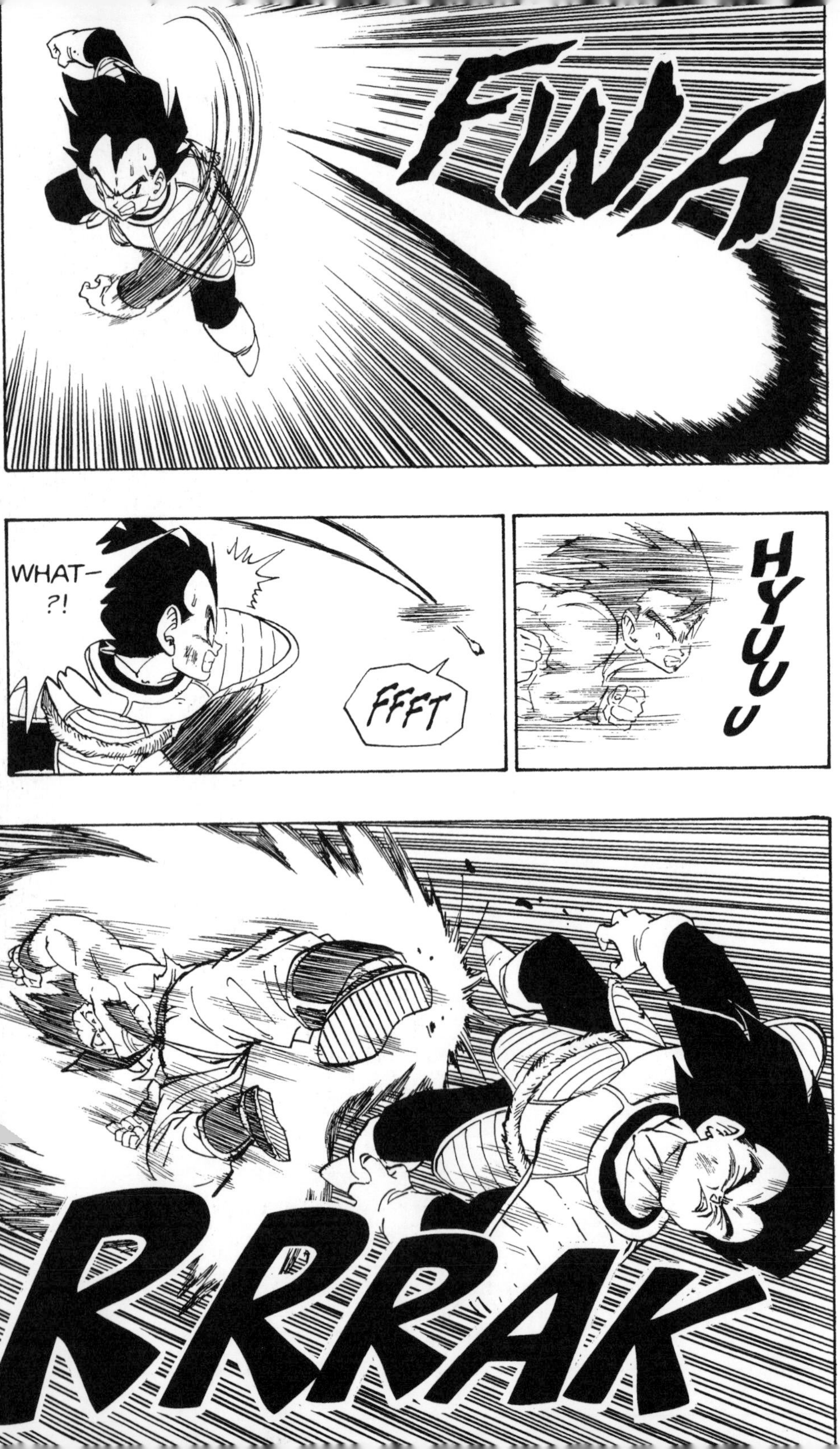
FWA
HYUUUU
WHAT— ?!
FFFT
RRRAK

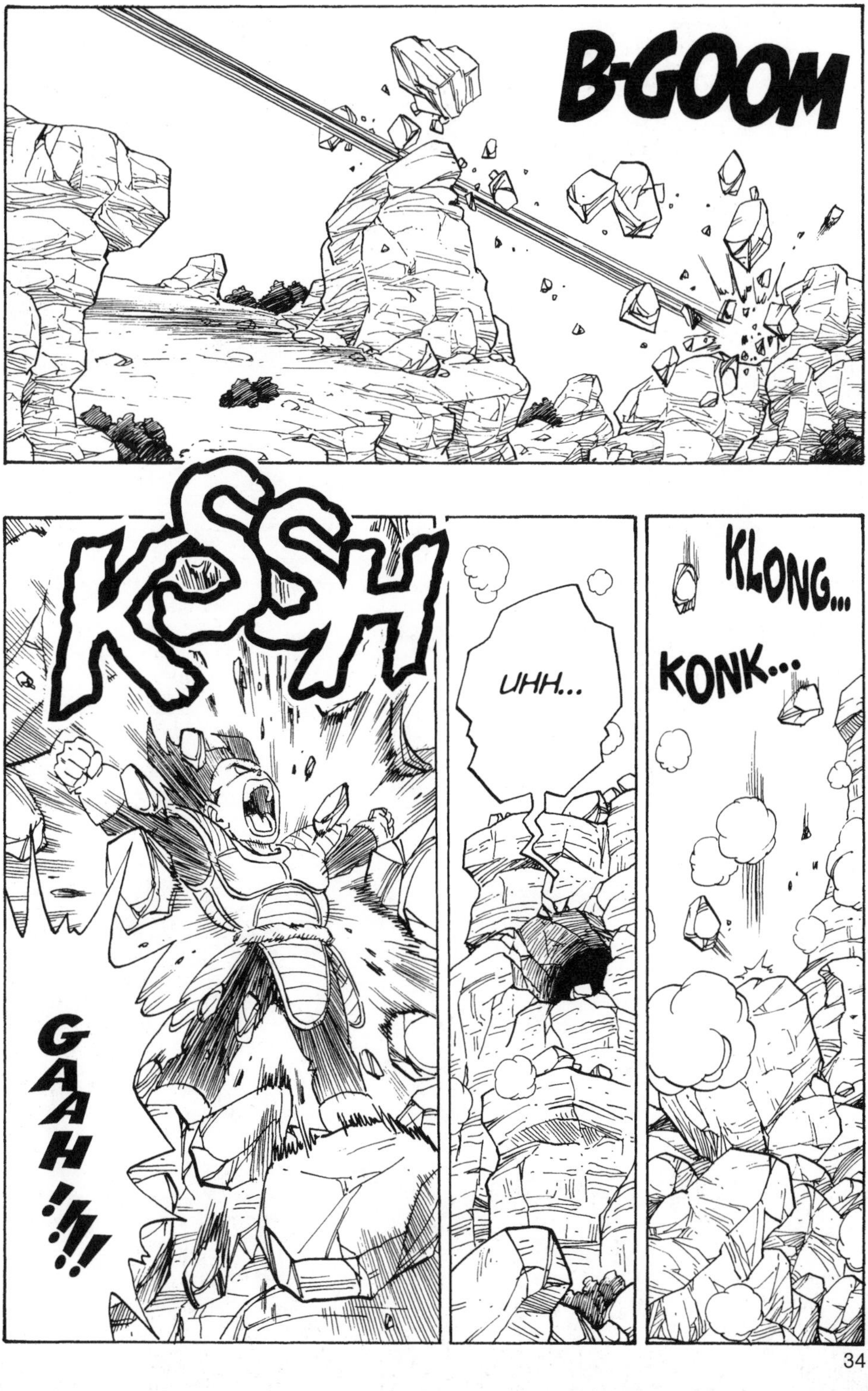
B-GOOM
KLONG...
KONK...
UHH...
KSSH
GAAH!!!!

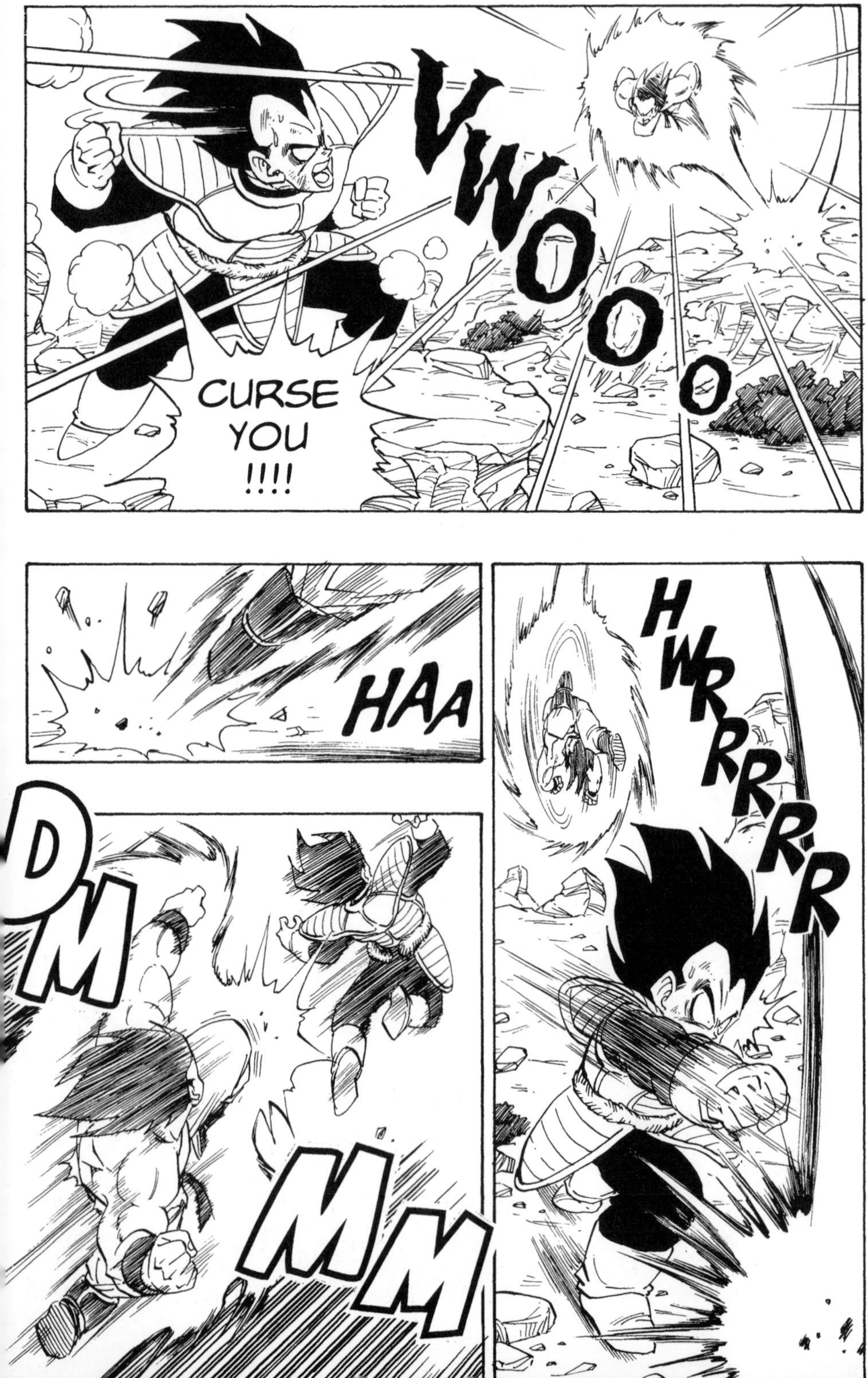
VWOOOO
CURSE YOU !!!!
HWRRRRRR
HAA
DMMM

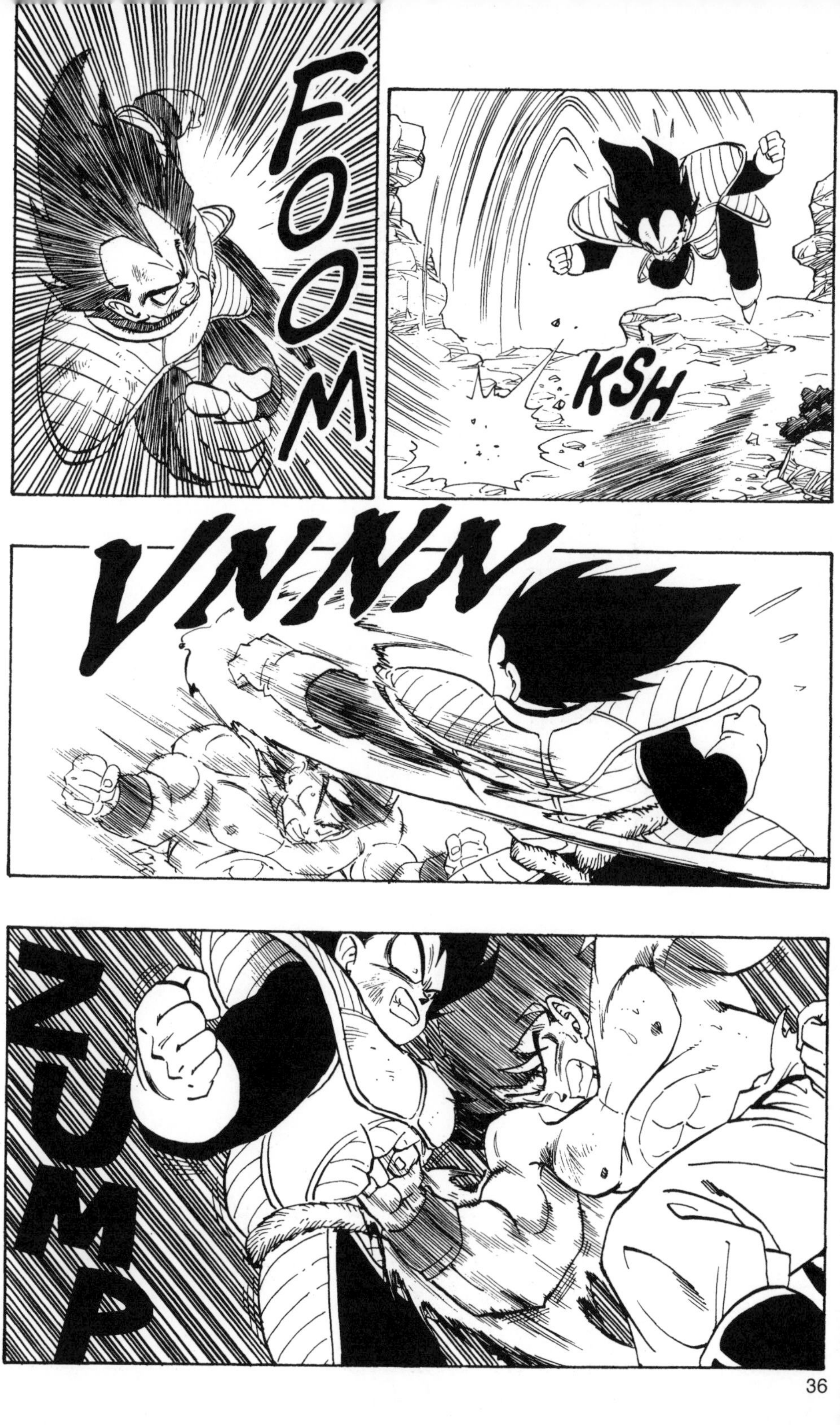
KSH
FOOM
VNNN
NUMP

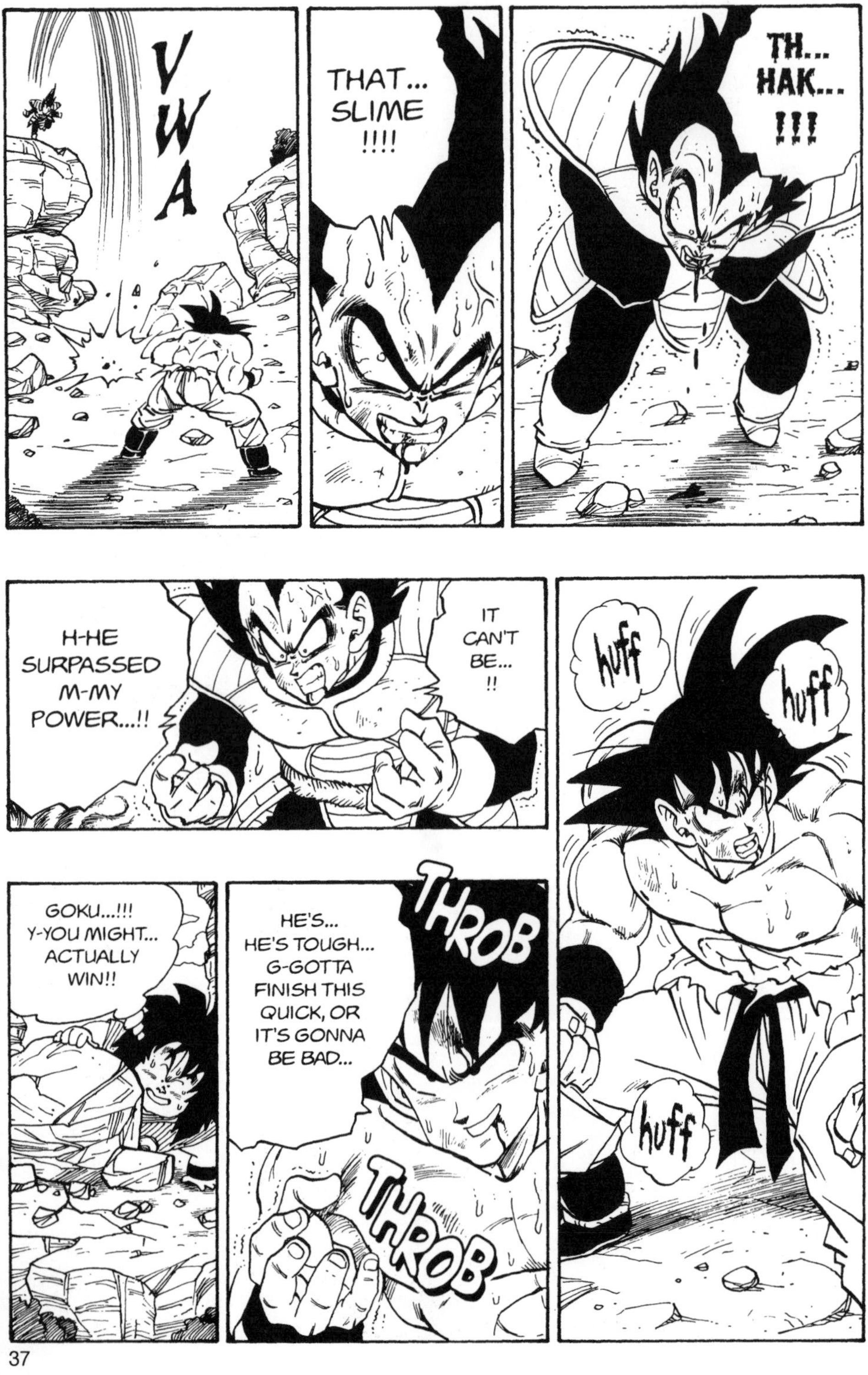
TH... HAK... !!!
THAT... SLIME !!!!
VWA
huff
huff
huff
IT CAN'T BE... !!
H-HE SURPASSED M-MY POWER...!!
THROB
HE'S... HE'S TOUGH... G-GOTTA FINISH THIS QUICK, OR IT'S GONNA BE BAD...
THROB
GOKU...!!! Y-YOU MIGHT... ACTUALLY WIN!!

# DBZ:37 • Battle in the Red Zone!

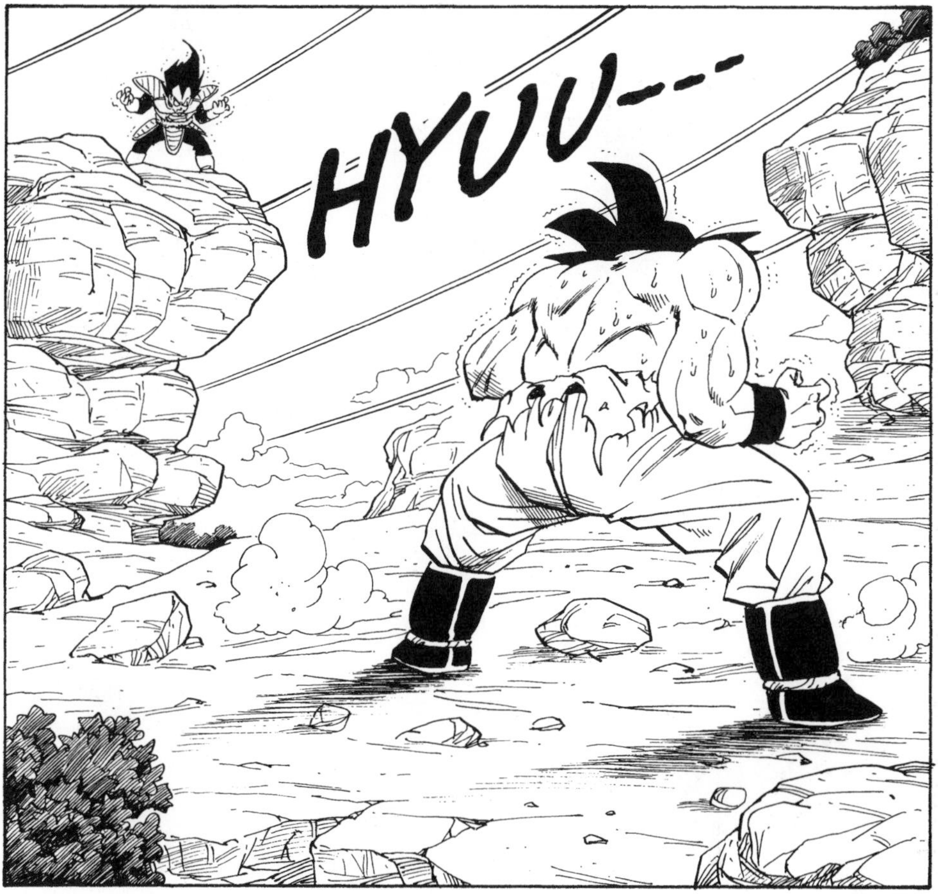
HYUU---

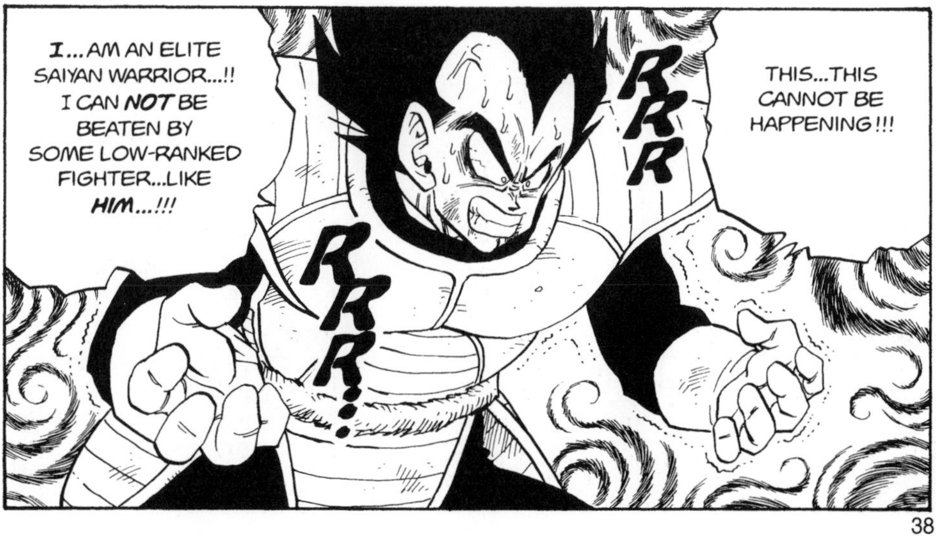
THIS...THIS CANNOT BE HAPPENING!!!
RRR
I...AM AN ELITE SAIYAN WARRIOR...!! I CAN **NOT** BE BEATEN BY SOME LOW-RANKED FIGHTER...LIKE **HIM**...!!!
RRR!!

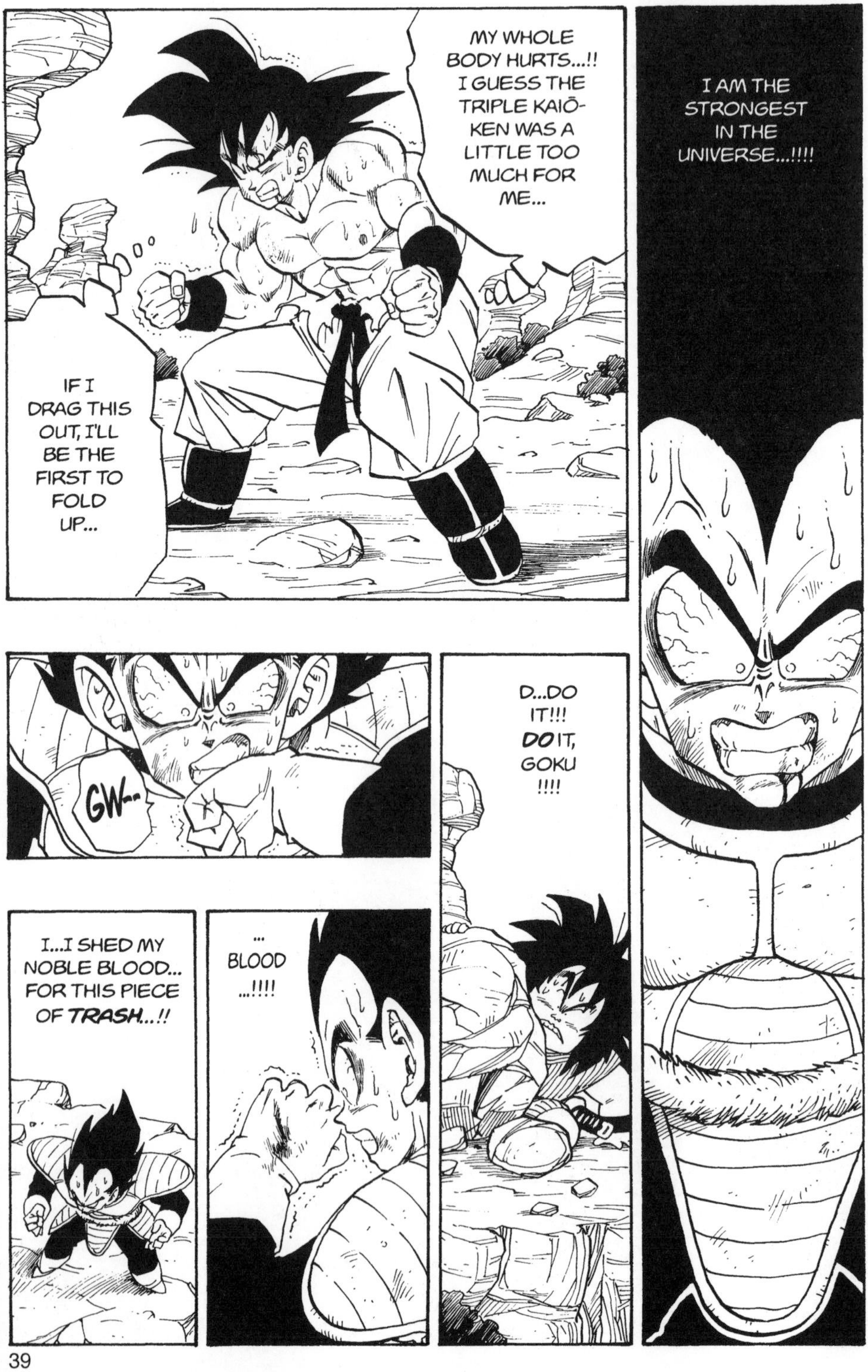
I AM THE STRONGEST IN THE UNIVERSE...!!!!
MY WHOLE BODY HURTS...!! I GUESS THE TRIPLE KAIŌ-KEN WAS A LITTLE TOO MUCH FOR ME...
IF I DRAG THIS OUT, I'LL BE THE FIRST TO FOLD UP...
D...DO IT!!! **DO** IT, GOKU !!!!
GW--
... BLOOD ...!!!!
I...I SHED MY NOBLE BLOOD... FOR THIS PIECE OF ***TRASH***...!!

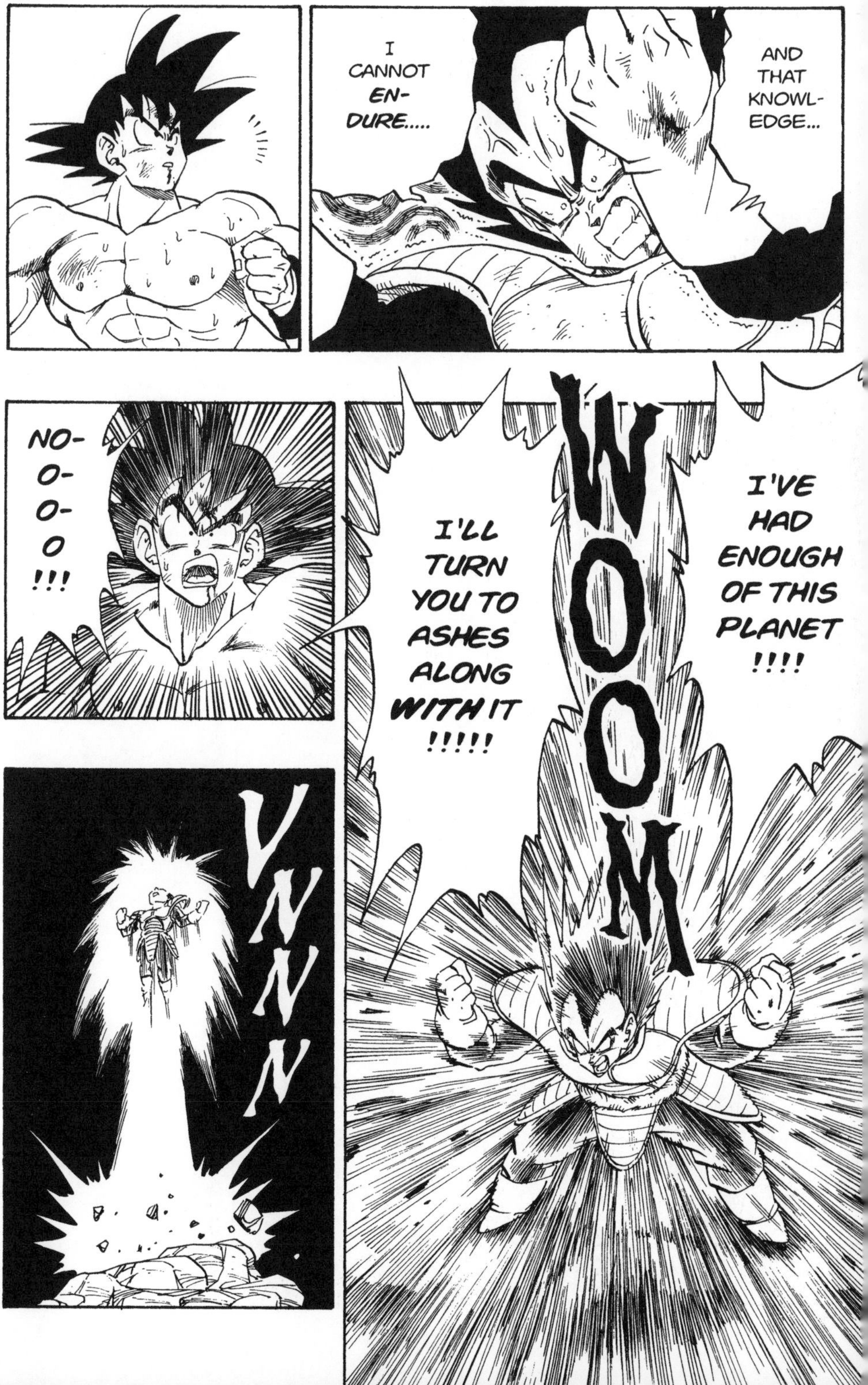
AND THAT KNOWL- EDGE...
I CANNOT EN- DURE.....
I'VE HAD ENOUGH OF THIS PLANET !!!!
WOOM
I'LL TURN YOU TO ASHES ALONG WITH IT !!!!!
NO- O- O- O !!!
VNNN

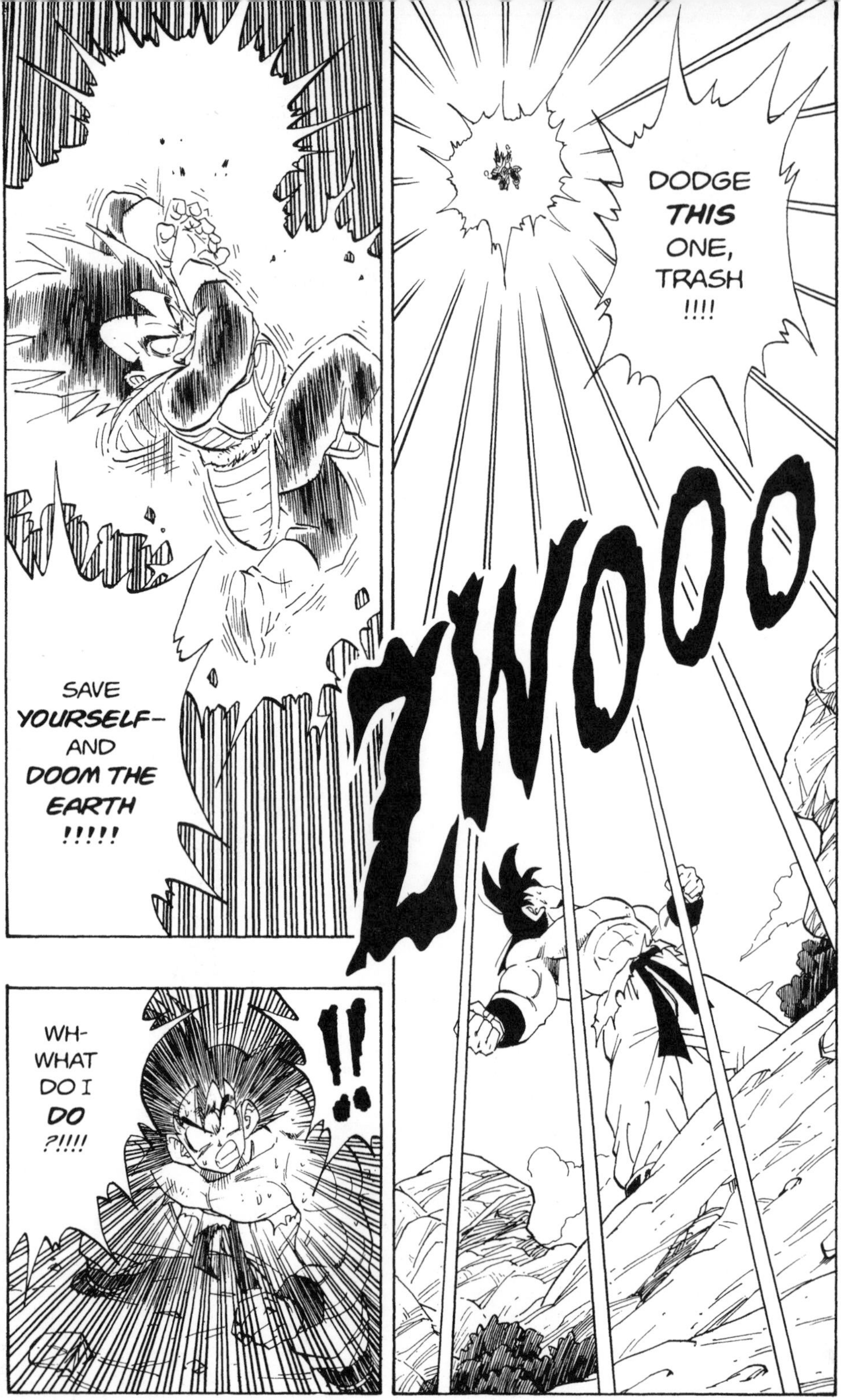
DODGE THIS ONE, TRASH !!!!
ZWOOO
SAVE YOURSELF—AND DOOM THE EARTH !!!!!
WH-WHAT DO I DO ?!!!!
!!

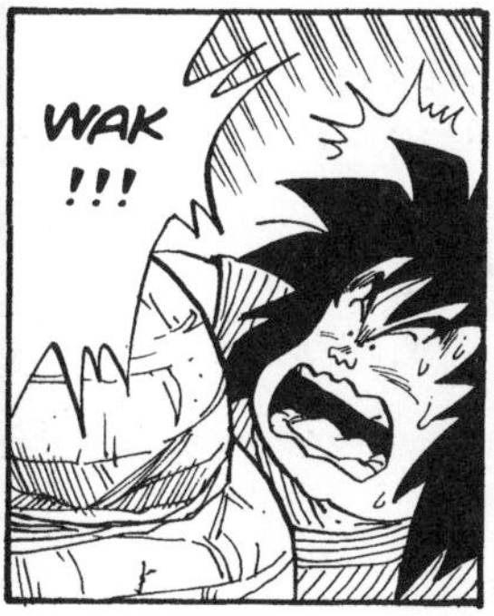
WAK
!!!
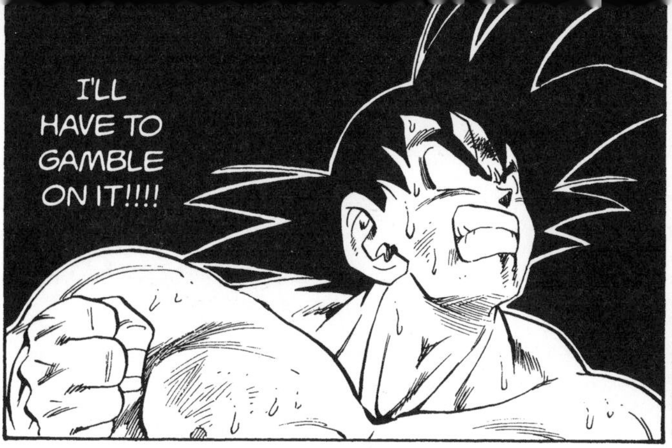
I'LL HAVE TO GAMBLE ON IT!!!!
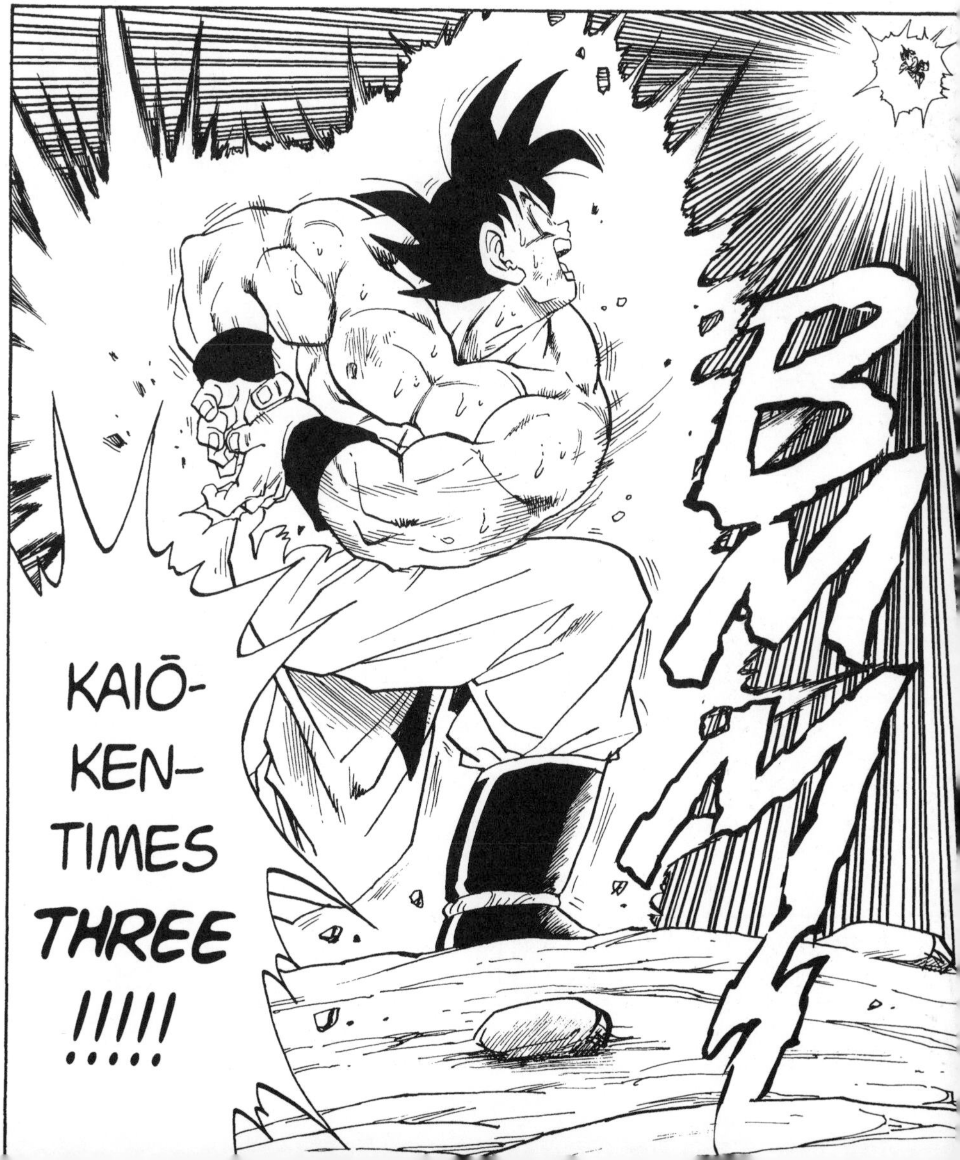
KAIŌ-KEN-TIMES THREE
!!!!!

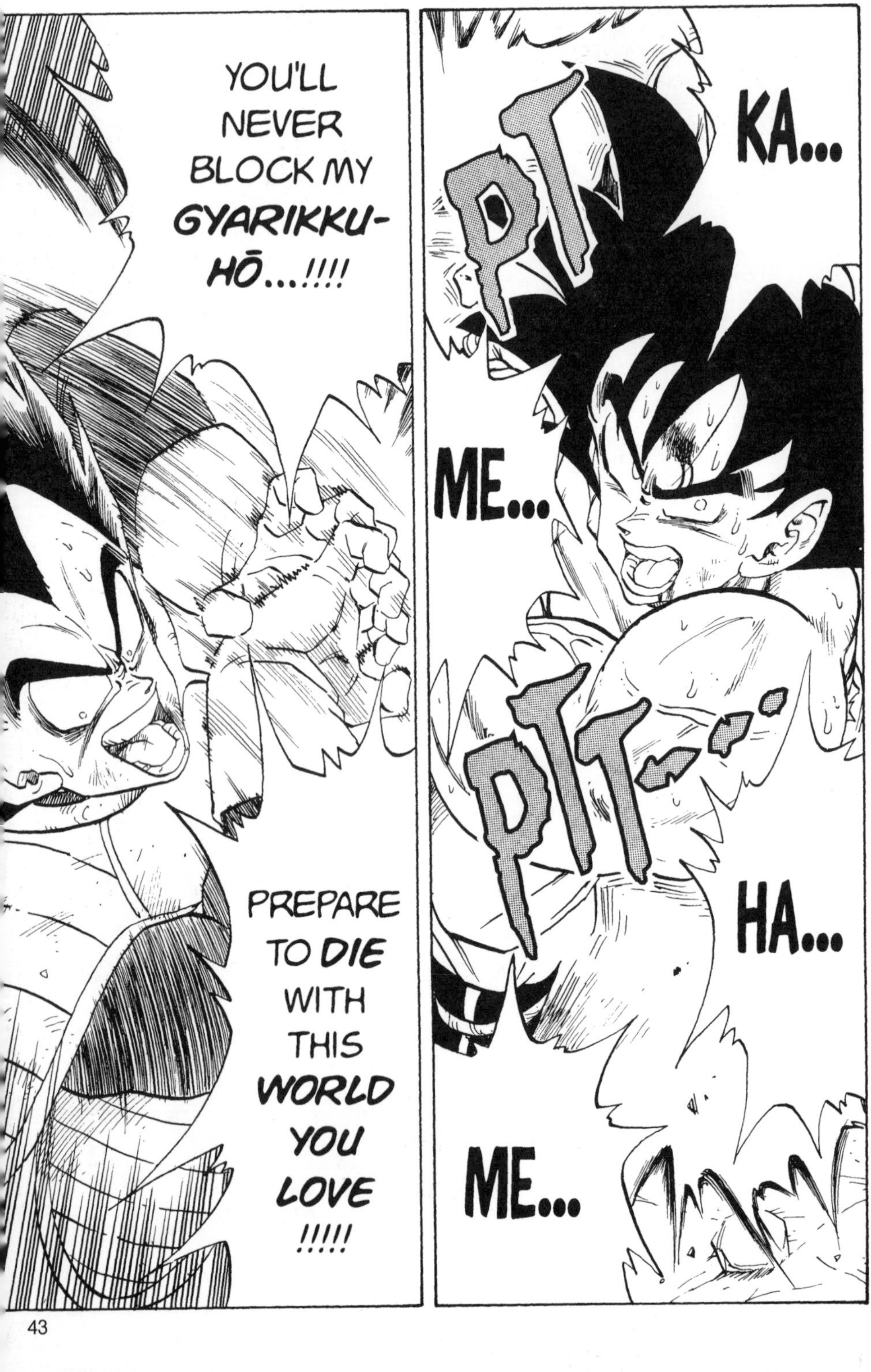
KA...
PIT
ME...
PIT...
HA...
ME...
YOU'LL NEVER BLOCK MY GYARIKKU-HŌ...!!!!
PREPARE TO DIE WITH THIS WORLD YOU LOVE !!!!!

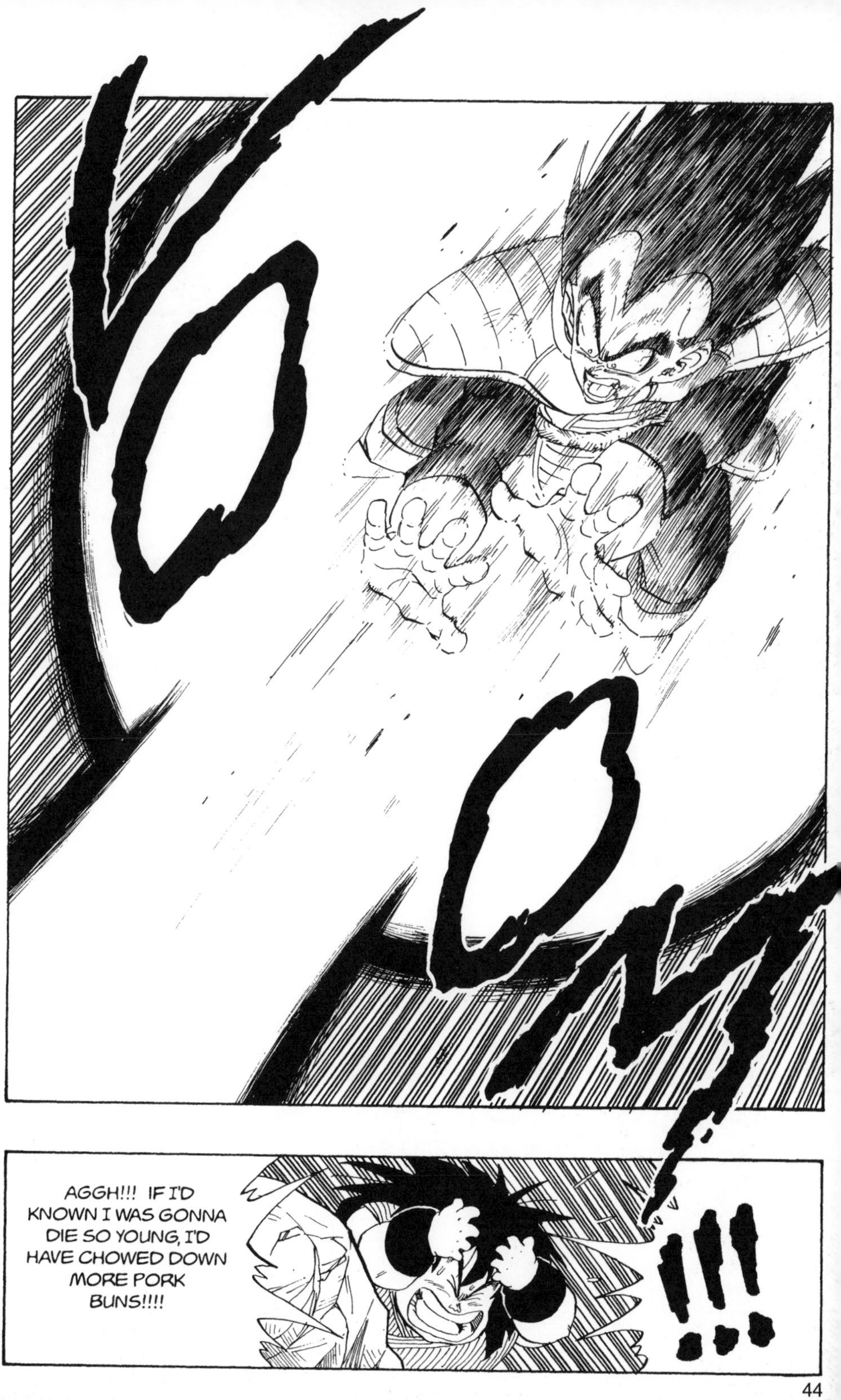
AGGH!!! IF I'D KNOWN I WAS GONNA DIE SO YOUNG, I'D HAVE CHOWED DOWN MORE PORK BUNS!!!!

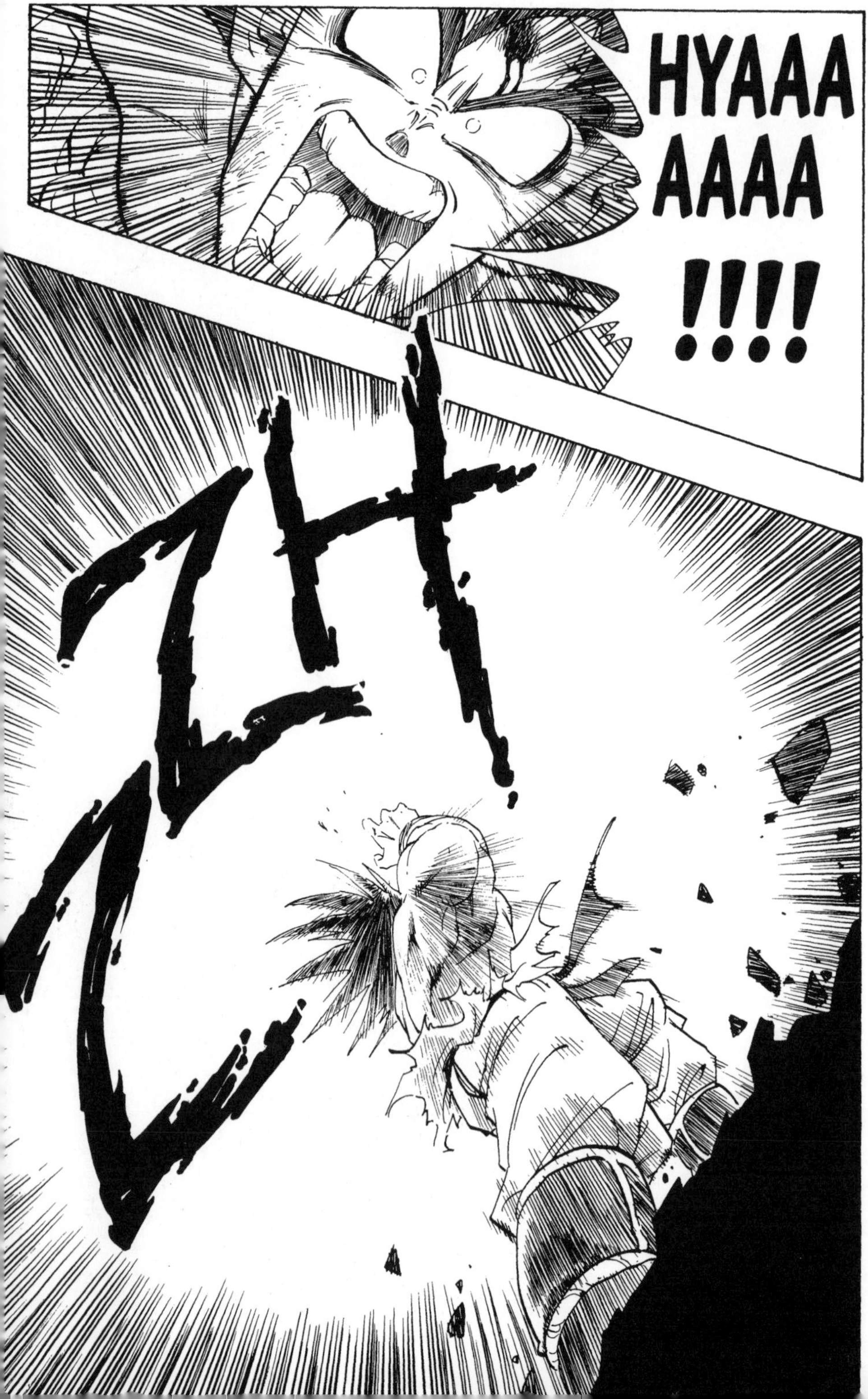
HYAAA
AAAA
!!!!

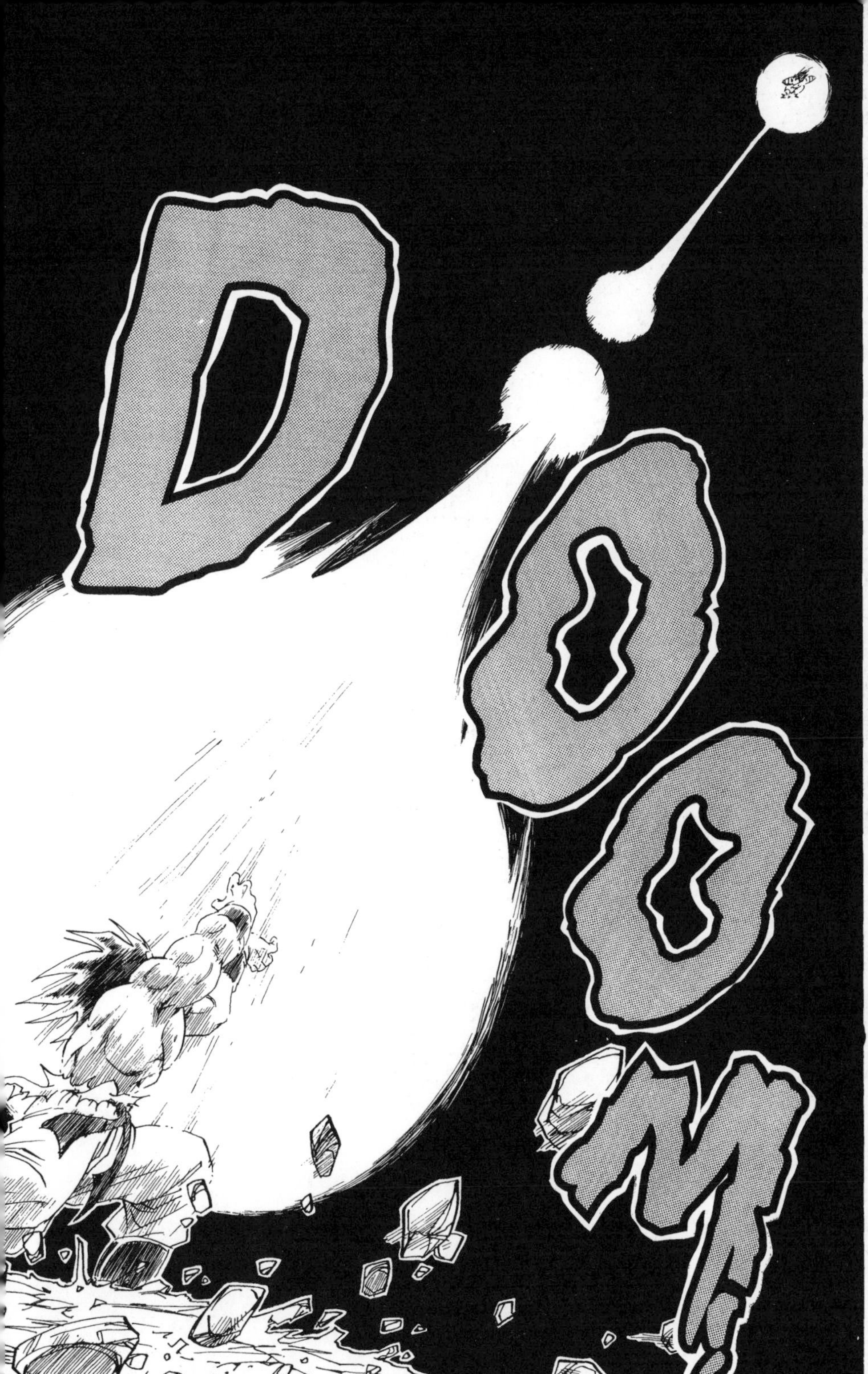
DOOM

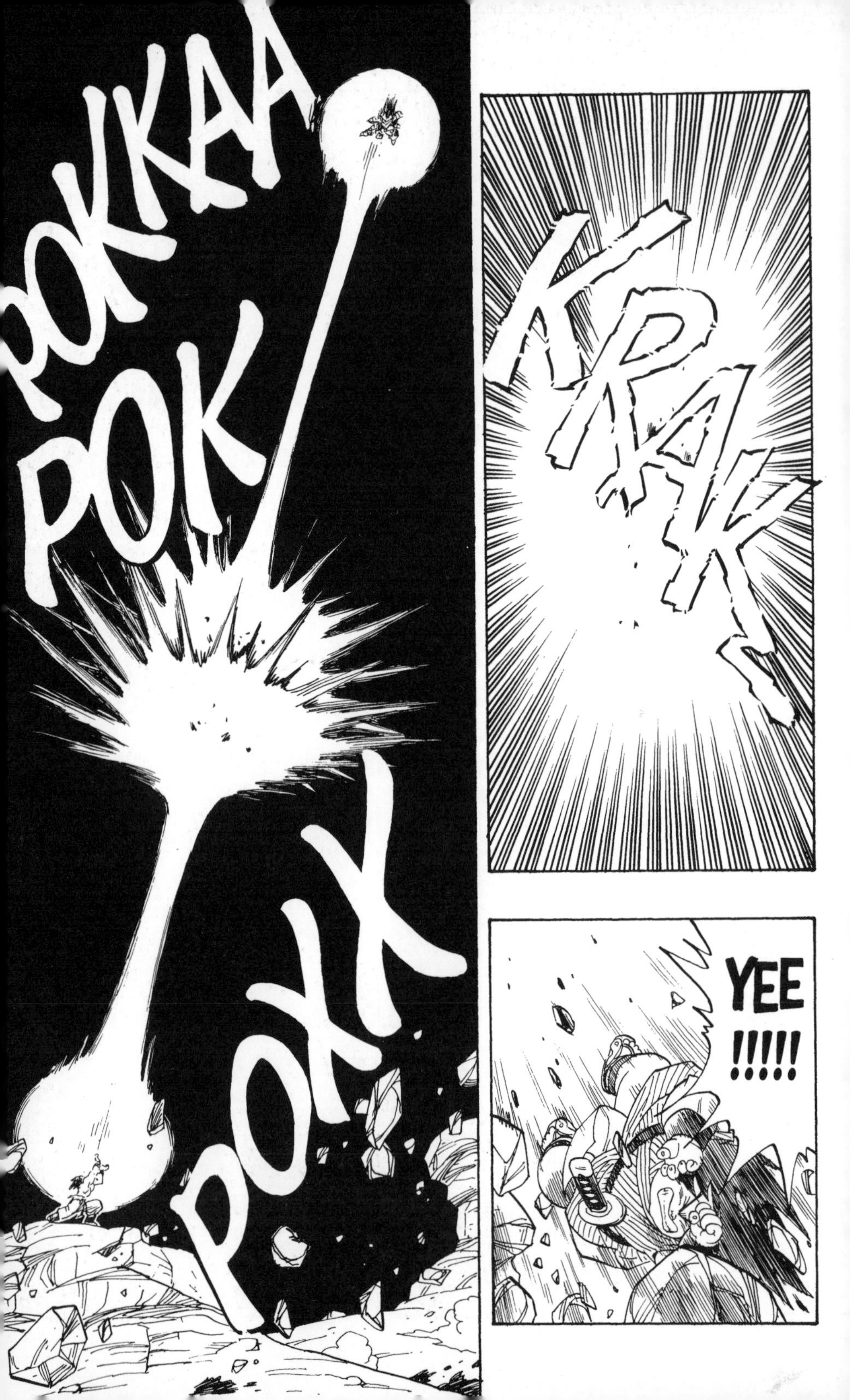

KRAAK
YEE
!!!!!
POKKAA
POK
POK

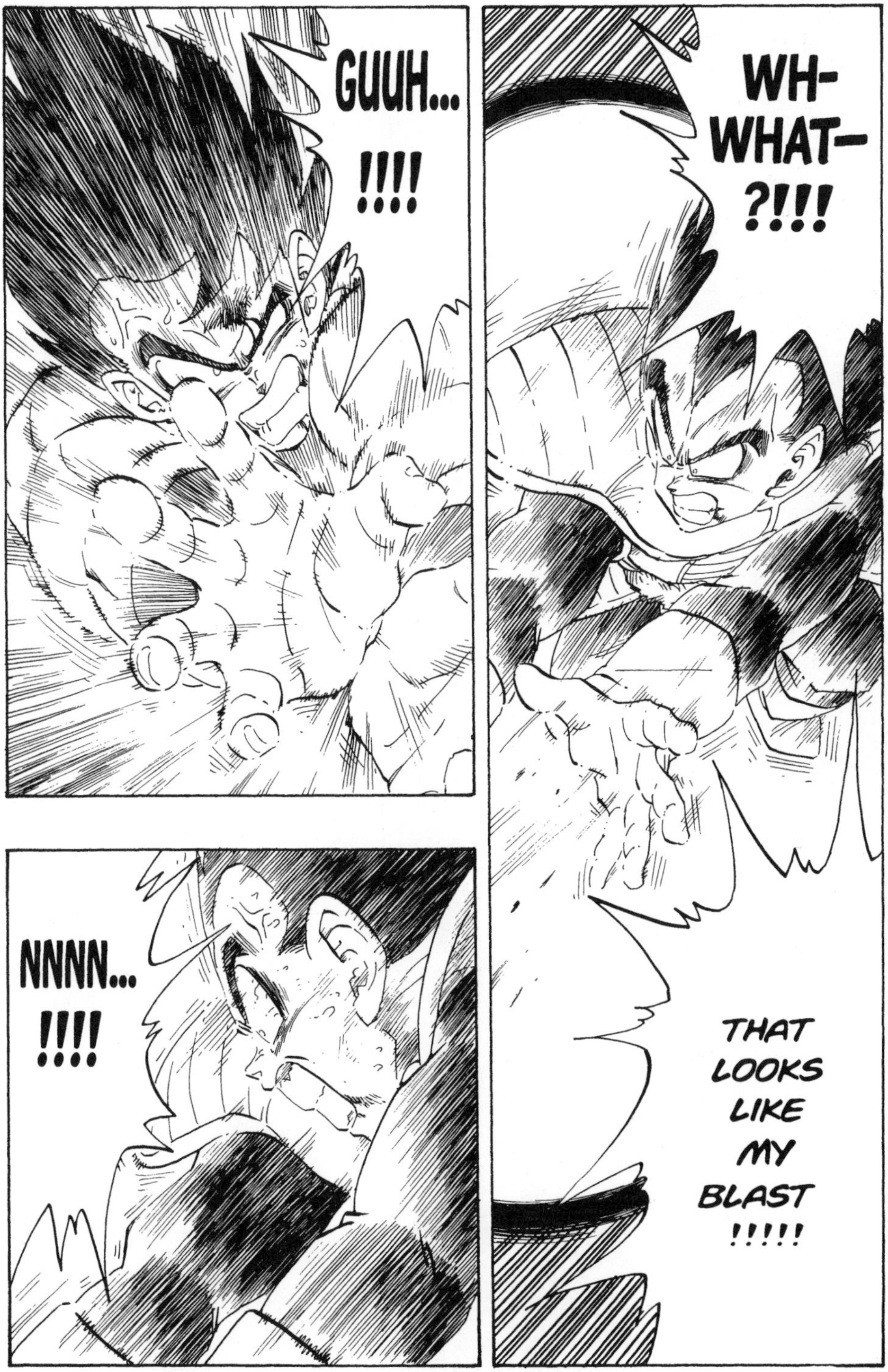
WH-WHAT-?!!!
THAT LOOKS LIKE MY BLAST!!!!!
GUUH... !!!!
NNNN... !!!!

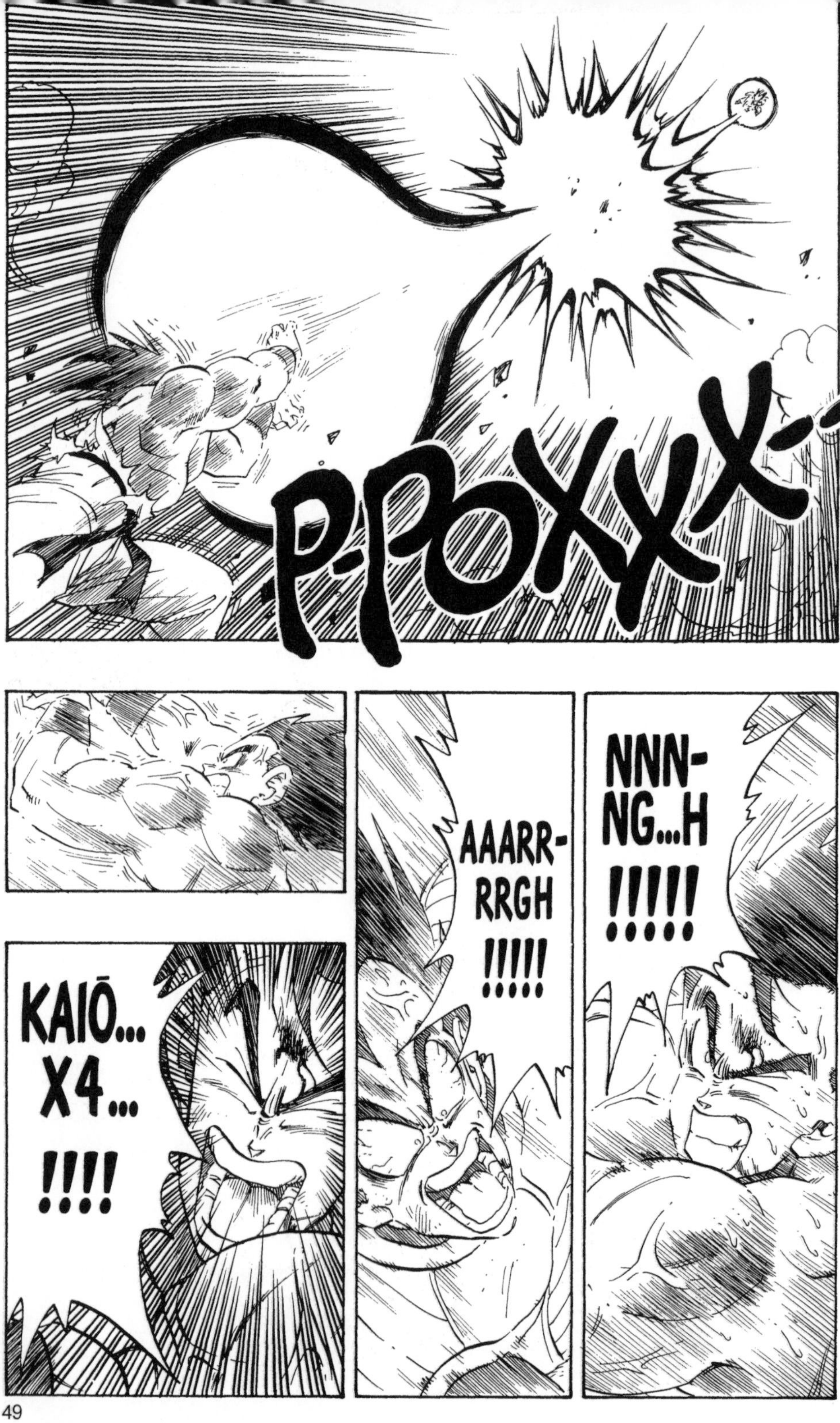
P-POXXX
NNN-NG...H!!!!!
AAARR-RRGH!!!!!
KAIŌ... X4... !!!!

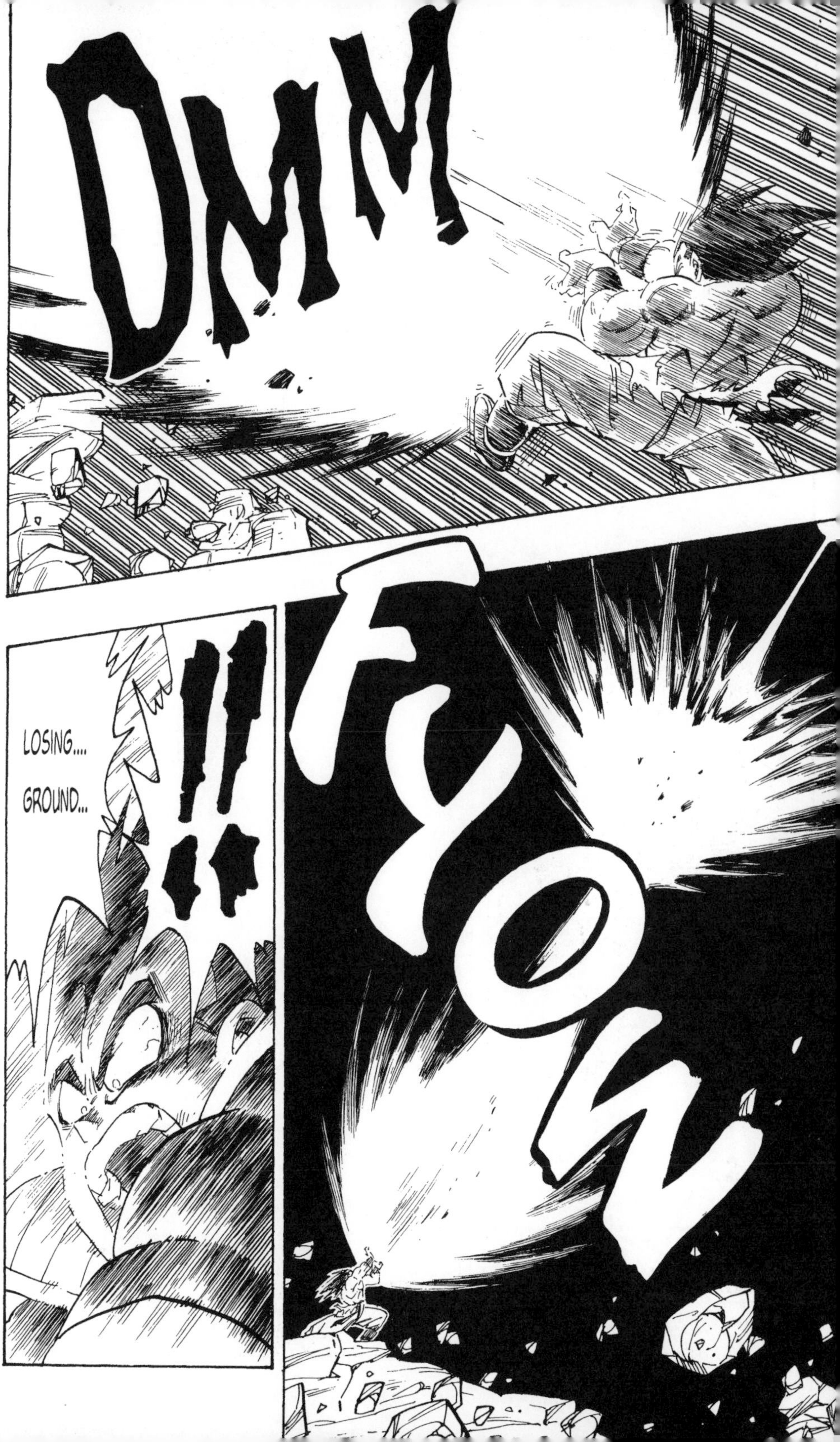
DMM
!!
LOSING....
GROUND...

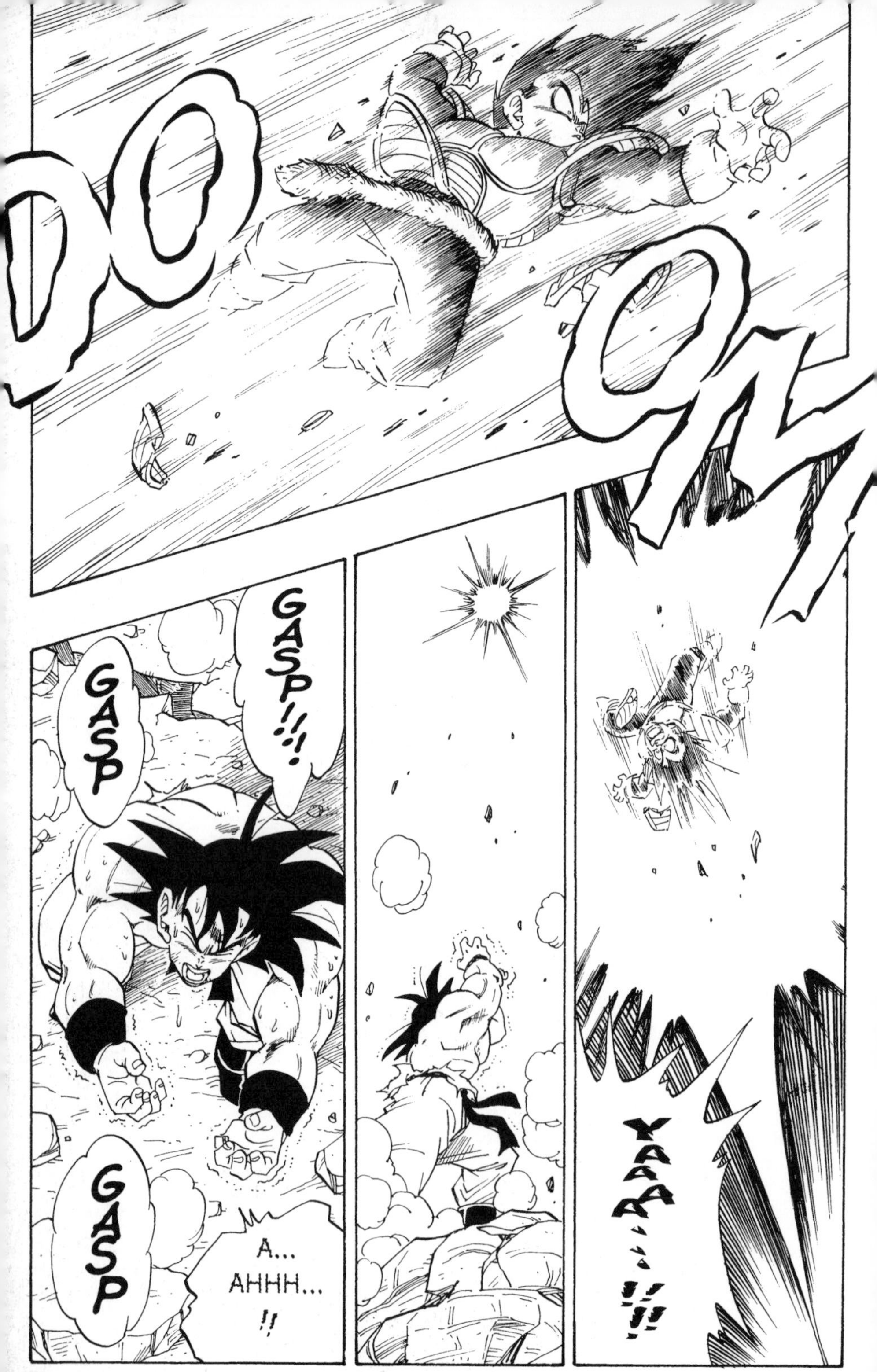
DOOON
YAAAA...!!!
GASP!!!
GASP
A... AHHH...!!
GASP

# DBZ:38 • The Moon

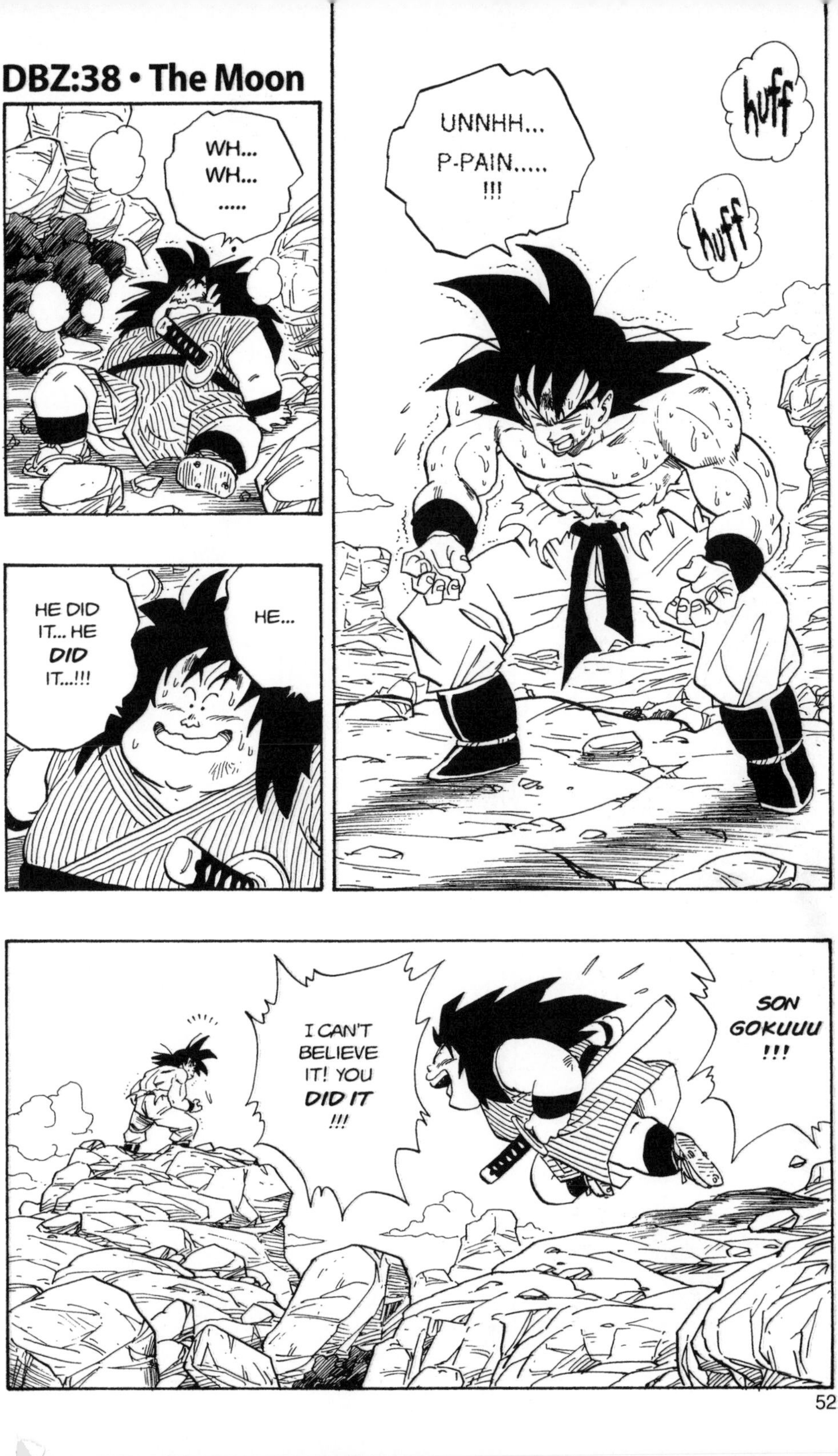
huff
huff
UNNHH... P-PAIN..... !!!
WH... WH... .....
HE...
HE DID IT... HE DID IT...!!!
SON GOKUUU !!!
I CAN'T BELIEVE IT! YOU DID IT !!!

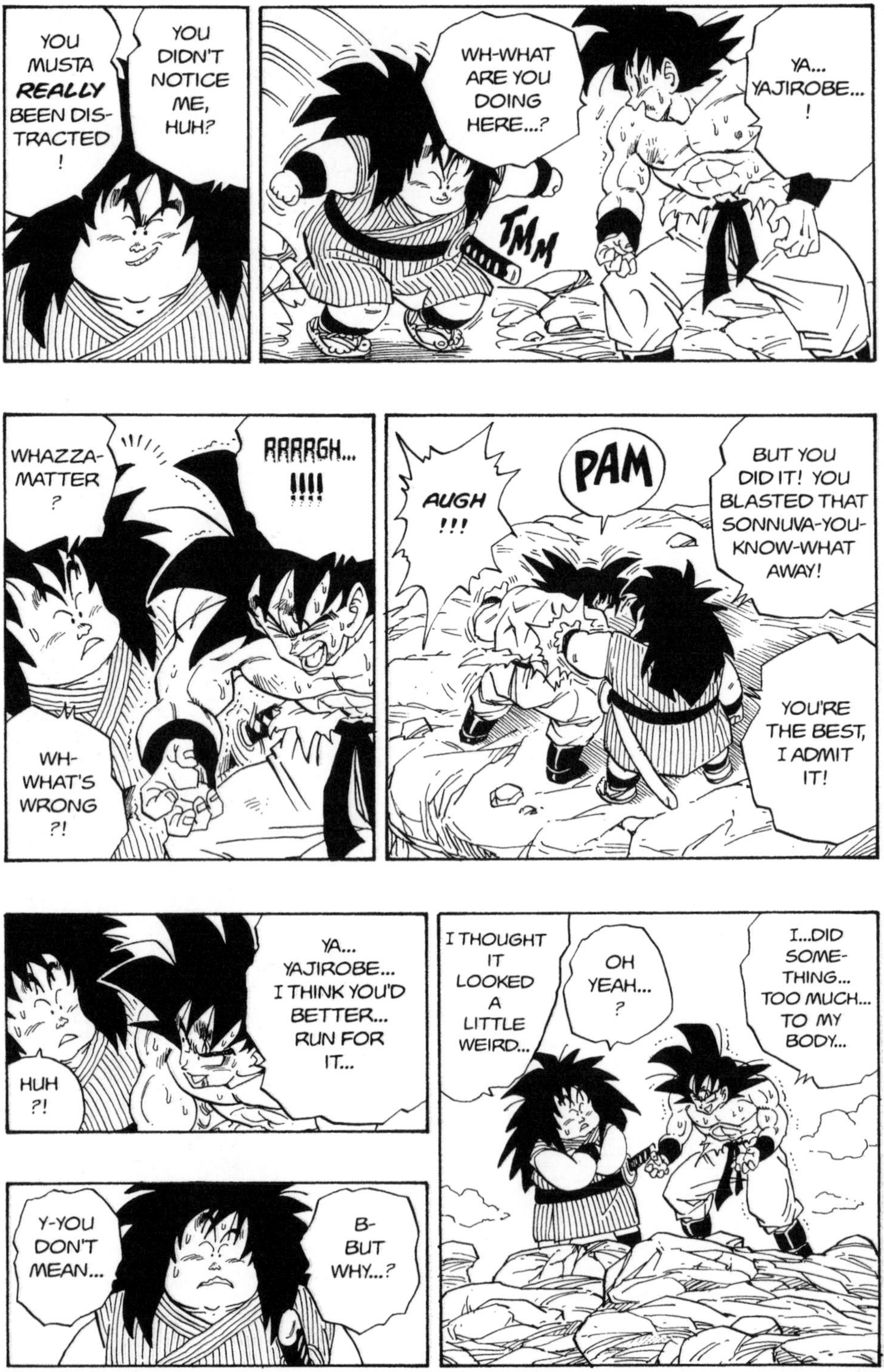

YA... YAJIROBE... !
WH-WHAT ARE YOU DOING HERE...?
TMM
YOU DIDN'T NOTICE ME, HUH?
YOU MUSTA **REALLY** BEEN DIS-TRACTED !
BUT YOU DID IT! YOU BLASTED THAT SONNUVA-YOU-KNOW-WHAT AWAY!
PAM
AUGH !!!
YOU'RE THE BEST, I ADMIT IT!
RRRRGH... !!!!
WHAZZA-MATTER ?
WH-WHAT'S WRONG ?!
I...DID SOME-THING... TOO MUCH... TO MY BODY...
OH YEAH... ?
I THOUGHT IT LOOKED A LITTLE WEIRD...
YA... YAJIROBE... I THINK YOU'D BETTER... RUN FOR IT...
HUH ?!
B-BUT WHY...?
Y-YOU DON'T MEAN...

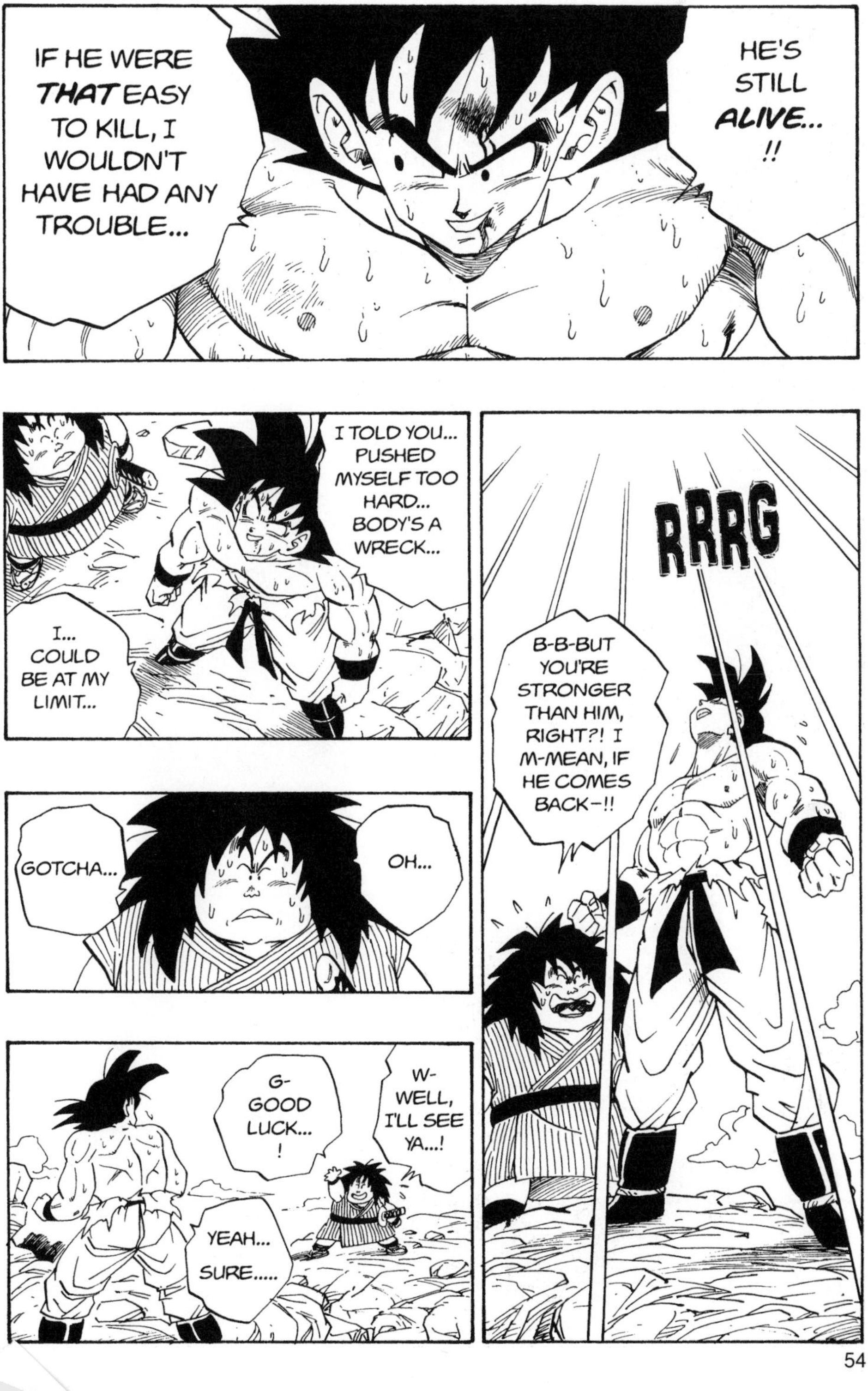
HE'S STILL ALIVE... !!
IF HE WERE THAT EASY TO KILL, I WOULDN'T HAVE HAD ANY TROUBLE...
RRRG
B-B-BUT YOU'RE STRONGER THAN HIM, RIGHT?! I M-MEAN, IF HE COMES BACK-!!
I TOLD YOU... PUSHED MYSELF TOO HARD... BODY'S A WRECK...
I... COULD BE AT MY LIMIT...
OH...
GOTCHA...
W-WELL, I'LL SEE YA...!
G-GOOD LUCK...!
YEAH... SURE.....

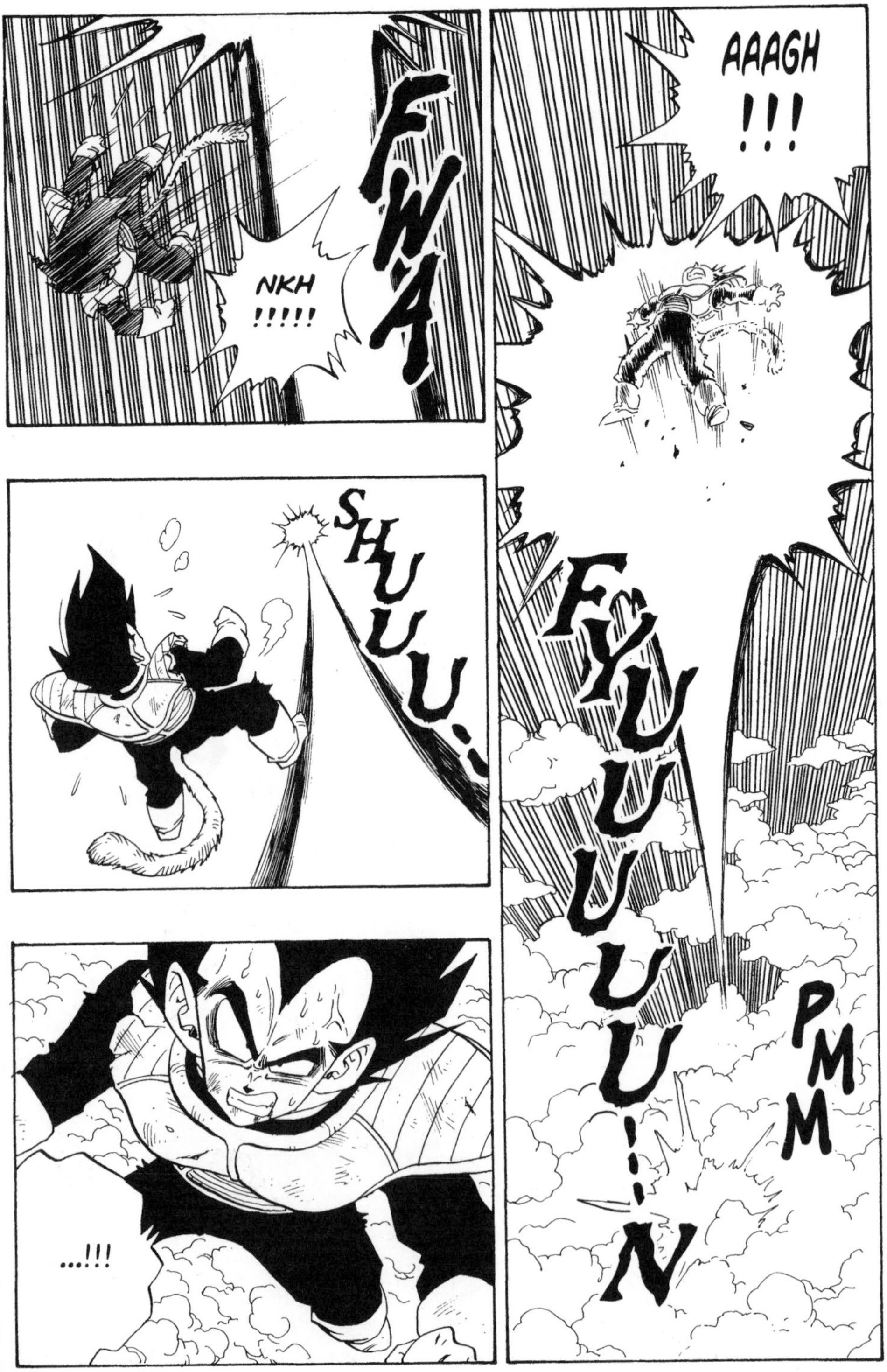
AAAGH !!!
FYUUUUU...N
PMM
FWA
NKH !!!!!
SHUUU...
...!!!

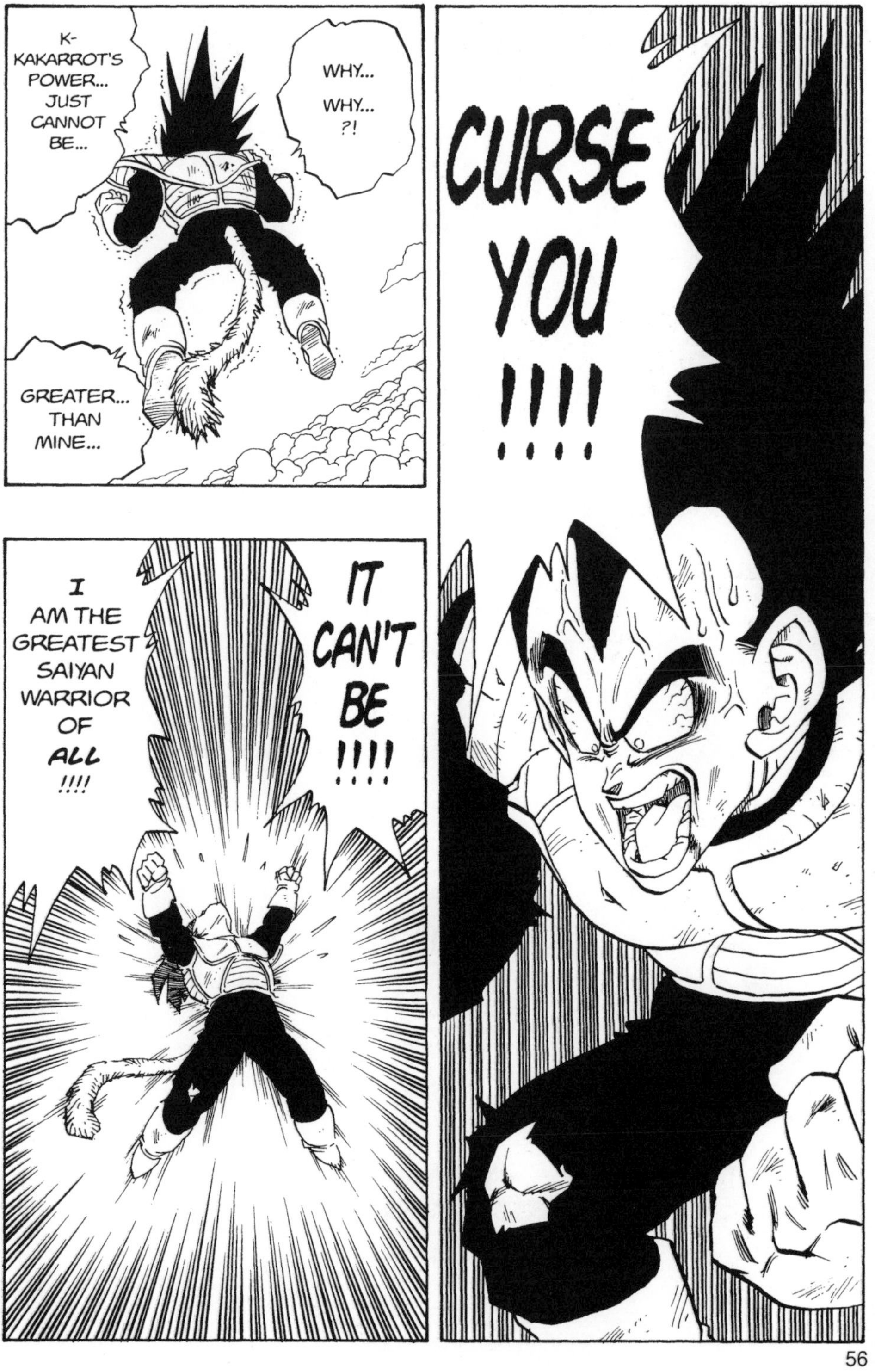
CURSE YOU !!!!
K-KAKARROT'S POWER... JUST CANNOT BE...
WHY... WHY...?!
GREATER... THAN MINE...
IT CAN'T BE !!!!
I AM THE GREATEST SAIYAN WARRIOR OF ALL !!!!

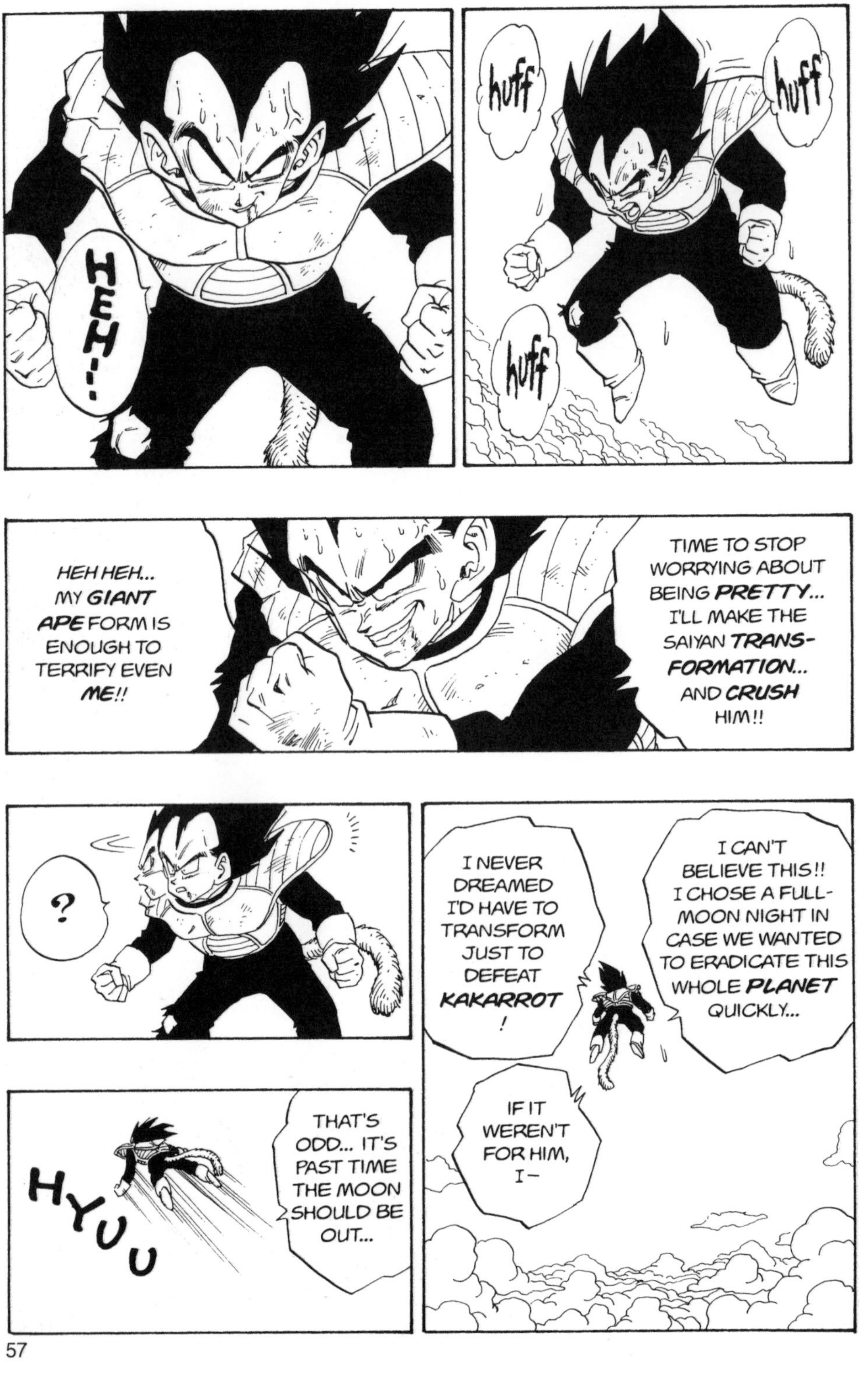
huff
huff
huff
HEH!!
TIME TO STOP WORRYING ABOUT BEING **PRETTY**... I'LL MAKE THE SAIYAN **TRANSFORMATION**... AND **CRUSH** HIM!!
HEH HEH... MY **GIANT APE** FORM IS ENOUGH TO TERRIFY EVEN **ME**!!
I CAN'T BELIEVE THIS!! I CHOSE A FULL-MOON NIGHT IN CASE WE WANTED TO ERADICATE THIS WHOLE **PLANET** QUICKLY...
I NEVER DREAMED I'D HAVE TO TRANSFORM JUST TO DEFEAT **KAKARROT**!
IF IT WEREN'T FOR HIM, I—
?
THAT'S ODD... IT'S PAST TIME THE MOON SHOULD BE OUT...
HYUU

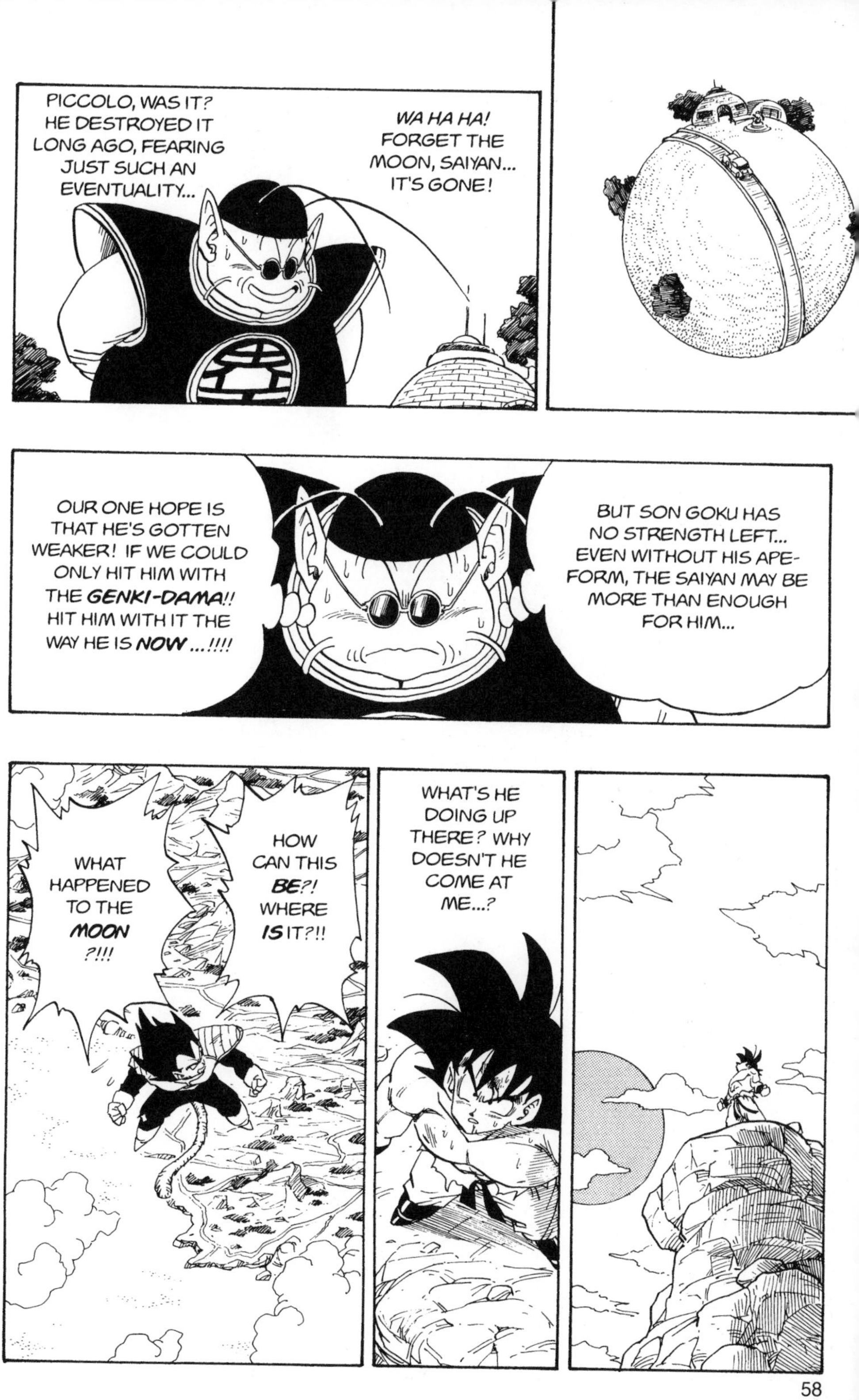
WA HA HA! FORGET THE MOON, SAIYAN... IT'S GONE!
PICCOLO, WAS IT? HE DESTROYED IT LONG AGO, FEARING JUST SUCH AN EVENTUALITY...
BUT SON GOKU HAS NO STRENGTH LEFT... EVEN WITHOUT HIS APE-FORM, THE SAIYAN MAY BE MORE THAN ENOUGH FOR HIM...
OUR ONE HOPE IS THAT HE'S GOTTEN WEAKER! IF WE COULD ONLY HIT HIM WITH THE GENKI-DAMA!! HIT HIM WITH IT THE WAY HE IS NOW...!!!!
WHAT'S HE DOING UP THERE? WHY DOESN'T HE COME AT ME...?
HOW CAN THIS BE?! WHERE IS IT?!!
WHAT HAPPENED TO THE MOON?!!!

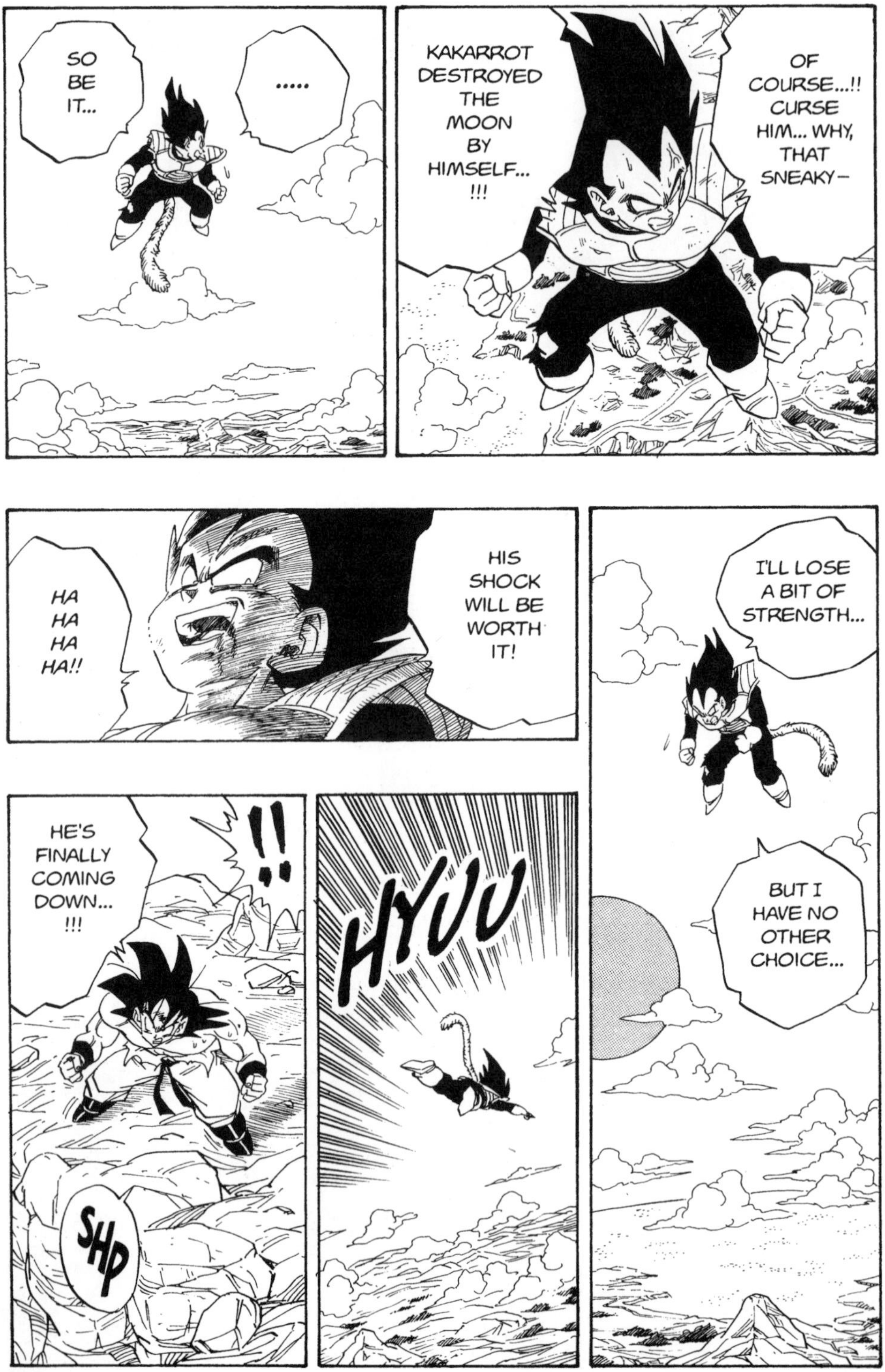
OF COURSE...!! CURSE HIM... WHY, THAT SNEAKY—
KAKARROT DESTROYED THE MOON BY HIMSELF... !!!
.....
SO BE IT...
I'LL LOSE A BIT OF STRENGTH...
BUT I HAVE NO OTHER CHOICE...
HIS SHOCK WILL BE WORTH IT!
HA HA HA HA!!
HYUU
!!
HE'S FINALLY COMING DOWN... !!!
SHP

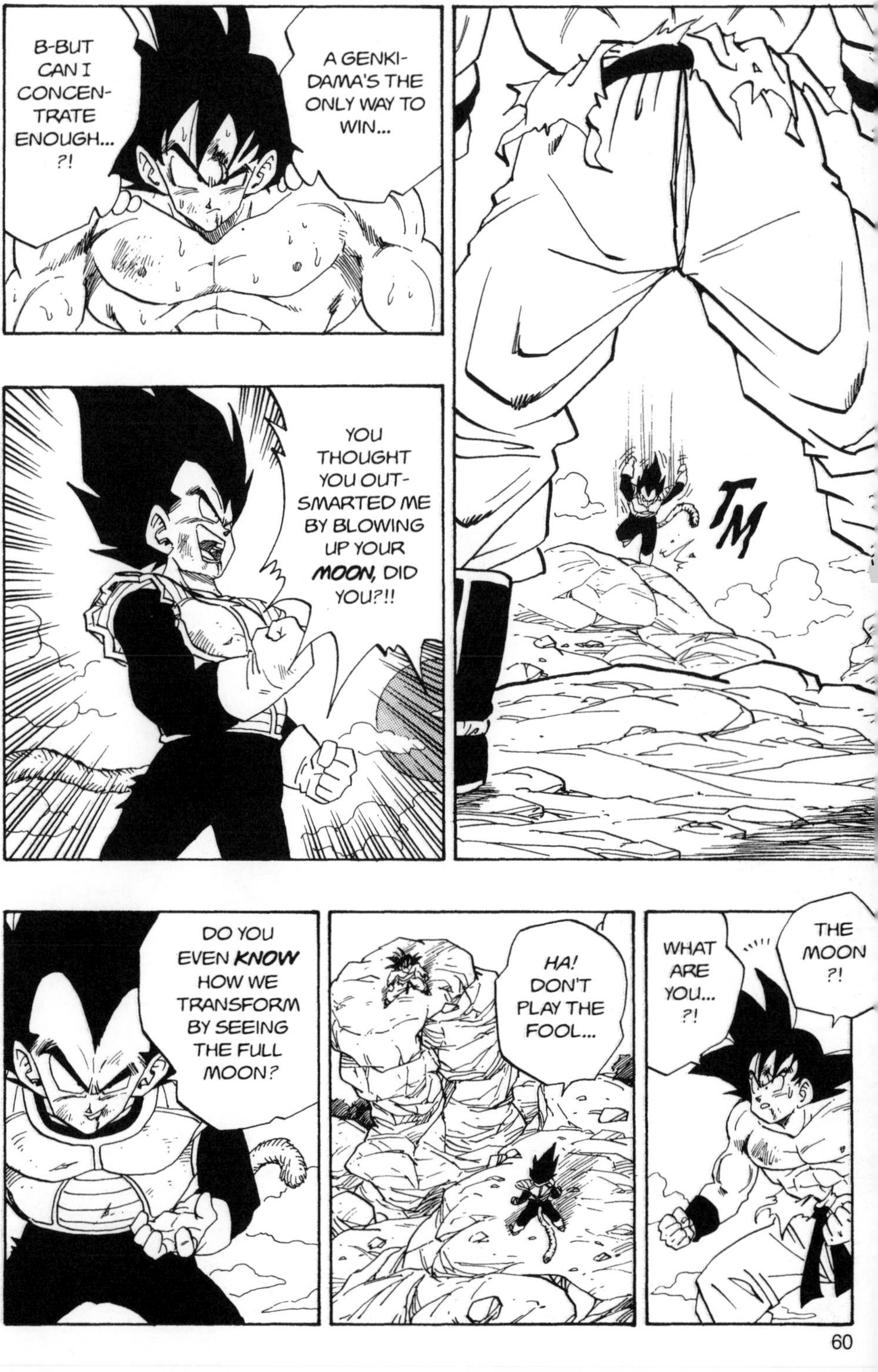
TM
A GENKI-DAMA'S THE ONLY WAY TO WIN...
B-BUT CAN I CONCENTRATE ENOUGH...?!
YOU THOUGHT YOU OUT-SMARTED ME BY BLOWING UP YOUR MOON, DID YOU?!!
THE MOON ?!
WHAT ARE YOU...?!
HA! DON'T PLAY THE FOOL...
DO YOU EVEN KNOW HOW WE TRANSFORM BY SEEING THE FULL MOON?

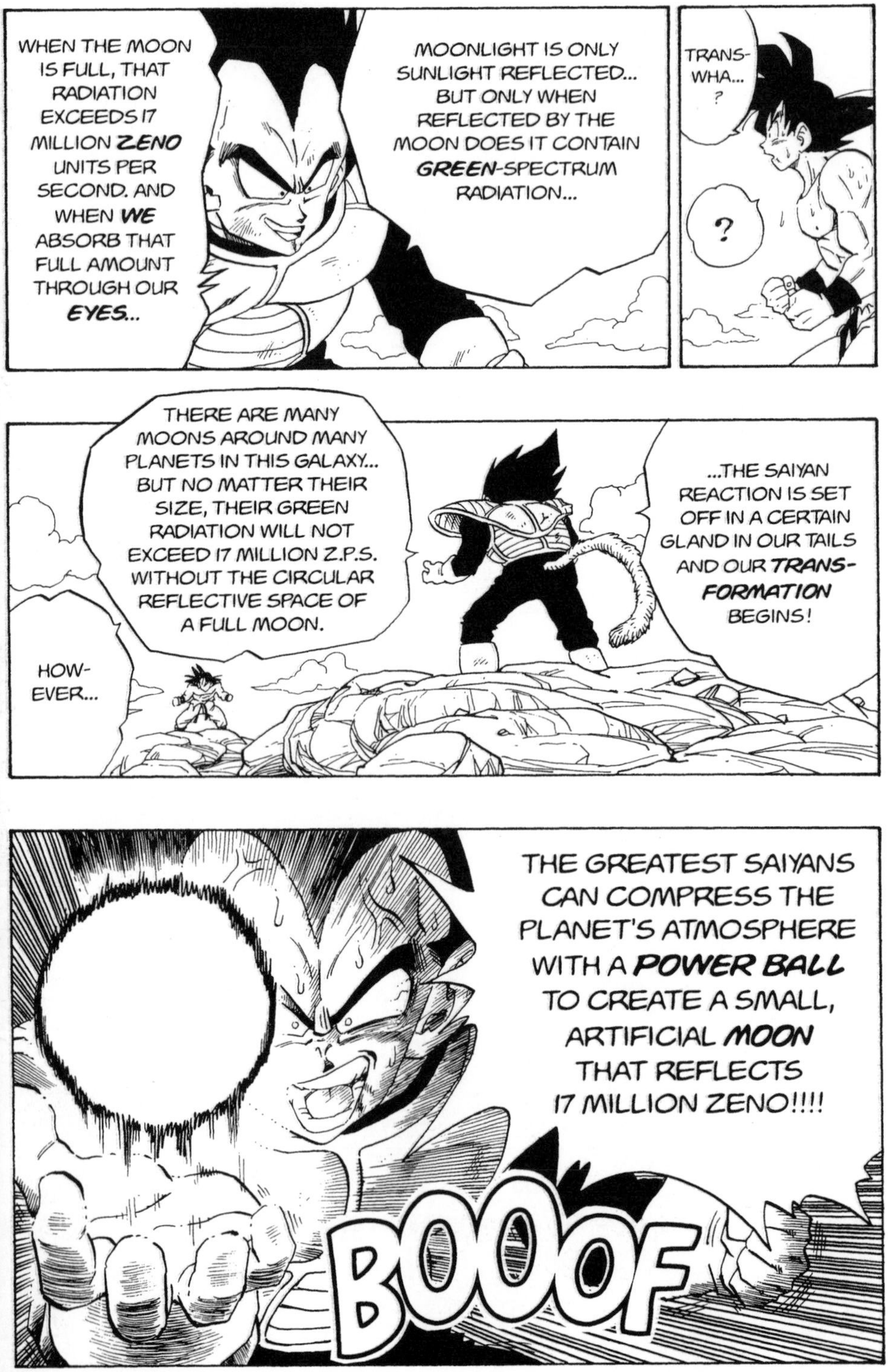
TRANS-WHA... ?
?
MOONLIGHT IS ONLY SUNLIGHT REFLECTED... BUT ONLY WHEN REFLECTED BY THE MOON DOES IT CONTAIN GREEN-SPECTRUM RADIATION...
WHEN THE MOON IS FULL, THAT RADIATION EXCEEDS 17 MILLION ZENO UNITS PER SECOND. AND WHEN WE ABSORB THAT FULL AMOUNT THROUGH OUR EYES...
...THE SAIYAN REACTION IS SET OFF IN A CERTAIN GLAND IN OUR TAILS AND OUR TRANSFORMATION BEGINS!
THERE ARE MANY MOONS AROUND MANY PLANETS IN THIS GALAXY... BUT NO MATTER THEIR SIZE, THEIR GREEN RADIATION WILL NOT EXCEED 17 MILLION Z.P.S. WITHOUT THE CIRCULAR REFLECTIVE SPACE OF A FULL MOON.
HOW-EVER...
THE GREATEST SAIYANS CAN COMPRESS THE PLANET'S ATMOSPHERE WITH A POWER BALL TO CREATE A SMALL, ARTIFICIAL MOON THAT REFLECTS 17 MILLION ZENO!!!!
BOOOF

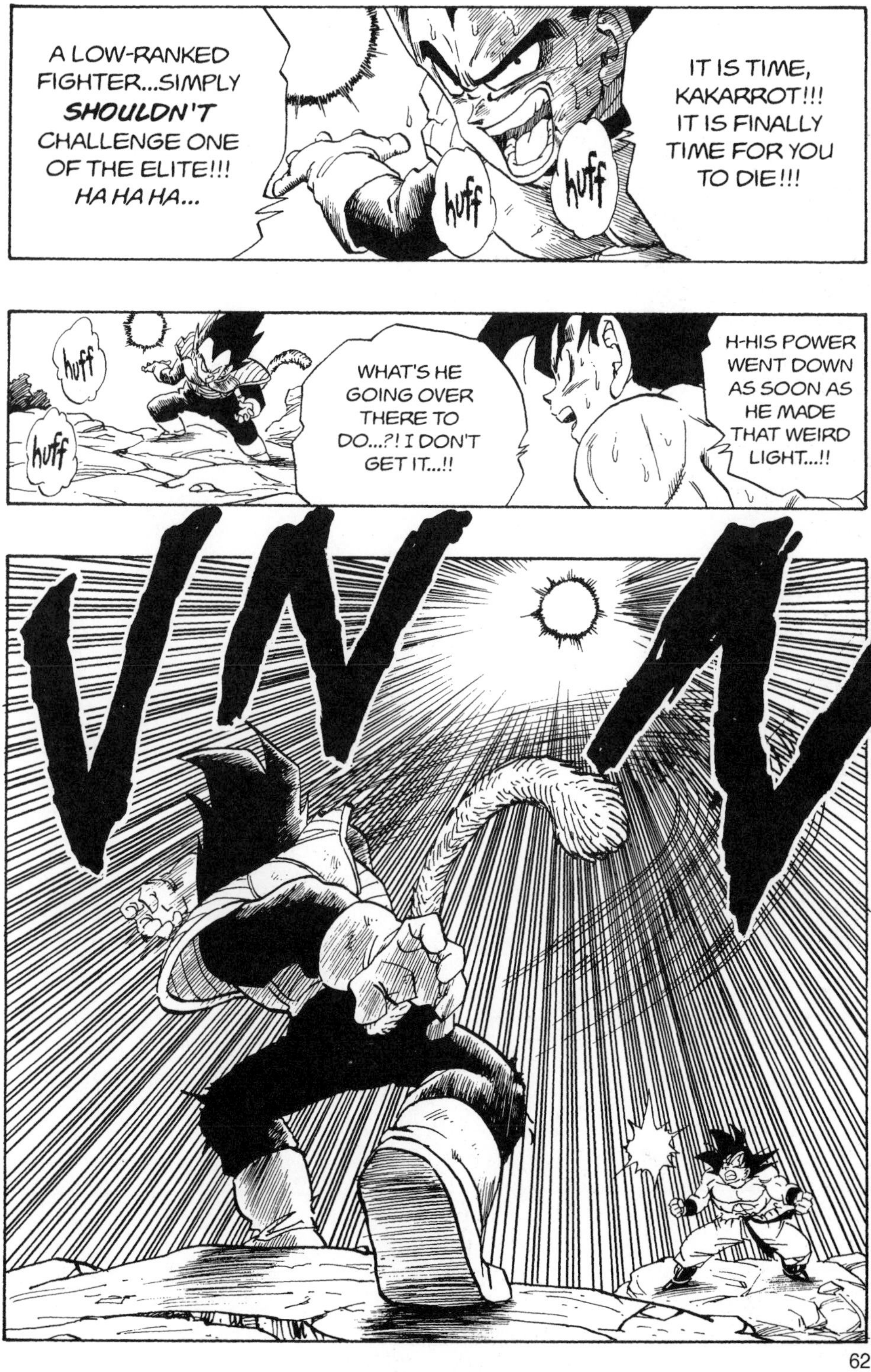
IT IS TIME, KAKARROT!!! IT IS FINALLY TIME FOR YOU TO DIE!!!
huff
huff
A LOW-RANKED FIGHTER...SIMPLY **SHOULDN'T** CHALLENGE ONE OF THE ELITE!!! *HA HA HA...*
H-HIS POWER WENT DOWN AS SOON AS HE MADE THAT WEIRD LIGHT...!!
WHAT'S HE GOING OVER THERE TO DO...?! I DON'T GET IT...!!
huff
huff
VNN

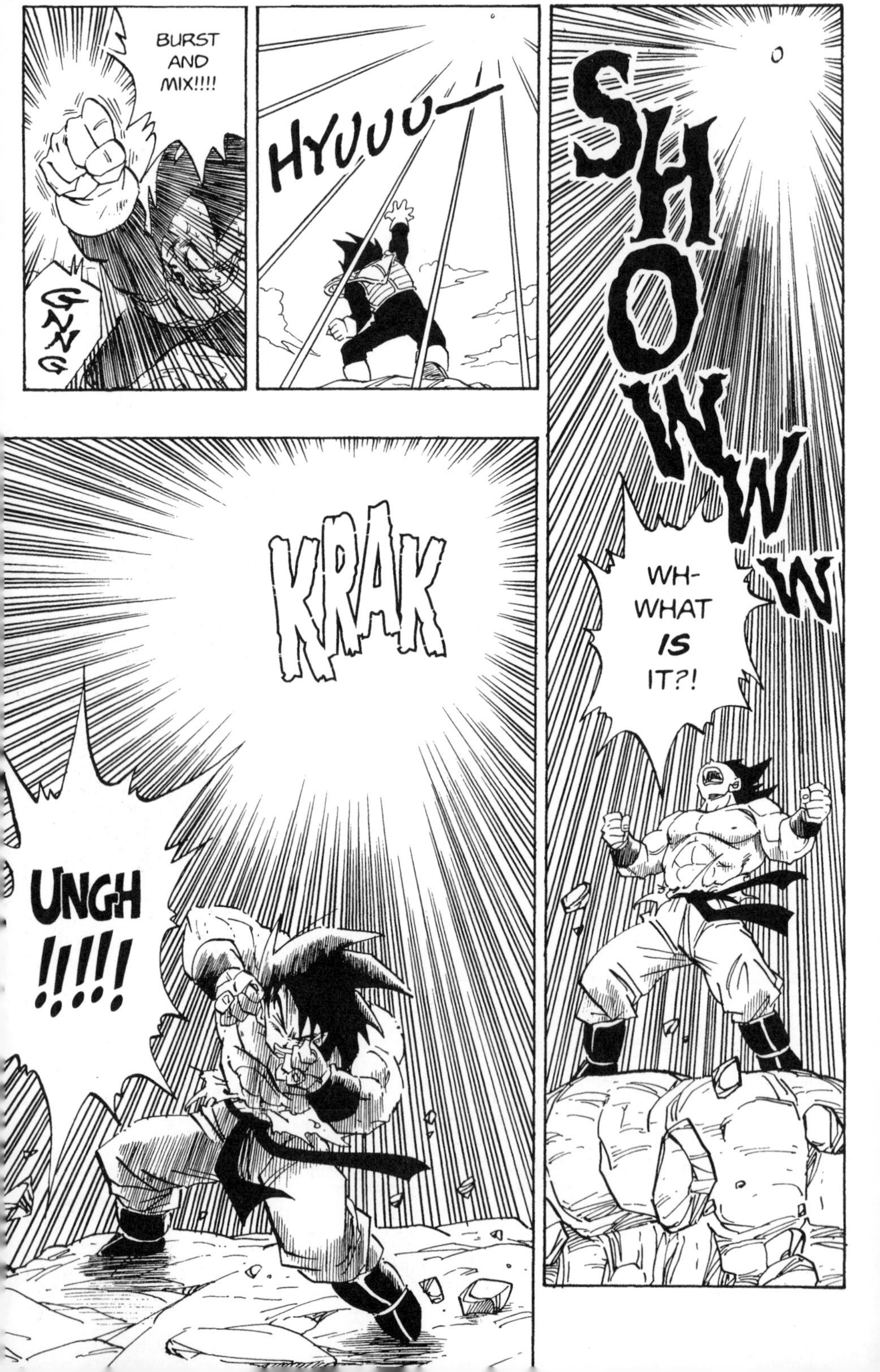
SHOWWW
WH- WHAT IS IT?!
HYUUU—
BURST AND MIX!!!!
GNNG
KRAK
UNGH !!!!!

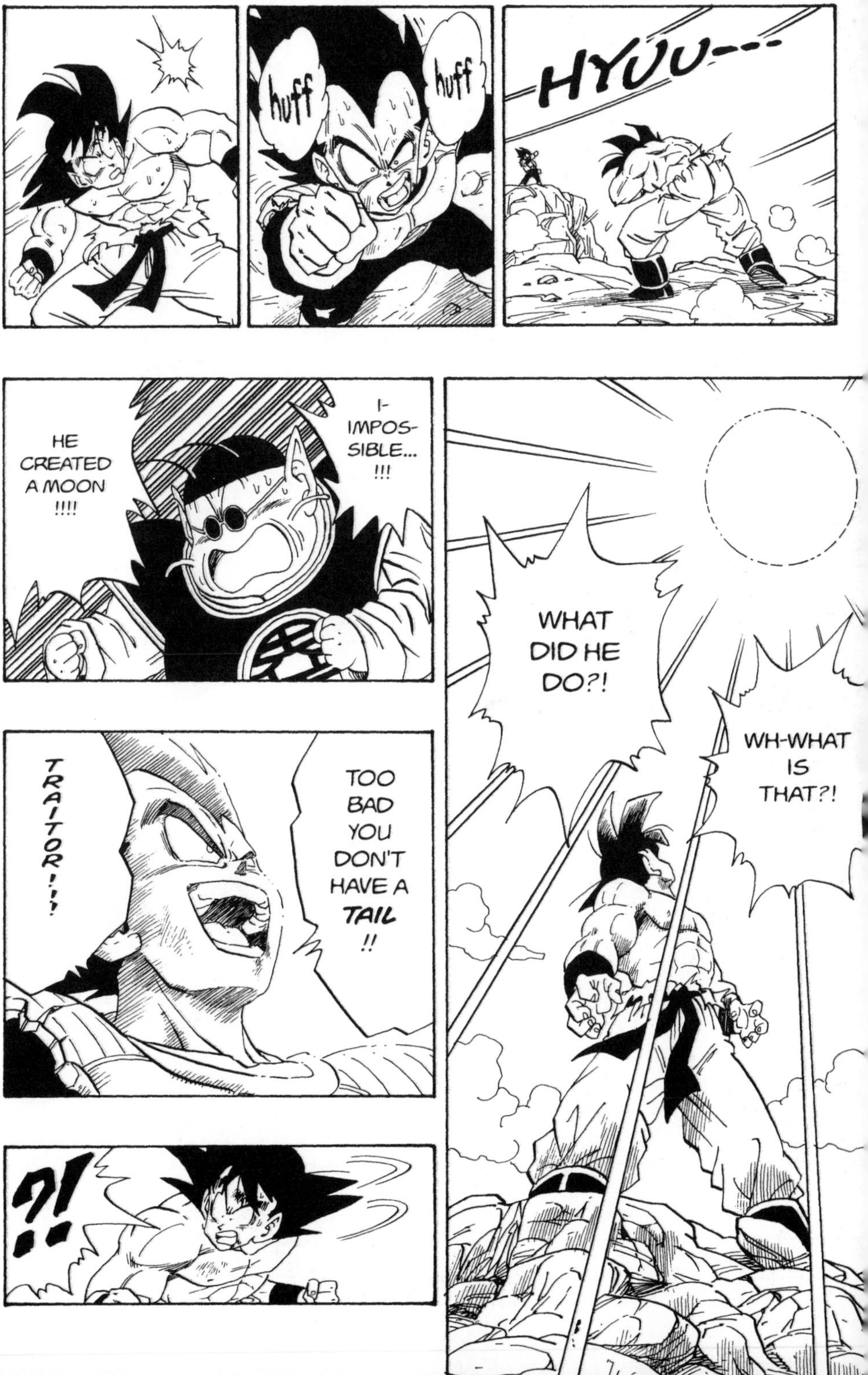
HYUU---
huff
huff
WHAT DID HE DO?!
WH-WHAT IS THAT?!
I-IMPOSSIBLE...!!!
HE CREATED A MOON!!!!
TOO BAD YOU DON'T HAVE A TAIL!!
TRAITOR!!?
?!

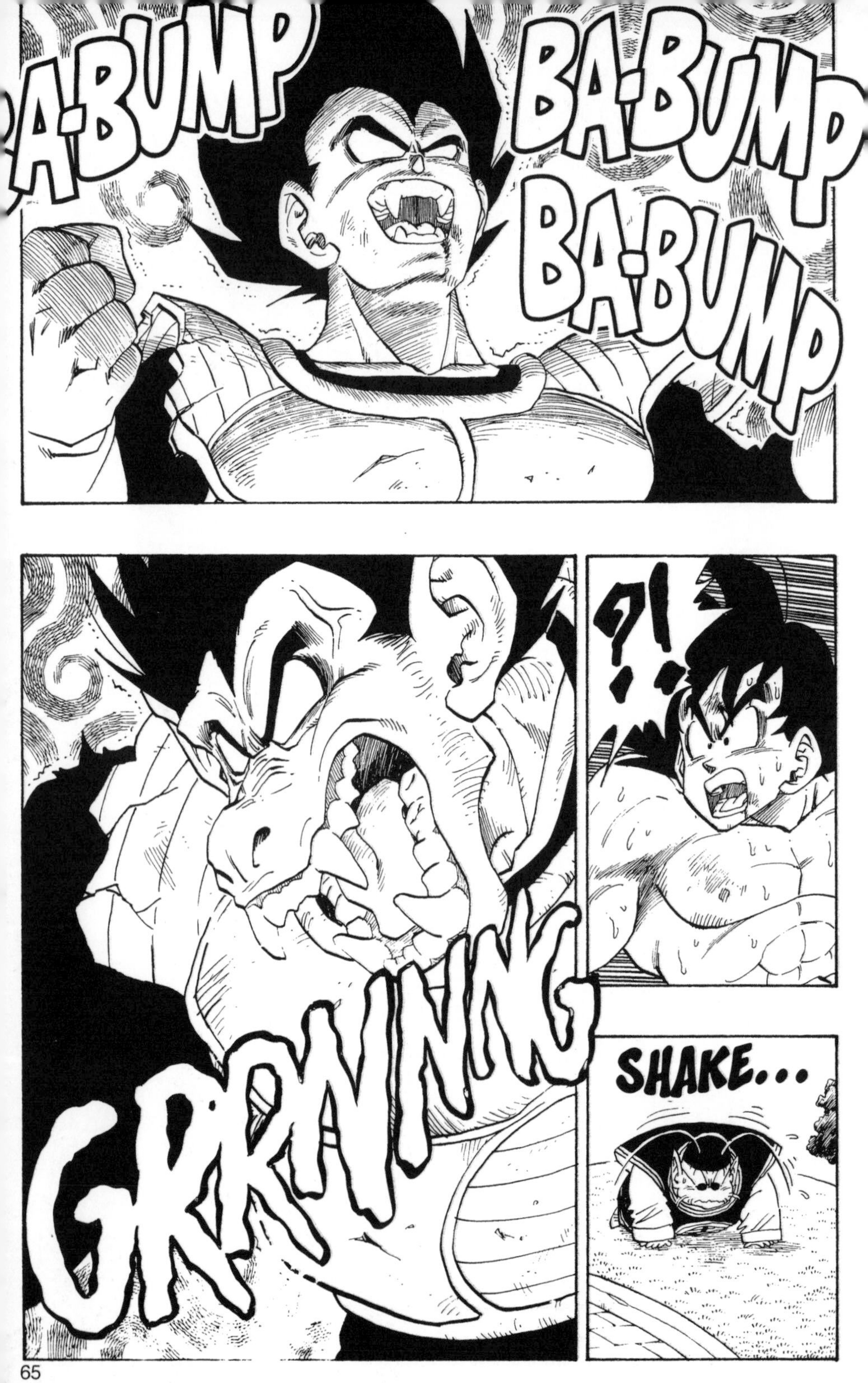
BA-BUMP
BA-BUMP
A-BUMP
?!
SHAKE...
GRRNNNG

# DBZ:39 • The Energy Sphere

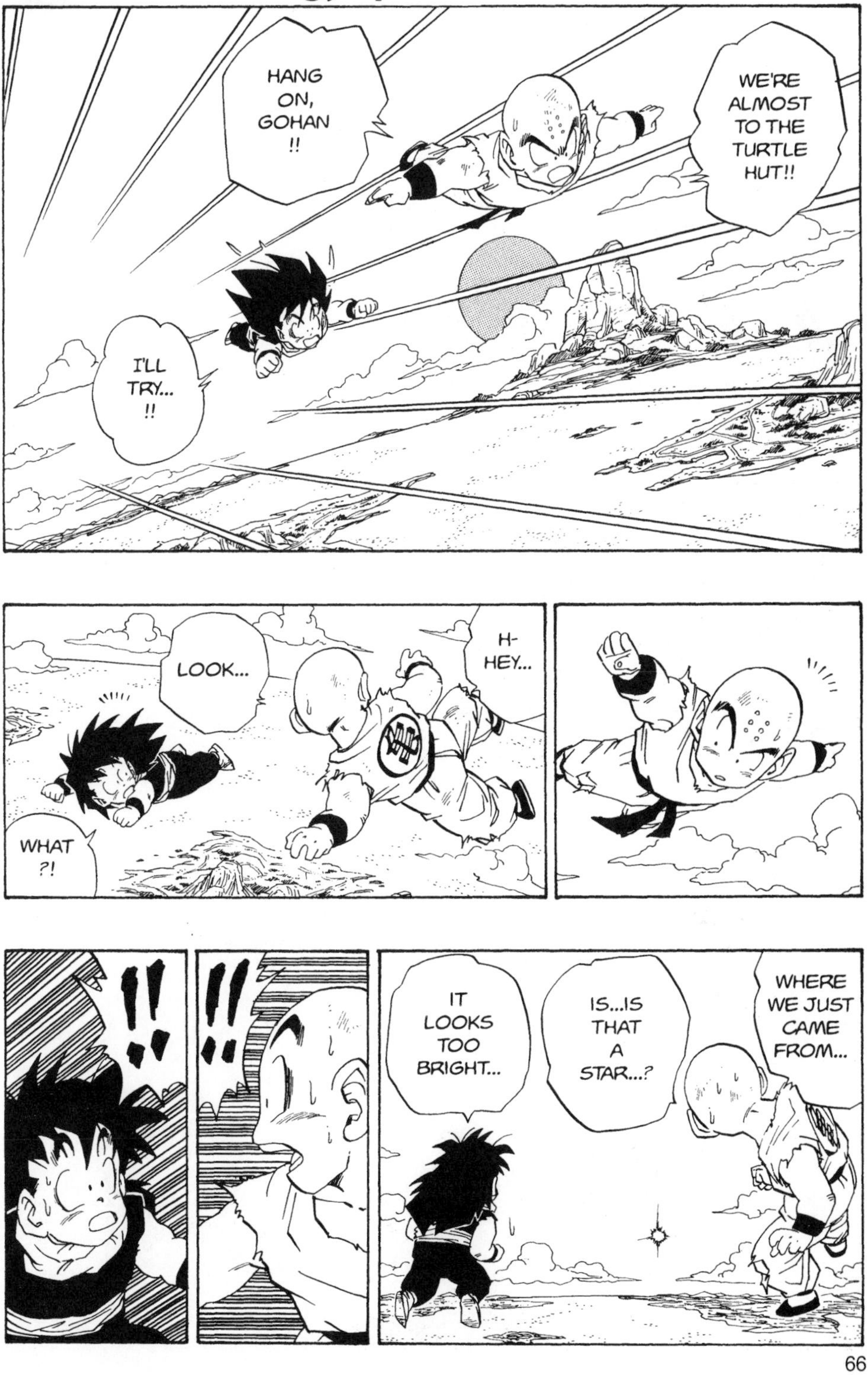
WE'RE ALMOST TO THE TURTLE HUT!!
HANG ON, GOHAN !!
I'LL TRY... !!
H-HEY...
LOOK...
WHAT ?!
WHERE WE JUST CAME FROM...
IS...IS THAT A STAR...?
IT LOOKS TOO BRIGHT...
!!
!!

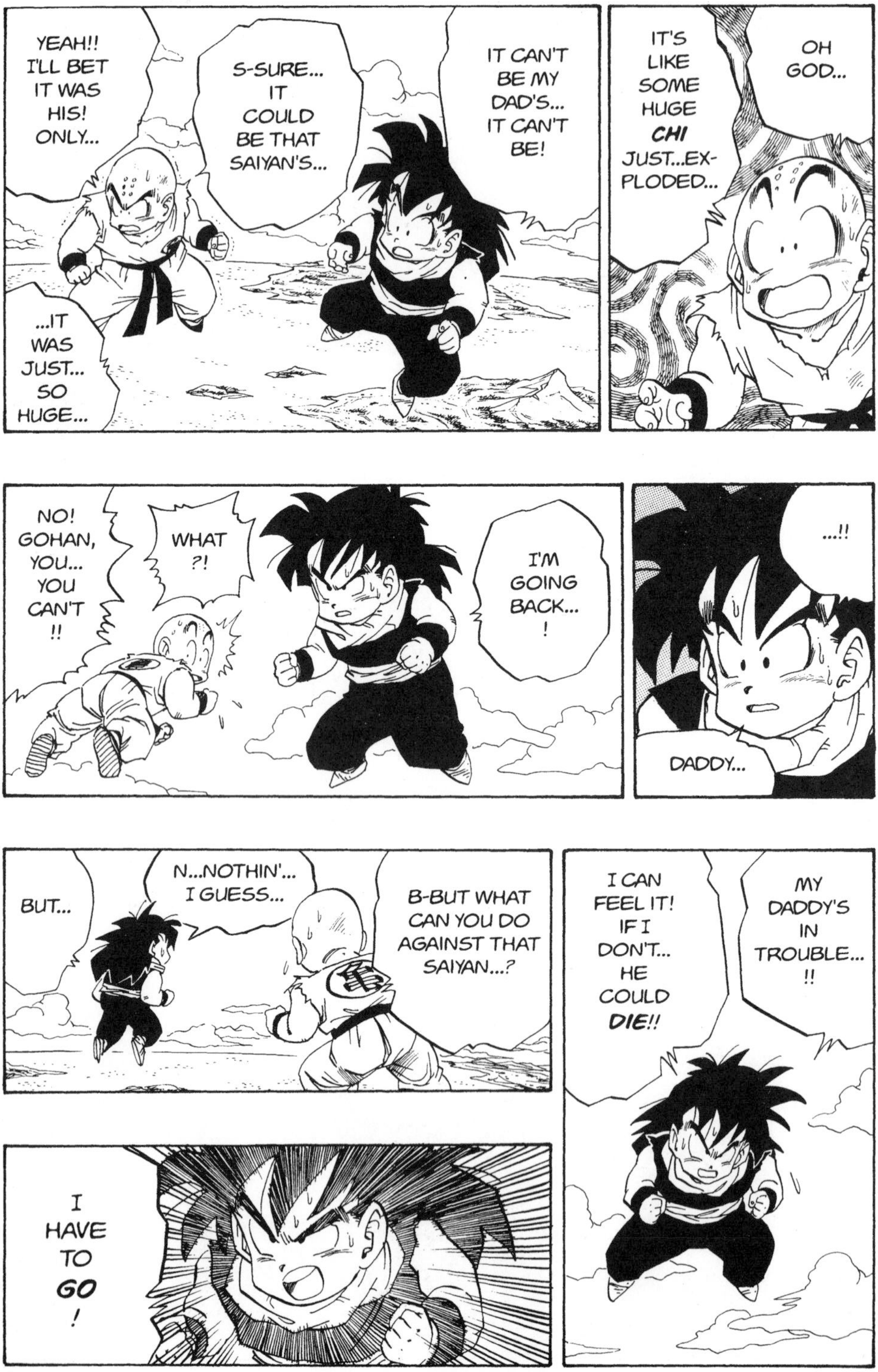
OH GOD...
IT'S LIKE SOME HUGE CHI JUST...EX-PLODED...
IT CAN'T BE MY DAD'S... IT CAN'T BE!
S-SURE... IT COULD BE THAT SAIYAN'S...
YEAH!! I'LL BET IT WAS HIS! ONLY...
...IT WAS JUST... SO HUGE...
...!!
DADDY...
I'M GOING BACK...!
WHAT ?!
NO! GOHAN, YOU... YOU CAN'T !!
MY DADDY'S IN TROUBLE... !!
I CAN FEEL IT! IF I DON'T... HE COULD DIE!!
B-BUT WHAT CAN YOU DO AGAINST THAT SAIYAN...?
N...NOTHIN'... I GUESS...
BUT...
I HAVE TO GO !

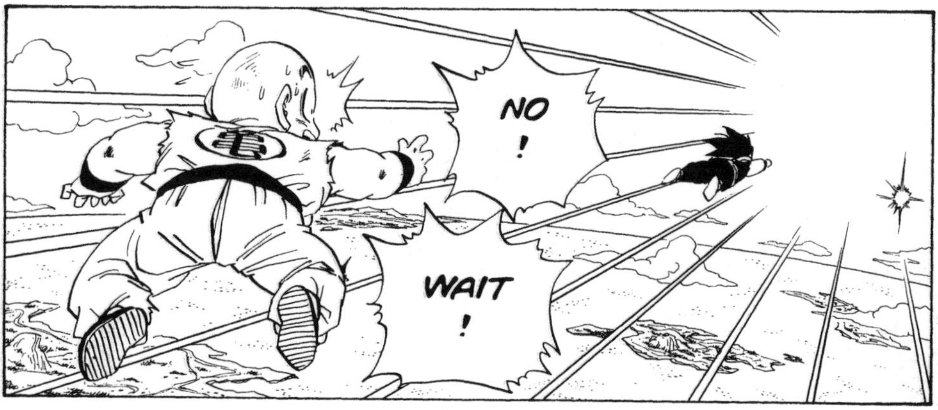
NO !
WAIT !

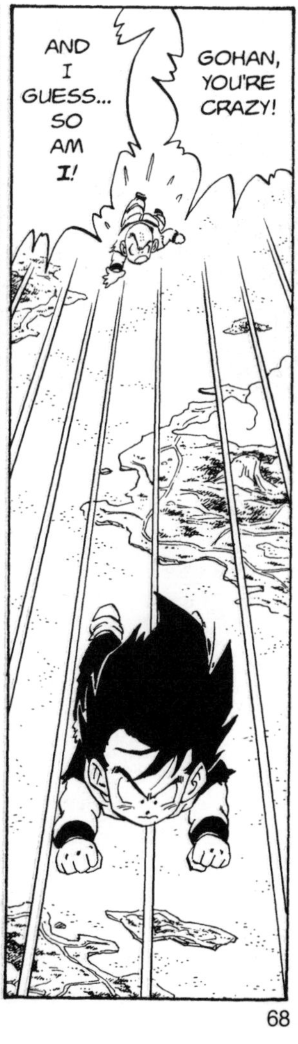
GOHAN, YOU'RE CRAZY!
AND I GUESS... SO AM I!

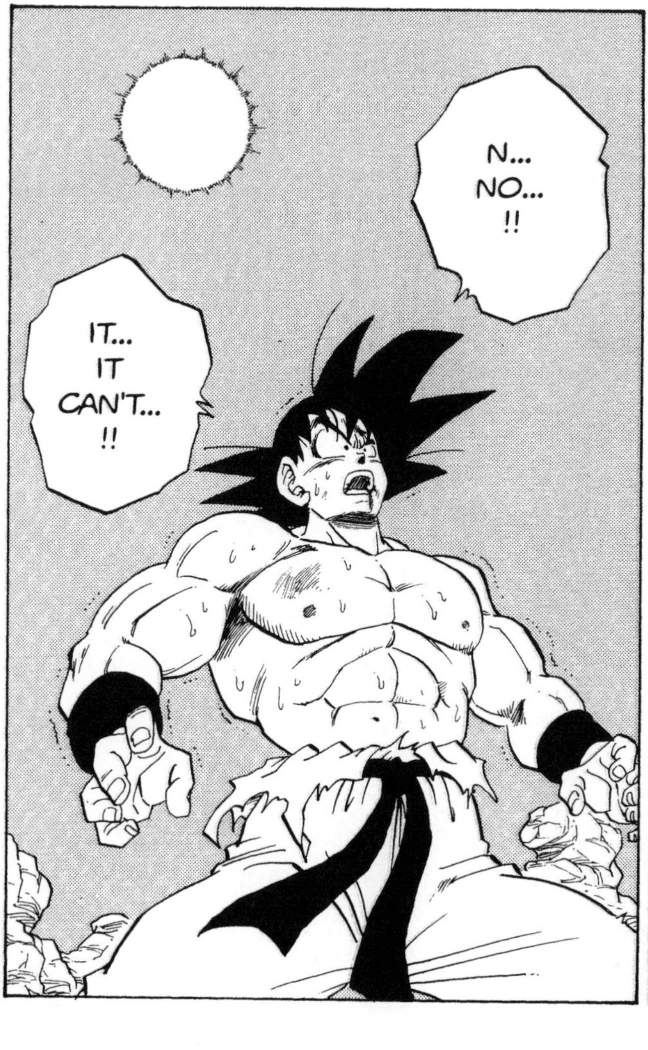
N... NO... !!
IT... IT CAN'T... !!

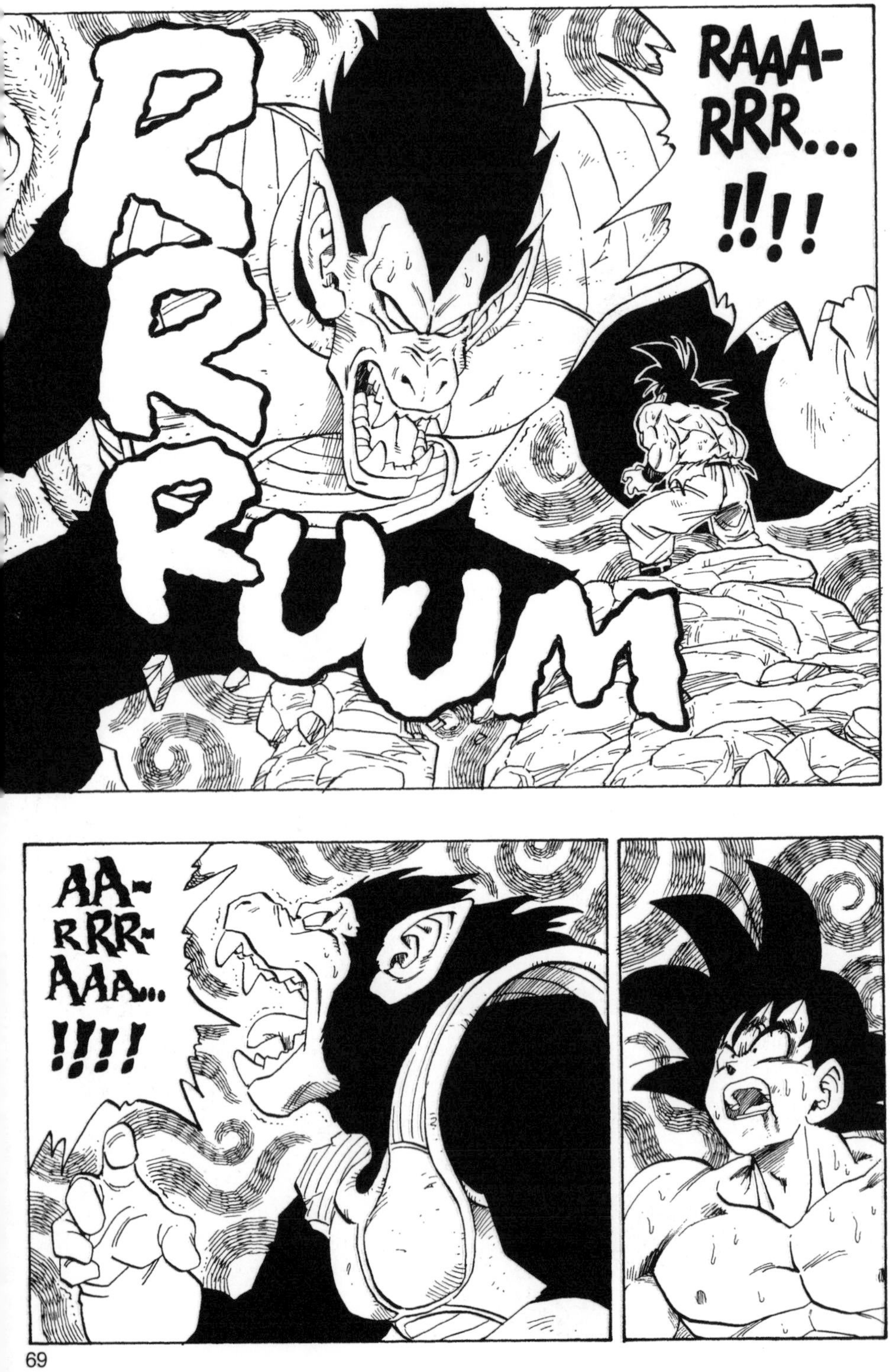
RAAA-RRR...!!!!
RRRUUM
AA-RRR-AAA...!!!!

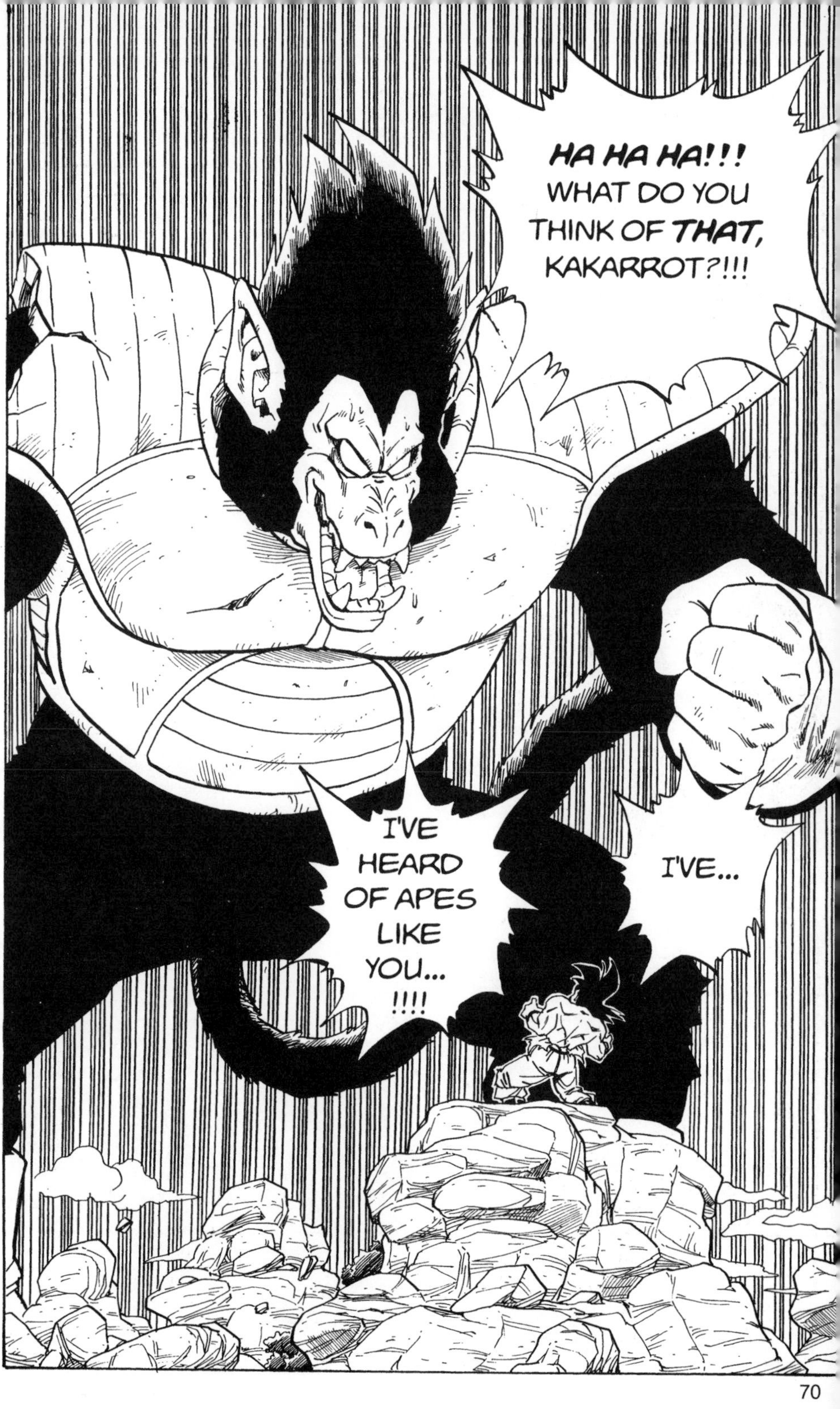
HA HA HA!!! WHAT DO YOU THINK OF THAT, KAKARROT?!!!
I'VE...
I'VE HEARD OF APES LIKE YOU... !!!!

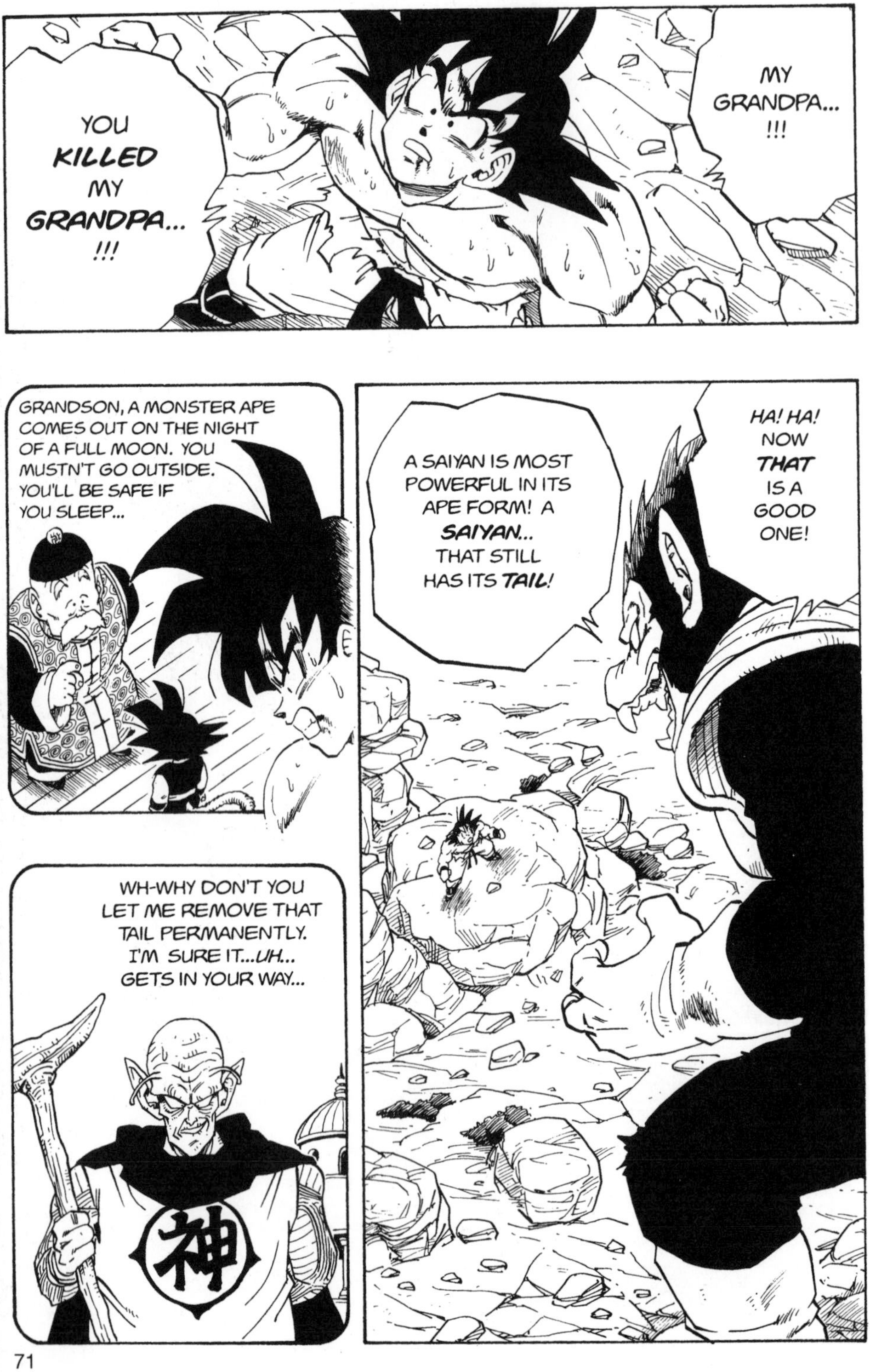
MY GRANDPA... !!!
YOU KILLED MY GRANDPA... !!!
HA! HA! NOW THAT IS A GOOD ONE!
A SAIYAN IS MOST POWERFUL IN ITS APE FORM! A SAIYAN... THAT STILL HAS ITS TAIL!
GRANDSON, A MONSTER APE COMES OUT ON THE NIGHT OF A FULL MOON. YOU MUSTN'T GO OUTSIDE. YOU'LL BE SAFE IF YOU SLEEP...
WH-WHY DON'T YOU LET ME REMOVE THAT TAIL PERMANENTLY. I'M SURE IT...UH... GETS IN YOUR WAY...
神

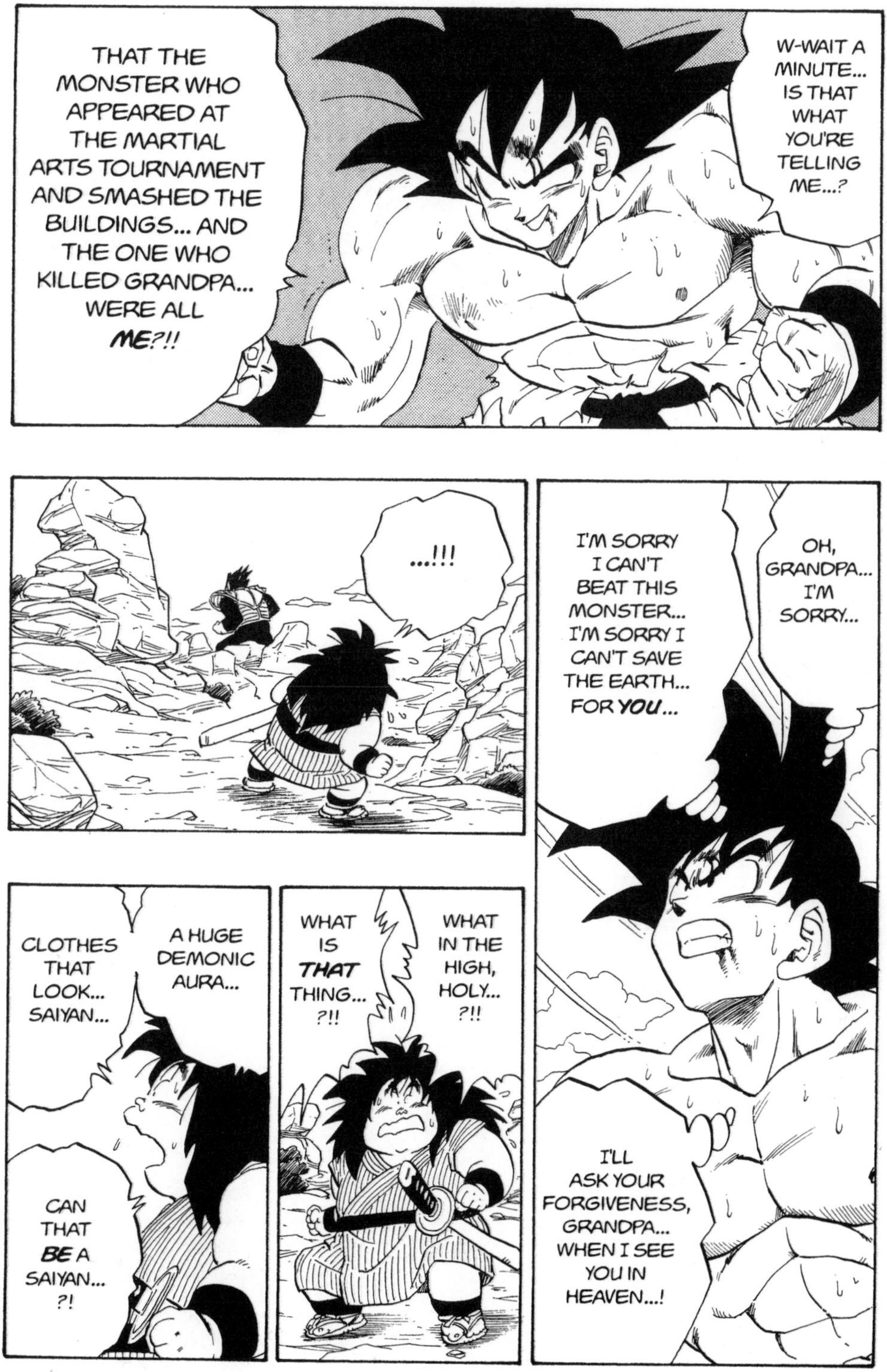
W-WAIT A MINUTE... IS THAT WHAT YOU'RE TELLING ME...?
THAT THE MONSTER WHO APPEARED AT THE MARTIAL ARTS TOURNAMENT AND SMASHED THE BUILDINGS... AND THE ONE WHO KILLED GRANDPA... WERE ALL ***ME***?!!
OH, GRANDPA... I'M SORRY...
I'M SORRY I CAN'T BEAT THIS MONSTER... I'M SORRY I CAN'T SAVE THE EARTH... FOR ***YOU***...
I'LL ASK YOUR FORGIVENESS, GRANDPA... WHEN I SEE YOU IN HEAVEN...!
...!!!
WHAT IN THE HIGH, HOLY... ?!!
WHAT IS ***THAT*** THING... ?!!
A HUGE DEMONIC AURA...
CLOTHES THAT LOOK... SAIYAN...
CAN THAT ***BE*** A SAIYAN... ?!

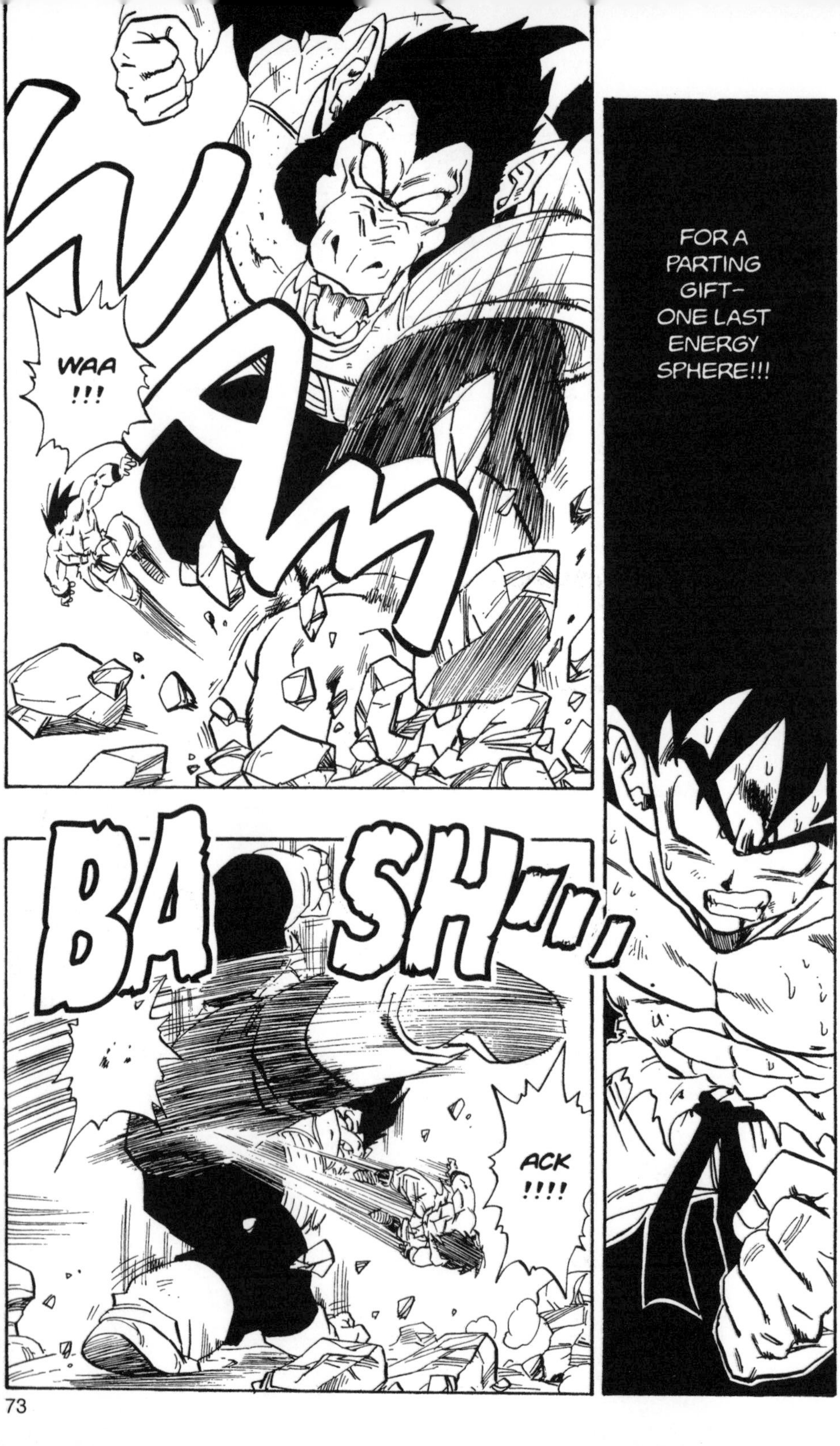
FOR A PARTING GIFT— ONE LAST ENERGY SPHERE!!!
WAM
WAA !!!
BASH...
ACK !!!!

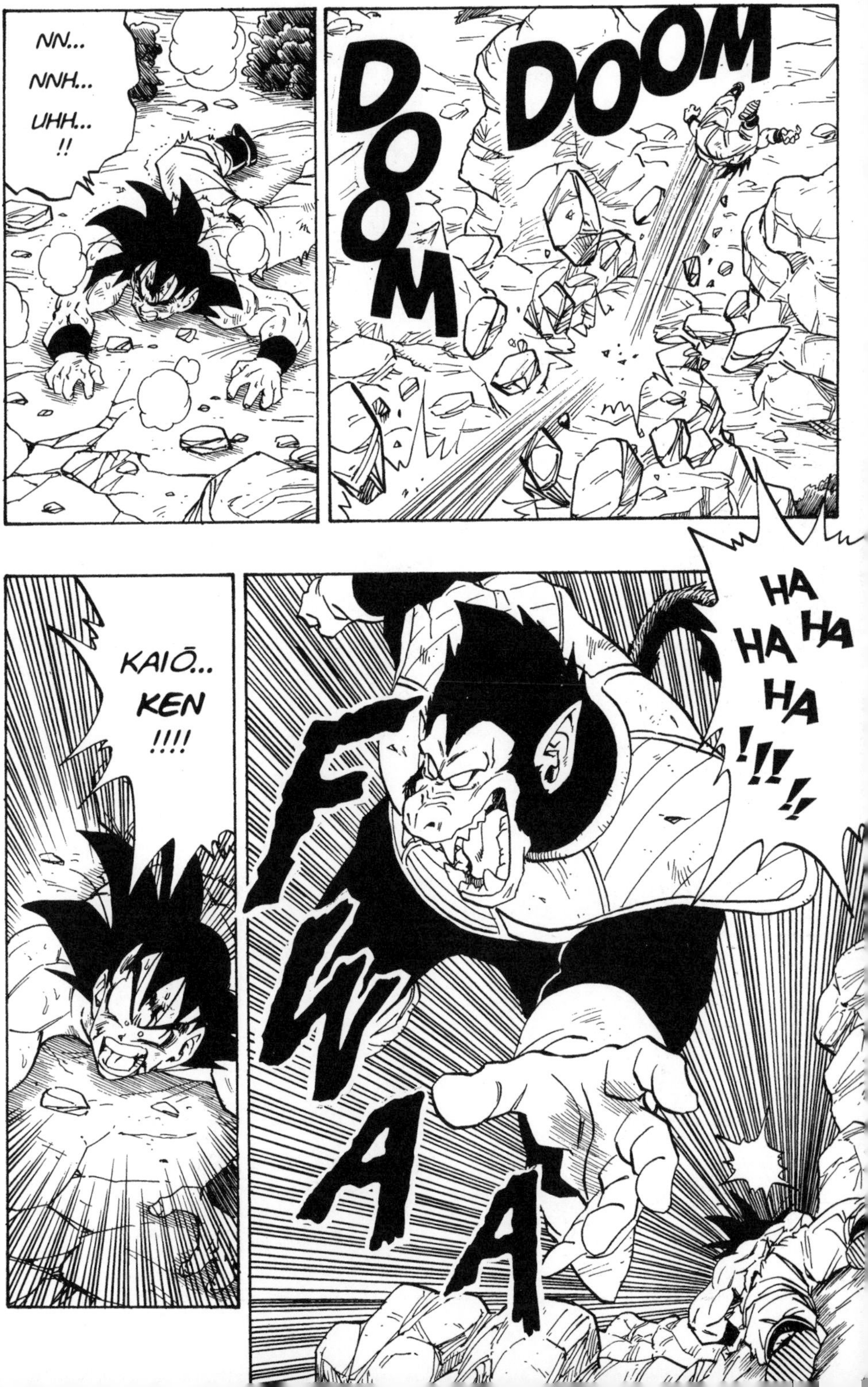
DOOM
DOOM
NN... NNH... UHH... !!
HA HA HA HA HA !!!!!
FWAA
KAIŌ... KEN !!!!

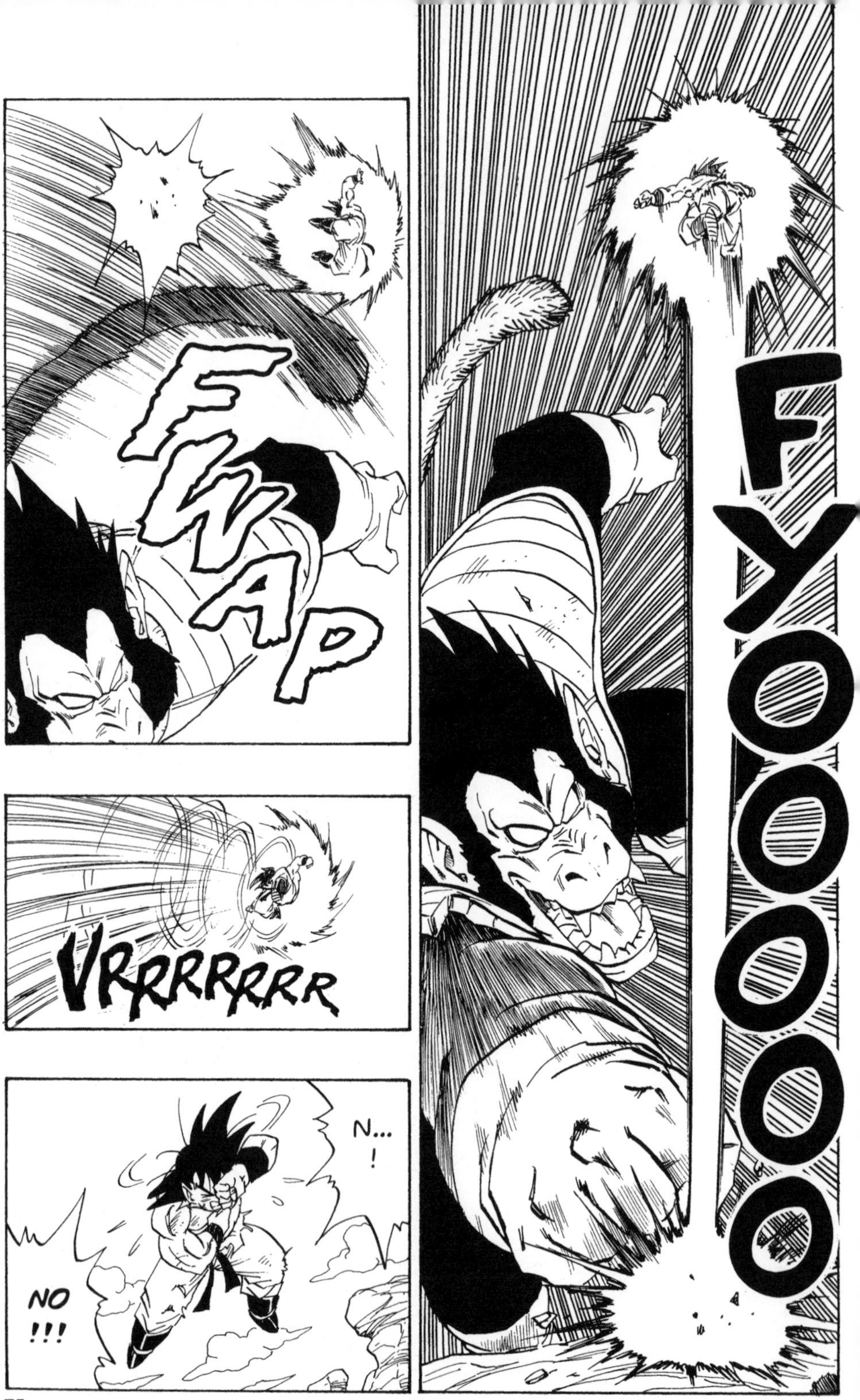
FYOOOOO
FWAP
VRRRRRRR
N...
!
NO
!!!

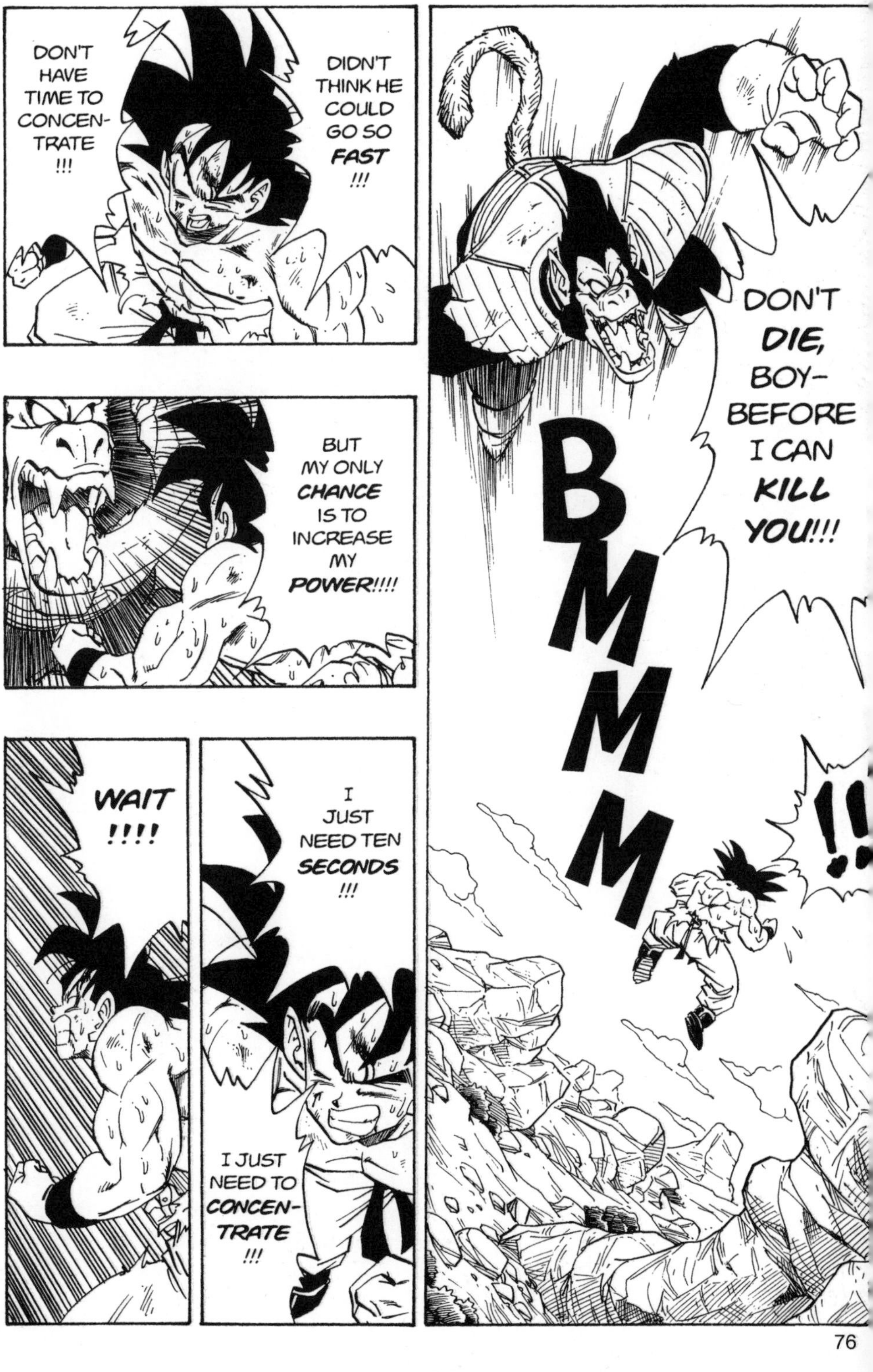
DON'T DIE, BOY– BEFORE I CAN KILL YOU!!!
BMMMM
!!
DIDN'T THINK HE COULD GO SO FAST !!!
DON'T HAVE TIME TO CONCEN-TRATE !!!
BUT MY ONLY CHANCE IS TO INCREASE MY POWER!!!!
I JUST NEED TEN SECONDS !!!
I JUST NEED TO CONCEN-TRATE !!!
WAIT !!!!

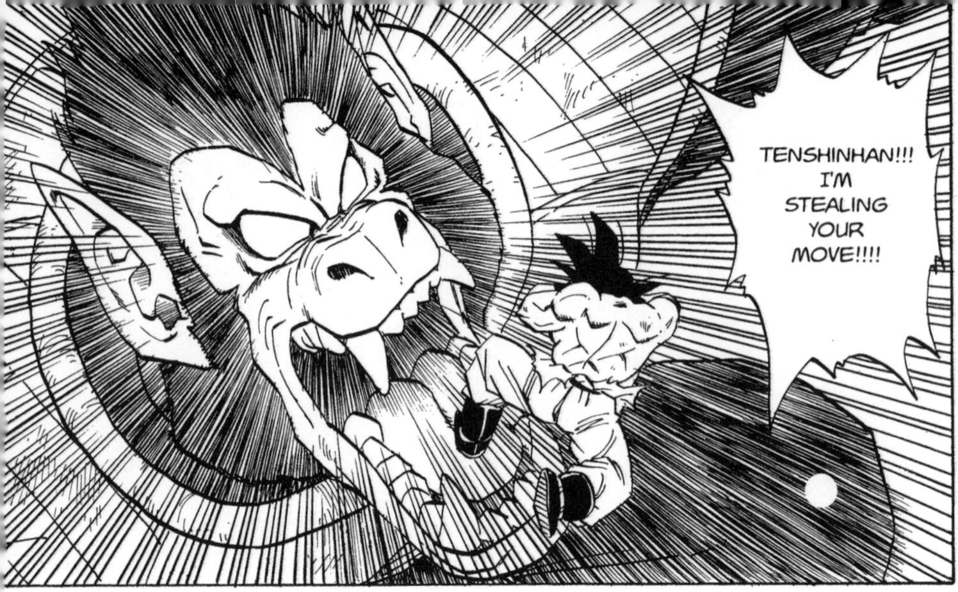
TENSHINHAN!!! I'M STEALING YOUR MOVE!!!!

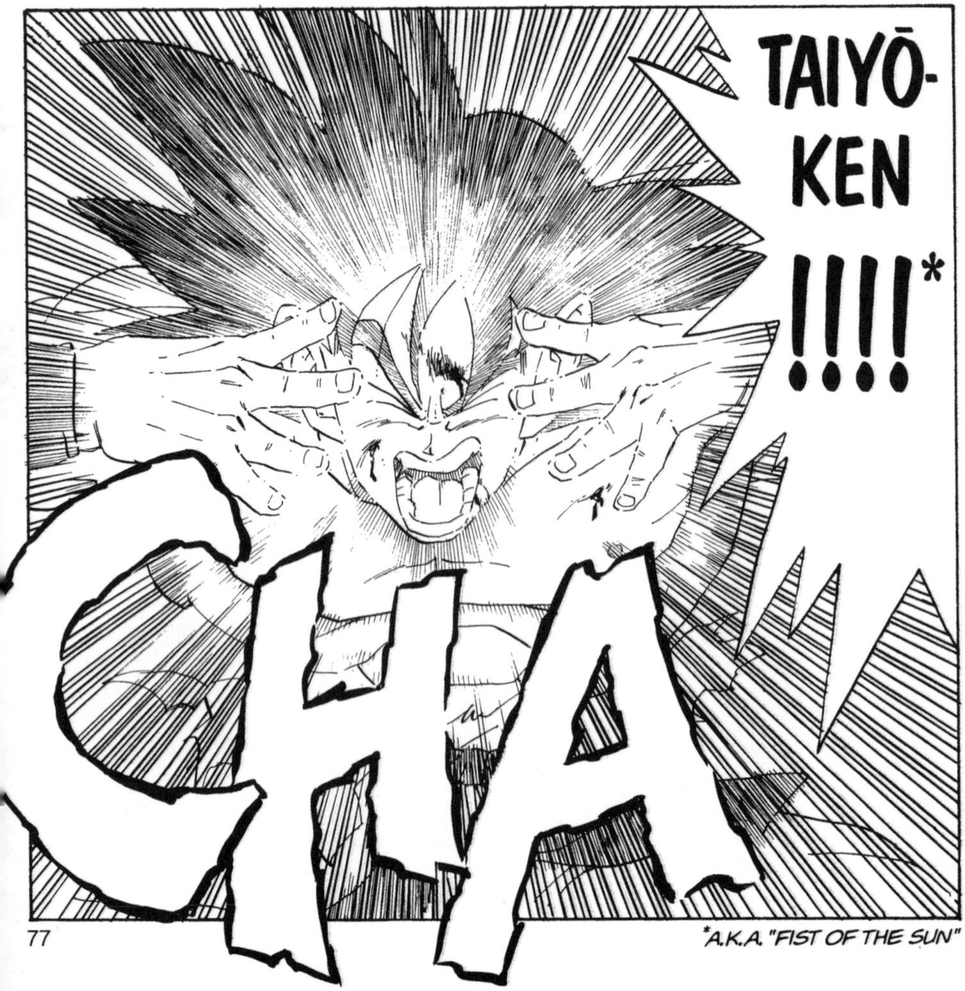
TAIYŌ-KEN !!!!!*
CHA

*A.K.A. "FIST OF THE SUN"

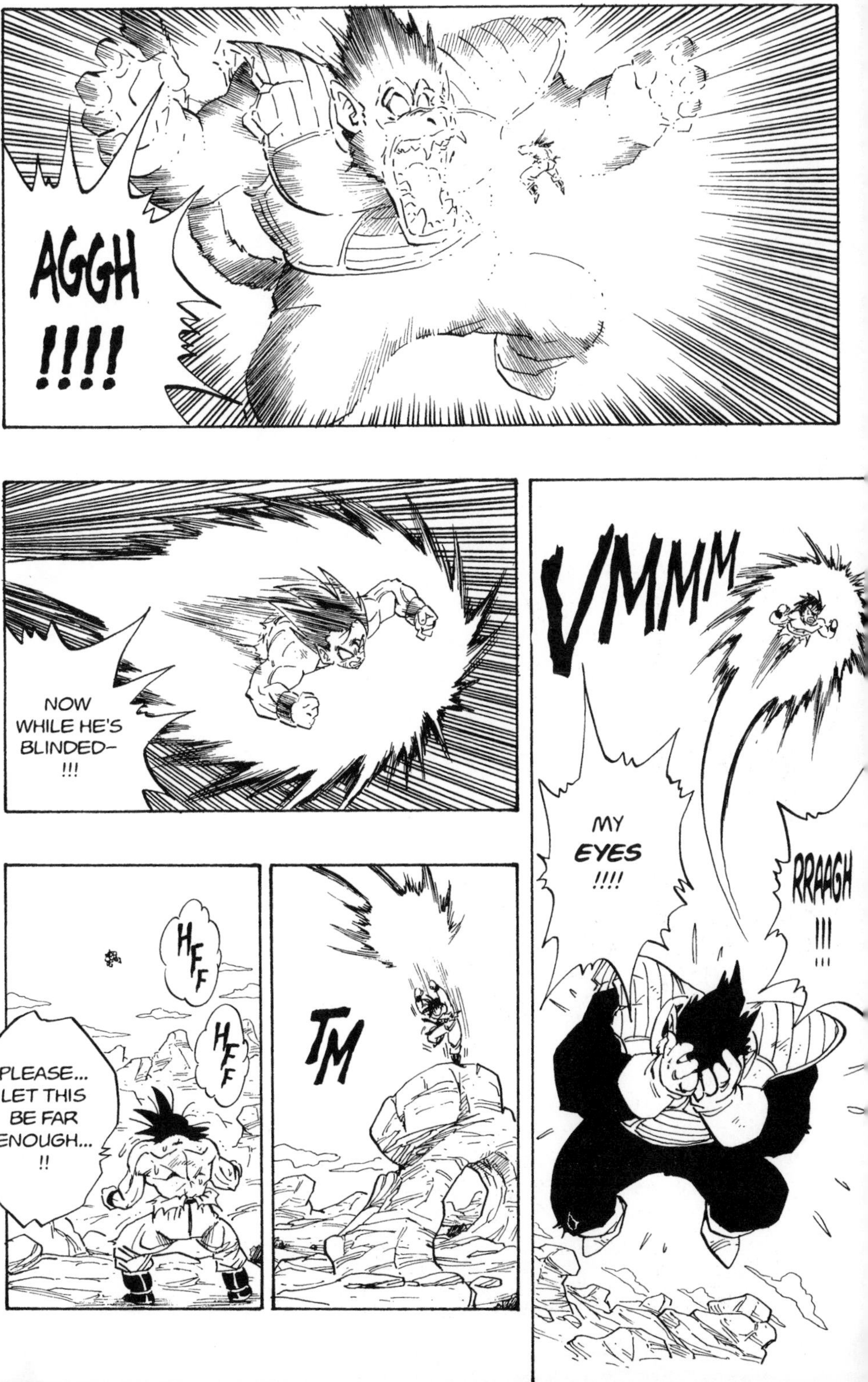
AGGH
!!!!
VMMM
MY EYES !!!!
RRAAGH !!!
NOW WHILE HE'S BLINDED— !!!
TM
HFF
HFF
PLEASE... LET THIS BE FAR ENOUGH... !!

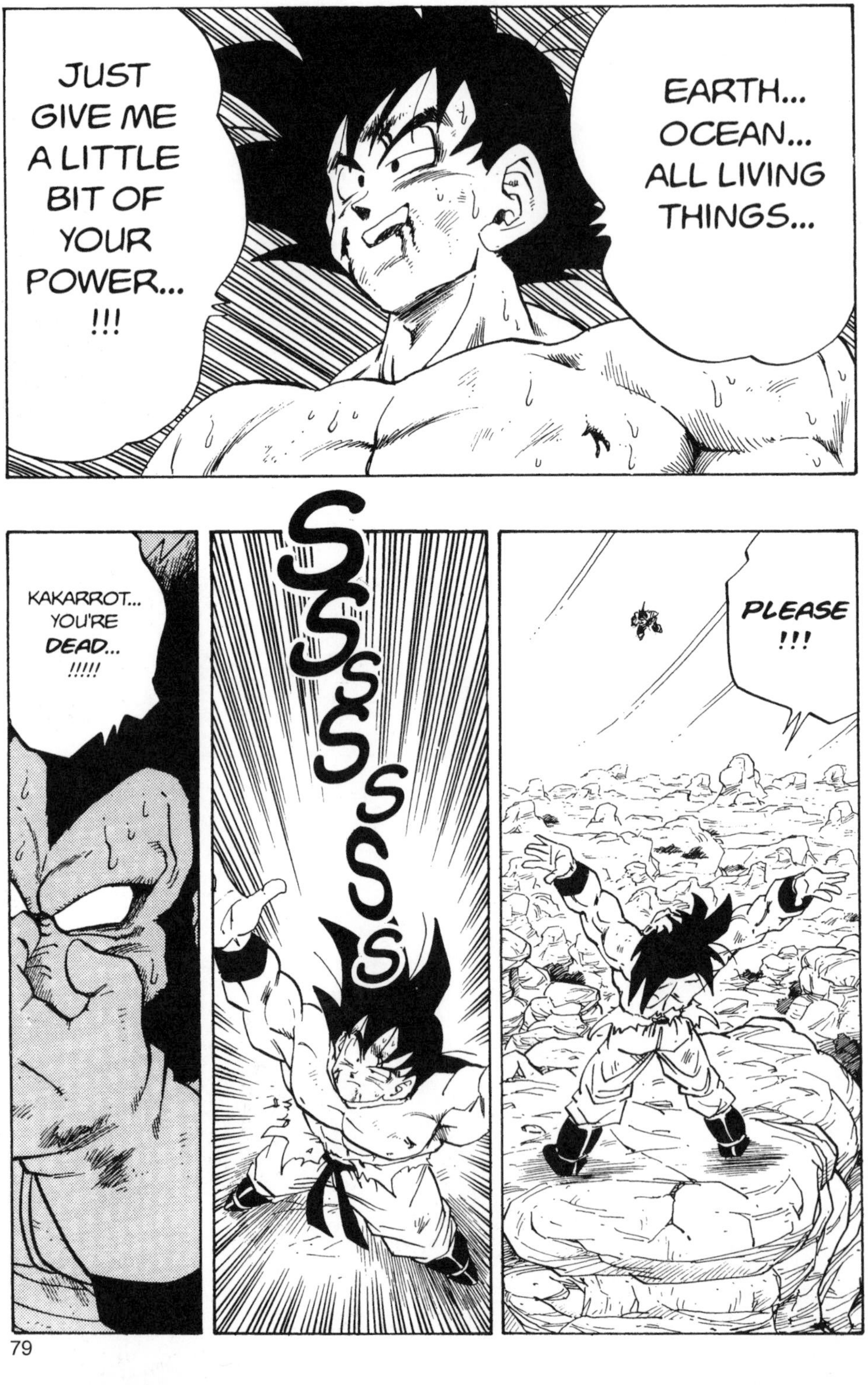
EARTH... OCEAN... ALL LIVING THINGS...
JUST GIVE ME A LITTLE BIT OF YOUR POWER... !!!
PLEASE !!!
SSSSSSS
KAKARROT... YOU'RE *DEAD*... !!!!!

# DBZ:40 • All That Power…

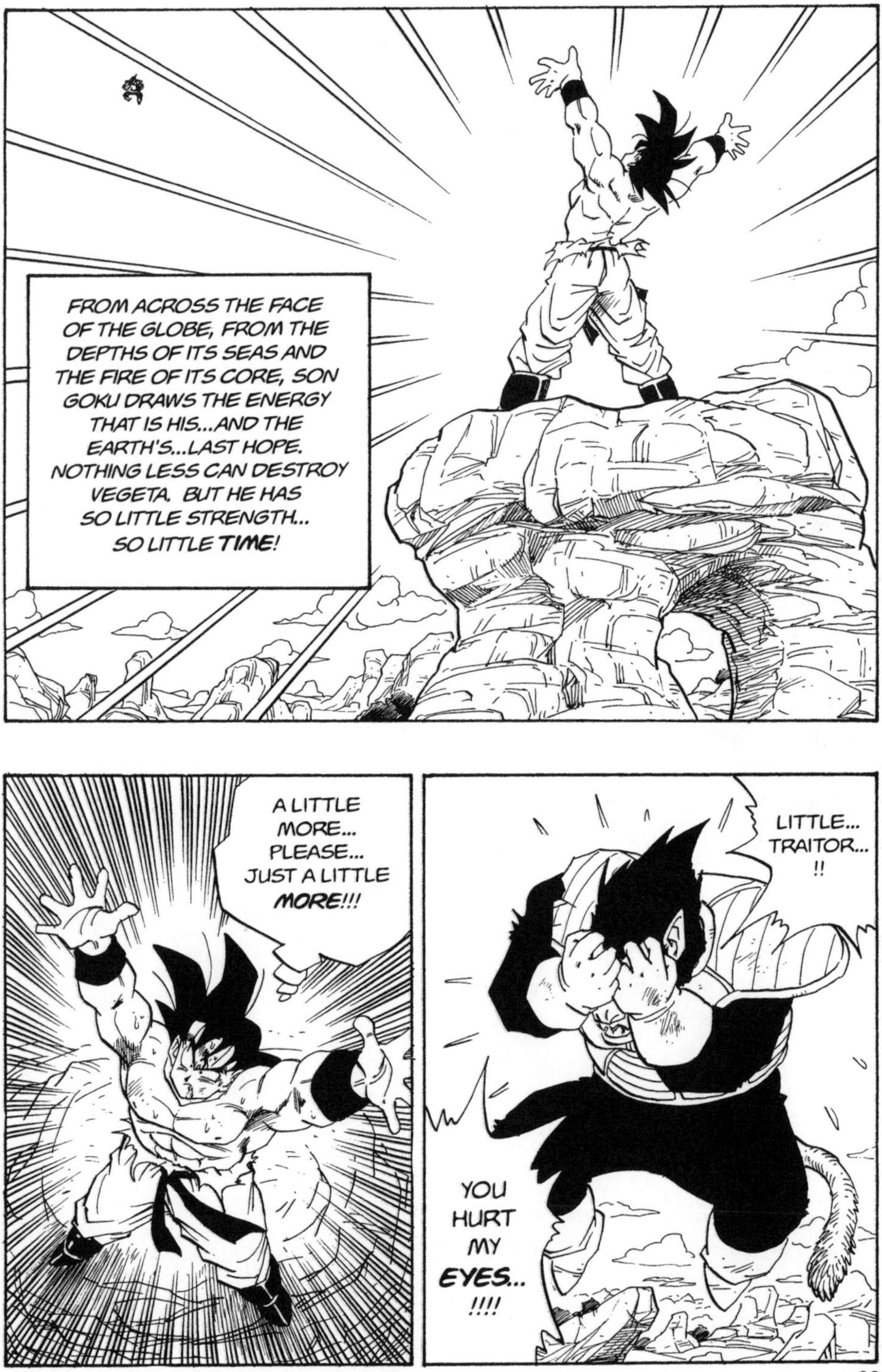

FROM ACROSS THE FACE OF THE GLOBE, FROM THE DEPTHS OF ITS SEAS AND THE FIRE OF ITS CORE, SON GOKU DRAWS THE ENERGY THAT IS HIS...AND THE EARTH'S...LAST HOPE. NOTHING LESS CAN DESTROY VEGETA. BUT HE HAS SO LITTLE STRENGTH... SO LITTLE ***TIME***!
LITTLE... TRAITOR... !!
YOU HURT MY ***EYES...*** !!!!
A LITTLE MORE... PLEASE... JUST A LITTLE ***MORE***!!!

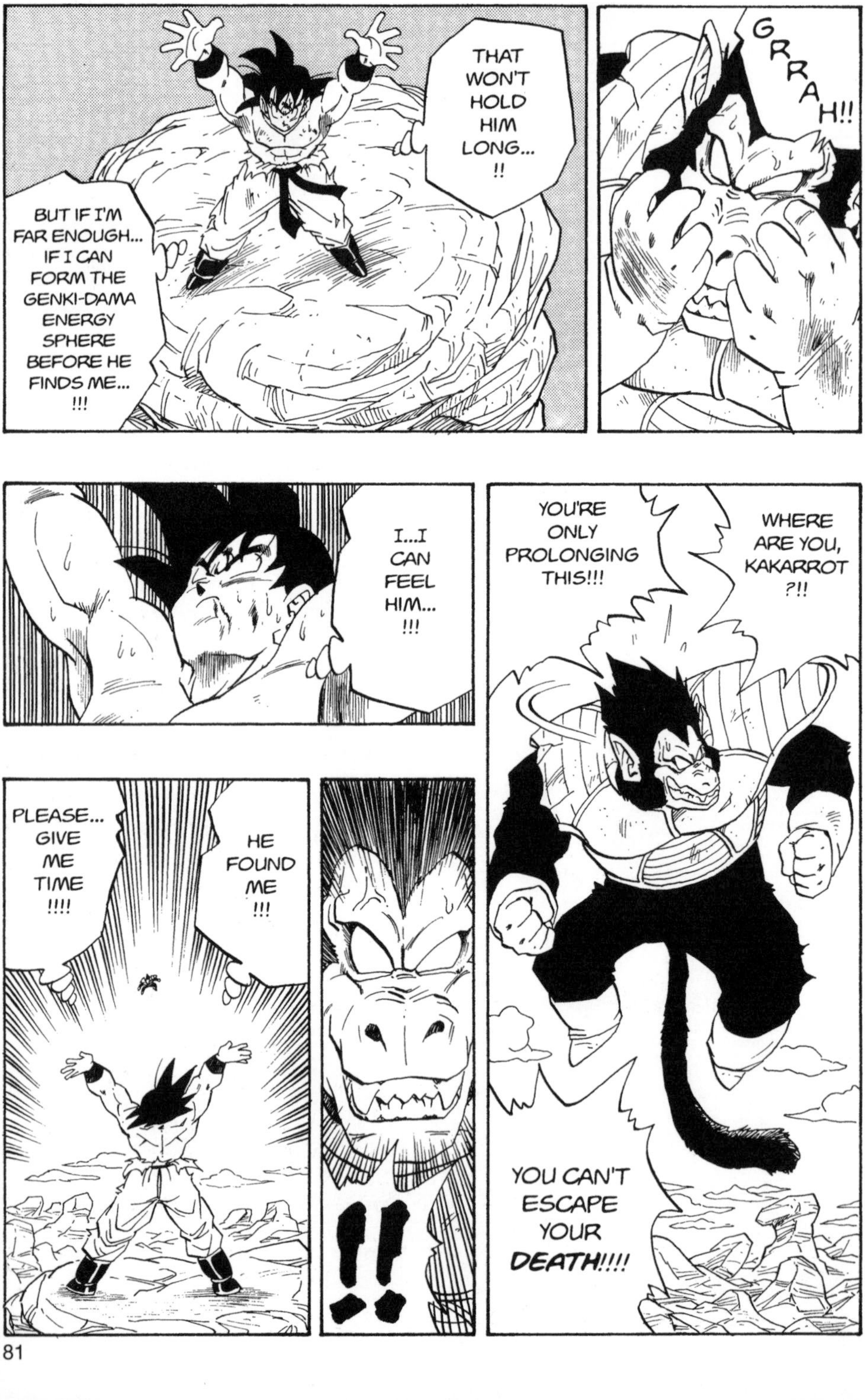
GRRAAH!!
THAT WON'T HOLD HIM LONG... !!
BUT IF I'M FAR ENOUGH... IF I CAN FORM THE GENKI-DAMA ENERGY SPHERE BEFORE HE FINDS ME... !!!
WHERE ARE YOU, KAKARROT ?!!
YOU'RE ONLY PROLONGING THIS!!!
YOU CAN'T ESCAPE YOUR **DEATH**!!!!
I...I CAN FEEL HIM... !!!
!!
HE FOUND ME !!!
PLEASE... GIVE ME TIME !!!!

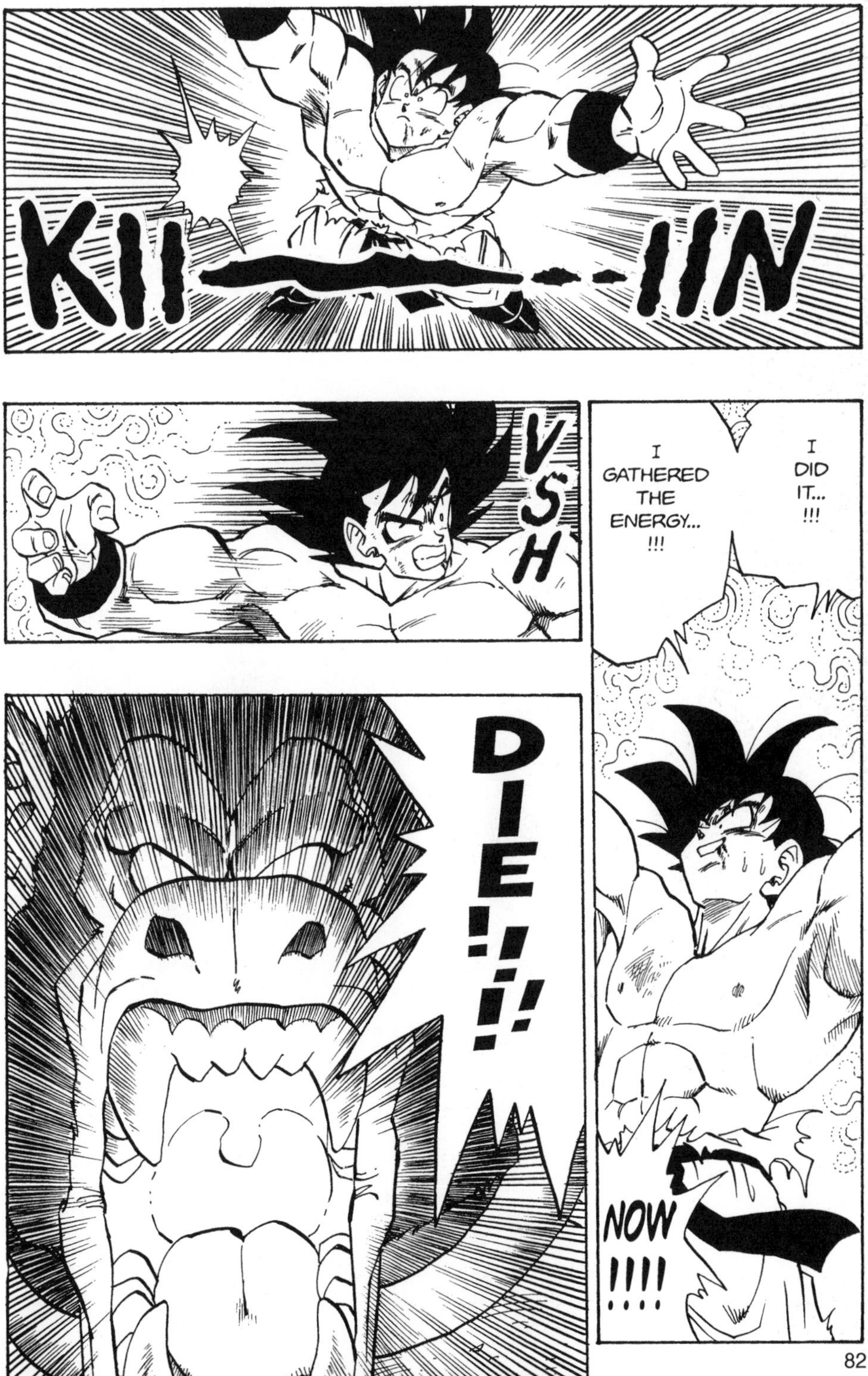
KII——IIN
I DID IT... !!!
I GATHERED THE ENERGY... !!!
NOW !!!!
VSH
DIE!!!!

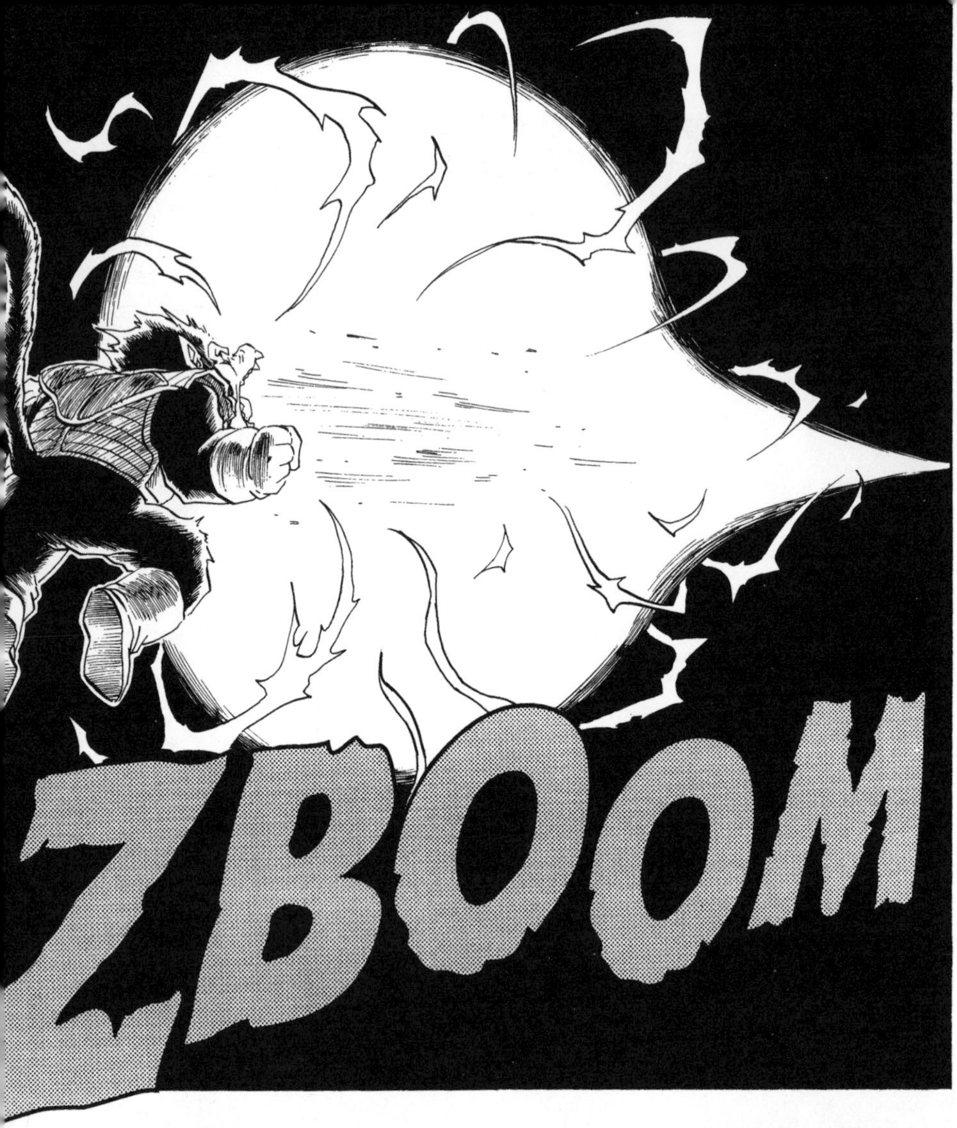
ZBOOM
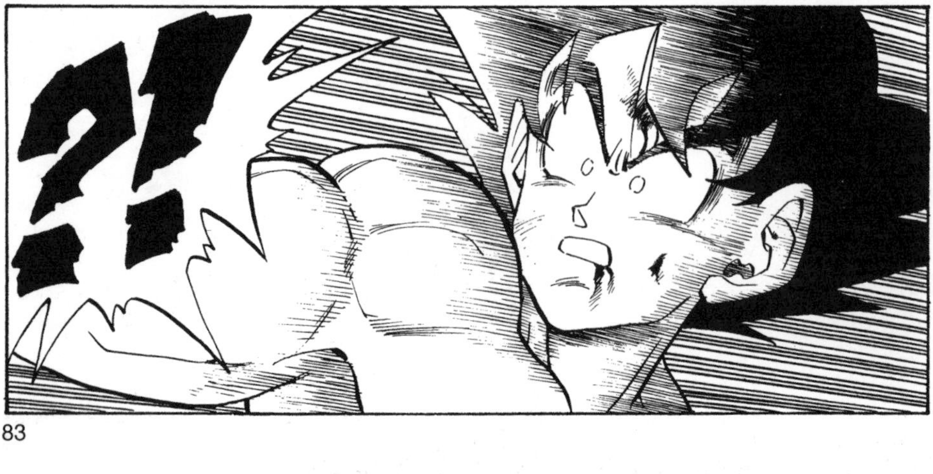
?!

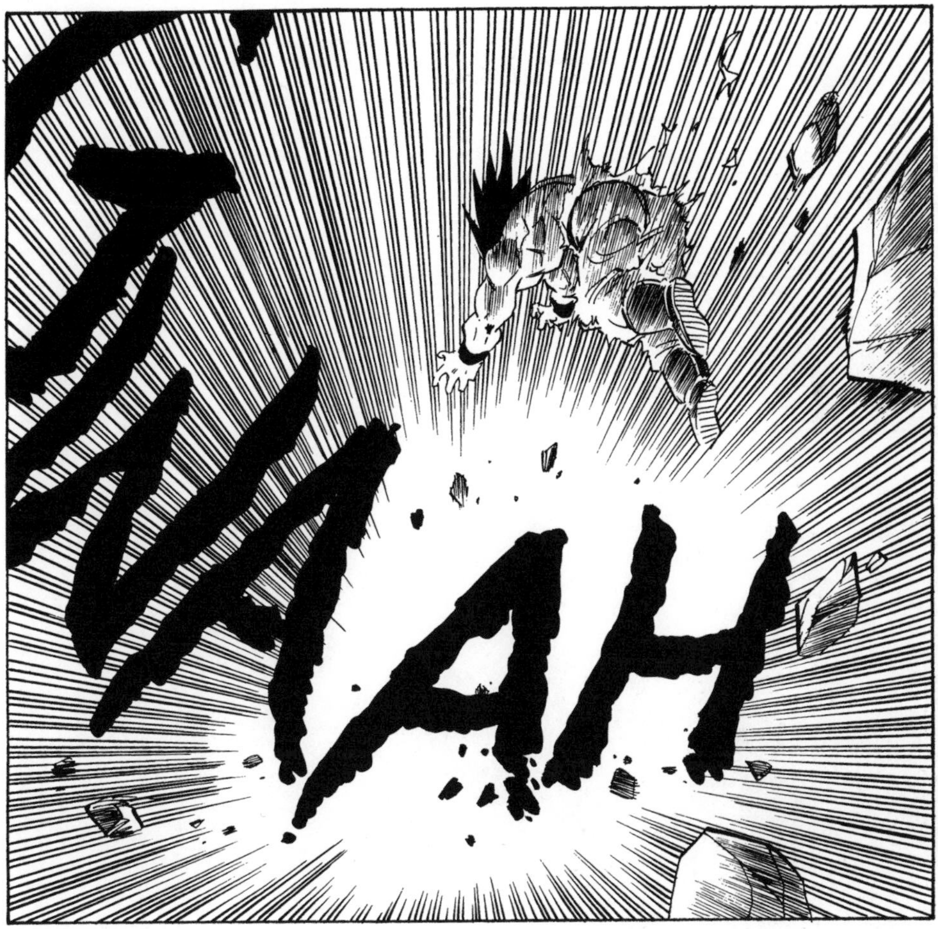

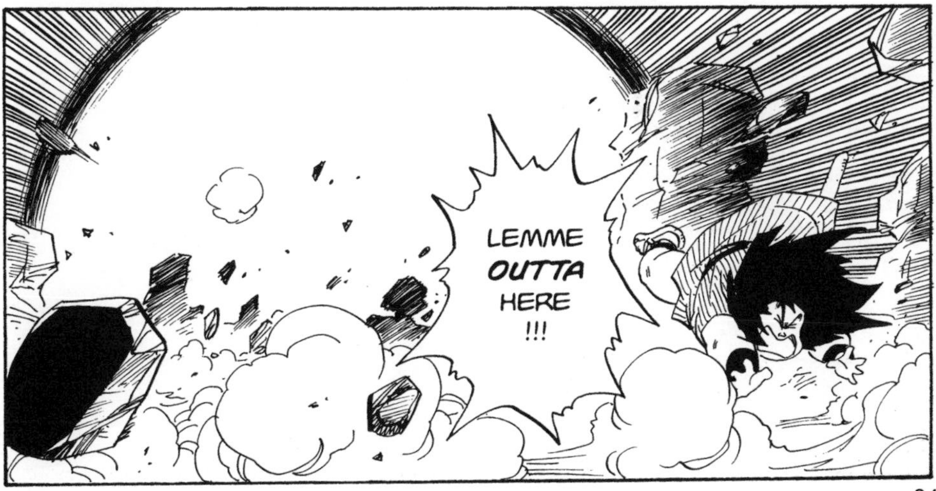
LEMME **OUTTA** HERE !!!

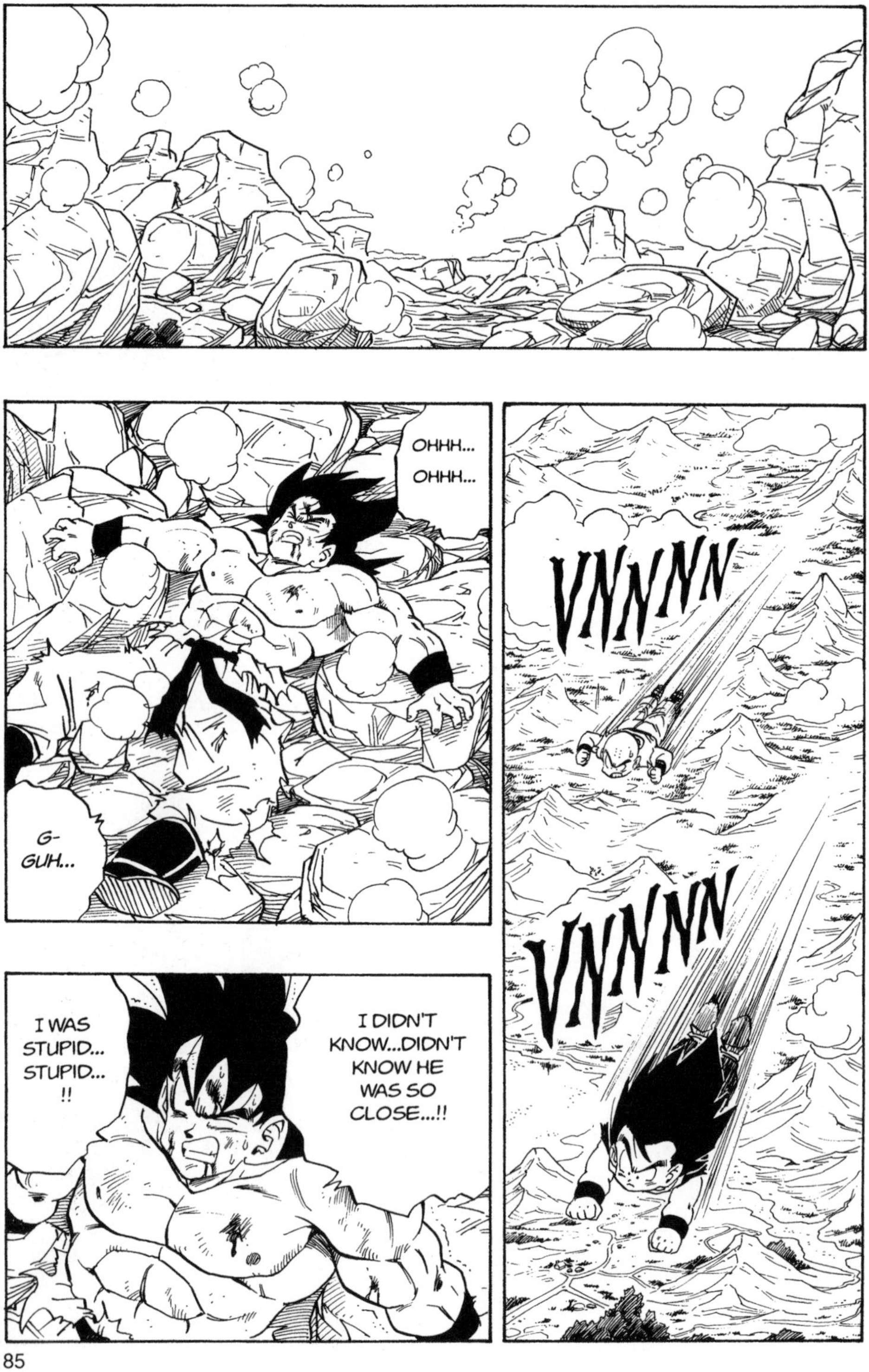
VNNNNN
VNNNNN
OHHH... OHHH...
G-GUH...
I DIDN'T KNOW...DIDN'T KNOW HE WAS SO CLOSE...!!
I WAS STUPID... STUPID... !!

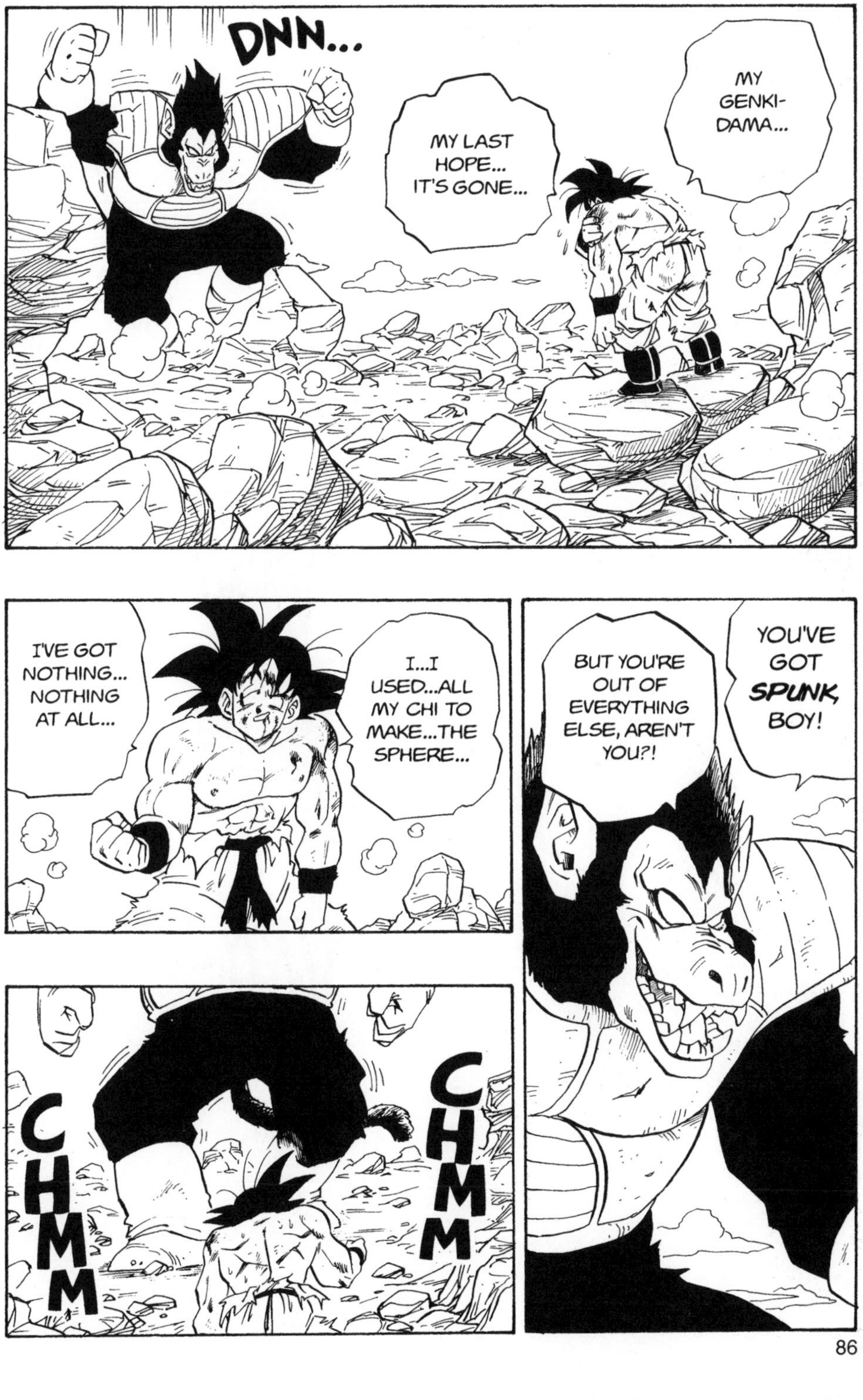
MY GENKI-DAMA...
MY LAST HOPE... IT'S GONE...
DNN...
YOU'VE GOT **SPUNK**, BOY!
BUT YOU'RE OUT OF EVERYTHING ELSE, AREN'T YOU?!
I...I USED...ALL MY CHI TO MAKE...THE SPHERE...
I'VE GOT NOTHING... NOTHING AT ALL...
CHMM
CHMM

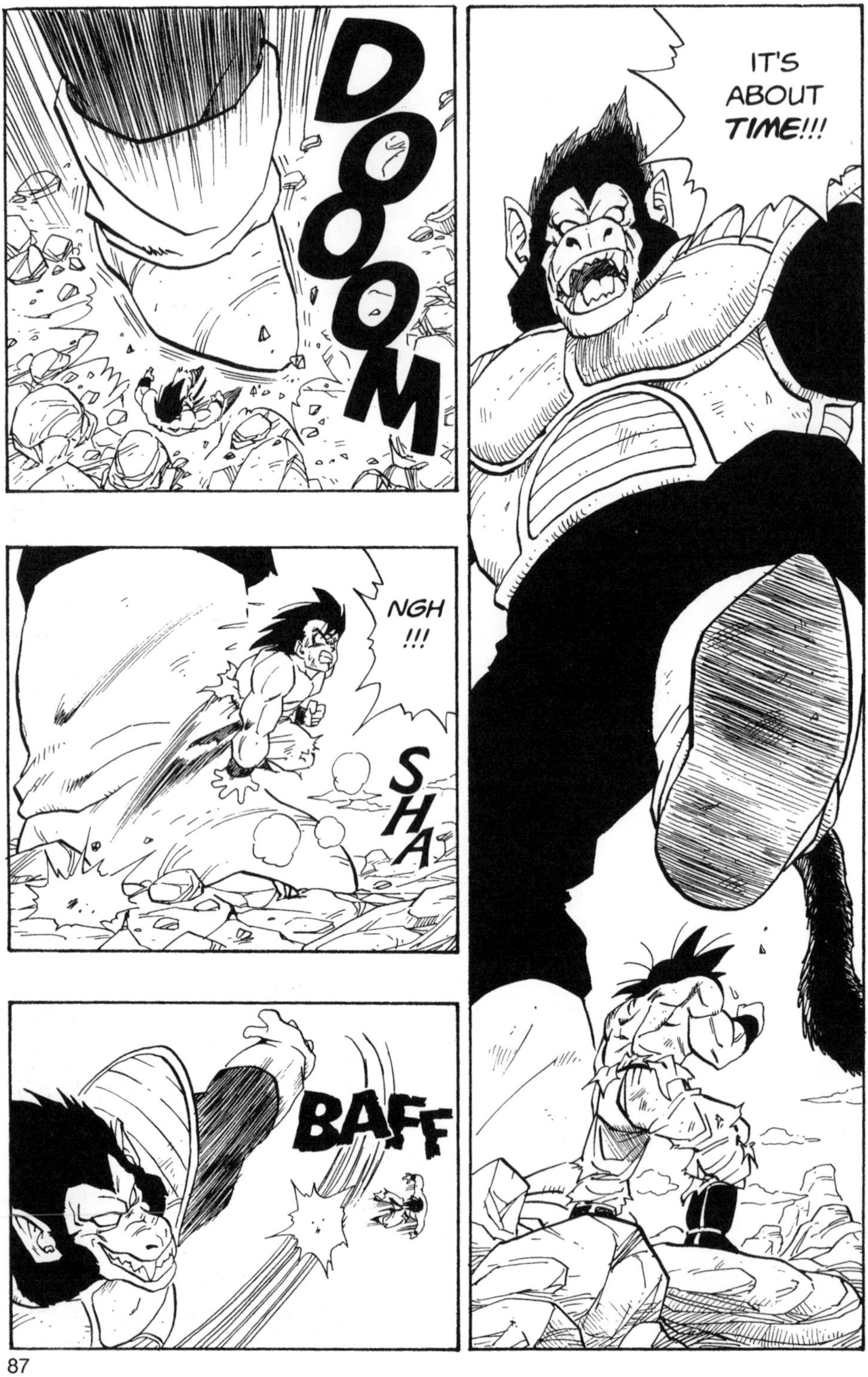
IT'S ABOUT TIME!!!
DOOOM
NGH !!!
SHA
BAFF

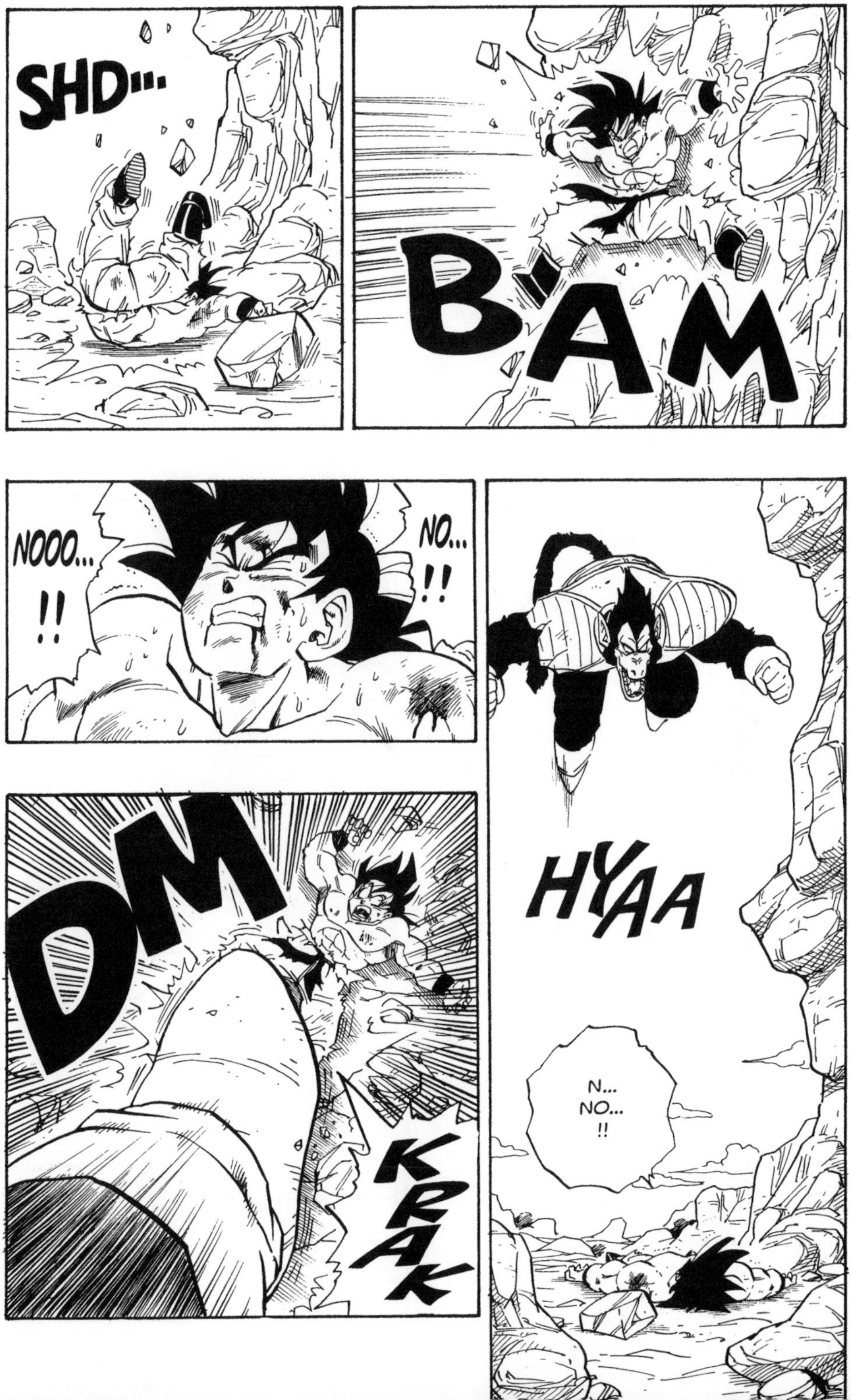
BAM
SHD...
HYAA
N... NO... !!
NO... !!
NOOO... !!
DM
KRAK

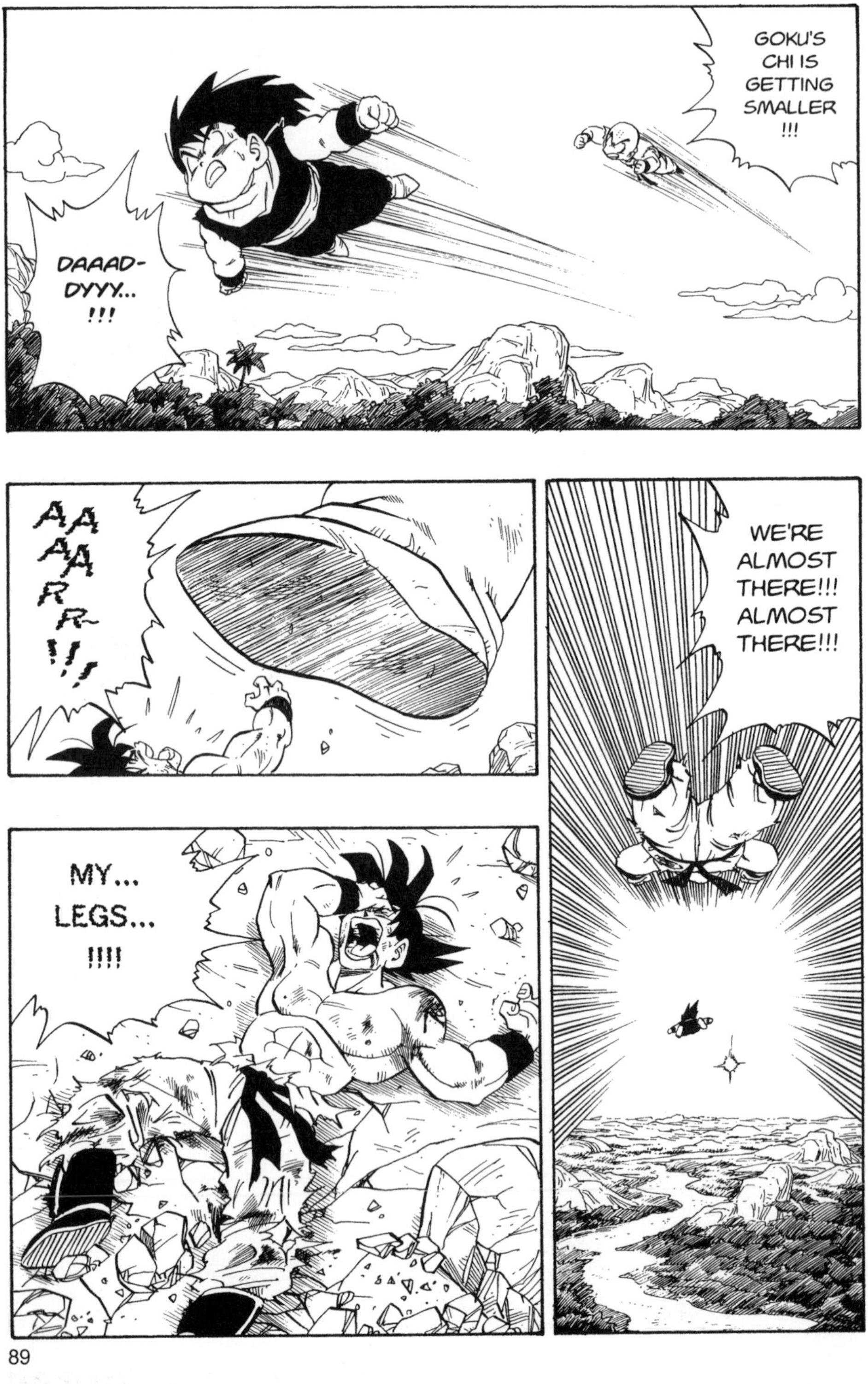
GOKU'S CHI IS GETTING SMALLER !!!
DAAAD-DYYY... !!!
WE'RE ALMOST THERE!!! ALMOST THERE!!!
AAAARR~!!!
MY... LEGS... !!!!

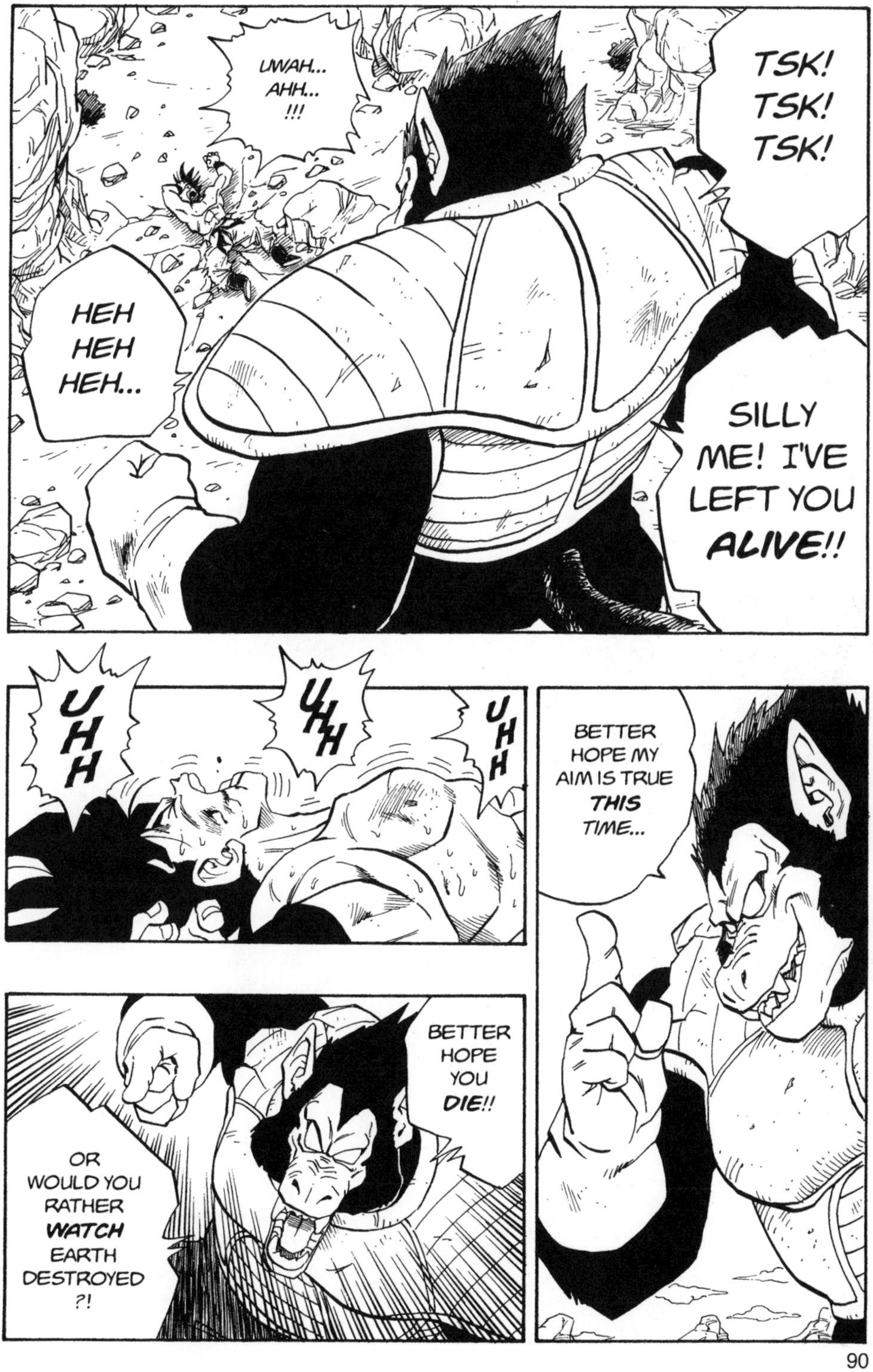
TSK! TSK! TSK!
UWAH... AHH... !!!
SILLY ME! I'VE LEFT YOU ALIVE!!
HEH HEH HEH...
BETTER HOPE MY AIM IS TRUE THIS TIME...
UHH
UHH
UHH
BETTER HOPE YOU DIE!!
OR WOULD YOU RATHER WATCH EARTH DESTROYED ?!

SH-SHUT UP... VEGETA... YOU BEAT ME... YOU WERE STRONGER THAN WHAT I...OR ANYBODY ELSE... THOUGHT ...
huff
B...BUT IF YOU THINK... THIS IS SOME-THING TO BE PROUD OF...Y...YOU'RE GONNA LEARN...
huff
YOU'RE GONNA PAY... SOMEDAY...
HAHH!!!!
VMM

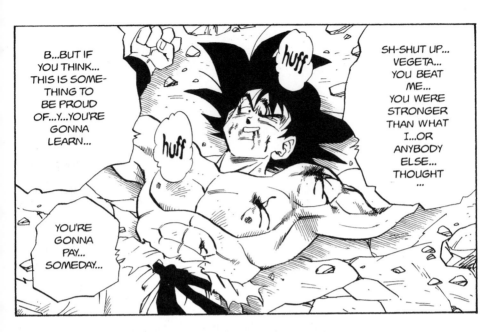

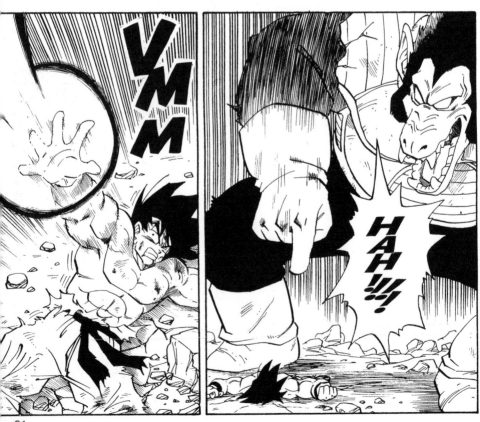

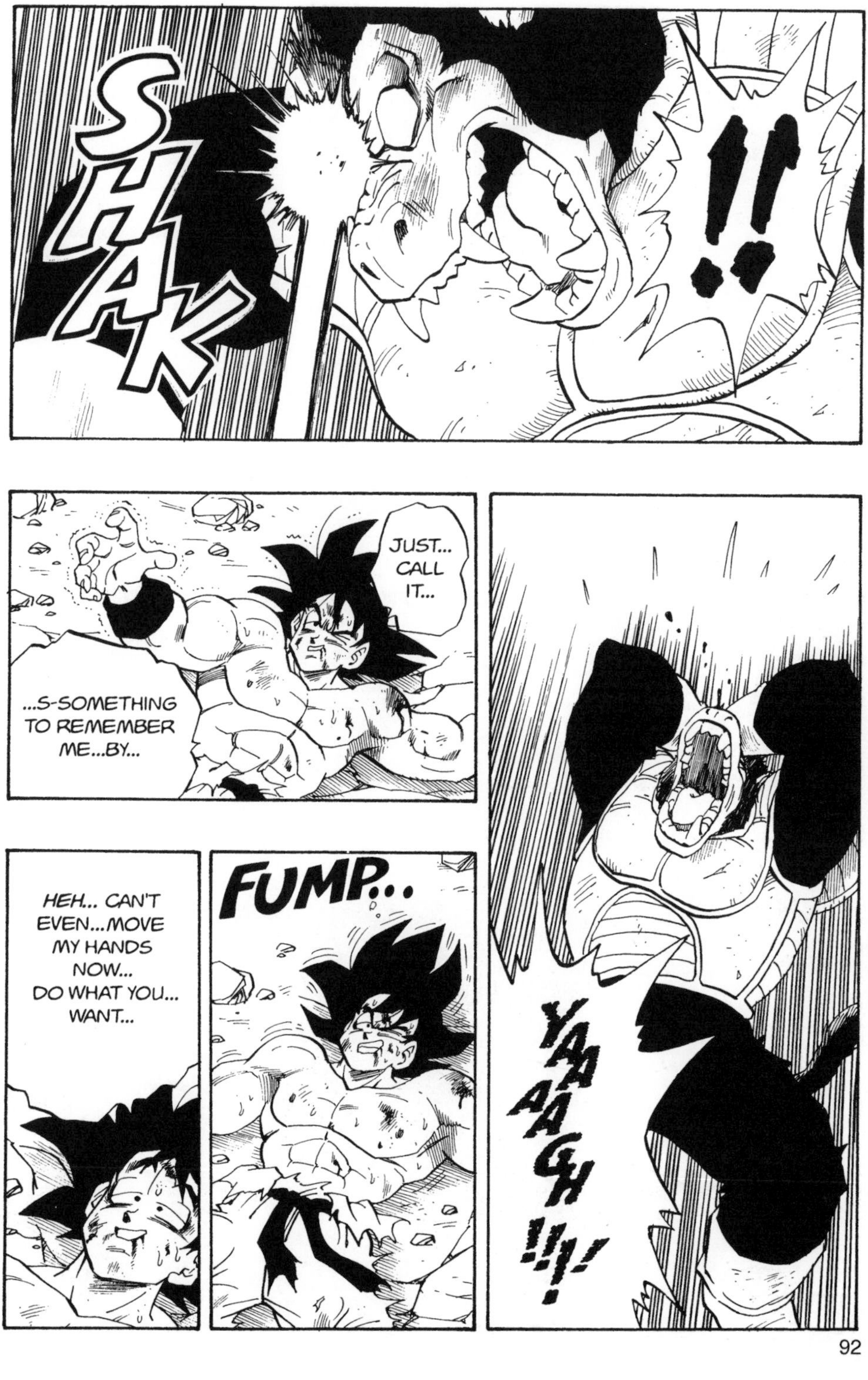
!!
SHAK
YAAAAGH!!!!
JUST... CALL IT...
...S-SOMETHING TO REMEMBER ME...BY...
FUMP...
HEH... CAN'T EVEN...MOVE MY HANDS NOW... DO WHAT YOU... WANT...

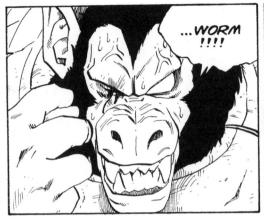

...WORM
!!!!

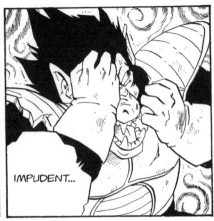

IMPUDENT...

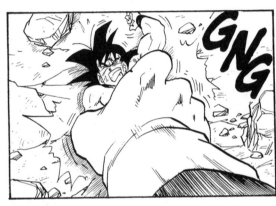

GNG

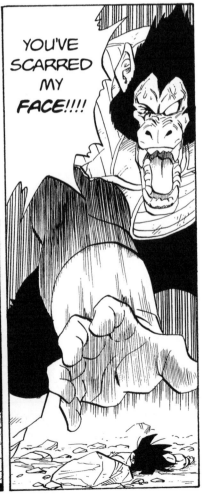

YOU'VE
SCARRED
MY
*FACE*!!!!

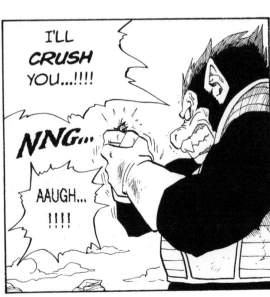

I'LL
*CRUSH*
YOU...!!!!

NNG...

AAUGH...
!!!!

# DBZ:41 • The Last Heartbeat

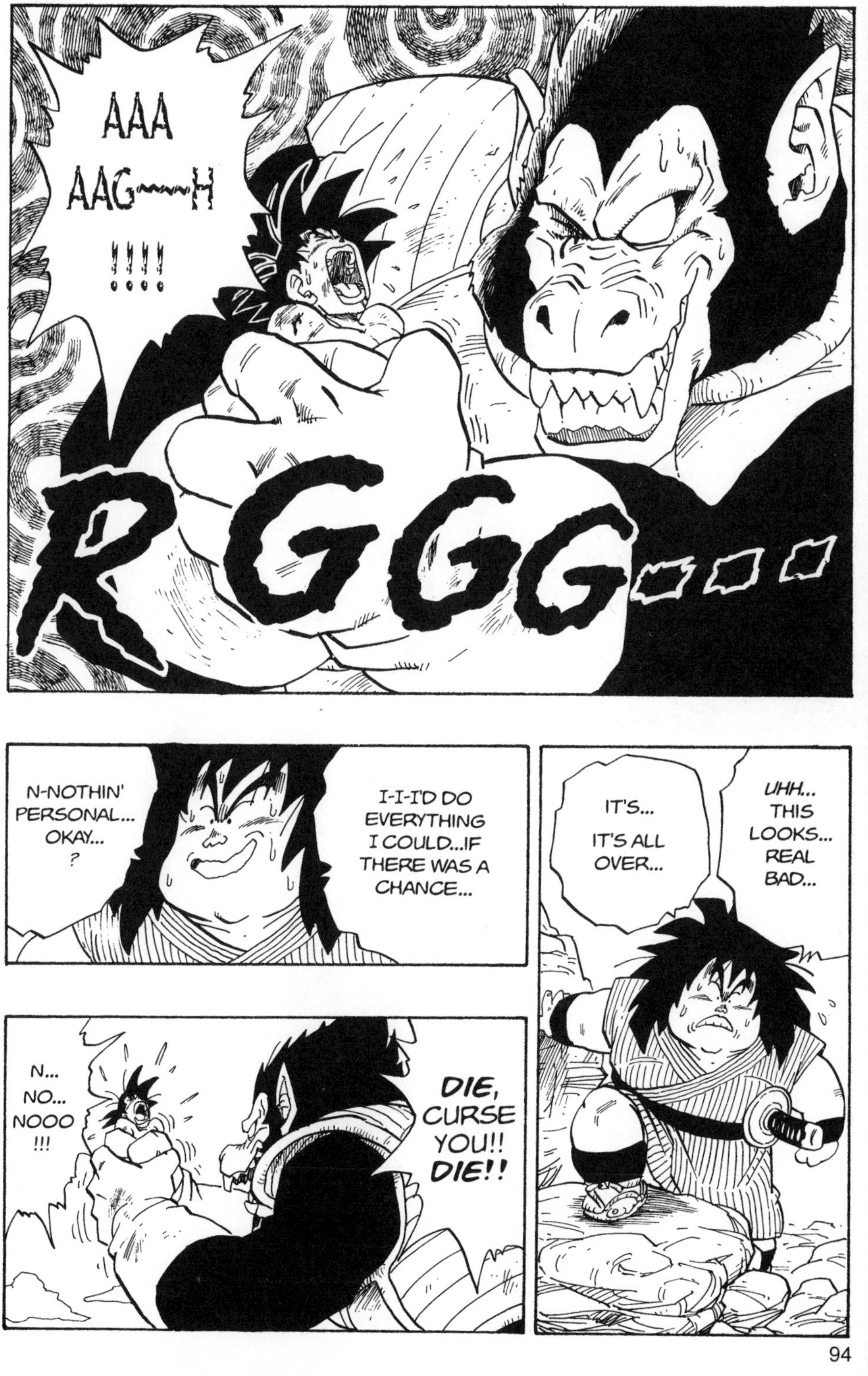
AAA AAG~~~H !!!!
RGGG...
UHH... THIS LOOKS... REAL BAD...
IT'S... IT'S ALL OVER...
I-I-I'D DO EVERYTHING I COULD...IF THERE WAS A CHANCE...
N-NOTHIN' PERSONAL... OKAY... ?
DIE, CURSE YOU!! DIE!!
N... NO... NOOO !!!

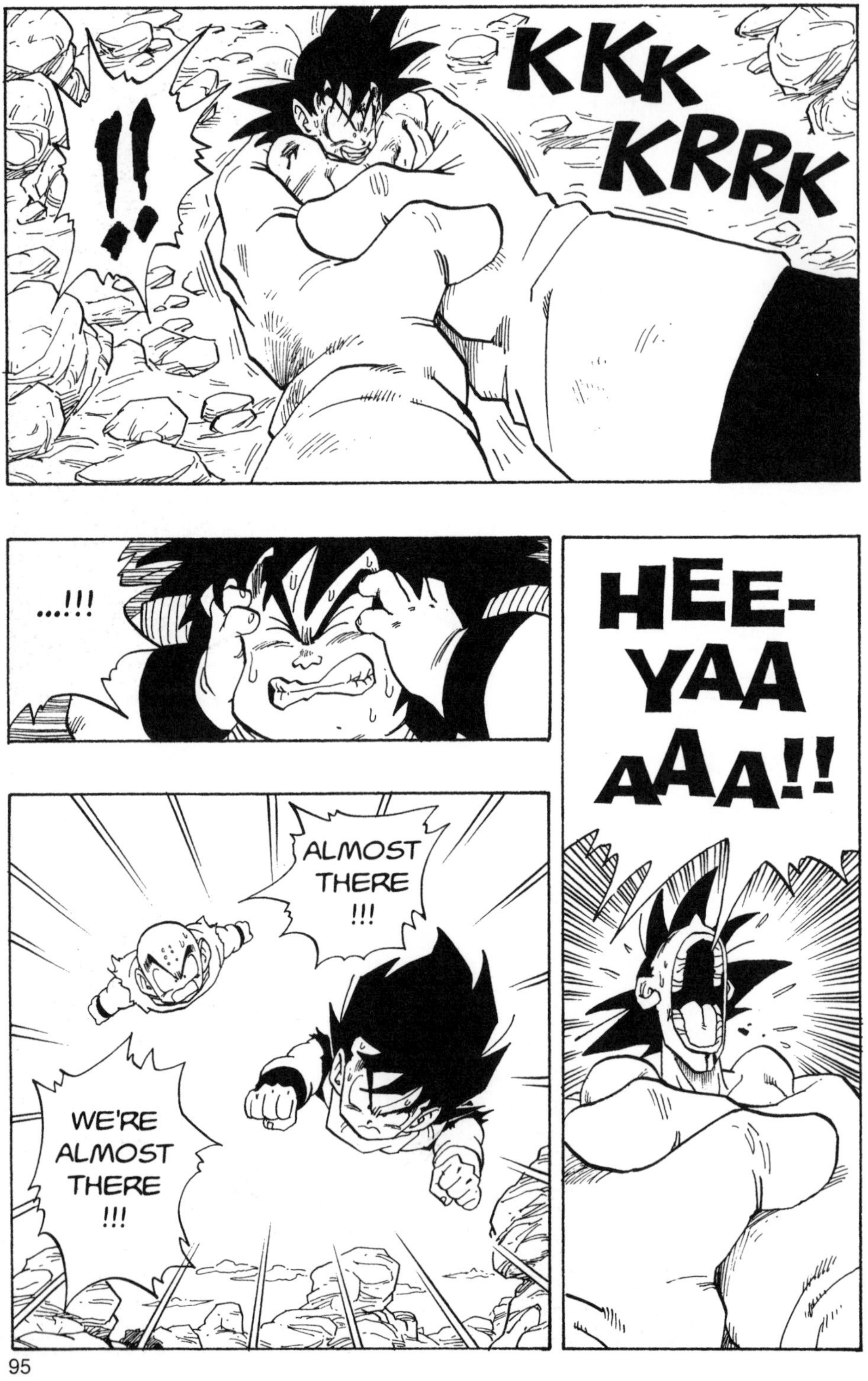
KKK KRRK
!!
HEE-YAA AAA!!
...!!!
ALMOST THERE !!!
WE'RE ALMOST THERE !!!

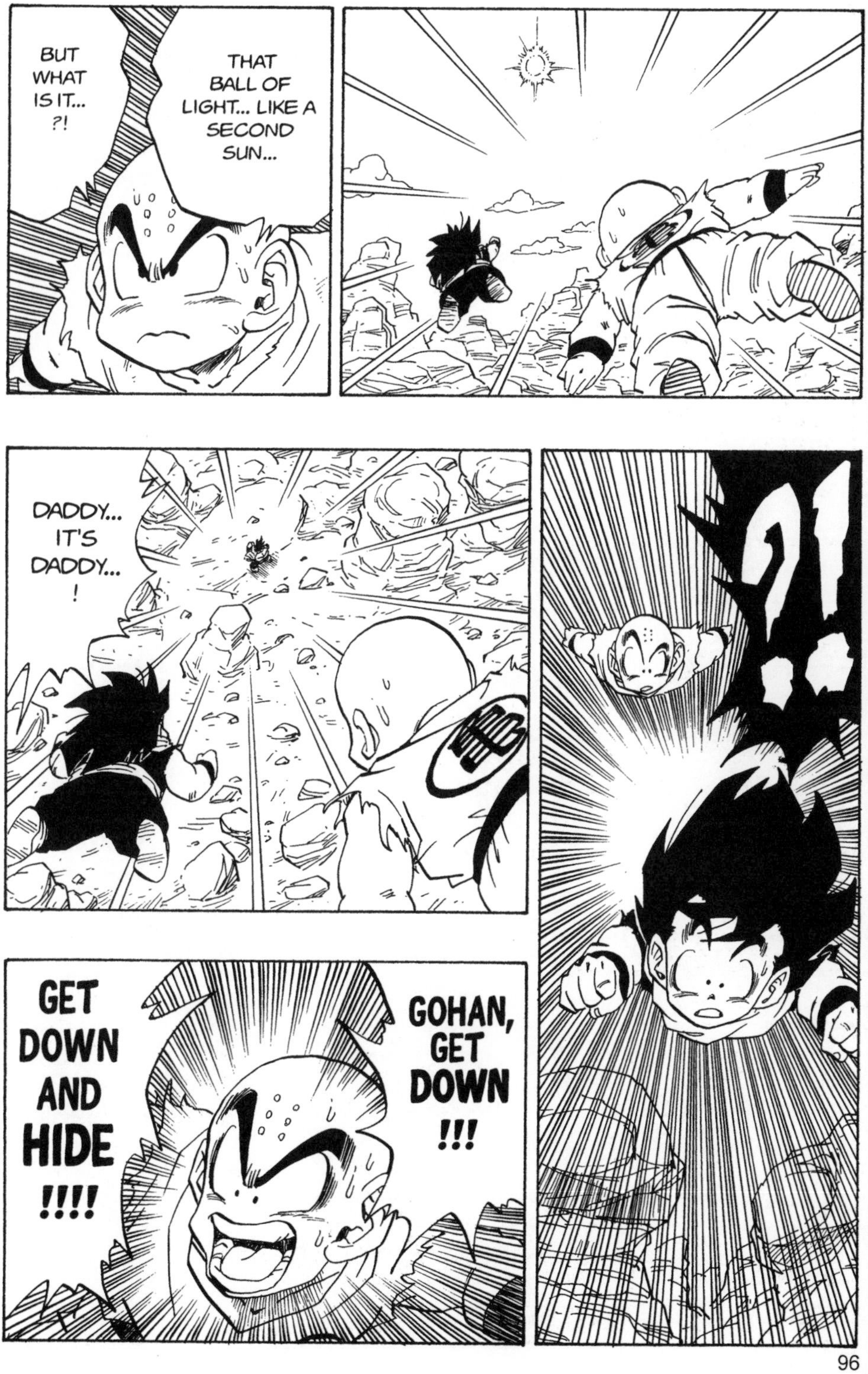
THAT BALL OF LIGHT... LIKE A SECOND SUN...
BUT WHAT IS IT... ?!
?!
DADDY... IT'S DADDY... !
GOHAN, GET DOWN !!!
GET DOWN AND HIDE !!!!

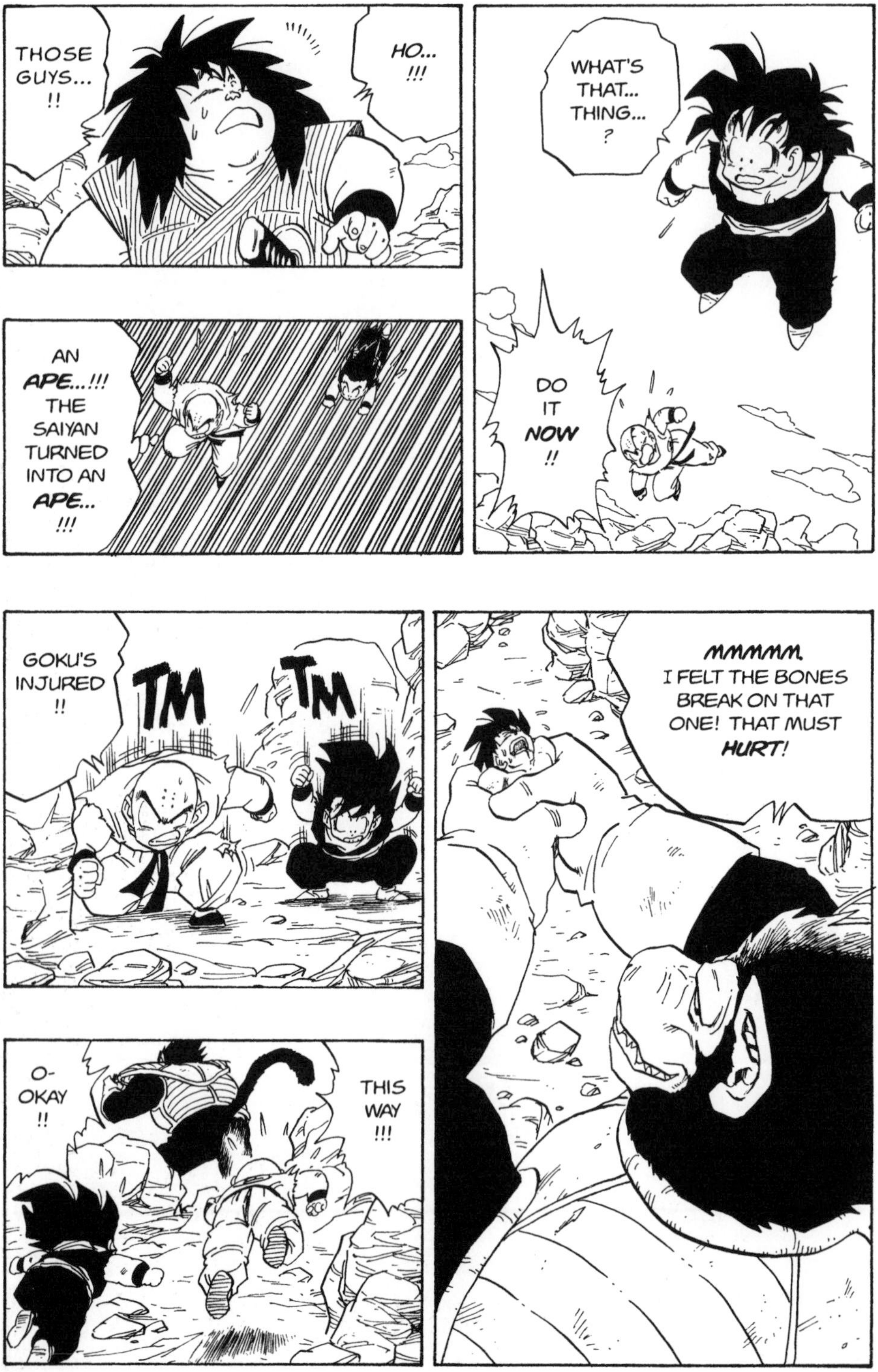

WHAT'S THAT... THING... ?
DO IT NOW !!
HO... !!!
THOSE GUYS... !!
AN APE...!!! THE SAIYAN TURNED INTO AN APE... !!!
MMMMM. I FELT THE BONES BREAK ON THAT ONE! THAT MUST HURT!
GOKU'S INJURED !!
TM
TM
THIS WAY !!!
O-OKAY !!

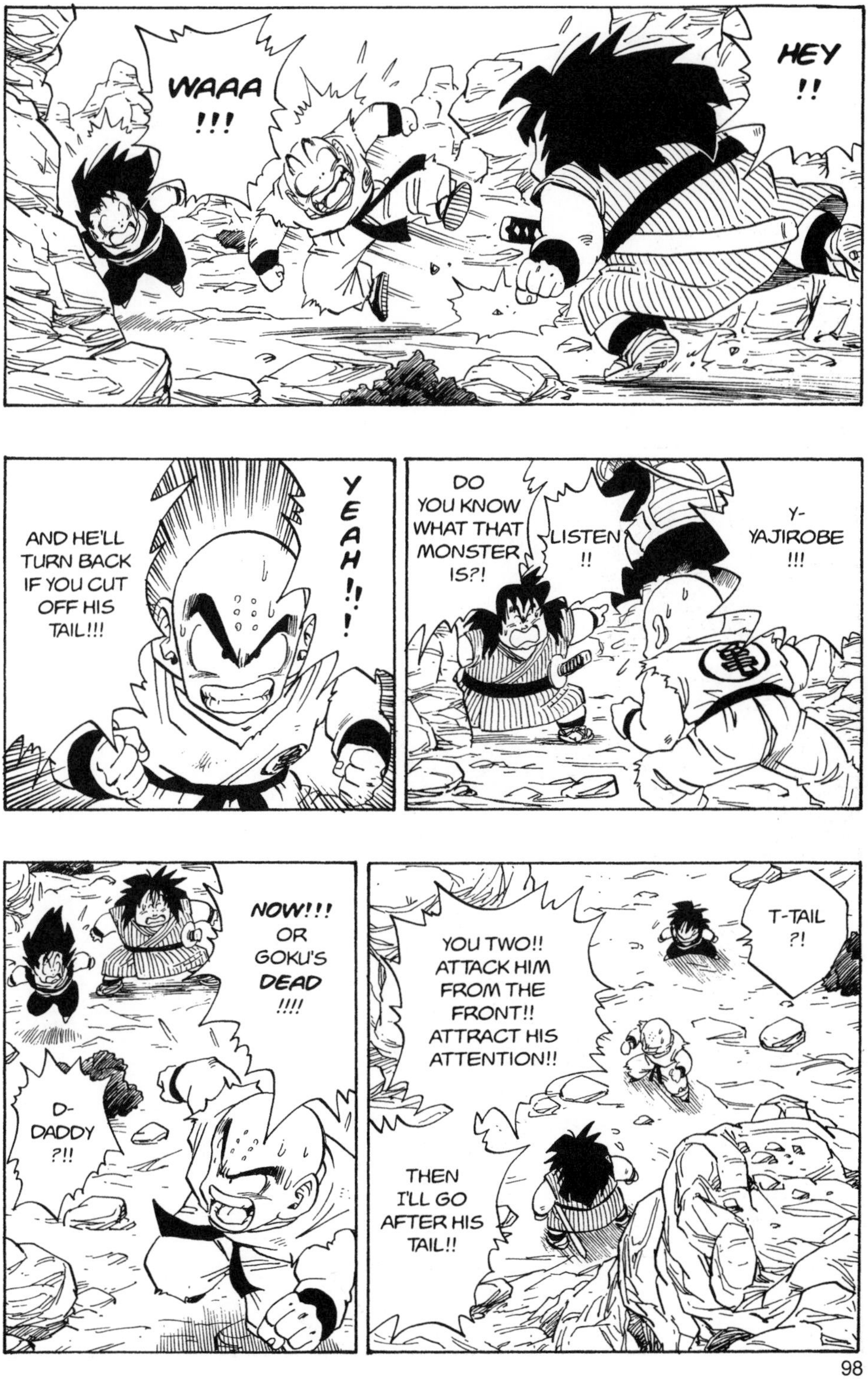
HEY !!
WAAA !!!
Y- YAJIROBE !!!
LISTEN !!
DO YOU KNOW WHAT THAT MONSTER IS?!
YEAH!!!
AND HE'LL TURN BACK IF YOU CUT OFF HIS TAIL!!!
T-TAIL ?!
YOU TWO!! ATTACK HIM FROM THE FRONT!! ATTRACT HIS ATTENTION!!
THEN I'LL GO AFTER HIS TAIL!!
NOW!!! OR GOKU'S DEAD !!!!
D-DADDY ?!!

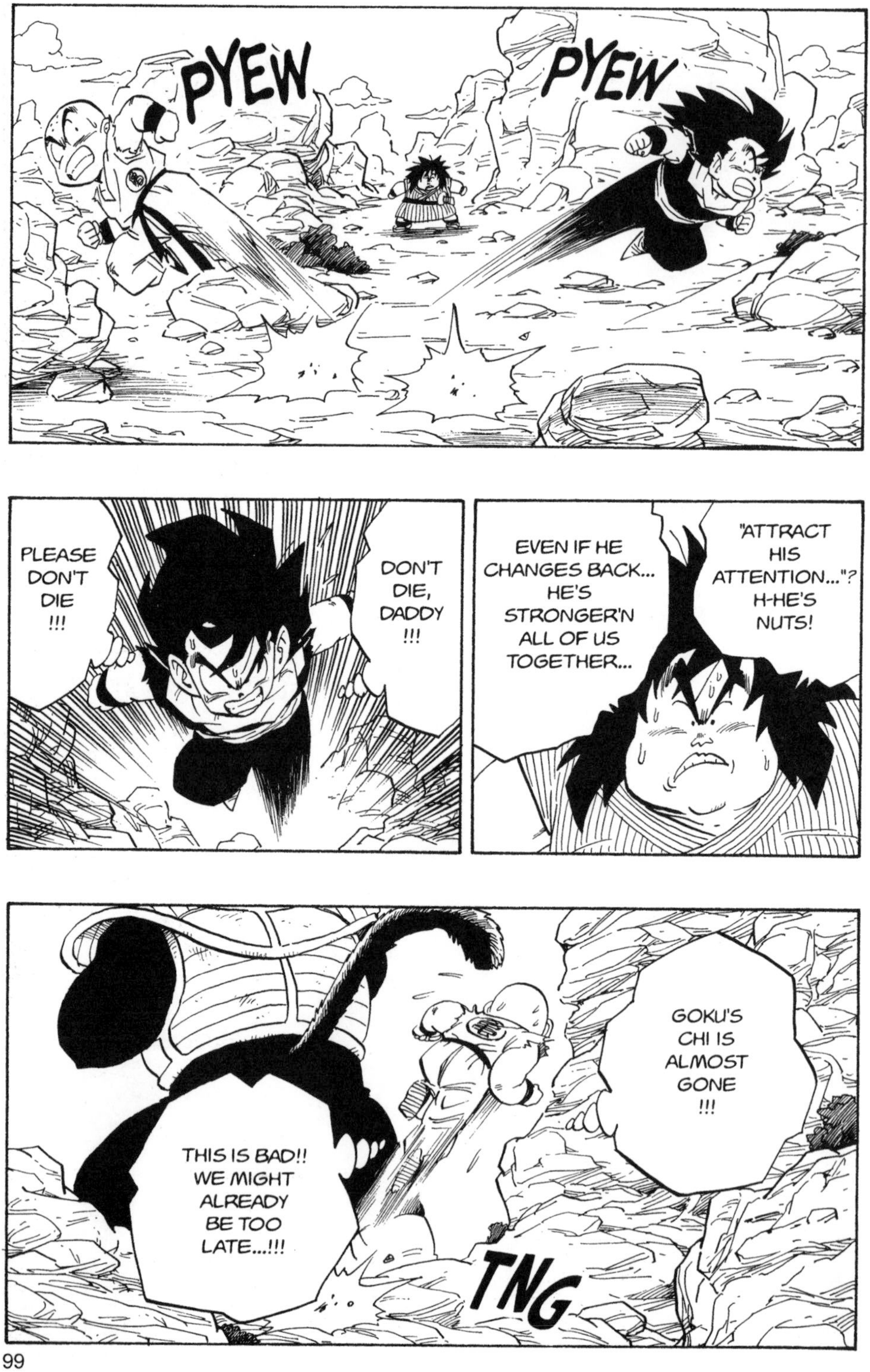
PYEW
PYEW
"ATTRACT HIS ATTENTION..."? H-HE'S NUTS!
EVEN IF HE CHANGES BACK... HE'S STRONGER'N ALL OF US TOGETHER...
DON'T DIE, DADDY !!!
PLEASE DON'T DIE !!!
GOKU'S CHI IS ALMOST GONE !!!
THIS IS BAD!! WE MIGHT ALREADY BE TOO LATE...!!!
TNG

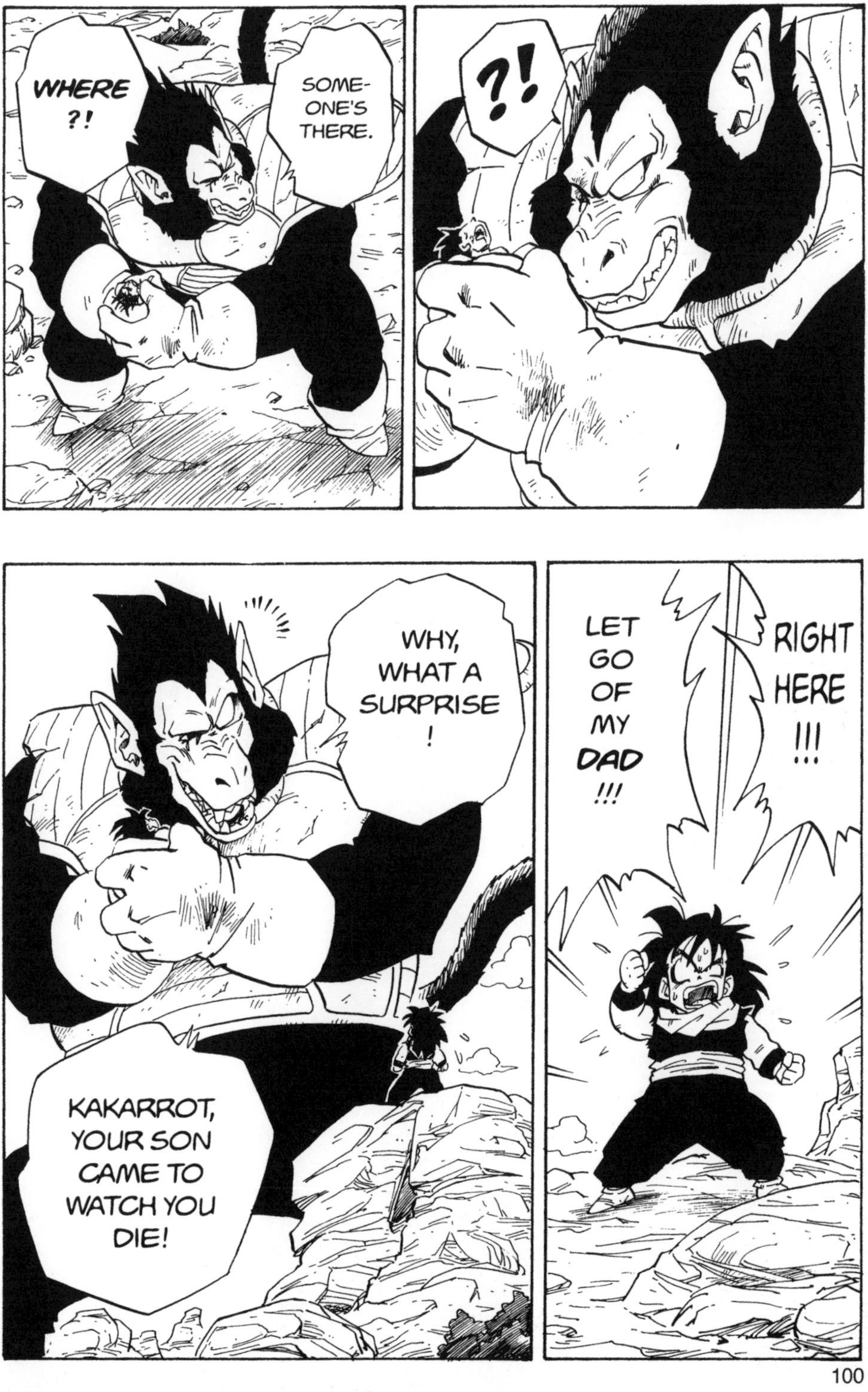
?!
SOME-ONE'S THERE.
WHERE ?!
RIGHT HERE !!!
LET GO OF MY DAD !!!
WHY, WHAT A SURPRISE !
KAKARROT, YOUR SON CAME TO WATCH YOU DIE!

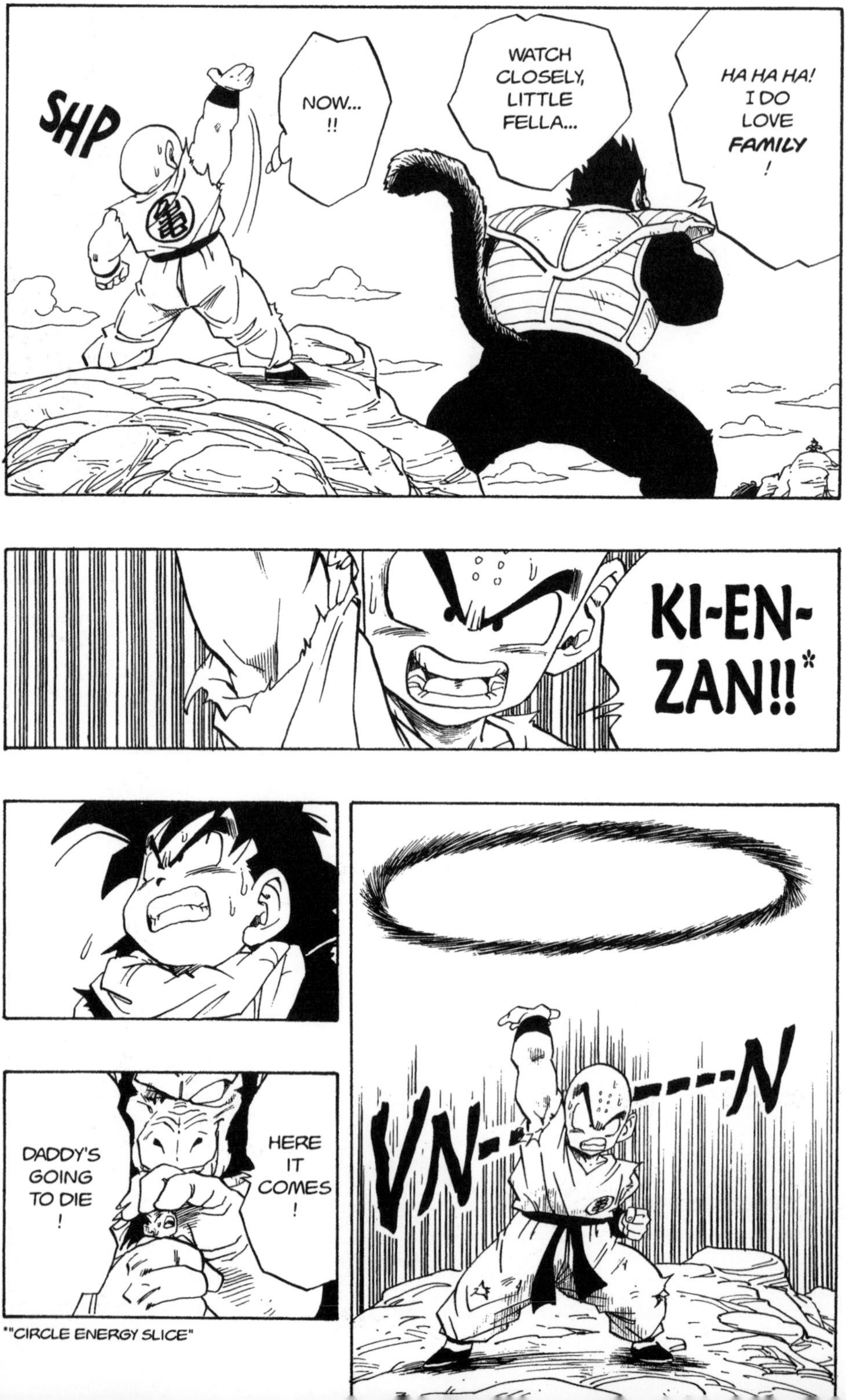
HA HA HA! I DO LOVE FAMILY!
WATCH CLOSELY, LITTLE FELLA...
NOW... !!
SHP
KI-EN-ZAN!!*
VN----N
HERE IT COMES!
DADDY'S GOING TO DIE!

*"CIRCLE ENERGY SLICE"

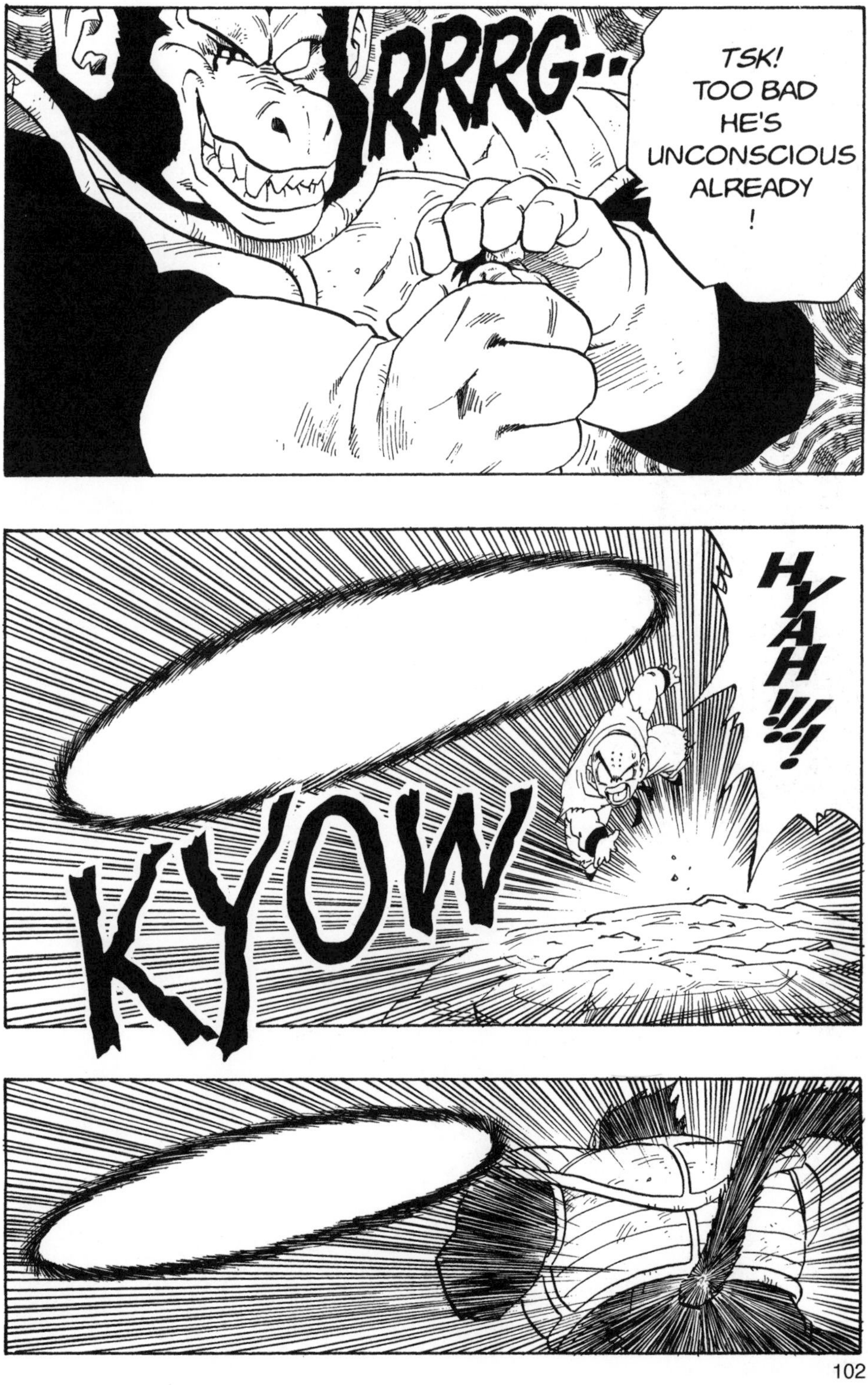
TSK! TOO BAD HE'S UNCONSCIOUS ALREADY !
RRRG..
HYAH!!!!
KYOW

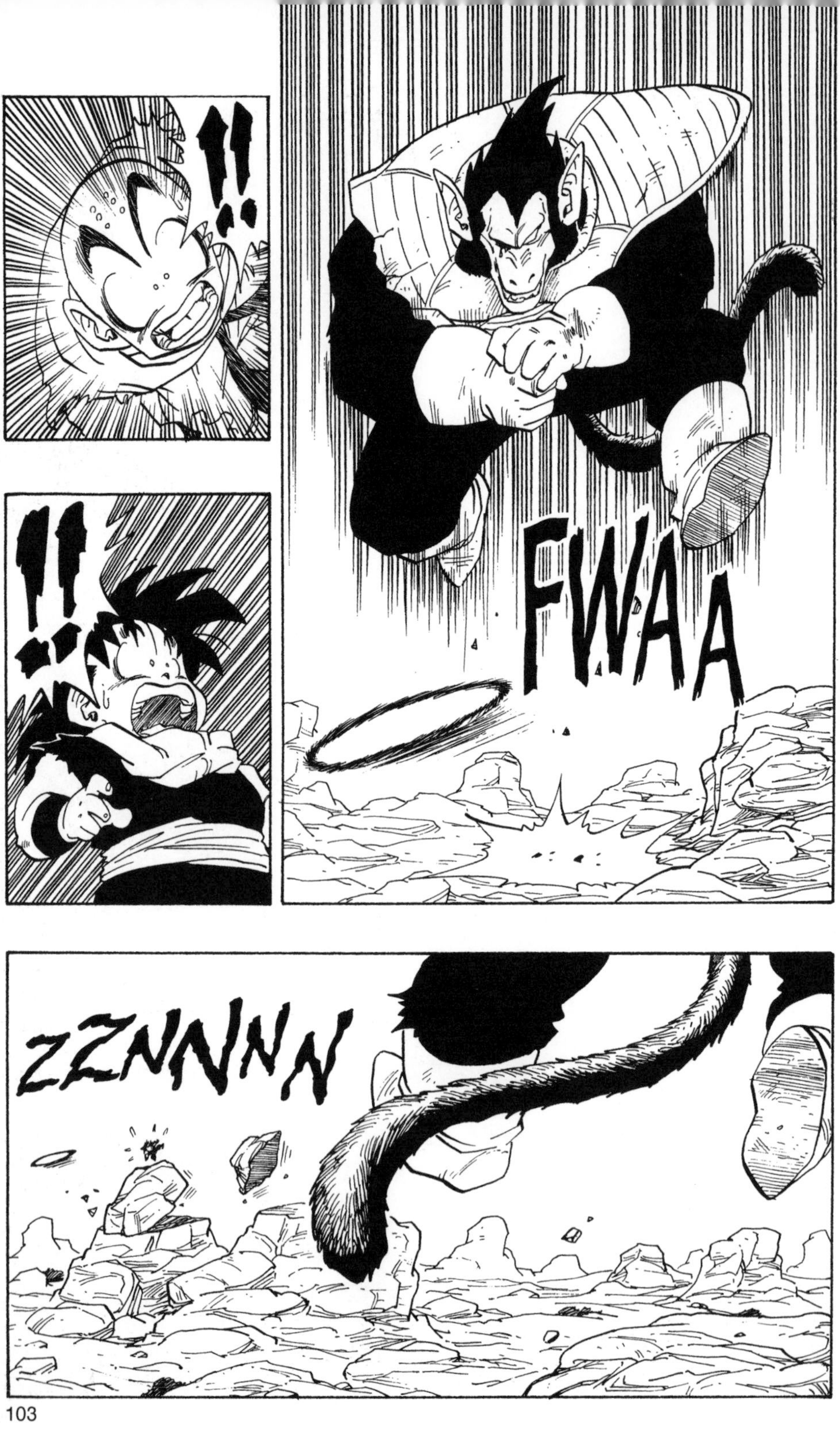
FWAA
!!
!!
ZZNNNN

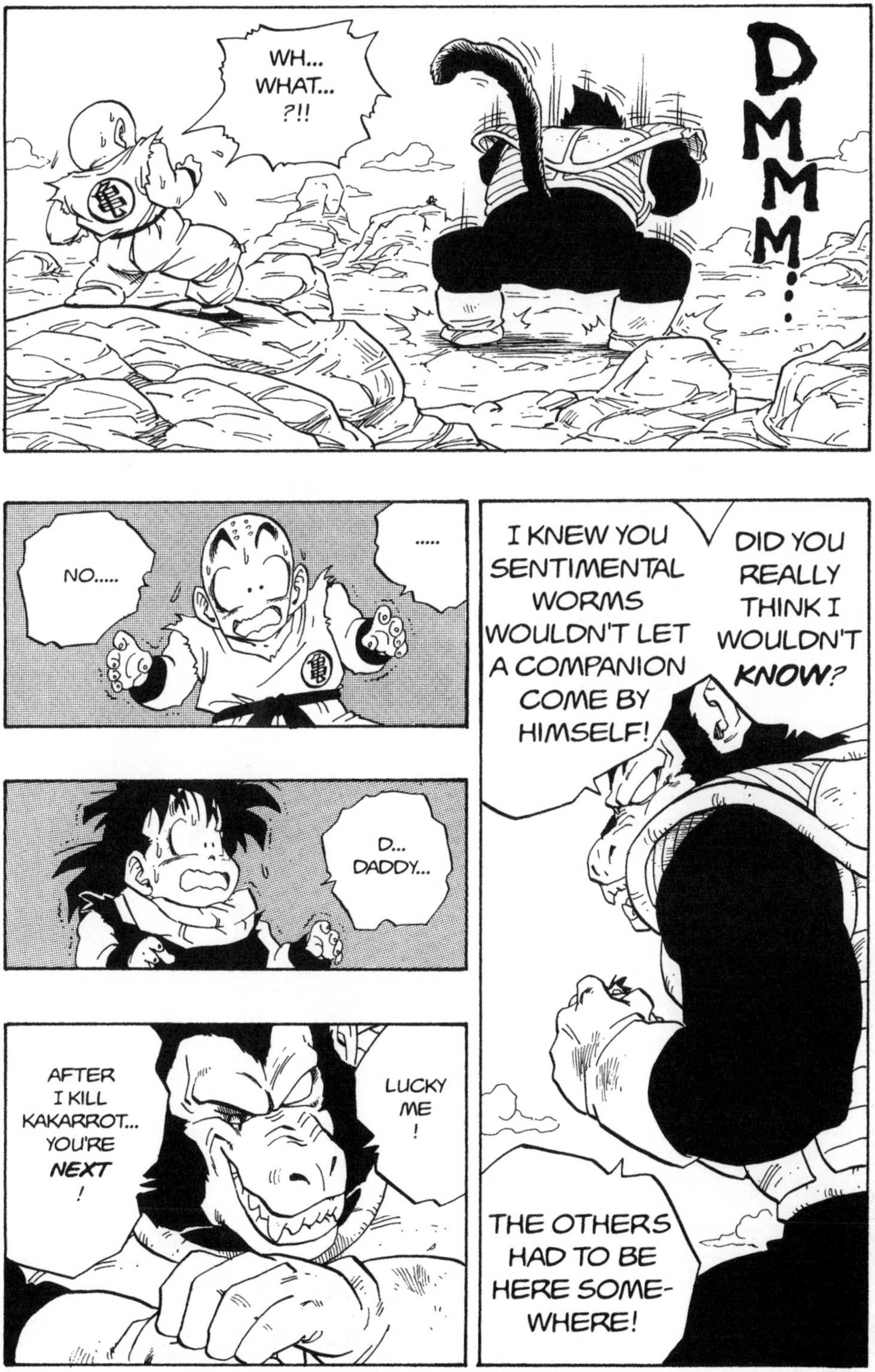
DMMM...
WH... WHAT... ?!!
DID YOU REALLY THINK I WOULDN'T ***KNOW***?
I KNEW YOU SENTIMENTAL WORMS WOULDN'T LET A COMPANION COME BY HIMSELF!
THE OTHERS HAD TO BE HERE SOME-WHERE!
.....
NO.....
D... DADDY...
LUCKY ME!
AFTER I KILL KAKARROT... YOU'RE ***NEXT***!

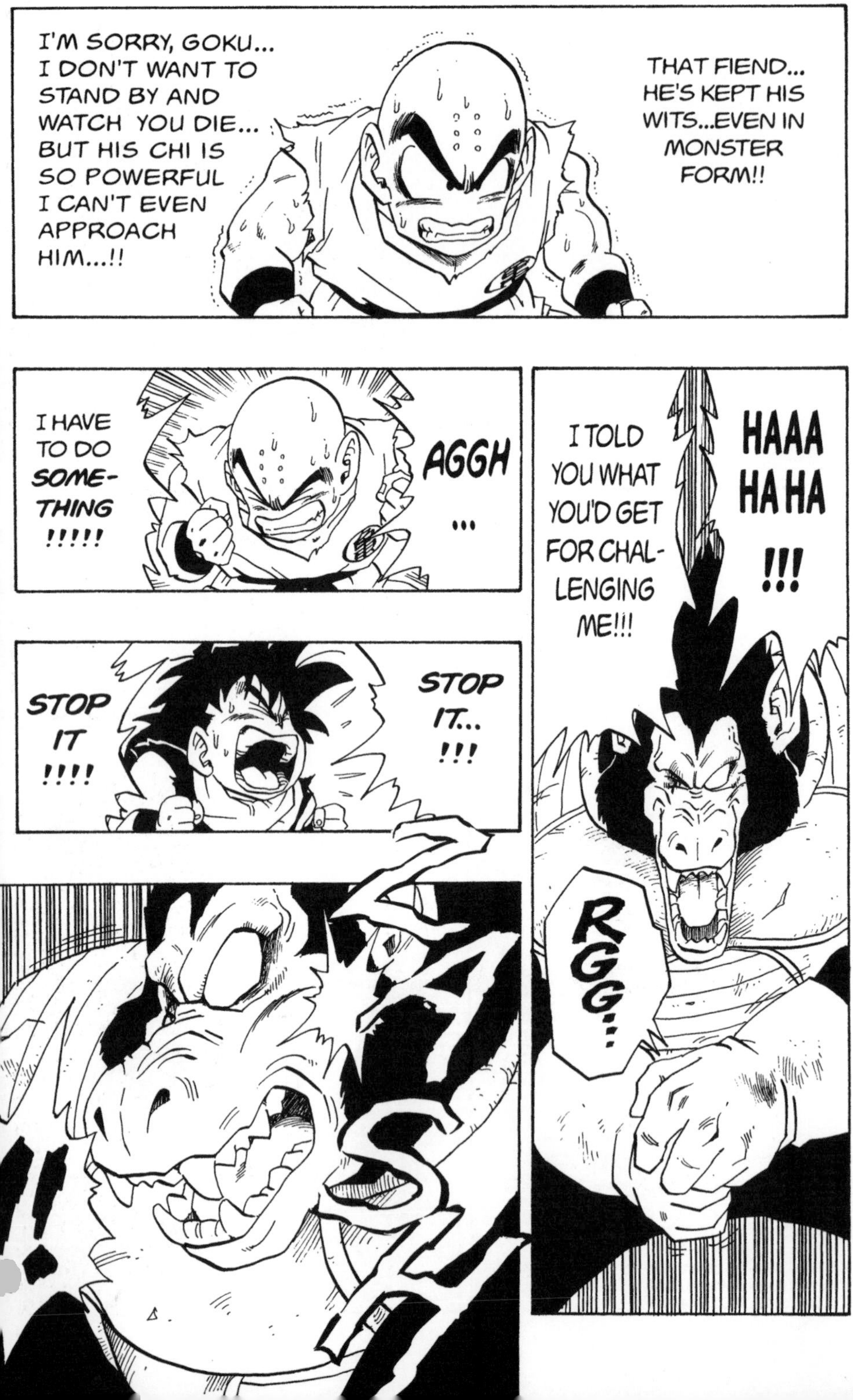
THAT FIEND... HE'S KEPT HIS WITS...EVEN IN MONSTER FORM!!
I'M SORRY, GOKU... I DON'T WANT TO STAND BY AND WATCH YOU DIE... BUT HIS CHI IS SO POWERFUL I CAN'T EVEN APPROACH HIM...!!
HAAA HA HA !!!
I TOLD YOU WHAT YOU'D GET FOR CHAL-LENGING ME!!!
RGG...
AGGH ...
I HAVE TO DO SOME-THING !!!!!
STOP IT... !!!
STOP IT !!!!
ZASH
!!

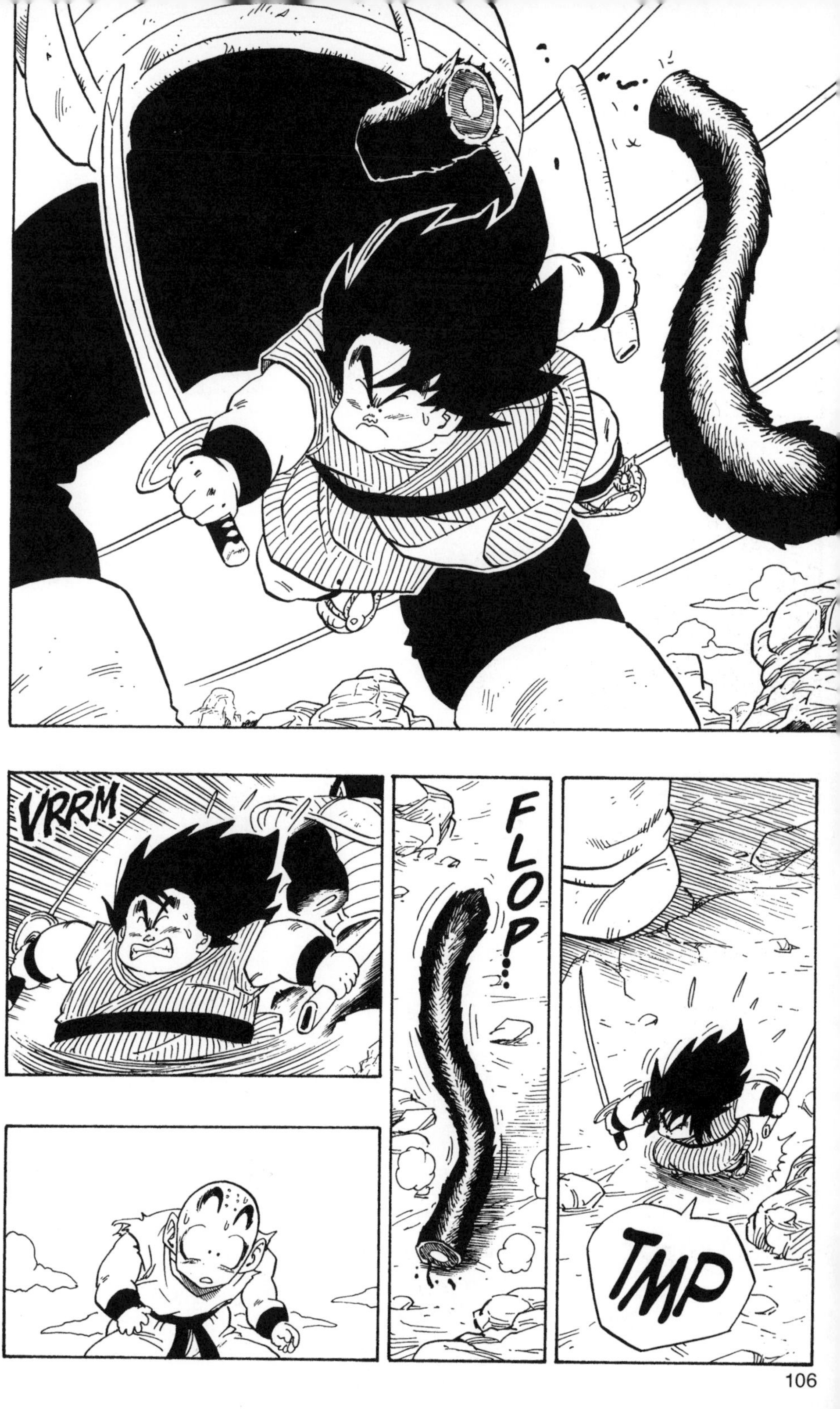
TMP
FLOP...
VRRM

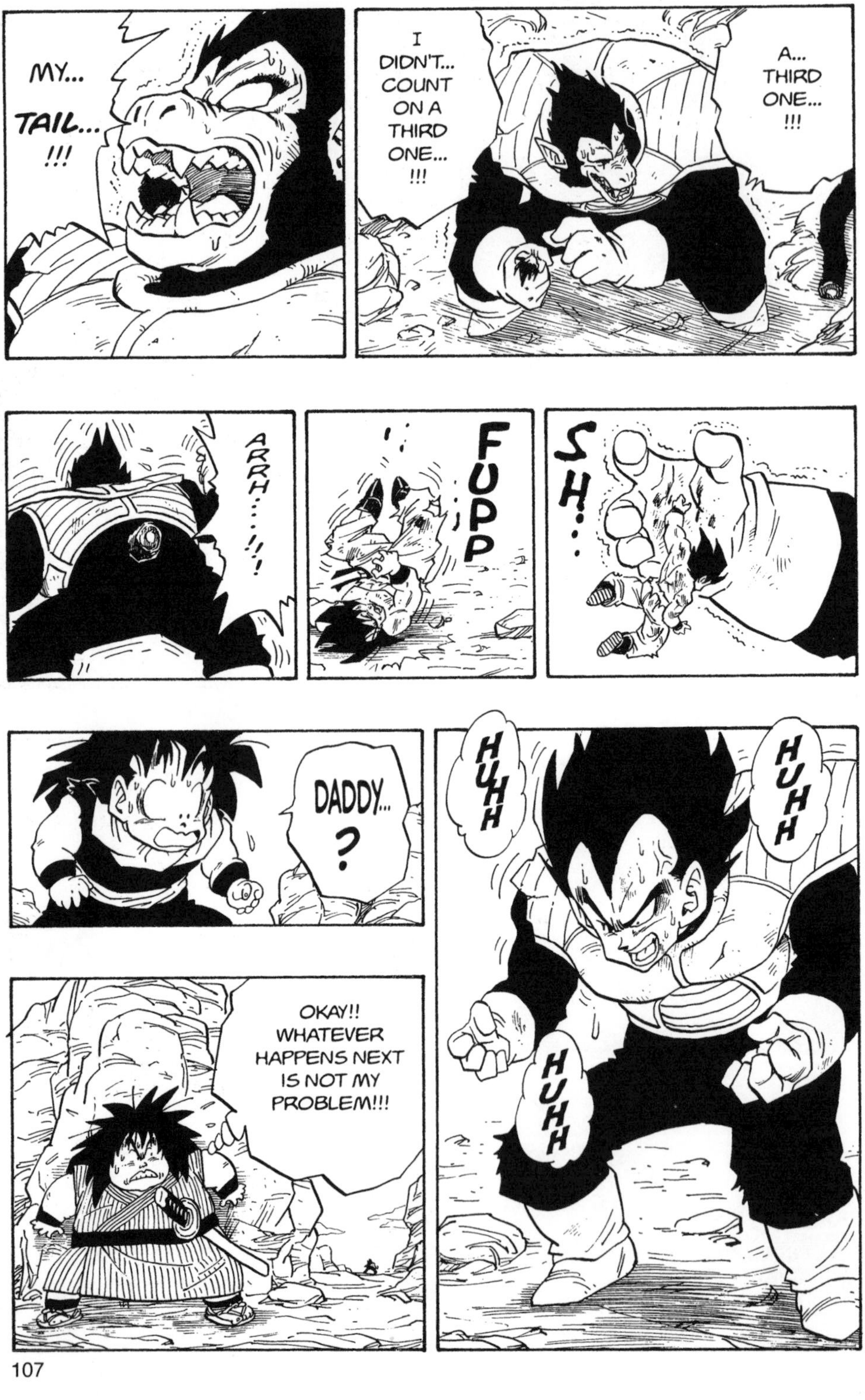
A... THIRD ONE... !!!
I DIDN'T... COUNT ON A THIRD ONE... !!!
MY... TAIL... !!!
SH...
FUPP
ARRH...!!!
HUHH
HUHH
HUHH
DADDY... ?
OKAY!! WHATEVER HAPPENS NEXT IS NOT MY PROBLEM!!!

# DBZ:42 • Least Resistance

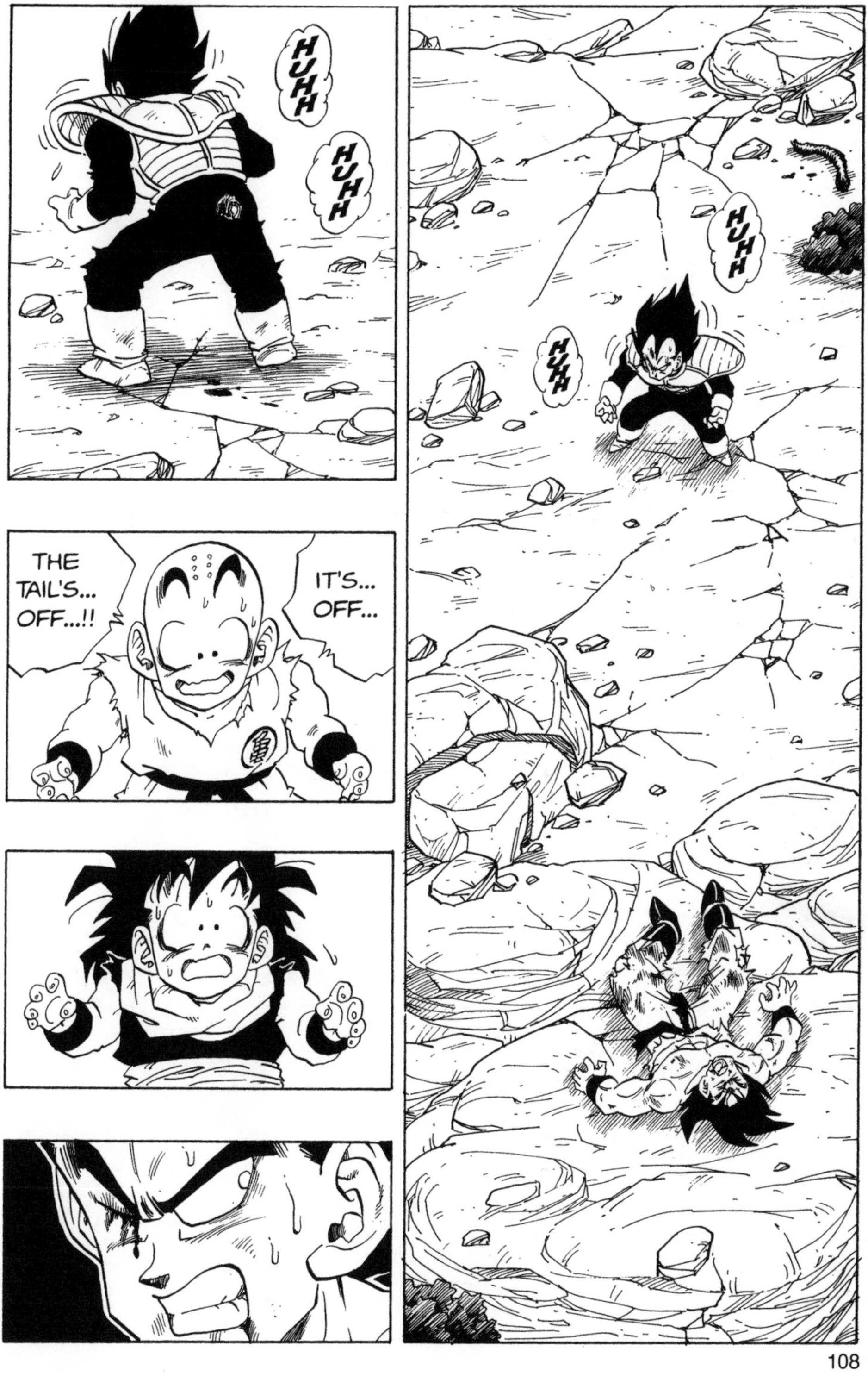
HUHH
HUHH
HUHH
HUHH
IT'S... OFF...
THE TAIL'S... OFF...!!

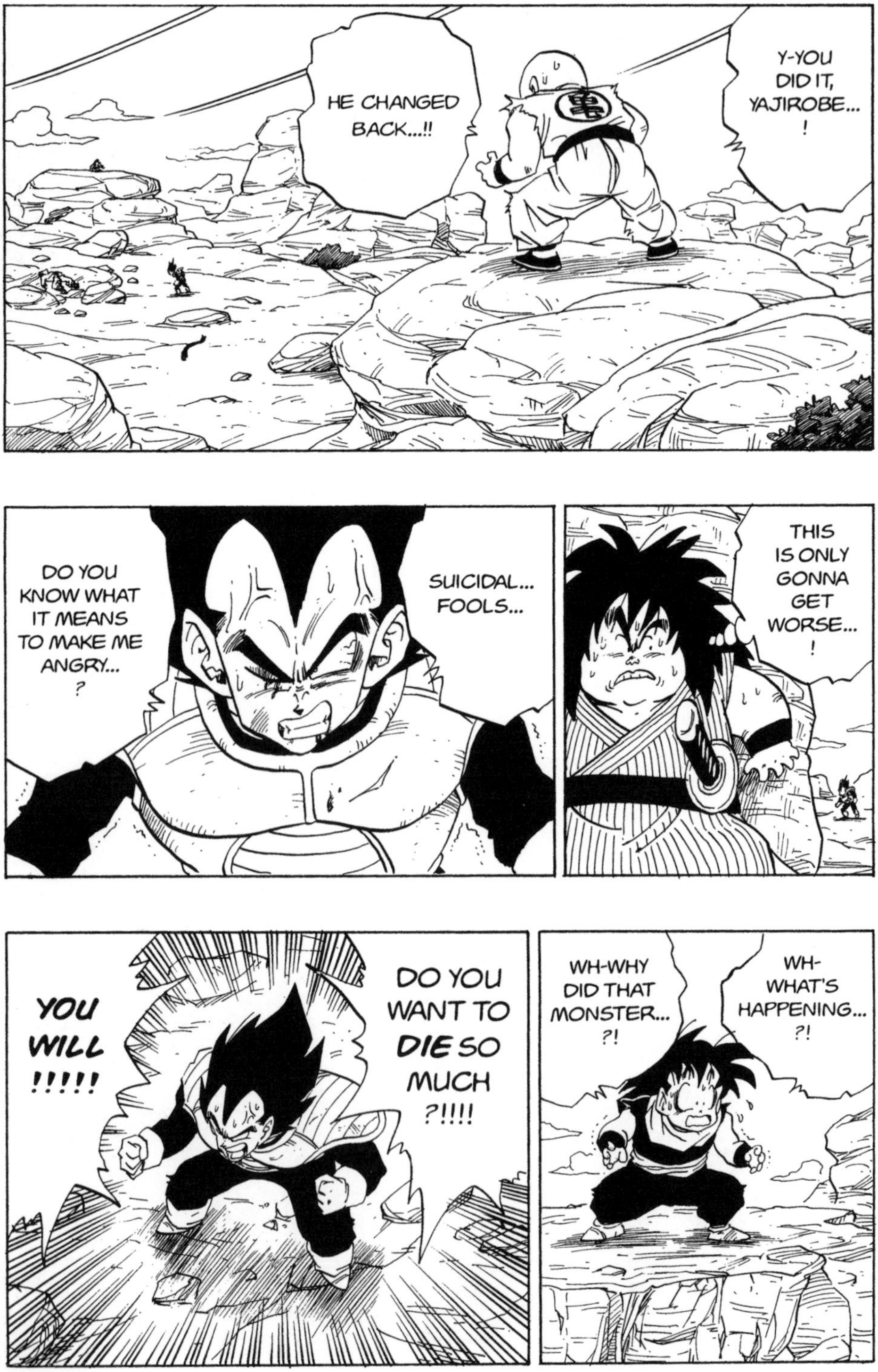
Y-YOU DID IT, YAJIROBE...!
HE CHANGED BACK...!!
THIS IS ONLY GONNA GET WORSE...!
SUICIDAL... FOOLS...
DO YOU KNOW WHAT IT MEANS TO MAKE ME ANGRY...?
WH-WHAT'S HAPPENING...?!
WH-WHY DID THAT MONSTER...?!
DO YOU WANT TO DIE SO MUCH?!!!!
YOU WILL!!!!!

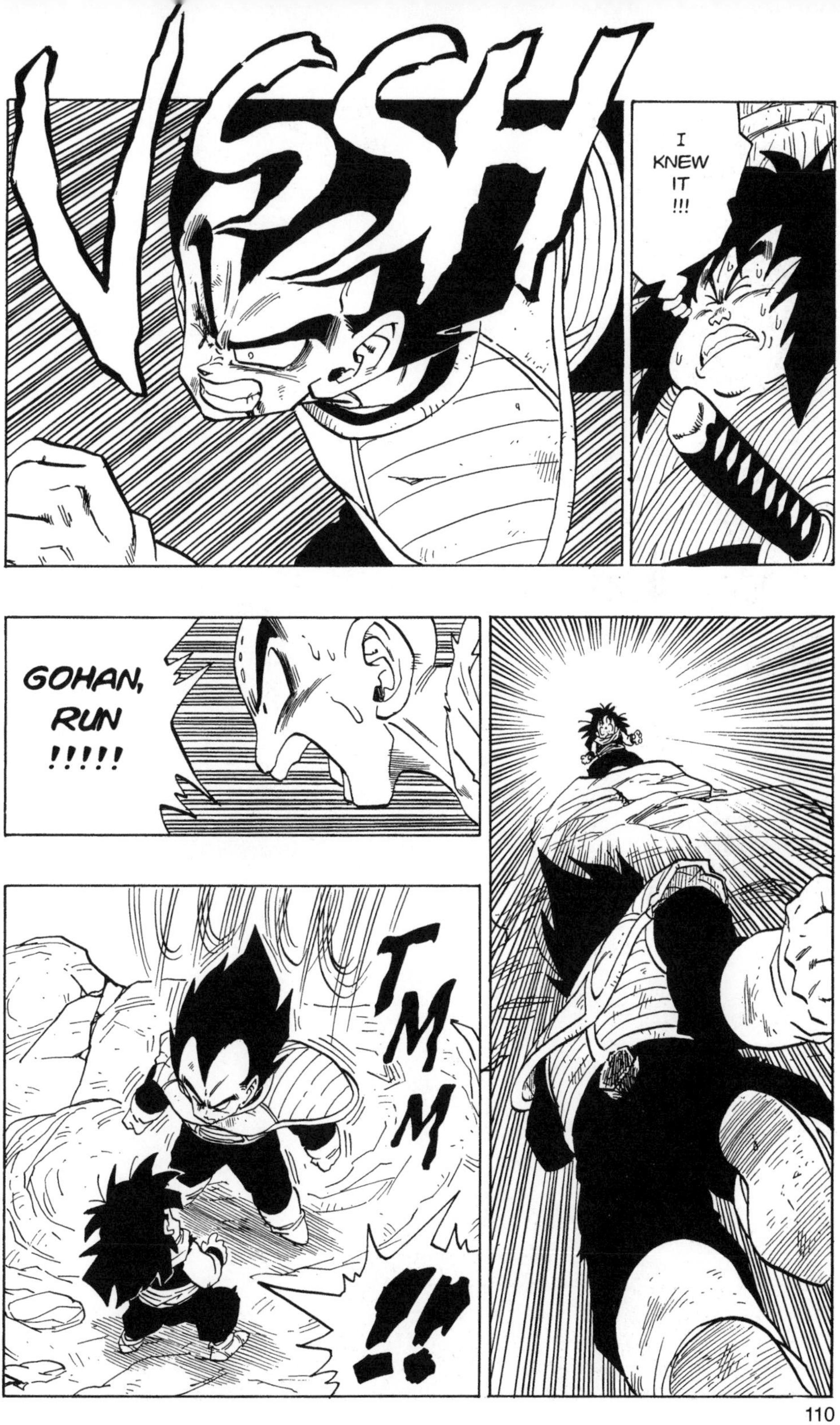

I KNEW IT !!!
VSSH
GOHAN, RUN !!!!!
TMM !!

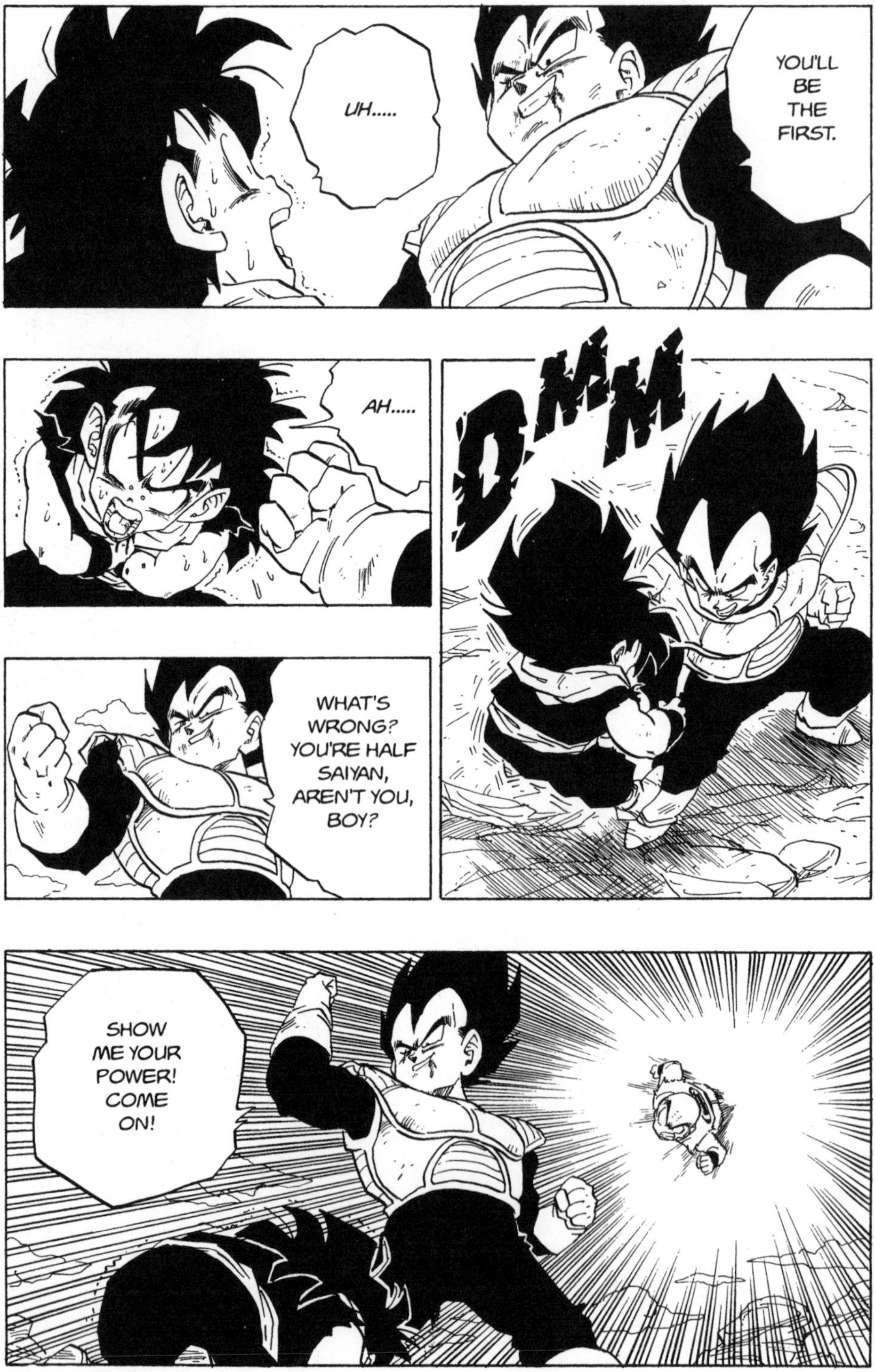
YOU'LL BE THE FIRST.
UH.....
DMM
AH.....
WHAT'S WRONG? YOU'RE HALF SAIYAN, AREN'T YOU, BOY?
SHOW ME YOUR POWER! COME ON!

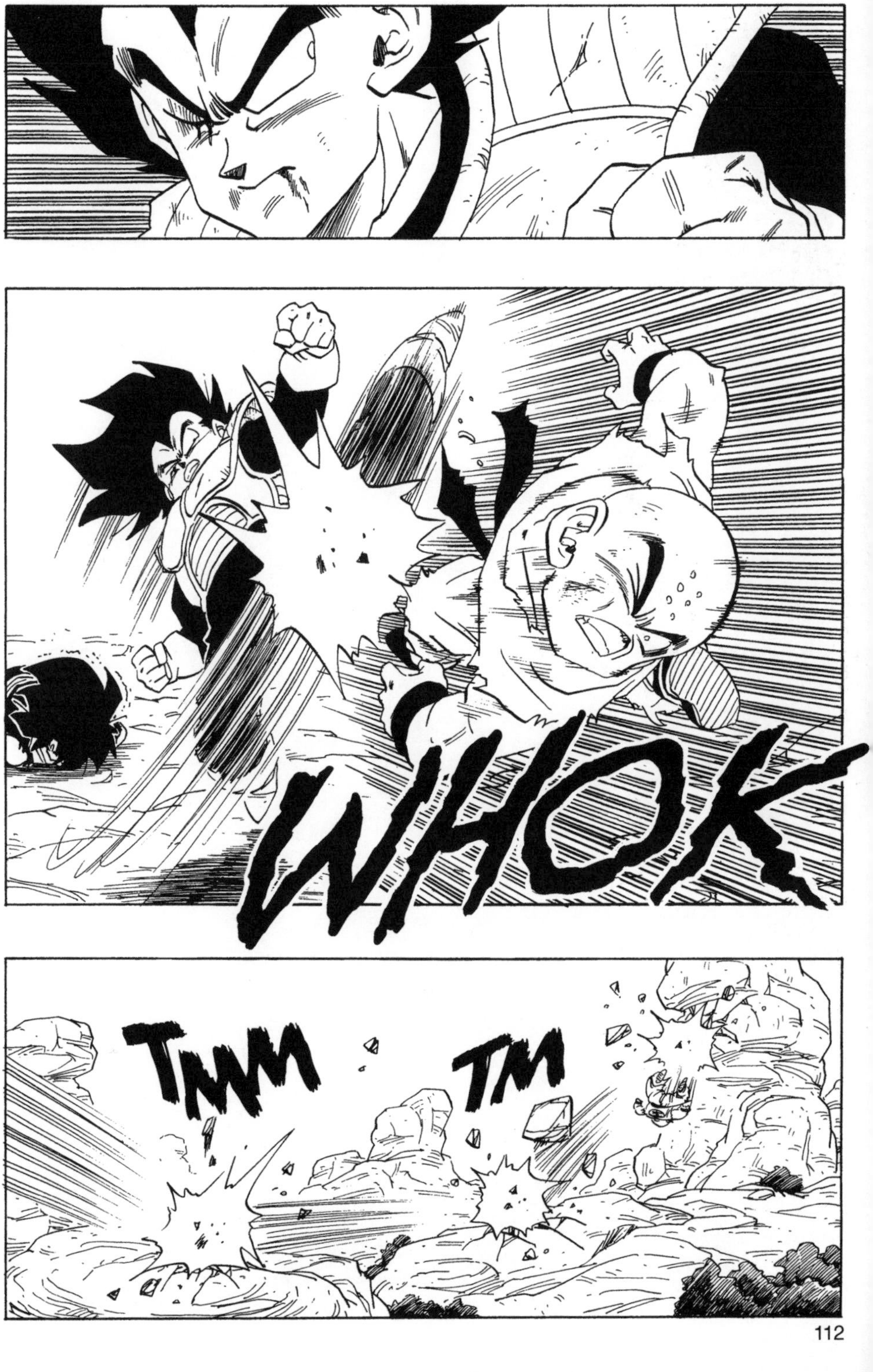
WHOK
TM
TMM

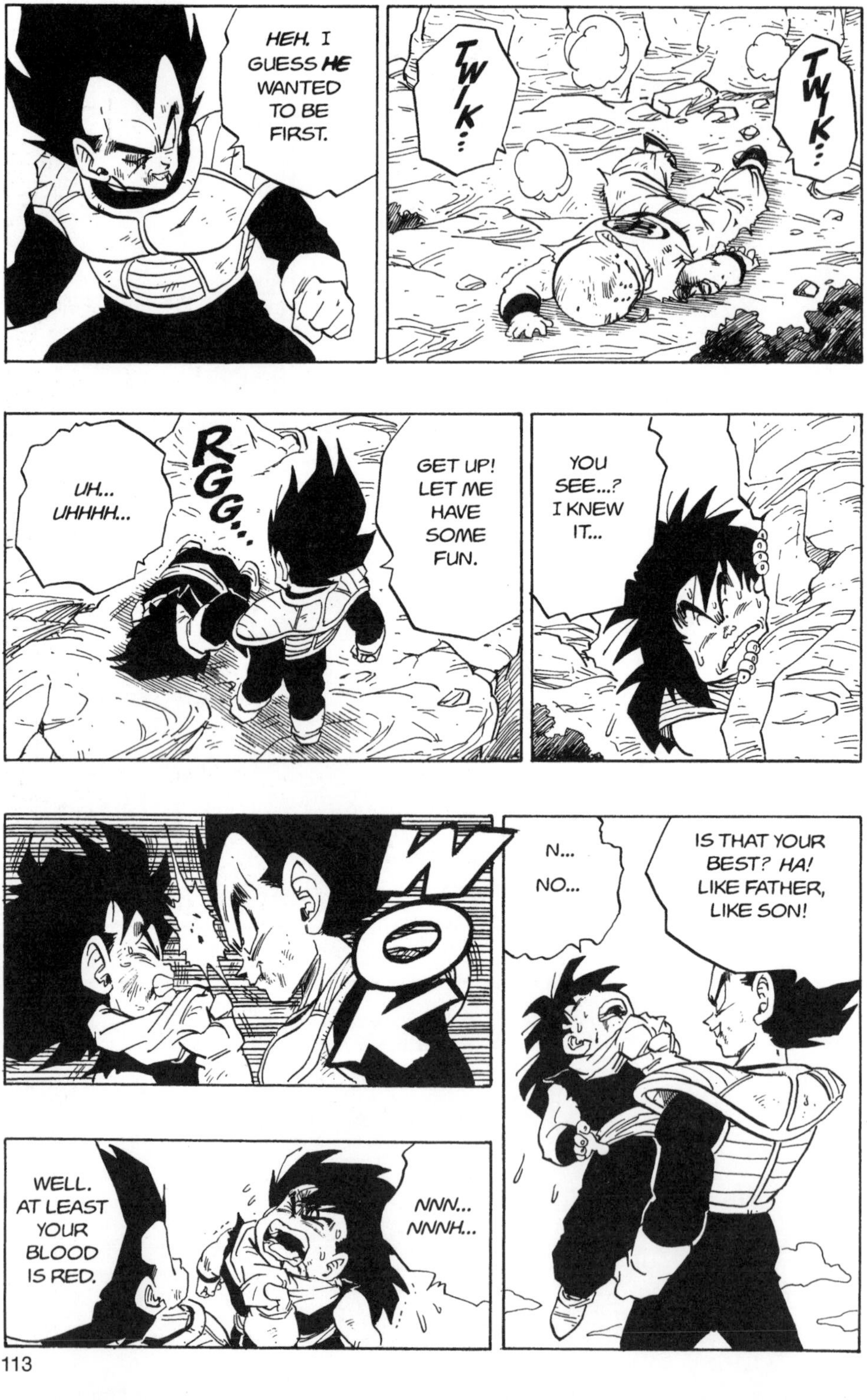
TWIK...
TWIK...
HEH. I GUESS HE WANTED TO BE FIRST.
YOU SEE...? I KNEW IT...
GET UP! LET ME HAVE SOME FUN.
RGG...
UH... UHHHH...
IS THAT YOUR BEST? HA! LIKE FATHER, LIKE SON!
N... NO...
WOK
NNN... NNNH...
WELL. AT LEAST YOUR BLOOD IS RED.

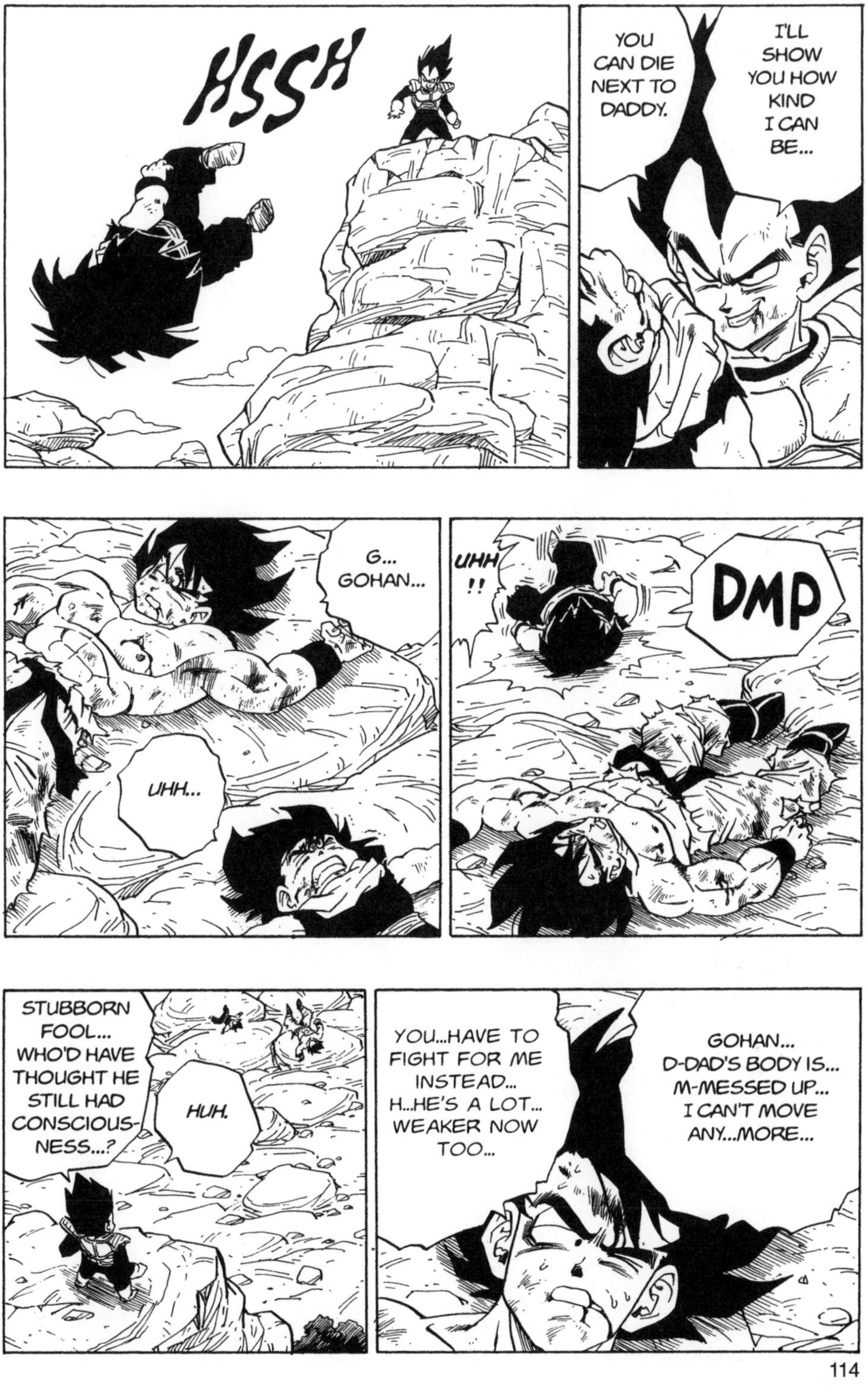
I'LL SHOW YOU HOW KIND I CAN BE...
YOU CAN DIE NEXT TO DADDY.
HSSH
DMP
UHH !!
G... GOHAN...
UHH...
GOHAN... D-DAD'S BODY IS... M-MESSED UP... I CAN'T MOVE ANY...MORE...
YOU...HAVE TO FIGHT FOR ME INSTEAD... H...HE'S A LOT... WEAKER NOW TOO...
HUH.
STUBBORN FOOL... WHO'D HAVE THOUGHT HE STILL HAD CONSCIOUSNESS...?

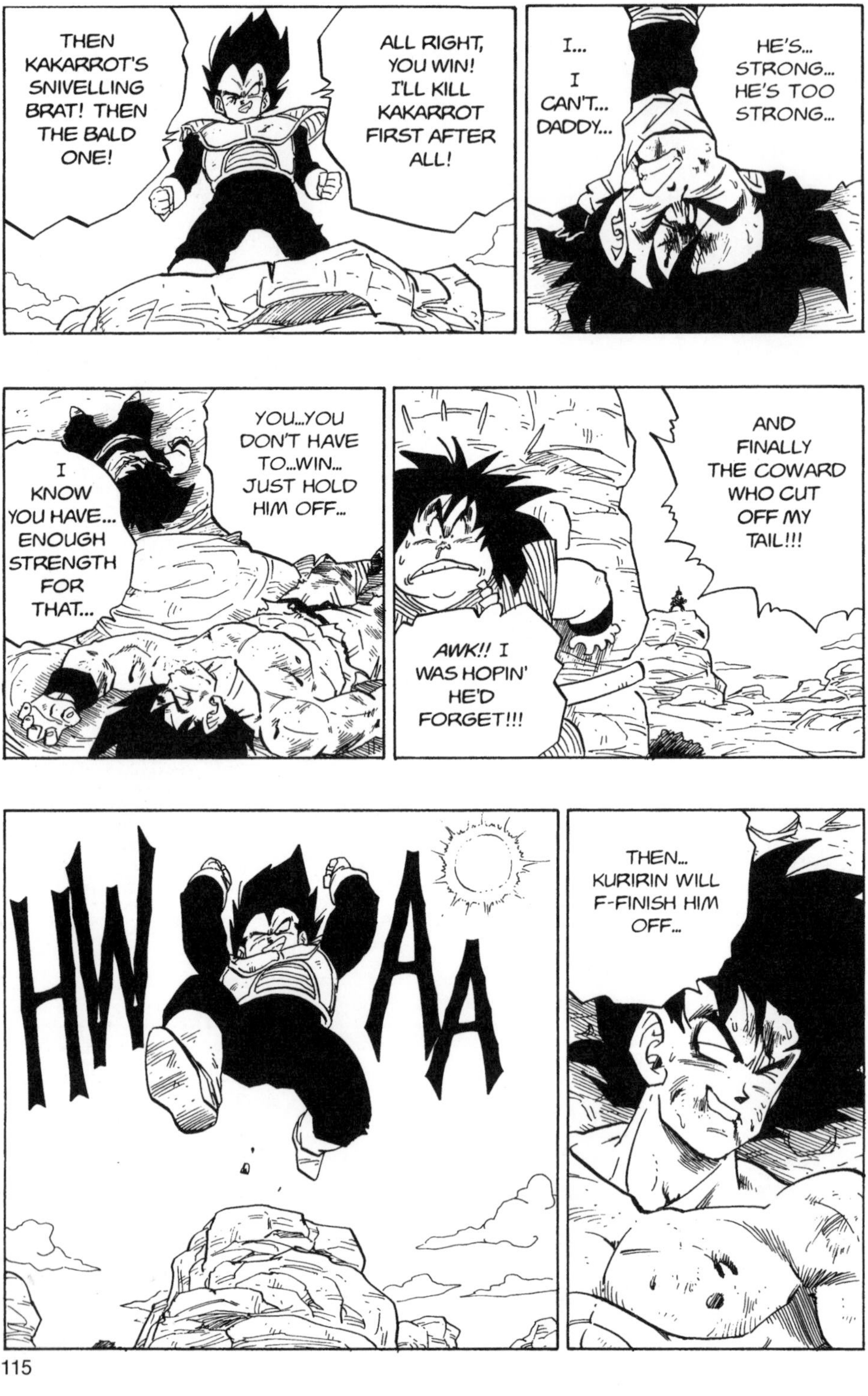
HE'S... STRONG... HE'S TOO STRONG...
I... I CAN'T... DADDY...
ALL RIGHT, YOU WIN! I'LL KILL KAKARROT FIRST AFTER ALL!
THEN KAKARROT'S SNIVELLING BRAT! THEN THE BALD ONE!
AND FINALLY THE COWARD WHO CUT OFF MY TAIL!!!
AWK!! I WAS HOPIN' HE'D FORGET!!!
YOU...YOU DON'T HAVE TO...WIN... JUST HOLD HIM OFF...
I KNOW YOU HAVE... ENOUGH STRENGTH FOR THAT...
THEN... KURIRIN WILL F-FINISH HIM OFF...
HWAA

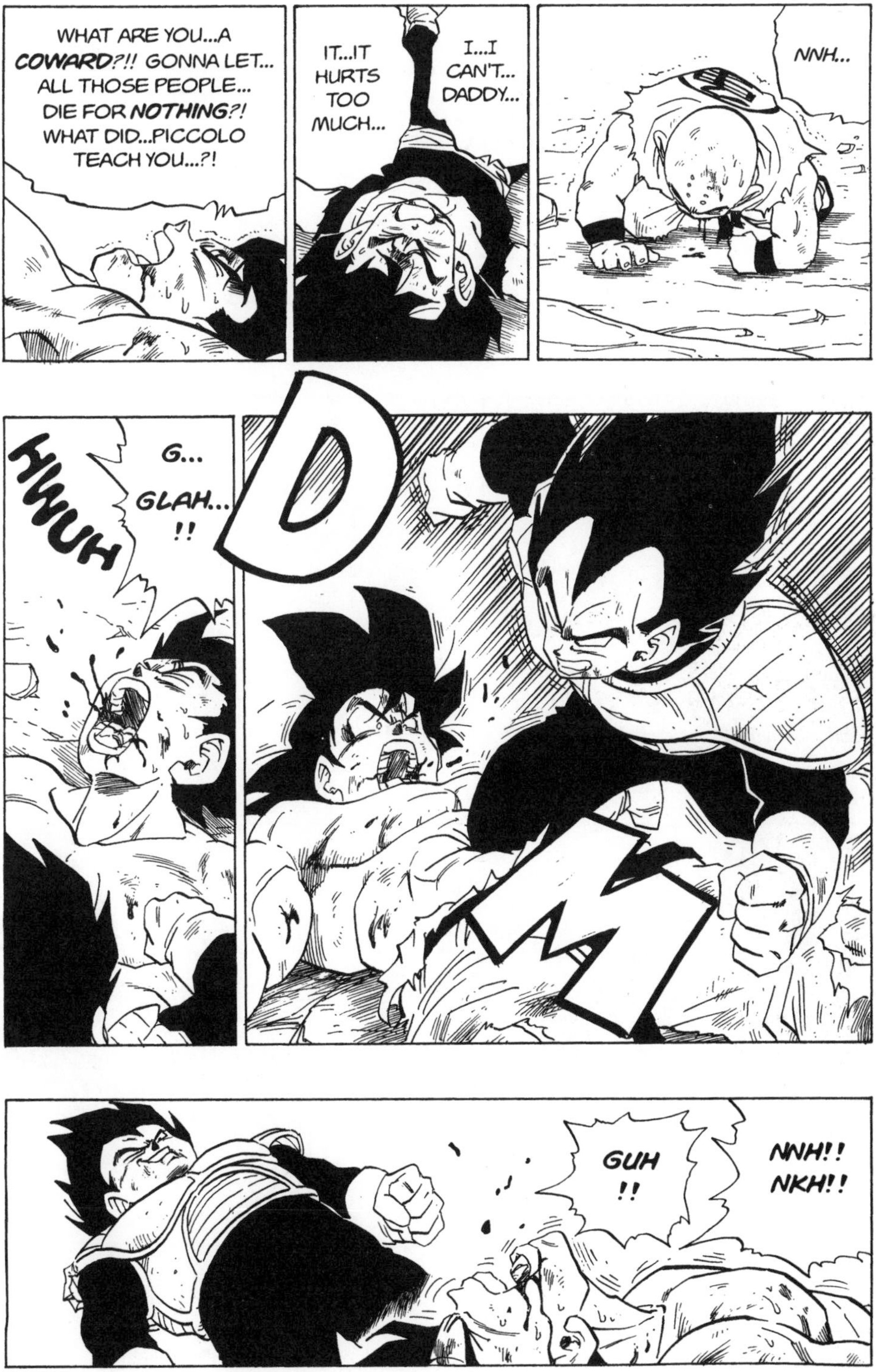
NNH...
I...I CAN'T... DADDY...
IT...IT HURTS TOO MUCH...
WHAT ARE YOU...A COWARD?!! GONNA LET... ALL THOSE PEOPLE... DIE FOR NOTHING?! WHAT DID...PICCOLO TEACH YOU...?!
D
M
HWUH
G... GLAH... !!
NNH!! NKH!!
GUH !!

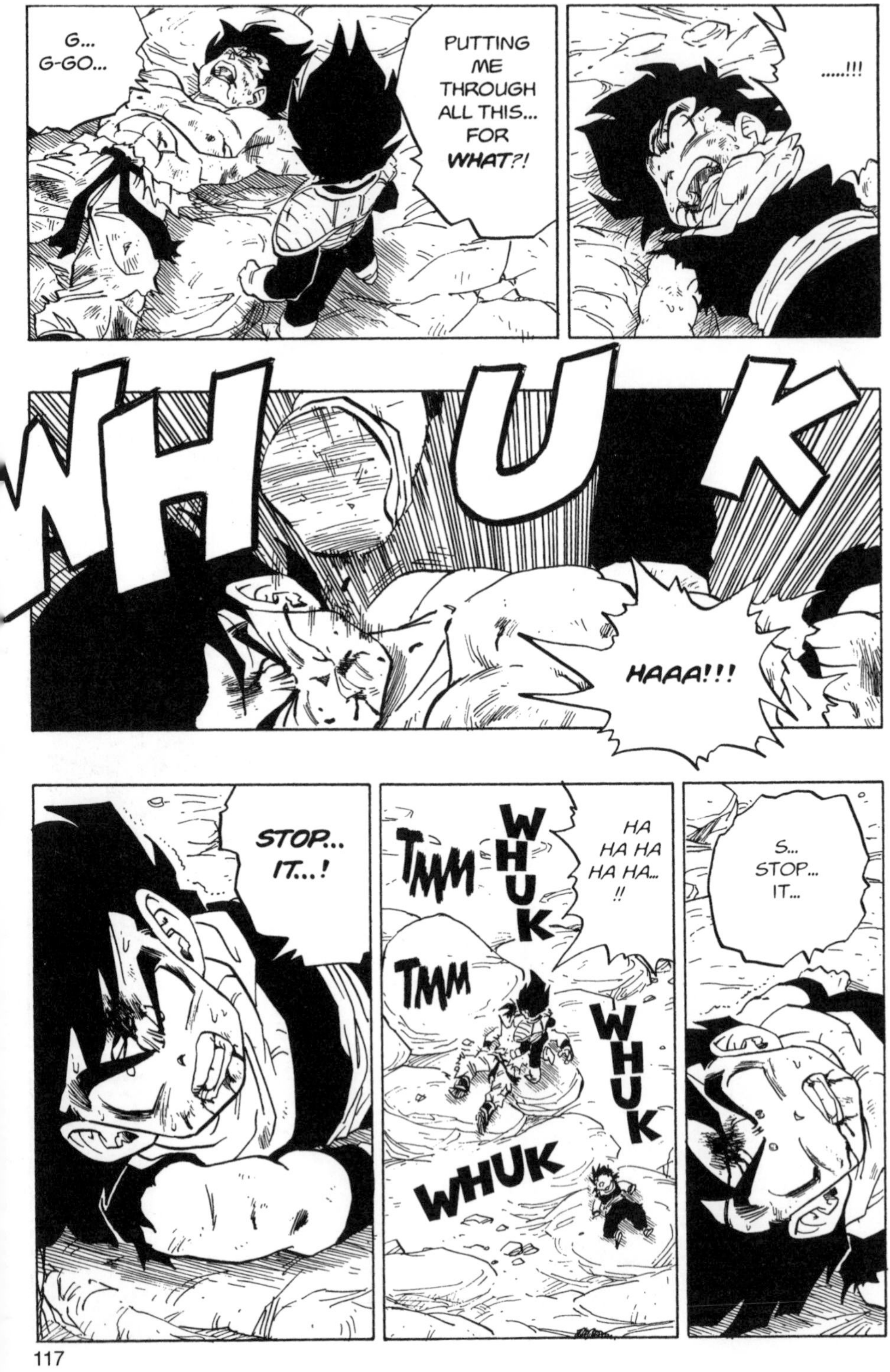
......!!!
PUTTING ME THROUGH ALL THIS... FOR WHAT?!
G... G-GO...
WHUK
HAAA!!!
S... STOP... IT...
HA HA HA HA HA... !!
WHUK
TMM
TMM
WHUK
WHUK
STOP... IT...!

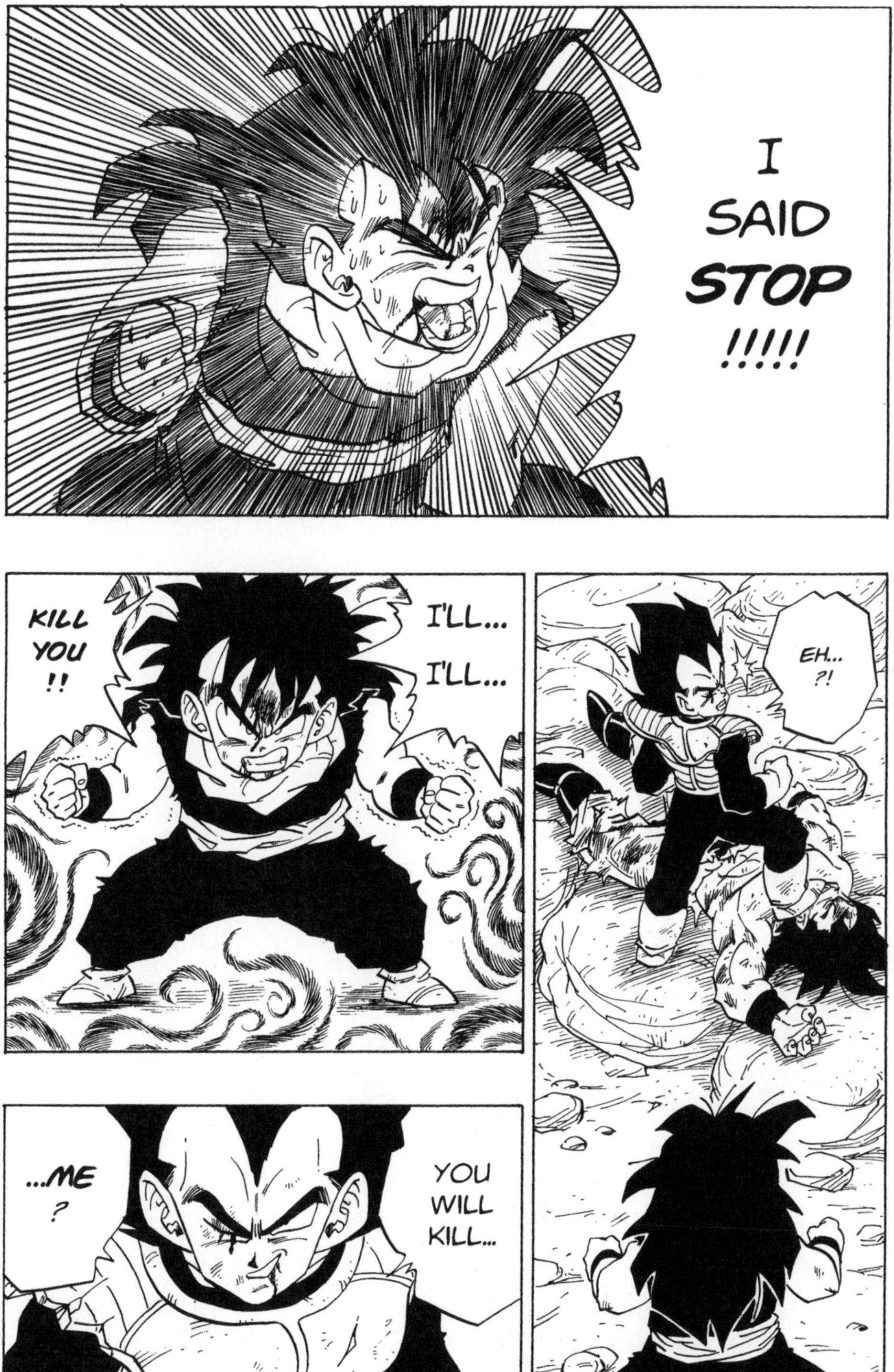
I SAID STOP !!!!!
EH... ?!
I'LL... I'LL...
KILL YOU !!
YOU WILL KILL...
...ME ?

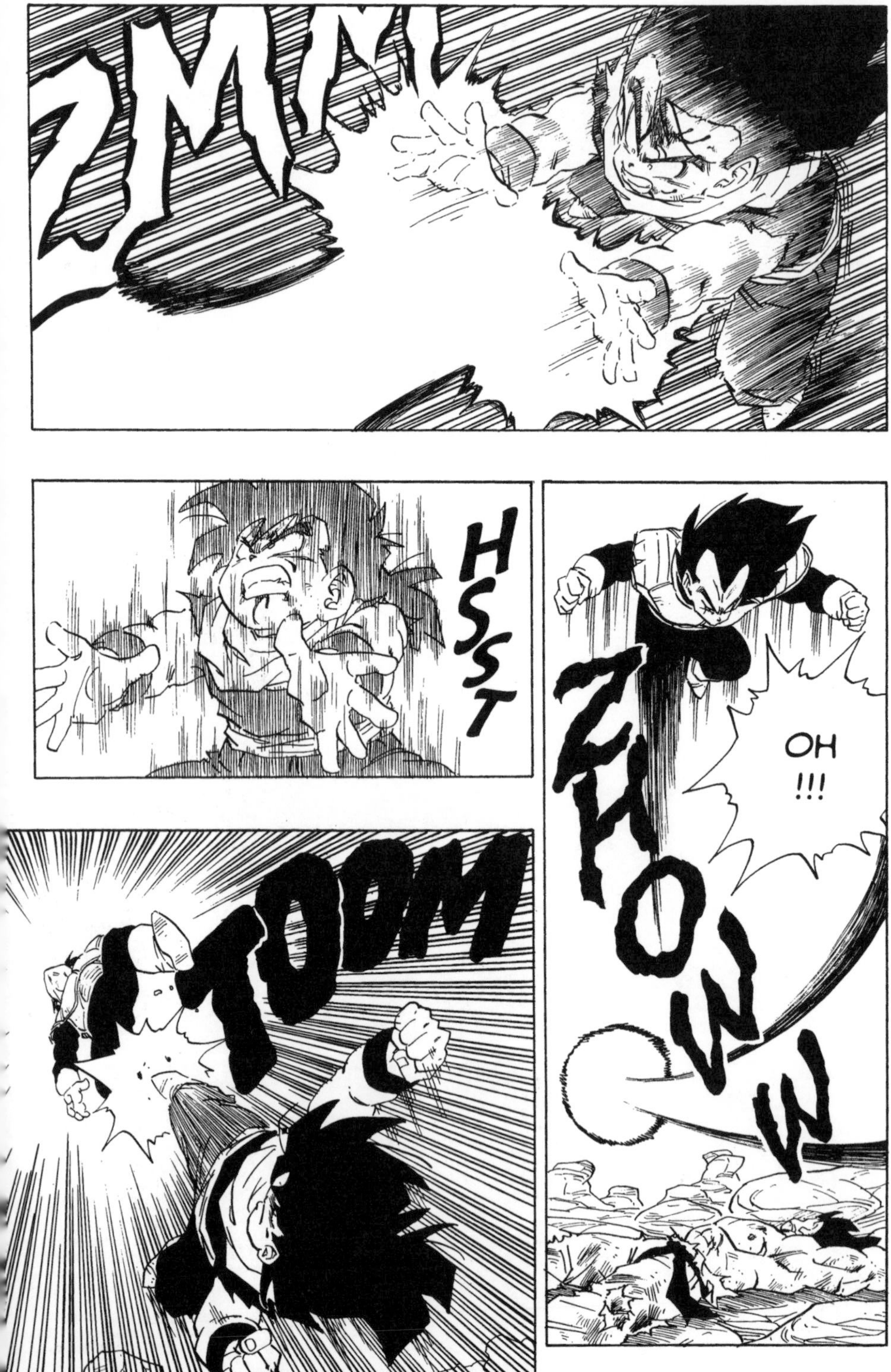
OH !!!
ZHOWWW
HSST
TOOM

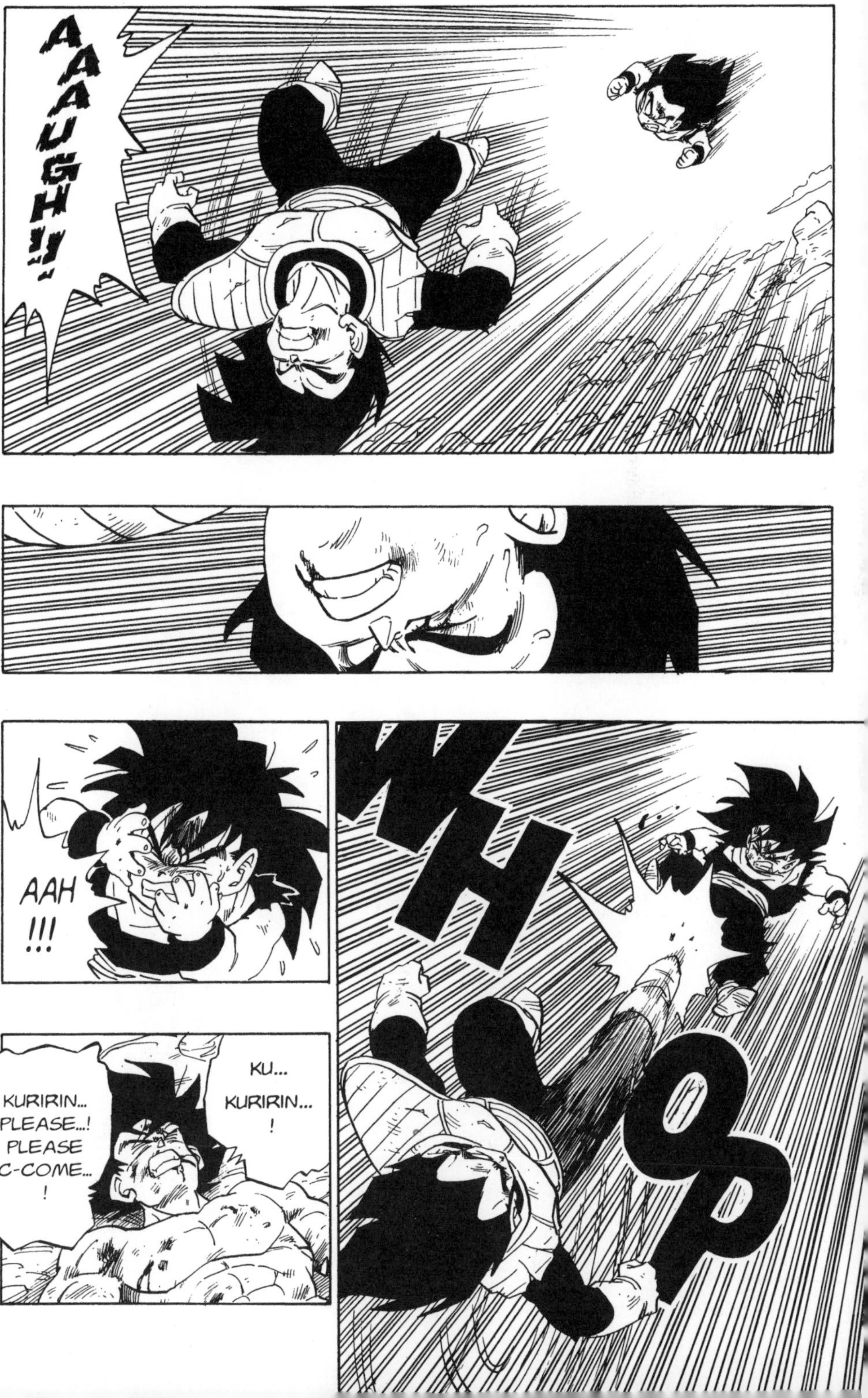
AAAUGH!!
AAH !!!
KU... KURIRIN... !
KURIRIN... PLEASE...! PLEASE C-COME... !

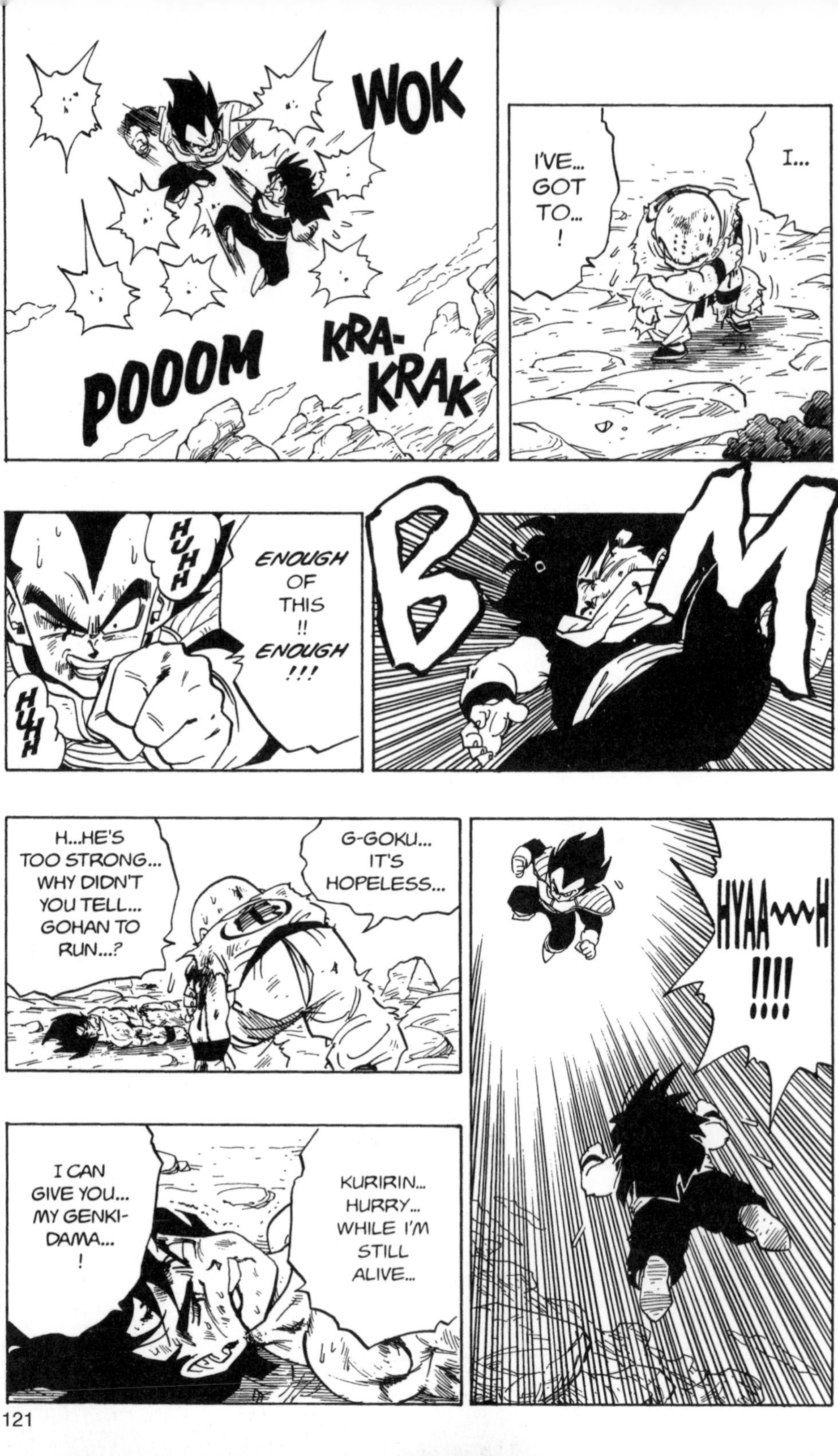

I...
I'VE... GOT TO... !
WOK
POOOM
KRA-KRAK
BAM
HUHH
ENOUGH OF THIS !! ENOUGH !!!
HUHH
HYAA~~H !!!!
G-GOKU... IT'S HOPELESS...
H...HE'S TOO STRONG... WHY DIDN'T YOU TELL... GOHAN TO RUN...?
KURIRIN... HURRY... WHILE I'M STILL ALIVE...
I CAN GIVE YOU... MY GENKI-DAMA... !

# DBZ:43 · Once More...the Sphere!

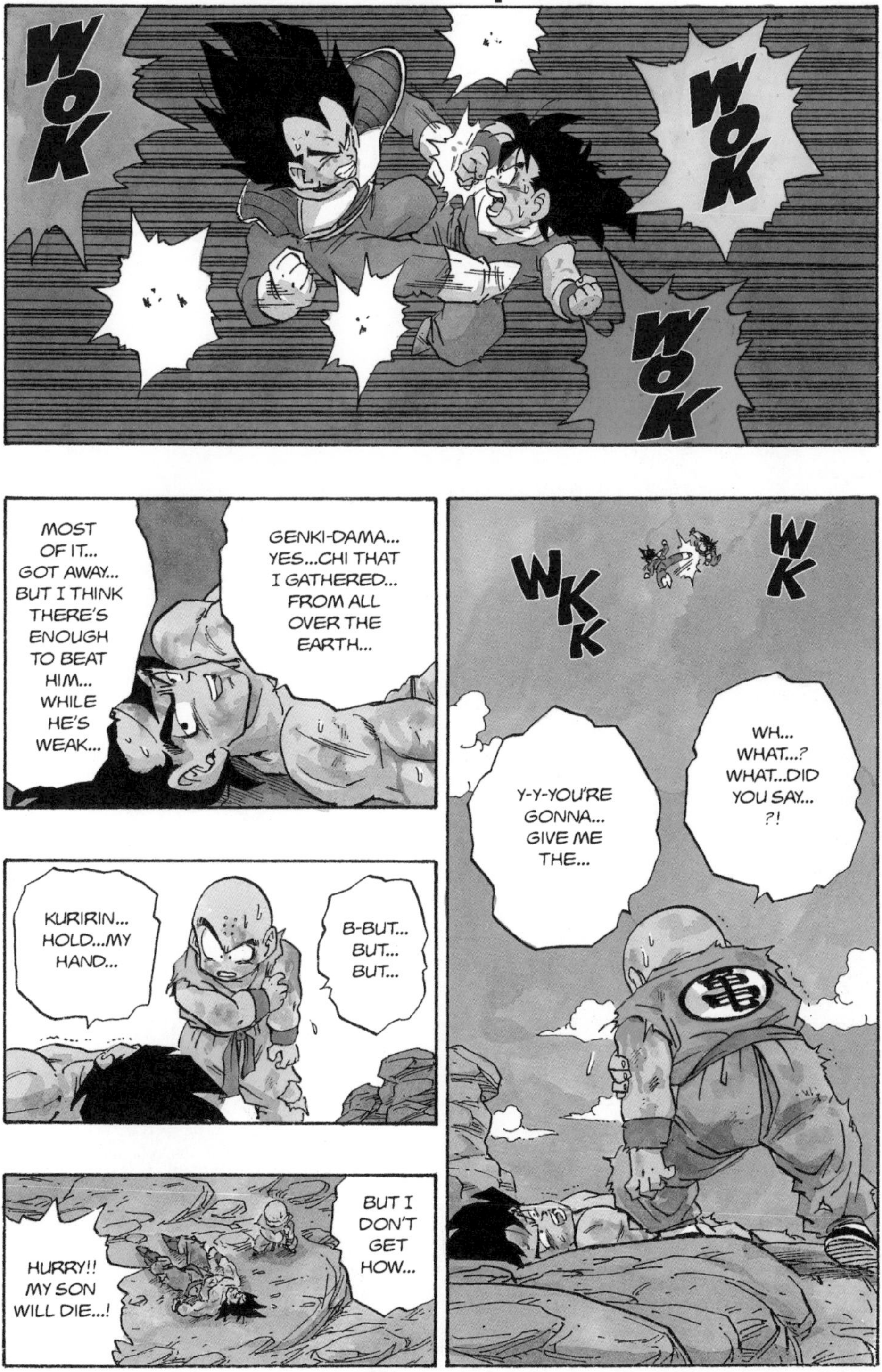
WOK
WOK
WOK
WK
WKK
WH... WHAT...? WHAT...DID YOU SAY... ?!
Y-Y-YOU'RE GONNA... GIVE ME THE...
GENKI-DAMA... YES...CHI THAT I GATHERED... FROM ALL OVER THE EARTH...
MOST OF IT... GOT AWAY... BUT I THINK THERE'S ENOUGH TO BEAT HIM... WHILE HE'S WEAK...
B-BUT... BUT... BUT...
KURIRIN... HOLD...MY HAND...
BUT I DON'T GET HOW...
HURRY!! MY SON WILL DIE...!

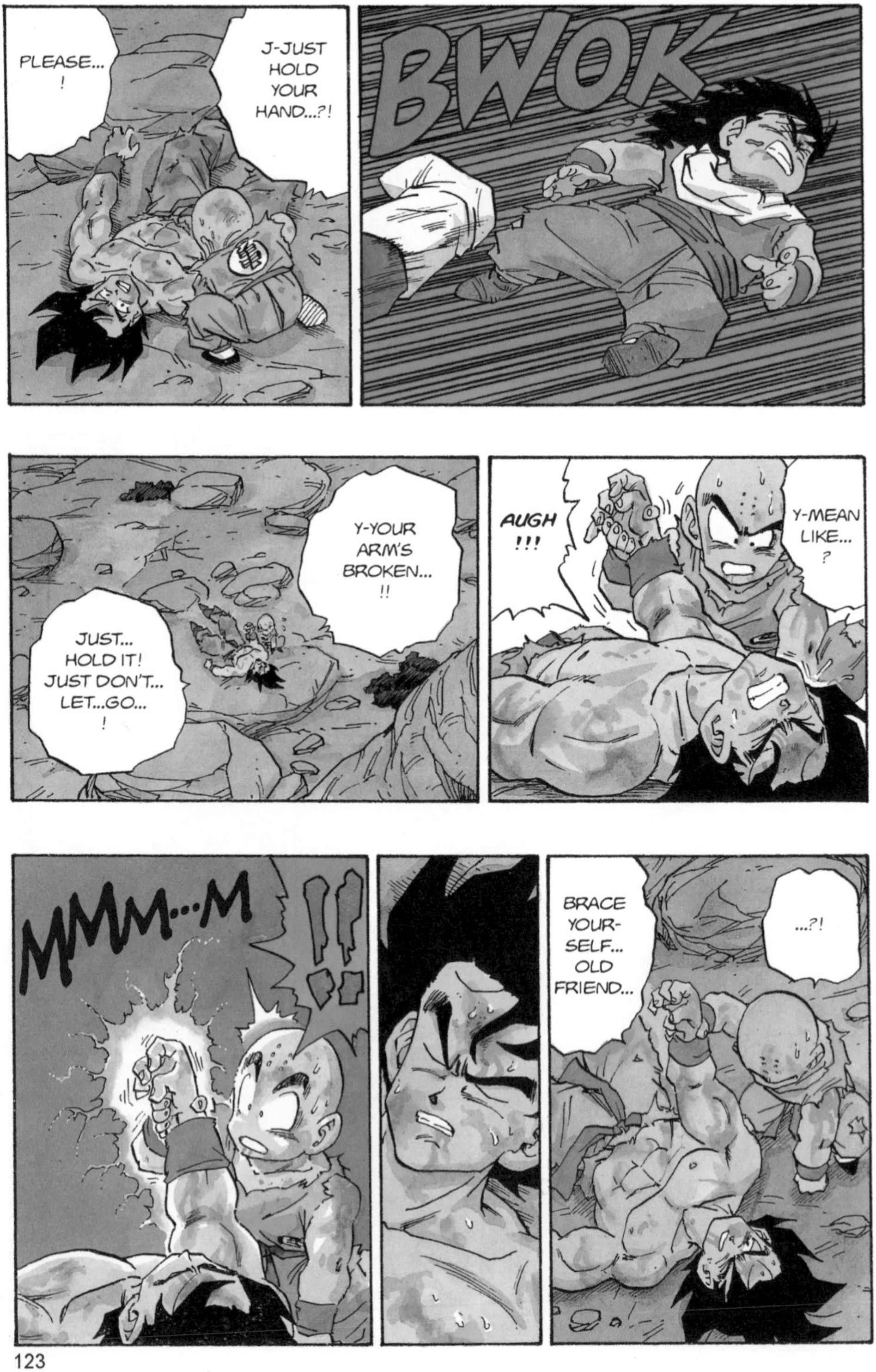
BWOK
J-JUST HOLD YOUR HAND...?!
PLEASE... !
Y-MEAN LIKE... ?
AUGH !!!
Y-YOUR ARM'S BROKEN... !!
JUST... HOLD IT! JUST DON'T... LET...GO... !
...?!
BRACE YOUR-SELF... OLD FRIEND...
!!
MMM...M

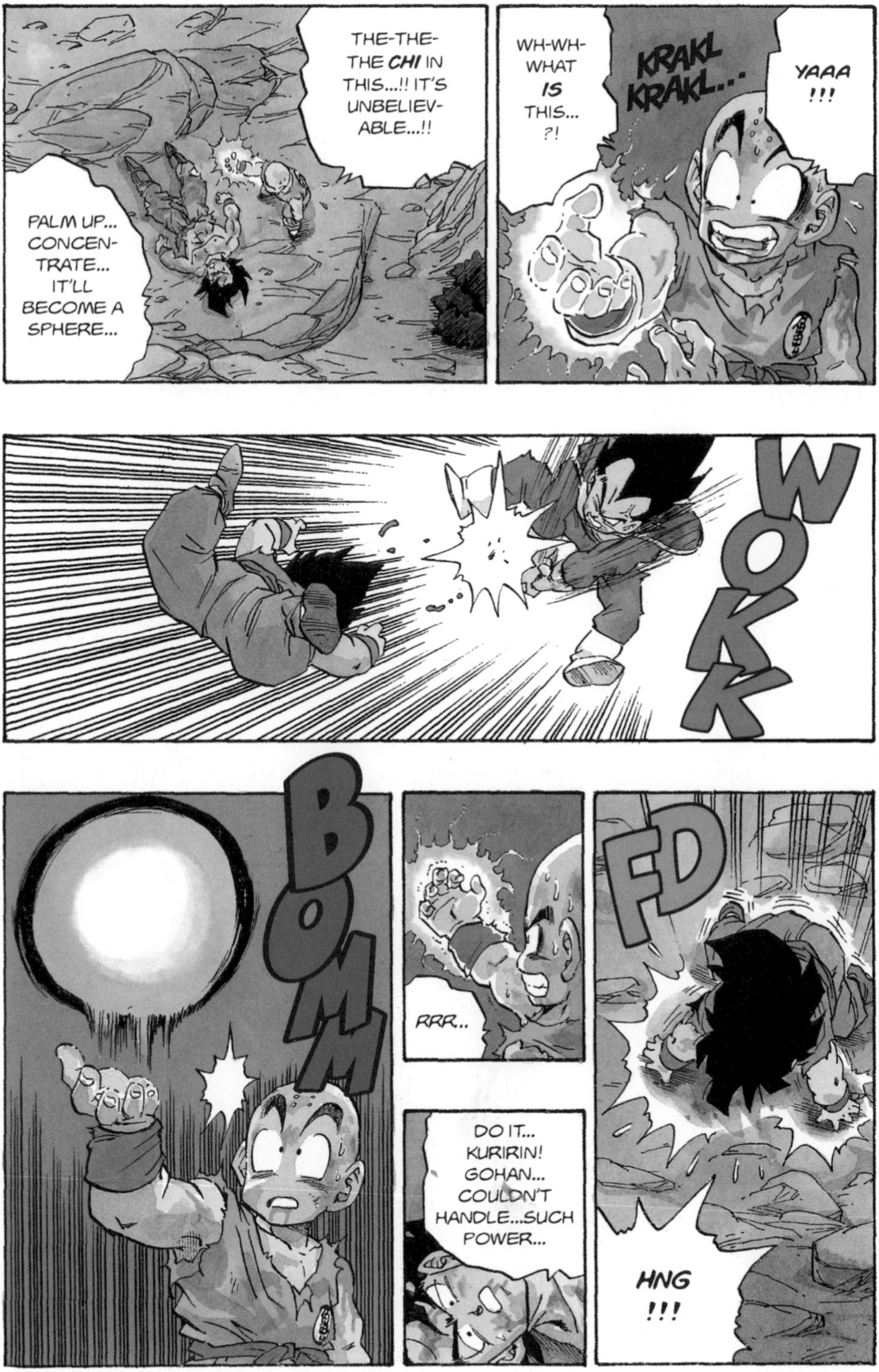
YAAA !!!
KRAKL KRAKL...
WH-WH-WHAT IS THIS...?!
THE-THE-THE CHI IN THIS...!! IT'S UNBELIEVABLE...!!
PALM UP... CONCENTRATE... IT'LL BECOME A SPHERE...
WOKK
FD
HNG !!!
RRR...
DO IT... KURIRIN! GOHAN... COULDN'T HANDLE...SUCH POWER...
BOMM

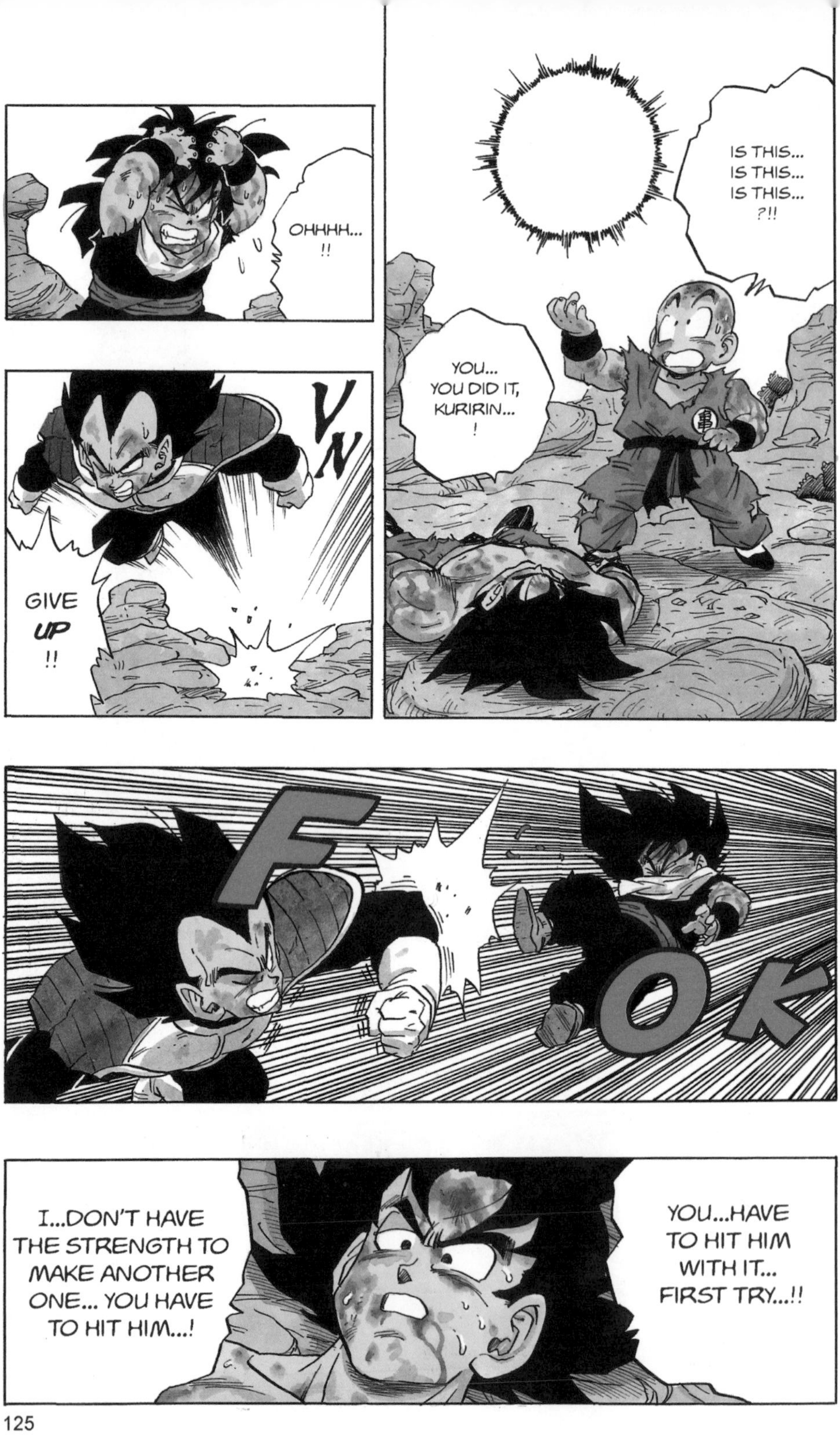
IS THIS... IS THIS... IS THIS... ?!!
YOU... YOU DID IT, KURIRIN... !
OHHHH... !!
VN
GIVE UP !!
FOK
YOU...HAVE TO HIT HIM WITH IT... FIRST TRY...!!
I...DON'T HAVE THE STRENGTH TO MAKE ANOTHER ONE... YOU HAVE TO HIT HIM...!

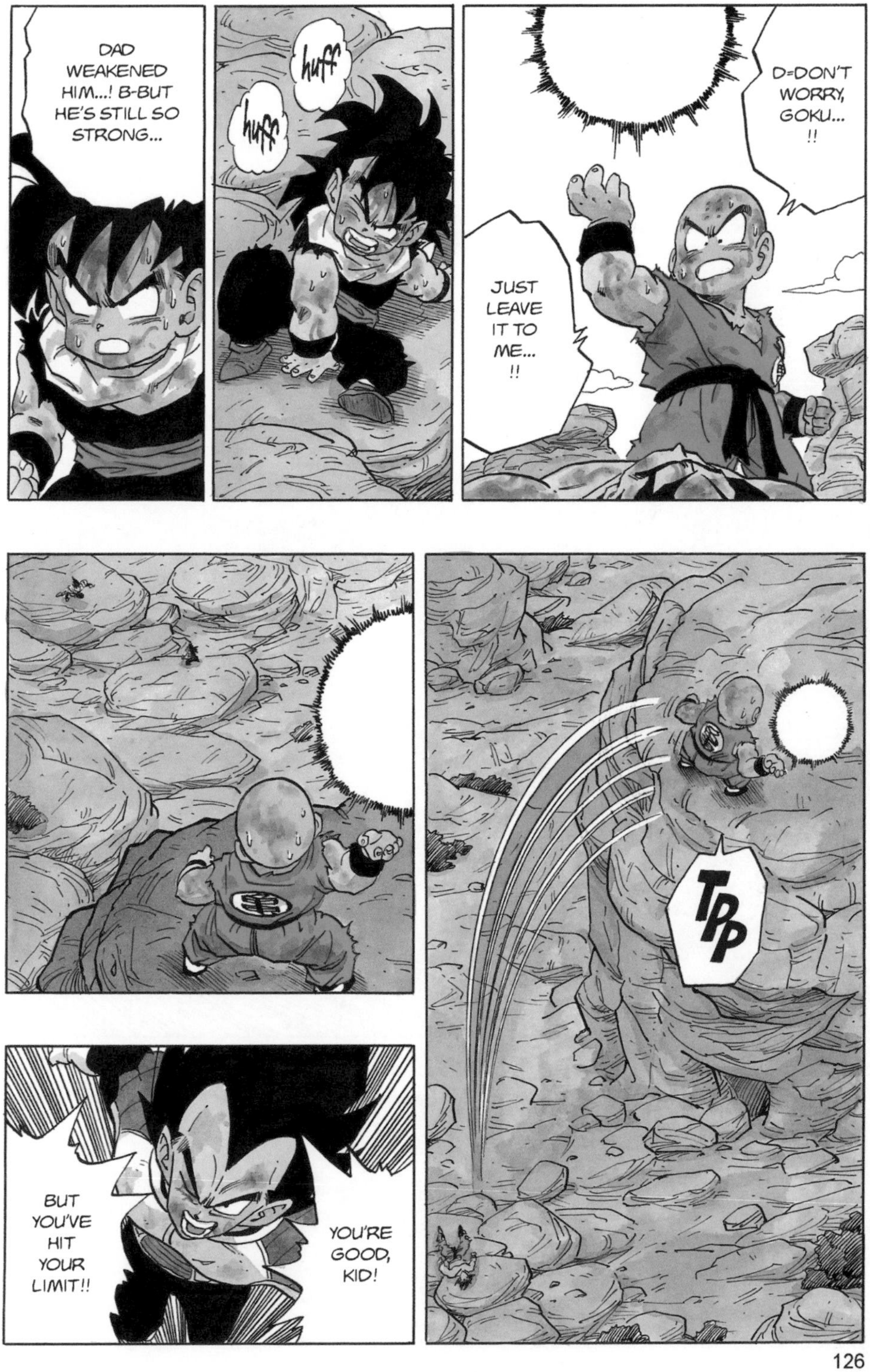
D=DON'T WORRY, GOKU... !!
JUST LEAVE IT TO ME... !!
huff
huff
DAD WEAKENED HIM...! B-BUT HE'S STILL SO STRONG...
TPP
YOU'RE GOOD, KID!
BUT YOU'VE HIT YOUR LIMIT!!

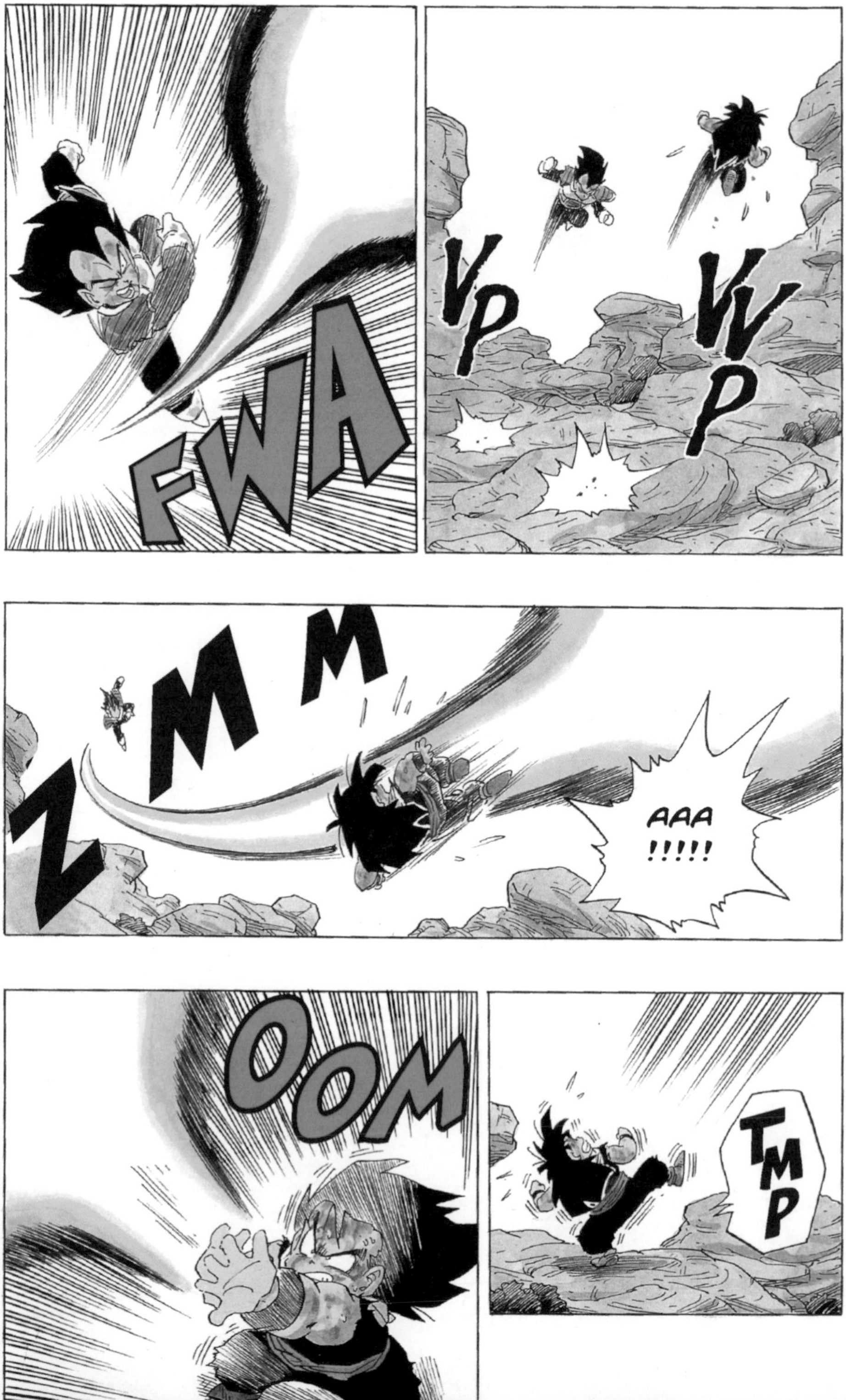
VWP
VP
FWA
AAA !!!!!
ZMMM
TMP
OOM

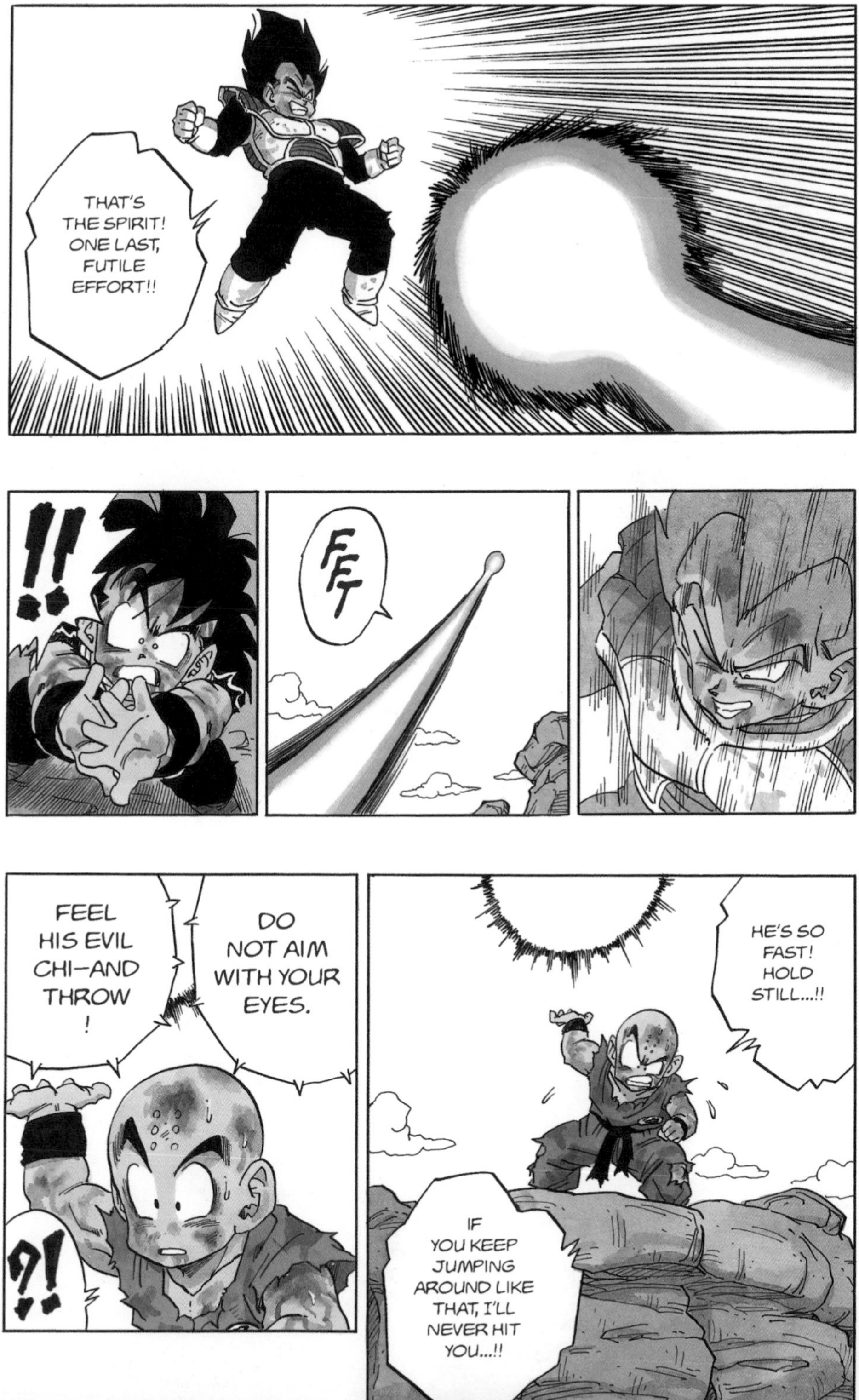
THAT'S THE SPIRIT! ONE LAST, FUTILE EFFORT!!
FFT
!!
HE'S SO FAST! HOLD STILL...!!
IF YOU KEEP JUMPING AROUND LIKE THAT, I'LL NEVER HIT YOU...!!
DO NOT AIM WITH YOUR EYES.
FEEL HIS EVIL CHI—AND THROW!
?!

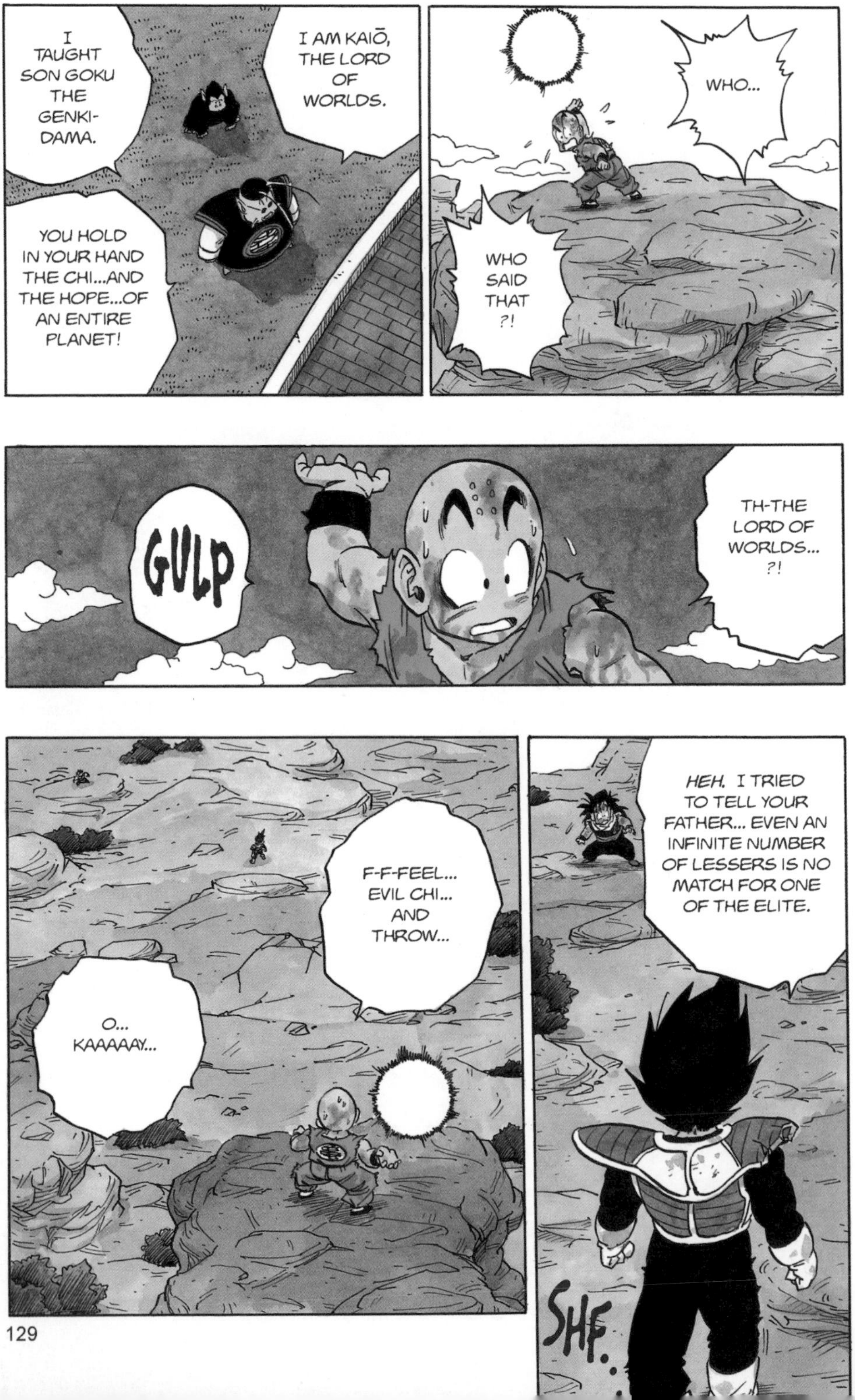
WHO...
WHO SAID THAT?!
I AM KAIŌ, THE LORD OF WORLDS.
I TAUGHT SON GOKU THE GENKI-DAMA.
YOU HOLD IN YOUR HAND THE CHI...AND THE HOPE...OF AN ENTIRE PLANET!
TH-THE LORD OF WORLDS...?!
GULP
*HEH.* I TRIED TO TELL YOUR FATHER... EVEN AN INFINITE NUMBER OF LESSERS IS NO MATCH FOR ONE OF THE ELITE.
SHF...
F-F-FEEL... EVIL CHI... AND THROW...
O... KAAAAAY...

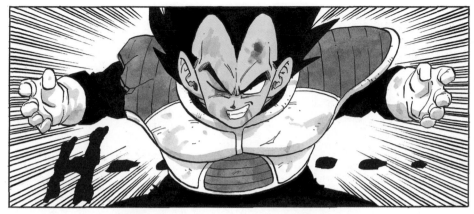

H------

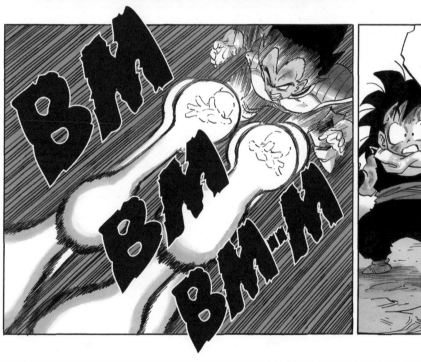

BM
BM
BM-M

....!!

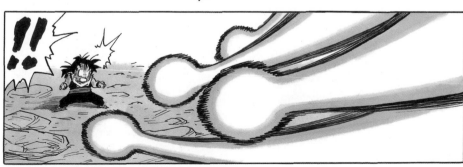

!!

130

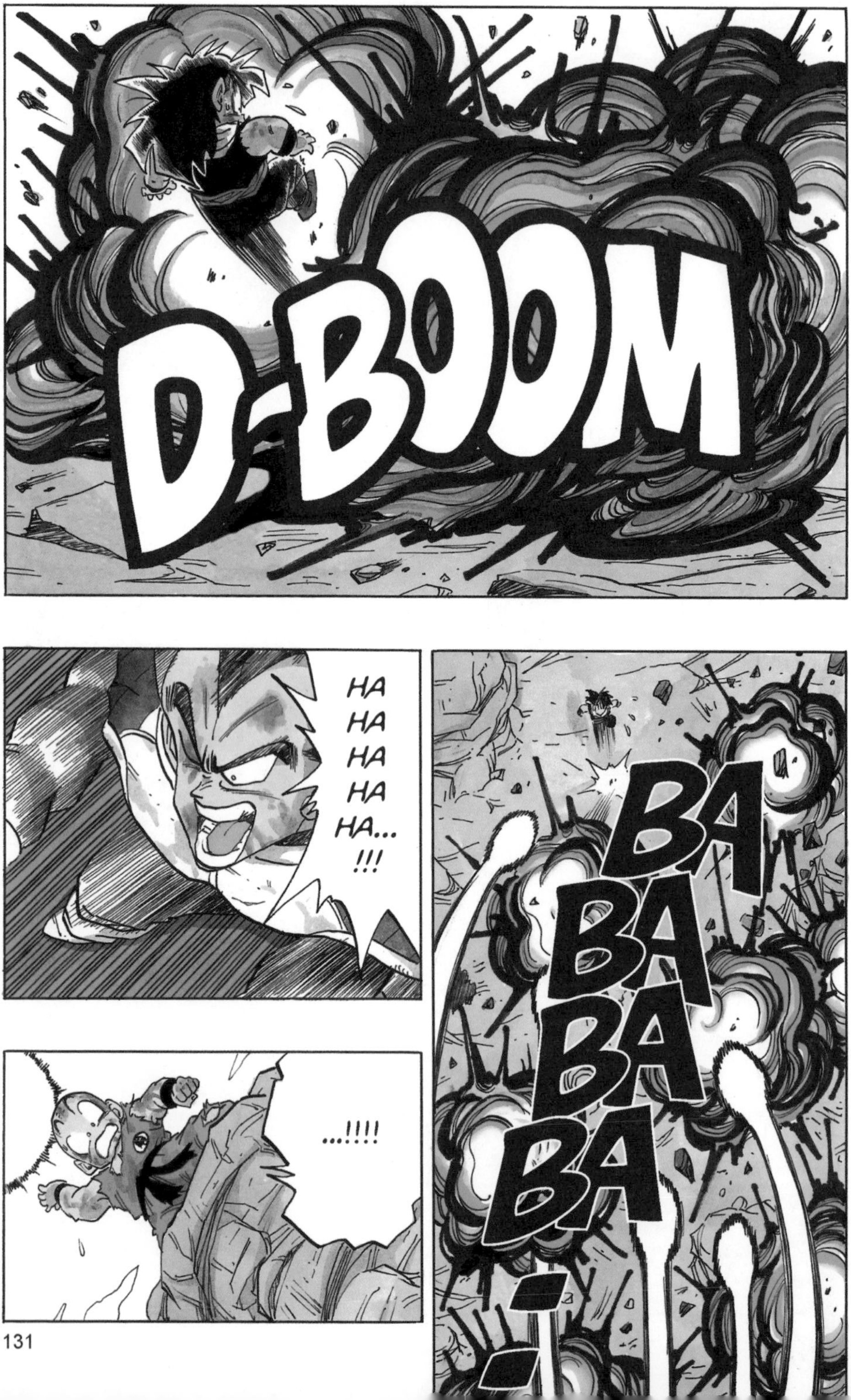
D-BOOM
BA BA BA BA BA...
HA HA HA HA HA... !!!
...!!!!

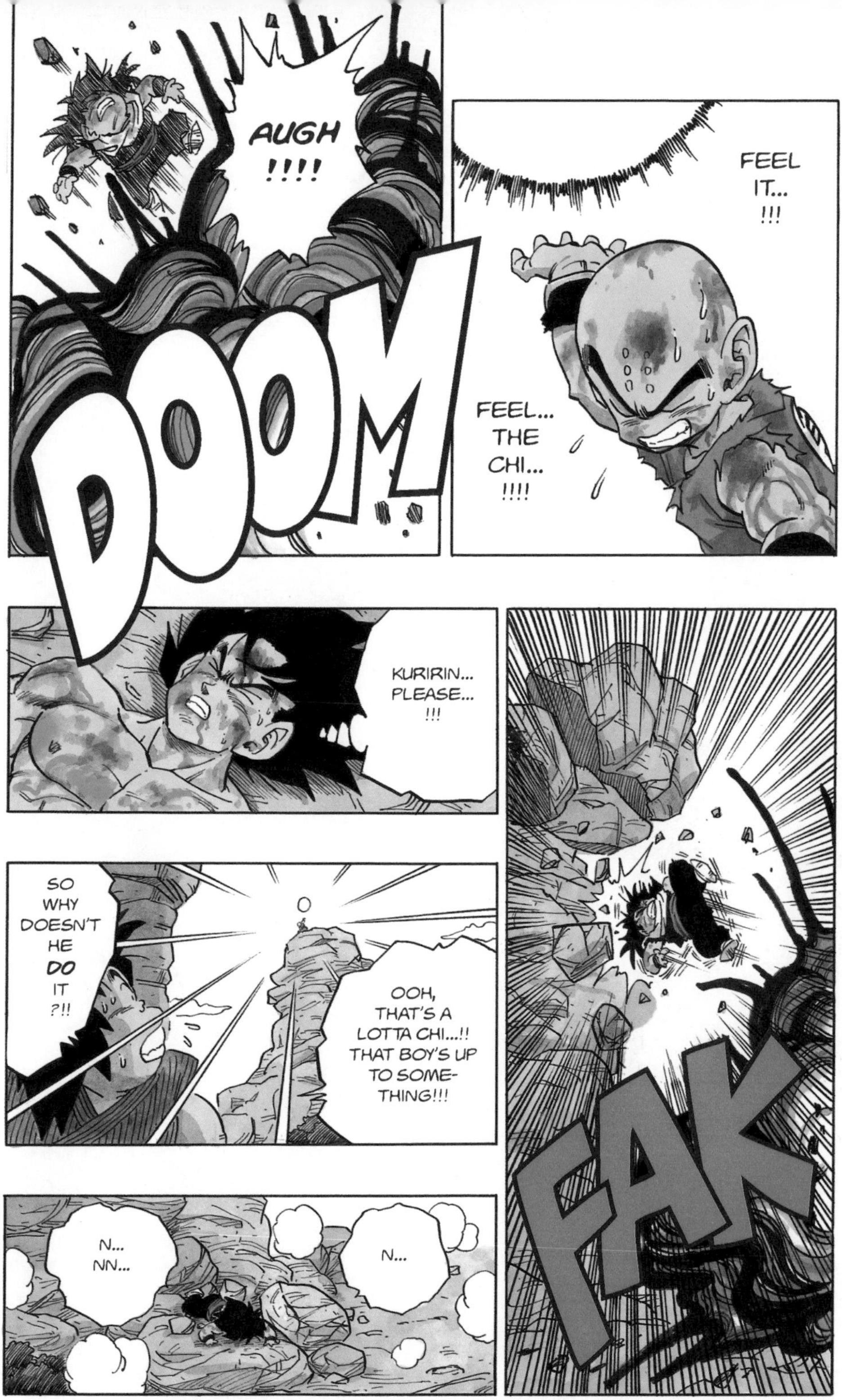

FEEL IT... !!!
FEEL... THE CHI... !!!!
AUGH !!!!
DOOM
FAK
KURIRIN... PLEASE... !!!
OOH, THAT'S A LOTTA CHI...!! THAT BOY'S UP TO SOME-THING!!!
SO WHY DOESN'T HE DO IT ?!!
N...
N... NN...

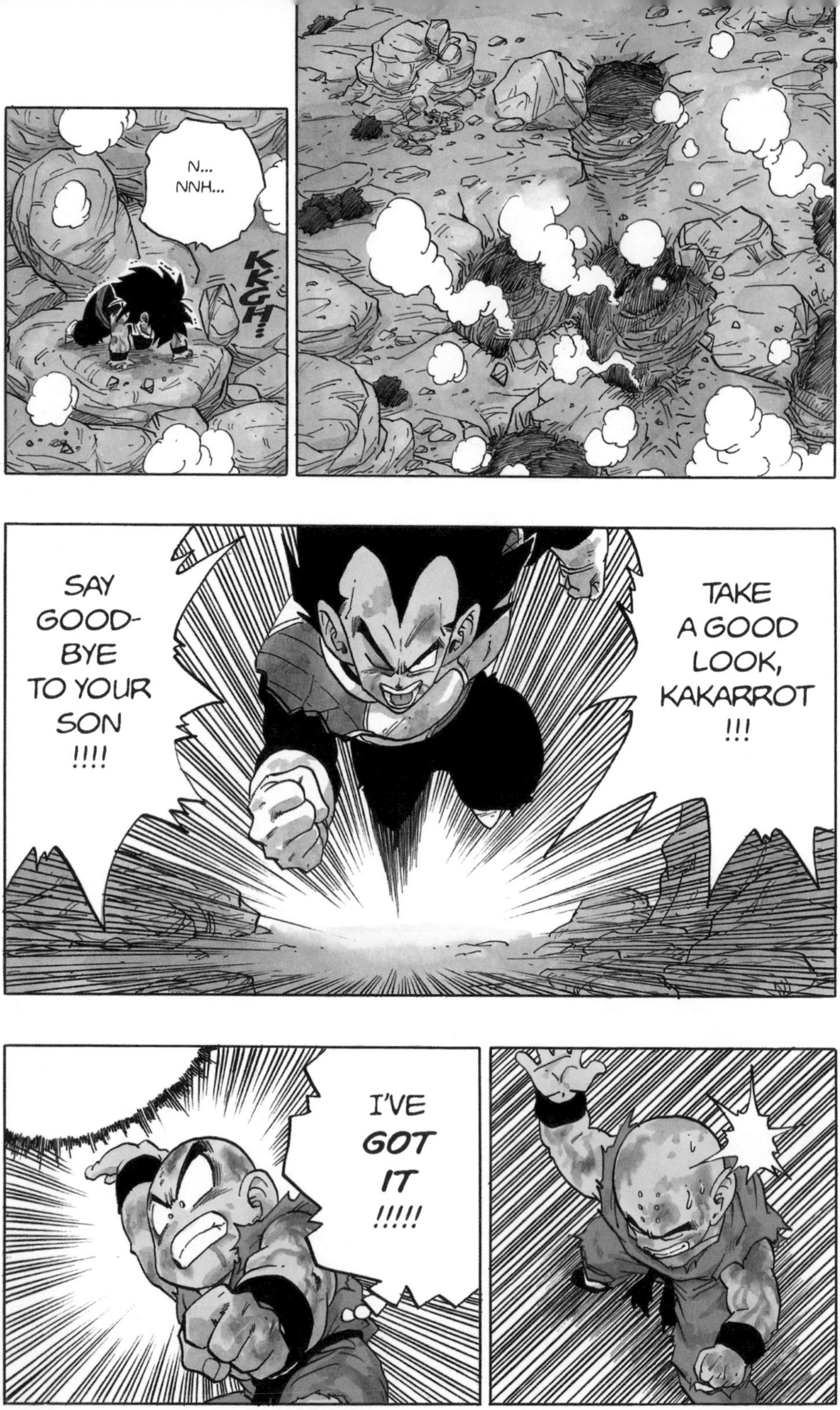
N... NNH...
KKGH!!
TAKE A GOOD LOOK, KAKARROT !!!
SAY GOOD-BYE TO YOUR SON !!!!
I'VE GOT IT !!!!!

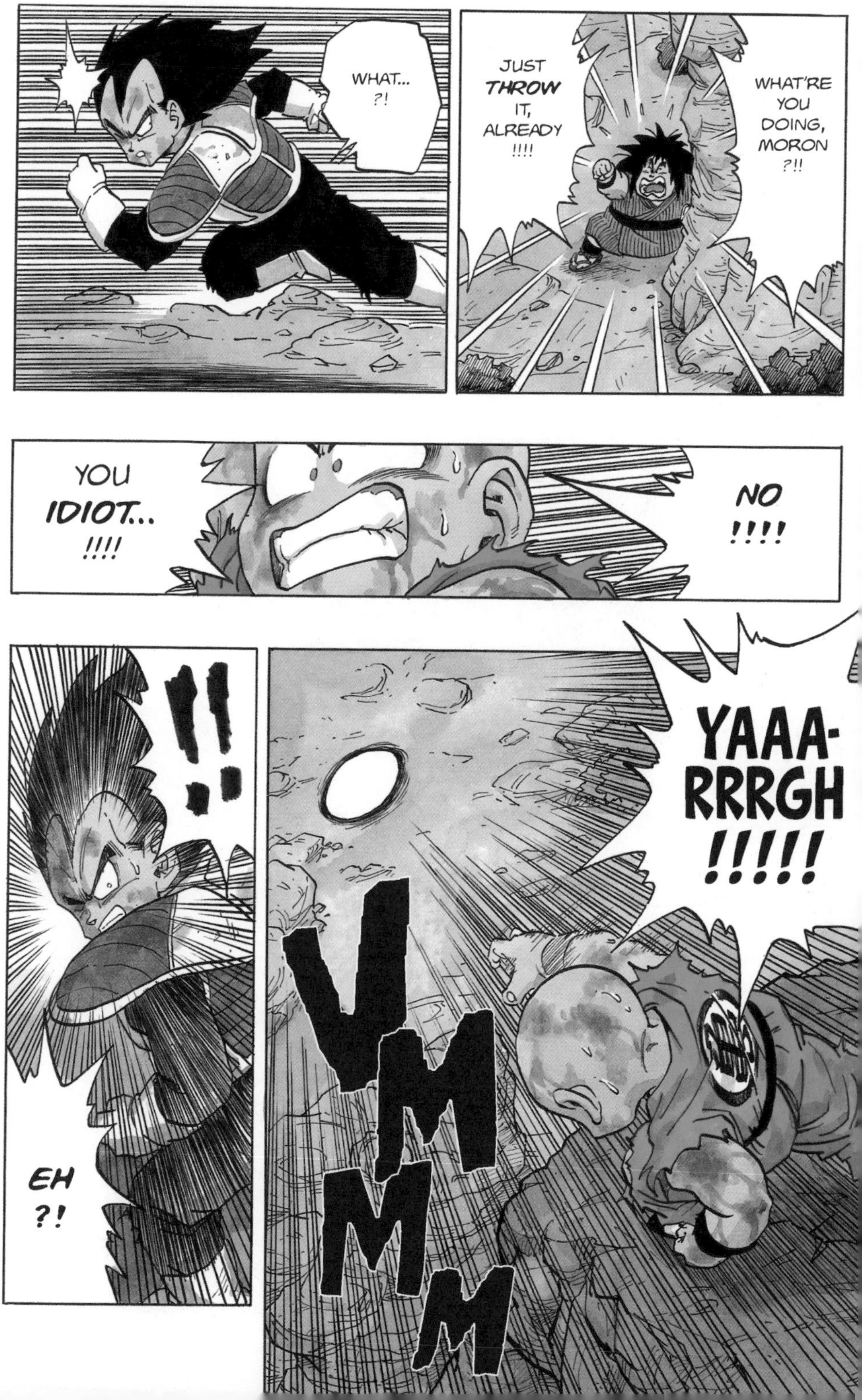
WHAT'RE YOU DOING, MORON ?!!
JUST THROW IT, ALREADY !!!!
WHAT... ?!
NO !!!!
YOU IDIOT... !!!!
YAAA-RRRGH !!!!!
VMMMM
!!
EH ?!

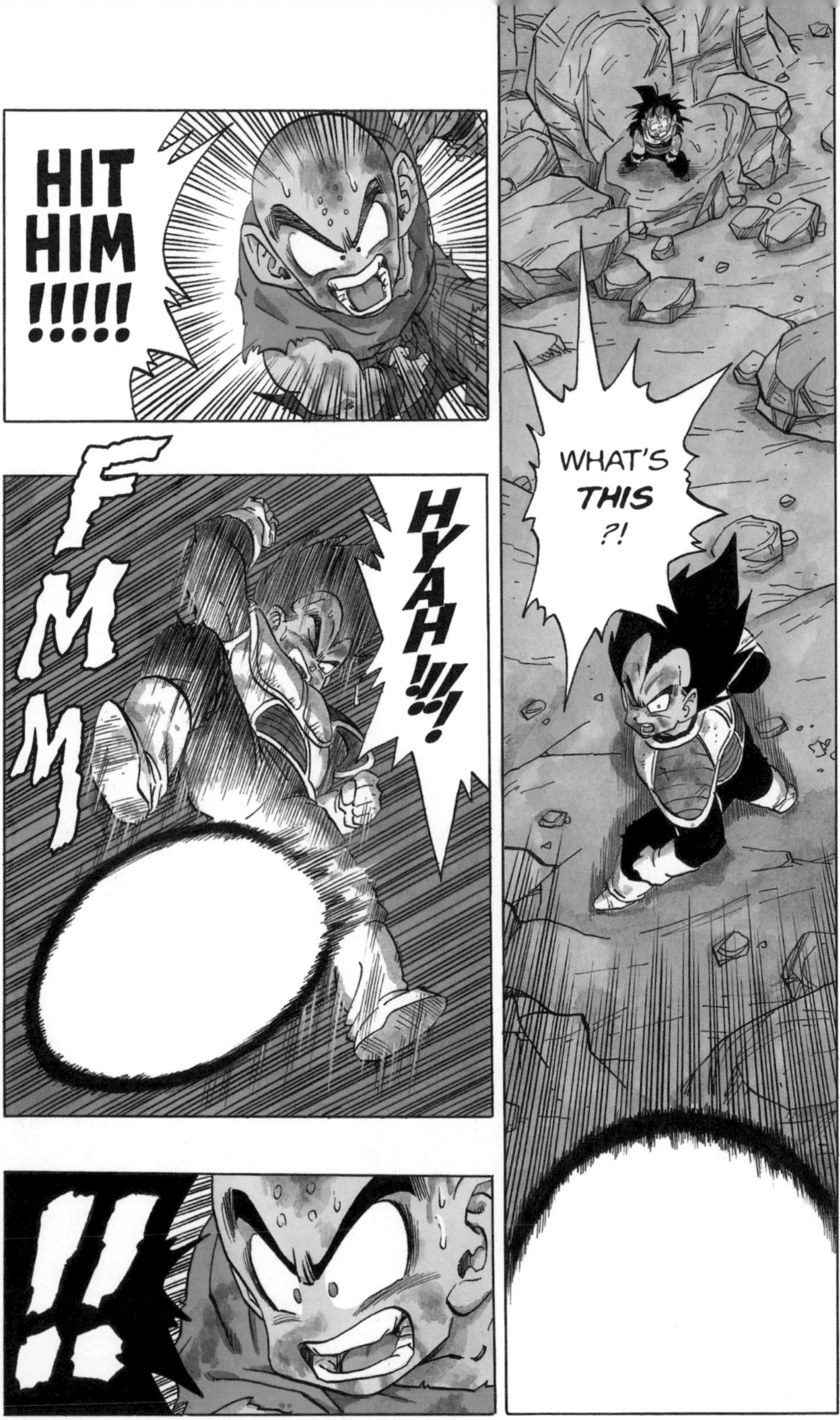
WHAT'S THIS ?!
HIT HIM !!!!!
HYAH!!!!
FMM
!!

## DBZ:43 • The Hopes of a Planet

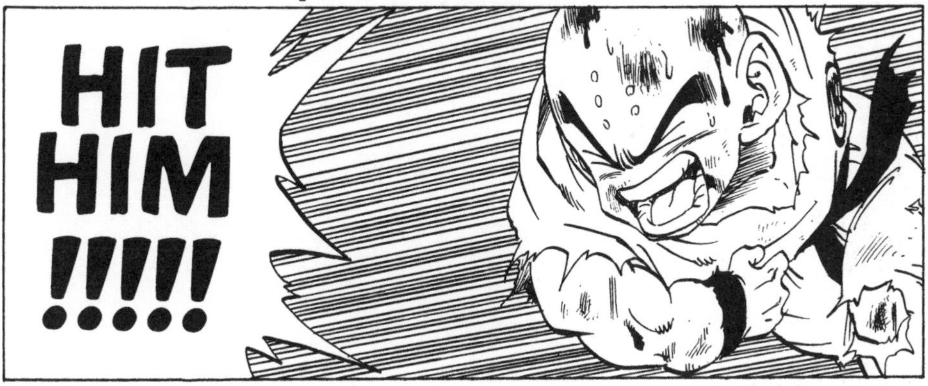
HIT HIM !!!!!

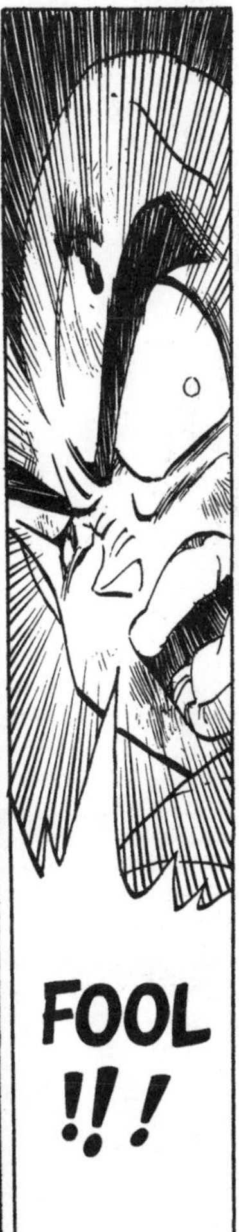
FOOL !!!

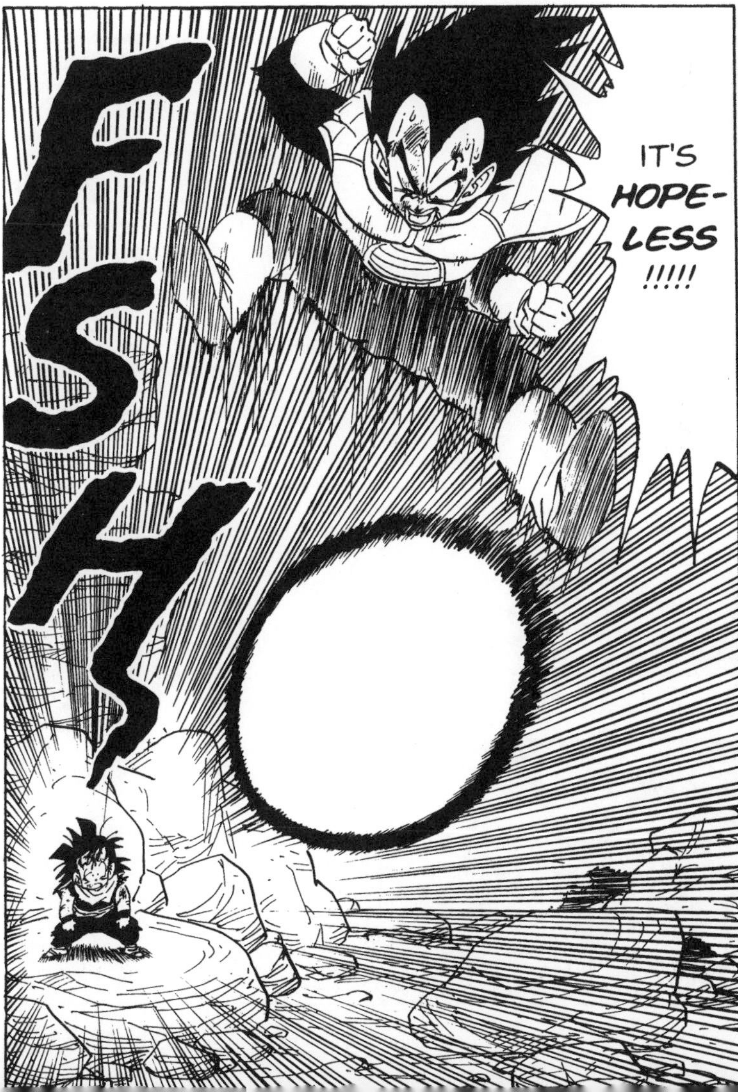
FSSH
IT'S HOPE-LESS !!!!!

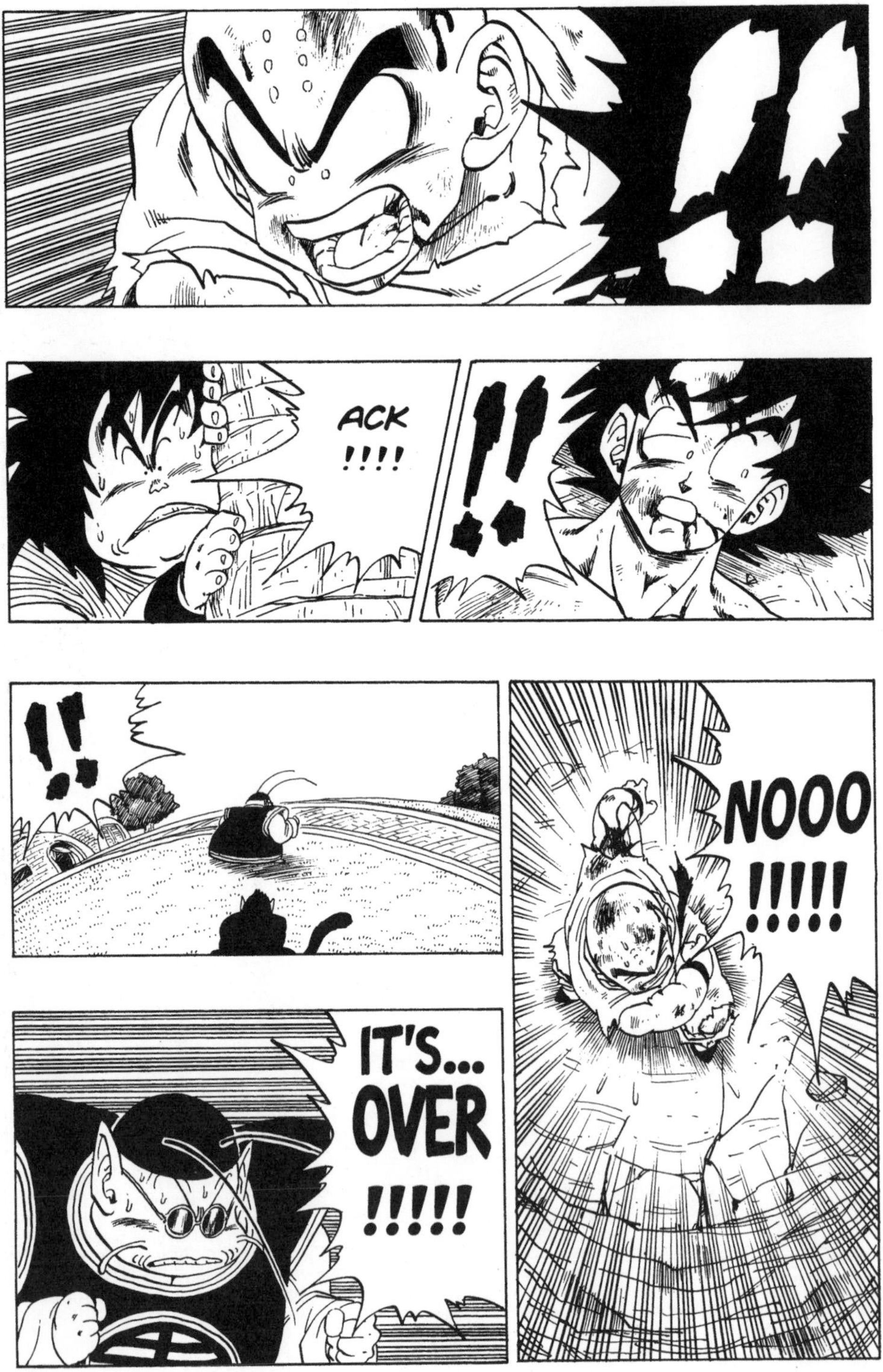
!!
!!
ACK !!!!
NOOO !!!!!
!!
IT'S... OVER !!!!!

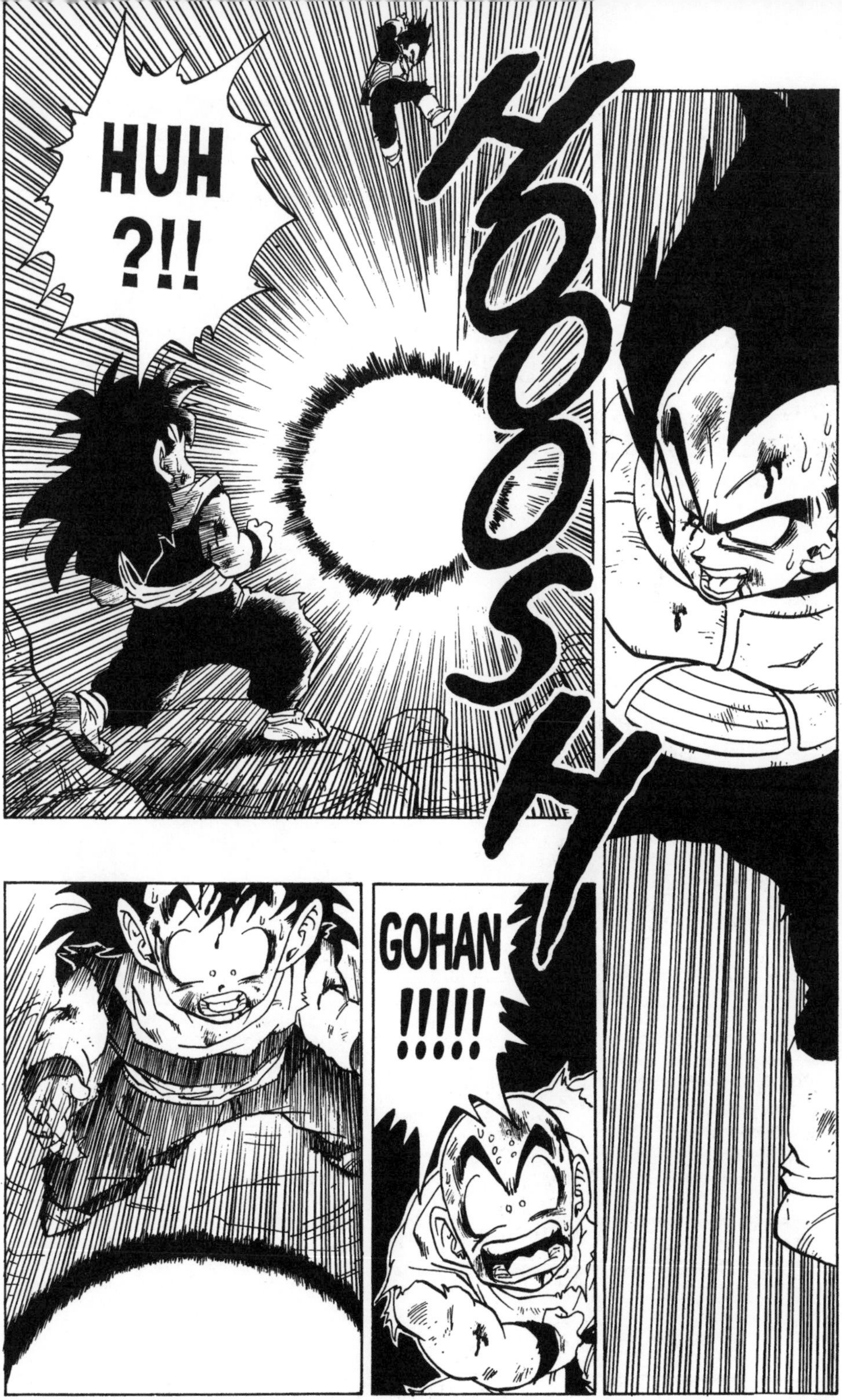
WHOOSH
HUH ?!!
GOHAN !!!!!

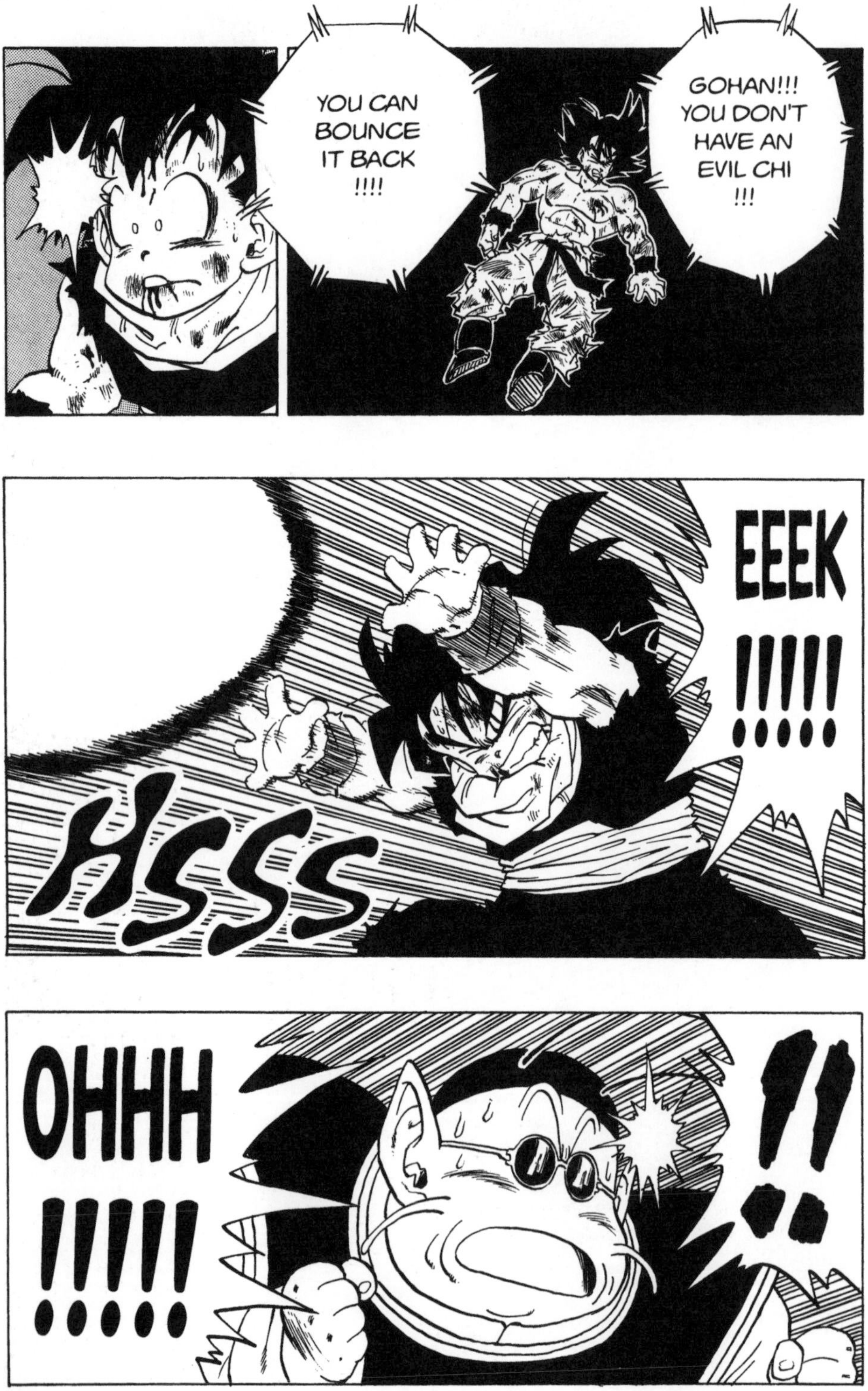
GOHAN!!! YOU DON'T HAVE AN EVIL CHI !!!
YOU CAN BOUNCE IT BACK !!!!
EEEK !!!!!!
HSSS
!!
OHHH !!!!!!

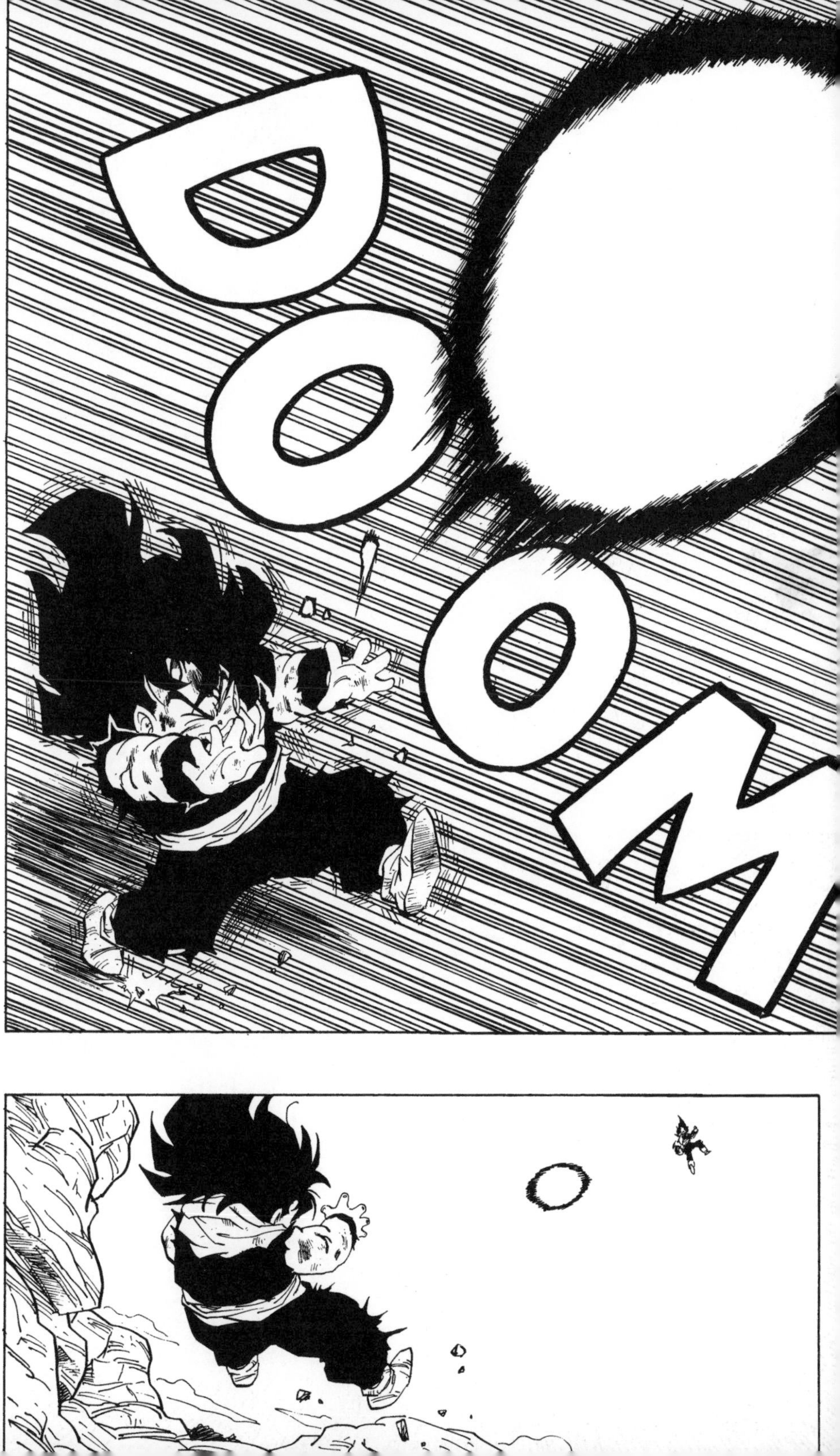
DOOM

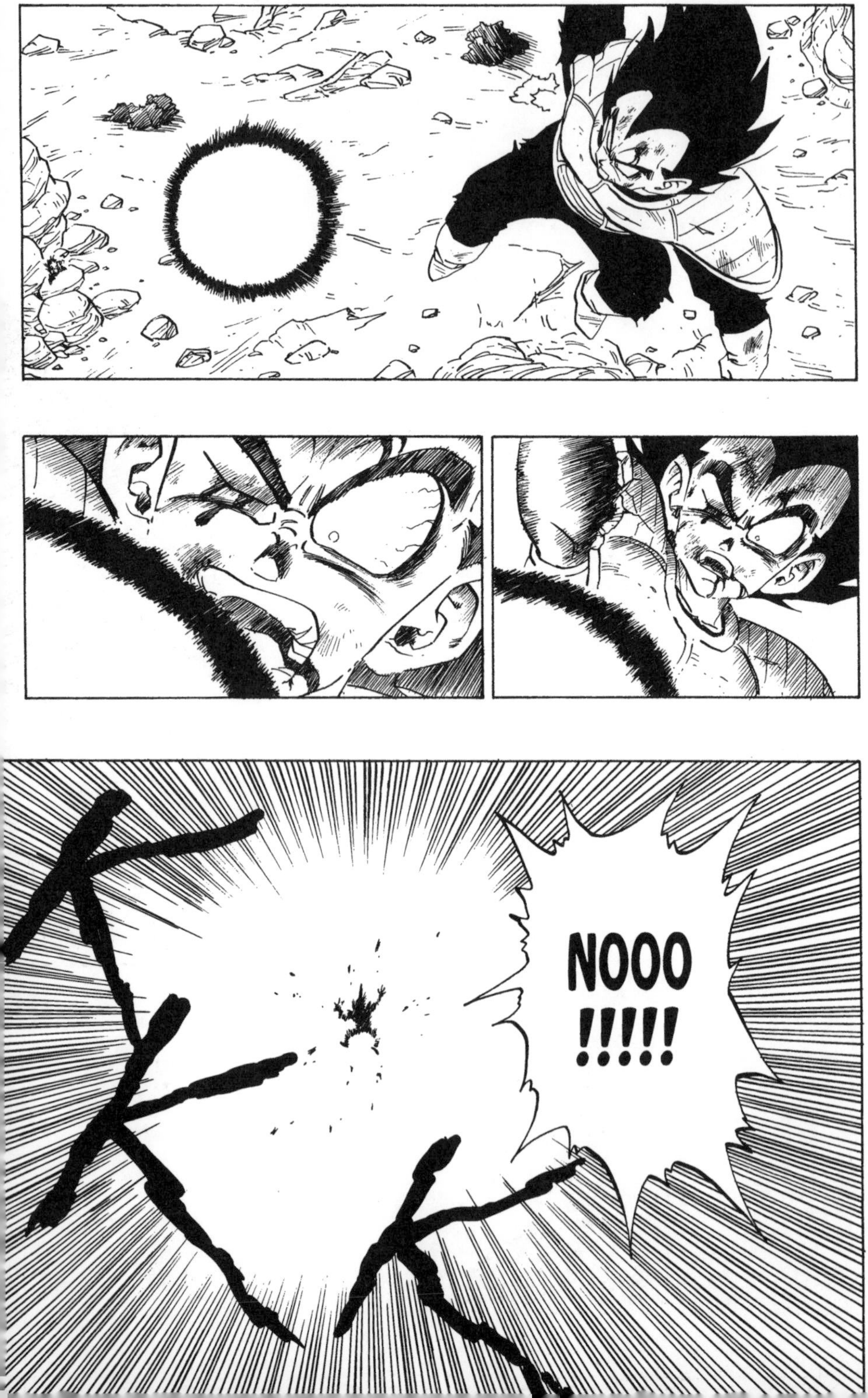
NOOO
!!!!!

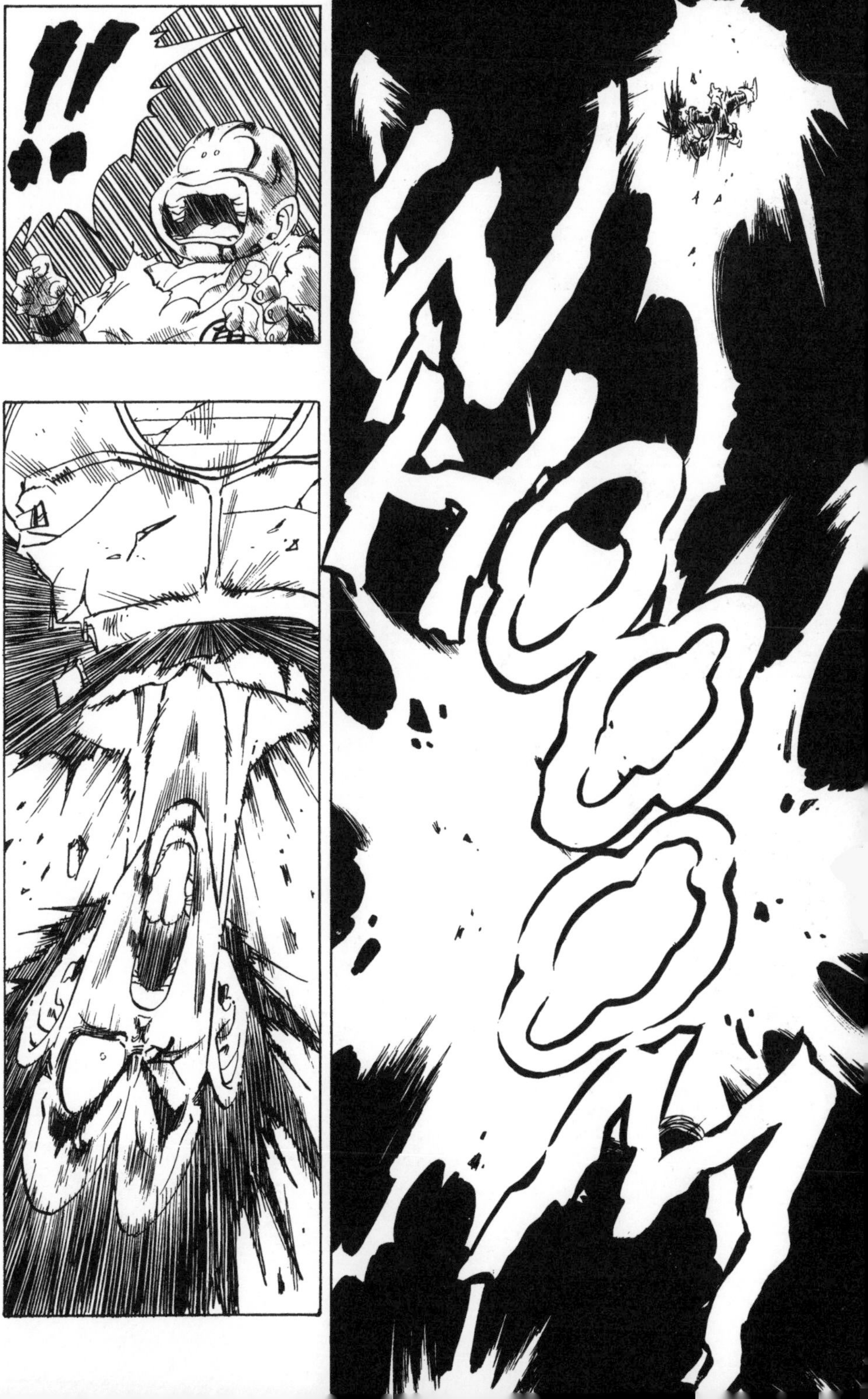
!!

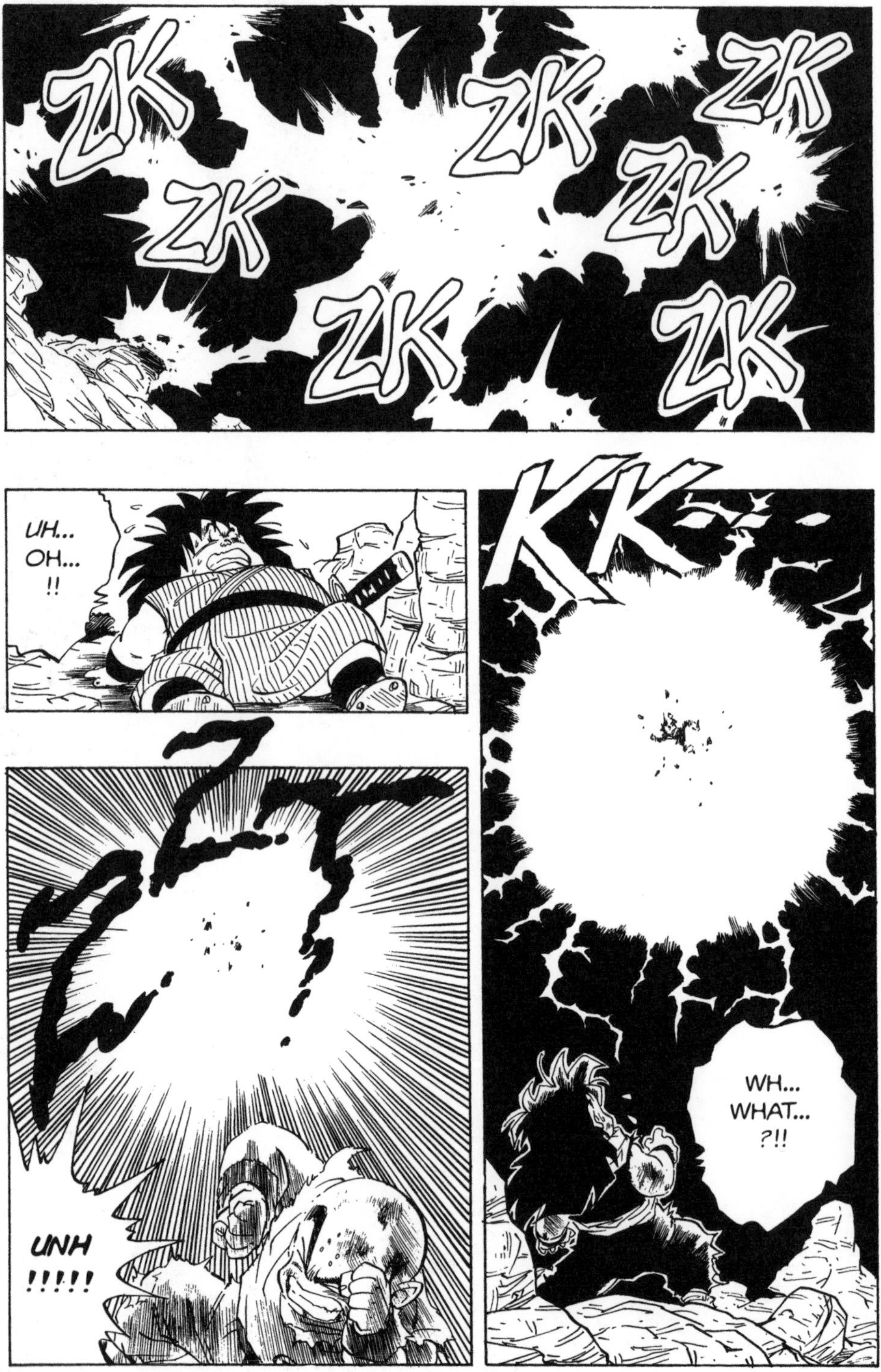
ZK ZK ZK ZK ZK ZK ZK
KK
WH... WHAT... ?!!
UH... OH... !!
UNH !!!!!

BWOOOSH
YAAAAA.....!!!
UH.....
UH...
THEY DID IT !!!!

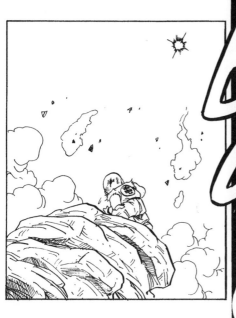

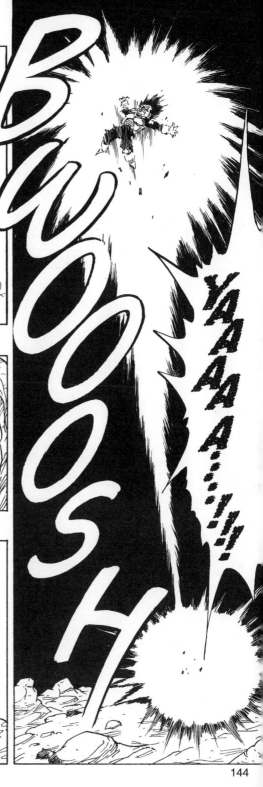

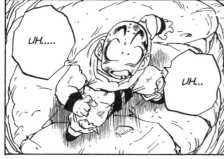

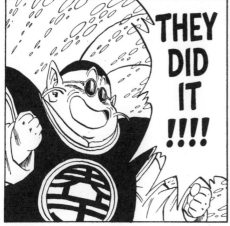

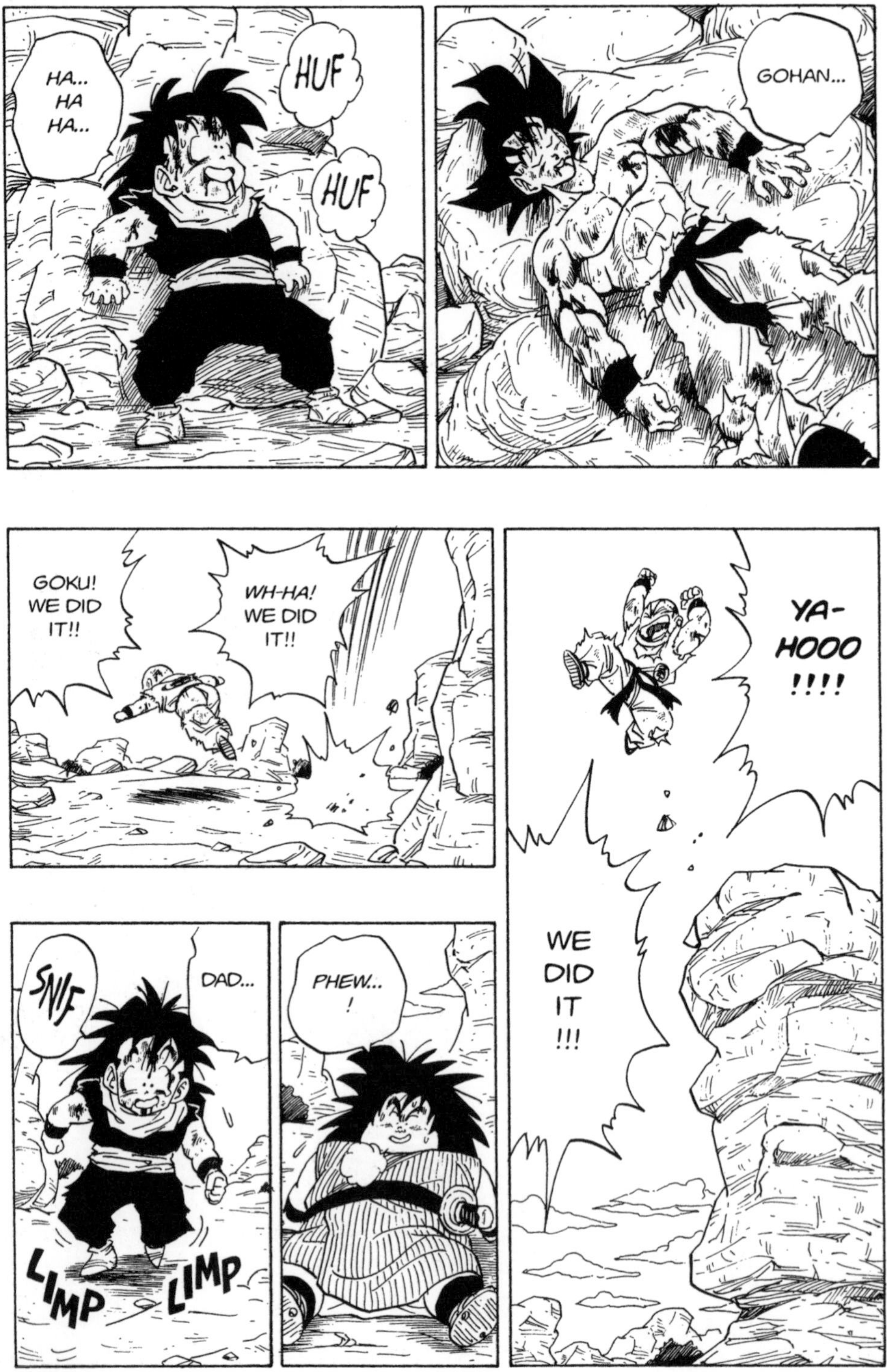
GOHAN...
HUF
HUF
HA... HA HA...
YA-HOOO!!!!
WE DID IT!!!
WH-HA! WE DID IT!!
GOKU! WE DID IT!!
PHEW...!
DAD...
SNIF
LIMP
LIMP

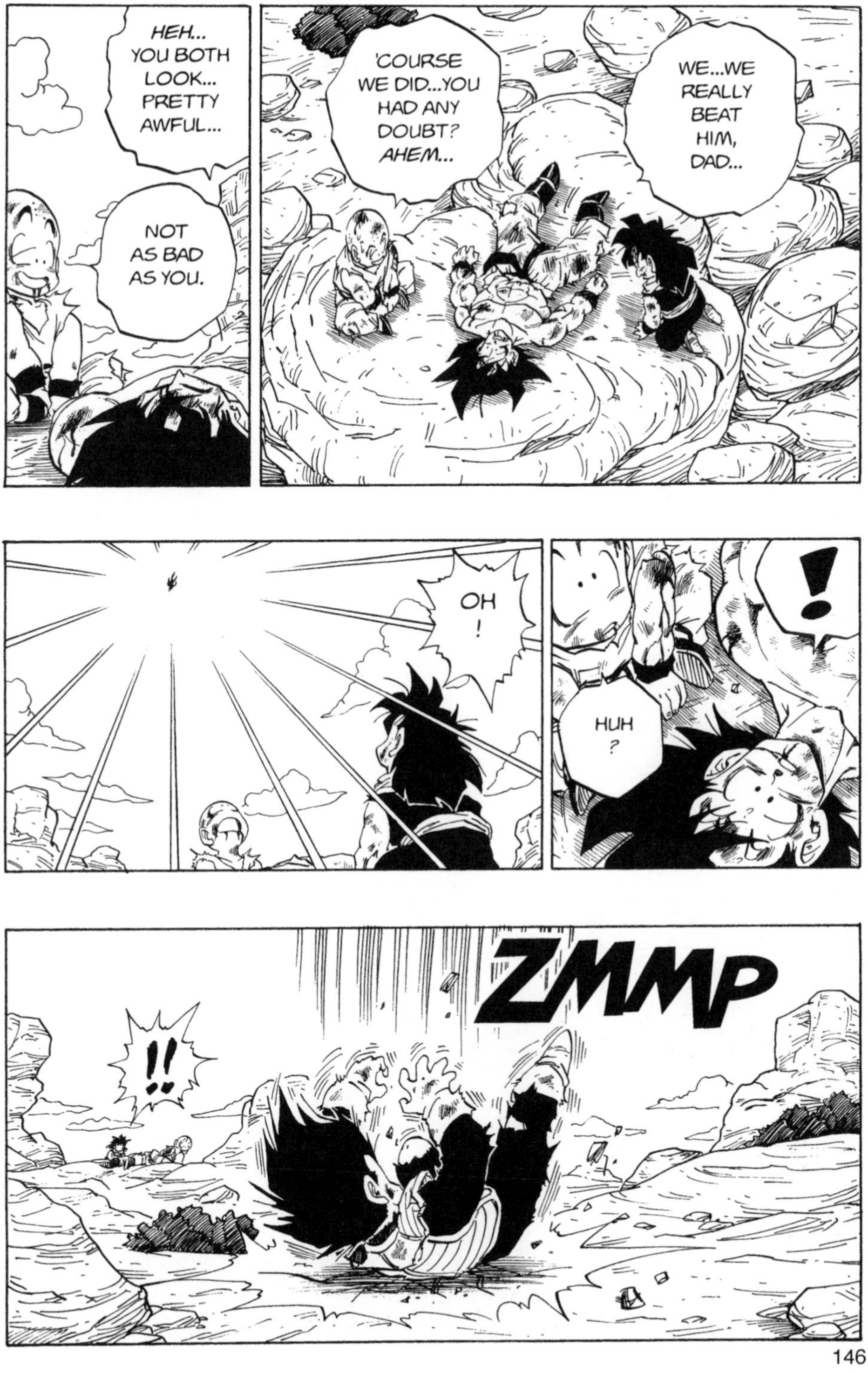
WE...WE REALLY BEAT HIM, DAD...
'COURSE WE DID...YOU HAD ANY DOUBT? AHEM...
HEH... YOU BOTH LOOK... PRETTY AWFUL...
NOT AS BAD AS YOU.
!
HUH?
OH!
ZMMP
!!

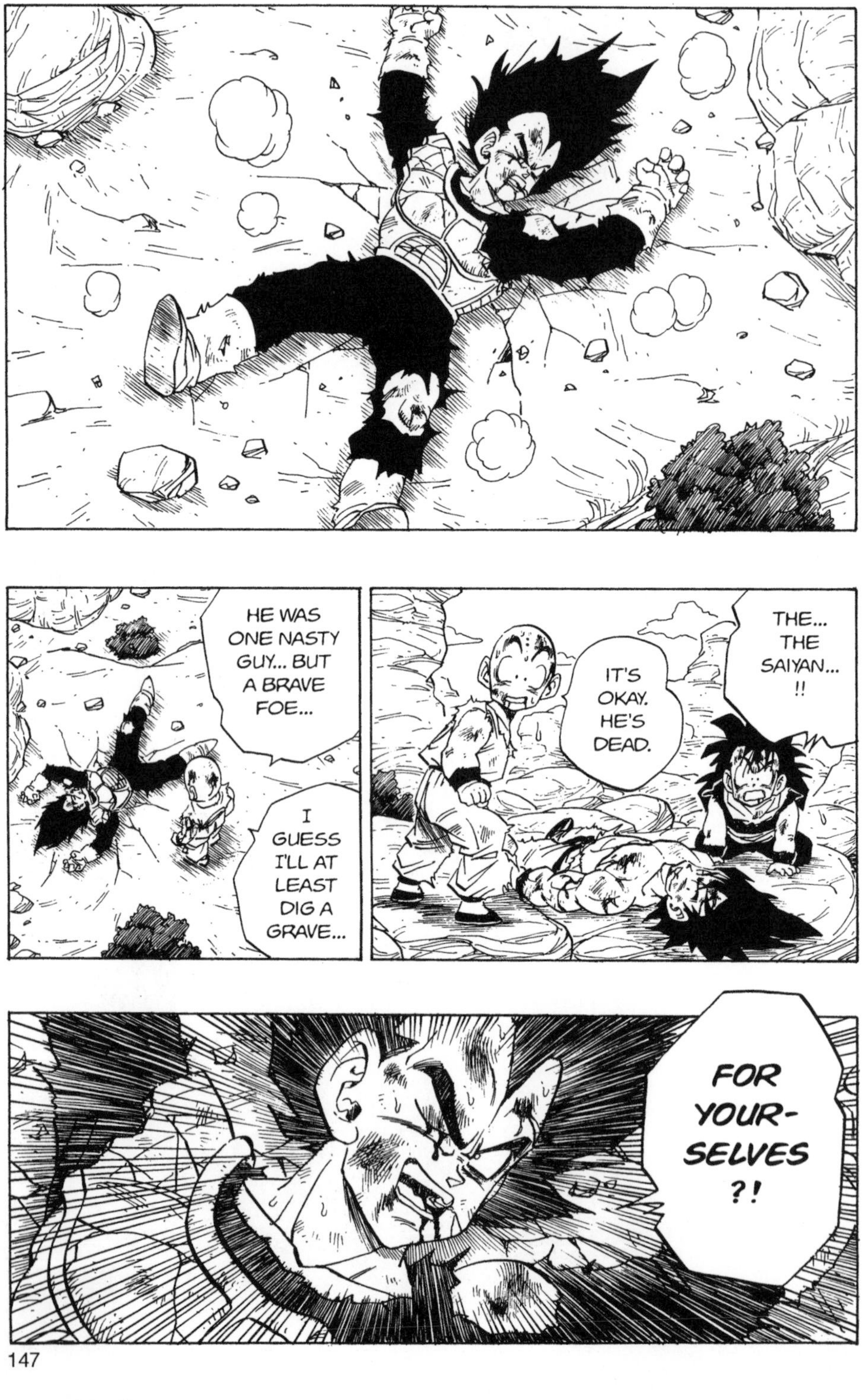
THE... THE SAIYAN... !!
IT'S OKAY. HE'S DEAD.
HE WAS ONE NASTY GUY... BUT A BRAVE FOE...
I GUESS I'LL AT LEAST DIG A GRAVE...
FOR YOUR-SELVES ?!

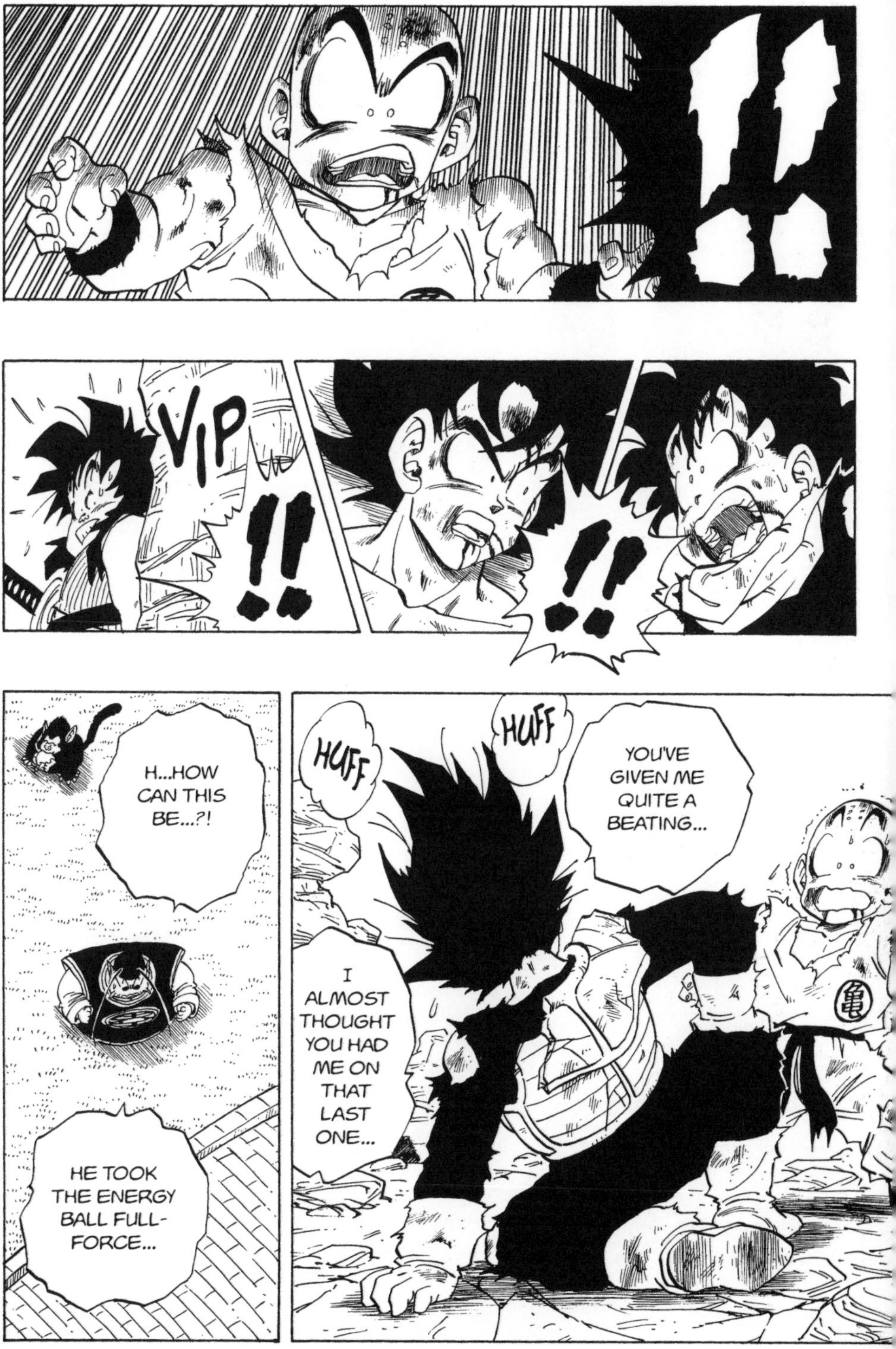
!!
!!
VIP
!!
YOU'VE GIVEN ME QUITE A BEATING...
HUFF
HUFF
I ALMOST THOUGHT YOU HAD ME ON THAT LAST ONE...
H...HOW CAN THIS BE...?!
HE TOOK THE ENERGY BALL FULL-FORCE...

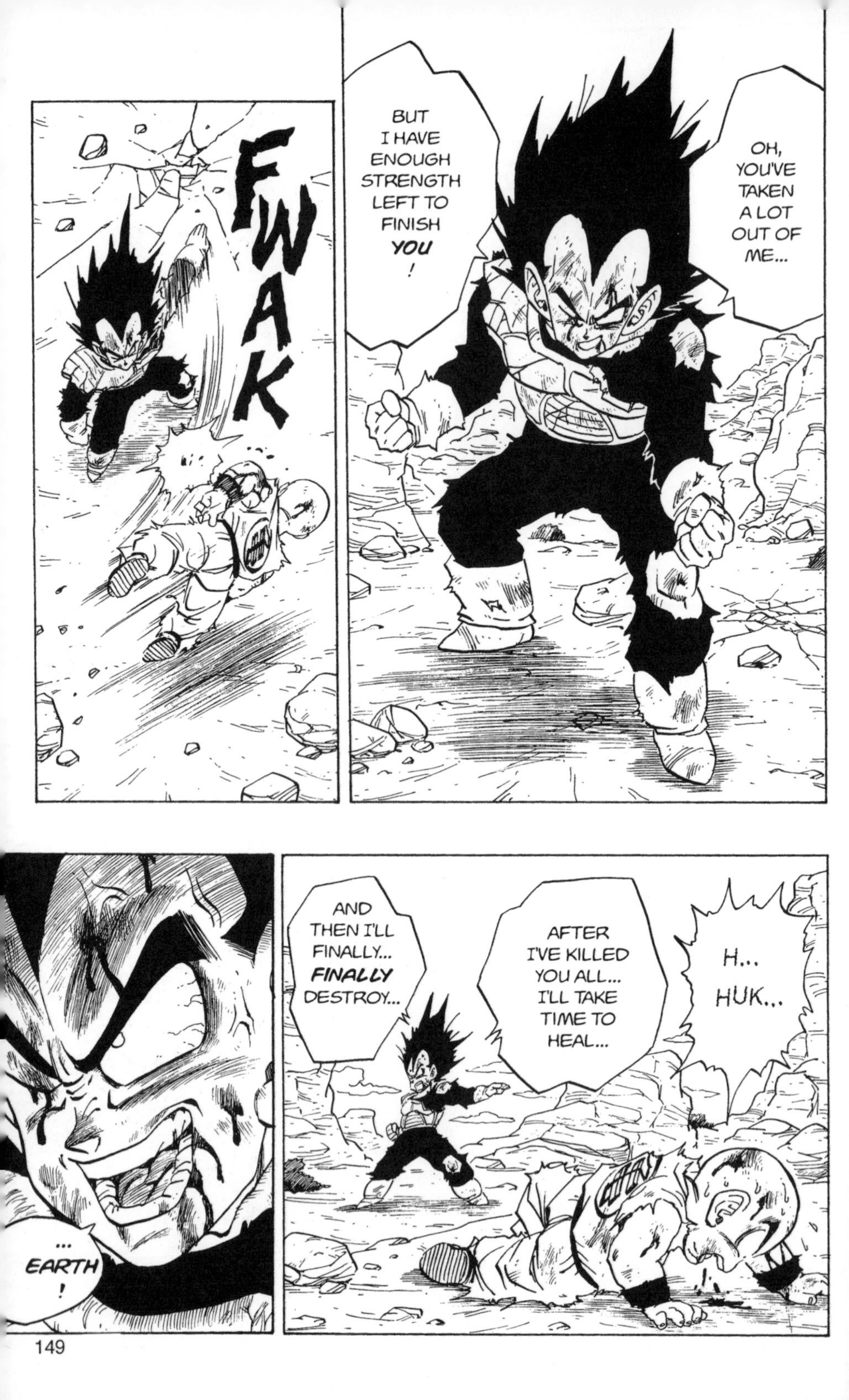
OH, YOU'VE TAKEN A LOT OUT OF ME...
BUT I HAVE ENOUGH STRENGTH LEFT TO FINISH YOU!
FWAK
H... HUK...
AFTER I'VE KILLED YOU ALL... I'LL TAKE TIME TO HEAL...
AND THEN I'LL FINALLY... FINALLY DESTROY...
...EARTH!

# DBZ:45 • The Worn-out Warriors

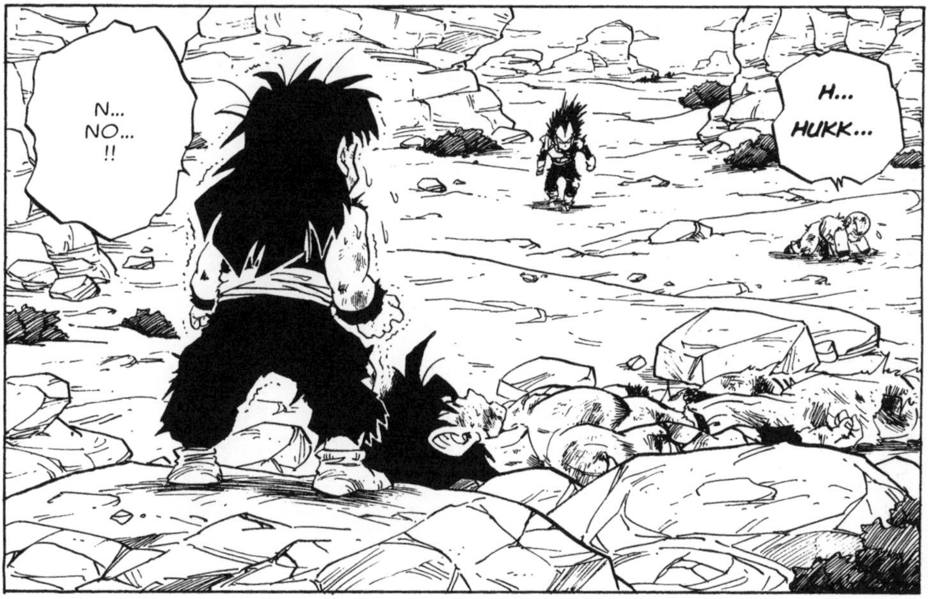
H... HUKK...
N... NO... !!

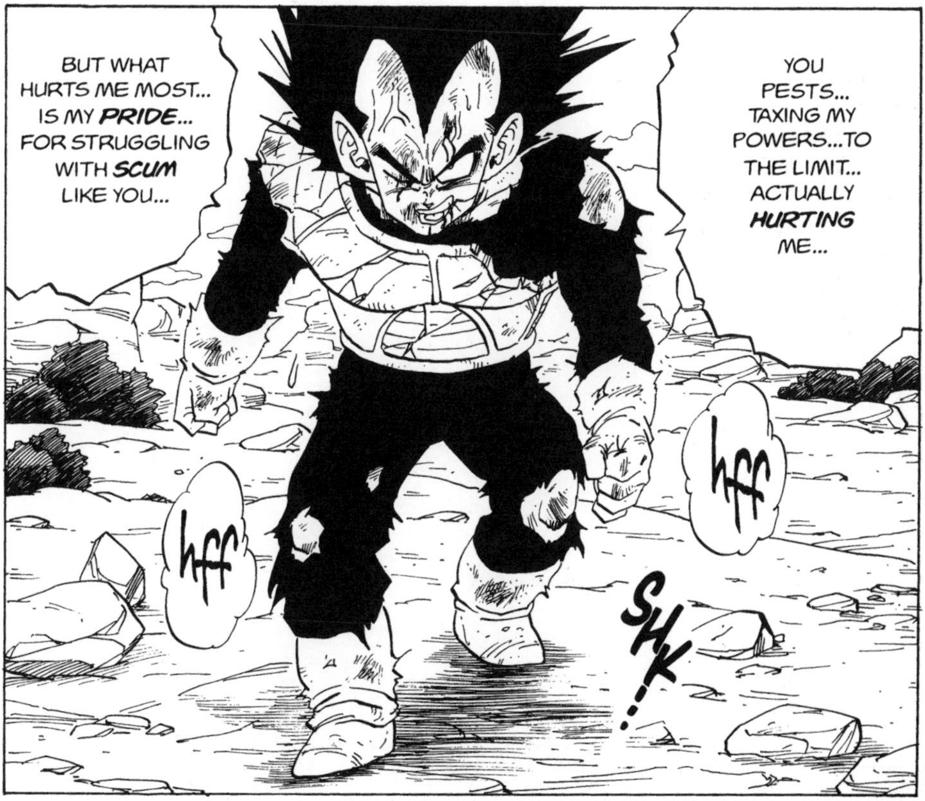
YOU PESTS... TAXING MY POWERS...TO THE LIMIT... ACTUALLY HURTING ME...
BUT WHAT HURTS ME MOST... IS MY PRIDE... FOR STRUGGLING WITH SCUM LIKE YOU...
hff
hff
SHK...

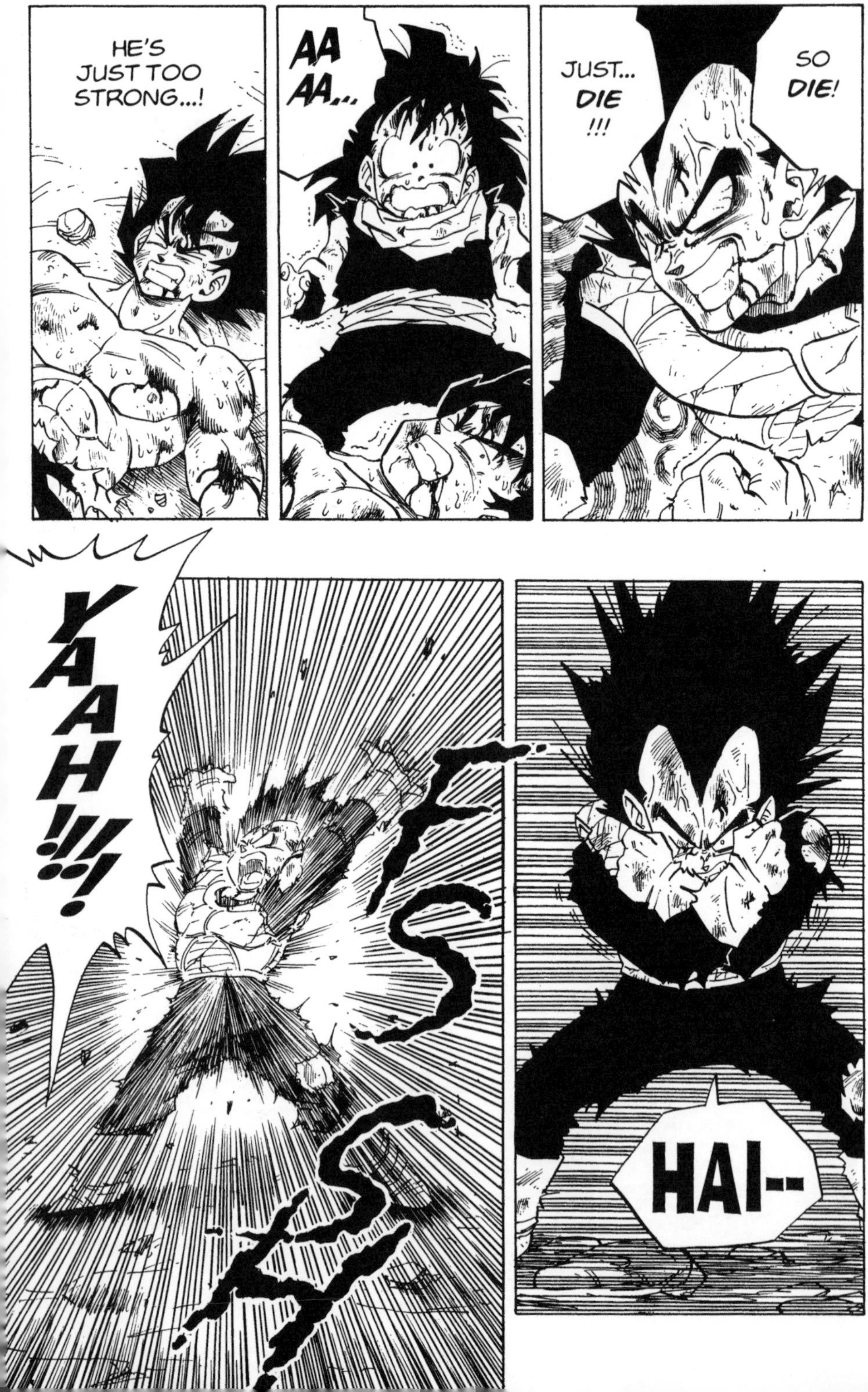
SO DIE!
JUST... DIE !!!
AA AA...
HE'S JUST TOO STRONG...!
HAI--
YAAH!!!!

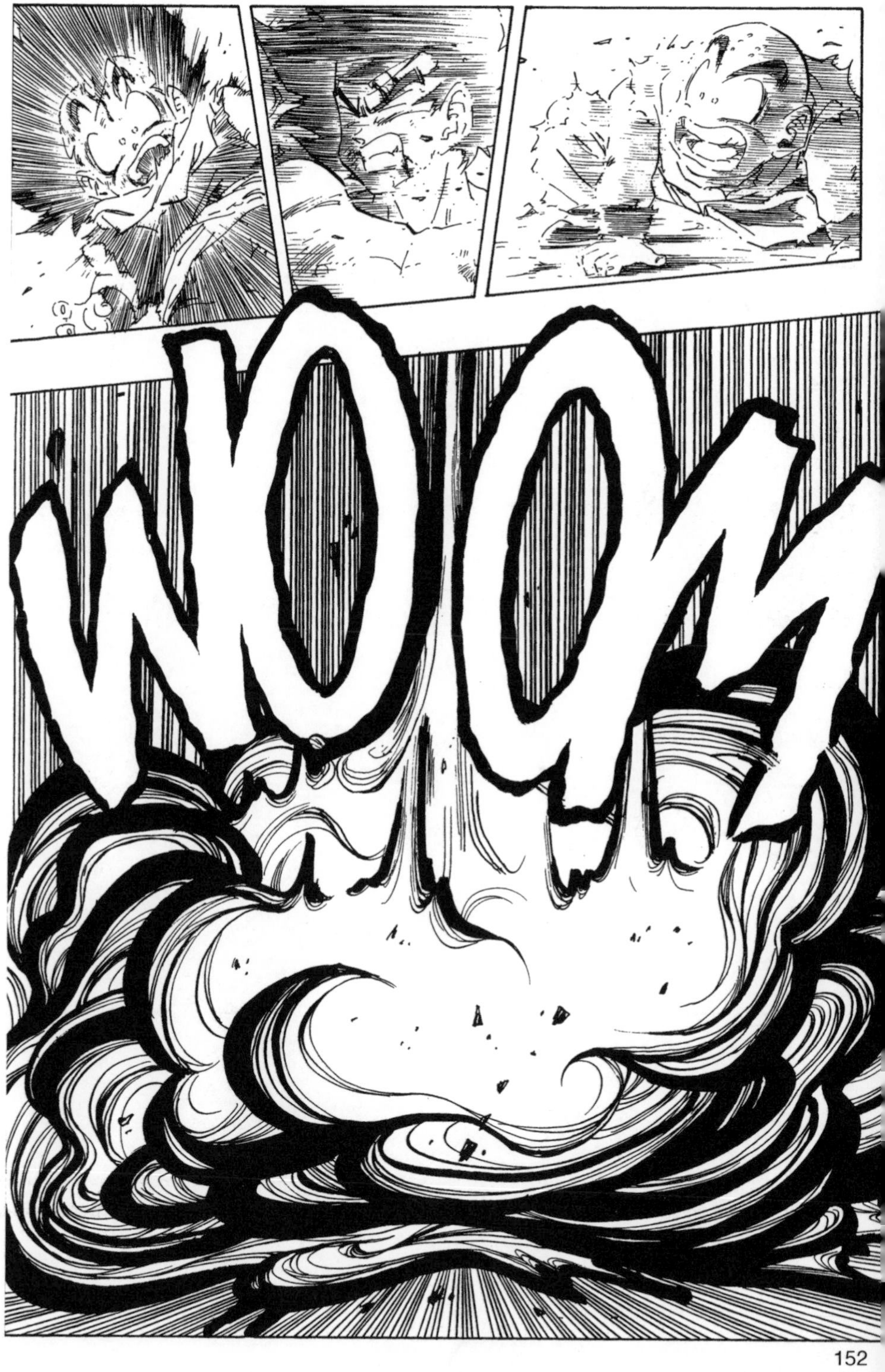
WOOM

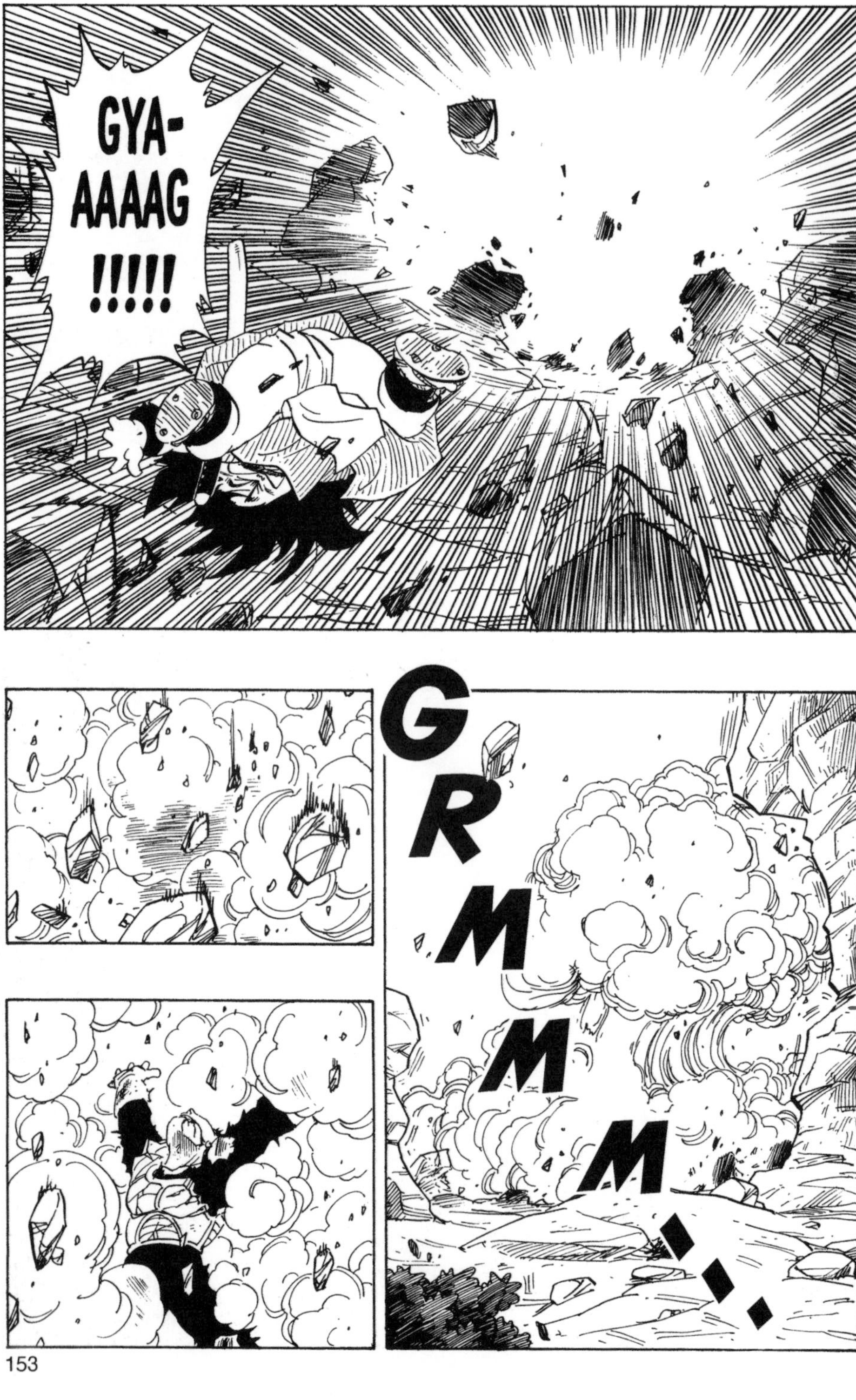
GYA-AAAAG!!!!!!
GRMMM...

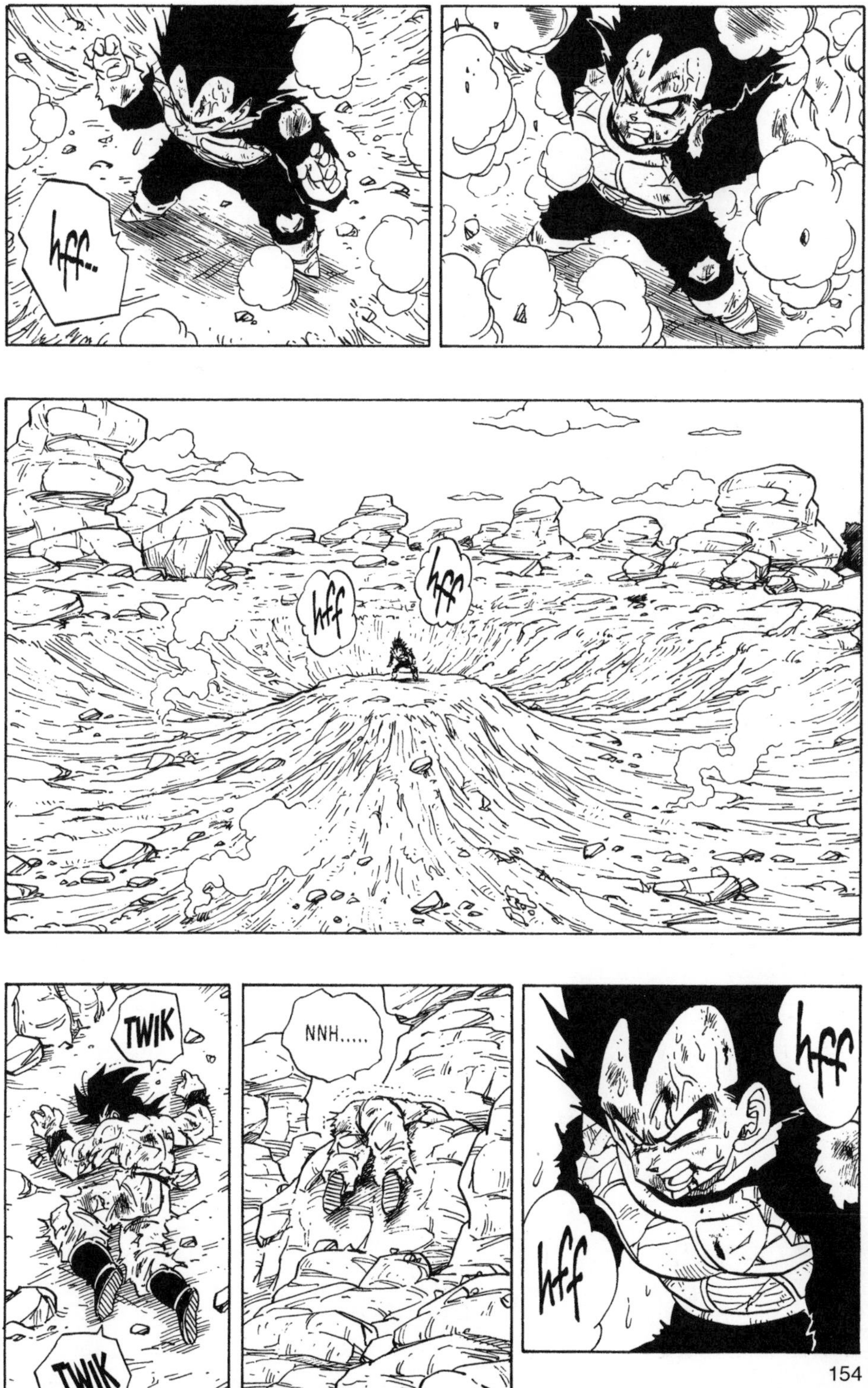
hff..
hff
hff
hff
hff
NNH.....
TWIK
TWIK

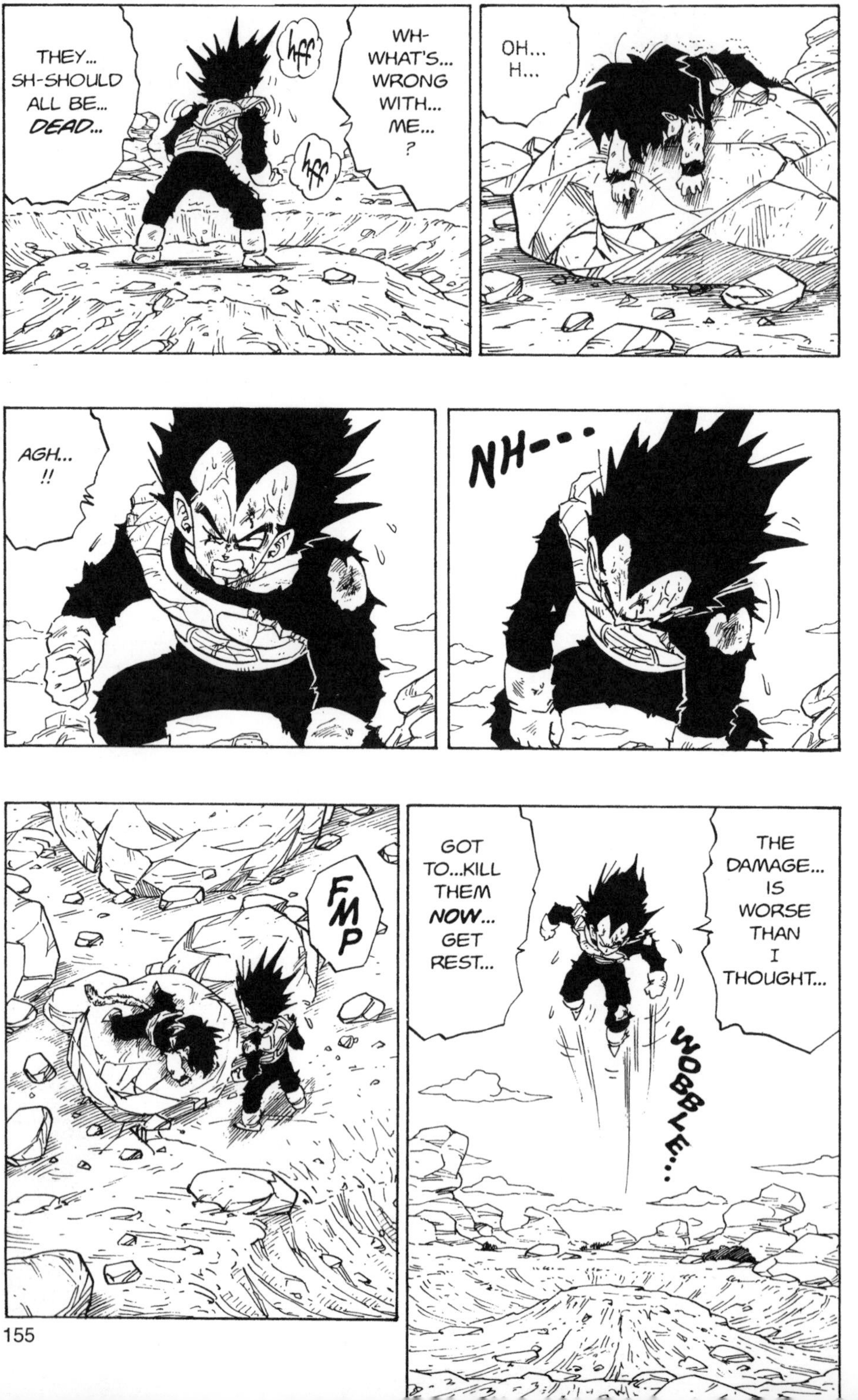

OH... H...
WH- WHAT'S... WRONG WITH... ME... ?
hff
hff
THEY... SH-SHOULD ALL BE... DEAD...
NH---
AGH... !!
THE DAMAGE... IS WORSE THAN I THOUGHT...
GOT TO...KILL THEM NOW... GET REST...
WOBBLE...
FMP

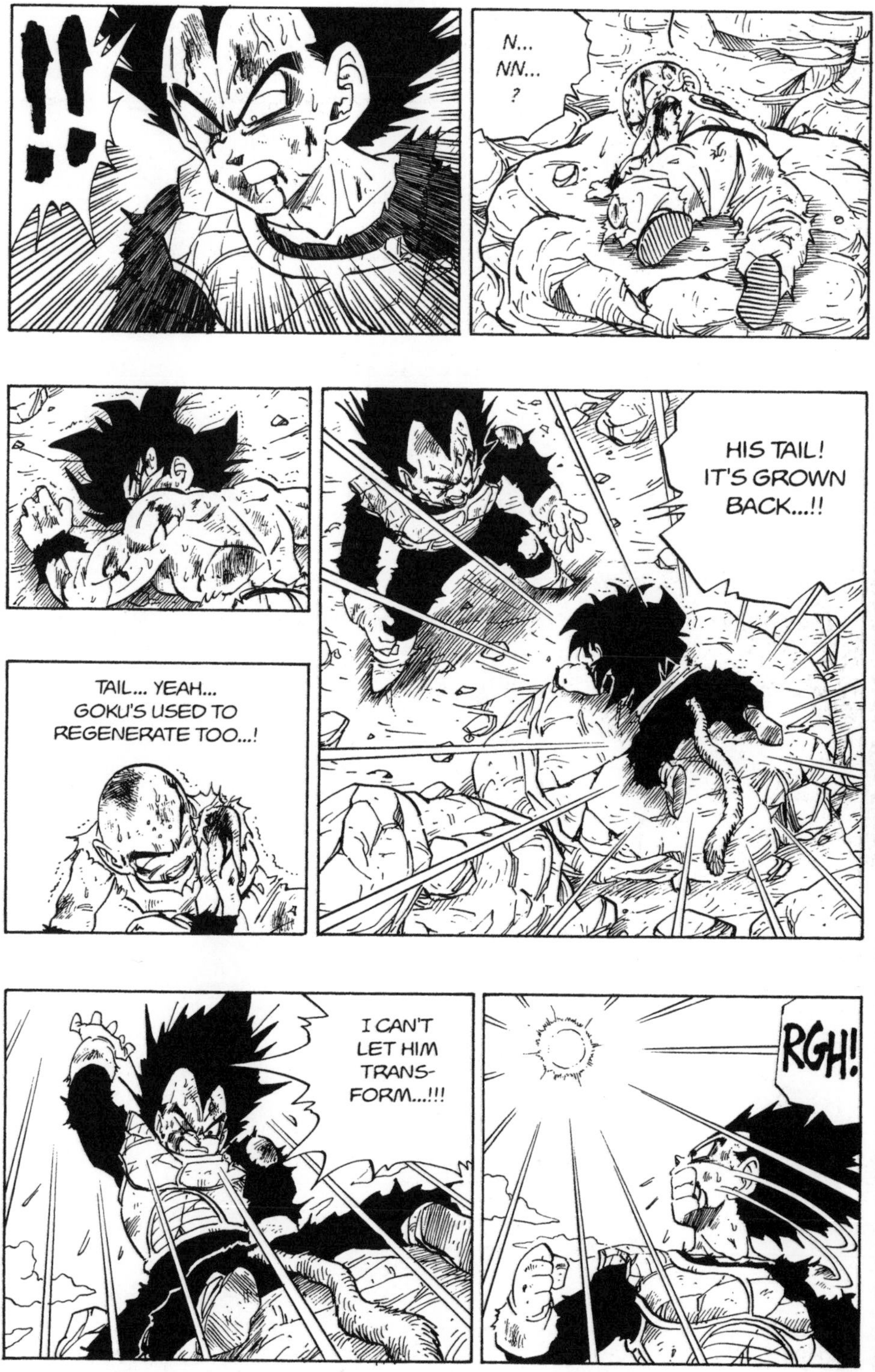
N... NN... ?
!!
HIS TAIL! IT'S GROWN BACK...!!
TAIL... YEAH... GOKU'S USED TO REGENERATE TOO...!
RGH!
I CAN'T LET HIM TRANS-FORM...!!!

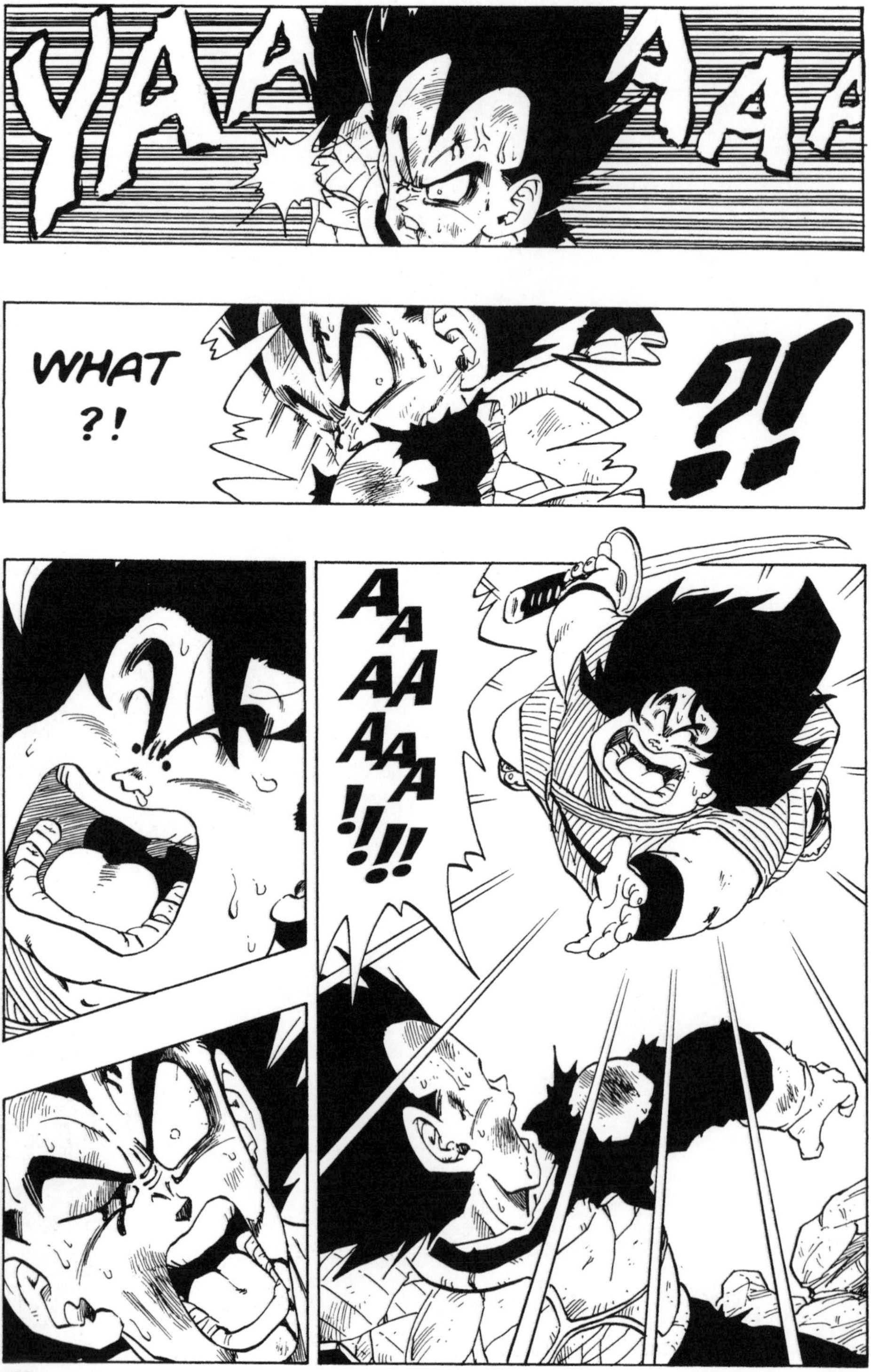
YAAAAA
WHAT ?!
?!!
AAAAAAA!!!!!

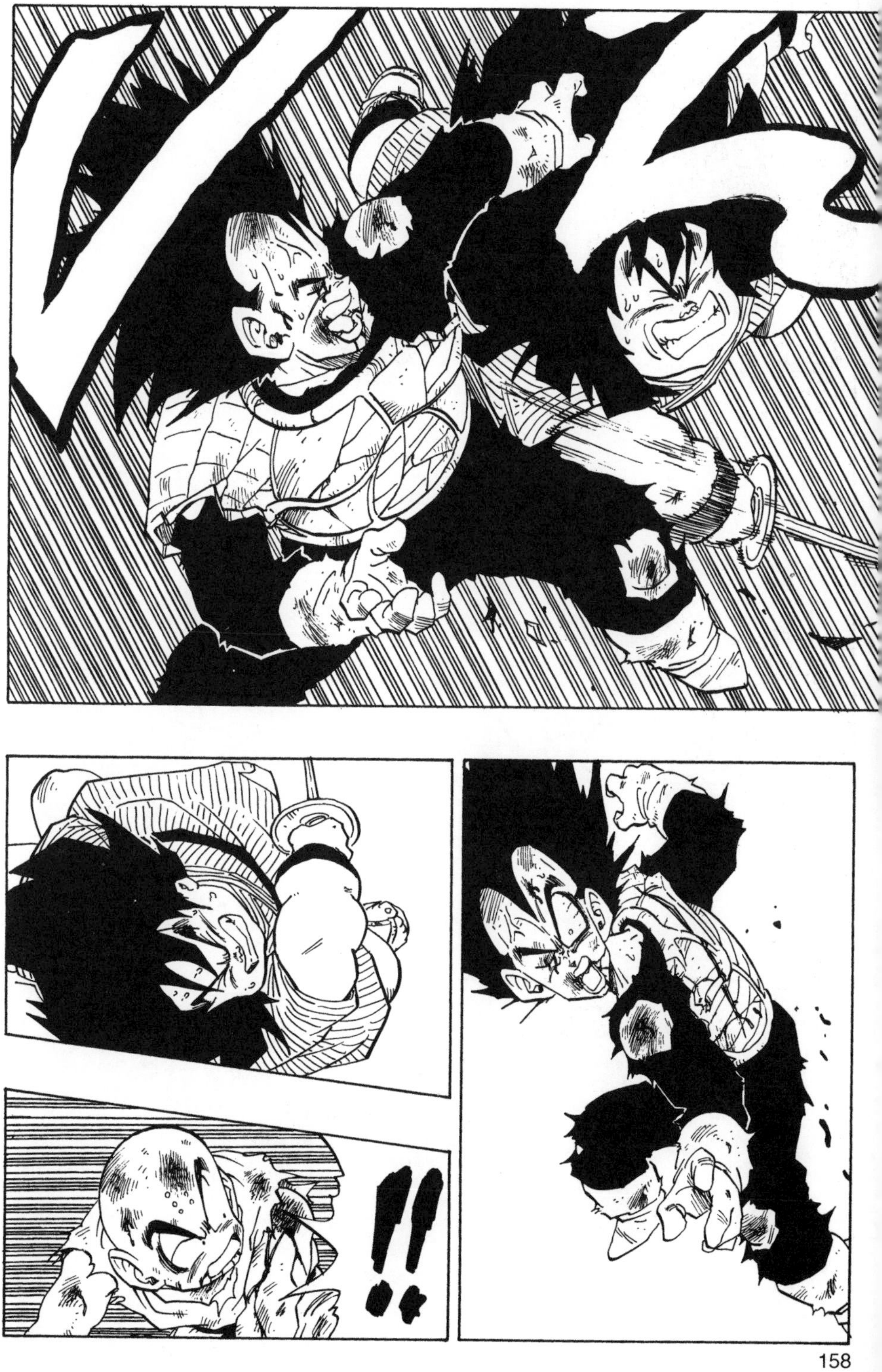
!!

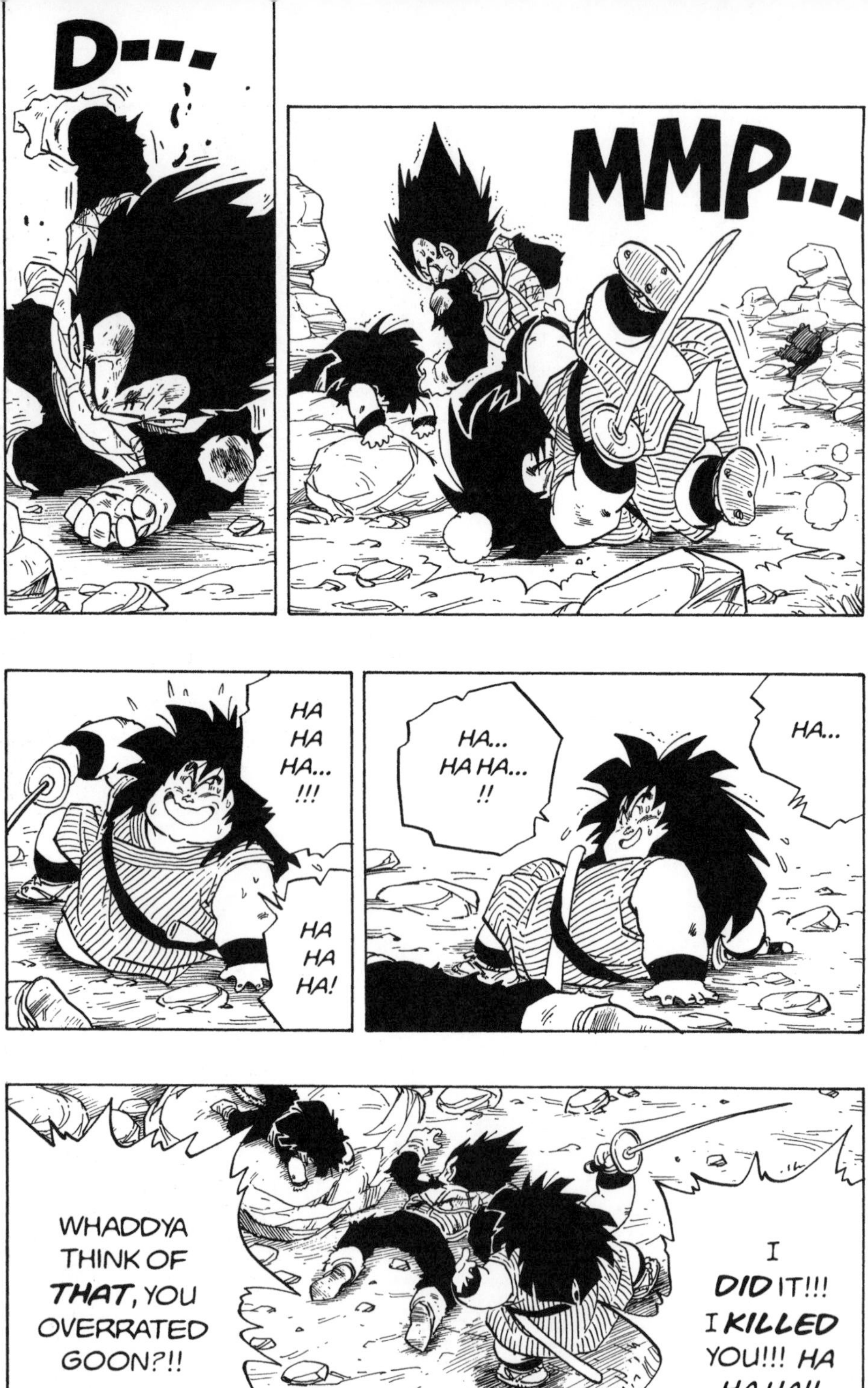
MMP...
D-...
HA...
HA... HA HA... !!
HA HA HA... !!!
HA HA HA!
I DID IT!!! I KILLED YOU!!! HA HA HA!!
WHADDYA THINK OF THAT, YOU OVERRATED GOON?!!

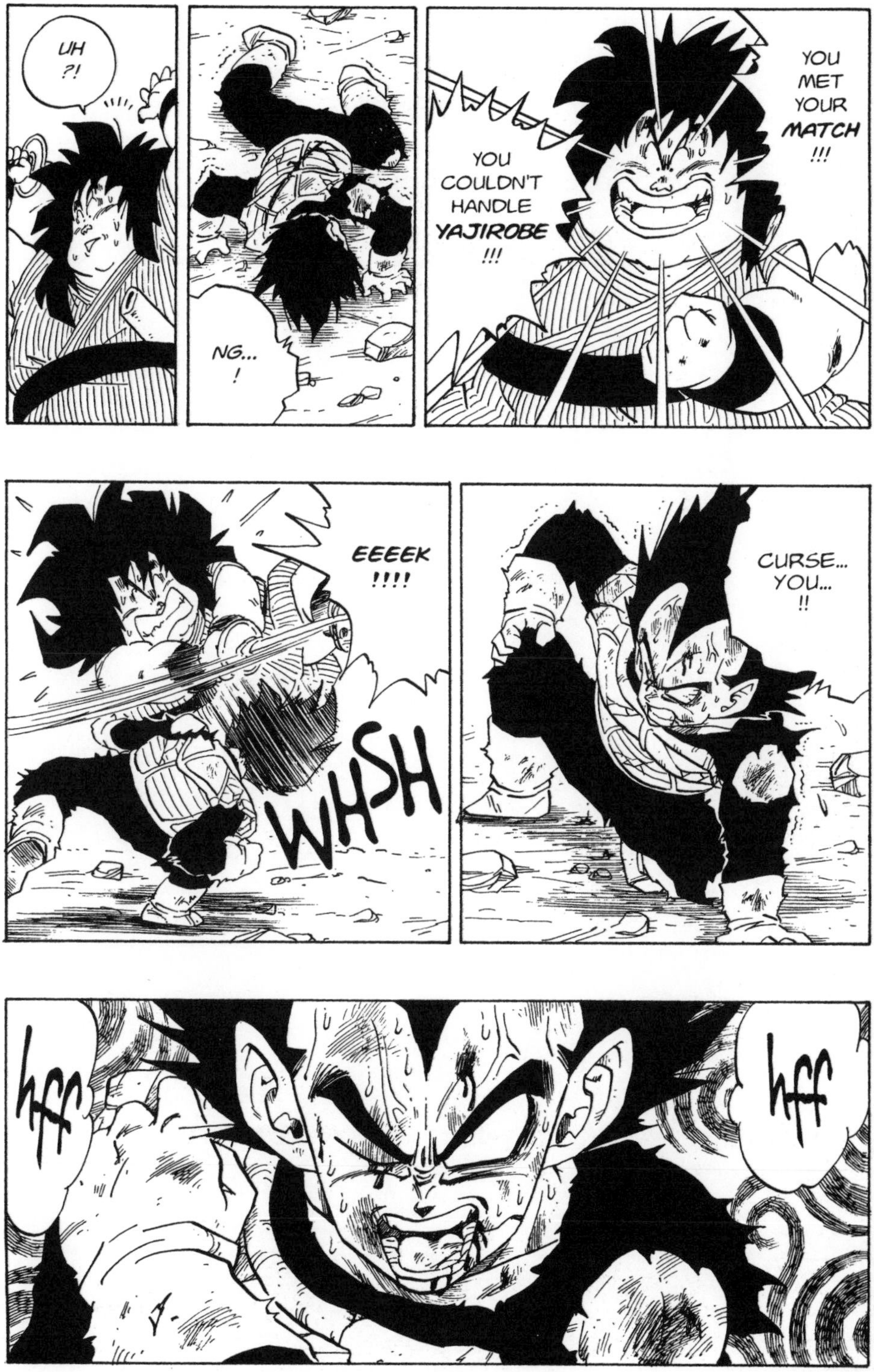
YOU MET YOUR MATCH !!!
YOU COULDN'T HANDLE YAJIROBE !!!
NG... !
UH ?!
CURSE... YOU... !!
EEEEK !!!!
WHSH
hff
hff

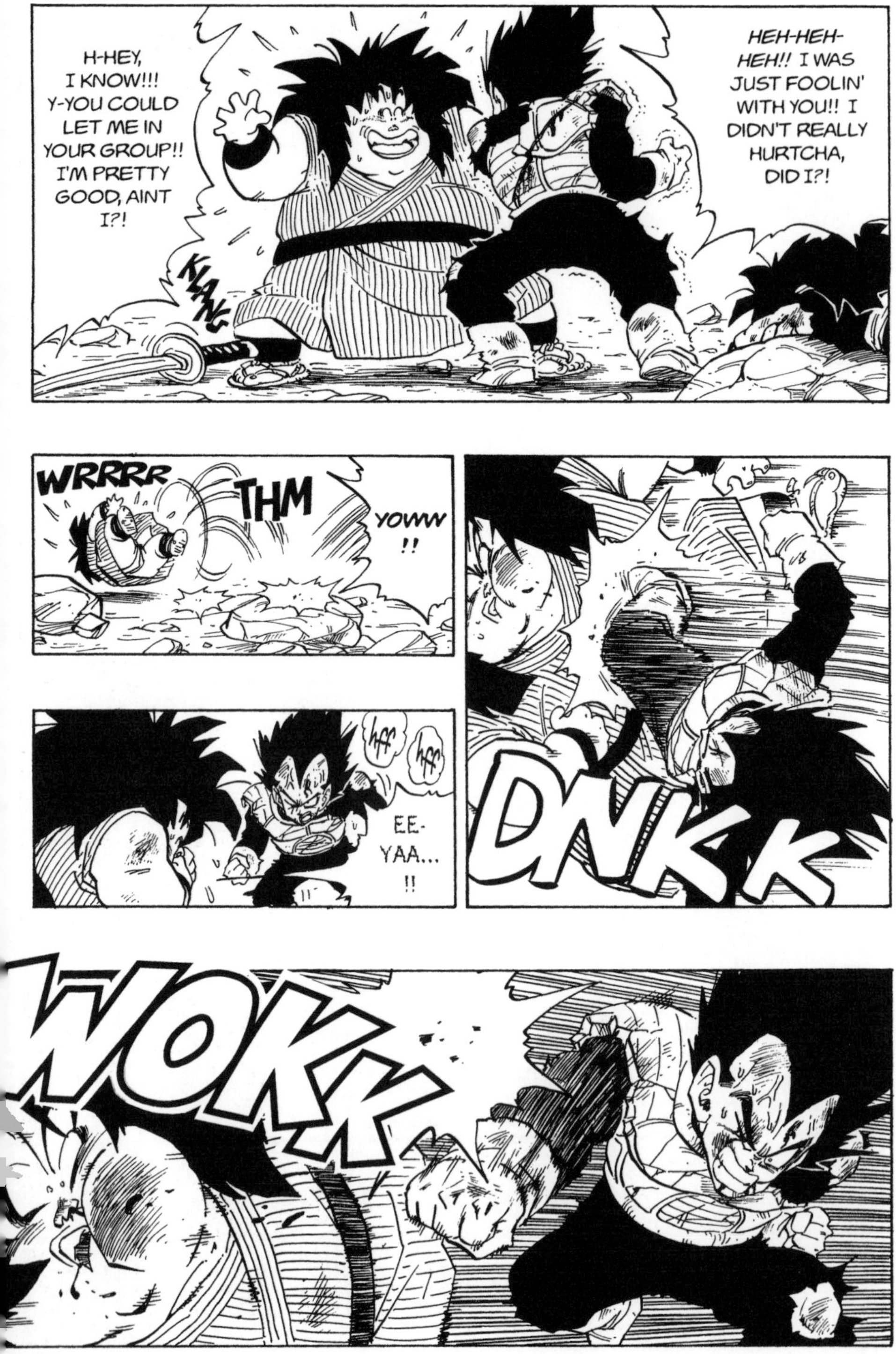
HEH-HEH-HEH!! I WAS JUST FOOLIN' WITH YOU!! I DIDN'T REALLY HURTCHA, DID I?!
H-HEY, I KNOW!!! Y-YOU COULD LET ME IN YOUR GROUP!! I'M PRETTY GOOD, AINT I?!
KLANG
DNKK
WRRRR
THM
YOWW !!
hff
hff
EE- YAA... !!
WOKK

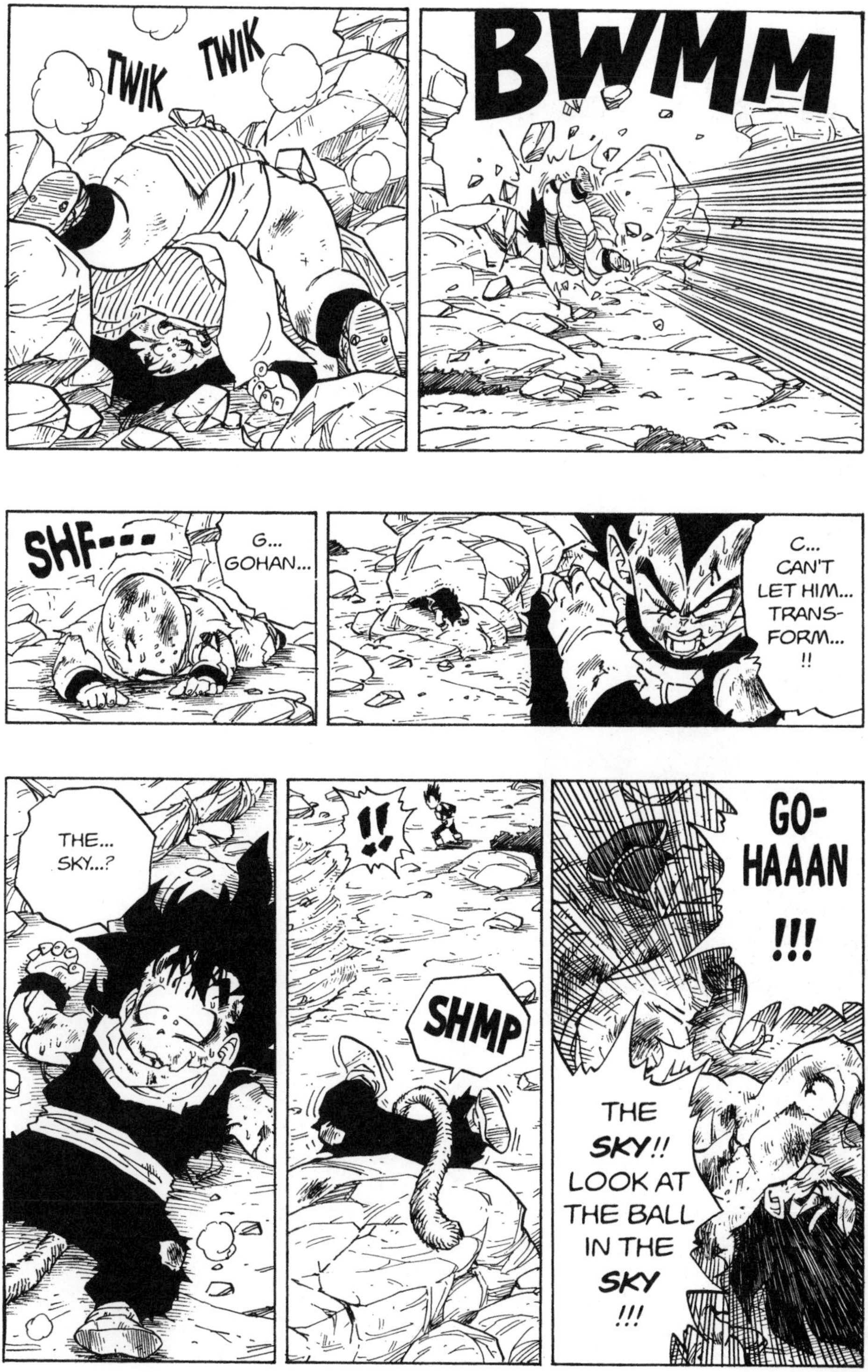
BWMM
TWIK
TWIK
C... CAN'T LET HIM... TRANS-FORM... !!
G... GOHAN...
SHF---
GO-HAAAN!!!
THE SKY!! LOOK AT THE BALL IN THE SKY!!!
!!
SHMP
THE... SKY...?

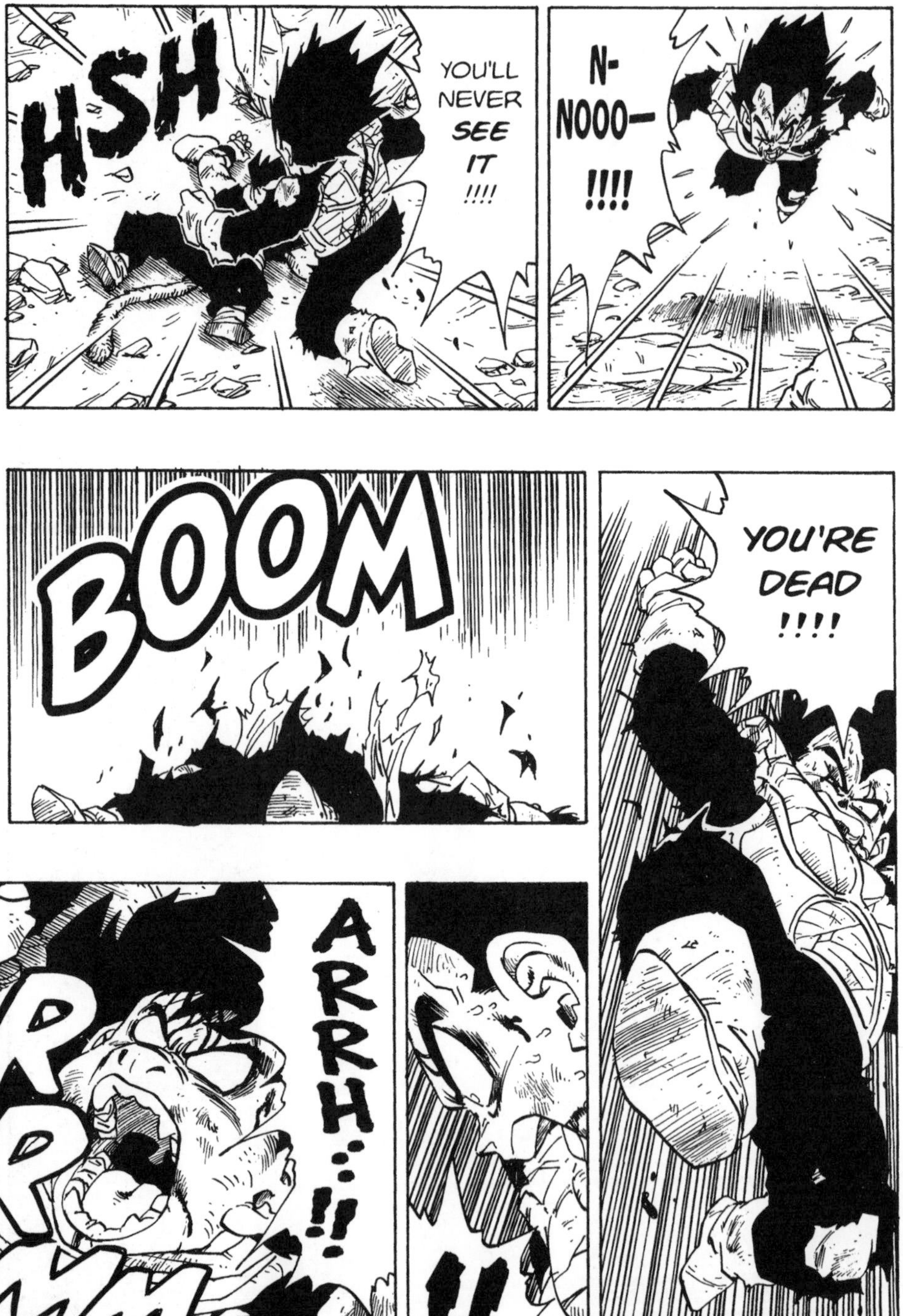

N-
NOOO—
!!!!
HSH
YOU'LL NEVER SEE IT !!!!
YOU'RE DEAD !!!!
BOOM
!!
ARRH...!!
RRMM...

# DBZ : 45 • Monkey in the Moon

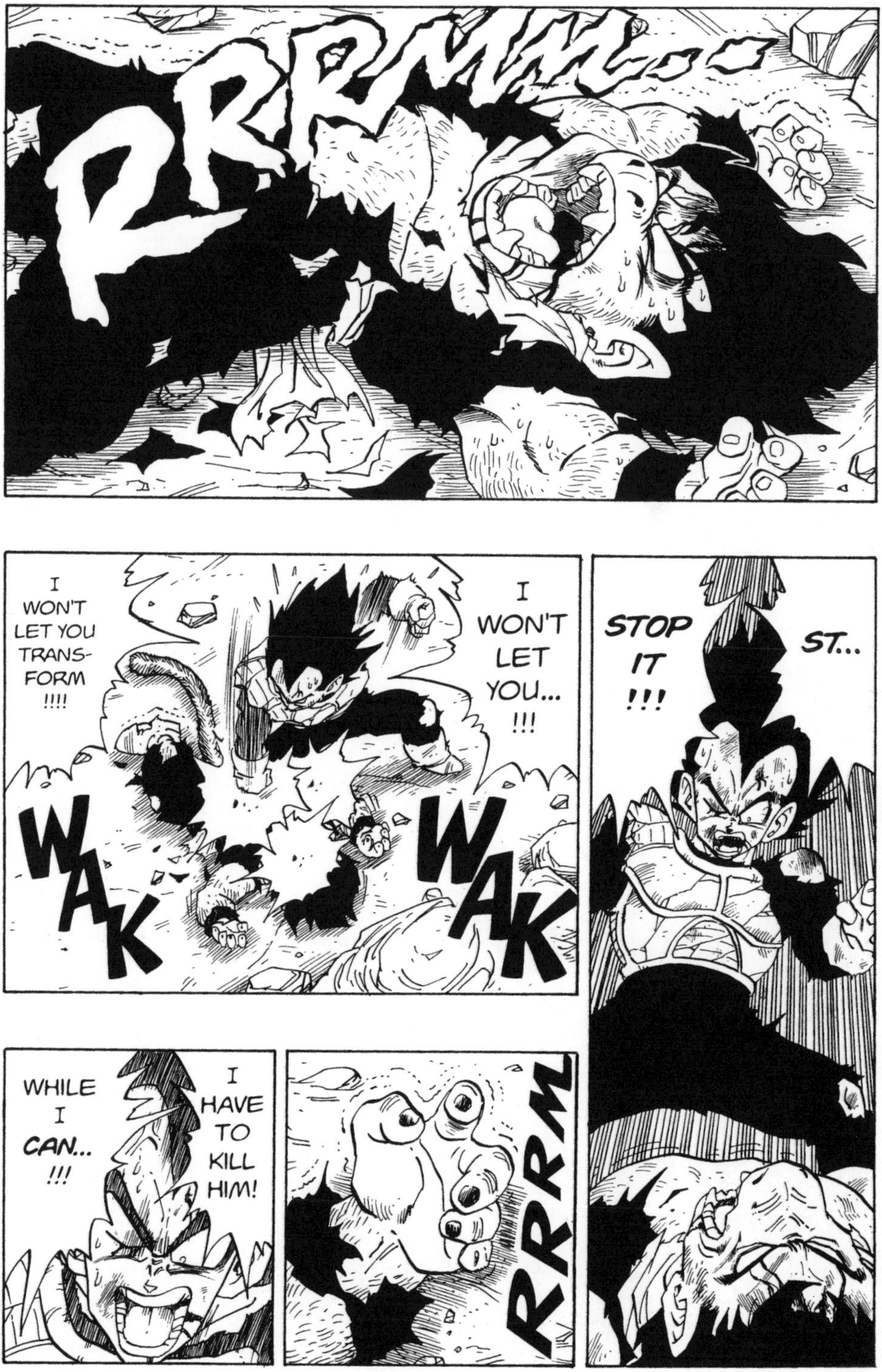
PRRMM...
ST...
STOP IT!!!
I WON'T LET YOU...!!!
I WON'T LET YOU TRANSFORM!!!!
WAK
WAK
RRRM
I HAVE TO KILL HIM!
WHILE I CAN...!!!

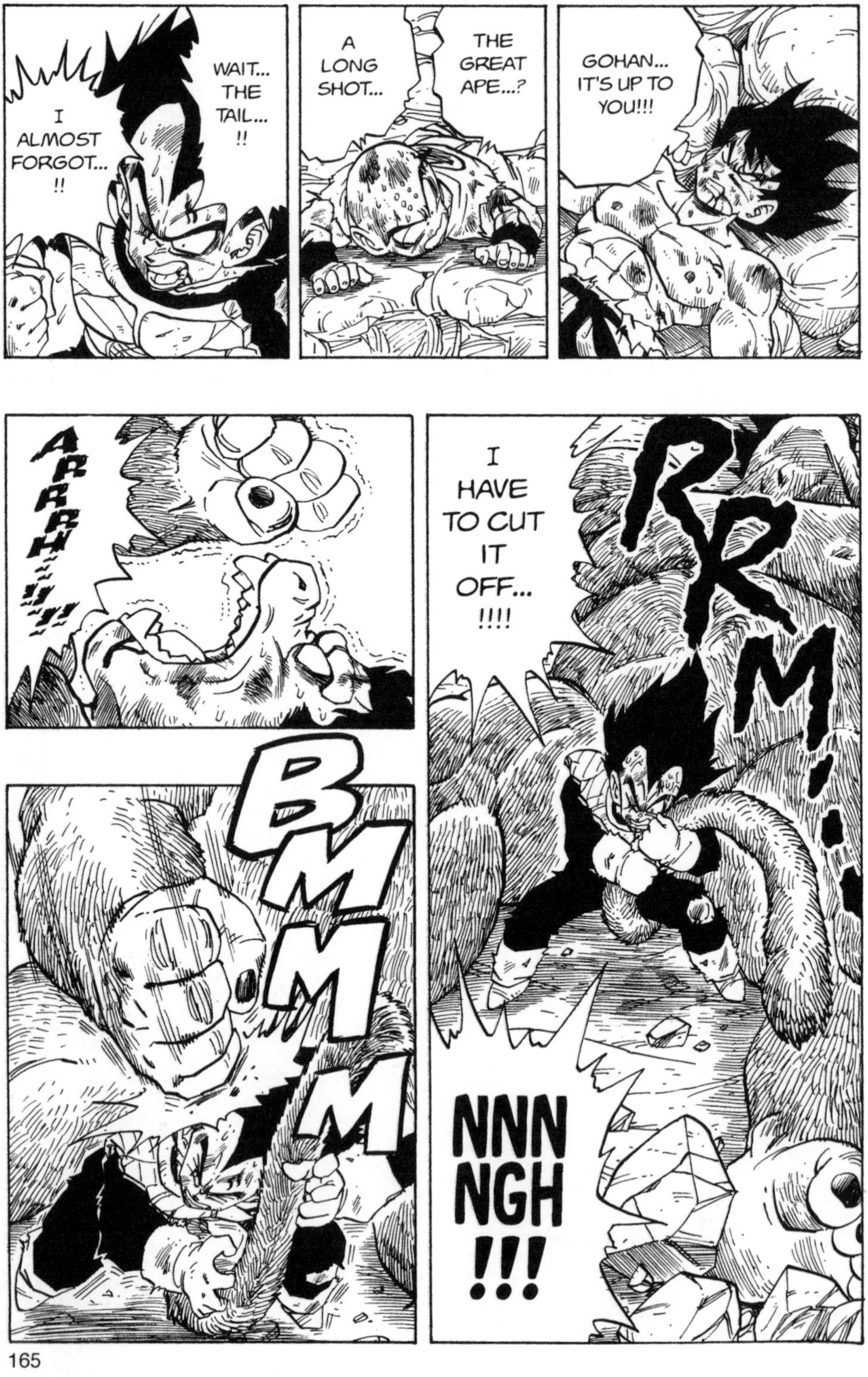
GOHAN... IT'S UP TO YOU!!!
THE GREAT APE...?
A LONG SHOT...
WAIT... THE TAIL... !!
I ALMOST FORGOT... !!
I HAVE TO CUT IT OFF... !!!!
RRM...
NNNNGH!!!
ARRRH...!!!
BMMM

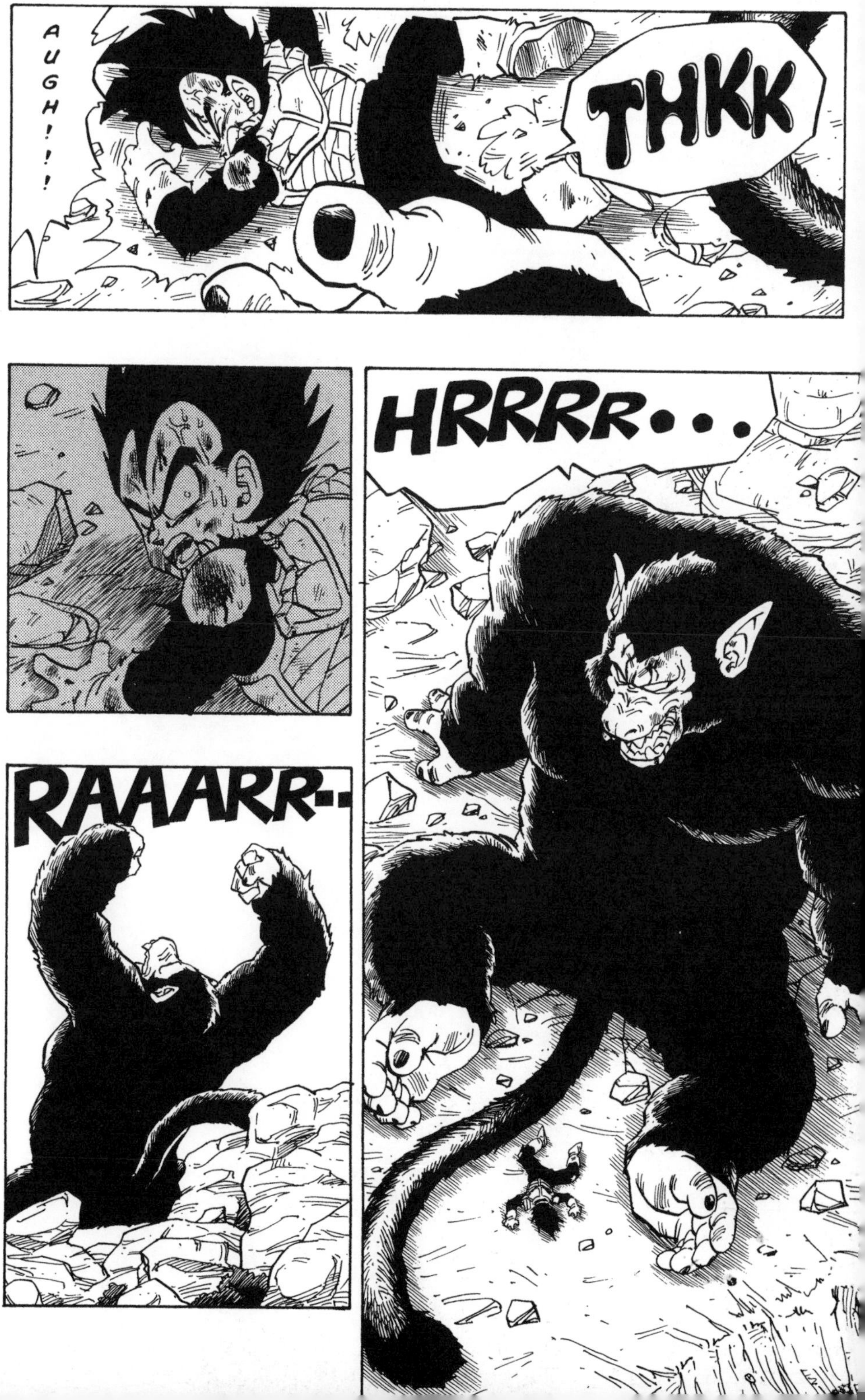
THKK
AUGH!!!
HRRRR...
RAAARR-..

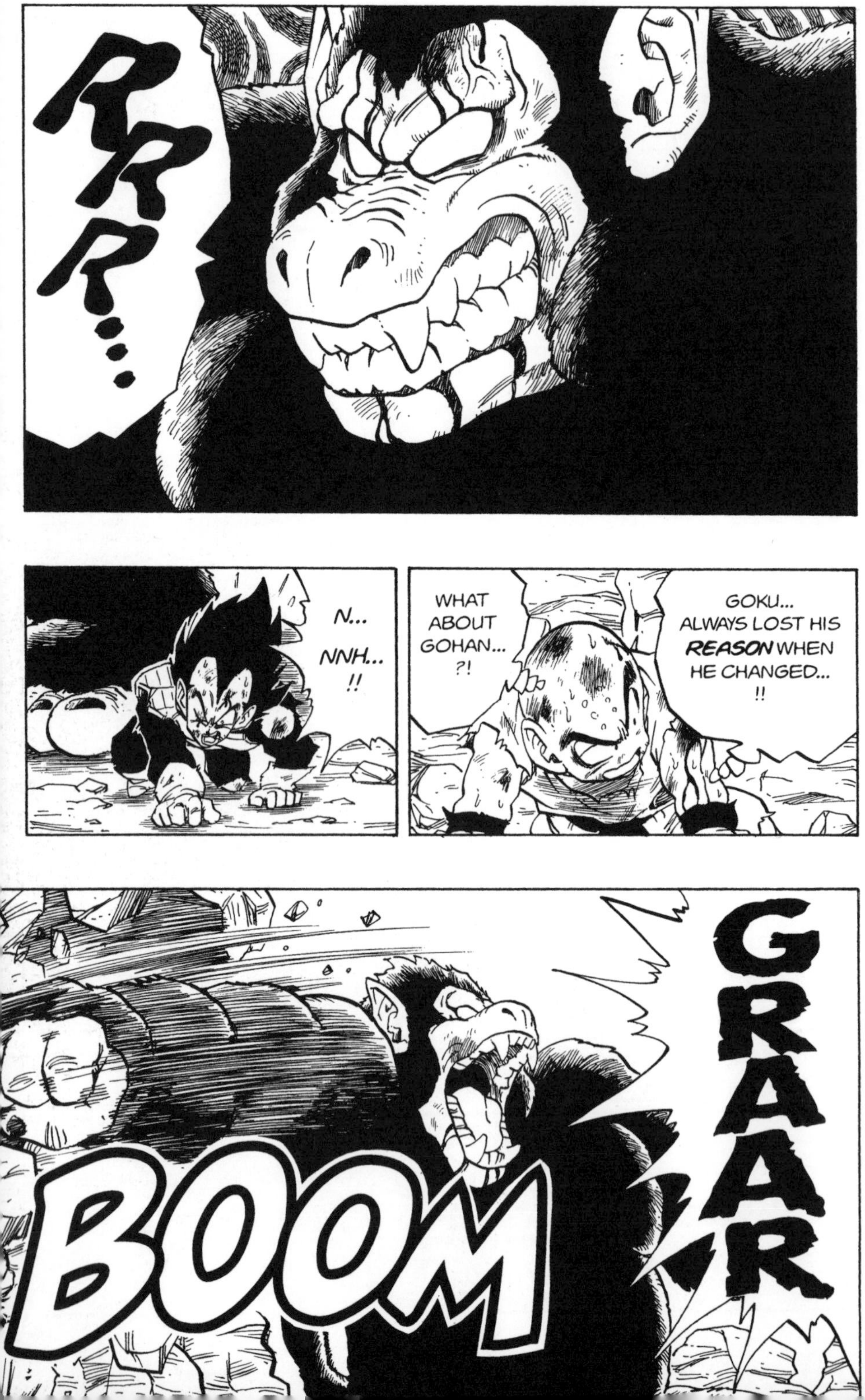
RRR...
GOKU... ALWAYS LOST HIS **REASON** WHEN HE CHANGED... !!
WHAT ABOUT GOHAN... ?!
N... NNH... !!
GRAAR
BOOM

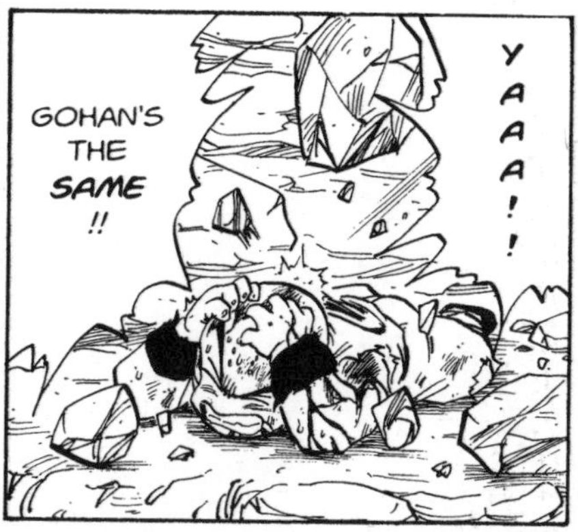
GOHAN'S THE SAME !!
YAAAA!!
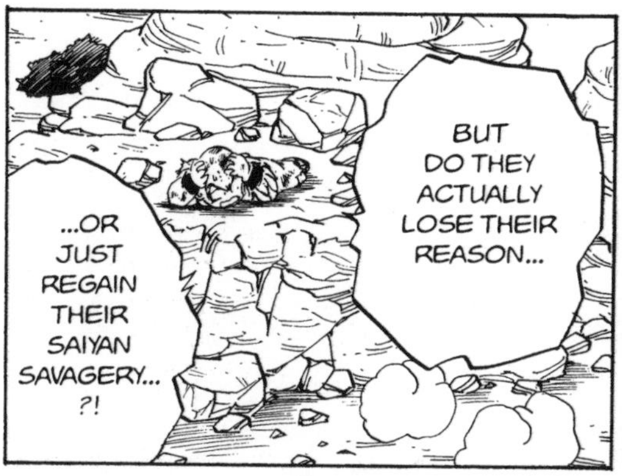
BUT DO THEY ACTUALLY LOSE THEIR REASON...
...OR JUST REGAIN THEIR SAIYAN SAVAGERY... ?!
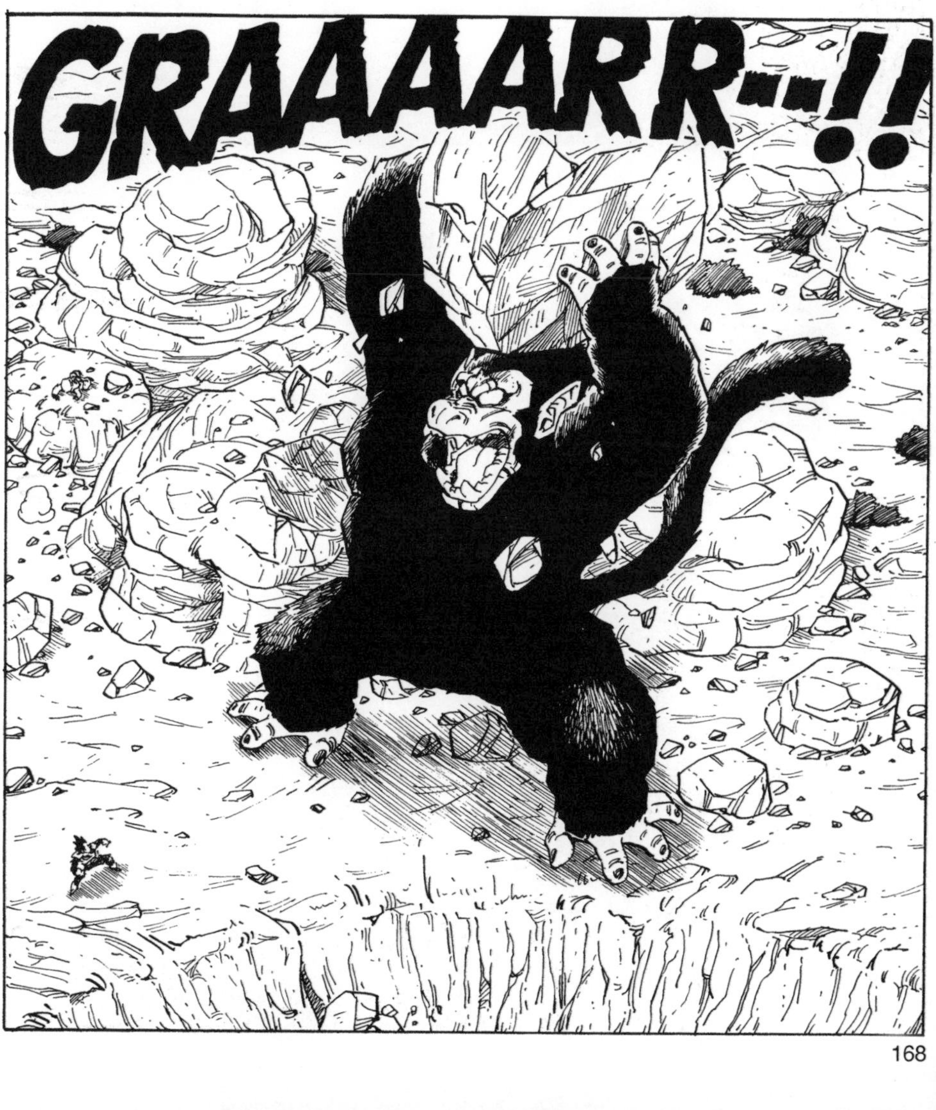
GRAAARR..!!

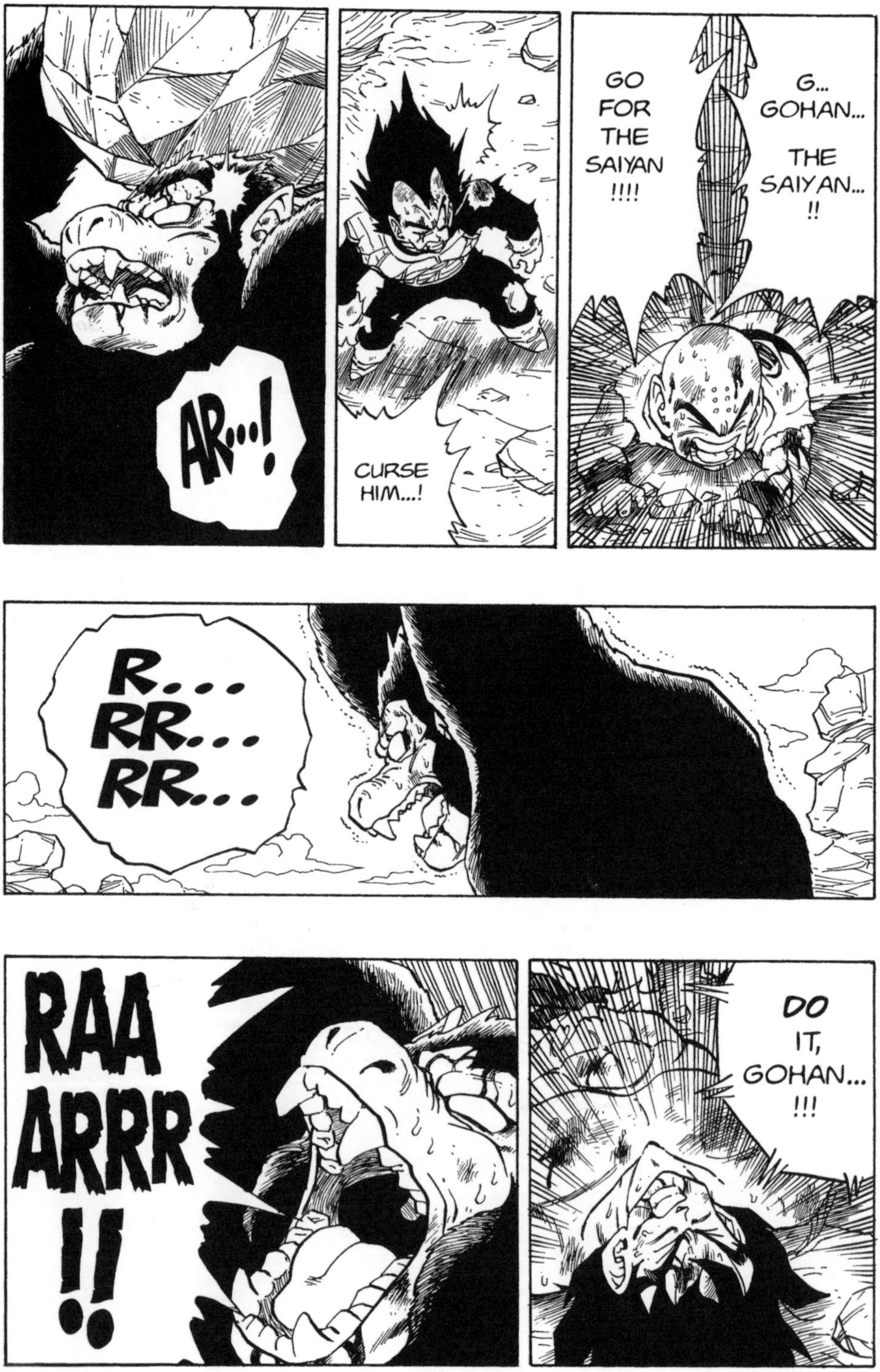
G... GOHAN... THE SAIYAN... !!
GO FOR THE SAIYAN !!!!
CURSE HIM...!
AR...!
R... RR... RR...
DO IT, GOHAN... !!!
RAA ARRR !!

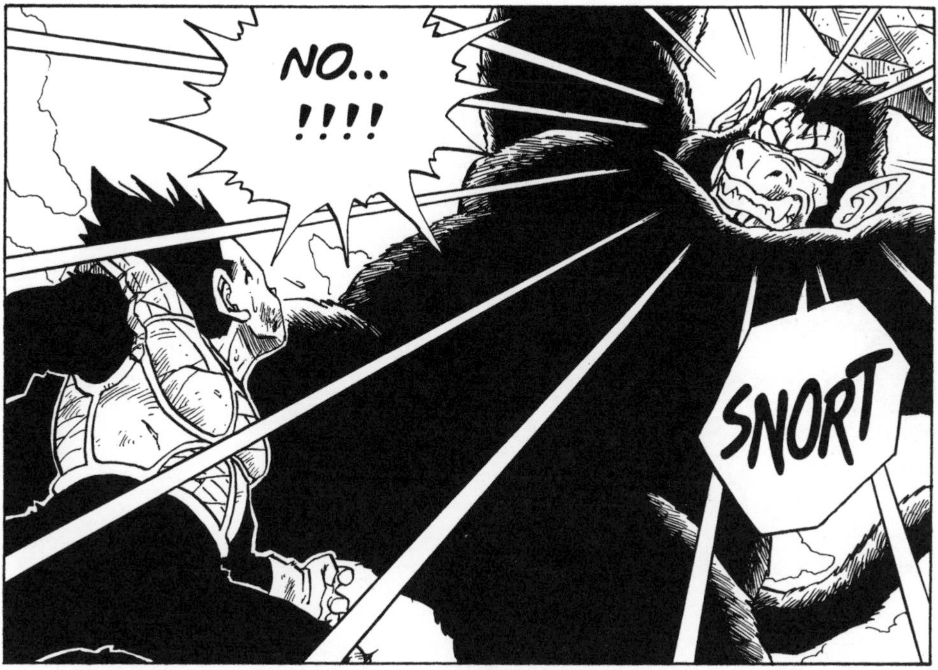
NO... !!!!
SNORT
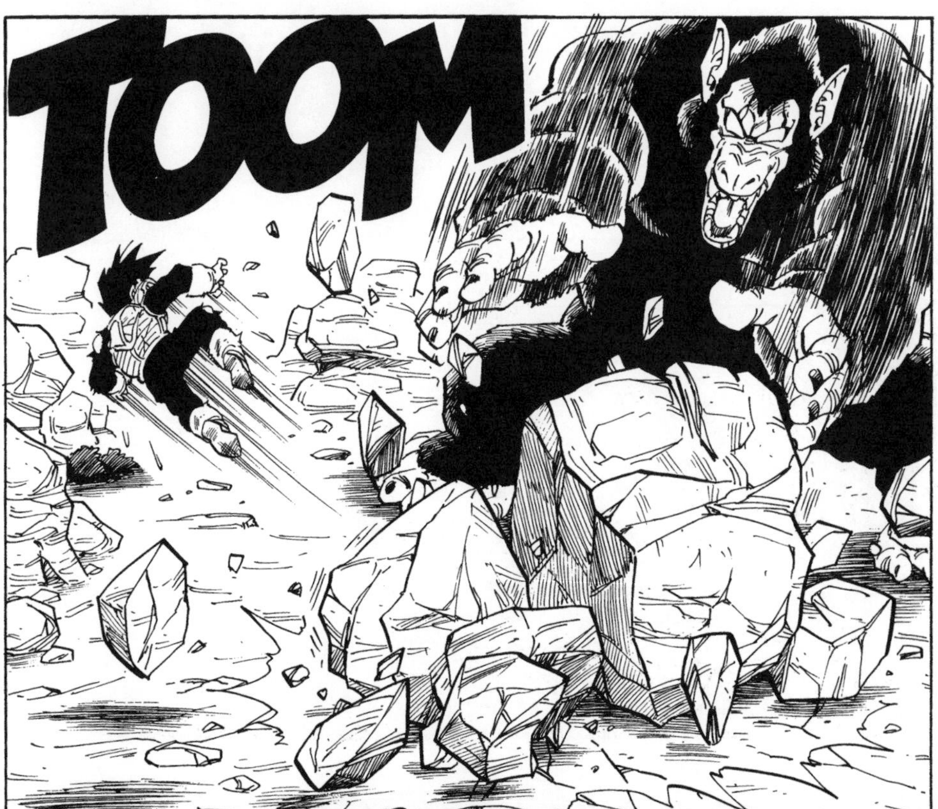
TOOM

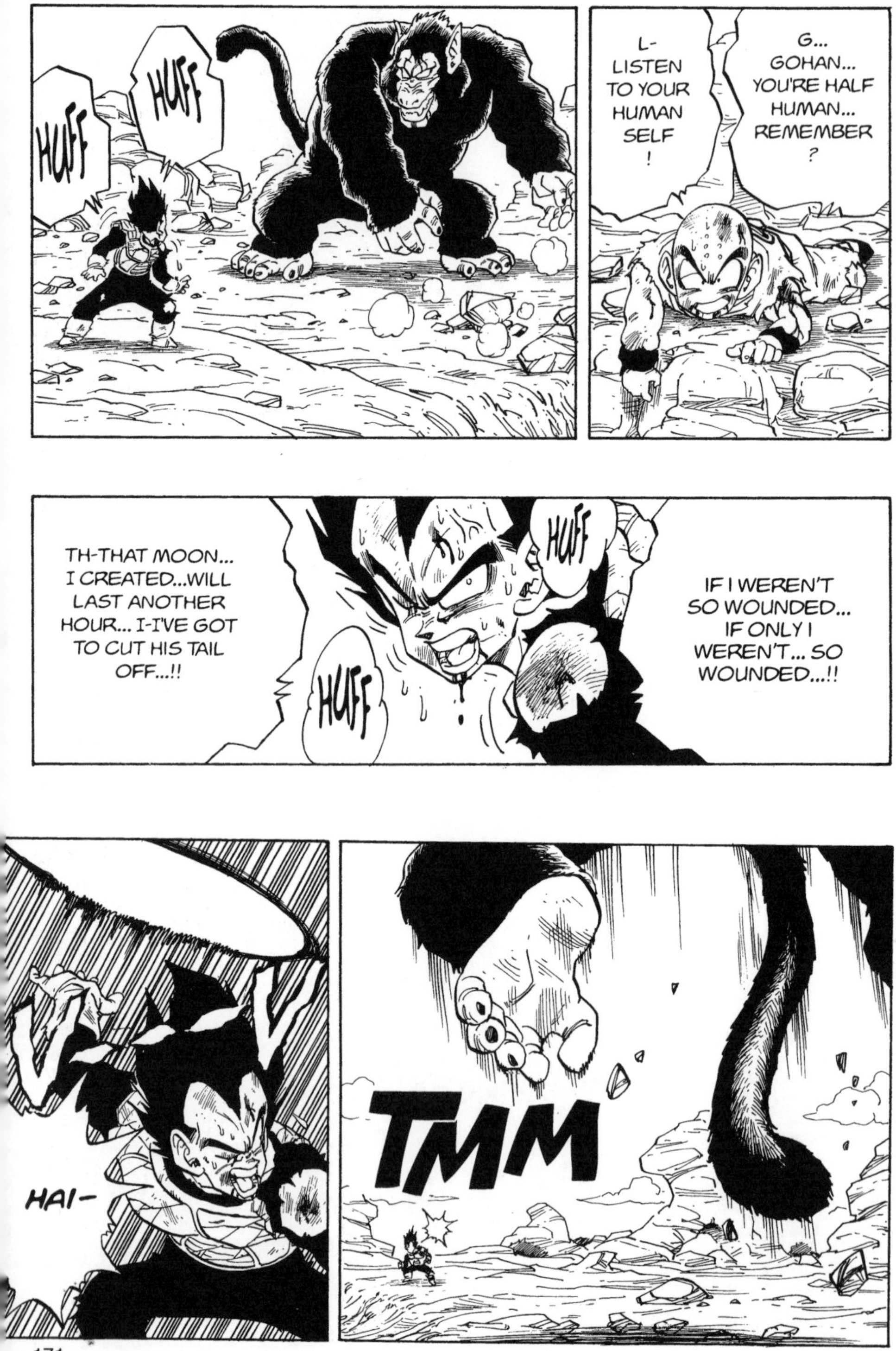
G... GOHAN... YOU'RE HALF HUMAN... REMEMBER?
L- LISTEN TO YOUR HUMAN SELF!
HUFF
HUFF
HUFF
IF I WEREN'T SO WOUNDED... IF ONLY I WEREN'T... SO WOUNDED...!!
TH-THAT MOON... I CREATED...WILL LAST ANOTHER HOUR... I-I'VE GOT TO CUT HIS TAIL OFF...!!
HUFF
TMM
HAI-

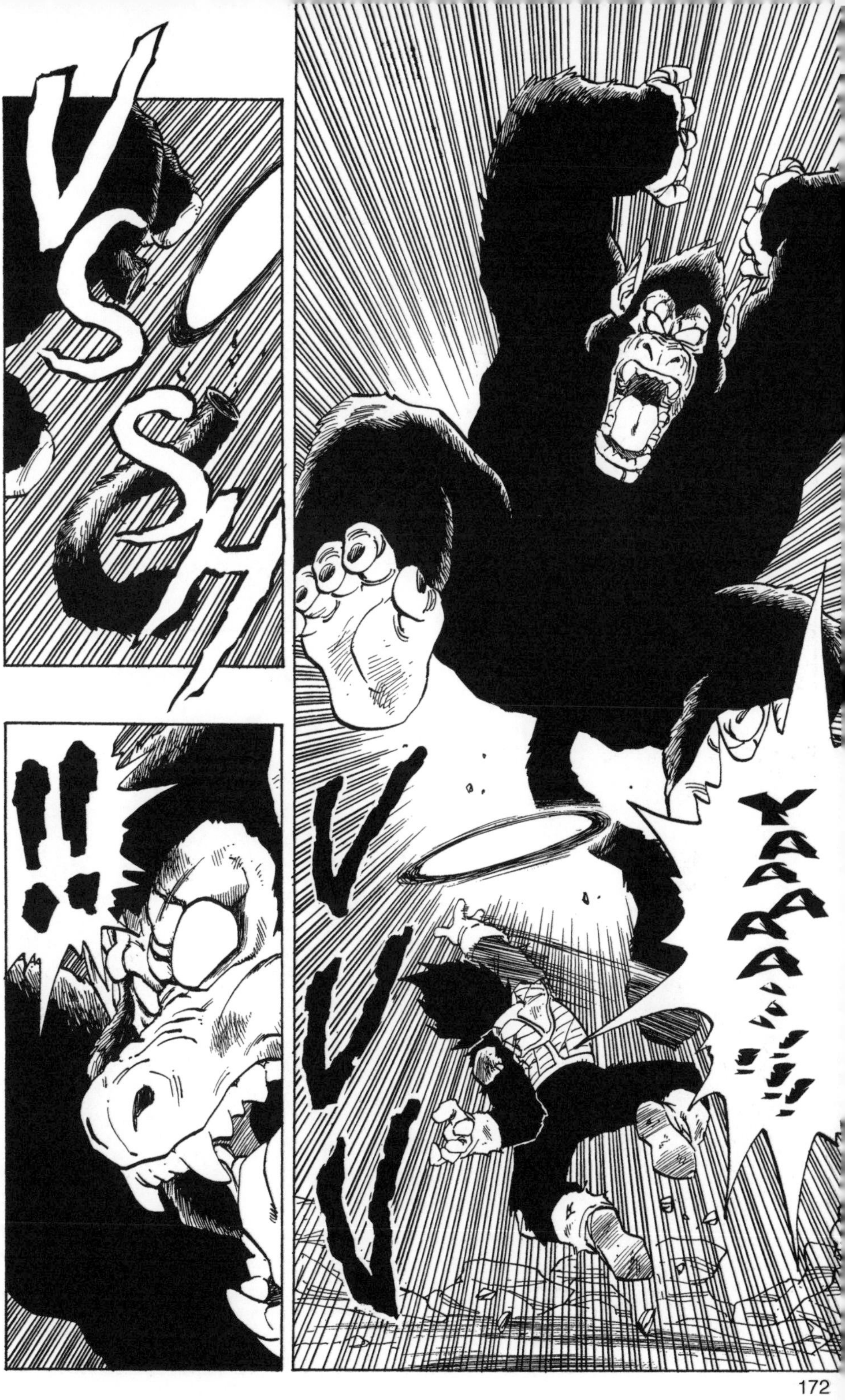
YAAAAA!!
VSSH
!!

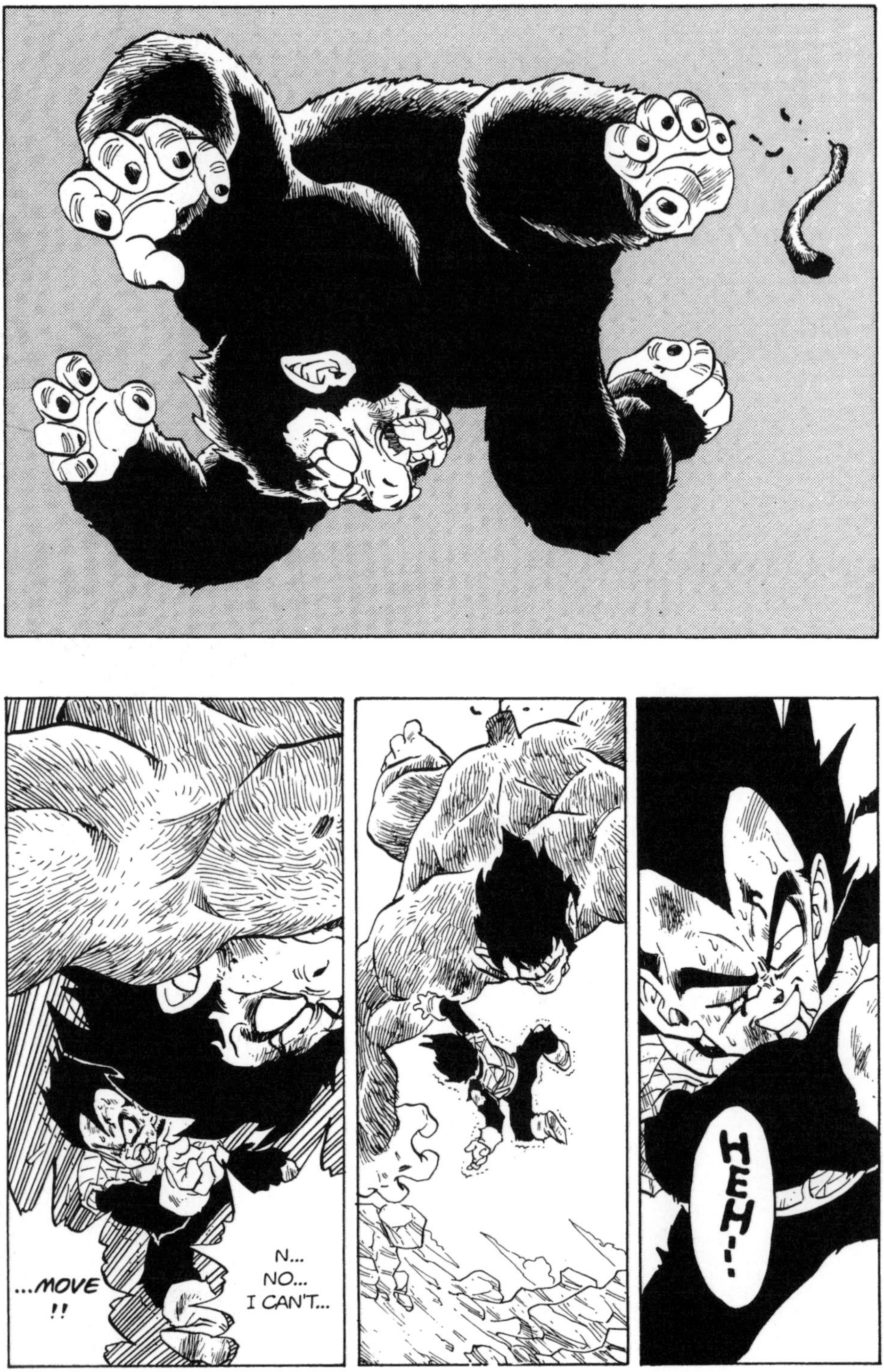
HEH!!
N... NO... I CAN'T...
...MOVE !!

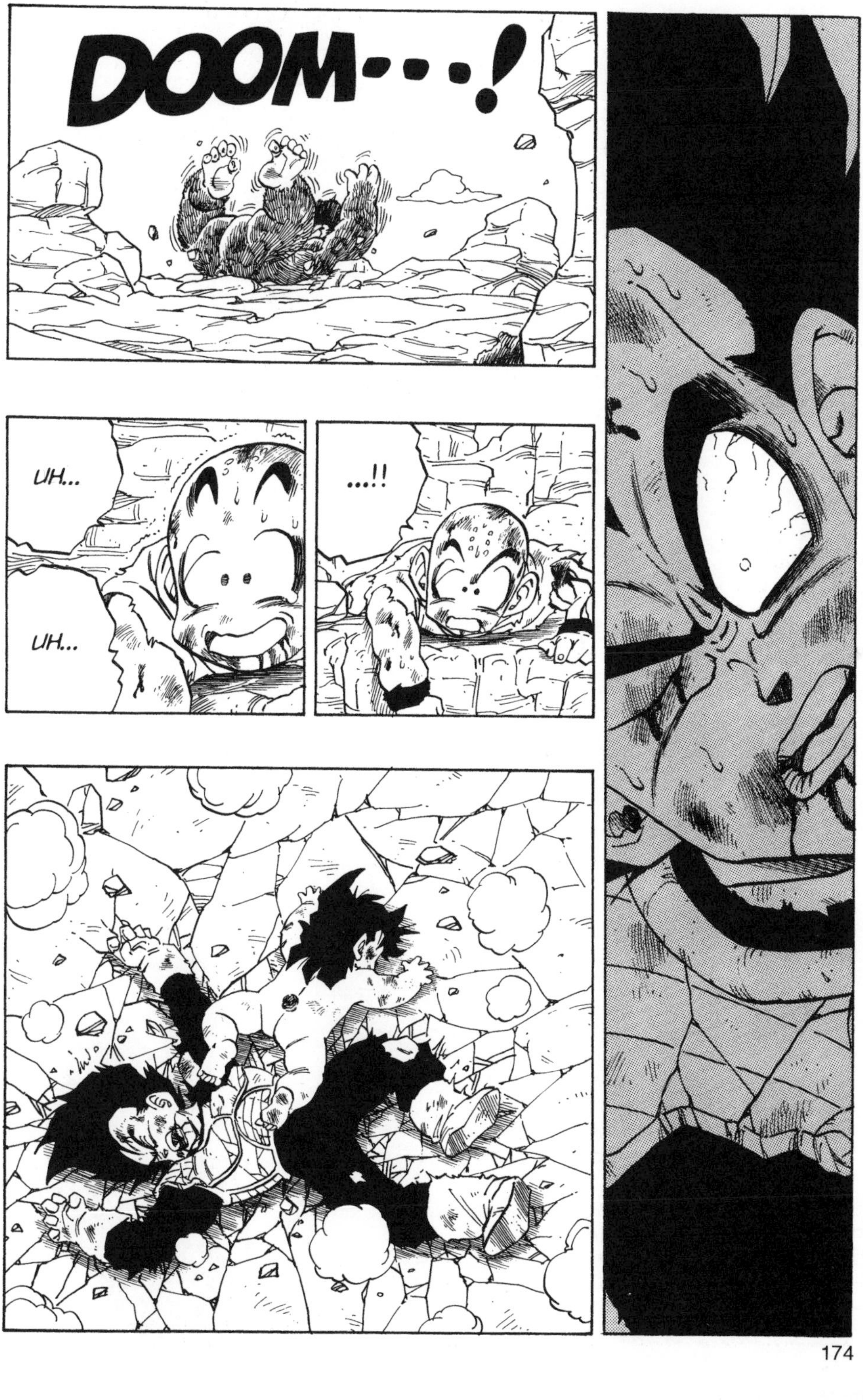
DOOM...!
...!!
UH...
UH...

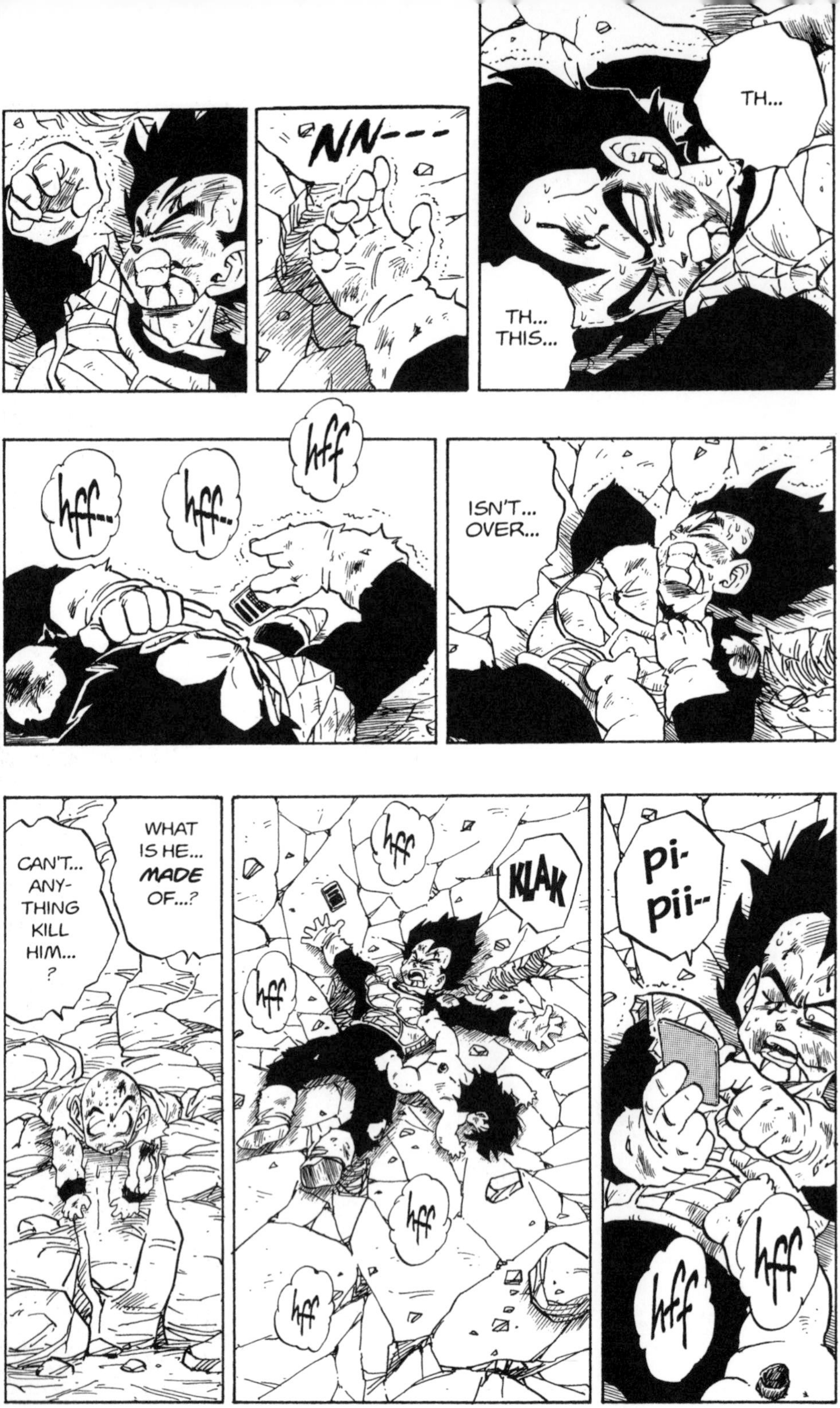
TH...
TH... THIS...
NN---
ISN'T... OVER...
hff
hff...
hff...
Pi-pii--
hff
hff
hff
KLAK
hff
hff
hff
WHAT IS HE... *MADE* OF...?
CAN'T... ANYTHING KILL HIM... ?

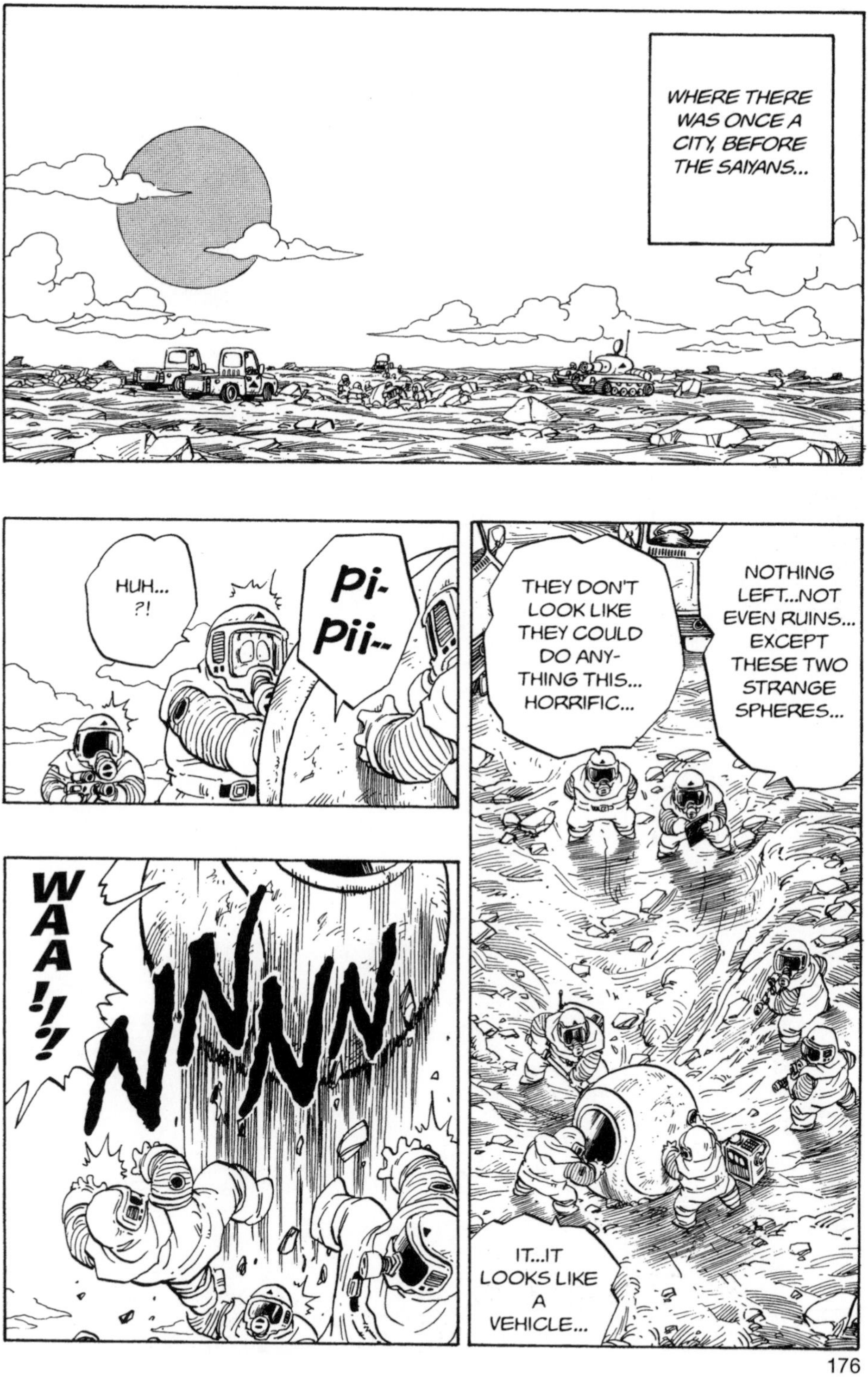
WHERE THERE WAS ONCE A CITY, BEFORE THE SAIYANS...
NOTHING LEFT...NOT EVEN RUINS... EXCEPT THESE TWO STRANGE SPHERES...
THEY DON'T LOOK LIKE THEY COULD DO ANY-THING THIS... HORRIFIC...
IT...IT LOOKS LIKE A VEHICLE...
Pi-Pii--
HUH... ?!
WAAA!!?!
NNNN

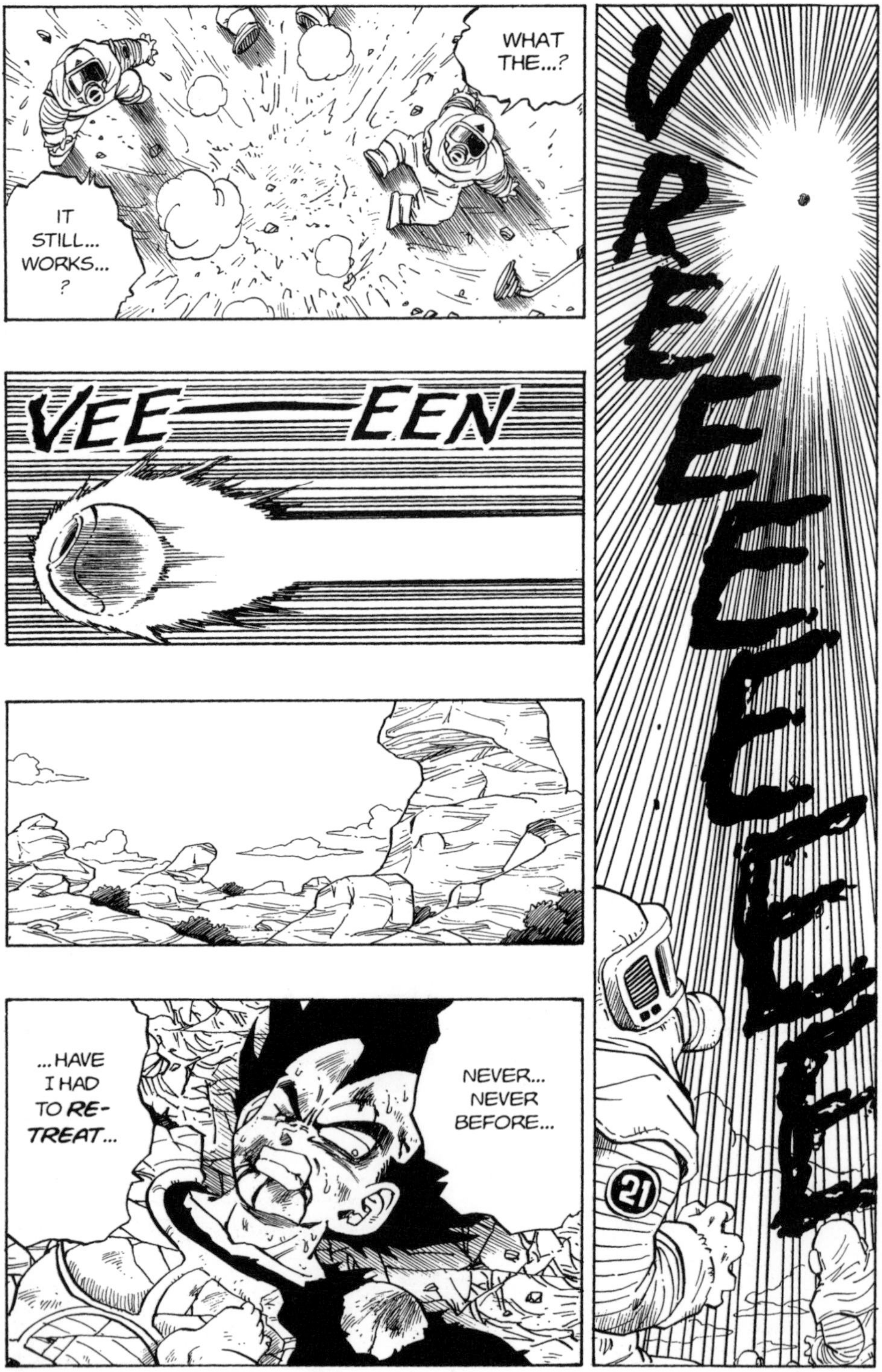
VREEEEEEEE
WHAT THE...?
IT STILL... WORKS... ?
VEE——EEN
NEVER... NEVER BEFORE...
...HAVE I HAD TO ***RE-TREAT***...

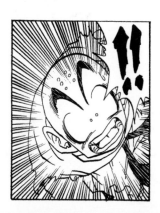

# DragonBallZ

VOLUME 5

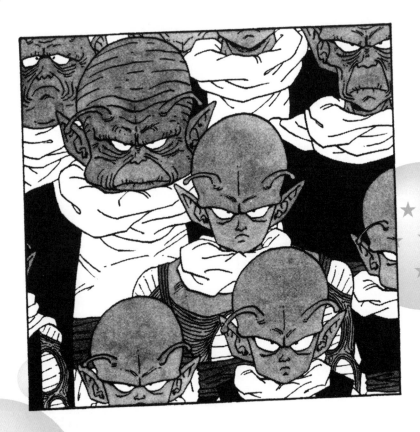

## DRAGON BALL IN SPACE

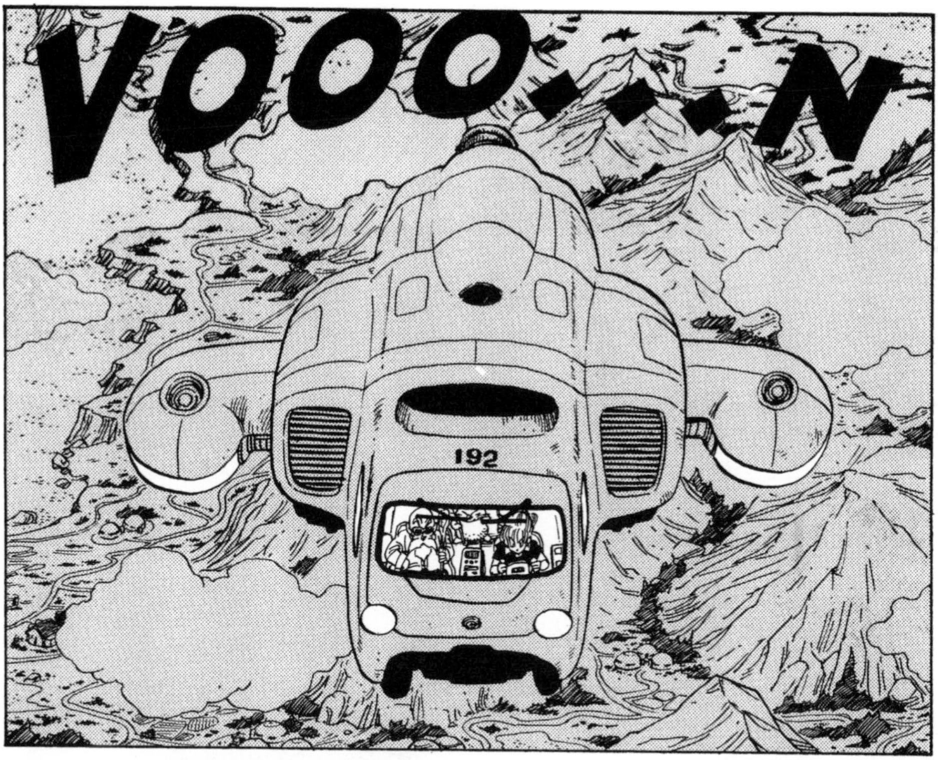
VOOO--N

## DBZ:47 • Goku's Request

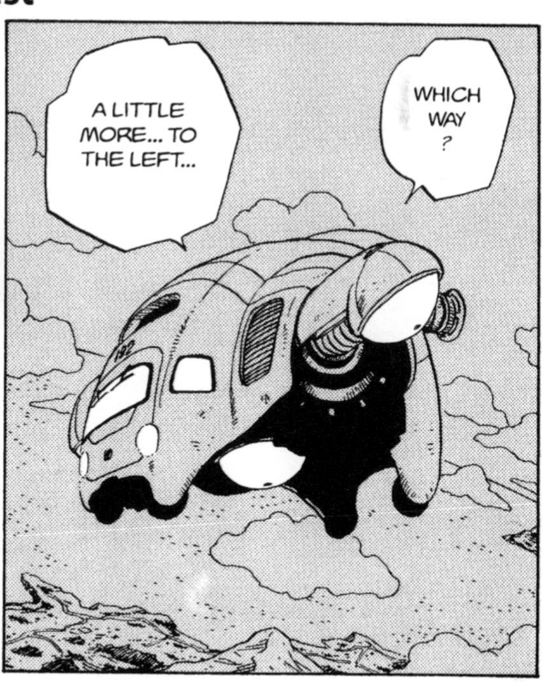
WHICH WAY ?
A LITTLE MORE... TO THE LEFT...

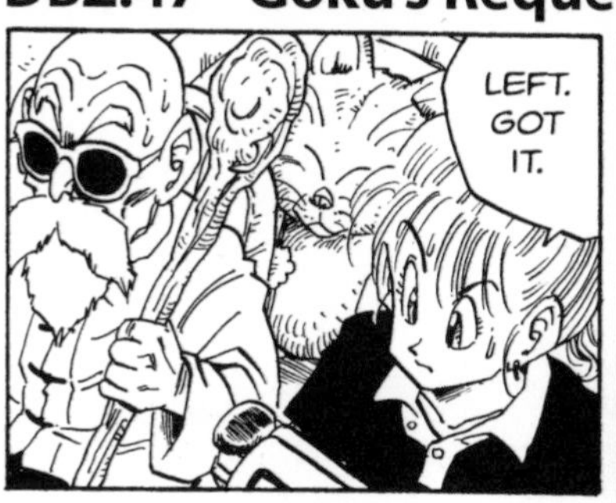
LEFT. GOT IT.

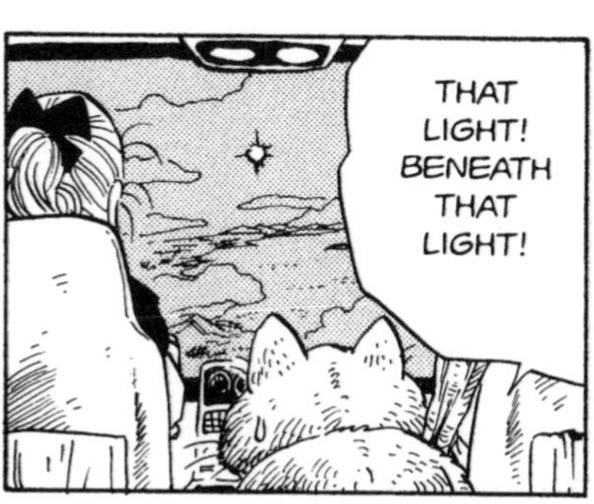
THAT LIGHT! BENEATH THAT LIGHT!

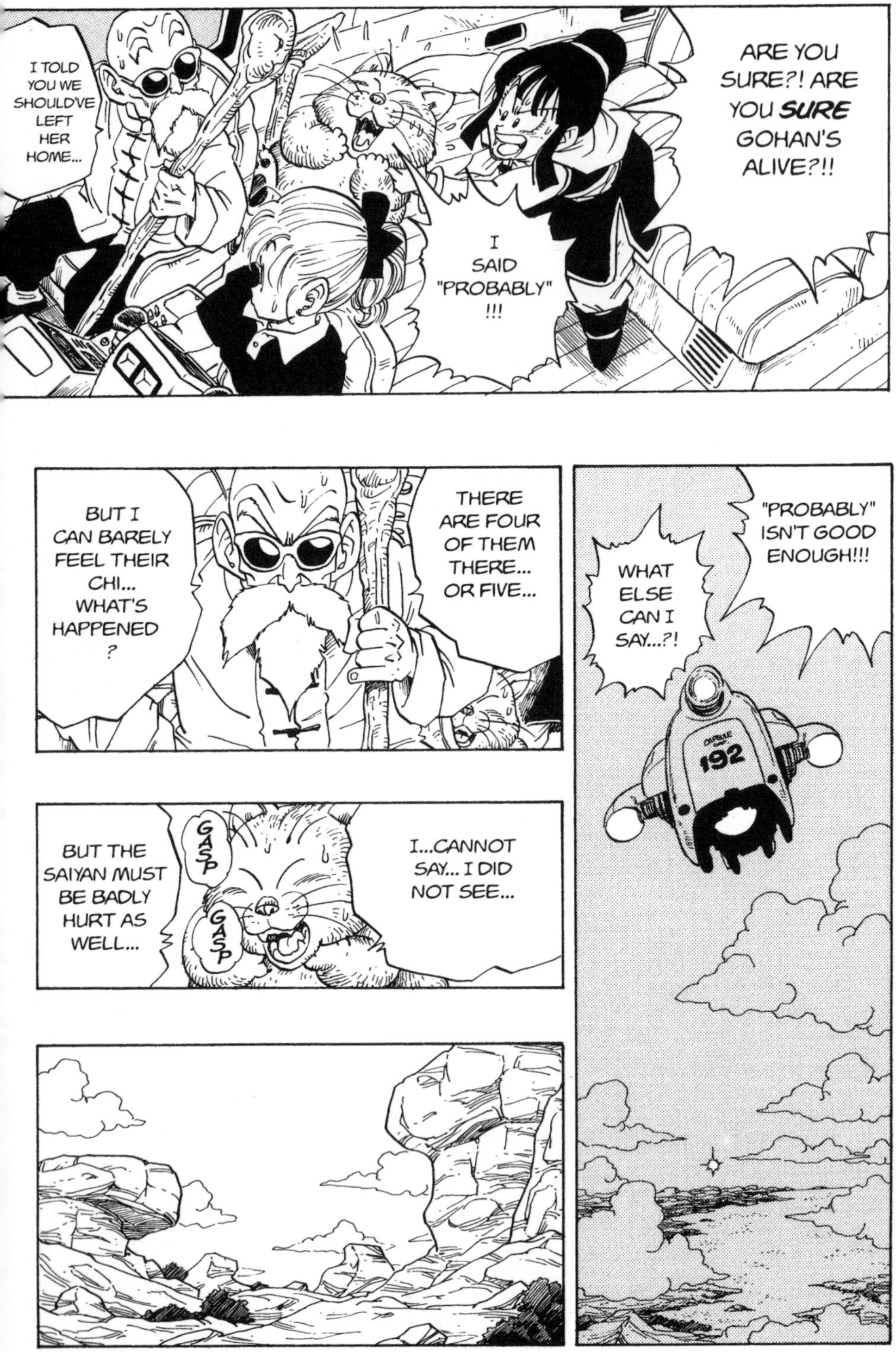
ARE YOU SURE?! ARE YOU **SURE** GOHAN'S ALIVE?!!
I SAID "PROBABLY" !!!
I TOLD YOU WE SHOULD'VE LEFT HER HOME...
"PROBABLY" ISN'T GOOD ENOUGH!!!
WHAT ELSE CAN I SAY...?!
192
THERE ARE FOUR OF THEM THERE... OR FIVE...
BUT I CAN BARELY FEEL THEIR CHI... WHAT'S HAPPENED ?
I...CANNOT SAY... I DID NOT SEE...
GASP
GASP
BUT THE SAIYAN MUST BE BADLY HURT AS WELL...

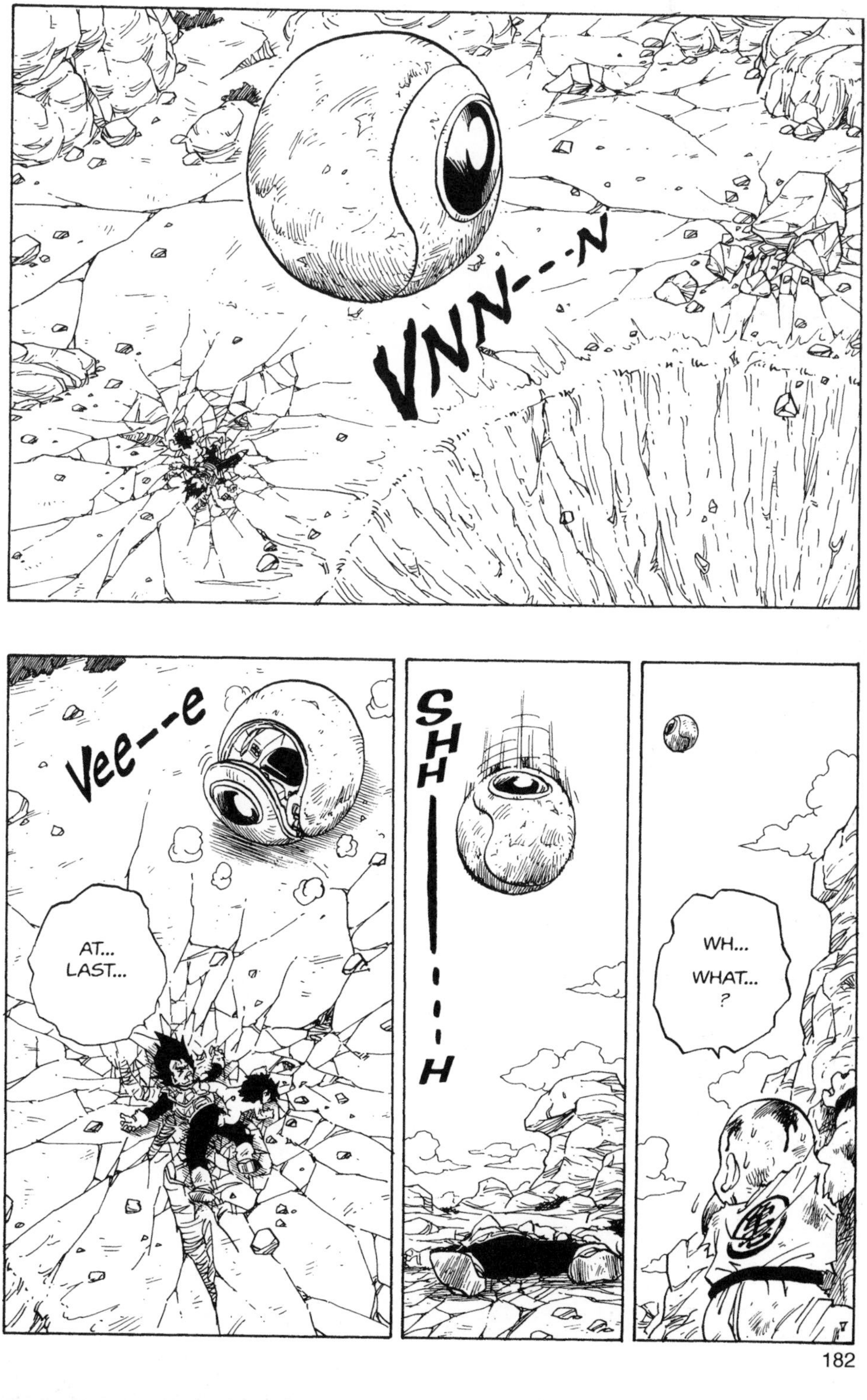
VNN--N
WH... WHAT...?
SHH---H
Vee--e
AT... LAST...

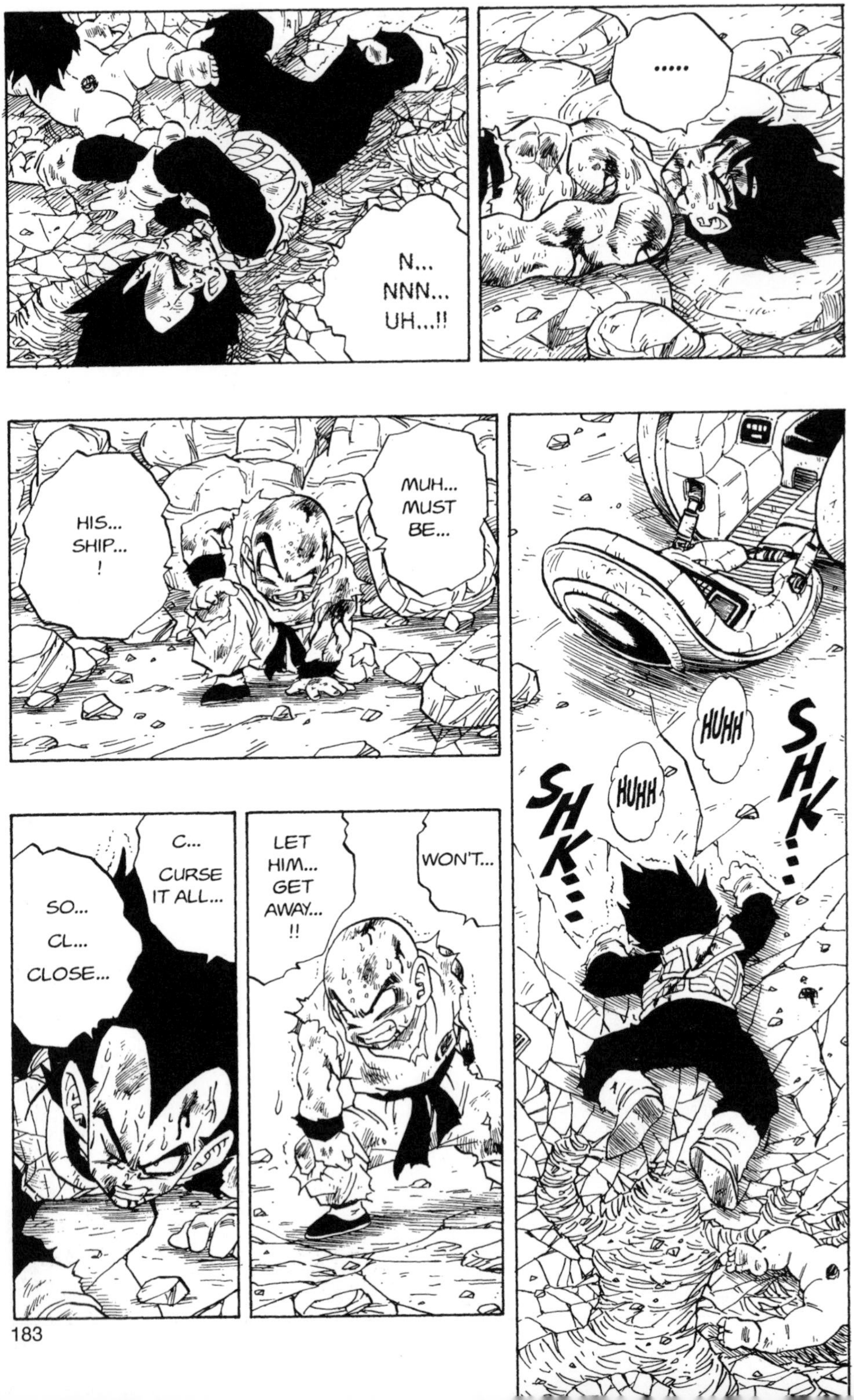
......
N... NNN... UH...!!
HUHH
HUHH
SHK...
SHK...
MUH... MUST BE...
HIS... SHIP... !
WON'T...
LET HIM... GET AWAY... !!
C... CURSE IT ALL...
SO... CL... CLOSE...

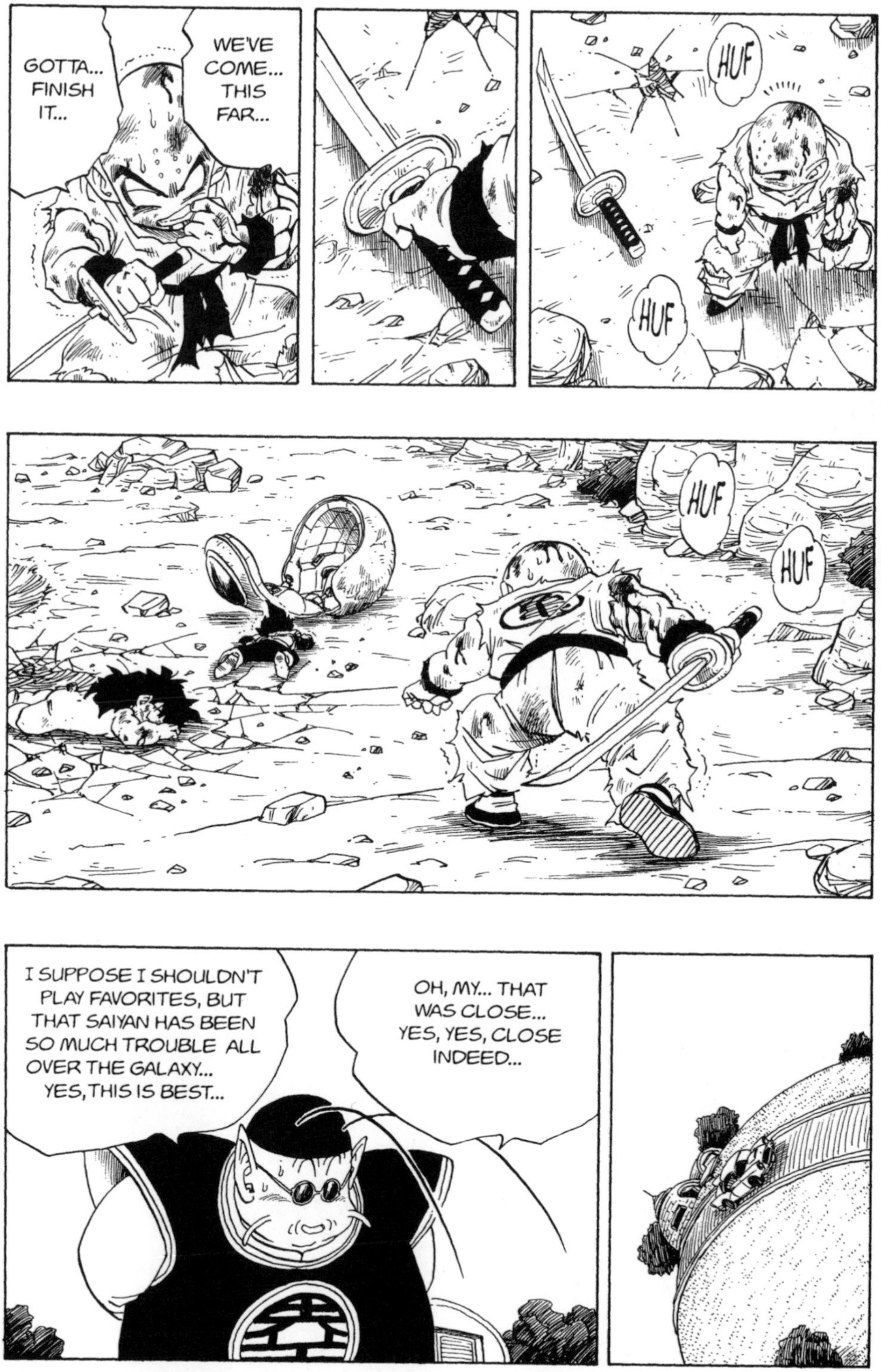
HUF
HUF
WE'VE COME... THIS FAR...
GOTTA... FINISH IT...
HUF
HUF
OH, MY... THAT WAS CLOSE... YES, YES, CLOSE INDEED...
I SUPPOSE I SHOULDN'T PLAY FAVORITES, BUT THAT SAIYAN HAS BEEN SO MUCH TROUBLE ALL OVER THE GALAXY... YES, THIS IS BEST...

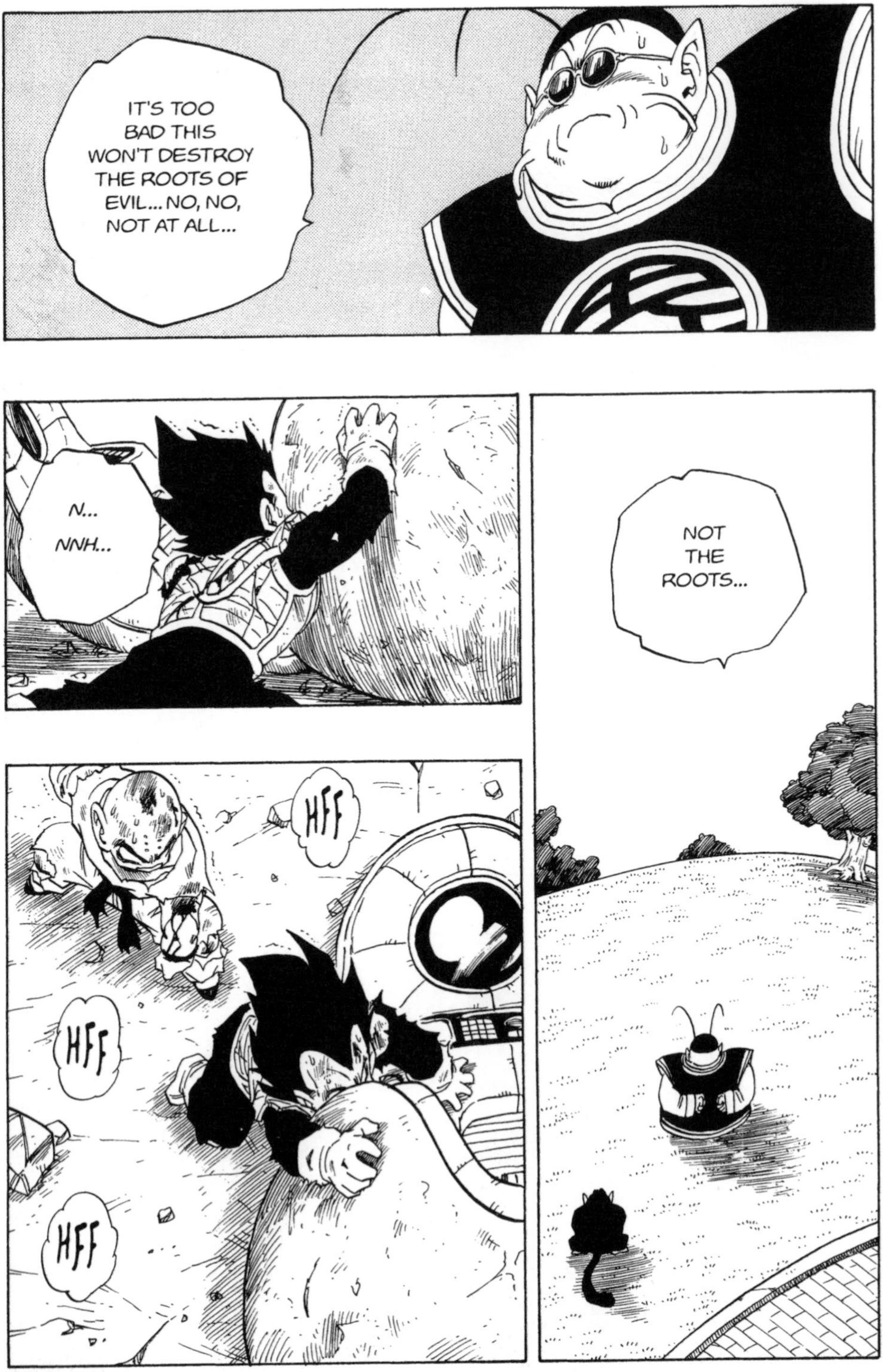
IT'S TOO BAD THIS WON'T DESTROY THE ROOTS OF EVIL... NO, NO, NOT AT ALL...
NOT THE ROOTS...
N... NNH...
HFF
HFF
HFF

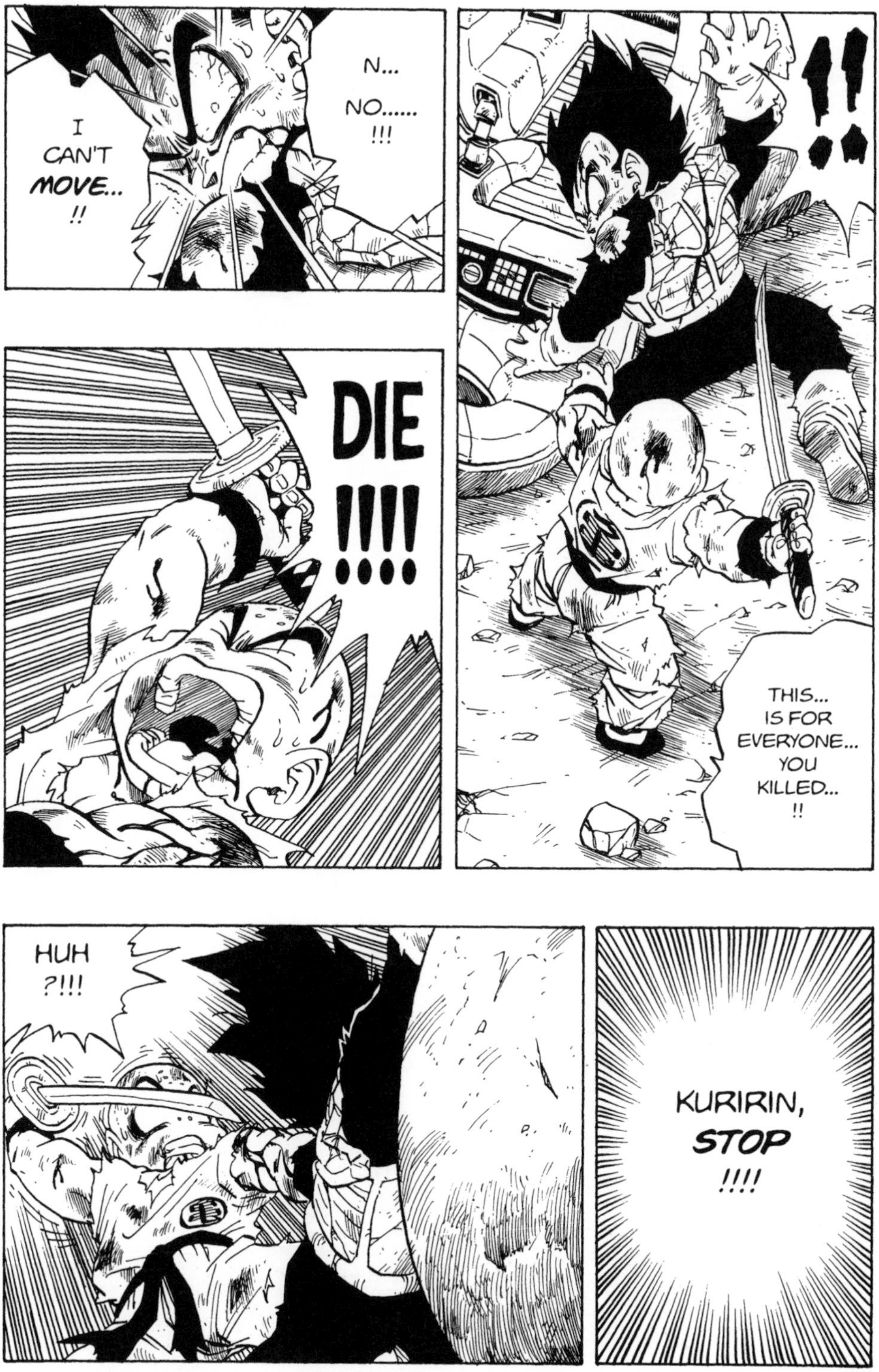
!!
THIS... IS FOR EVERYONE... YOU KILLED...!!
N... NO......!!!
I CAN'T MOVE...!!
DIE!!!!
KURIRIN, STOP!!!!
HUH?!!!

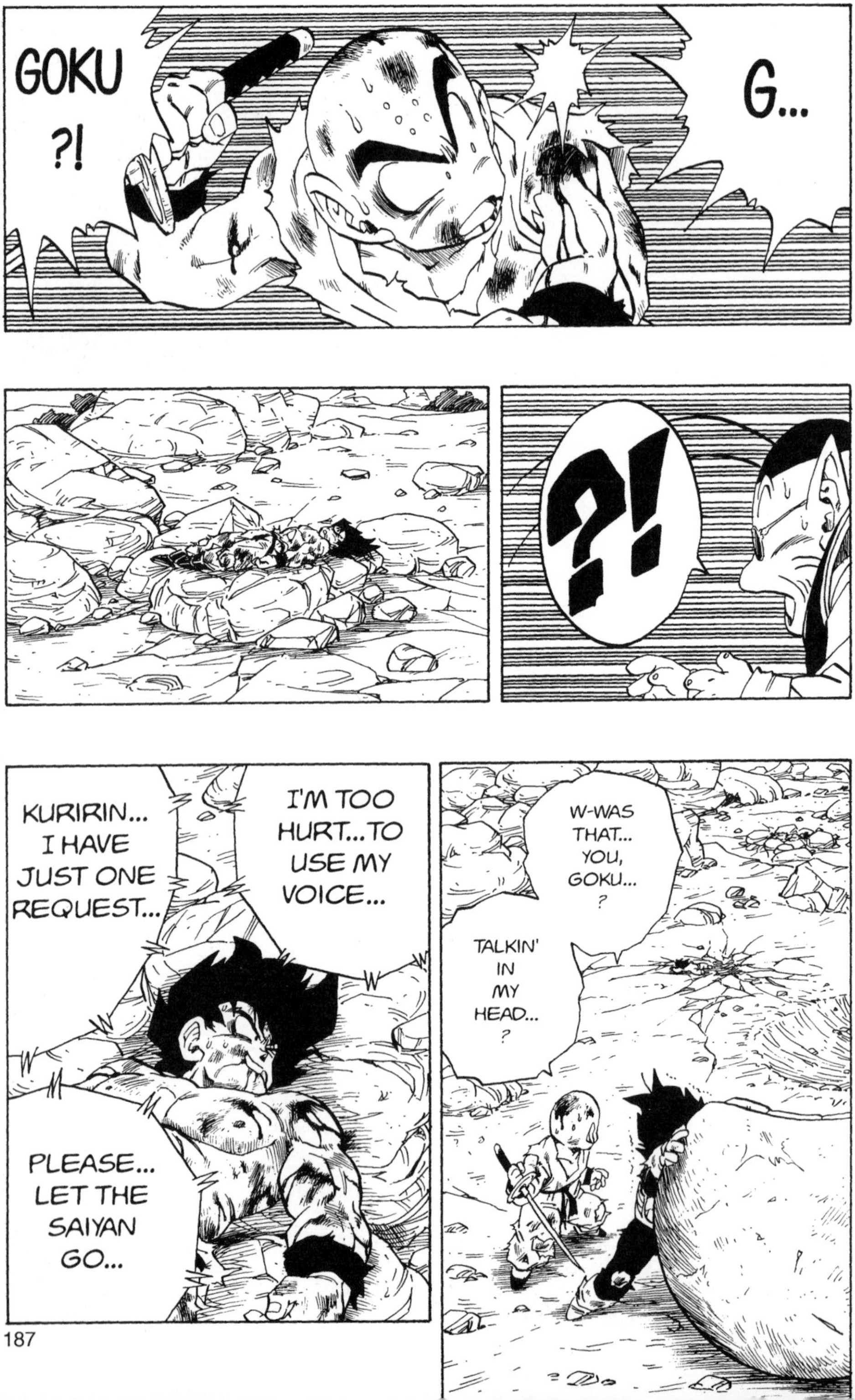
G...
GOKU ?!
?!
W-WAS THAT... YOU, GOKU... ?
TALKIN' IN MY HEAD... ?
I'M TOO HURT... TO USE MY VOICE...
KURIRIN... I HAVE JUST ONE REQUEST...
PLEASE... LET THE SAIYAN GO...

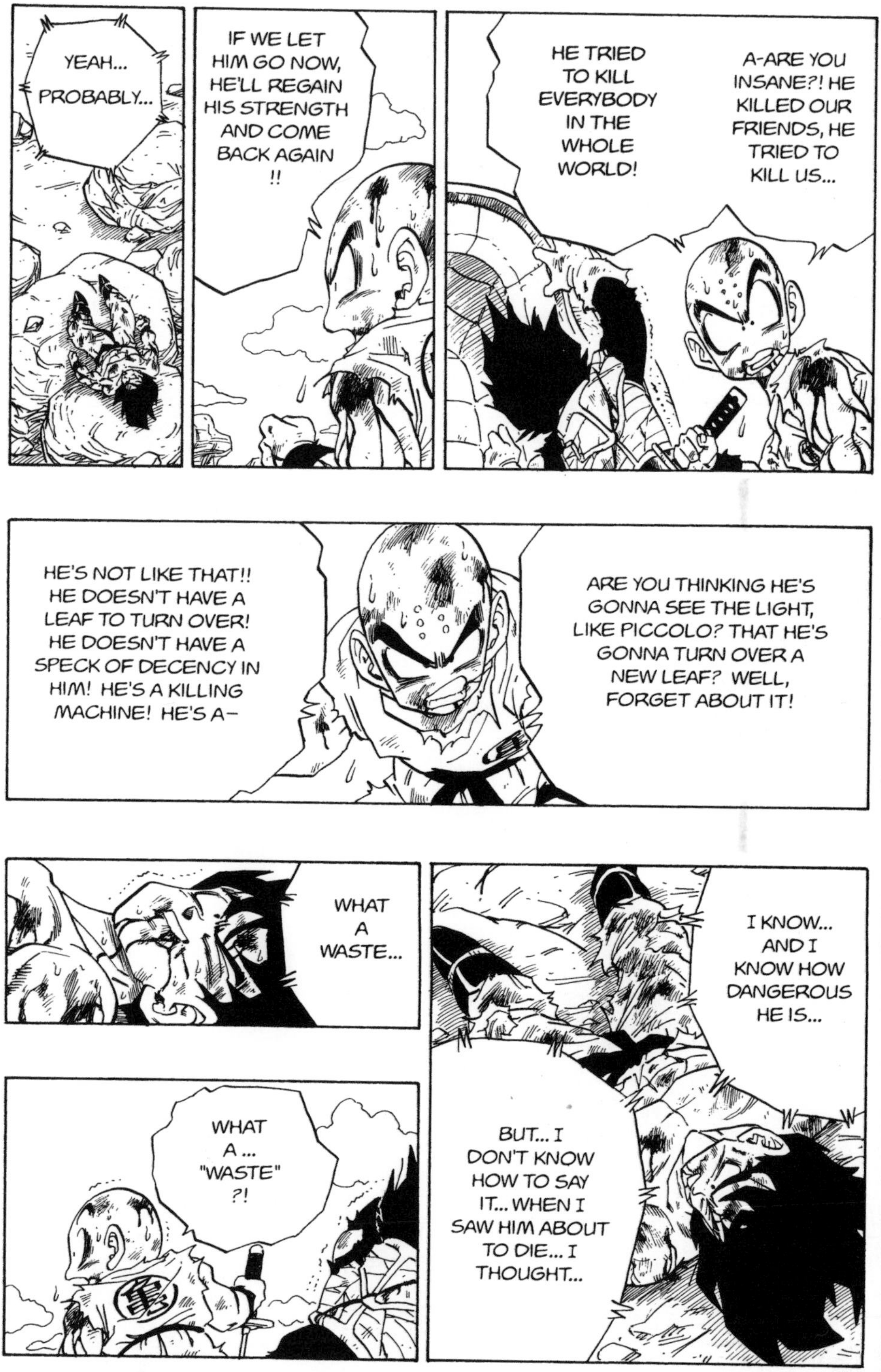
A-ARE YOU INSANE?! HE KILLED OUR FRIENDS, HE TRIED TO KILL US...
HE TRIED TO KILL EVERYBODY IN THE WHOLE WORLD!
IF WE LET HIM GO NOW, HE'LL REGAIN HIS STRENGTH AND COME BACK AGAIN !!
YEAH... PROBABLY...
ARE YOU THINKING HE'S GONNA SEE THE LIGHT, LIKE PICCOLO? THAT HE'S GONNA TURN OVER A NEW LEAF? WELL, FORGET ABOUT IT!
HE'S NOT LIKE THAT!! HE DOESN'T HAVE A LEAF TO TURN OVER! HE DOESN'T HAVE A SPECK OF DECENCY IN HIM! HE'S A KILLING MACHINE! HE'S A–
I KNOW... AND I KNOW HOW DANGEROUS HE IS...
BUT... I DON'T KNOW HOW TO SAY IT... WHEN I SAW HIM ABOUT TO DIE... I THOUGHT...
WHAT A WASTE...
WHAT A ... "WASTE" ?!

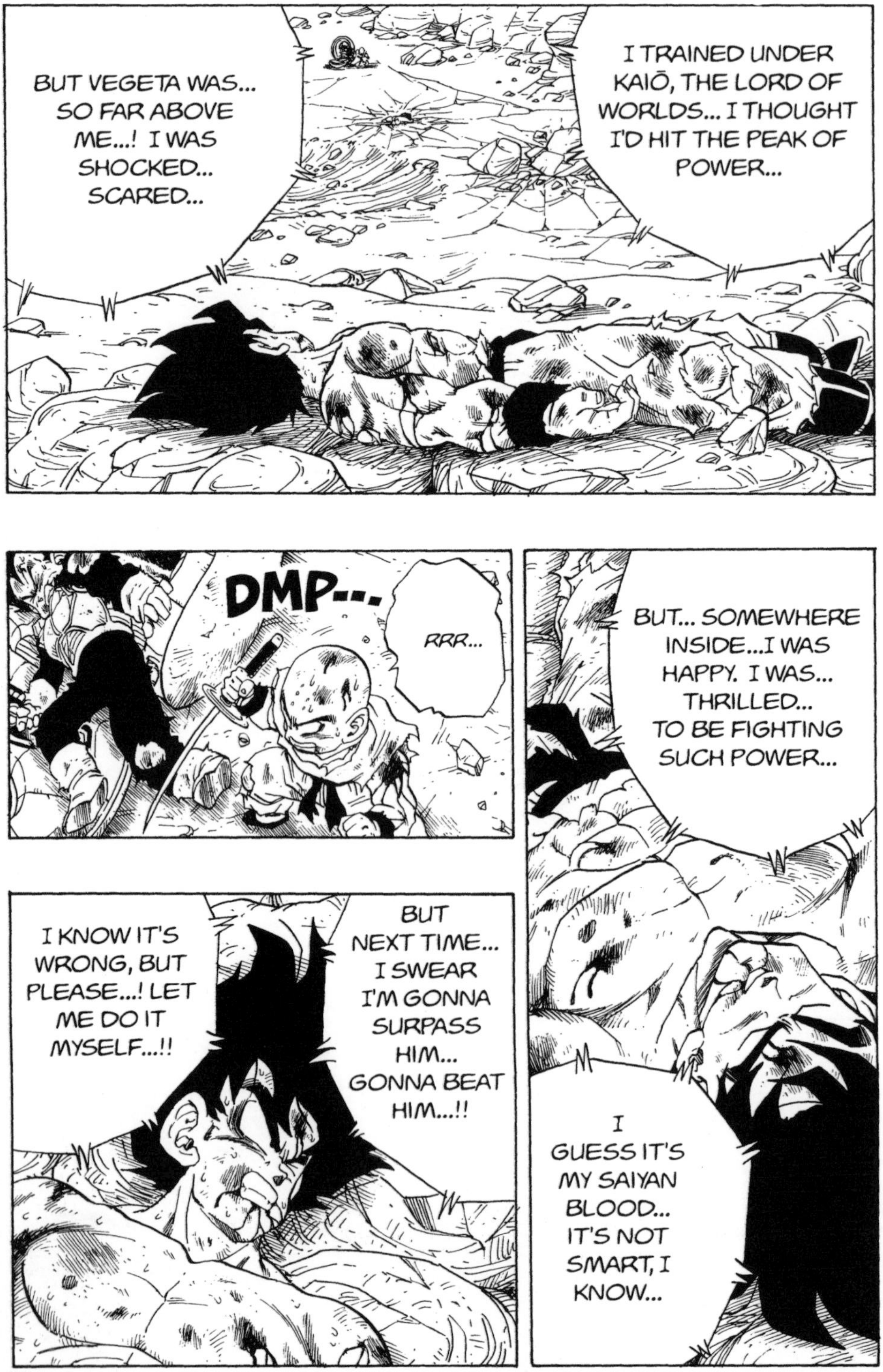

I TRAINED UNDER KAIŌ, THE LORD OF WORLDS... I THOUGHT I'D HIT THE PEAK OF POWER...
BUT VEGETA WAS... SO FAR ABOVE ME...! I WAS SHOCKED... SCARED...
BUT... SOMEWHERE INSIDE...I WAS HAPPY. I WAS... THRILLED... TO BE FIGHTING SUCH POWER...
I GUESS IT'S MY SAIYAN BLOOD... IT'S NOT SMART, I KNOW...
RRR...
DMP...
BUT NEXT TIME... I SWEAR I'M GONNA SURPASS HIM... GONNA BEAT HIM...!!
I KNOW IT'S WRONG, BUT PLEASE...! LET ME DO IT MYSELF...!!

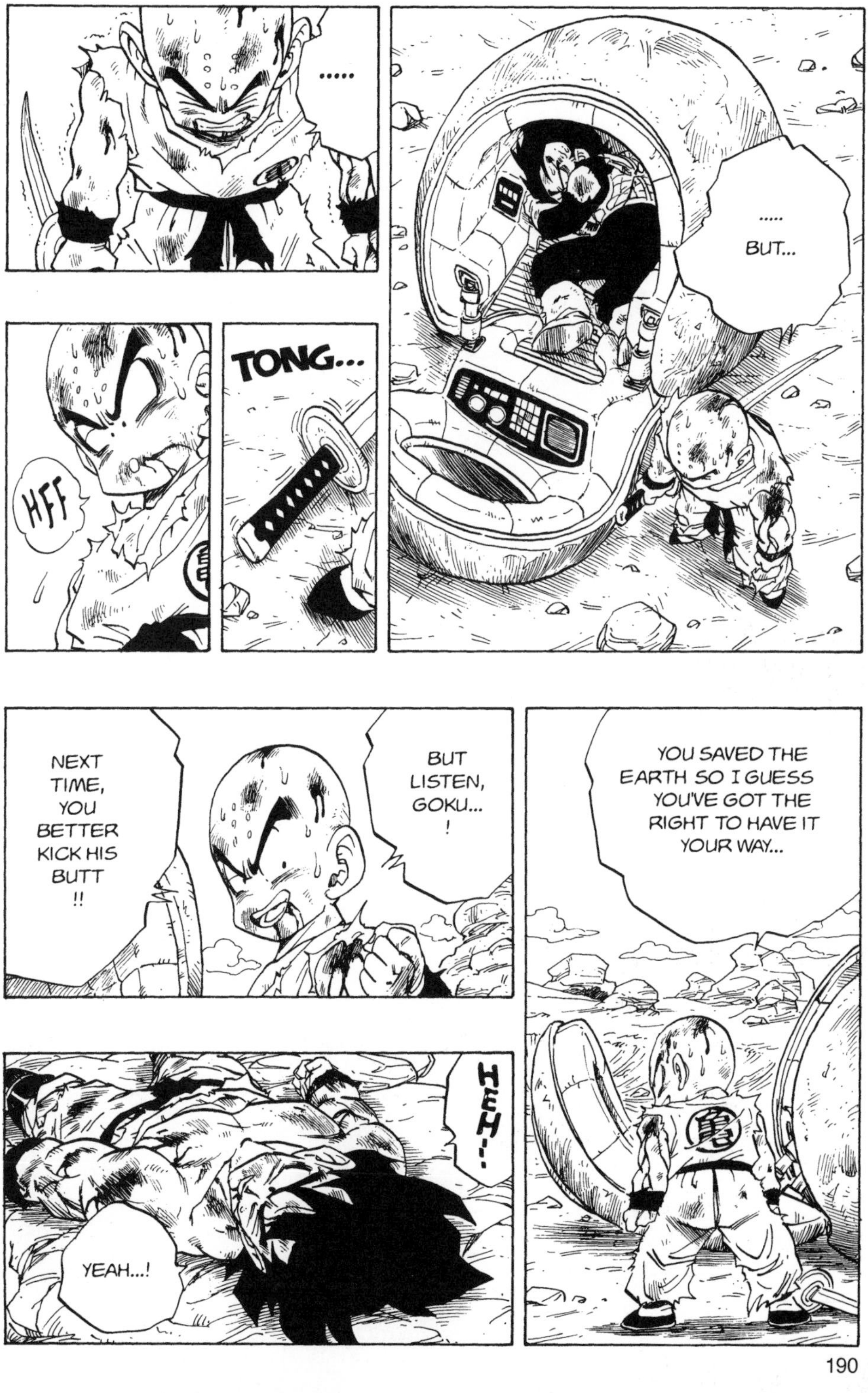

.....
BUT...
......
TONG...
HFF
YOU SAVED THE EARTH SO I GUESS YOU'VE GOT THE RIGHT TO HAVE IT YOUR WAY...
BUT LISTEN, GOKU... !
NEXT TIME, YOU BETTER KICK HIS BUTT !!
HEH!!
YEAH...!

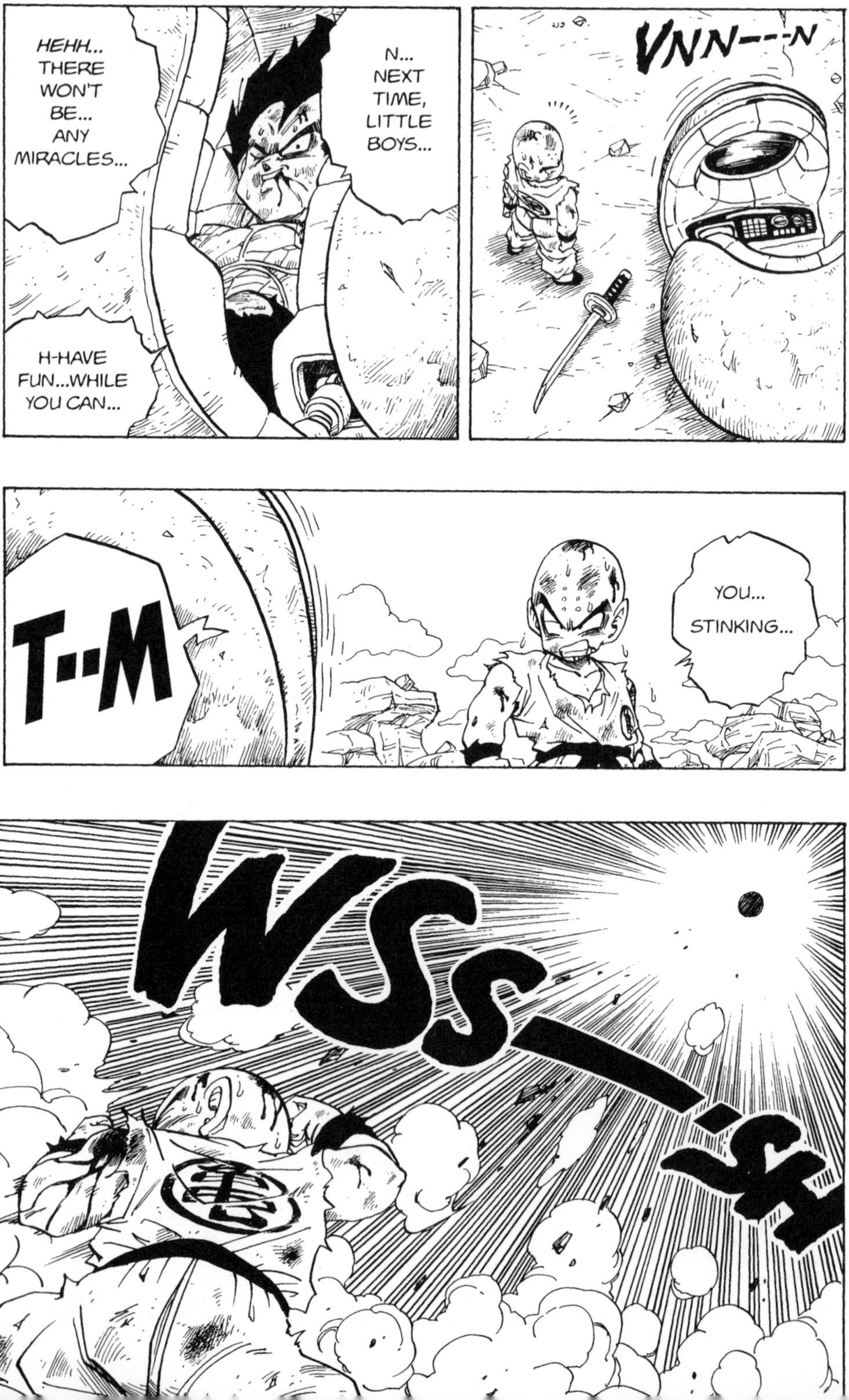
VNN---N
N... NEXT TIME, LITTLE BOYS...
HEHH... THERE WON'T BE... ANY MIRACLES...
H-HAVE FUN...WHILE YOU CAN...
YOU... STINKING...
T--M
WSS--SH

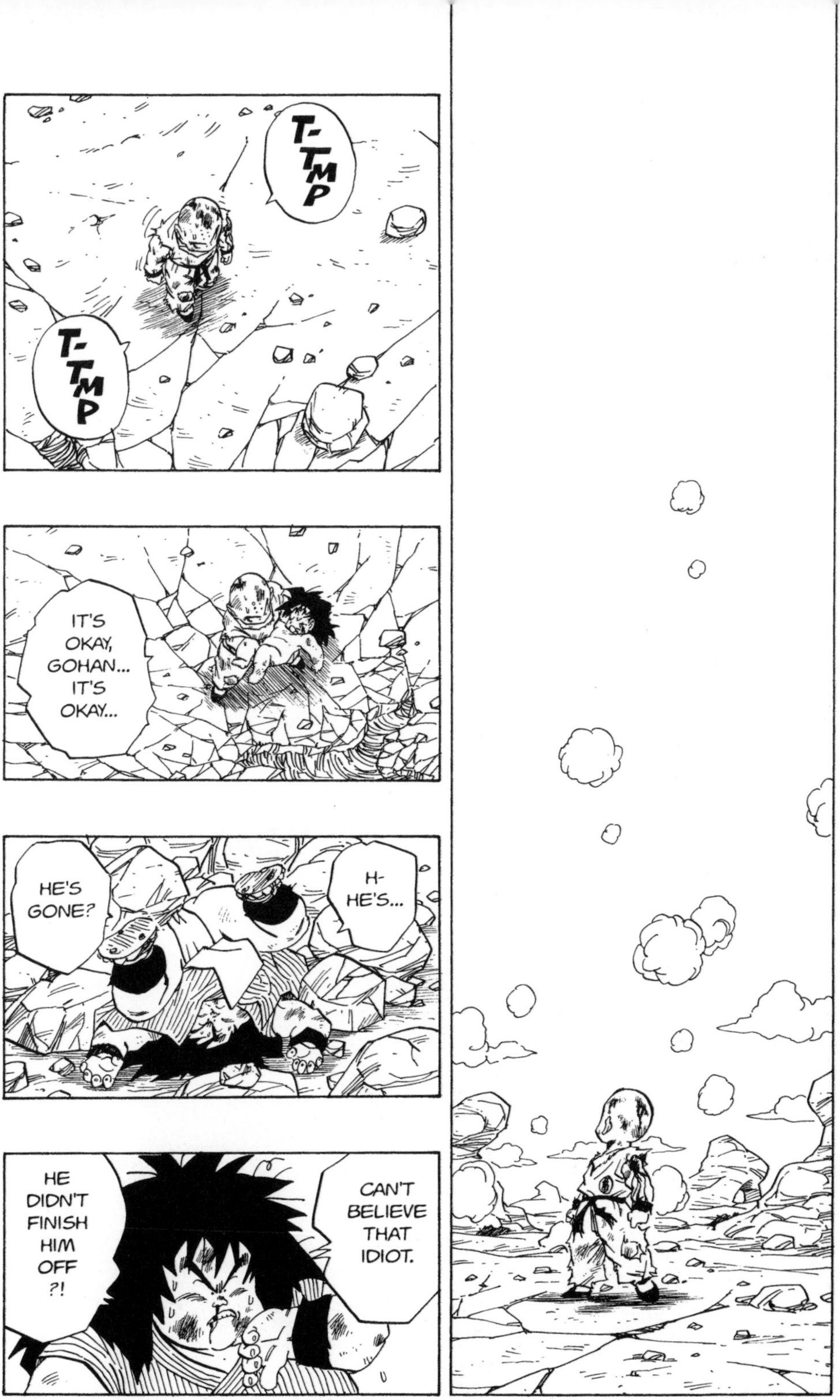
T-TMP
T-TMP
IT'S OKAY, GOHAN... IT'S OKAY...
H- HE'S...
HE'S GONE?
CAN'T BELIEVE THAT IDIOT.
HE DIDN'T FINISH HIM OFF ?!

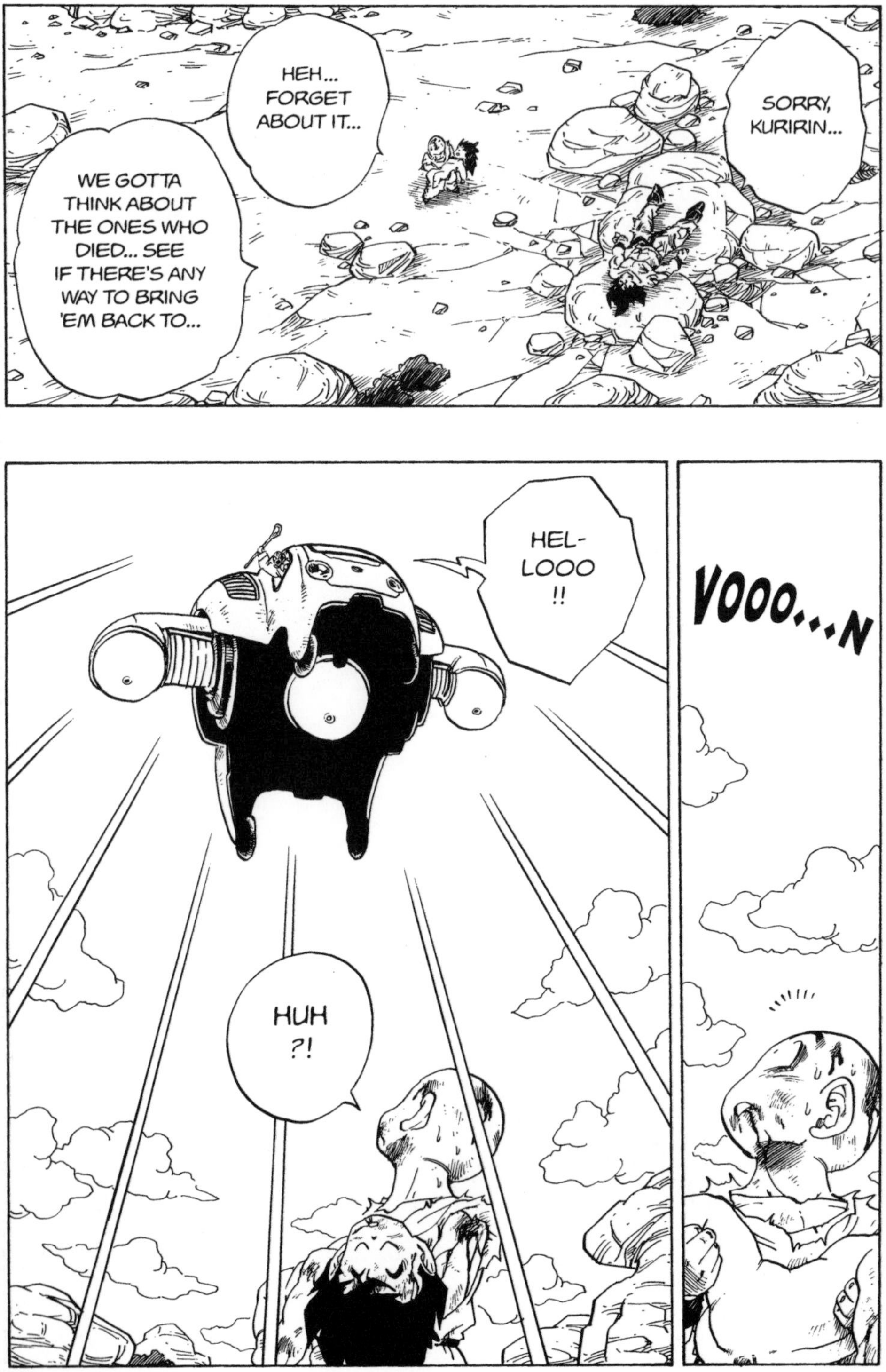
SORRY, KURIRIN...
HEH... FORGET ABOUT IT...
WE GOTTA THINK ABOUT THE ONES WHO DIED... SEE IF THERE'S ANY WAY TO BRING 'EM BACK TO...
VOOO...N
HEL-LOOO !!
HUH ?!

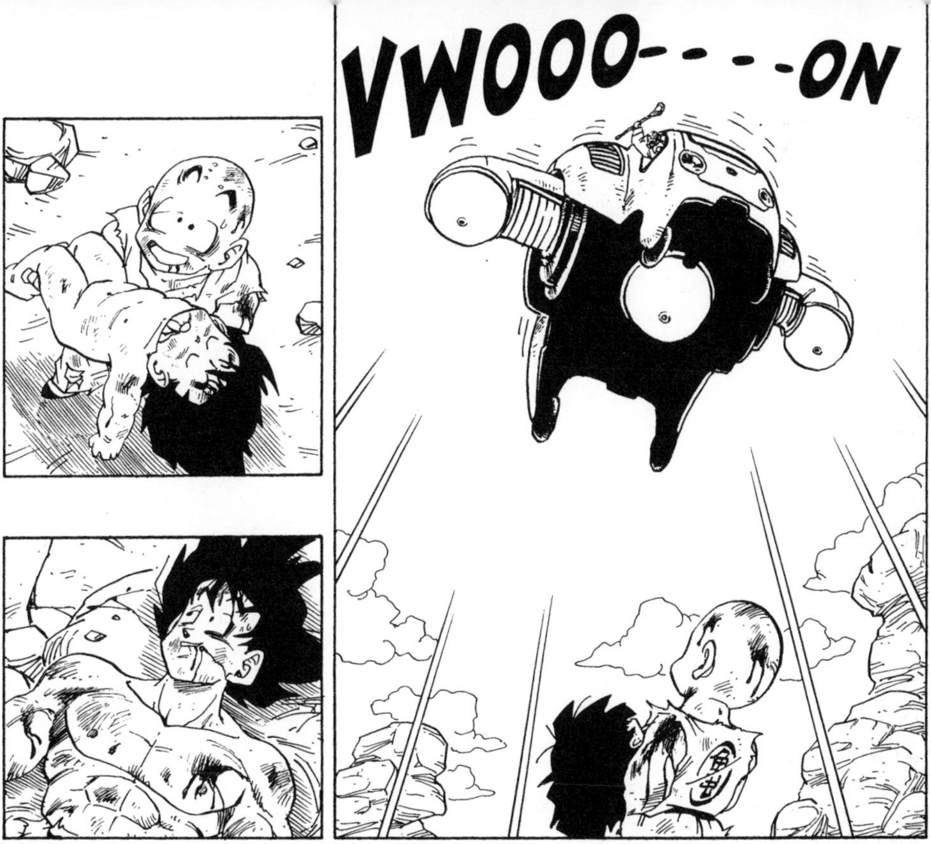
VWOOO- - - -ON

## DBZ:48 • The Bittersweet End

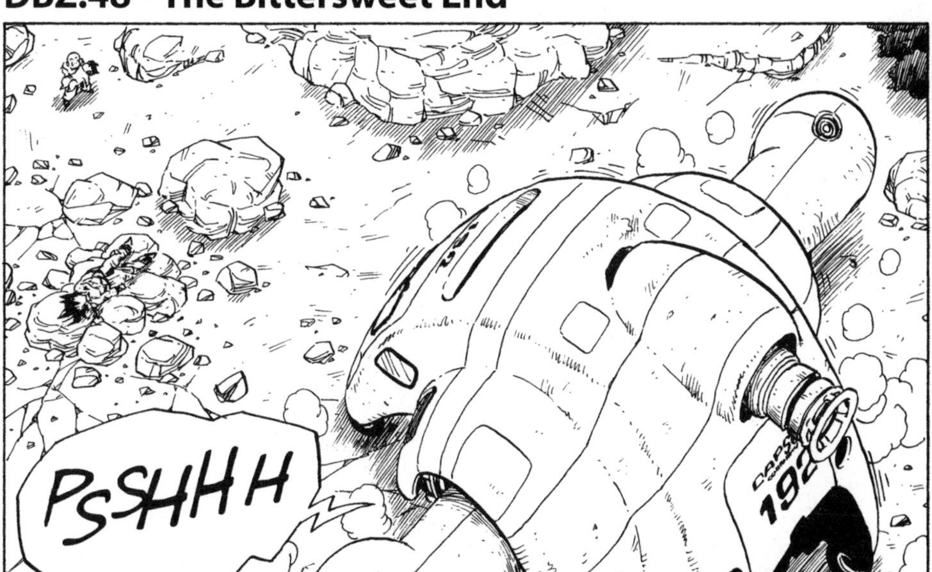
PSHHH

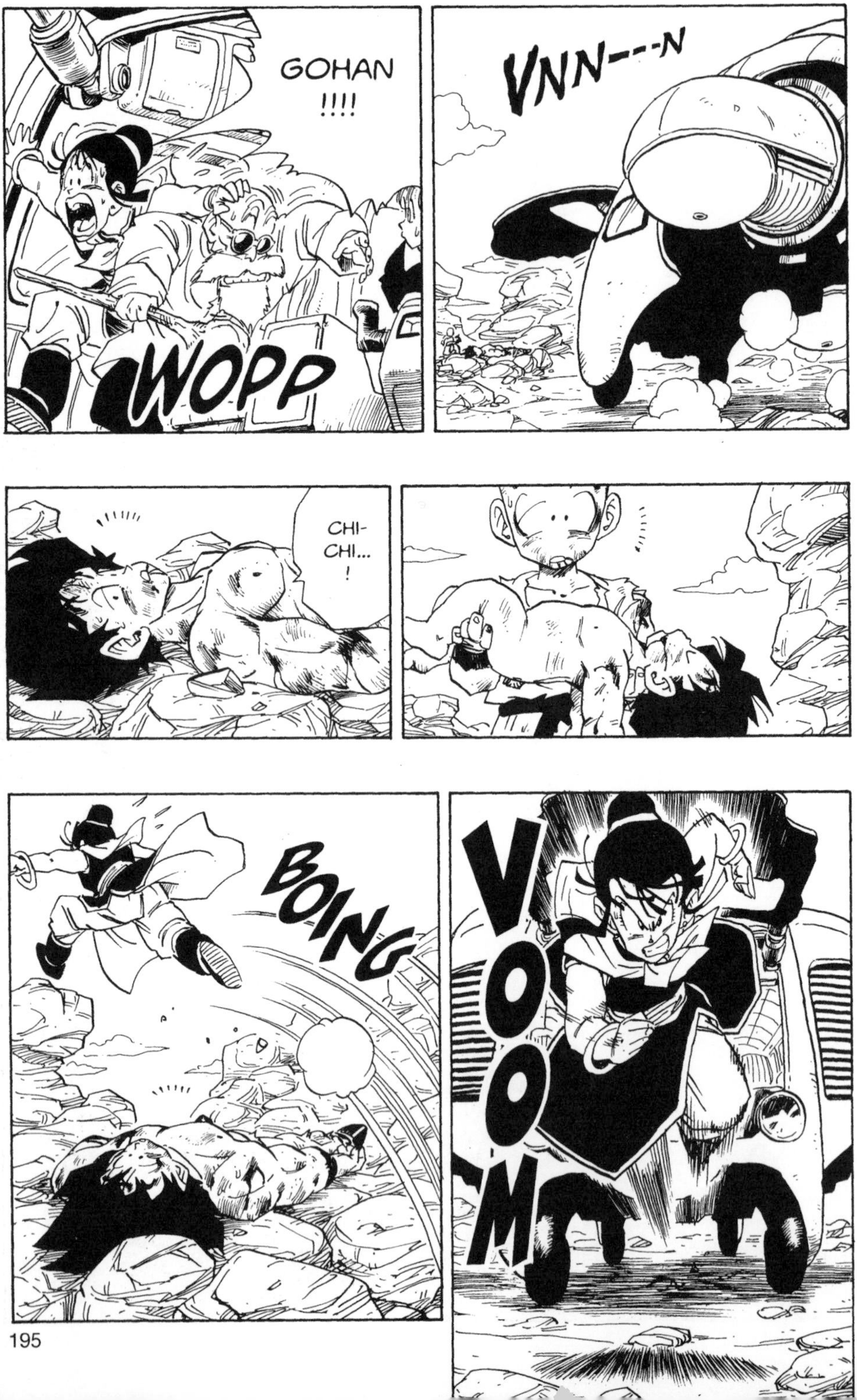
VNN---N
GOHAN !!!!
WOPP
CHI-CHI... !
VOOM
BOING

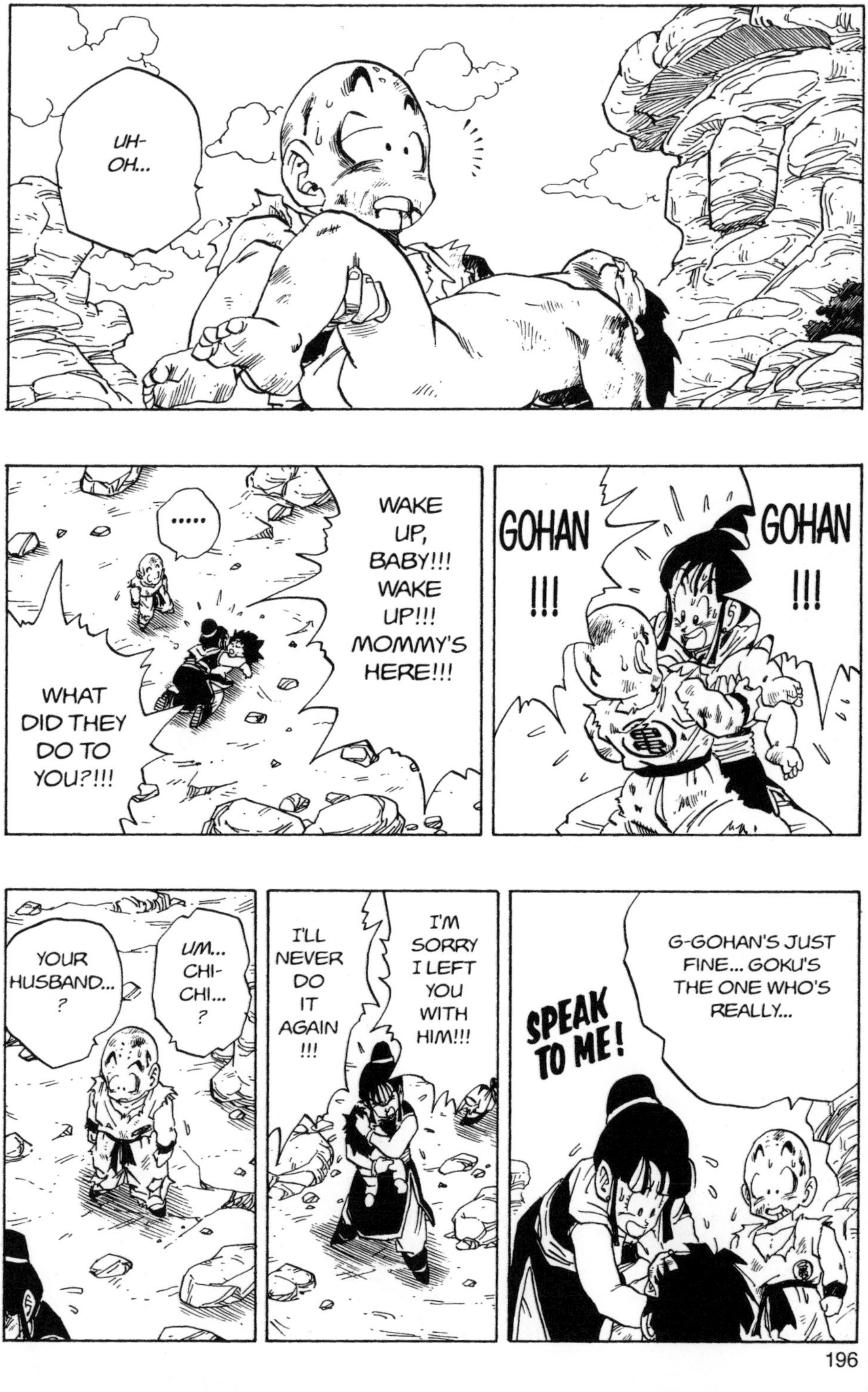
UH-OH...
GOHAN!!!
GOHAN!!!
WAKE UP, BABY!!! WAKE UP!!! MOMMY'S HERE!!!
......
WHAT DID THEY DO TO YOU?!!!
G-GOHAN'S JUST FINE... GOKU'S THE ONE WHO'S REALLY...
SPEAK TO ME!
I'M SORRY I LEFT YOU WITH HIM!!!
I'LL NEVER DO IT AGAIN!!!
UM... CHI-CHI...?
YOUR HUSBAND...?

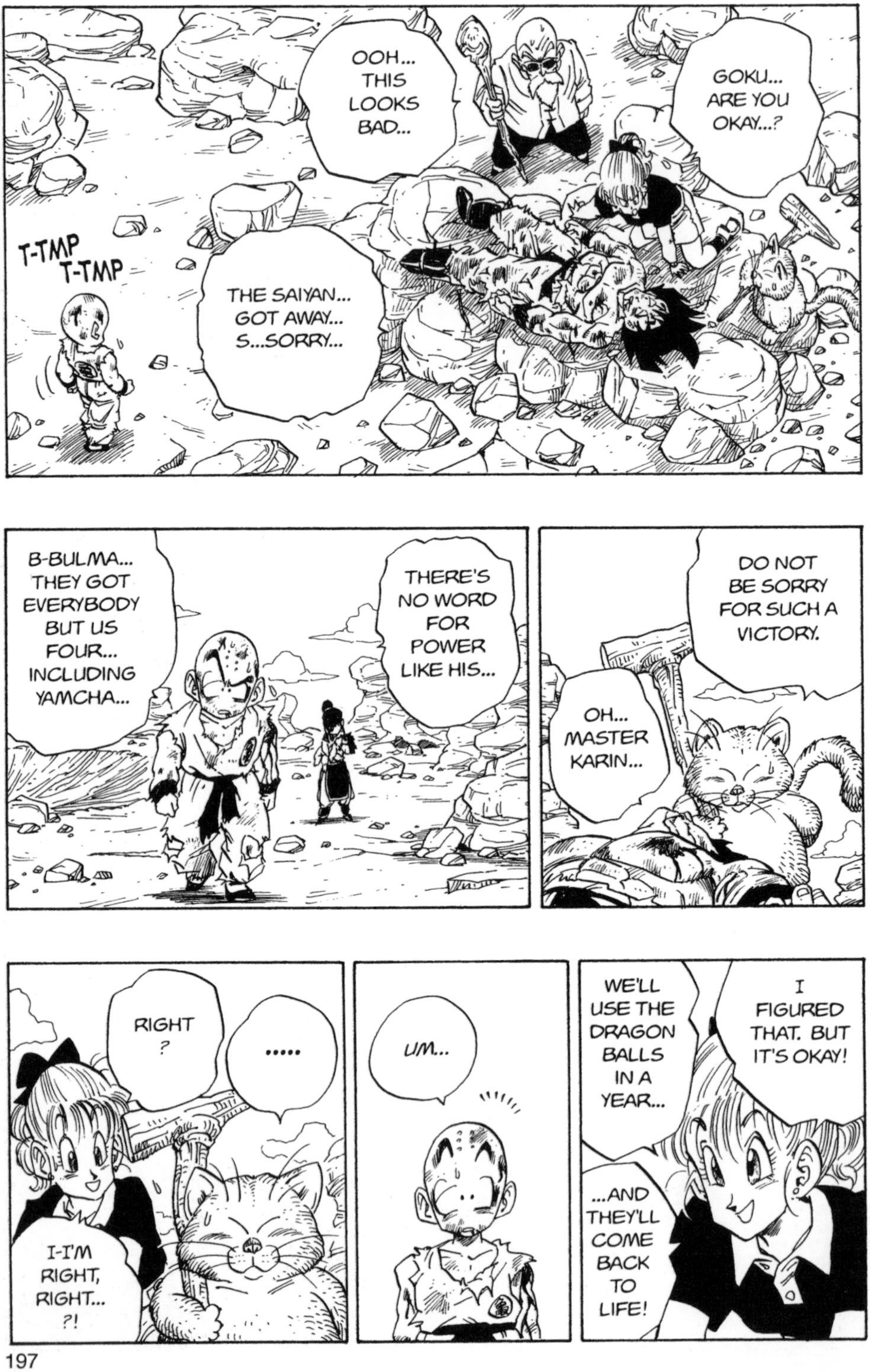
GOKU... ARE YOU OKAY...?
OOH... THIS LOOKS BAD...
THE SAIYAN... GOT AWAY... S...SORRY...
T-TMP T-TMP
DO NOT BE SORRY FOR SUCH A VICTORY.
OH... MASTER KARIN...
THERE'S NO WORD FOR POWER LIKE HIS...
B-BULMA... THEY GOT EVERYBODY BUT US FOUR... INCLUDING YAMCHA...
I FIGURED THAT. BUT IT'S OKAY!
WE'LL USE THE DRAGON BALLS IN A YEAR...
...AND THEY'LL COME BACK TO LIFE!
UM...
.....
RIGHT ?
I-I'M RIGHT, RIGHT... ?!

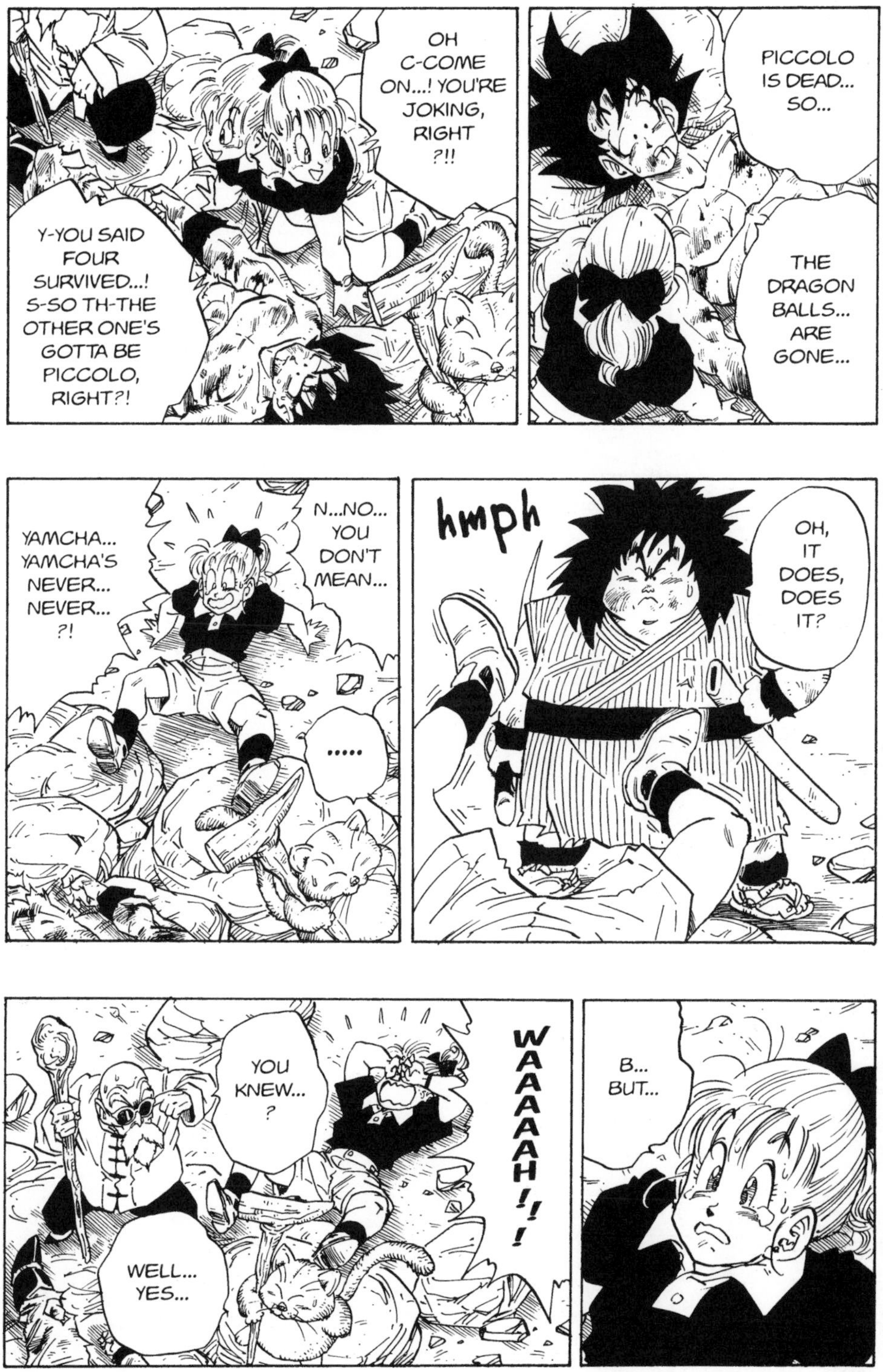
PICCOLO IS DEAD... SO...
THE DRAGON BALLS... ARE GONE...
OH C-COME ON...! YOU'RE JOKING, RIGHT ?!!
Y-YOU SAID FOUR SURVIVED...! S-SO TH-THE OTHER ONE'S GOTTA BE PICCOLO, RIGHT?!
hmph
OH, IT DOES, DOES IT?
N...NO... YOU DON'T MEAN...
YAMCHA... YAMCHA'S NEVER... NEVER... ?!
.....
B... BUT...
WAAAAAH!!!
YOU KNEW... ?
WELL... YES...

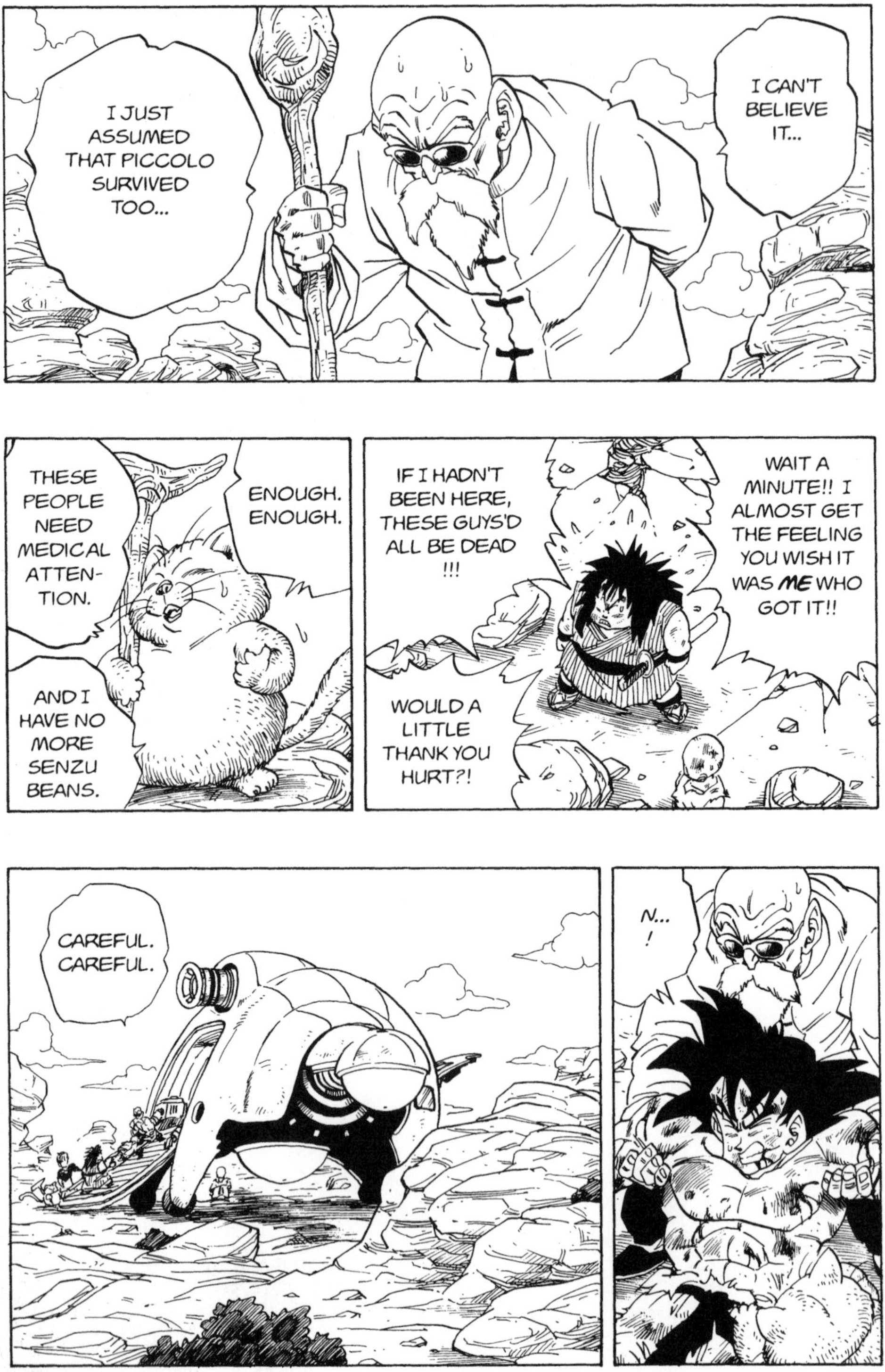
I CAN'T BELIEVE IT...
I JUST ASSUMED THAT PICCOLO SURVIVED TOO...
WAIT A MINUTE!! I ALMOST GET THE FEELING YOU WISH IT WAS *ME* WHO GOT IT!!
IF I HADN'T BEEN HERE, THESE GUYS'D ALL BE DEAD !!!
WOULD A LITTLE THANK YOU HURT?!
ENOUGH. ENOUGH.
THESE PEOPLE NEED MEDICAL ATTEN-TION.
AND I HAVE NO MORE SENZU BEANS.
N... !
CAREFUL. CAREFUL.

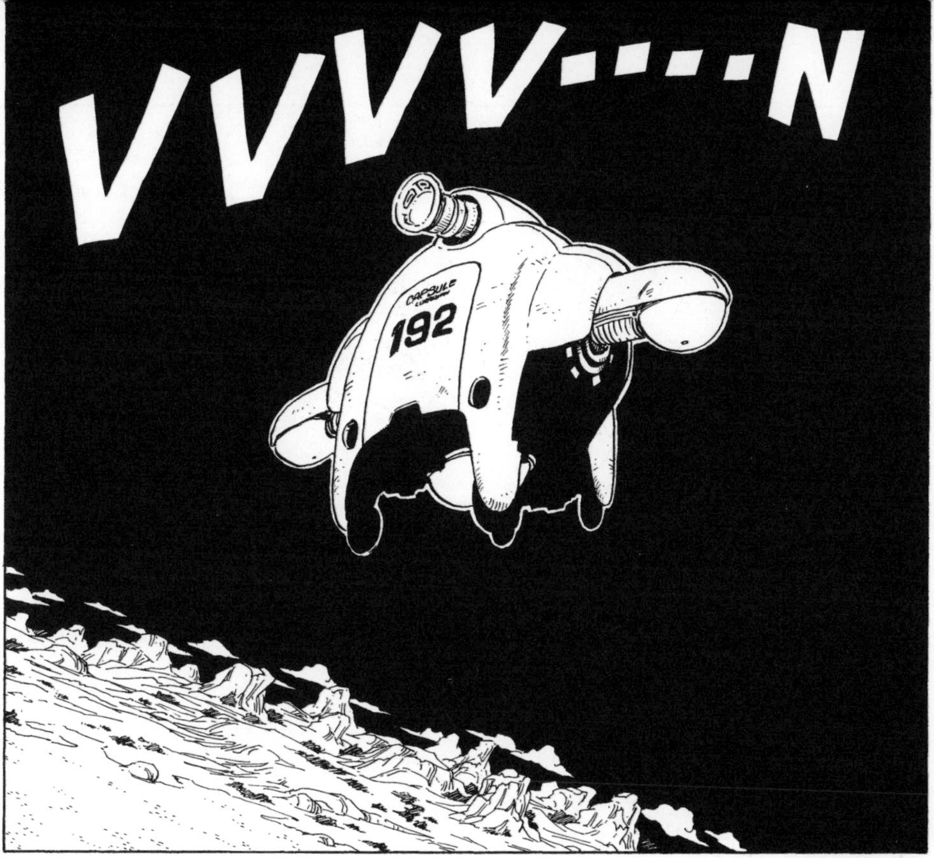
VVVV....N
CAPSULE
192

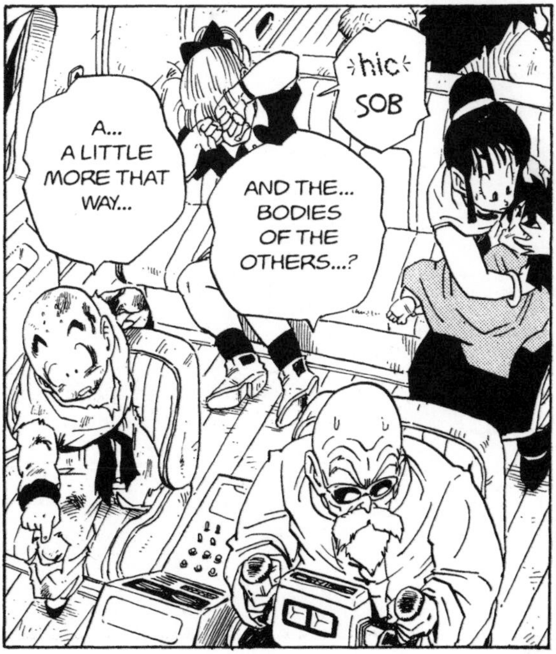
hic SOB
A... A LITTLE MORE THAT WAY...
AND THE... BODIES OF THE OTHERS...?

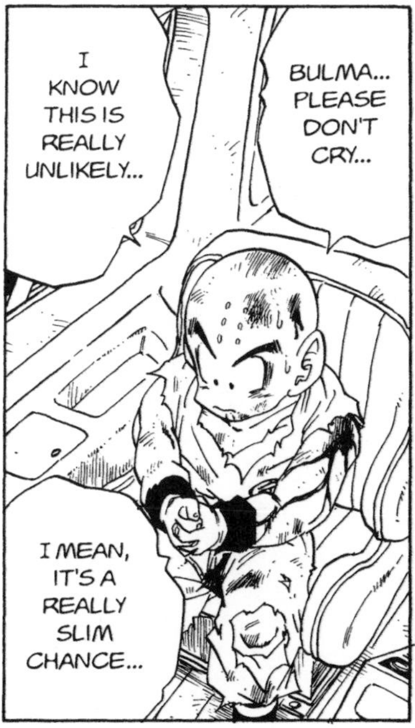
BULMA... PLEASE DON'T CRY...
I KNOW THIS IS REALLY UNLIKELY...
I MEAN, IT'S A REALLY SLIM CHANCE...

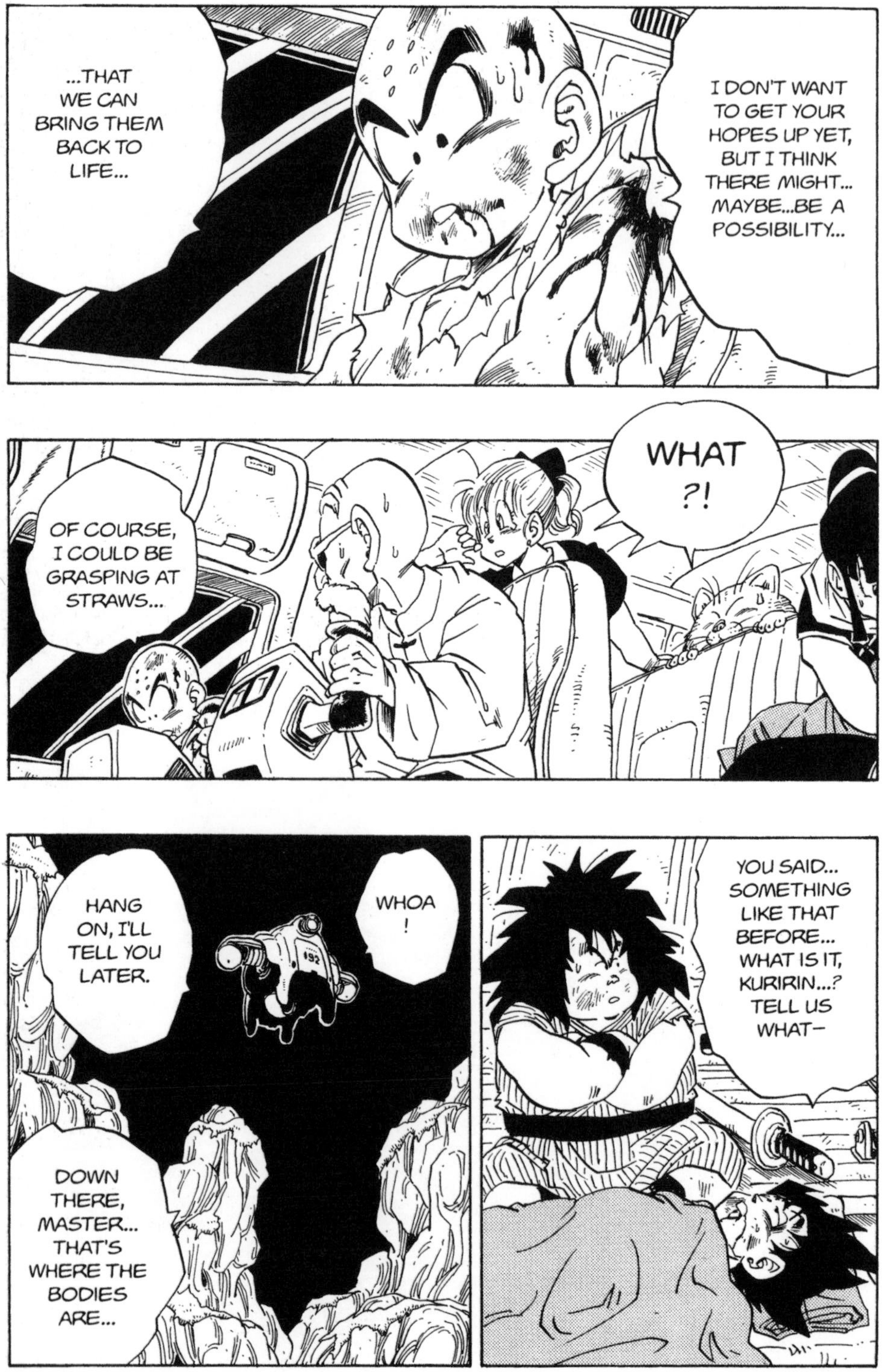
I DON'T WANT TO GET YOUR HOPES UP YET, BUT I THINK THERE MIGHT... MAYBE...BE A POSSIBILITY...
...THAT WE CAN BRING THEM BACK TO LIFE...
WHAT ?!
OF COURSE, I COULD BE GRASPING AT STRAWS...
YOU SAID... SOMETHING LIKE THAT BEFORE... WHAT IS IT, KURIRIN...? TELL US WHAT—
WHOA !
HANG ON, I'LL TELL YOU LATER.
DOWN THERE, MASTER... THAT'S WHERE THE BODIES ARE...

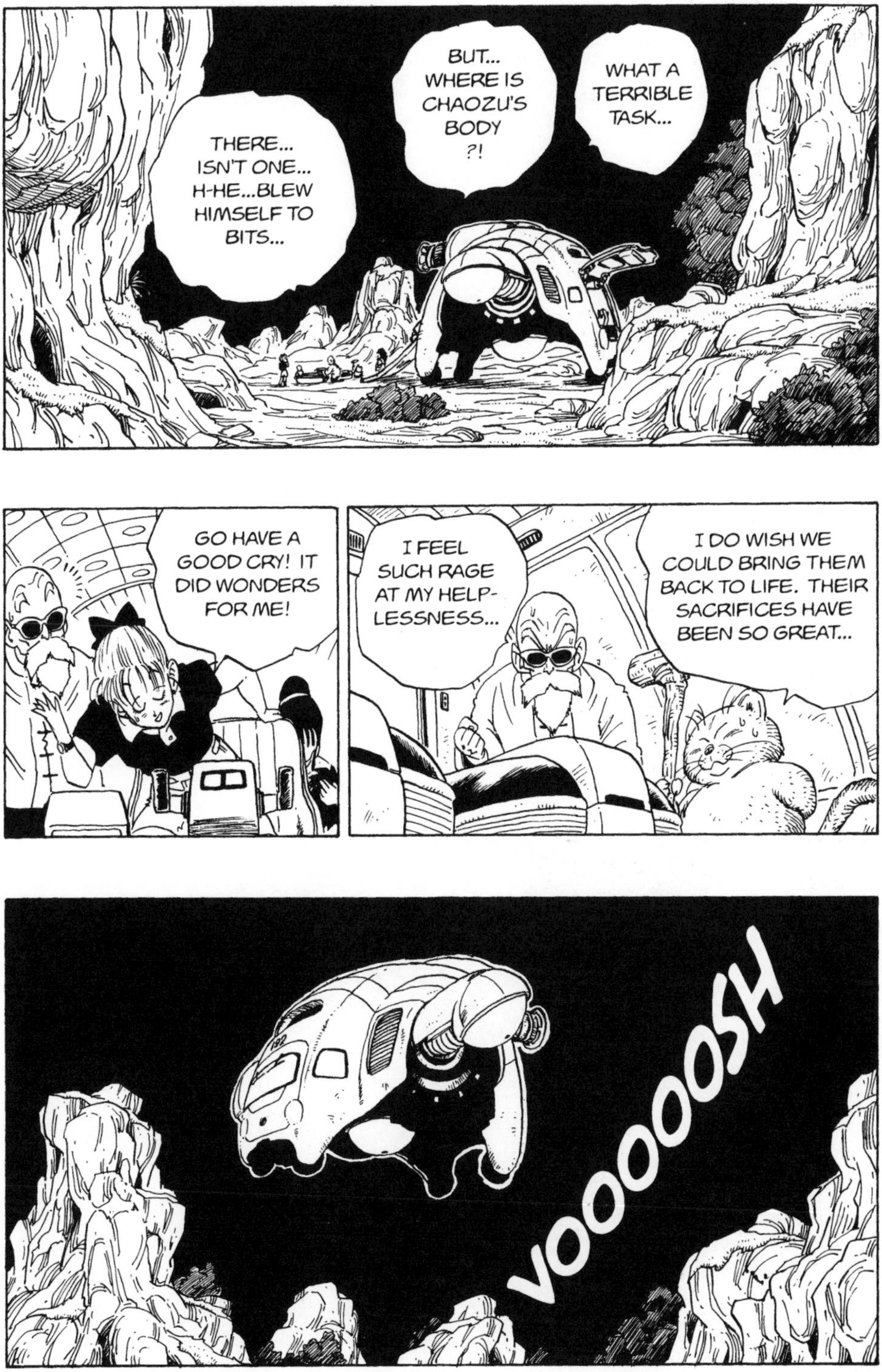
WHAT A TERRIBLE TASK...
BUT... WHERE IS CHAOZU'S BODY ?!
THERE... ISN'T ONE... H-HE...BLEW HIMSELF TO BITS...
I DO WISH WE COULD BRING THEM BACK TO LIFE. THEIR SACRIFICES HAVE BEEN SO GREAT...
I FEEL SUCH RAGE AT MY HELP-LESSNESS...
GO HAVE A GOOD CRY! IT DID WONDERS FOR ME!
VOOOOOSH

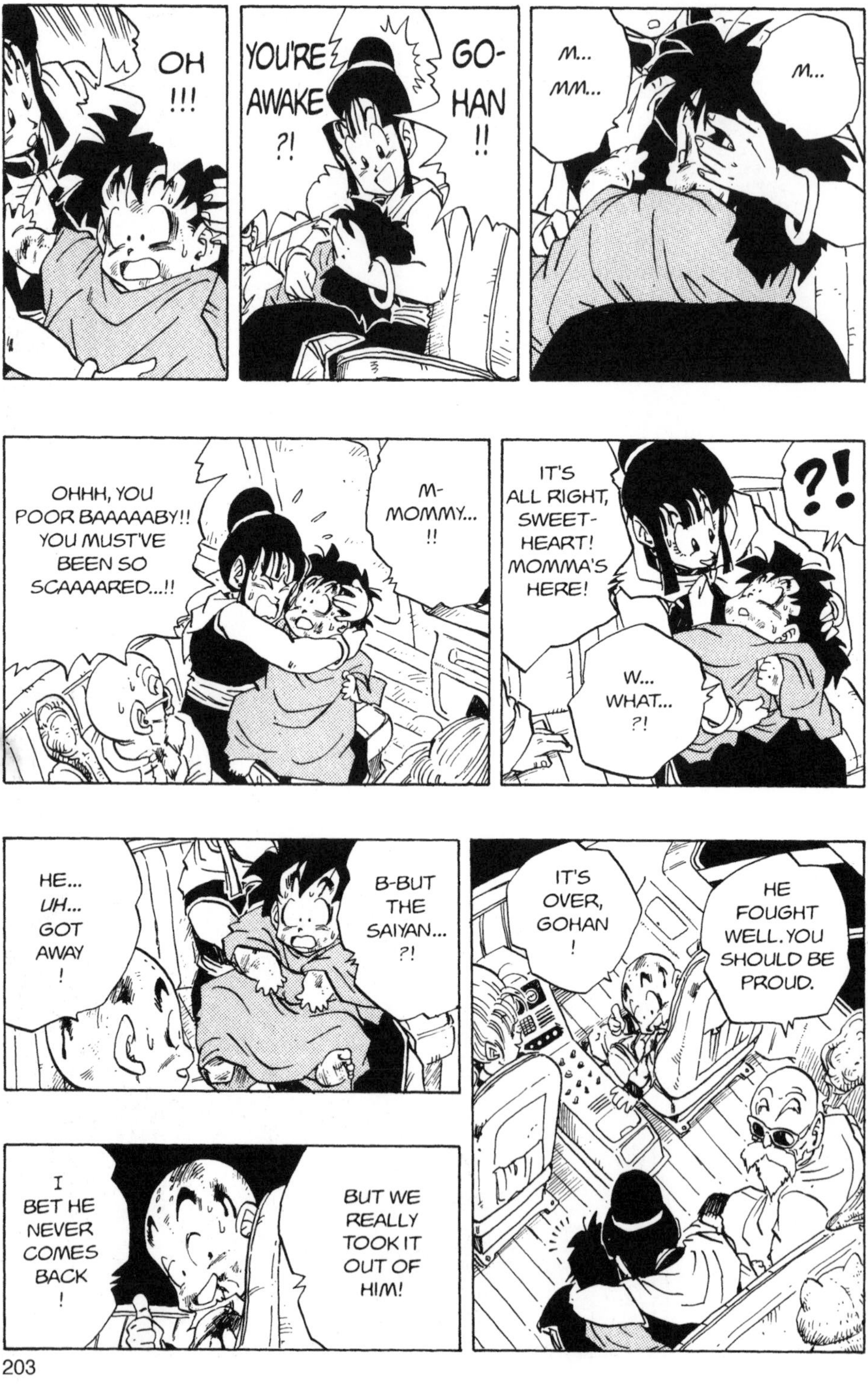
M...
M...
MM...
GO-HAN!!
YOU'RE AWAKE?!
OH!!!
?!
IT'S ALL RIGHT, SWEET-HEART! MOMMA'S HERE!
W... WHAT...?!
M-MOMMY...!!
OHHH, YOU POOR BAAAAABY!! YOU MUST'VE BEEN SO SCAAAARED...!!
HE FOUGHT WELL. YOU SHOULD BE PROUD.
IT'S OVER, GOHAN!
B-BUT THE SAIYAN...?!
HE... UH... GOT AWAY!
BUT WE REALLY TOOK IT OUT OF HIM!
I BET HE NEVER COMES BACK!

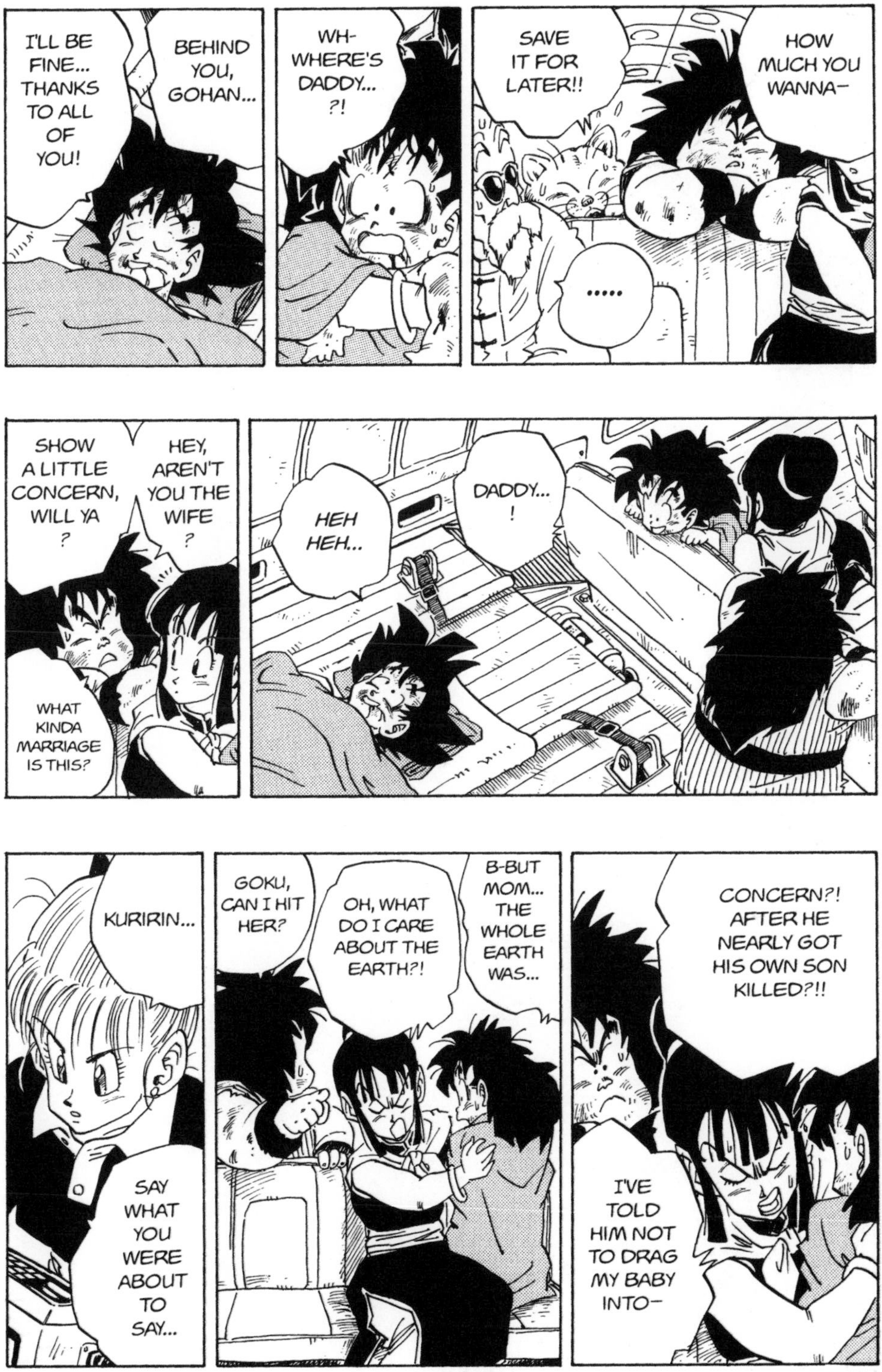
HOW MUCH YOU WANNA–
SAVE IT FOR LATER!!
......
WH- WHERE'S DADDY...?!
BEHIND YOU, GOHAN...
I'LL BE FINE... THANKS TO ALL OF YOU!
DADDY...!
HEH HEH...
HEY, AREN'T YOU THE WIFE?
SHOW A LITTLE CONCERN, WILL YA?
WHAT KINDA MARRIAGE IS THIS?
CONCERN?! AFTER HE NEARLY GOT HIS OWN SON KILLED?!!
I'VE TOLD HIM NOT TO DRAG MY BABY INTO–
B-BUT MOM... THE WHOLE EARTH WAS...
OH, WHAT DO I CARE ABOUT THE EARTH?!
GOKU, CAN I HIT HER?
KURIRIN...
SAY WHAT YOU WERE ABOUT TO SAY...

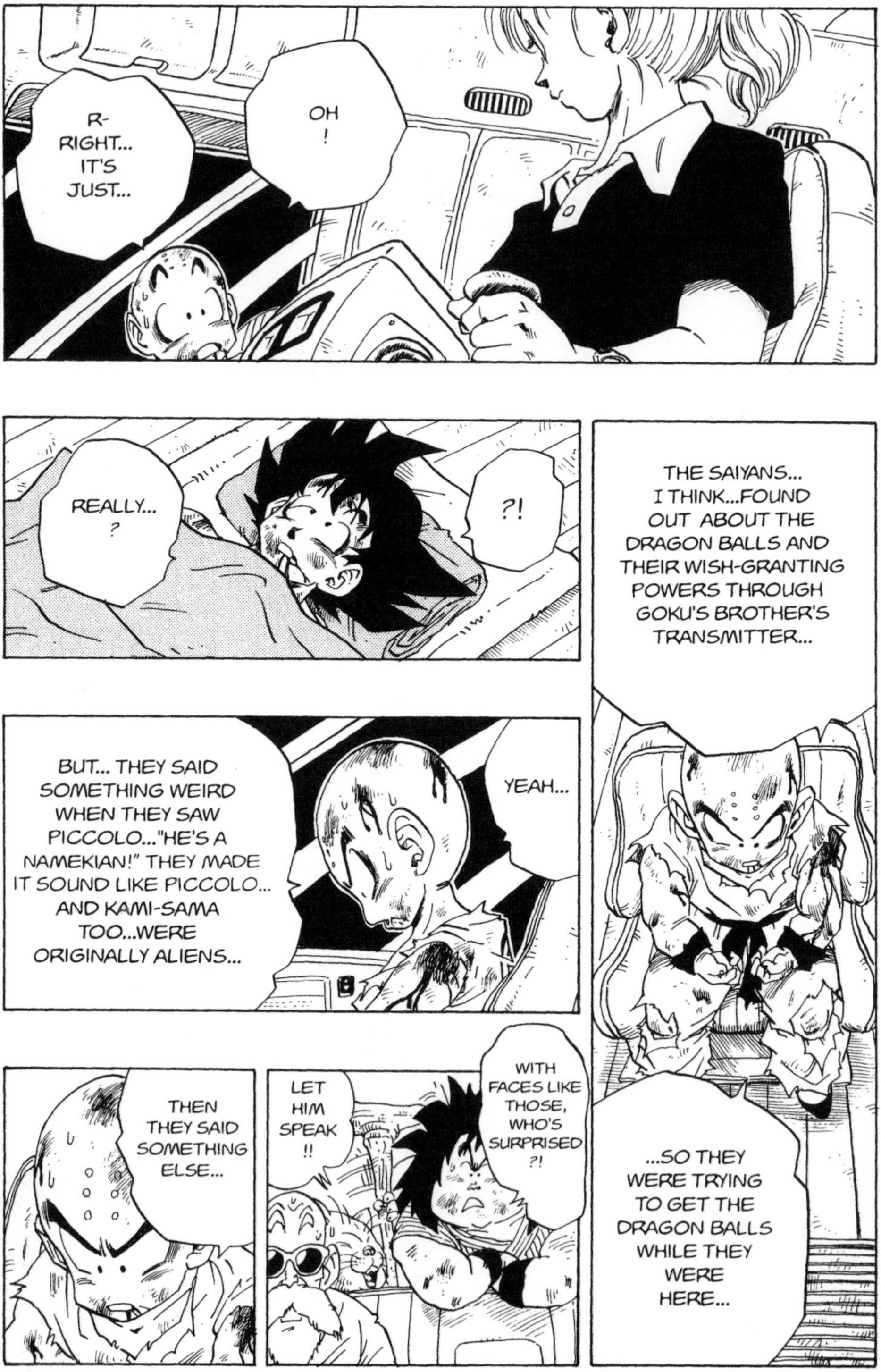
OH !
R- RIGHT... IT'S JUST...
THE SAIYANS... I THINK...FOUND OUT ABOUT THE DRAGON BALLS AND THEIR WISH-GRANTING POWERS THROUGH GOKU'S BROTHER'S TRANSMITTER...
...SO THEY WERE TRYING TO GET THE DRAGON BALLS WHILE THEY WERE HERE...
?!
REALLY... ?
YEAH...
BUT... THEY SAID SOMETHING WEIRD WHEN THEY SAW PICCOLO..."HE'S A NAMEKIAN!" THEY MADE IT SOUND LIKE PICCOLO... AND KAMI-SAMA TOO...WERE ORIGINALLY ALIENS...
WITH FACES LIKE THOSE, WHO'S SURPRISED ?!
LET HIM SPEAK !!
THEN THEY SAID SOMETHING ELSE...

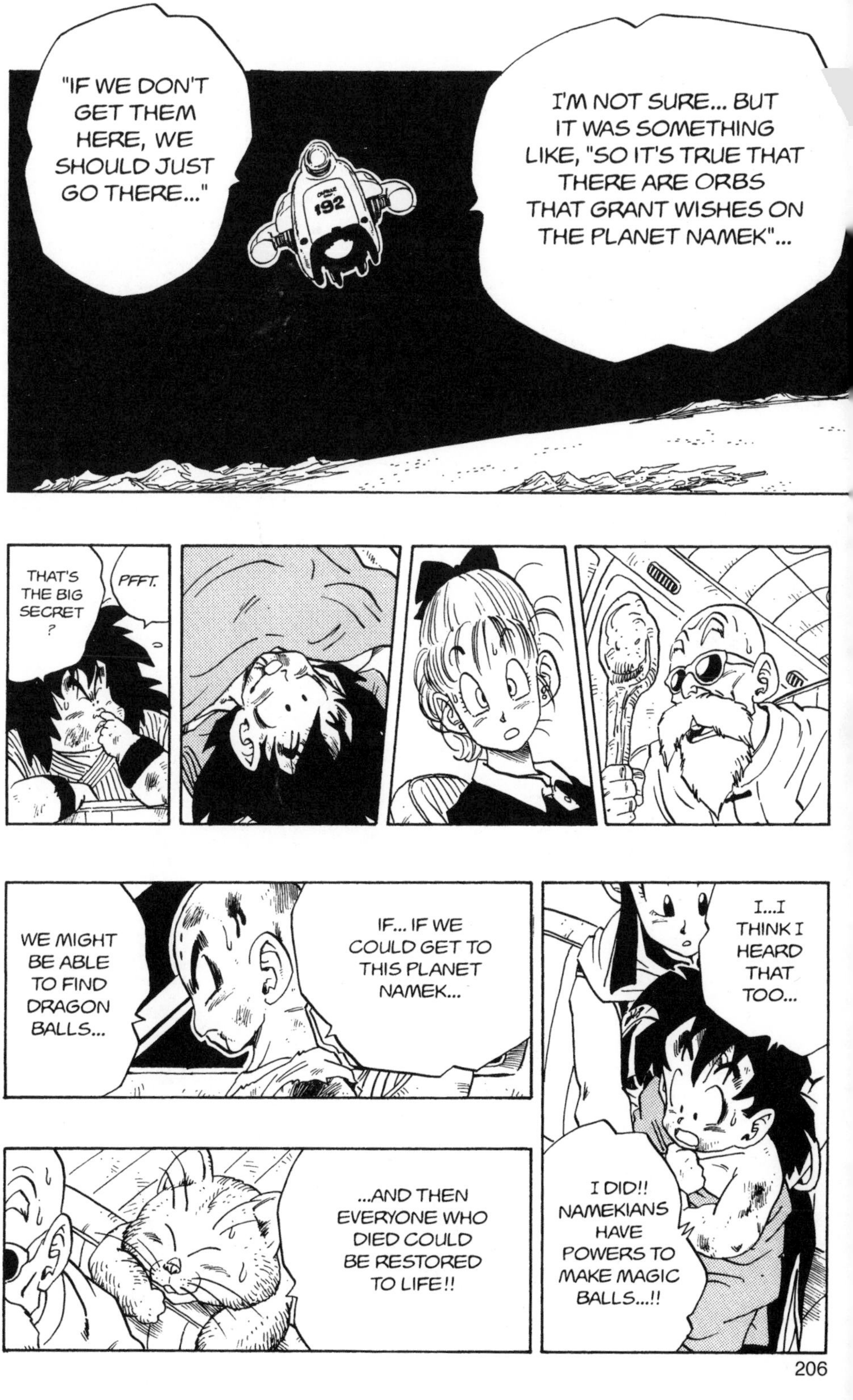
I'M NOT SURE... BUT IT WAS SOMETHING LIKE, "SO IT'S TRUE THAT THERE ARE ORBS THAT GRANT WISHES ON THE PLANET NAMEK"...
"IF WE DON'T GET THEM HERE, WE SHOULD JUST GO THERE..."
192
PFFT.
THAT'S THE BIG SECRET?
I...I THINK I HEARD THAT TOO...
I DID!! NAMEKIANS HAVE POWERS TO MAKE MAGIC BALLS...!!
IF... IF WE COULD GET TO THIS PLANET NAMEK...
WE MIGHT BE ABLE TO FIND DRAGON BALLS...
...AND THEN EVERYONE WHO DIED COULD BE RESTORED TO LIFE!!

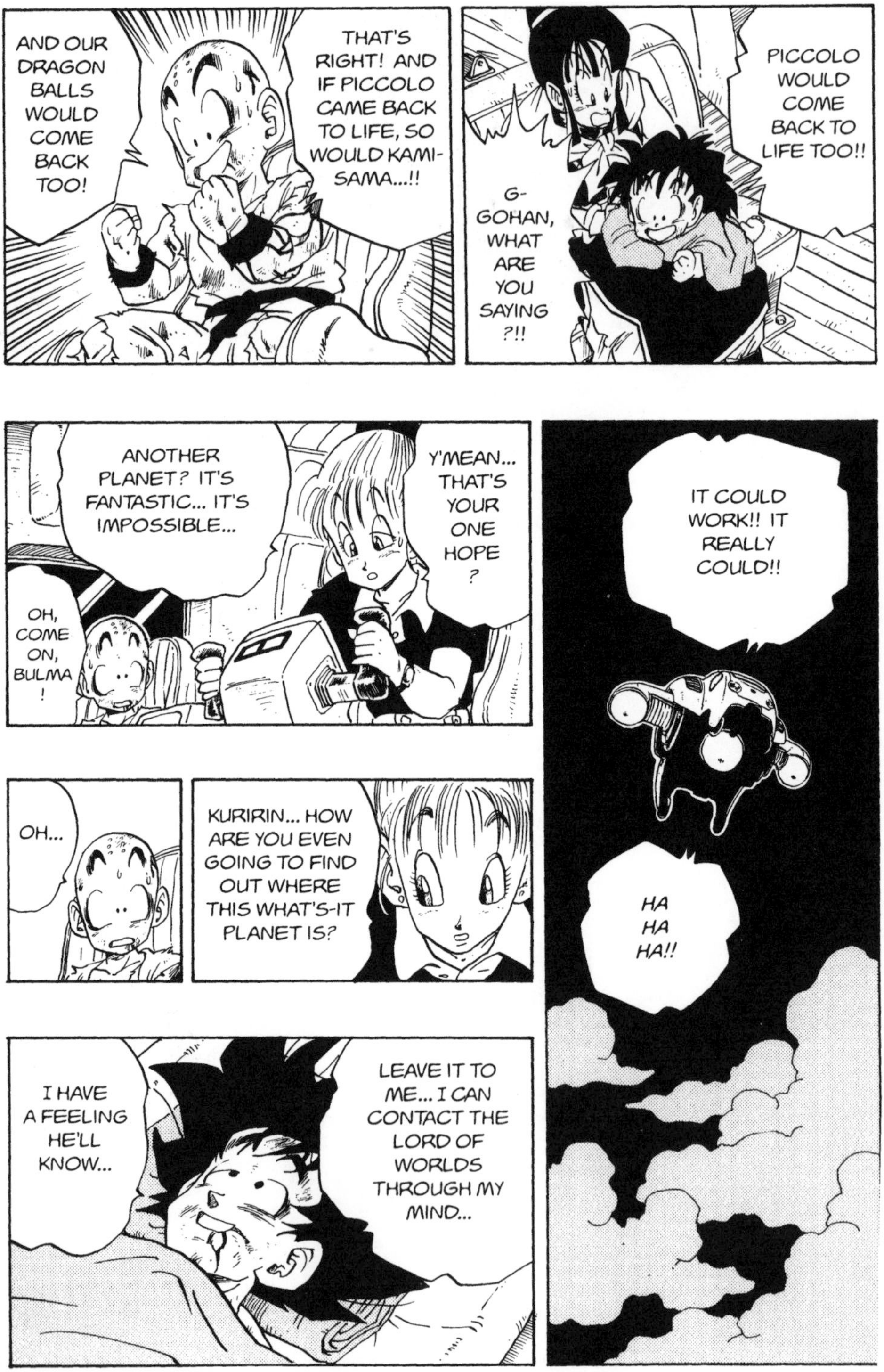
PICCOLO WOULD COME BACK TO LIFE TOO!!
G-GOHAN, WHAT ARE YOU SAYING?!!
THAT'S RIGHT! AND IF PICCOLO CAME BACK TO LIFE, SO WOULD KAMI-SAMA...!!
AND OUR DRAGON BALLS WOULD COME BACK TOO!
IT COULD WORK!! IT REALLY COULD!!
HA HA HA!!
Y'MEAN... THAT'S YOUR ONE HOPE?
ANOTHER PLANET? IT'S FANTASTIC... IT'S IMPOSSIBLE...
OH, COME ON, BULMA!
KURIRIN... HOW ARE YOU EVEN GOING TO FIND OUT WHERE THIS WHAT'S-IT PLANET IS?
OH...
LEAVE IT TO ME... I CAN CONTACT THE LORD OF WORLDS THROUGH MY MIND...
I HAVE A FEELING HE'LL KNOW...

# DBZ:49 • Destination Namek

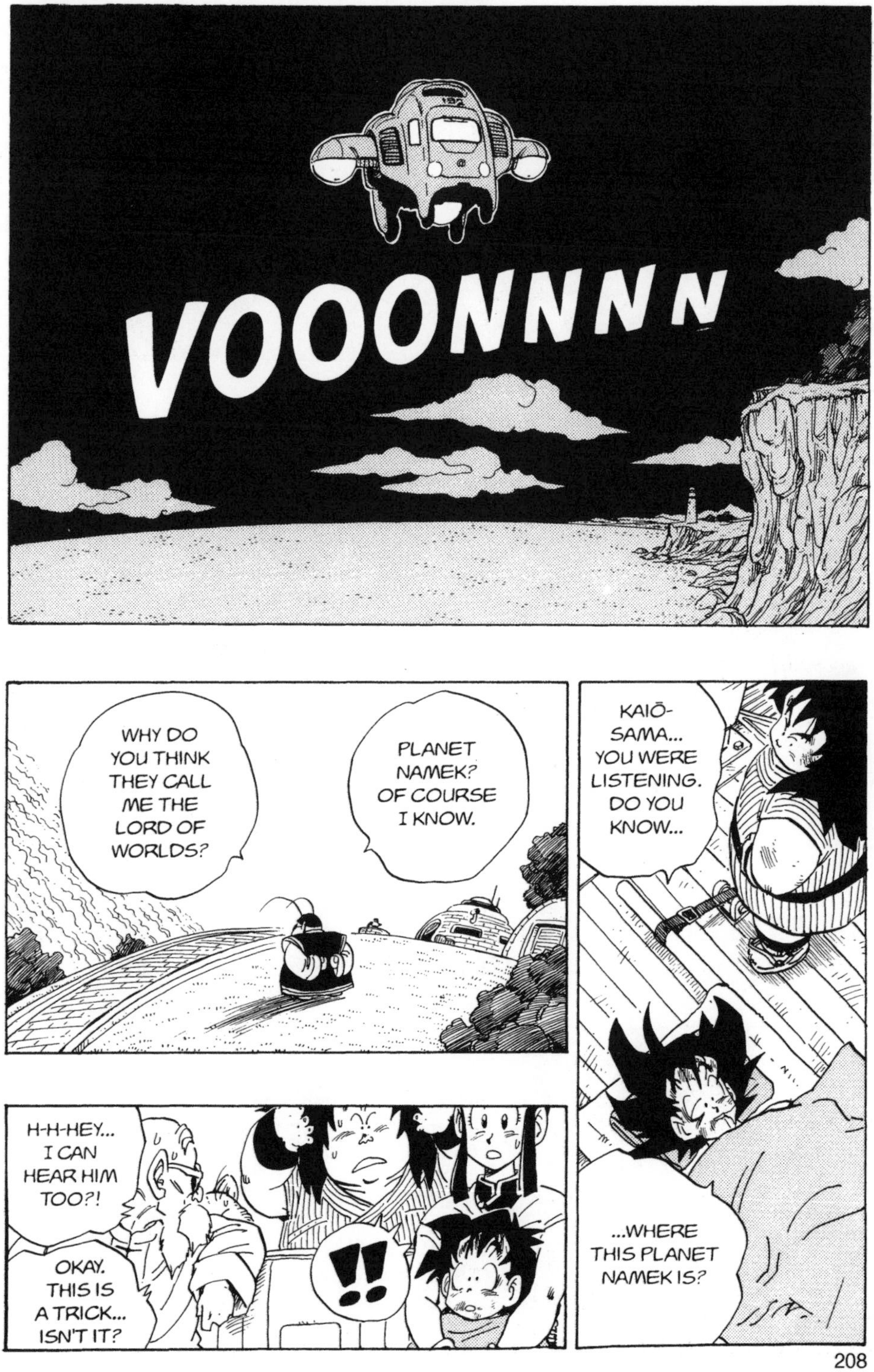
VOOONNNN
KAIŌ-SAMA... YOU WERE LISTENING. DO YOU KNOW...
...WHERE THIS PLANET NAMEK IS?
PLANET NAMEK? OF COURSE I KNOW.
WHY DO YOU THINK THEY CALL ME THE LORD OF WORLDS?
!!
H-H-HEY... I CAN HEAR HIM TOO?!
OKAY. THIS IS A TRICK... ISN'T IT?

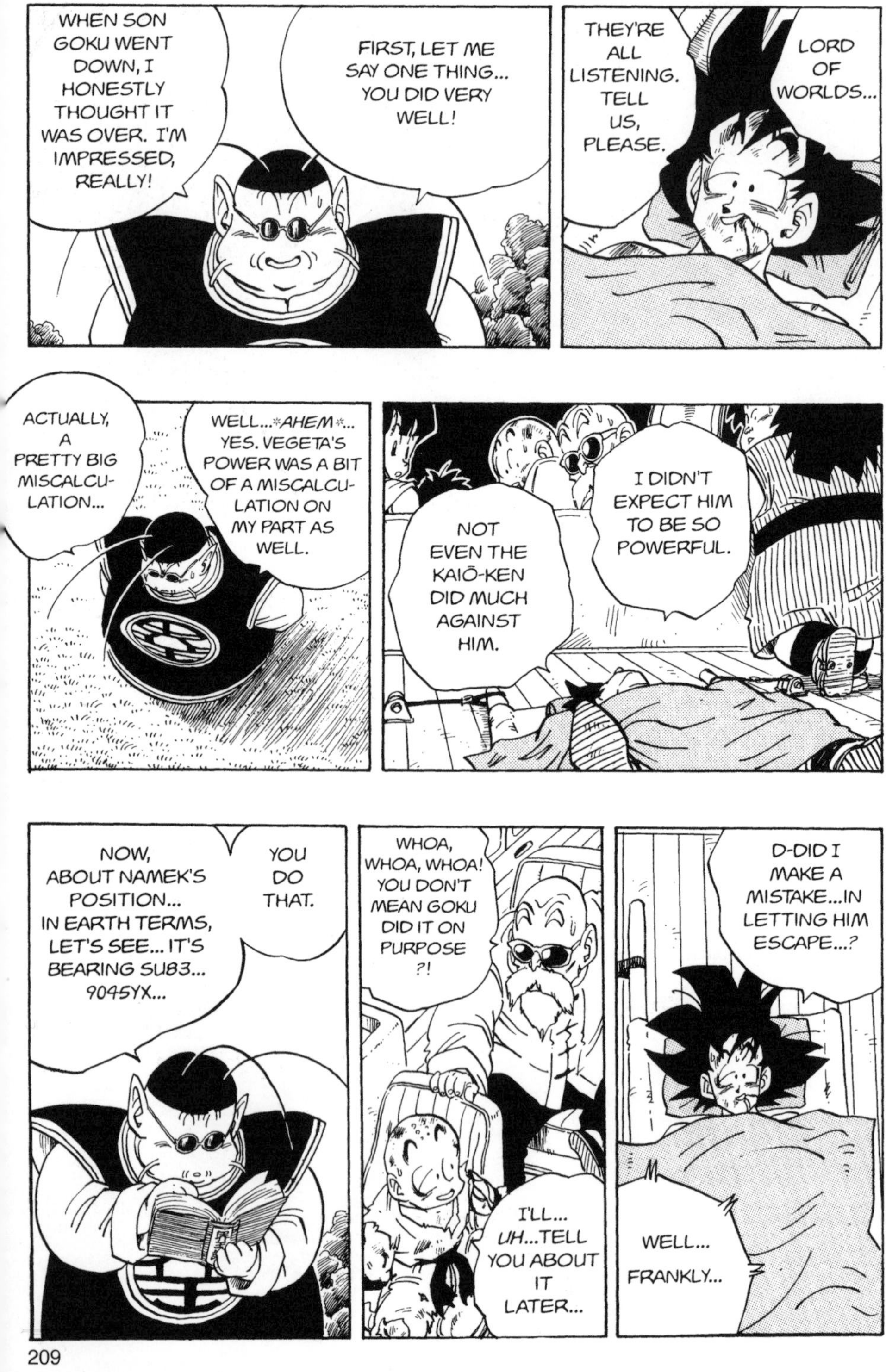
LORD OF WORLDS...
THEY'RE ALL LISTENING. TELL US, PLEASE.
FIRST, LET ME SAY ONE THING... YOU DID VERY WELL!
WHEN SON GOKU WENT DOWN, I HONESTLY THOUGHT IT WAS OVER. I'M IMPRESSED, REALLY!
I DIDN'T EXPECT HIM TO BE SO POWERFUL.
NOT EVEN THE KAIŌ-KEN DID MUCH AGAINST HIM.
WELL...*AHEM*... YES. VEGETA'S POWER WAS A BIT OF A MISCALCULATION ON MY PART AS WELL.
ACTUALLY, A PRETTY BIG MISCALCULATION...
D-DID I MAKE A MISTAKE...IN LETTING HIM ESCAPE...?
WELL... FRANKLY...
WHOA, WHOA, WHOA! YOU DON'T MEAN GOKU DID IT ON PURPOSE?!
I'LL... UH...TELL YOU ABOUT IT LATER...
YOU DO THAT.
NOW, ABOUT NAMEK'S POSITION... IN EARTH TERMS, LET'S SEE... IT'S BEARING SU83... 9045YX...

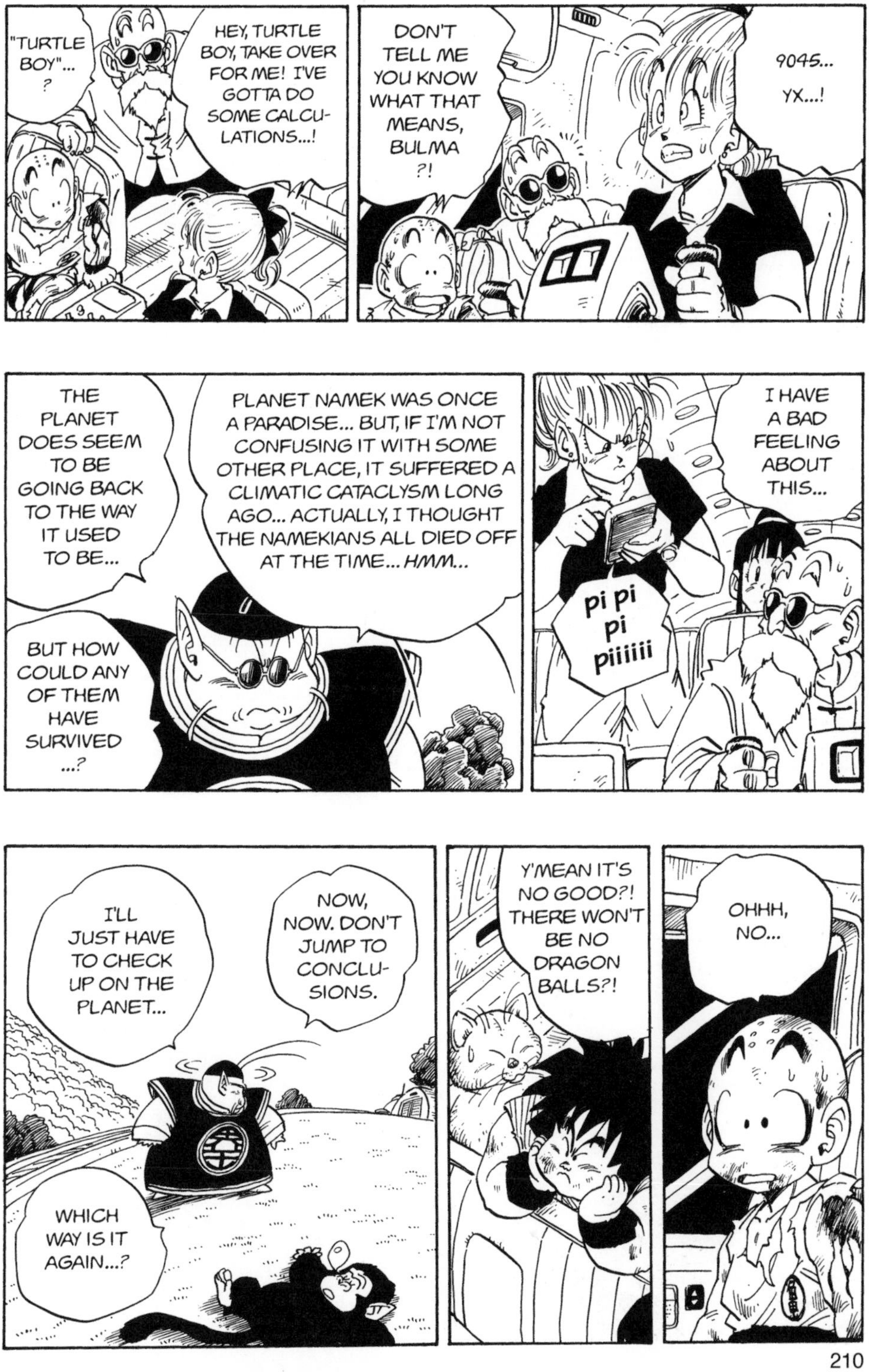
9045...
YX...!
DON'T TELL ME YOU KNOW WHAT THAT MEANS, BULMA ?!
HEY, TURTLE BOY, TAKE OVER FOR ME! I'VE GOTTA DO SOME CALCU-LATIONS...!
"TURTLE BOY"... ?
I HAVE A BAD FEELING ABOUT THIS...
pi pi pi piiiiii
PLANET NAMEK WAS ONCE A PARADISE... BUT, IF I'M NOT CONFUSING IT WITH SOME OTHER PLACE, IT SUFFERED A CLIMATIC CATACLYSM LONG AGO... ACTUALLY, I THOUGHT THE NAMEKIANS ALL DIED OFF AT THE TIME... HMM...
THE PLANET DOES SEEM TO BE GOING BACK TO THE WAY IT USED TO BE...
BUT HOW COULD ANY OF THEM HAVE SURVIVED ...?
OHHH, NO...
Y'MEAN IT'S NO GOOD?! THERE WON'T BE NO DRAGON BALLS?!
NOW, NOW. DON'T JUMP TO CONCLU-SIONS.
I'LL JUST HAVE TO CHECK UP ON THE PLANET...
WHICH WAY IS IT AGAIN...?

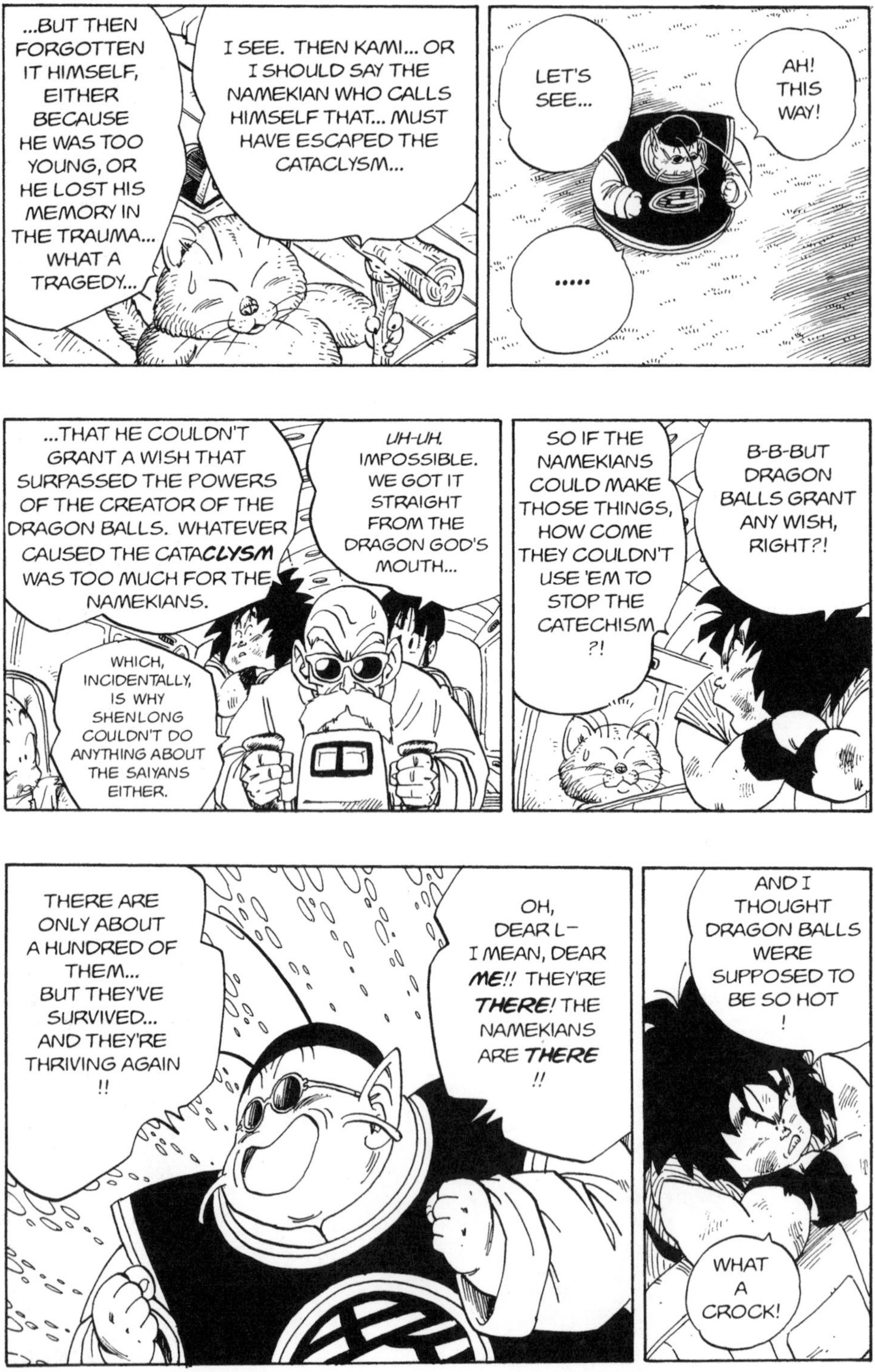
AH! THIS WAY!
LET'S SEE...
.....
I SEE. THEN KAMI... OR I SHOULD SAY THE NAMEKIAN WHO CALLS HIMSELF THAT... MUST HAVE ESCAPED THE CATACLYSM...
...BUT THEN FORGOTTEN IT HIMSELF, EITHER BECAUSE HE WAS TOO YOUNG, OR HE LOST HIS MEMORY IN THE TRAUMA... WHAT A TRAGEDY...
B-B-BUT DRAGON BALLS GRANT ANY WISH, RIGHT?!
SO IF THE NAMEKIANS COULD MAKE THOSE THINGS, HOW COME THEY COULDN'T USE 'EM TO STOP THE CATECHISM ?!
UH-UH. IMPOSSIBLE. WE GOT IT STRAIGHT FROM THE DRAGON GOD'S MOUTH...
...THAT HE COULDN'T GRANT A WISH THAT SURPASSED THE POWERS OF THE CREATOR OF THE DRAGON BALLS. WHATEVER CAUSED THE CATACLYSM WAS TOO MUCH FOR THE NAMEKIANS.
WHICH, INCIDENTALLY, IS WHY SHENLONG COULDN'T DO ANYTHING ABOUT THE SAIYANS EITHER.
AND I THOUGHT DRAGON BALLS WERE SUPPOSED TO BE SO HOT !
WHAT A CROCK!
OH, DEAR L— I MEAN, DEAR ME!! THEY'RE THERE! THE NAMEKIANS ARE THERE !!
THERE ARE ONLY ABOUT A HUNDRED OF THEM... BUT THEY'VE SURVIVED... AND THEY'RE THRIVING AGAIN !!

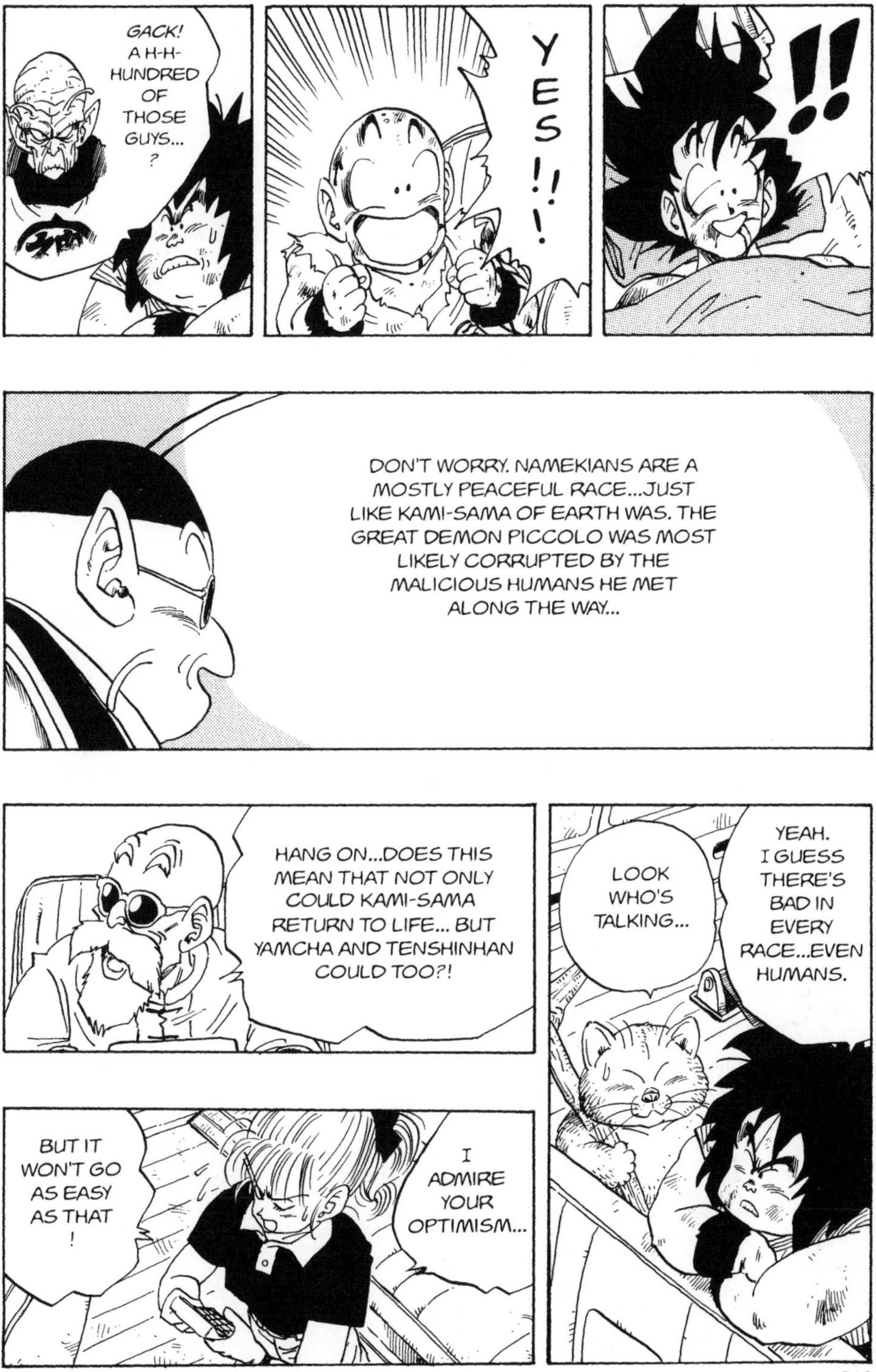
!!
YES!!!
GACK! A H-H-HUNDRED OF THOSE GUYS...?
DON'T WORRY. NAMEKIANS ARE A MOSTLY PEACEFUL RACE...JUST LIKE KAMI-SAMA OF EARTH WAS. THE GREAT DEMON PICCOLO WAS MOST LIKELY CORRUPTED BY THE MALICIOUS HUMANS HE MET ALONG THE WAY...
YEAH. I GUESS THERE'S BAD IN EVERY RACE...EVEN HUMANS.
LOOK WHO'S TALKING...
HANG ON...DOES THIS MEAN THAT NOT ONLY COULD KAMI-SAMA RETURN TO LIFE... BUT YAMCHA AND TENSHINHAN COULD TOO?!
I ADMIRE YOUR OPTIMISM...
BUT IT WON'T GO AS EASY AS THAT!

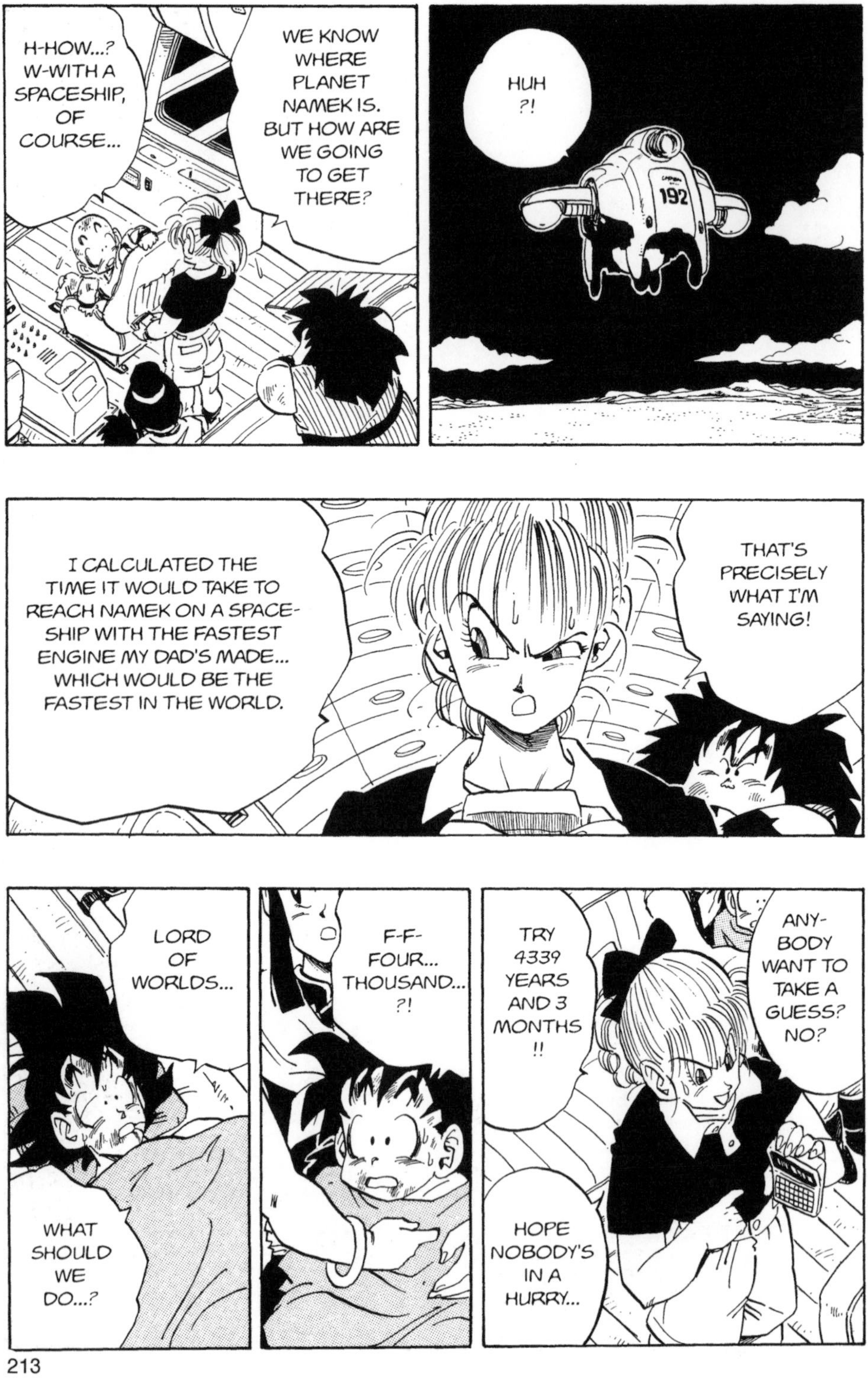

HUH ?!
WE KNOW WHERE PLANET NAMEK IS. BUT HOW ARE WE GOING TO GET THERE?
H-HOW...? W-WITH A SPACESHIP, OF COURSE...
THAT'S PRECISELY WHAT I'M SAYING!
I CALCULATED THE TIME IT WOULD TAKE TO REACH NAMEK ON A SPACE-SHIP WITH THE FASTEST ENGINE MY DAD'S MADE... WHICH WOULD BE THE FASTEST IN THE WORLD.
ANY-BODY WANT TO TAKE A GUESS? NO?
TRY 4339 YEARS AND 3 MONTHS !!
HOPE NOBODY'S IN A HURRY...
F-F-FOUR... THOUSAND... ?!
LORD OF WORLDS...
WHAT SHOULD WE DO...?

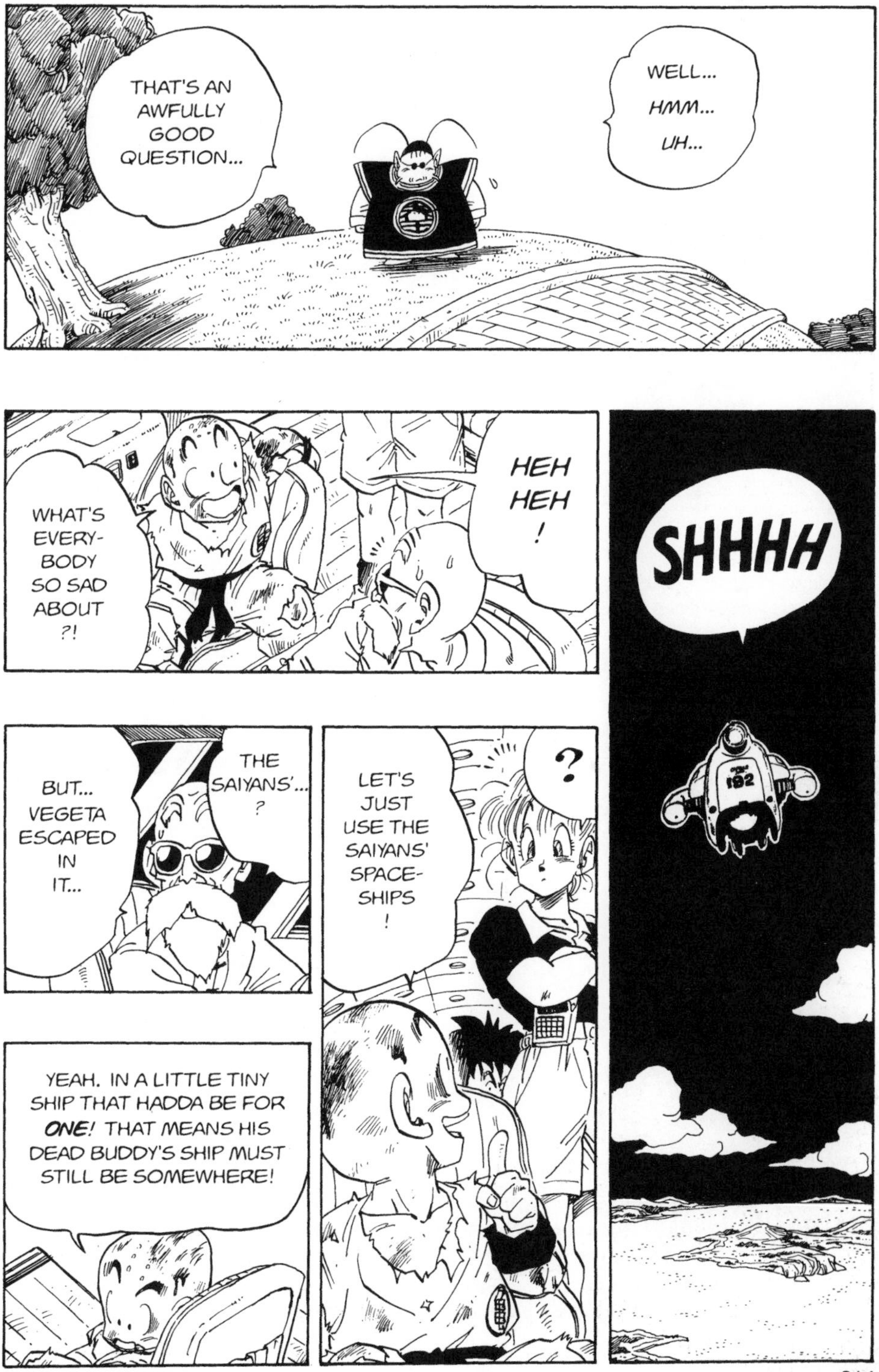
WELL... HMM... UH...
THAT'S AN AWFULLY GOOD QUESTION...
SHHHH
HEH HEH!
WHAT'S EVERYBODY SO SAD ABOUT?!
?
LET'S JUST USE THE SAIYANS' SPACESHIPS!
THE SAIYANS'...?
BUT... VEGETA ESCAPED IN IT...
YEAH. IN A LITTLE TINY SHIP THAT HADDA BE FOR *ONE!* THAT MEANS HIS DEAD BUDDY'S SHIP MUST STILL BE SOMEWHERE!

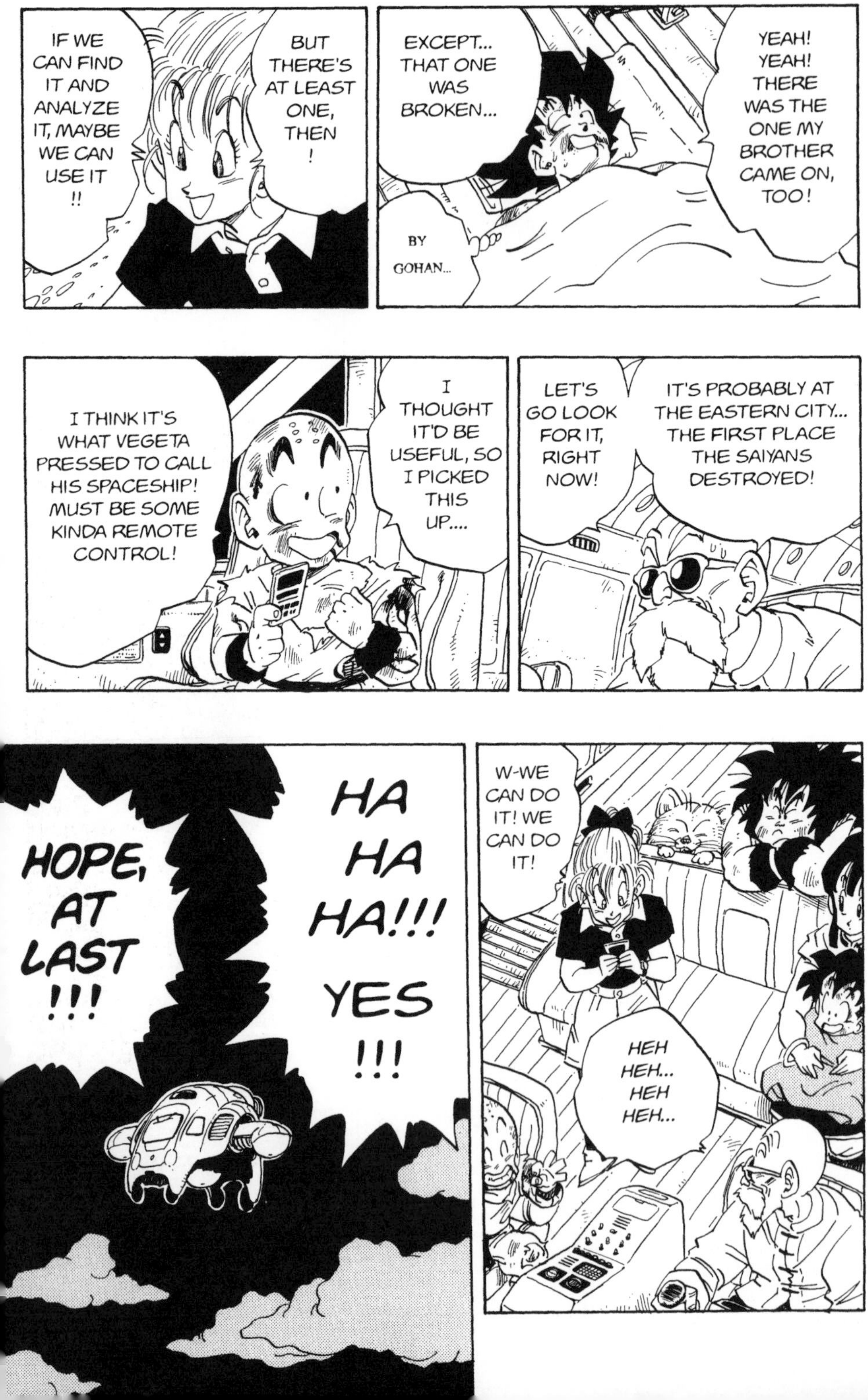
YEAH! YEAH! THERE WAS THE ONE MY BROTHER CAME ON, TOO!
EXCEPT... THAT ONE WAS BROKEN...
BY GOHAN...
BUT THERE'S AT LEAST ONE, THEN!
IF WE CAN FIND IT AND ANALYZE IT, MAYBE WE CAN USE IT!!
IT'S PROBABLY AT THE EASTERN CITY... THE FIRST PLACE THE SAIYANS DESTROYED!
LET'S GO LOOK FOR IT, RIGHT NOW!
I THOUGHT IT'D BE USEFUL, SO I PICKED THIS UP....
I THINK IT'S WHAT VEGETA PRESSED TO CALL HIS SPACESHIP! MUST BE SOME KINDA REMOTE CONTROL!
W-WE CAN DO IT! WE CAN DO IT!
HEH HEH... HEH HEH...
HA HA HA!!! YES!!!
HOPE, AT LAST!!!

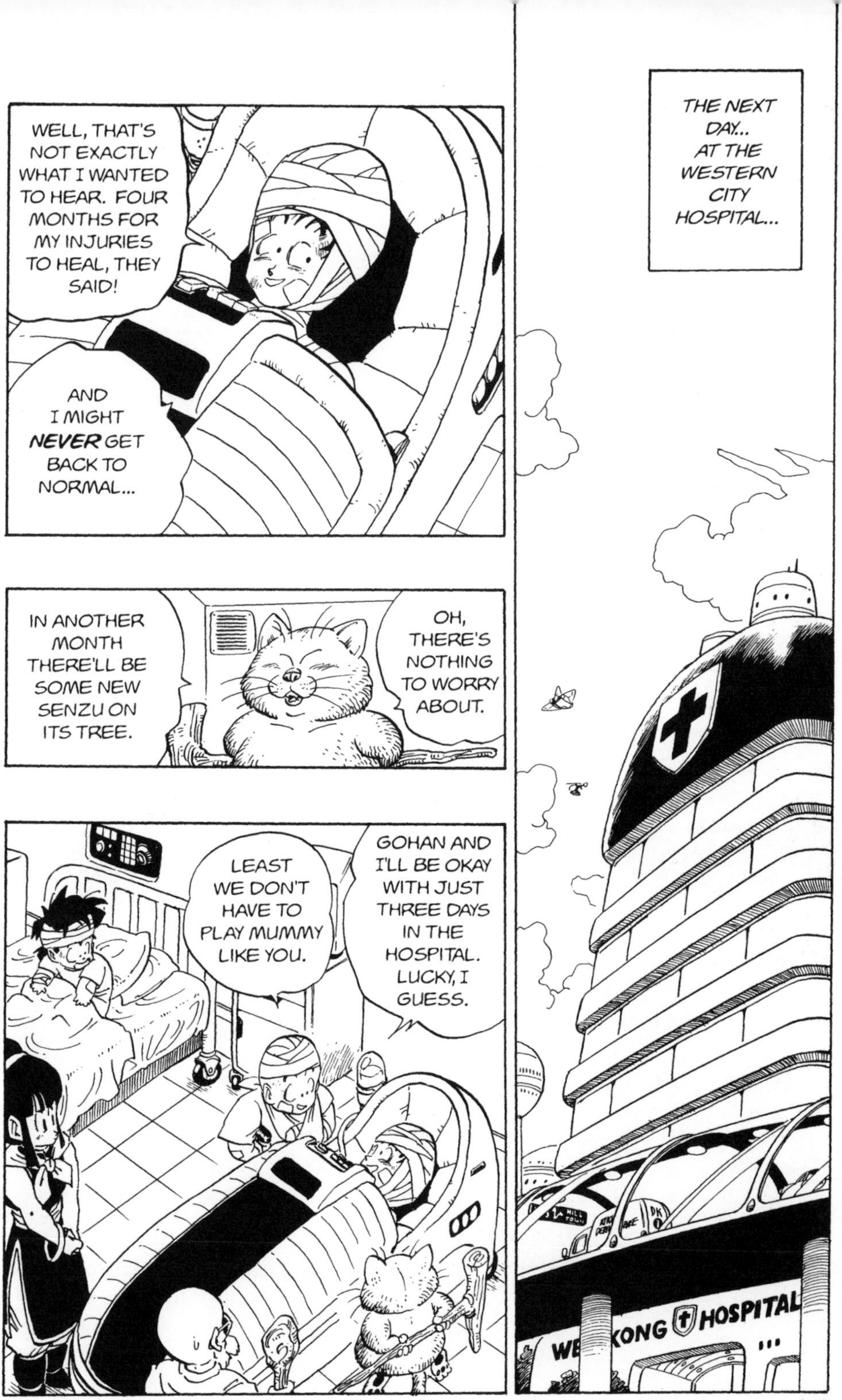
THE NEXT DAY... AT THE WESTERN CITY HOSPITAL...
WELL, THAT'S NOT EXACTLY WHAT I WANTED TO HEAR. FOUR MONTHS FOR MY INJURIES TO HEAL, THEY SAID!
AND I MIGHT ***NEVER*** GET BACK TO NORMAL...
OH, THERE'S NOTHING TO WORRY ABOUT.
IN ANOTHER MONTH THERE'LL BE SOME NEW SENZU ON ITS TREE.
GOHAN AND I'LL BE OKAY WITH JUST THREE DAYS IN THE HOSPITAL. LUCKY, I GUESS.
LEAST WE DON'T HAVE TO PLAY MUMMY LIKE YOU.

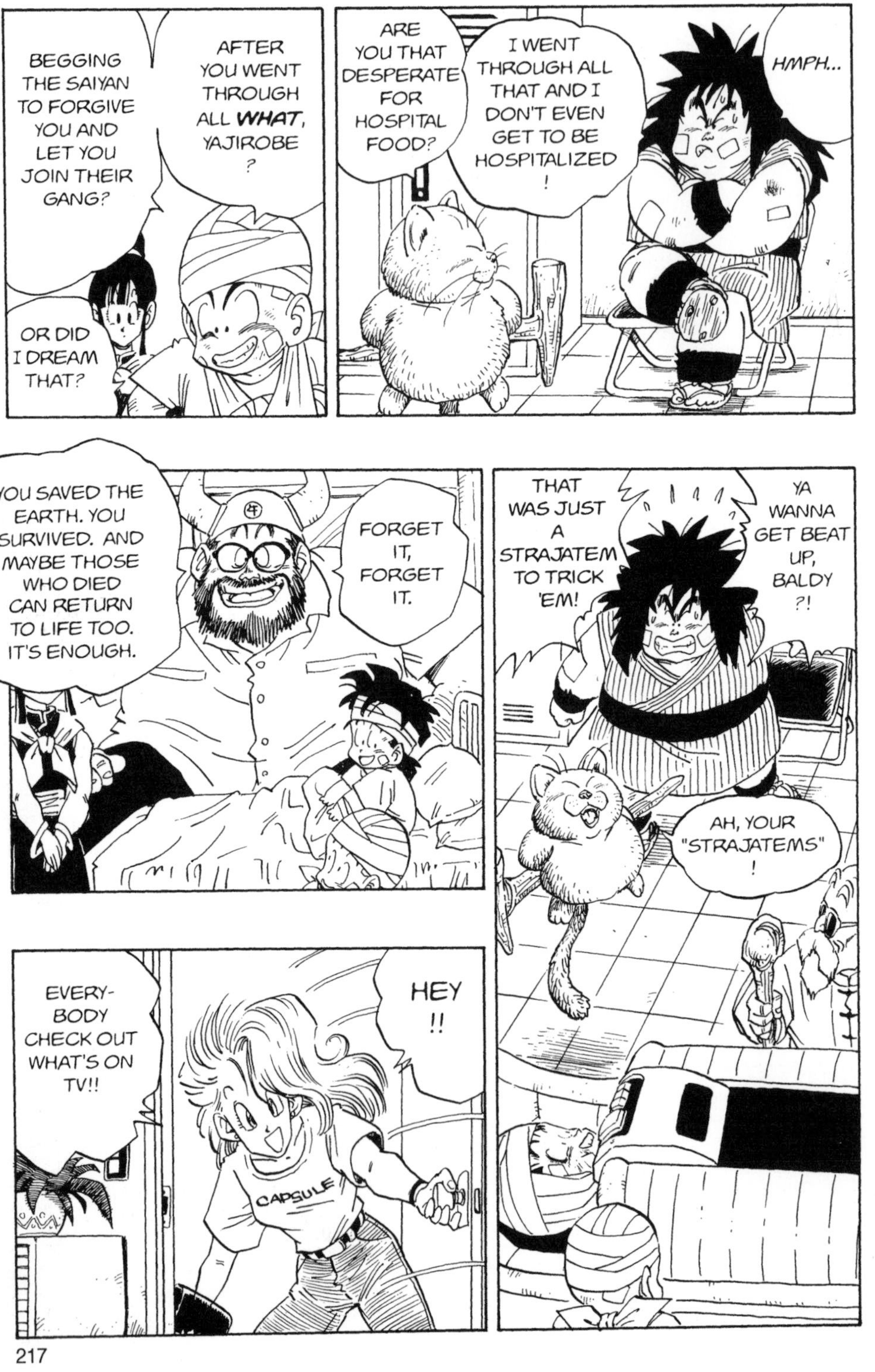
HMPH...
I WENT THROUGH ALL THAT AND I DON'T EVEN GET TO BE HOSPITALIZED!
ARE YOU THAT DESPERATE FOR HOSPITAL FOOD?
AFTER YOU WENT THROUGH ALL **WHAT**, YAJIROBE?
BEGGING THE SAIYAN TO FORGIVE YOU AND LET YOU JOIN THEIR GANG?
OR DID I DREAM THAT?
YA WANNA GET BEAT UP, BALDY?!
THAT WAS JUST A STRAJATEM TO TRICK 'EM!
AH, YOUR "STRAJATEMS"!
FORGET IT, FORGET IT.
YOU SAVED THE EARTH. YOU SURVIVED. AND MAYBE THOSE WHO DIED CAN RETURN TO LIFE TOO. IT'S ENOUGH.
HEY!!
EVERYBODY CHECK OUT WHAT'S ON TV!!
CAPSULE

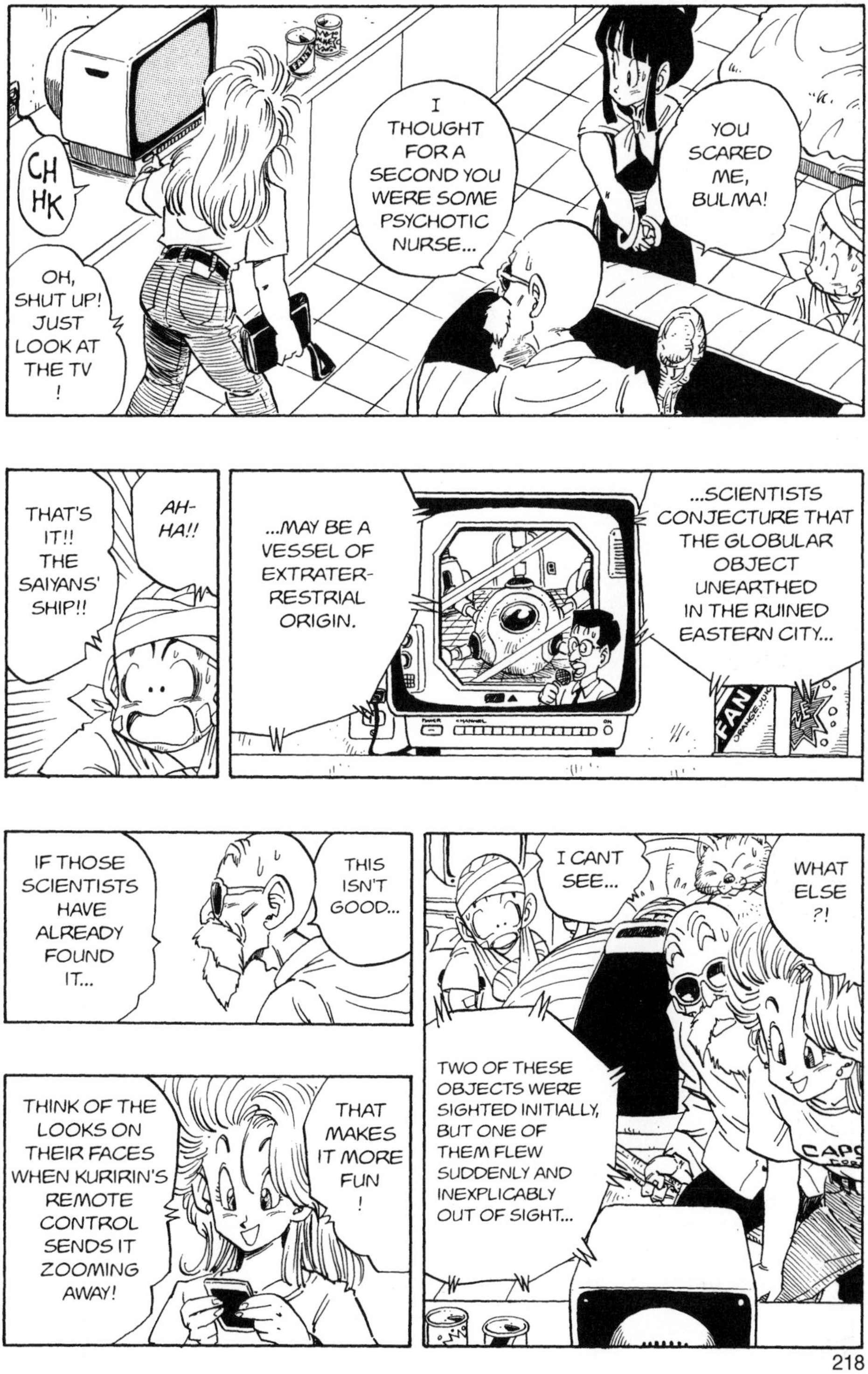
YOU SCARED ME, BULMA!
I THOUGHT FOR A SECOND YOU WERE SOME PSYCHOTIC NURSE...
CH HK
OH, SHUT UP! JUST LOOK AT THE TV!
...SCIENTISTS CONJECTURE THAT THE GLOBULAR OBJECT UNEARTHED IN THE RUINED EASTERN CITY...
...MAY BE A VESSEL OF EXTRATER-RESTRIAL ORIGIN.
AH-HA!!
THAT'S IT!! THE SAIYANS' SHIP!!
WHAT ELSE?!
I CANT SEE...
TWO OF THESE OBJECTS WERE SIGHTED INITIALLY, BUT ONE OF THEM FLEW SUDDENLY AND INEXPLICABLY OUT OF SIGHT...
THIS ISN'T GOOD...
IF THOSE SCIENTISTS HAVE ALREADY FOUND IT...
THAT MAKES IT MORE FUN!
THINK OF THE LOOKS ON THEIR FACES WHEN KURIRIN'S REMOTE CONTROL SENDS IT ZOOMING AWAY!

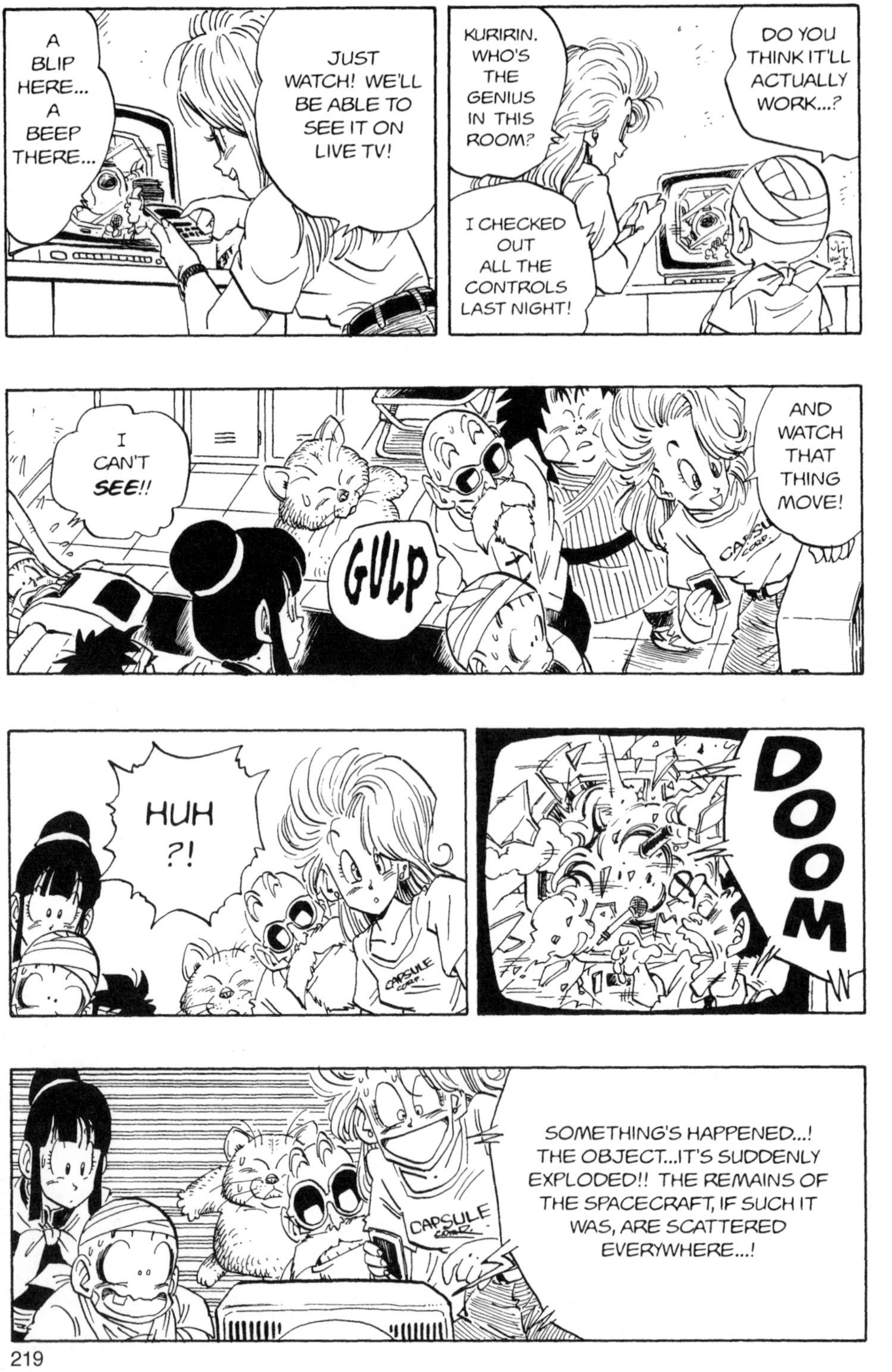
DO YOU THINK IT'LL ACTUALLY WORK...?
KURIRIN. WHO'S THE GENIUS IN THIS ROOM?
I CHECKED OUT ALL THE CONTROLS LAST NIGHT!
JUST WATCH! WE'LL BE ABLE TO SEE IT ON LIVE TV!
A BLIP HERE... A BEEP THERE...
AND WATCH THAT THING MOVE!
GULP
I CAN'T **SEE**!!
DOOM
HUH ?!
SOMETHING'S HAPPENED...! THE OBJECT...IT'S SUDDENLY EXPLODED!! THE REMAINS OF THE SPACECRAFT, IF SUCH IT WAS, ARE SCATTERED EVERYWHERE...!

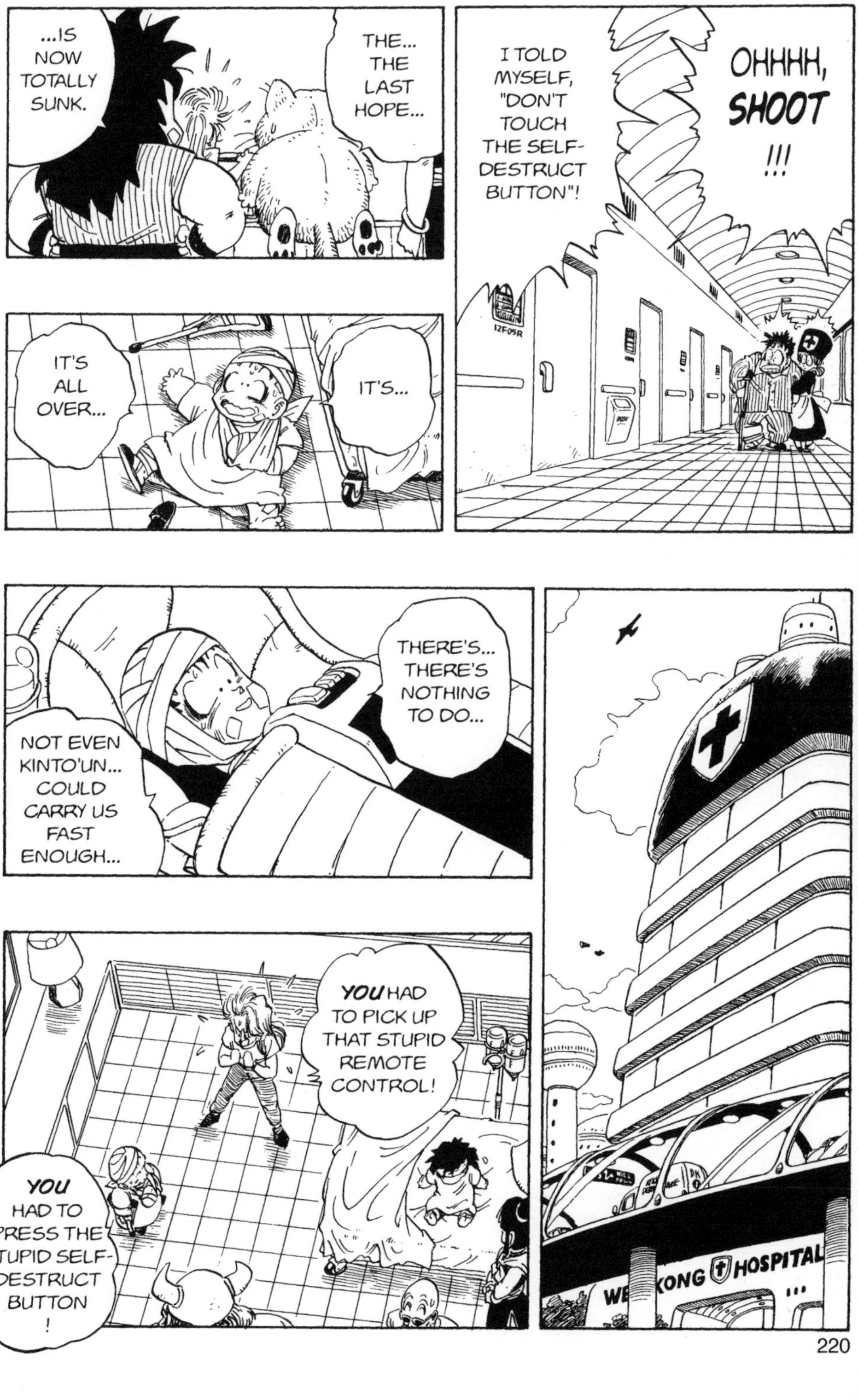
OHHHH, SHOOT !!!
I TOLD MYSELF, "DON'T TOUCH THE SELF-DESTRUCT BUTTON"!
12F05R
THE... THE LAST HOPE...
...IS NOW TOTALLY SUNK.
IT'S...
IT'S ALL OVER...
WE KONG HOSPITAL
...
THERE'S... THERE'S NOTHING TO DO...
NOT EVEN KINTO'UN... COULD CARRY US FAST ENOUGH...
YOU HAD TO PICK UP THAT STUPID REMOTE CONTROL!
YOU HAD TO PRESS THE STUPID SELF-DESTRUCT BUTTON !

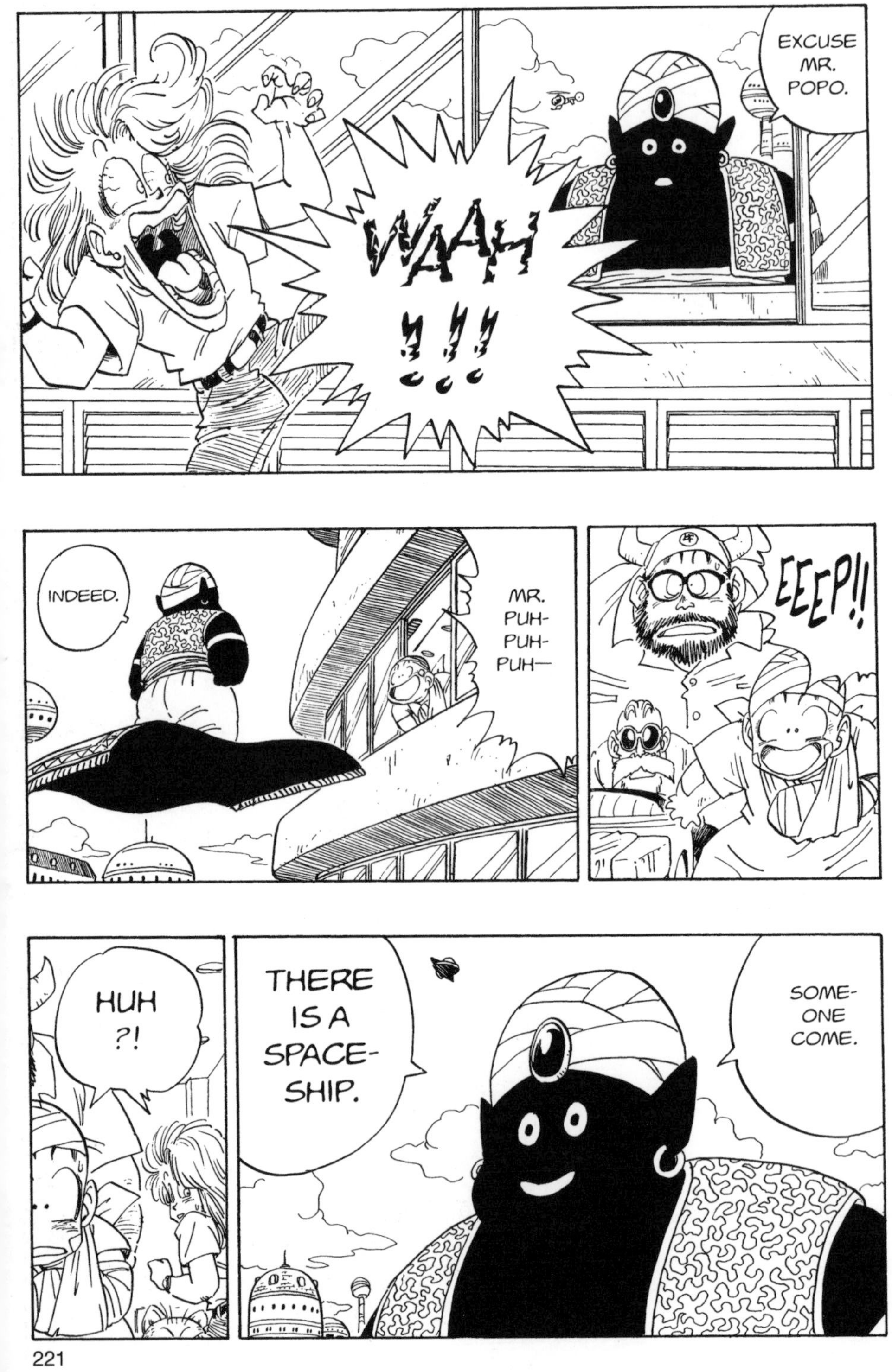
EXCUSE MR. POPO.
WAAH!!!
EEEP!!
MR. PUH-PUH-PUH—
INDEED.
SOME-ONE COME.
THERE IS A SPACE-SHIP.
HUH?!

# DBZ:50 • The Mysterious Spaceship

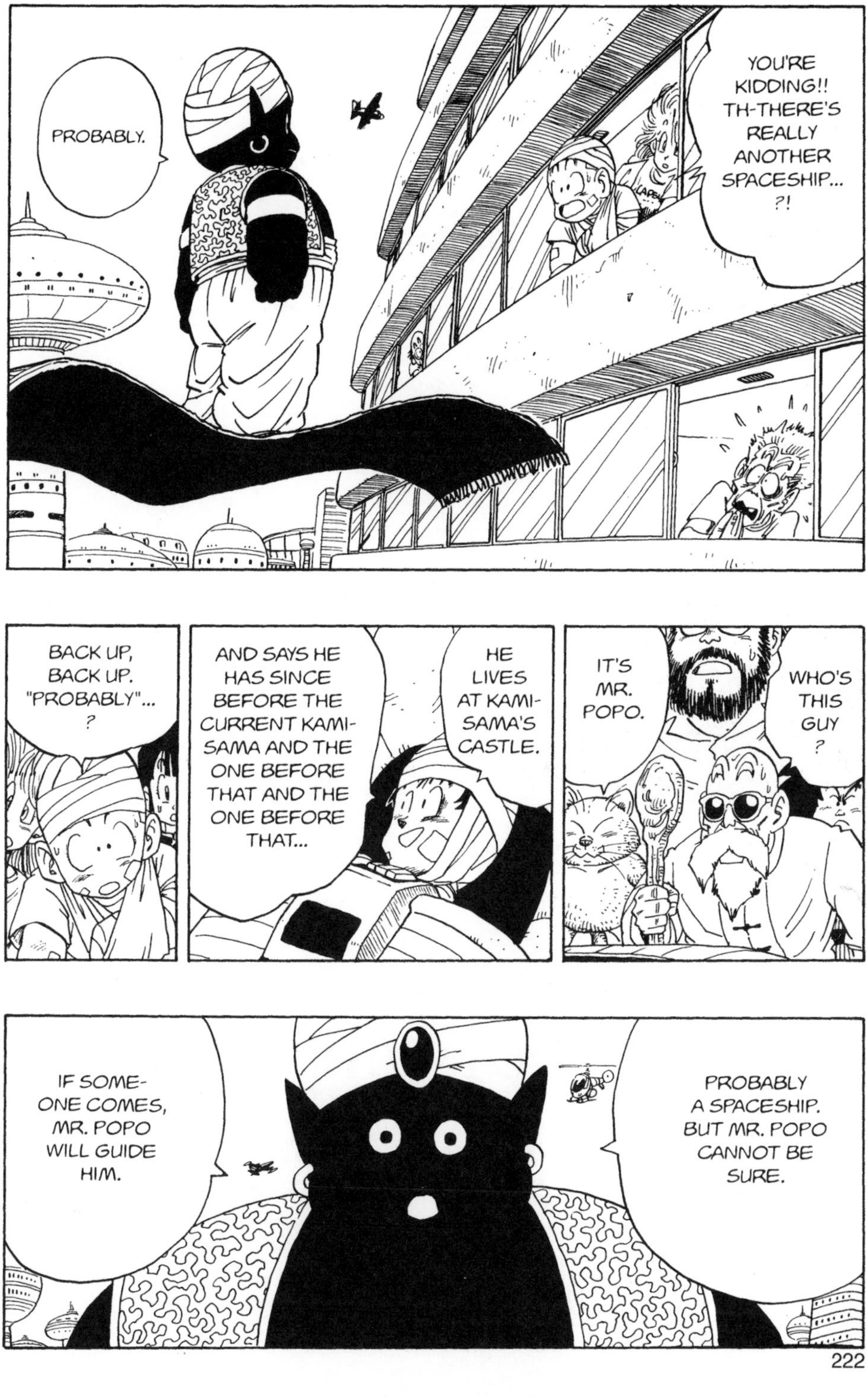
YOU'RE KIDDING!! TH-THERE'S REALLY ANOTHER SPACESHIP... ?!
PROBABLY.
WHO'S THIS GUY ?
IT'S MR. POPO.
HE LIVES AT KAMI-SAMA'S CASTLE.
AND SAYS HE HAS SINCE BEFORE THE CURRENT KAMI-SAMA AND THE ONE BEFORE THAT AND THE ONE BEFORE THAT...
BACK UP, BACK UP. "PROBABLY"... ?
PROBABLY A SPACESHIP. BUT MR. POPO CANNOT BE SURE.
IF SOME-ONE COMES, MR. POPO WILL GUIDE HIM.

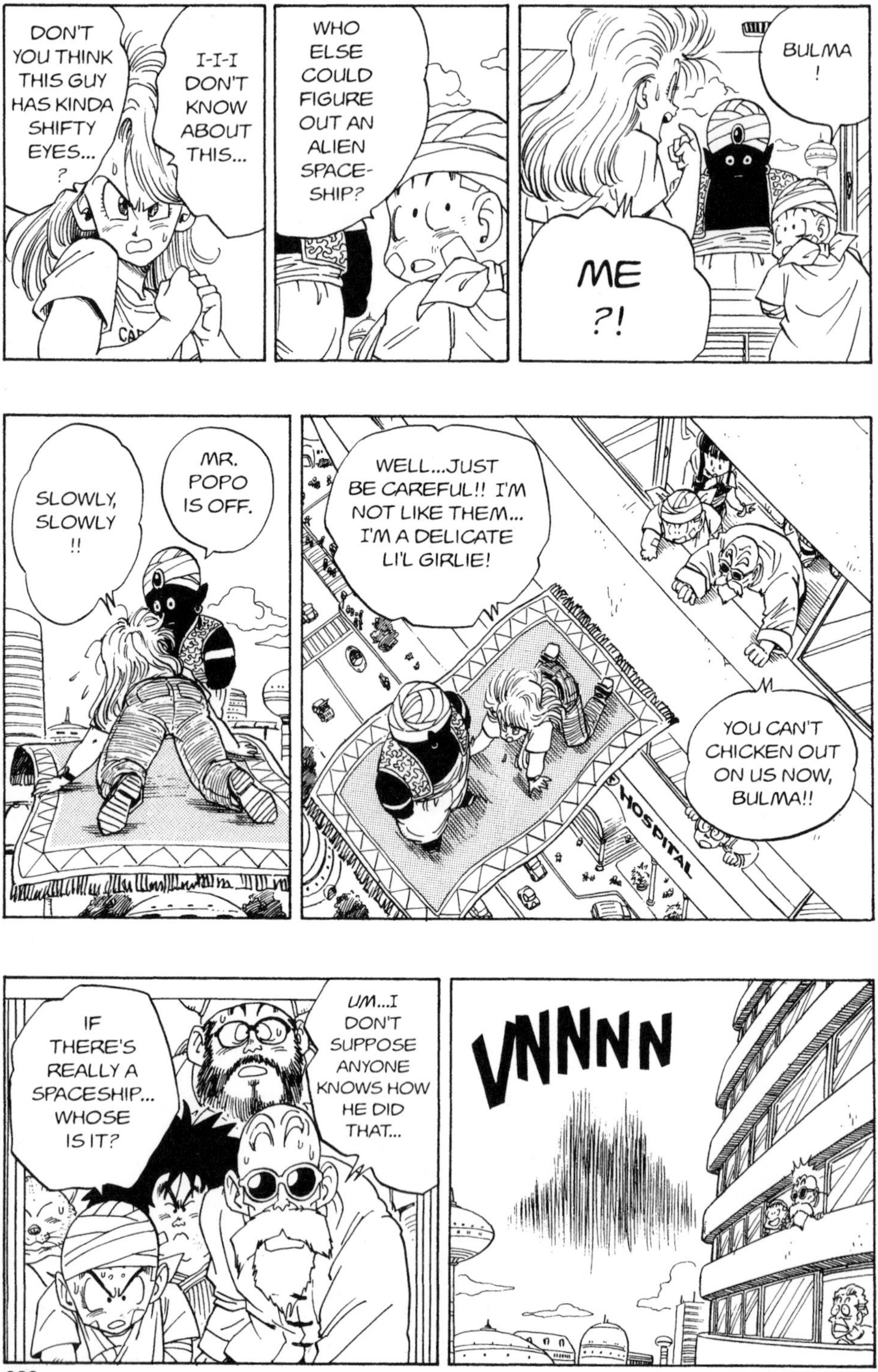

BULMA!
ME ?!
WHO ELSE COULD FIGURE OUT AN ALIEN SPACE-SHIP?
I-I-I DON'T KNOW ABOUT THIS...
DON'T YOU THINK THIS GUY HAS KINDA SHIFTY EYES...?
WELL...JUST BE CAREFUL!! I'M NOT LIKE THEM... I'M A DELICATE LI'L GIRLIE!
HOSPITAL
YOU CAN'T CHICKEN OUT ON US NOW, BULMA!!
MR. POPO IS OFF.
SLOWLY, SLOWLY!!
VNNNN
UM...I DON'T SUPPOSE ANYONE KNOWS HOW HE DID THAT...
IF THERE'S REALLY A SPACESHIP... WHOSE IS IT?

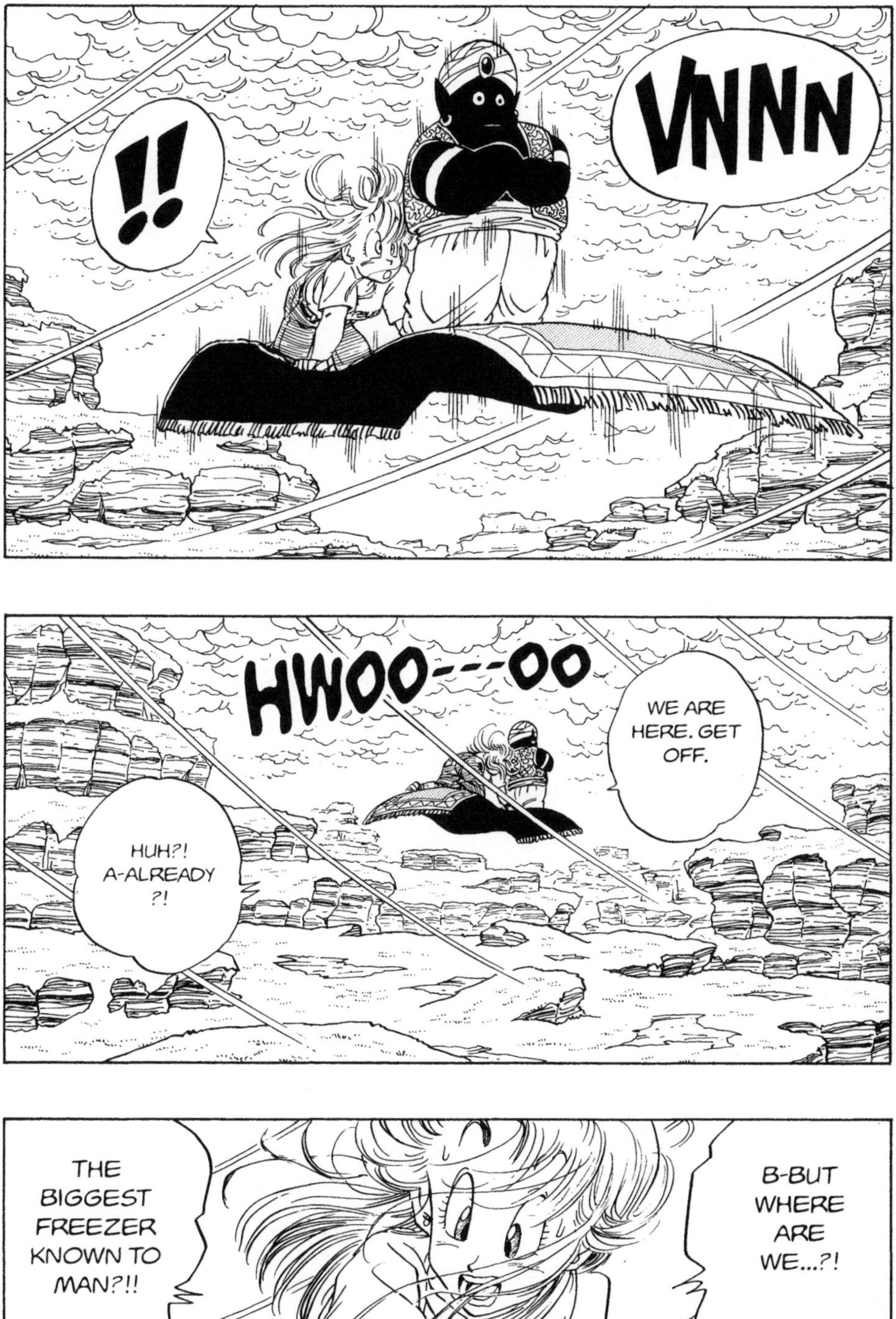
VNNN
!!
HWOO---OO
WE ARE HERE. GET OFF.
HUH?! A-ALREADY ?!
B-BUT WHERE ARE WE...?!
THE BIGGEST FREEZER KNOWN TO MAN?!!

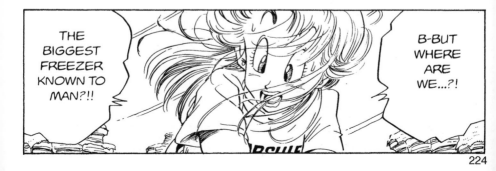

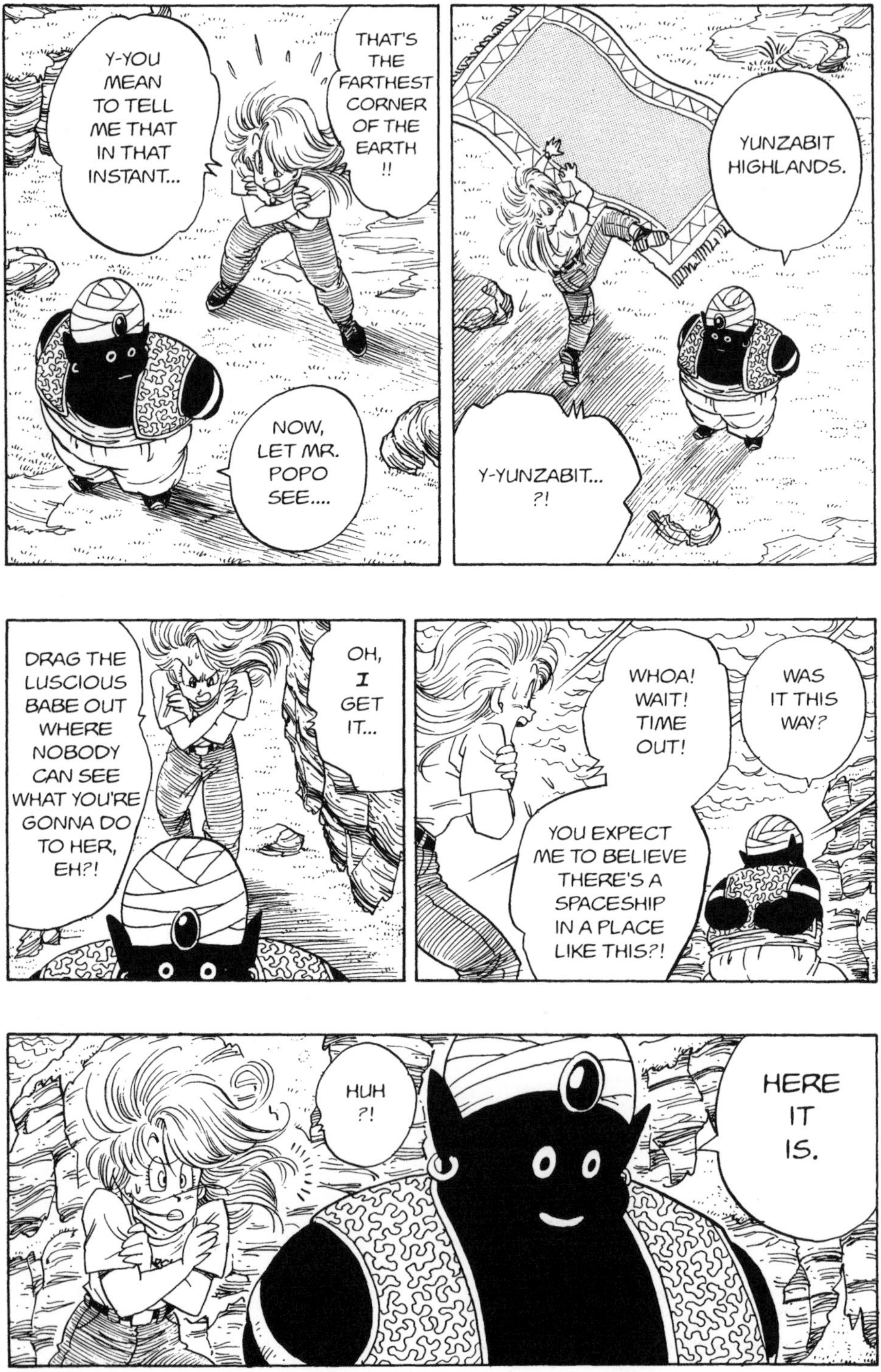
YUNZABIT HIGHLANDS.
Y-YUNZABIT... ?!
THAT'S THE FARTHEST CORNER OF THE EARTH !!
Y-YOU MEAN TO TELL ME THAT IN THAT INSTANT...
NOW, LET MR. POPO SEE....
WAS IT THIS WAY?
WHOA! WAIT! TIME OUT!
YOU EXPECT ME TO BELIEVE THERE'S A SPACESHIP IN A PLACE LIKE THIS?!
OH, I GET IT...
DRAG THE LUSCIOUS BABE OUT WHERE NOBODY CAN SEE WHAT YOU'RE GONNA DO TO HER, EH?!
HERE IT IS.
HUH ?!

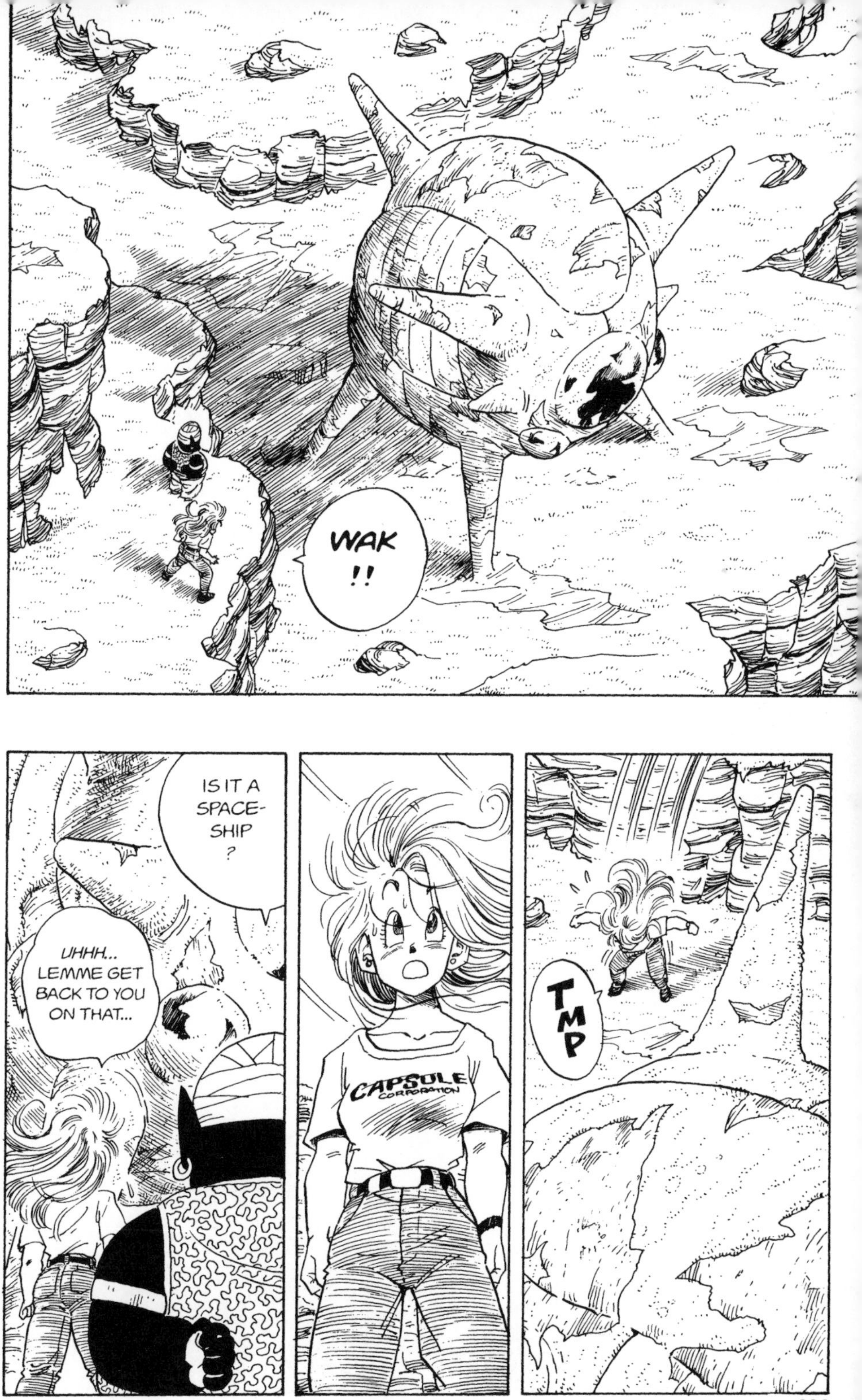
WAK !!
TMP
IS IT A SPACE-SHIP ?
UHHH... LEMME GET BACK TO YOU ON THAT...

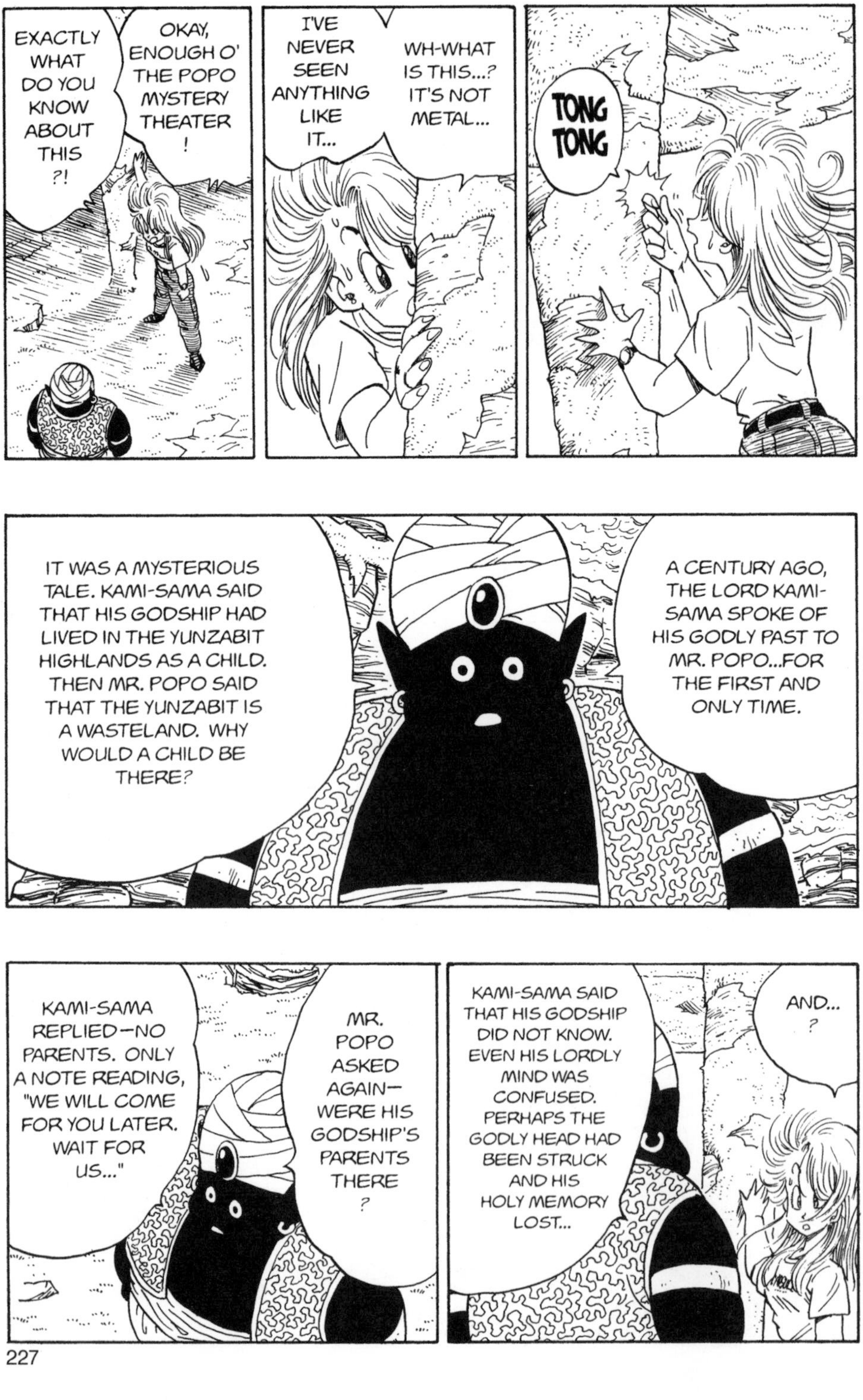
TONG TONG
WH-WHAT IS THIS...? IT'S NOT METAL...
I'VE NEVER SEEN ANYTHING LIKE IT...
OKAY, ENOUGH O' THE POPO MYSTERY THEATER!
EXACTLY WHAT DO YOU KNOW ABOUT THIS?!
A CENTURY AGO, THE LORD KAMI-SAMA SPOKE OF HIS GODLY PAST TO MR. POPO...FOR THE FIRST AND ONLY TIME.
IT WAS A MYSTERIOUS TALE. KAMI-SAMA SAID THAT HIS GODSHIP HAD LIVED IN THE YUNZABIT HIGHLANDS AS A CHILD. THEN MR. POPO SAID THAT THE YUNZABIT IS A WASTELAND. WHY WOULD A CHILD BE THERE?
AND...?
KAMI-SAMA SAID THAT HIS GODSHIP DID NOT KNOW. EVEN HIS LORDLY MIND WAS CONFUSED. PERHAPS THE GODLY HEAD HAD BEEN STRUCK AND HIS HOLY MEMORY LOST...
MR. POPO ASKED AGAIN—WERE HIS GODSHIP'S PARENTS THERE?
KAMI-SAMA REPLIED—NO PARENTS. ONLY A NOTE READING, "WE WILL COME FOR YOU LATER. WAIT FOR US..."

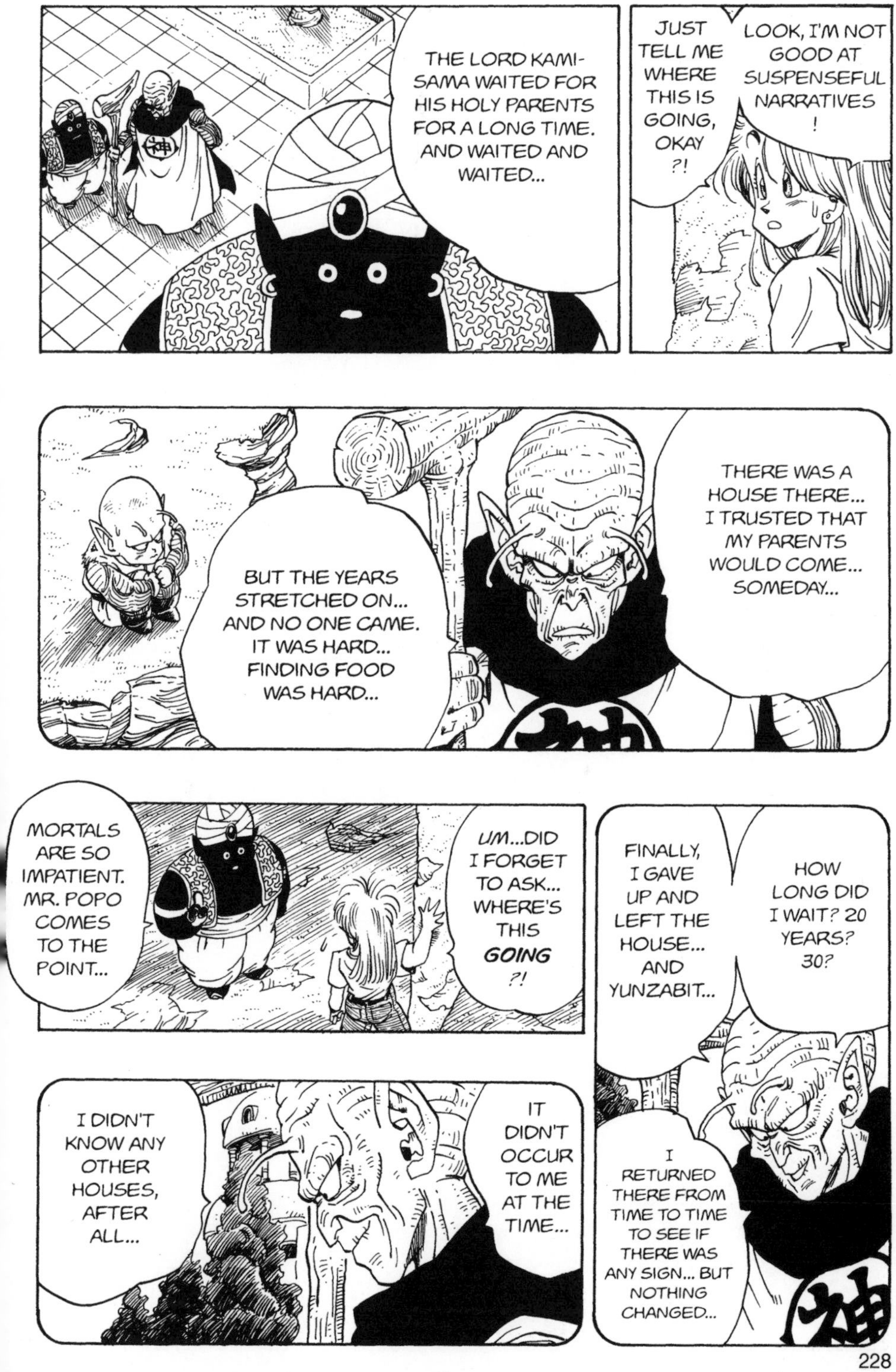
LOOK, I'M NOT GOOD AT SUSPENSEFUL NARRATIVES!
JUST TELL ME WHERE THIS IS GOING, OKAY?!
THE LORD KAMI-SAMA WAITED FOR HIS HOLY PARENTS FOR A LONG TIME. AND WAITED AND WAITED...
THERE WAS A HOUSE THERE... I TRUSTED THAT MY PARENTS WOULD COME... SOMEDAY...
BUT THE YEARS STRETCHED ON... AND NO ONE CAME. IT WAS HARD... FINDING FOOD WAS HARD...
HOW LONG DID I WAIT? 20 YEARS? 30?
FINALLY, I GAVE UP AND LEFT THE HOUSE... AND YUNZABIT...
I RETURNED THERE FROM TIME TO TIME TO SEE IF THERE WAS ANY SIGN... BUT NOTHING CHANGED...
UM...DID I FORGET TO ASK... WHERE'S THIS *GOING*?!
MORTALS ARE SO IMPATIENT. MR. POPO COMES TO THE POINT...
IT DIDN'T OCCUR TO ME AT THE TIME...
I DIDN'T KNOW ANY OTHER HOUSES, AFTER ALL...

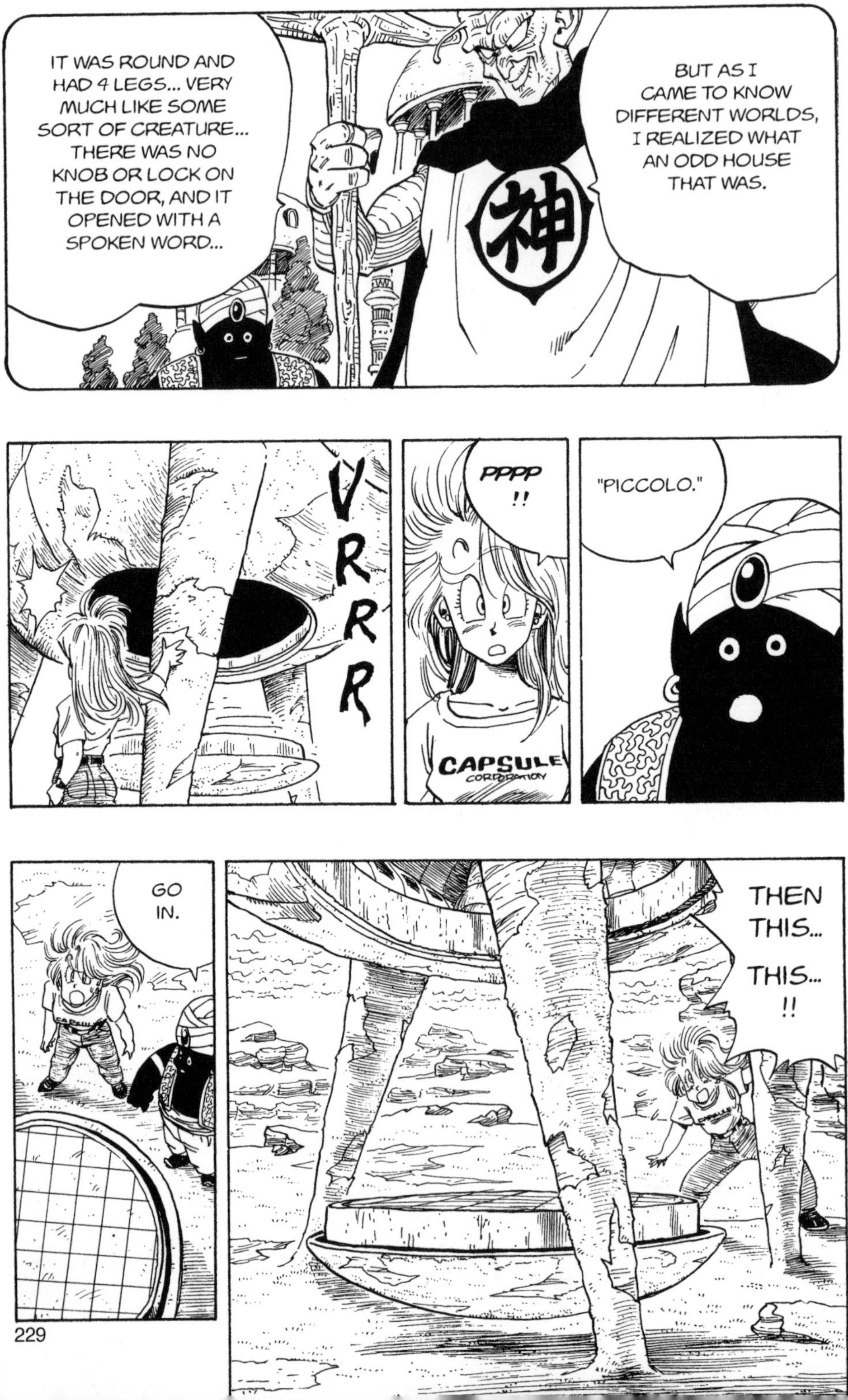
BUT AS I CAME TO KNOW DIFFERENT WORLDS, I REALIZED WHAT AN ODD HOUSE THAT WAS.
IT WAS ROUND AND HAD 4 LEGS... VERY MUCH LIKE SOME SORT OF CREATURE... THERE WAS NO KNOB OR LOCK ON THE DOOR, AND IT OPENED WITH A SPOKEN WORD...
"PICCOLO."
PPPP !!
VRRR
THEN THIS...
THIS... !!
GO IN.

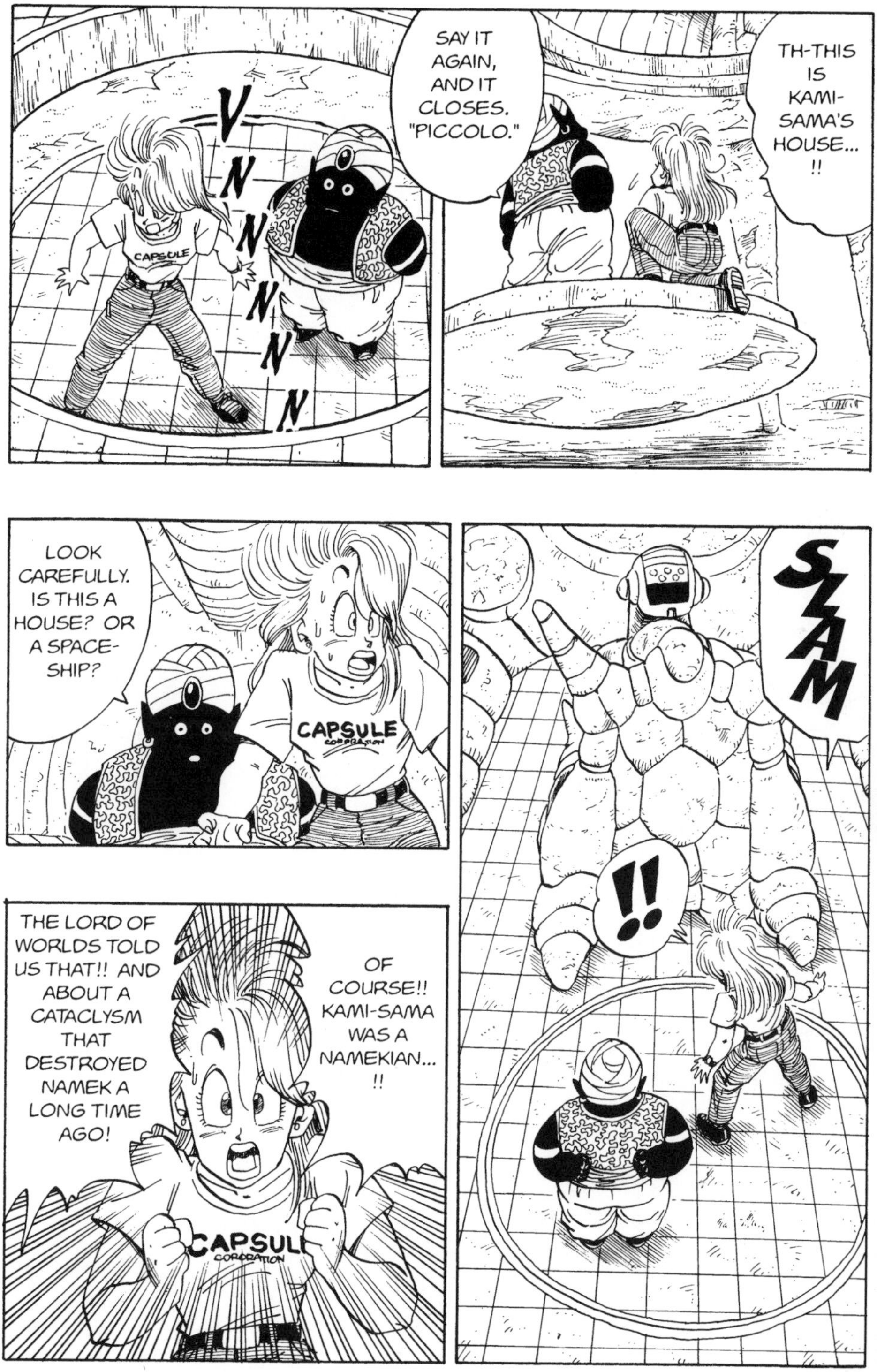

TH-THIS IS KAMI-SAMA'S HOUSE...!!
SAY IT AGAIN, AND IT CLOSES. "PICCOLO."
VNNNNNN
SLAM
!!
LOOK CAREFULLY. IS THIS A HOUSE? OR A SPACE-SHIP?
CAPSULE
OF COURSE!! KAMI-SAMA WAS A NAMEKIAN...!!
THE LORD OF WORLDS TOLD US THAT!! AND ABOUT A CATACLYSM THAT DESTROYED NAMEK A LONG TIME AGO!
CAPSULE CORPORATION

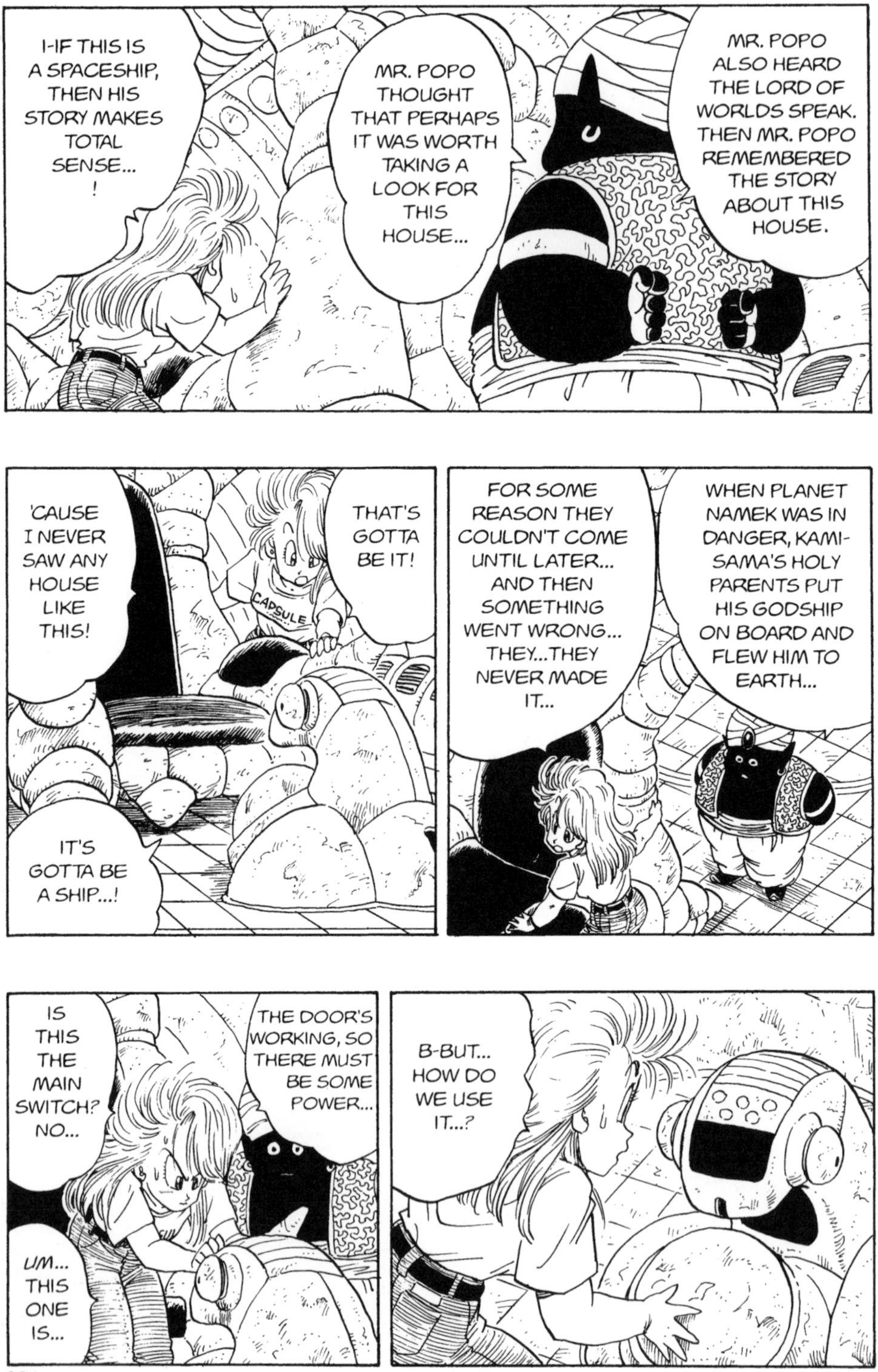
MR. POPO ALSO HEARD THE LORD OF WORLDS SPEAK. THEN MR. POPO REMEMBERED THE STORY ABOUT THIS HOUSE.
MR. POPO THOUGHT THAT PERHAPS IT WAS WORTH TAKING A LOOK FOR THIS HOUSE...
I-IF THIS IS A SPACESHIP, THEN HIS STORY MAKES TOTAL SENSE... !
WHEN PLANET NAMEK WAS IN DANGER, KAMI-SAMA'S HOLY PARENTS PUT HIS GODSHIP ON BOARD AND FLEW HIM TO EARTH...
FOR SOME REASON THEY COULDN'T COME UNTIL LATER... AND THEN SOMETHING WENT WRONG... THEY...THEY NEVER MADE IT...
THAT'S GOTTA BE IT!
'CAUSE I NEVER SAW ANY HOUSE LIKE THIS!
CAPSULE
IT'S GOTTA BE A SHIP...!
B-BUT... HOW DO WE USE IT...?
THE DOOR'S WORKING, SO THERE MUST BE SOME POWER...
IS THIS THE MAIN SWITCH? NO...
UM... THIS ONE IS...

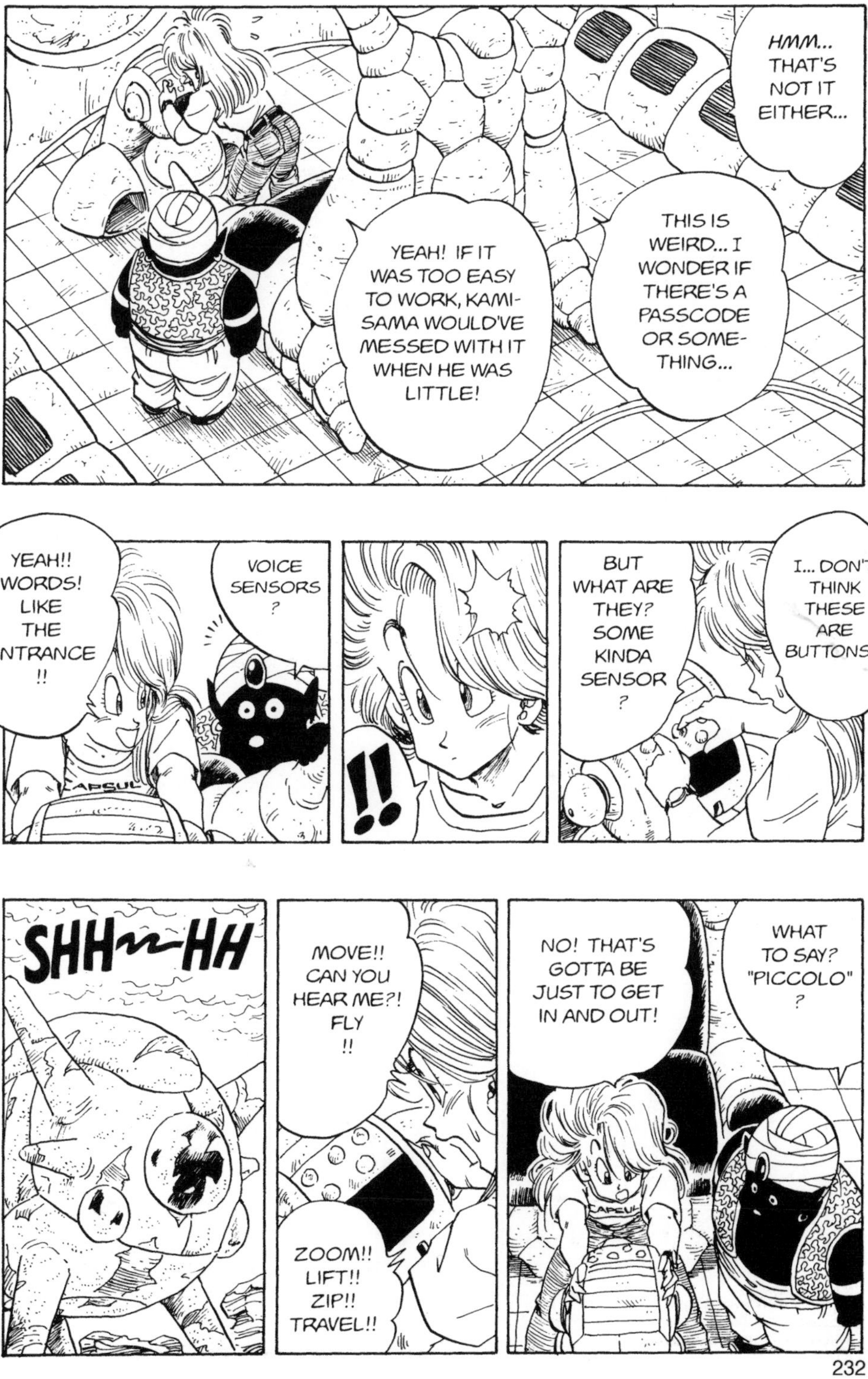
HMM... THAT'S NOT IT EITHER...
THIS IS WEIRD... I WONDER IF THERE'S A PASSCODE OR SOMETHING...
YEAH! IF IT WAS TOO EASY TO WORK, KAMI-SAMA WOULD'VE MESSED WITH IT WHEN HE WAS LITTLE!
I... DON'T THINK THESE ARE BUTTONS...
BUT WHAT ARE THEY? SOME KINDA SENSOR ?
!!
VOICE SENSORS ?
YEAH!! WORDS! LIKE THE ENTRANCE !!
WHAT TO SAY? "PICCOLO" ?
NO! THAT'S GOTTA BE JUST TO GET IN AND OUT!
MOVE!! CAN YOU HEAR ME?! FLY !!
ZOOM!! LIFT!! ZIP!! TRAVEL!!
SHH~HH

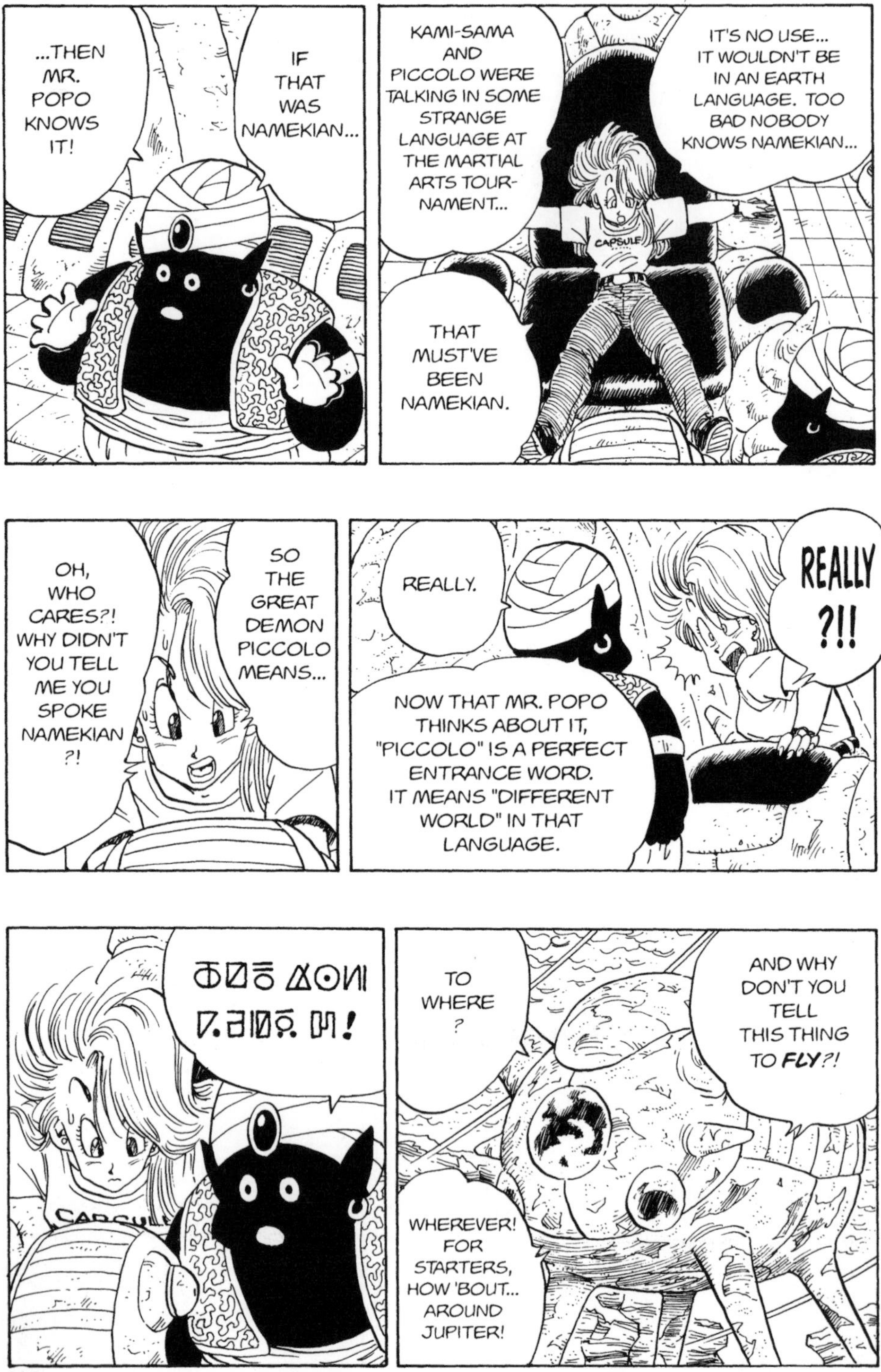
IT'S NO USE... IT WOULDN'T BE IN AN EARTH LANGUAGE. TOO BAD NOBODY KNOWS NAMEKIAN...
KAMI-SAMA AND PICCOLO WERE TALKING IN SOME STRANGE LANGUAGE AT THE MARTIAL ARTS TOURNAMENT...
THAT MUST'VE BEEN NAMEKIAN.
IF THAT WAS NAMEKIAN...
...THEN MR. POPO KNOWS IT!
REALLY ?!!
REALLY.
NOW THAT MR. POPO THINKS ABOUT IT, "PICCOLO" IS A PERFECT ENTRANCE WORD. IT MEANS "DIFFERENT WORLD" IN THAT LANGUAGE.
SO THE GREAT DEMON PICCOLO MEANS...
OH, WHO CARES?! WHY DIDN'T YOU TELL ME YOU SPOKE NAMEKIAN ?!
AND WHY DON'T YOU TELL THIS THING TO FLY?!
TO WHERE ?
WHEREVER! FOR STARTERS, HOW 'BOUT... AROUND JUPITER!

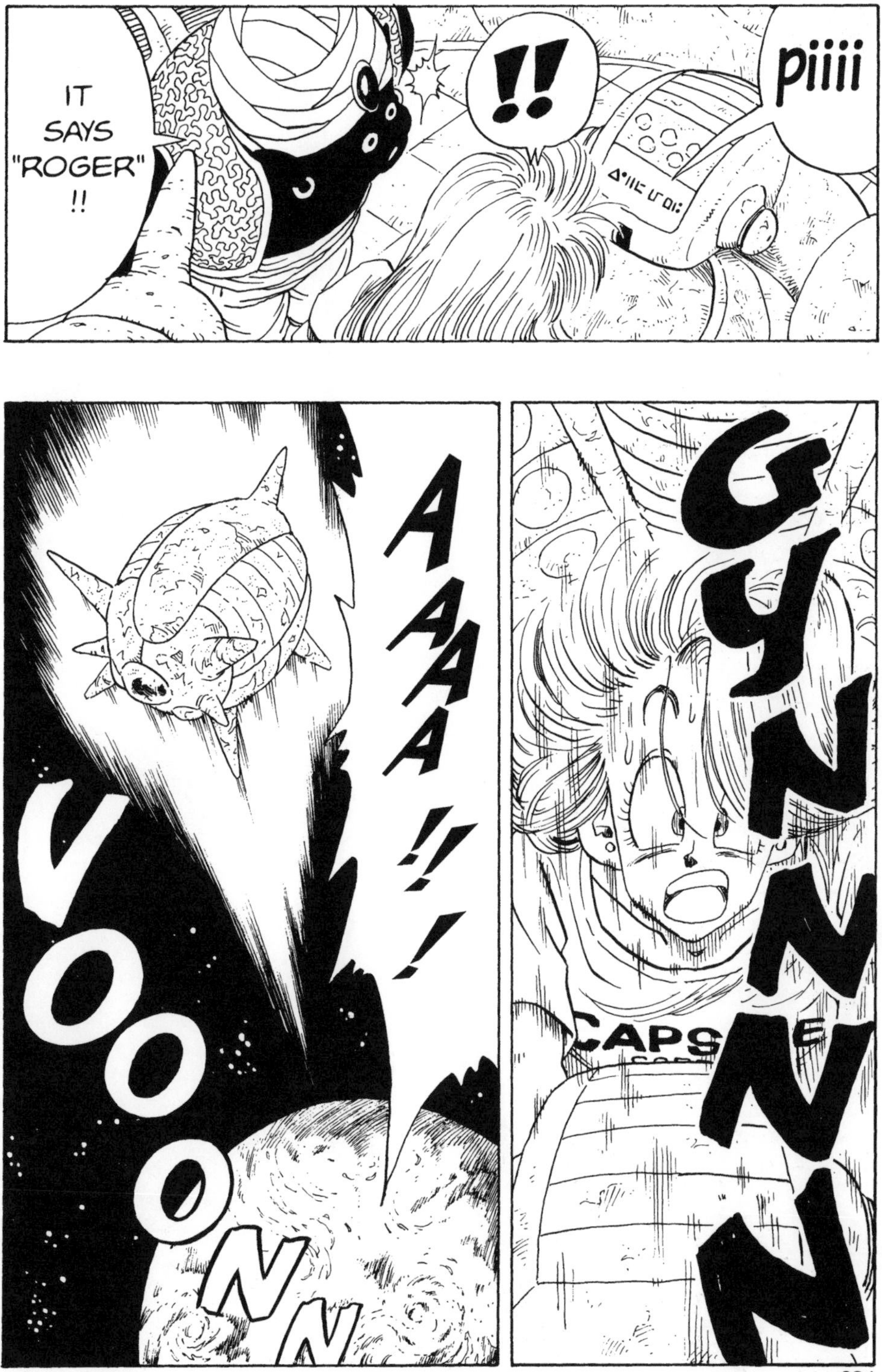
piiii
!!
IT SAYS "ROGER" !!
GYNNNN
CAPS E
AAAA!!!
VOOONN

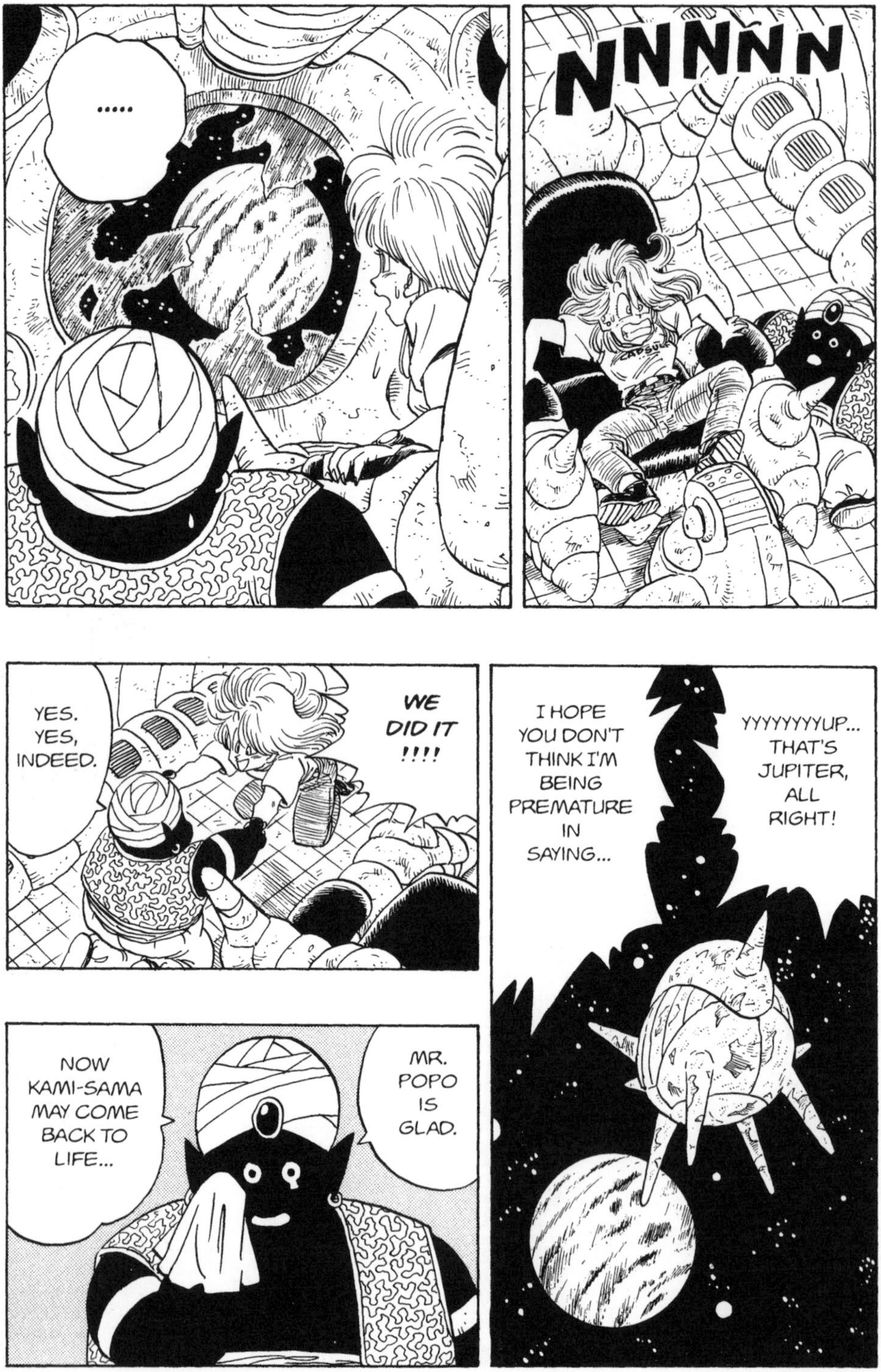
NNNNN
......
YYYYYYYYUP... THAT'S JUPITER, ALL RIGHT!
I HOPE YOU DON'T THINK I'M BEING PREMATURE IN SAYING...
WE DID IT !!!!
YES. YES, INDEED.
MR. POPO IS GLAD.
NOW KAMI-SAMA MAY COME BACK TO LIFE...

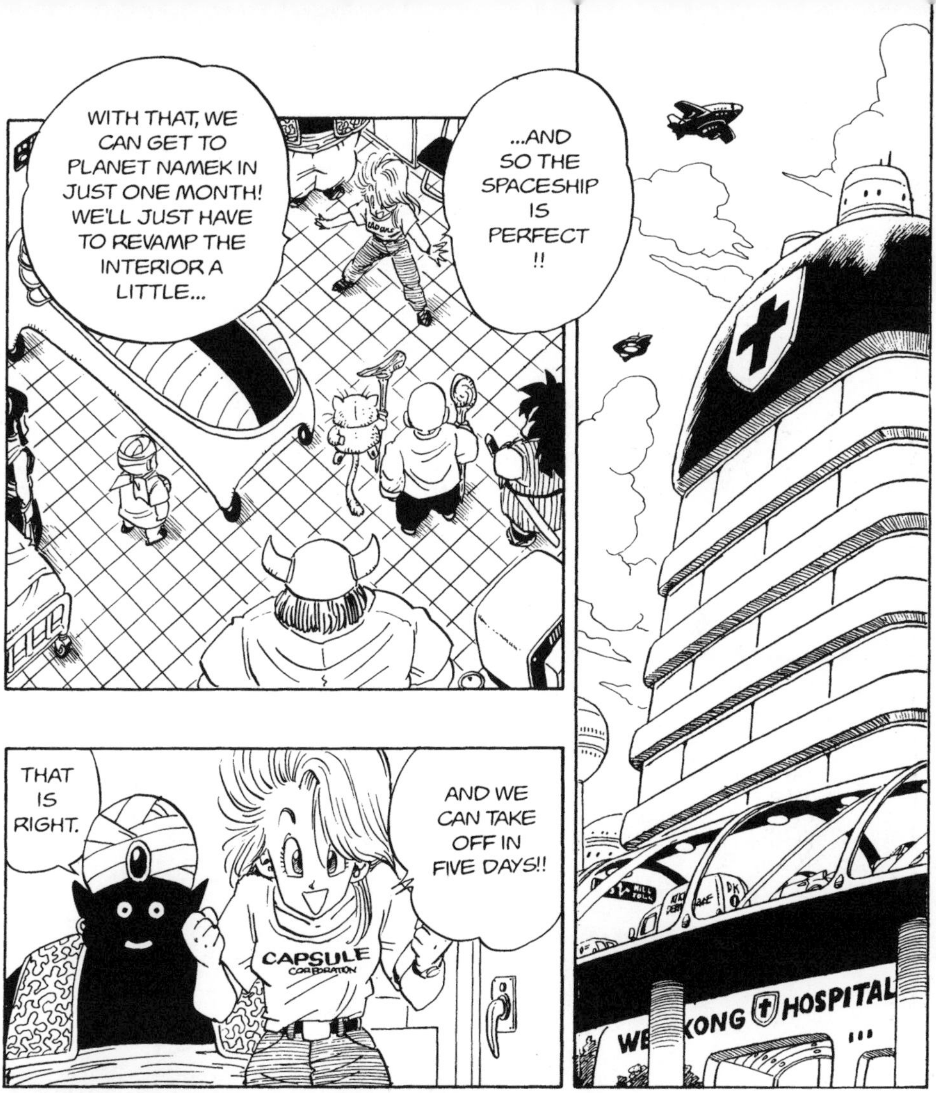
HOSPITAL
...AND SO THE SPACESHIP IS PERFECT!!
WITH THAT, WE CAN GET TO PLANET NAMEK IN JUST ONE MONTH! WE'LL JUST HAVE TO REVAMP THE INTERIOR A LITTLE...
AND WE CAN TAKE OFF IN FIVE DAYS!!
THAT IS RIGHT.
CAPSULE CORPORATION

## DBZ:51 • 3...2...1...Lift Off!

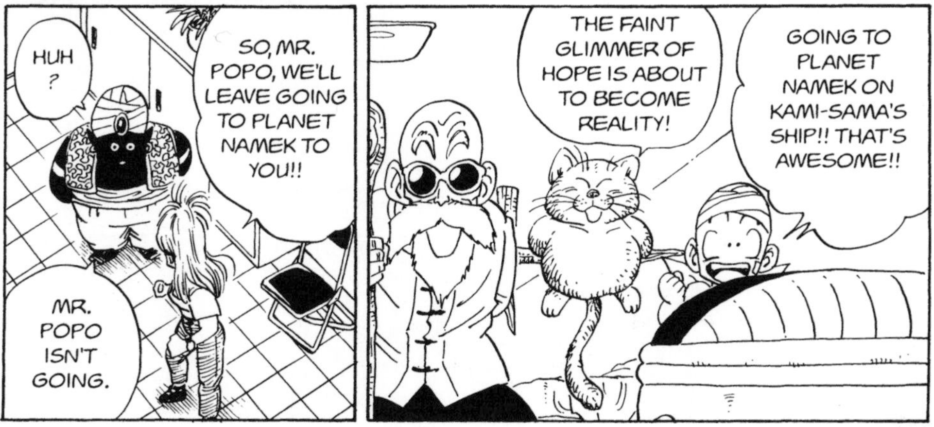
GOING TO PLANET NAMEK ON KAMI-SAMA'S SHIP!! THAT'S AWESOME!!
THE FAINT GLIMMER OF HOPE IS ABOUT TO BECOME REALITY!
SO, MR. POPO, WE'LL LEAVE GOING TO PLANET NAMEK TO YOU!!
HUH ?
MR. POPO ISN'T GOING.

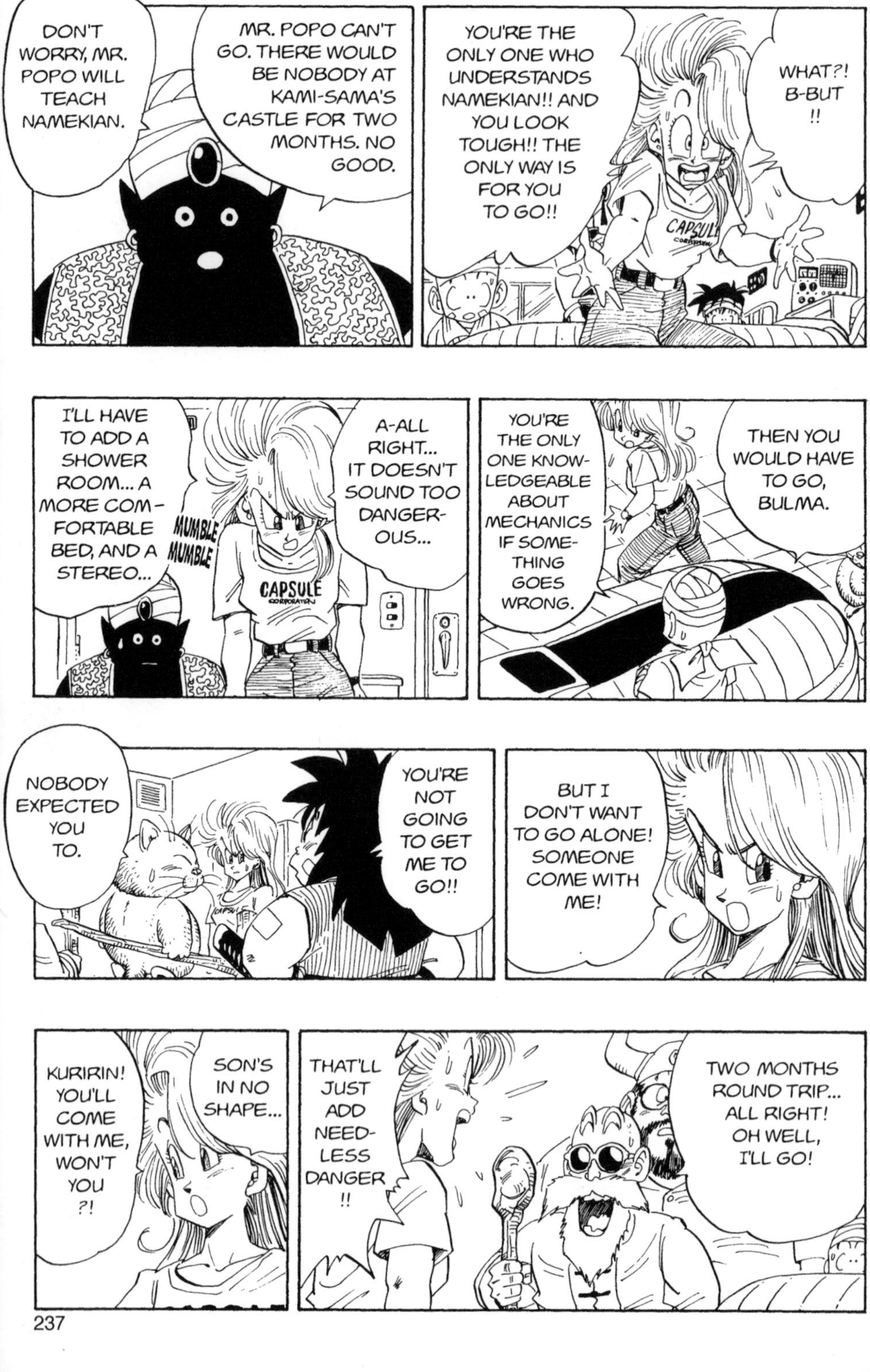
WHAT?! B-BUT !!
YOU'RE THE ONLY ONE WHO UNDERSTANDS NAMEKIAN!! AND YOU LOOK TOUGH!! THE ONLY WAY IS FOR YOU TO GO!!
MR. POPO CAN'T GO. THERE WOULD BE NOBODY AT KAMI-SAMA'S CASTLE FOR TWO MONTHS. NO GOOD.
DON'T WORRY, MR. POPO WILL TEACH NAMEKIAN.
THEN YOU WOULD HAVE TO GO, BULMA.
YOU'RE THE ONLY ONE KNOWLEDGEABLE ABOUT MECHANICS IF SOMETHING GOES WRONG.
A-ALL RIGHT... IT DOESN'T SOUND TOO DANGEROUS...
MUMBLE MUMBLE
I'LL HAVE TO ADD A SHOWER ROOM... A MORE COMFORTABLE BED, AND A STEREO...
BUT I DON'T WANT TO GO ALONE! SOMEONE COME WITH ME!
YOU'RE NOT GOING TO GET ME TO GO!!
NOBODY EXPECTED YOU TO.
TWO MONTHS ROUND TRIP... ALL RIGHT! OH WELL, I'LL GO!
THAT'LL JUST ADD NEEDLESS DANGER !!
SON'S IN NO SHAPE...
KURIRIN! YOU'LL COME WITH ME, WON'T YOU ?!

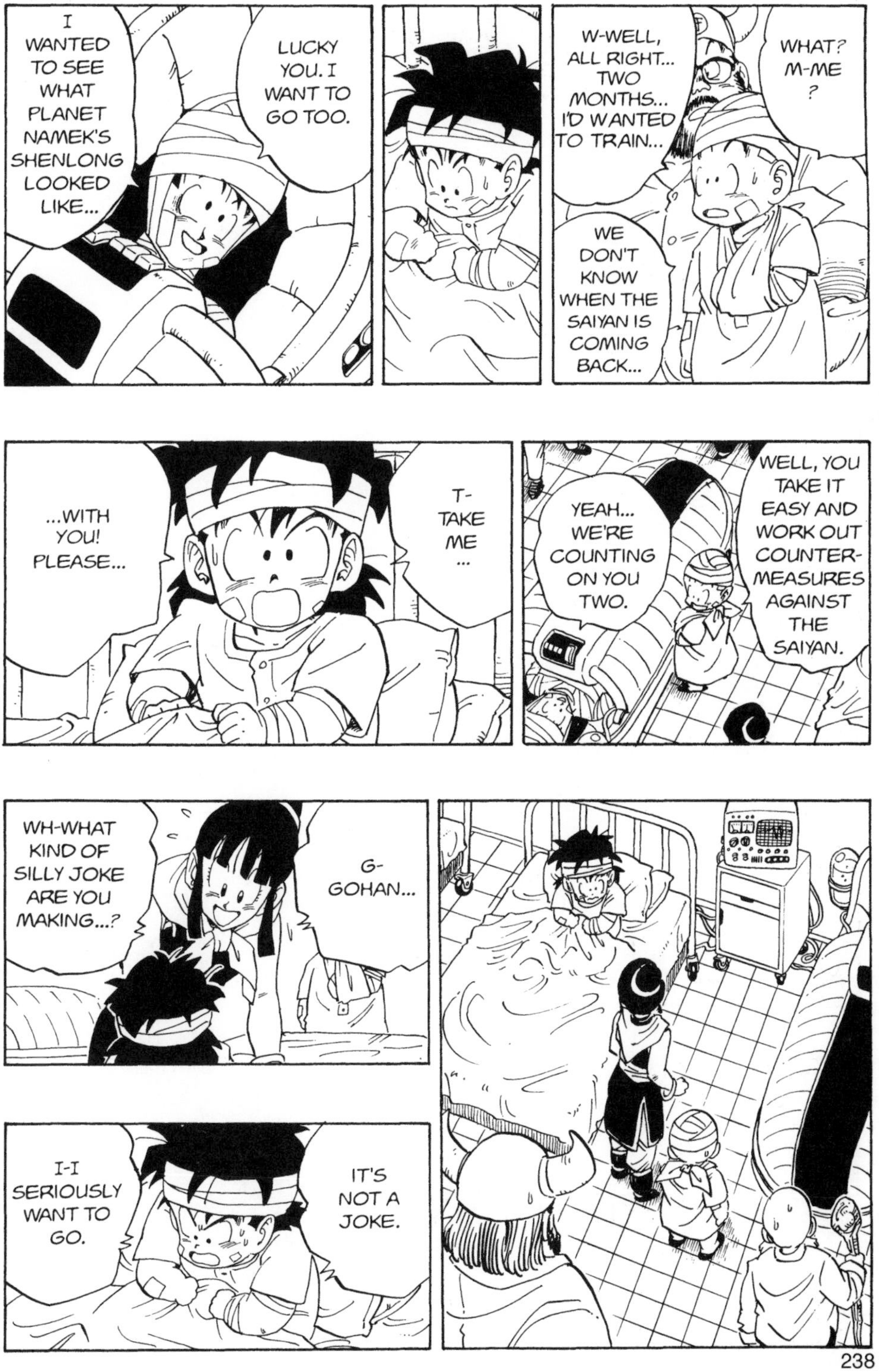
WHAT? M-ME ?
W-WELL, ALL RIGHT... TWO MONTHS... I'D WANTED TO TRAIN...
WE DON'T KNOW WHEN THE SAIYAN IS COMING BACK...
LUCKY YOU. I WANT TO GO TOO.
I WANTED TO SEE WHAT PLANET NAMEK'S SHENLONG LOOKED LIKE...
WELL, YOU TAKE IT EASY AND WORK OUT COUNTER-MEASURES AGAINST THE SAIYAN.
YEAH... WE'RE COUNTING ON YOU TWO.
T- TAKE ME ...
...WITH YOU! PLEASE...
G- GOHAN...
WH-WHAT KIND OF SILLY JOKE ARE YOU MAKING...?
IT'S NOT A JOKE.
I-I SERIOUSLY WANT TO GO.

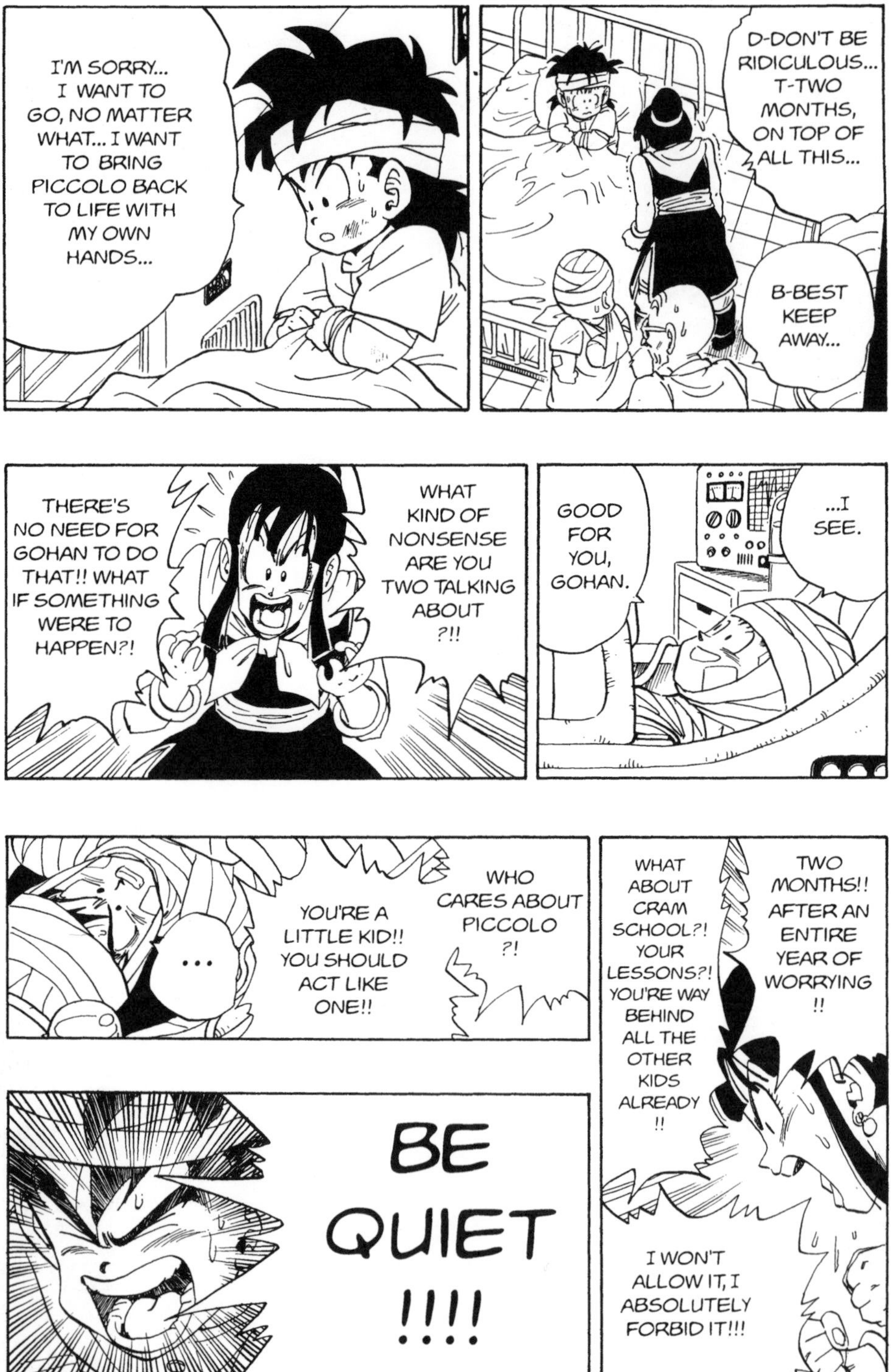
D-DON'T BE RIDICULOUS... T-TWO MONTHS, ON TOP OF ALL THIS...
B-BEST KEEP AWAY...
I'M SORRY... I WANT TO GO, NO MATTER WHAT... I WANT TO BRING PICCOLO BACK TO LIFE WITH MY OWN HANDS...
...I SEE.
GOOD FOR YOU, GOHAN.
WHAT KIND OF NONSENSE ARE YOU TWO TALKING ABOUT ?!!
THERE'S NO NEED FOR GOHAN TO DO THAT!! WHAT IF SOMETHING WERE TO HAPPEN?!
TWO MONTHS!! AFTER AN ENTIRE YEAR OF WORRYING !!
WHAT ABOUT CRAM SCHOOL?! YOUR LESSONS?! YOU'RE WAY BEHIND ALL THE OTHER KIDS ALREADY !!
I WON'T ALLOW IT, I ABSOLUTELY FORBID IT!!!
WHO CARES ABOUT PICCOLO ?!
YOU'RE A LITTLE KID!! YOU SHOULD ACT LIKE ONE!!
...
BE QUIET !!!!

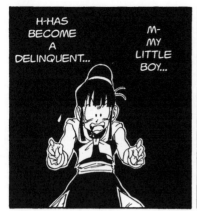

OOOOOH
M- MY LITTLE BOY...
H-HAS BECOME A DELINQUENT...
M-MOM... NOW... NOW'S NOT THE TIME TO BE SAYING SUCH THINGS...
EVERYONE... WE ALL FOUGHT FOR THE EARTH... WE HAVE TO BRING THOSE WHO DIED BACK TO LIFE... AND FIGHT THE SAIYAN AGAIN...
I CAN... I CAN FIGHT TOO...!
I HAVE TO DO SOMETHING... !!
HEE HEE. THAT KID SAYS GOOD STUFF SOMETIMES.
YOU LOSE, CHI-CHI...
LET GOHAN FLY INTO SPACE WITH YOUR BLESSING.

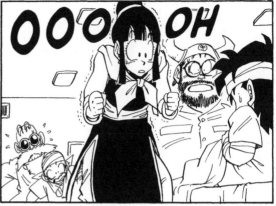

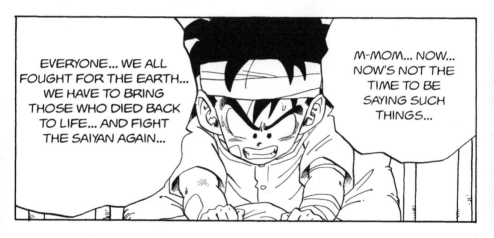

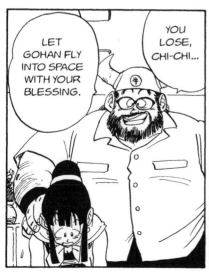

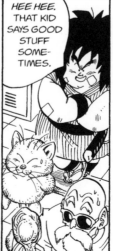

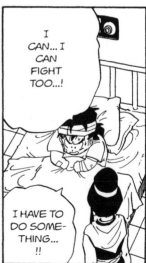

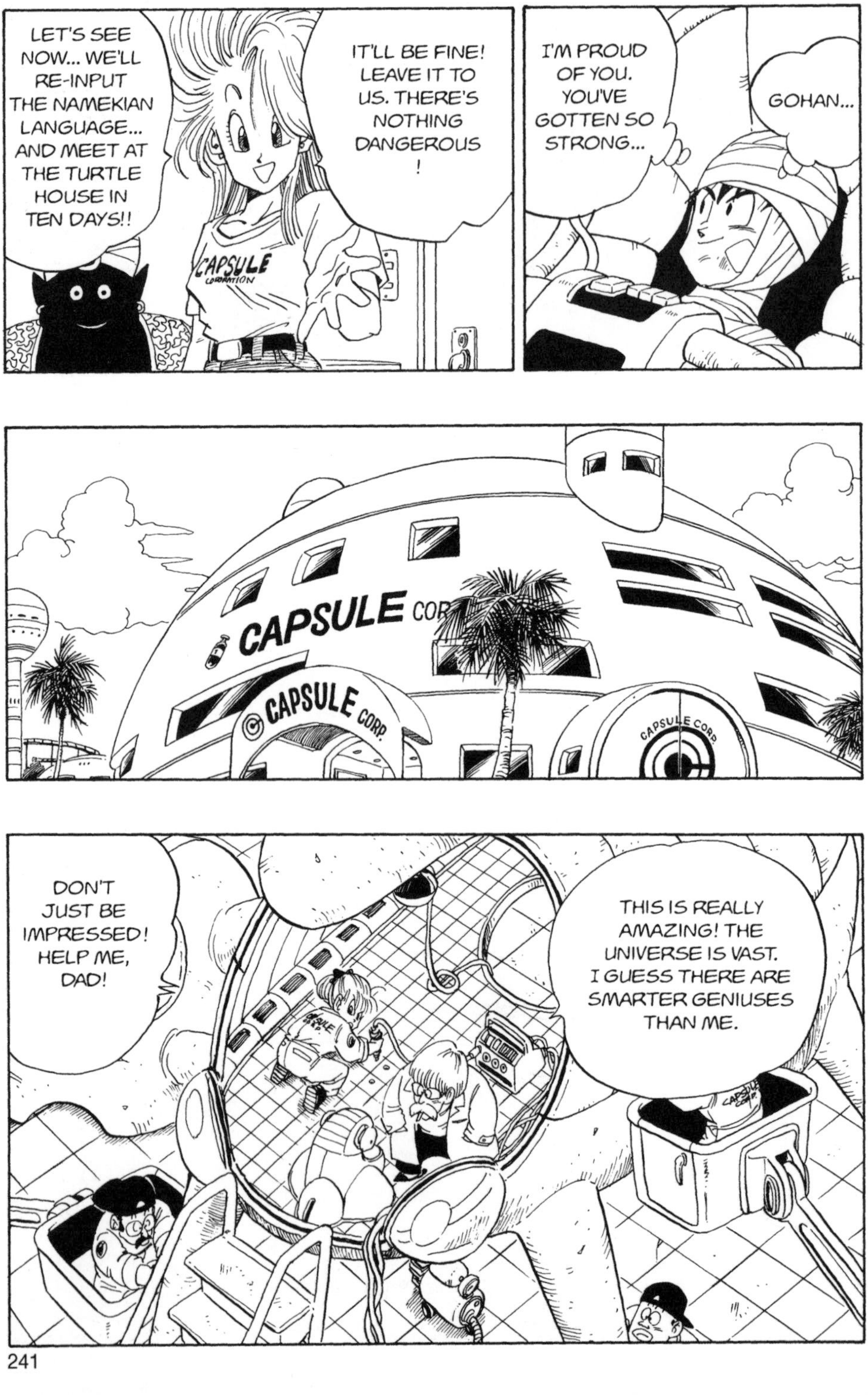
GOHAN...
I'M PROUD OF YOU. YOU'VE GOTTEN SO STRONG...
IT'LL BE FINE! LEAVE IT TO US. THERE'S NOTHING DANGEROUS!
LET'S SEE NOW... WE'LL RE-INPUT THE NAMEKIAN LANGUAGE... AND MEET AT THE TURTLE HOUSE IN TEN DAYS!!
CAPSULE CORPORATION
CAPSULE CORP
CAPSULE CORP.
CAPSULE CORP
THIS IS REALLY AMAZING! THE UNIVERSE IS VAST. I GUESS THERE ARE SMARTER GENIUSES THAN ME.
DON'T JUST BE IMPRESSED! HELP ME, DAD!

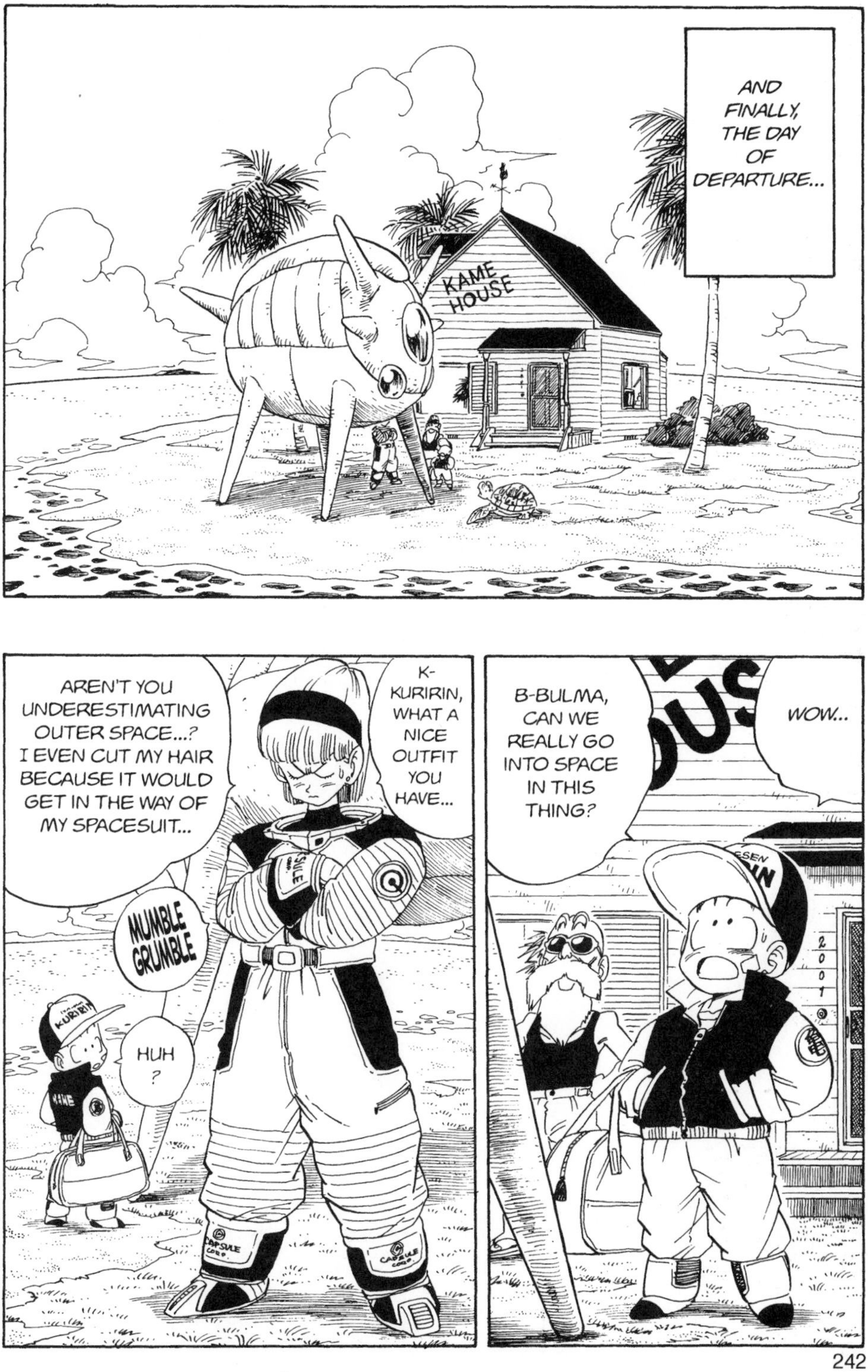
AND FINALLY, THE DAY OF DEPARTURE...
KAME HOUSE
WOW...
B-BULMA, CAN WE REALLY GO INTO SPACE IN THIS THING?
K-KURIRIN, WHAT A NICE OUTFIT YOU HAVE...
AREN'T YOU UNDERESTIMATING OUTER SPACE...? I EVEN CUT MY HAIR BECAUSE IT WOULD GET IN THE WAY OF MY SPACESUIT...
MUMBLE GRUMBLE
HUH?

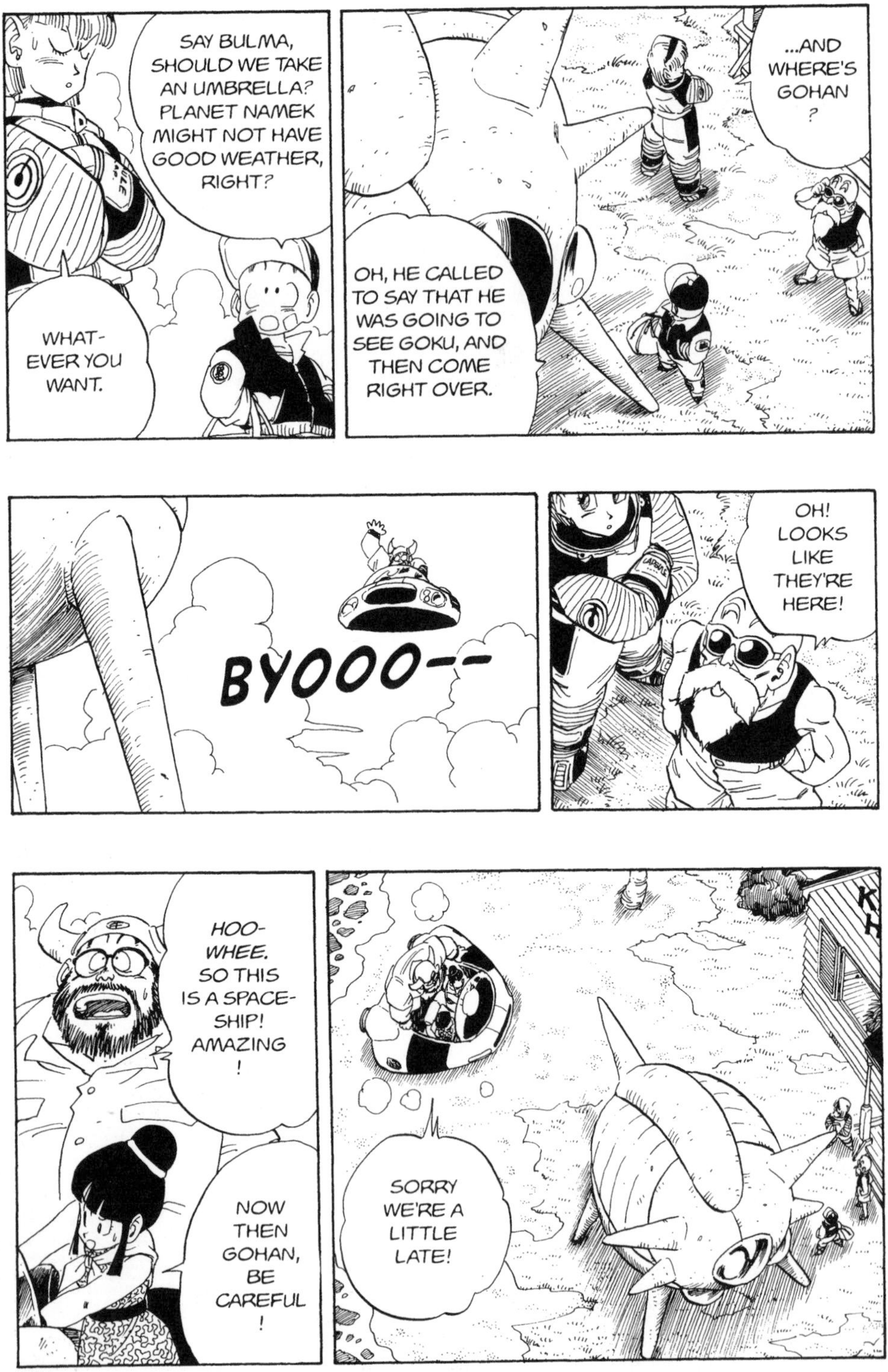
...AND WHERE'S GOHAN ?
OH, HE CALLED TO SAY THAT HE WAS GOING TO SEE GOKU, AND THEN COME RIGHT OVER.
SAY BULMA, SHOULD WE TAKE AN UMBRELLA? PLANET NAMEK MIGHT NOT HAVE GOOD WEATHER, RIGHT?
WHAT-EVER YOU WANT.
OH! LOOKS LIKE THEY'RE HERE!
BYOOO--
SORRY WE'RE A LITTLE LATE!
HOO-WHEE. SO THIS IS A SPACE-SHIP! AMAZING !
NOW THEN GOHAN, BE CAREFUL !

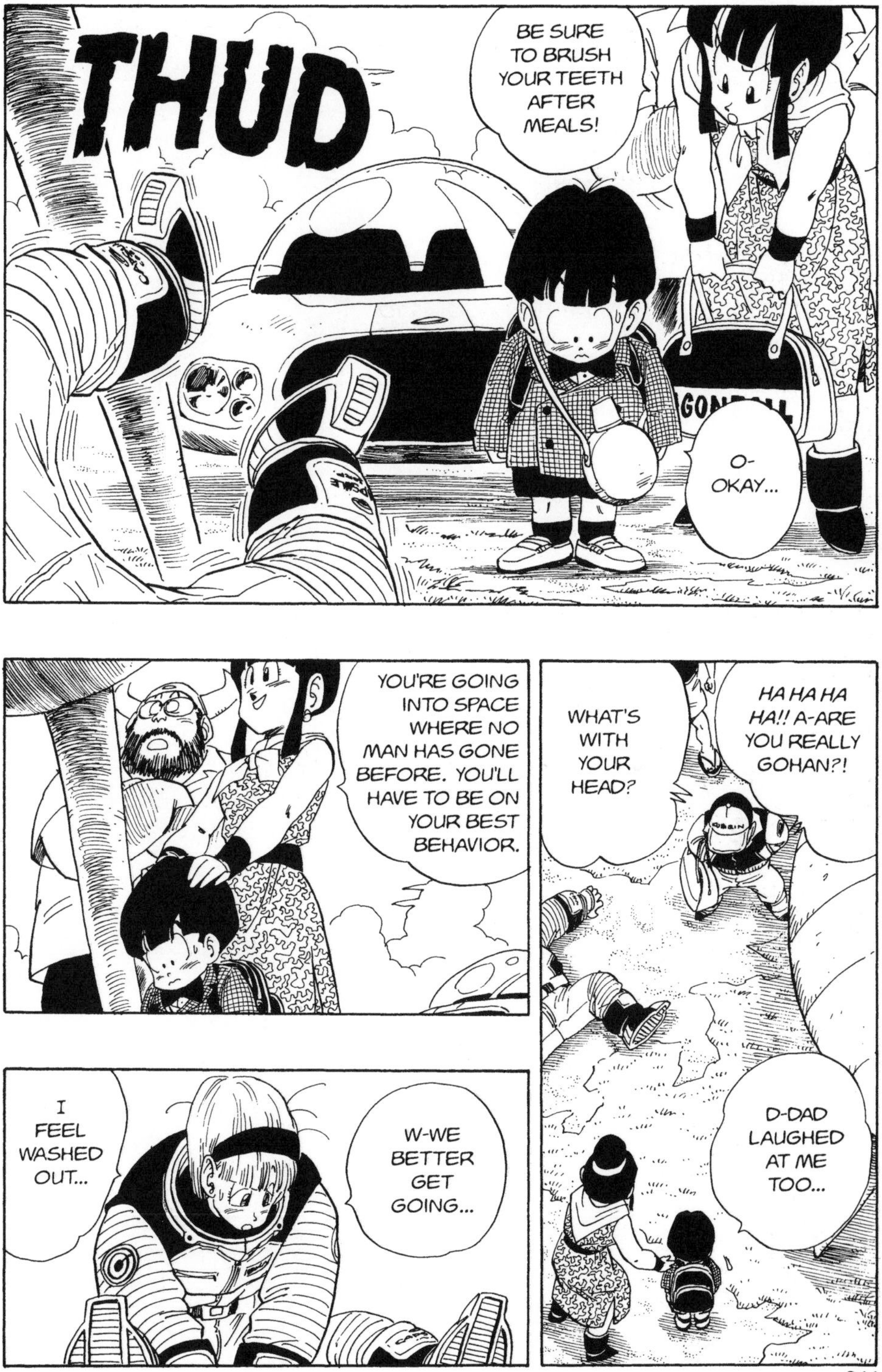
BE SURE TO BRUSH YOUR TEETH AFTER MEALS!
THUD
O-OKAY...
HA HA HA HA!! A-ARE YOU REALLY GOHAN?!
WHAT'S WITH YOUR HEAD?
D-DAD LAUGHED AT ME TOO...
YOU'RE GOING INTO SPACE WHERE NO MAN HAS GONE BEFORE. YOU'LL HAVE TO BE ON YOUR BEST BEHAVIOR.
W-WE BETTER GET GOING...
I FEEL WASHED OUT...

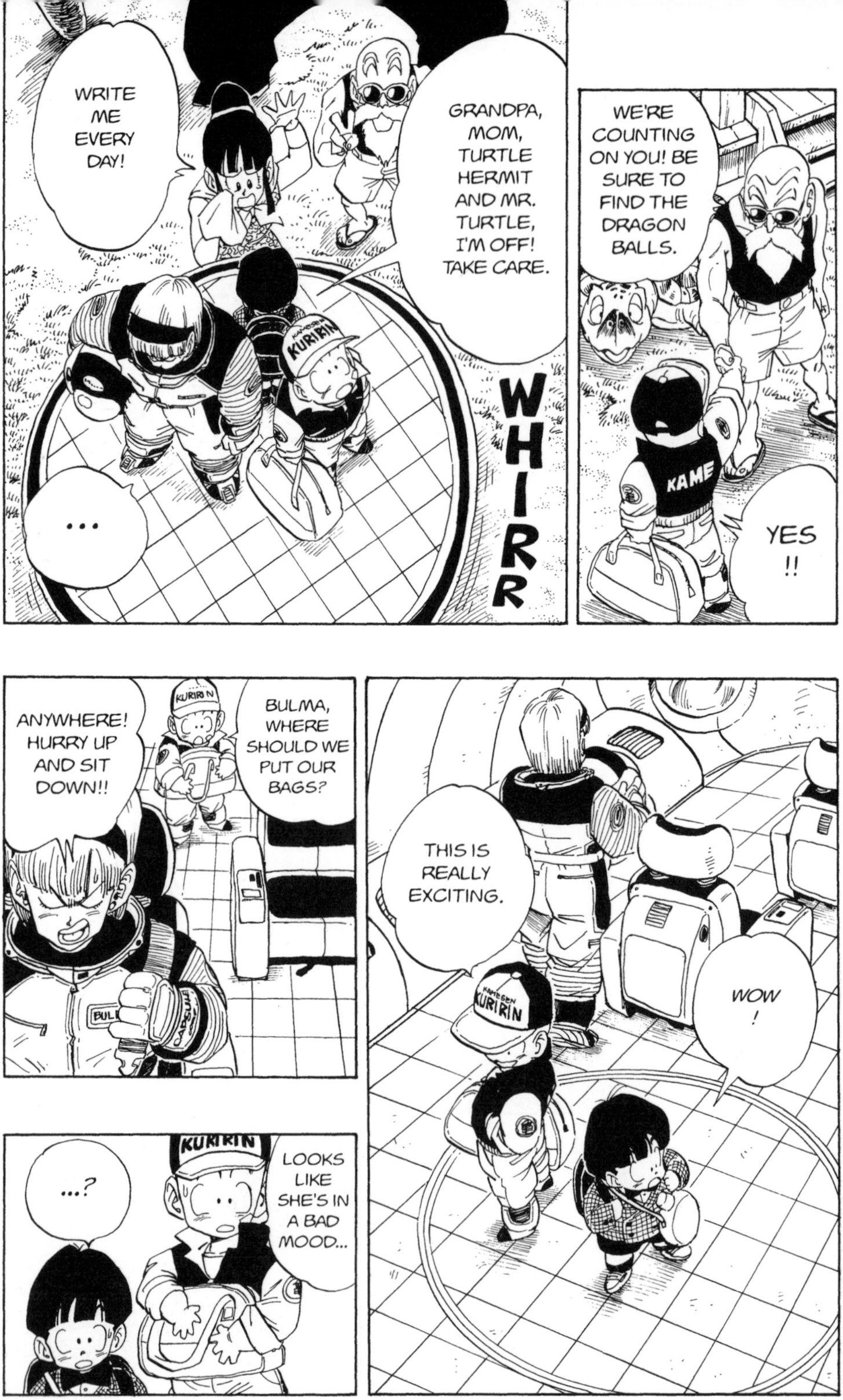

WE'RE COUNTING ON YOU! BE SURE TO FIND THE DRAGON BALLS.
YES !!
GRANDPA, MOM, TURTLE HERMIT AND MR. TURTLE, I'M OFF! TAKE CARE.
WRITE ME EVERY DAY!
WHIRR
...
THIS IS REALLY EXCITING.
WOW !
BULMA, WHERE SHOULD WE PUT OUR BAGS?
ANYWHERE! HURRY UP AND SIT DOWN!!
LOOKS LIKE SHE'S IN A BAD MOOD...
...?

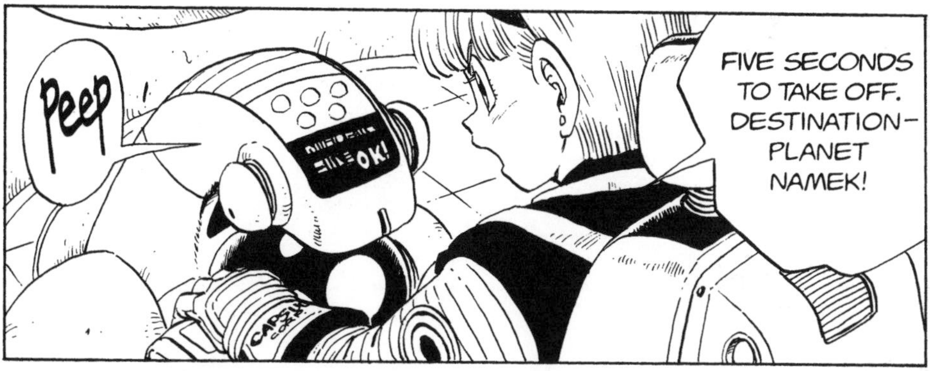
FIVE SECONDS TO TAKE OFF. DESTINATION–PLANET NAMEK!
Peep
OK!
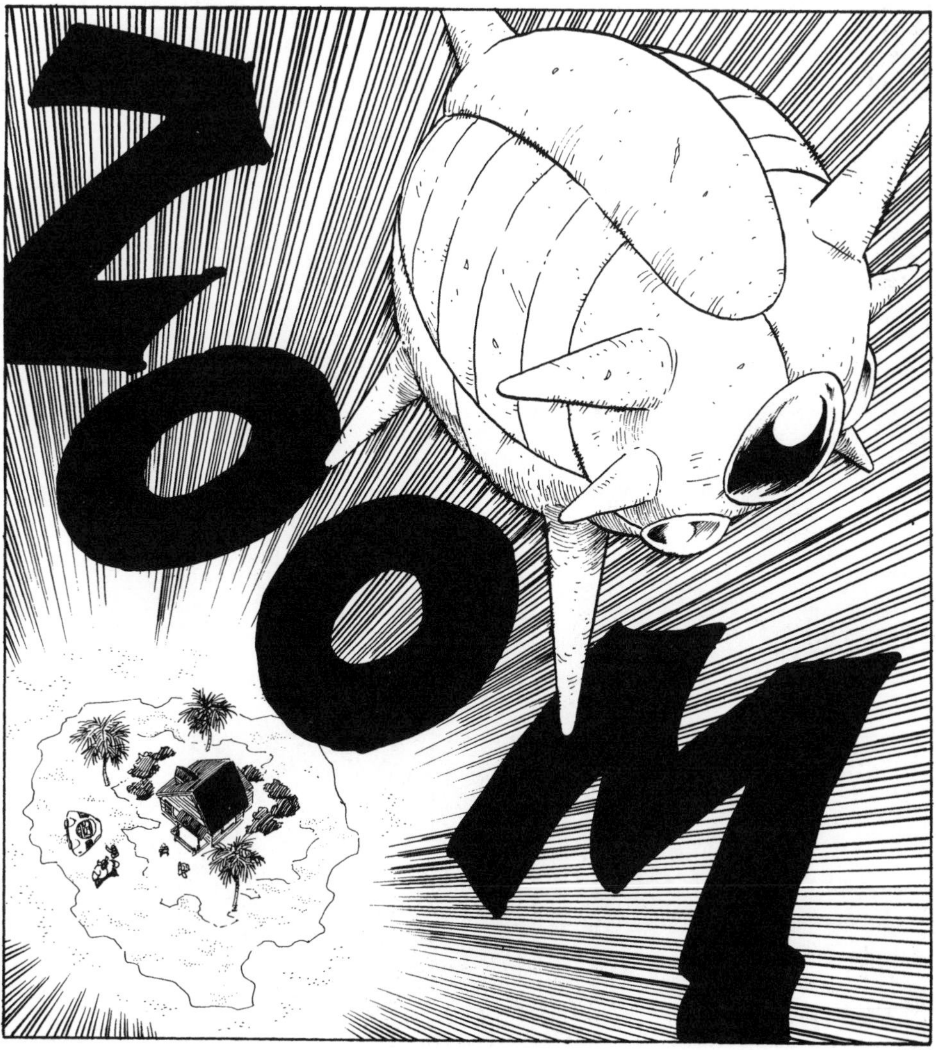
ZOOM

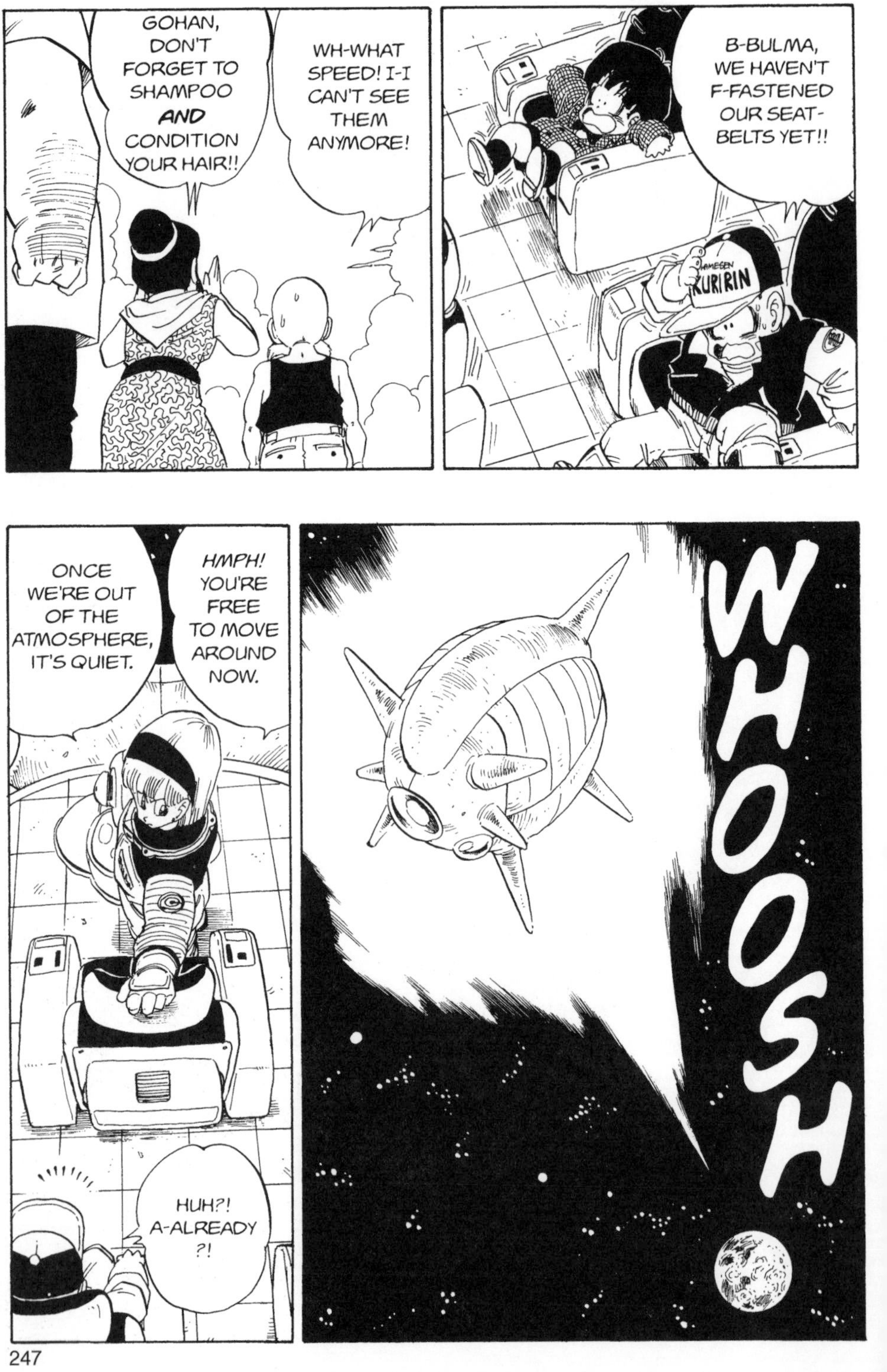
B-BULMA, WE HAVEN'T F-FASTENED OUR SEAT-BELTS YET!!
KURIRIN
WH-WHAT SPEED! I-I CAN'T SEE THEM ANYMORE!
GOHAN, DON'T FORGET TO SHAMPOO AND CONDITION YOUR HAIR!!
WHOOSH
HMPH! YOU'RE FREE TO MOVE AROUND NOW.
ONCE WE'RE OUT OF THE ATMOSPHERE, IT'S QUIET.
HUH?! A-ALREADY ?!

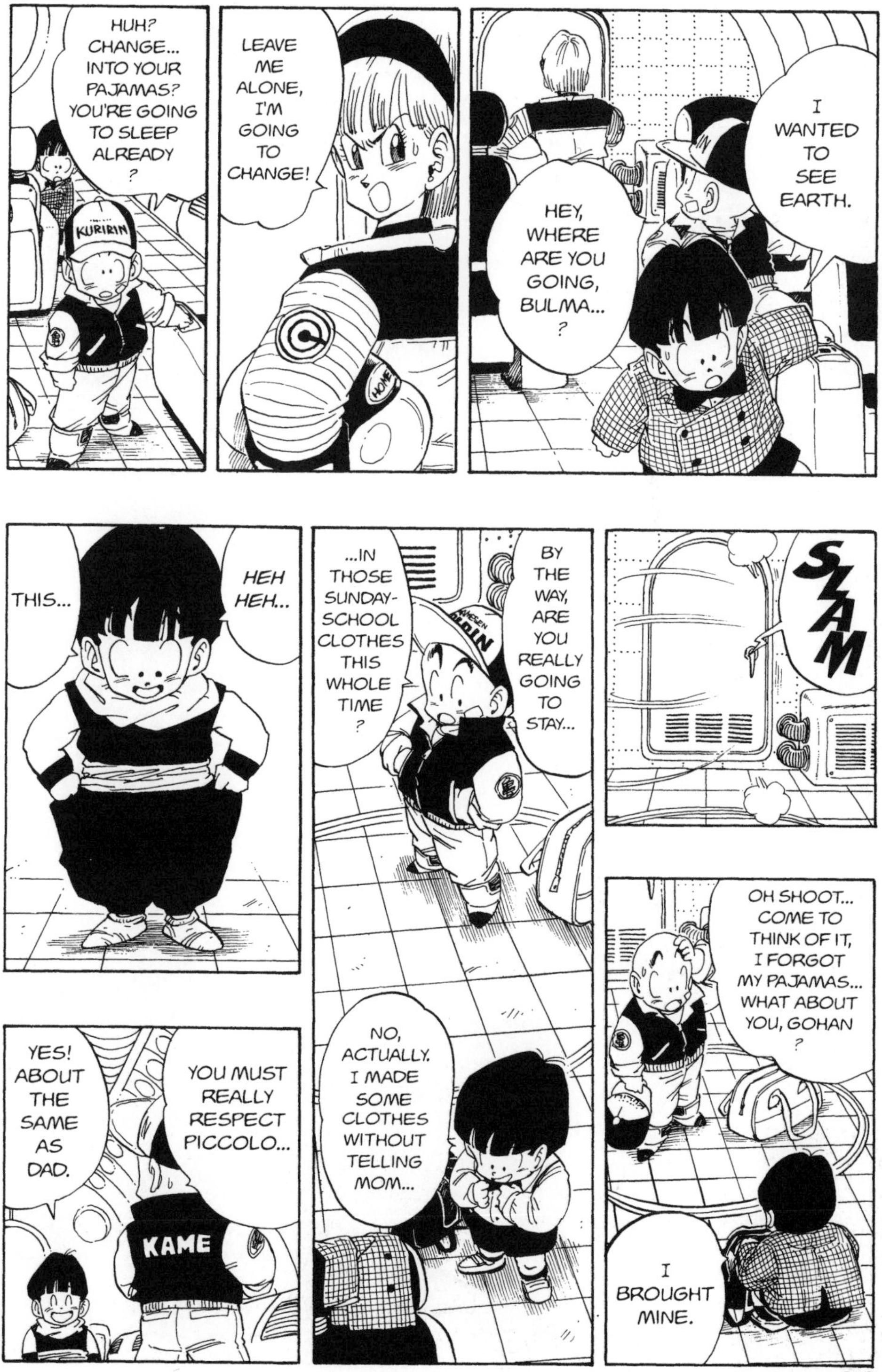
I WANTED TO SEE EARTH.
HEY, WHERE ARE YOU GOING, BULMA...?
LEAVE ME ALONE, I'M GOING TO CHANGE!
HUH? CHANGE... INTO YOUR PAJAMAS? YOU'RE GOING TO SLEEP ALREADY?
SLAM
OH SHOOT... COME TO THINK OF IT, I FORGOT MY PAJAMAS... WHAT ABOUT YOU, GOHAN?
I BROUGHT MINE.
BY THE WAY, ARE YOU REALLY GOING TO STAY...
...IN THOSE SUNDAY-SCHOOL CLOTHES THIS WHOLE TIME?
NO, ACTUALLY. I MADE SOME CLOTHES WITHOUT TELLING MOM...
HEH HEH...
THIS...
YOU MUST REALLY RESPECT PICCOLO...
YES! ABOUT THE SAME AS DAD.
KAME

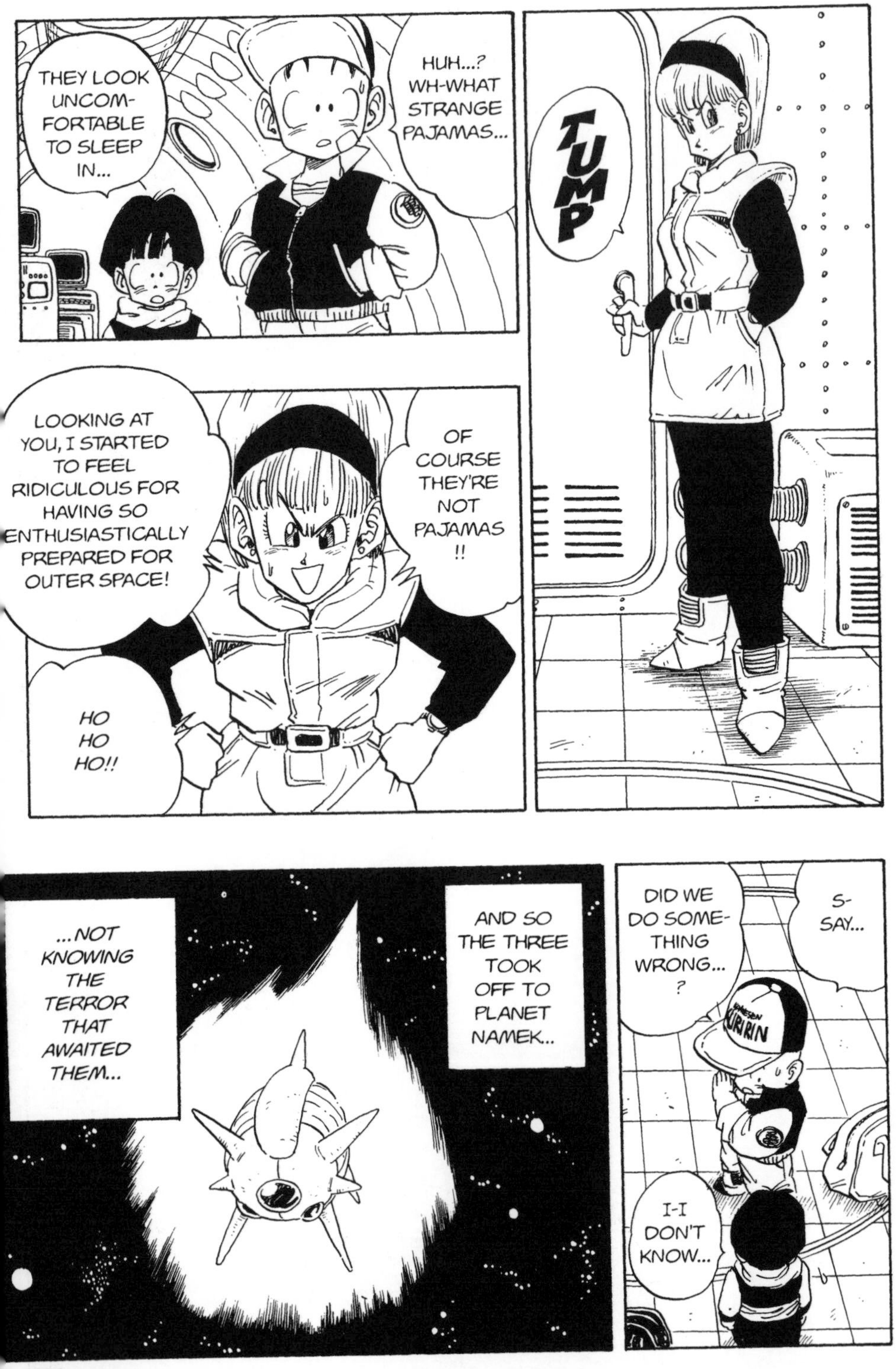
TUMP
HUH...? WH-WHAT STRANGE PAJAMAS...
THEY LOOK UNCOM-FORTABLE TO SLEEP IN...
OF COURSE THEY'RE NOT PAJAMAS !!
LOOKING AT YOU, I STARTED TO FEEL RIDICULOUS FOR HAVING SO ENTHUSIASTICALLY PREPARED FOR OUTER SPACE!
HO HO HO!!
S-SAY...
DID WE DO SOME-THING WRONG...?
KURIRIN
I-I DON'T KNOW...
AND SO THE THREE TOOK OFF TO PLANET NAMEK...
...NOT KNOWING THE TERROR THAT AWAITED THEM...

# DBZ:52 • The Return of Vegeta

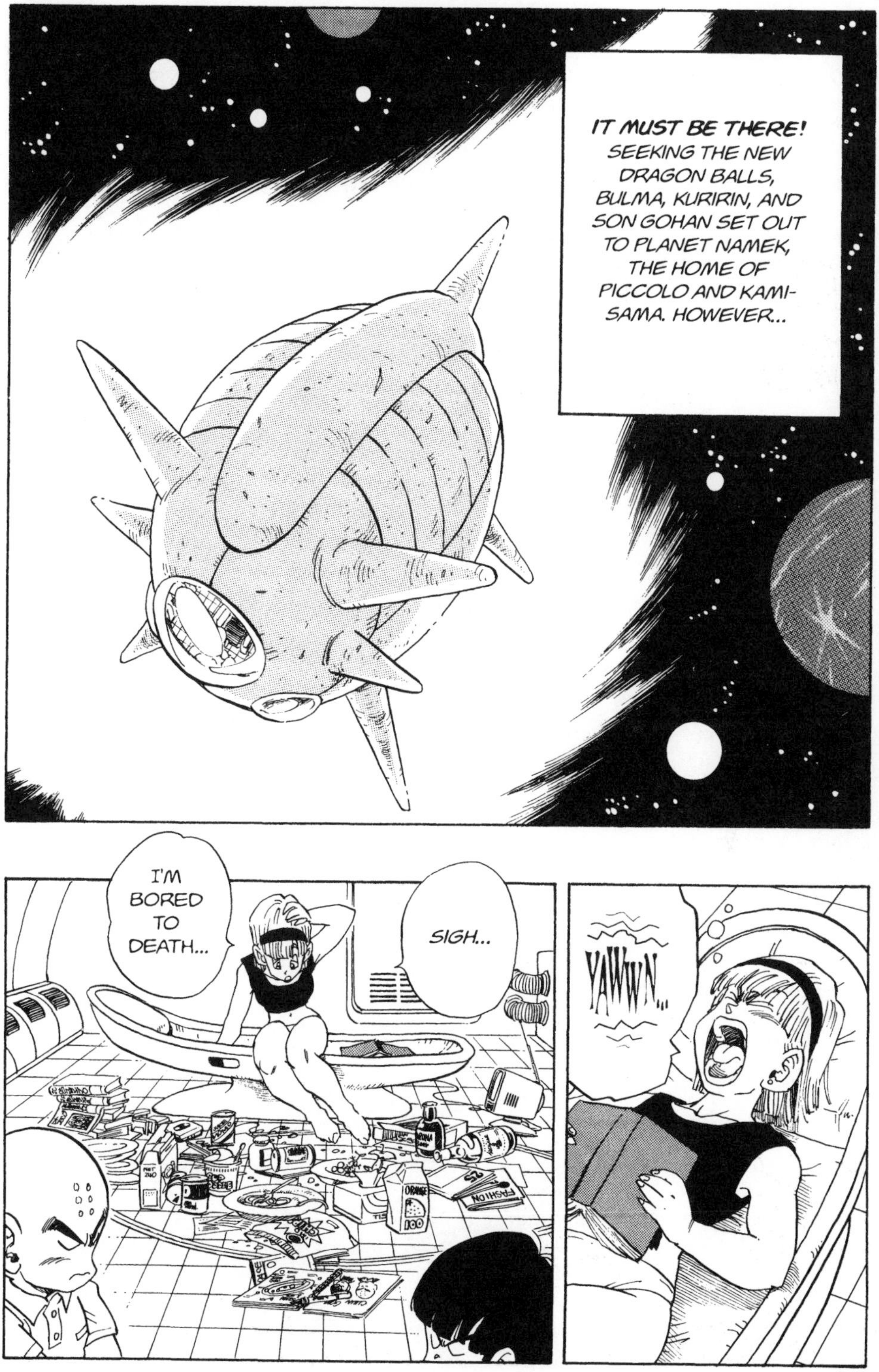
IT MUST BE THERE! SEEKING THE NEW DRAGON BALLS, BULMA, KURIRIN, AND SON GOHAN SET OUT TO PLANET NAMEK, THE HOME OF PICCOLO AND KAMI-SAMA. HOWEVER...
YAWWN...
SIGH...
I'M BORED TO DEATH...

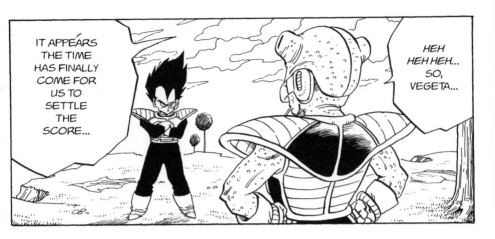

HEH HEH HEH... SO, VEGETA...
IT APPEARS THE TIME HAS FINALLY COME FOR US TO SETTLE THE SCORE...
HEH
YOU'VE BEEN SLACKING OFF... WITH THAT POWER LEVEL, YOU HAVE NO CHANCE.
HAVEN'T I...? WELL THEN, I'LL HAVE TO SHOW YOU MY NEW DISCOVERY...
SOMETHING INTERESTING I LEARNED WHEN I WENT TO EARTH...
FEH!
HOW TO RUN AWAY QUICKLY?
NO. HOW TO CONCEAL MY **TRUE POWER**!!!!

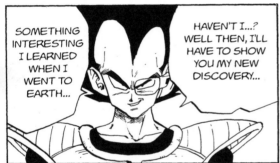

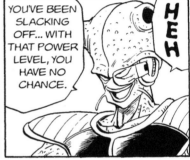

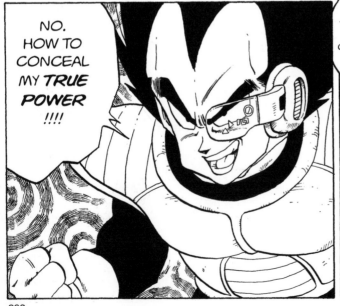

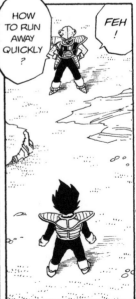

# DBZ:55 • Vegeta's True Power!

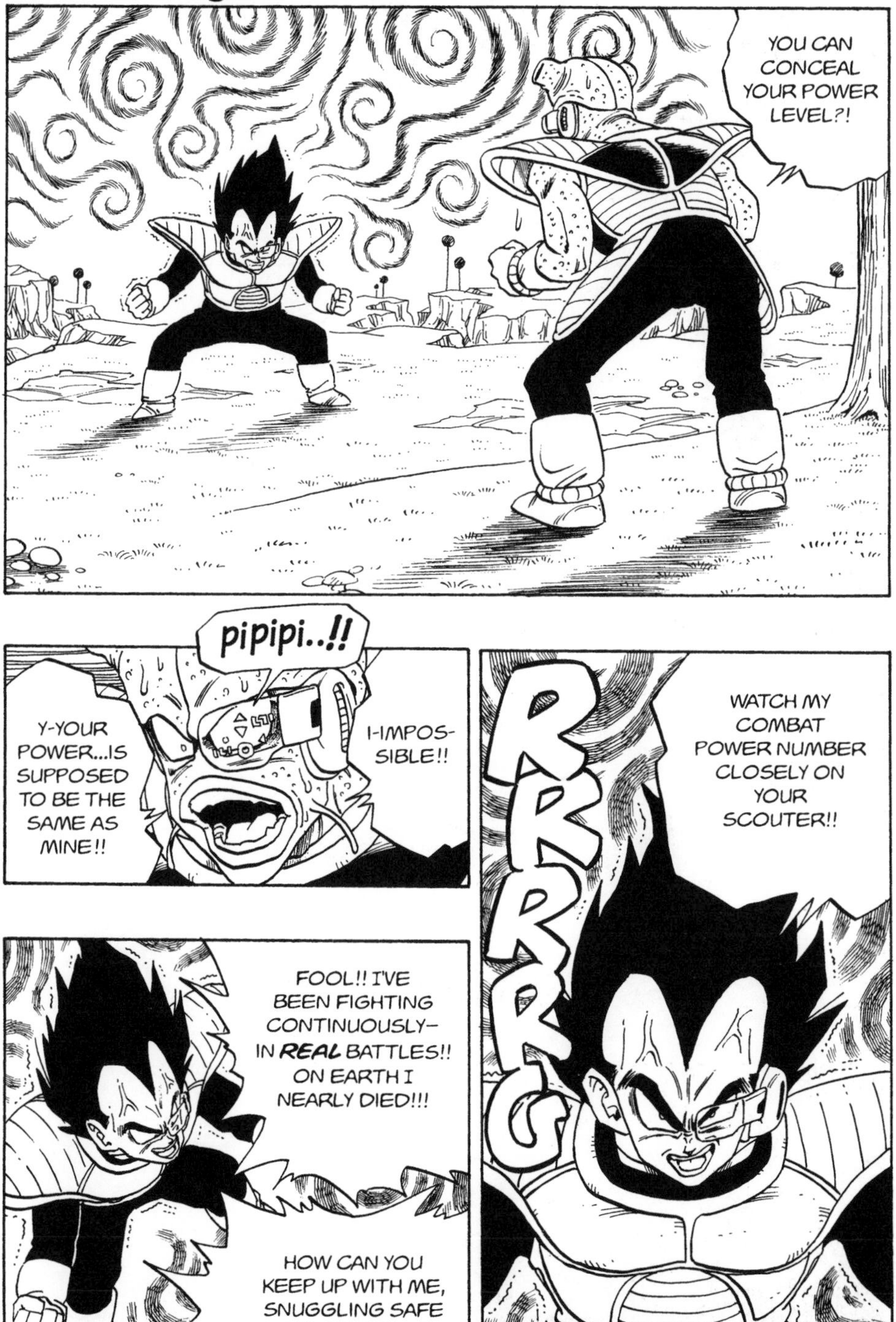
YOU CAN CONCEAL YOUR POWER LEVEL?!
WATCH MY COMBAT POWER NUMBER CLOSELY ON YOUR SCOUTER!!
RRRRG
pipipi..!!
I-IMPOSSIBLE!!
Y-YOUR POWER...IS SUPPOSED TO BE THE SAME AS MINE!!
FOOL!! I'VE BEEN FIGHTING CONTINUOUSLY— IN ***REAL*** BATTLES!! ON EARTH I NEARLY DIED!!!
HOW CAN YOU KEEP UP WITH ME, SNUGGLING SAFE AND SOUND AT FREEZA'S?!

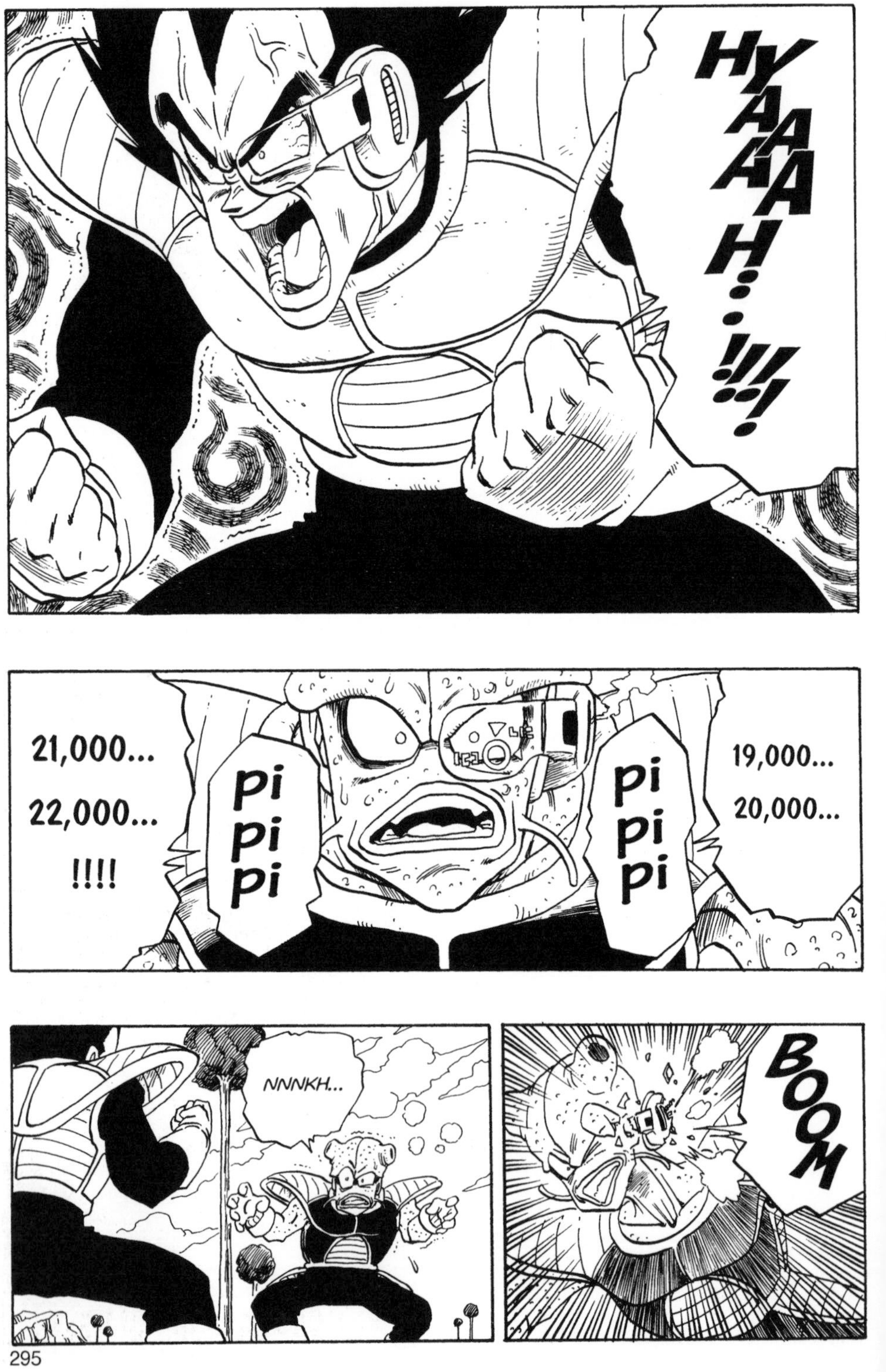
HYAAAAH...!!!!
19,000...
20,000...
pi
pi
pi
pi
pi
pi
21,000...
22,000...
!!!!
BOOM
NNNKH...

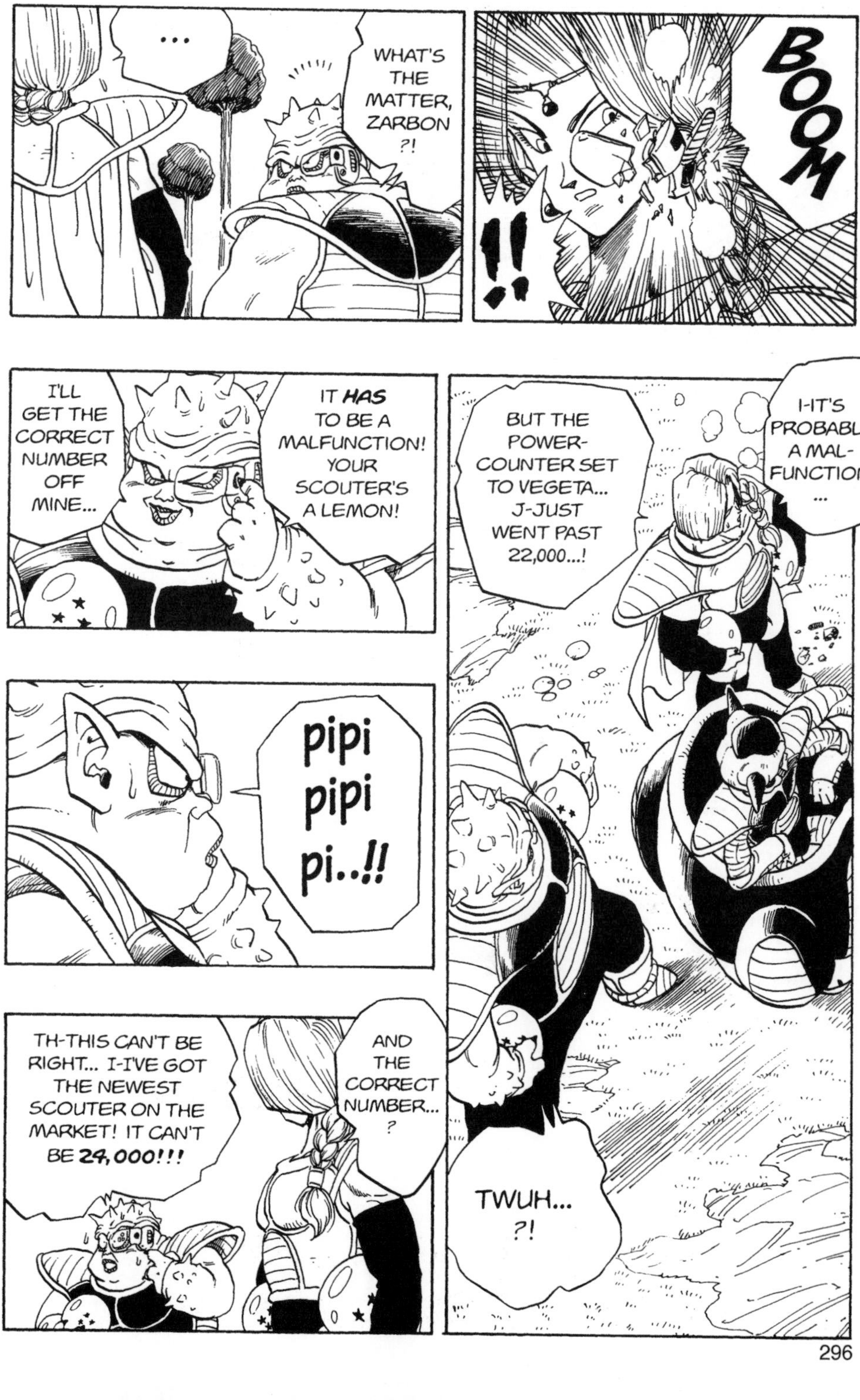
BOOM
!!
...
WHAT'S THE MATTER, ZARBON ?!
I-IT'S PROBABLY A MAL-FUNCTION ...
BUT THE POWER-COUNTER SET TO VEGETA... J-JUST WENT PAST 22,000...!
TWUH... ?!
IT **HAS** TO BE A MALFUNCTION! YOUR SCOUTER'S A LEMON!
I'LL GET THE CORRECT NUMBER OFF MINE...
pipi pipi pi..!!
AND THE CORRECT NUMBER... ?
TH-THIS CAN'T BE RIGHT... I-I'VE GOT THE NEWEST SCOUTER ON THE MARKET! IT CAN'T BE **24,000**!!!

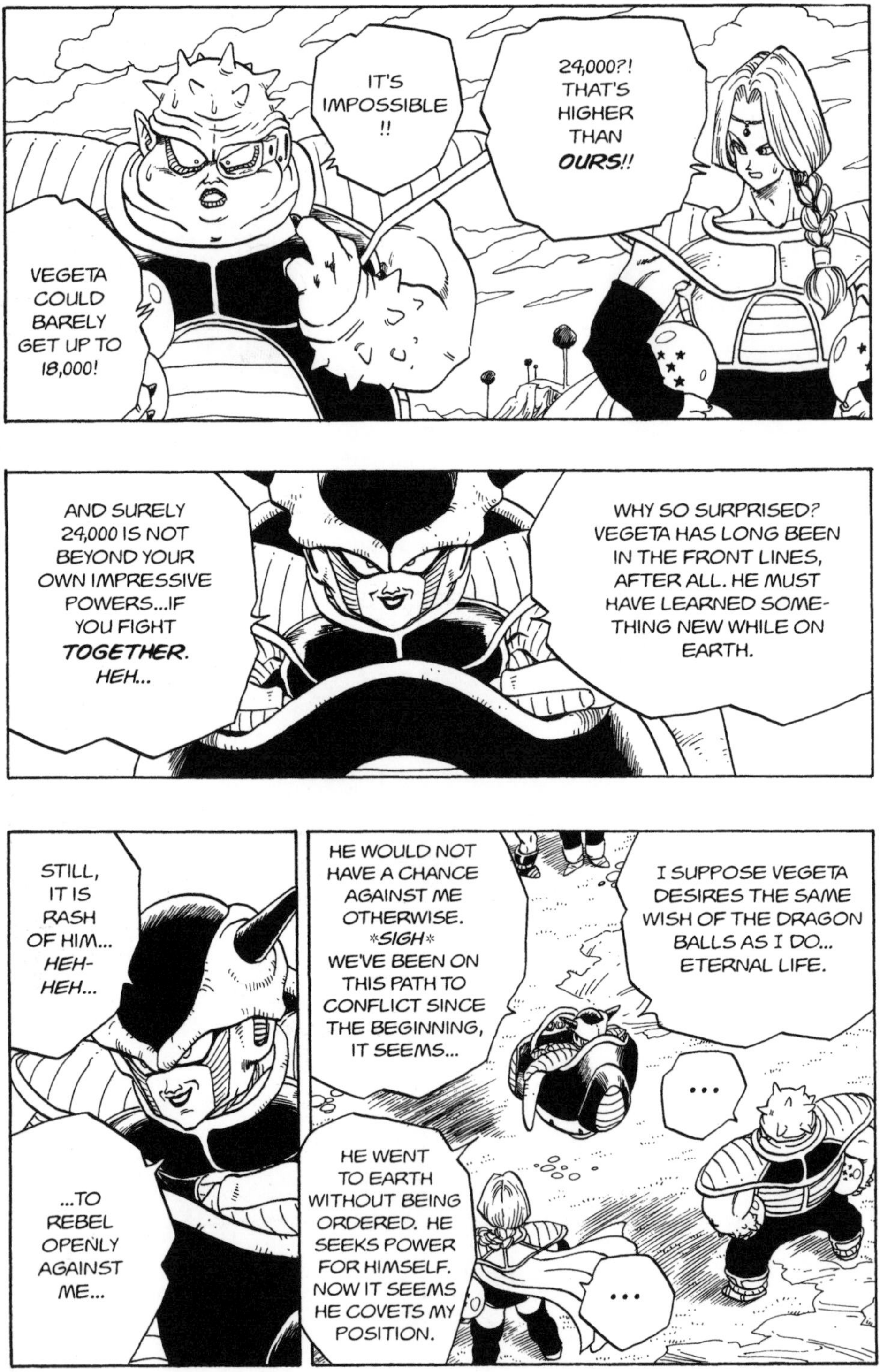
24,000?! THAT'S HIGHER THAN **OURS**!!
IT'S IMPOSSIBLE !!
VEGETA COULD BARELY GET UP TO 18,000!
WHY SO SURPRISED? VEGETA HAS LONG BEEN IN THE FRONT LINES, AFTER ALL. HE MUST HAVE LEARNED SOME-THING NEW WHILE ON EARTH.
AND SURELY 24,000 IS NOT BEYOND YOUR OWN IMPRESSIVE POWERS...IF YOU FIGHT ***TOGETHER***. *HEH...*
I SUPPOSE VEGETA DESIRES THE SAME WISH OF THE DRAGON BALLS AS I DO... ETERNAL LIFE.
HE WOULD NOT HAVE A CHANCE AGAINST ME OTHERWISE. **SIGH** WE'VE BEEN ON THIS PATH TO CONFLICT SINCE THE BEGINNING, IT SEEMS...
...
HE WENT TO EARTH WITHOUT BEING ORDERED. HE SEEKS POWER FOR HIMSELF. NOW IT SEEMS HE COVETS MY POSITION.
...
STILL, IT IS RASH OF HIM... *HEH-HEH...*
...TO REBEL OPENLY AGAINST ME...

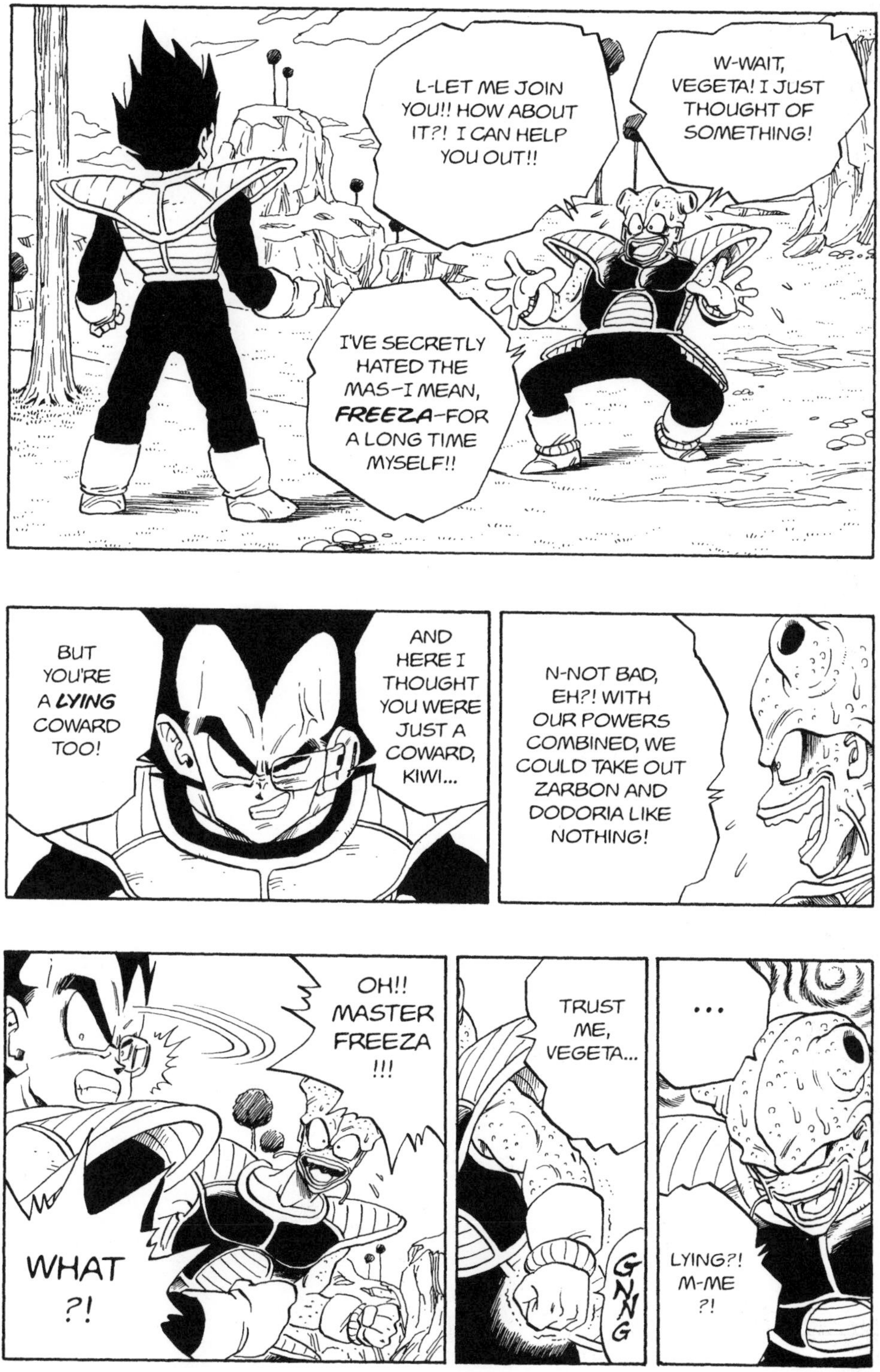
W-WAIT, VEGETA! I JUST THOUGHT OF SOMETHING!
L-LET ME JOIN YOU!! HOW ABOUT IT?! I CAN HELP YOU OUT!!
I'VE SECRETLY HATED THE MAS—I MEAN, FREEZA—FOR A LONG TIME MYSELF!!
N-NOT BAD, EH?! WITH OUR POWERS COMBINED, WE COULD TAKE OUT ZARBON AND DODORIA LIKE NOTHING!
AND HERE I THOUGHT YOU WERE JUST A COWARD, KIWI...
BUT YOU'RE A LYING COWARD TOO!
...
LYING?! M-ME ?!
TRUST ME, VEGETA...
GNNG
OH!! MASTER FREEZA !!!
WHAT ?!

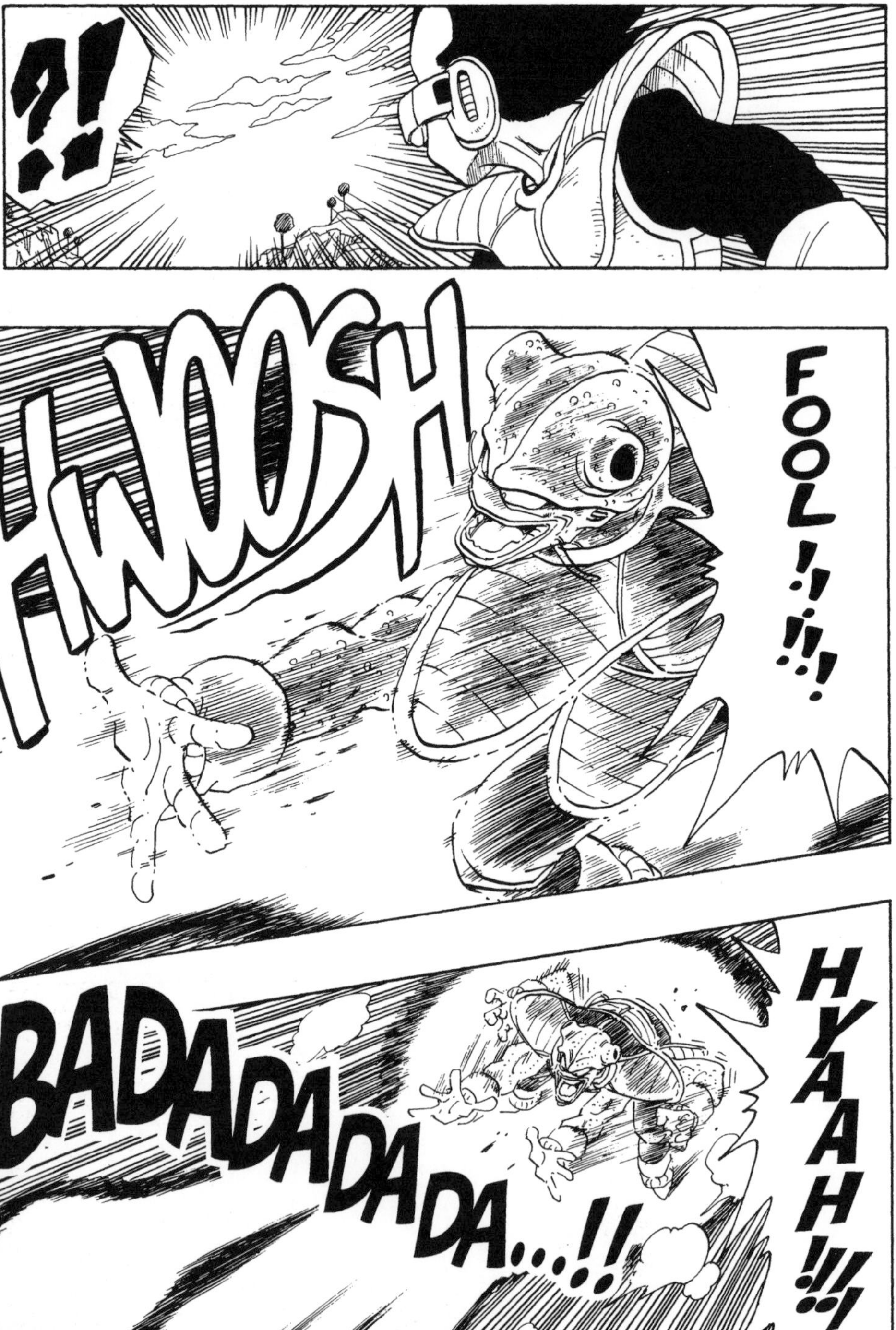
?!
FWOOSH
FOOL!!!!
HYAAH!!!
BADADADADADA...!!

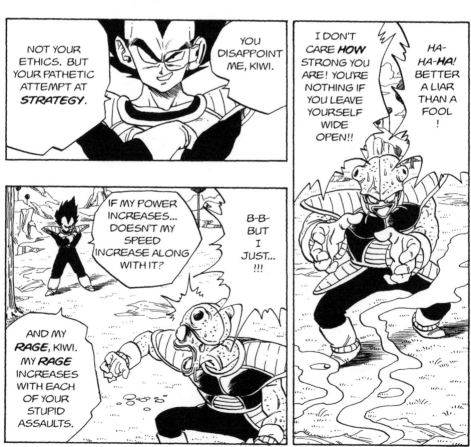

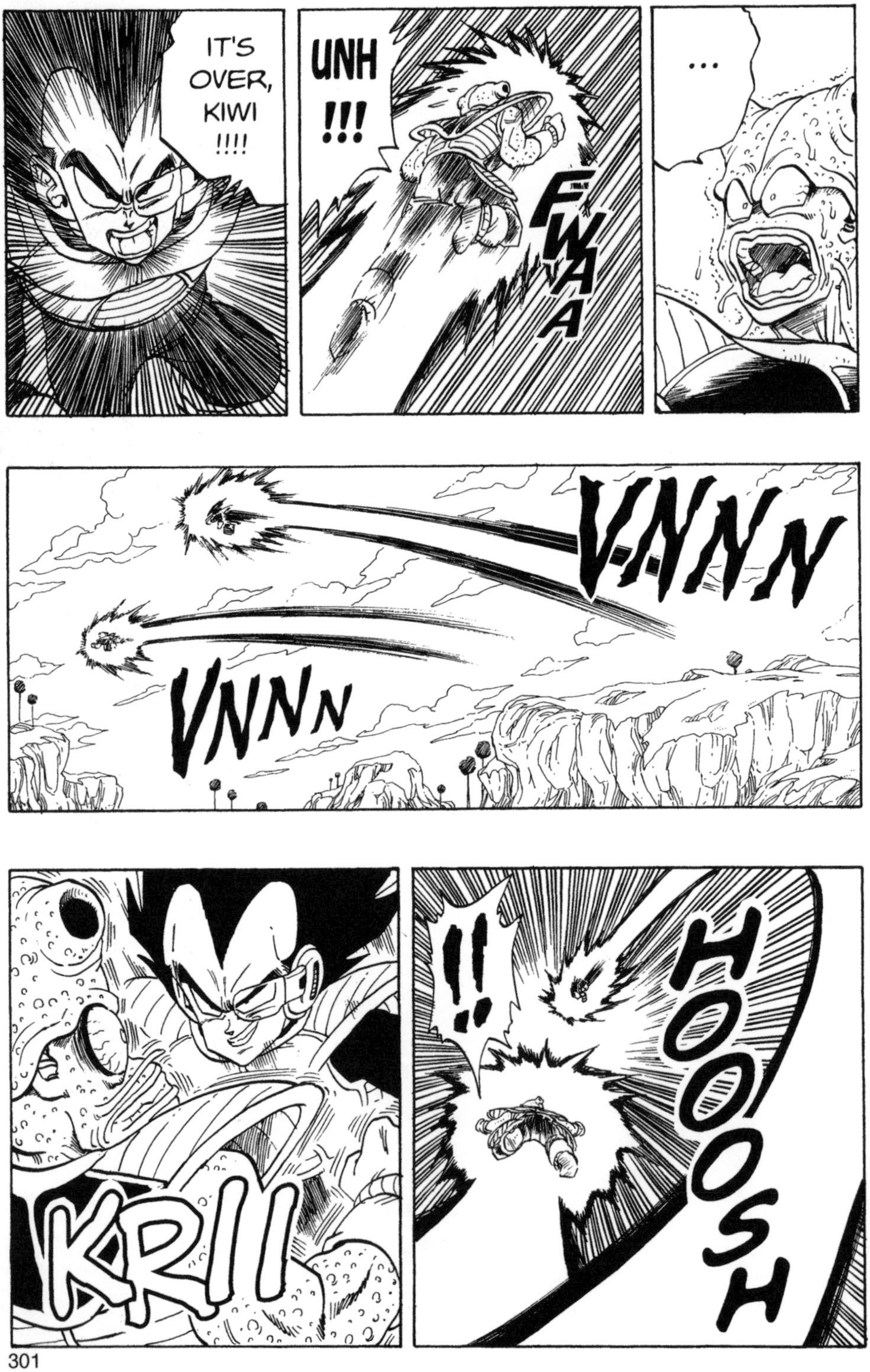
...
UNH !!!
FWAA
IT'S OVER, KIWI !!!!
VNNN
VNNn
!!
HOOOSH
KRII

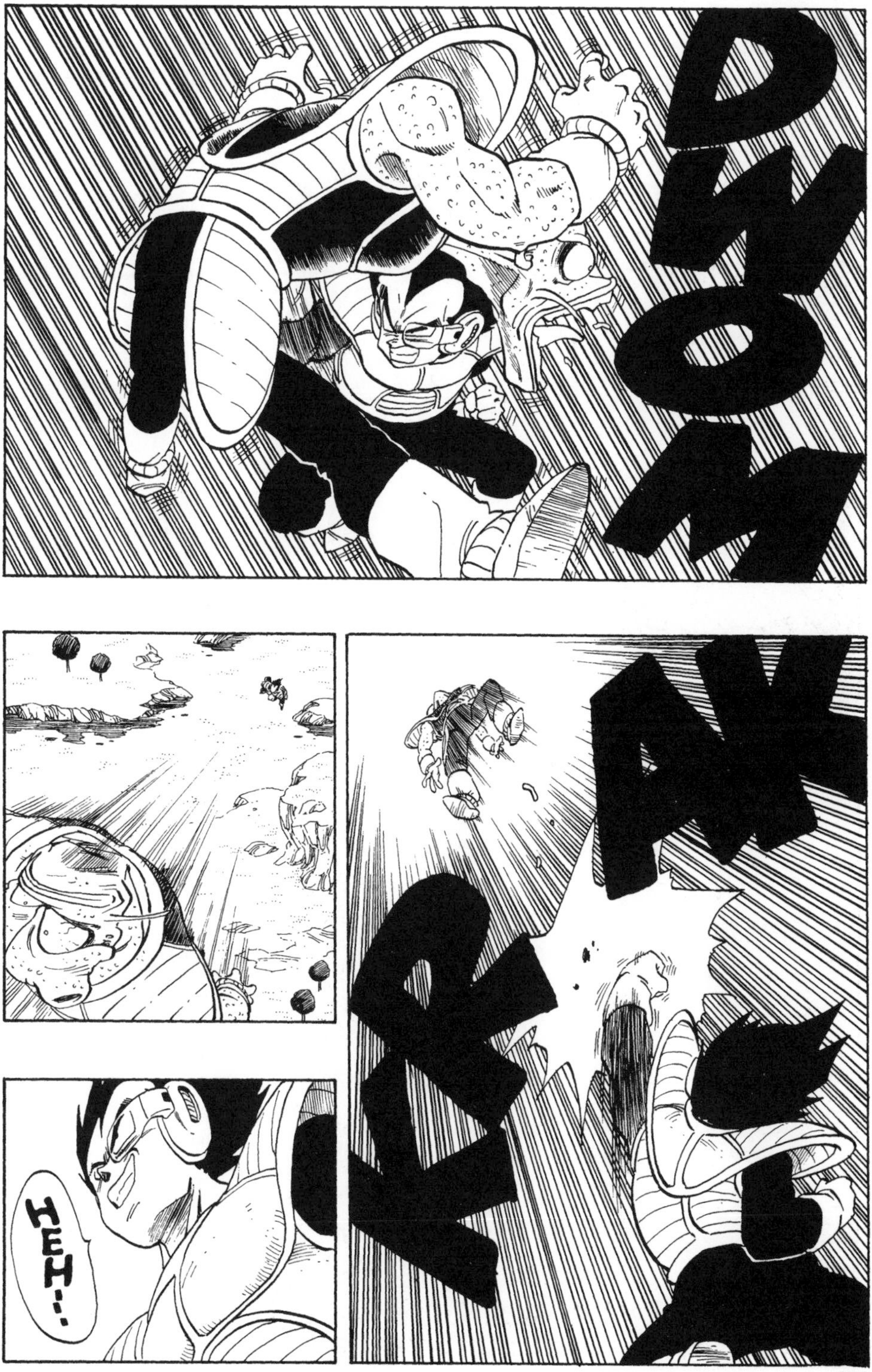
KRAK
HEH..

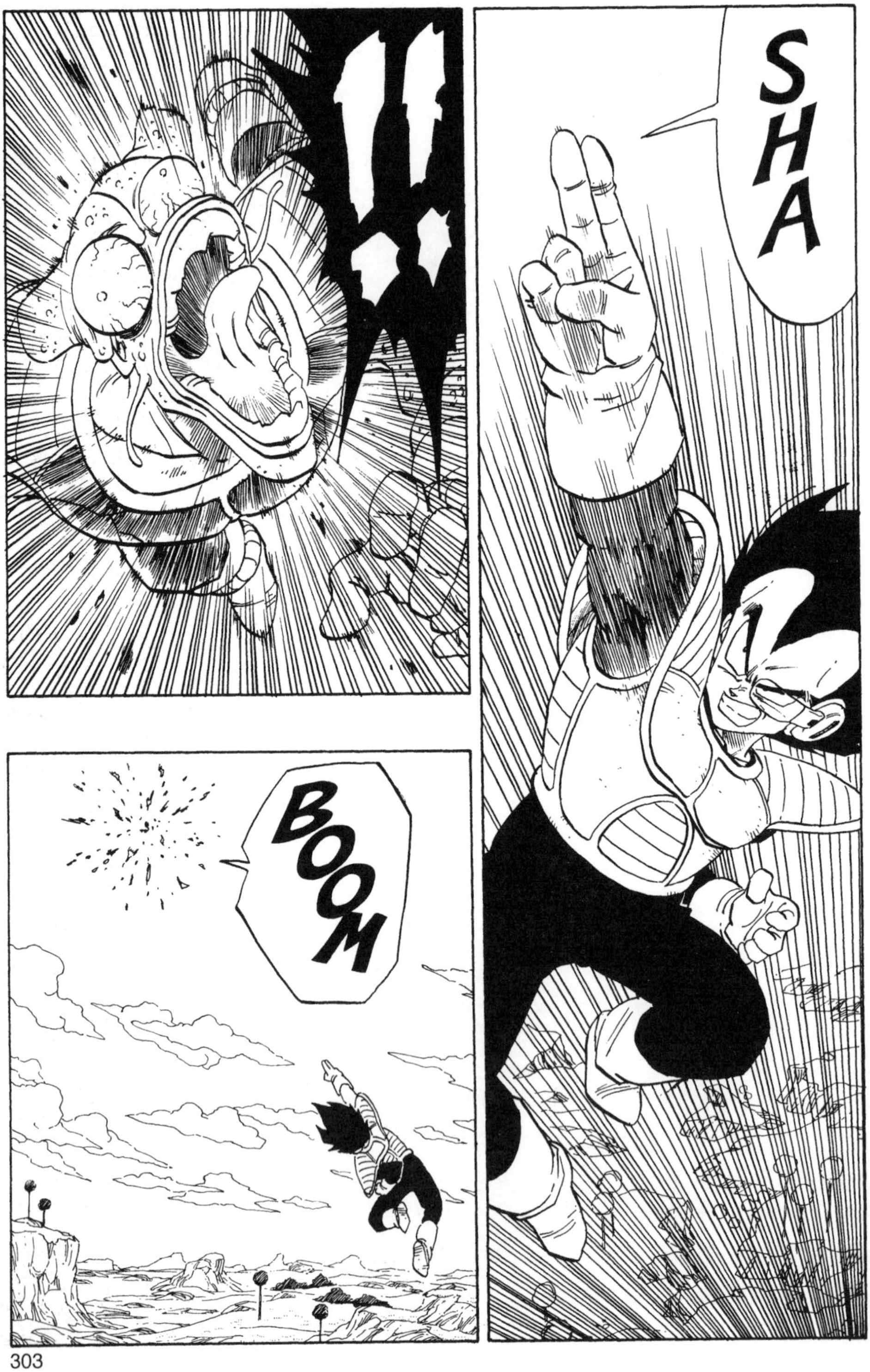
SHA
!!
BOOM

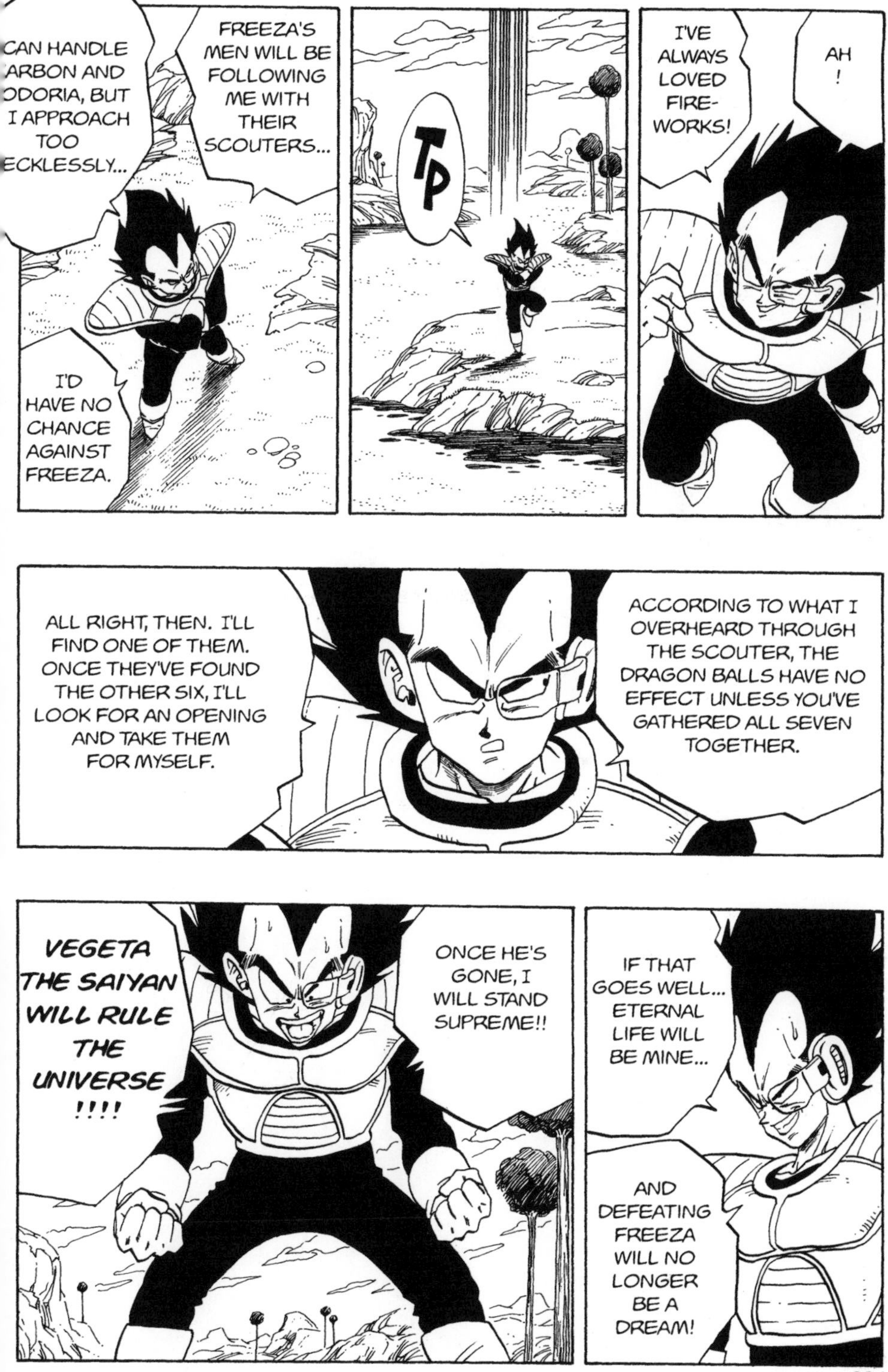
AH!
I'VE ALWAYS LOVED FIRE-WORKS!
TP
FREEZA'S MEN WILL BE FOLLOWING ME WITH THEIR SCOUTERS...
CAN HANDLE ARBON AND ODORIA, BUT I APPROACH TOO ECKLESSLY...
I'D HAVE NO CHANCE AGAINST FREEZA.
ACCORDING TO WHAT I OVERHEARD THROUGH THE SCOUTER, THE DRAGON BALLS HAVE NO EFFECT UNLESS YOU'VE GATHERED ALL SEVEN TOGETHER.
ALL RIGHT, THEN. I'LL FIND ONE OF THEM. ONCE THEY'VE FOUND THE OTHER SIX, I'LL LOOK FOR AN OPENING AND TAKE THEM FOR MYSELF.
IF THAT GOES WELL... ETERNAL LIFE WILL BE MINE...
AND DEFEATING FREEZA WILL NO LONGER BE A DREAM!
ONCE HE'S GONE, I WILL STAND SUPREME!!
VEGETA THE SAIYAN WILL RULE THE UNIVERSE!!!!

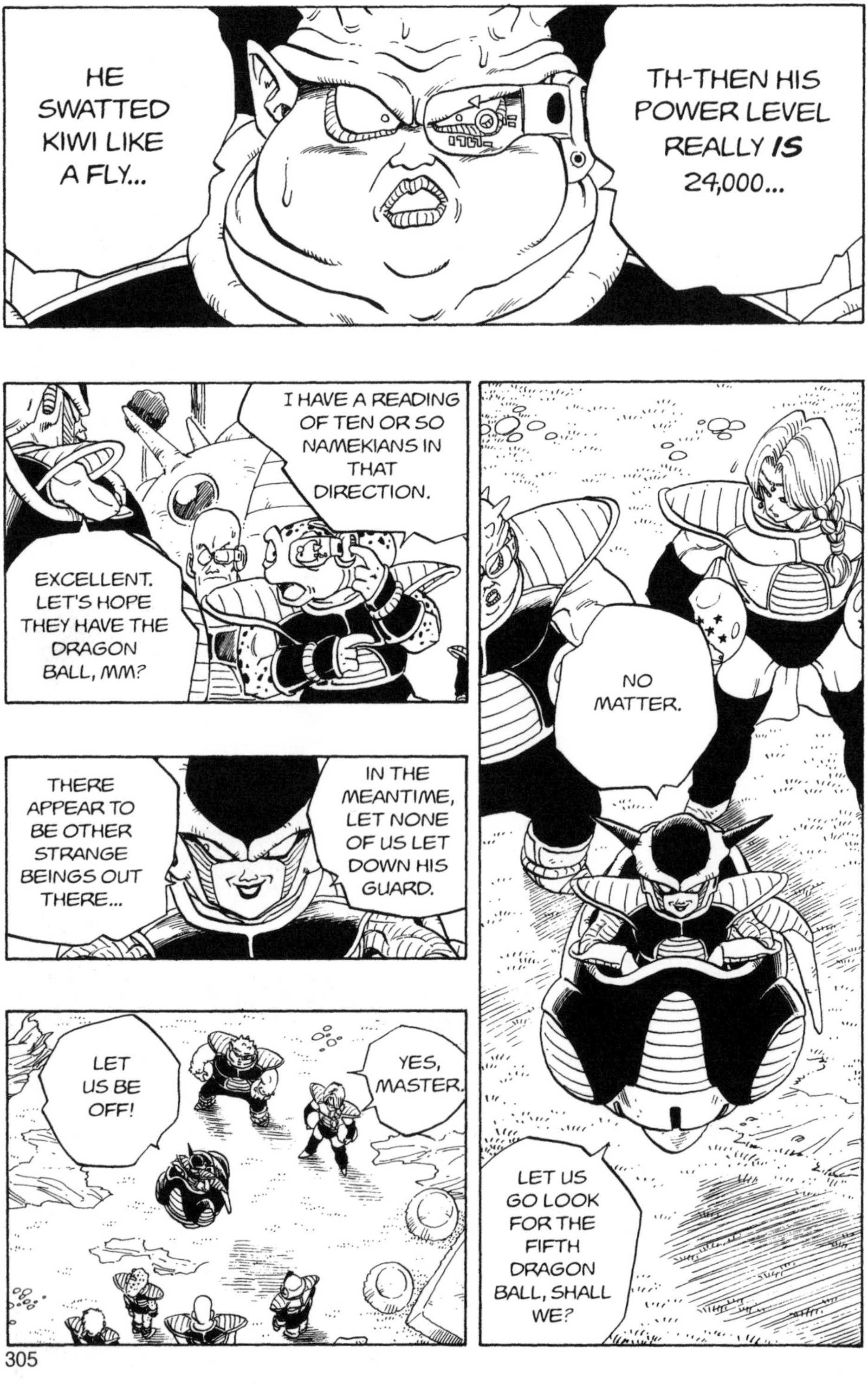
TH-THEN HIS POWER LEVEL REALLY **IS** 24,000...
HE SWATTED KIWI LIKE A FLY...
NO MATTER.
LET US GO LOOK FOR THE FIFTH DRAGON BALL, SHALL WE?
I HAVE A READING OF TEN OR SO NAMEKIANS IN THAT DIRECTION.
EXCELLENT. LET'S HOPE THEY HAVE THE DRAGON BALL, MM?
IN THE MEANTIME, LET NONE OF US LET DOWN HIS GUARD.
THERE APPEAR TO BE OTHER STRANGE BEINGS OUT THERE...
YES, MASTER.
LET US BE OFF!

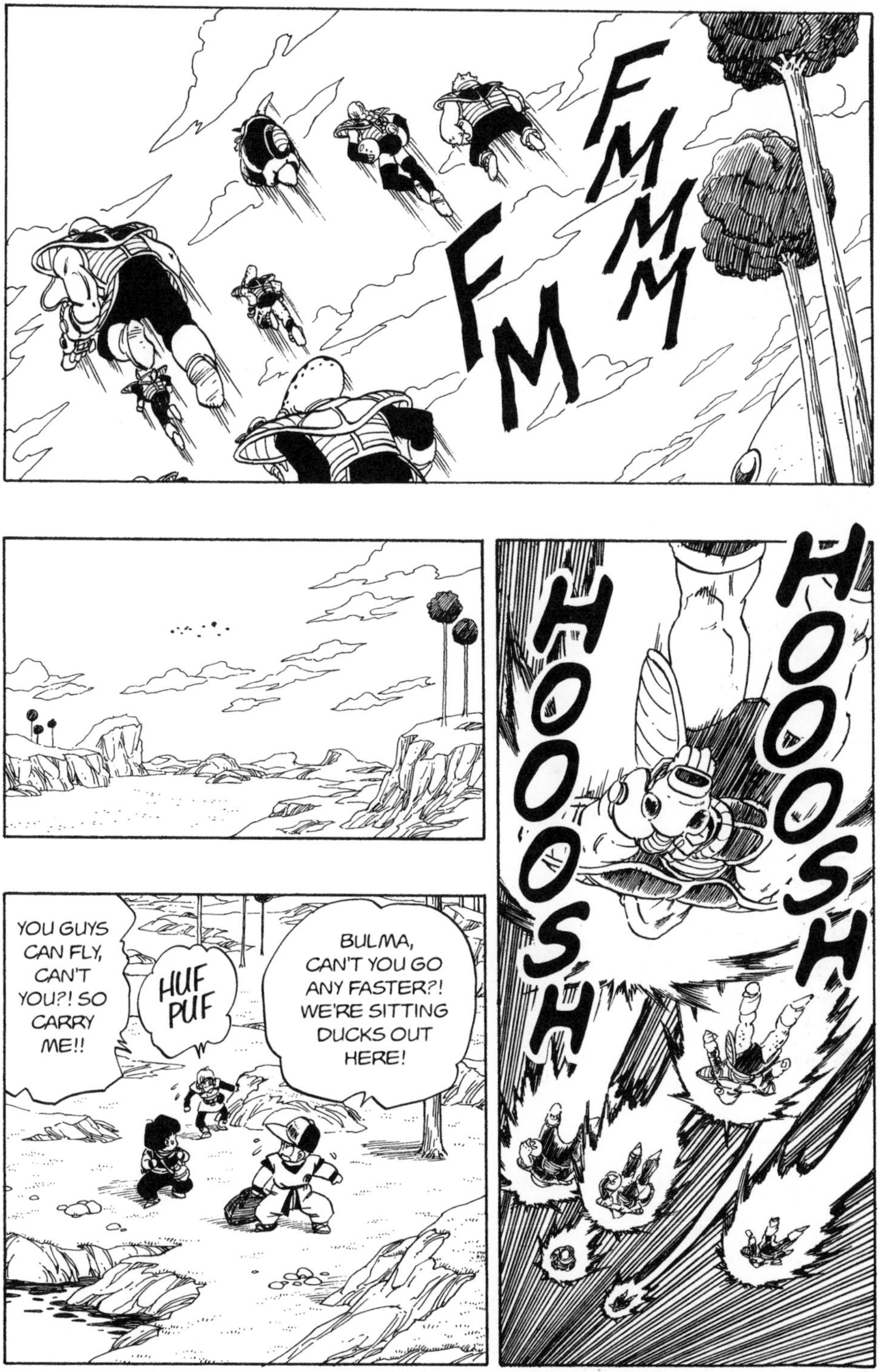
FMMM
FM
HOOOOSH
HOOOOSH
BULMA, CAN'T YOU GO ANY FASTER?! WE'RE SITTING DUCKS OUT HERE!
HUF PUF
YOU GUYS CAN FLY, CAN'T YOU?! SO CARRY ME!!

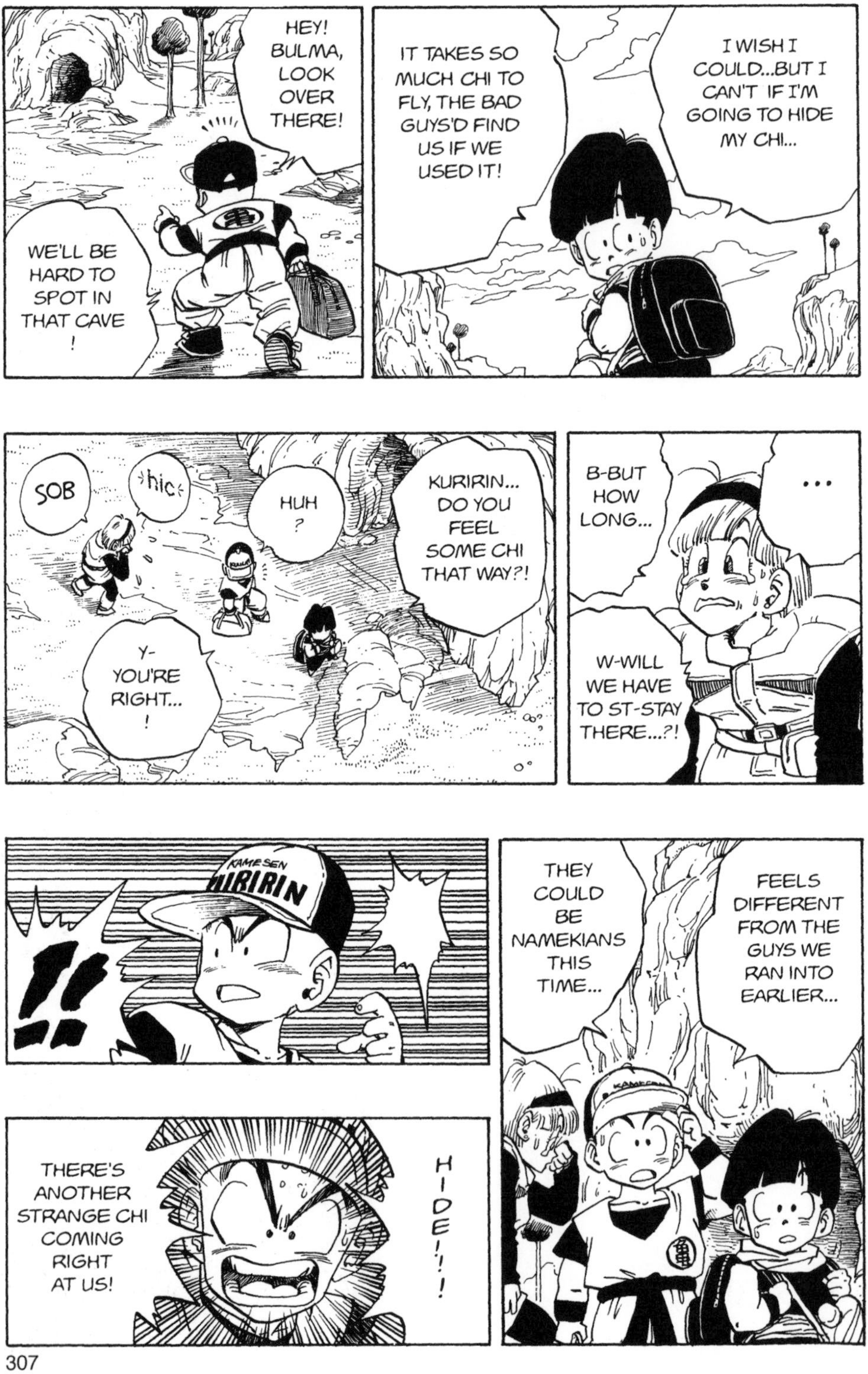

I WISH I COULD...BUT I CAN'T IF I'M GOING TO HIDE MY CHI...
IT TAKES SO MUCH CHI TO FLY, THE BAD GUYS'D FIND US IF WE USED IT!
HEY! BULMA, LOOK OVER THERE!
WE'LL BE HARD TO SPOT IN THAT CAVE!
...
B-BUT HOW LONG...
W-WILL WE HAVE TO ST-STAY THERE...?!
KURIRIN... DO YOU FEEL SOME CHI THAT WAY?!
HUH?
hic
SOB
Y-YOU'RE RIGHT...!
FEELS DIFFERENT FROM THE GUYS WE RAN INTO EARLIER...
THEY COULD BE NAMEKIANS THIS TIME...
KAME SEN
HIDE!!!
THERE'S ANOTHER STRANGE CHI COMING RIGHT AT US!

# DBZ:56 • Goku Returns! Again!

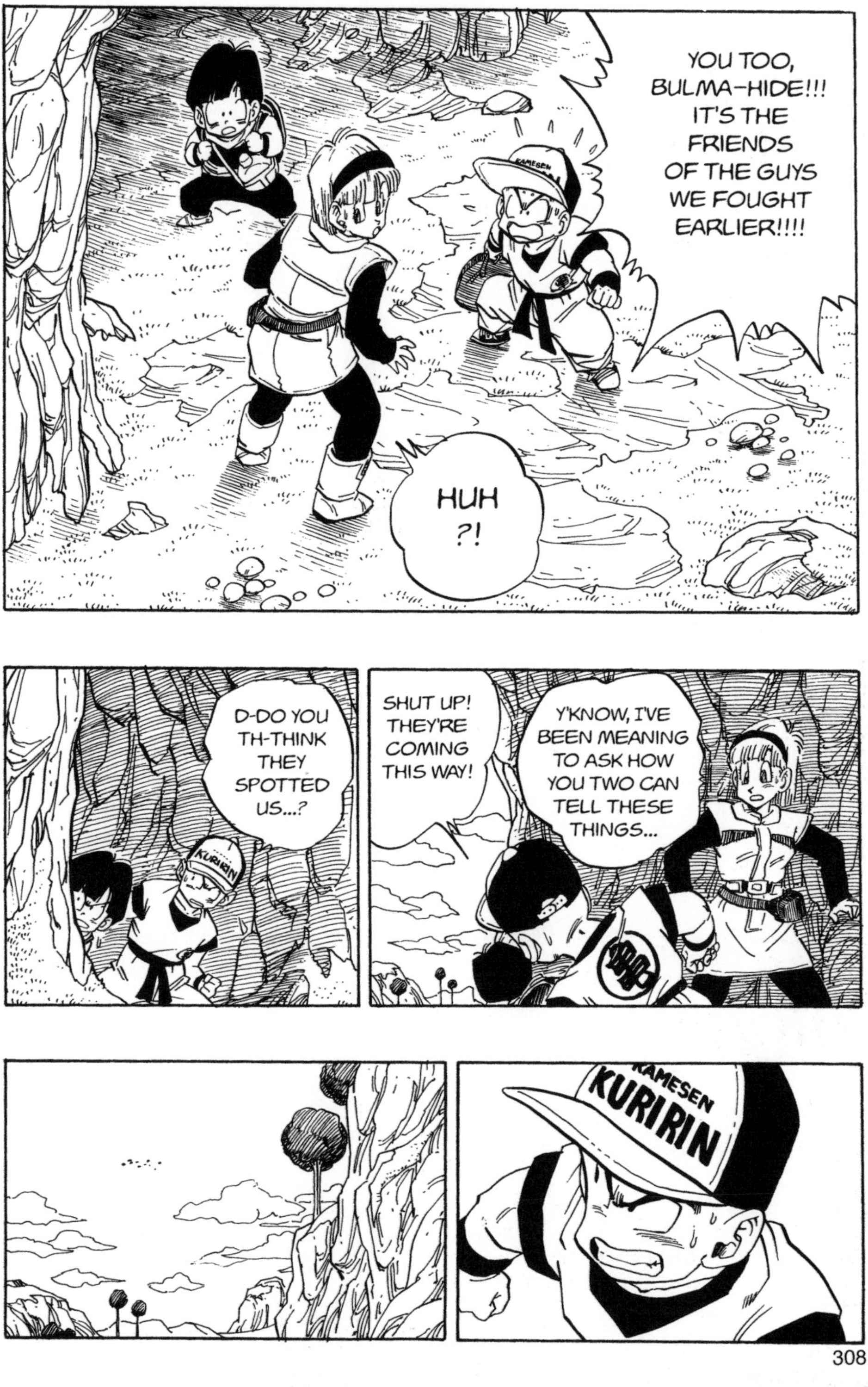
YOU TOO, BULMA-HIDE!!! IT'S THE FRIENDS OF THE GUYS WE FOUGHT EARLIER!!!!
HUH ?!
KAMESEN
Y'KNOW, I'VE BEEN MEANING TO ASK HOW YOU TWO CAN TELL THESE THINGS...
SHUT UP! THEY'RE COMING THIS WAY!
D-DO YOU TH-THINK THEY SPOTTED US...?
KURIRIN
KAMESEN KURIRIN

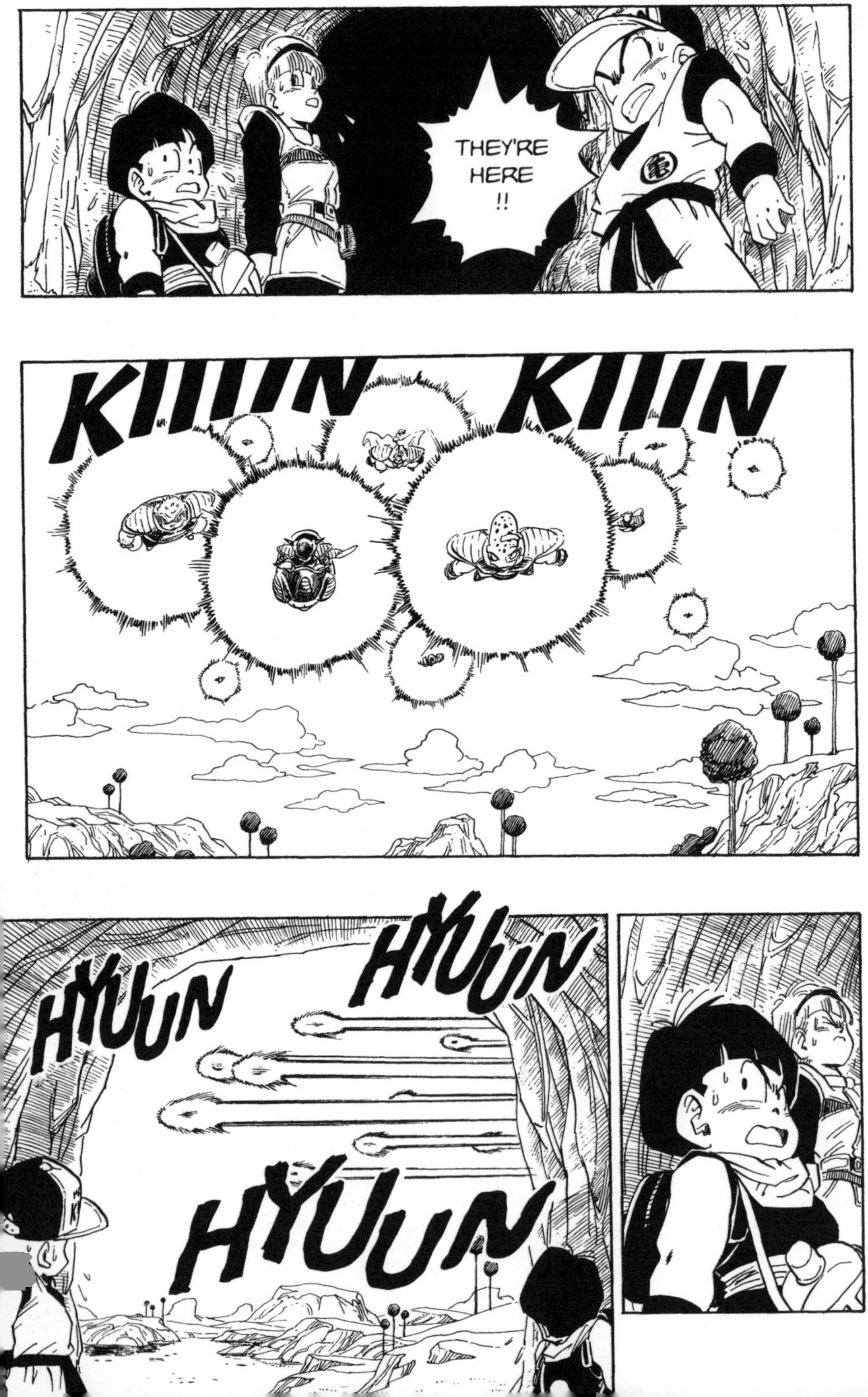
THEY'RE HERE !!
KIIIN KIIIN
HYUUN
HYUUN
HYUUN

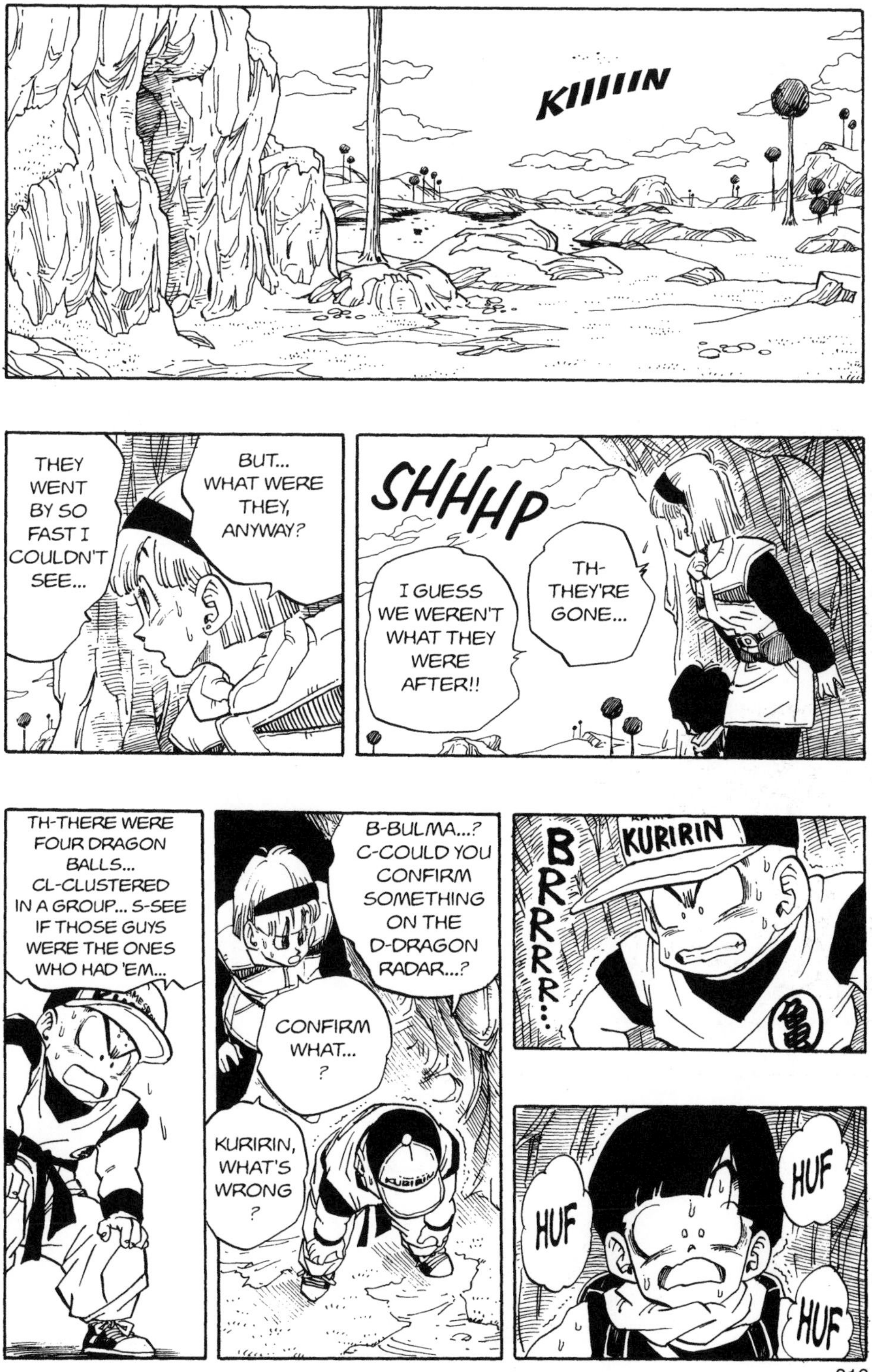
KIIIIIN
SHHHP
TH- THEY'RE GONE...
I GUESS WE WEREN'T WHAT THEY WERE AFTER!!
BUT... WHAT WERE THEY, ANYWAY?
THEY WENT BY SO FAST I COULDN'T SEE...
KURIRIN
BRRRR...
HUF
HUF
HUF
B-BULMA...? C-COULD YOU CONFIRM SOMETHING ON THE D-DRAGON RADAR...?
CONFIRM WHAT... ?
KURIRIN, WHAT'S WRONG ?
TH-THERE WERE FOUR DRAGON BALLS... CL-CLUSTERED IN A GROUP... S-SEE IF THOSE GUYS WERE THE ONES WHO HAD 'EM...

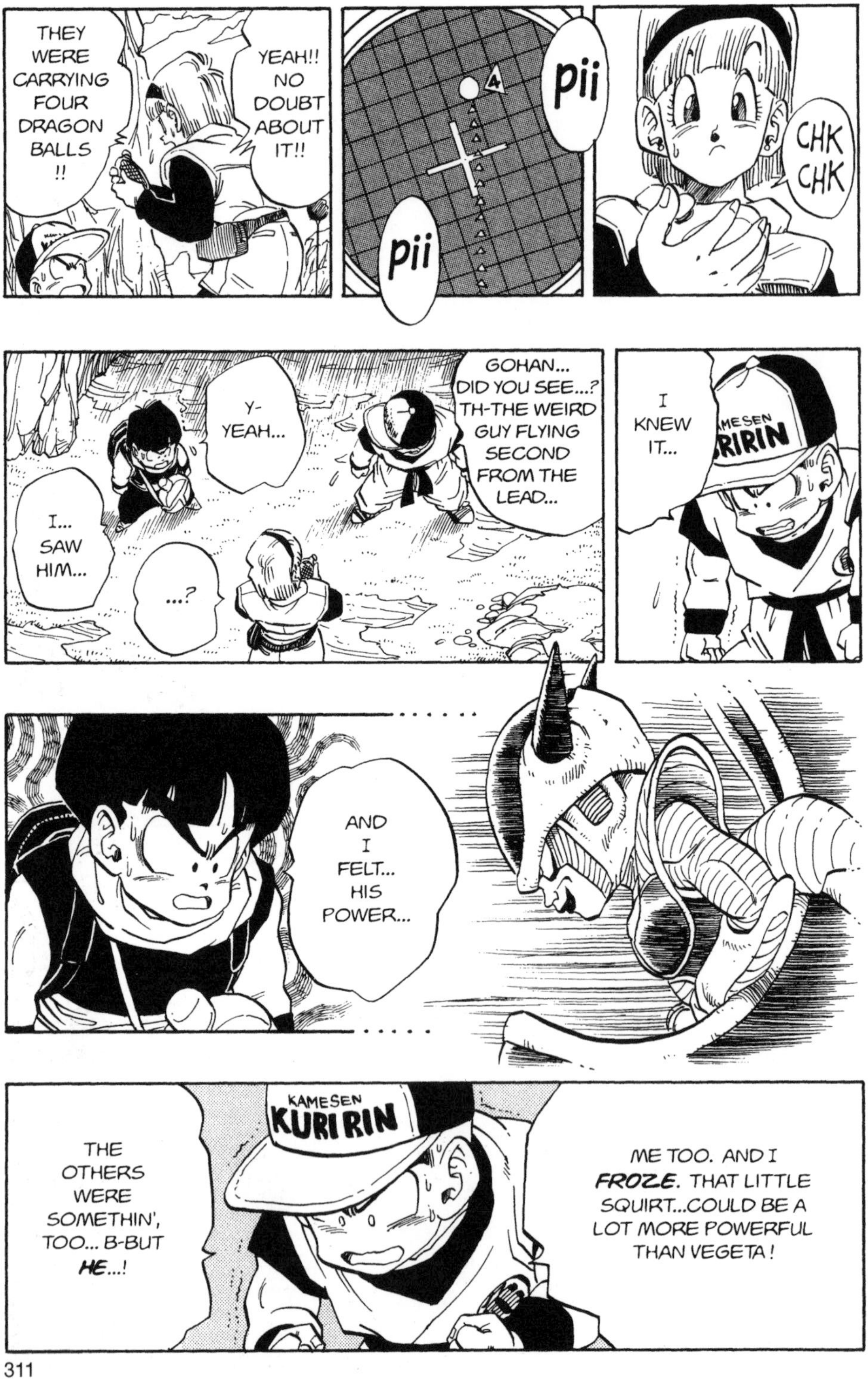
CHK CHK
pii
pii
YEAH!! NO DOUBT ABOUT IT!!
THEY WERE CARRYING FOUR DRAGON BALLS !!
I KNEW IT...
GOHAN... DID YOU SEE...? TH-THE WEIRD GUY FLYING SECOND FROM THE LEAD...
Y-YEAH...
I... SAW HIM...
...?
AND I FELT... HIS POWER...
ME TOO. AND I *FROZE*. THAT LITTLE SQUIRT...COULD BE A LOT MORE POWERFUL THAN VEGETA !
KAMESEN KURIRIN
THE OTHERS WERE SOMETHIN', TOO... B-BUT *HE*...!

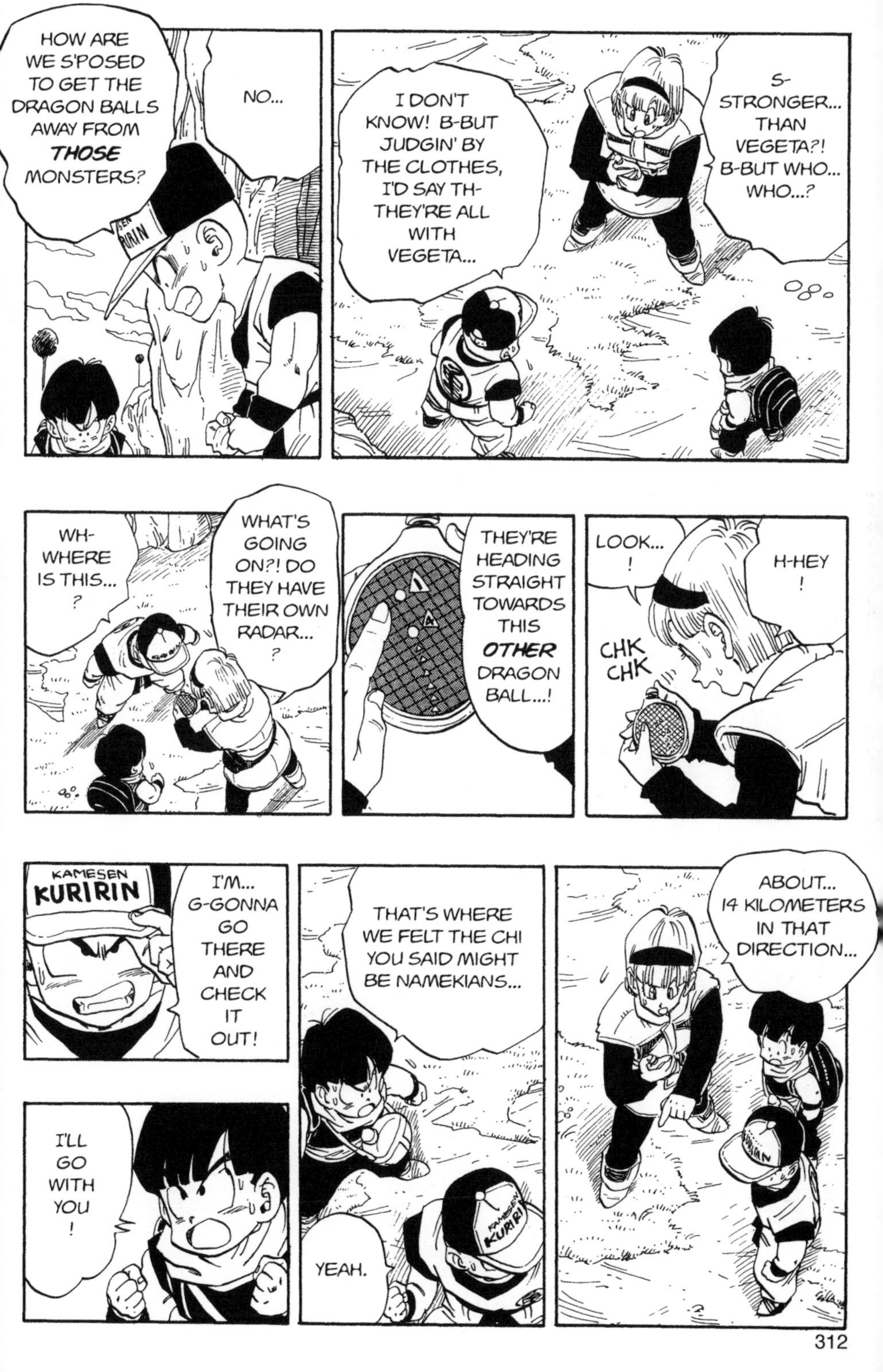
S-STRONGER... THAN VEGETA?! B-BUT WHO... WHO...?
I DON'T KNOW! B-BUT JUDGIN' BY THE CLOTHES, I'D SAY TH-THEY'RE ALL WITH VEGETA...
NO...
HOW ARE WE S'POSED TO GET THE DRAGON BALLS AWAY FROM THOSE MONSTERS?
H-HEY!
LOOK...!
CHK CHK
THEY'RE HEADING STRAIGHT TOWARDS THIS OTHER DRAGON BALL...!
WHAT'S GOING ON?! DO THEY HAVE THEIR OWN RADAR...?
WH-WHERE IS THIS...?
ABOUT... 14 KILOMETERS IN THAT DIRECTION...
THAT'S WHERE WE FELT THE CHI YOU SAID MIGHT BE NAMEKIANS...
YEAH.
KAMESEN KURIRIN
I'M... G-GONNA GO THERE AND CHECK IT OUT!
I'LL GO WITH YOU!

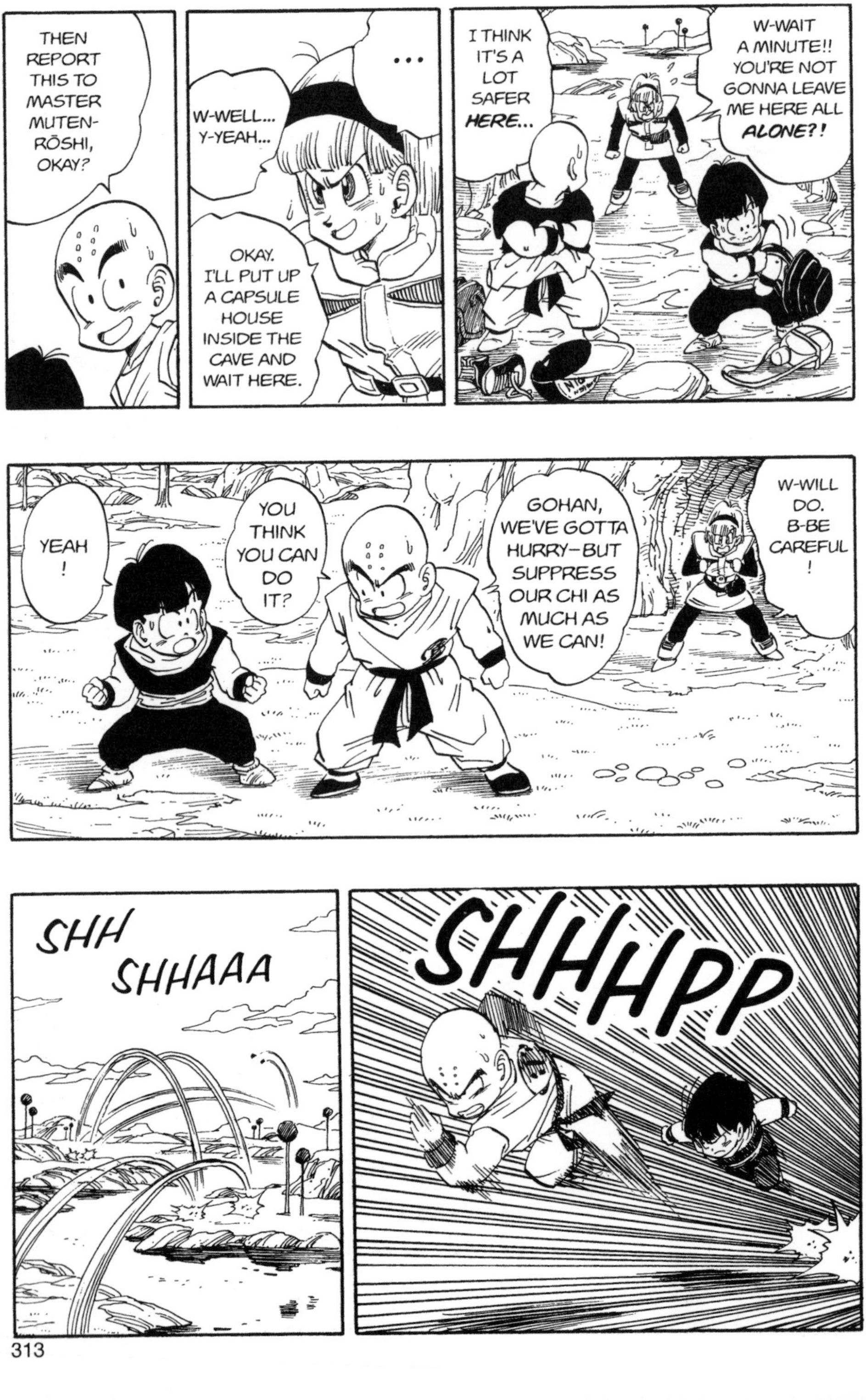
THEN REPORT THIS TO MASTER MUTEN-RŌSHI, OKAY?
...
W-WELL... Y-YEAH...
OKAY. I'LL PUT UP A CAPSULE HOUSE INSIDE THE CAVE AND WAIT HERE.
I THINK IT'S A LOT SAFER ***HERE***...
W-WAIT A MINUTE!! YOU'RE NOT GONNA LEAVE ME HERE ALL ***ALONE?!***
GOHAN, WE'VE GOTTA HURRY—BUT SUPPRESS OUR CHI AS MUCH AS WE CAN!
YOU THINK YOU CAN DO IT?
YEAH!
W-WILL DO. B-BE CAREFUL!
SHH SHHAAA
SHHHPP

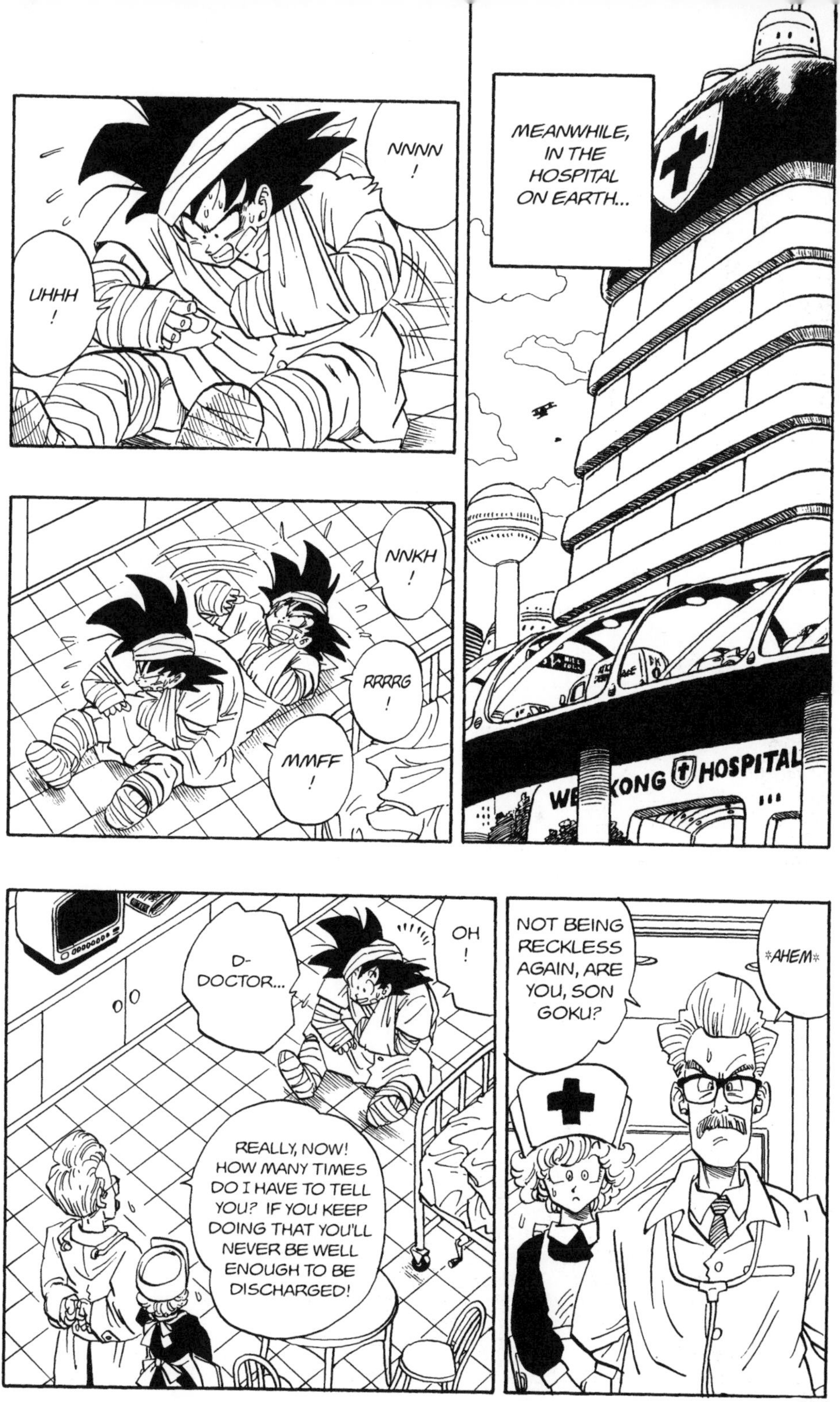
MEANWHILE, IN THE HOSPITAL ON EARTH...
KONG HOSPITAL
NNNN!
UHHH!
NNKH!
RRRRG!
MMFF!
*AHEM*
NOT BEING RECKLESS AGAIN, ARE YOU, SON GOKU?
OH!
D-DOCTOR...
REALLY, NOW! HOW MANY TIMES DO I HAVE TO TELL YOU? IF YOU KEEP DOING THAT YOU'LL NEVER BE WELL ENOUGH TO BE DISCHARGED!

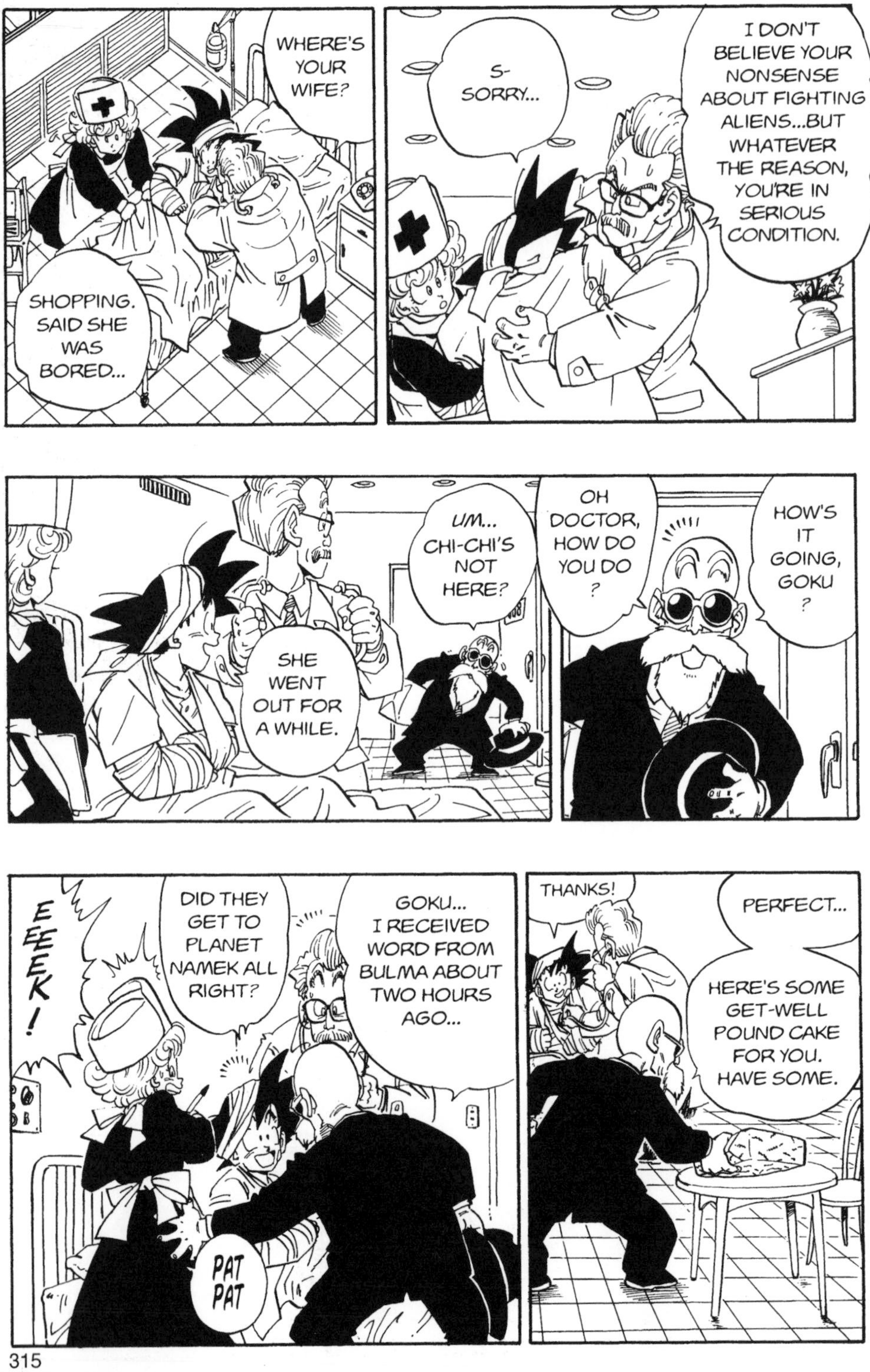
WHERE'S YOUR WIFE?
SHOPPING. SAID SHE WAS BORED...
I DON'T BELIEVE YOUR NONSENSE ABOUT FIGHTING ALIENS...BUT WHATEVER THE REASON, YOU'RE IN SERIOUS CONDITION.
S- SORRY...
UM... CHI-CHI'S NOT HERE?
SHE WENT OUT FOR A WHILE.
HOW'S IT GOING, GOKU ?
OH DOCTOR, HOW DO YOU DO ?
EEEEK!
DID THEY GET TO PLANET NAMEK ALL RIGHT?
GOKU... I RECEIVED WORD FROM BULMA ABOUT TWO HOURS AGO...
PAT PAT
PERFECT...
HERE'S SOME GET-WELL POUND CAKE FOR YOU. HAVE SOME.
THANKS!

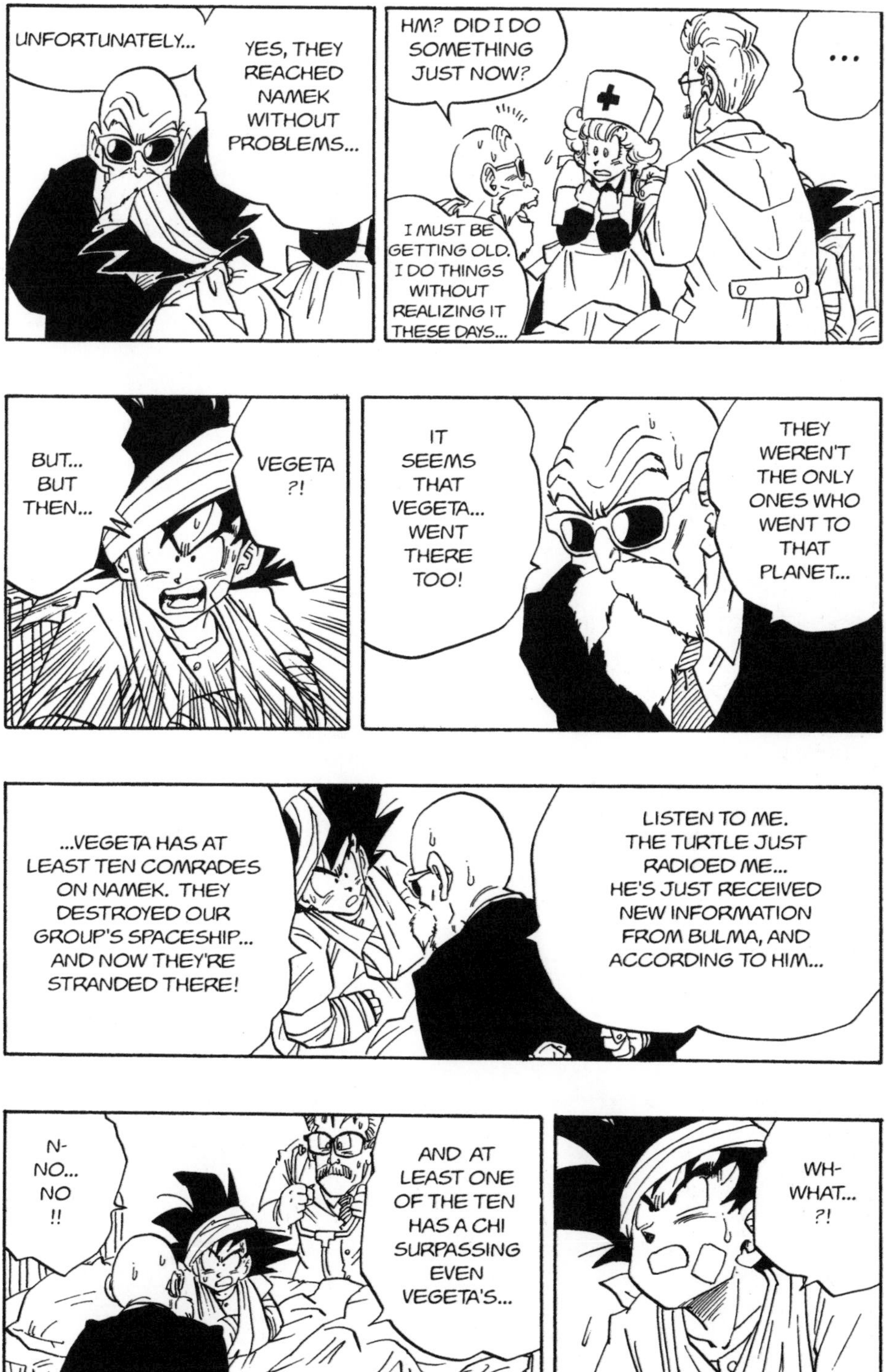
...
HM? DID I DO SOMETHING JUST NOW?
I MUST BE GETTING OLD. I DO THINGS WITHOUT REALIZING IT THESE DAYS...
YES, THEY REACHED NAMEK WITHOUT PROBLEMS...
UNFORTUNATELY...
THEY WEREN'T THE ONLY ONES WHO WENT TO THAT PLANET...
IT SEEMS THAT VEGETA... WENT THERE TOO!
VEGETA ?!
BUT... BUT THEN...
LISTEN TO ME. THE TURTLE JUST RADIOED ME... HE'S JUST RECEIVED NEW INFORMATION FROM BULMA, AND ACCORDING TO HIM...
...VEGETA HAS AT LEAST TEN COMRADES ON NAMEK. THEY DESTROYED OUR GROUP'S SPACESHIP... AND NOW THEY'RE STRANDED THERE!
WH- WHAT... ?!
AND AT LEAST ONE OF THE TEN HAS A CHI SURPASSING EVEN VEGETA'S...
N- NO... NO !!

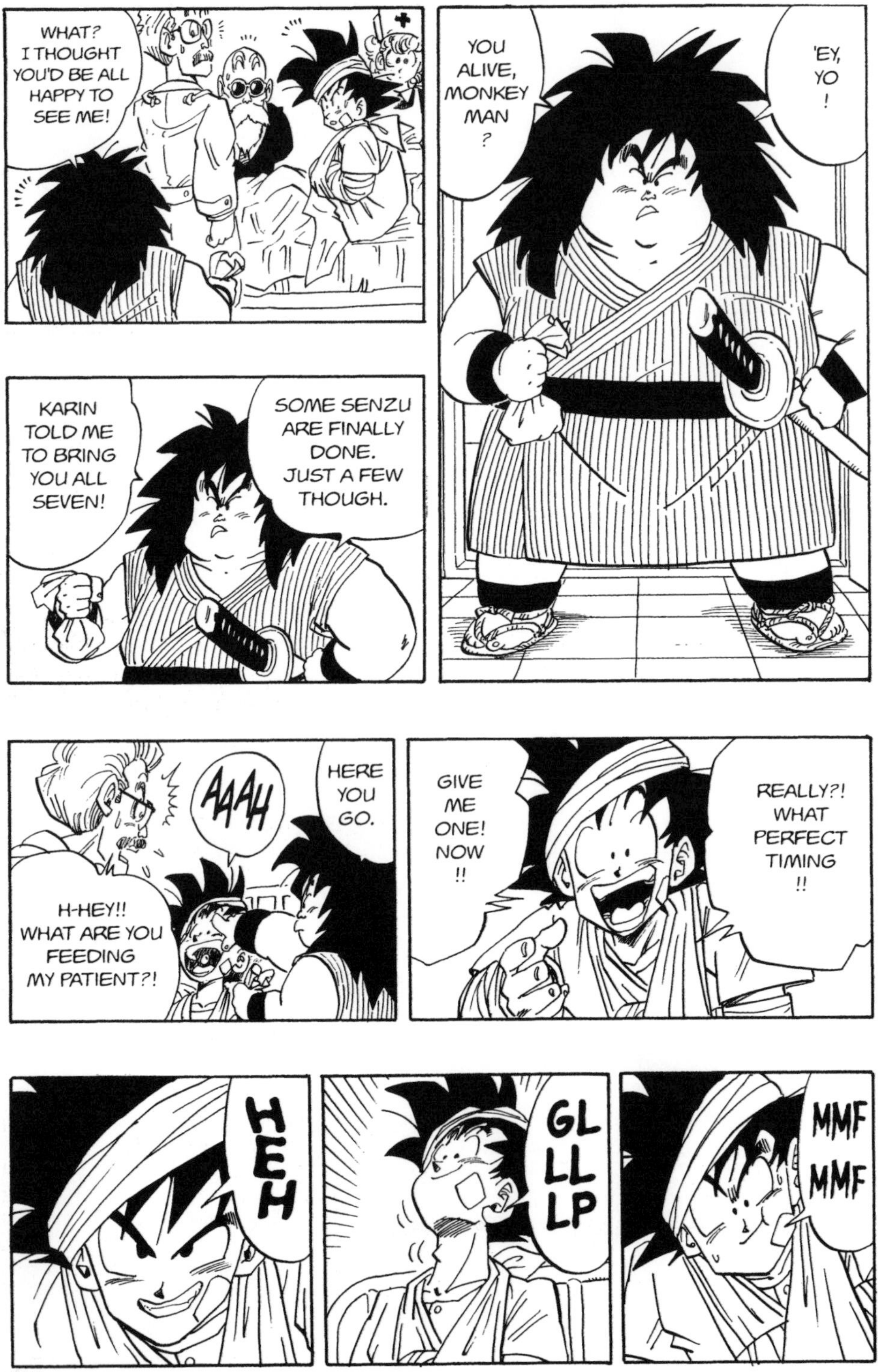
'EY, YO!
YOU ALIVE, MONKEY MAN?
WHAT? I THOUGHT YOU'D BE ALL HAPPY TO SEE ME!
SOME SENZU ARE FINALLY DONE. JUST A FEW THOUGH.
KARIN TOLD ME TO BRING YOU ALL SEVEN!
REALLY?! WHAT PERFECT TIMING!!
GIVE ME ONE! NOW!!
HERE YOU GO.
AAAH
H-HEY!! WHAT ARE YOU FEEDING MY PATIENT?!
MMF MMF
GL LL LP
HEH

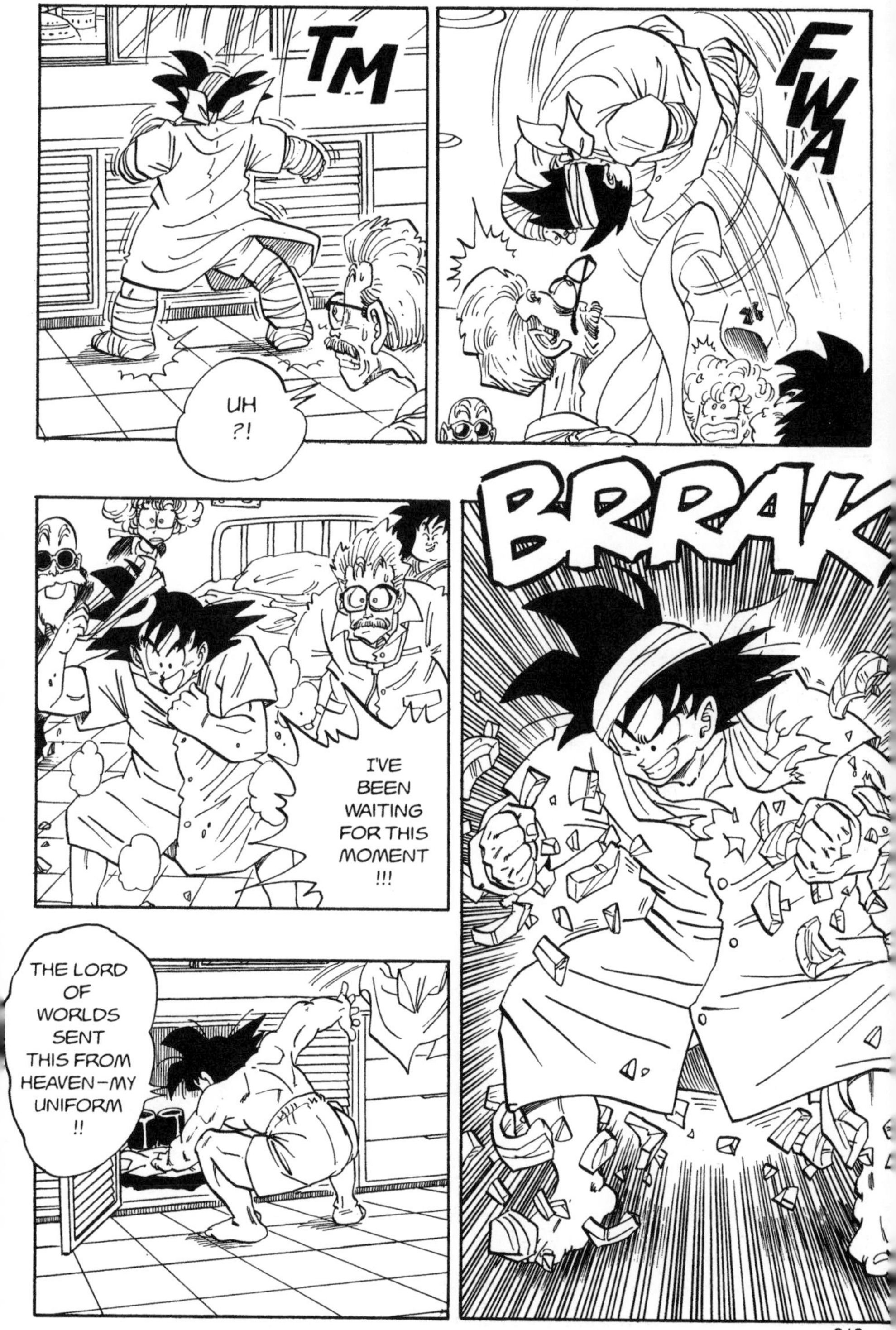
FWA
TM
UH ?!
BRRAK
I'VE BEEN WAITING FOR THIS MOMENT !!!
THE LORD OF WORLDS SENT THIS FROM HEAVEN—MY UNIFORM !!

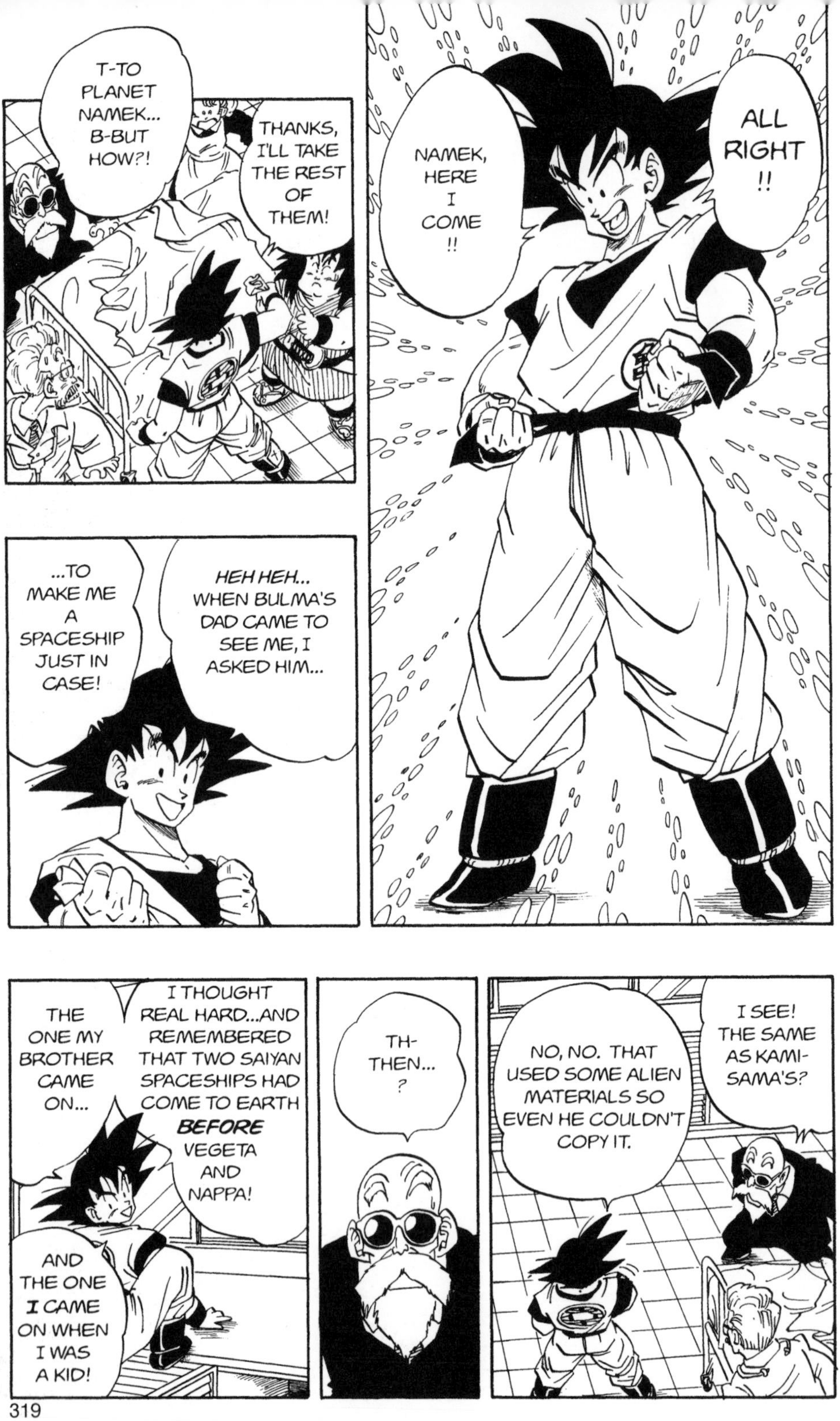
ALL RIGHT !!
NAMEK, HERE I COME !!
THANKS, I'LL TAKE THE REST OF THEM!
T-TO PLANET NAMEK... B-BUT HOW?!
*HEH HEH...* WHEN BULMA'S DAD CAME TO SEE ME, I ASKED HIM...
...TO MAKE ME A SPACESHIP JUST IN CASE!
I SEE! THE SAME AS KAMI-SAMA'S?
NO, NO. THAT USED SOME ALIEN MATERIALS SO EVEN HE COULDN'T COPY IT.
TH-THEN... ?
I THOUGHT REAL HARD...AND REMEMBERED THAT TWO SAIYAN SPACESHIPS HAD COME TO EARTH ***BEFORE*** VEGETA AND NAPPA!
THE ONE MY BROTHER CAME ON...
AND THE ONE **I** CAME ON WHEN I WAS A KID!

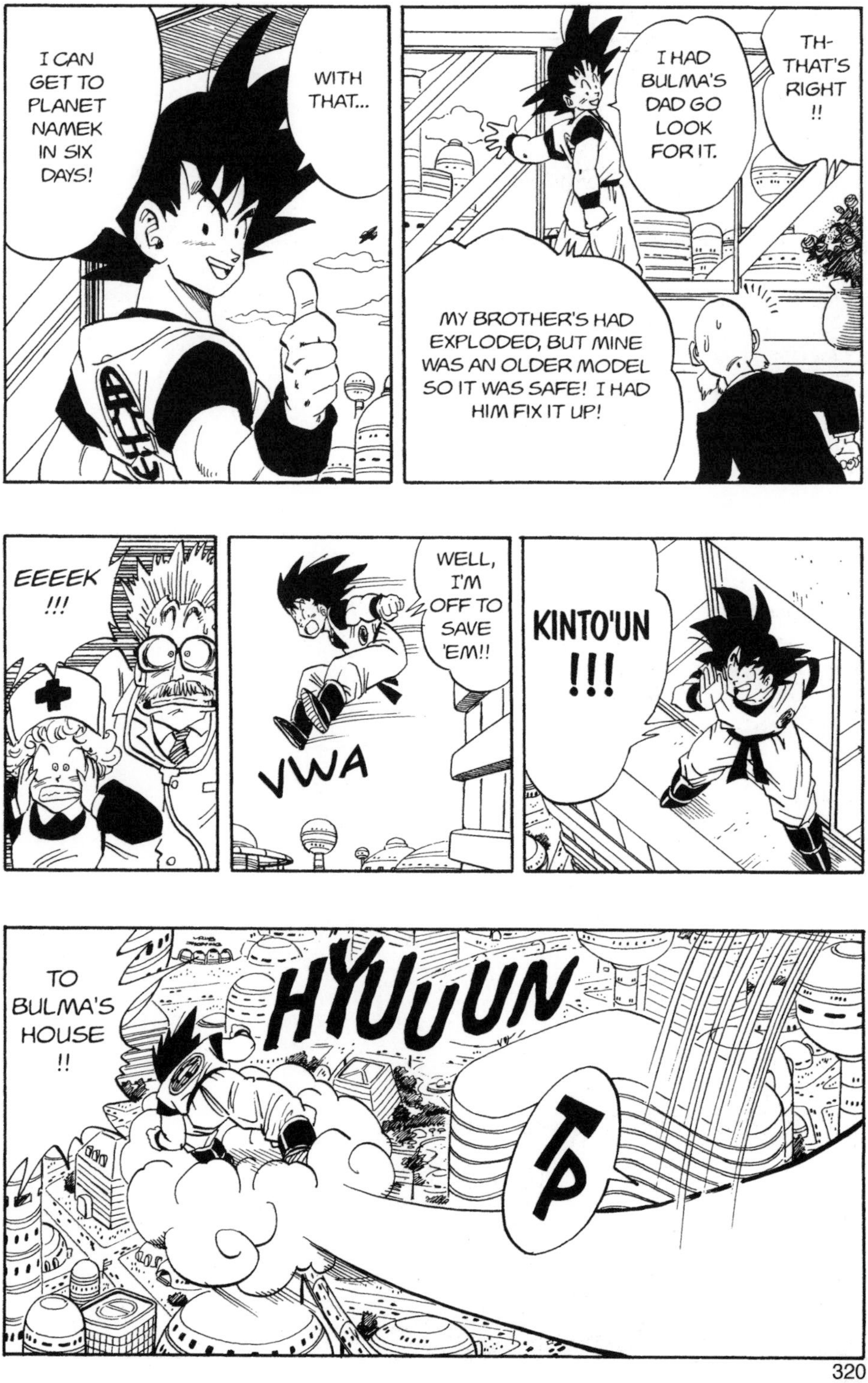
TH- THAT'S RIGHT !!
I HAD BULMA'S DAD GO LOOK FOR IT.
MY BROTHER'S HAD EXPLODED, BUT MINE WAS AN OLDER MODEL SO IT WAS SAFE! I HAD HIM FIX IT UP!
WITH THAT...
I CAN GET TO PLANET NAMEK IN SIX DAYS!
KINTO'UN !!!
WELL, I'M OFF TO SAVE 'EM!!
VWA
EEEEK !!!
HYUUUN
TO BULMA'S HOUSE !!
TP

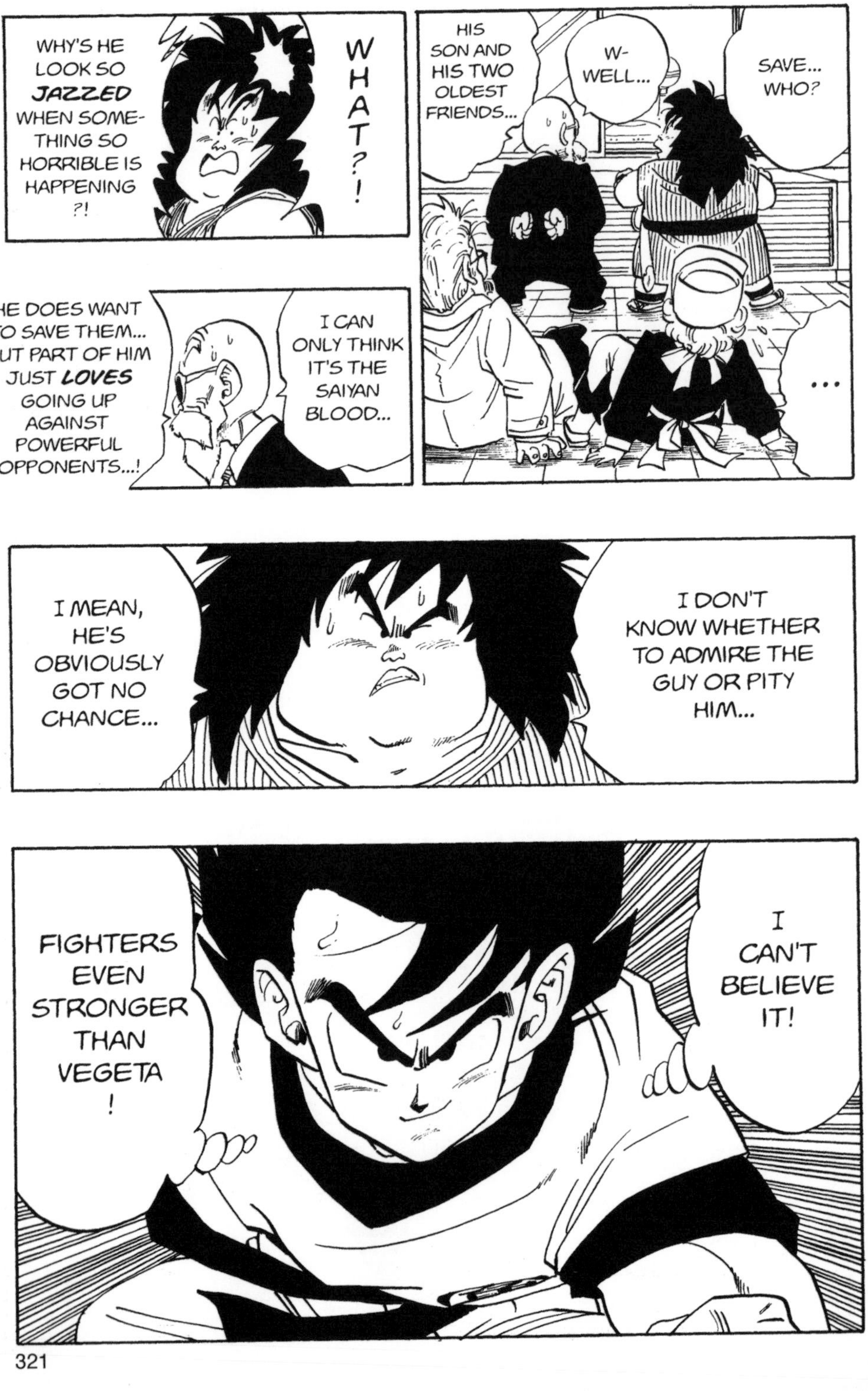
SAVE... WHO?
W- WELL...
HIS SON AND HIS TWO OLDEST FRIENDS...
...
WHAT?!
WHY'S HE LOOK SO JAZZED WHEN SOMETHING SO HORRIBLE IS HAPPENING?!
I CAN ONLY THINK IT'S THE SAIYAN BLOOD...
HE DOES WANT TO SAVE THEM... BUT PART OF HIM JUST LOVES GOING UP AGAINST POWERFUL OPPONENTS...!
I DON'T KNOW WHETHER TO ADMIRE THE GUY OR PITY HIM...
I MEAN, HE'S OBVIOUSLY GOT NO CHANCE...
I CAN'T BELIEVE IT!
FIGHTERS EVEN STRONGER THAN VEGETA!

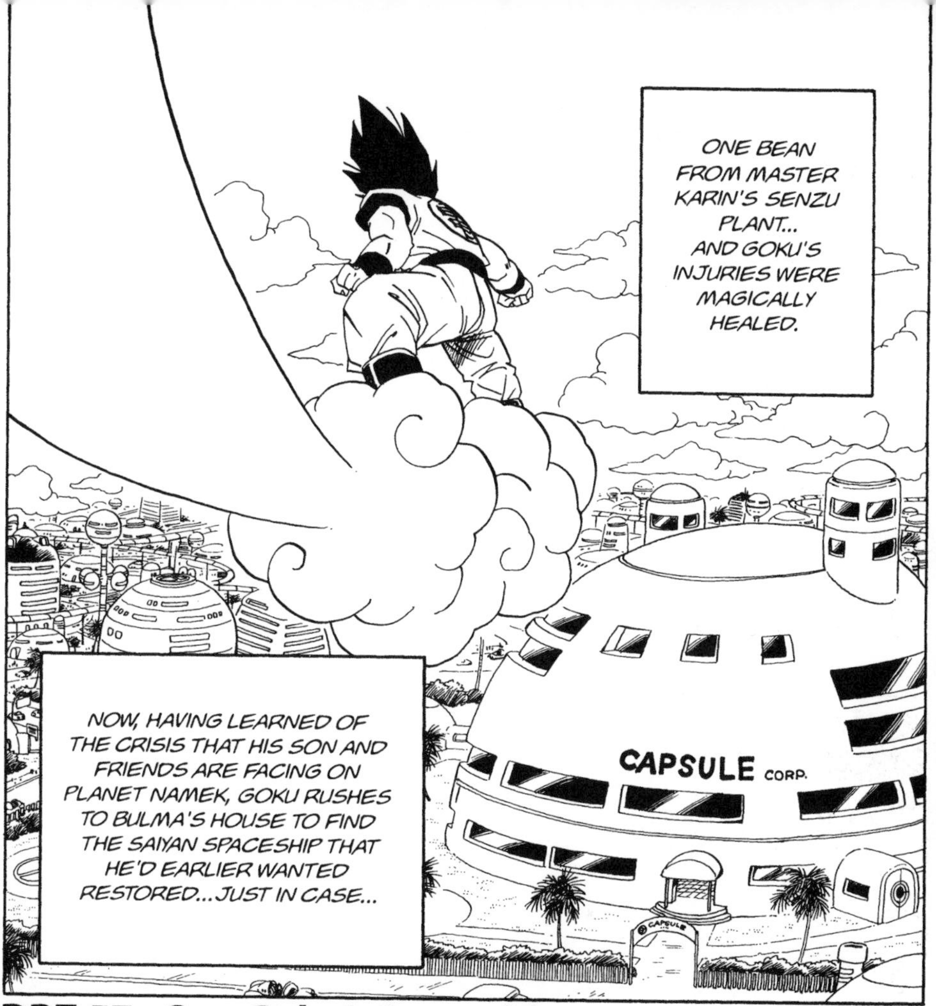
ONE BEAN FROM MASTER KARIN'S SENZU PLANT... AND GOKU'S INJURIES WERE MAGICALLY HEALED.
NOW, HAVING LEARNED OF THE CRISIS THAT HIS SON AND FRIENDS ARE FACING ON PLANET NAMEK, GOKU RUSHES TO BULMA'S HOUSE TO FIND THE SAIYAN SPACESHIP THAT HE'D EARLIER WANTED RESTORED...JUST IN CASE...
CAPSULE CORP.

## DBZ:57 • Son Goku's Spaceship

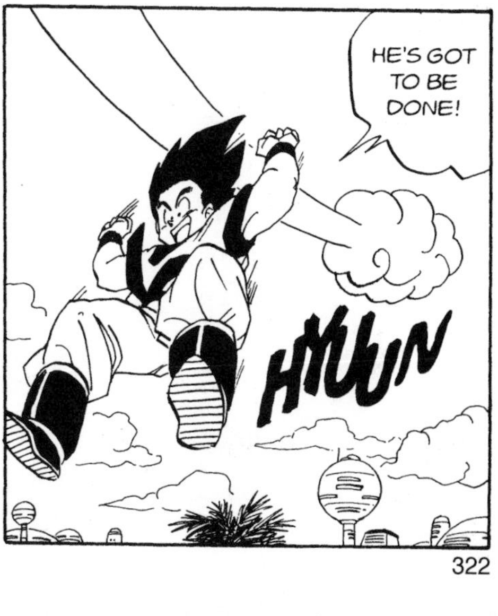
HE'S GOT TO BE DONE!
HYUUN

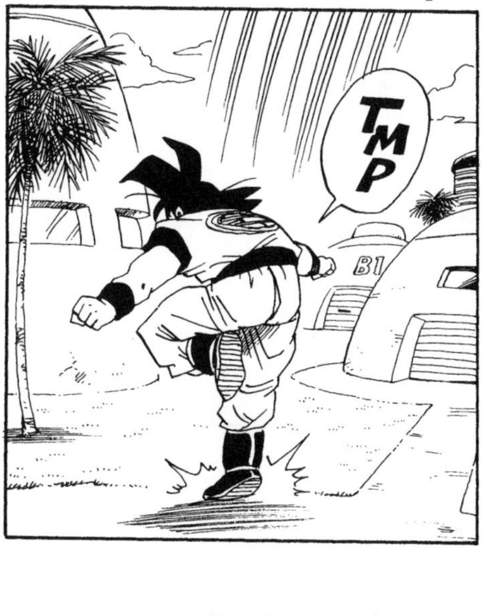
TMP
B1

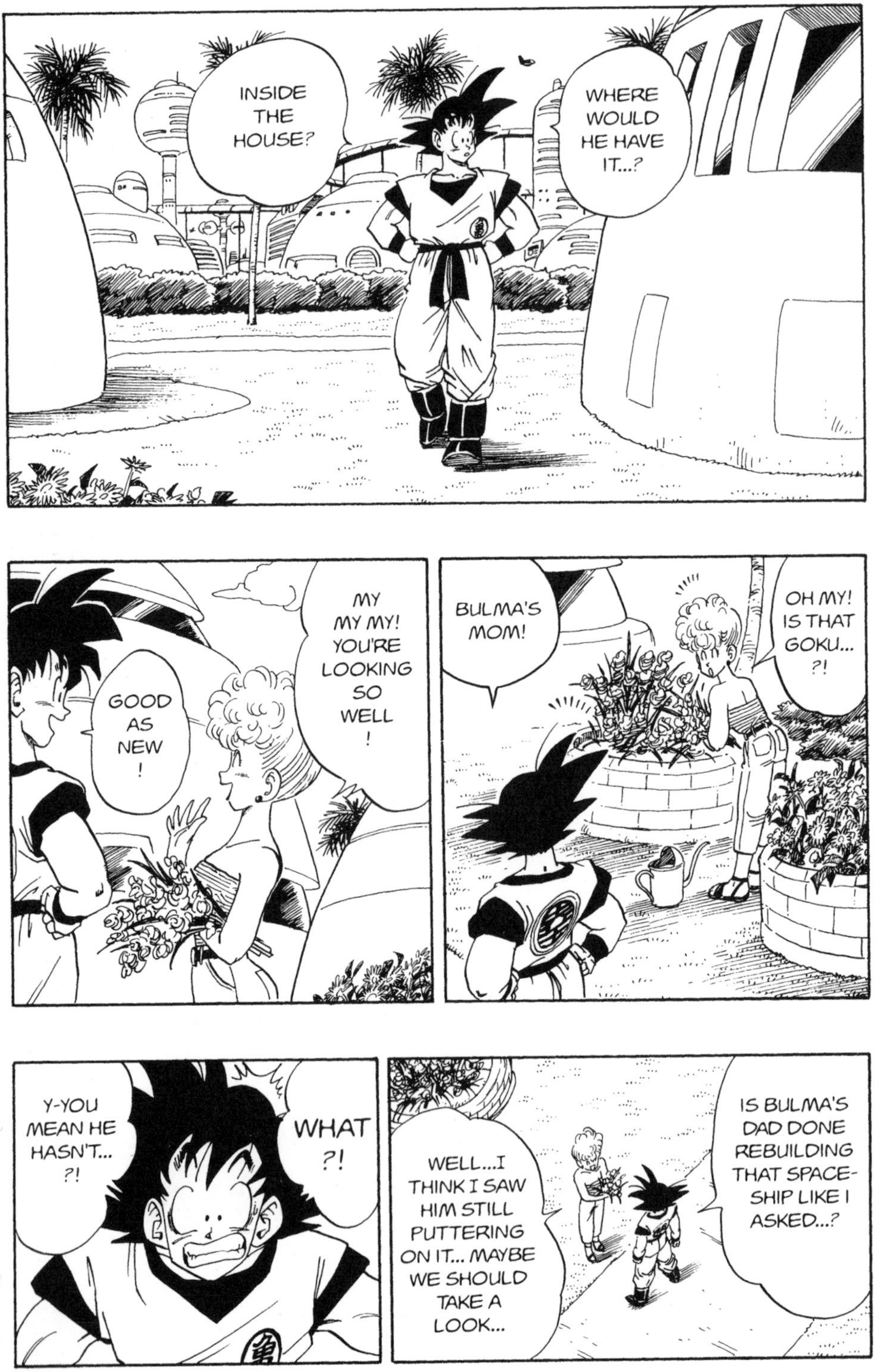
WHERE WOULD HE HAVE IT...?
INSIDE THE HOUSE?
OH MY! IS THAT GOKU...?!
BULMA'S MOM!
MY MY MY! YOU'RE LOOKING SO WELL!
GOOD AS NEW!
IS BULMA'S DAD DONE REBUILDING THAT SPACE-SHIP LIKE I ASKED...?
WELL...I THINK I SAW HIM STILL PUTTERING ON IT... MAYBE WE SHOULD TAKE A LOOK...
WHAT?!
Y-YOU MEAN HE HASN'T...?!

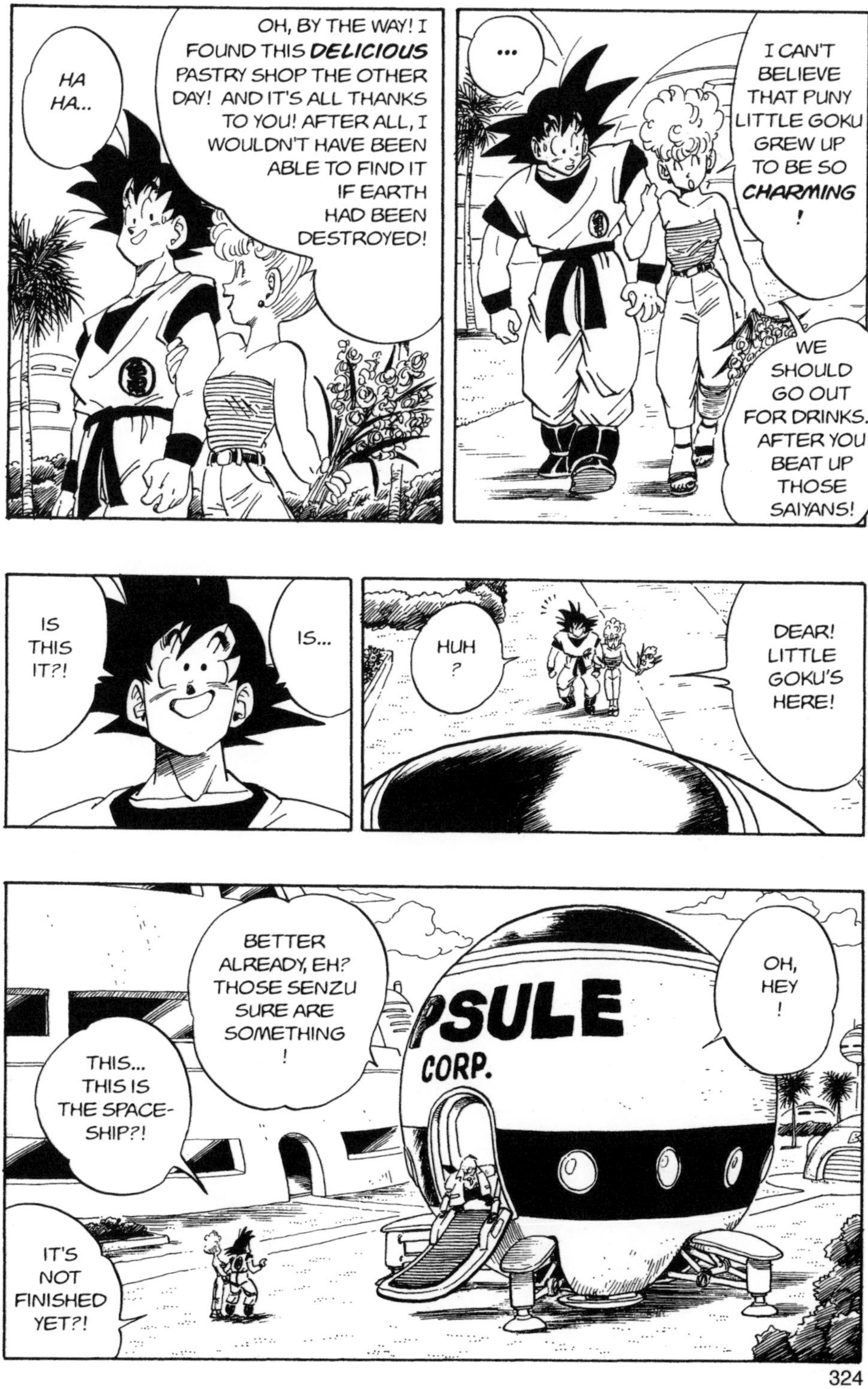
I CAN'T BELIEVE THAT PUNY LITTLE GOKU GREW UP TO BE SO **CHARMING**!
...
WE SHOULD GO OUT FOR DRINKS... AFTER YOU BEAT UP THOSE SAIYANS!
OH, BY THE WAY! I FOUND THIS **DELICIOUS** PASTRY SHOP THE OTHER DAY! AND IT'S ALL THANKS TO YOU! AFTER ALL, I WOULDN'T HAVE BEEN ABLE TO FIND IT IF EARTH HAD BEEN DESTROYED!
HA HA...
DEAR! LITTLE GOKU'S HERE!
HUH?
IS...
IS THIS IT?!
OH, HEY!
PSULE
CORP.
BETTER ALREADY, EH? THOSE SENZU SURE ARE SOMETHING!
THIS... THIS IS THE SPACE-SHIP?!
IT'S NOT FINISHED YET?!

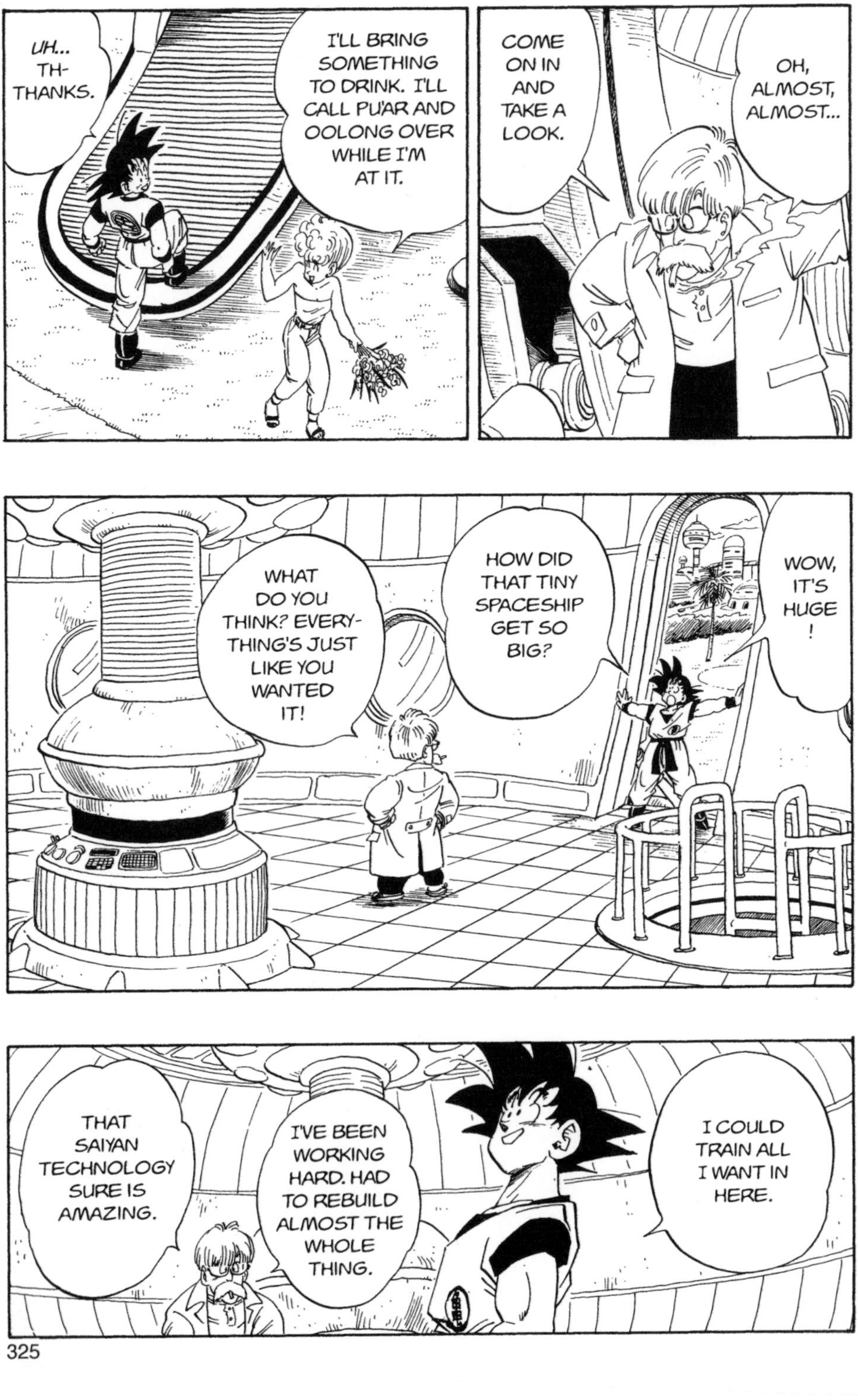
OH, ALMOST, ALMOST...
COME ON IN AND TAKE A LOOK.
I'LL BRING SOMETHING TO DRINK. I'LL CALL PU'AR AND OOLONG OVER WHILE I'M AT IT.
UH... TH-THANKS.
WOW, IT'S HUGE!
HOW DID THAT TINY SPACESHIP GET SO BIG?
WHAT DO YOU THINK? EVERY-THING'S JUST LIKE YOU WANTED IT!
I COULD TRAIN ALL I WANT IN HERE.
I'VE BEEN WORKING HARD. HAD TO REBUILD ALMOST THE WHOLE THING.
THAT SAIYAN TECHNOLOGY SURE IS AMAZING.

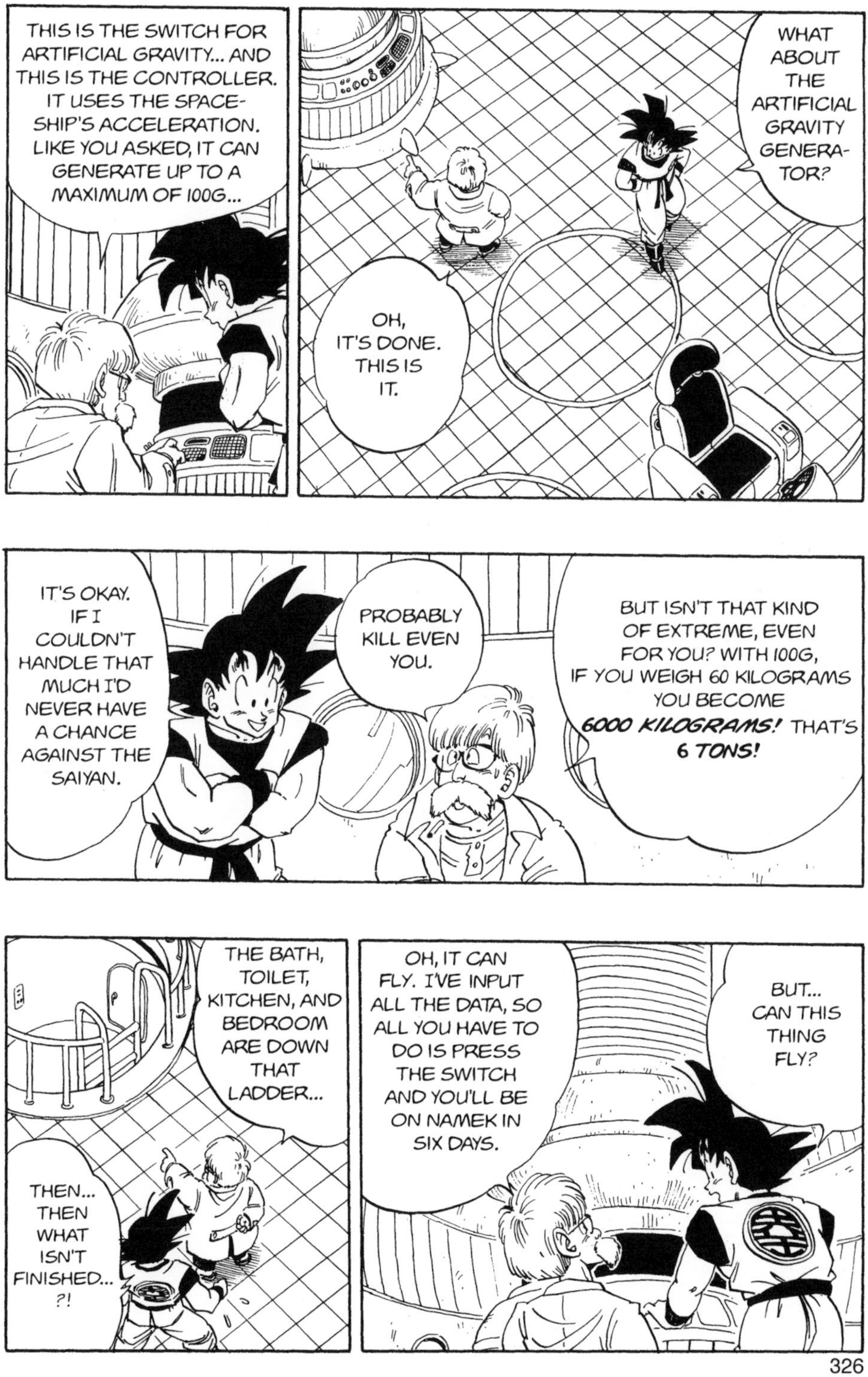
WHAT ABOUT THE ARTIFICIAL GRAVITY GENERATOR?
OH, IT'S DONE. THIS IS IT.
THIS IS THE SWITCH FOR ARTIFICIAL GRAVITY... AND THIS IS THE CONTROLLER. IT USES THE SPACE-SHIP'S ACCELERATION. LIKE YOU ASKED, IT CAN GENERATE UP TO A MAXIMUM OF 100G...
BUT ISN'T THAT KIND OF EXTREME, EVEN FOR YOU? WITH 100G, IF YOU WEIGH 60 KILOGRAMS YOU BECOME **6000 KILOGRAMS!** THAT'S **6 TONS!**
PROBABLY KILL EVEN YOU.
IT'S OKAY. IF I COULDN'T HANDLE THAT MUCH I'D NEVER HAVE A CHANCE AGAINST THE SAIYAN.
BUT... CAN THIS THING FLY?
OH, IT CAN FLY. I'VE INPUT ALL THE DATA, SO ALL YOU HAVE TO DO IS PRESS THE SWITCH AND YOU'LL BE ON NAMEK IN SIX DAYS.
THE BATH, TOILET, KITCHEN, AND BEDROOM ARE DOWN THAT LADDER...
THEN... THEN WHAT ISN'T FINISHED... ?!

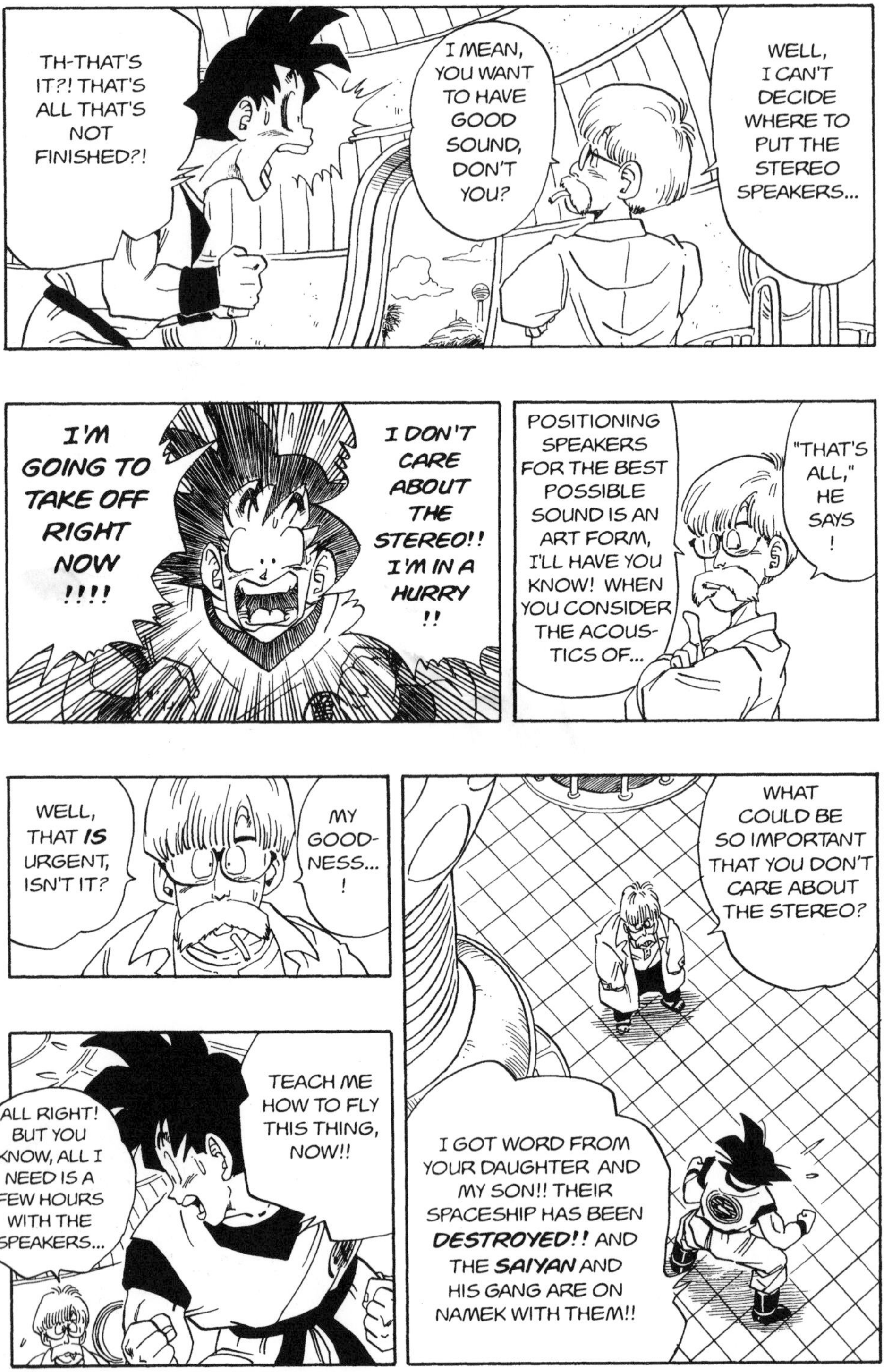
WELL, I CAN'T DECIDE WHERE TO PUT THE STEREO SPEAKERS...
I MEAN, YOU WANT TO HAVE GOOD SOUND, DON'T YOU?
TH-THAT'S IT?! THAT'S ALL THAT'S NOT FINISHED?!
"THAT'S ALL," HE SAYS !
POSITIONING SPEAKERS FOR THE BEST POSSIBLE SOUND IS AN ART FORM, I'LL HAVE YOU KNOW! WHEN YOU CONSIDER THE ACOUS-TICS OF...
I DON'T CARE ABOUT THE STEREO!! I'M IN A HURRY !!
I'M GOING TO TAKE OFF RIGHT NOW !!!!
WHAT COULD BE SO IMPORTANT THAT YOU DON'T CARE ABOUT THE STEREO?
I GOT WORD FROM YOUR DAUGHTER AND MY SON!! THEIR SPACESHIP HAS BEEN **DESTROYED!!** AND THE **SAIYAN** AND HIS GANG ARE ON NAMEK WITH THEM!!
MY GOOD-NESS... !
WELL, THAT **IS** URGENT, ISN'T IT?
TEACH ME HOW TO FLY THIS THING, NOW!!
ALL RIGHT! BUT YOU KNOW, ALL I NEED IS A FEW HOURS WITH THE SPEAKERS...

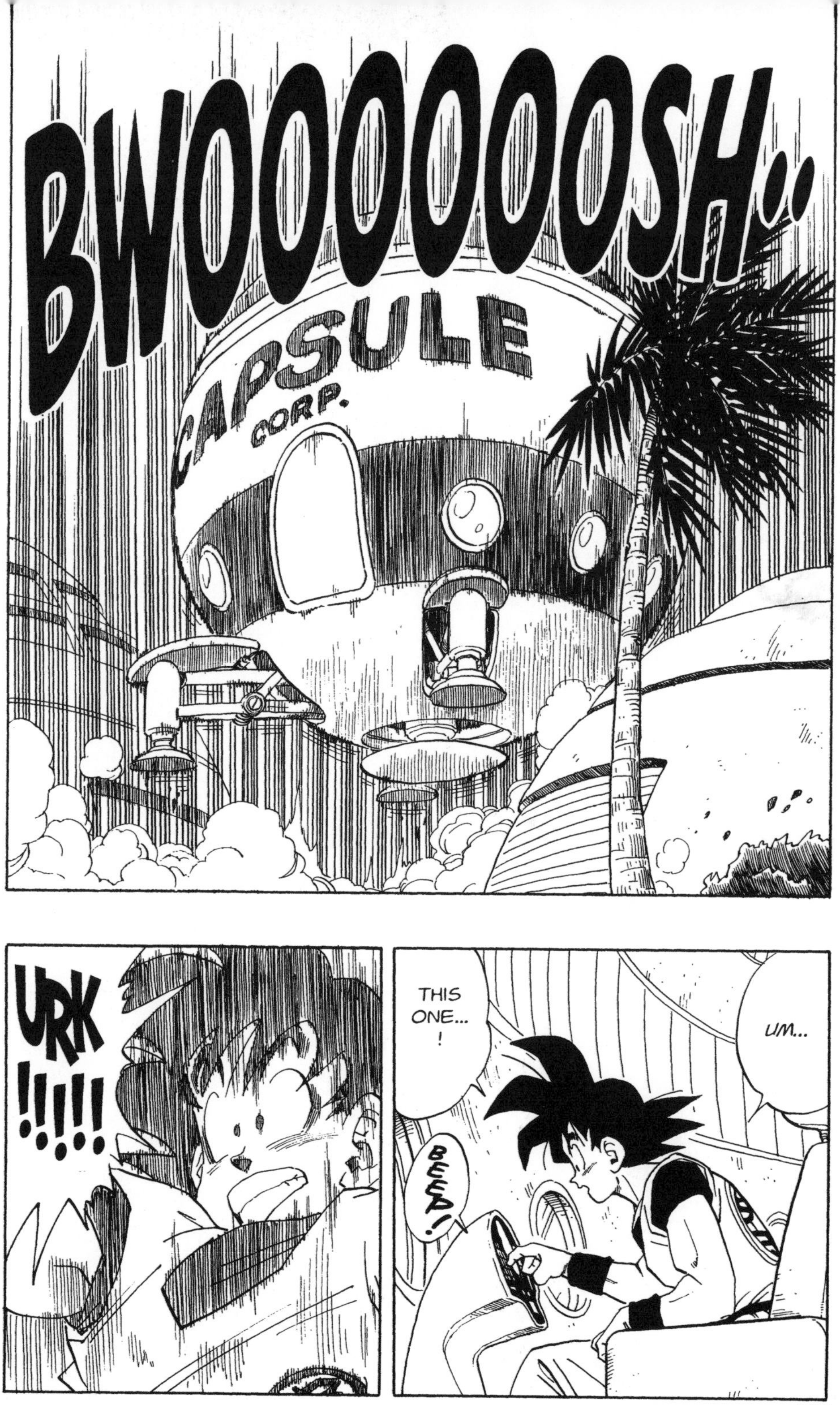
BWOOOOOSH..
CAPSULE
CORP.
UM...
THIS ONE...!
BEEP!
URK!!!!!

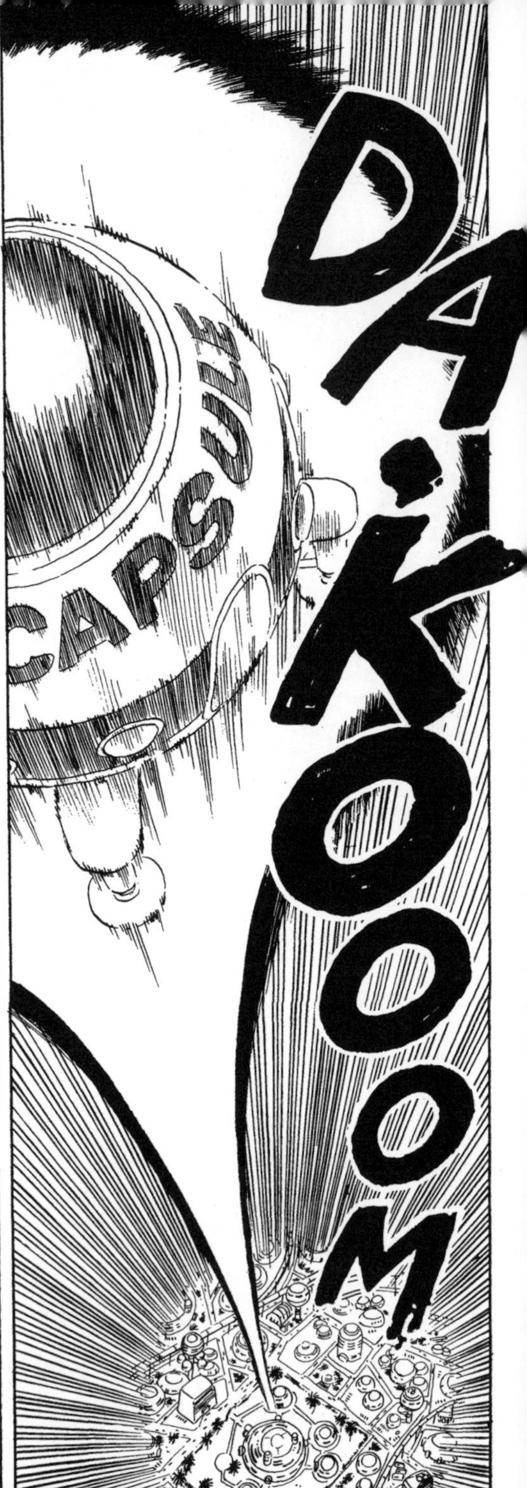
CAPSULE
DA-KOOM

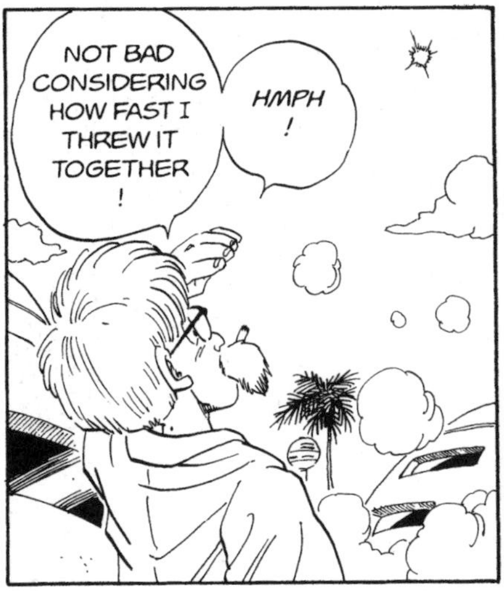
HMPH!
NOT BAD CONSIDERING HOW FAST I THREW IT TOGETHER!

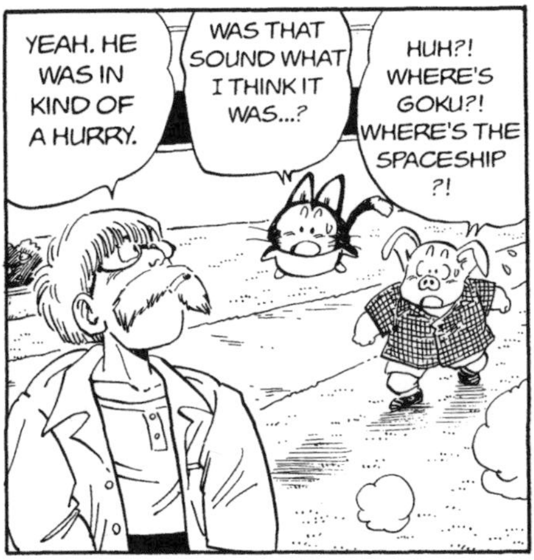
HUH?! WHERE'S GOKU?! WHERE'S THE SPACESHIP?!
WAS THAT SOUND WHAT I THINK IT WAS...?
YEAH. HE WAS IN KIND OF A HURRY.

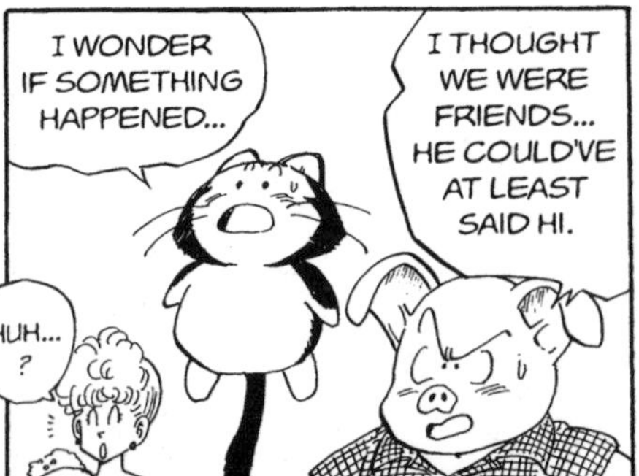
I THOUGHT WE WERE FRIENDS... HE COULD'VE AT LEAST SAID HI.
I WONDER IF SOMETHING HAPPENED...
HUH...?

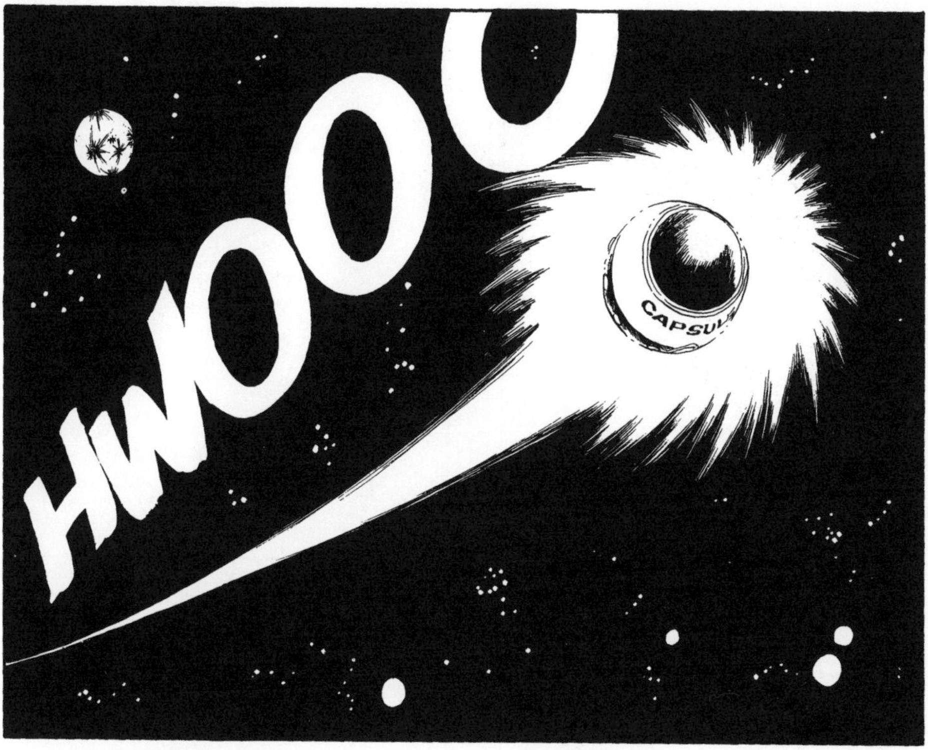
HWOOO
CAPSUL

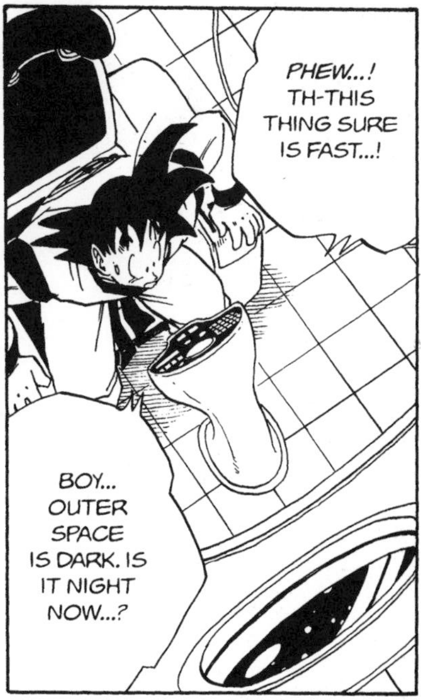
*PHEW...!* TH-THIS THING SURE IS FAST...!
BOY... OUTER SPACE IS DARK. IS IT NIGHT NOW...?

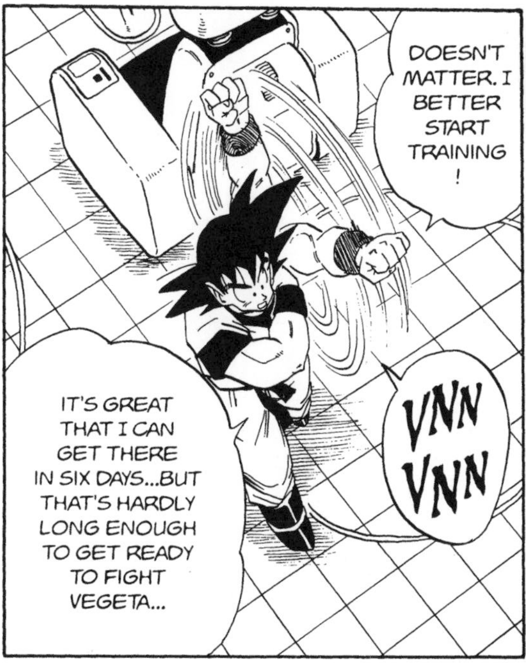
DOESN'T MATTER. I BETTER START TRAINING!
VNN VNN
IT'S GREAT THAT I CAN GET THERE IN SIX DAYS...BUT THAT'S HARDLY LONG ENOUGH TO GET READY TO FIGHT VEGETA...

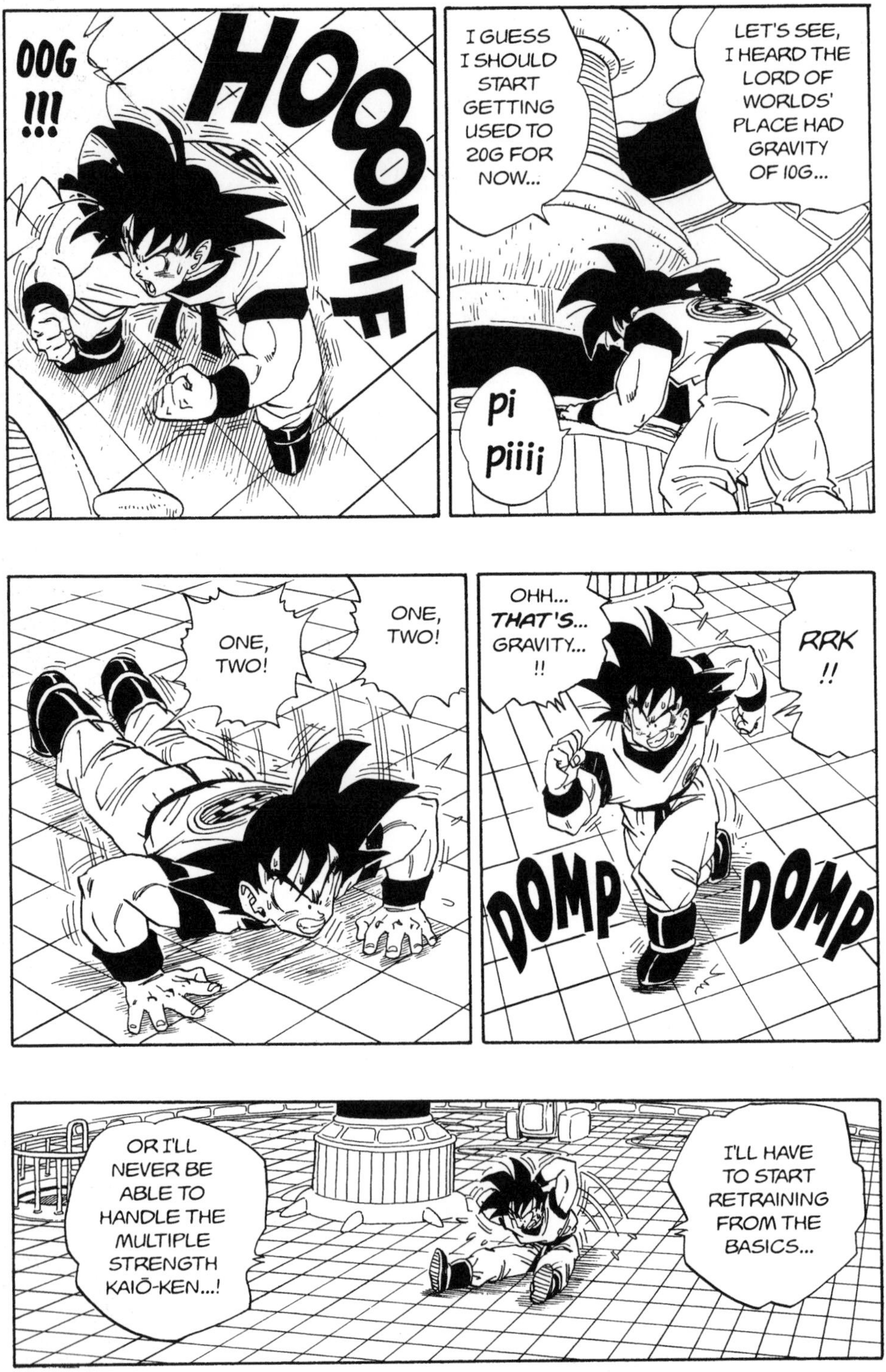

LET'S SEE, I HEARD THE LORD OF WORLDS' PLACE HAD GRAVITY OF 10G...
I GUESS I SHOULD START GETTING USED TO 20G FOR NOW...
pi piiii
HOOOMF
OOG !!!
RRK !!
OHH... *THAT'S*... GRAVITY... !!
DOMP
DOMP
ONE, TWO!
ONE, TWO!
I'LL HAVE TO START RETRAINING FROM THE BASICS...
OR I'LL NEVER BE ABLE TO HANDLE THE MULTIPLE STRENGTH KAIŌ-KEN...!

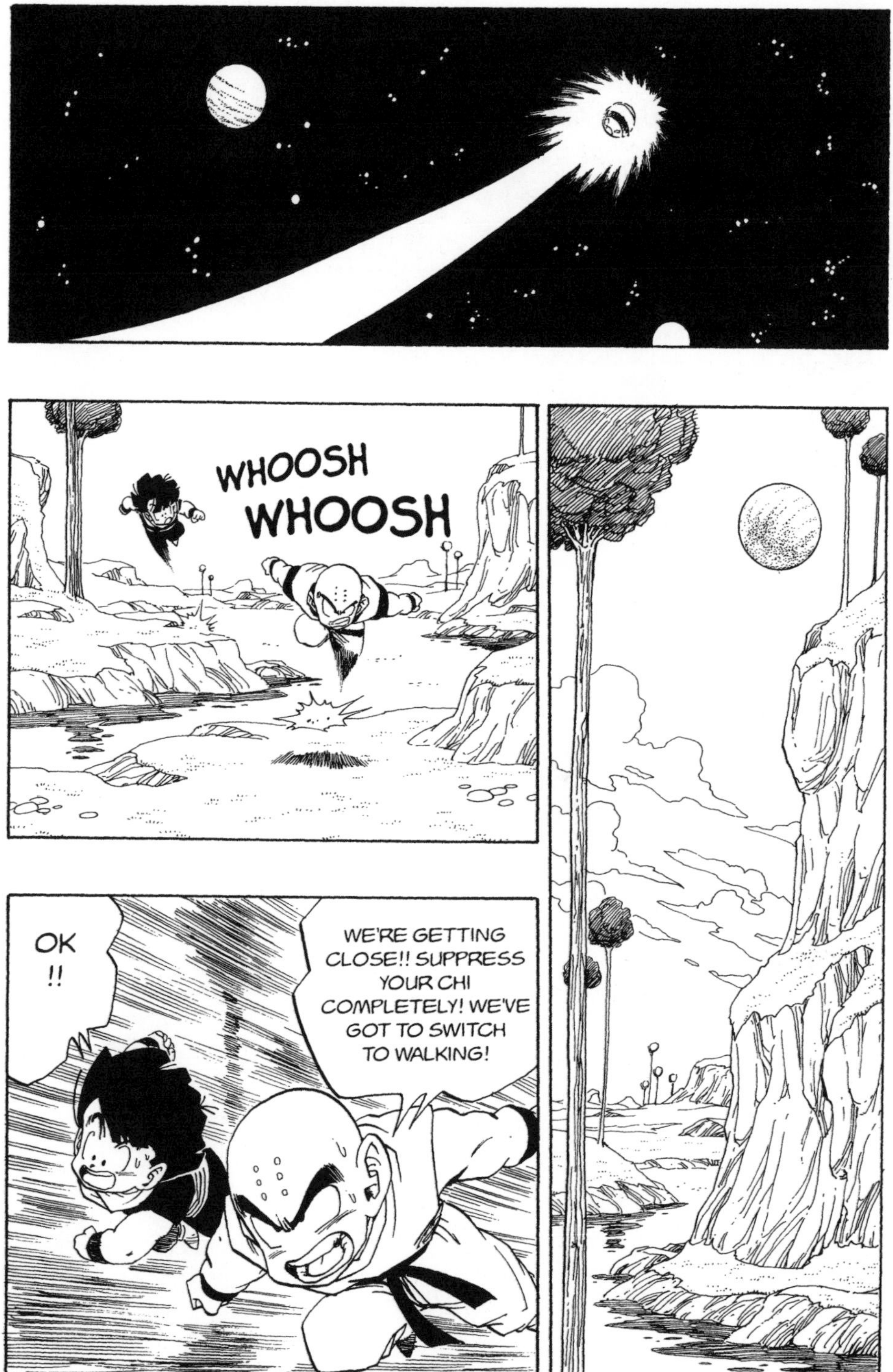
WHOOSH
WHOOSH
WE'RE GETTING CLOSE!! SUPPRESS YOUR CHI COMPLETELY! WE'VE GOT TO SWITCH TO WALKING!
OK !!

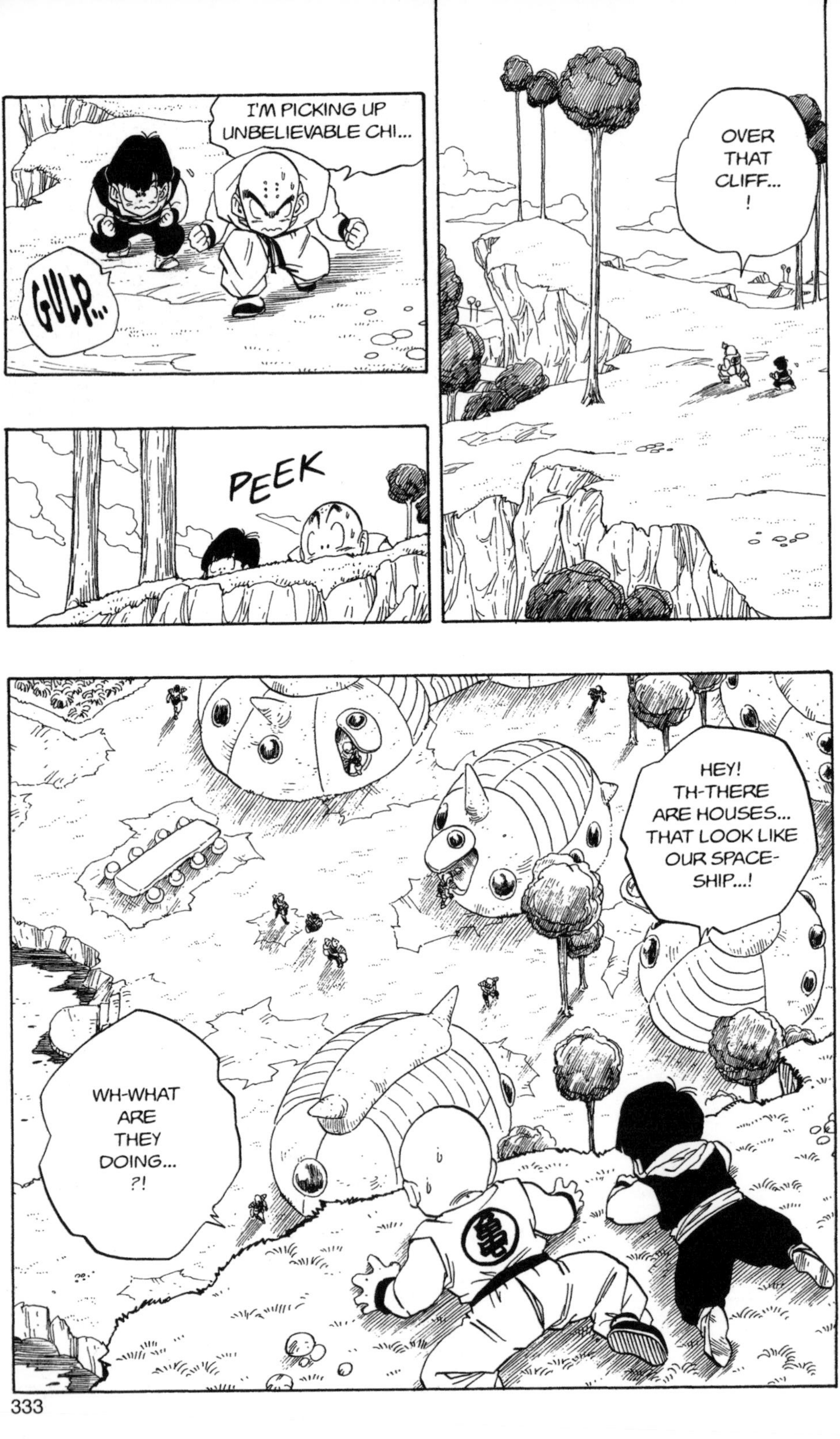
OVER THAT CLIFF... !
I'M PICKING UP UNBELIEVABLE CHI...
GULP...
PEEK
HEY! TH-THERE ARE HOUSES... THAT LOOK LIKE OUR SPACE-SHIP...!
WH-WHAT ARE THEY DOING... ?!

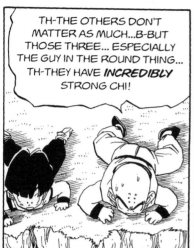

TH-THE OTHERS DON'T MATTER AS MUCH...B-BUT THOSE THREE... ESPECIALLY THE GUY IN THE ROUND THING... TH-THEY HAVE *INCREDIBLY* STRONG CHI!

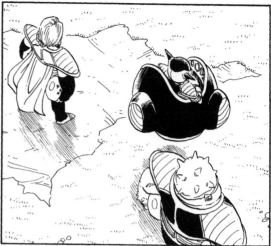

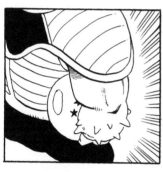

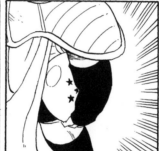

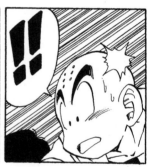

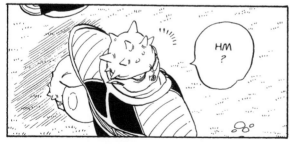

HM?

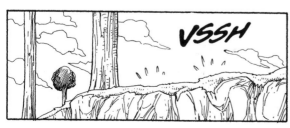

*VSSH*

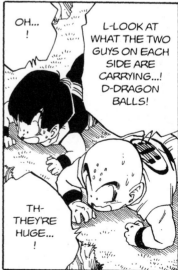

OH...!

L-LOOK AT WHAT THE TWO GUYS ON EACH SIDE ARE CARRYING...! D-DRAGON BALLS!

TH-THEY'RE HUGE...!

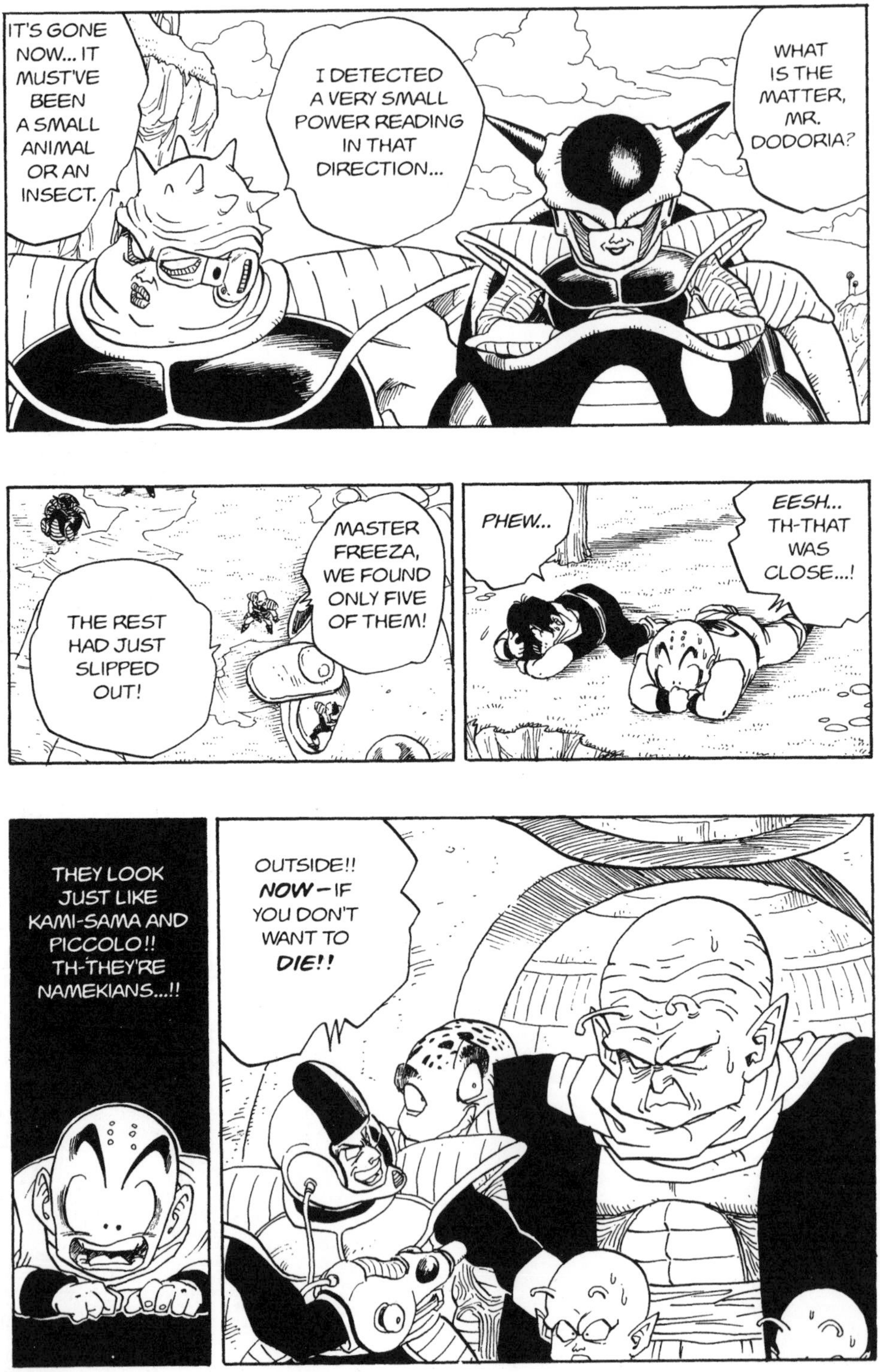
WHAT IS THE MATTER, MR. DODORIA?
I DETECTED A VERY SMALL POWER READING IN THAT DIRECTION...
IT'S GONE NOW... IT MUST'VE BEEN A SMALL ANIMAL OR AN INSECT.
EESH... TH-THAT WAS CLOSE...!
PHEW...
MASTER FREEZA, WE FOUND ONLY FIVE OF THEM!
THE REST HAD JUST SLIPPED OUT!
OUTSIDE!! NOW—IF YOU DON'T WANT TO DIE!!
THEY LOOK JUST LIKE KAMI-SAMA AND PICCOLO!! TH-THEY'RE NAMEKIANS...!!

# DBZ : 58 • Namekian Fear

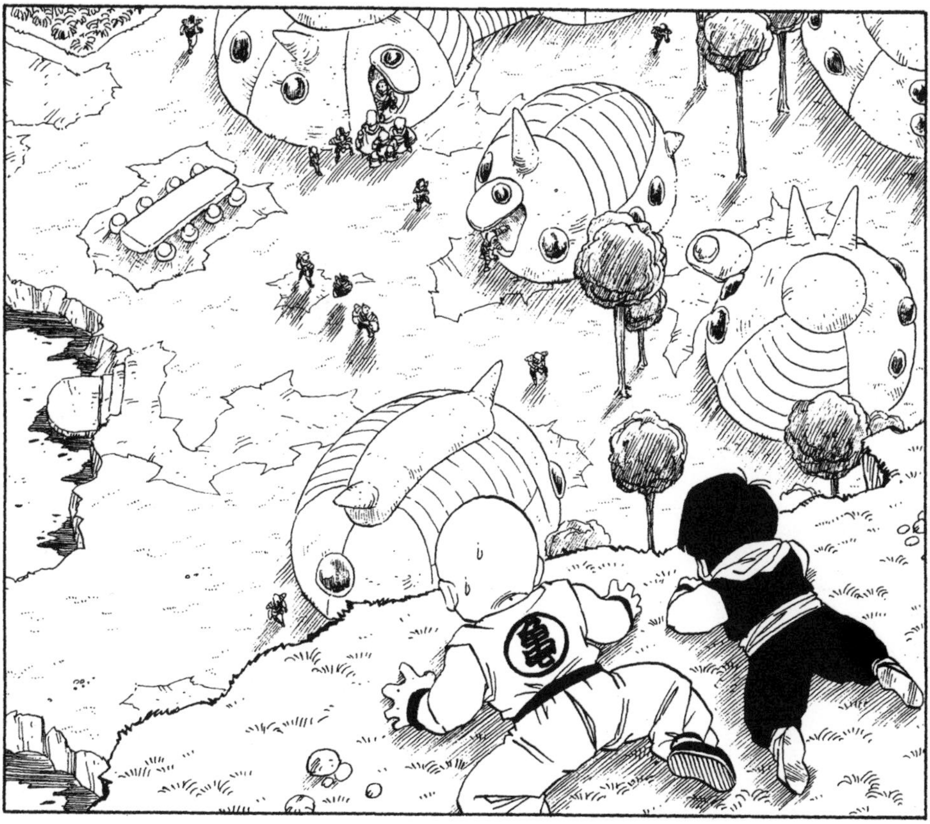

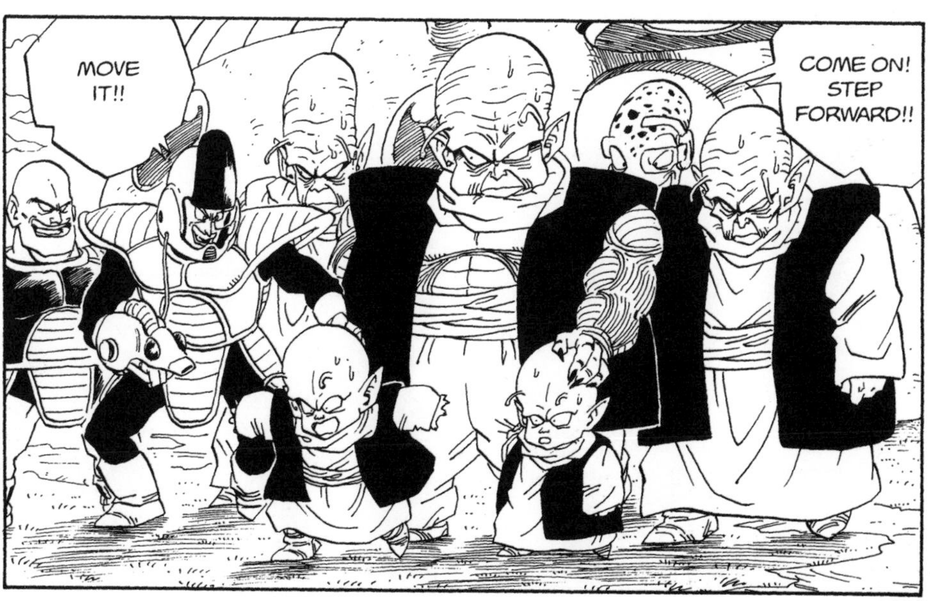
COME ON! STEP FORWARD!!
MOVE IT!!

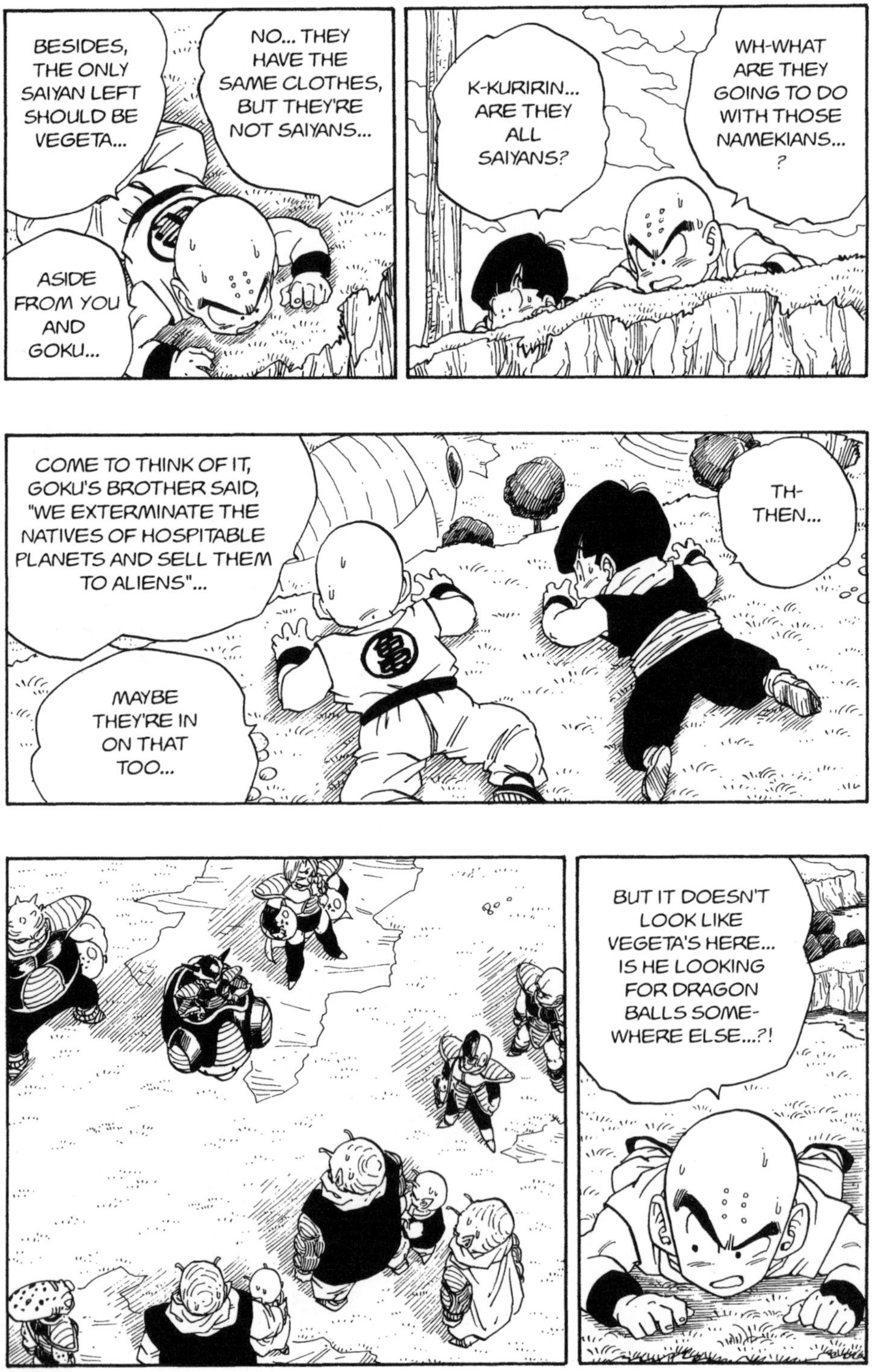
WH-WHAT ARE THEY GOING TO DO WITH THOSE NAMEKIANS...?
K-KURIRIN... ARE THEY ALL SAIYANS?
NO... THEY HAVE THE SAME CLOTHES, BUT THEY'RE NOT SAIYANS...
BESIDES, THE ONLY SAIYAN LEFT SHOULD BE VEGETA...
ASIDE FROM YOU AND GOKU...
TH- THEN...
COME TO THINK OF IT, GOKU'S BROTHER SAID, "WE EXTERMINATE THE NATIVES OF HOSPITABLE PLANETS AND SELL THEM TO ALIENS"...
MAYBE THEY'RE IN ON THAT TOO...
BUT IT DOESN'T LOOK LIKE VEGETA'S HERE... IS HE LOOKING FOR DRAGON BALLS SOME-WHERE ELSE...?!

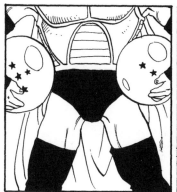

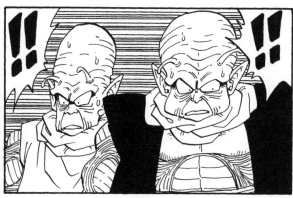

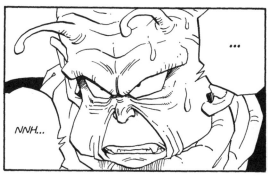

!!
!!
...
NNH...
I AM CALLED FREEZA. AS YOU CAN SEE, I AM COLLECTING YOUR DRAGON BALLS.
WHERE ARE THE OTHERS, BY THE WAY? WE HAD NOTED THAT THERE WERE TEN OF YOU...

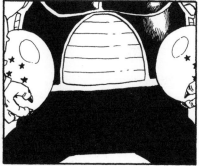

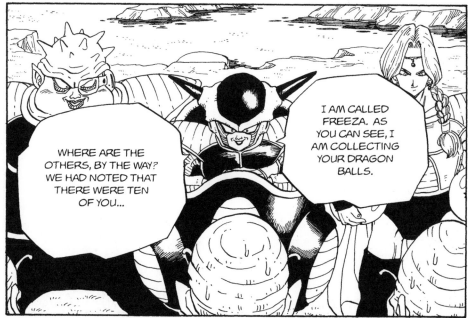

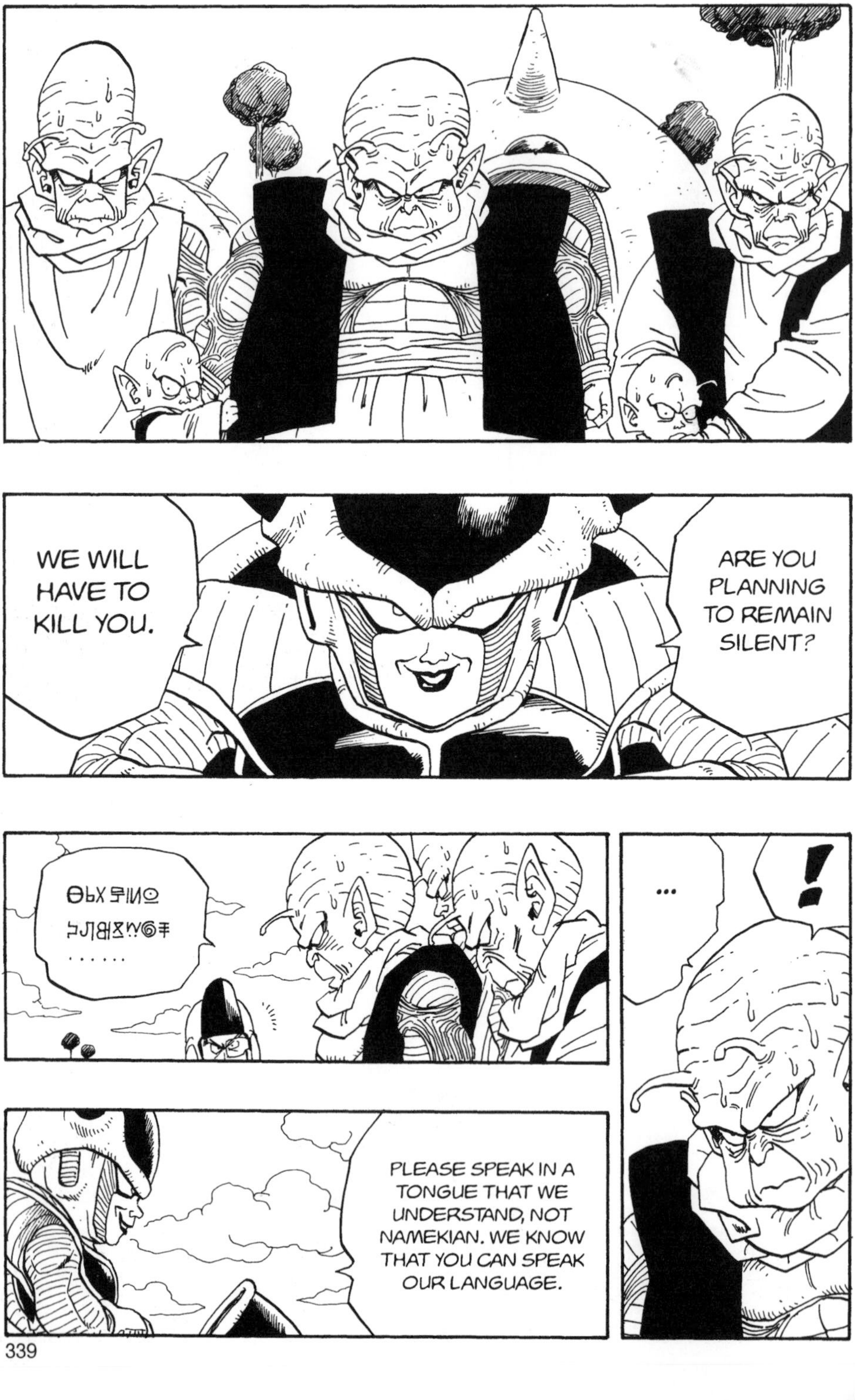

ARE YOU PLANNING TO REMAIN SILENT?
WE WILL HAVE TO KILL YOU.
!
...
PLEASE SPEAK IN A TONGUE THAT WE UNDERSTAND, NOT NAMEKIAN. WE KNOW THAT YOU CAN SPEAK OUR LANGUAGE.

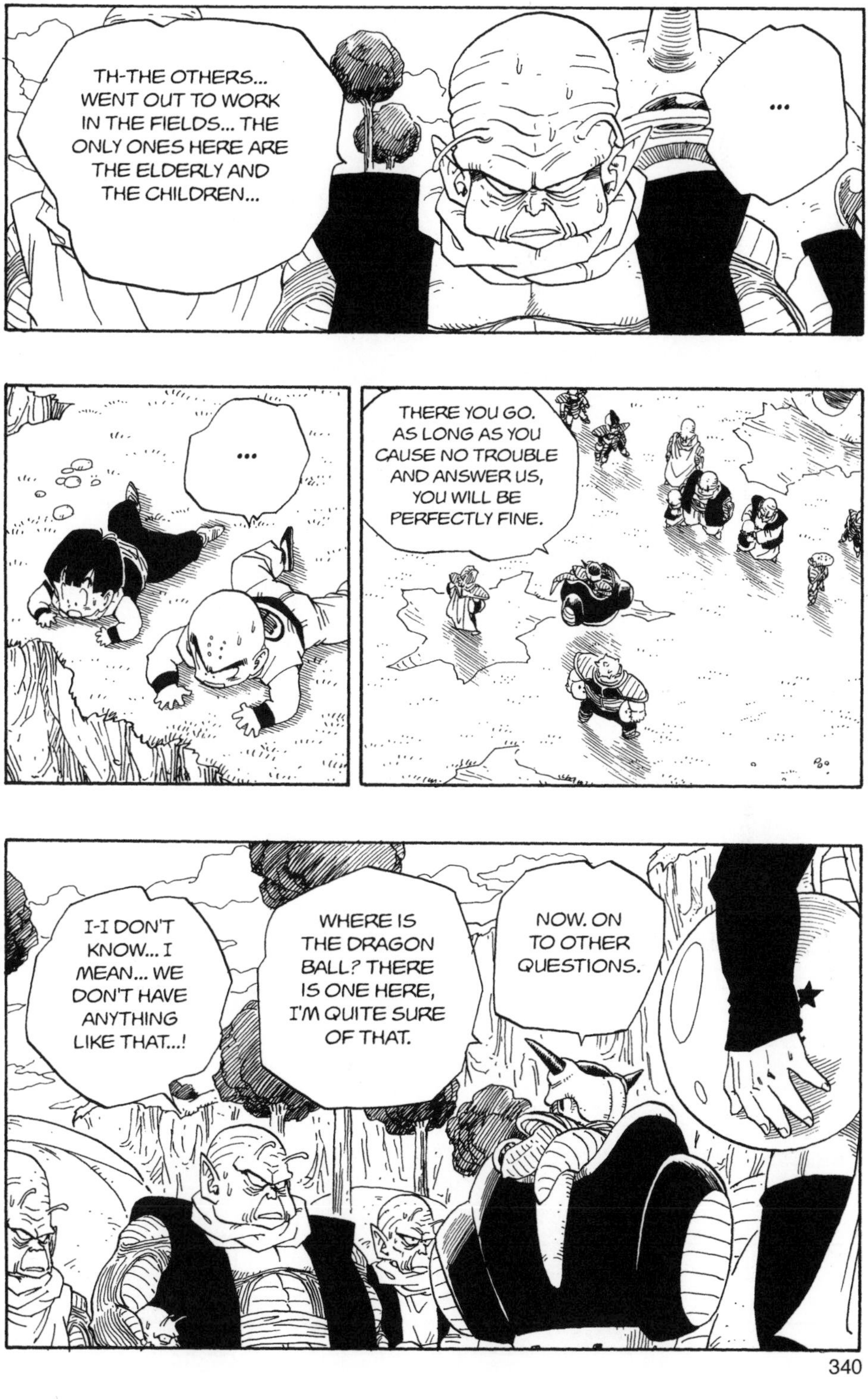
...
TH-THE OTHERS... WENT OUT TO WORK IN THE FIELDS... THE ONLY ONES HERE ARE THE ELDERLY AND THE CHILDREN...
THERE YOU GO. AS LONG AS YOU CAUSE NO TROUBLE AND ANSWER US, YOU WILL BE PERFECTLY FINE.
...
NOW. ON TO OTHER QUESTIONS.
WHERE IS THE DRAGON BALL? THERE IS ONE HERE, I'M QUITE SURE OF THAT.
I-I DON'T KNOW... I MEAN... WE DON'T HAVE ANYTHING LIKE THAT...!

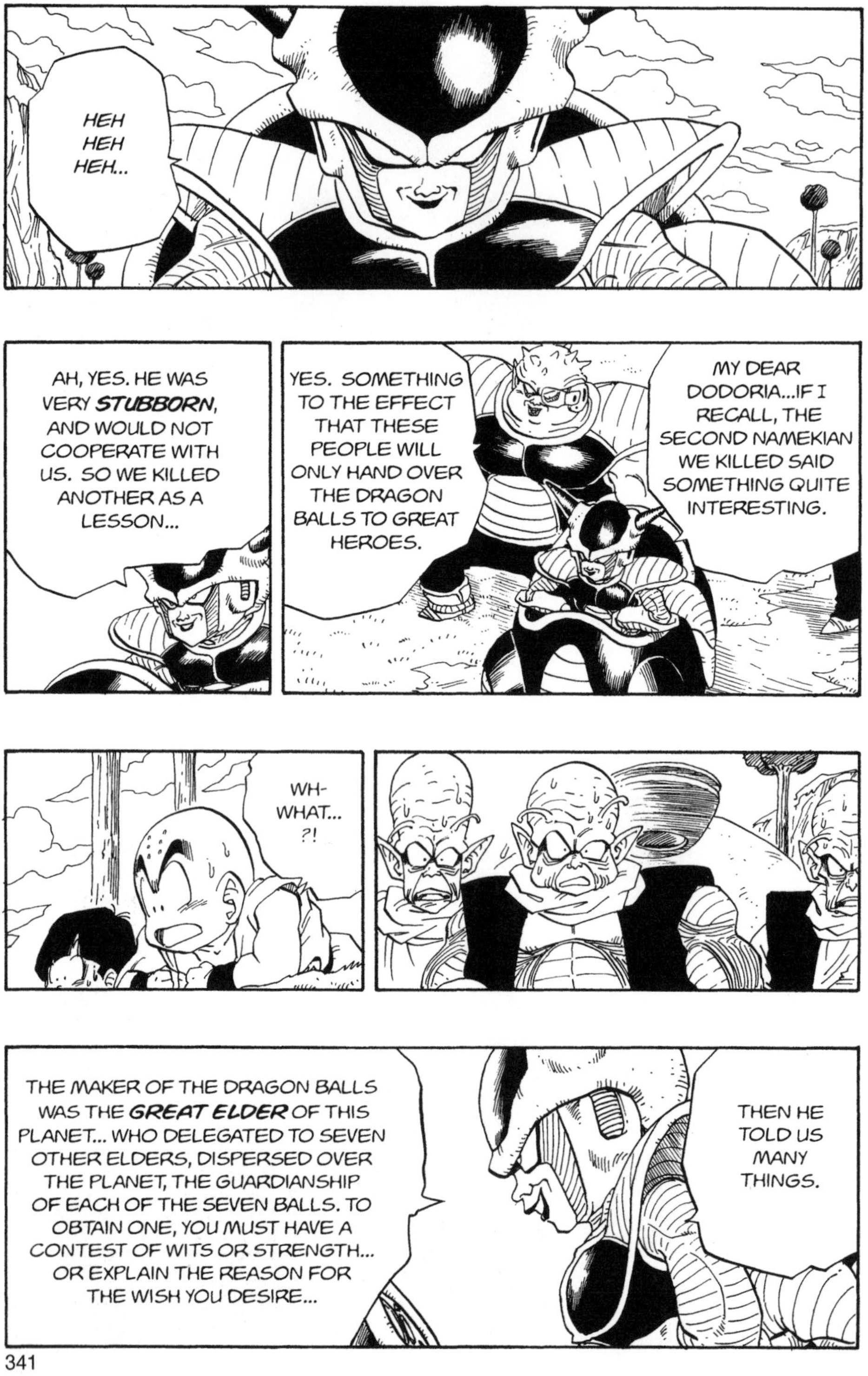
HEH HEH HEH...
MY DEAR DODORIA...IF I RECALL, THE SECOND NAMEKIAN WE KILLED SAID SOMETHING QUITE INTERESTING.
YES. SOMETHING TO THE EFFECT THAT THESE PEOPLE WILL ONLY HAND OVER THE DRAGON BALLS TO GREAT HEROES.
AH, YES. HE WAS VERY STUBBORN, AND WOULD NOT COOPERATE WITH US. SO WE KILLED ANOTHER AS A LESSON...
WH- WHAT... ?!
THEN HE TOLD US MANY THINGS.
THE MAKER OF THE DRAGON BALLS WAS THE GREAT ELDER OF THIS PLANET... WHO DELEGATED TO SEVEN OTHER ELDERS, DISPERSED OVER THE PLANET, THE GUARDIANSHIP OF EACH OF THE SEVEN BALLS. TO OBTAIN ONE, YOU MUST HAVE A CONTEST OF WITS OR STRENGTH... OR EXPLAIN THE REASON FOR THE WISH YOU DESIRE...

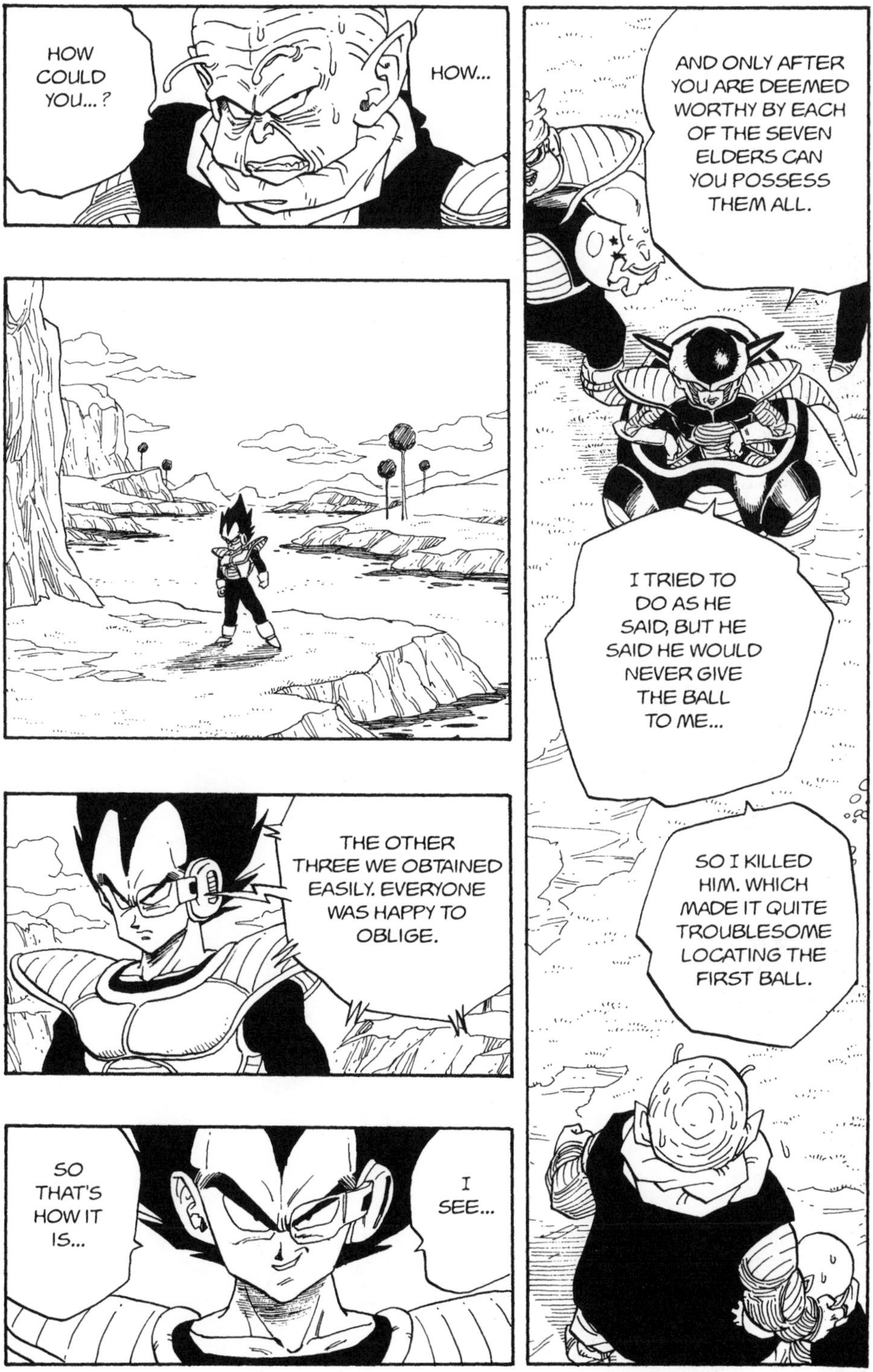
AND ONLY AFTER YOU ARE DEEMED WORTHY BY EACH OF THE SEVEN ELDERS CAN YOU POSSESS THEM ALL.
I TRIED TO DO AS HE SAID, BUT HE SAID HE WOULD NEVER GIVE THE BALL TO ME...
SO I KILLED HIM. WHICH MADE IT QUITE TROUBLESOME LOCATING THE FIRST BALL.
HOW...
HOW COULD YOU...?
THE OTHER THREE WE OBTAINED EASILY. EVERYONE WAS HAPPY TO OBLIGE.
I SEE...
SO THAT'S HOW IT IS...

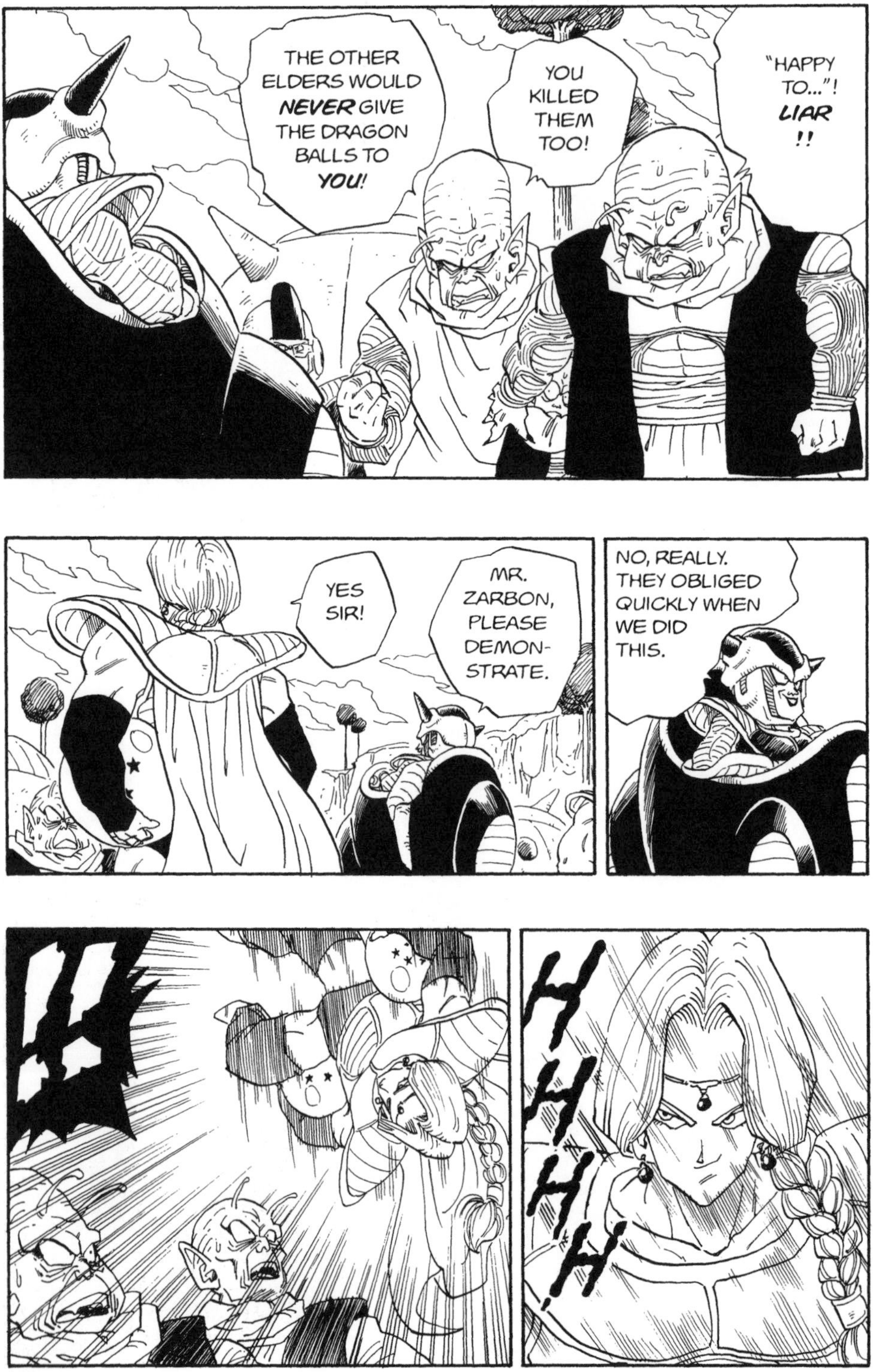
"HAPPY TO..."! LIAR!!
YOU KILLED THEM TOO!
THE OTHER ELDERS WOULD NEVER GIVE THE DRAGON BALLS TO YOU!
NO, REALLY. THEY OBLIGED QUICKLY WHEN WE DID THIS.
MR. ZARBON, PLEASE DEMONSTRATE.
YES SIR!
HHHHH!
!!

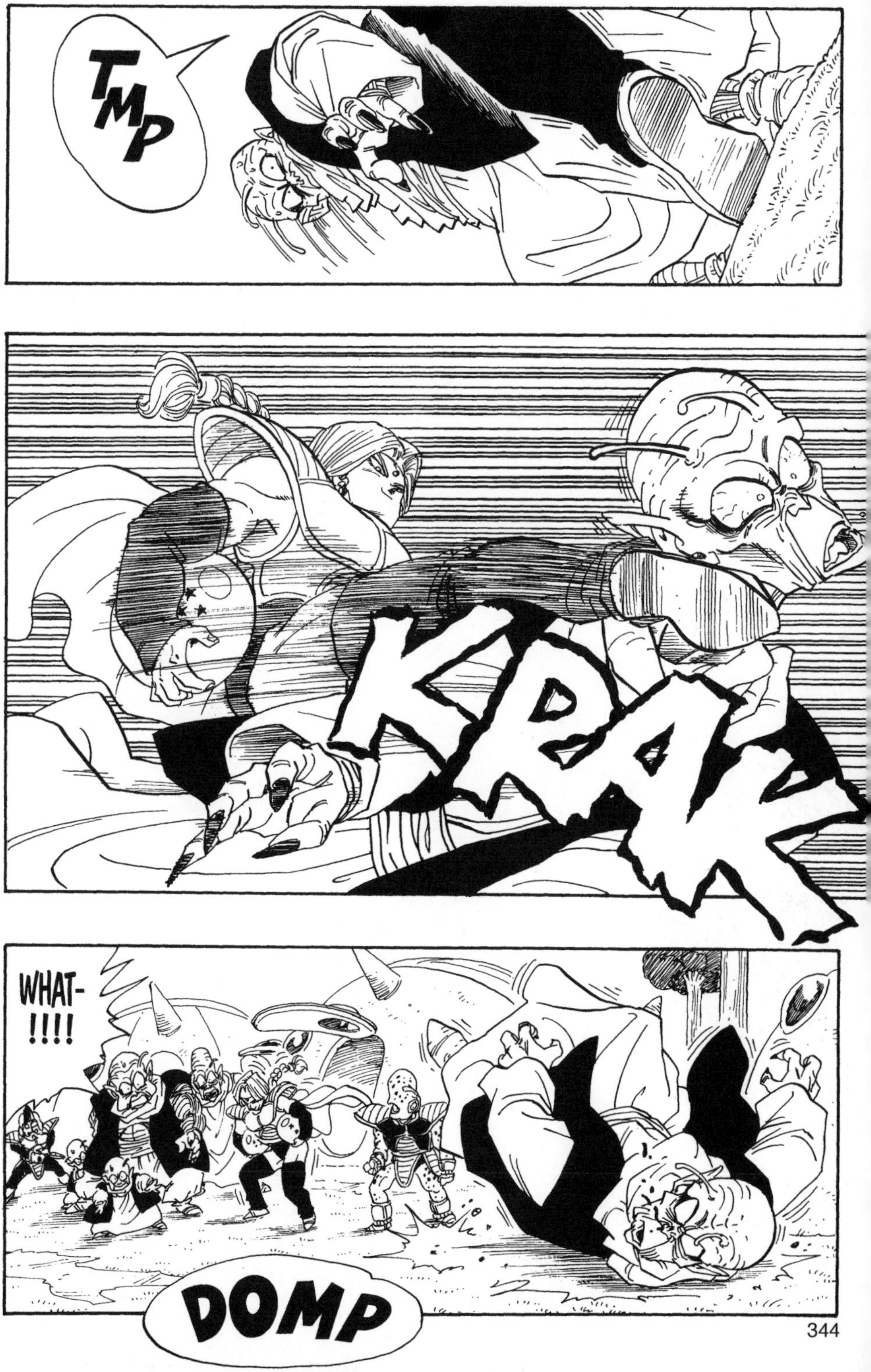
TMP
KRA
WHAT-!!!!
DOMP

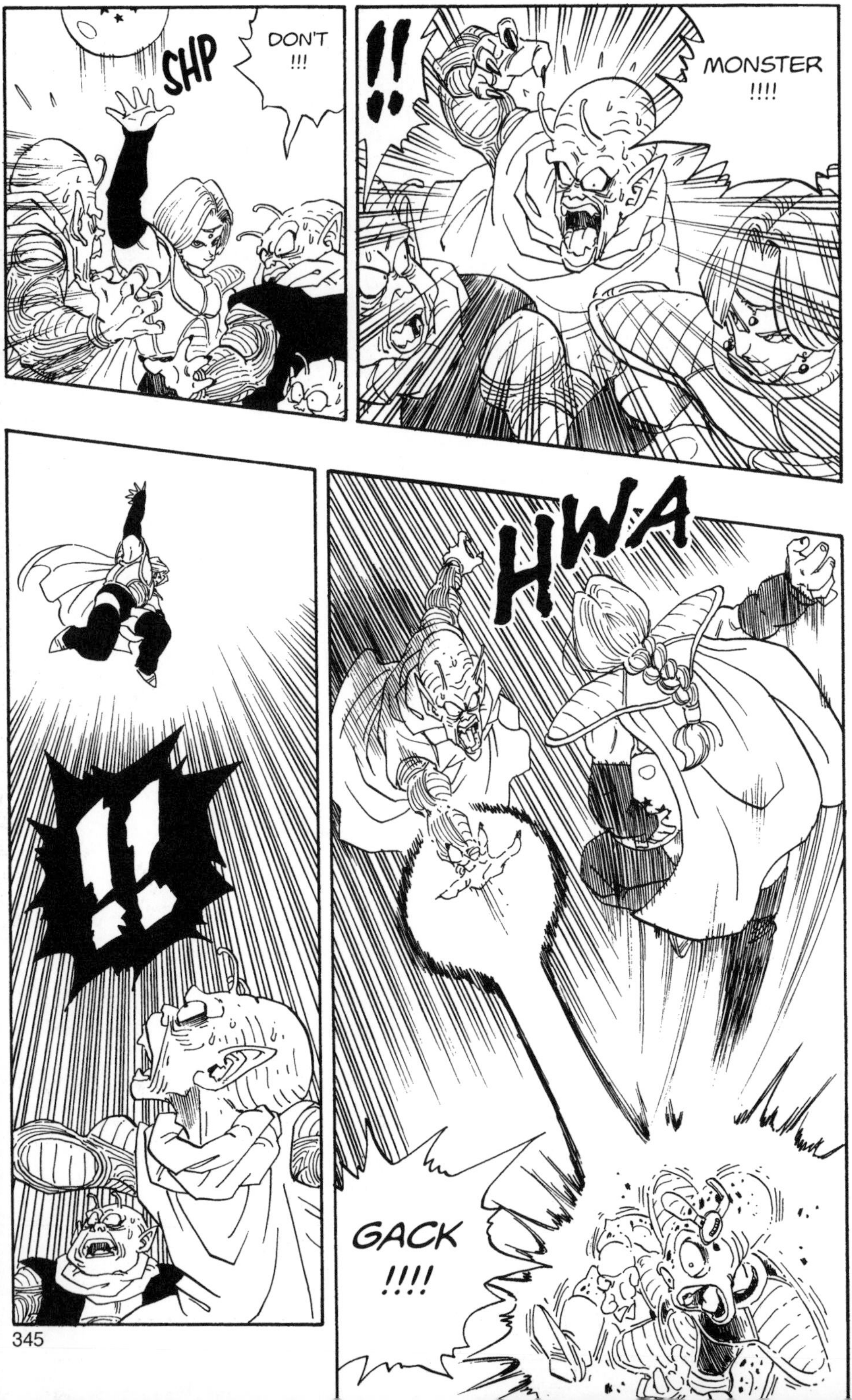
!!
MONSTER !!!!
SHP
DON'T !!!
HWA
GACK !!!!
!!

BWOOM
GA...
TMP
fap

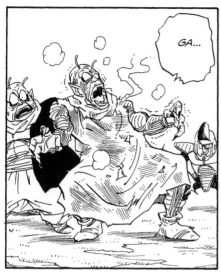

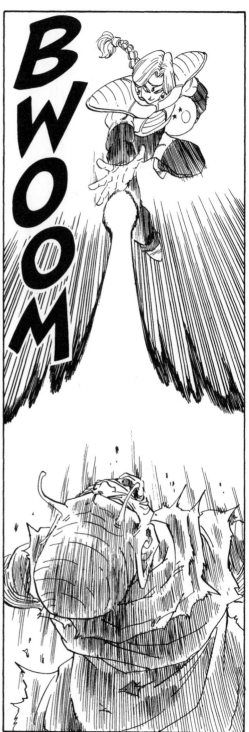

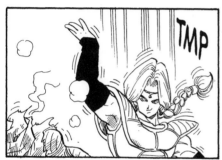

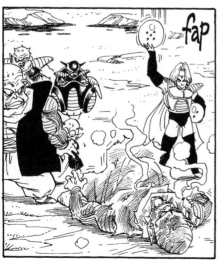

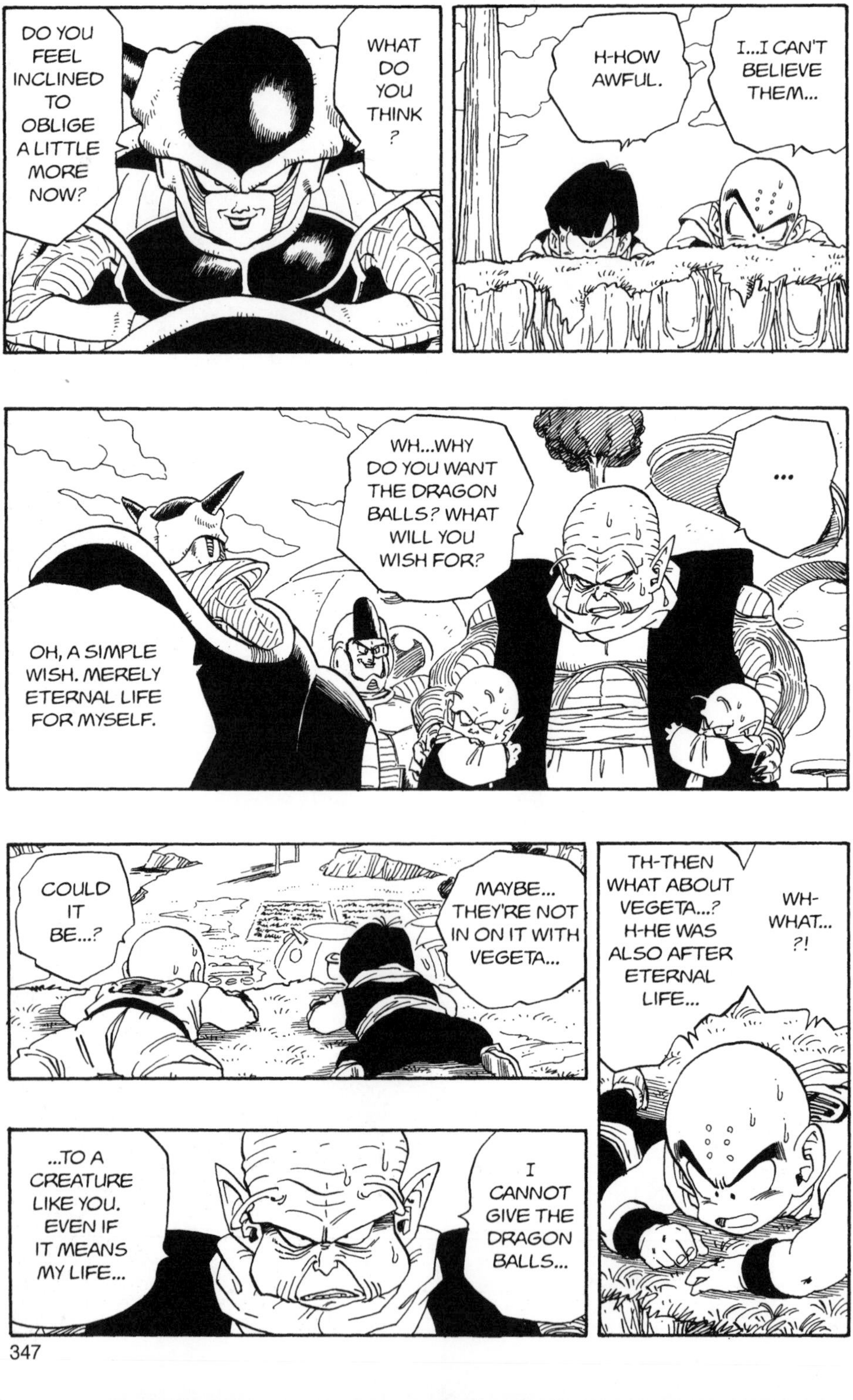
I...I CAN'T BELIEVE THEM...
H-HOW AWFUL.
WHAT DO YOU THINK?
DO YOU FEEL INCLINED TO OBLIGE A LITTLE MORE NOW?
...
WH...WHY DO YOU WANT THE DRAGON BALLS? WHAT WILL YOU WISH FOR?
OH, A SIMPLE WISH. MERELY ETERNAL LIFE FOR MYSELF.
WH- WHAT...?!
TH-THEN WHAT ABOUT VEGETA...? H-HE WAS ALSO AFTER ETERNAL LIFE...
MAYBE... THEY'RE NOT IN ON IT WITH VEGETA...
COULD IT BE...?
I CANNOT GIVE THE DRAGON BALLS...
...TO A CREATURE LIKE YOU. EVEN IF IT MEANS MY LIFE...

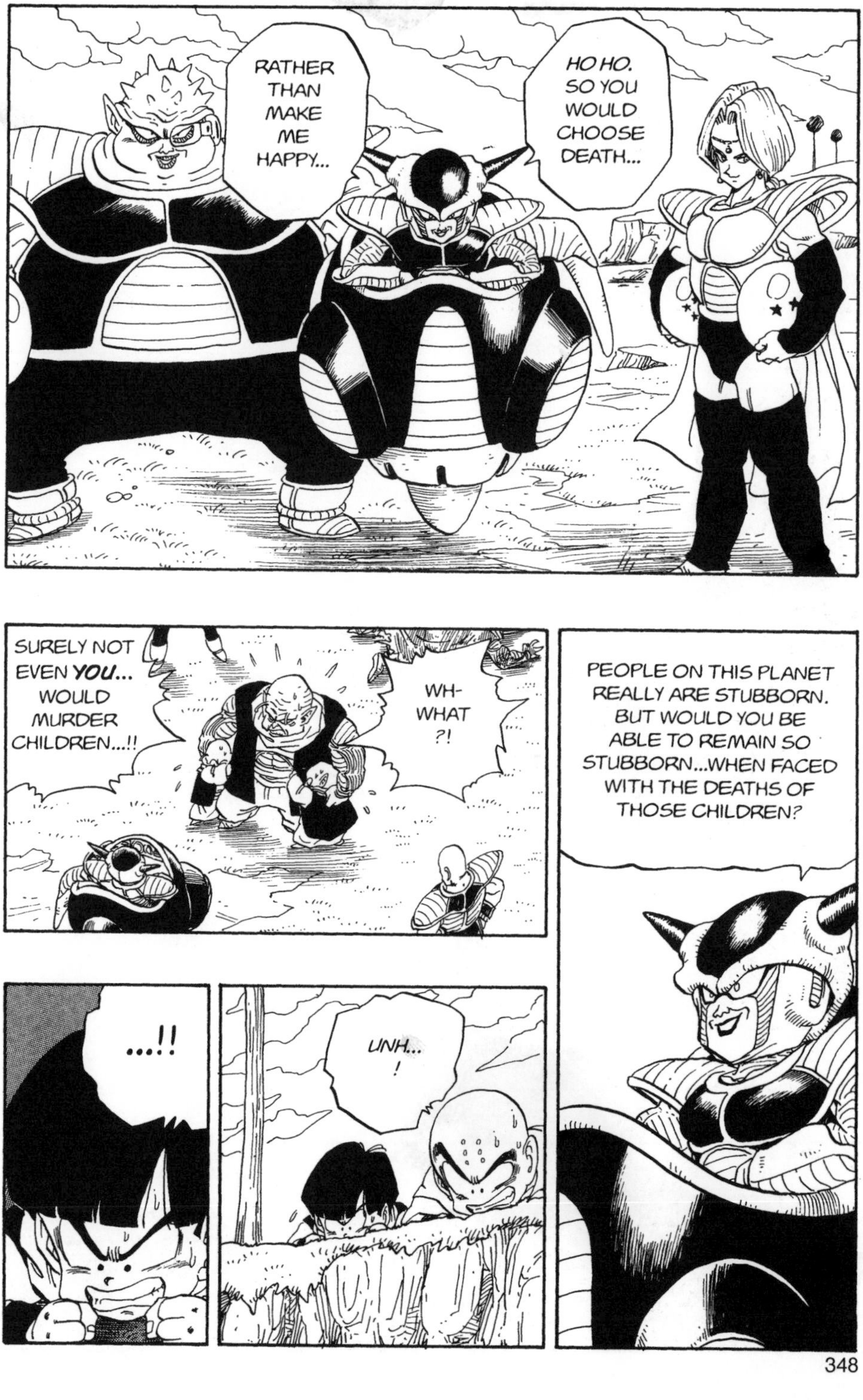
HO HO. SO YOU WOULD CHOOSE DEATH...
RATHER THAN MAKE ME HAPPY...
PEOPLE ON THIS PLANET REALLY ARE STUBBORN. BUT WOULD YOU BE ABLE TO REMAIN SO STUBBORN...WHEN FACED WITH THE DEATHS OF THOSE CHILDREN?
WH-WHAT?!
SURELY NOT EVEN ***YOU***... WOULD MURDER CHILDREN...!!
UNH...!
...!!

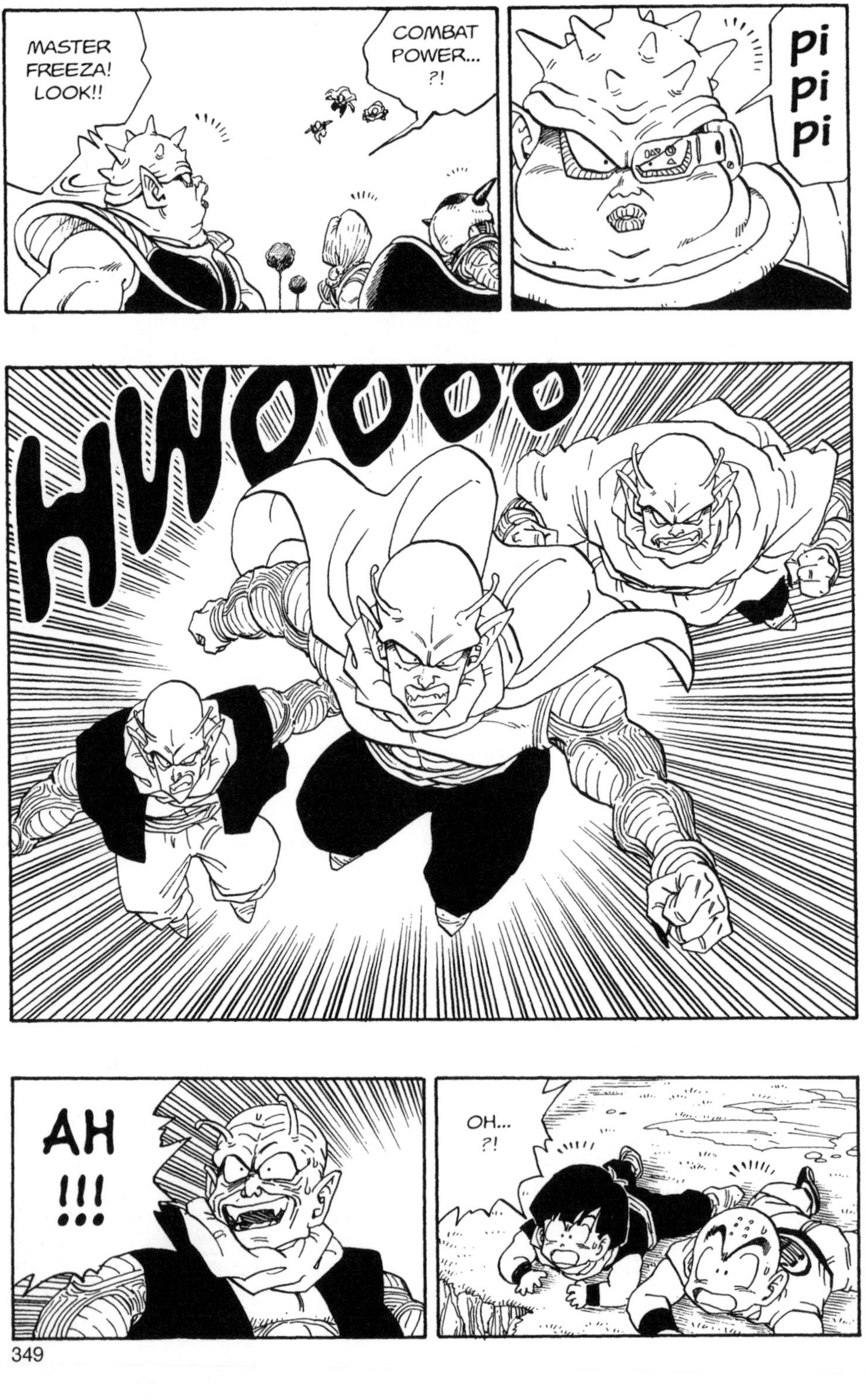
pi
pi
pi
COMBAT POWER... ?!
MASTER FREEZA! LOOK!!
HWOOOO
OH... ?!
AH !!!

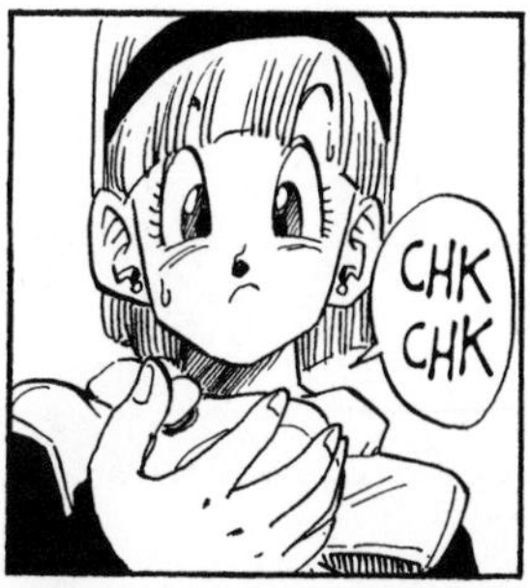
CHK
CHK

# DragonBallZ

VOLUME 6

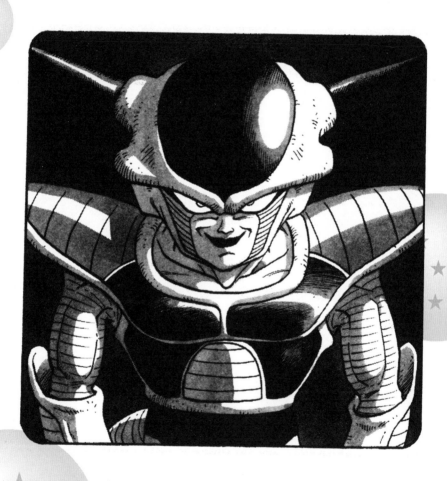

## BATTLEFIELD NAMEK

# DBZ:59 • Showdown!

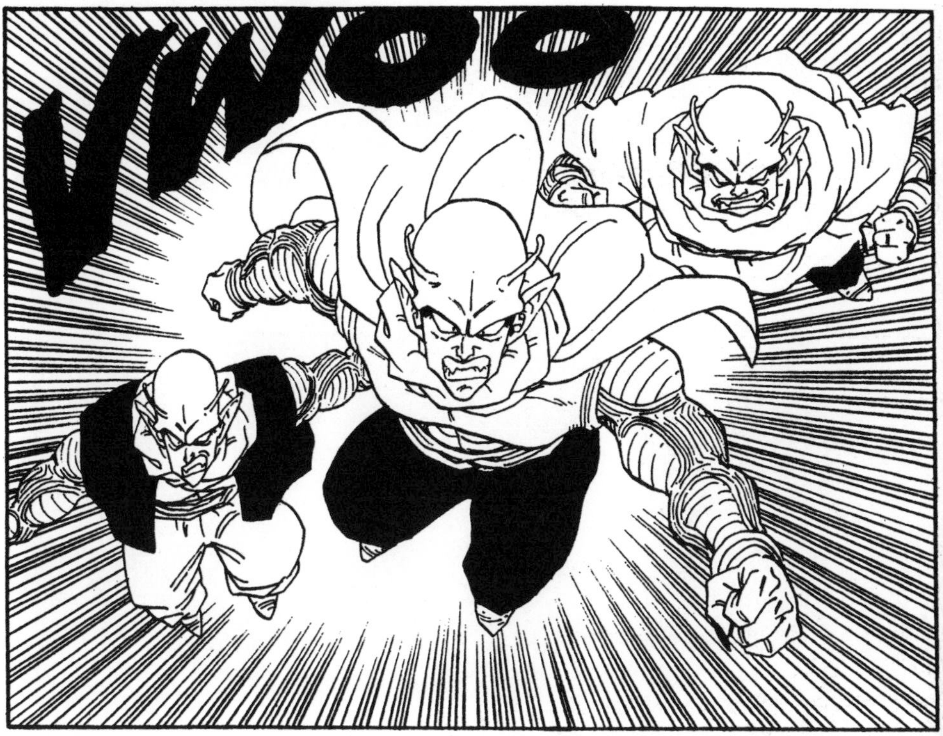
VWOO

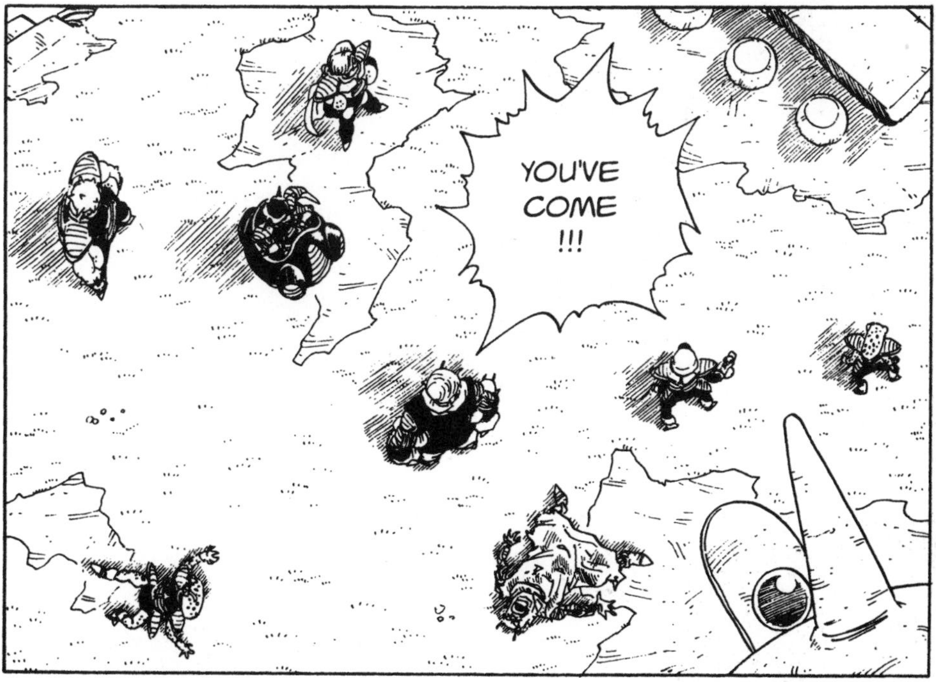
YOU'VE COME !!!

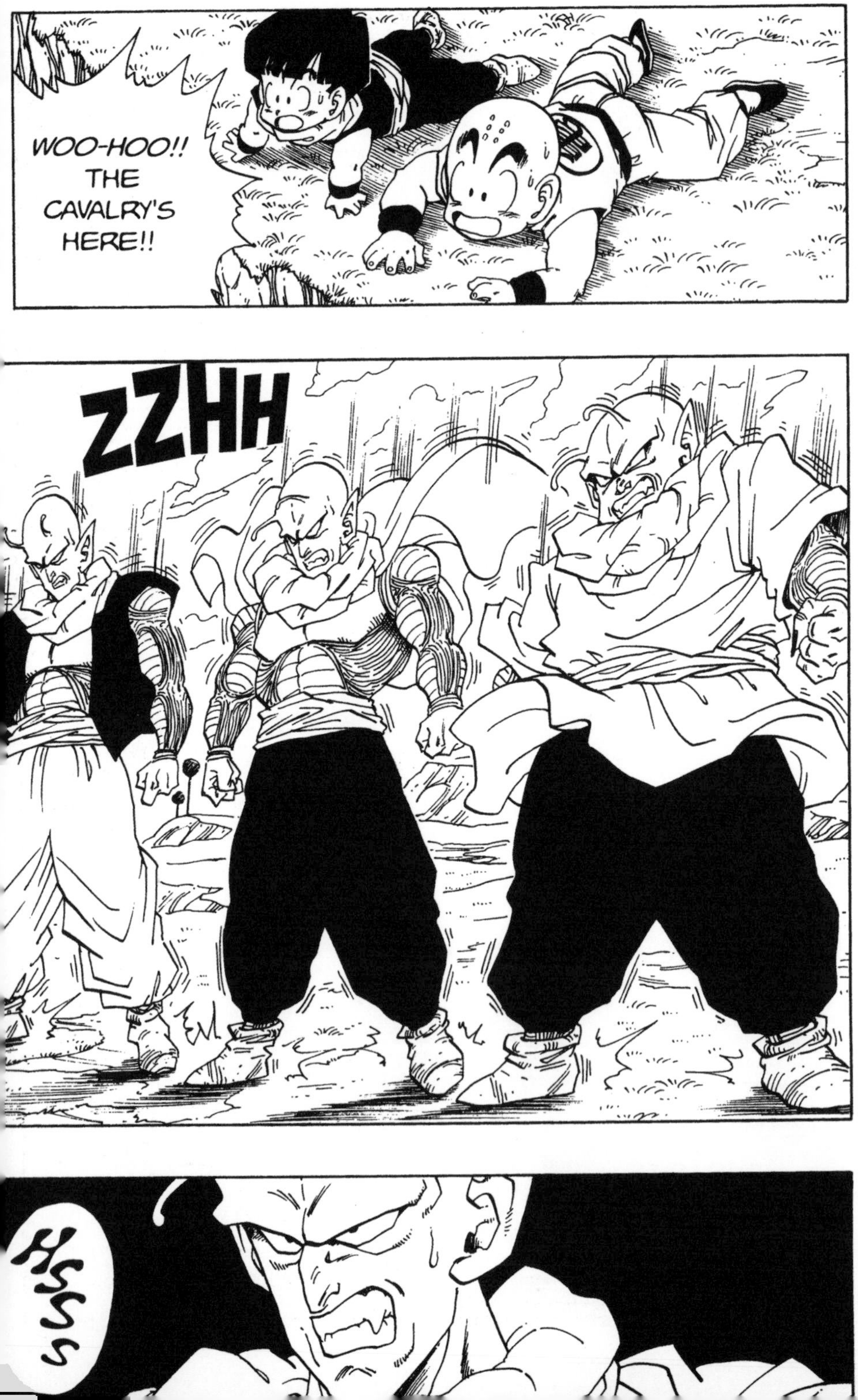
WOO-HOO!! THE CAVALRY'S HERE!!
ZZHH
HSSS

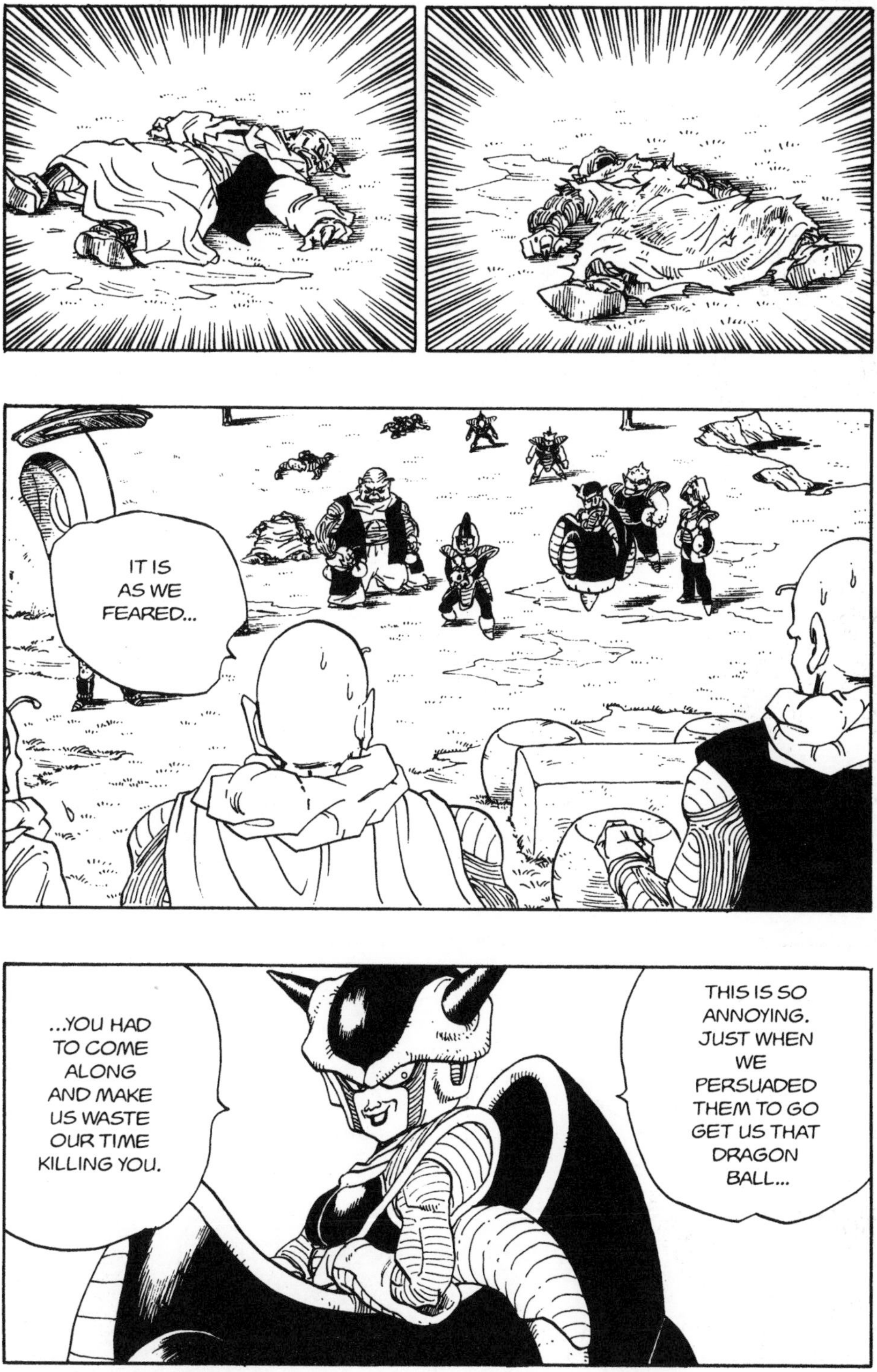
IT IS AS WE FEARED...
THIS IS SO ANNOYING. JUST WHEN WE PERSUADED THEM TO GO GET US THAT DRAGON BALL...
...YOU HAD TO COME ALONG AND MAKE US WASTE OUR TIME KILLING YOU.

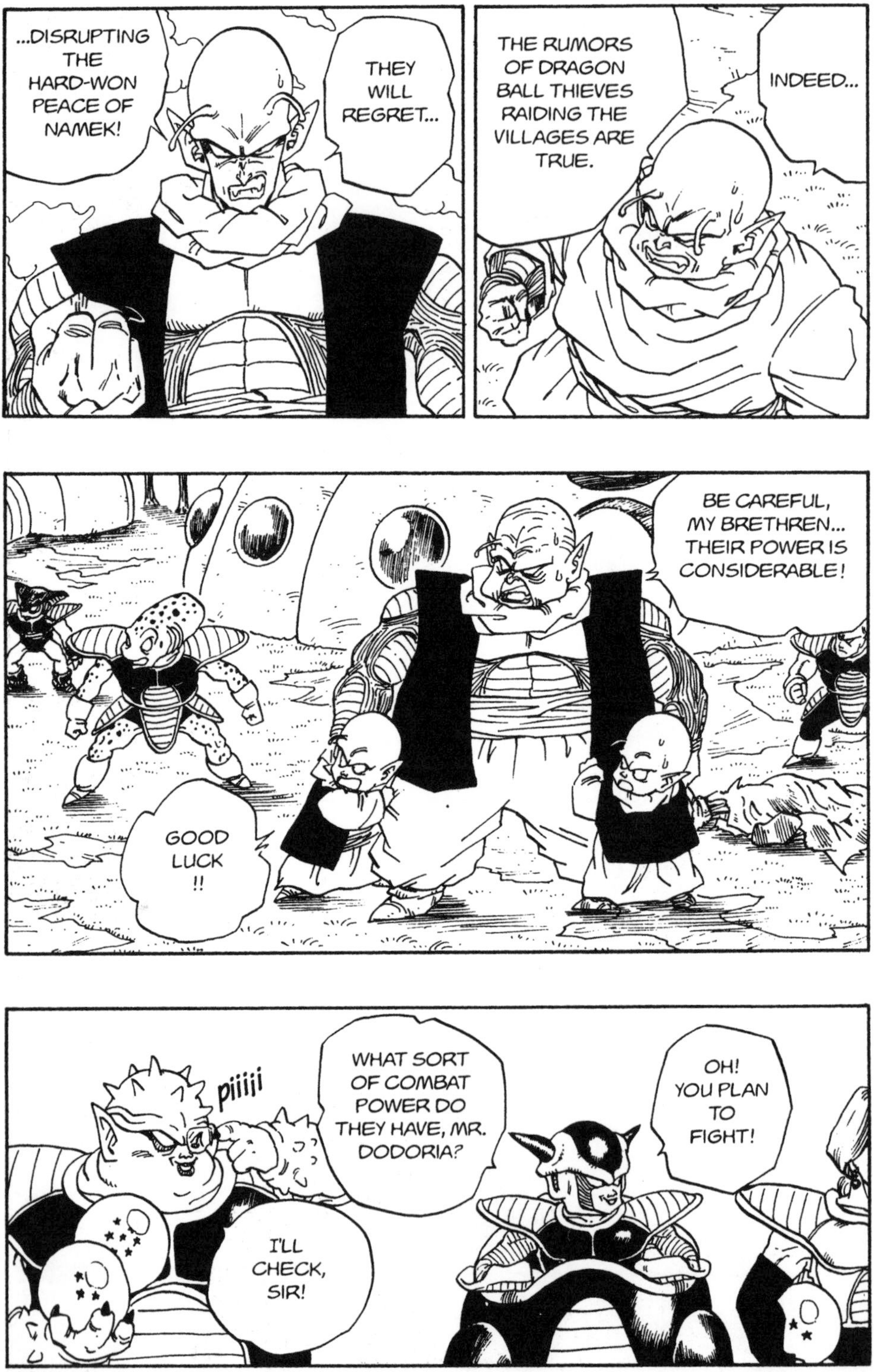
INDEED...
THE RUMORS OF DRAGON BALL THIEVES RAIDING THE VILLAGES ARE TRUE.
THEY WILL REGRET...
...DISRUPTING THE HARD-WON PEACE OF NAMEK!
BE CAREFUL, MY BRETHREN... THEIR POWER IS CONSIDERABLE!
GOOD LUCK !!
OH! YOU PLAN TO FIGHT!
WHAT SORT OF COMBAT POWER DO THEY HAVE, MR. DODORIA?
piiiji
I'LL CHECK, SIR!

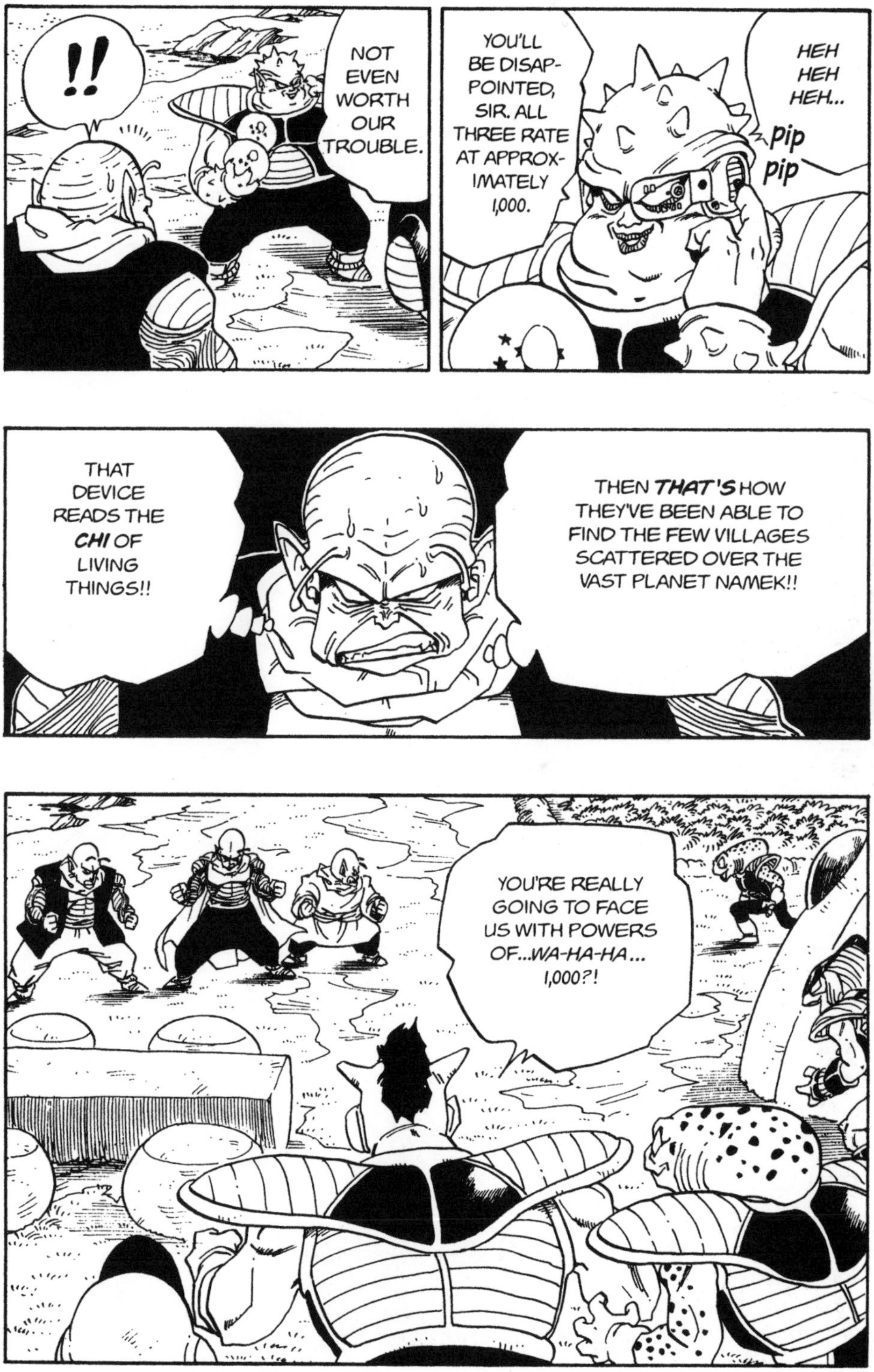
HEH HEH HEH...
pip pip
YOU'LL BE DISAP-POINTED, SIR. ALL THREE RATE AT APPROX-IMATELY 1,000.
NOT EVEN WORTH OUR TROUBLE.
!!
THEN THAT'S HOW THEY'VE BEEN ABLE TO FIND THE FEW VILLAGES SCATTERED OVER THE VAST PLANET NAMEK!!
THAT DEVICE READS THE CHI OF LIVING THINGS!!
YOU'RE REALLY GOING TO FACE US WITH POWERS OF...WA-HA-HA... 1,000?!

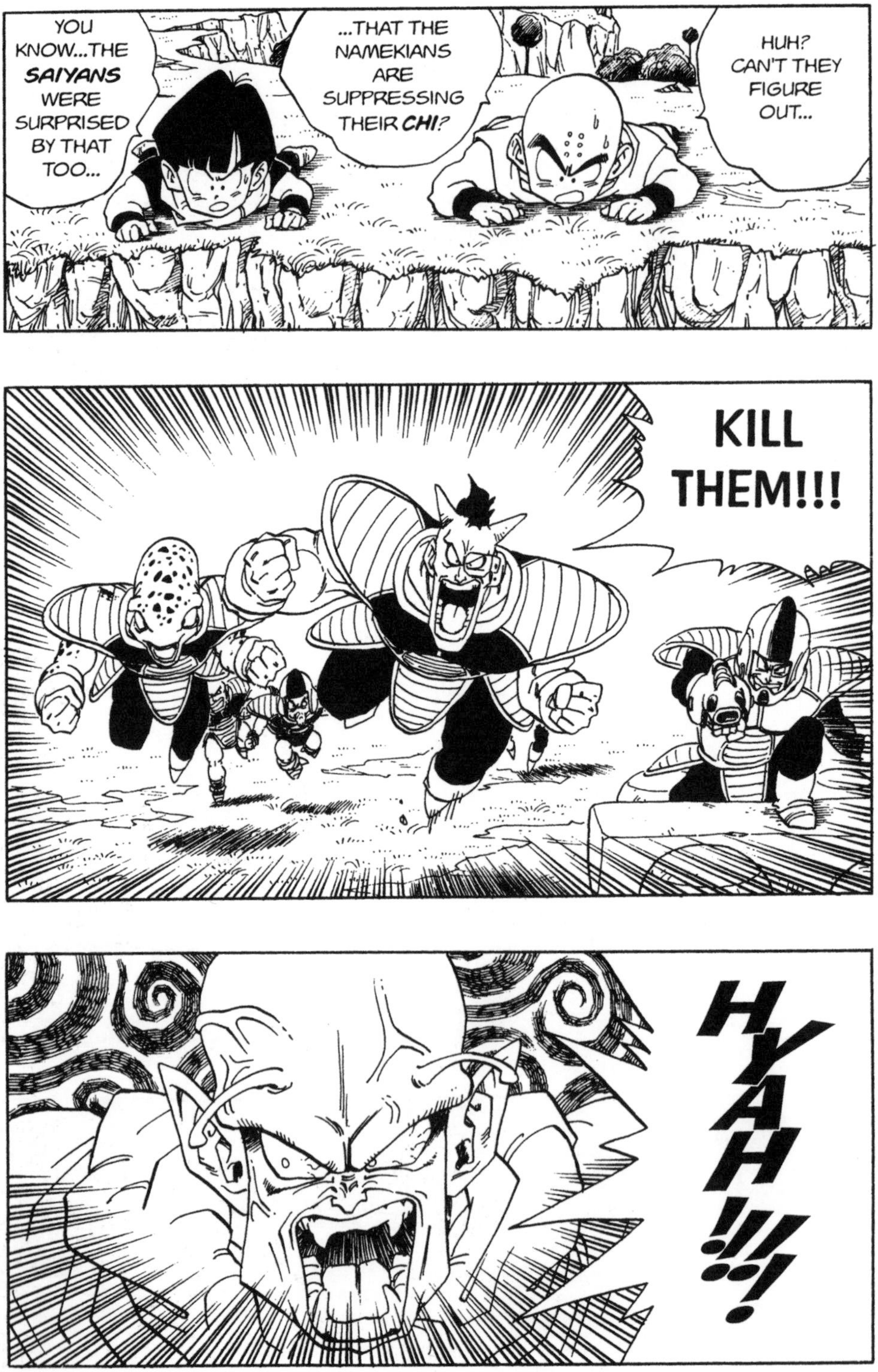
HUH? CAN'T THEY FIGURE OUT...
...THAT THE NAMEKIANS ARE SUPPRESSING THEIR CHI?
YOU KNOW...THE SAIYANS WERE SURPRISED BY THAT TOO...
KILL THEM!!!
HYAH!!!!

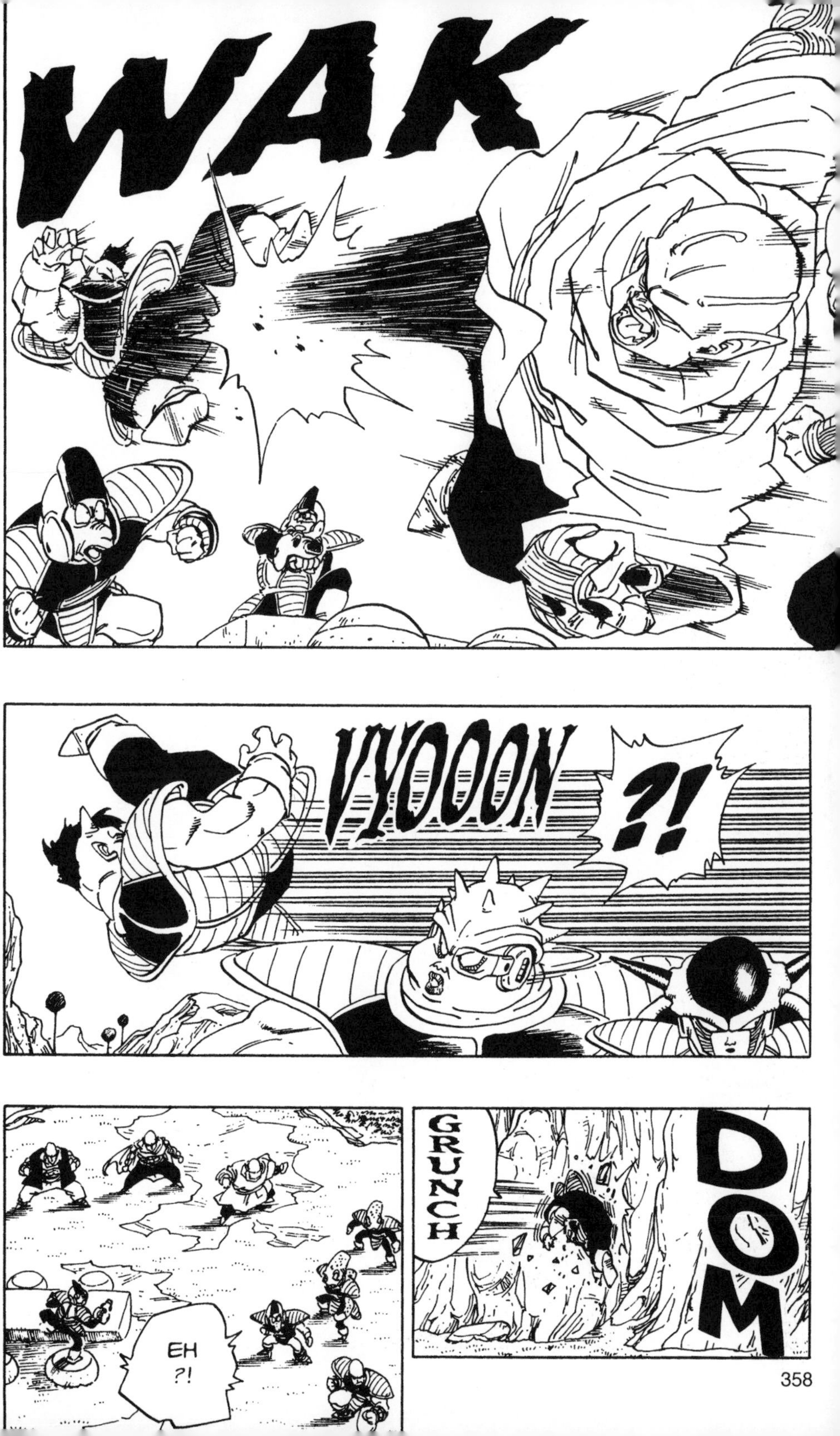
WAK
VYOOON
?!
DOM
GRUNCH
EH ?!

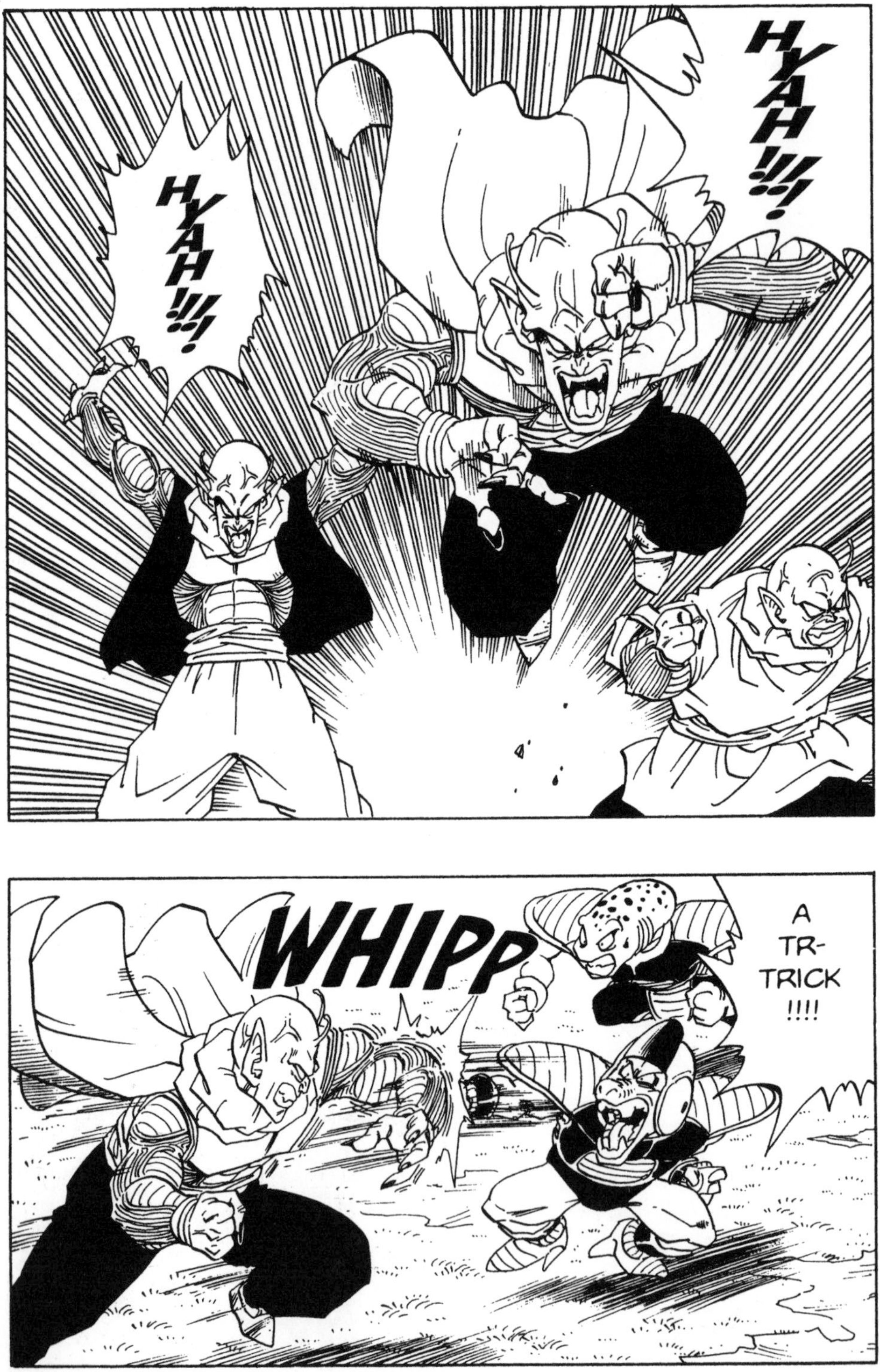
HYAH!!!!
HYAH!!!!
A TR-TRICK!!!!
WHIPP

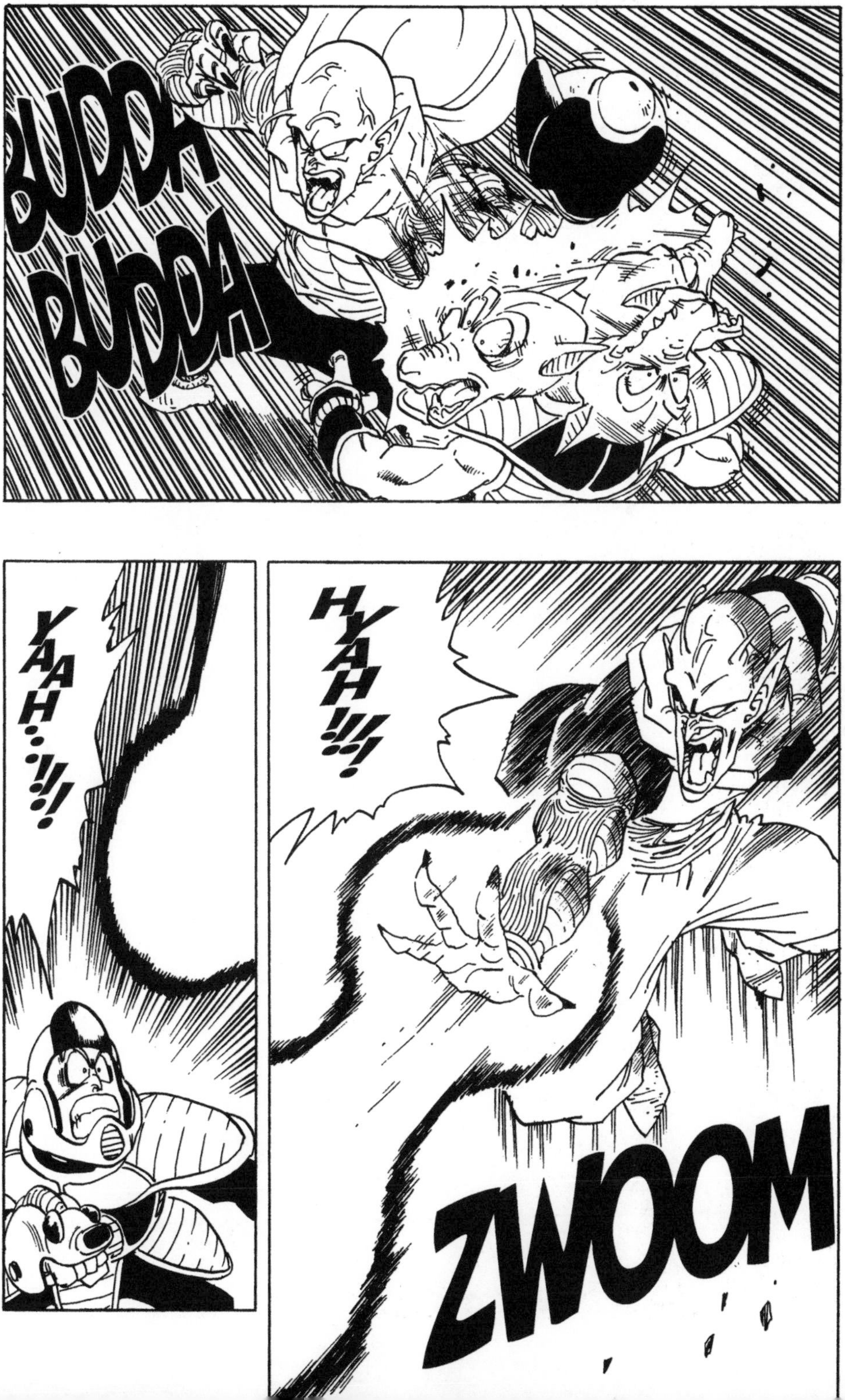
BUDDA BUDDA
HYAH!!!!
ZWOOM
YAAH...!!!

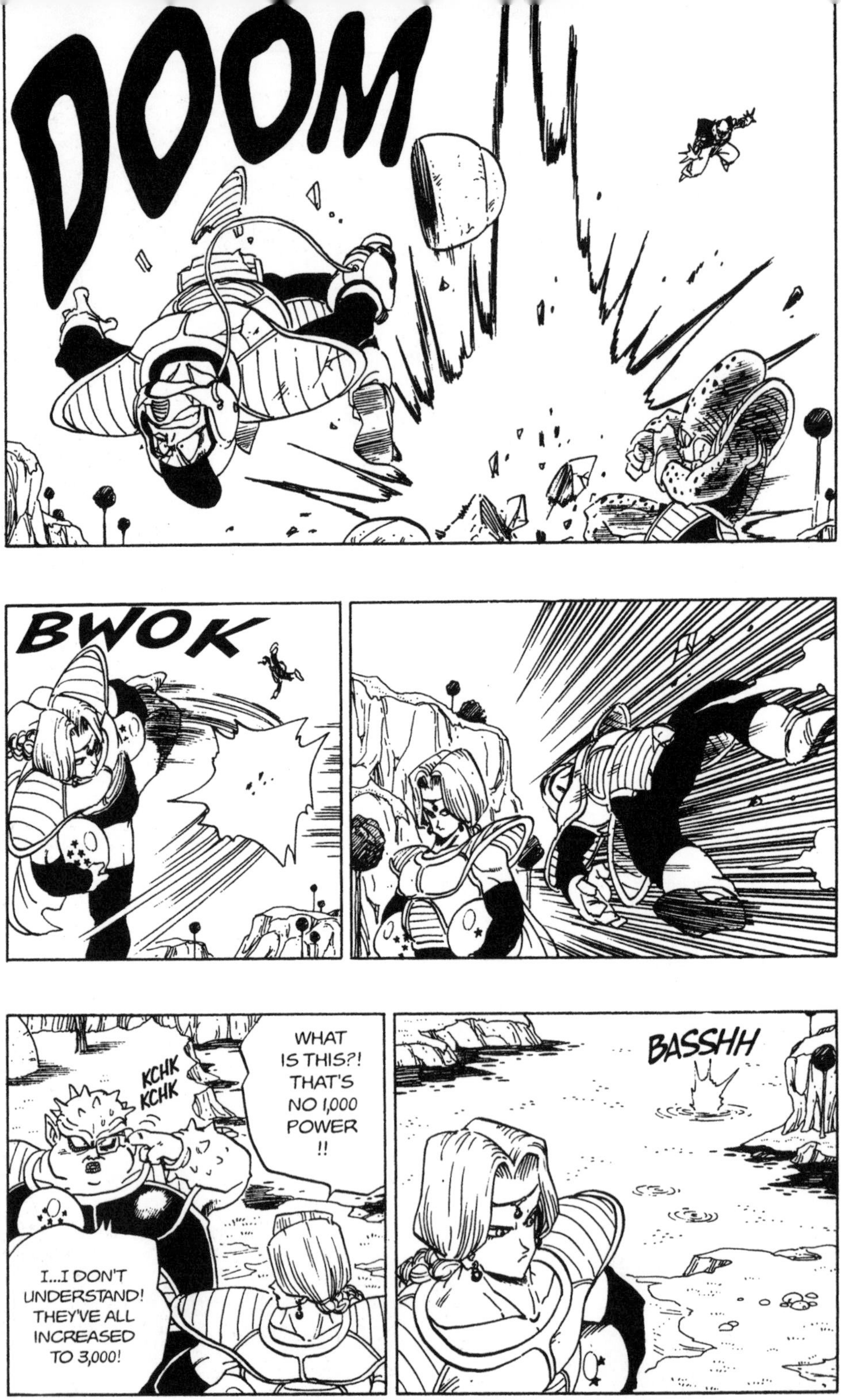
DOOM
BWOK
BASSHH
WHAT IS THIS?! THAT'S NO 1,000 POWER !!
KCHK KCHK
I...I DON'T UNDERSTAND! THEY'VE ALL INCREASED TO 3,000!

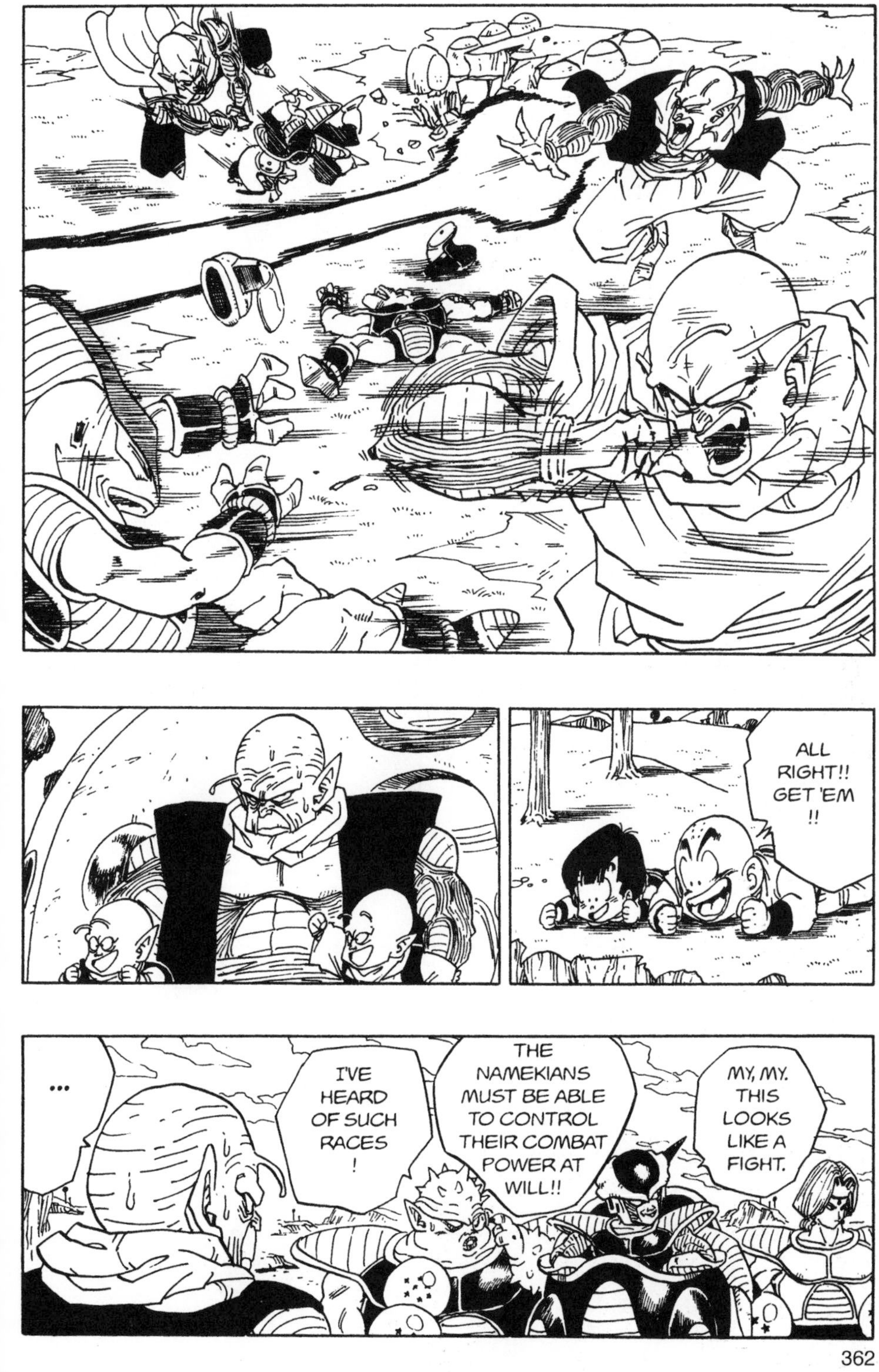
ALL RIGHT!! GET 'EM !!
MY, MY. THIS LOOKS LIKE A FIGHT.
THE NAMEKIANS MUST BE ABLE TO CONTROL THEIR COMBAT POWER AT WILL!!
I'VE HEARD OF SUCH RACES !
...

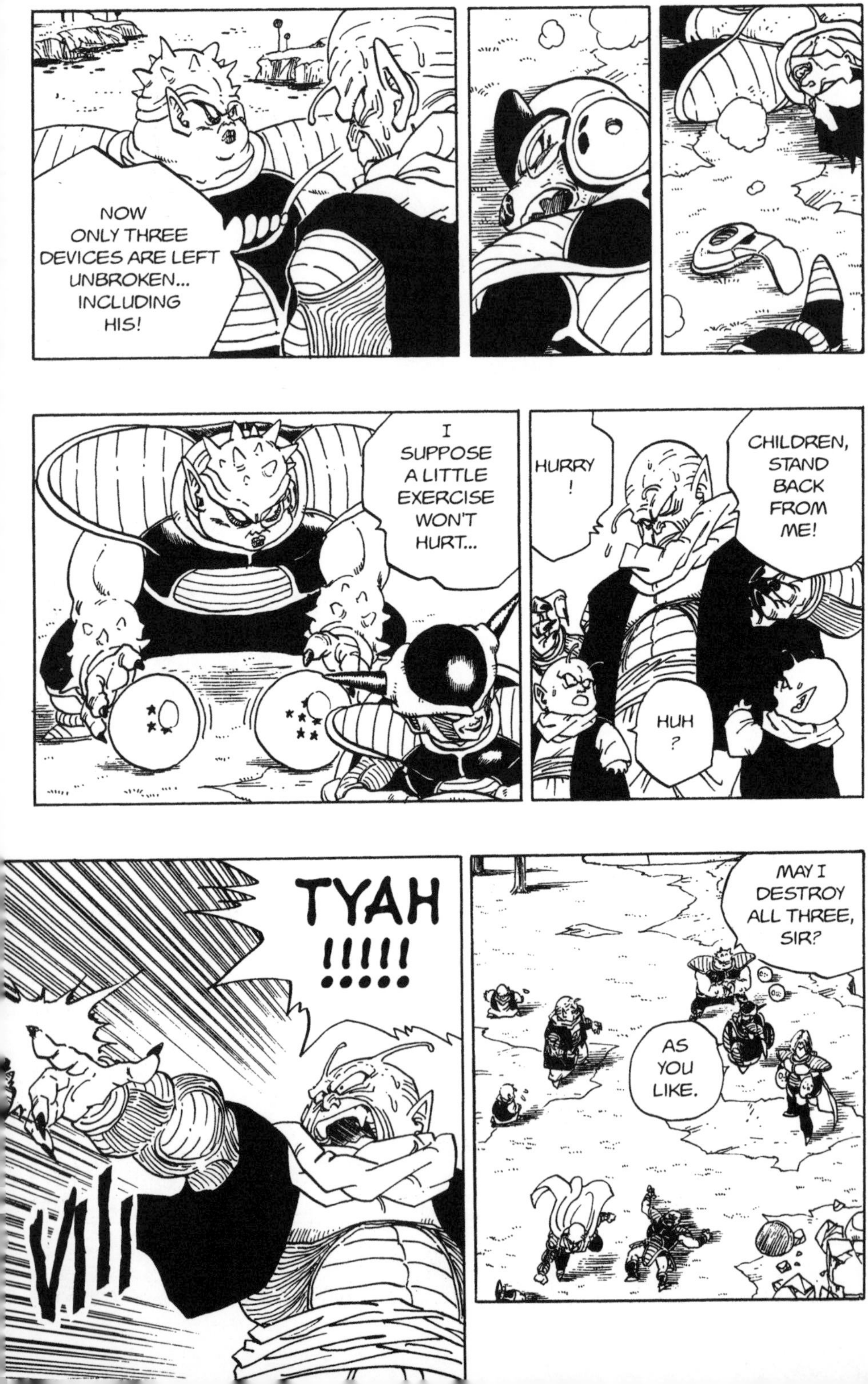
NOW ONLY THREE DEVICES ARE LEFT UNBROKEN... INCLUDING HIS!
CHILDREN, STAND BACK FROM ME!
HURRY!
HUH?
I SUPPOSE A LITTLE EXERCISE WON'T HURT...
MAY I DESTROY ALL THREE, SIR?
AS YOU LIKE.
TYAH!!!!!

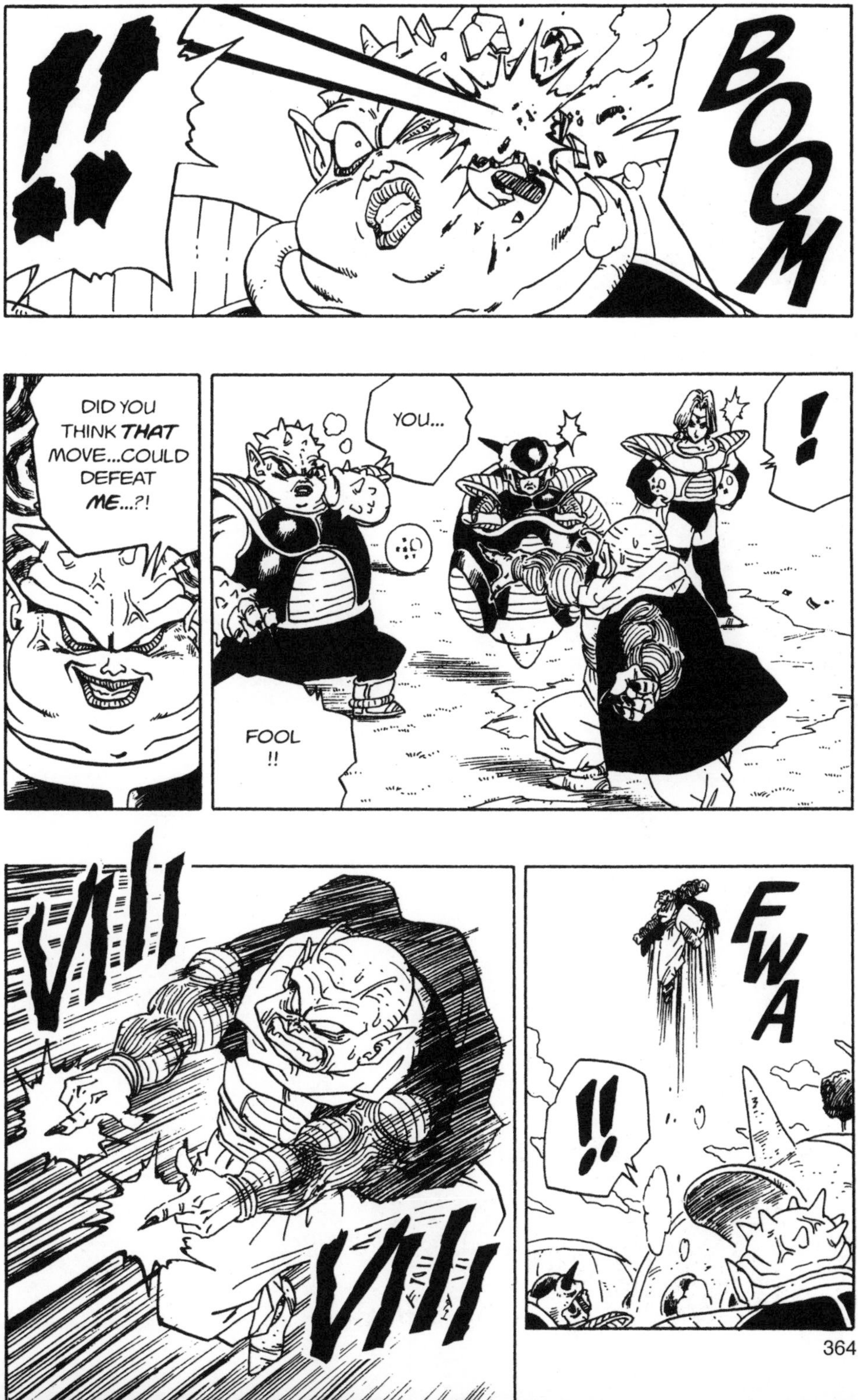
BOOM
!!
!
YOU...
FOOL !!
DID YOU THINK THAT MOVE...COULD DEFEAT ME...?!
FWA
!!
VIII
VIII

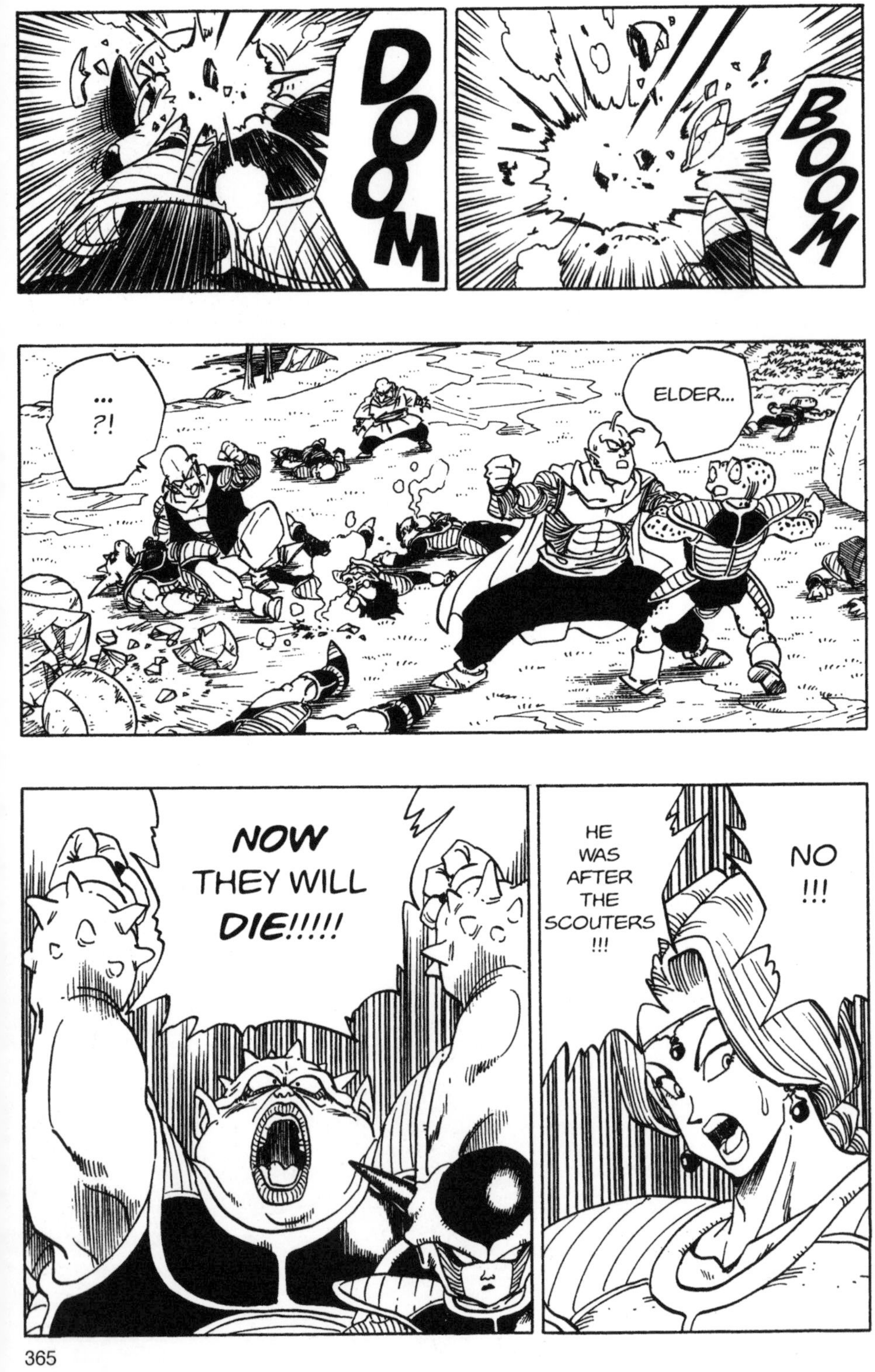
BOOM
DOOM
ELDER...
... ?!
NO !!!
HE WAS AFTER THE SCOUTERS !!!
NOW THEY WILL DIE!!!!!

# DBZ:60 • Ten Seconds of Death

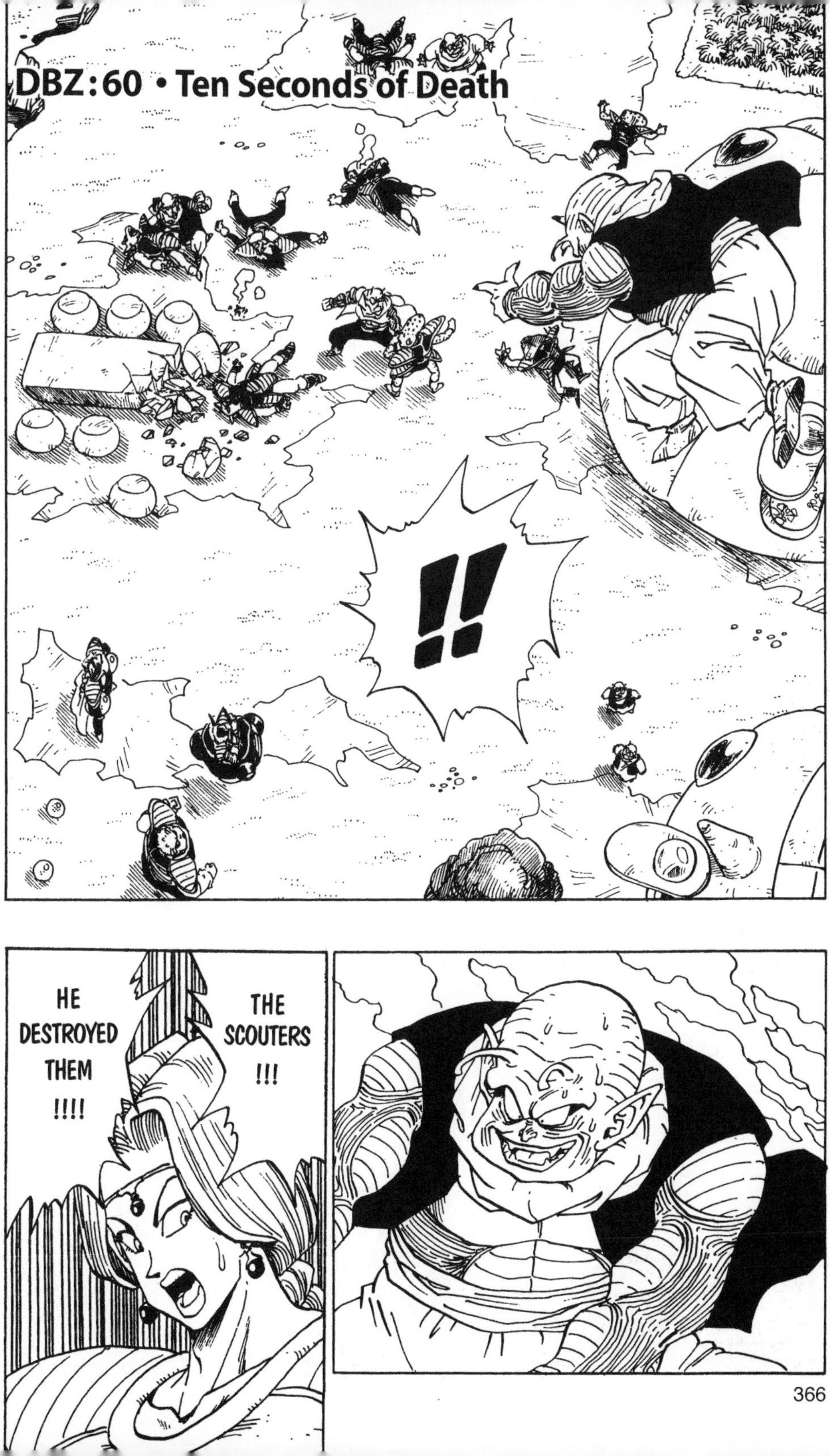
!!
THE SCOUTERS !!!
HE DESTROYED THEM !!!!

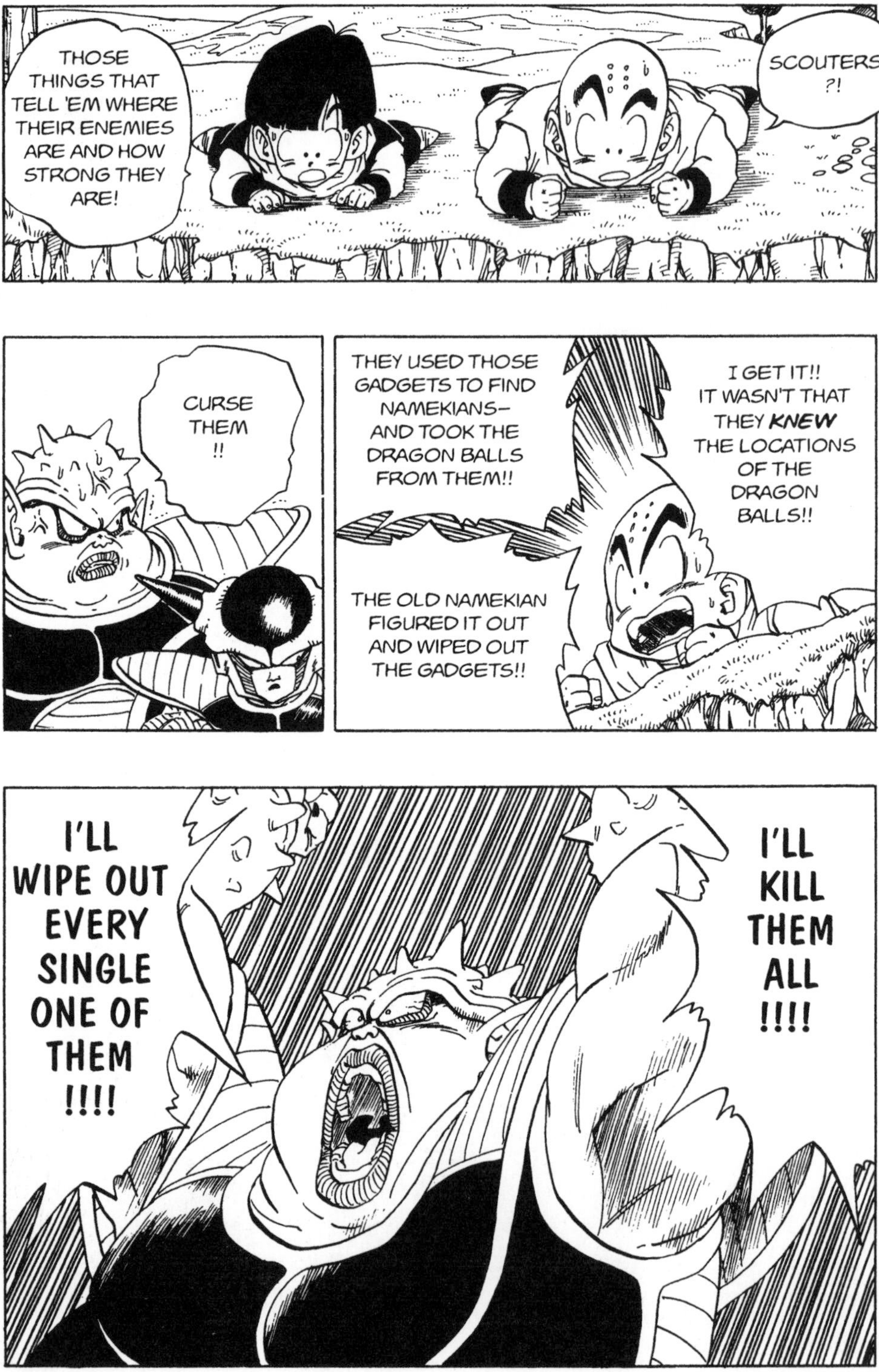
SCOUTERS... ?!
THOSE THINGS THAT TELL 'EM WHERE THEIR ENEMIES ARE AND HOW STRONG THEY ARE!
I GET IT!! IT WASN'T THAT THEY *KNEW* THE LOCATIONS OF THE DRAGON BALLS!!
THEY USED THOSE GADGETS TO FIND NAMEKIANS— AND TOOK THE DRAGON BALLS FROM THEM!!
THE OLD NAMEKIAN FIGURED IT OUT AND WIPED OUT THE GADGETS!!
CURSE THEM !!
I'LL KILL THEM ALL !!!!
I'LL WIPE OUT EVERY SINGLE ONE OF THEM !!!!

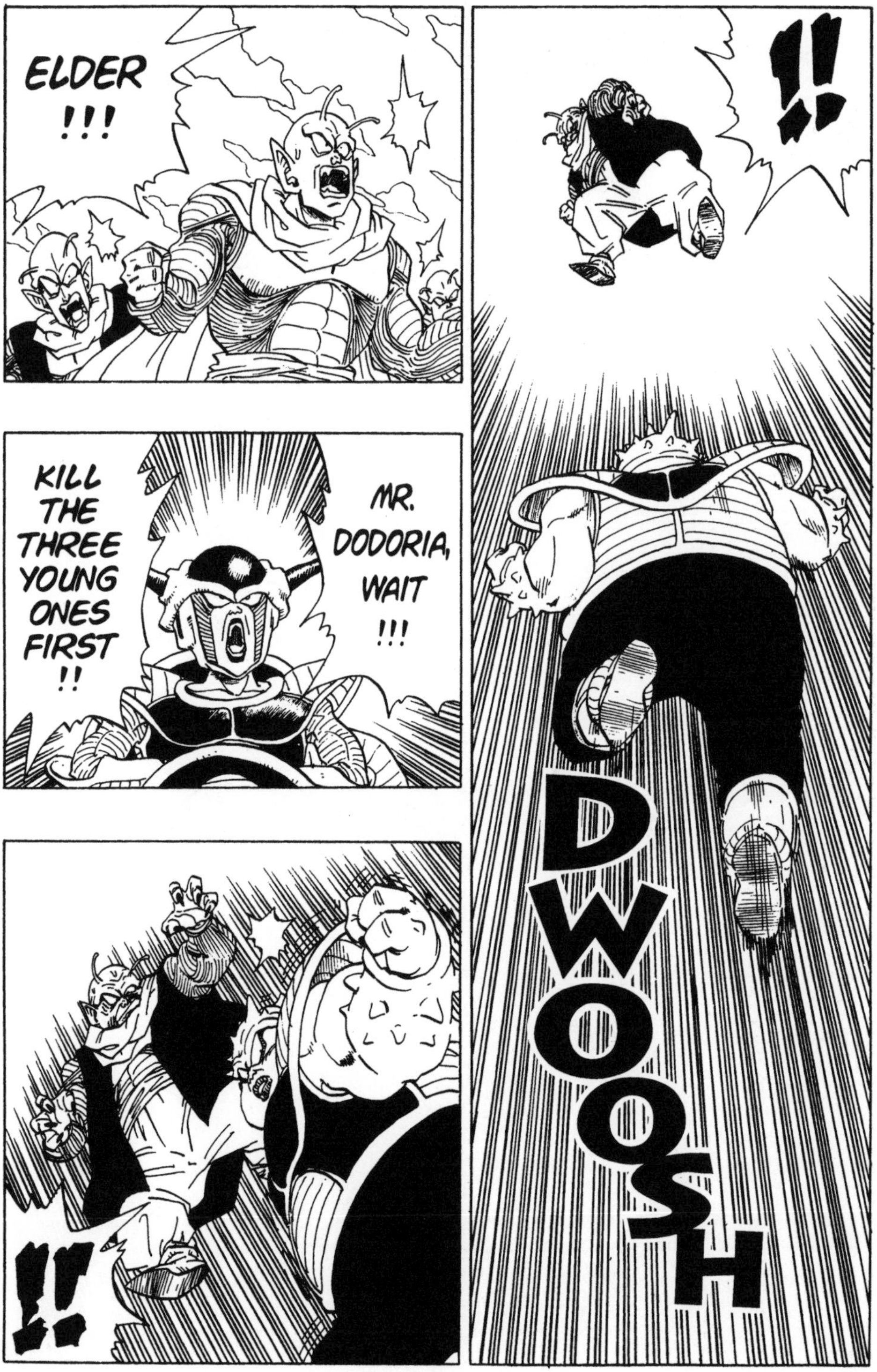
!!
DWOOSH
ELDER !!!
MR. DODORIA, WAIT !!!
KILL THE THREE YOUNG ONES FIRST !!
!!

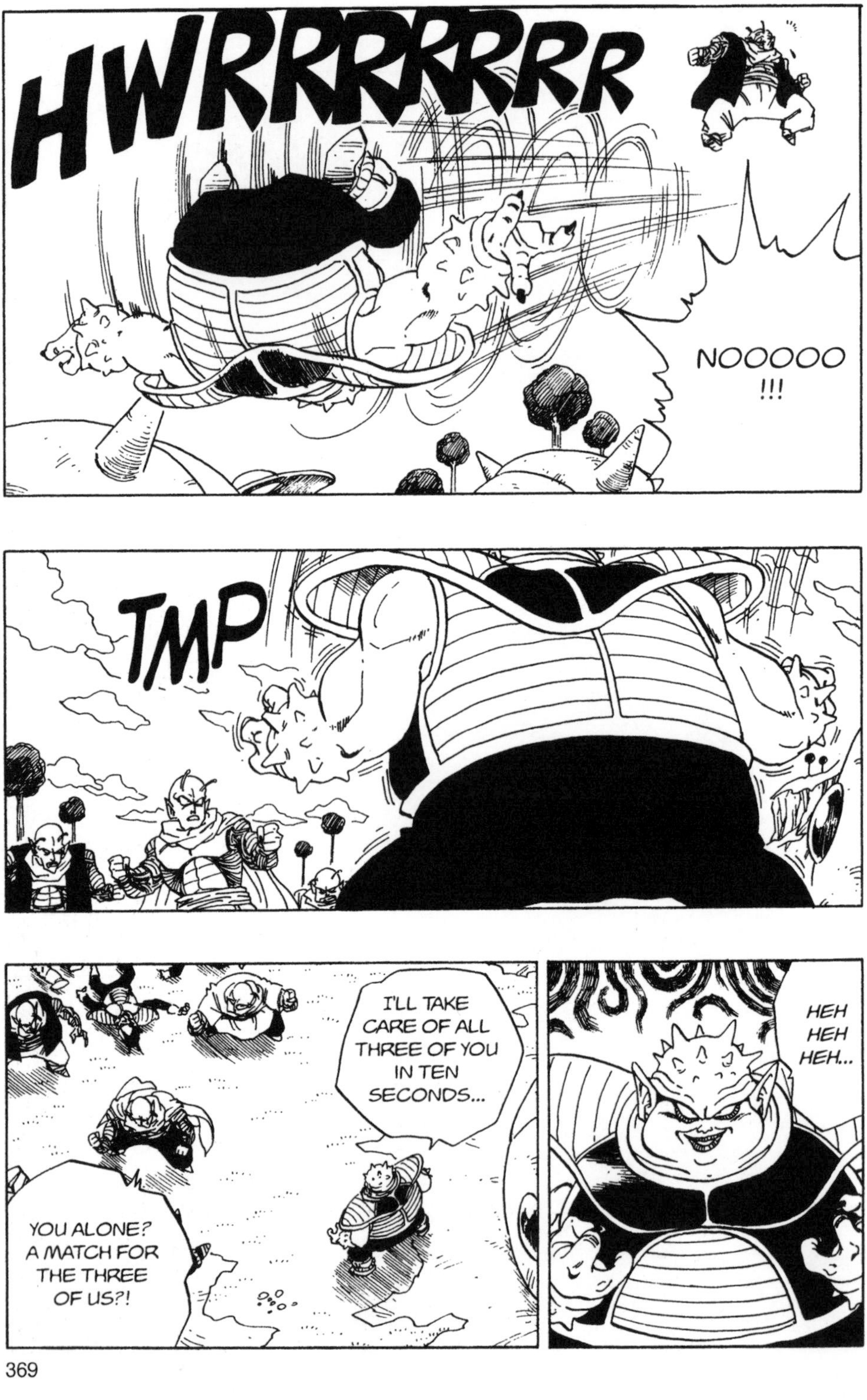
HWRRRRRRR
NOOOOO !!!
TMP
HEH HEH HEH...
I'LL TAKE CARE OF ALL THREE OF YOU IN TEN SECONDS...
YOU ALONE? A MATCH FOR THE THREE OF US?!

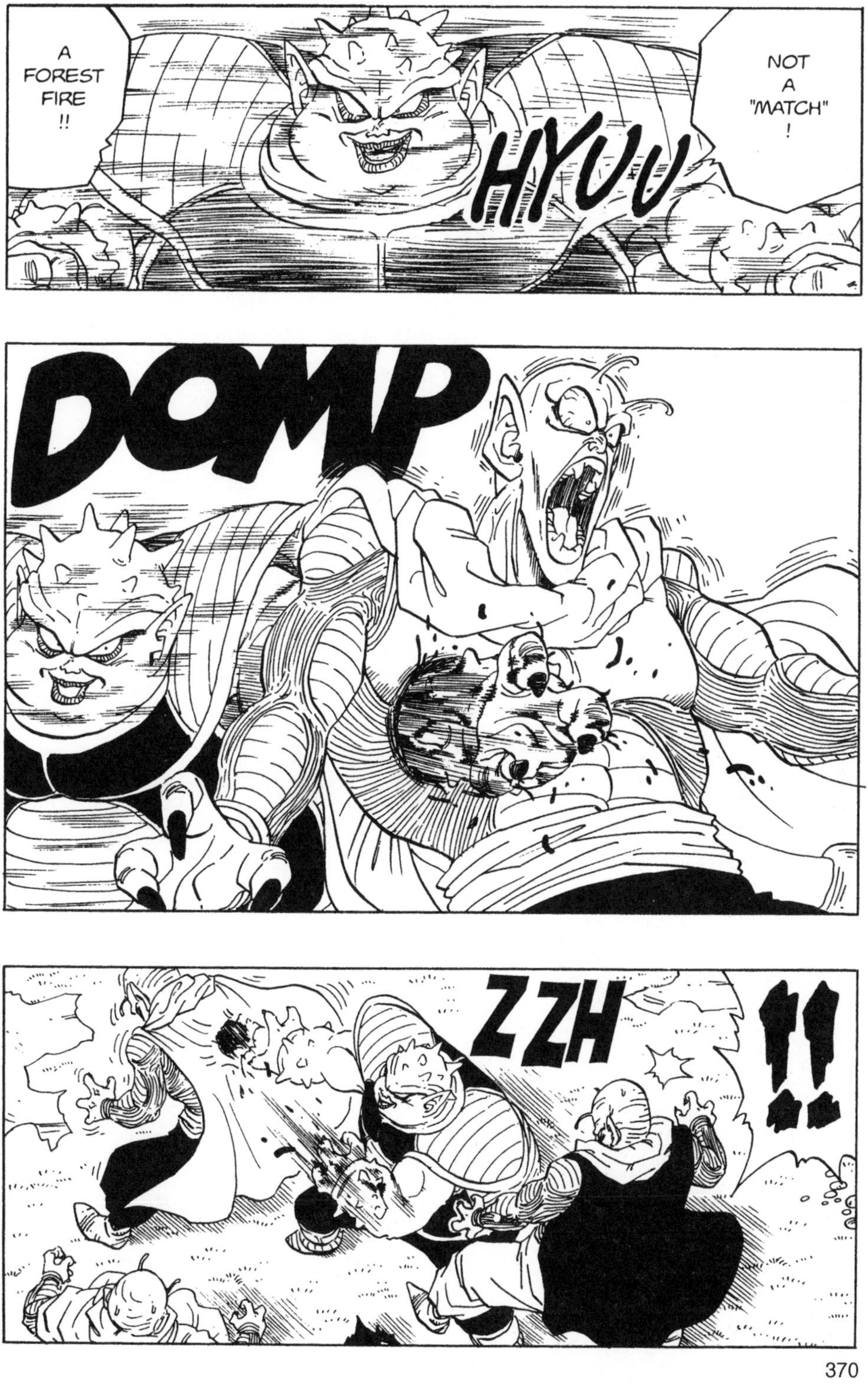
NOT A "MATCH" !
A FOREST FIRE !!
HYUU
DOMP
!!
ZZH

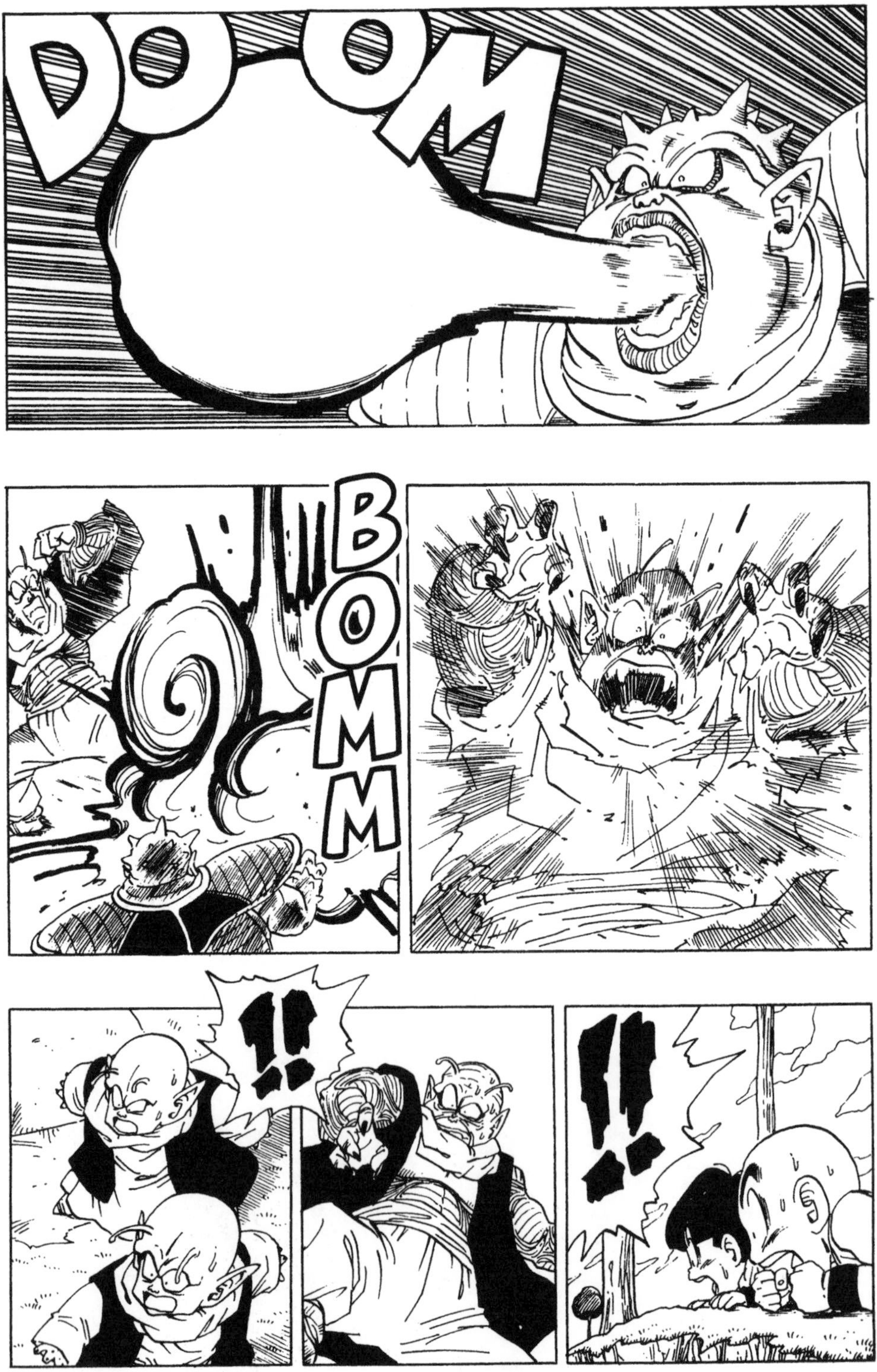
DOOOM
BOMM
!!
!!

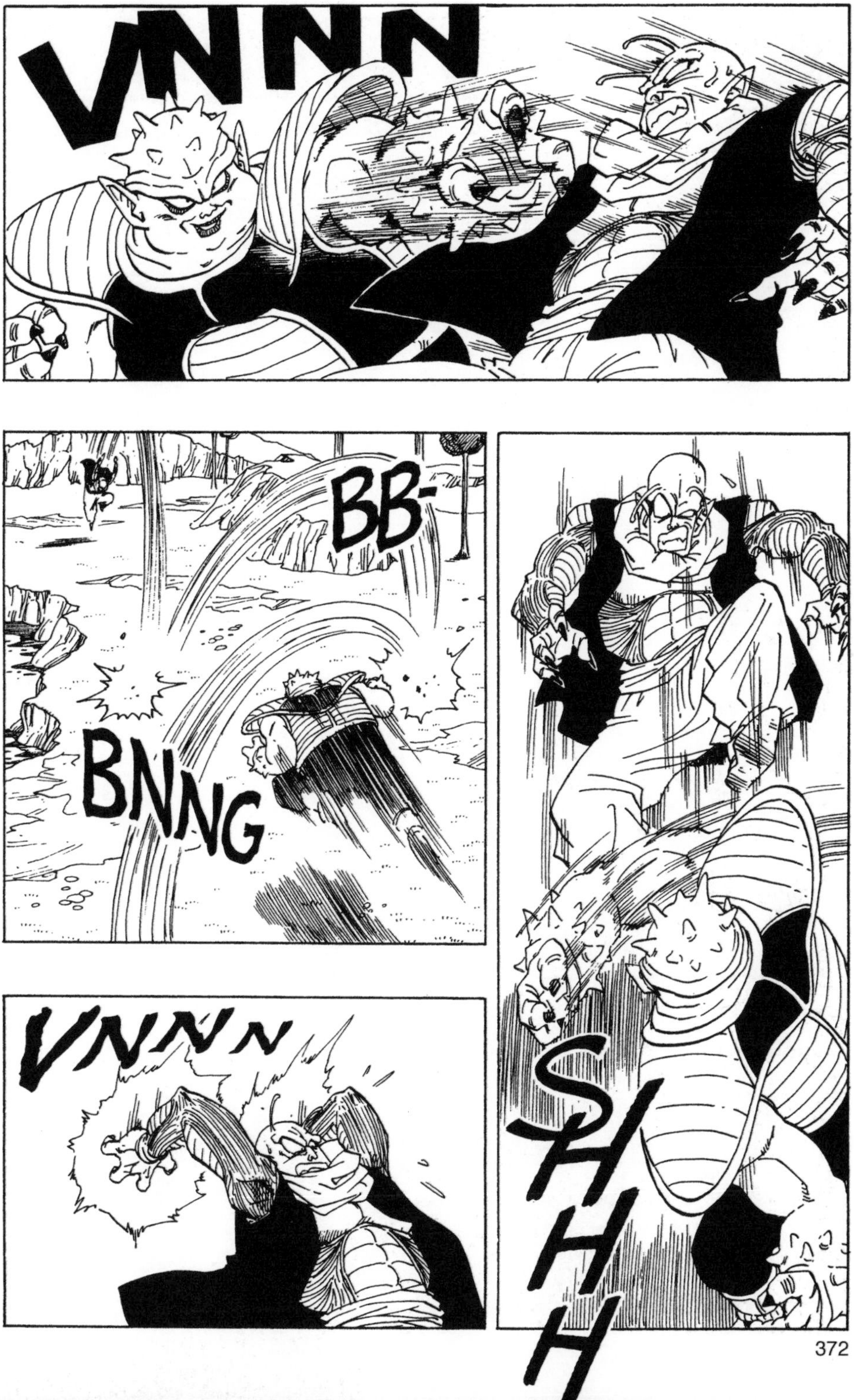
VNNN
SHHH
BB-
BNNG
VNNNN

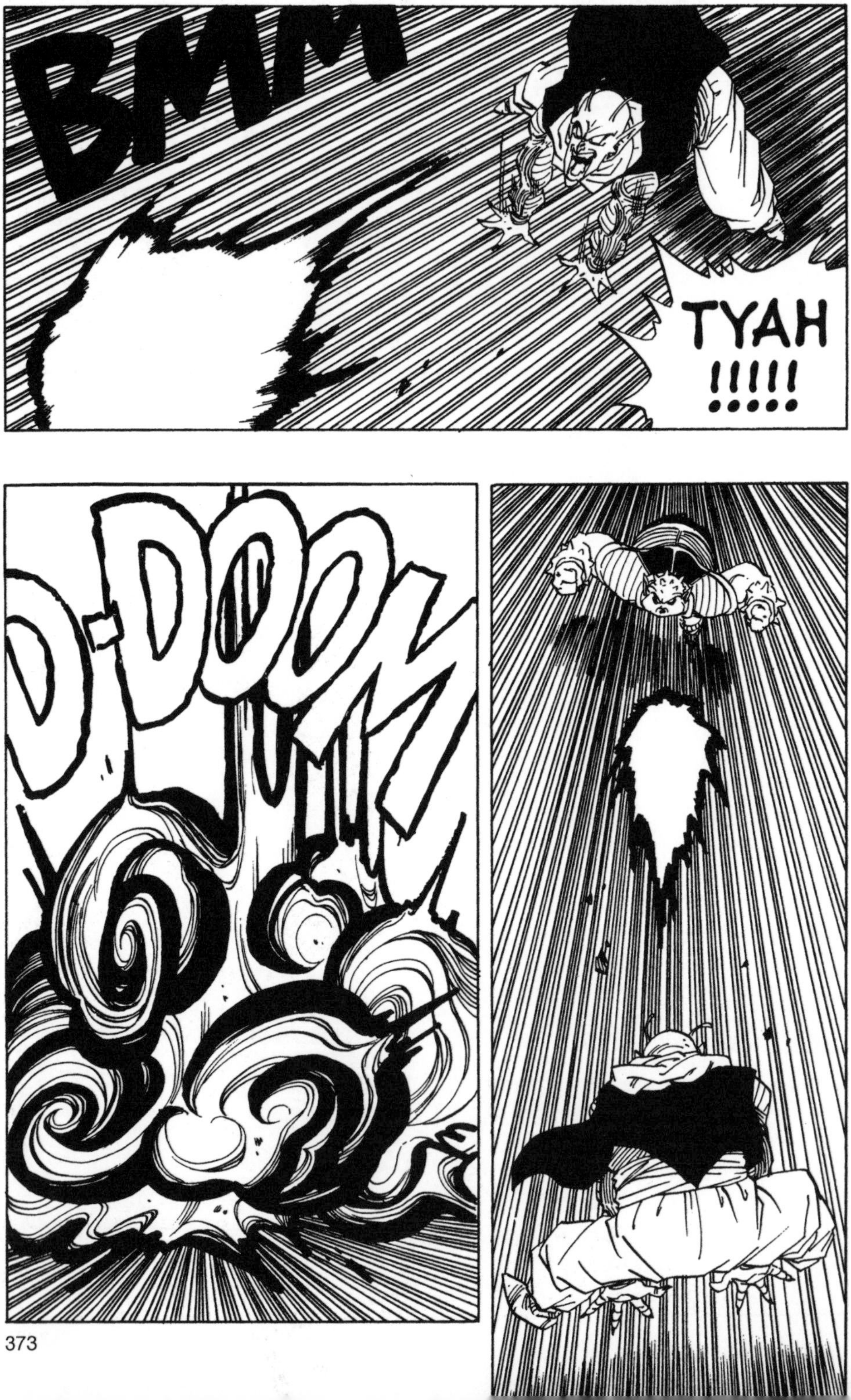
TYAH !!!!!
BMM
D-DOOM

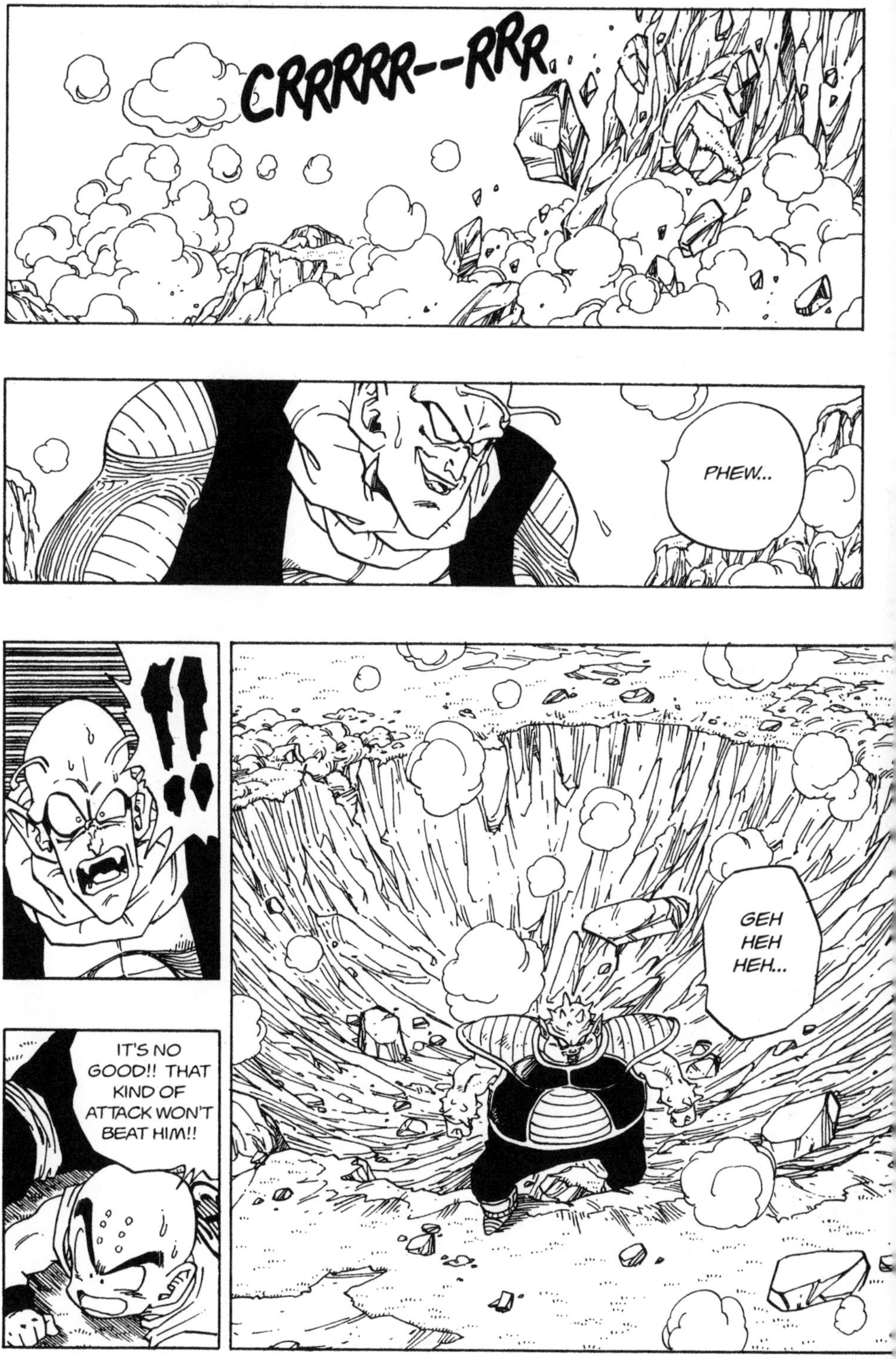
CRRRRR--RRR
PHEW...
GEH HEH HEH...
!!
IT'S NO GOOD!! THAT KIND OF ATTACK WON'T BEAT HIM!!

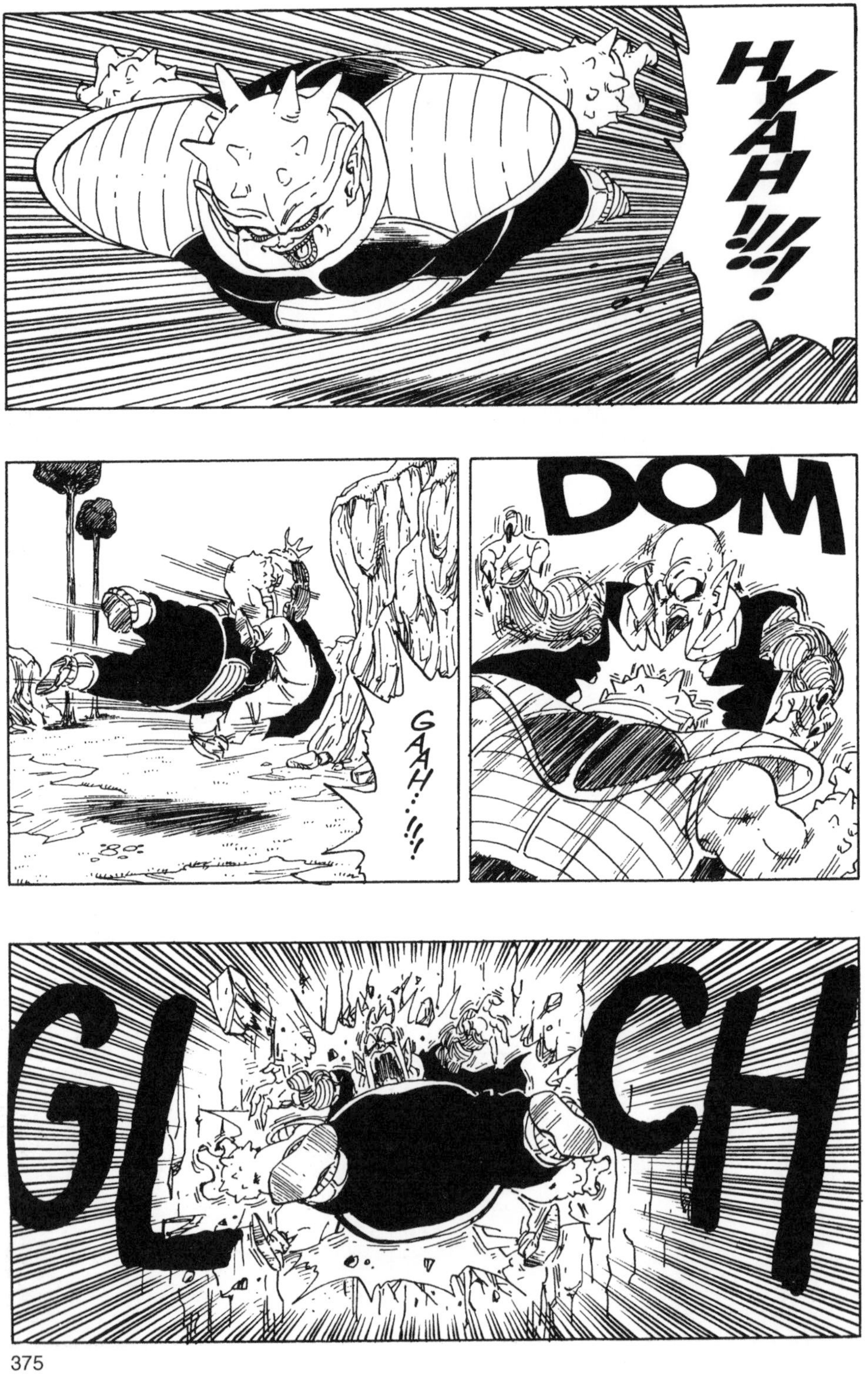
HYAH!!!!
DOM
GAAH...!!!
GL CH

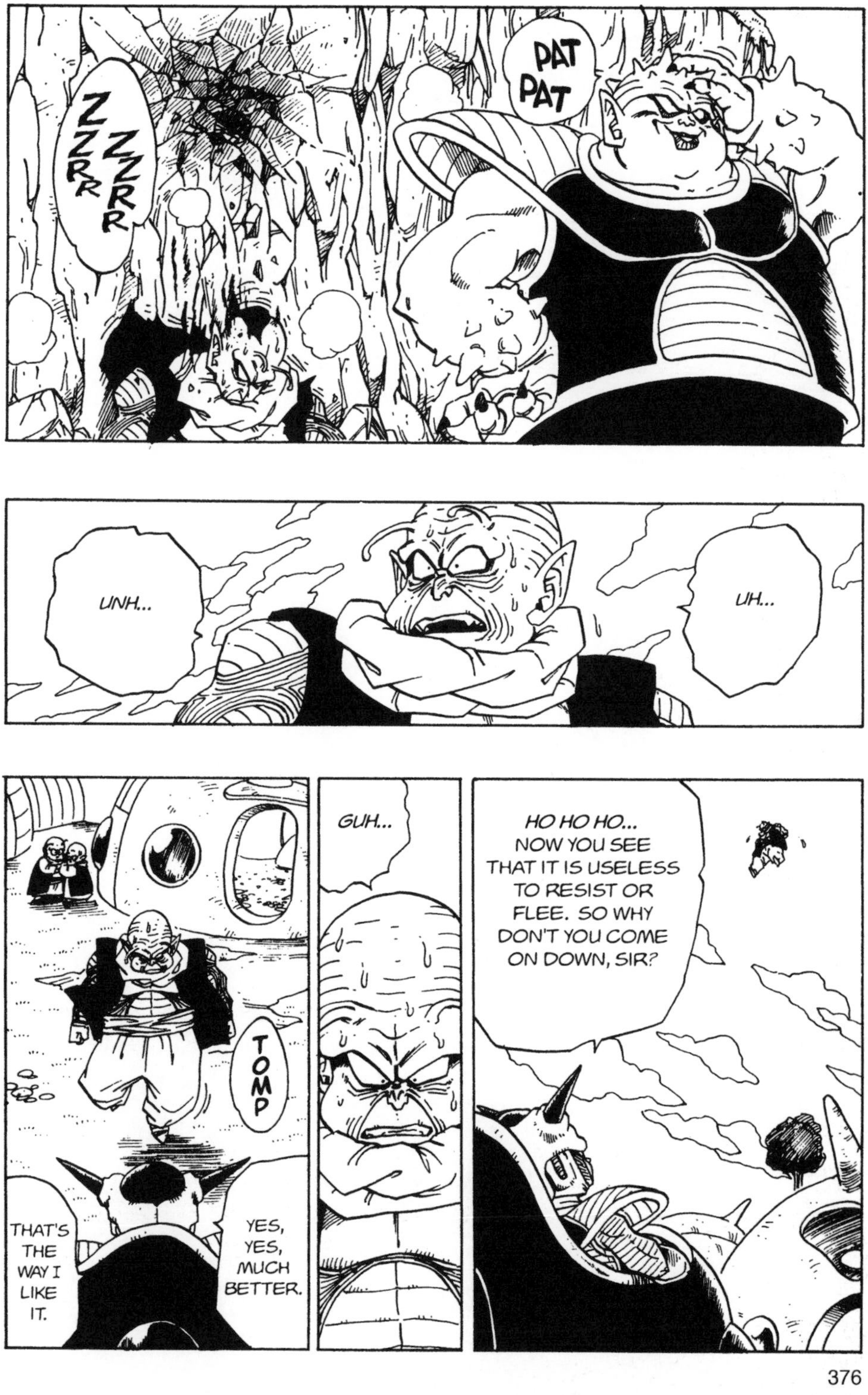
PAT PAT
ZZZRR
ZZZRR
UH...
UNH...
HO HO HO... NOW YOU SEE THAT IT IS USELESS TO RESIST OR FLEE. SO WHY DON'T YOU COME ON DOWN, SIR?
GUH...
TOMP
YES, YES, MUCH BETTER.
THAT'S THE WAY I LIKE IT.

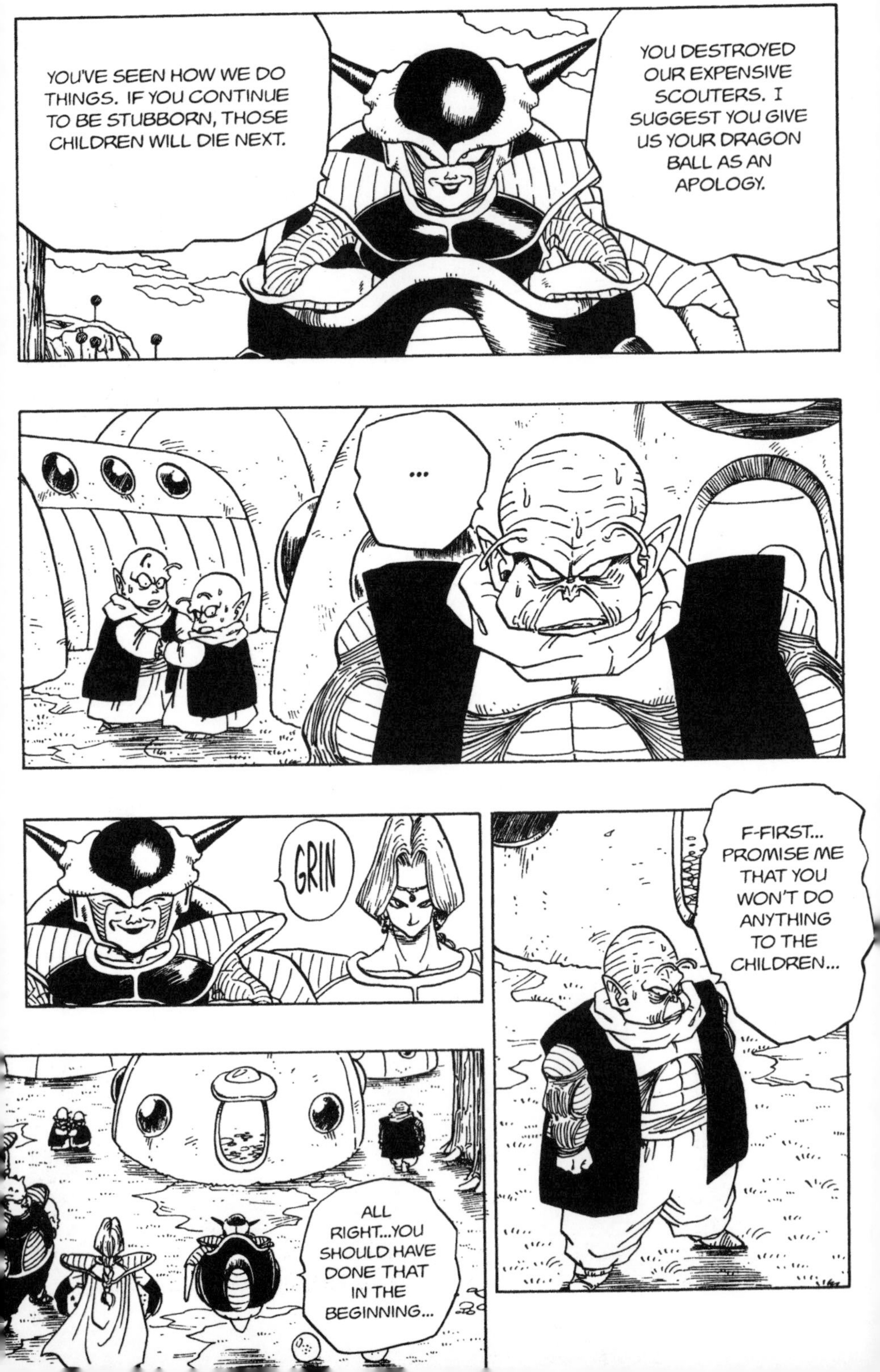
YOU DESTROYED OUR EXPENSIVE SCOUTERS. I SUGGEST YOU GIVE US YOUR DRAGON BALL AS AN APOLOGY.
YOU'VE SEEN HOW WE DO THINGS. IF YOU CONTINUE TO BE STUBBORN, THOSE CHILDREN WILL DIE NEXT.
...
F-FIRST... PROMISE ME THAT YOU WON'T DO ANYTHING TO THE CHILDREN...
GRIN
ALL RIGHT...YOU SHOULD HAVE DONE THAT IN THE BEGINNING...

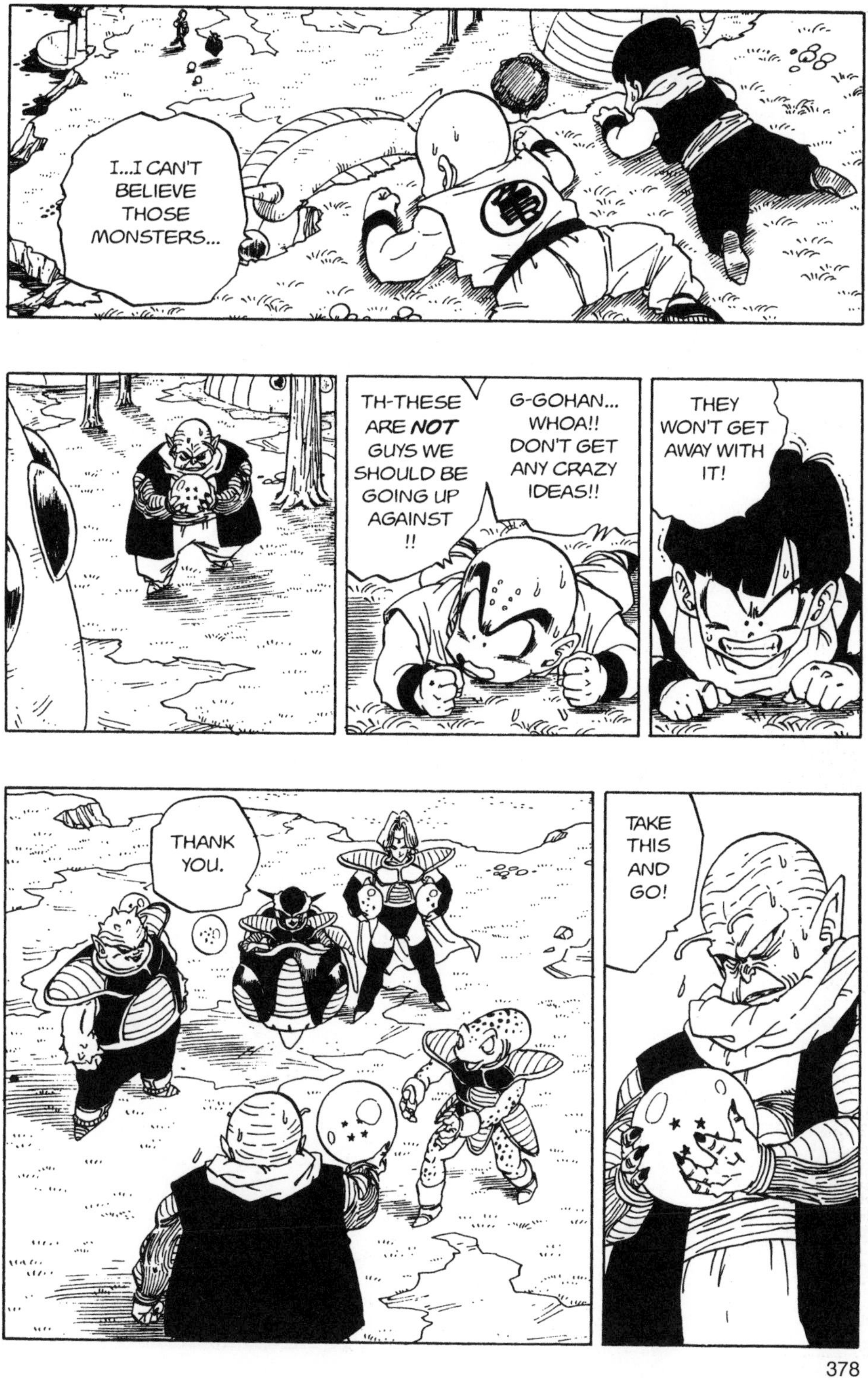
I...I CAN'T BELIEVE THOSE MONSTERS...
THEY WON'T GET AWAY WITH IT!
G-GOHAN... WHOA!! DON'T GET ANY CRAZY IDEAS!!
TH-THESE ARE ***NOT*** GUYS WE SHOULD BE GOING UP AGAINST !!
TAKE THIS AND GO!
THANK YOU.

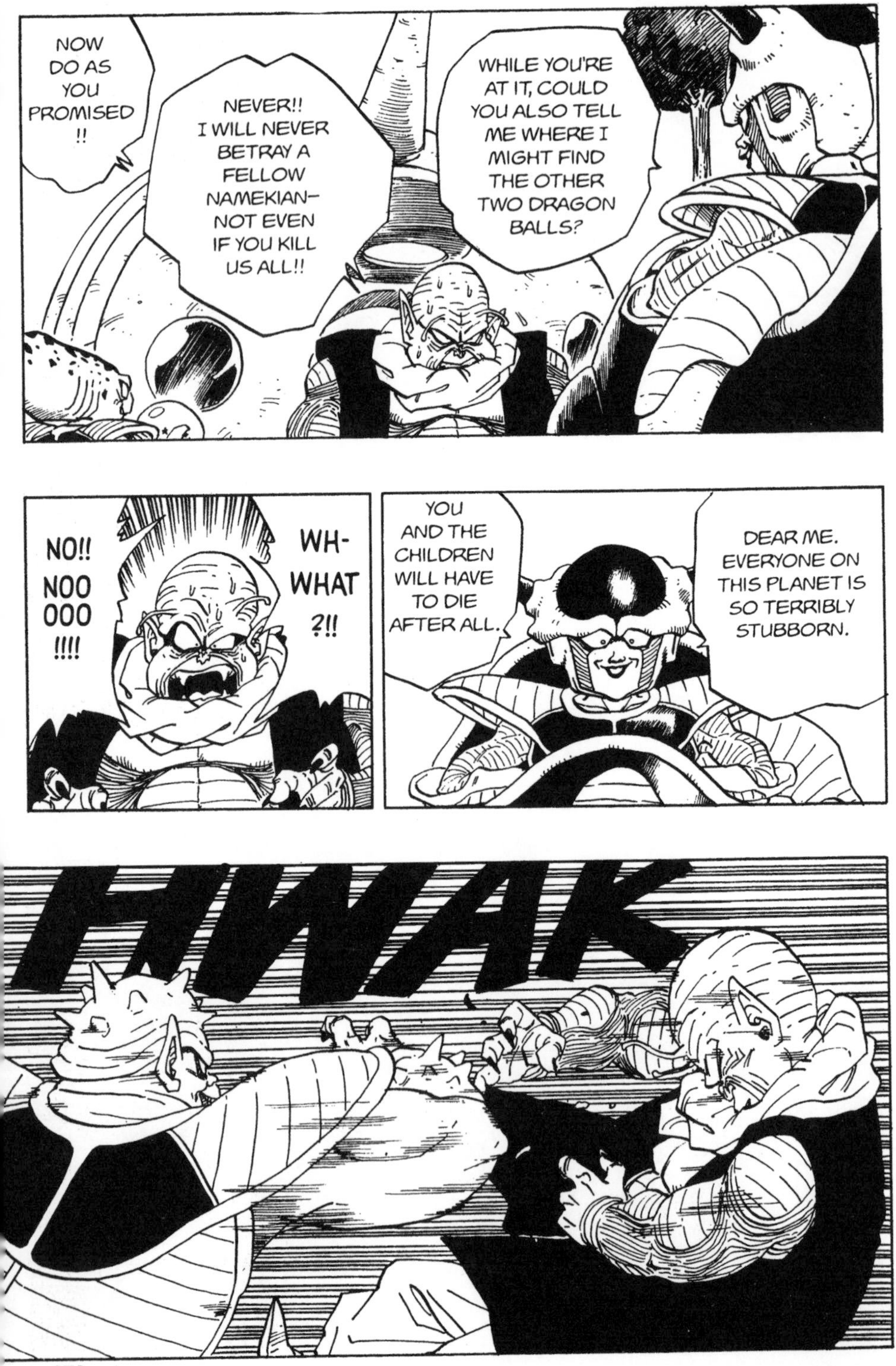
WHILE YOU'RE AT IT, COULD YOU ALSO TELL ME WHERE I MIGHT FIND THE OTHER TWO DRAGON BALLS?
NEVER!! I WILL NEVER BETRAY A FELLOW NAMEKIAN— NOT EVEN IF YOU KILL US ALL!!
NOW DO AS YOU PROMISED !!
DEAR ME. EVERYONE ON THIS PLANET IS SO TERRIBLY STUBBORN.
YOU AND THE CHILDREN WILL HAVE TO DIE AFTER ALL.
WH- WHAT ?!!
NO!! NOO OOO !!!!
HWAK

# DBZ:61 • Son Gohan Snaps!

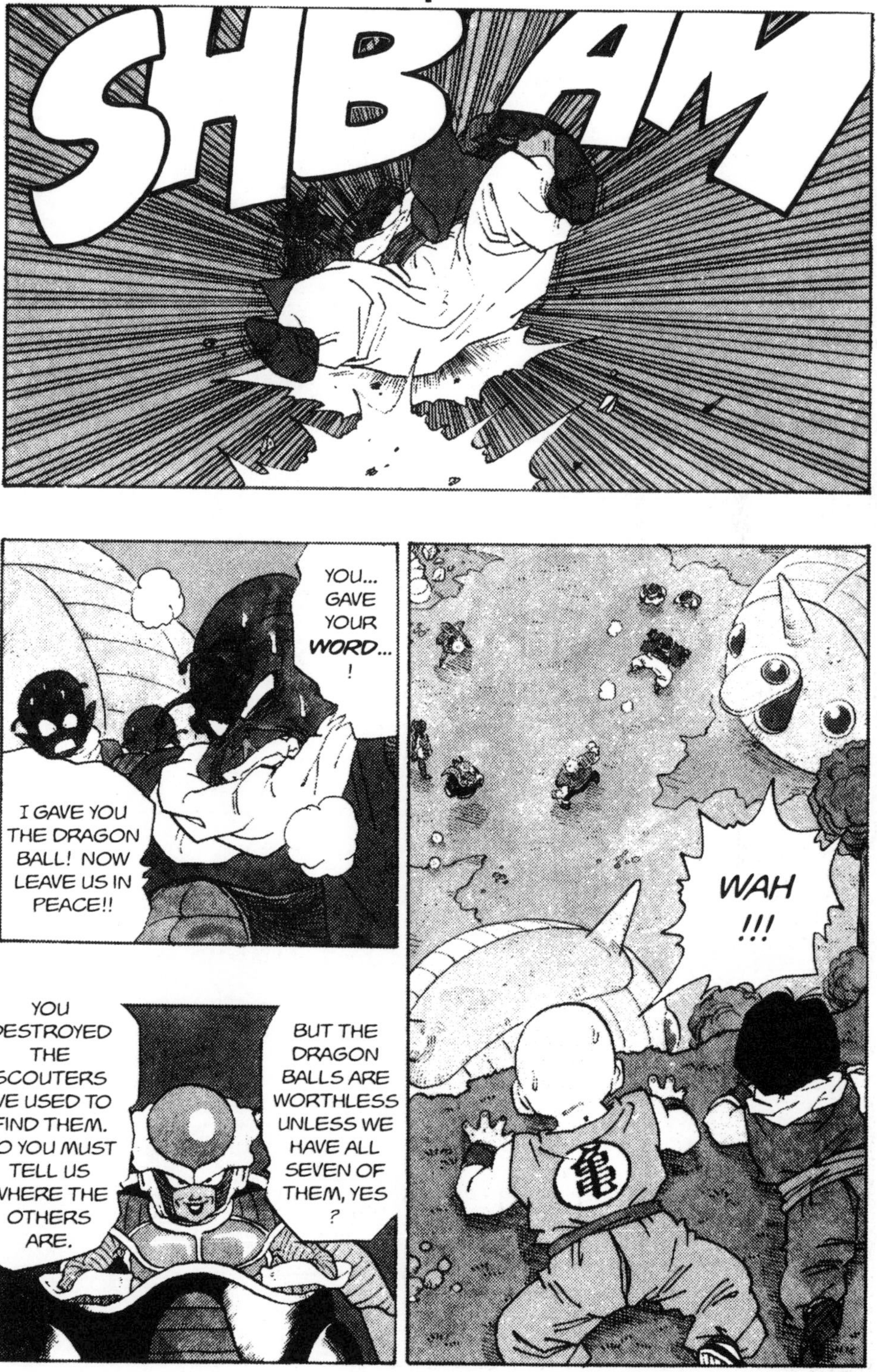
SHBAM
WAH !!!
YOU... GAVE YOUR WORD... !
I GAVE YOU THE DRAGON BALL! NOW LEAVE US IN PEACE!!
BUT THE DRAGON BALLS ARE WORTHLESS UNLESS WE HAVE ALL SEVEN OF THEM, YES ?
YOU DESTROYED THE SCOUTERS WE USED TO FIND THEM. SO YOU MUST TELL US WHERE THE OTHERS ARE.

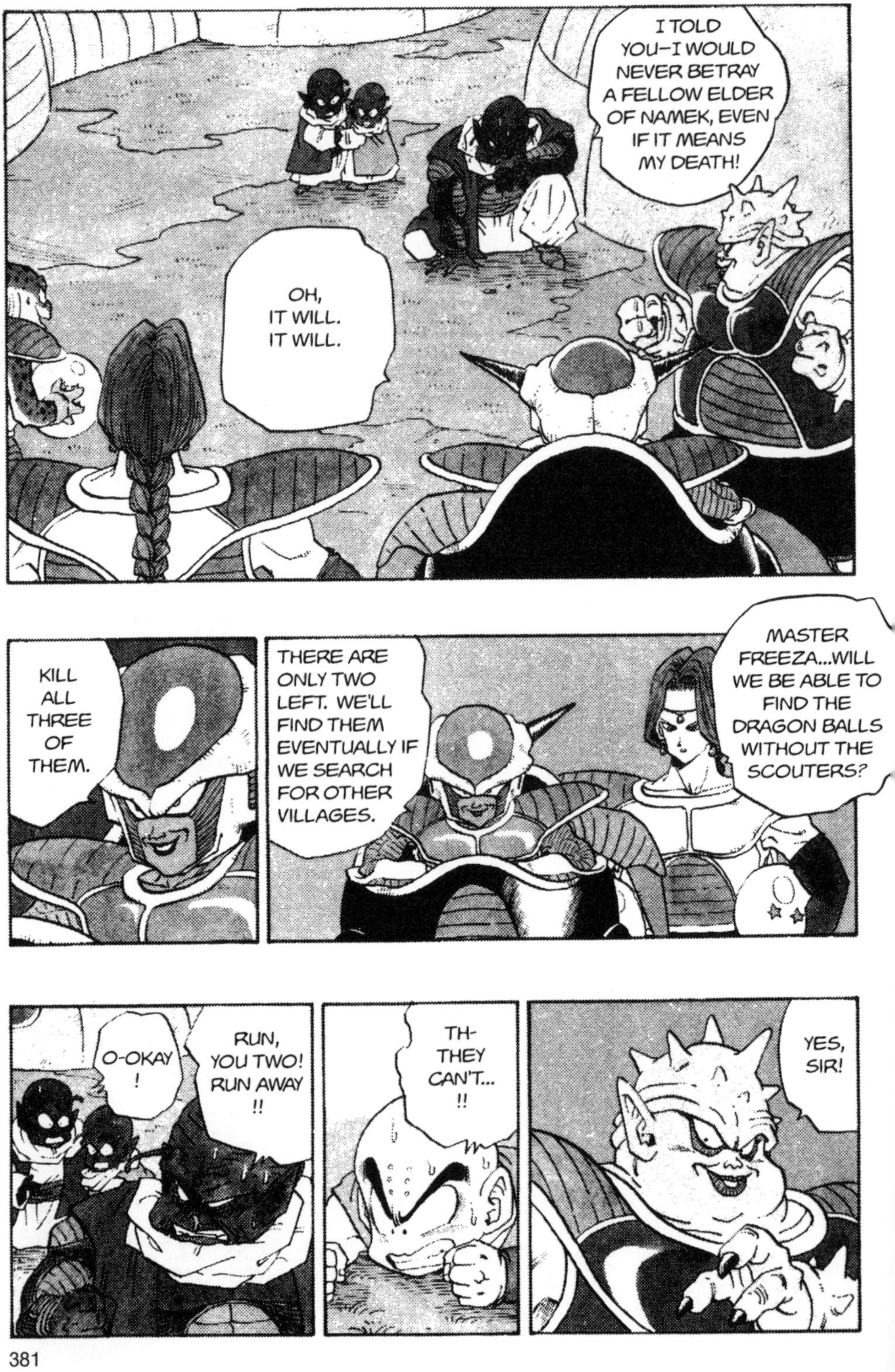
I TOLD YOU—I WOULD NEVER BETRAY A FELLOW ELDER OF NAMEK, EVEN IF IT MEANS MY DEATH!
OH, IT WILL. IT WILL.
MASTER FREEZA...WILL WE BE ABLE TO FIND THE DRAGON BALLS WITHOUT THE SCOUTERS?
THERE ARE ONLY TWO LEFT. WE'LL FIND THEM EVENTUALLY IF WE SEARCH FOR OTHER VILLAGES.
KILL ALL THREE OF THEM.
YES, SIR!
TH- THEY CAN'T... !!
RUN, YOU TWO! RUN AWAY !!
O-OKAY !

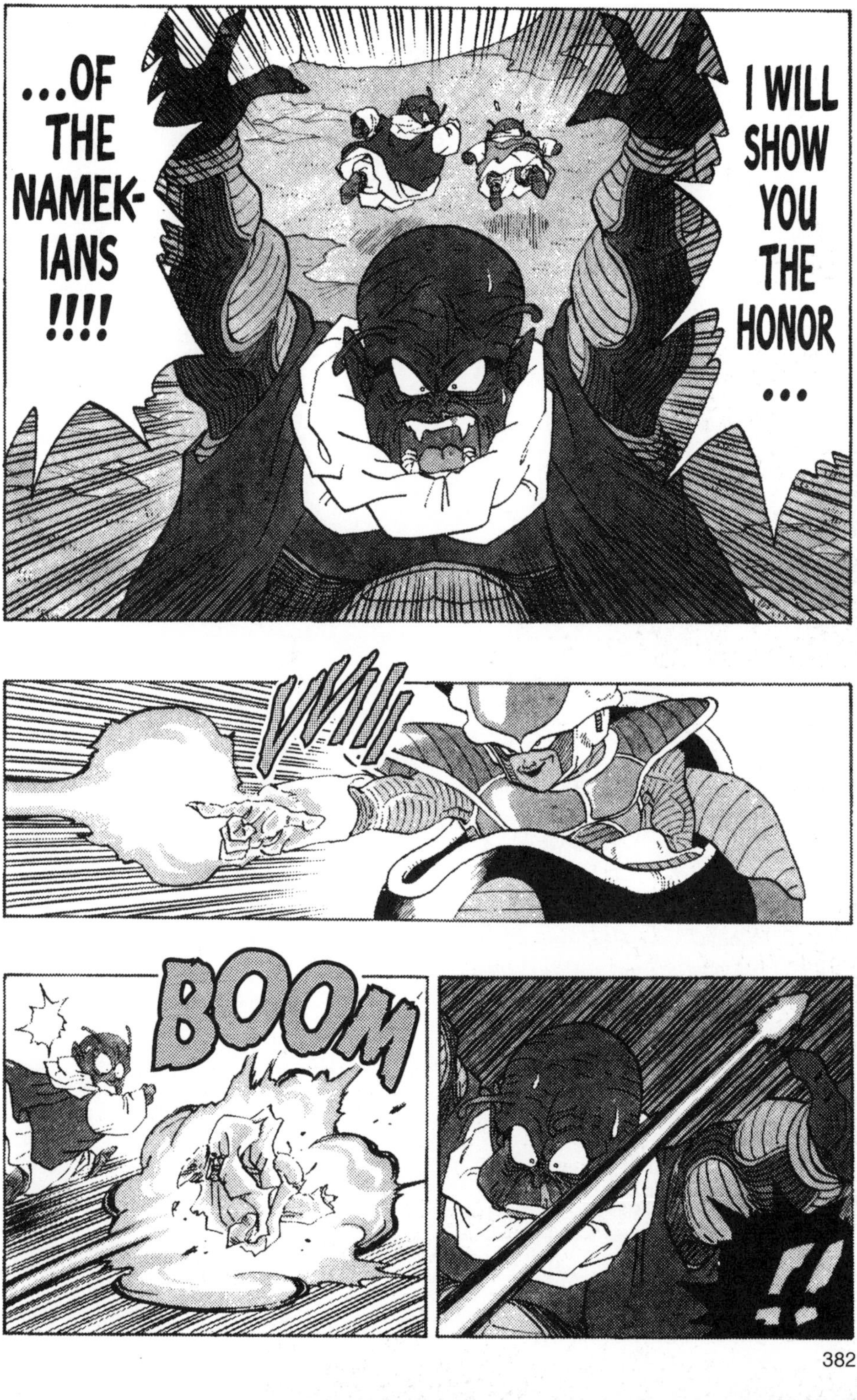
I WILL SHOW YOU THE HONOR...
...OF THE NAMEK-IANS!!!!
VWII
!?
BOOM

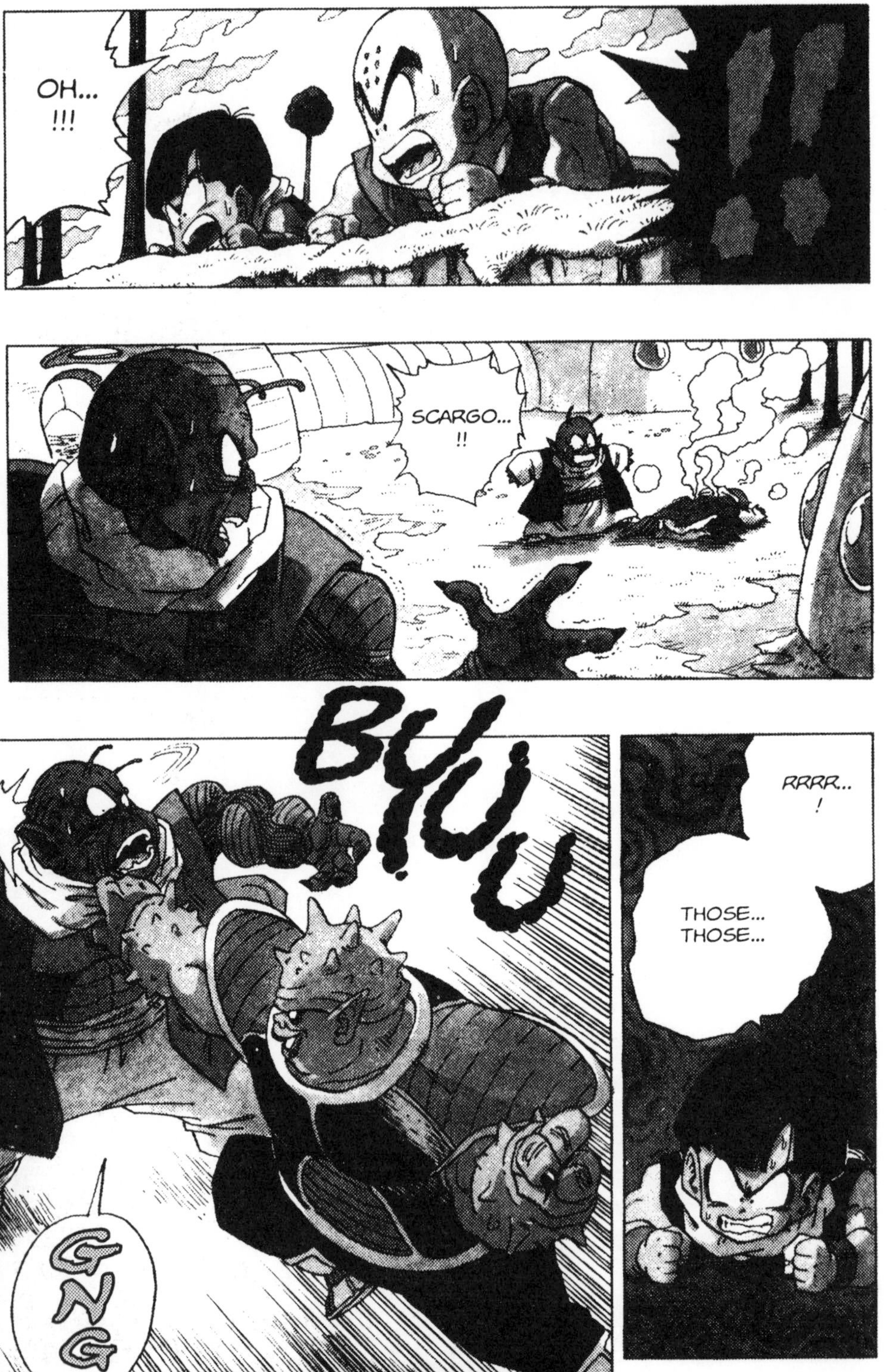
OH... !!!
SCARGO... !!
RRRR... !
THOSE... THOSE...
BYUU
GNG

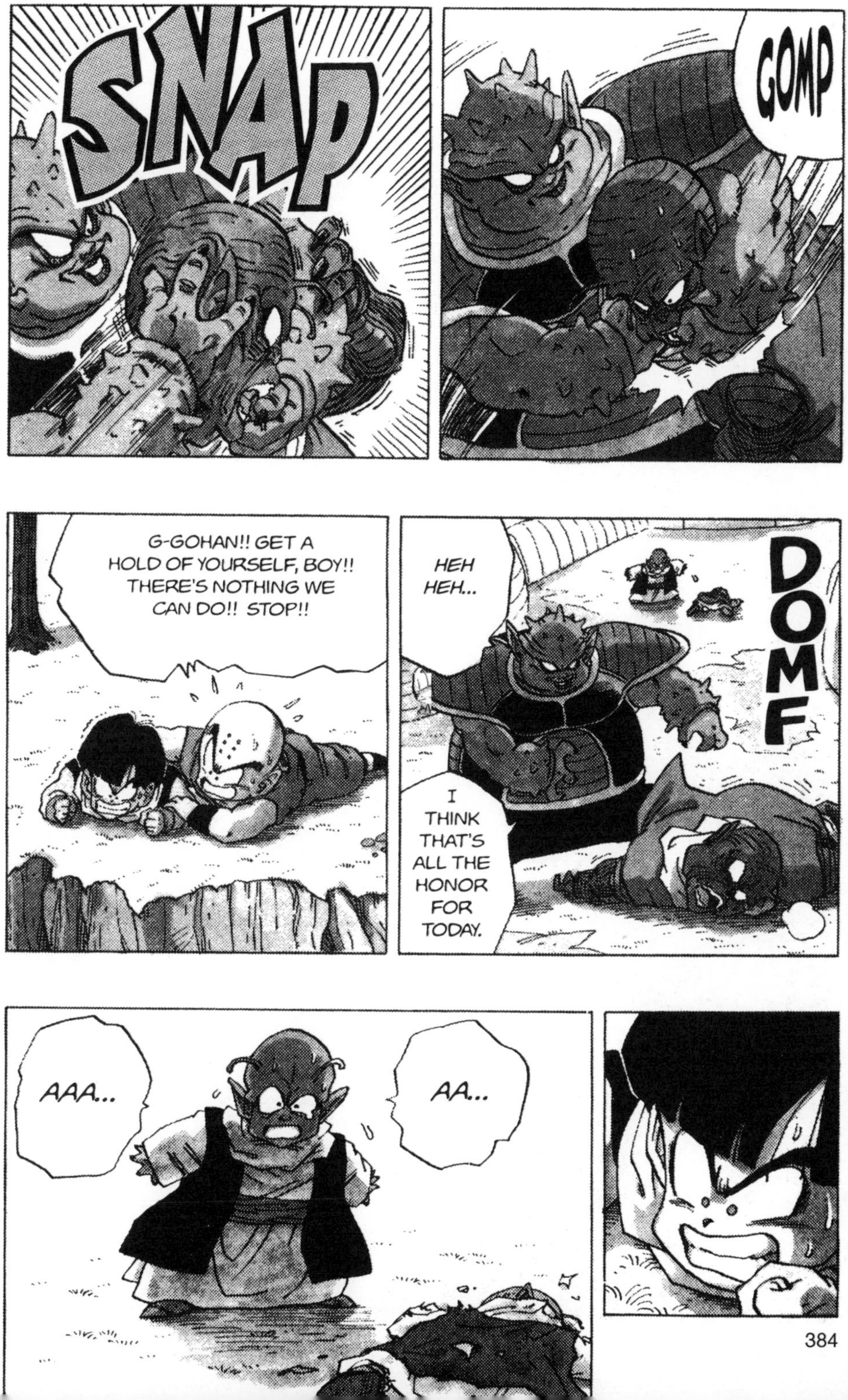
GOMP
SNAP
HEH HEH...
DOMF
I THINK THAT'S ALL THE HONOR FOR TODAY.
G-GOHAN!! GET A HOLD OF YOURSELF, BOY!! THERE'S NOTHING WE CAN DO!! STOP!!
AA...
AAA...

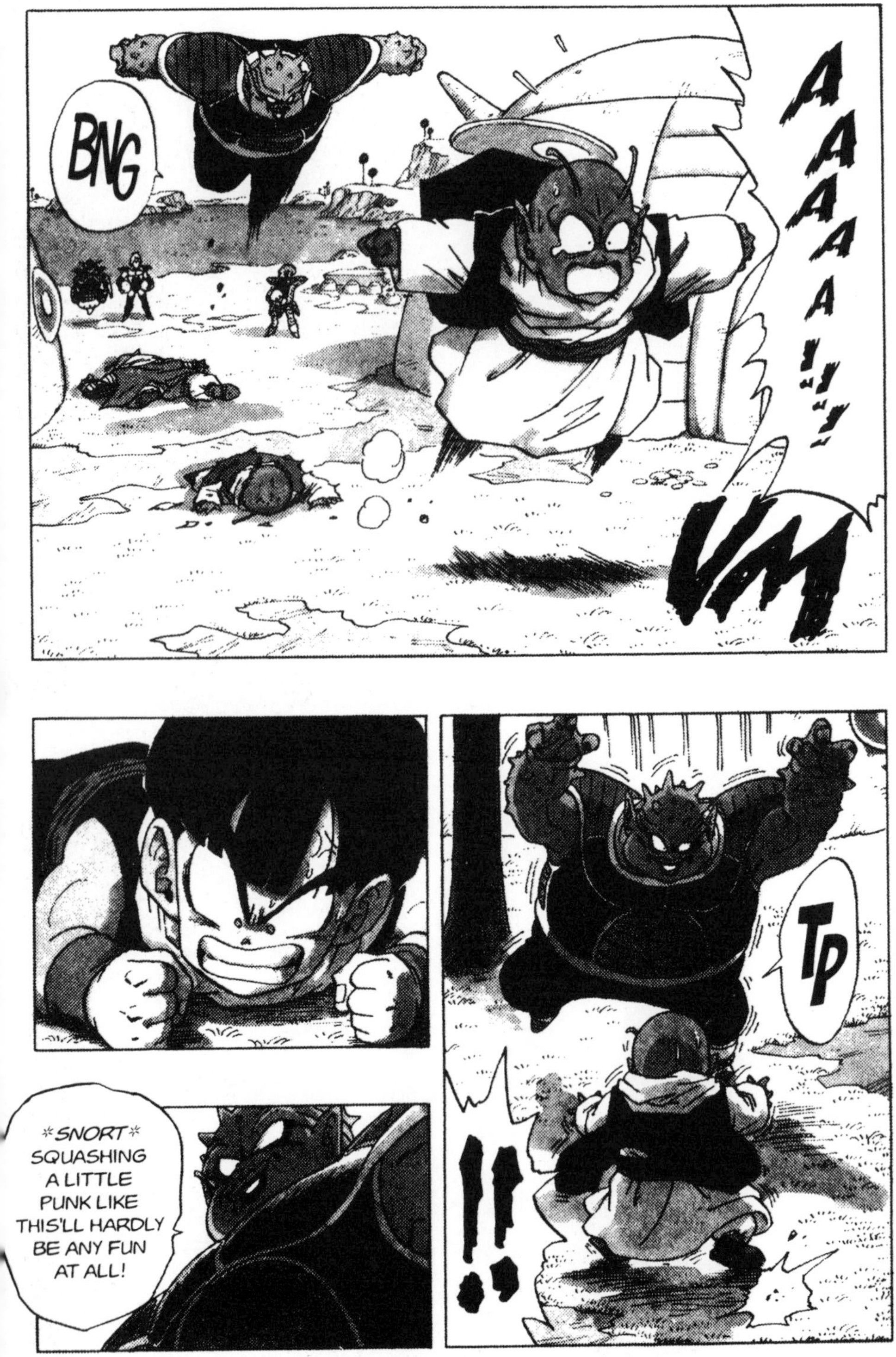
AAAAA!!!!!
VM
BNG
TP
!!
*SNORT* SQUASHING A LITTLE PUNK LIKE THIS'LL HARDLY BE ANY FUN AT ALL!

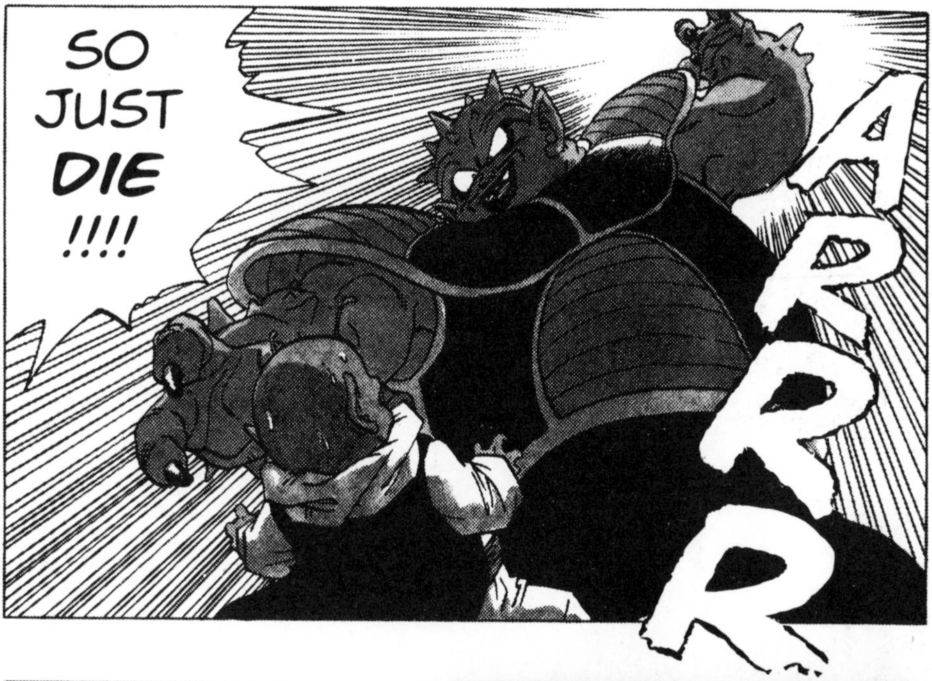
ARRR
SO JUST DIE !!!!
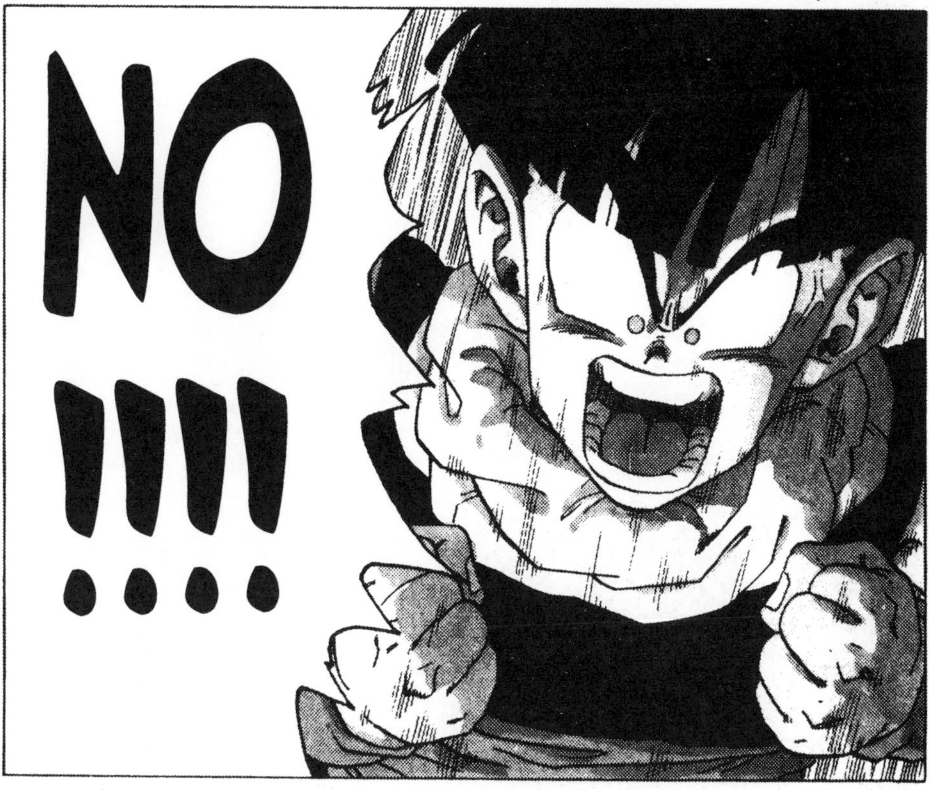
NO !!!!

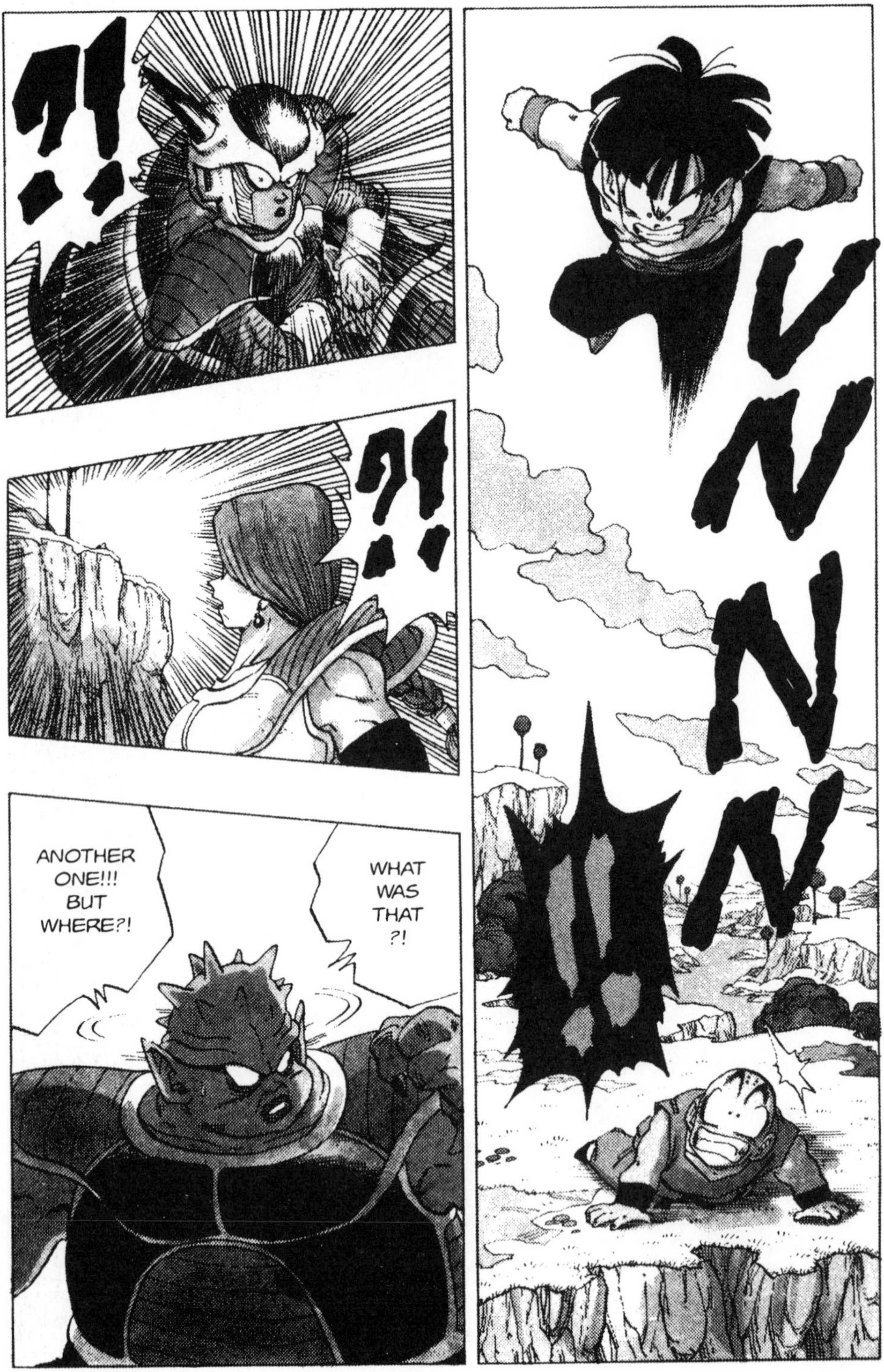
!!
?!
?!
WHAT WAS THAT ?!
ANOTHER ONE!!! BUT WHERE?!

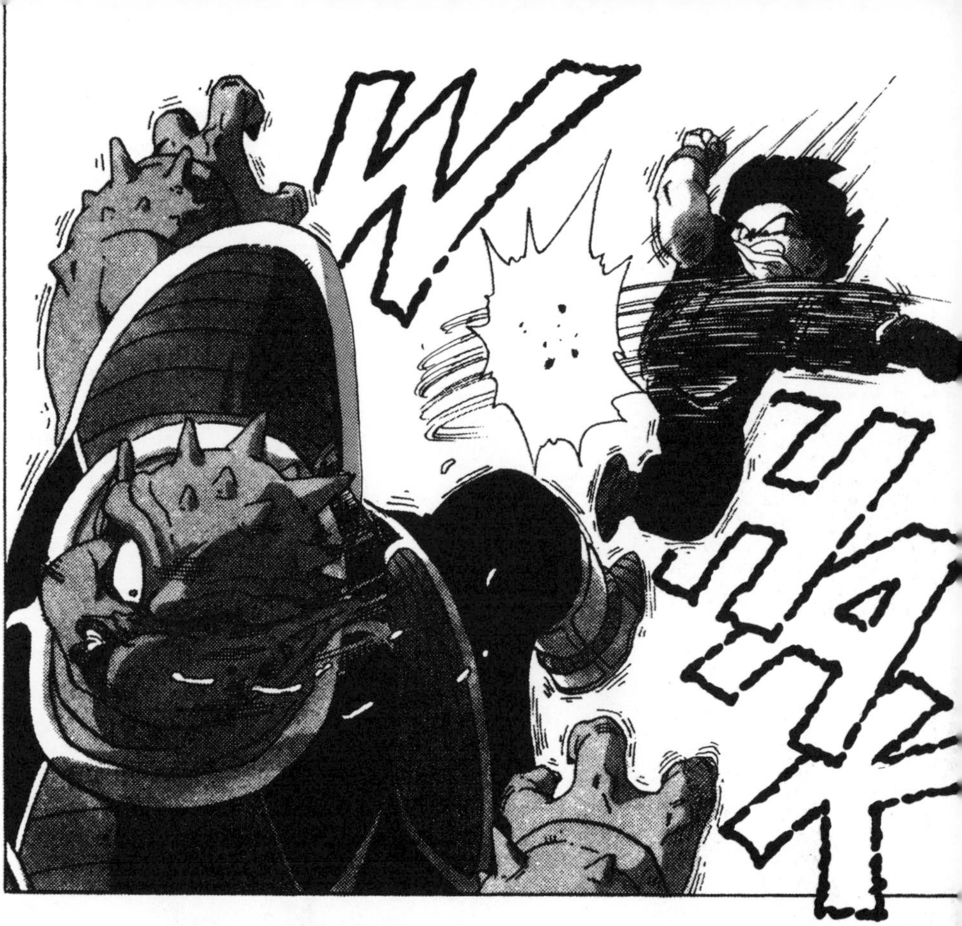
WHAK

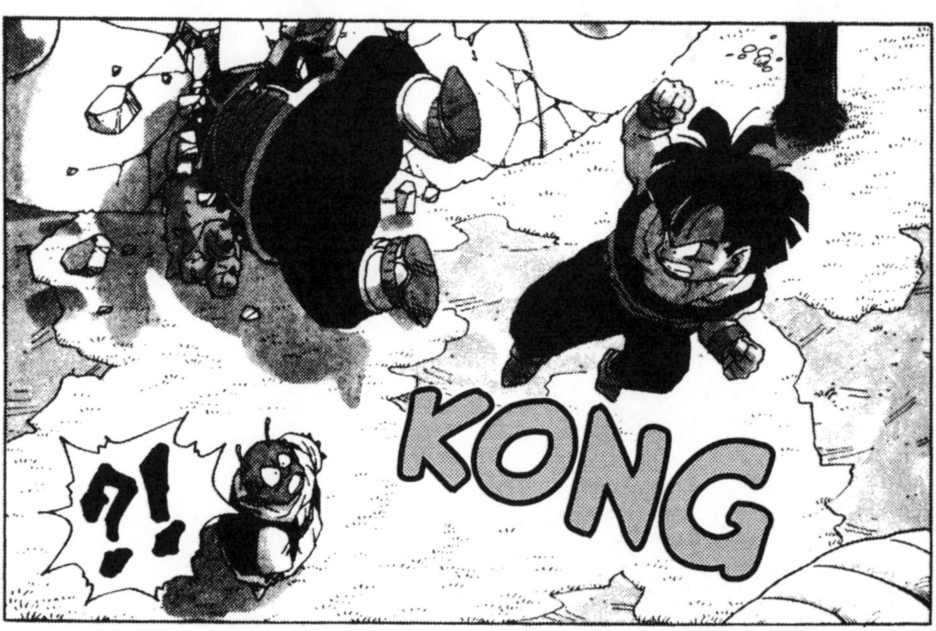
KONG
?!

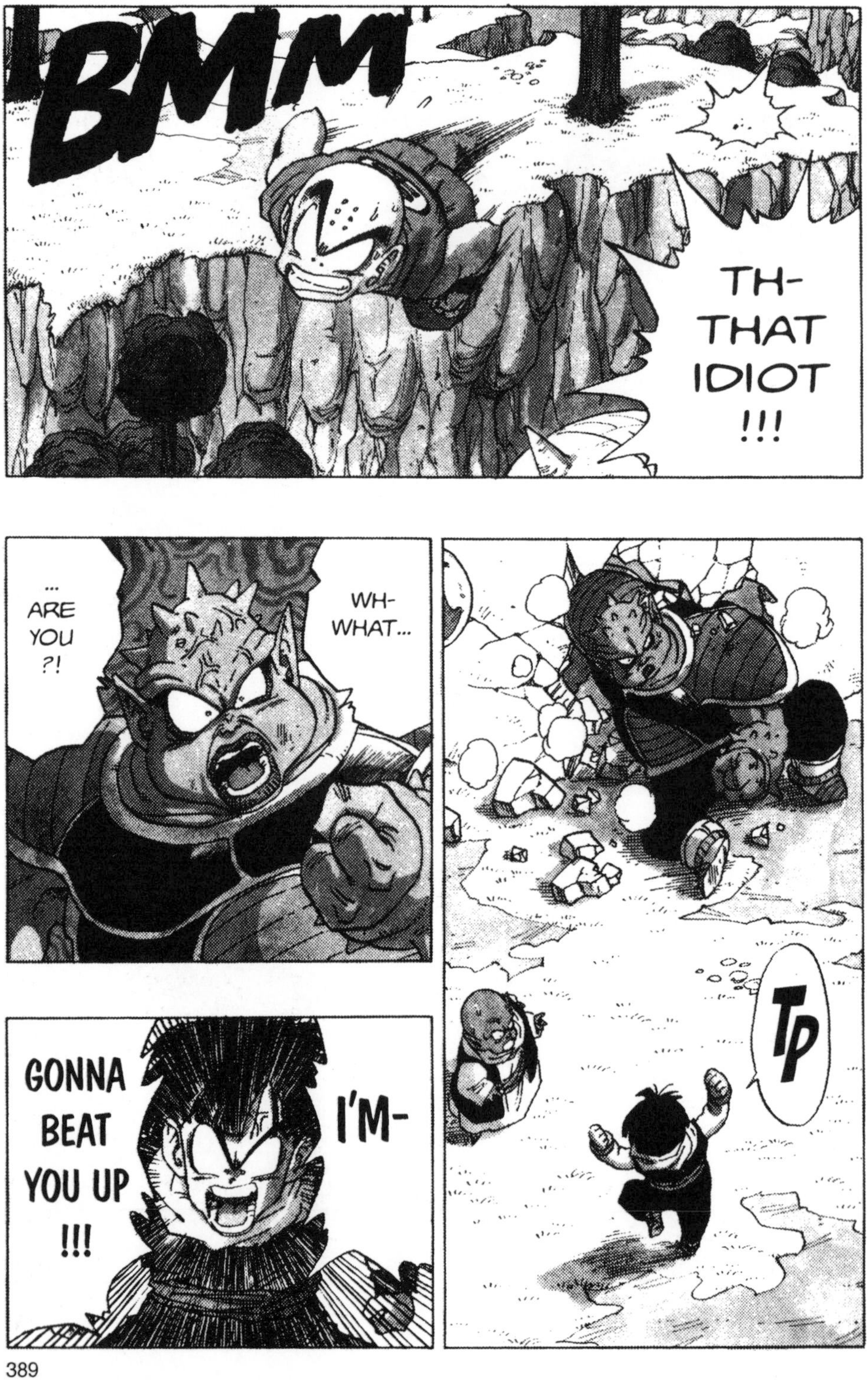
BMM
TH- THAT IDIOT !!!
TP
WH- WHAT...
... ARE YOU ?!
I'M-
GONNA BEAT YOU UP !!!

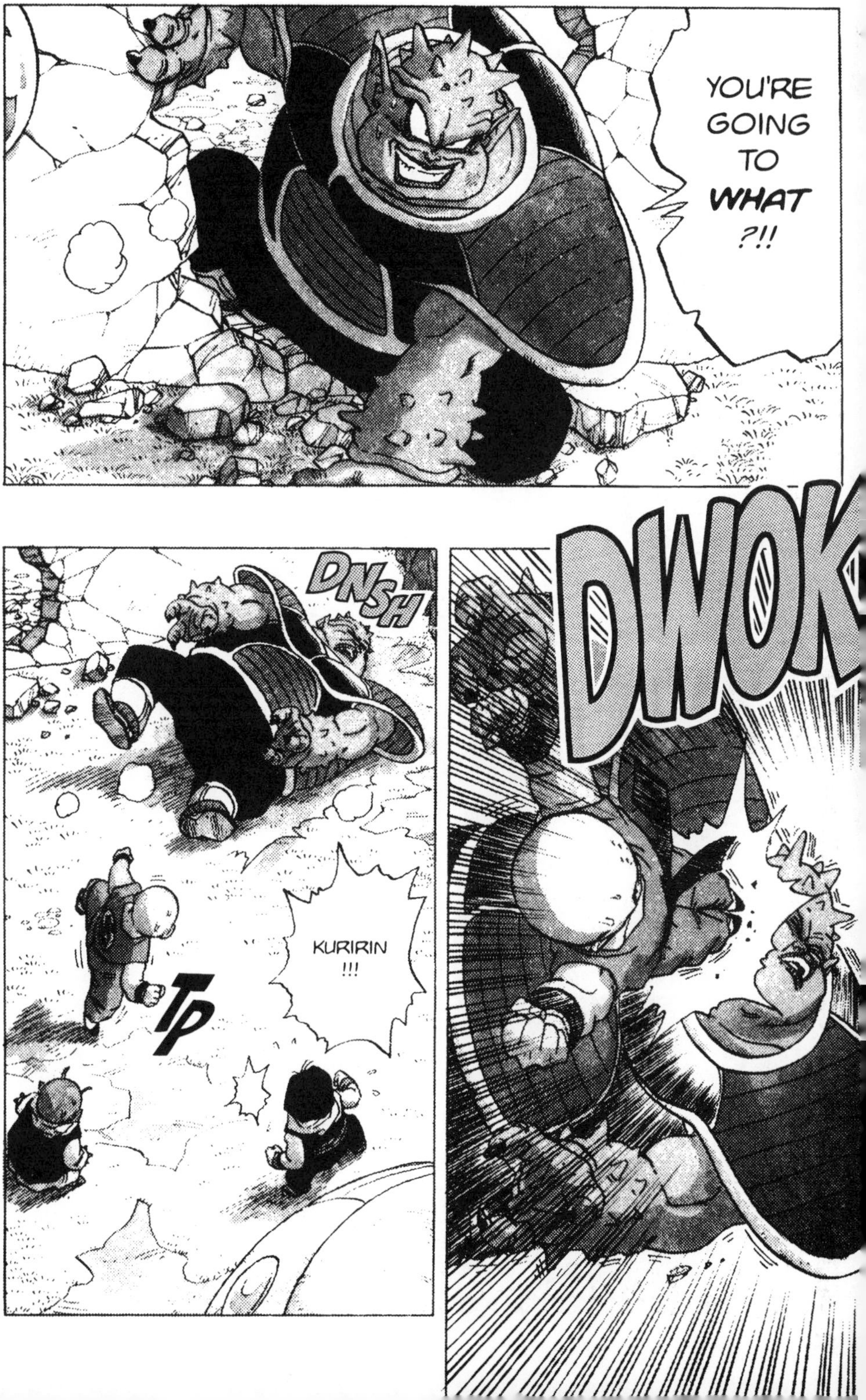
YOU'RE GOING TO WHAT ?!!
DWOK
DNSH
KURIRIN !!!
TP

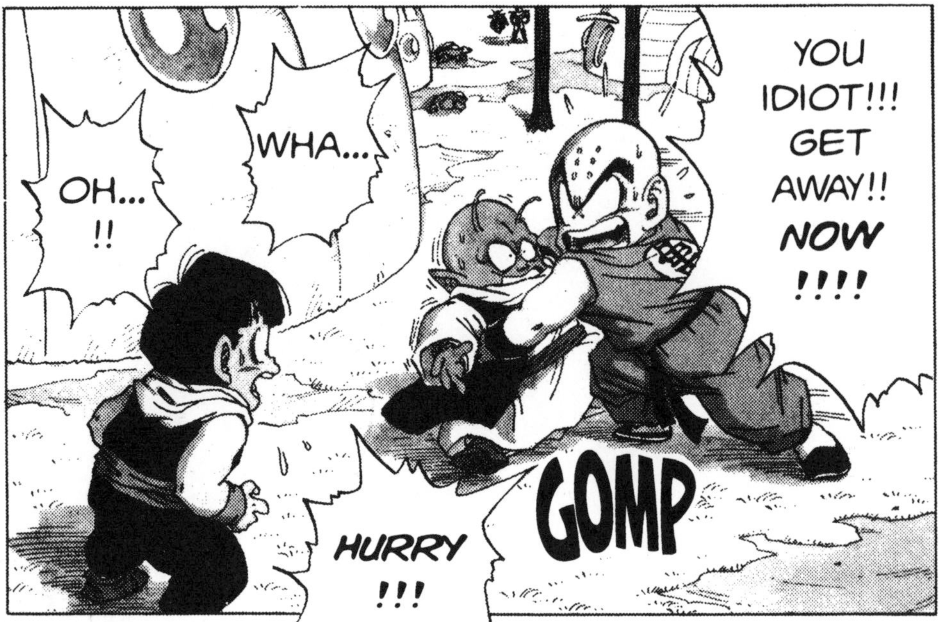
YOU IDIOT!!! GET AWAY!! NOW !!!!
WHA...
OH... !!
GOMP
HURRY !!!

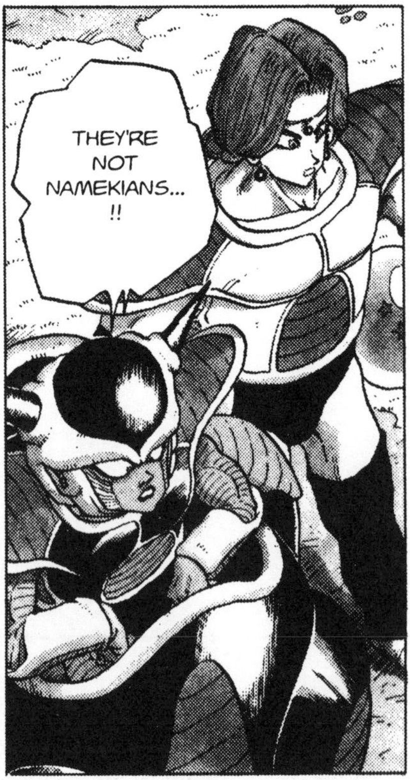
THEY'RE NOT NAMEKIANS... !!

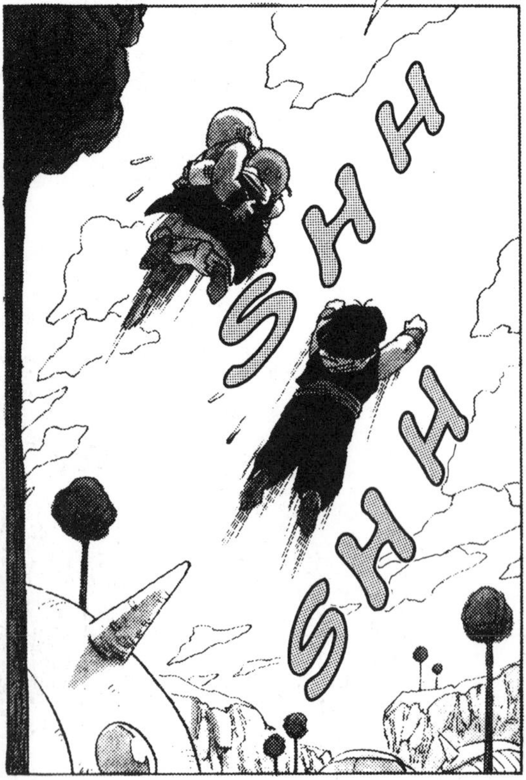
SHHH
SHHH

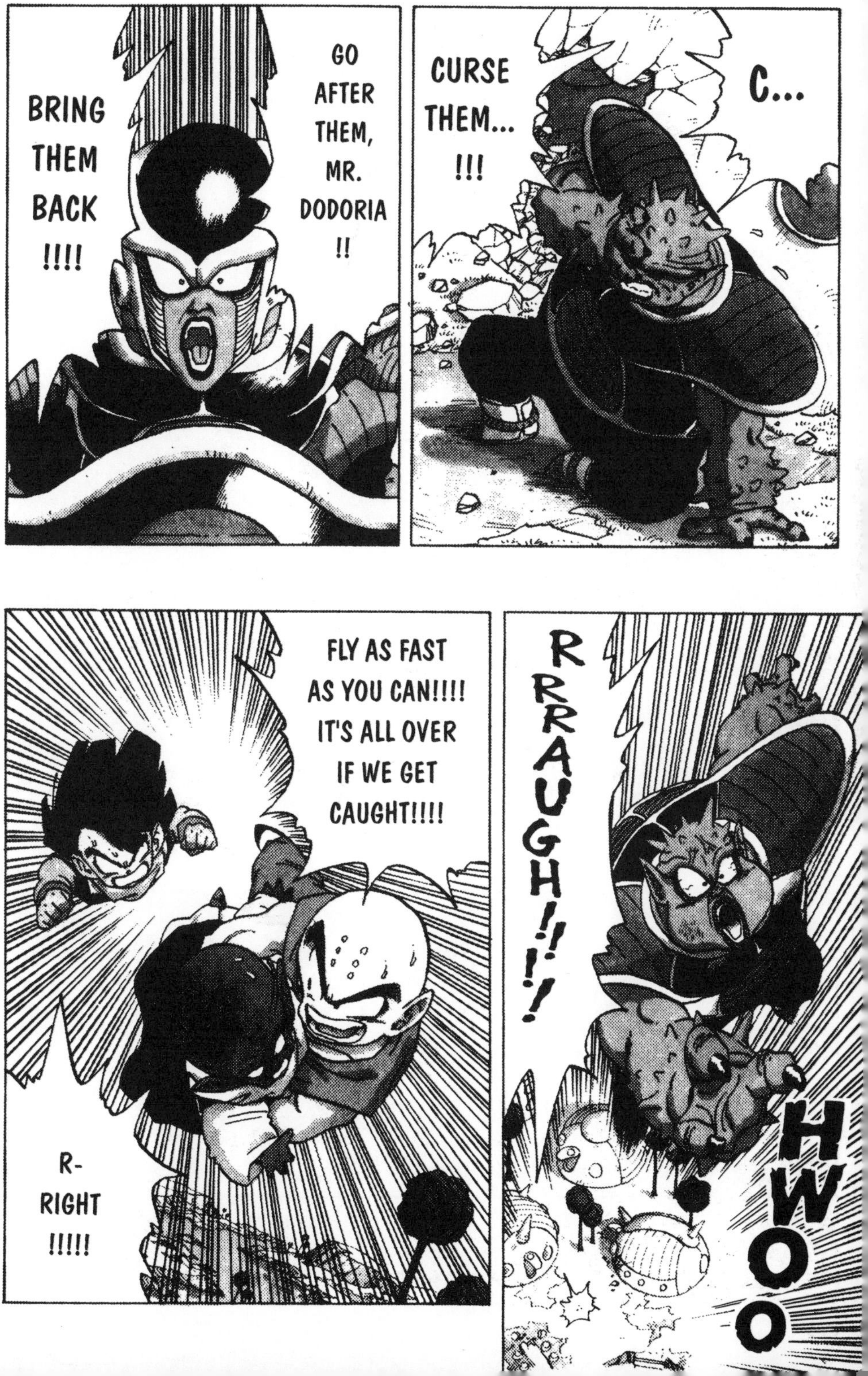
C...
CURSE THEM... !!!
GO AFTER THEM, MR. DODORIA !!
BRING THEM BACK !!!!
RRRAUGH!!!!!
HWOO
FLY AS FAST AS YOU CAN!!!! IT'S ALL OVER IF WE GET CAUGHT!!!!
R-RIGHT !!!!!

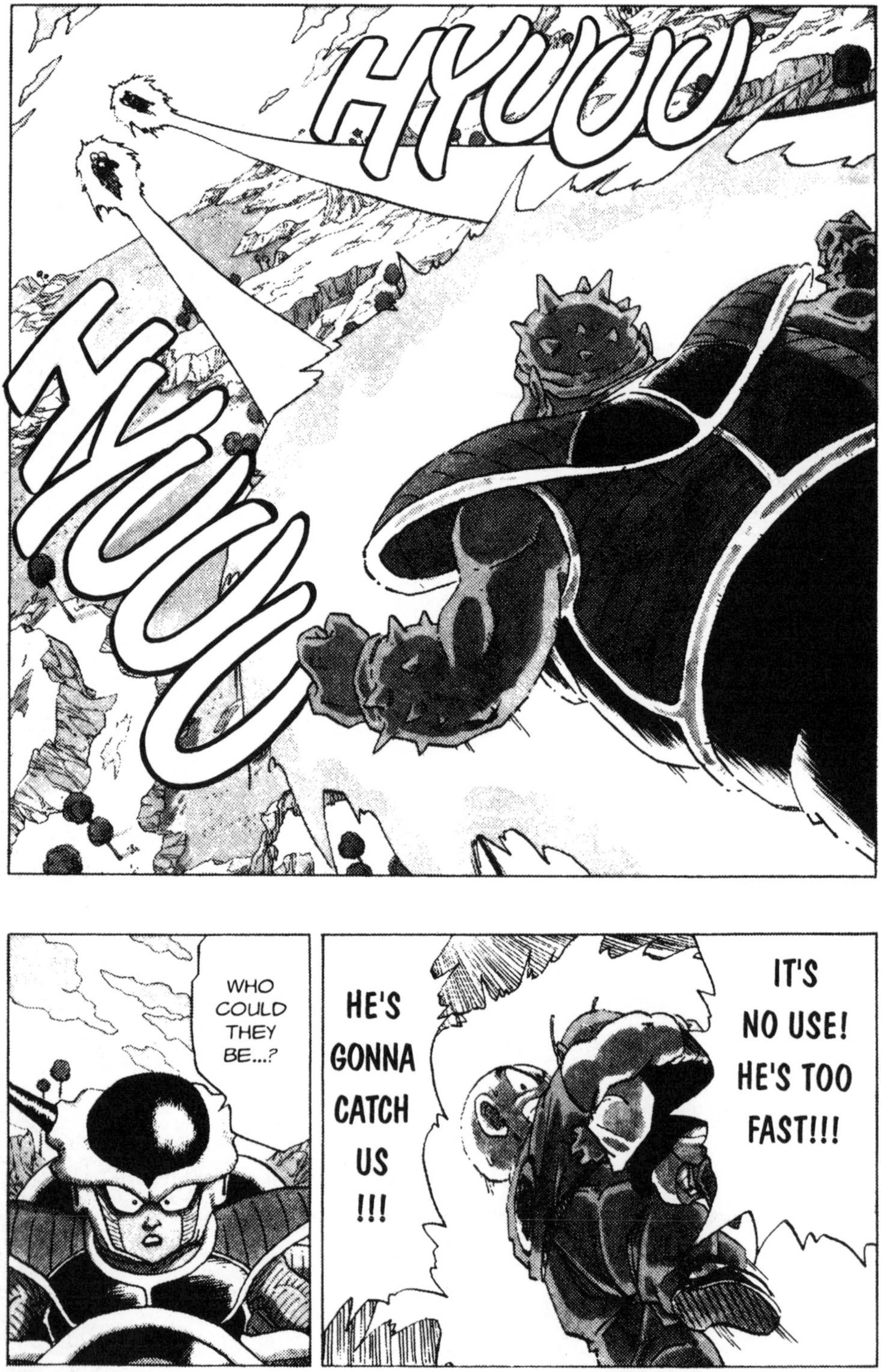
HYUUU
HYUUUU
IT'S NO USE! HE'S TOO FAST!!!
HE'S GONNA CATCH US !!!
WHO COULD THEY BE...?

# DBZ:62 • Death in Flight

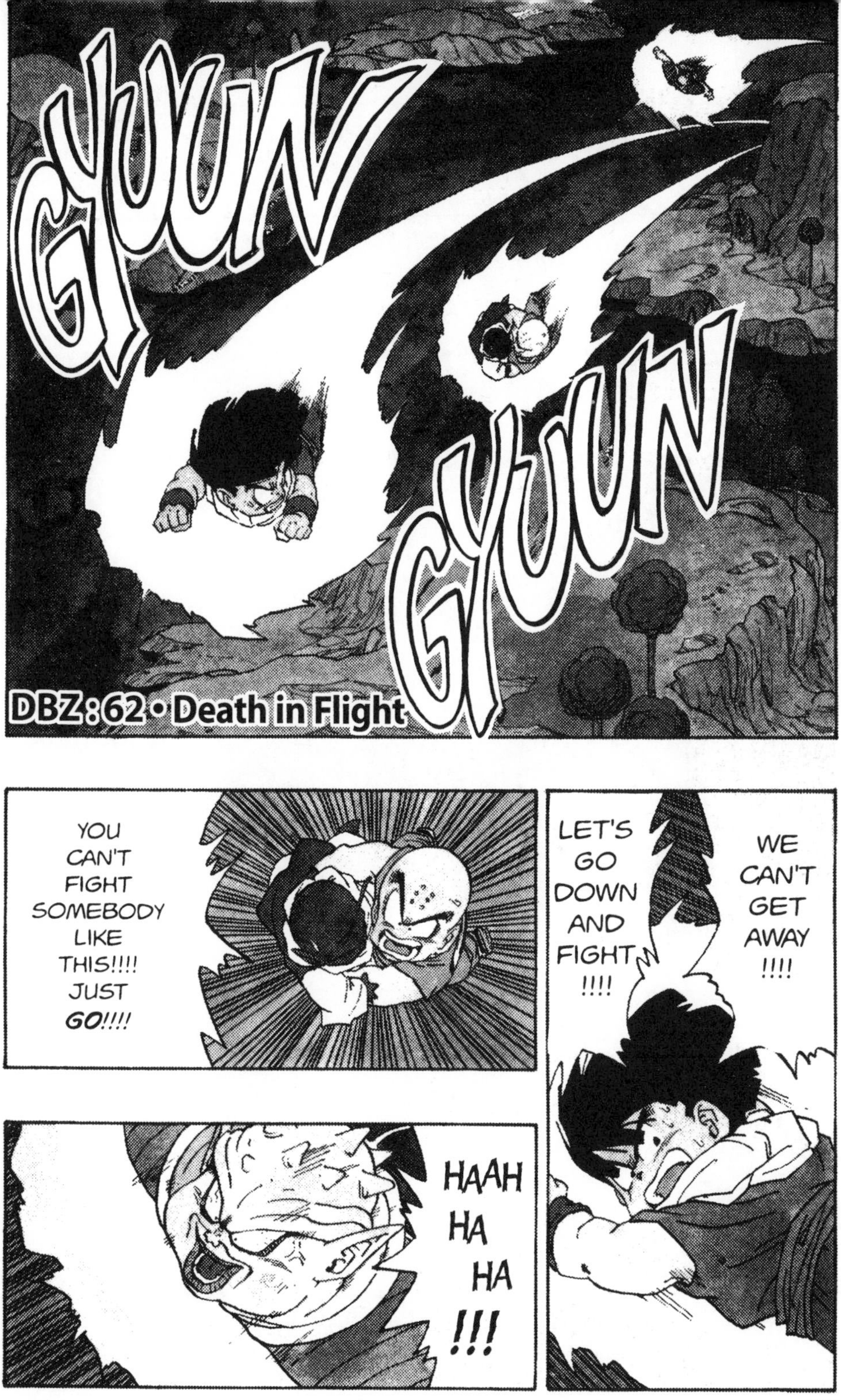
GYUUN
GYUUN
WE CAN'T GET AWAY!!!!
LET'S GO DOWN AND FIGHT!!!!
YOU CAN'T FIGHT SOMEBODY LIKE THIS!!!! JUST *GO*!!!!
HAAH HA HA!!!

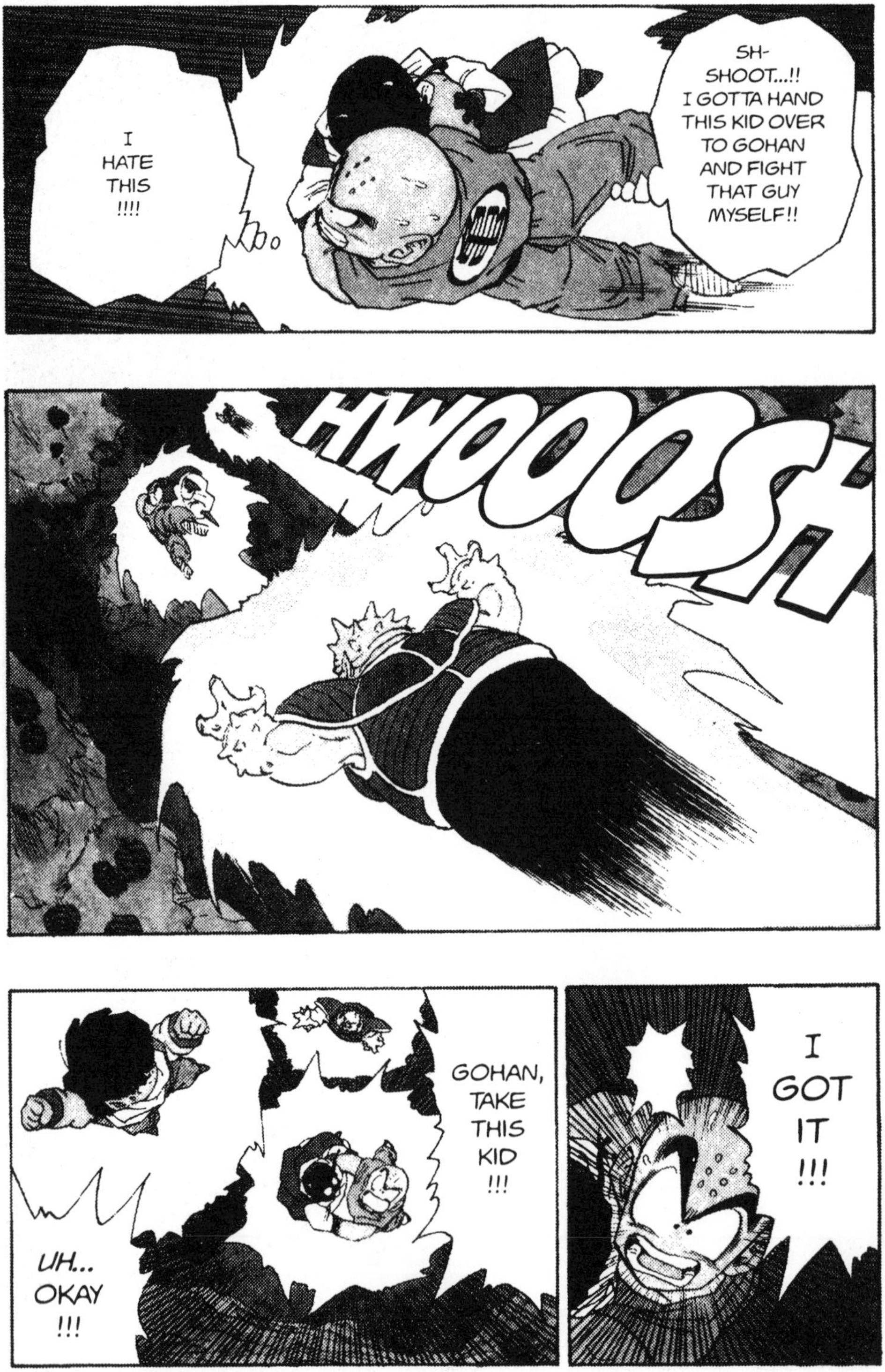
SH- SHOOT...!! I GOTTA HAND THIS KID OVER TO GOHAN AND FIGHT THAT GUY MYSELF!!
I HATE THIS !!!!
HWOOOSH
I GOT IT !!!
GOHAN, TAKE THIS KID !!!
UH... OKAY !!!

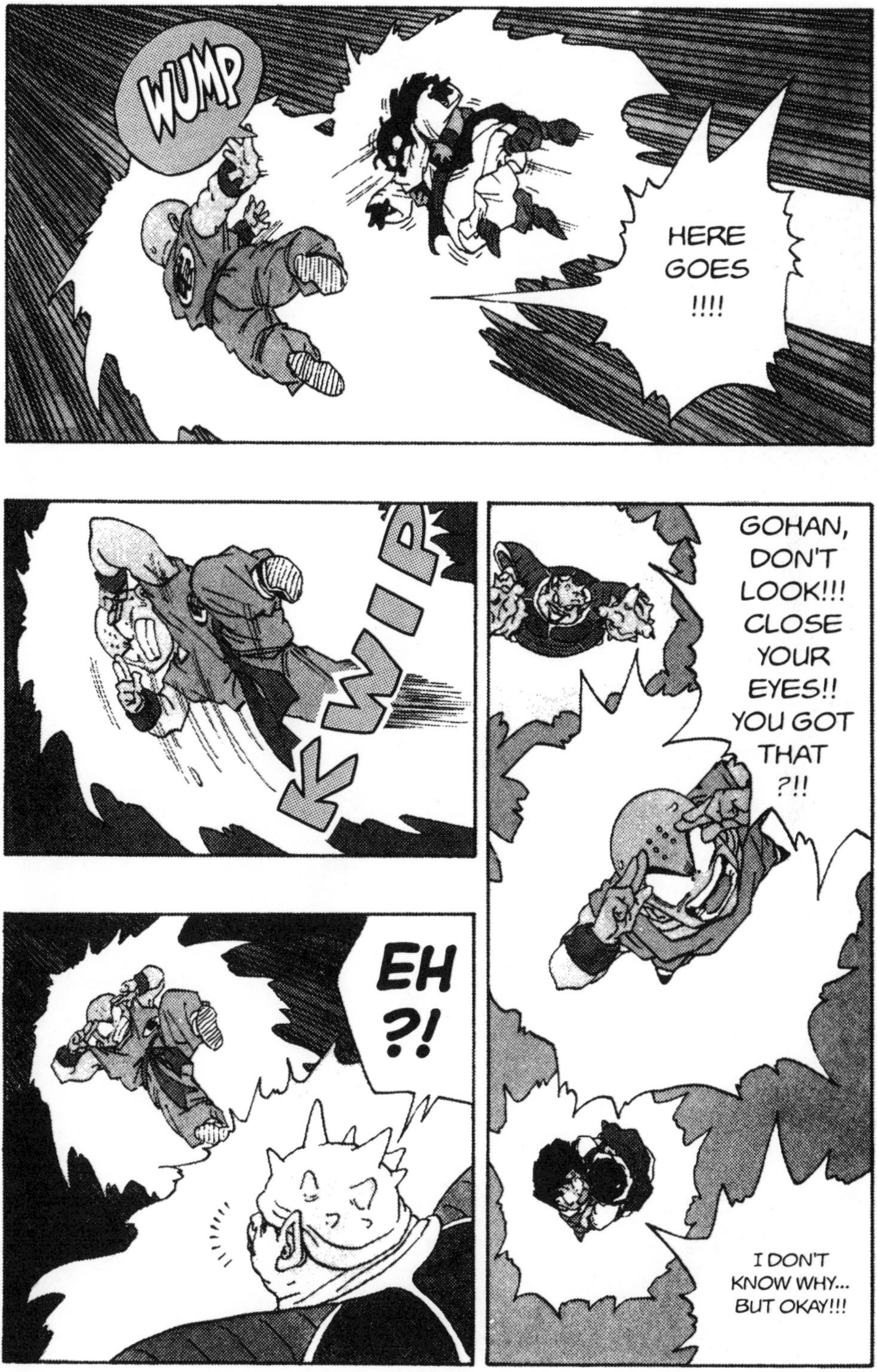
WUMP
HERE GOES !!!!
GOHAN, DON'T LOOK!!! CLOSE YOUR EYES!! YOU GOT THAT ?!!
I DON'T KNOW WHY... BUT OKAY!!!
KWIP
EH ?!

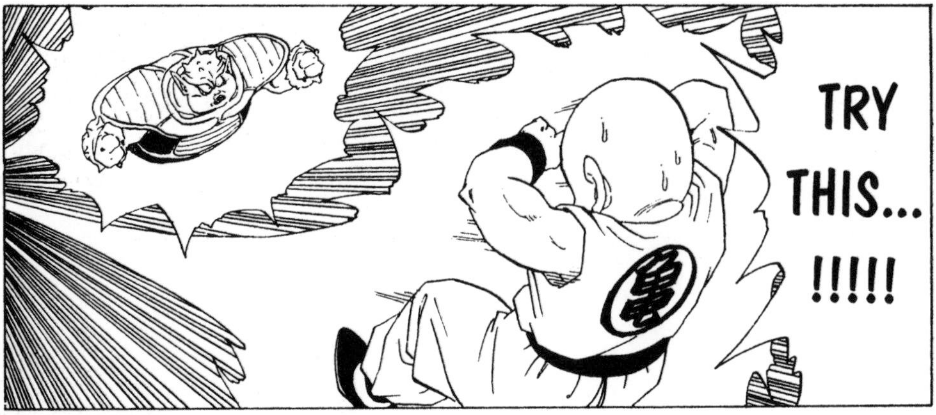
TRY THIS... !!!!!
TAIYŌ-KEN !!!!!*

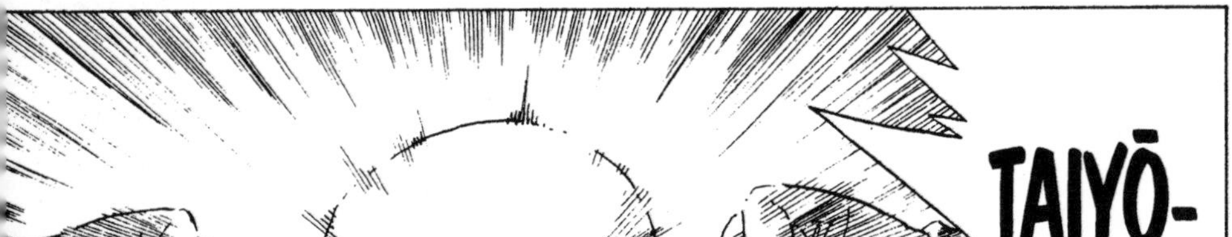

*A.K.A. "FIST OF THE SUN!"

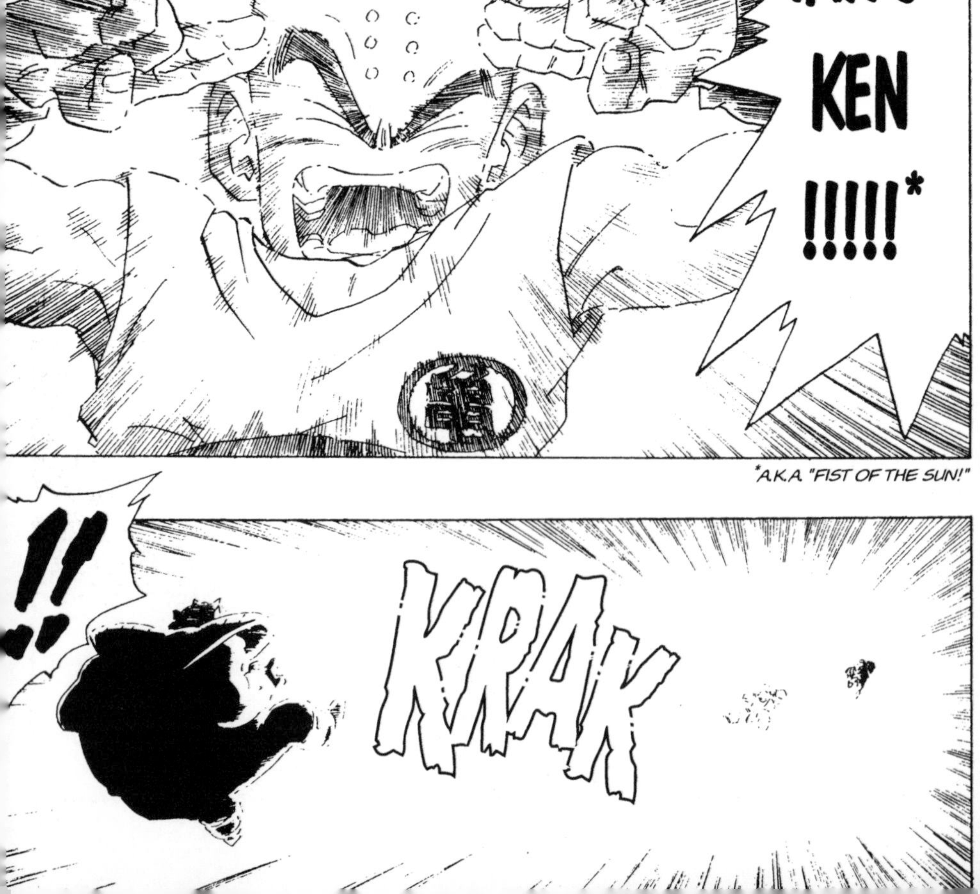
!!
KRAK

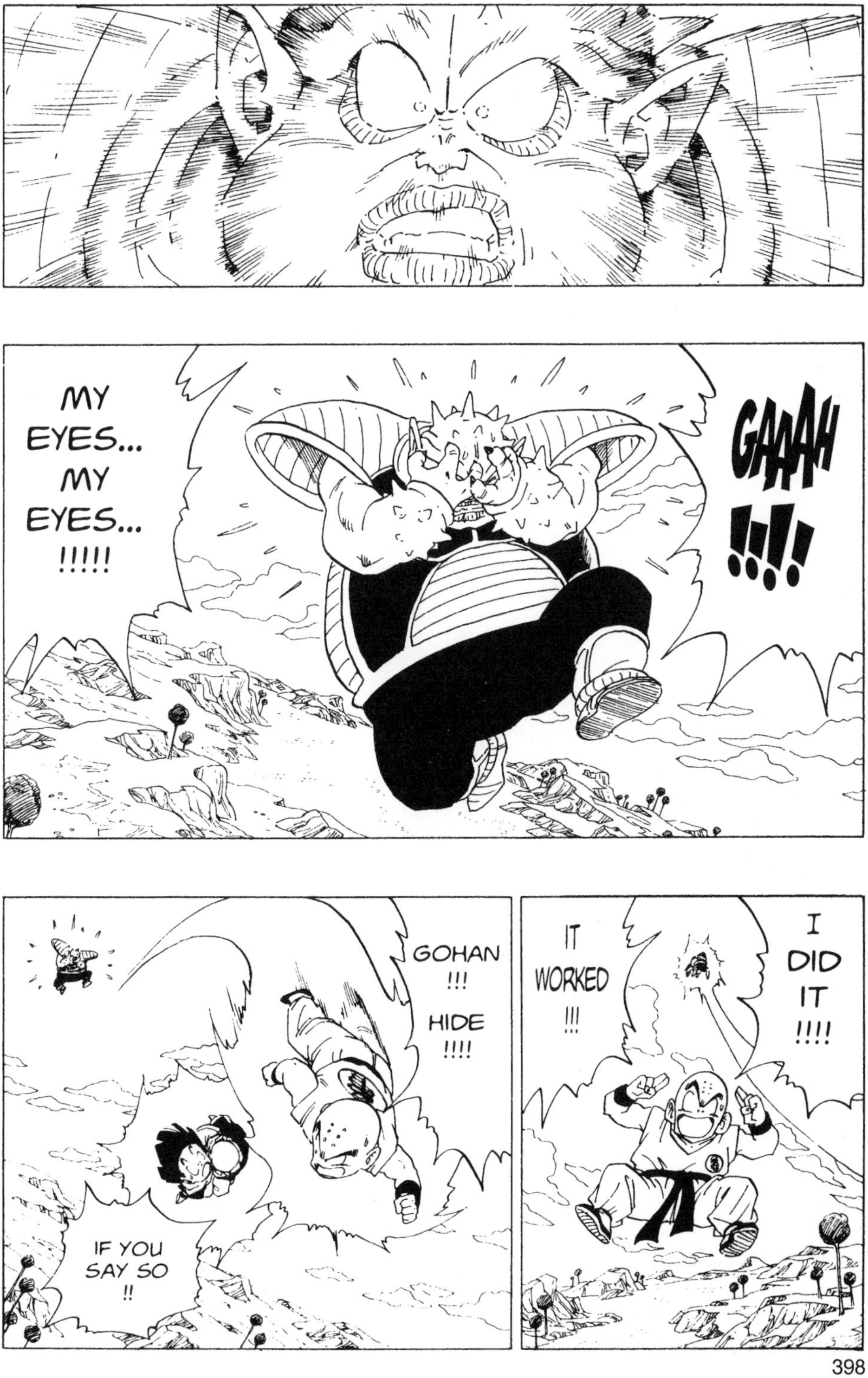
GAAAH !!!!
MY EYES... MY EYES... !!!!!
I DID IT !!!!
IT WORKED !!!
GOHAN !!! HIDE !!!!
IF YOU SAY SO !!

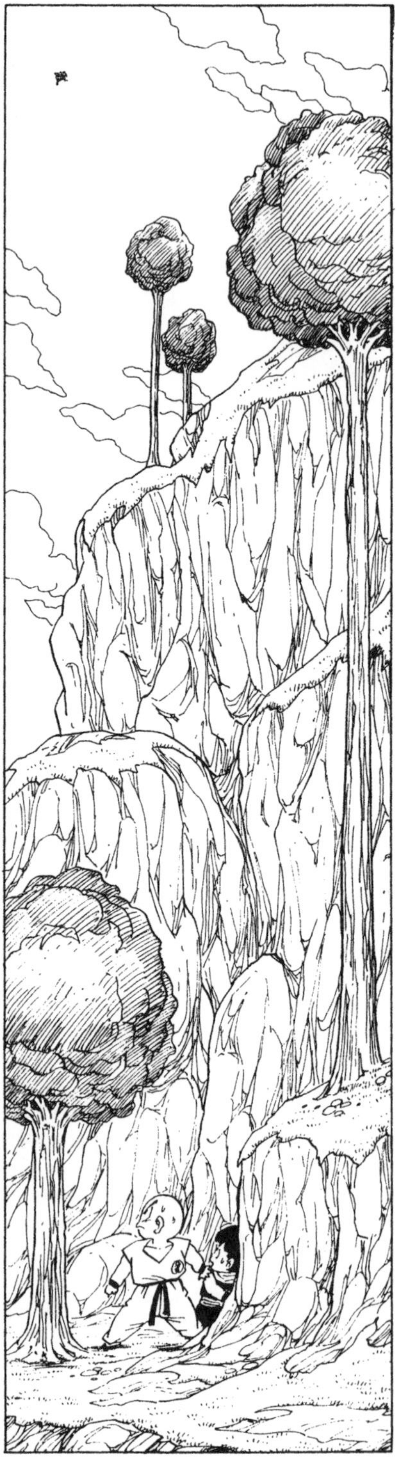

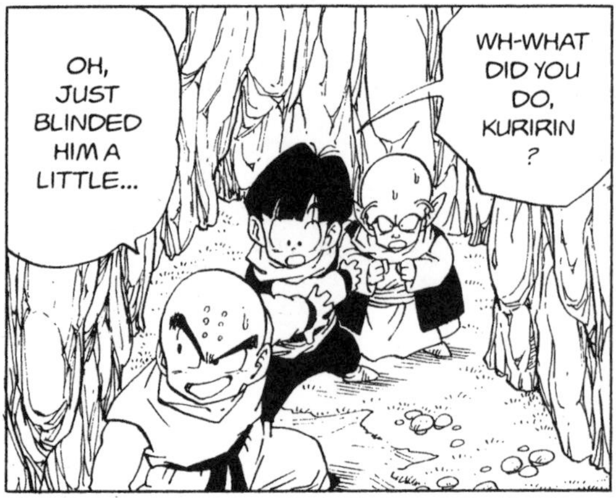
WH-WHAT DID YOU DO, KURIRIN ?
OH, JUST BLINDED HIM A LITTLE...

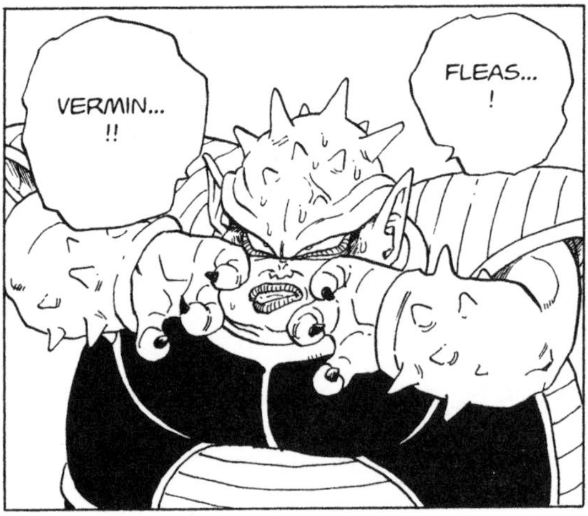
FLEAS... !
VERMIN... !!

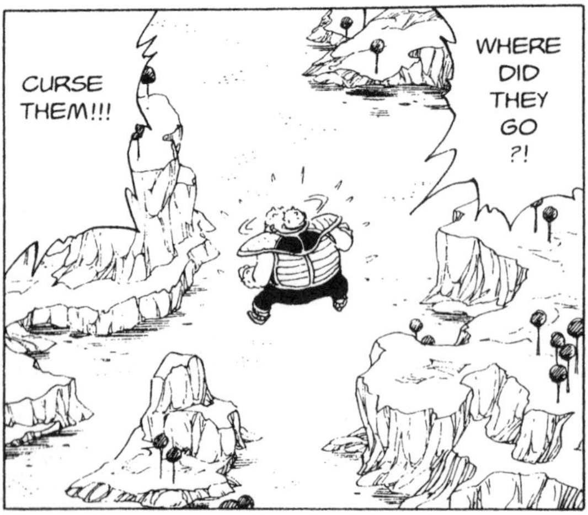
WHERE DID THEY GO ?!
CURSE THEM!!!

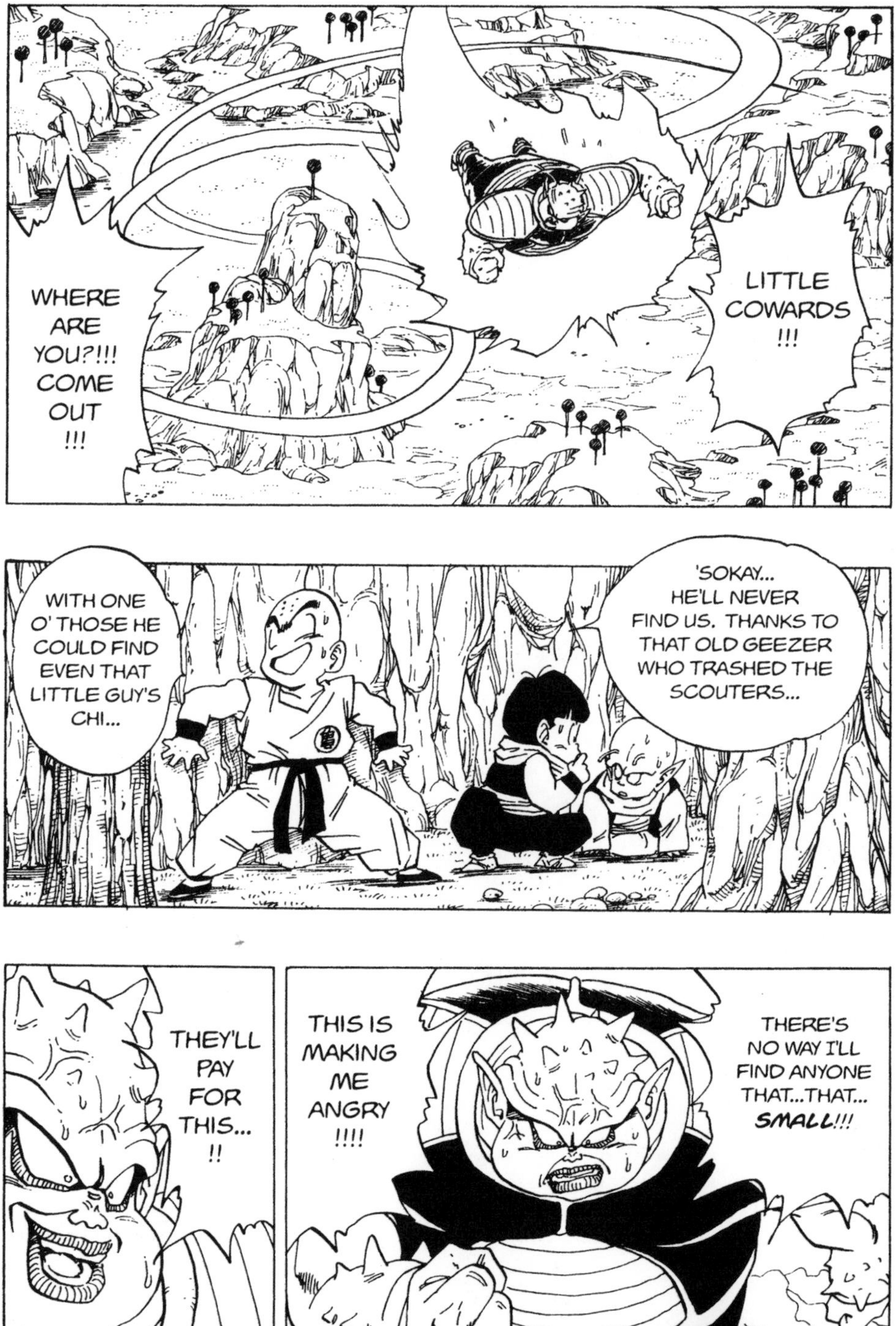
LITTLE COWARDS!!!
WHERE ARE YOU?!!! COME OUT!!!
'SOKAY... HE'LL NEVER FIND US. THANKS TO THAT OLD GEEZER WHO TRASHED THE SCOUTERS...
WITH ONE O' THOSE HE COULD FIND EVEN THAT LITTLE GUY'S CHI...
THERE'S NO WAY I'LL FIND ANYONE THAT...THAT... ***SMALL***!!!
THIS IS MAKING ME ANGRY!!!!
THEY'LL PAY FOR THIS...!!

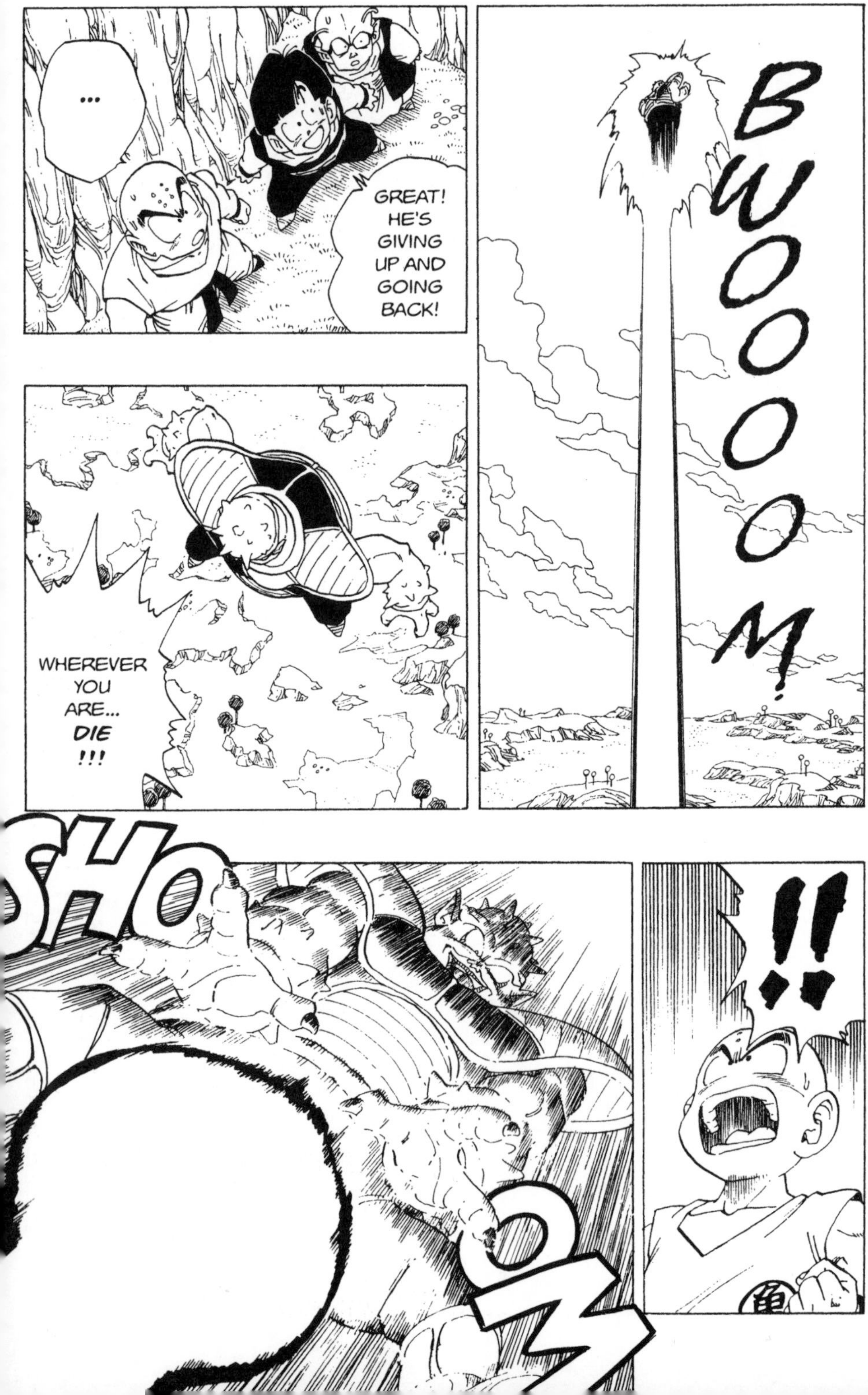
BWOOOOOM
GREAT! HE'S GIVING UP AND GOING BACK!
...
WHEREVER YOU ARE... DIE !!!
!!
SHO
OM

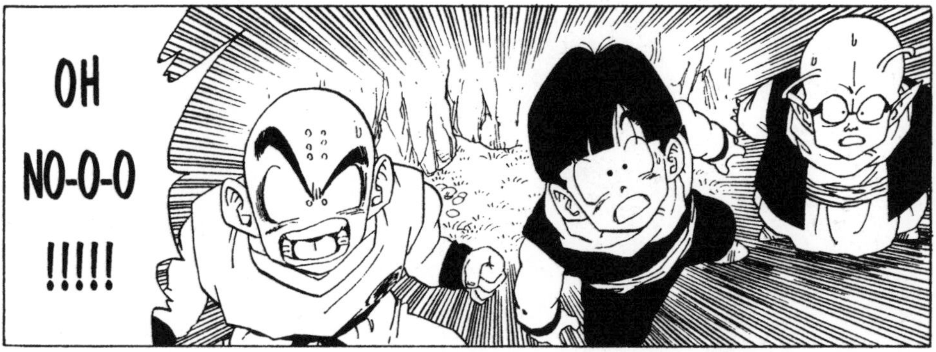
OH NO-O-O !!!!!
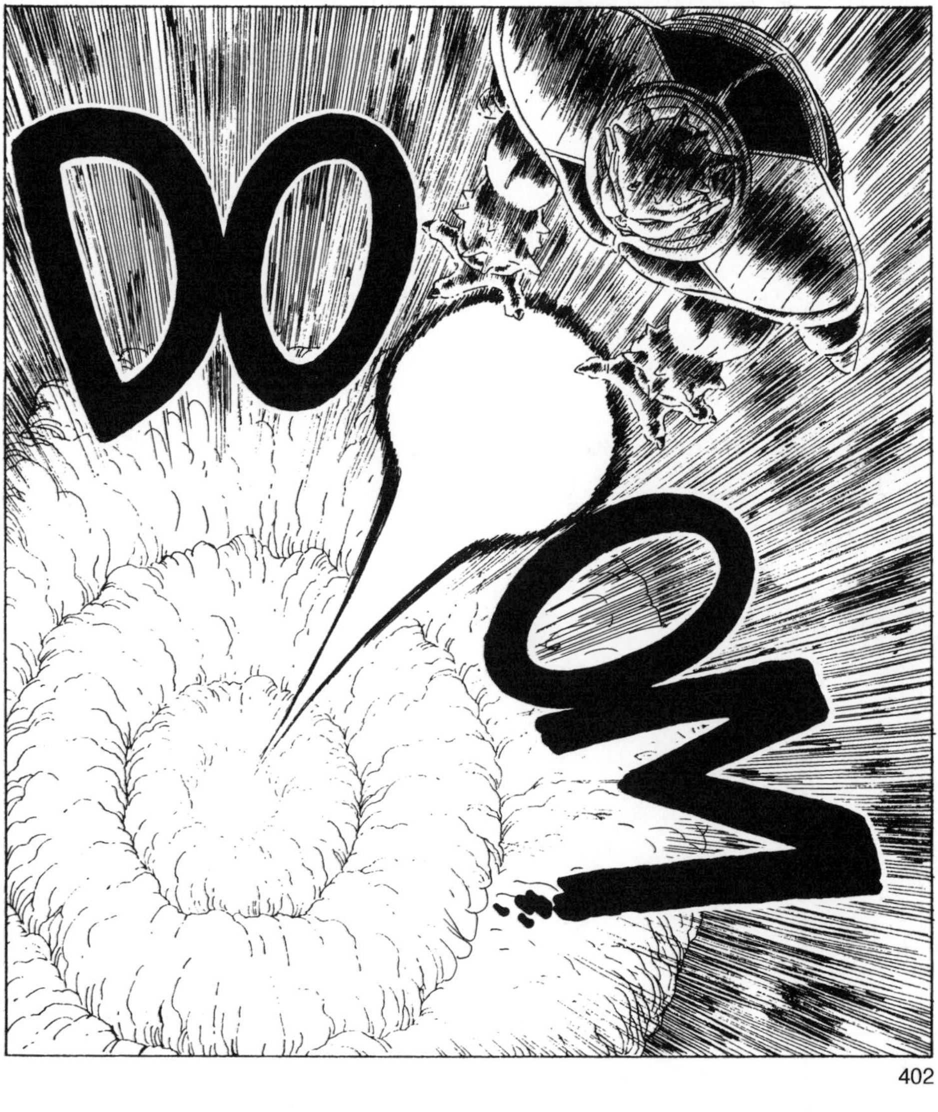
DOOM

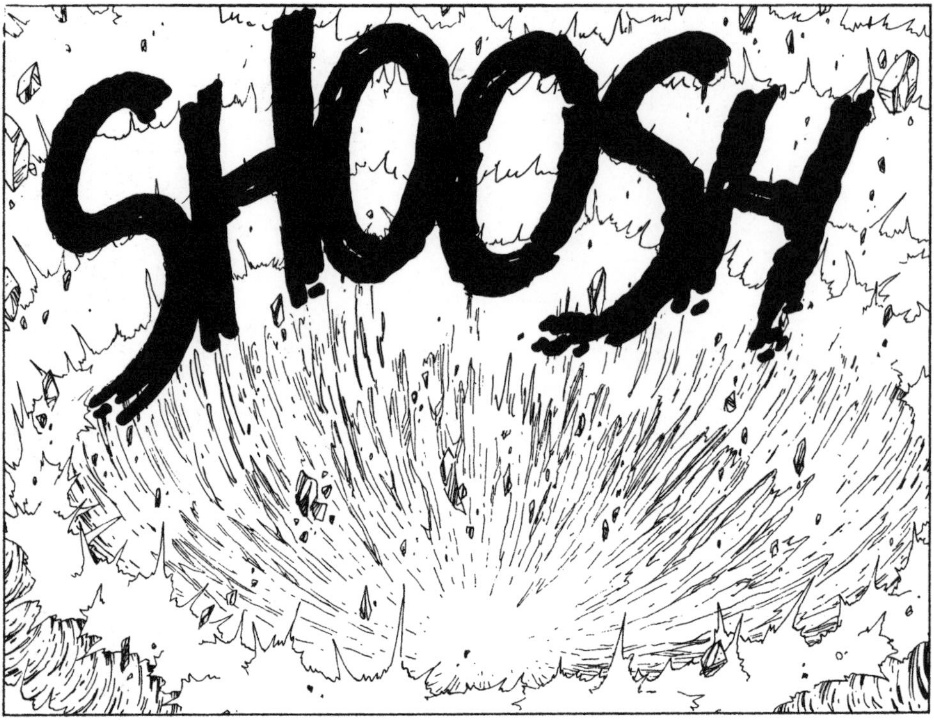
SHOOSH

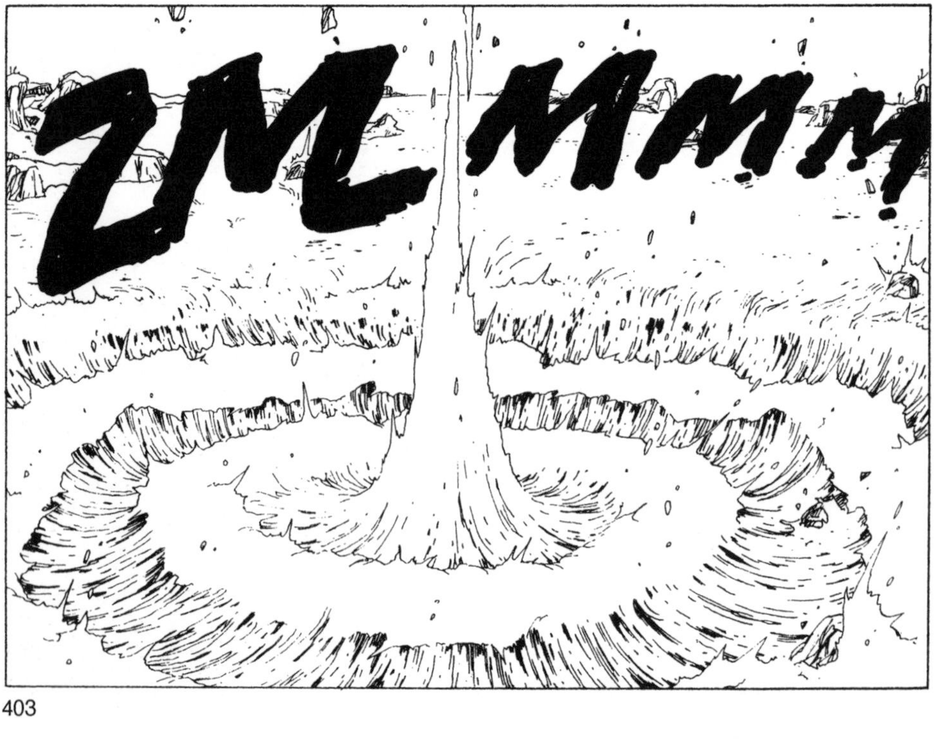
ZMMMM

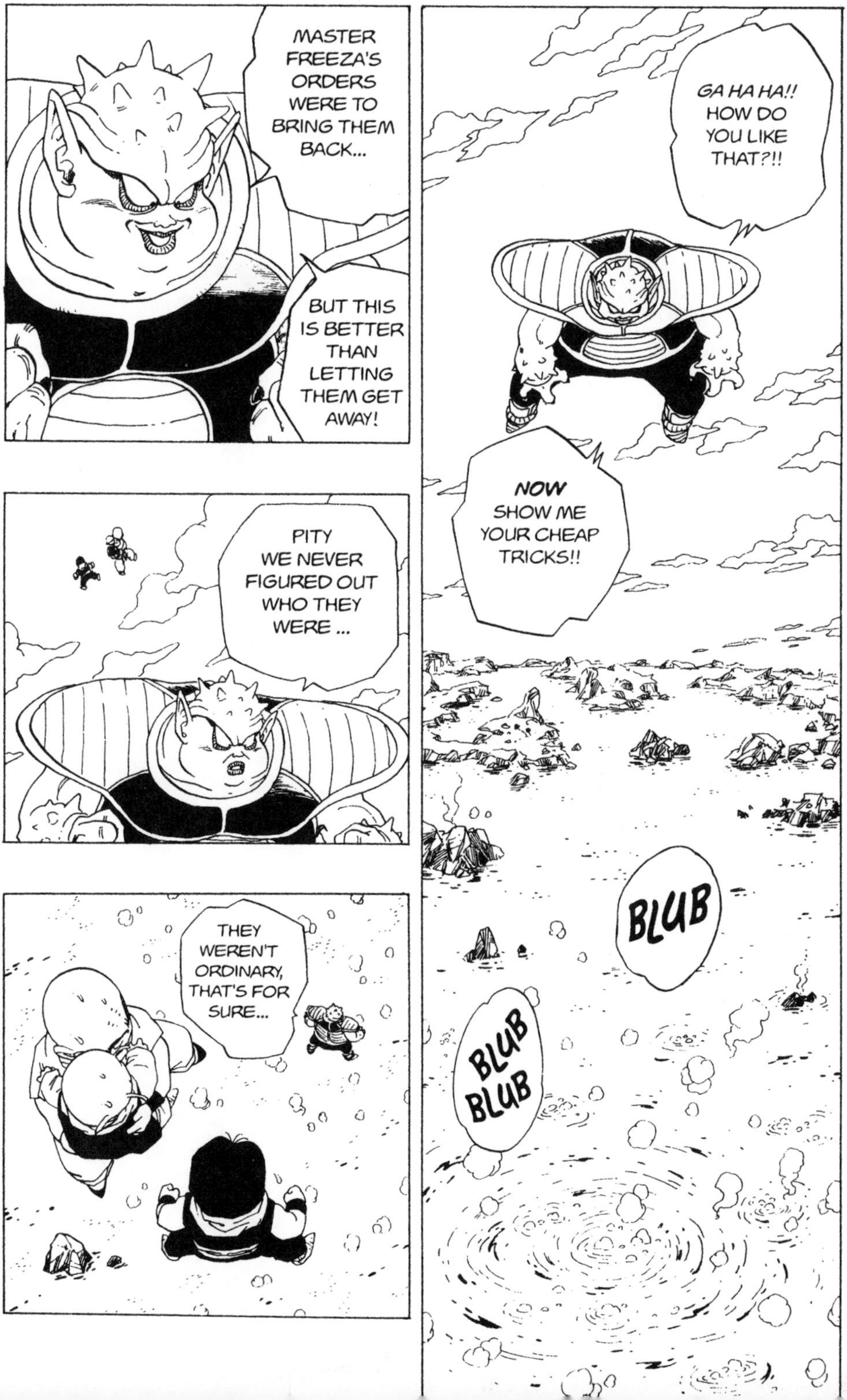

GA HA HA!! HOW DO YOU LIKE THAT?!!
NOW SHOW ME YOUR CHEAP TRICKS!!
BLUB
BLUB BLUB
MASTER FREEZA'S ORDERS WERE TO BRING THEM BACK...
BUT THIS IS BETTER THAN LETTING THEM GET AWAY!
PITY WE NEVER FIGURED OUT WHO THEY WERE ...
THEY WEREN'T ORDINARY, THAT'S FOR SURE...

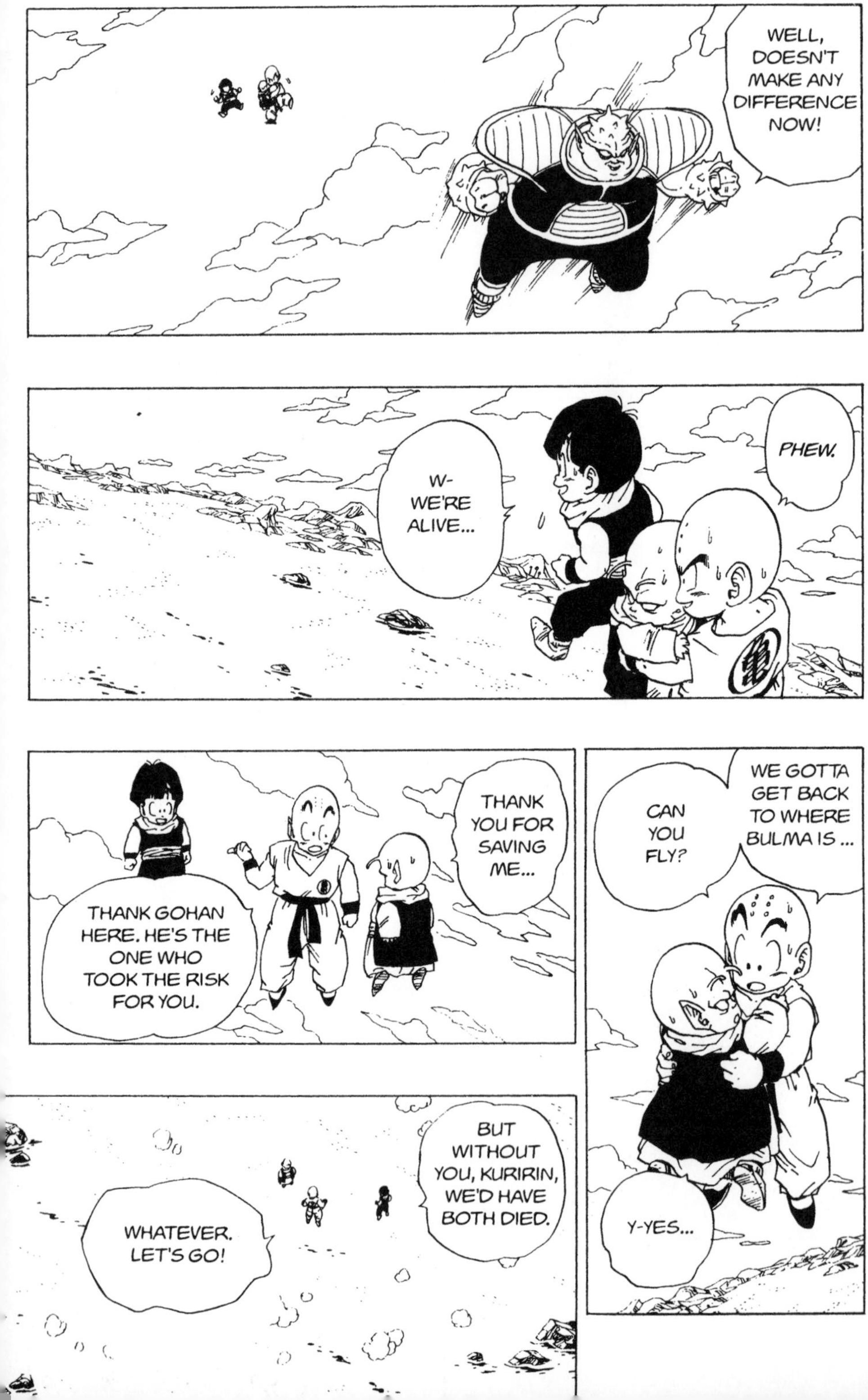
WELL, DOESN'T MAKE ANY DIFFERENCE NOW!
PHEW.
W- WE'RE ALIVE...
WE GOTTA GET BACK TO WHERE BULMA IS...
CAN YOU FLY?
Y-YES...
THANK YOU FOR SAVING ME...
THANK GOHAN HERE. HE'S THE ONE WHO TOOK THE RISK FOR YOU.
BUT WITHOUT YOU, KURIRIN, WE'D HAVE BOTH DIED.
WHATEVER. LET'S GO!

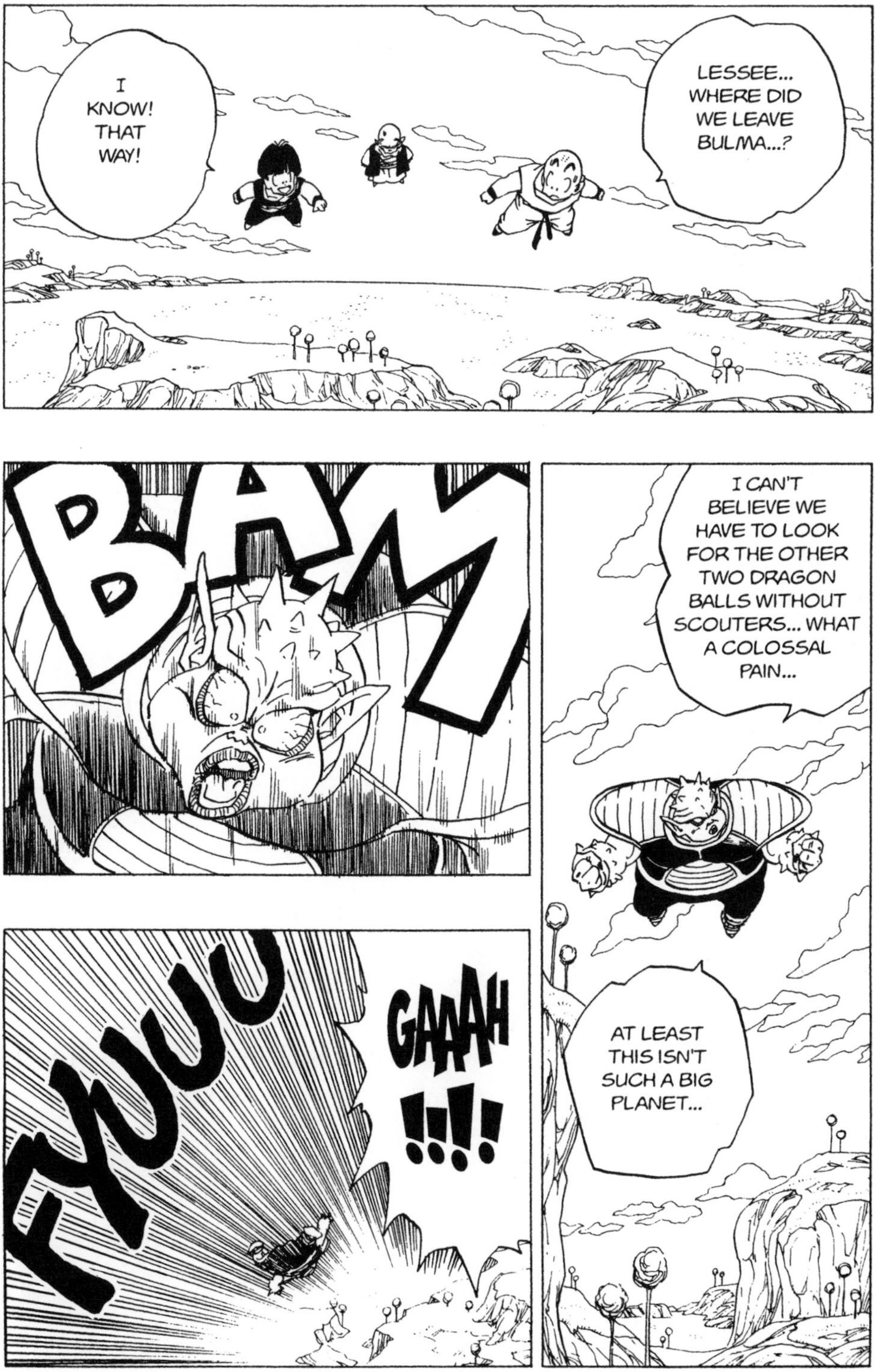
LESSEE... WHERE DID WE LEAVE BULMA...?
I KNOW! THAT WAY!
I CAN'T BELIEVE WE HAVE TO LOOK FOR THE OTHER TWO DRAGON BALLS WITHOUT SCOUTERS... WHAT A COLOSSAL PAIN...
AT LEAST THIS ISN'T SUCH A BIG PLANET...
BAM
GAAAH !!!!
FYUUU

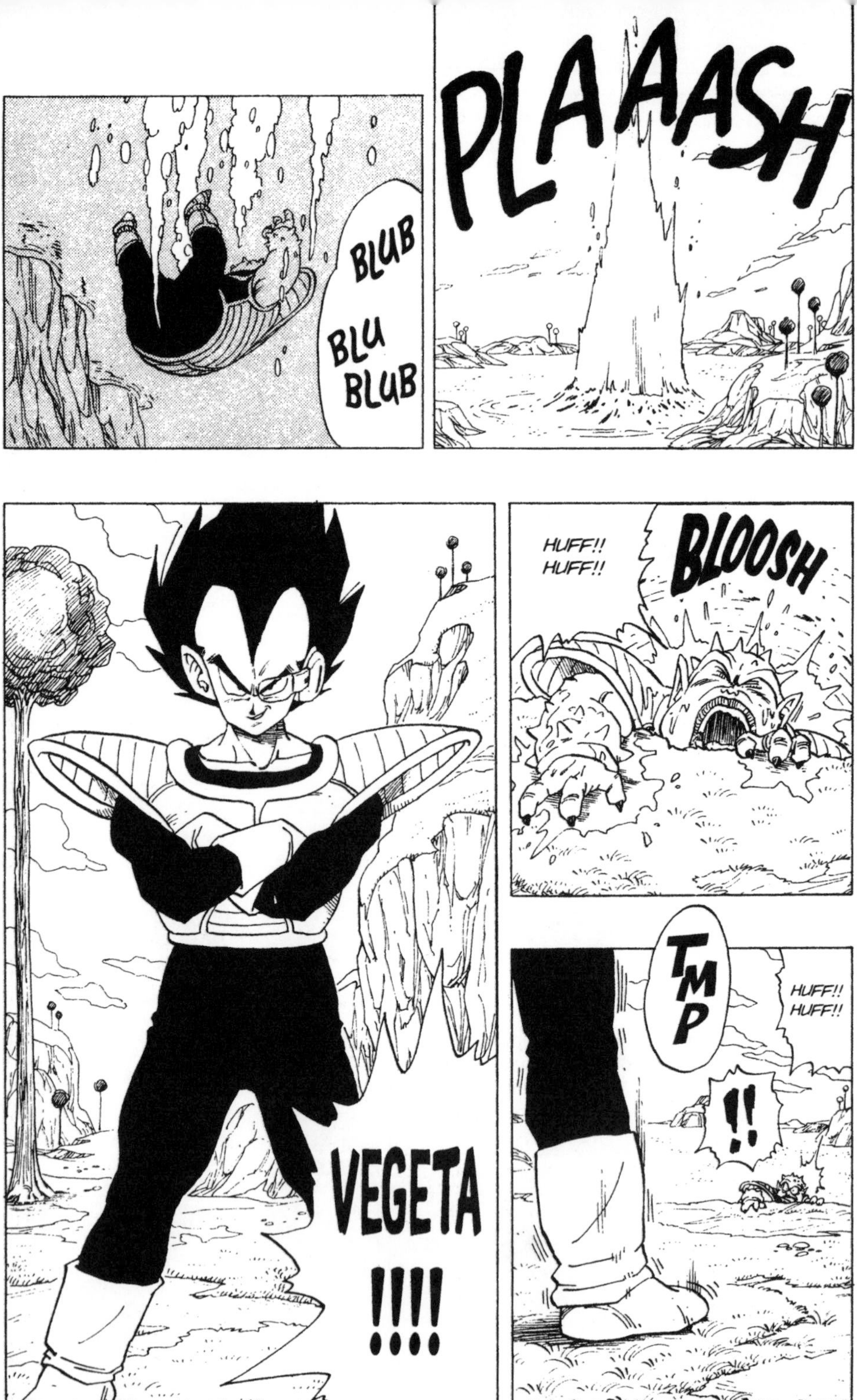
PLAAASH
BLUB
BLU BLUB
HUFF!! HUFF!!
BLOOSH
TMP
HUFF!! HUFF!!
!!
VEGETA !!!!

# DBZ:63 • Vegeta vs. Dodoria

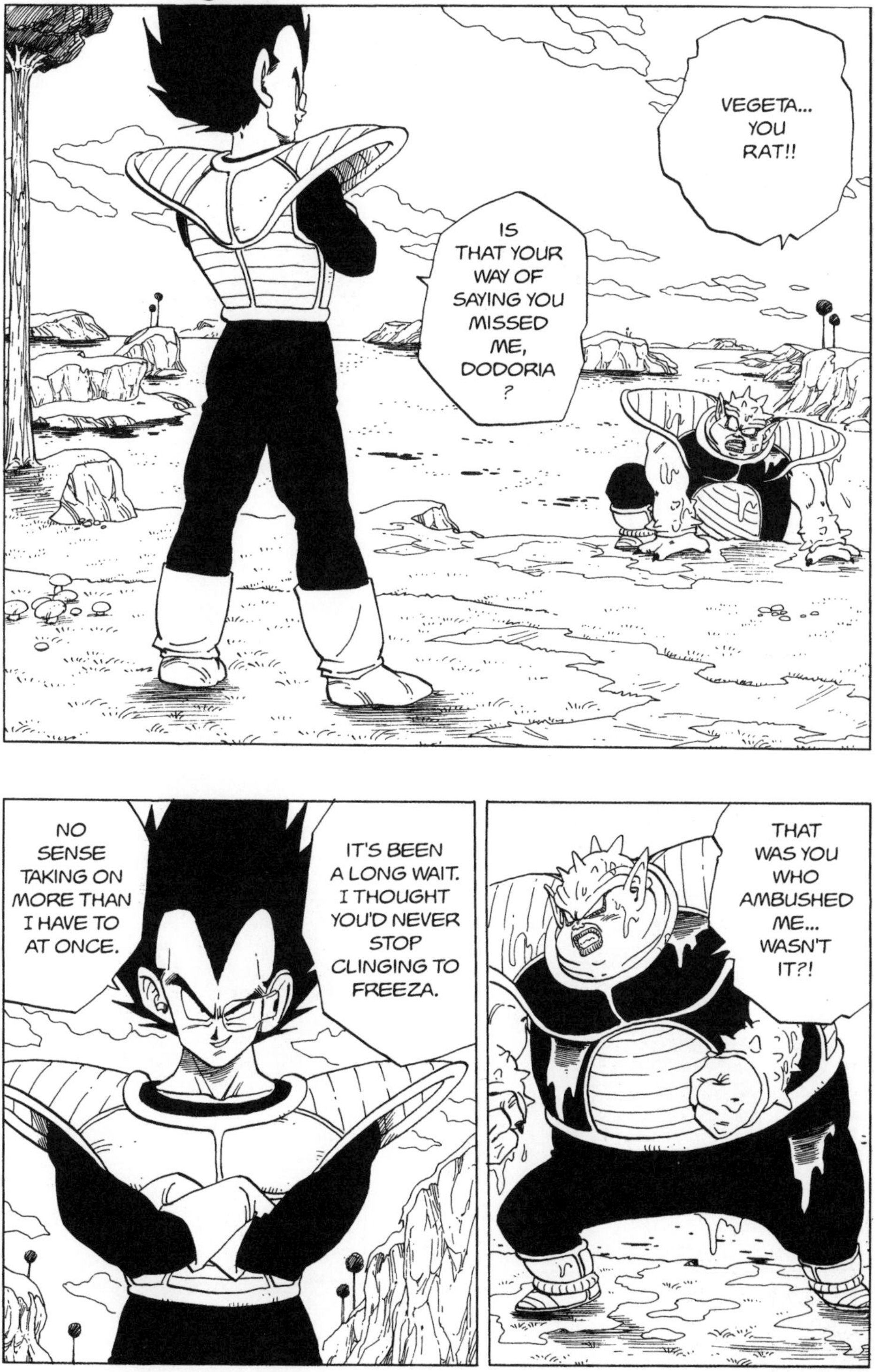
VEGETA... YOU RAT!!
IS THAT YOUR WAY OF SAYING YOU MISSED ME, DODORIA?
THAT WAS YOU WHO AMBUSHED ME... WASN'T IT?!
IT'S BEEN A LONG WAIT. I THOUGHT YOU'D NEVER STOP CLINGING TO FREEZA.
NO SENSE TAKING ON MORE THAN I HAVE TO AT ONCE.

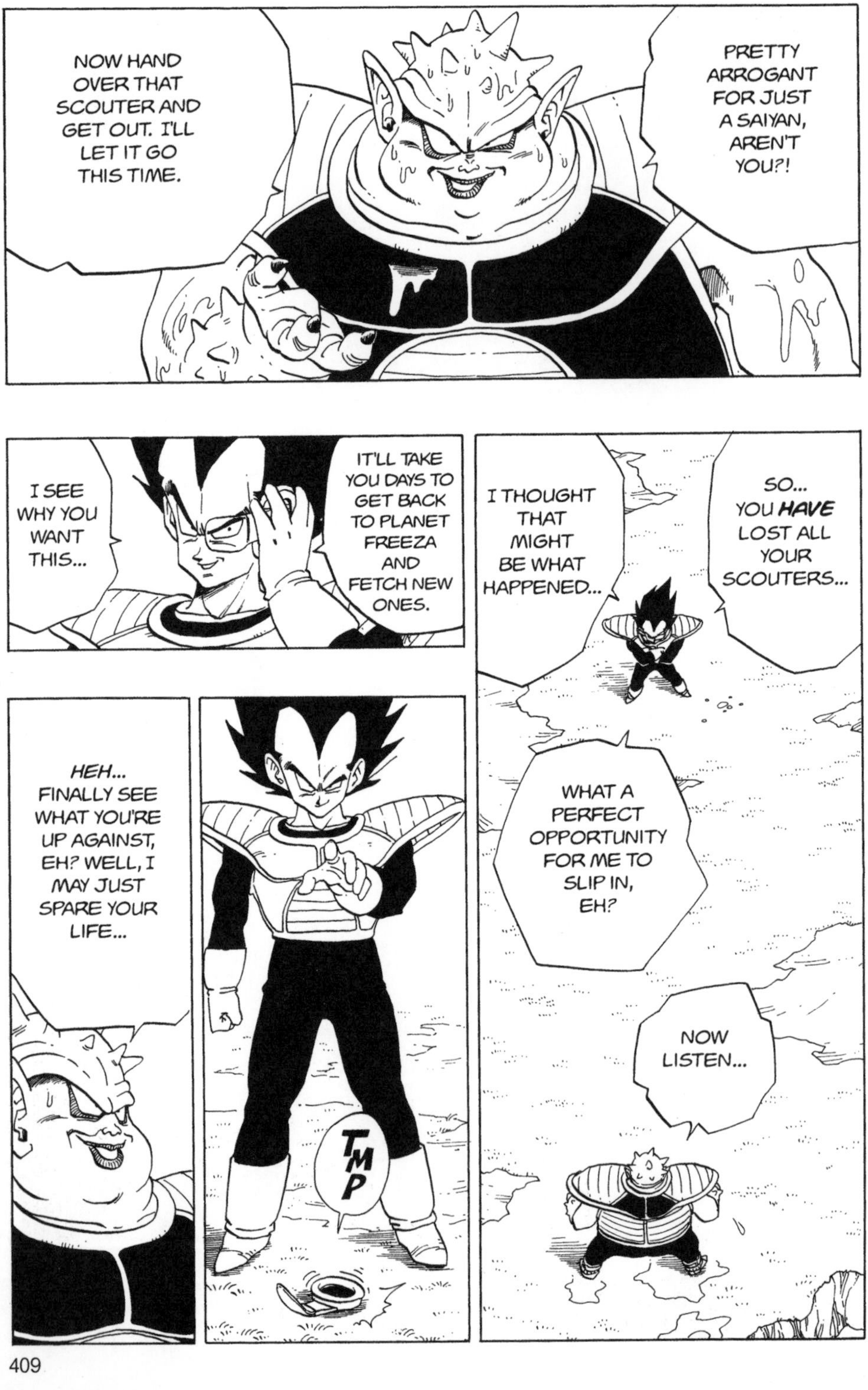
PRETTY ARROGANT FOR JUST A SAIYAN, AREN'T YOU?!
NOW HAND OVER THAT SCOUTER AND GET OUT. I'LL LET IT GO THIS TIME.
SO... YOU **HAVE** LOST ALL YOUR SCOUTERS...
I THOUGHT THAT MIGHT BE WHAT HAPPENED...
WHAT A PERFECT OPPORTUNITY FOR ME TO SLIP IN, EH?
NOW LISTEN...
IT'LL TAKE YOU DAYS TO GET BACK TO PLANET FREEZA AND FETCH NEW ONES.
I SEE WHY YOU WANT THIS...
TMP
*HEH...* FINALLY SEE WHAT YOU'RE UP AGAINST, EH? WELL, I *MAY* JUST SPARE YOUR LIFE...

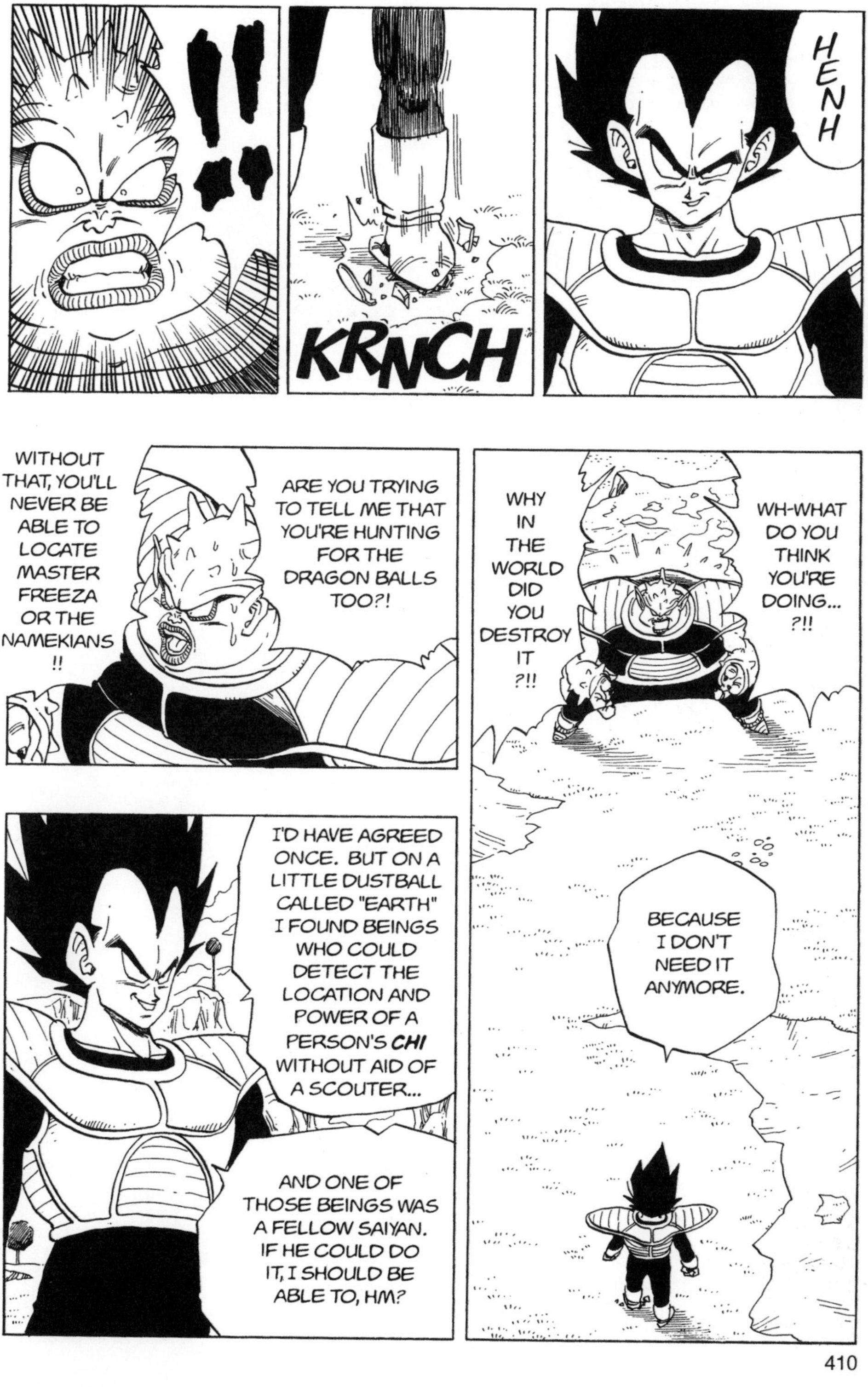
HENH
KRNCH
!!
WH-WHAT DO YOU THINK YOU'RE DOING... ?!!
WHY IN THE WORLD DID YOU DESTROY IT ?!!
BECAUSE I DON'T NEED IT ANYMORE.
ARE YOU TRYING TO TELL ME THAT YOU'RE HUNTING FOR THE DRAGON BALLS TOO?!
WITHOUT THAT, YOU'LL NEVER BE ABLE TO LOCATE MASTER FREEZA OR THE NAMEKIANS !!
I'D HAVE AGREED ONCE. BUT ON A LITTLE DUSTBALL CALLED "EARTH" I FOUND BEINGS WHO COULD DETECT THE LOCATION AND POWER OF A PERSON'S *CHI* WITHOUT AID OF A SCOUTER...
AND ONE OF THOSE BEINGS WAS A FELLOW SAIYAN. IF HE COULD DO IT, I SHOULD BE ABLE TO, HM?

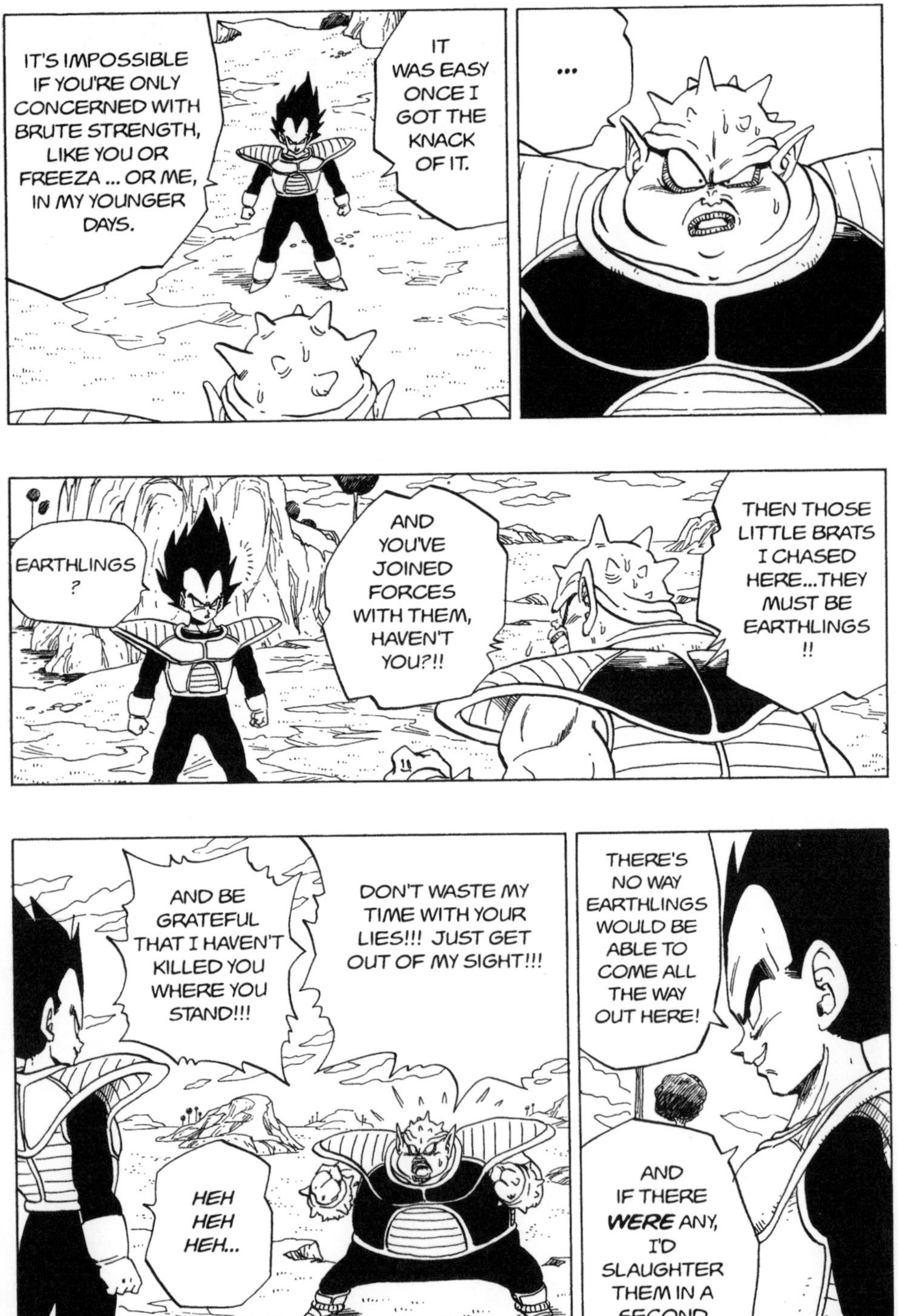
...
IT WAS EASY ONCE I GOT THE KNACK OF IT.
IT'S IMPOSSIBLE IF YOU'RE ONLY CONCERNED WITH BRUTE STRENGTH, LIKE YOU OR FREEZA ... OR ME, IN MY YOUNGER DAYS.
THEN THOSE LITTLE BRATS I CHASED HERE...THEY MUST BE EARTHLINGS !!
AND YOU'VE JOINED FORCES WITH THEM, HAVEN'T YOU?!!
EARTHLINGS ?
THERE'S NO WAY EARTHLINGS WOULD BE ABLE TO COME ALL THE WAY OUT HERE!
AND IF THERE ***WERE*** ANY, I'D SLAUGHTER THEM IN A SECOND !!
DON'T WASTE MY TIME WITH YOUR LIES!!! JUST GET OUT OF MY SIGHT!!!
AND BE GRATEFUL THAT I HAVEN'T KILLED YOU WHERE YOU STAND!!!
HEH HEH HEH...

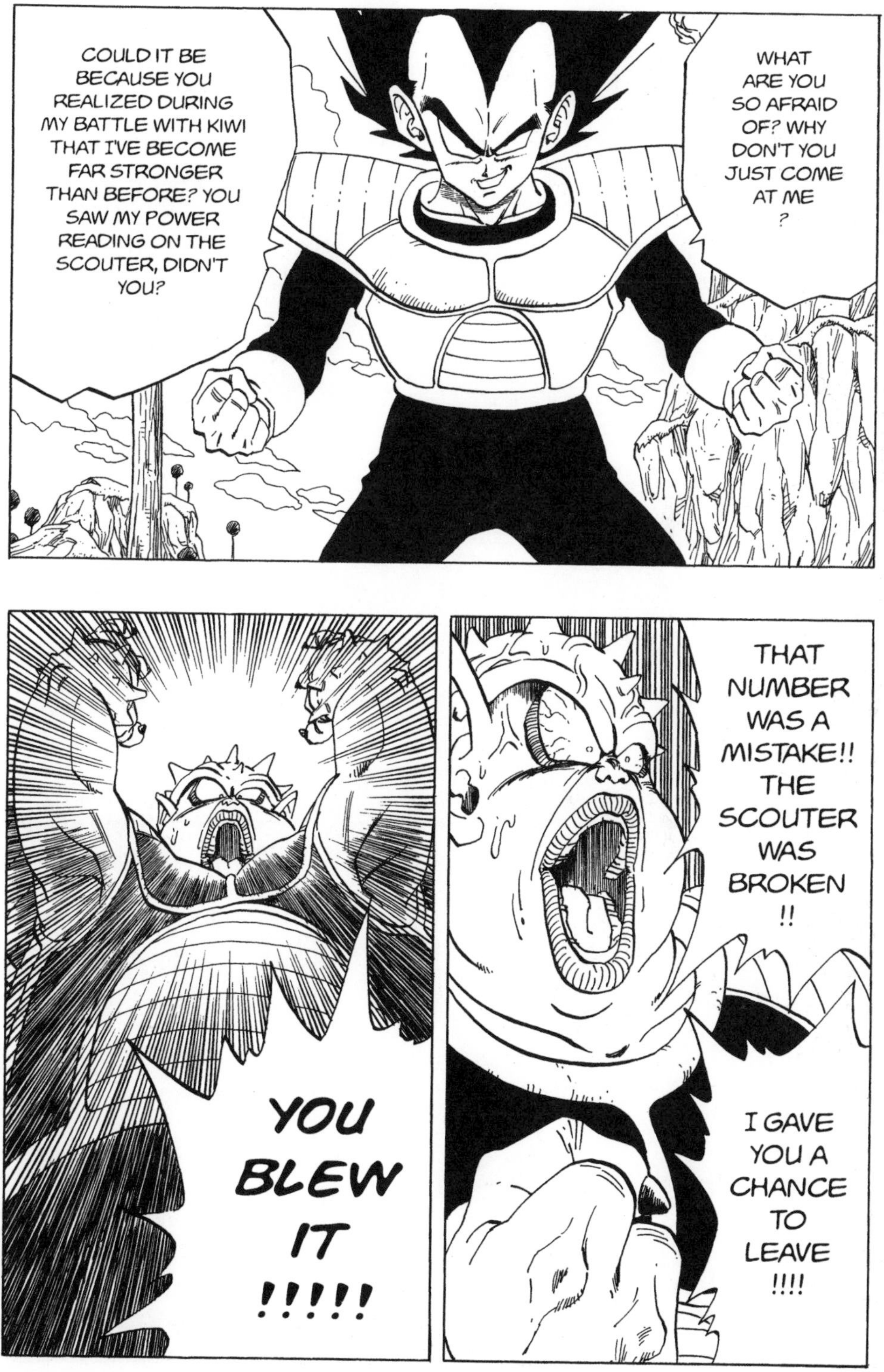
WHAT ARE YOU SO AFRAID OF? WHY DON'T YOU JUST COME AT ME ?
COULD IT BE BECAUSE YOU REALIZED DURING MY BATTLE WITH KIWI THAT I'VE BECOME FAR STRONGER THAN BEFORE? YOU SAW MY POWER READING ON THE SCOUTER, DIDN'T YOU?
THAT NUMBER WAS A MISTAKE!! THE SCOUTER WAS BROKEN !!
I GAVE YOU A CHANCE TO LEAVE !!!!
YOU BLEW IT !!!!!

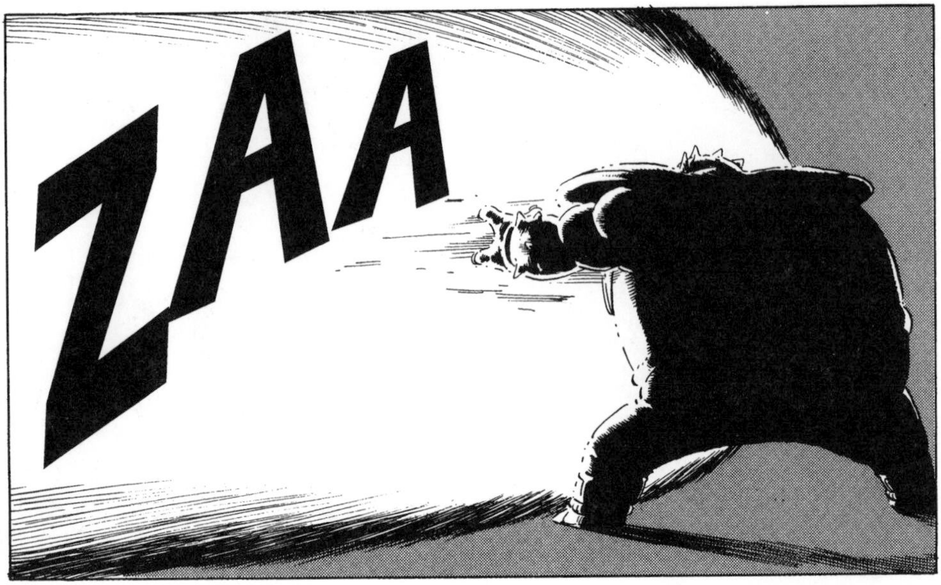
ZAA
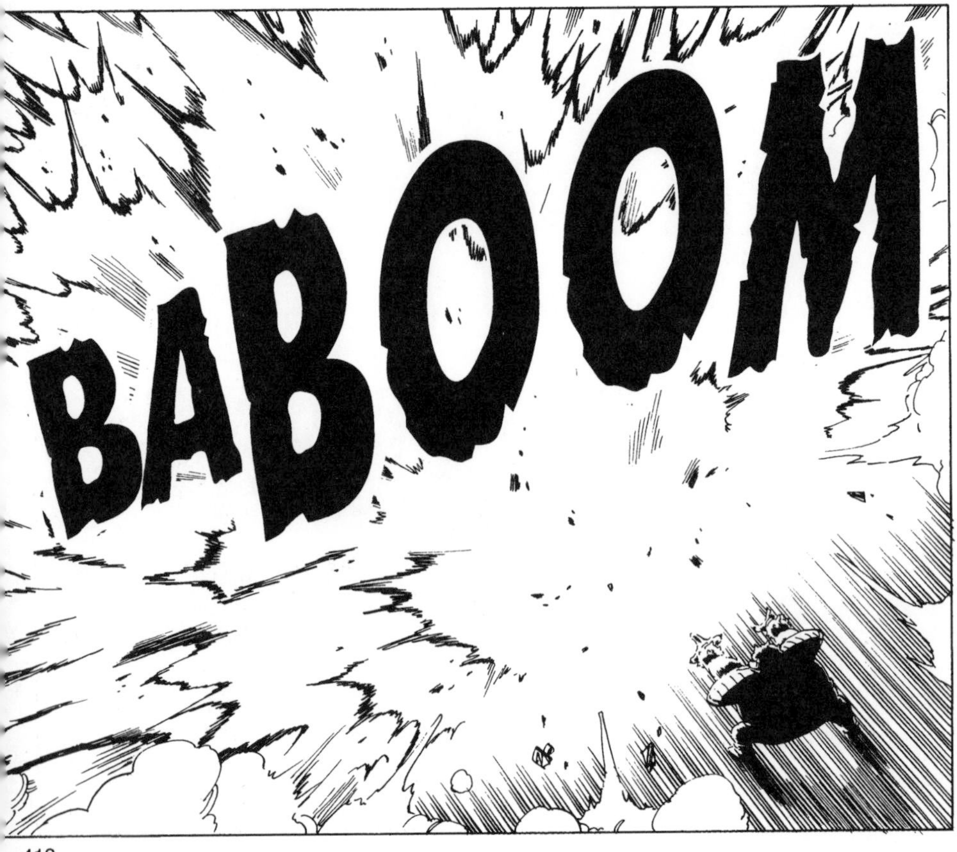
BABOOM

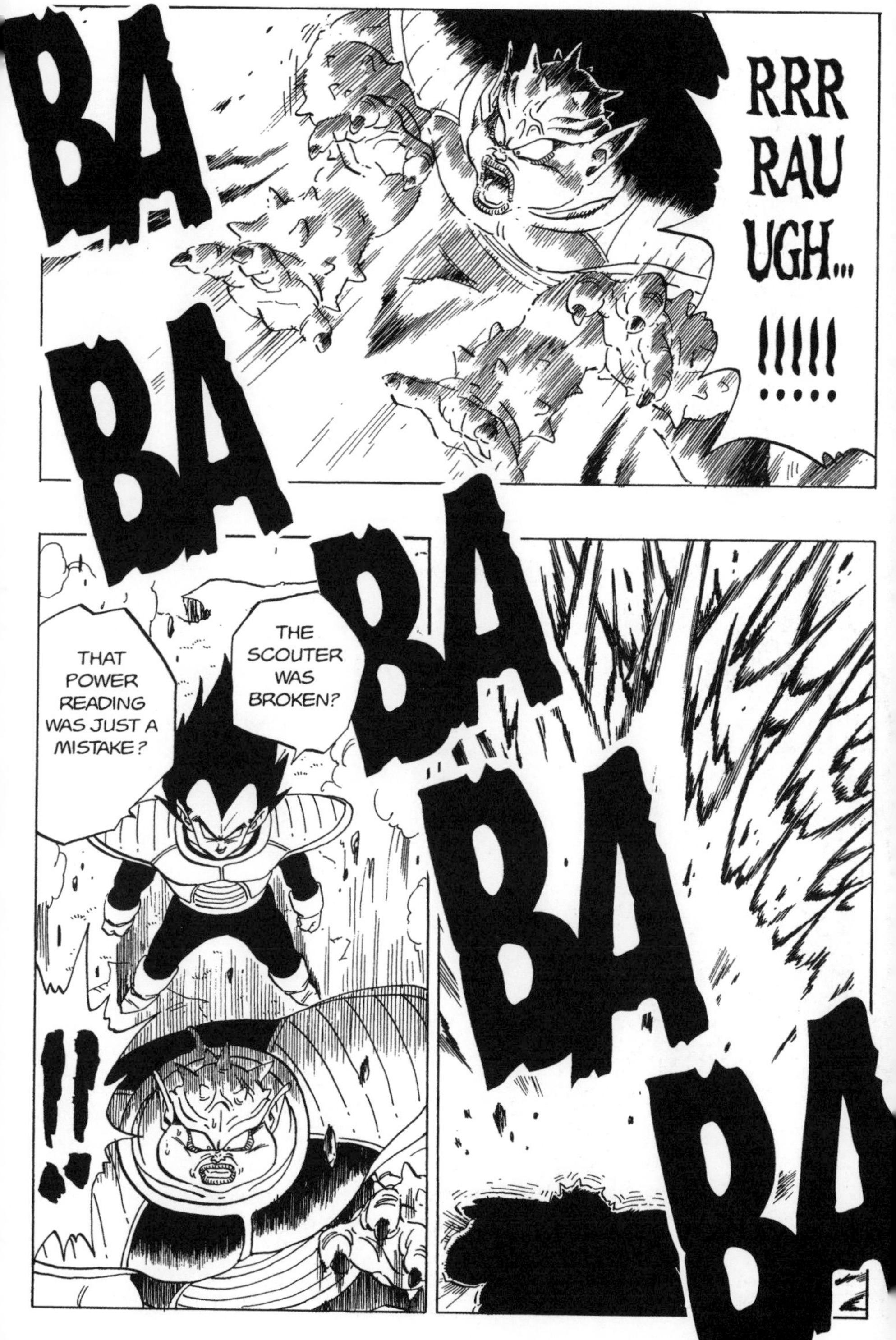
RRR RAUGH... !!!!!!
BA
BA
BA
BA
BA
THE SCOUTER WAS BROKEN?
THAT POWER READING WAS JUST A MISTAKE?
!!

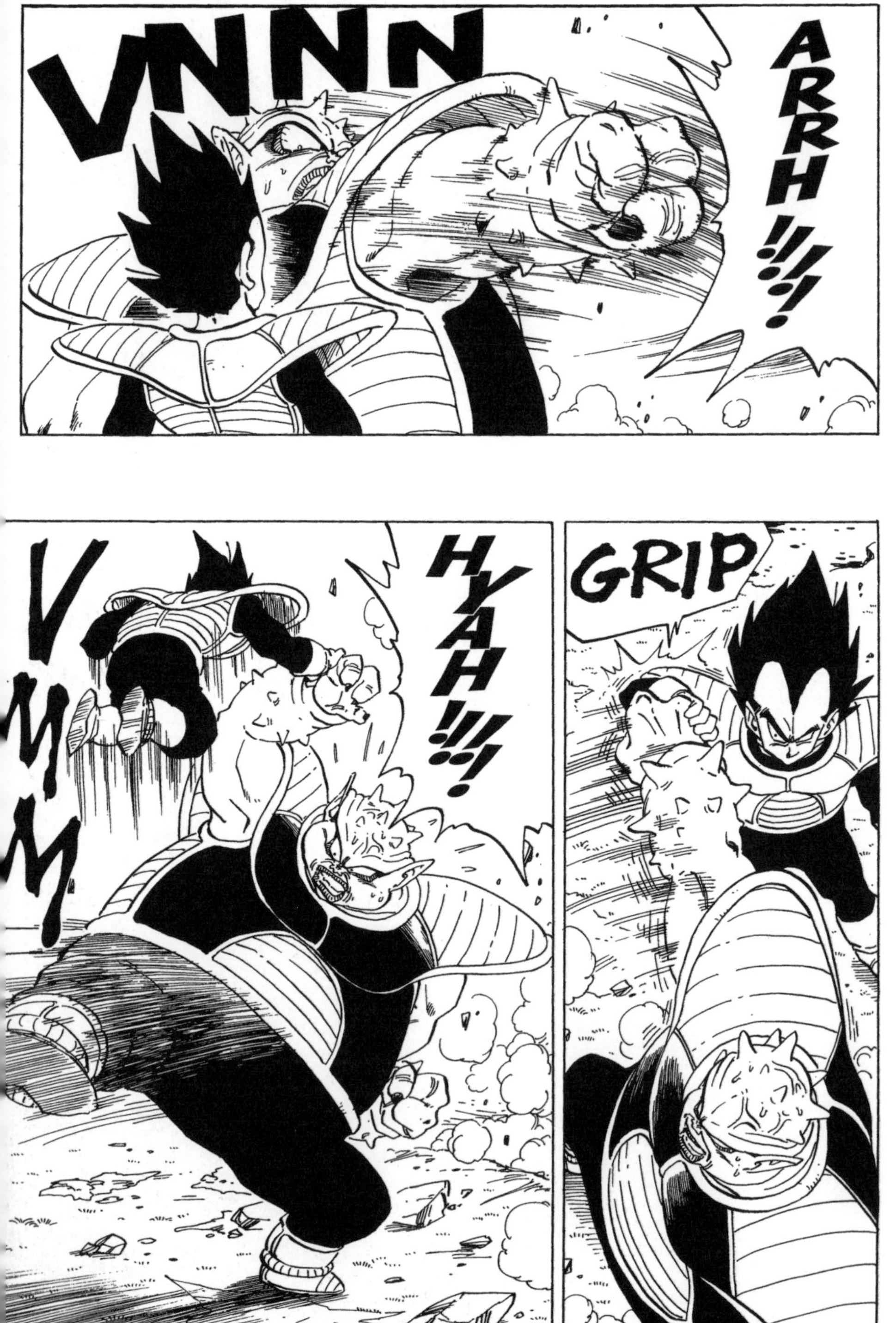
ARRH!!!!
VNNN
GRIP
HYAH!!!!
VMMM

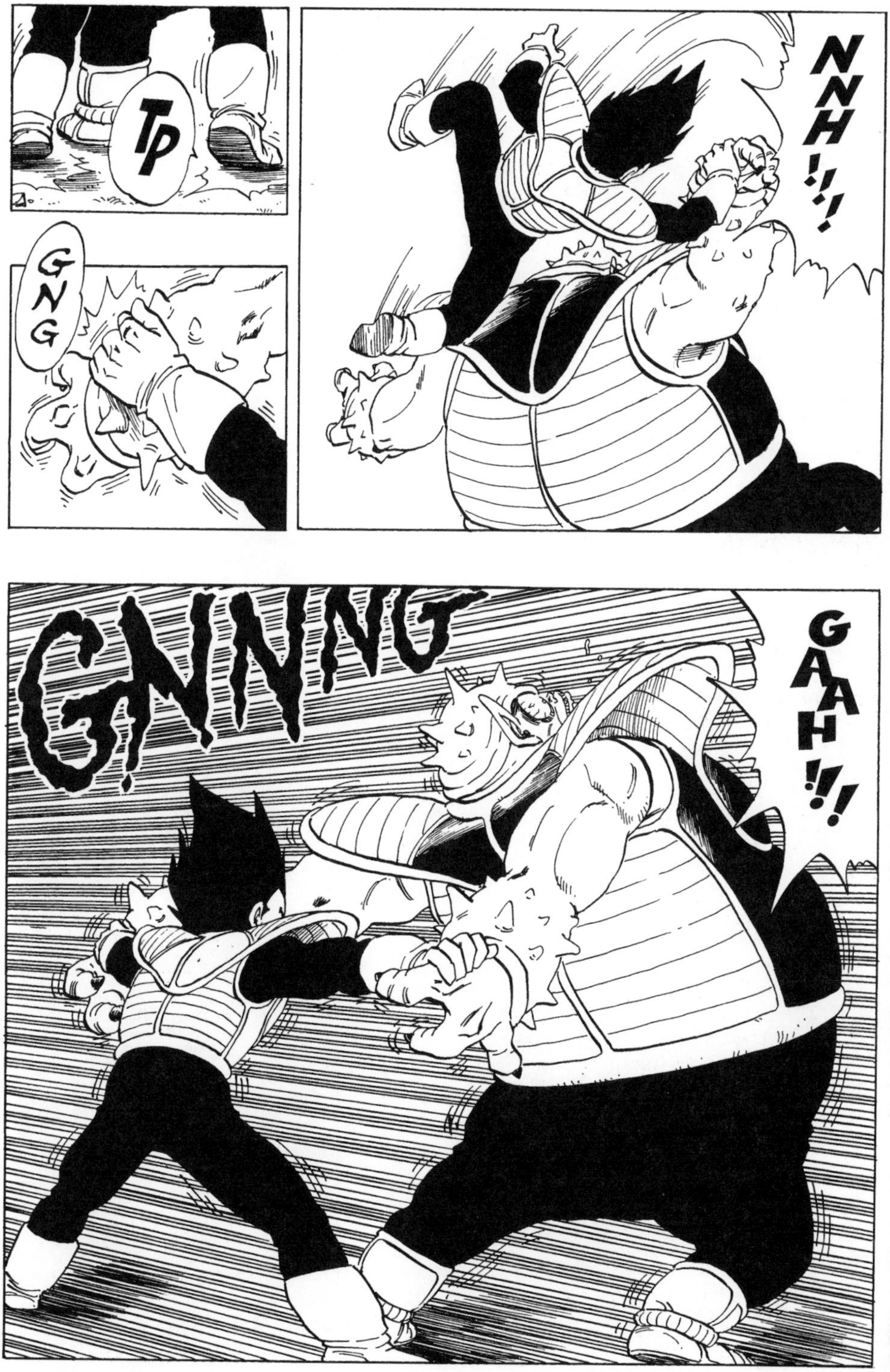
NNH!!!
TP
GNG
GAAH!!!
GNNNG

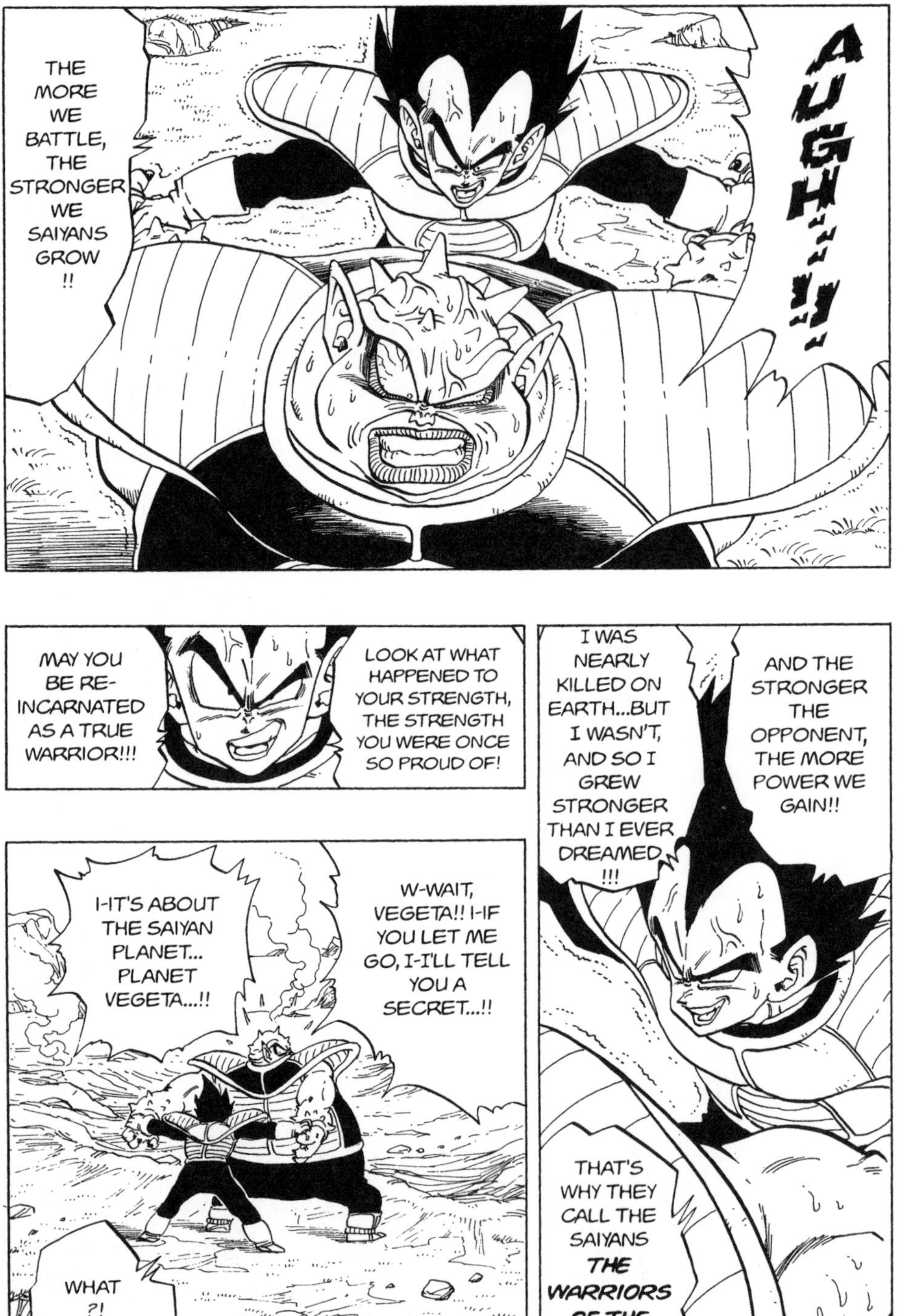
AUGH...!!
THE MORE WE BATTLE, THE STRONGER WE SAIYANS GROW !!
AND THE STRONGER THE OPPONENT, THE MORE POWER WE GAIN!!
I WAS NEARLY KILLED ON EARTH...BUT I WASN'T, AND SO I GREW STRONGER THAN I EVER DREAMED !!!
THAT'S WHY THEY CALL THE SAIYANS ***THE WARRIORS OF THE UNIVERSE*** !!!
LOOK AT WHAT HAPPENED TO YOUR STRENGTH, THE STRENGTH YOU WERE ONCE SO PROUD OF!
MAY YOU BE RE-INCARNATED AS A TRUE WARRIOR!!!
W-WAIT, VEGETA!! I-IF YOU LET ME GO, I-I'LL TELL YOU A SECRET...!!
I-IT'S ABOUT THE SAIYAN PLANET... PLANET VEGETA...!!
WHAT ?!

PLANET VEGETA?! WHAT IS THERE ABOUT PLANET VEGETA THAT I DON'T KNOW ?!
MMF !!!
YOU...YOU WOULDN'T KILL ME AFTER I TELL YOU... WOULD YOU?
IF YOU DON'T TELL ME, I'LL KILL YOU RIGHT NOW !!!
SAY IT !!!!
Y-YOUR PLANET... IT WASN'T DESTROYED BY A...
...BY A METEOR... LIKE MASTER FREEZA... SAID...
WHAT... ?!
TH-THE STRENGTH OF INDIVIDUAL SAIYANS IS NO MATCH FOR M-MASTER FREEZA...
...BUT IF MANY SAIYANS UNITED... IT WOULD BE DIFFICULT EVEN FOR HIM TO DEAL WITH...

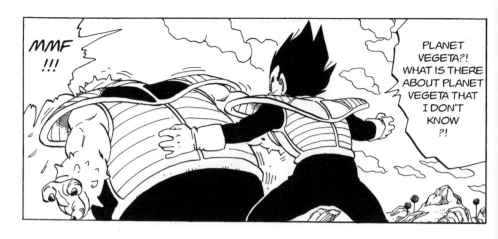

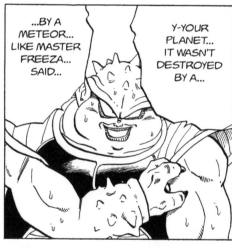

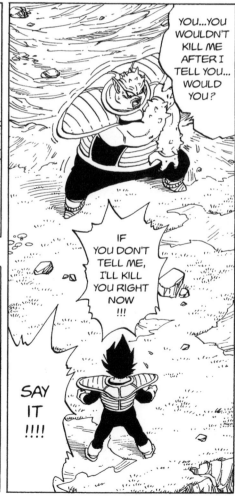

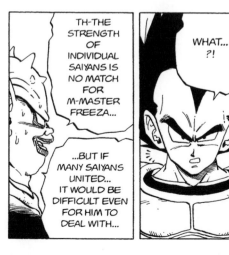

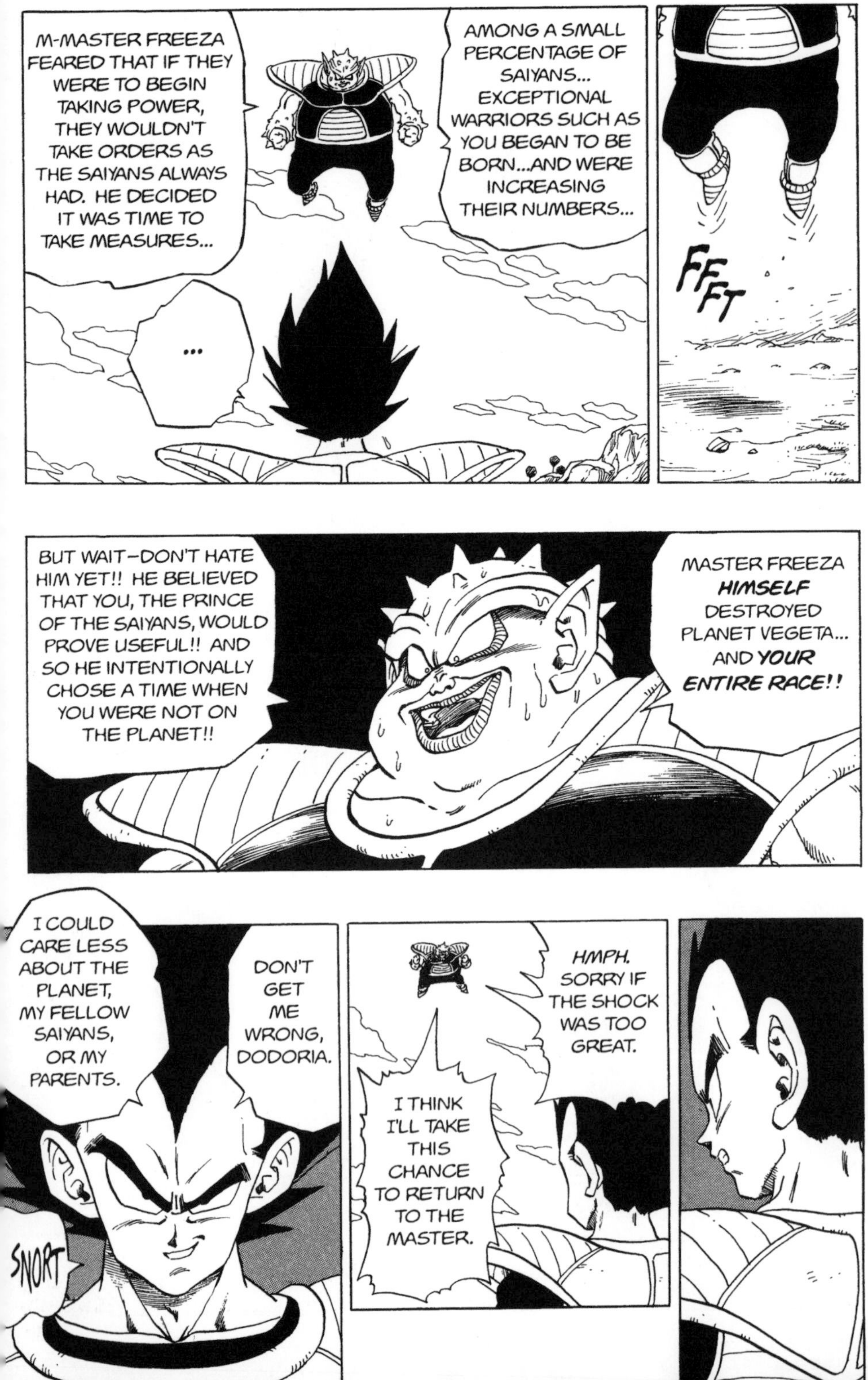
FFFT
AMONG A SMALL PERCENTAGE OF SAIYANS... EXCEPTIONAL WARRIORS SUCH AS YOU BEGAN TO BE BORN...AND WERE INCREASING THEIR NUMBERS...
M-MASTER FREEZA FEARED THAT IF THEY WERE TO BEGIN TAKING POWER, THEY WOULDN'T TAKE ORDERS AS THE SAIYANS ALWAYS HAD. HE DECIDED IT WAS TIME TO TAKE MEASURES...
...
MASTER FREEZA HIMSELF DESTROYED PLANET VEGETA... AND YOUR ENTIRE RACE!!
BUT WAIT—DON'T HATE HIM YET!! HE BELIEVED THAT YOU, THE PRINCE OF THE SAIYANS, WOULD PROVE USEFUL!! AND SO HE INTENTIONALLY CHOSE A TIME WHEN YOU WERE NOT ON THE PLANET!!
HMPH. SORRY IF THE SHOCK WAS TOO GREAT.
I THINK I'LL TAKE THIS CHANCE TO RETURN TO THE MASTER.
DON'T GET ME WRONG, DODORIA.
I COULD CARE LESS ABOUT THE PLANET, MY FELLOW SAIYANS, OR MY PARENTS.
SNORT

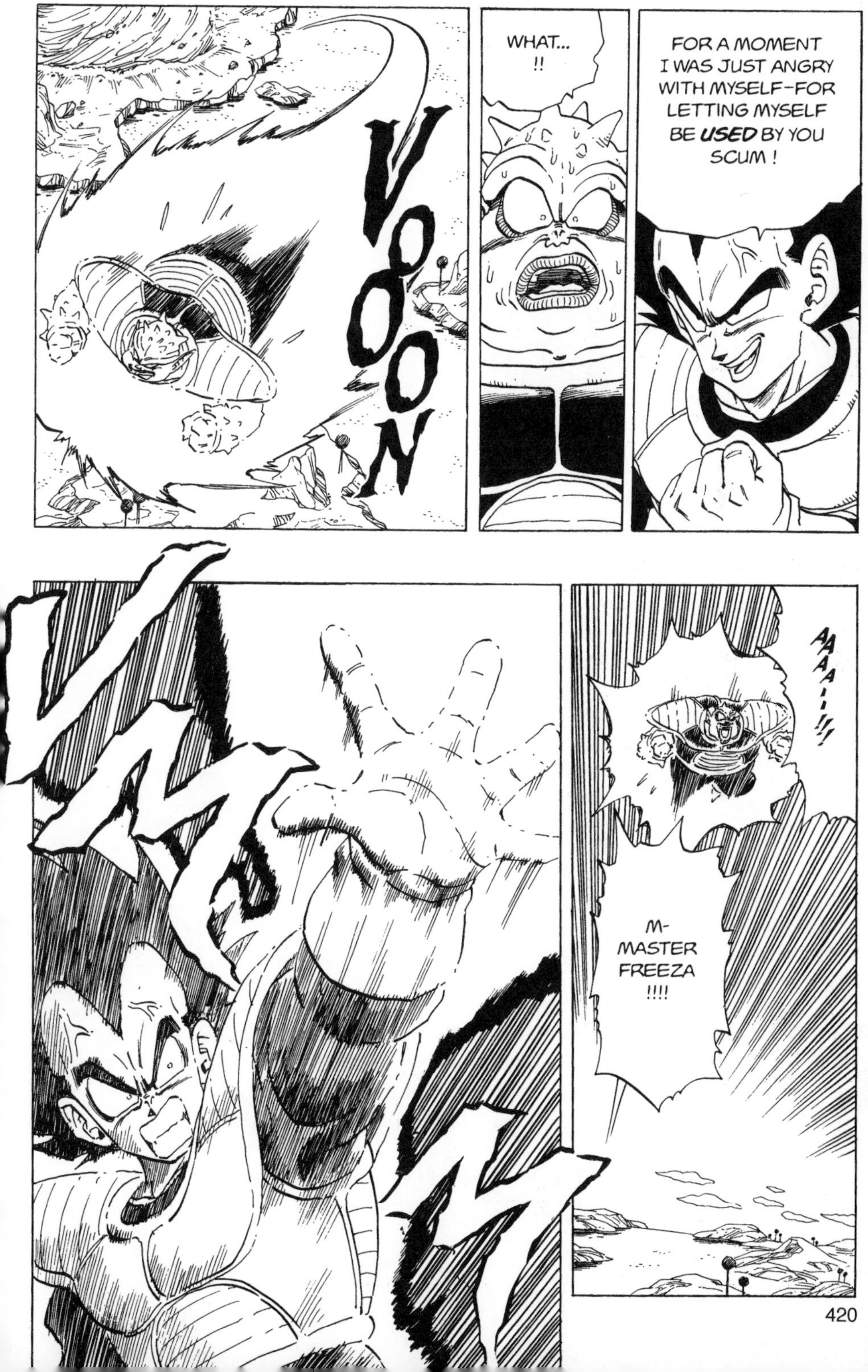
FOR A MOMENT I WAS JUST ANGRY WITH MYSELF--FOR LETTING MYSELF BE ***USED*** BY YOU SCUM !
WHAT... !!
VOOON
AAAAII!!!
M-MASTER FREEZA !!!!

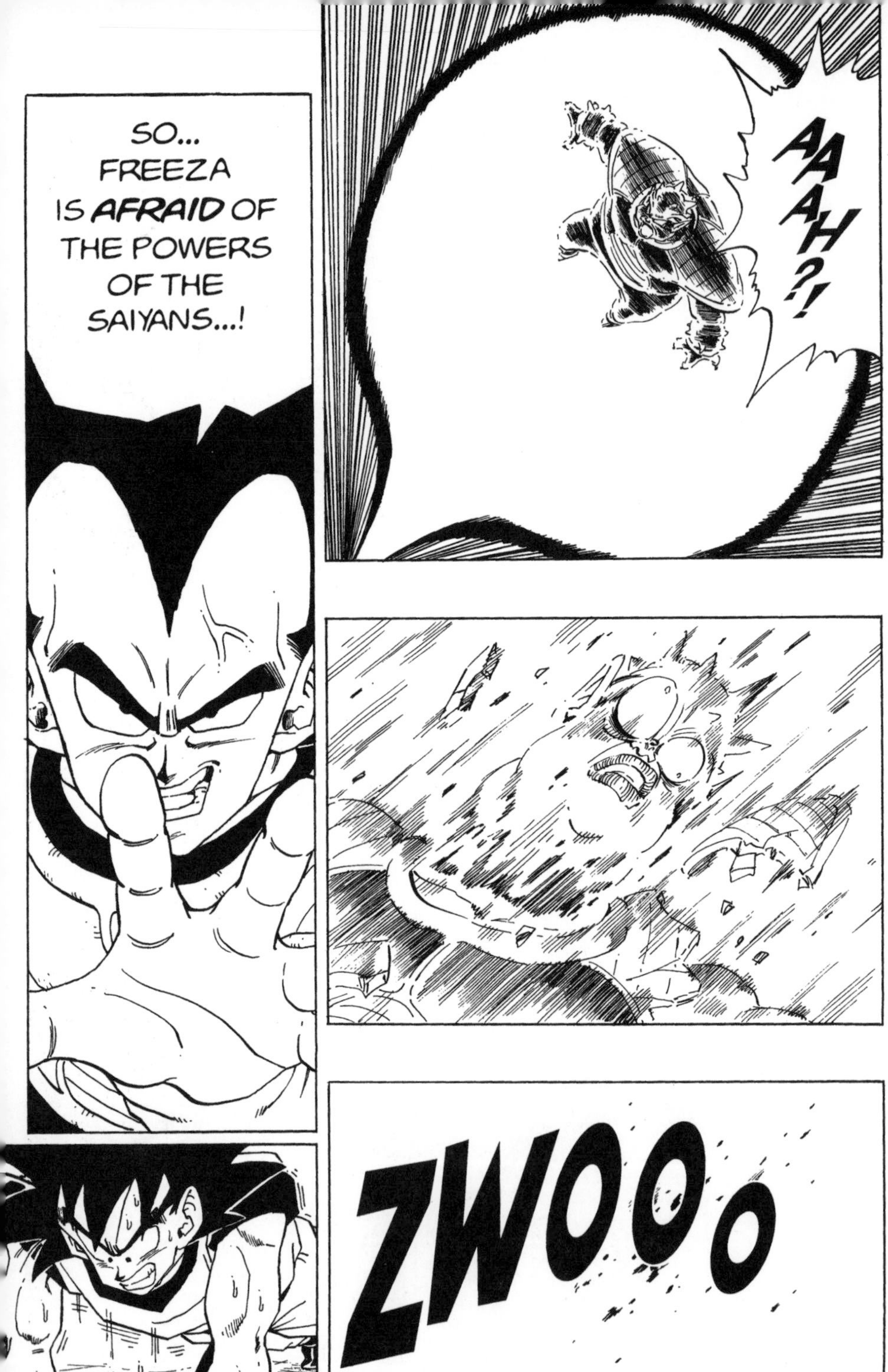
AAAH?!
ZWOOOO
SO... FREEZA IS *AFRAID* OF THE POWERS OF THE SAIYANS...!

# DBZ:64 • Hide and Seek

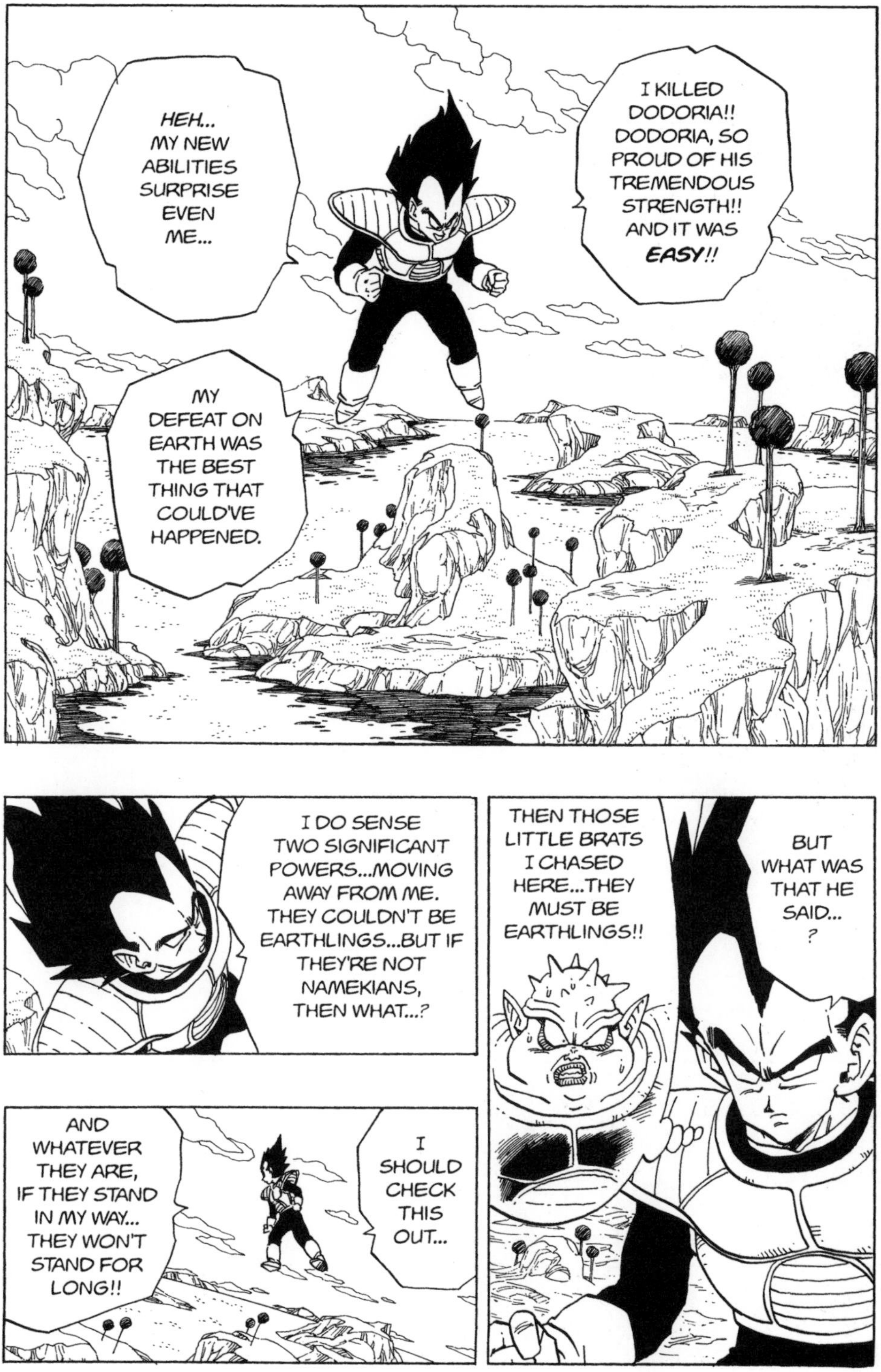
I KILLED DODORIA!! DODORIA, SO PROUD OF HIS TREMENDOUS STRENGTH!! AND IT WAS *EASY*!!
HEH... MY NEW ABILITIES SURPRISE EVEN ME...
MY DEFEAT ON EARTH WAS THE BEST THING THAT COULD'VE HAPPENED.
BUT WHAT WAS THAT HE SAID...?
THEN THOSE LITTLE BRATS I CHASED HERE...THEY MUST BE EARTHLINGS!!
I DO SENSE TWO SIGNIFICANT POWERS...MOVING AWAY FROM ME. THEY COULDN'T BE EARTHLINGS...BUT IF THEY'RE NOT NAMEKIANS, THEN WHAT...?
I SHOULD CHECK THIS OUT...
AND WHATEVER THEY ARE, IF THEY STAND IN MY WAY... THEY WON'T STAND FOR LONG!!

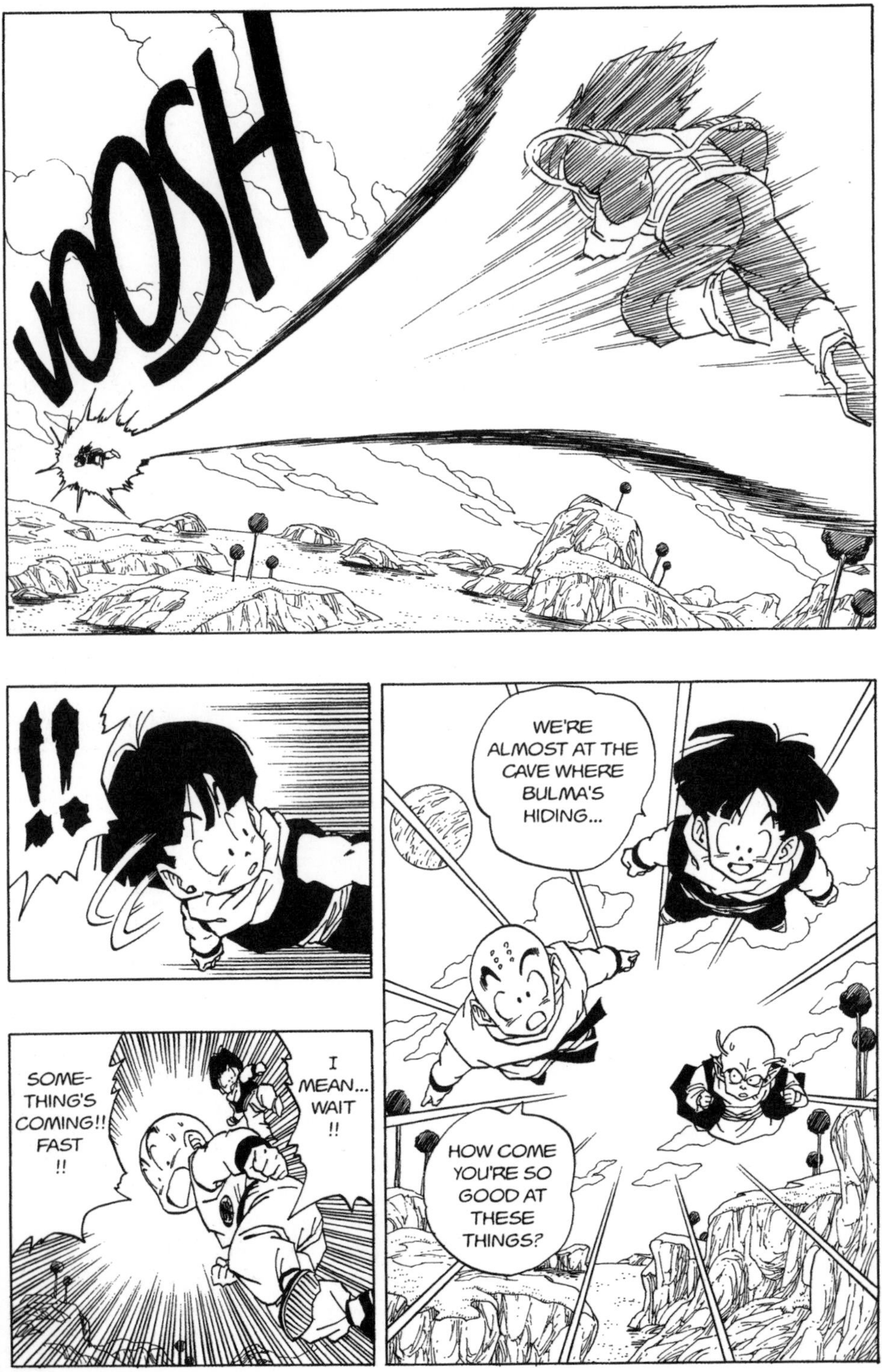
VOOSH
WE'RE ALMOST AT THE CAVE WHERE BULMA'S HIDING...
HOW COME YOU'RE SO GOOD AT THESE THINGS?
!!
I MEAN... WAIT !!
SOME-THING'S COMING!! FAST !!

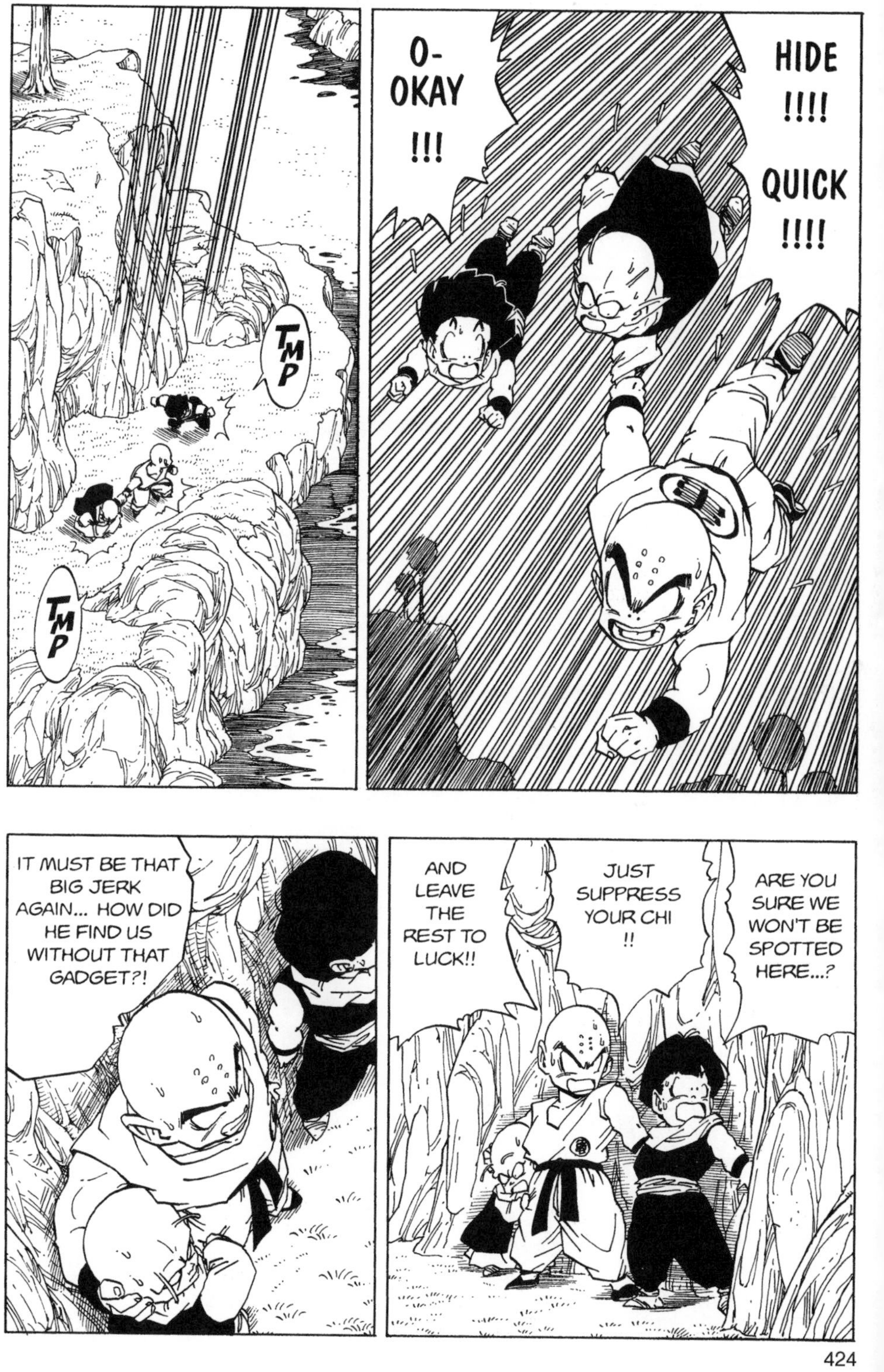
HIDE!!!! QUICK!!!!
O-OKAY!!!
TMP
TMP
ARE YOU SURE WE WON'T BE SPOTTED HERE...?
JUST SUPPRESS YOUR CHI!!
AND LEAVE THE REST TO LUCK!!
IT MUST BE THAT BIG JERK AGAIN... HOW DID HE FIND US WITHOUT THAT GADGET?!

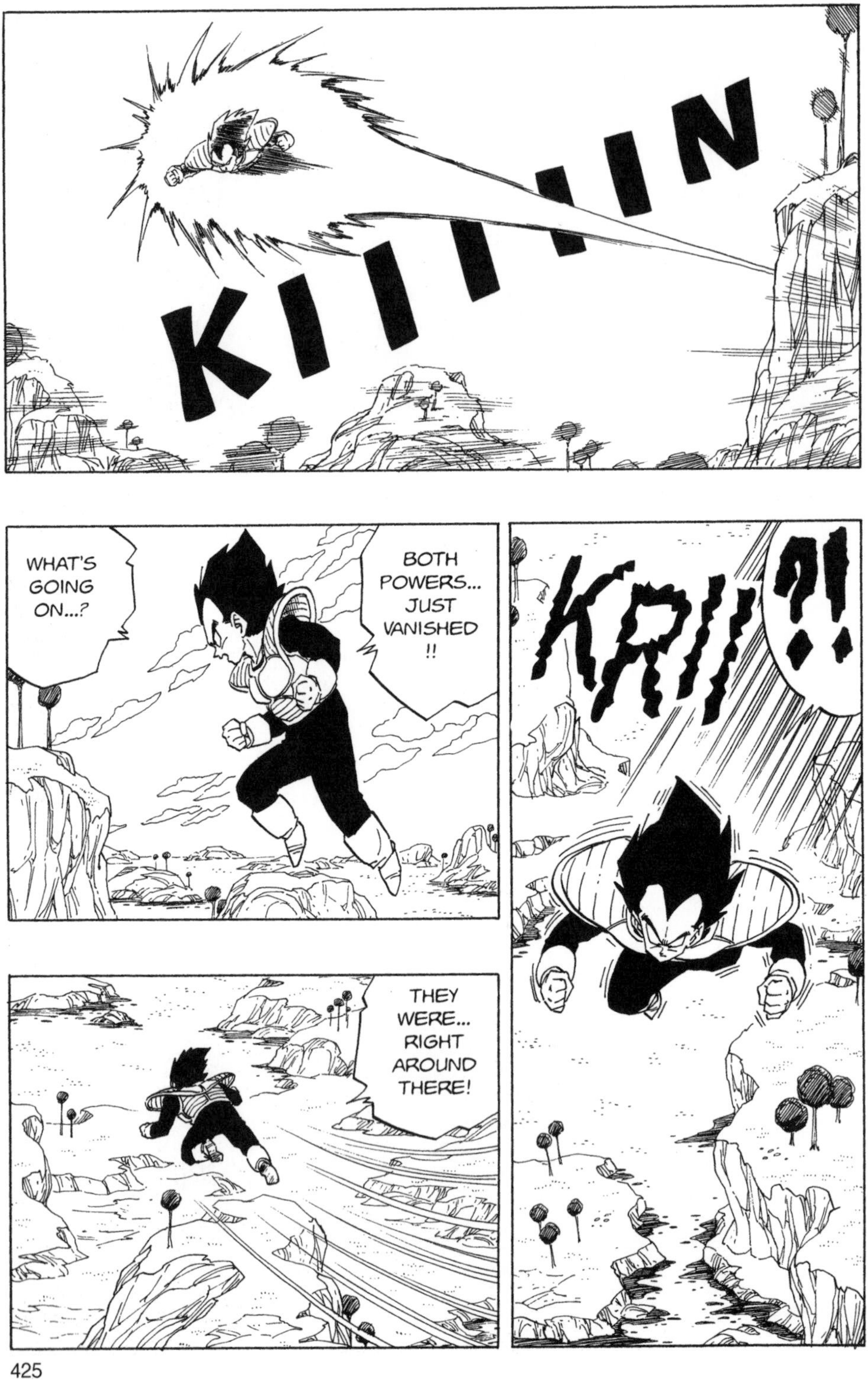
KIIIIIN
KRII?!
BOTH POWERS... JUST VANISHED!!
WHAT'S GOING ON...?
THEY WERE... RIGHT AROUND THERE!

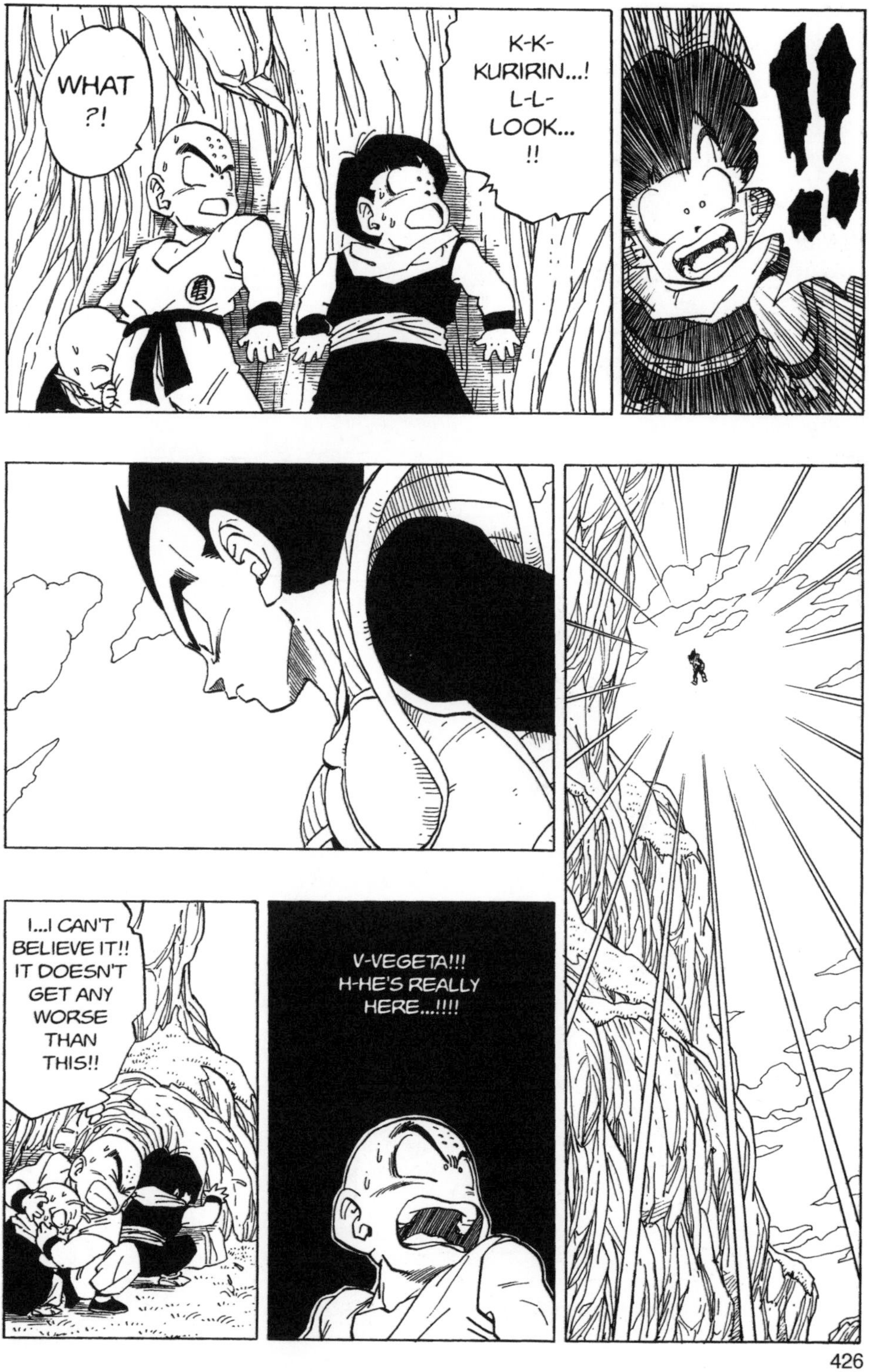
!!
K-K- KURIRIN...! L-L- LOOK... !!
WHAT ?!
V-VEGETA!!! H-HE'S REALLY HERE...!!!!
I...I CAN'T BELIEVE IT!! IT DOESN'T GET ANY WORSE THAN THIS!!

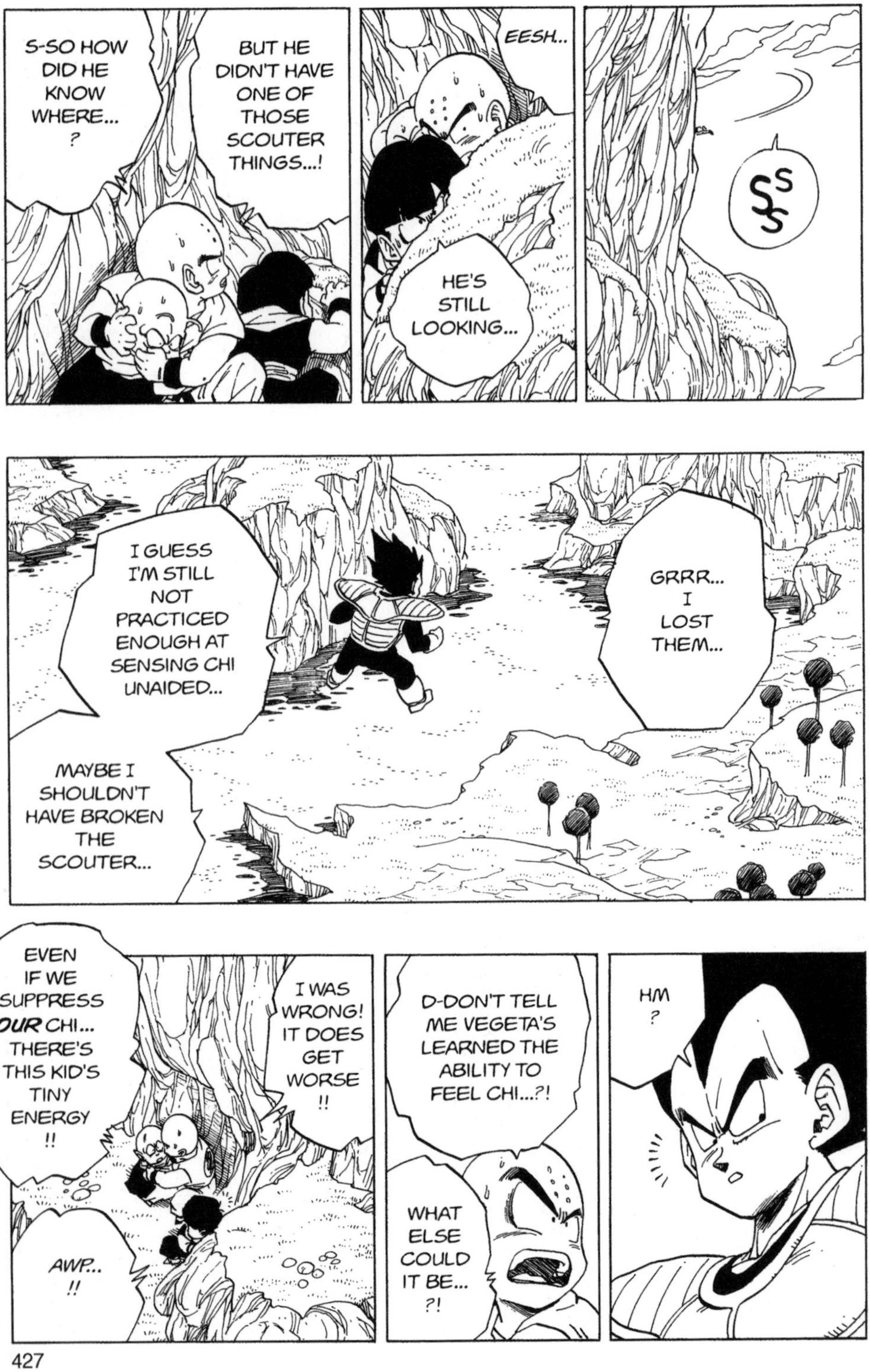
SSS
EESH...
HE'S STILL LOOKING...
BUT HE DIDN'T HAVE ONE OF THOSE SCOUTER THINGS...!
S-SO HOW DID HE KNOW WHERE...?
GRRR... I LOST THEM...
I GUESS I'M STILL NOT PRACTICED ENOUGH AT SENSING CHI UNAIDED...
MAYBE I SHOULDN'T HAVE BROKEN THE SCOUTER...
HM?
D-DON'T TELL ME VEGETA'S LEARNED THE ABILITY TO FEEL CHI...?!
WHAT ELSE COULD IT BE...?!
I WAS WRONG! IT DOES GET WORSE!!
EVEN IF WE SUPPRESS ***OUR*** CHI... THERE'S THIS KID'S TINY ENERGY!!
AWP...!!

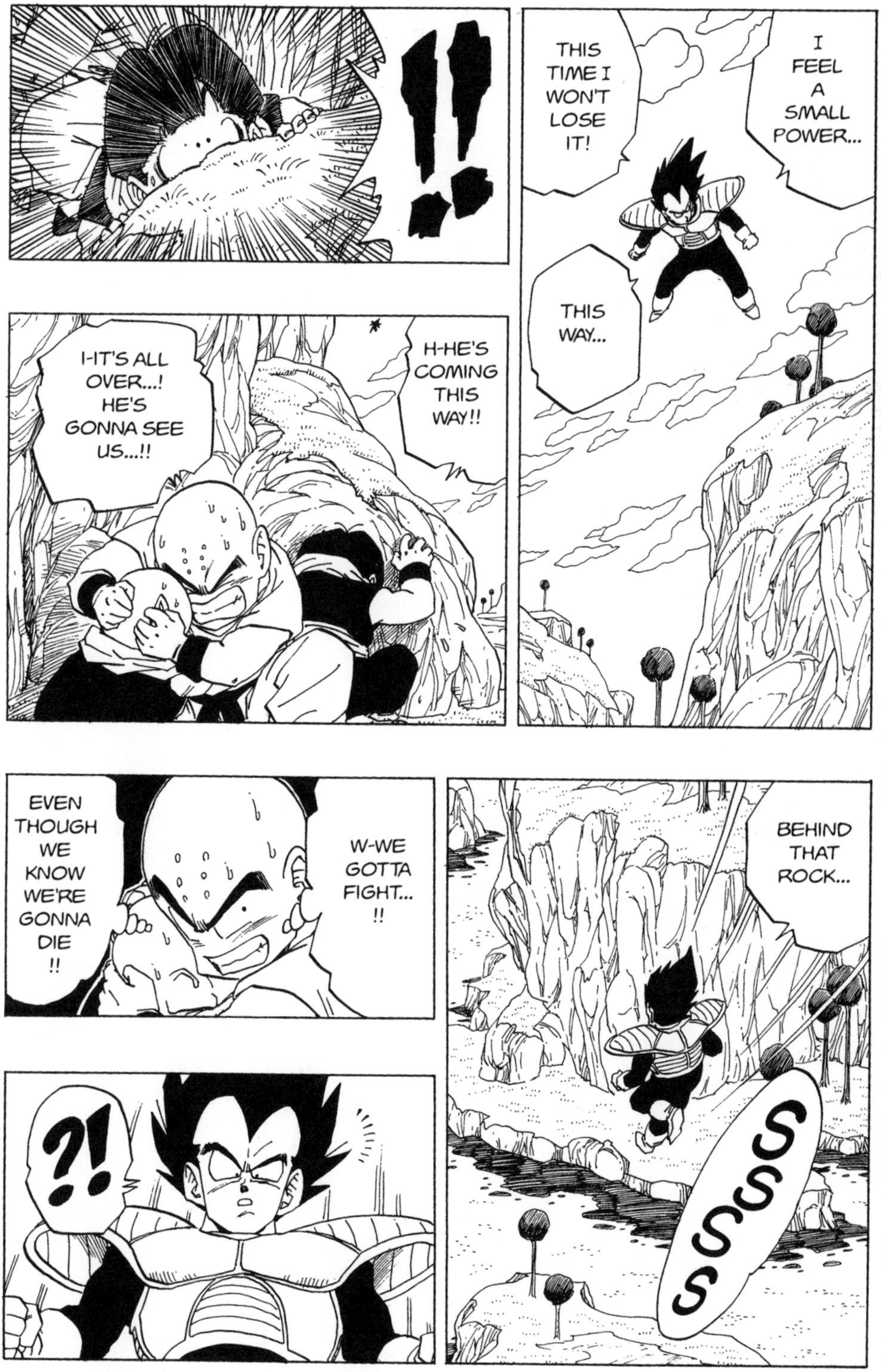
I FEEL A SMALL POWER...
THIS TIME I WON'T LOSE IT!
THIS WAY...
!!
H-HE'S COMING THIS WAY!!
I-IT'S ALL OVER...! HE'S GONNA SEE US...!!
BEHIND THAT ROCK...
SSSSS
W-WE GOTTA FIGHT... !!
EVEN THOUGH WE KNOW WE'RE GONNA DIE !!
?!

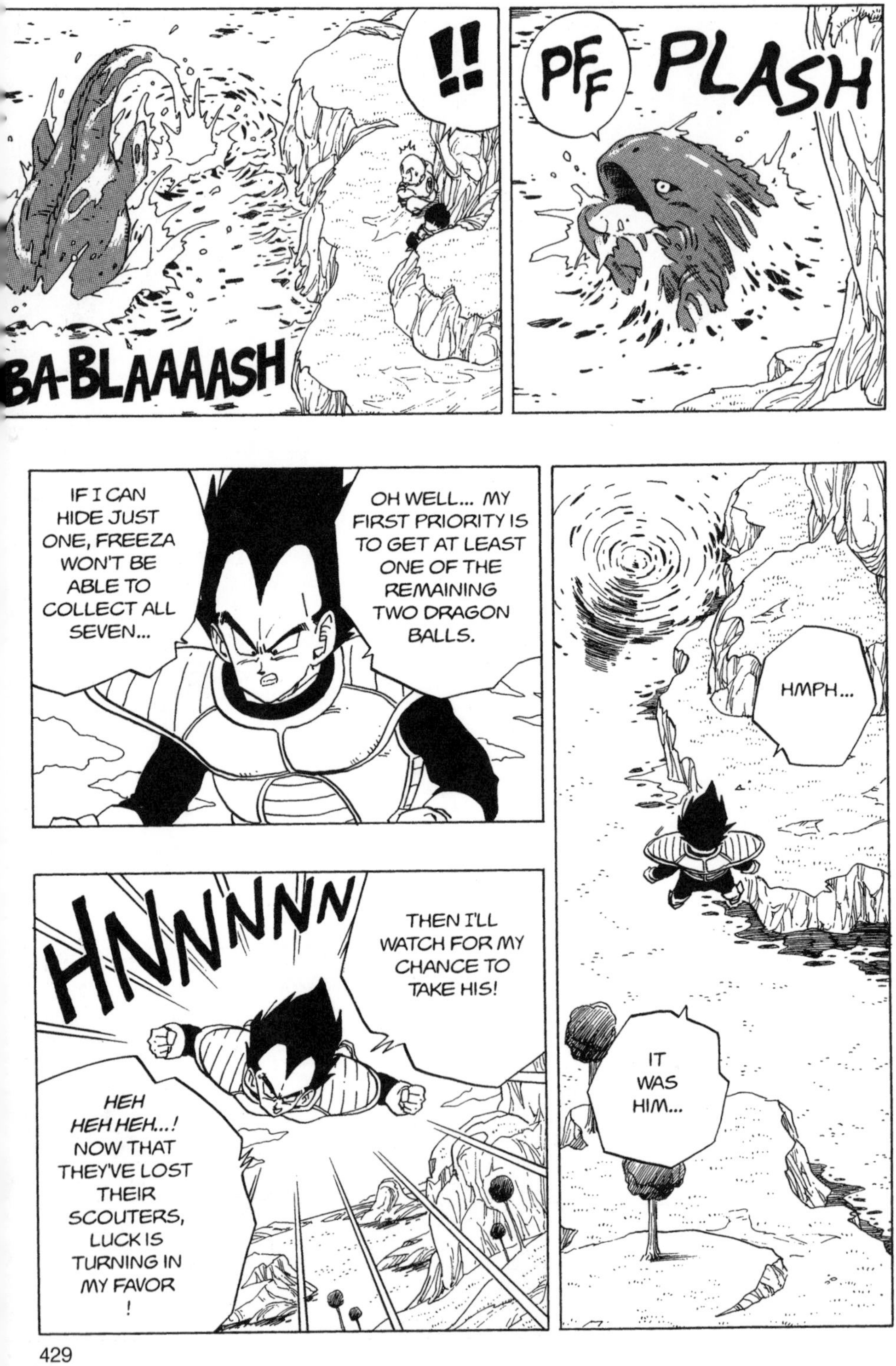
PFF
PLASH
!!
BA-BLAAAASH
HMPH...
IT WAS HIM...
OH WELL... MY FIRST PRIORITY IS TO GET AT LEAST ONE OF THE REMAINING TWO DRAGON BALLS.
IF I CAN HIDE JUST ONE, FREEZA WON'T BE ABLE TO COLLECT ALL SEVEN...
THEN I'LL WATCH FOR MY CHANCE TO TAKE HIS!
HNNNNNN
HEH HEH HEH...! NOW THAT THEY'VE LOST THEIR SCOUTERS, LUCK IS TURNING IN MY FAVOR!

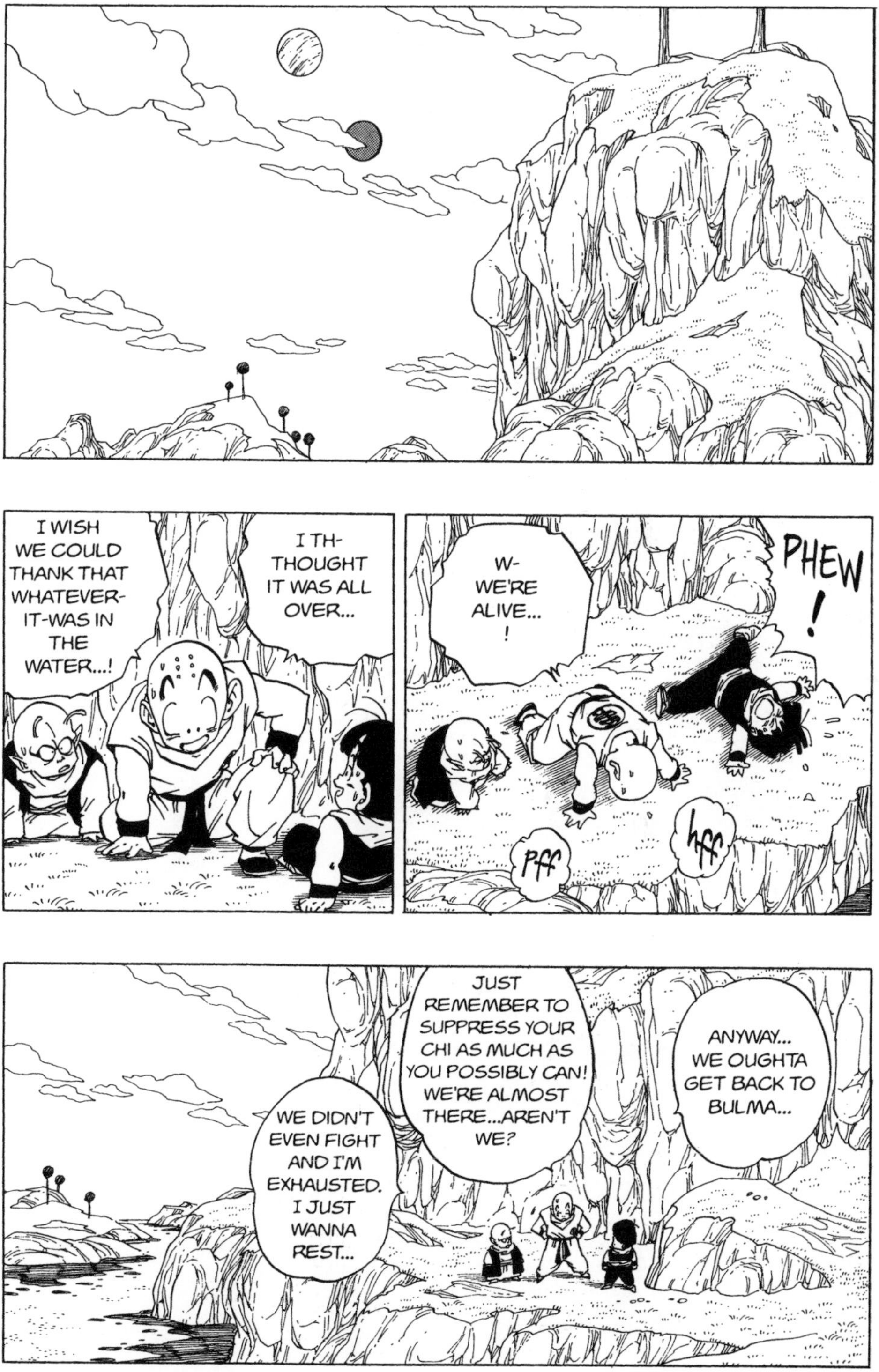
PHEW !
W- WE'RE ALIVE... !
hff
Pff
I TH- THOUGHT IT WAS ALL OVER...
I WISH WE COULD THANK THAT WHATEVER-IT-WAS IN THE WATER...!
ANYWAY... WE OUGHTA GET BACK TO BULMA...
JUST REMEMBER TO SUPPRESS YOUR CHI AS MUCH AS YOU POSSIBLY CAN! WE'RE ALMOST THERE...AREN'T WE?
WE DIDN'T EVEN FIGHT AND I'M EXHAUSTED. I JUST WANNA REST...

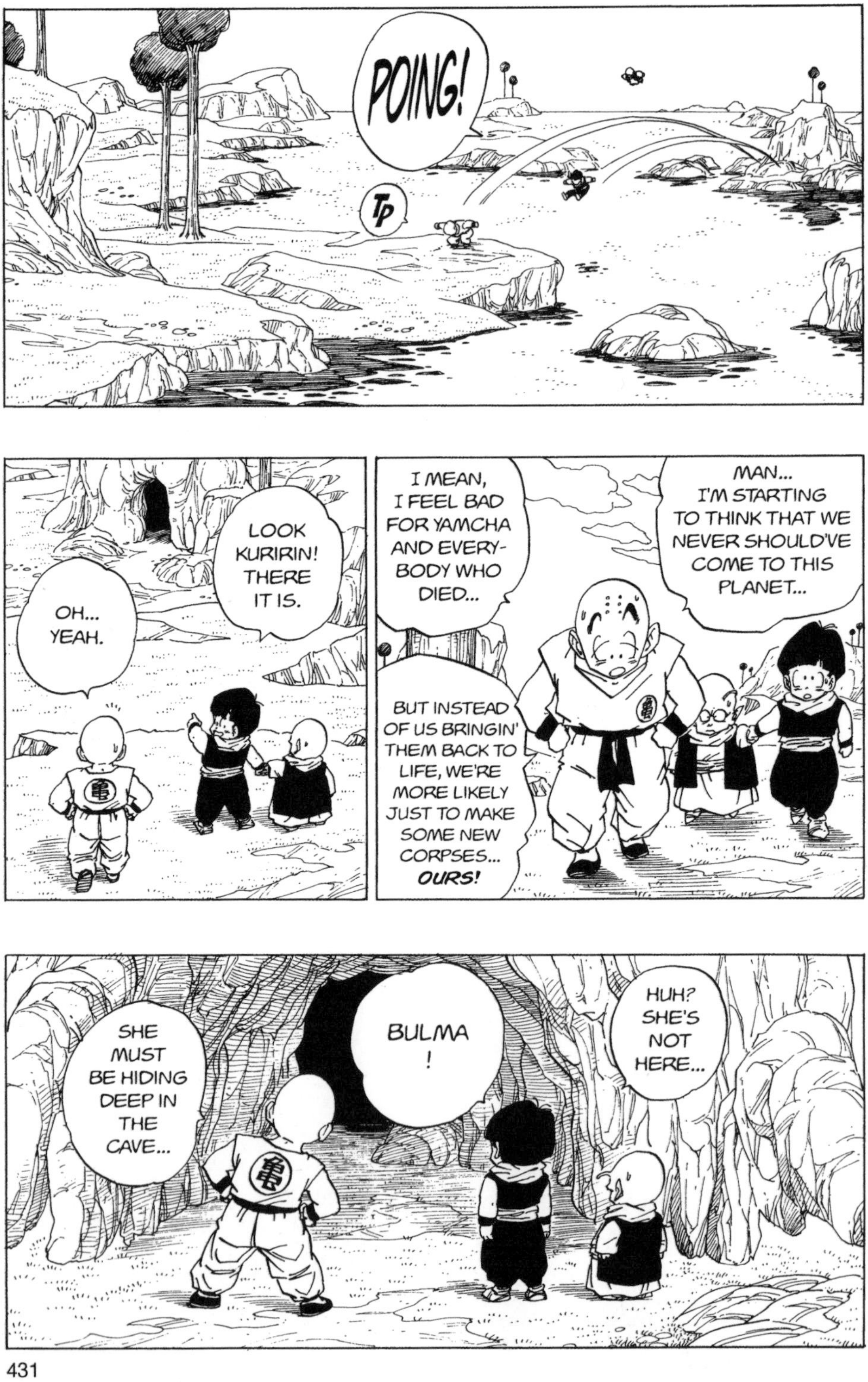
POING!
TP
MAN... I'M STARTING TO THINK THAT WE NEVER SHOULD'VE COME TO THIS PLANET...
I MEAN, I FEEL BAD FOR YAMCHA AND EVERYBODY WHO DIED...
BUT INSTEAD OF US BRINGIN' THEM BACK TO LIFE, WE'RE MORE LIKELY JUST TO MAKE SOME NEW CORPSES... **OURS!**
LOOK KURIRIN! THERE IT IS.
OH... YEAH.
HUH? SHE'S NOT HERE...
BULMA!
SHE MUST BE HIDING DEEP IN THE CAVE...

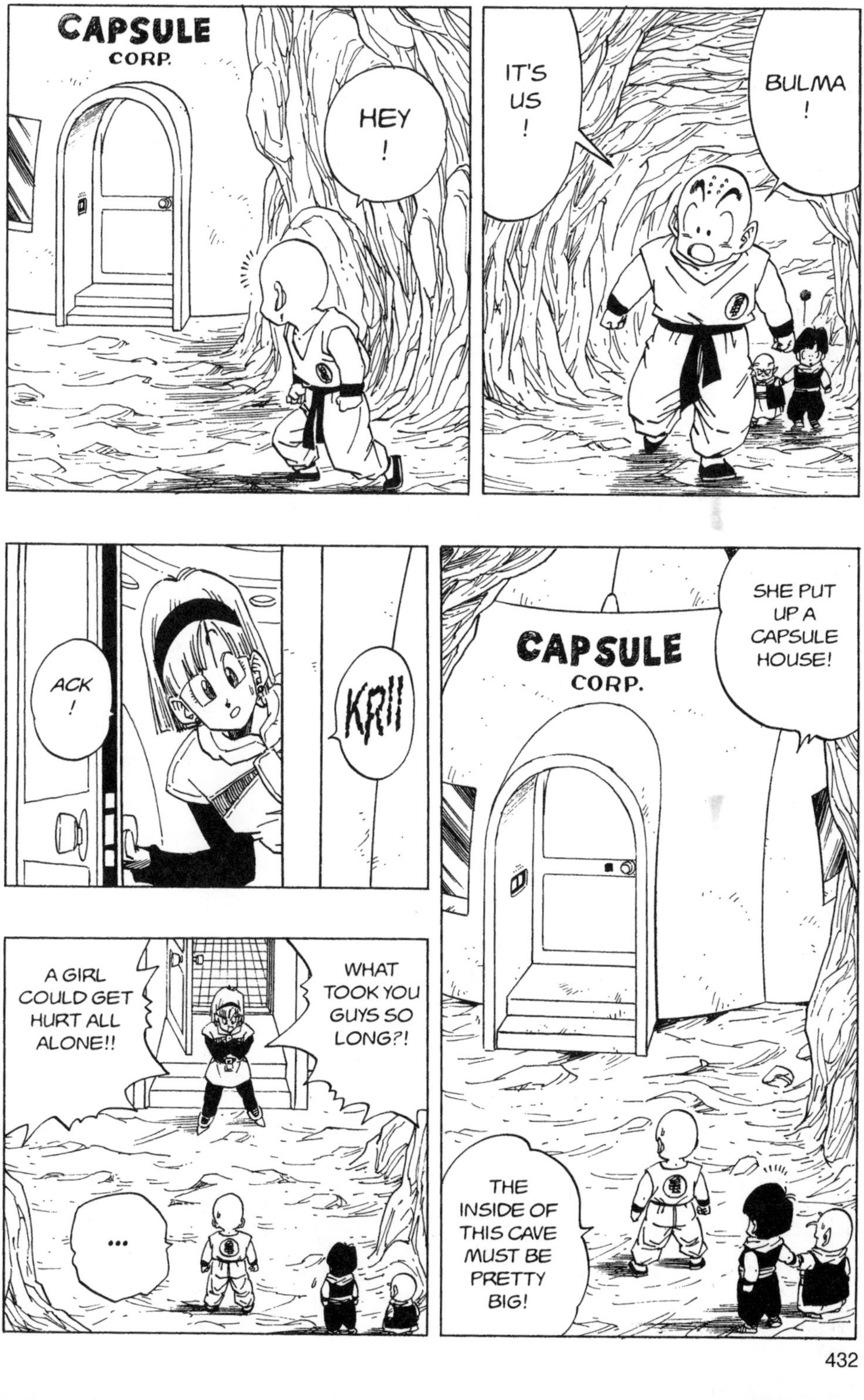
BULMA!
IT'S US!
CAPSULE CORP.
HEY!
SHE PUT UP A CAPSULE HOUSE!
CAPSULE CORP.
THE INSIDE OF THIS CAVE MUST BE PRETTY BIG!
KRII
ACK!
WHAT TOOK YOU GUYS SO LONG?!
A GIRL COULD GET HURT ALL ALONE!!
...

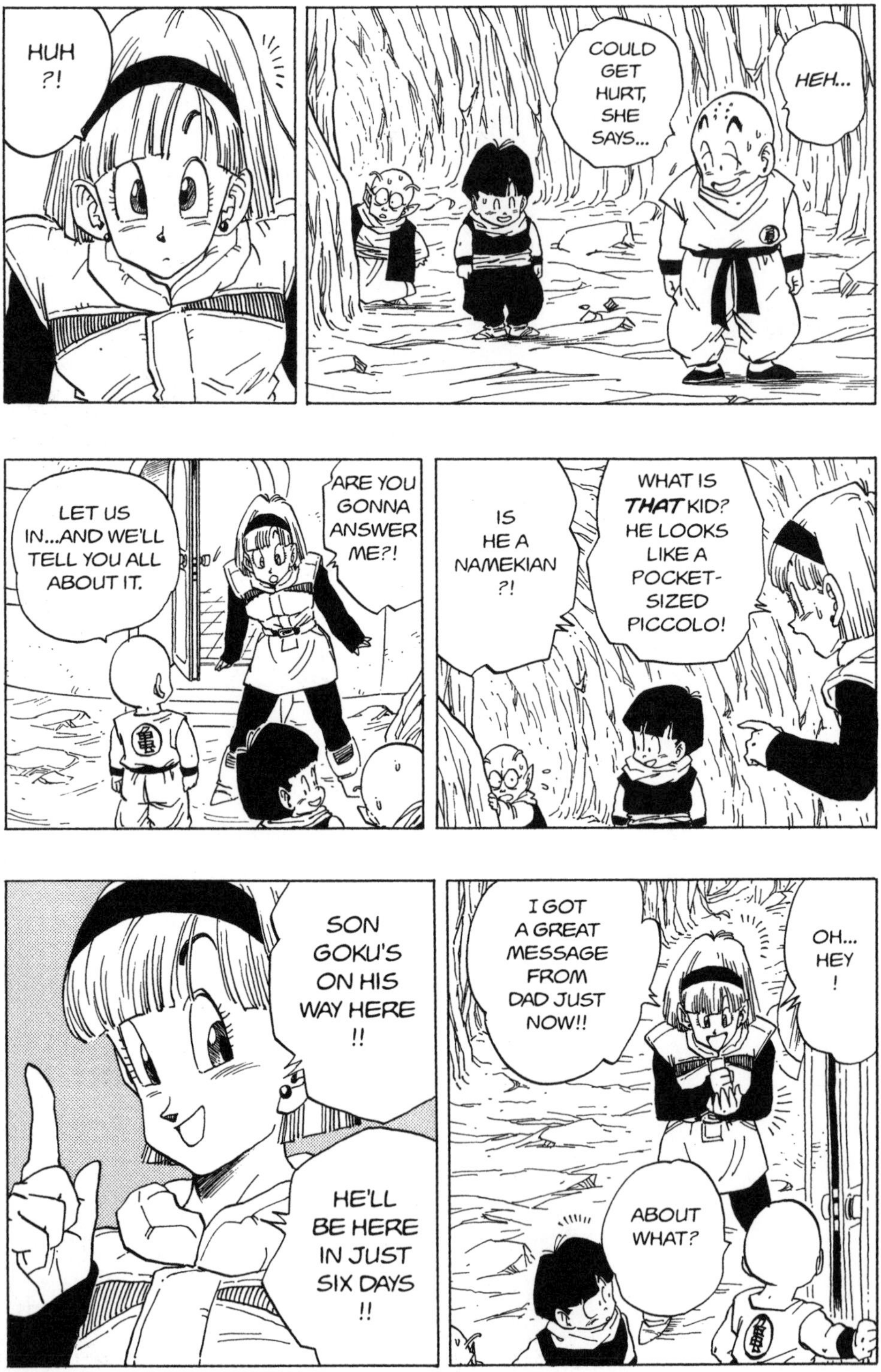
HEH...
COULD GET HURT, SHE SAYS...
HUH ?!
WHAT IS THAT KID? HE LOOKS LIKE A POCKET-SIZED PICCOLO!
IS HE A NAMEKIAN ?!
ARE YOU GONNA ANSWER ME?!
LET US IN...AND WE'LL TELL YOU ALL ABOUT IT.
OH... HEY !
I GOT A GREAT MESSAGE FROM DAD JUST NOW!!
ABOUT WHAT?
SON GOKU'S ON HIS WAY HERE !!
HE'LL BE HERE IN JUST SIX DAYS !!

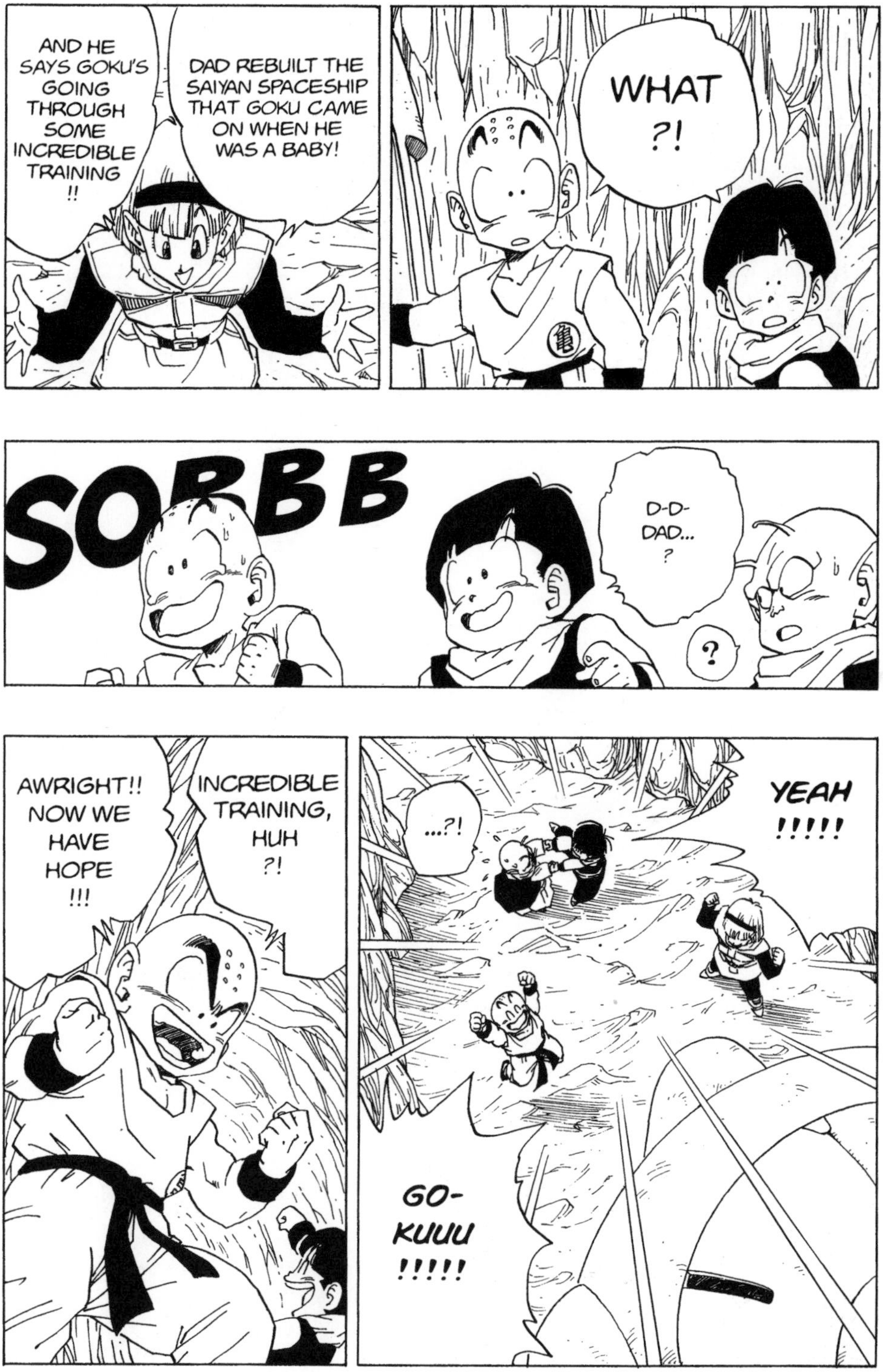
WHAT ?!
DAD REBUILT THE SAIYAN SPACESHIP THAT GOKU CAME ON WHEN HE WAS A BABY!
AND HE SAYS GOKU'S GOING THROUGH SOME INCREDIBLE TRAINING !!
D-D-DAD...?
?
SOBBB
YEAH !!!!!
...?!
GO-KUUU !!!!!
INCREDIBLE TRAINING, HUH ?!
AWRIGHT!! NOW WE HAVE HOPE !!!

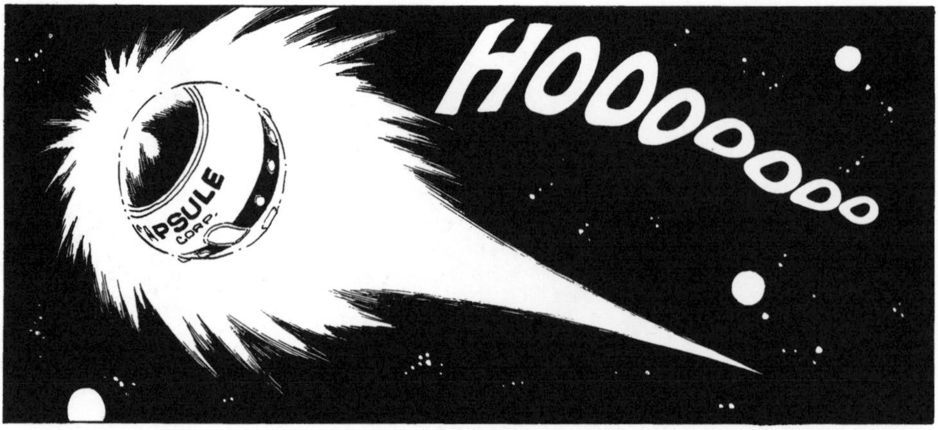
HOOOOOOOO
CAPSULE CORP.
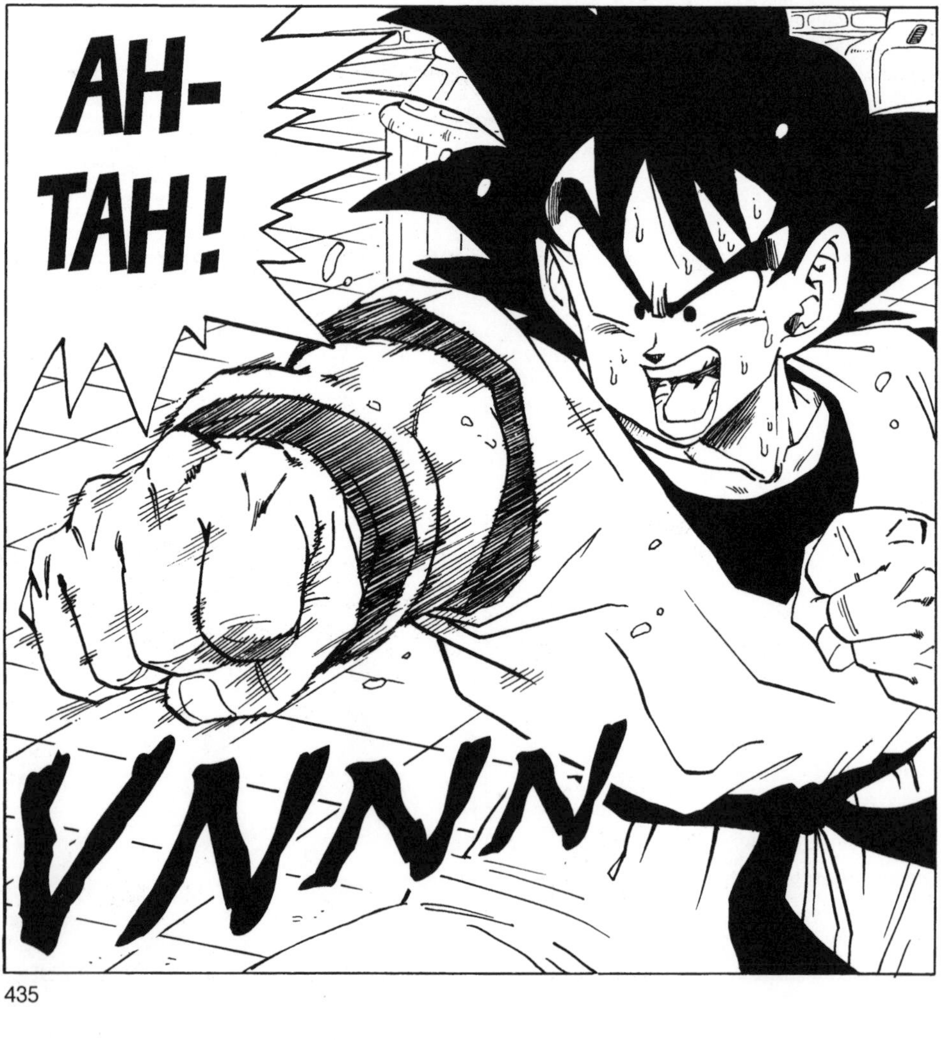
AH-TAH!
VNNN

# DBZ:65 • The Sixth Dragon Ball

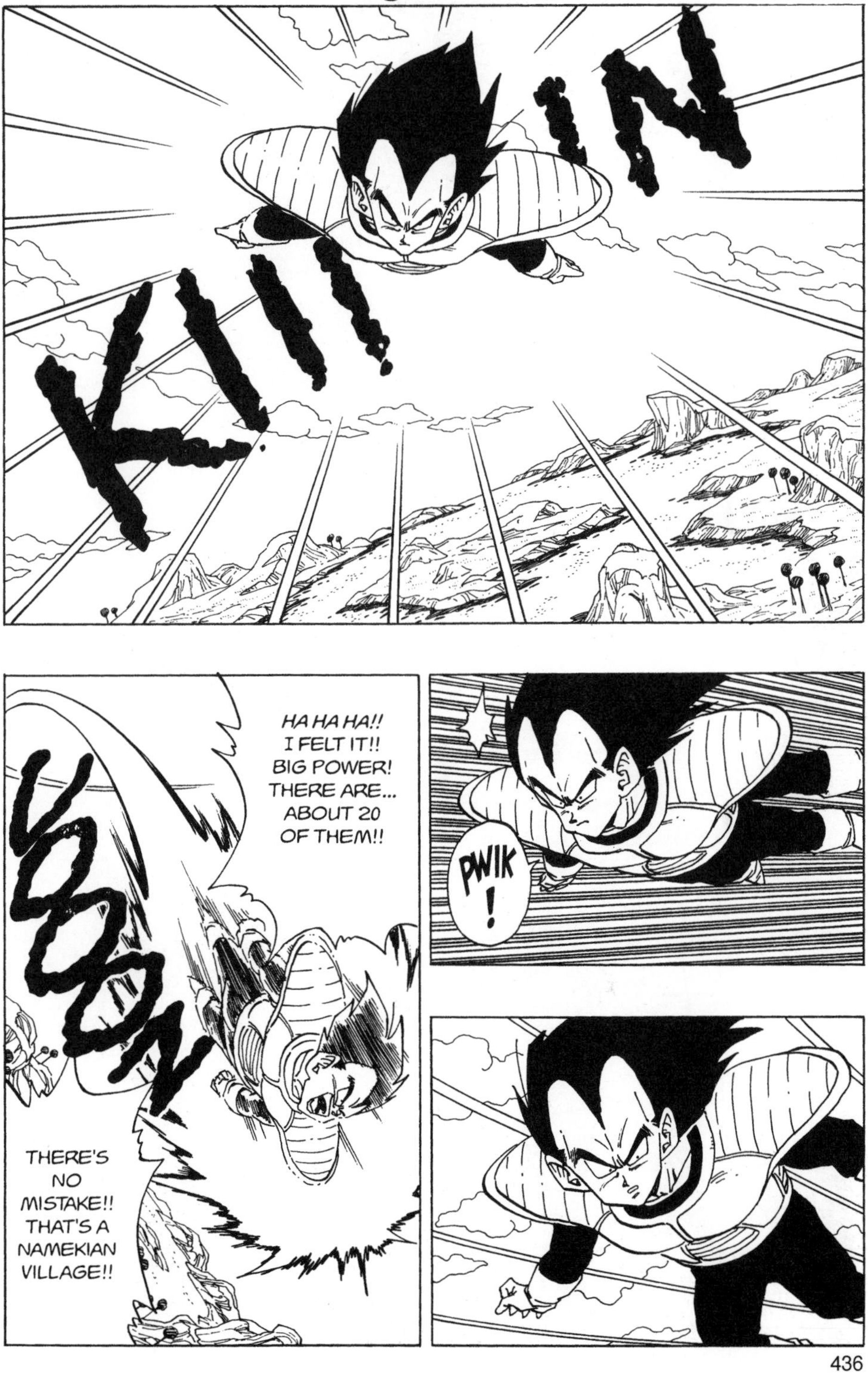
KIIIIN
PWIK!
HA HA HA!! I FELT IT!! BIG POWER! THERE ARE... ABOUT 20 OF THEM!!
THERE'S NO MISTAKE!! THAT'S A NAMEKIAN VILLAGE!!

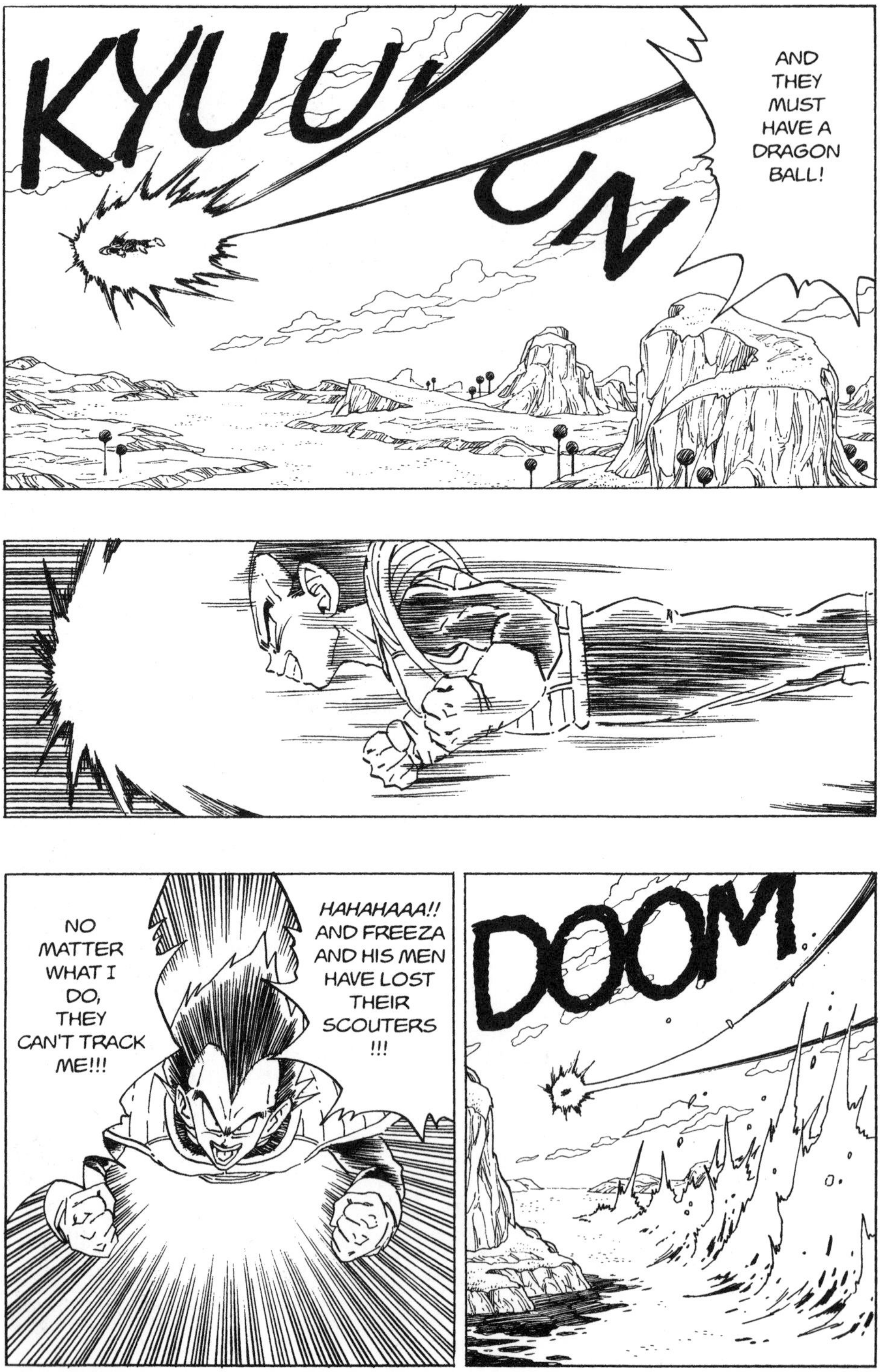
AND THEY MUST HAVE A DRAGON BALL!
KYUUUN
DOOM
*HAHAHAAA!!* AND FREEZA AND HIS MEN HAVE LOST THEIR SCOUTERS!!!
NO MATTER WHAT I DO, THEY CAN'T TRACK ME!!!

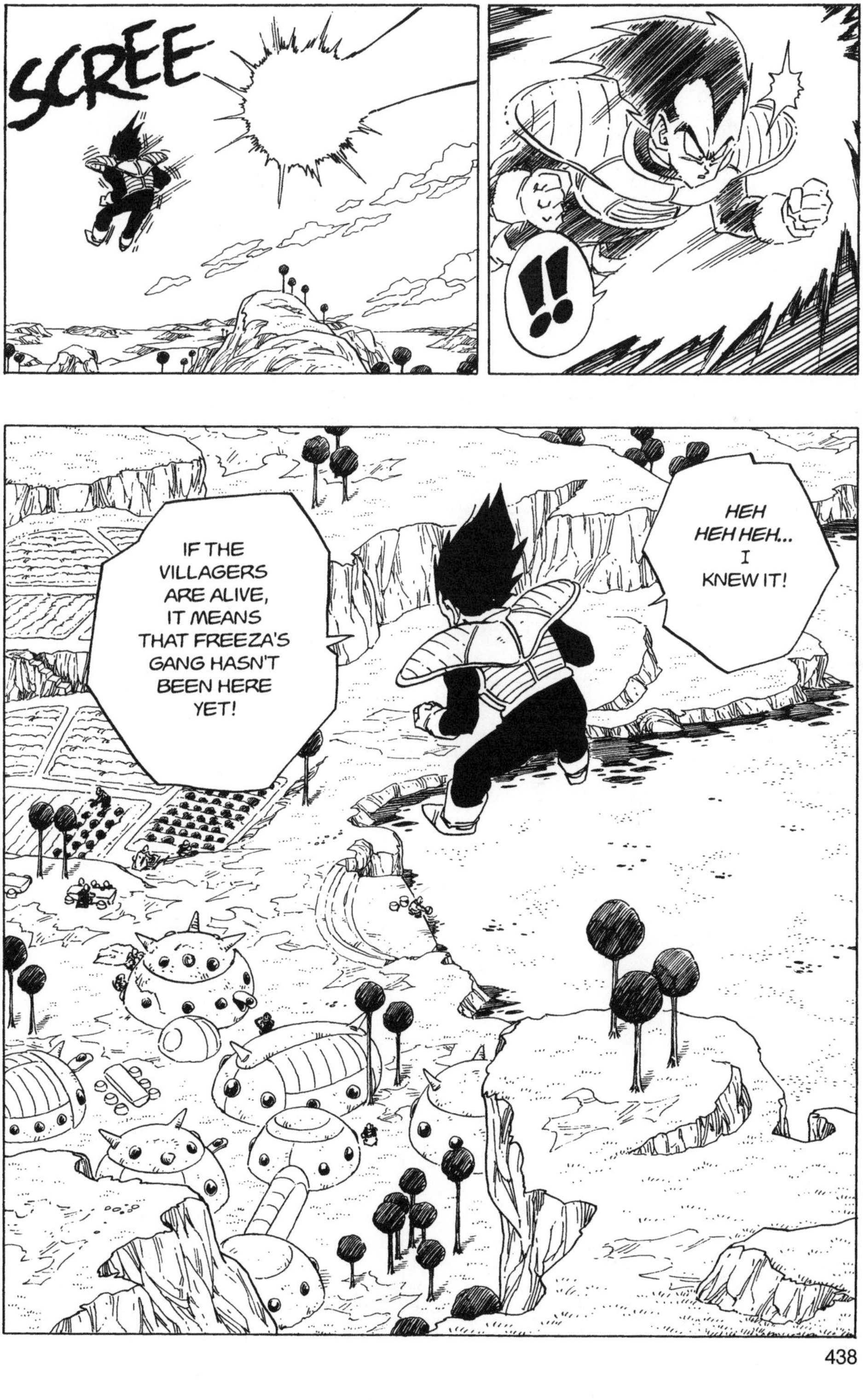
!!
SCREE
HEH HEH HEH... I KNEW IT!
IF THE VILLAGERS ARE ALIVE, IT MEANS THAT FREEZA'S GANG HASN'T BEEN HERE YET!

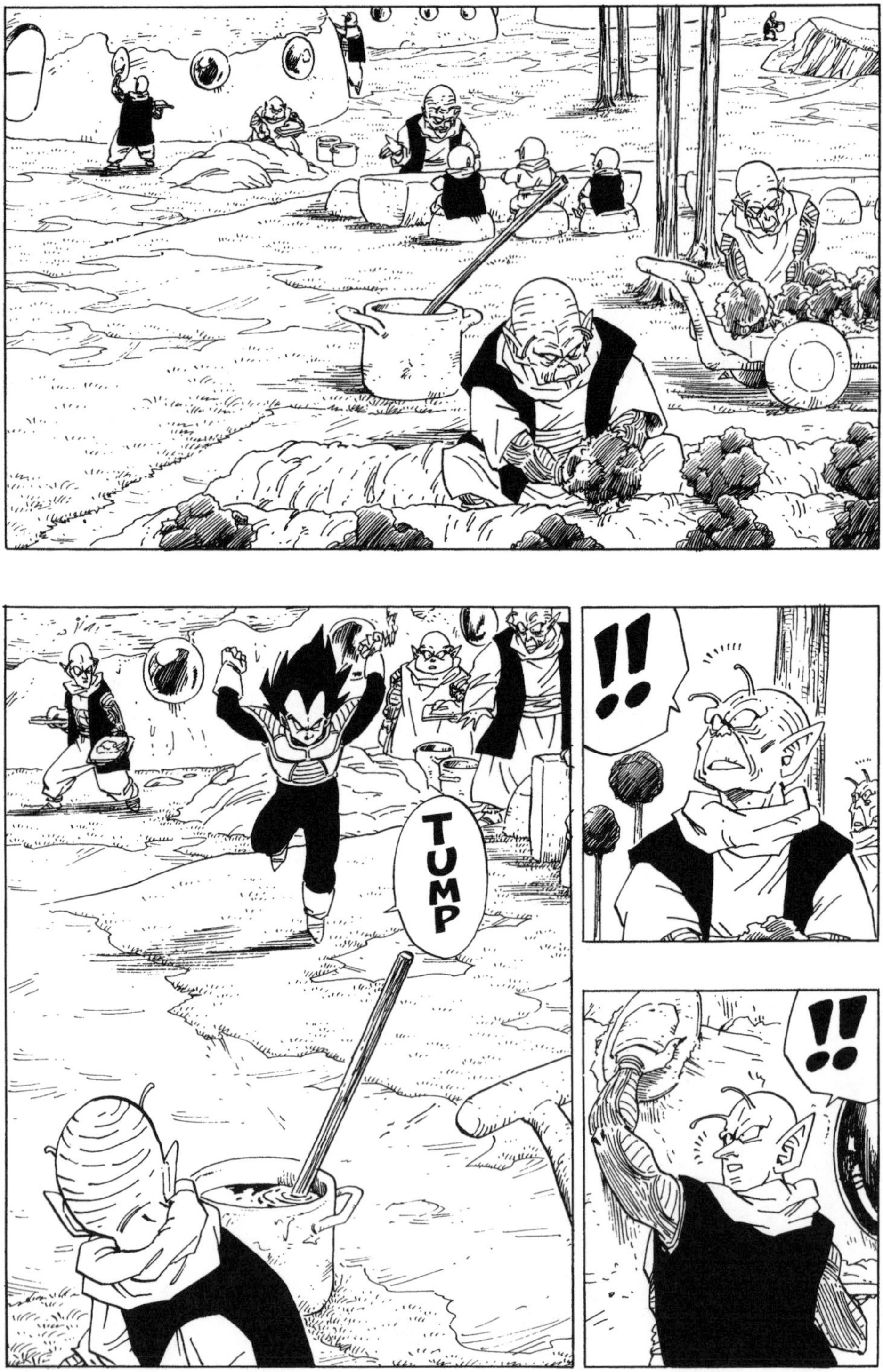
!!
!!
TUMP

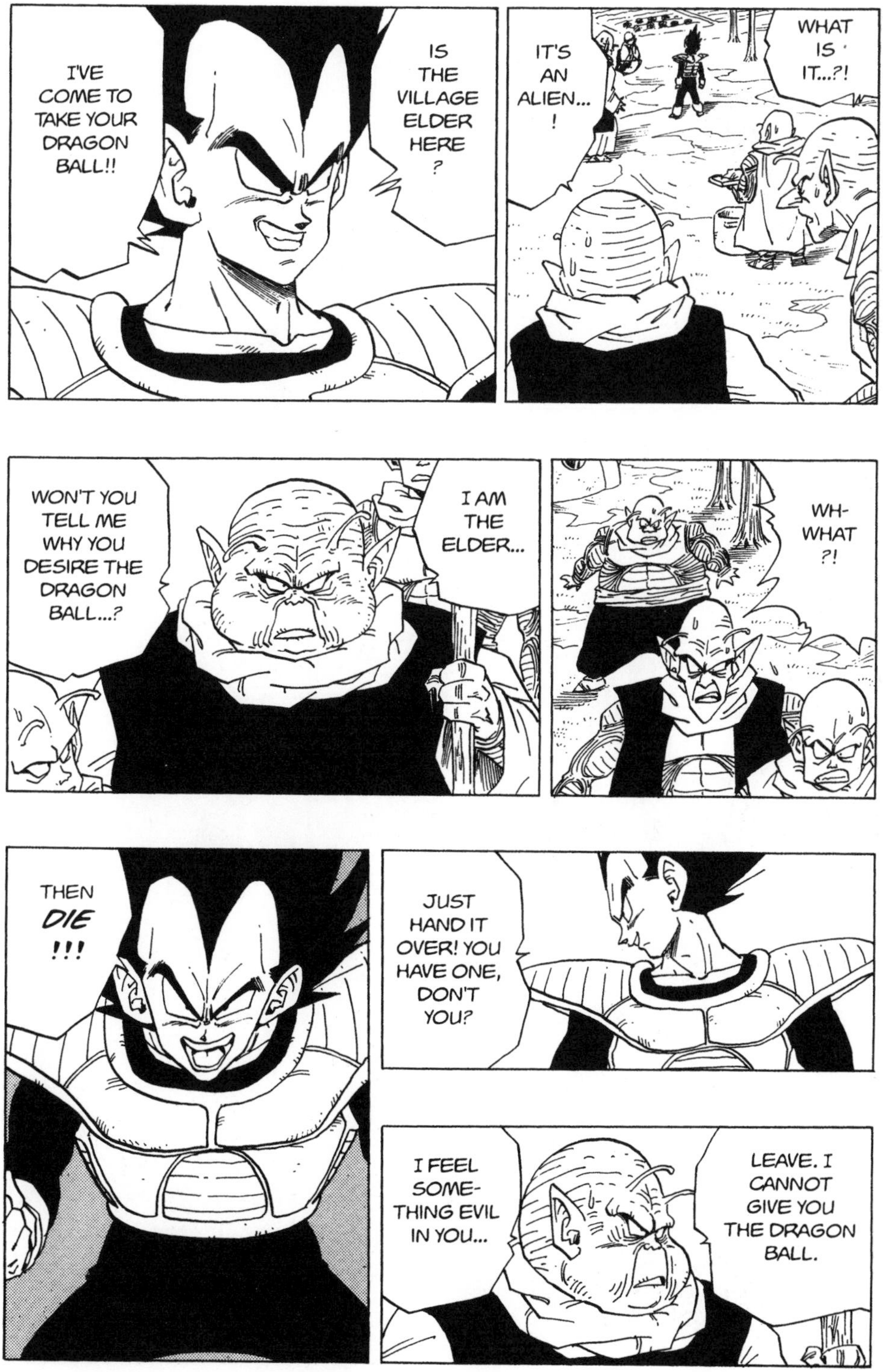
WHAT IS IT...?!
IT'S AN ALIEN...!
IS THE VILLAGE ELDER HERE?
I'VE COME TO TAKE YOUR DRAGON BALL!!
WH-WHAT?!
I AM THE ELDER...
WON'T YOU TELL ME WHY YOU DESIRE THE DRAGON BALL...?
JUST HAND IT OVER! YOU HAVE ONE, DON'T YOU?
LEAVE. I CANNOT GIVE YOU THE DRAGON BALL.
I FEEL SOME-THING EVIL IN YOU...
THEN *DIE*!!!

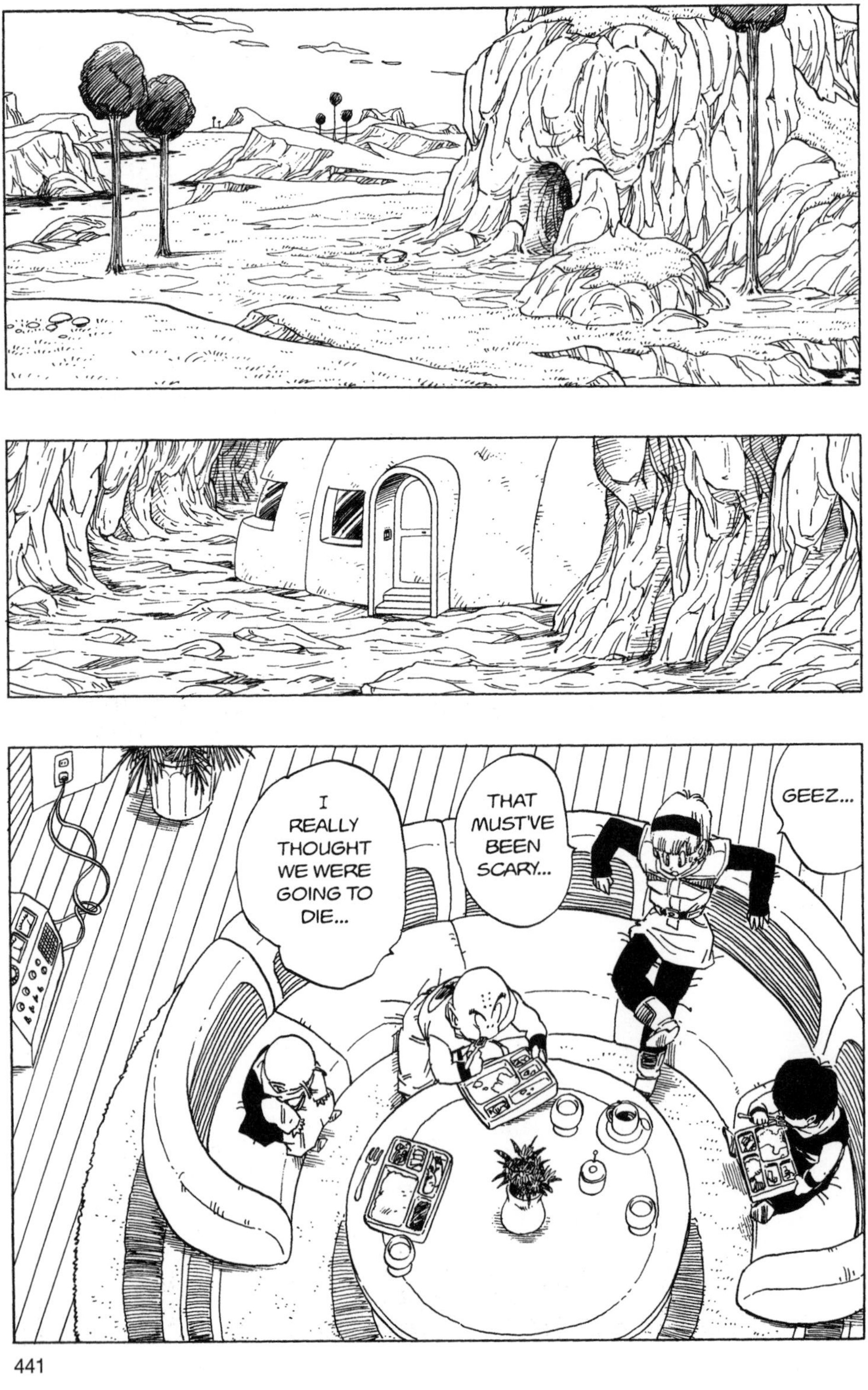
GEEZ...
THAT MUST'VE BEEN SCARY...
I REALLY THOUGHT WE WERE GOING TO DIE...

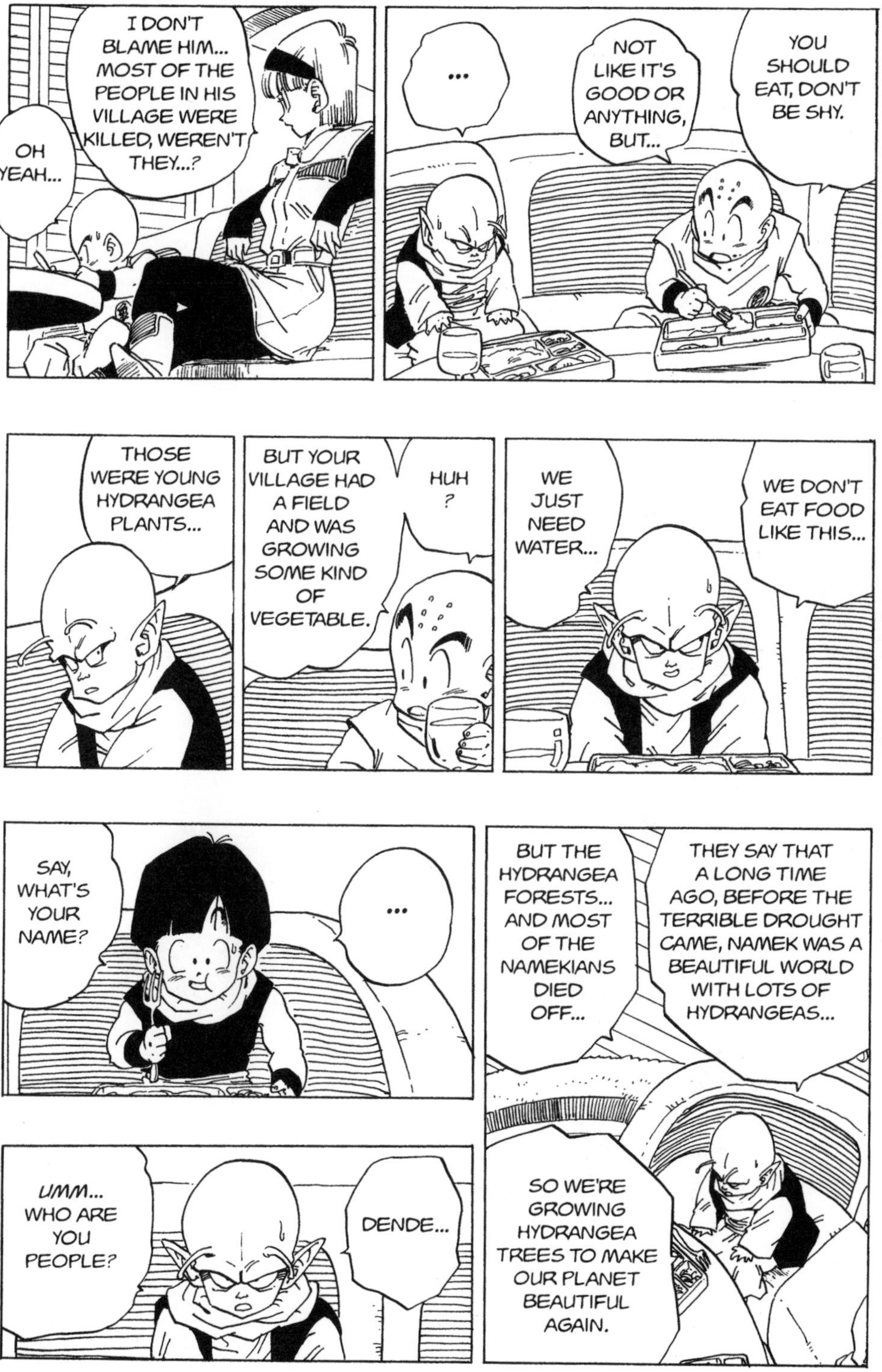
YOU SHOULD EAT, DON'T BE SHY.
NOT LIKE IT'S GOOD OR ANYTHING, BUT...
...
I DON'T BLAME HIM... MOST OF THE PEOPLE IN HIS VILLAGE WERE KILLED, WEREN'T THEY...?
OH YEAH...
WE DON'T EAT FOOD LIKE THIS...
WE JUST NEED WATER...
HUH ?
BUT YOUR VILLAGE HAD A FIELD AND WAS GROWING SOME KIND OF VEGETABLE.
THOSE WERE YOUNG HYDRANGEA PLANTS...
THEY SAY THAT A LONG TIME AGO, BEFORE THE TERRIBLE DROUGHT CAME, NAMEK WAS A BEAUTIFUL WORLD WITH LOTS OF HYDRANGEAS...
BUT THE HYDRANGEA FORESTS... AND MOST OF THE NAMEKIANS DIED OFF...
SO WE'RE GROWING HYDRANGEA TREES TO MAKE OUR PLANET BEAUTIFUL AGAIN.
...
SAY, WHAT'S YOUR NAME?
DENDE...
UMM... WHO ARE YOU PEOPLE?

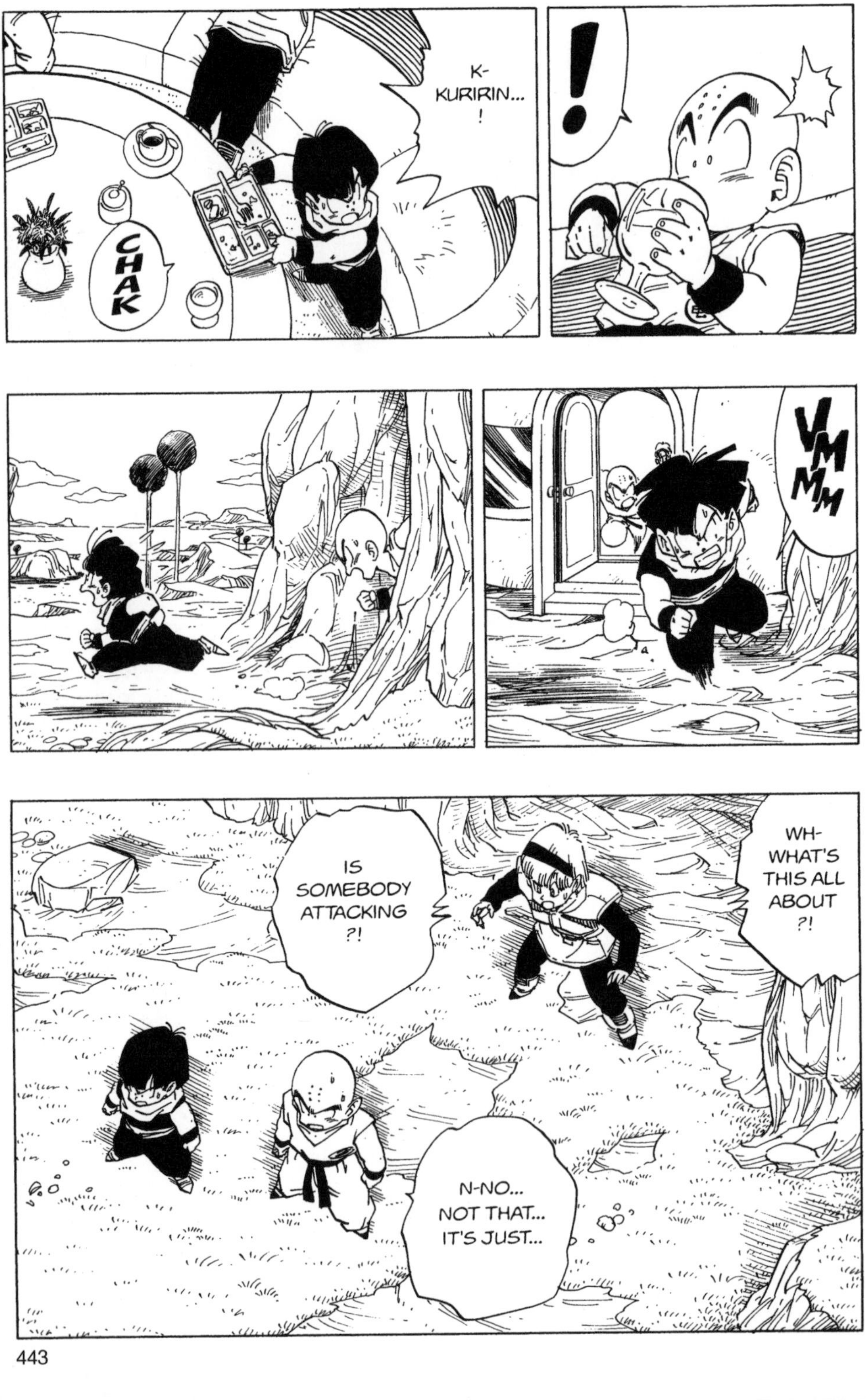
!
K-KURIRIN...!
CHAK
VMMM
WH-WHAT'S THIS ALL ABOUT?!
IS SOMEBODY ATTACKING?!
N-NO... NOT THAT... IT'S JUST...

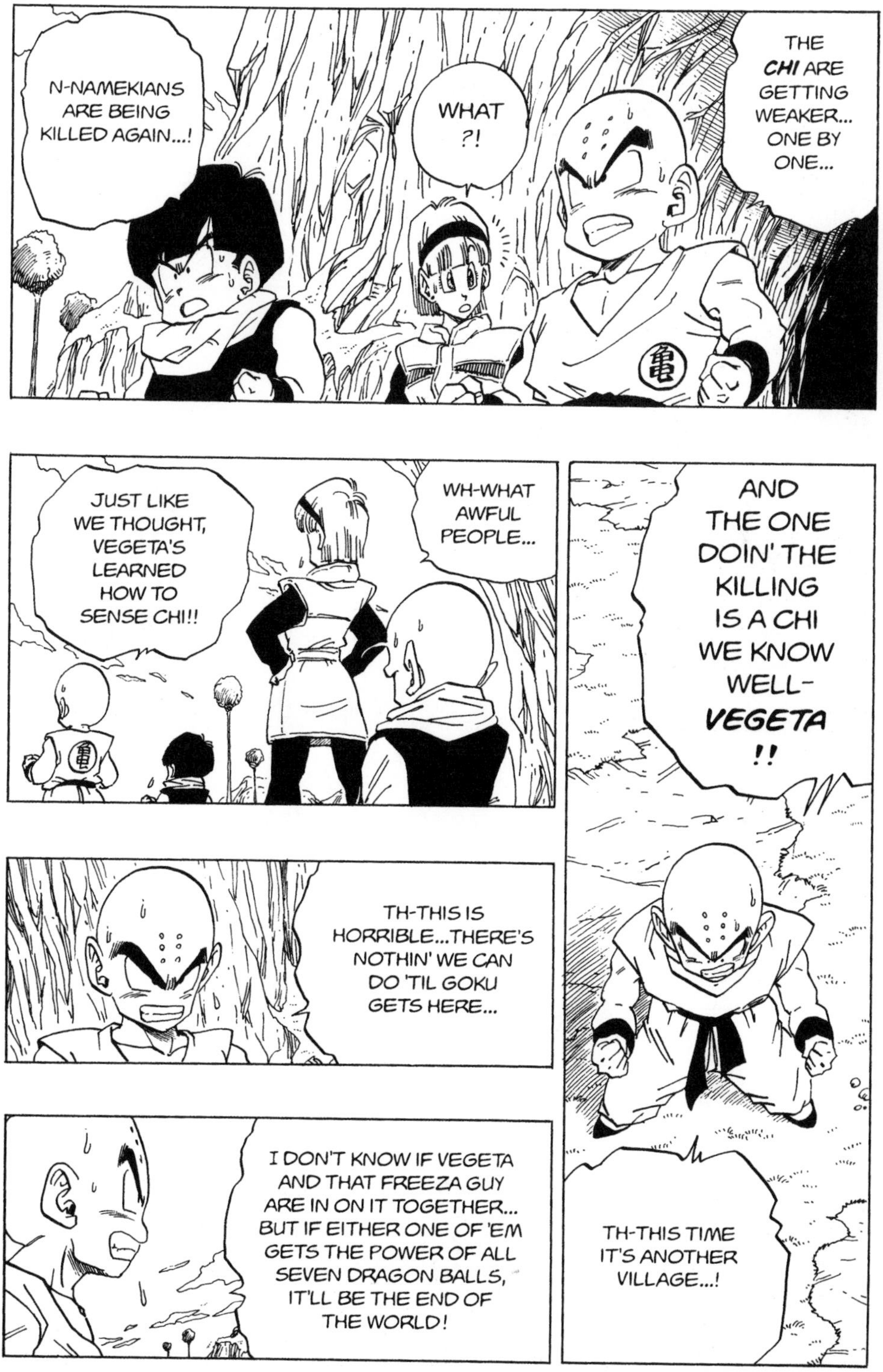
THE **CHI** ARE GETTING WEAKER... ONE BY ONE...
WHAT ?!
N-NAMEKIANS ARE BEING KILLED AGAIN...!
AND THE ONE DOIN' THE KILLING IS A CHI WE KNOW WELL- **VEGETA** !!
TH-THIS TIME IT'S ANOTHER VILLAGE...!
WH-WHAT AWFUL PEOPLE...
JUST LIKE WE THOUGHT, VEGETA'S LEARNED HOW TO SENSE CHI!!
TH-THIS IS HORRIBLE...THERE'S NOTHIN' WE CAN DO 'TIL GOKU GETS HERE...
I DON'T KNOW IF VEGETA AND THAT FREEZA GUY ARE IN ON IT TOGETHER... BUT IF EITHER ONE OF 'EM GETS THE POWER OF ALL SEVEN DRAGON BALLS, IT'LL BE THE END OF THE WORLD!

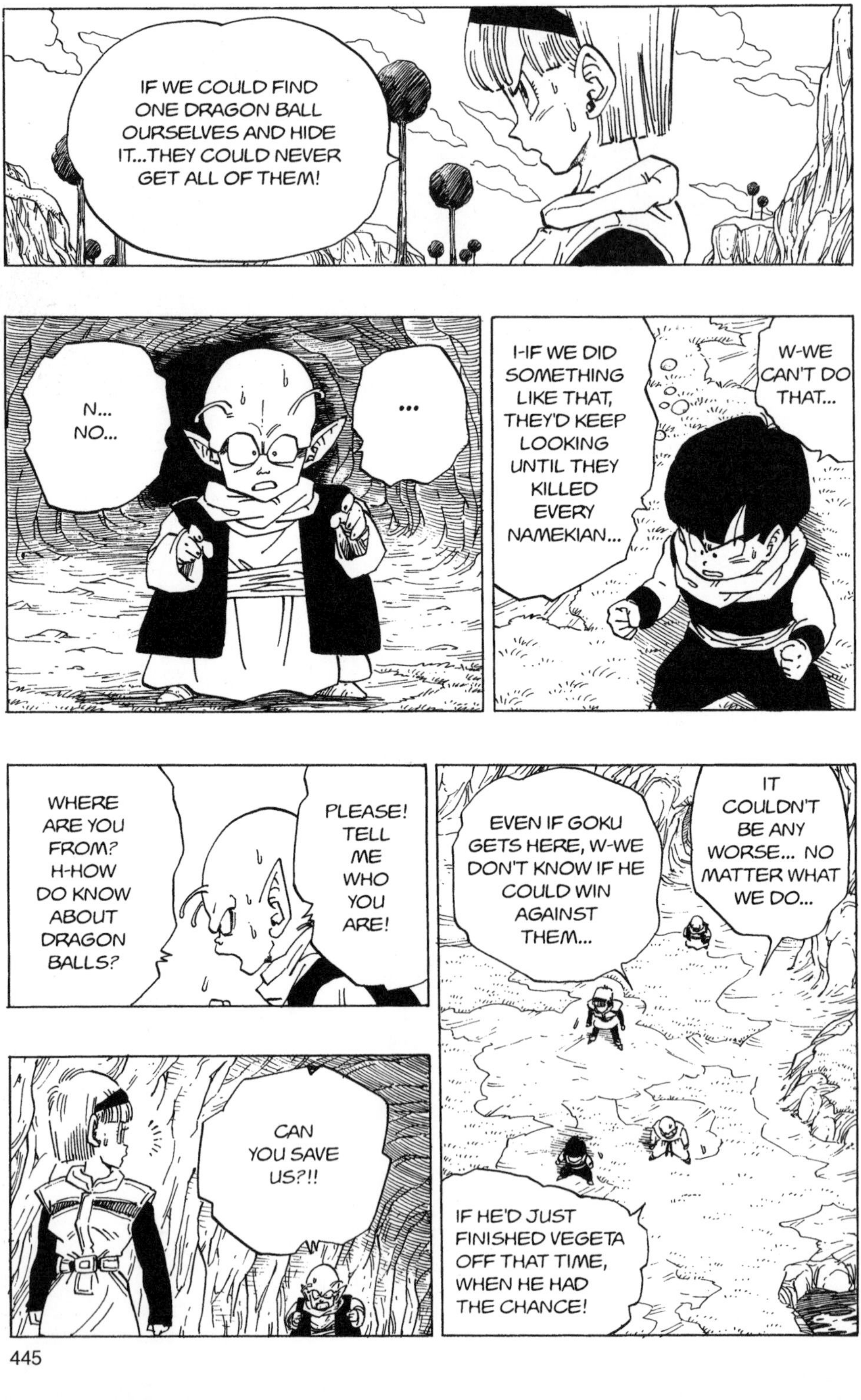
IF WE COULD FIND ONE DRAGON BALL OURSELVES AND HIDE IT...THEY COULD NEVER GET ALL OF THEM!
W-WE CAN'T DO THAT...
I-IF WE DID SOMETHING LIKE THAT, THEY'D KEEP LOOKING UNTIL THEY KILLED EVERY NAMEKIAN...
...
N... NO...
IT COULDN'T BE ANY WORSE... NO MATTER WHAT WE DO...
EVEN IF GOKU GETS HERE, W-WE DON'T KNOW IF HE COULD WIN AGAINST THEM...
IF HE'D JUST FINISHED VEGETA OFF THAT TIME, WHEN HE HAD THE CHANCE!
PLEASE! TELL ME WHO YOU ARE!
WHERE ARE YOU FROM? H-HOW DO KNOW ABOUT DRAGON BALLS?
CAN YOU SAVE US?!!

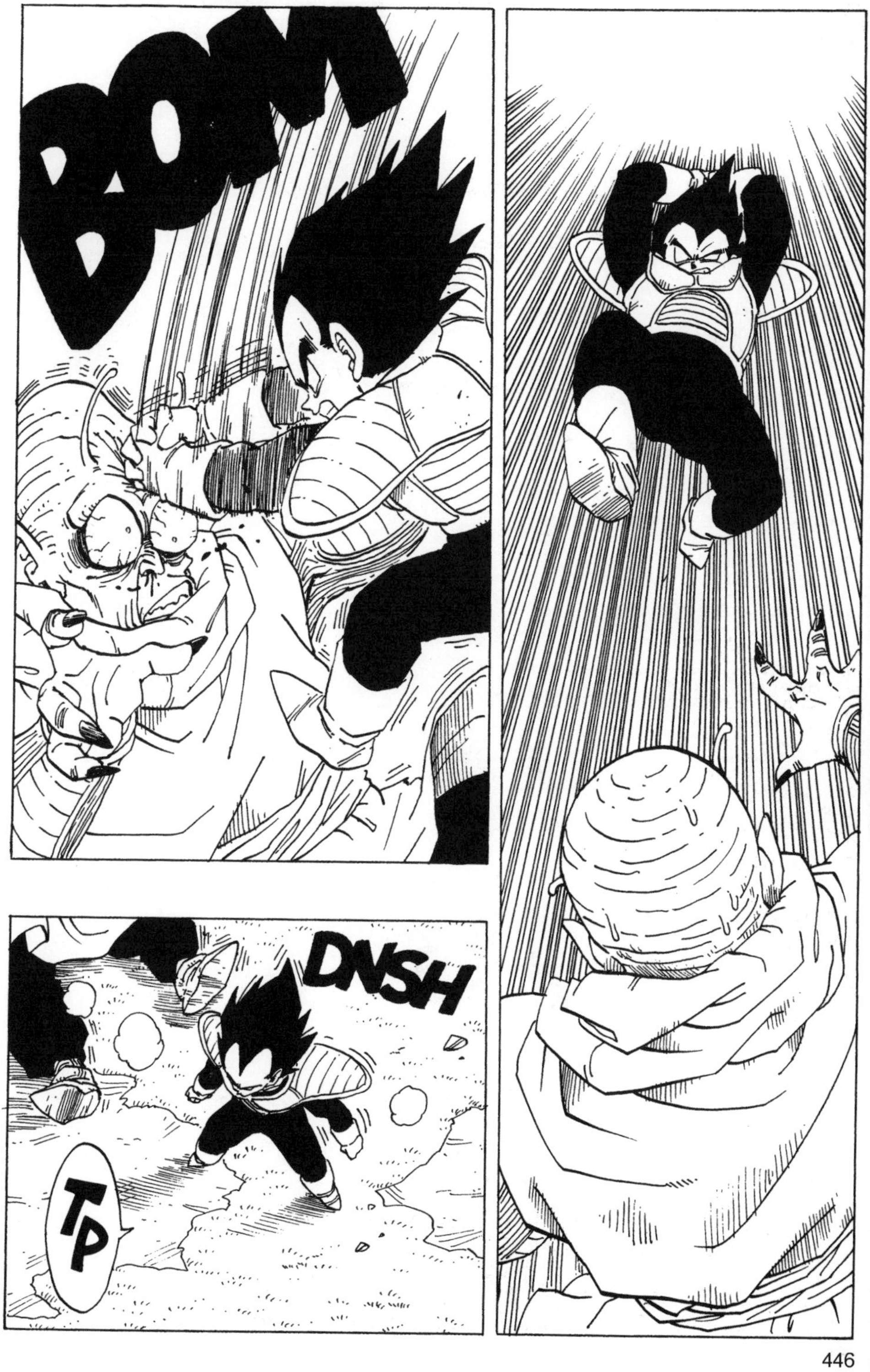
BOOM
DNSH
TP

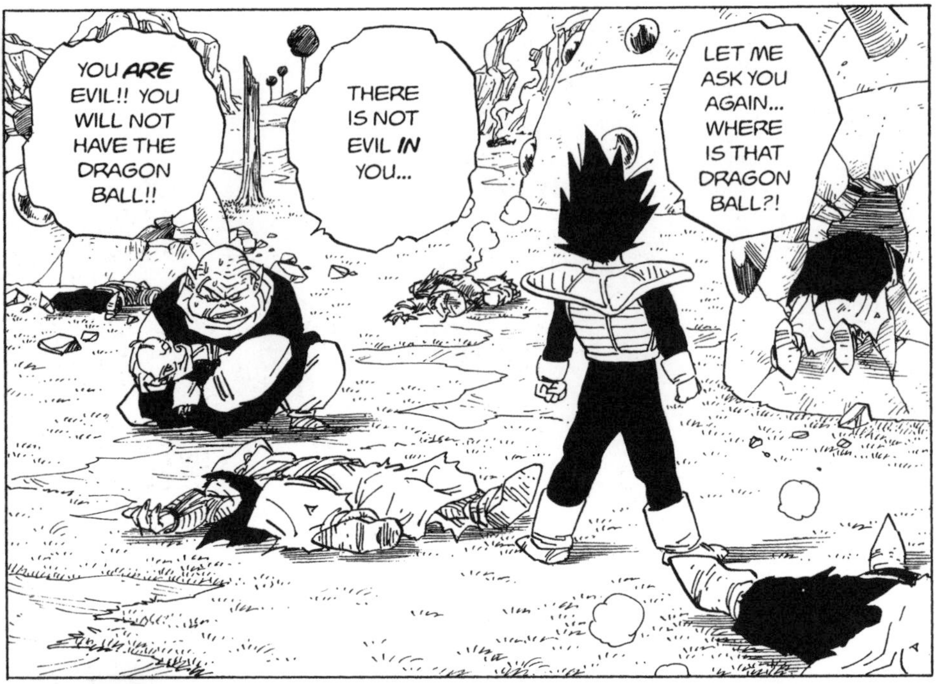
LET ME ASK YOU AGAIN... WHERE IS THAT DRAGON BALL?!
THERE IS NOT EVIL *IN* YOU...
YOU *ARE* EVIL!! YOU WILL NOT HAVE THE DRAGON BALL!!

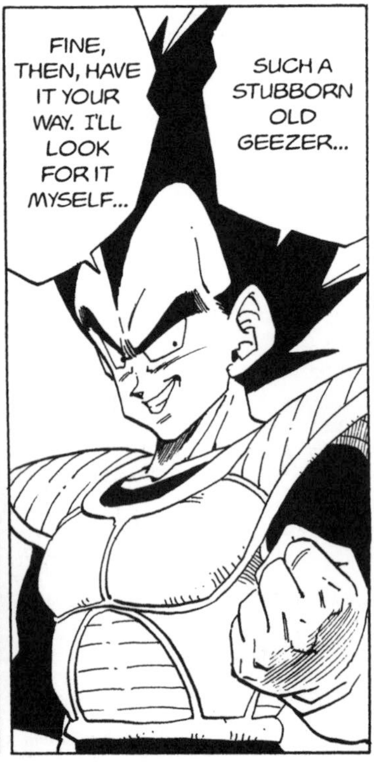
SUCH A STUBBORN OLD GEEZER...
FINE, THEN, HAVE IT YOUR WAY. I'LL LOOK FOR IT MYSELF...

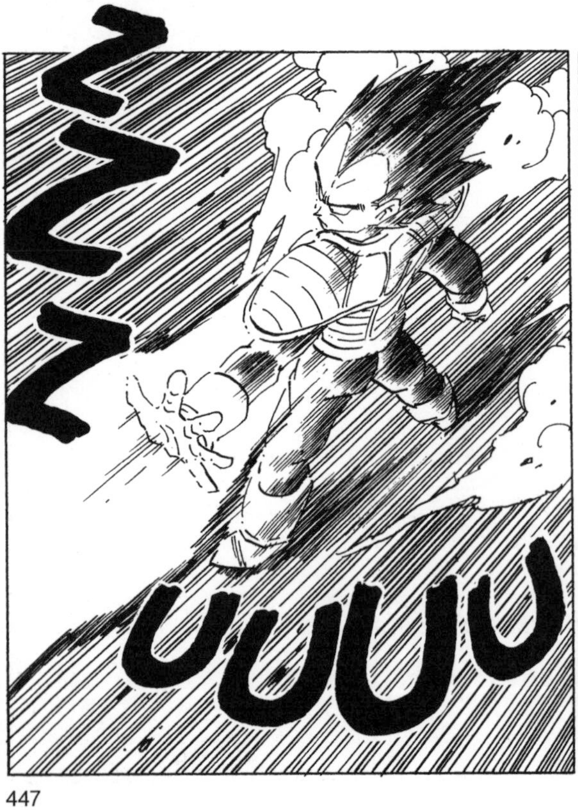
ZUUUUU

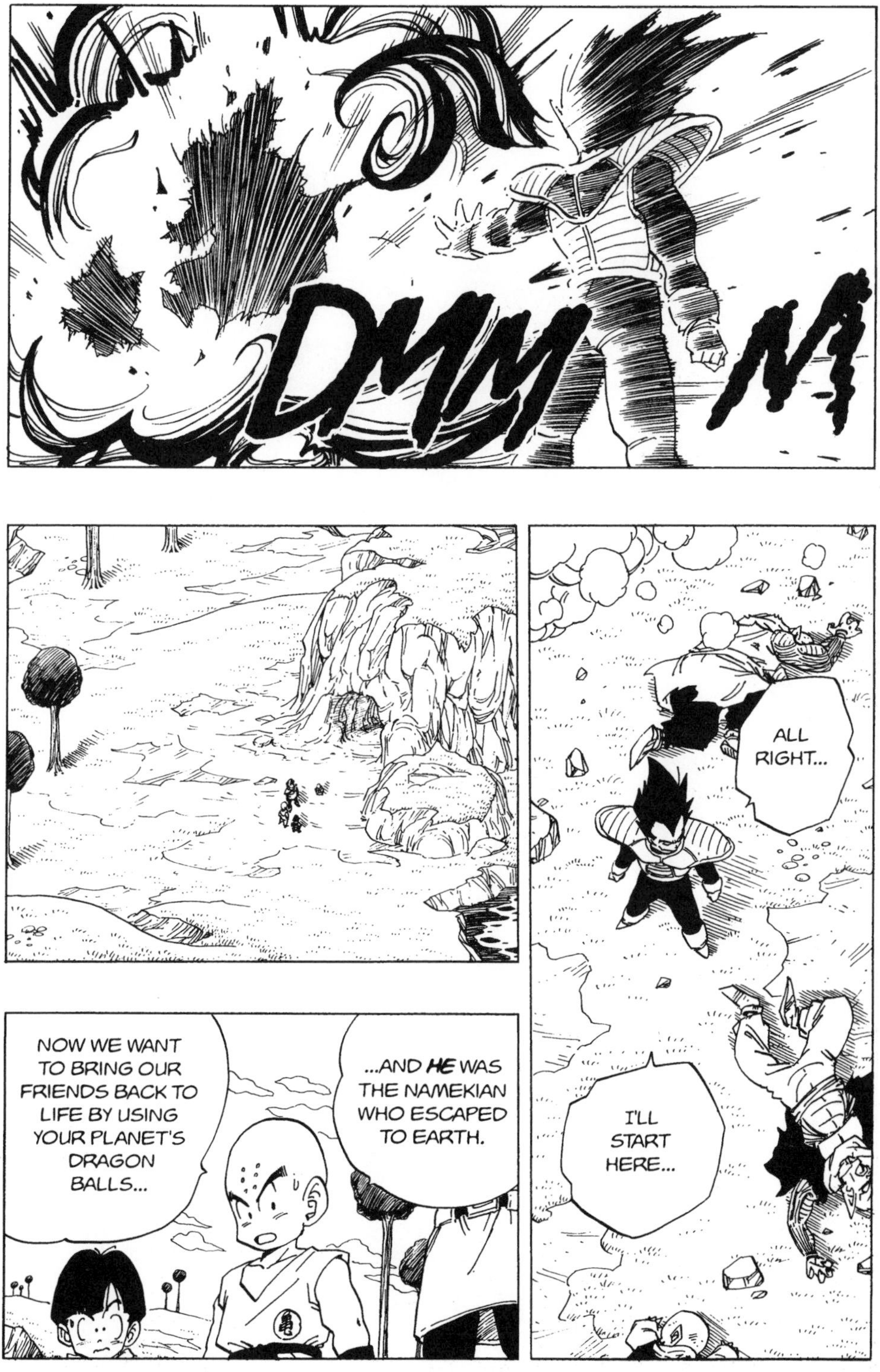
DMMM
ALL RIGHT...
I'LL START HERE...
...AND *HE* WAS THE NAMEKIAN WHO ESCAPED TO EARTH.
NOW WE WANT TO BRING OUR FRIENDS BACK TO LIFE BY USING YOUR PLANET'S DRAGON BALLS...

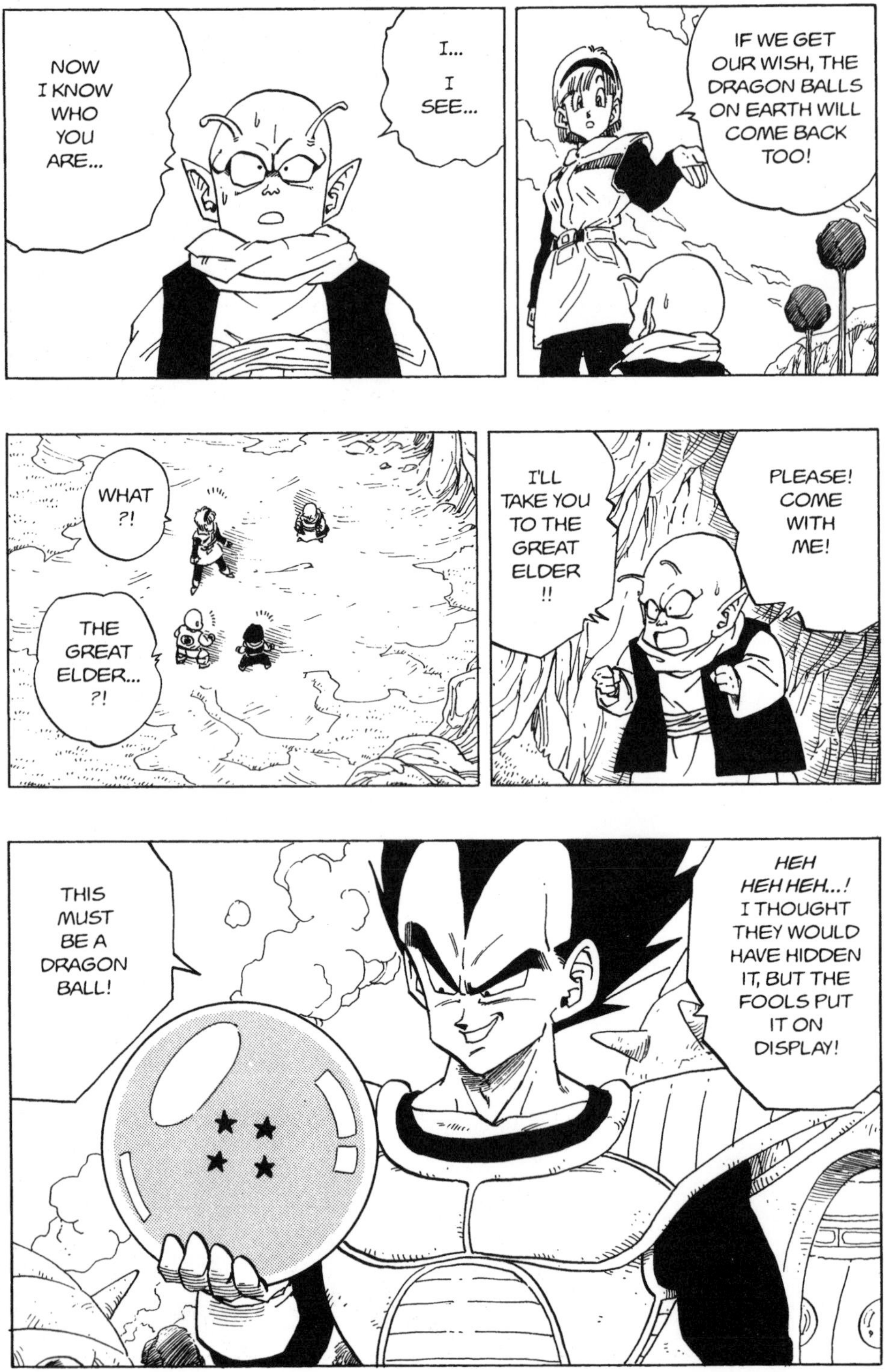
IF WE GET OUR WISH, THE DRAGON BALLS ON EARTH WILL COME BACK TOO!
I... I SEE...
NOW I KNOW WHO YOU ARE...
PLEASE! COME WITH ME!
I'LL TAKE YOU TO THE GREAT ELDER !!
WHAT ?!
THE GREAT ELDER... ?!
HEH HEH HEH...! I THOUGHT THEY WOULD HAVE HIDDEN IT, BUT THE FOOLS PUT IT ON DISPLAY!
THIS MUST BE A DRAGON BALL!

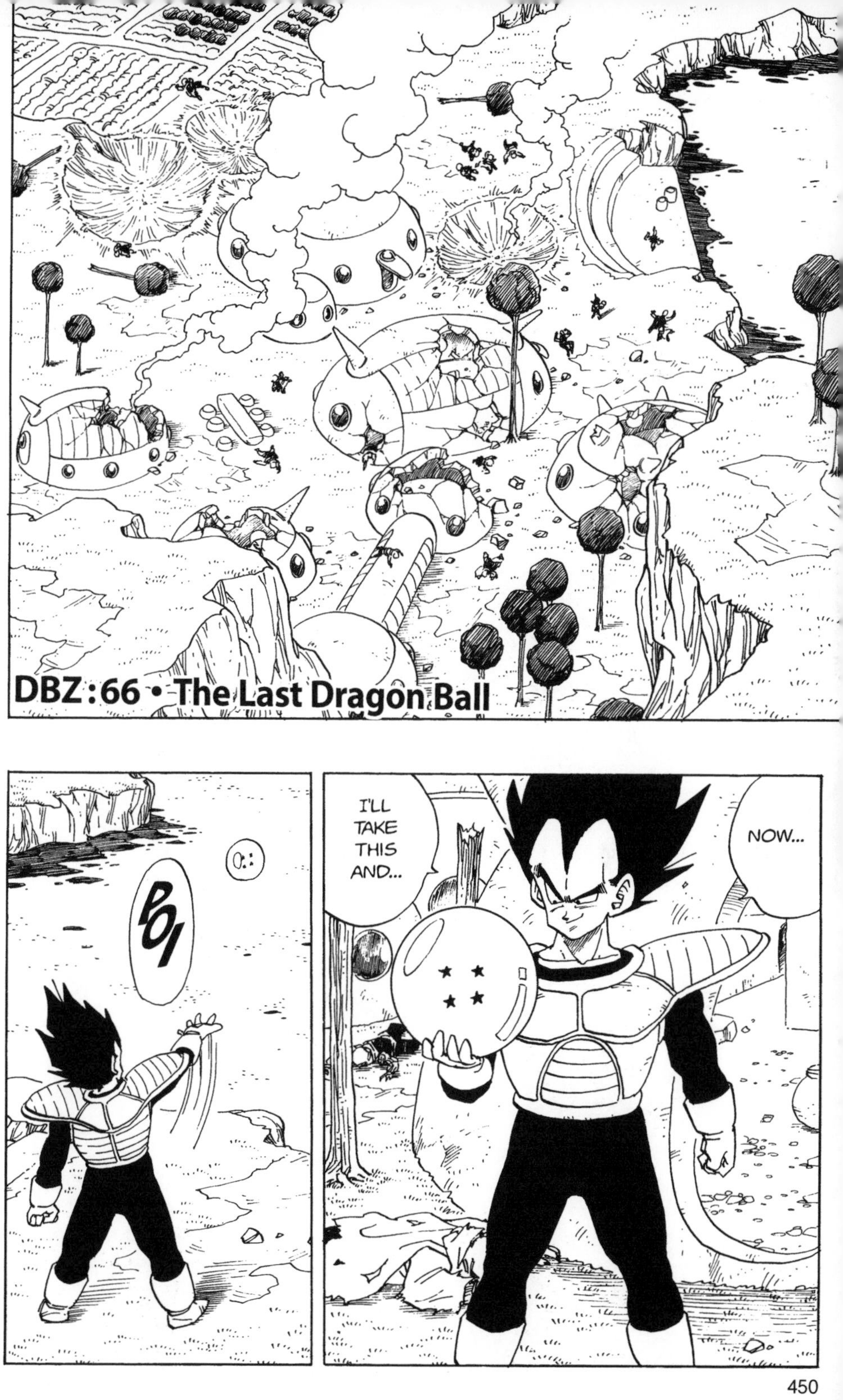
DBZ:66 • The Last Dragon Ball
NOW...
I'LL TAKE THIS AND...
POI

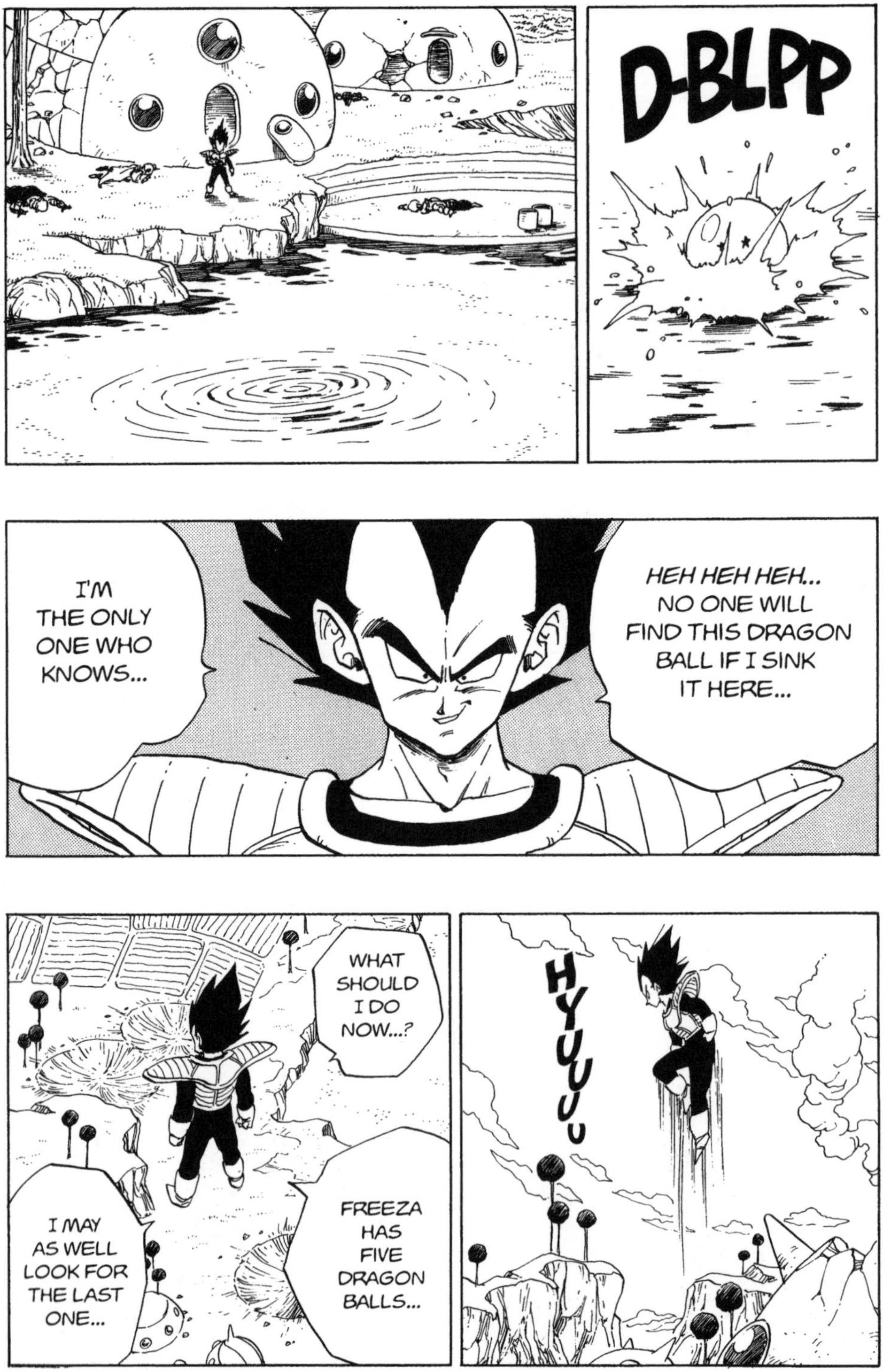
D-BLPP
HEH HEH HEH... NO ONE WILL FIND THIS DRAGON BALL IF I SINK IT HERE...
I'M THE ONLY ONE WHO KNOWS...
HYUUUU
WHAT SHOULD I DO NOW...?
FREEZA HAS FIVE DRAGON BALLS...
I MAY AS WELL LOOK FOR THE LAST ONE...

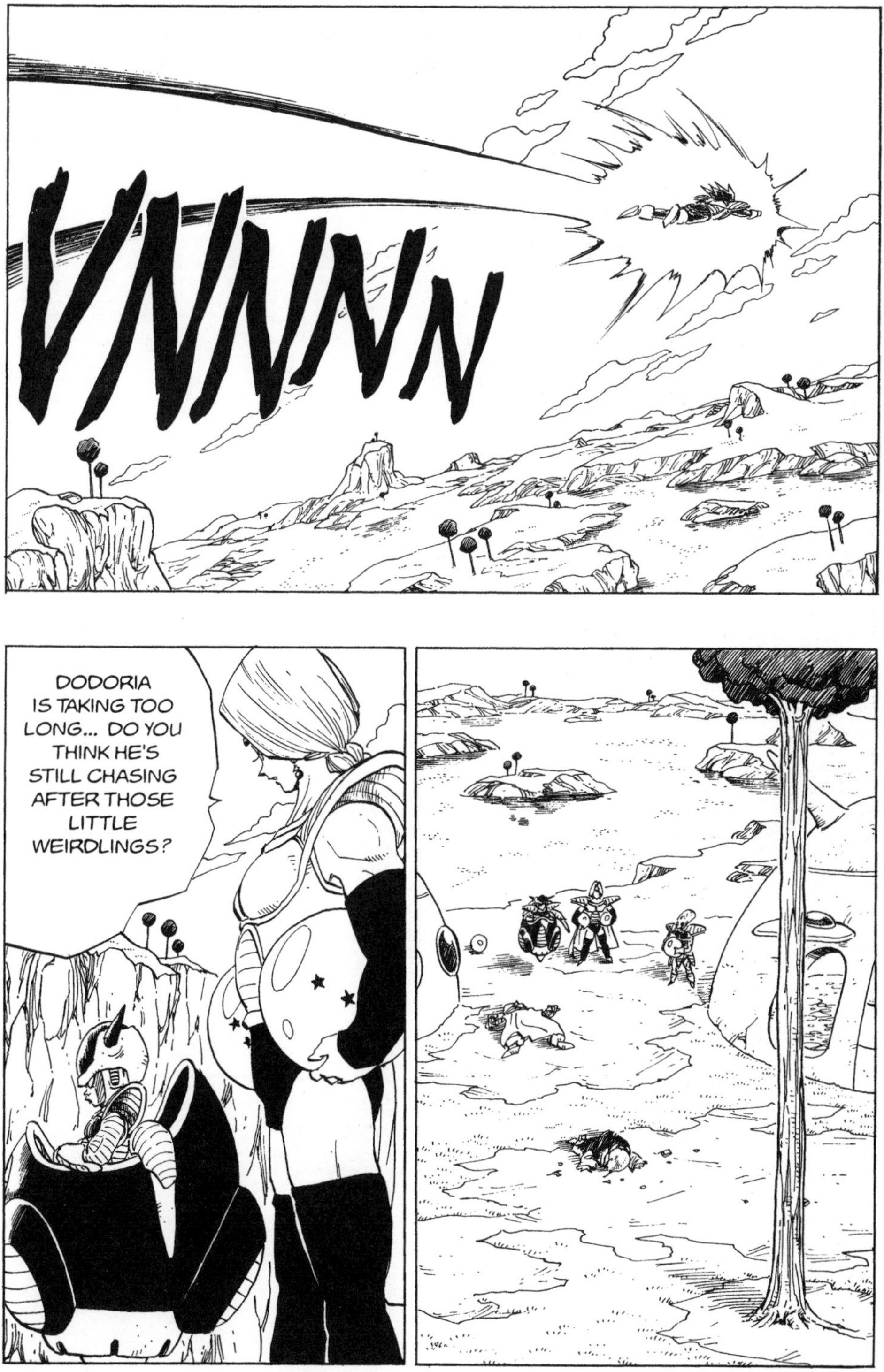
VNNNN
DODORIA IS TAKING TOO LONG... DO YOU THINK HE'S STILL CHASING AFTER THOSE LITTLE WEIRDLINGS?

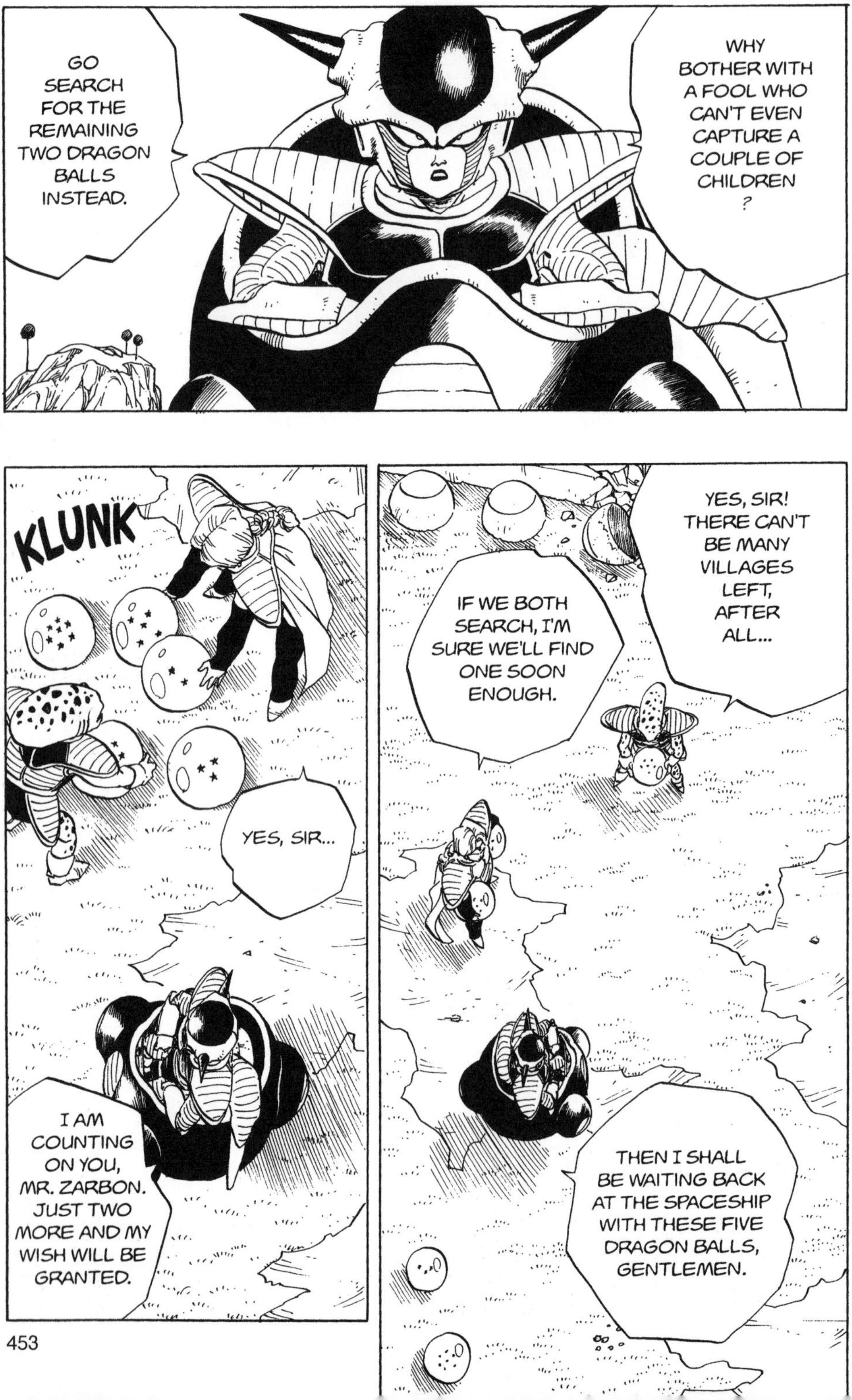
WHY BOTHER WITH A FOOL WHO CAN'T EVEN CAPTURE A COUPLE OF CHILDREN ?
GO SEARCH FOR THE REMAINING TWO DRAGON BALLS INSTEAD.
YES, SIR! THERE CAN'T BE MANY VILLAGES LEFT, AFTER ALL...
IF WE BOTH SEARCH, I'M SURE WE'LL FIND ONE SOON ENOUGH.
THEN I SHALL BE WAITING BACK AT THE SPACESHIP WITH THESE FIVE DRAGON BALLS, GENTLEMEN.
KLUNK
YES, SIR...
I AM COUNTING ON YOU, MR. ZARBON. JUST TWO MORE AND MY WISH WILL BE GRANTED.

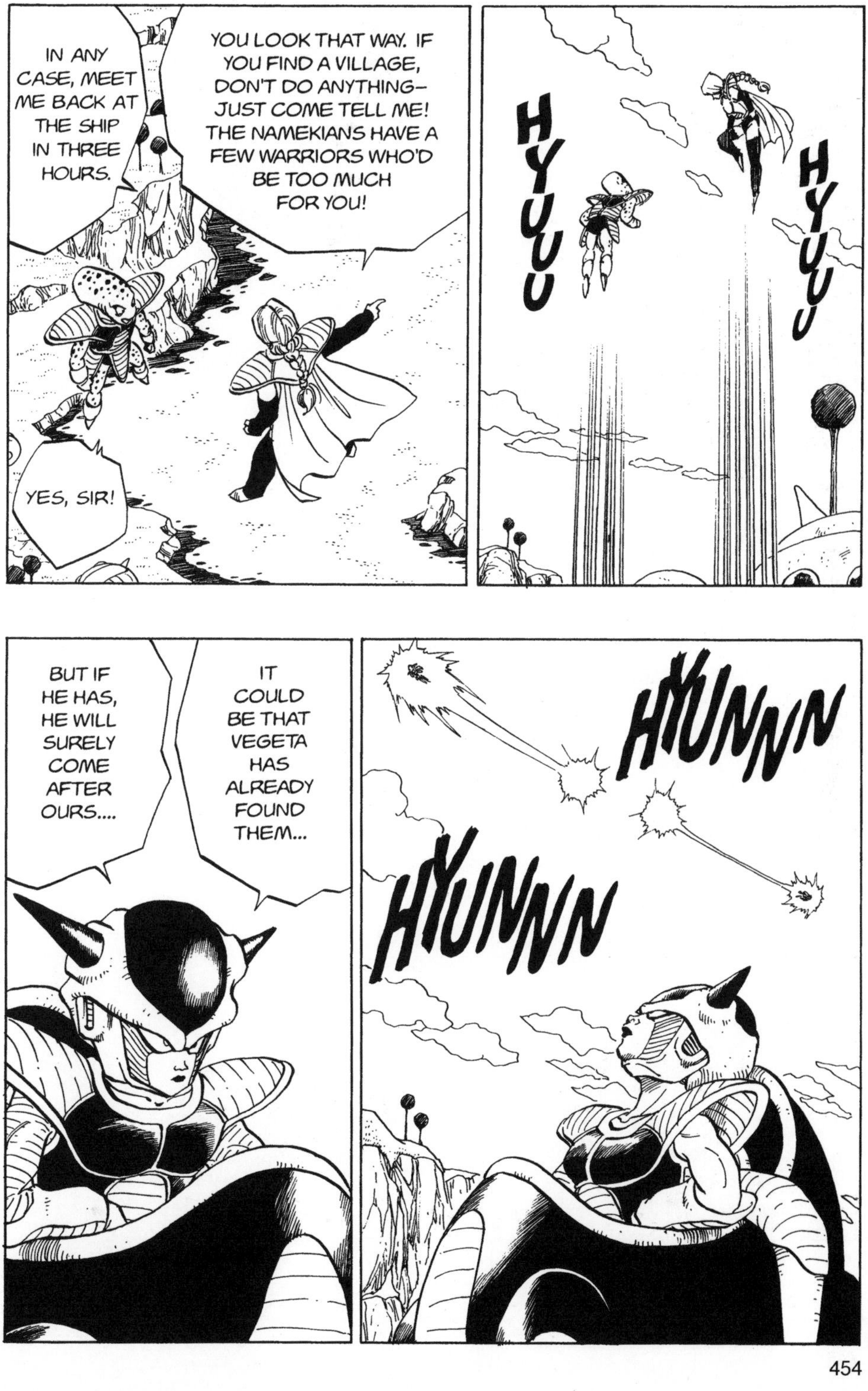
HYUUU
HYUUU
YOU LOOK THAT WAY. IF YOU FIND A VILLAGE, DON'T DO ANYTHING— JUST COME TELL ME! THE NAMEKIANS HAVE A FEW WARRIORS WHO'D BE TOO MUCH FOR YOU!
IN ANY CASE, MEET ME BACK AT THE SHIP IN THREE HOURS.
YES, SIR!
HYUNNN
HYUNNN
IT COULD BE THAT VEGETA HAS ALREADY FOUND THEM...
BUT IF HE HAS, HE WILL SURELY COME AFTER OURS....

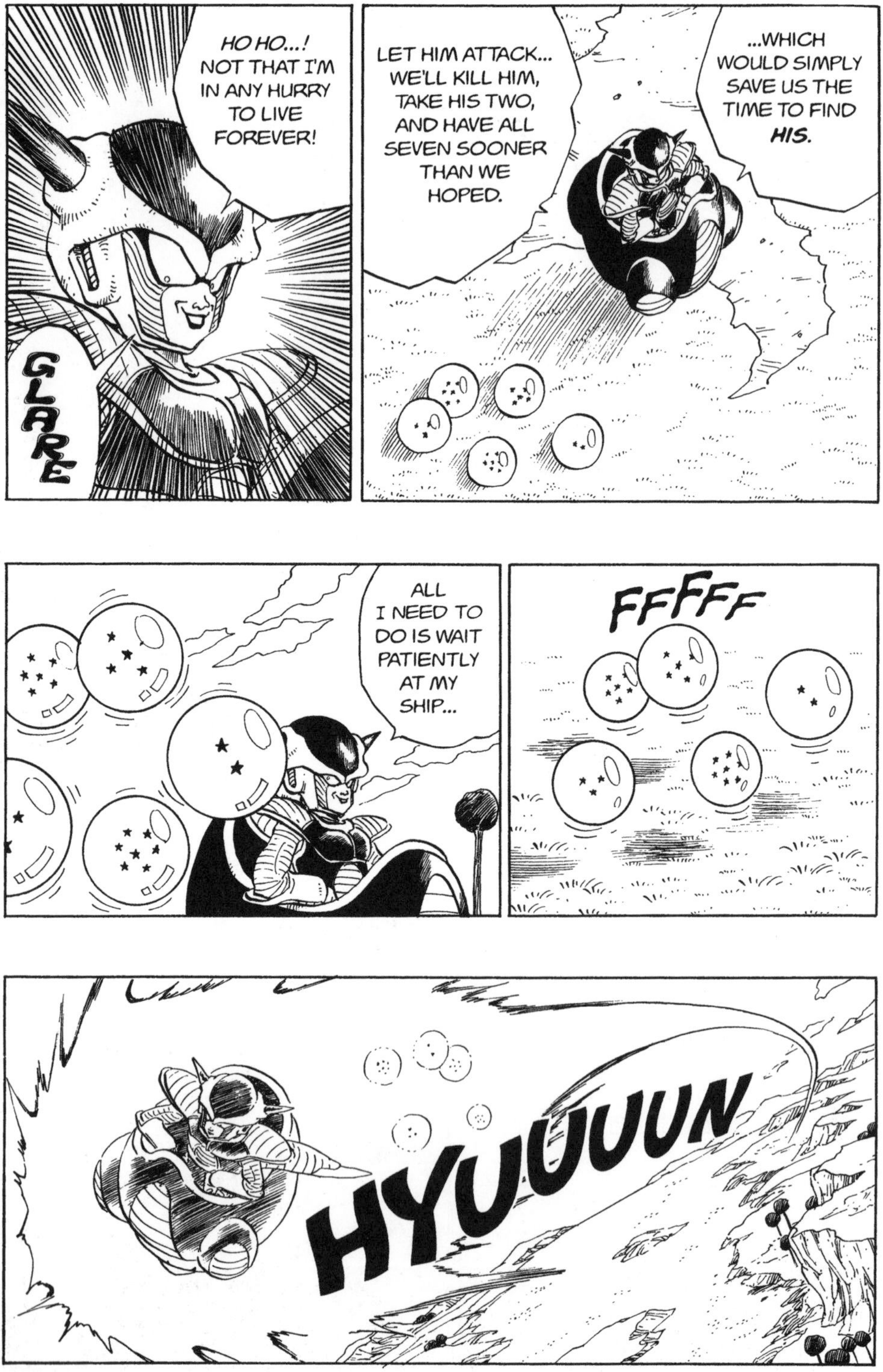
LET HIM ATTACK... WE'LL KILL HIM, TAKE HIS TWO, AND HAVE ALL SEVEN SOONER THAN WE HOPED.
...WHICH WOULD SIMPLY SAVE US THE TIME TO FIND ***HIS.***
*HO HO...!* NOT THAT I'M IN ANY HURRY TO LIVE FOREVER!
GLARE
FFFFF
ALL I NEED TO DO IS WAIT PATIENTLY AT MY SHIP...
HYUUUUN

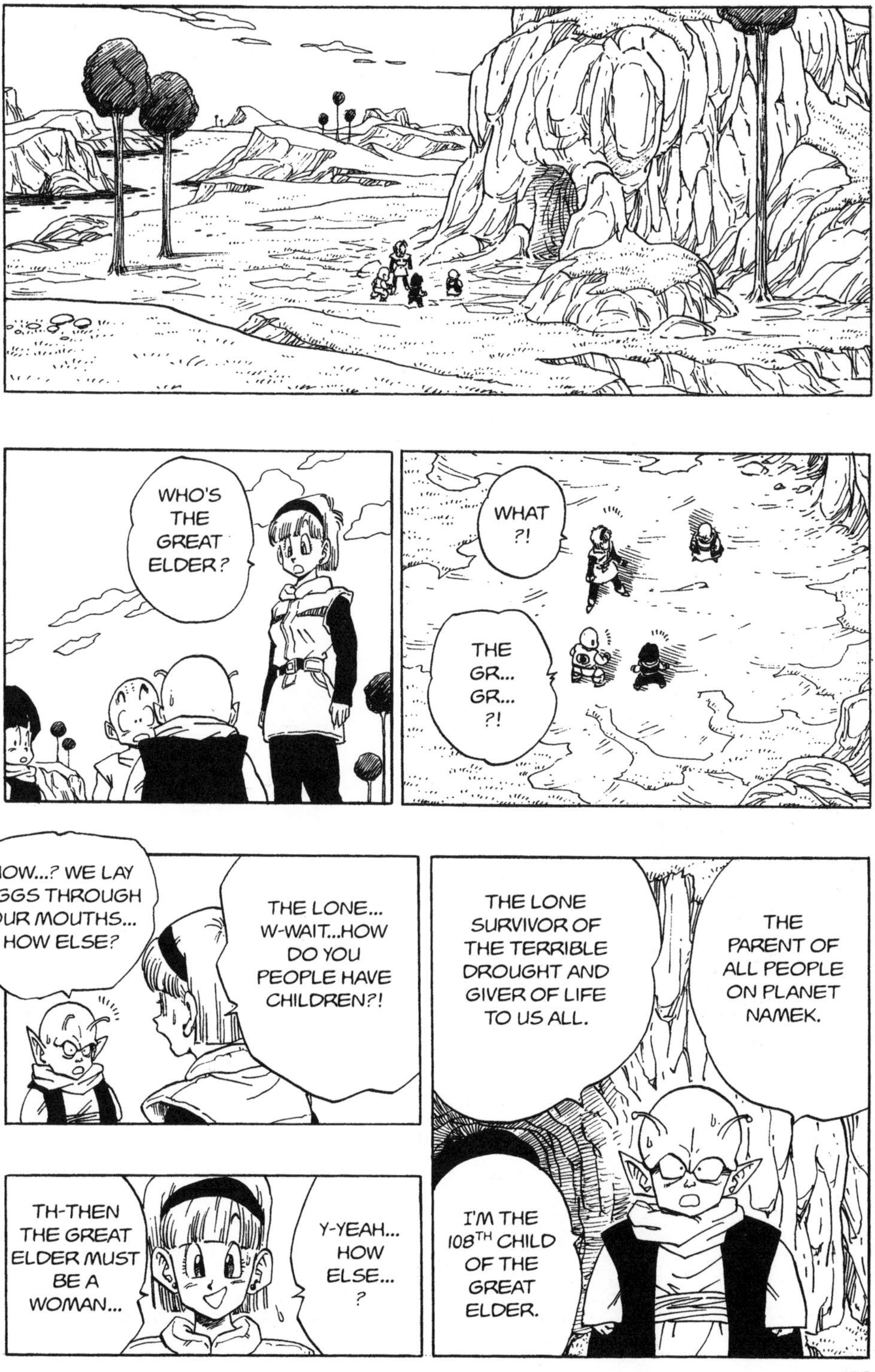
WHAT?!
THE GR... GR...?!
WHO'S THE GREAT ELDER?
THE PARENT OF ALL PEOPLE ON PLANET NAMEK.
THE LONE SURVIVOR OF THE TERRIBLE DROUGHT AND GIVER OF LIFE TO US ALL.
I'M THE 108TH CHILD OF THE GREAT ELDER.
THE LONE... W-WAIT...HOW DO YOU PEOPLE HAVE CHILDREN?!
HOW...? WE LAY EGGS THROUGH OUR MOUTHS... HOW ELSE?
TH-THEN THE GREAT ELDER MUST BE A WOMAN...
Y-YEAH... HOW ELSE...?

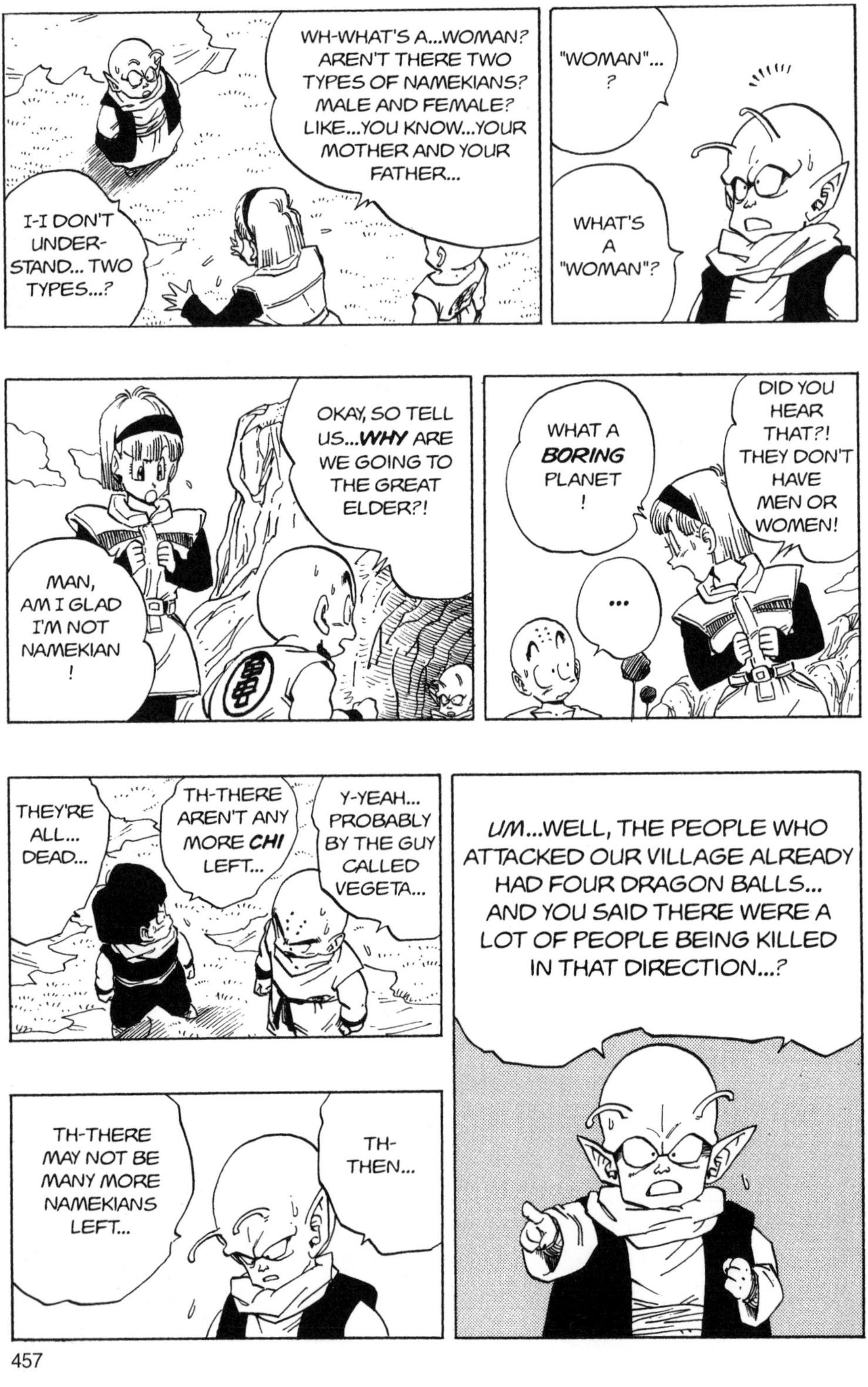
"WOMAN"... ?
WHAT'S A "WOMAN"?
WH-WHAT'S A...WOMAN? AREN'T THERE TWO TYPES OF NAMEKIANS? MALE AND FEMALE? LIKE...YOU KNOW...YOUR MOTHER AND YOUR FATHER...
I-I DON'T UNDER-STAND... TWO TYPES...?
DID YOU HEAR THAT?! THEY DON'T HAVE MEN OR WOMEN!
WHAT A BORING PLANET!
...
OKAY, SO TELL US...WHY ARE WE GOING TO THE GREAT ELDER?!
MAN, AM I GLAD I'M NOT NAMEKIAN!
UM...WELL, THE PEOPLE WHO ATTACKED OUR VILLAGE ALREADY HAD FOUR DRAGON BALLS... AND YOU SAID THERE WERE A LOT OF PEOPLE BEING KILLED IN THAT DIRECTION...?
Y-YEAH... PROBABLY BY THE GUY CALLED VEGETA...
TH-THERE AREN'T ANY MORE CHI LEFT...
THEY'RE ALL... DEAD...
TH- THEN...
TH-THERE MAY NOT BE MANY MORE NAMEKIANS LEFT...

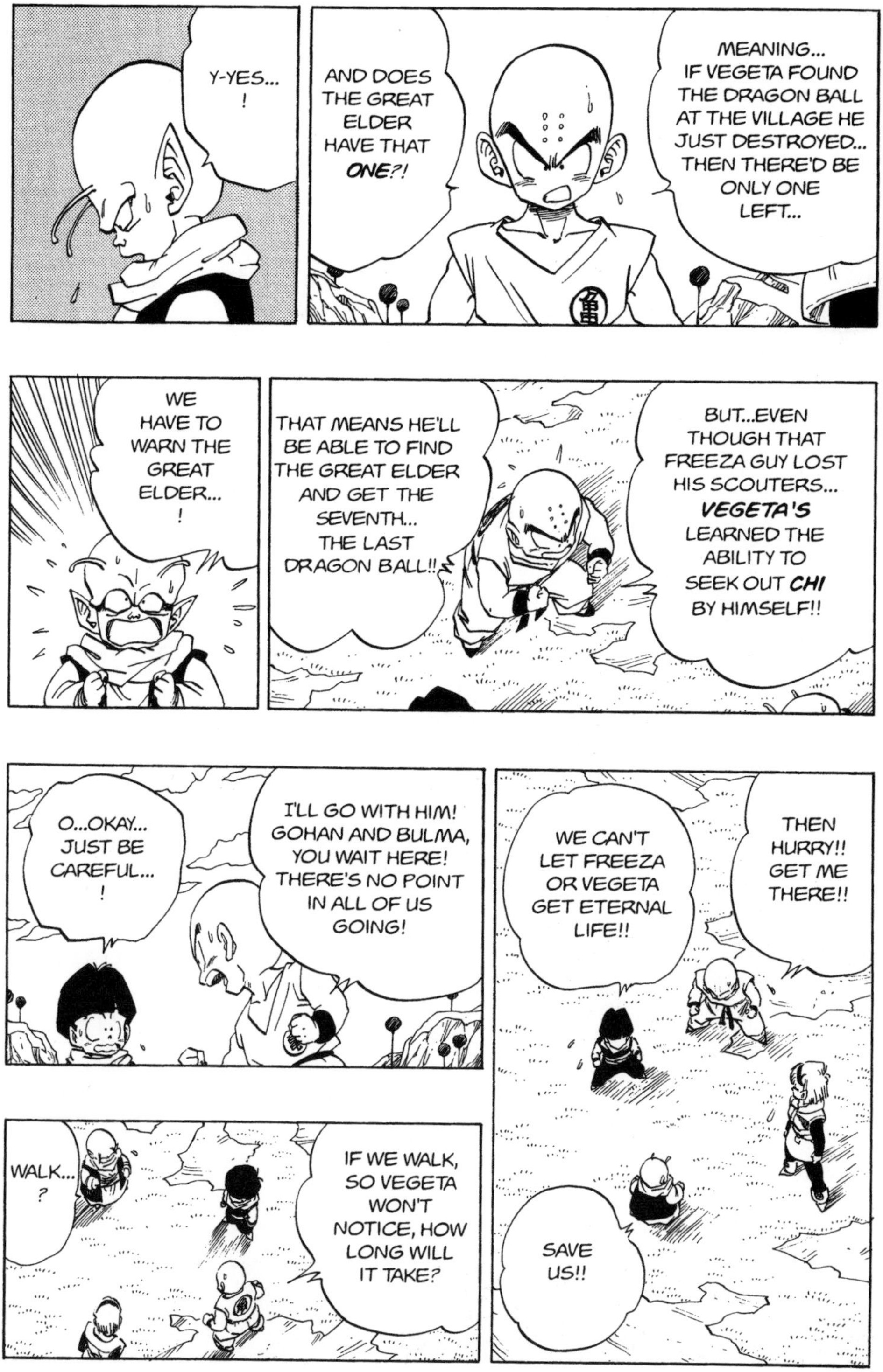
MEANING... IF VEGETA FOUND THE DRAGON BALL AT THE VILLAGE HE JUST DESTROYED... THEN THERE'D BE ONLY ONE LEFT...
AND DOES THE GREAT ELDER HAVE THAT *ONE*?!
Y-YES... !
BUT...EVEN THOUGH THAT FREEZA GUY LOST HIS SCOUTERS... **VEGETA'S** LEARNED THE ABILITY TO SEEK OUT ***CHI*** BY HIMSELF!!
THAT MEANS HE'LL BE ABLE TO FIND THE GREAT ELDER AND GET THE SEVENTH... THE LAST DRAGON BALL!!
WE HAVE TO WARN THE GREAT ELDER... !
THEN HURRY!! GET ME THERE!!
WE CAN'T LET FREEZA OR VEGETA GET ETERNAL LIFE!!
SAVE US!!
I'LL GO WITH HIM! GOHAN AND BULMA, YOU WAIT HERE! THERE'S NO POINT IN ALL OF US GOING!
O...OKAY... JUST BE CAREFUL... !
IF WE WALK, SO VEGETA WON'T NOTICE, HOW LONG WILL IT TAKE?
WALK... ?

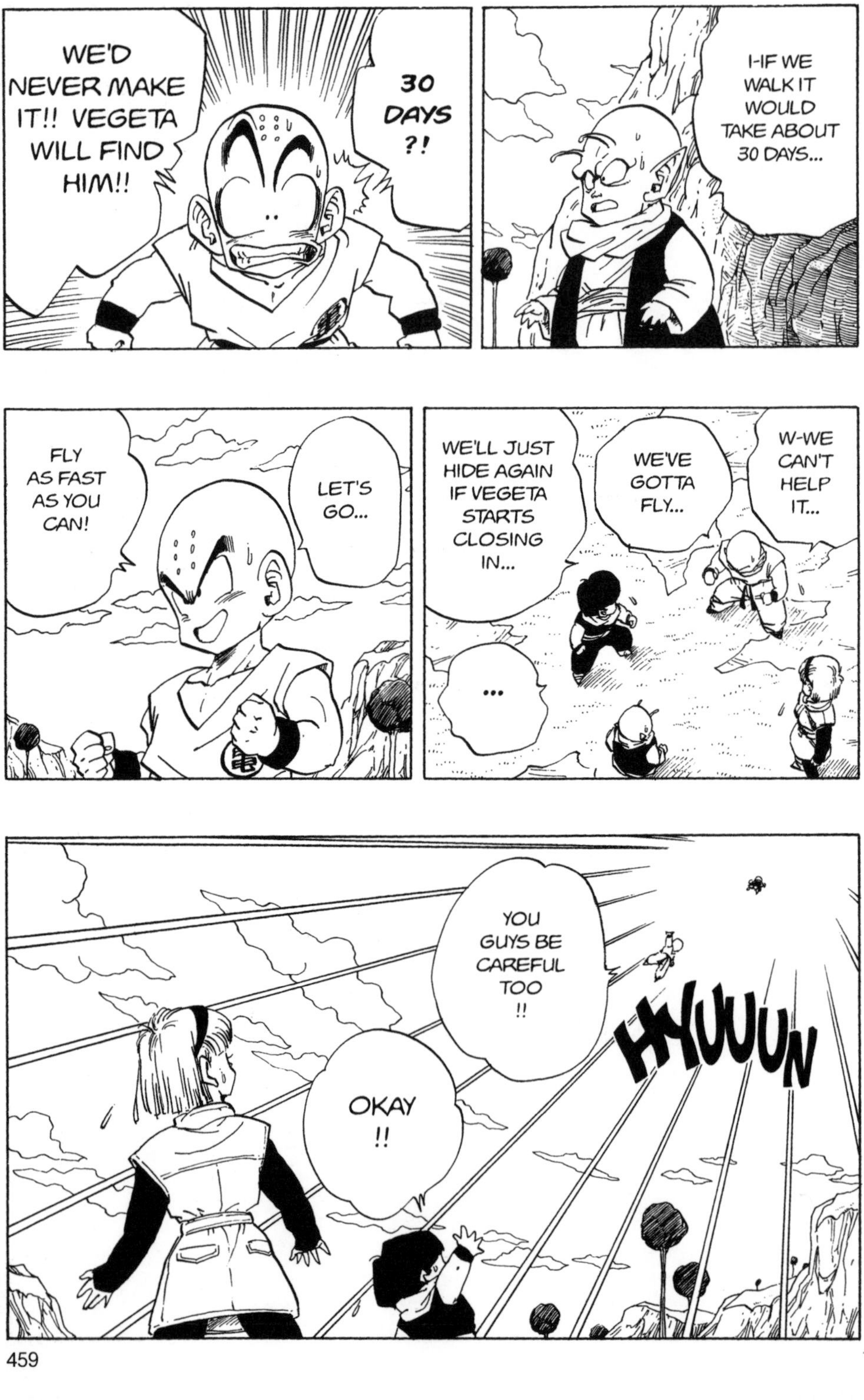
I-IF WE WALK IT WOULD TAKE ABOUT 30 DAYS...
30 DAYS ?!
WE'D NEVER MAKE IT!! VEGETA WILL FIND HIM!!
W-WE CAN'T HELP IT...
WE'VE GOTTA FLY...
WE'LL JUST HIDE AGAIN IF VEGETA STARTS CLOSING IN...
...
LET'S GO...
FLY AS FAST AS YOU CAN!
YOU GUYS BE CAREFUL TOO !!
HYUUUN
OKAY !!

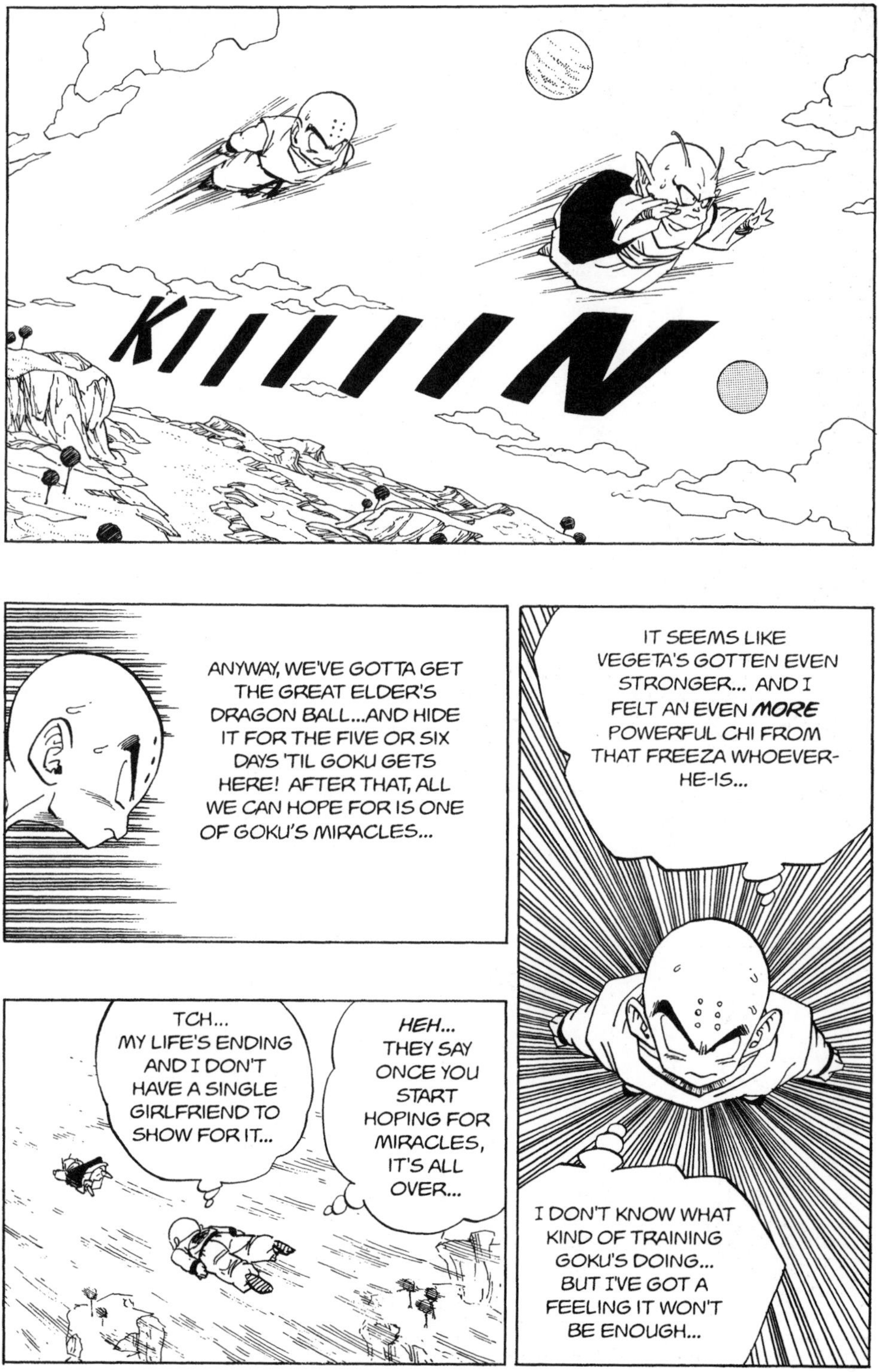
KIIIIN
IT SEEMS LIKE VEGETA'S GOTTEN EVEN STRONGER... AND I FELT AN EVEN **MORE** POWERFUL CHI FROM THAT FREEZA WHOEVER-HE-IS...
I DON'T KNOW WHAT KIND OF TRAINING GOKU'S DOING... BUT I'VE GOT A FEELING IT WON'T BE ENOUGH...
ANYWAY, WE'VE GOTTA GET THE GREAT ELDER'S DRAGON BALL...AND HIDE IT FOR THE FIVE OR SIX DAYS 'TIL GOKU GETS HERE! AFTER THAT, ALL WE CAN HOPE FOR IS ONE OF GOKU'S MIRACLES...
*HEH...* THEY SAY ONCE YOU START HOPING FOR MIRACLES, IT'S ALL OVER...
TCH... MY LIFE'S ENDING AND I DON'T HAVE A SINGLE GIRLFRIEND TO SHOW FOR IT...

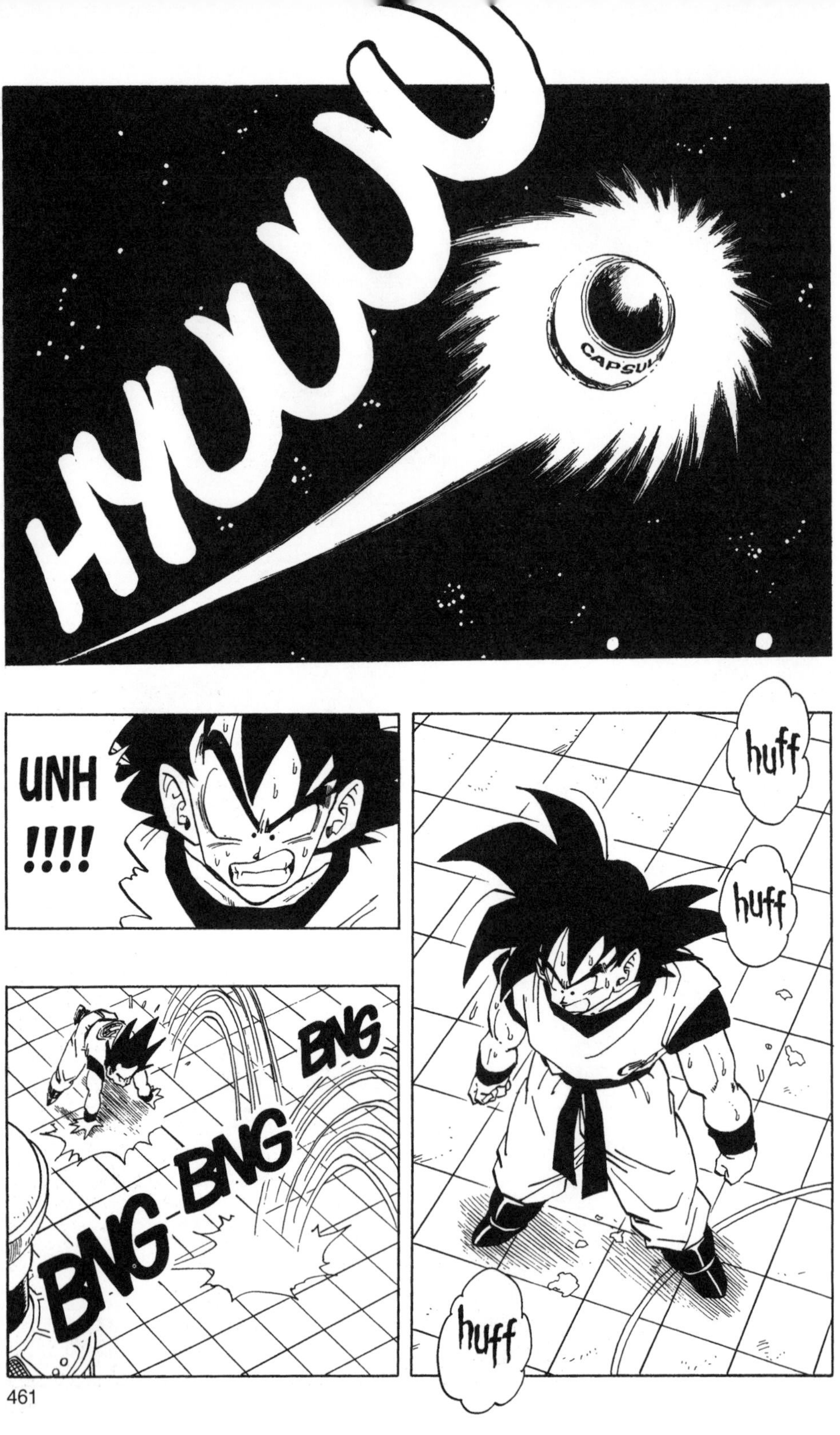
HYUUUU
CAPSUL
huff
huff
huff
UNH
!!!!
BNG-BNG-BNG

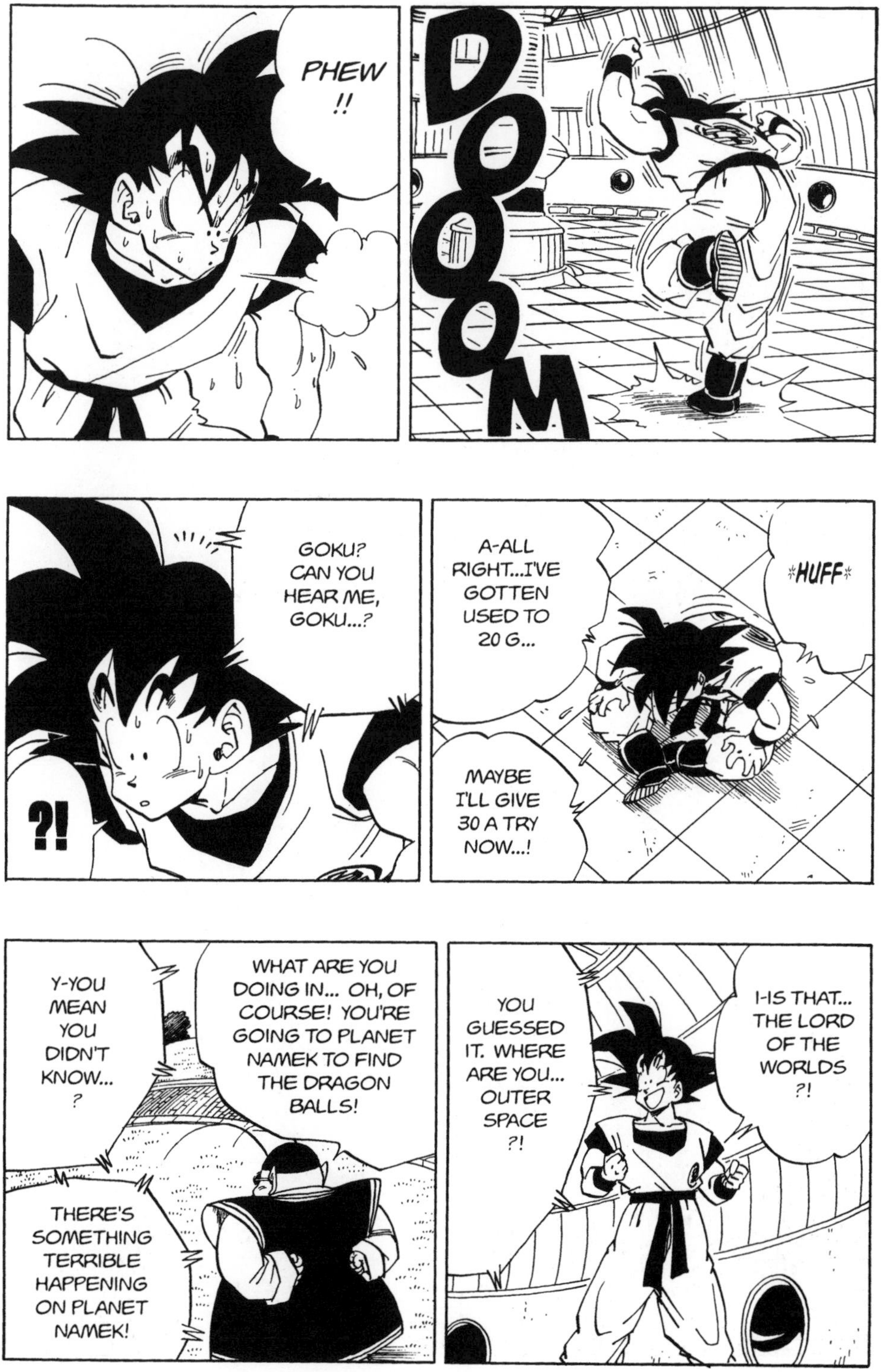
DOOOOM
PHEW !!
*HUFF*
A-ALL RIGHT...I'VE GOTTEN USED TO 20 G...
MAYBE I'LL GIVE 30 A TRY NOW...!
GOKU? CAN YOU HEAR ME, GOKU...?
?!
I-IS THAT... THE LORD OF THE WORLDS ?!
YOU GUESSED IT. WHERE ARE YOU... OUTER SPACE ?!
WHAT ARE YOU DOING IN... OH, OF COURSE! YOU'RE GOING TO PLANET NAMEK TO FIND THE DRAGON BALLS!
Y-YOU MEAN YOU DIDN'T KNOW... ?
THERE'S SOMETHING TERRIBLE HAPPENING ON PLANET NAMEK!

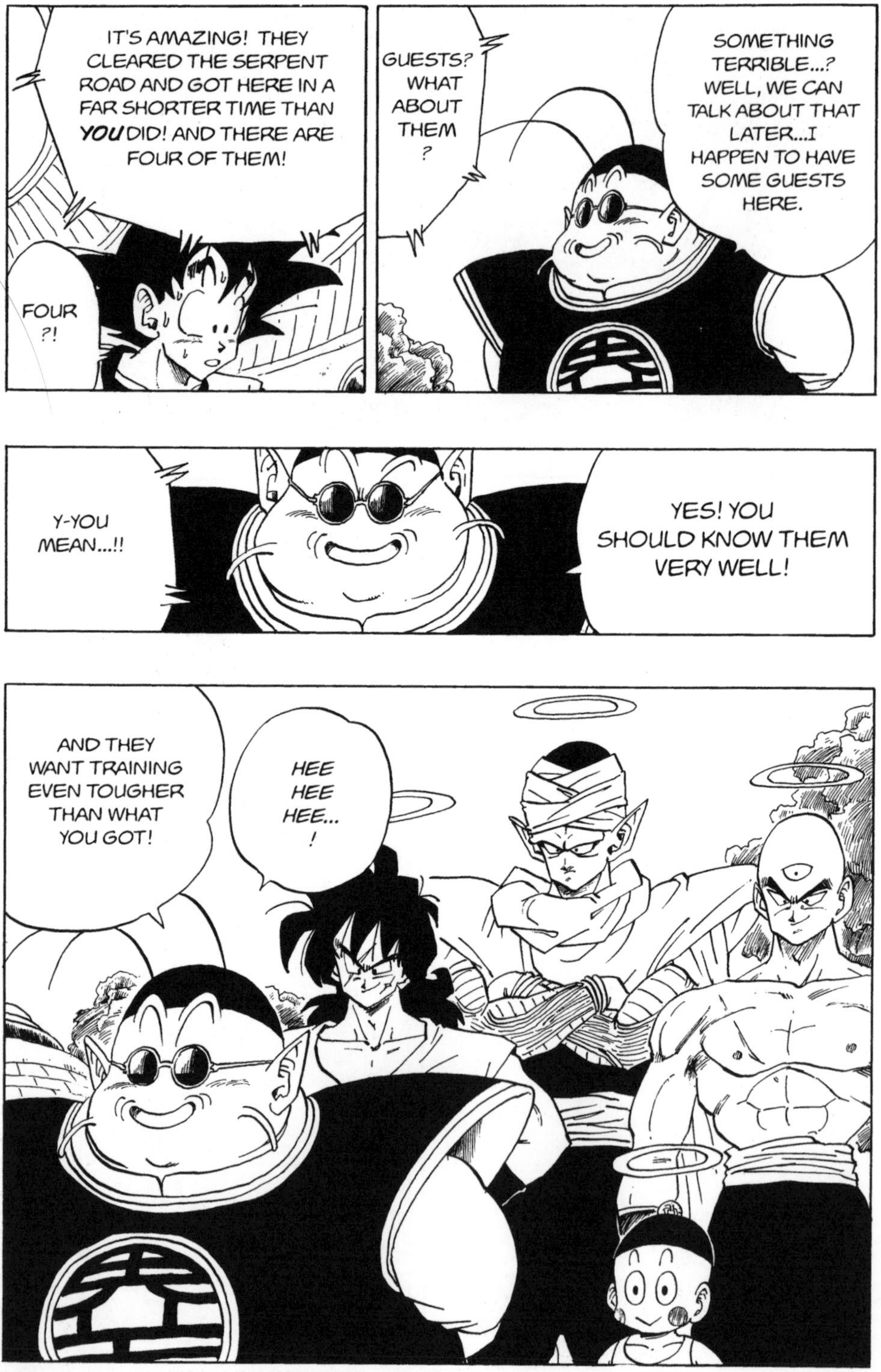
SOMETHING TERRIBLE...? WELL, WE CAN TALK ABOUT THAT LATER...I HAPPEN TO HAVE SOME GUESTS HERE.
GUESTS? WHAT ABOUT THEM ?
IT'S AMAZING! THEY CLEARED THE SERPENT ROAD AND GOT HERE IN A FAR SHORTER TIME THAN ***YOU*** DID! AND THERE ARE FOUR OF THEM!
FOUR ?!
Y-YOU MEAN...!!
YES! YOU SHOULD KNOW THEM VERY WELL!
AND THEY WANT TRAINING EVEN TOUGHER THAN WHAT YOU GOT!
HEE HEE HEE... !

# DBZ:67 • The Four Dead Heroes

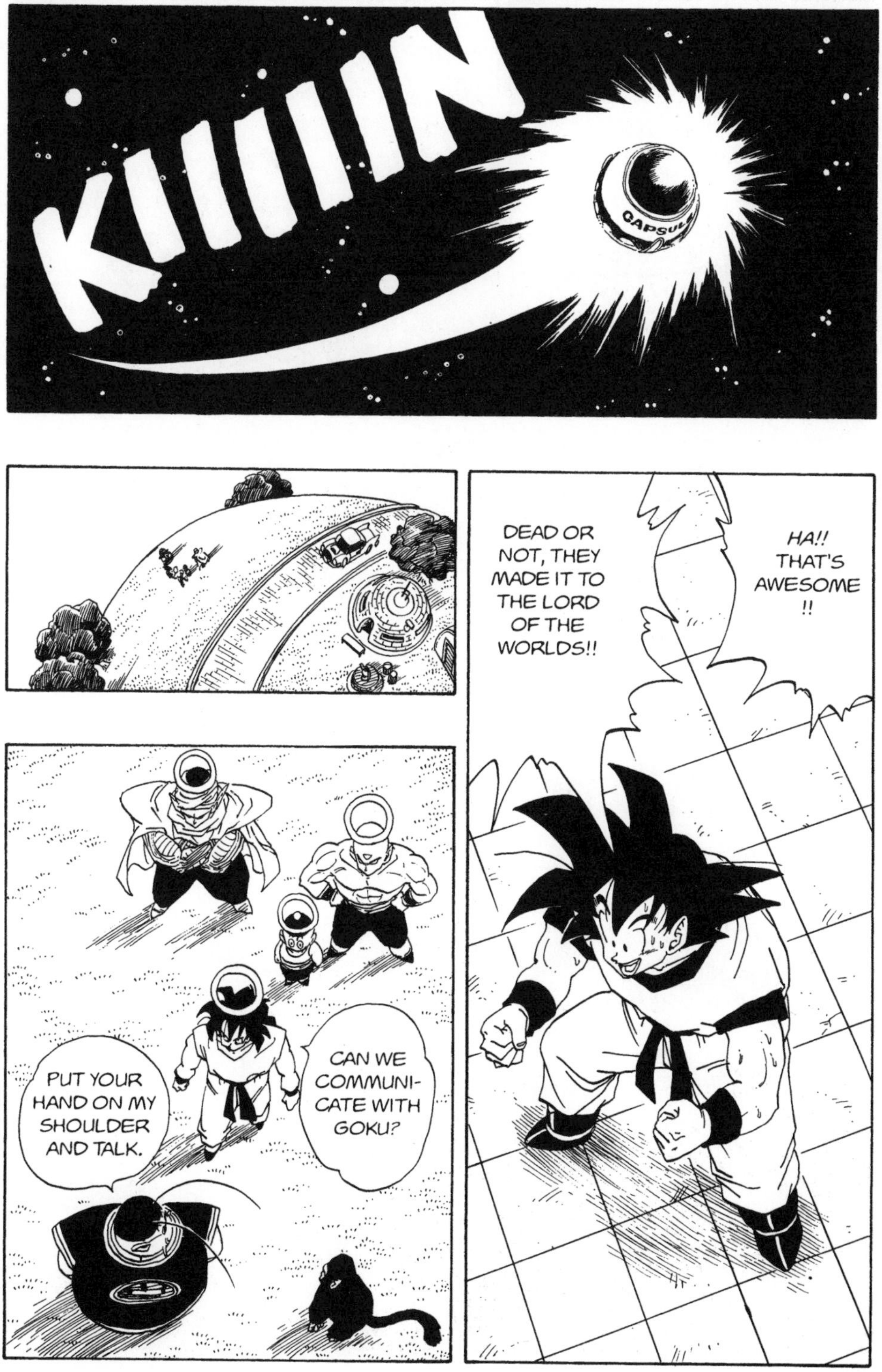

KIIIIN
CAPSULE
HA!! THAT'S AWESOME!!
DEAD OR NOT, THEY MADE IT TO THE LORD OF THE WORLDS!!
CAN WE COMMUNICATE WITH GOKU?
PUT YOUR HAND ON MY SHOULDER AND TALK.

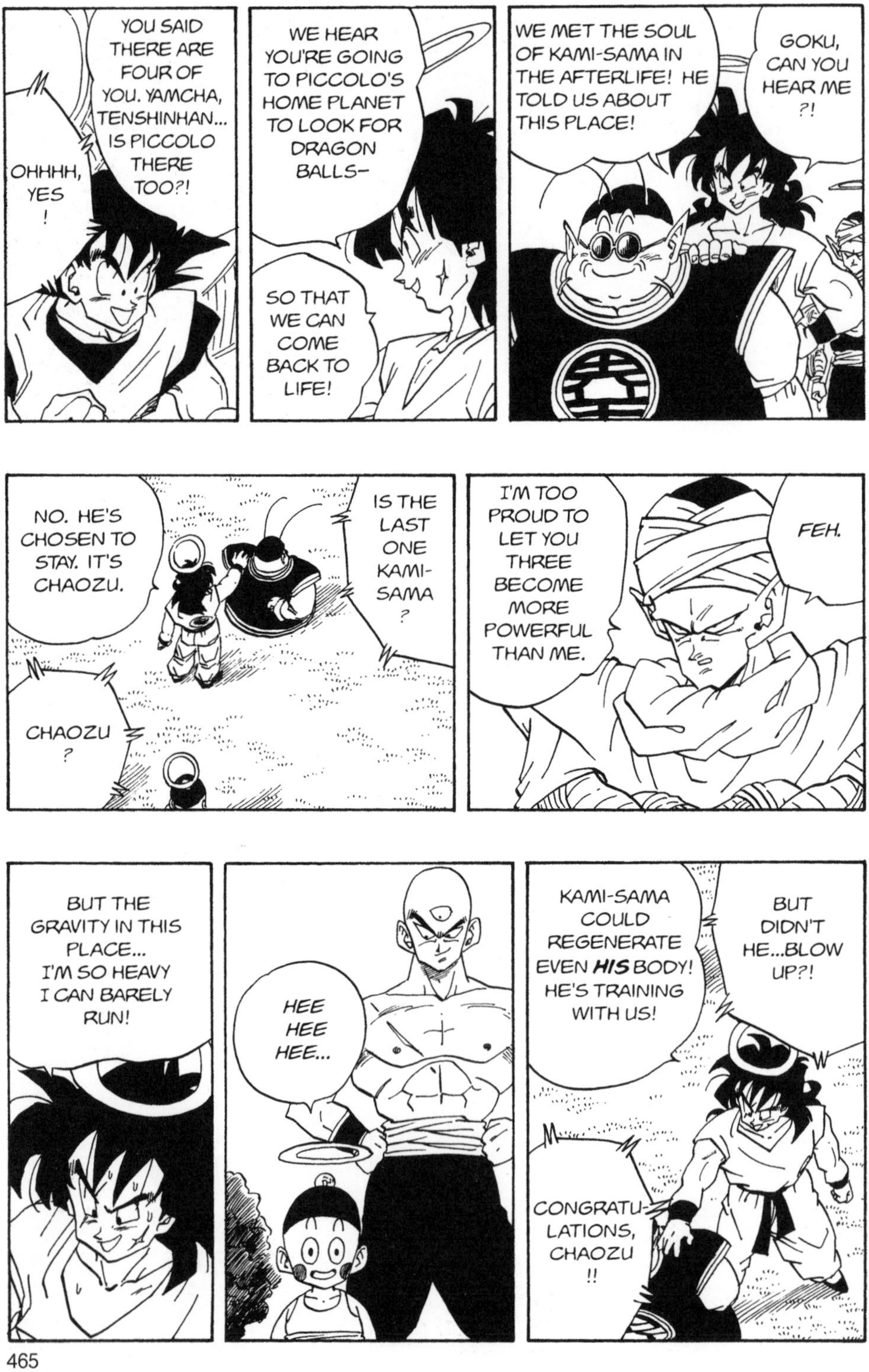
GOKU, CAN YOU HEAR ME ?!
WE MET THE SOUL OF KAMI-SAMA IN THE AFTERLIFE! HE TOLD US ABOUT THIS PLACE!
WE HEAR YOU'RE GOING TO PICCOLO'S HOME PLANET TO LOOK FOR DRAGON BALLS–
SO THAT WE CAN COME BACK TO LIFE!
YOU SAID THERE ARE FOUR OF YOU. YAMCHA, TENSHINHAN... IS PICCOLO THERE TOO?!
OHHHH, YES !
FEH.
I'M TOO PROUD TO LET YOU THREE BECOME MORE POWERFUL THAN ME.
IS THE LAST ONE KAMI-SAMA ?
NO. HE'S CHOSEN TO STAY. IT'S CHAOZU.
CHAOZU ?
BUT DIDN'T HE...BLOW UP?!
KAMI-SAMA COULD REGENERATE EVEN ***HIS*** BODY! HE'S TRAINING WITH US!
CONGRATULATIONS, CHAOZU !!
HEE HEE HEE...
BUT THE GRAVITY IN THIS PLACE... I'M SO HEAVY I CAN BARELY RUN!

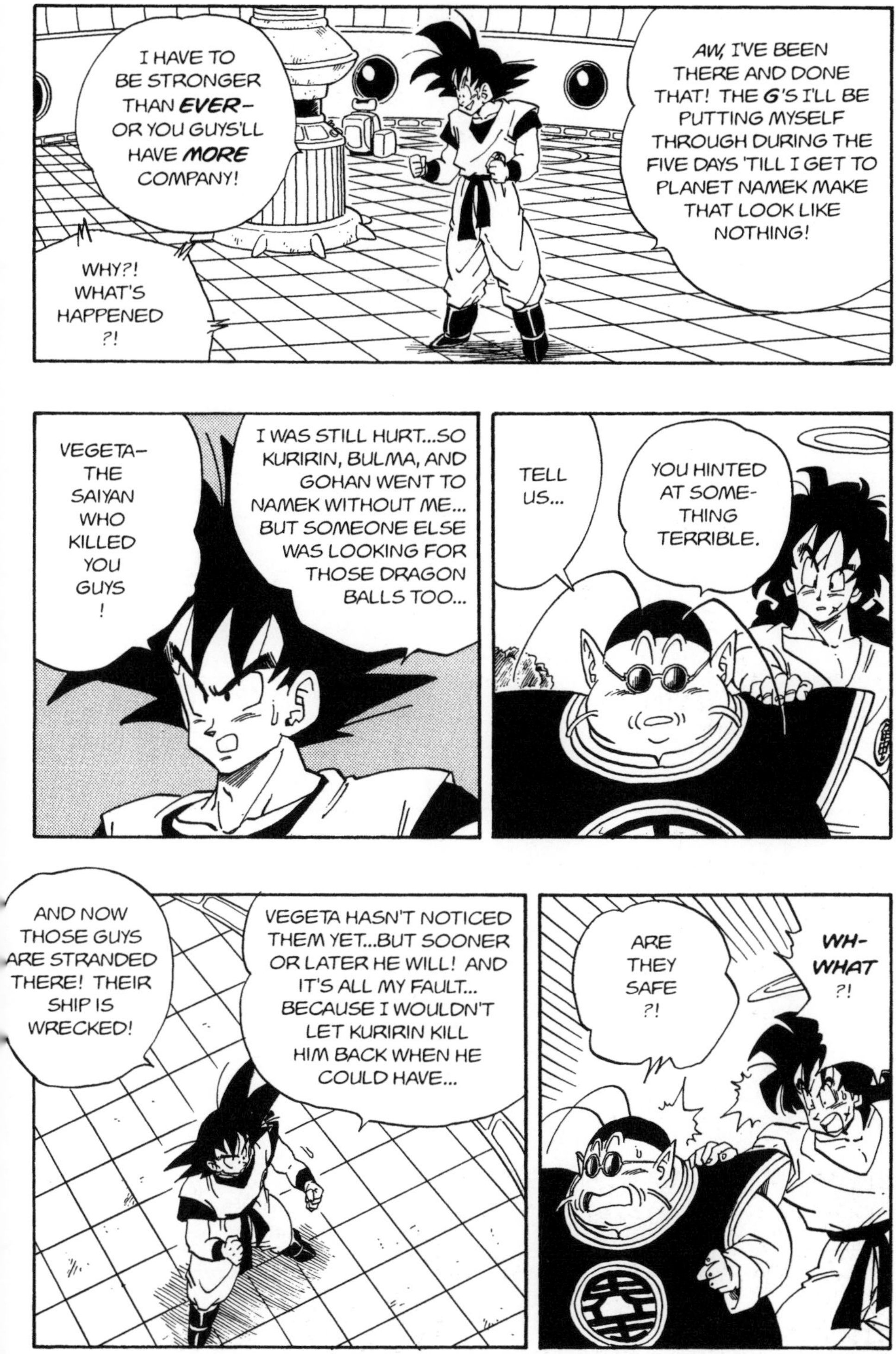
AW, I'VE BEEN THERE AND DONE THAT! THE G'S I'LL BE PUTTING MYSELF THROUGH DURING THE FIVE DAYS 'TILL I GET TO PLANET NAMEK MAKE THAT LOOK LIKE NOTHING!
I HAVE TO BE STRONGER THAN EVER— OR YOU GUYS'LL HAVE MORE COMPANY!
WHY?! WHAT'S HAPPENED ?!
YOU HINTED AT SOME-THING TERRIBLE.
TELL US...
I WAS STILL HURT...SO KURIRIN, BULMA, AND GOHAN WENT TO NAMEK WITHOUT ME... BUT SOMEONE ELSE WAS LOOKING FOR THOSE DRAGON BALLS TOO...
VEGETA— THE SAIYAN WHO KILLED YOU GUYS !
WH-WHAT ?!
ARE THEY SAFE ?!
VEGETA HASN'T NOTICED THEM YET...BUT SOONER OR LATER HE WILL! AND IT'S ALL MY FAULT... BECAUSE I WOULDN'T LET KURIRIN KILL HIM BACK WHEN HE COULD HAVE...
AND NOW THOSE GUYS ARE STRANDED THERE! THEIR SHIP IS WRECKED!

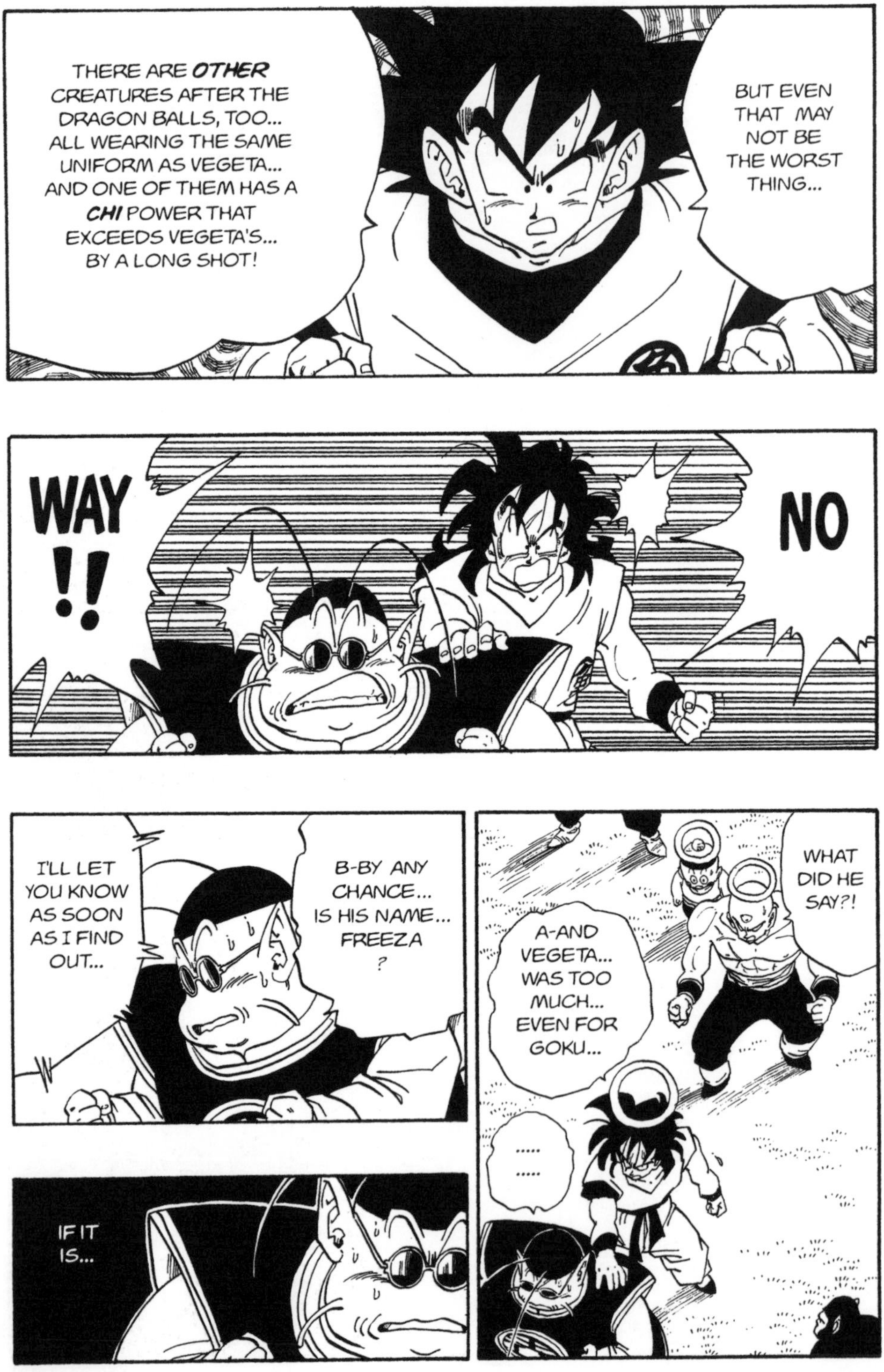
THERE ARE OTHER CREATURES AFTER THE DRAGON BALLS, TOO... ALL WEARING THE SAME UNIFORM AS VEGETA... AND ONE OF THEM HAS A CHI POWER THAT EXCEEDS VEGETA'S... BY A LONG SHOT!
BUT EVEN THAT MAY NOT BE THE WORST THING...
NO
WAY!!
WHAT DID HE SAY?!
A-AND VEGETA... WAS TOO MUCH... EVEN FOR GOKU...
..... .....
B-BY ANY CHANCE... IS HIS NAME... FREEZA ?
I'LL LET YOU KNOW AS SOON AS I FIND OUT...
IF IT IS...

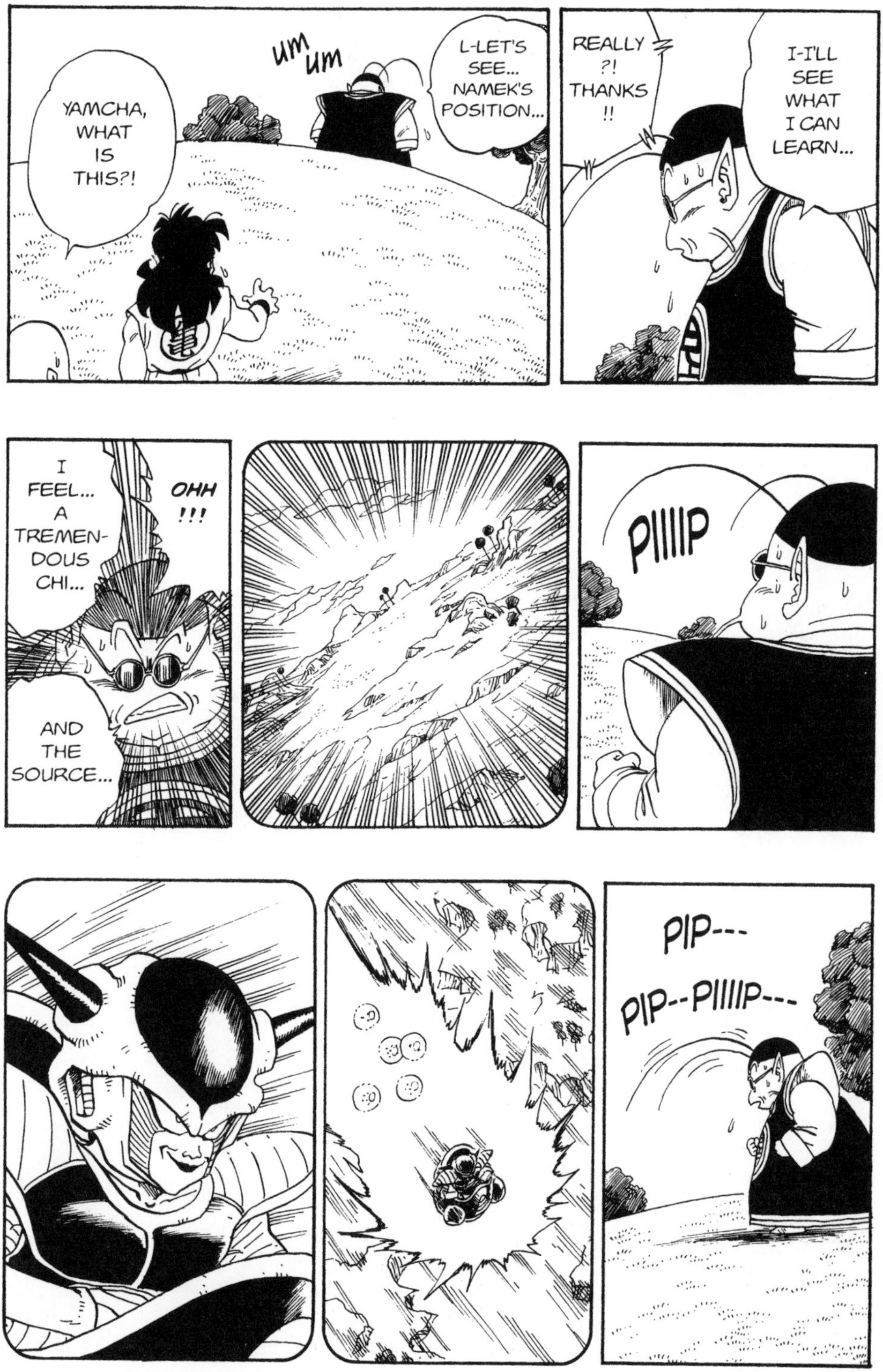
I-I'LL SEE WHAT I CAN LEARN...
REALLY ?! THANKS !!
L-LET'S SEE... NAMEK'S POSITION...
UM UM
YAMCHA, WHAT IS THIS?!
PIIIIP
OHH !!!
I FEEL... A TREMEN-DOUS CHI...
AND THE SOURCE...
PIP---
PIP--PIIIIP---

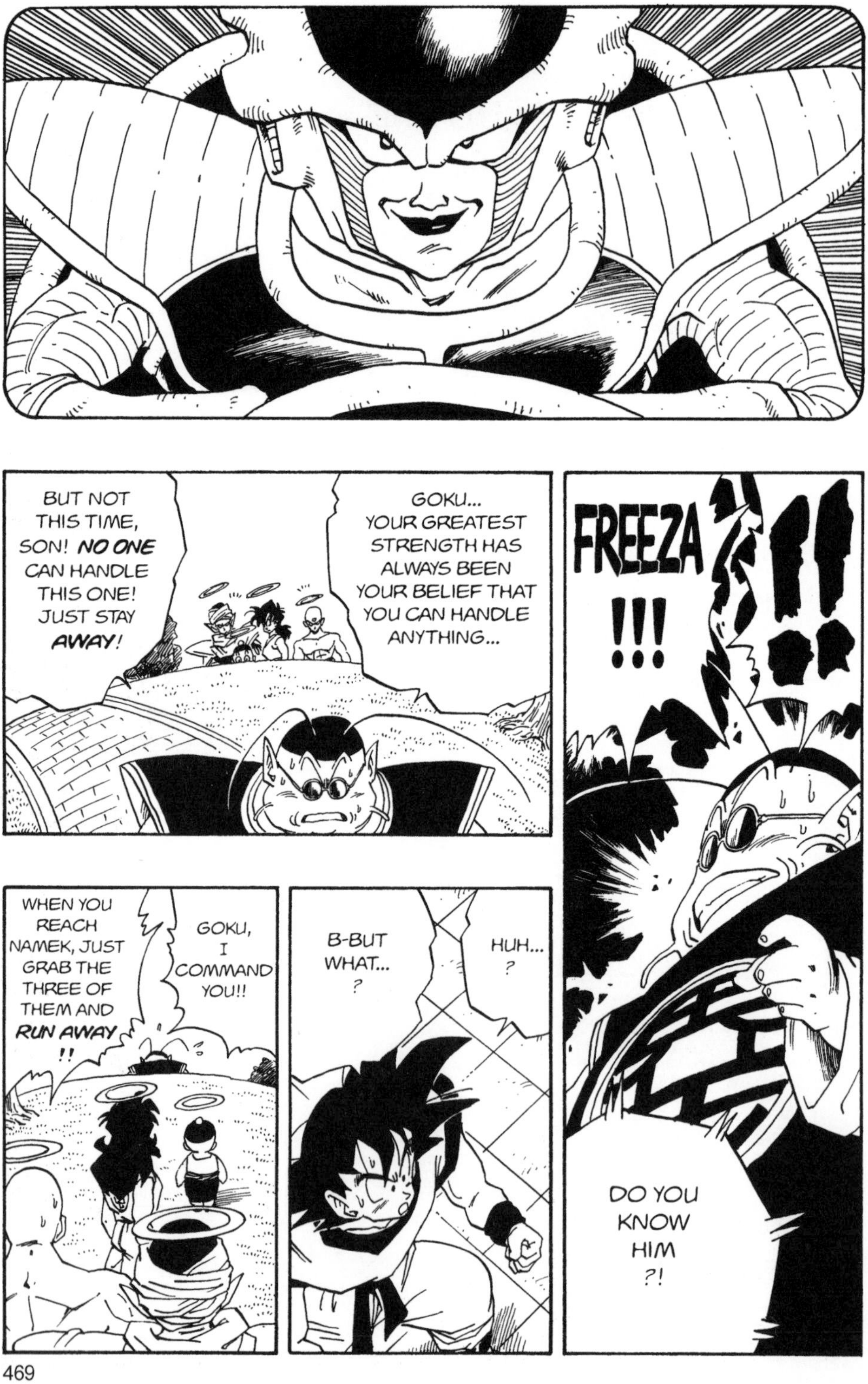
FREEZA!!!
DO YOU KNOW HIM?!
GOKU... YOUR GREATEST STRENGTH HAS ALWAYS BEEN YOUR BELIEF THAT YOU CAN HANDLE ANYTHING...
BUT NOT THIS TIME, SON! **NO ONE** CAN HANDLE THIS ONE! JUST STAY ***AWAY***!
HUH...?
B-BUT WHAT...?
GOKU, I COMMAND YOU!!
WHEN YOU REACH NAMEK, JUST GRAB THE THREE OF THEM AND ***RUN AWAY***!!

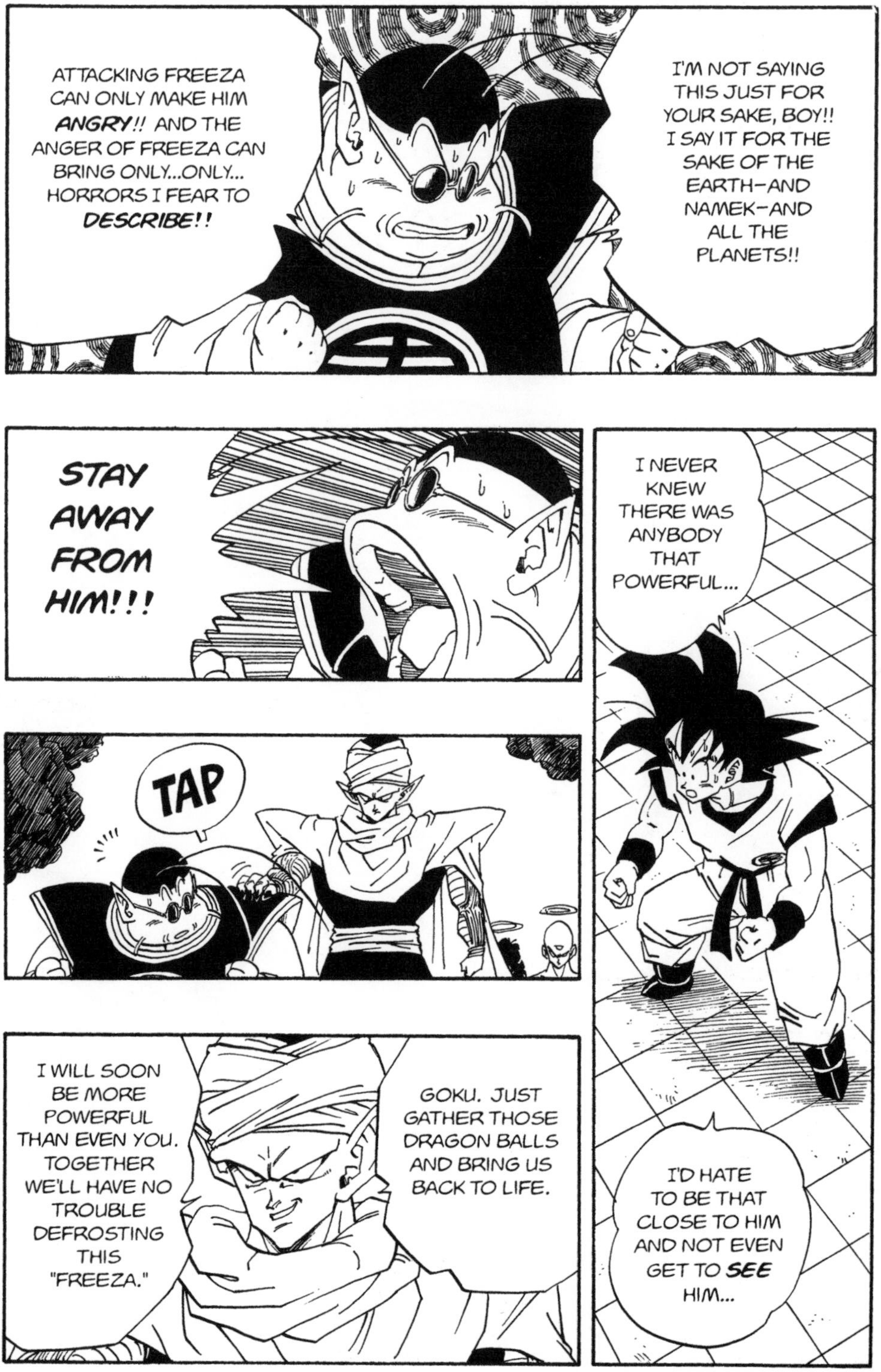
I'M NOT SAYING THIS JUST FOR YOUR SAKE, BOY!! I SAY IT FOR THE SAKE OF THE EARTH—AND NAMEK—AND ALL THE PLANETS!!
ATTACKING FREEZA CAN ONLY MAKE HIM ANGRY!! AND THE ANGER OF FREEZA CAN BRING ONLY...ONLY... HORRORS I FEAR TO DESCRIBE!!
I NEVER KNEW THERE WAS ANYBODY THAT POWERFUL...
I'D HATE TO BE THAT CLOSE TO HIM AND NOT EVEN GET TO SEE HIM...
STAY AWAY FROM HIM!!!
TAP
GOKU. JUST GATHER THOSE DRAGON BALLS AND BRING US BACK TO LIFE.
I WILL SOON BE MORE POWERFUL THAN EVEN YOU. TOGETHER WE'LL HAVE NO TROUBLE DEFROSTING THIS "FREEZA."

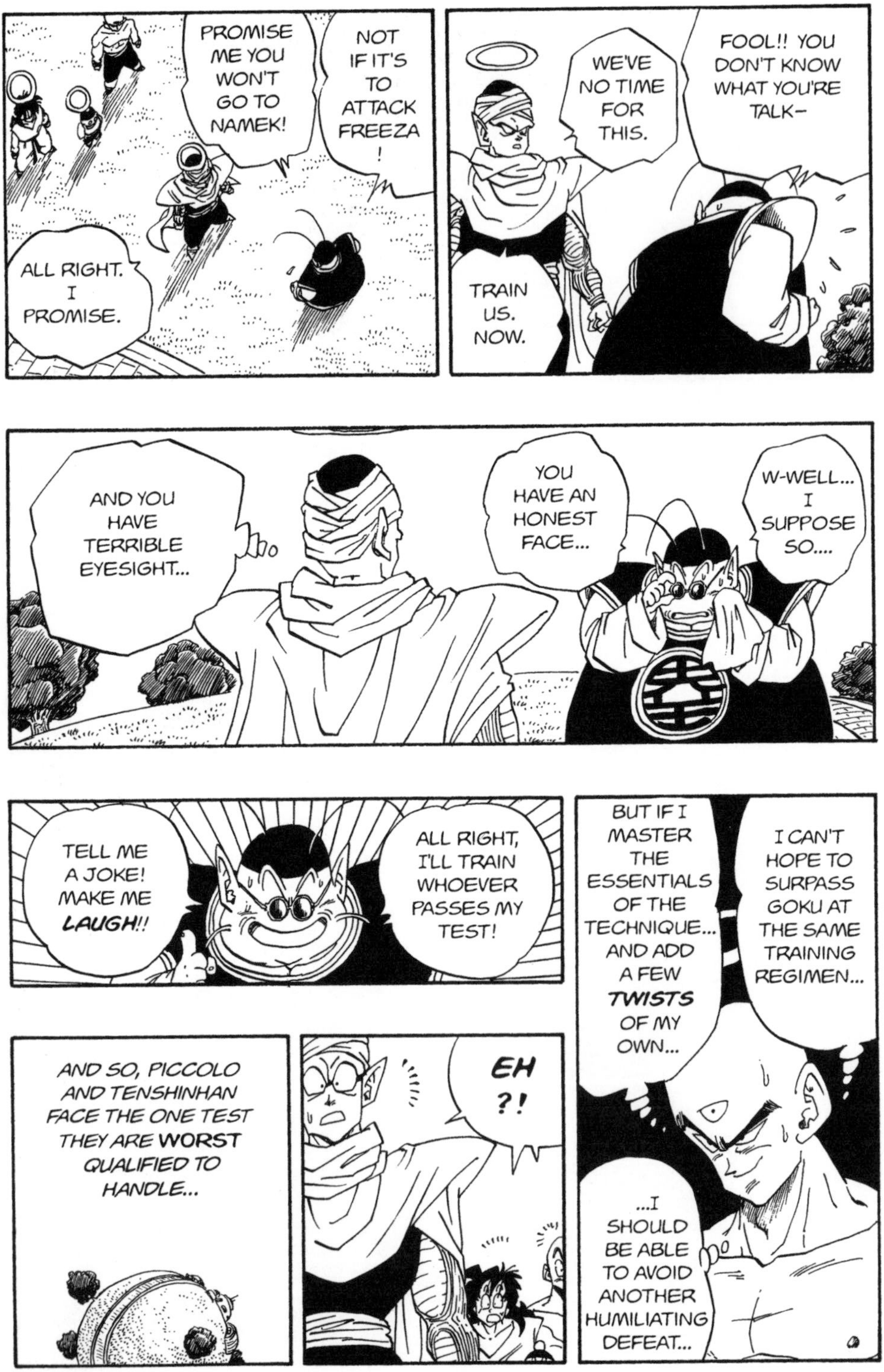
FOOL!! YOU DON'T KNOW WHAT YOU'RE TALK–
WE'VE NO TIME FOR THIS.
TRAIN US. NOW.
NOT IF IT'S TO ATTACK FREEZA!
PROMISE ME YOU WON'T GO TO NAMEK!
ALL RIGHT. I PROMISE.
W-WELL... I SUPPOSE SO....
YOU HAVE AN HONEST FACE...
AND YOU HAVE TERRIBLE EYESIGHT...
I CAN'T HOPE TO SURPASS GOKU AT THE SAME TRAINING REGIMEN...
BUT IF I MASTER THE ESSENTIALS OF THE TECHNIQUE... AND ADD A FEW **TWISTS** OF MY OWN...
...I SHOULD BE ABLE TO AVOID ANOTHER HUMILIATING DEFEAT...
ALL RIGHT, I'LL TRAIN WHOEVER PASSES MY TEST!
TELL ME A JOKE! MAKE ME ***LAUGH***!!
EH ?!
*AND SO, PICCOLO AND TENSHINHAN FACE THE ONE TEST THEY ARE* ***WORST*** *QUALIFIED TO HANDLE...*

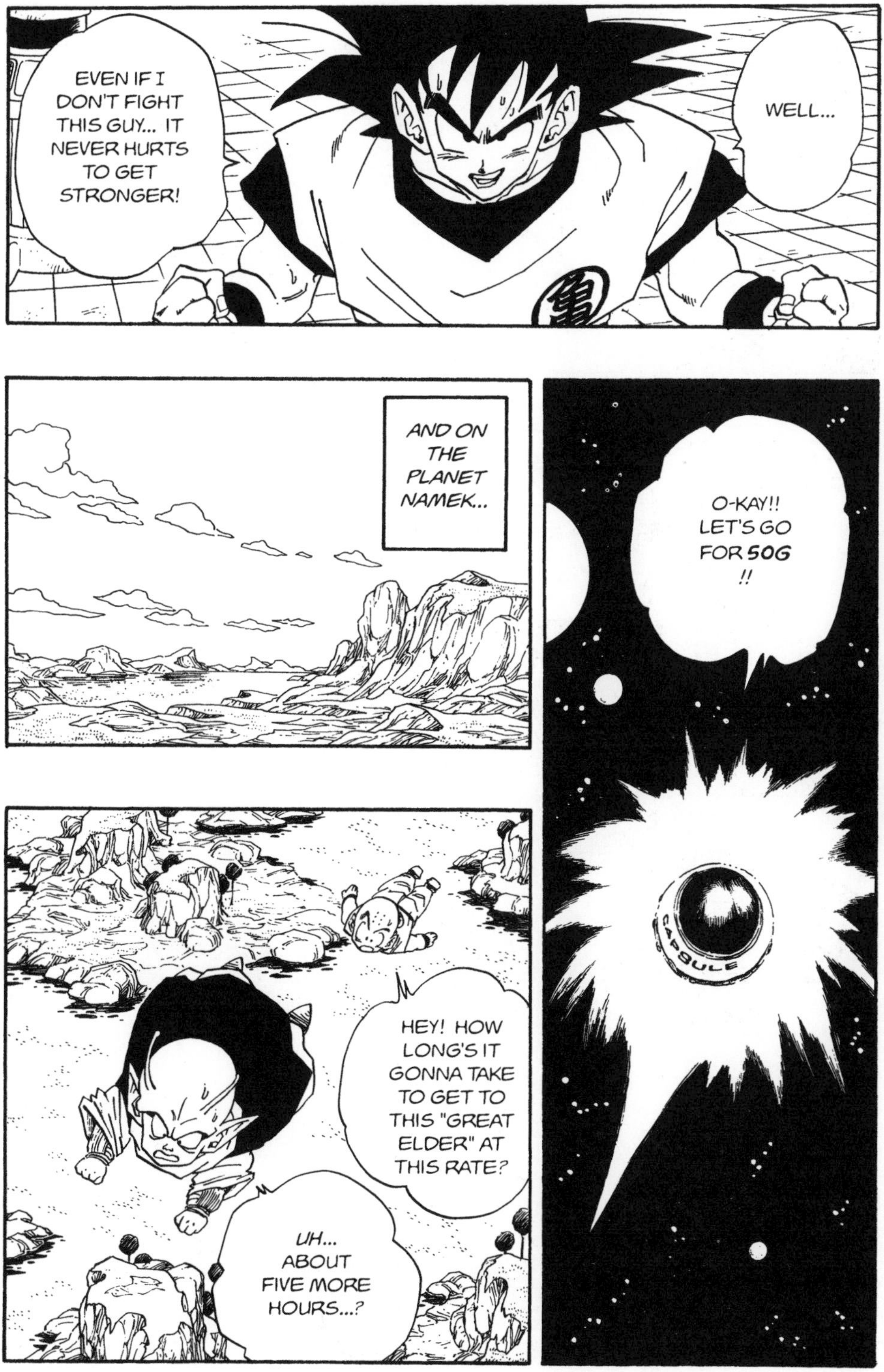
WELL...
EVEN IF I DON'T FIGHT THIS GUY... IT NEVER HURTS TO GET STRONGER!
O-KAY!! LET'S GO FOR 50G !!
CAPSULE
AND ON THE PLANET NAMEK...
HEY! HOW LONG'S IT GONNA TAKE TO GET TO THIS "GREAT ELDER" AT THIS RATE?
UH... ABOUT FIVE MORE HOURS...?

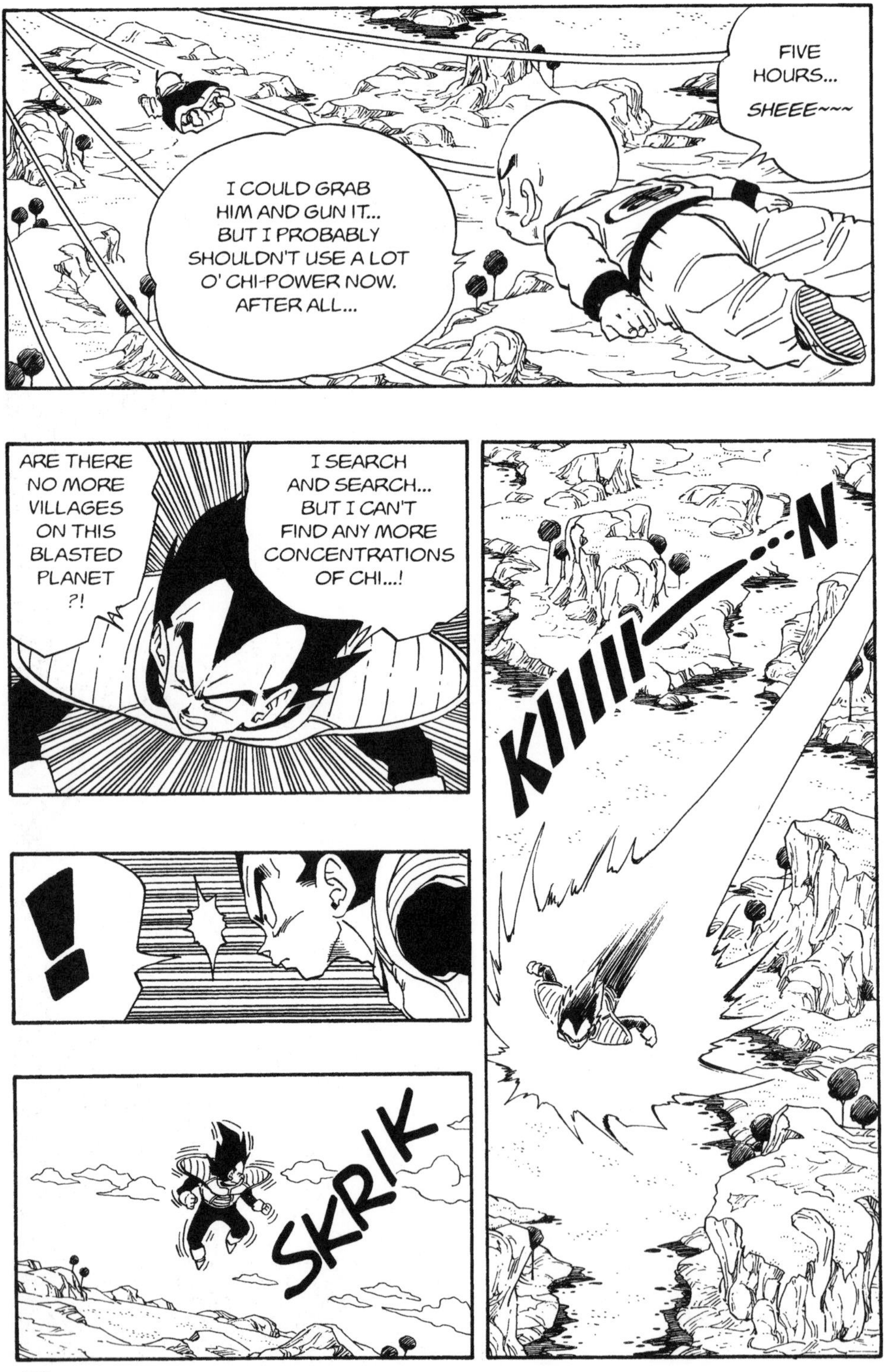
FIVE HOURS... SHEEE~~~
I COULD GRAB HIM AND GUN IT... BUT I PROBABLY SHOULDN'T USE A LOT O' CHI-POWER NOW. AFTER ALL...
KIIIII—···N
I SEARCH AND SEARCH... BUT I CAN'T FIND ANY MORE CONCENTRATIONS OF CHI...!
ARE THERE NO MORE VILLAGES ON THIS BLASTED PLANET ?!
!
SKRIK

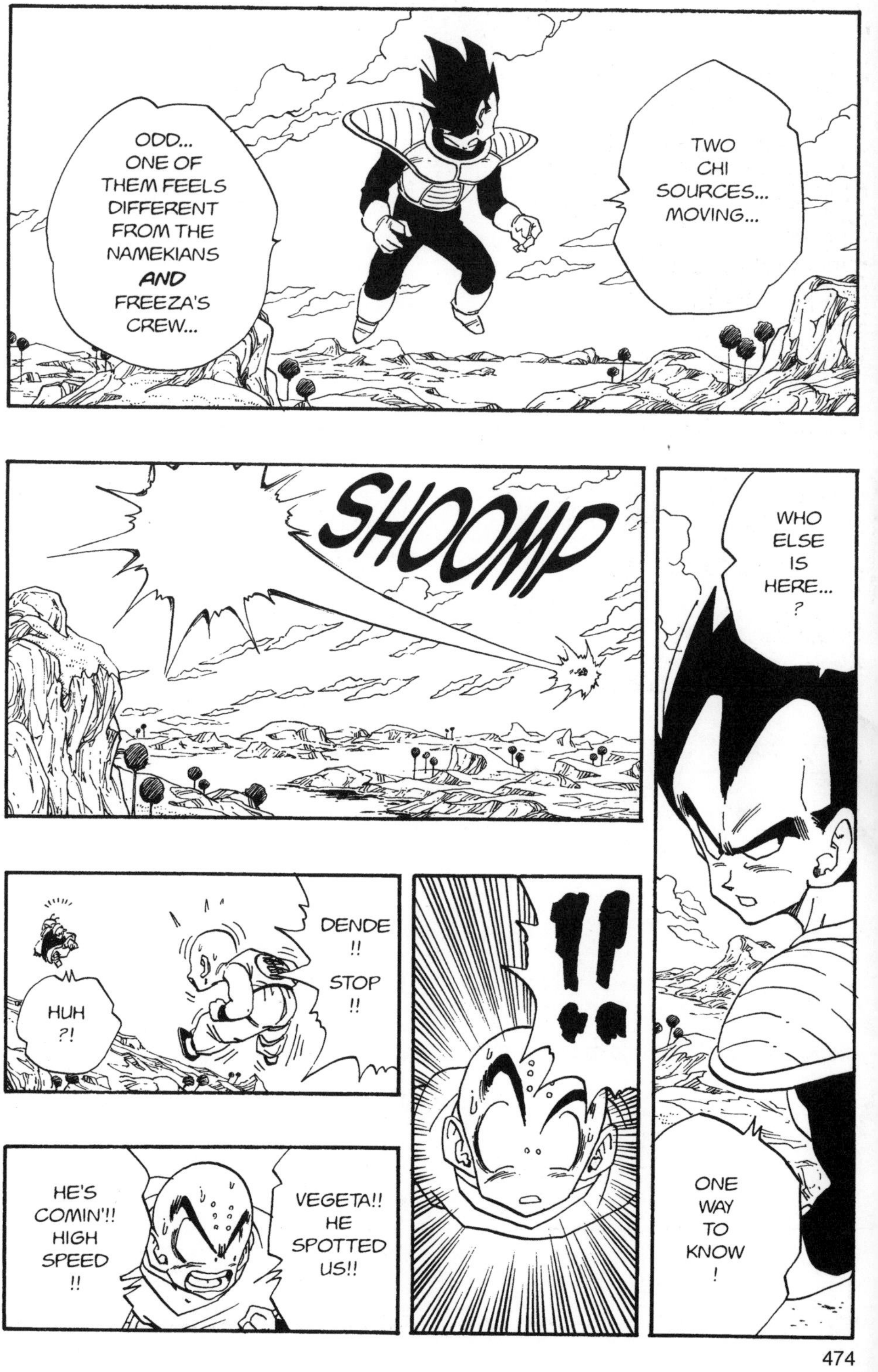
TWO CHI SOURCES... MOVING...
ODD... ONE OF THEM FEELS DIFFERENT FROM THE NAMEKIANS AND FREEZA'S CREW...
WHO ELSE IS HERE... ?
ONE WAY TO KNOW !
SHOOMP
!!
DENDE !! STOP !!
HUH ?!
VEGETA!! HE SPOTTED US!!
HE'S COMIN'!! HIGH SPEED !!

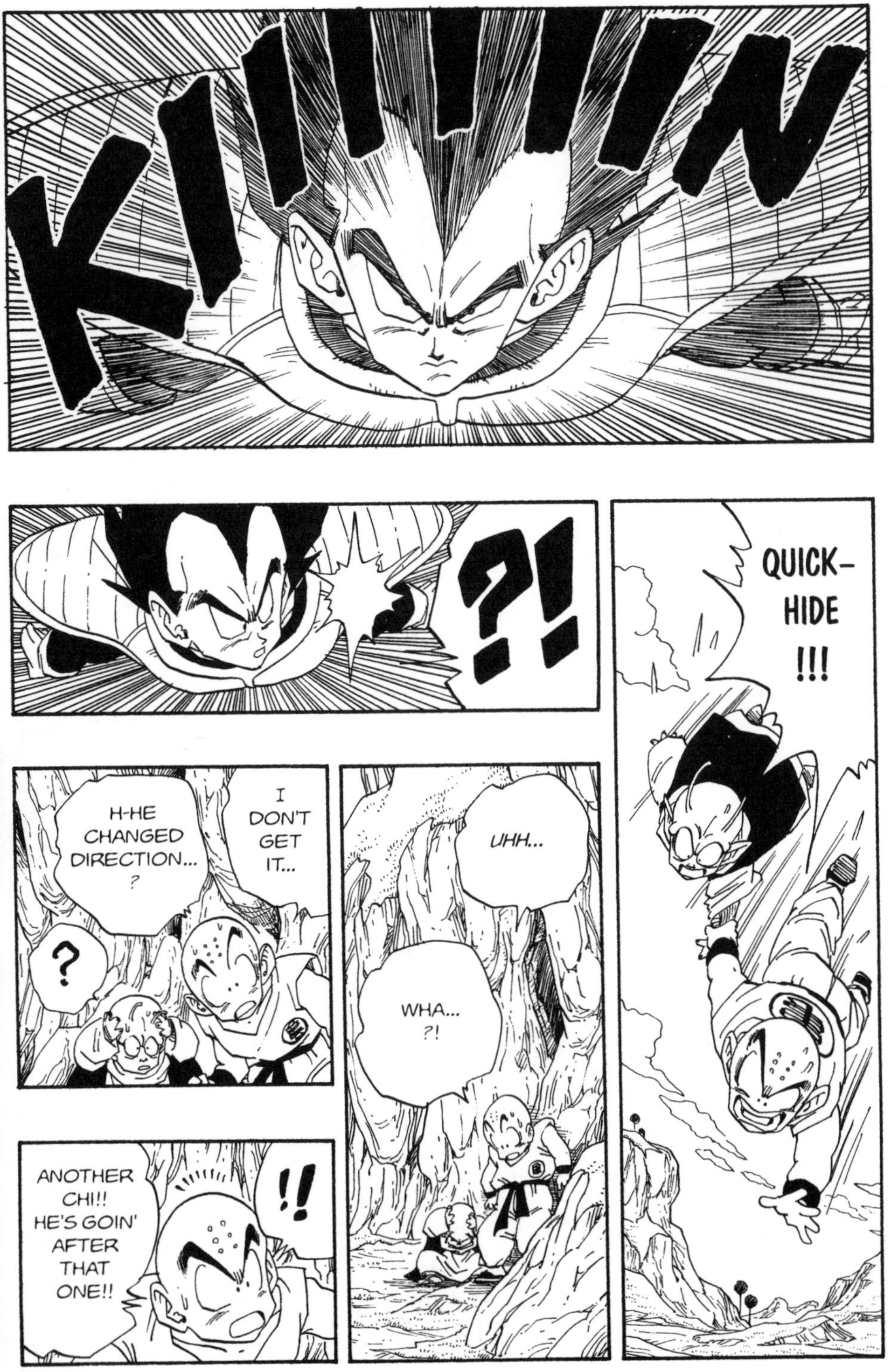
KIIIIIN
QUICK-HIDE !!!
?!
UHH...
WHA... ?!
I DON'T GET IT...
H-HE CHANGED DIRECTION... ?
?
!!
ANOTHER CHI!! HE'S GOIN' AFTER THAT ONE!!

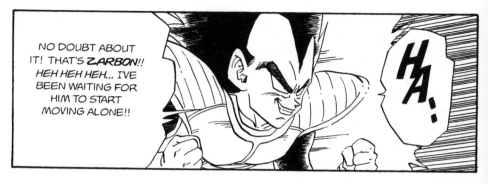

NO DOUBT ABOUT IT! THAT'S *ZARBON*!! *HEH HEH HEH... I'VE BEEN WAITING FOR HIM TO START MOVING ALONE!!*

HA..

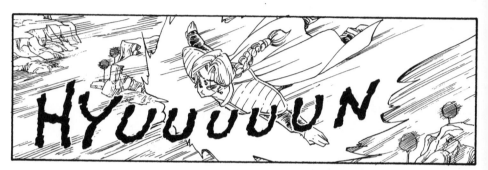

HYUUUUUN

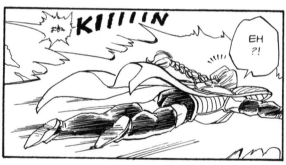

KIIIIIN

EH ?!

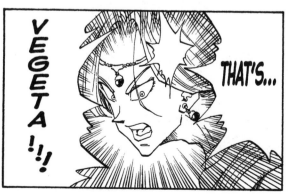

*VEGETA!!!*

THAT'S...

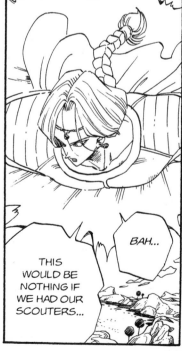

BAH...

THIS WOULD BE NOTHING IF WE HAD OUR SCOUTERS...

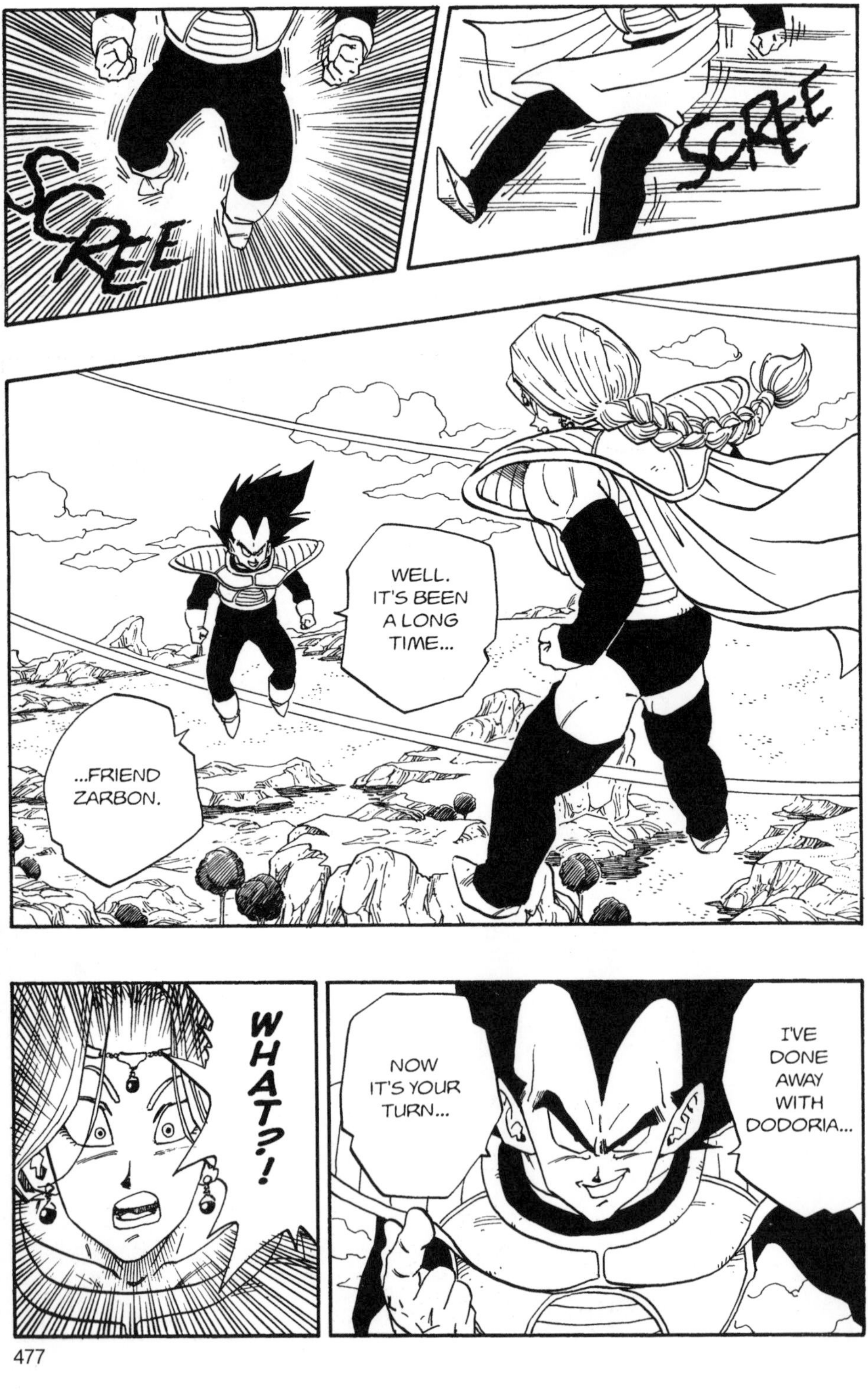
SCREE
SCREE
WELL. IT'S BEEN A LONG TIME...
...FRIEND ZARBON.
I'VE DONE AWAY WITH DODORIA...
NOW IT'S YOUR TURN...
WHAT?!

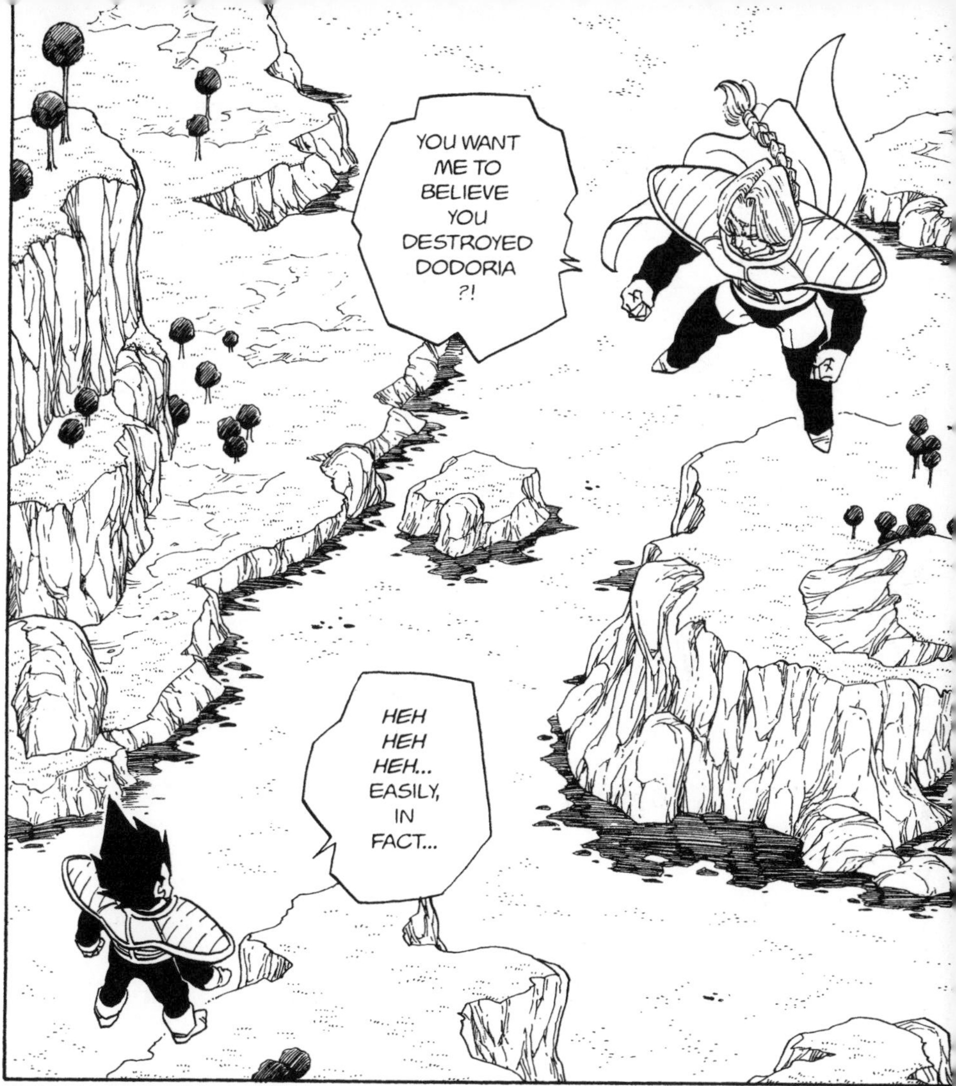
YOU WANT ME TO BELIEVE YOU DESTROYED DODORIA?!
HEH HEH HEH... EASILY, IN FACT...

## DBZ:68 • Vegeta vs. Zarbon

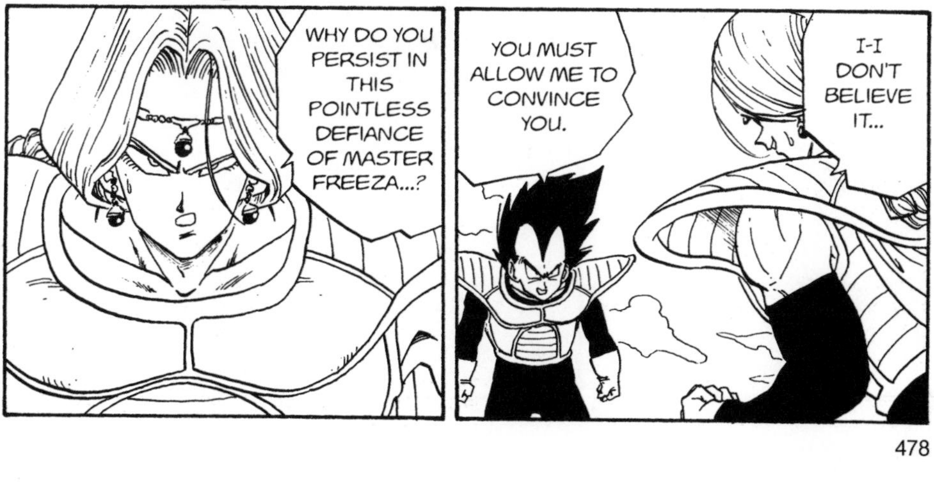
I-I DON'T BELIEVE IT...
YOU MUST ALLOW ME TO CONVINCE YOU.
WHY DO YOU PERSIST IN THIS POINTLESS DEFIANCE OF MASTER FREEZA...?

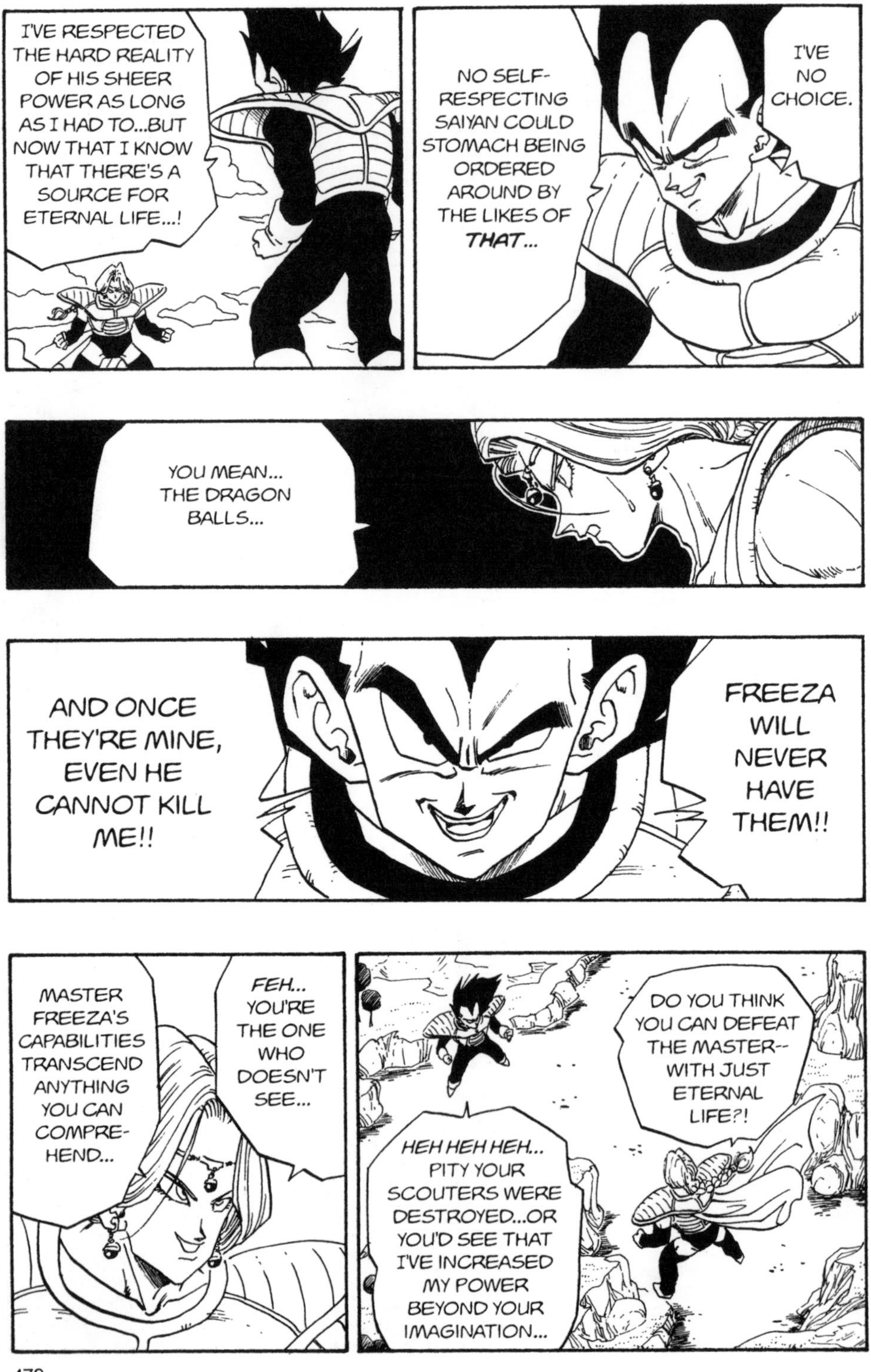
I'VE NO CHOICE.
NO SELF-RESPECTING SAIYAN COULD STOMACH BEING ORDERED AROUND BY THE LIKES OF *THAT*...
I'VE RESPECTED THE HARD REALITY OF HIS SHEER POWER AS LONG AS I HAD TO...BUT NOW THAT I KNOW THAT THERE'S A SOURCE FOR ETERNAL LIFE...!
YOU MEAN... THE DRAGON BALLS...
FREEZA WILL NEVER HAVE THEM!!
AND ONCE THEY'RE MINE, EVEN HE CANNOT KILL ME!!
DO YOU THINK YOU CAN DEFEAT THE MASTER--WITH JUST ETERNAL LIFE?!
*HEH HEH HEH...* PITY YOUR SCOUTERS WERE DESTROYED...OR YOU'D SEE THAT I'VE INCREASED MY POWER BEYOND YOUR IMAGINATION...
*FEH...* YOU'RE THE ONE WHO DOESN'T SEE...
MASTER FREEZA'S CAPABILITIES TRANSCEND ANYTHING YOU CAN COMPRE-HEND...

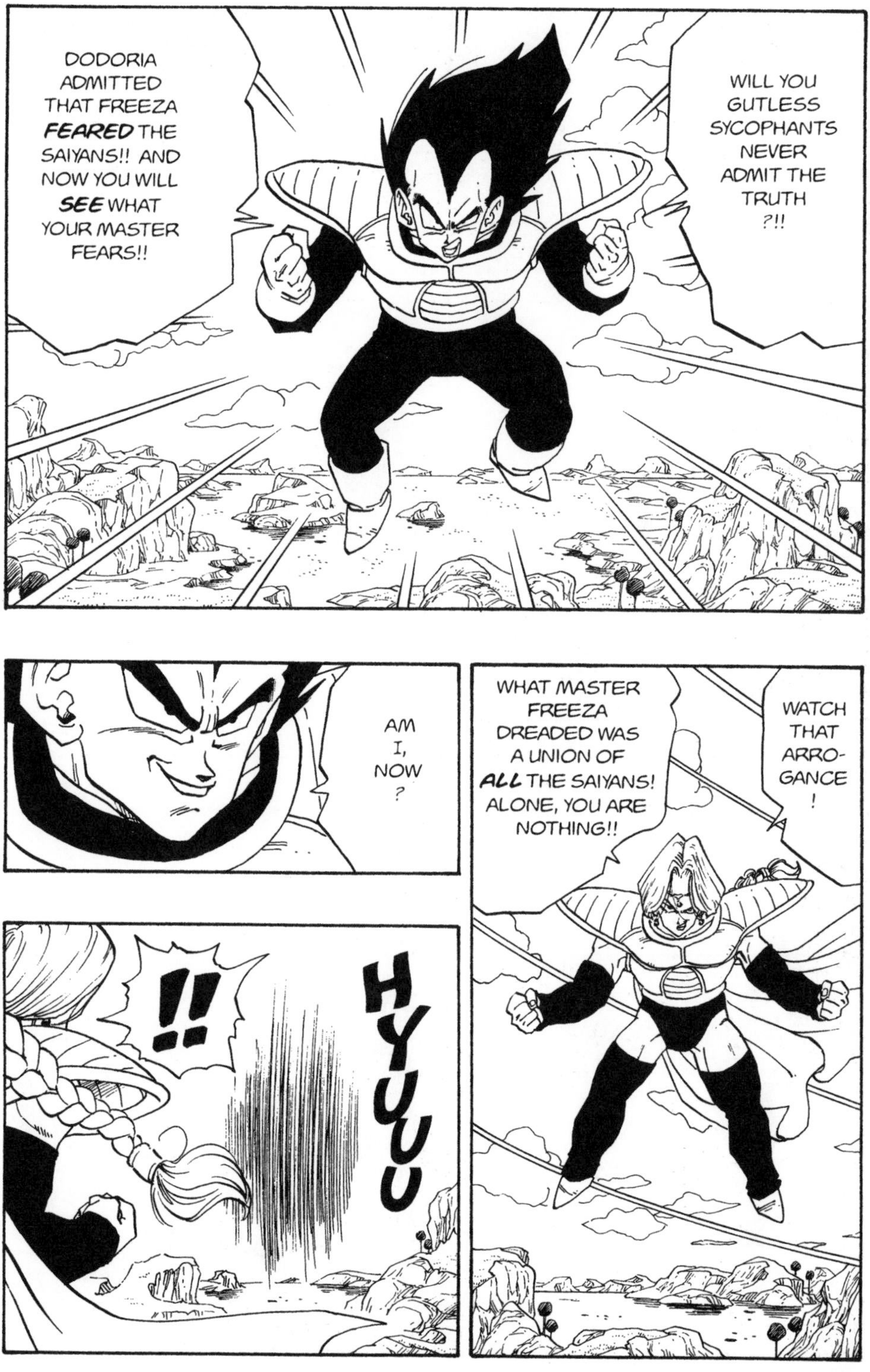
WILL YOU GUTLESS SYCOPHANTS NEVER ADMIT THE TRUTH ?!!
DODORIA ADMITTED THAT FREEZA **FEARED** THE SAIYANS!! AND NOW YOU WILL **SEE** WHAT YOUR MASTER FEARS!!
WATCH THAT ARRO-GANCE !
WHAT MASTER FREEZA DREADED WAS A UNION OF **ALL** THE SAIYANS! ALONE, YOU ARE NOTHING!!
AM I, NOW ?
!!
HYUUU

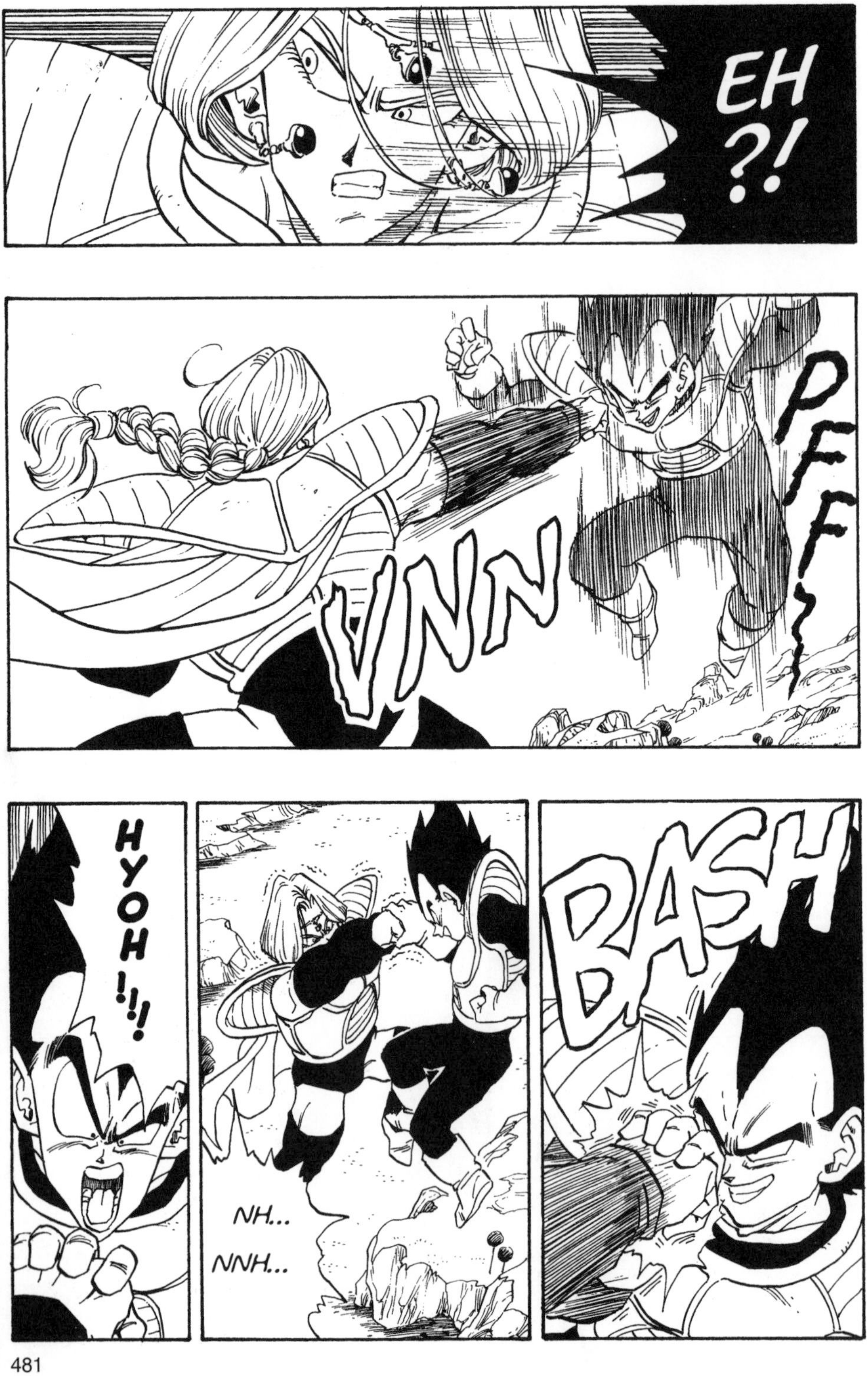
EH?!
PFFF
VNN
BASH
NH...
NNH...
HYOH!!!

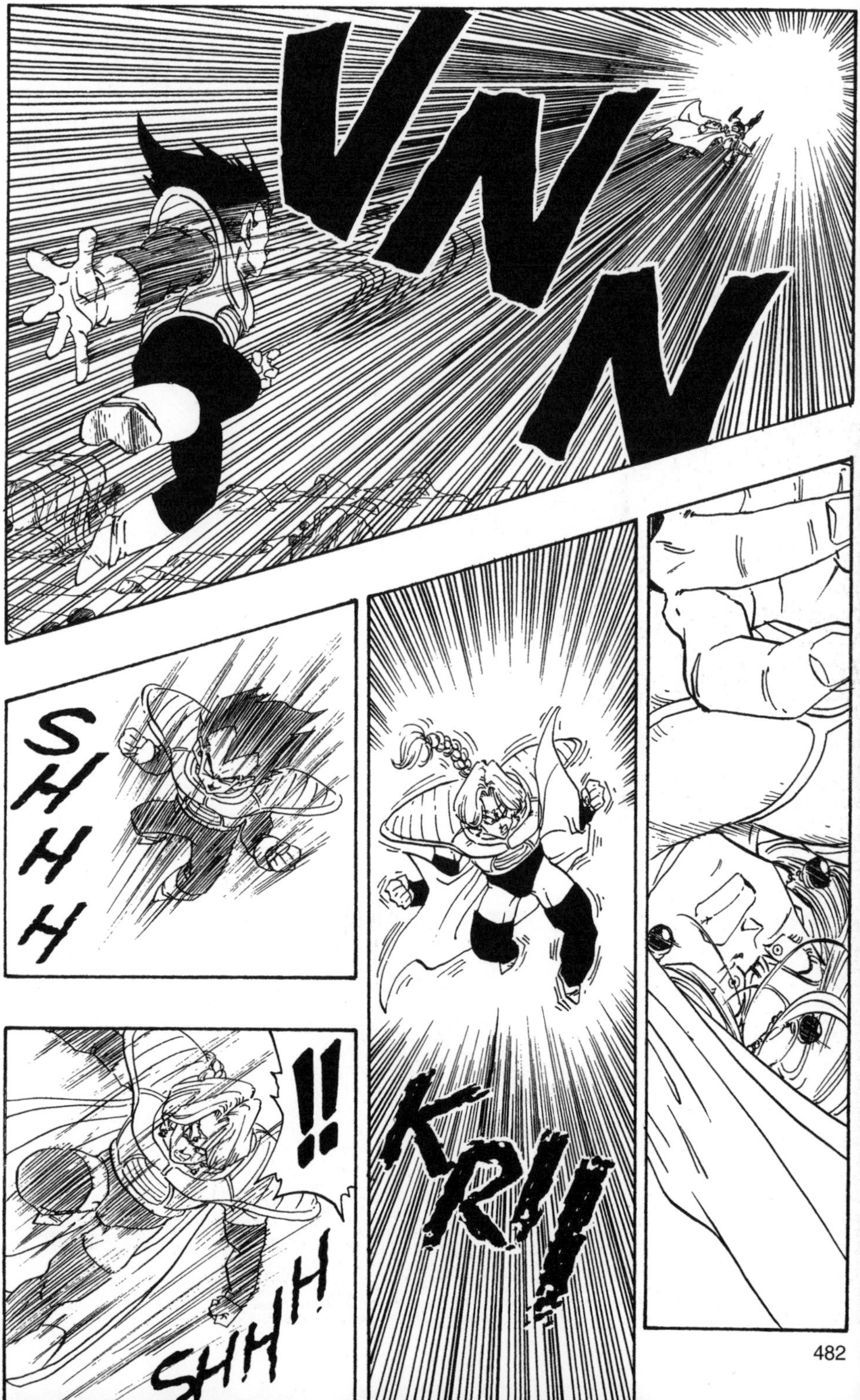
VWNN
KRII
SHHH
!!
SHHH!

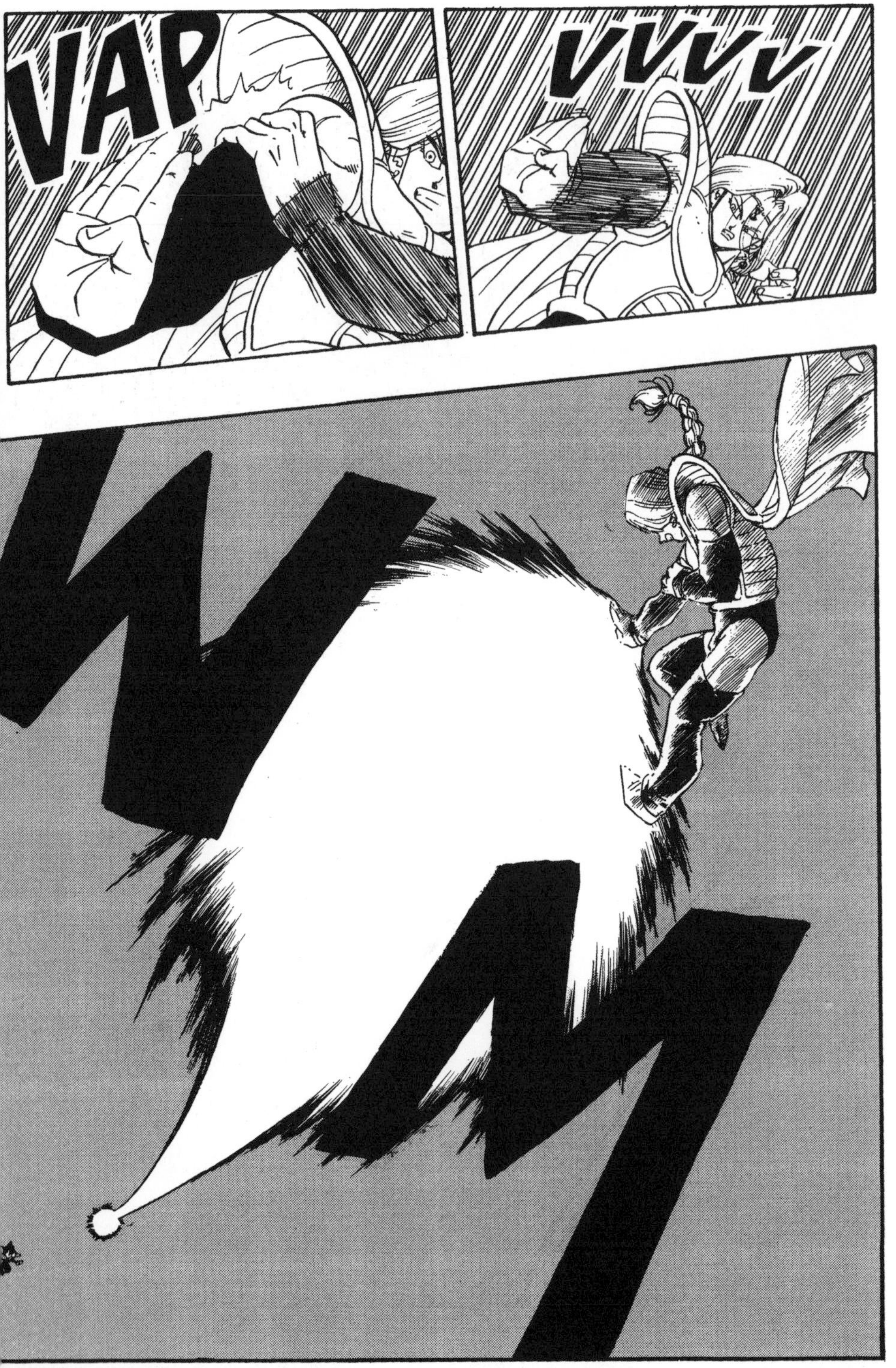
VVVV
VAP

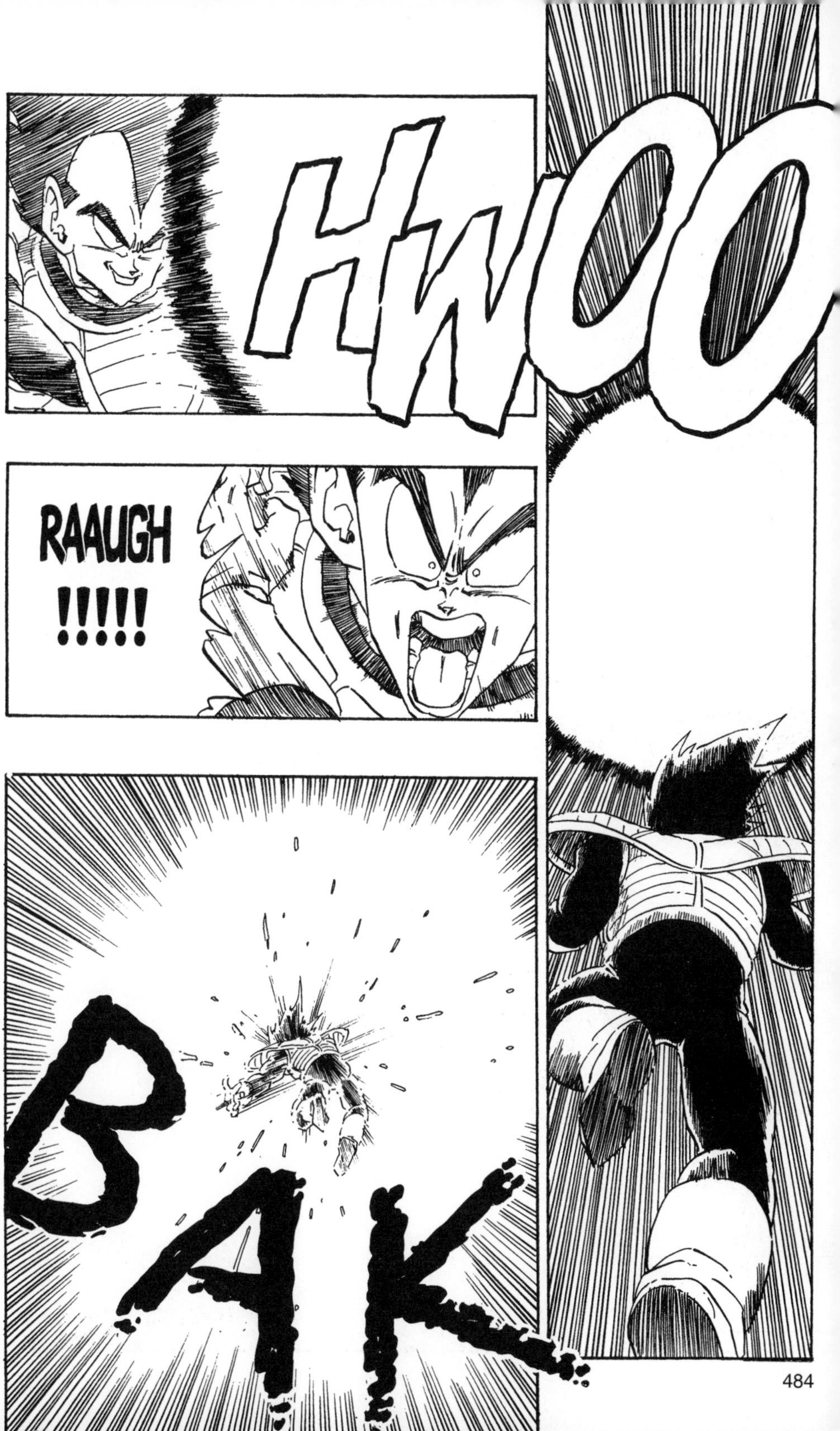
HWOOO
RAAUGH
!!!!!
BAK

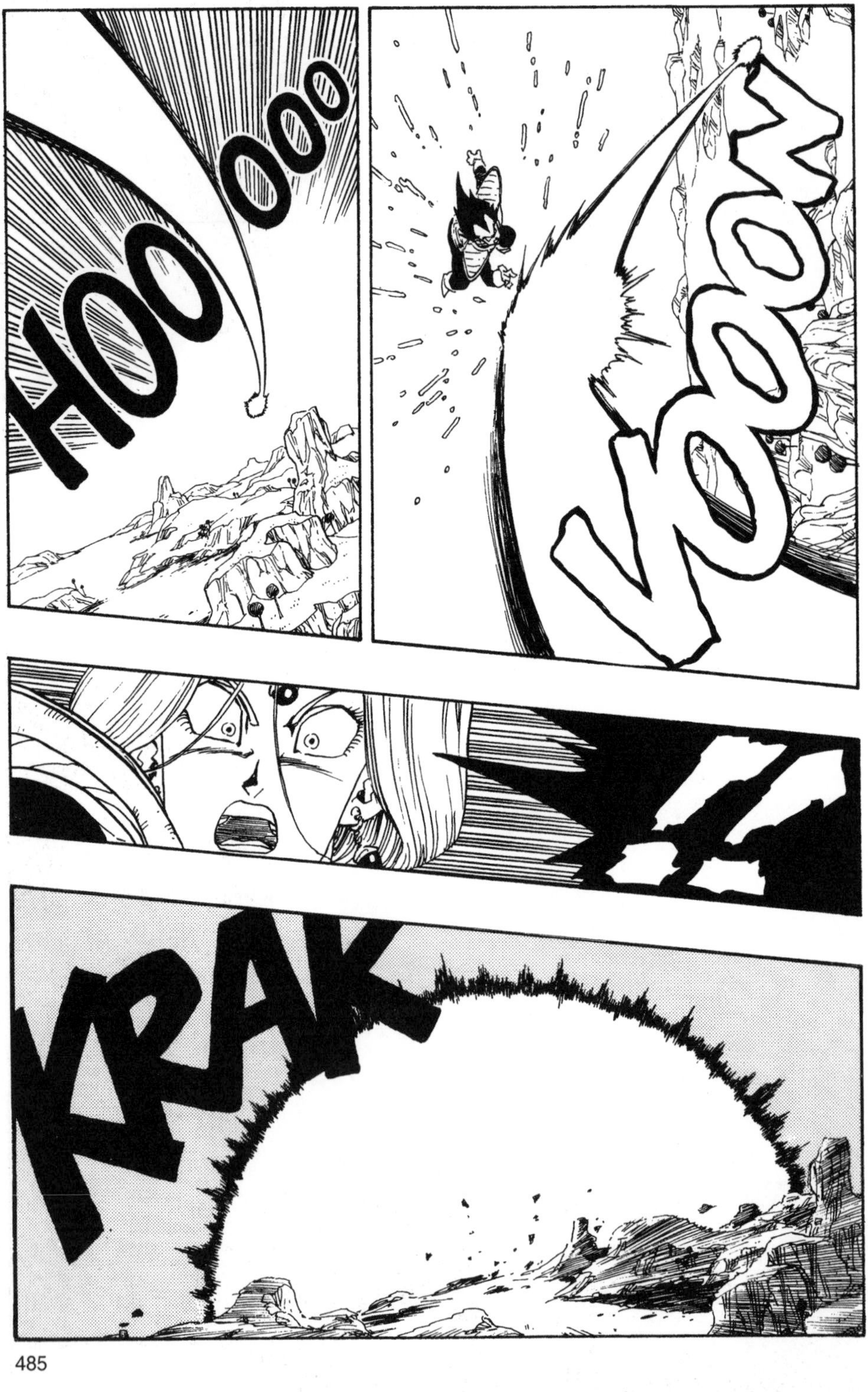
VOOOM
HOOOOOO
!!
KRAK

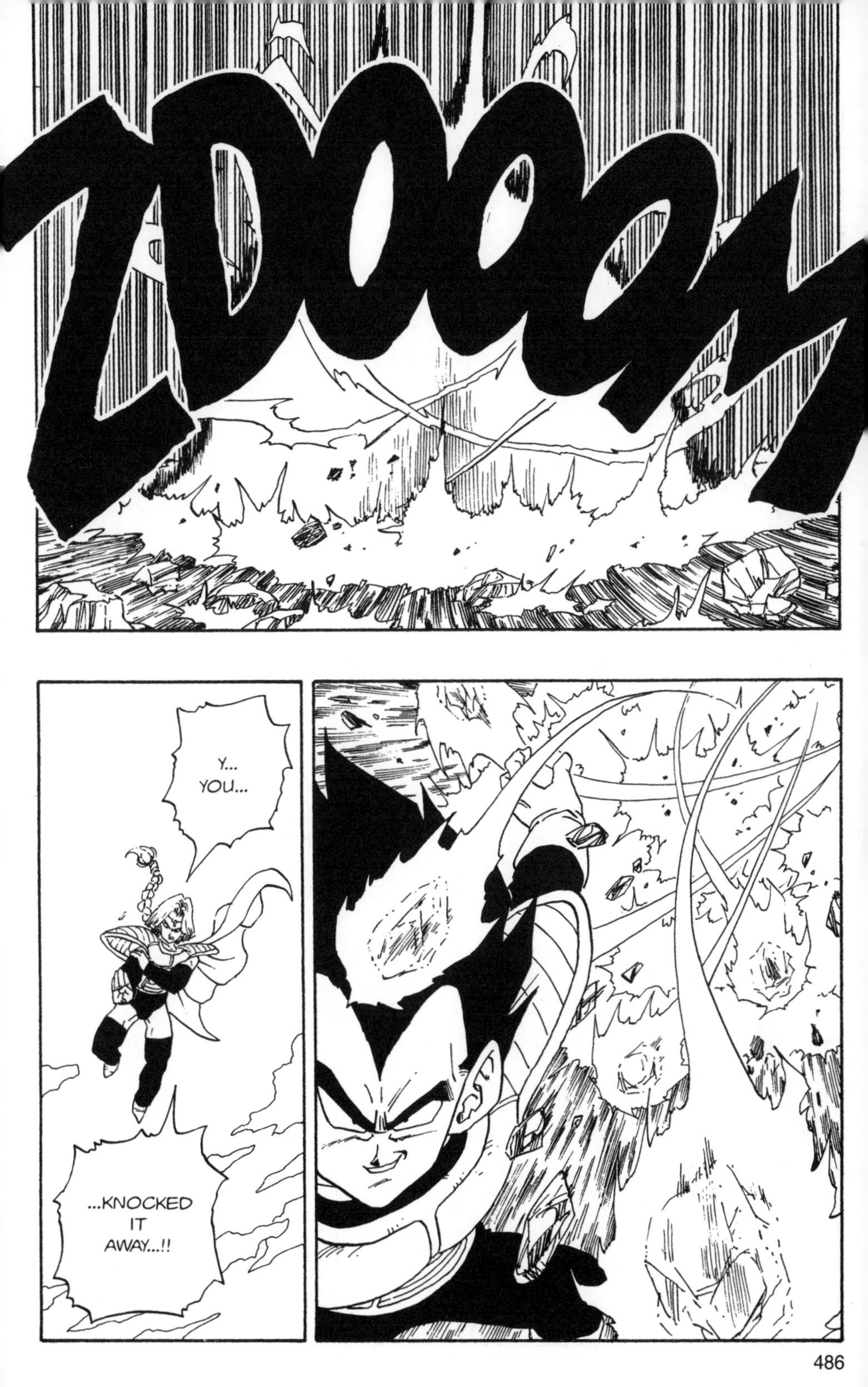
ZDOOOM
Y... YOU...
...KNOCKED IT AWAY...!!

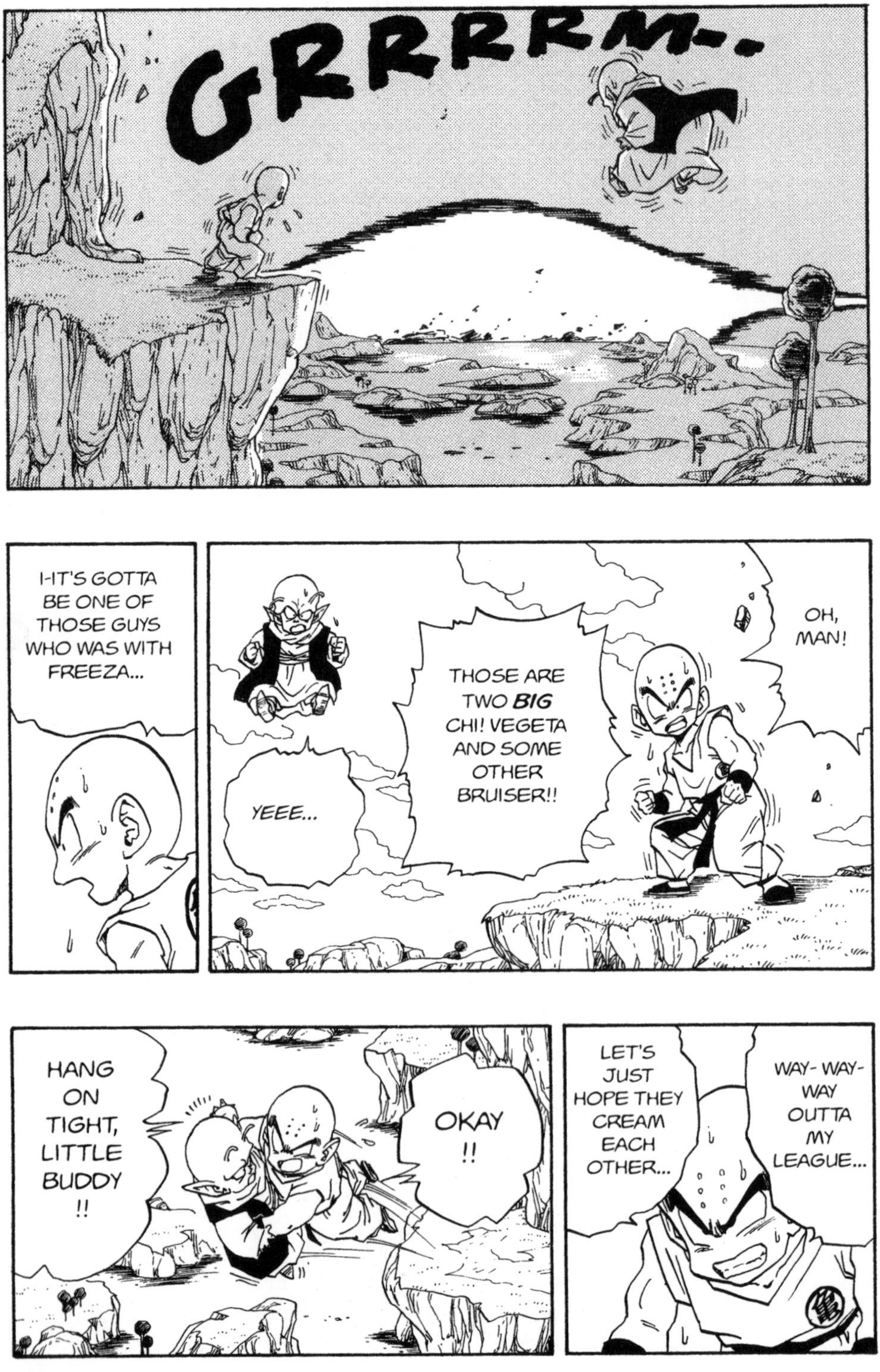
GRRRRM..
OH, MAN!
THOSE ARE TWO **BIG** CHI! VEGETA AND SOME OTHER BRUISER!!
YEEE...
I-IT'S GOTTA BE ONE OF THOSE GUYS WHO WAS WITH FREEZA...
WAY- WAY- WAY OUTTA MY LEAGUE...
LET'S JUST HOPE THEY CREAM EACH OTHER...
HANG ON TIGHT, LITTLE BUDDY !!
OKAY !!

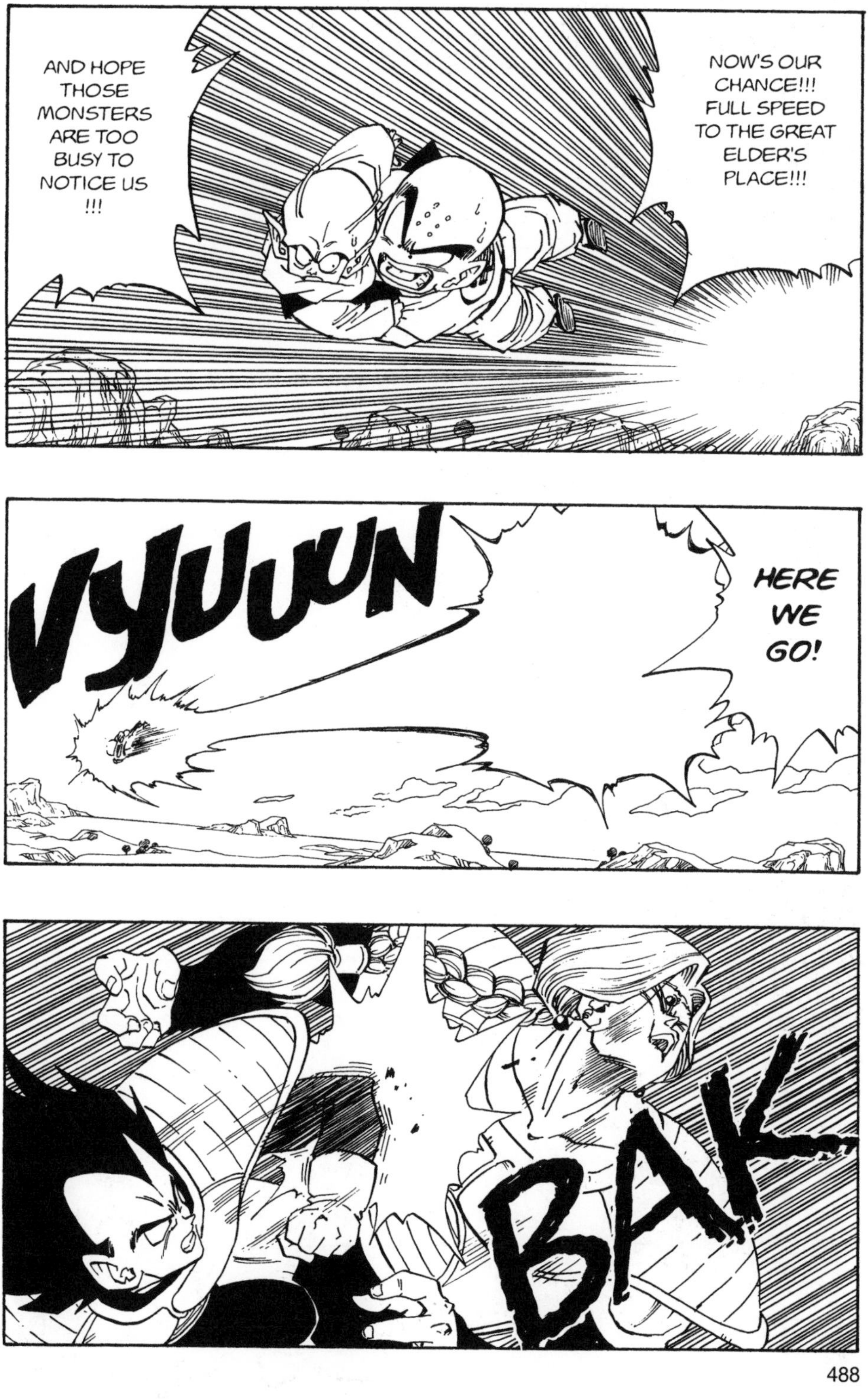
NOW'S OUR CHANCE!!! FULL SPEED TO THE GREAT ELDER'S PLACE!!!
AND HOPE THOSE MONSTERS ARE TOO BUSY TO NOTICE US !!!
HERE WE GO!
VYUUUN
BAK

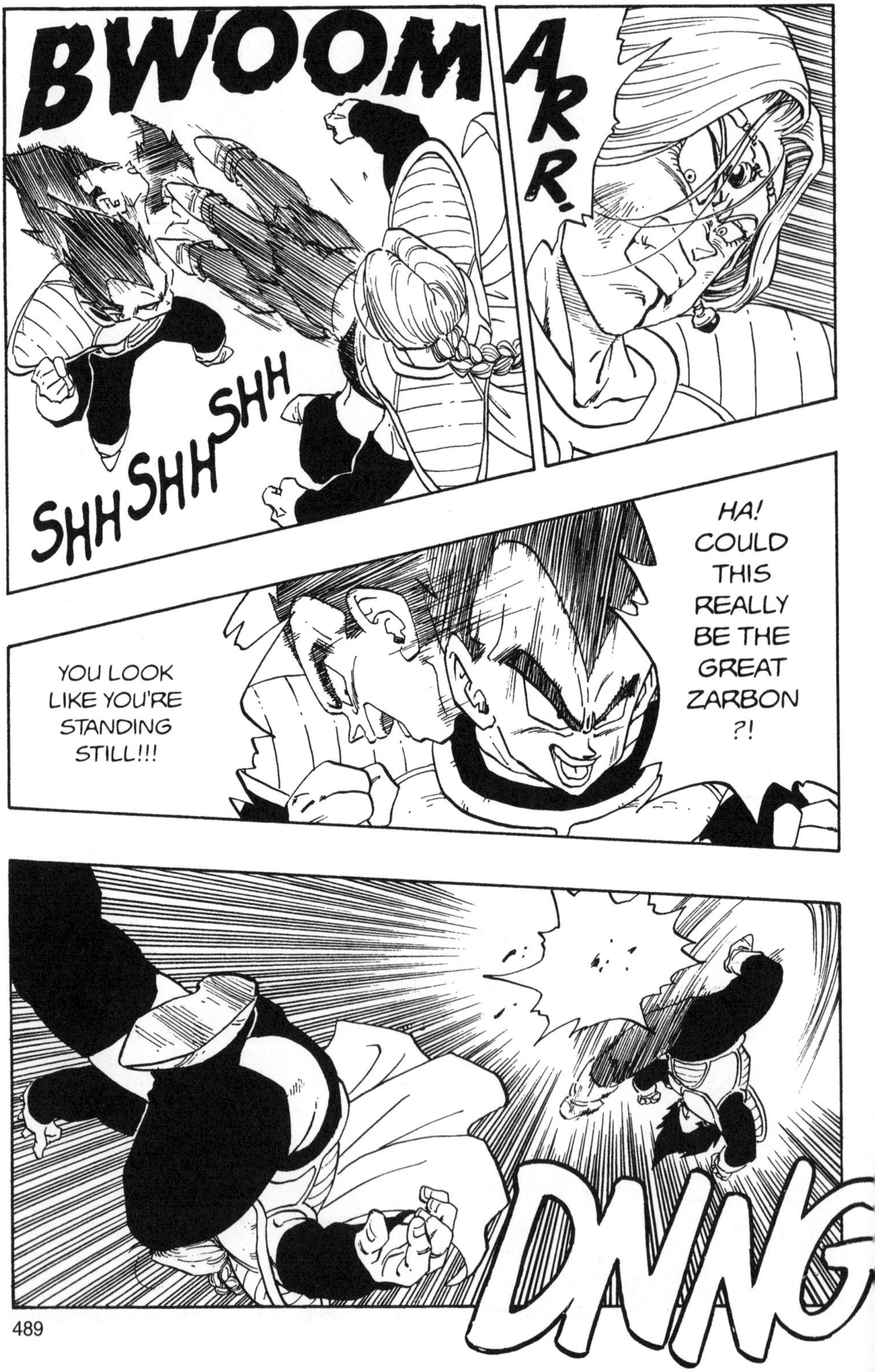
ARR.
BWOOM
SHH SHH SHH
HA! COULD THIS REALLY BE THE GREAT ZARBON ?!
YOU LOOK LIKE YOU'RE STANDING STILL!!!
DNNG

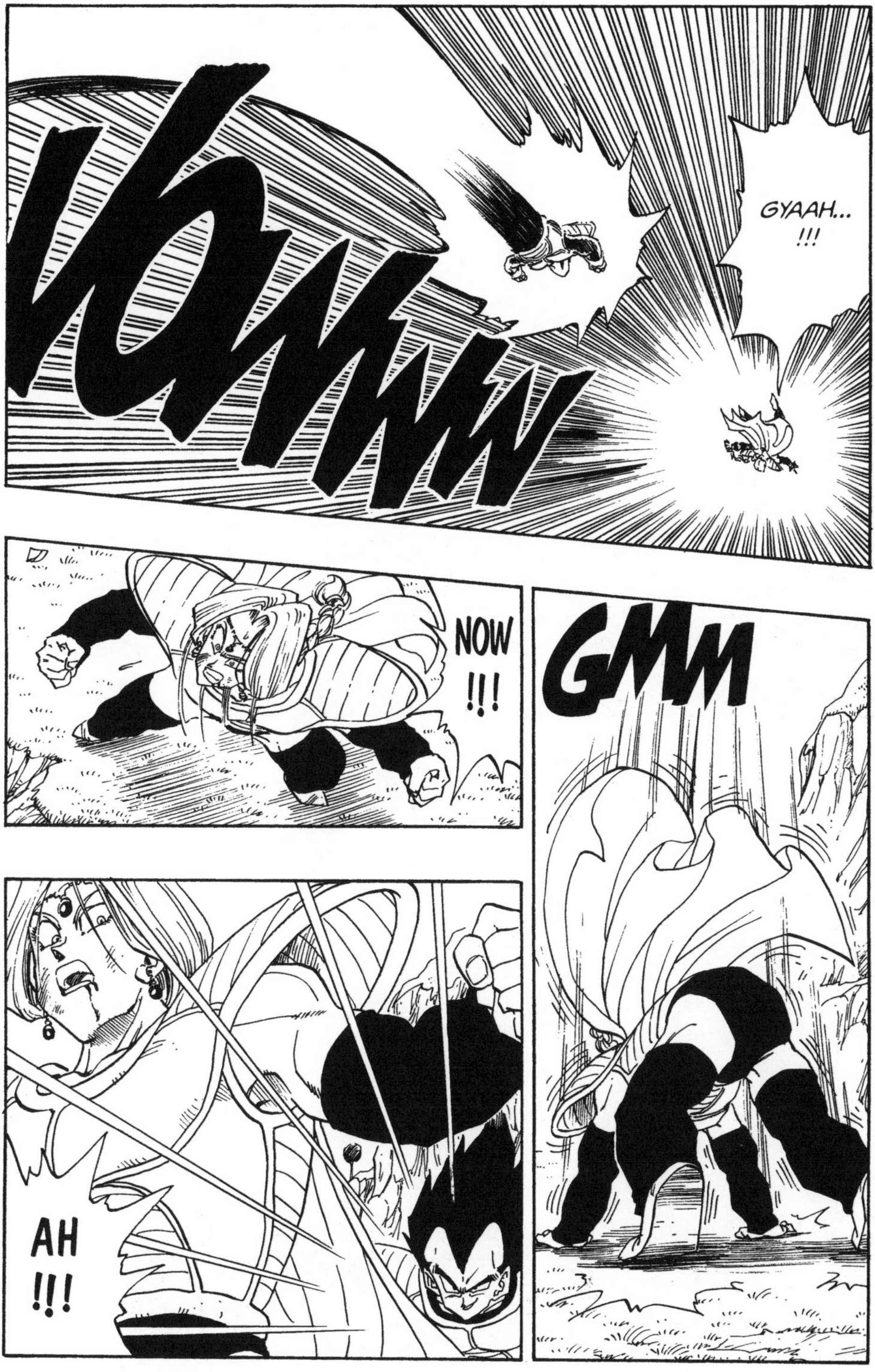
GYAAH... !!!
GMM
NOW !!!
AH !!!

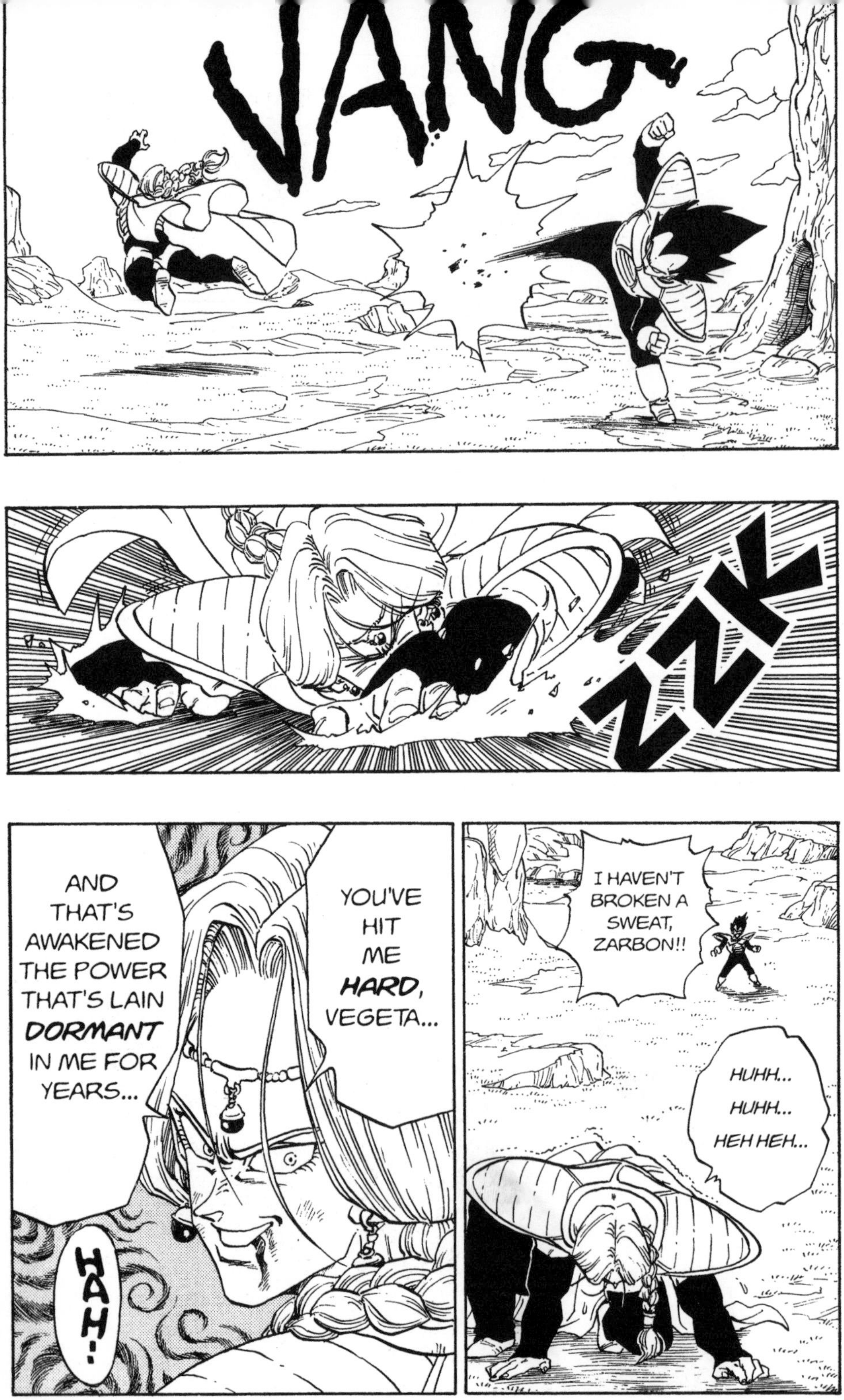
VANG
ZZZK
I HAVEN'T BROKEN A SWEAT, ZARBON!!
HUHH... HUHH... HEH HEH...
YOU'VE HIT ME HARD, VEGETA...
AND THAT'S AWAKENED THE POWER THAT'S LAIN DORMANT IN ME FOR YEARS...
HAH!

# DBZ:69 • Zarbon's True Power

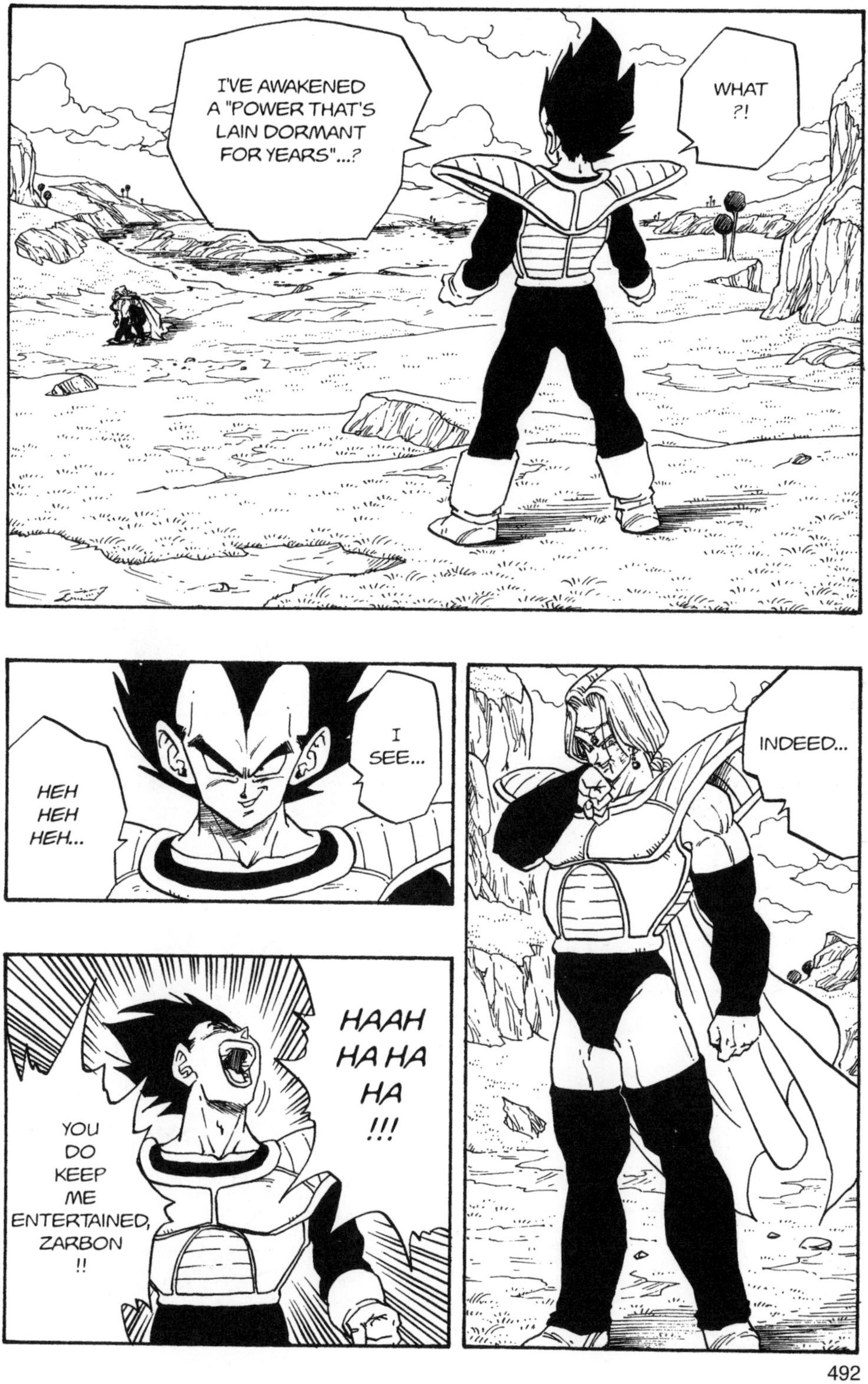
WHAT ?!
I'VE AWAKENED A "POWER THAT'S LAIN DORMANT FOR YEARS"...?
INDEED...
I SEE...
HEH HEH HEH...
HAAH HA HA HA !!!
YOU DO KEEP ME ENTERTAINED, ZARBON !!

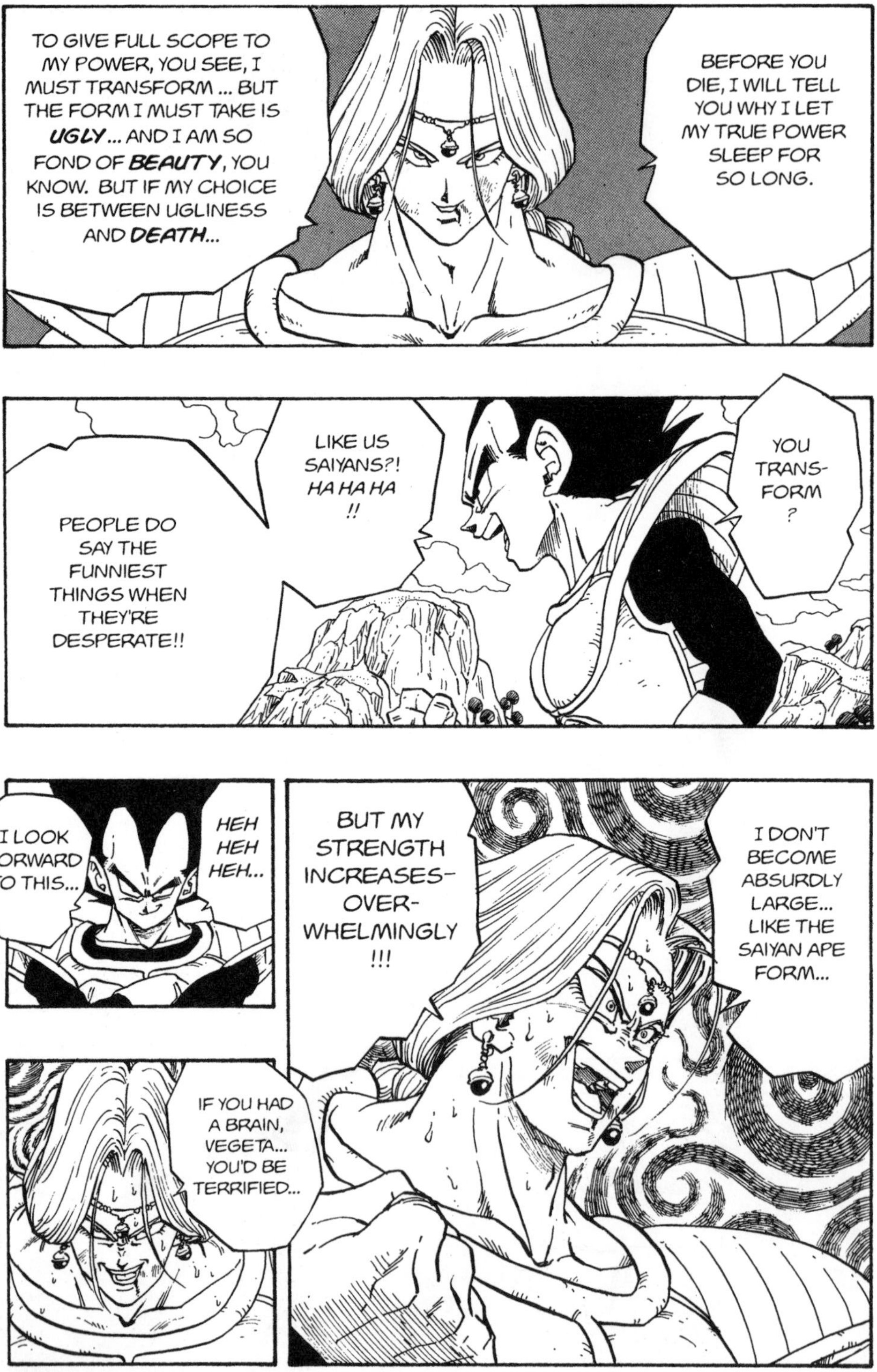

BEFORE YOU DIE, I WILL TELL YOU WHY I LET MY TRUE POWER SLEEP FOR SO LONG.
TO GIVE FULL SCOPE TO MY POWER, YOU SEE, I MUST TRANSFORM ... BUT THE FORM I MUST TAKE IS ***UGLY***... AND I AM SO FOND OF ***BEAUTY***, YOU KNOW. BUT IF MY CHOICE IS BETWEEN UGLINESS AND ***DEATH***...
YOU TRANS-FORM?
LIKE US SAIYANS?! *HA HA HA!!*
PEOPLE DO SAY THE FUNNIEST THINGS WHEN THEY'RE DESPERATE!!
I DON'T BECOME ABSURDLY LARGE... LIKE THE SAIYAN APE FORM...
BUT MY STRENGTH INCREASES-OVER-WHELMINGLY!!!
*HEH HEH HEH...*
I LOOK FORWARD TO THIS...
IF YOU HAD A BRAIN, VEGETA... YOU'D BE TERRIFIED...

DOOM
!!
DOOM
HAF

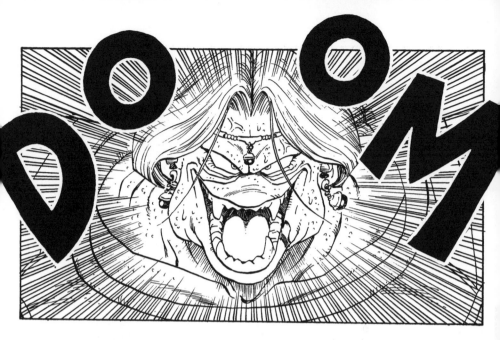

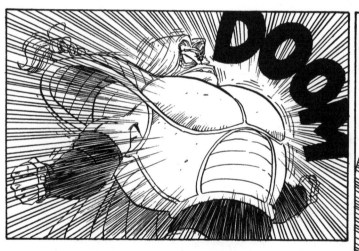

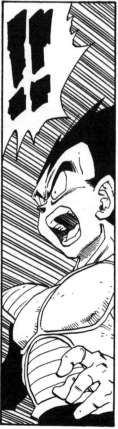

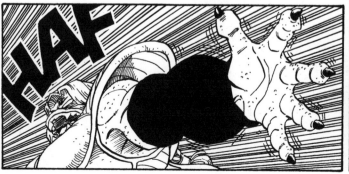

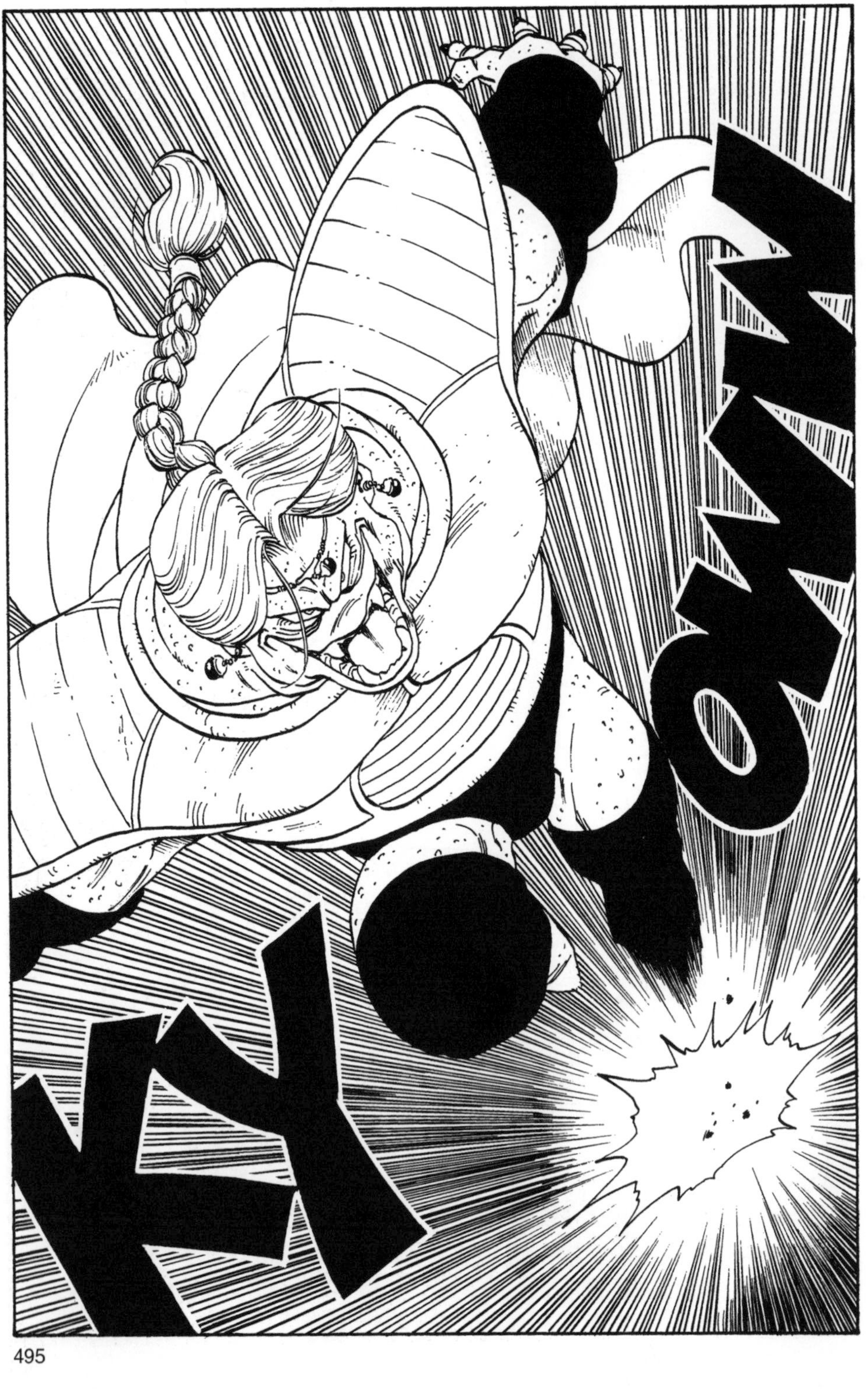
KYOWW

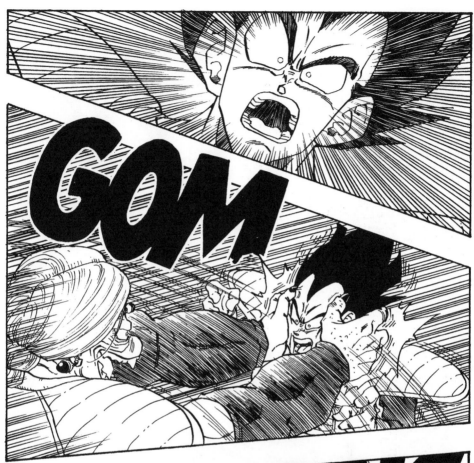

GOM.

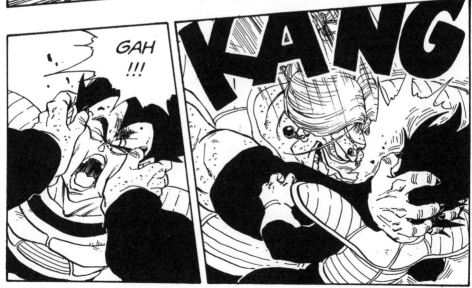

KANG

GAH
!!!

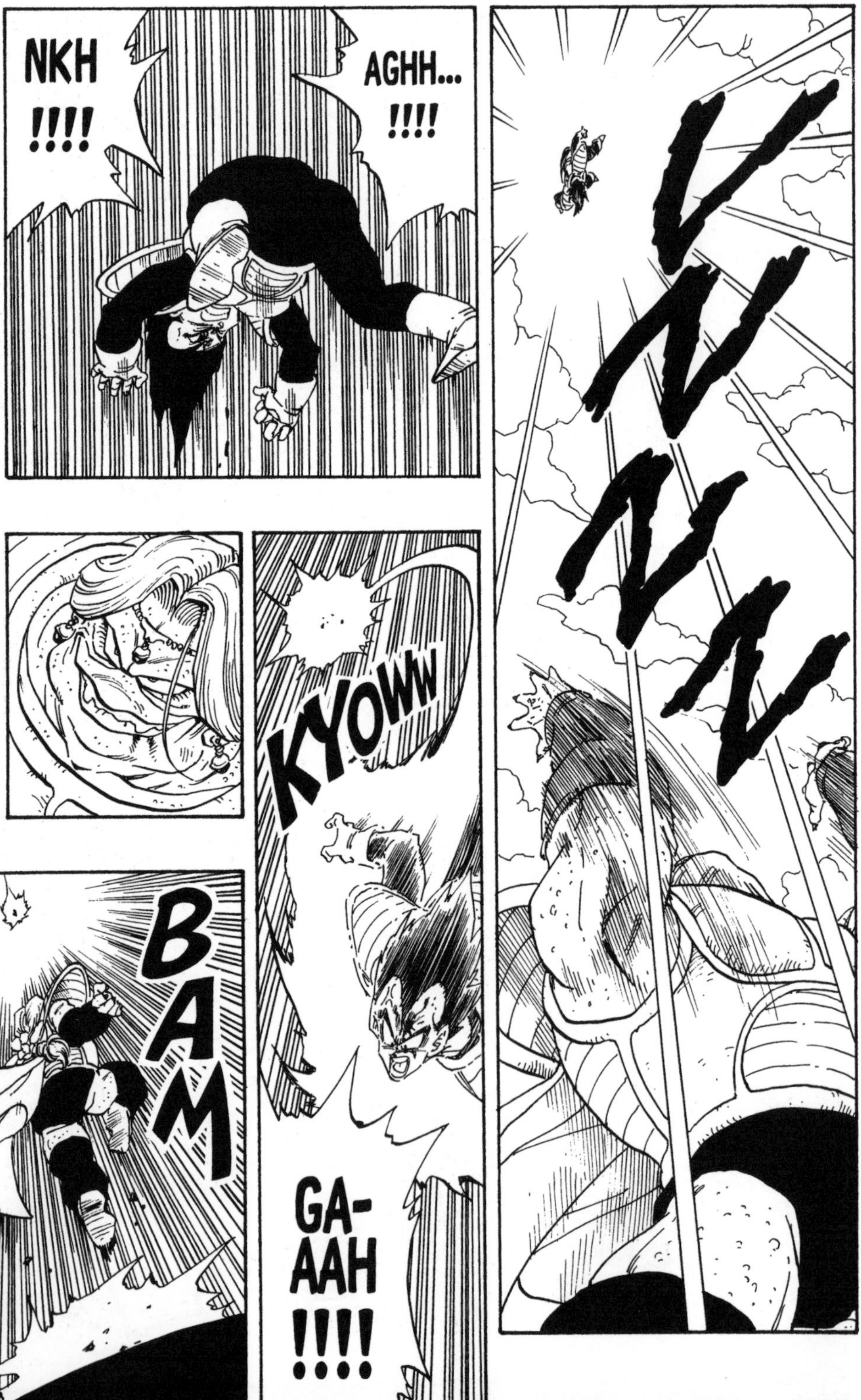
AGHH... !!!!
NKH !!!!
KYOWW
GA-AAH !!!!
BAM

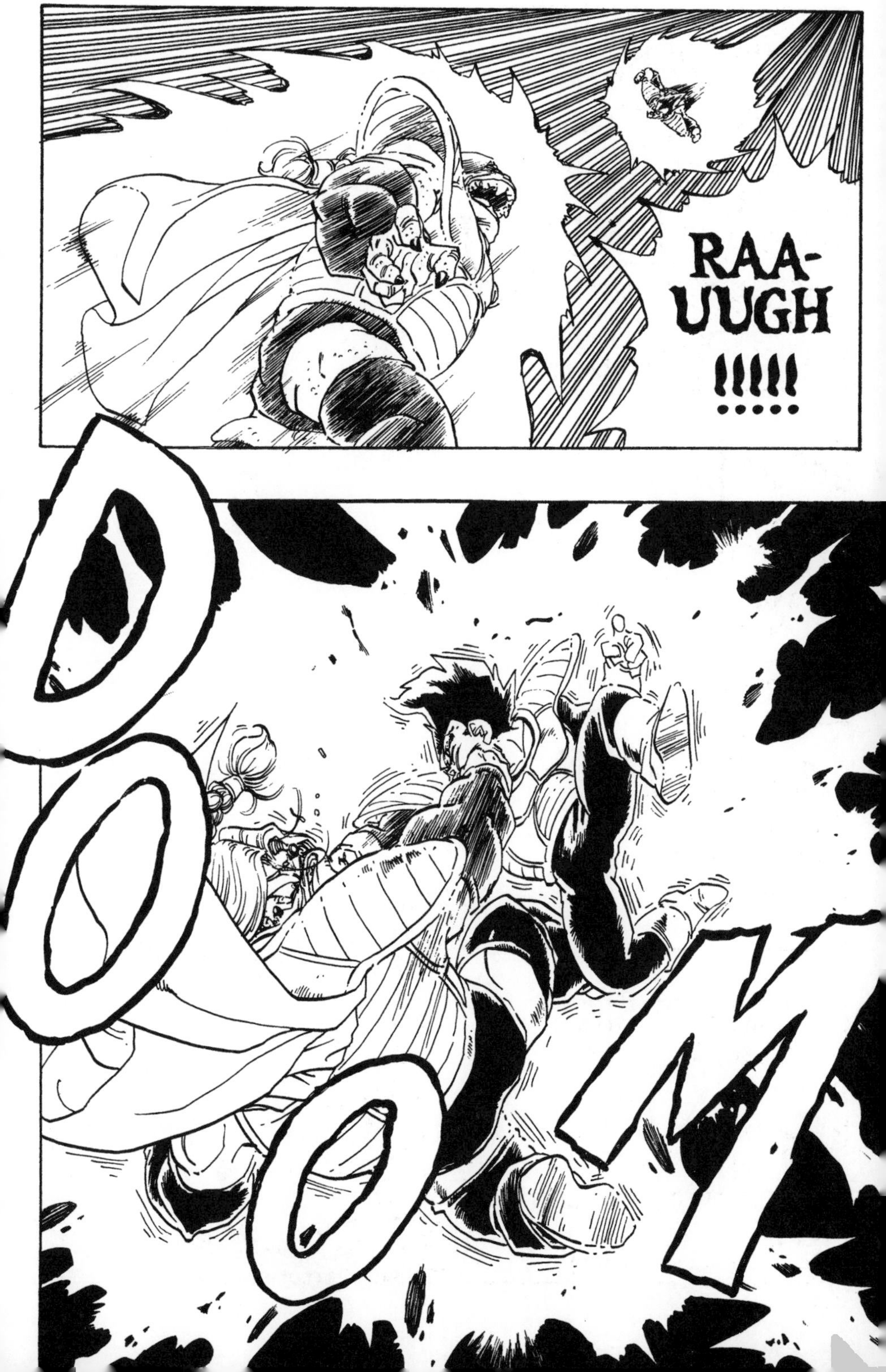
RAA-
UUGH
!!!!!
DOOM

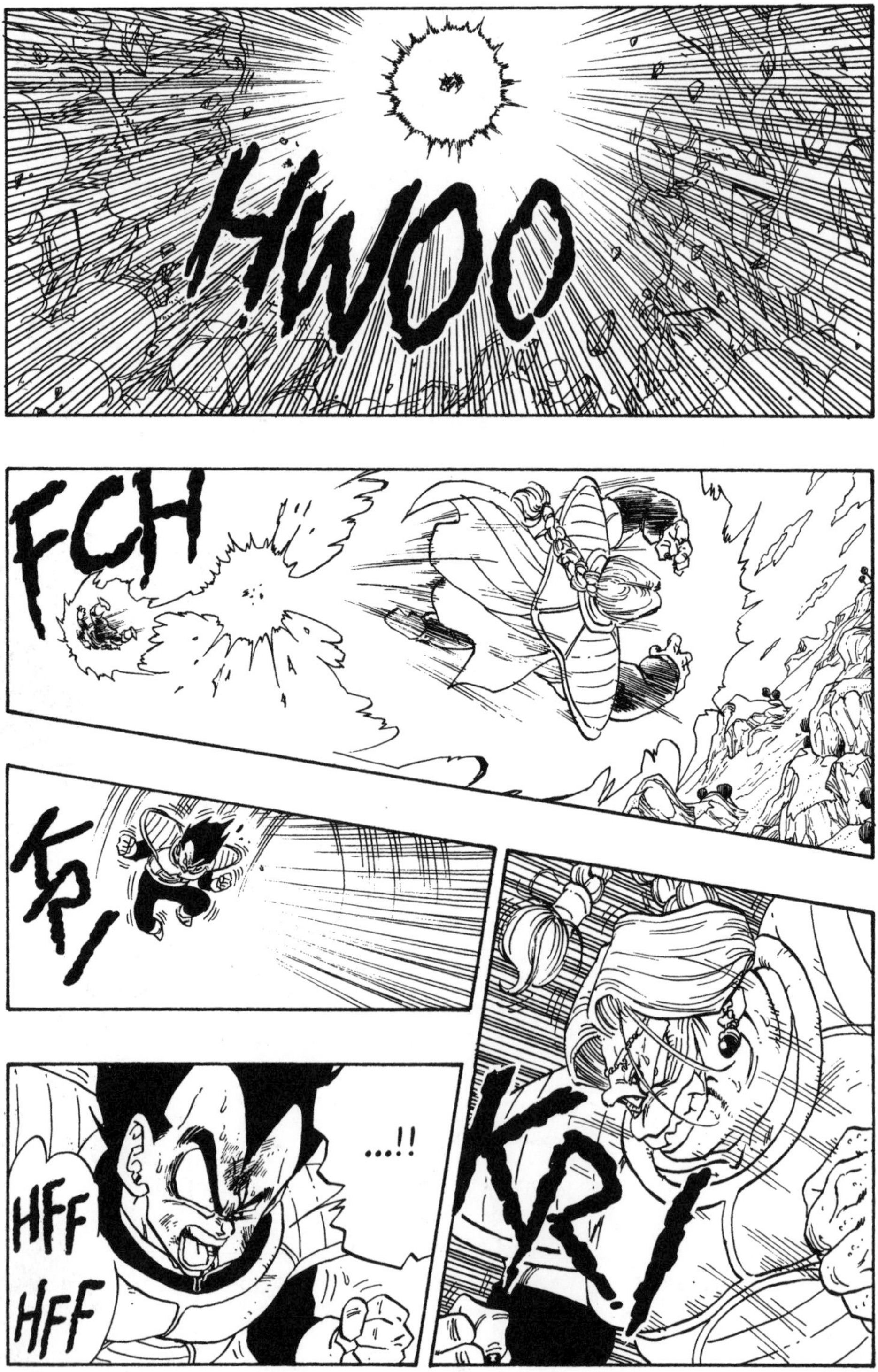
HWOO
FCH
KRI
KRI
...!!
HFF
HFF

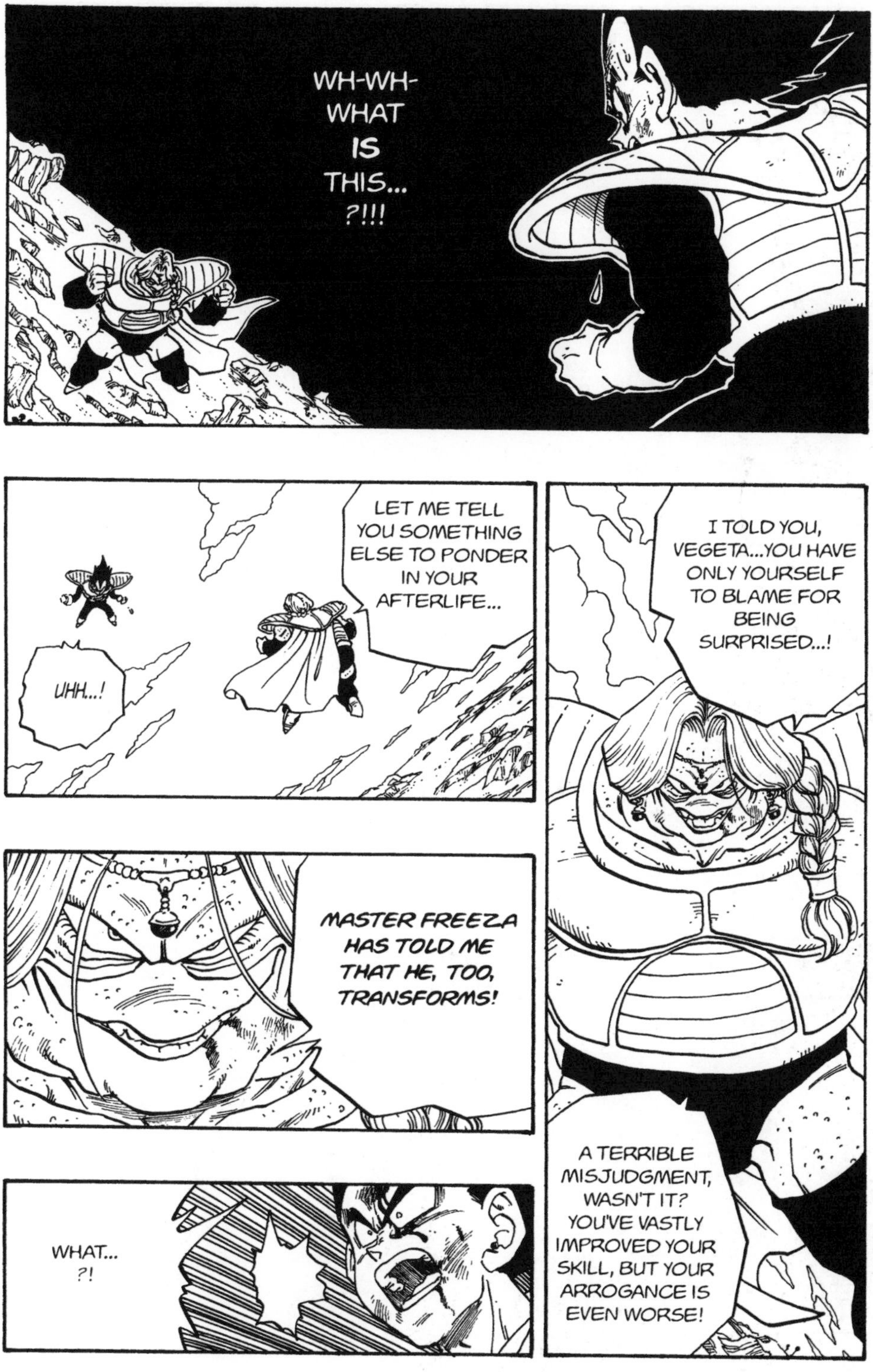
WH-WH-WHAT IS THIS...?!!!
I TOLD YOU, VEGETA...YOU HAVE ONLY YOURSELF TO BLAME FOR BEING SURPRISED...!
A TERRIBLE MISJUDGMENT, WASN'T IT? YOU'VE VASTLY IMPROVED YOUR SKILL, BUT YOUR ARROGANCE IS EVEN WORSE!
LET ME TELL YOU SOMETHING ELSE TO PONDER IN YOUR AFTERLIFE...
UHH...!
MASTER FREEZA HAS TOLD ME THAT HE, TOO, TRANSFORMS!
WHAT...?!

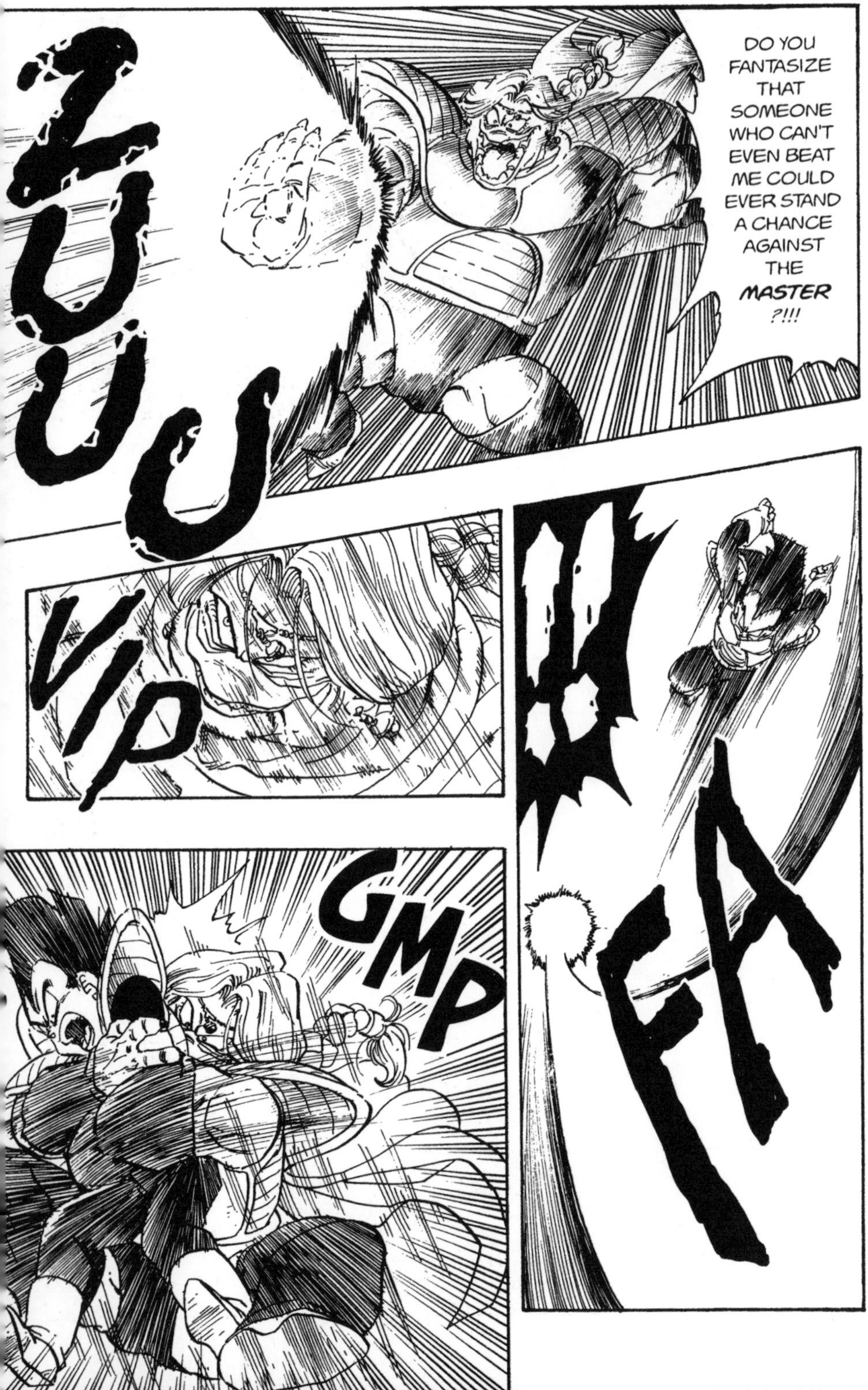
DO YOU FANTASIZE THAT SOMEONE WHO CAN'T EVEN BEAT ME COULD EVER STAND A CHANCE AGAINST THE *MASTER* ?!!!
ZUUU
!!
FA
VIP
GMP

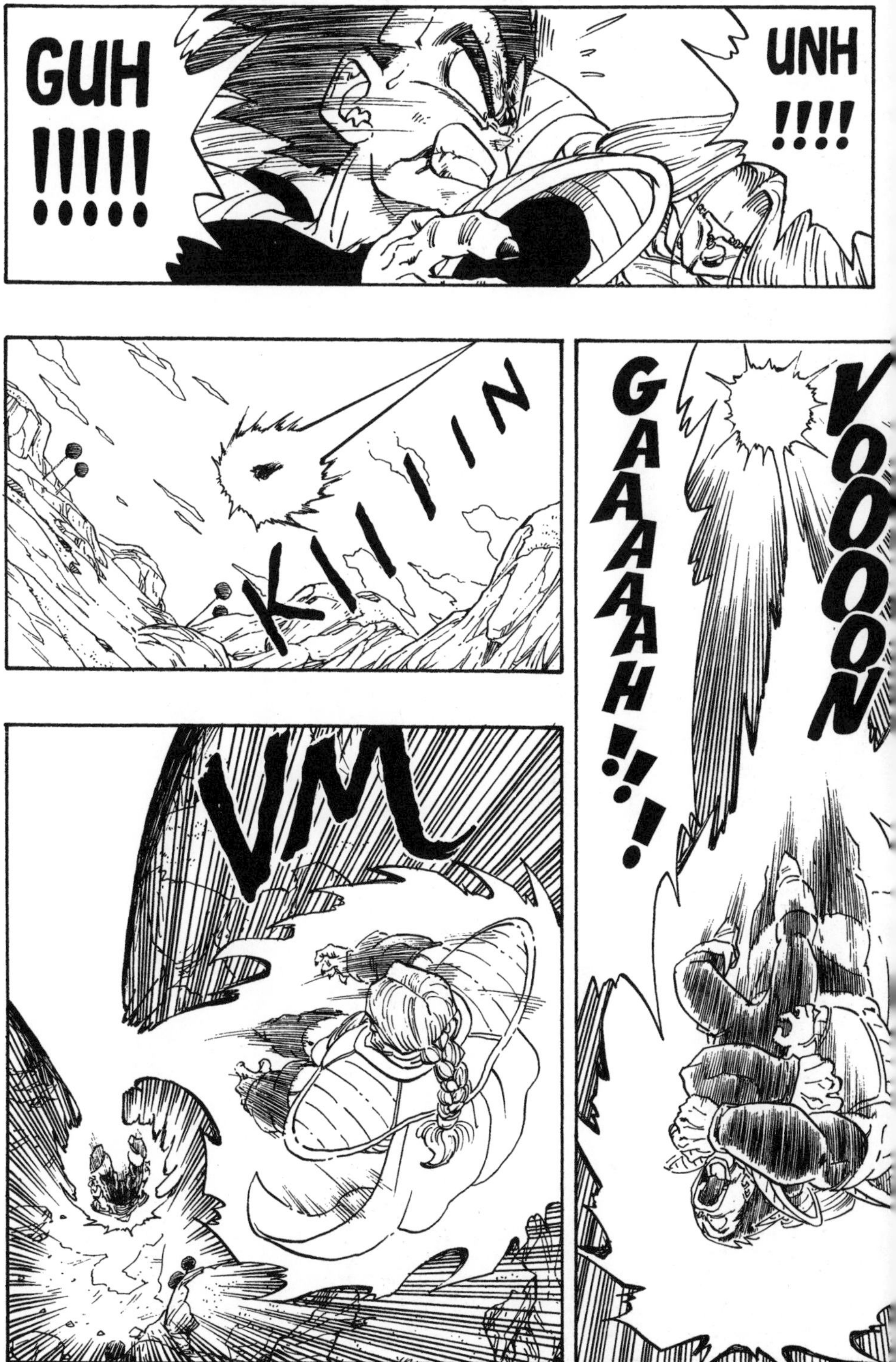
UNH !!!!
GUH !!!!!!
VOOOON
GAAAAAH!!!
KIIIIIN
VM

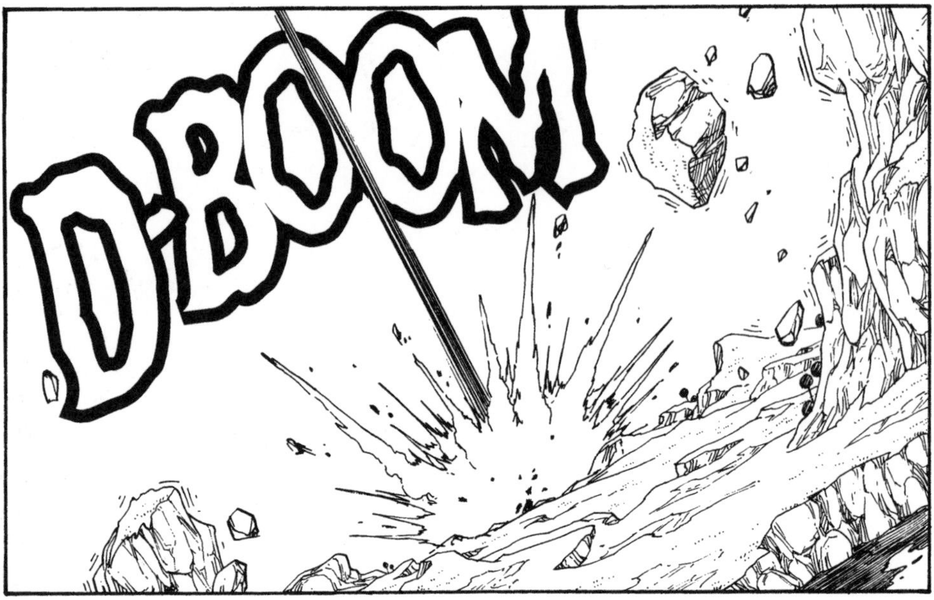
D-BOOM
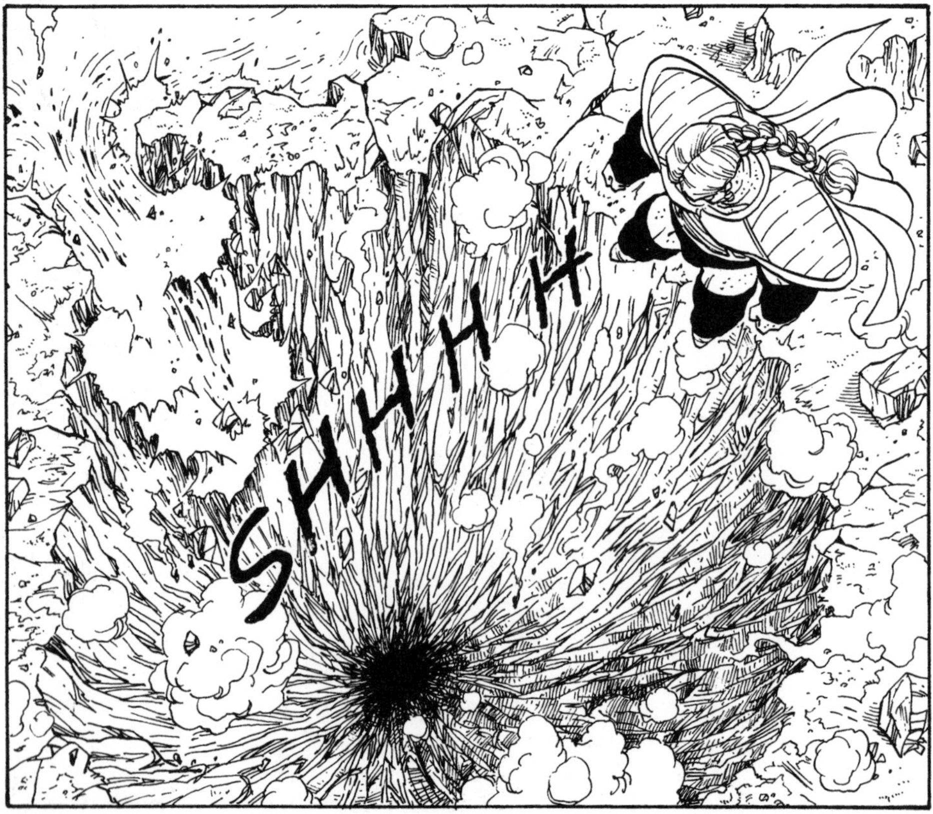
SHHHHH

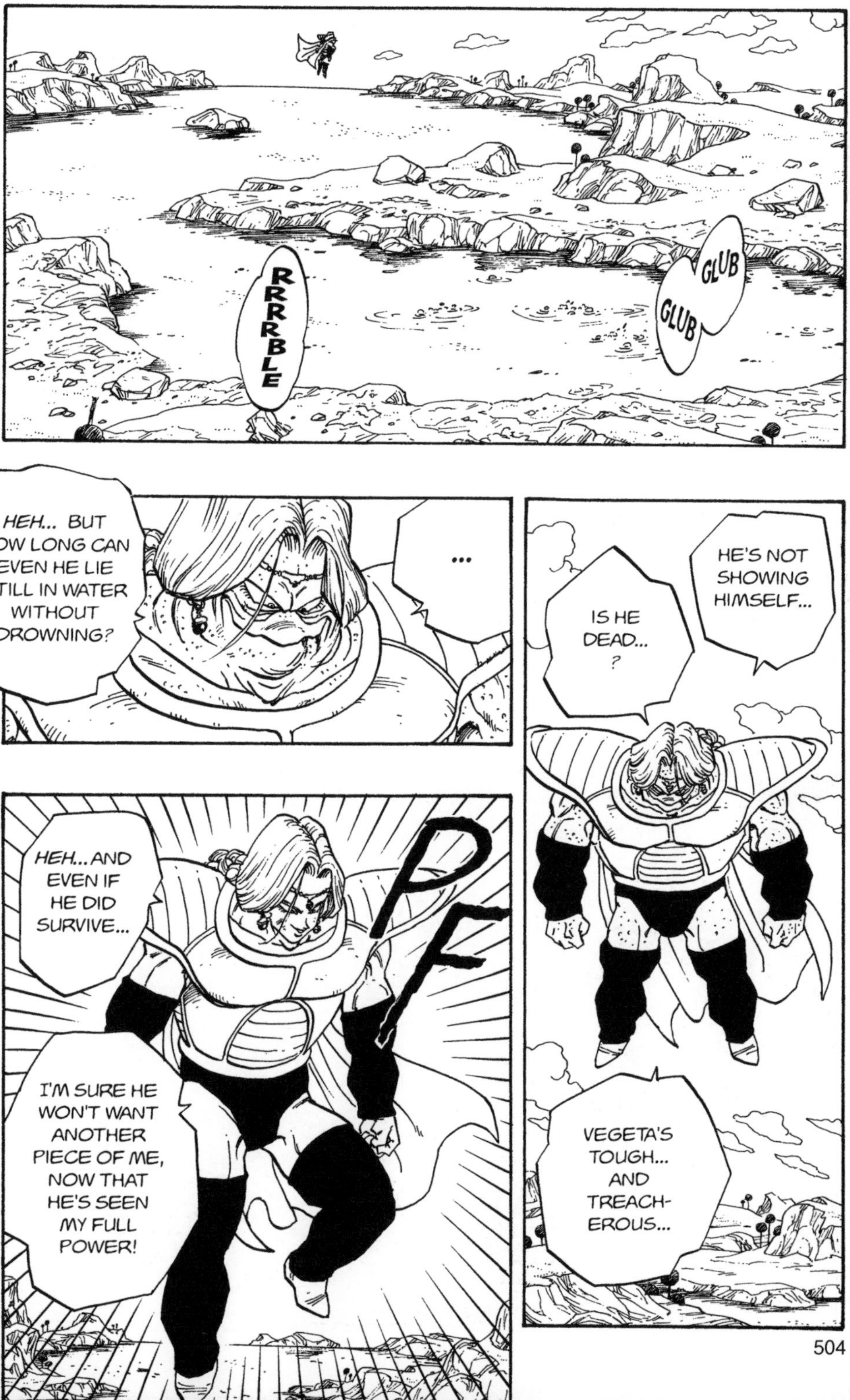
GLUB
GLUB
RRRRBLE
HE'S NOT SHOWING HIMSELF...
IS HE DEAD...?
VEGETA'S TOUGH... AND TREACH-EROUS...
...
HEH... BUT HOW LONG CAN EVEN HE LIE STILL IN WATER WITHOUT DROWNING?
PF
HEH...AND EVEN IF HE DID SURVIVE...
I'M SURE HE WON'T WANT ANOTHER PIECE OF ME, NOW THAT HE'S SEEN MY FULL POWER!

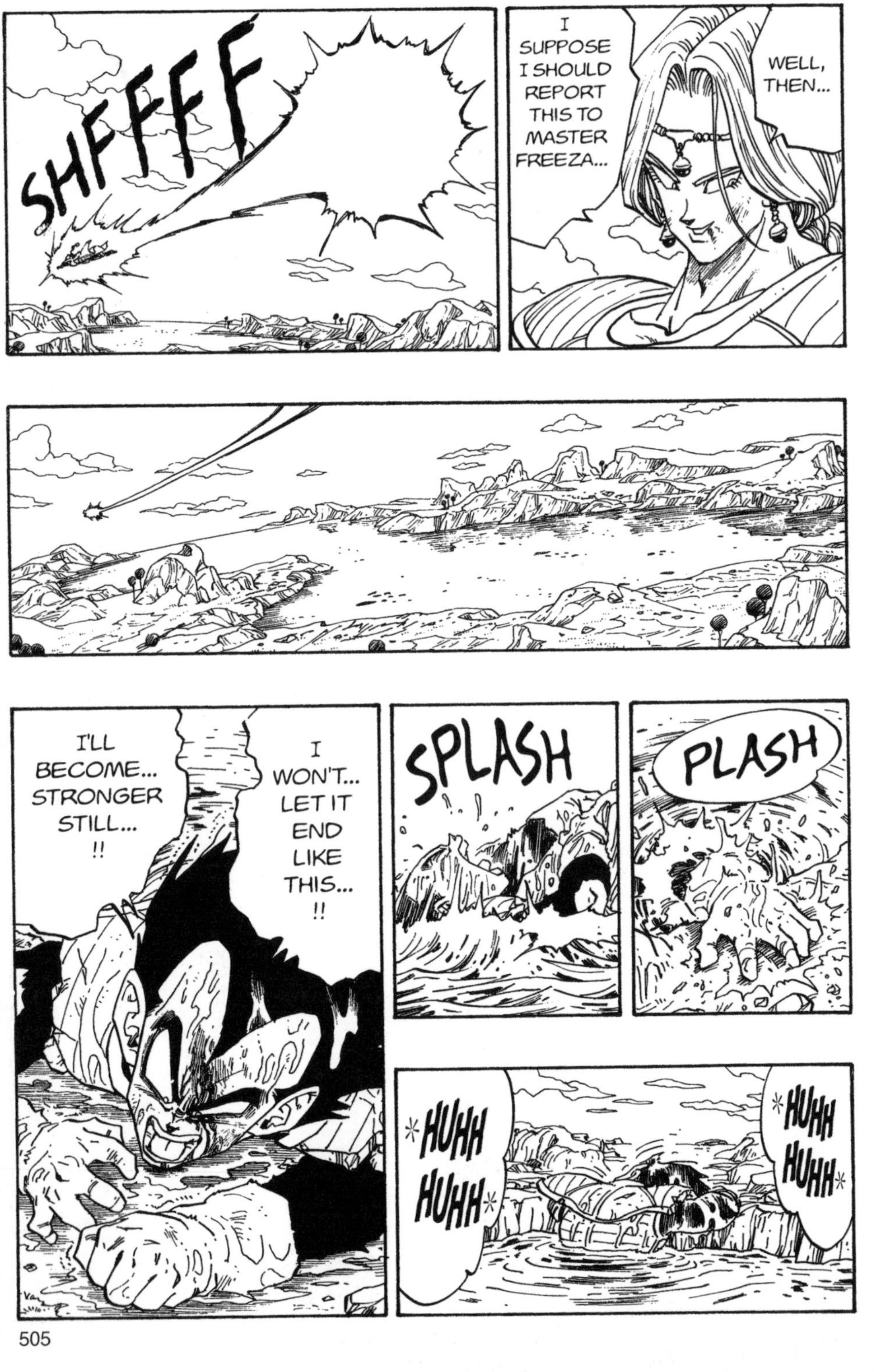
WELL, THEN...
I SUPPOSE I SHOULD REPORT THIS TO MASTER FREEZA...
SHFFFF
PLASH
SPLASH
*HUHH HUHH*
*HUHH HUHH*
I WON'T... LET IT END LIKE THIS... !!
I'LL BECOME... STRONGER STILL... !!

# DBZ:70 • The Great Elder's House

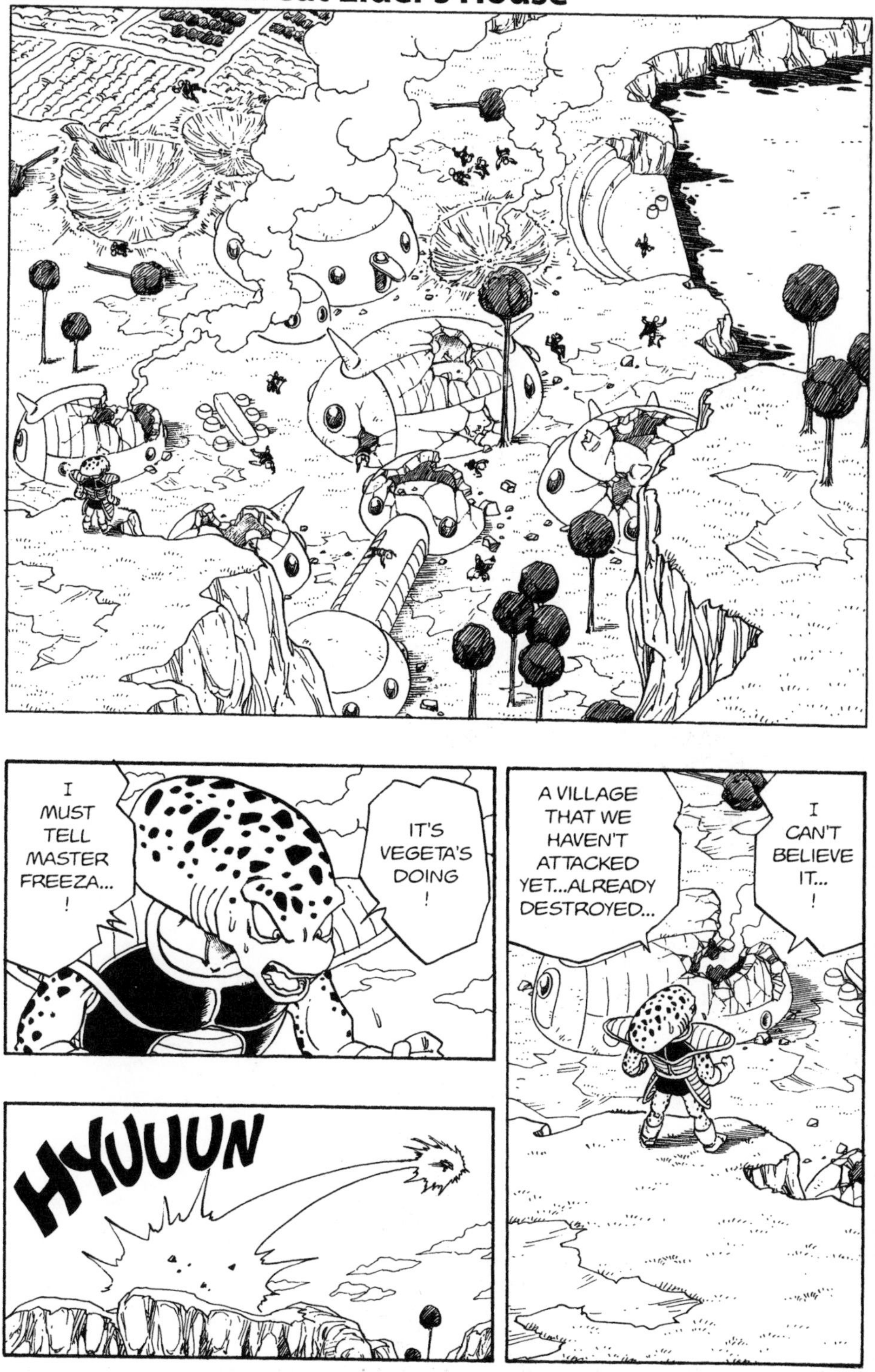
I CAN'T BELIEVE IT...!
A VILLAGE THAT WE HAVEN'T ATTACKED YET...ALREADY DESTROYED...
IT'S VEGETA'S DOING!
I MUST TELL MASTER FREEZA...!
HYUUUN

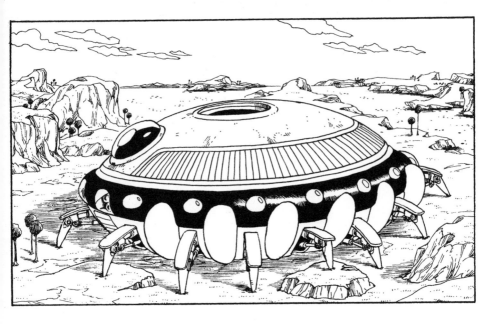

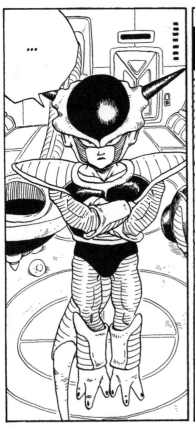

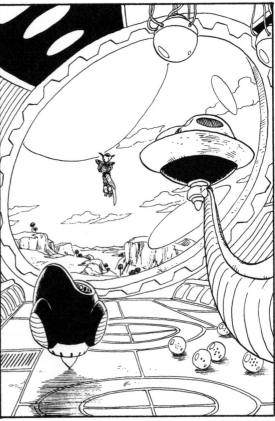

507

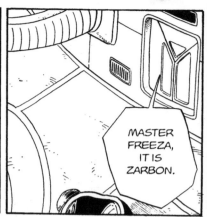

MASTER FREEZA, IT IS ZARBON.
COME IN, PLEASE.
VIIIIN
TP
DID YOU FIND A VILLAGE?
NO, I HAVEN'T YET... HOWEVER...
I DID DEFEAT VEGETA, MASTER.
AH. I TAKE IT, THEN, MR. ZARBON, THAT YOU TRANSFORMED FOR THE FIRST TIME IN A WHILE?
AND IS VEGETA DEAD?
I DID NOT CONFIRM THE CORPSE, SIR... BUT EVEN IF HE SURVIVED, HE SHOULD BE SERIOUSLY INJURED.
WHY DID YOU NOT CONFIRM IT?

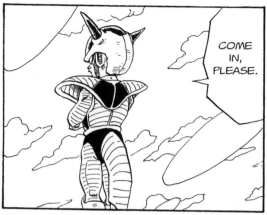

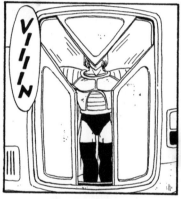

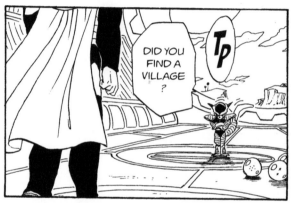

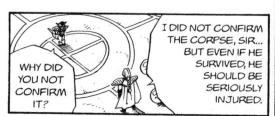

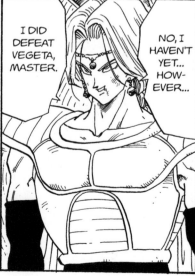

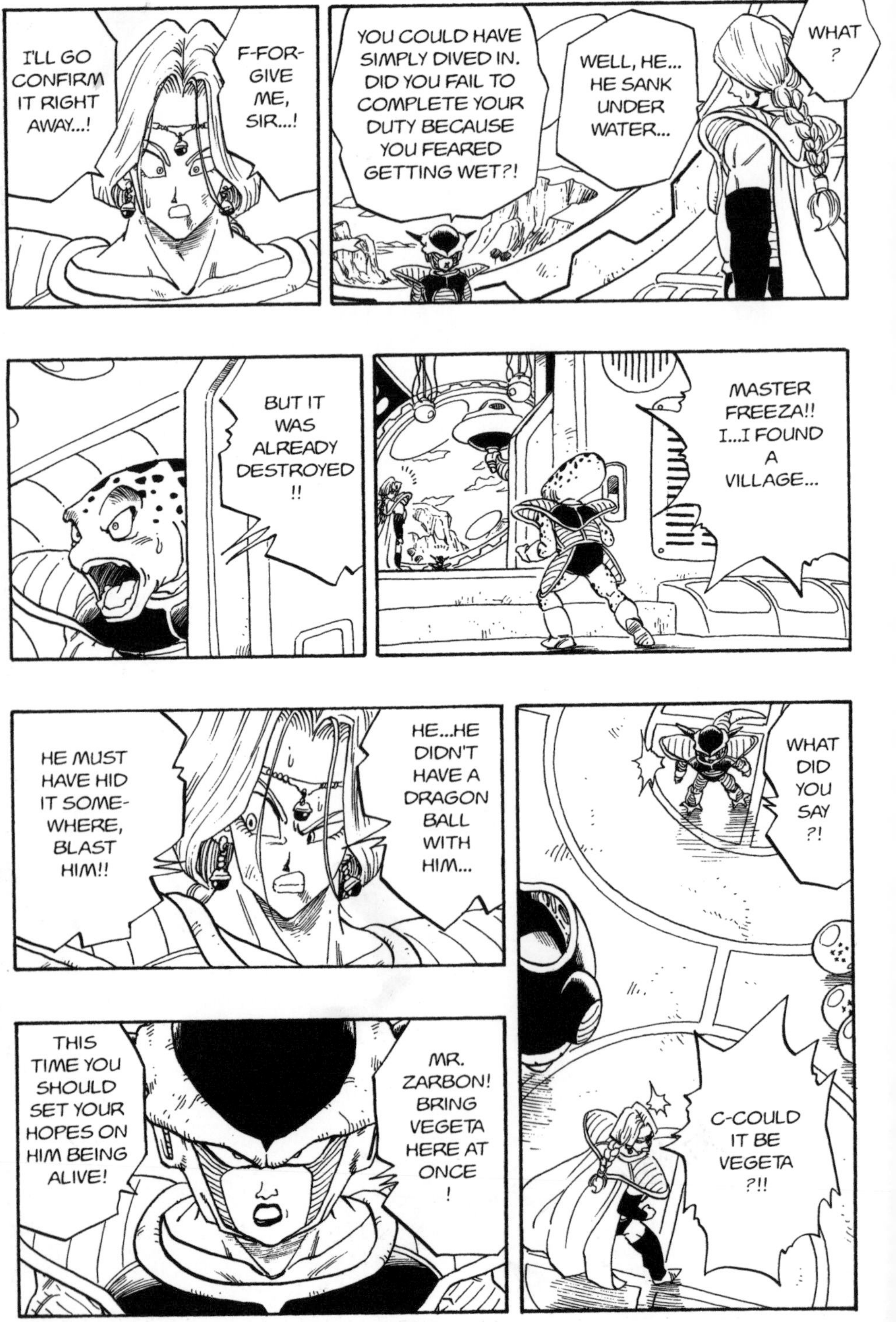
WHAT?
WELL, HE... HE SANK UNDER WATER...
YOU COULD HAVE SIMPLY DIVED IN. DID YOU FAIL TO COMPLETE YOUR DUTY BECAUSE YOU FEARED GETTING WET?!
F-FORGIVE ME, SIR...!
I'LL GO CONFIRM IT RIGHT AWAY...!
MASTER FREEZA!! I...I FOUND A VILLAGE...
BUT IT WAS ALREADY DESTROYED!!
WHAT DID YOU SAY?!
C-COULD IT BE VEGETA?!!
HE...HE DIDN'T HAVE A DRAGON BALL WITH HIM...
HE MUST HAVE HID IT SOMEWHERE, BLAST HIM!!
MR. ZARBON! BRING VEGETA HERE AT ONCE!
THIS TIME YOU SHOULD SET YOUR HOPES ON HIM BEING ALIVE!

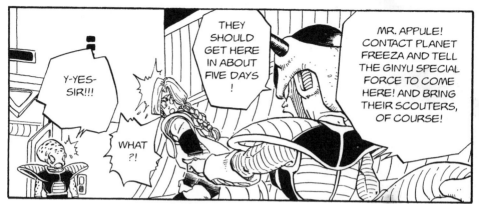

MR. APPULE! CONTACT PLANET FREEZA AND TELL THE GINYU SPECIAL FORCE TO COME HERE! AND BRING THEIR SCOUTERS, OF COURSE!
THEY SHOULD GET HERE IN ABOUT FIVE DAYS!
WHAT?!
Y-YES-SIR!!!
M-MASTER FREEZA, WH-WHY THE GINYU SPECIAL FORCE...?!
I'M AFRAID YOU WILL THINK ME IMPERTINENT TO SAY SO, BUT I FEEL THAT THERE IS NO NEED TO CALL THEM!
I HAVE AN ODD PREMONITION...
PREMONITION...?
I'VE BEEN THINKING IT OVER... I FEEL THAT A VERY POWERFUL SAIYAN IS DEVELOPING...AND MIGHT EVENTUALLY BECOME A GENUINE THREAT...
I HAD THOUGHT THAT IT WAS VEGETA AT FIRST, BUT THAT SEEMS LESS LIKELY NOW...

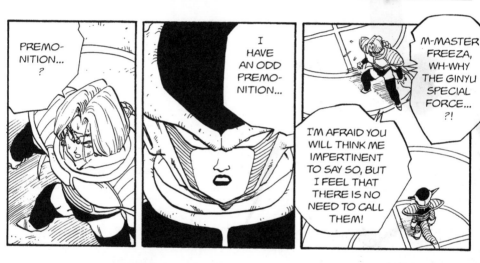

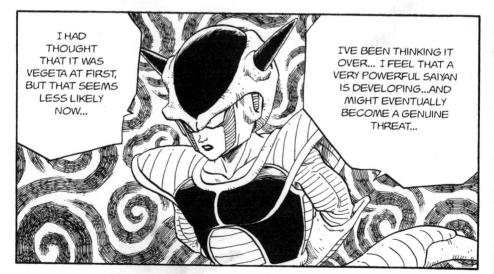

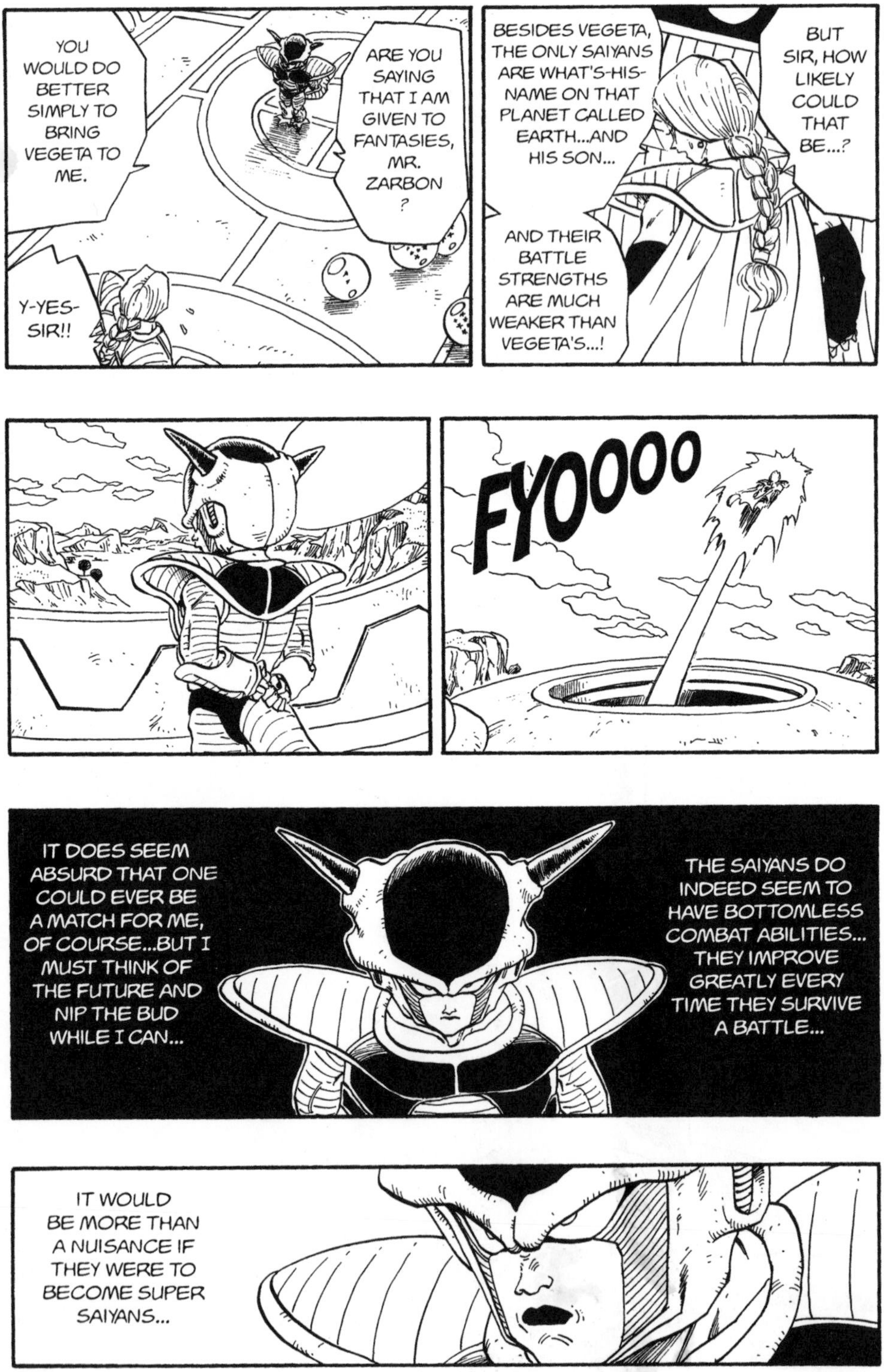
BUT SIR, HOW LIKELY COULD THAT BE...?
BESIDES VEGETA, THE ONLY SAIYANS ARE WHAT'S-HIS-NAME ON THAT PLANET CALLED EARTH...AND HIS SON...
AND THEIR BATTLE STRENGTHS ARE MUCH WEAKER THAN VEGETA'S...!
ARE YOU SAYING THAT I AM GIVEN TO FANTASIES, MR. ZARBON?
YOU WOULD DO BETTER SIMPLY TO BRING VEGETA TO ME.
Y-YES-SIR!!
FYOOOO
THE SAIYANS DO INDEED SEEM TO HAVE BOTTOMLESS COMBAT ABILITIES... THEY IMPROVE GREATLY EVERY TIME THEY SURVIVE A BATTLE...
IT DOES SEEM ABSURD THAT ONE COULD EVER BE A MATCH FOR ME, OF COURSE...BUT I MUST THINK OF THE FUTURE AND NIP THE BUD WHILE I CAN...
IT WOULD BE MORE THAN A NUISANCE IF THEY WERE TO BECOME SUPER SAIYANS...

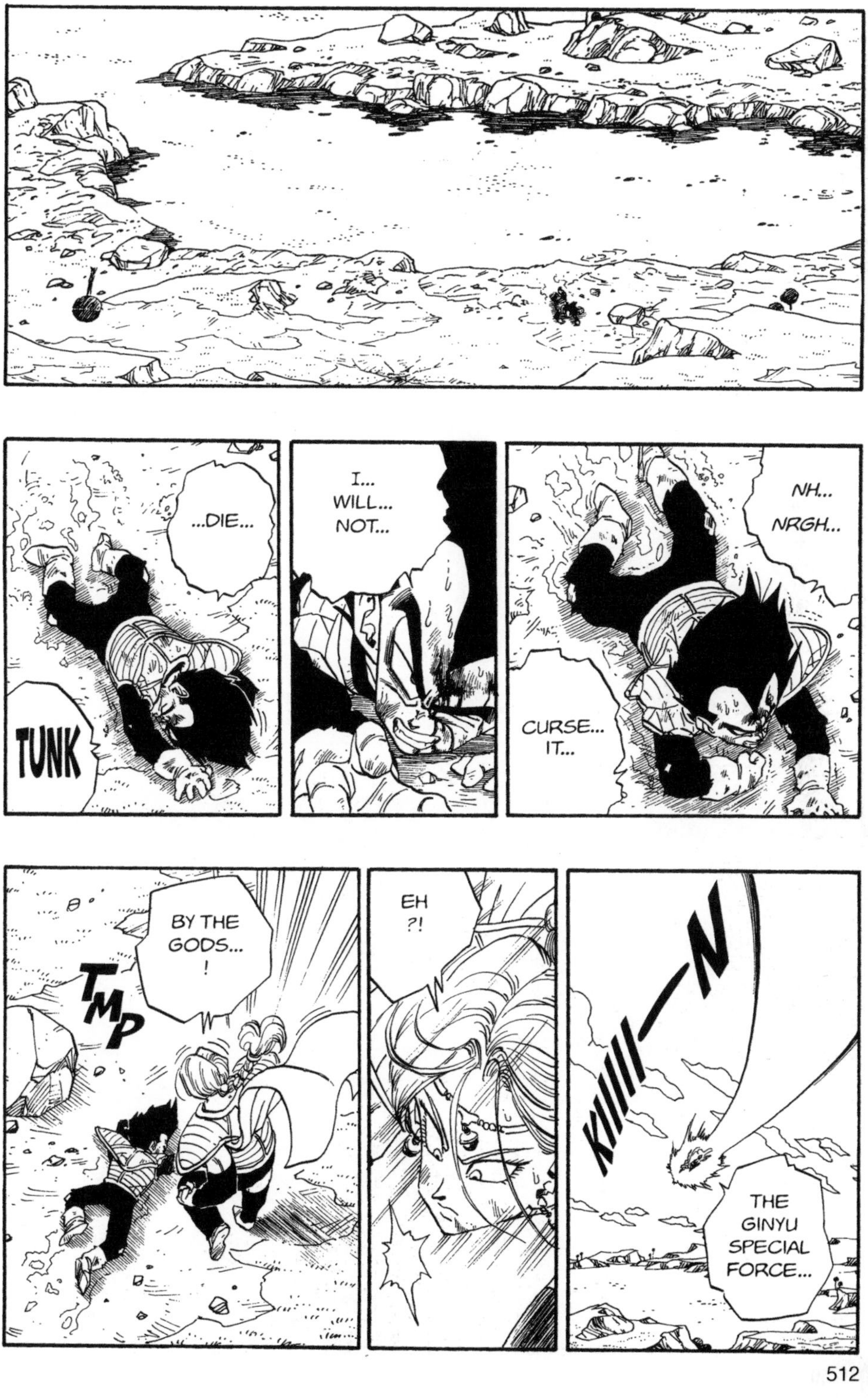
NH... NRGH...
CURSE... IT...
I... WILL... NOT...
...DIE...
TUNK
KIIIII—N
THE GINYU SPECIAL FORCE...
EH ?!
BY THE GODS... !
TMP

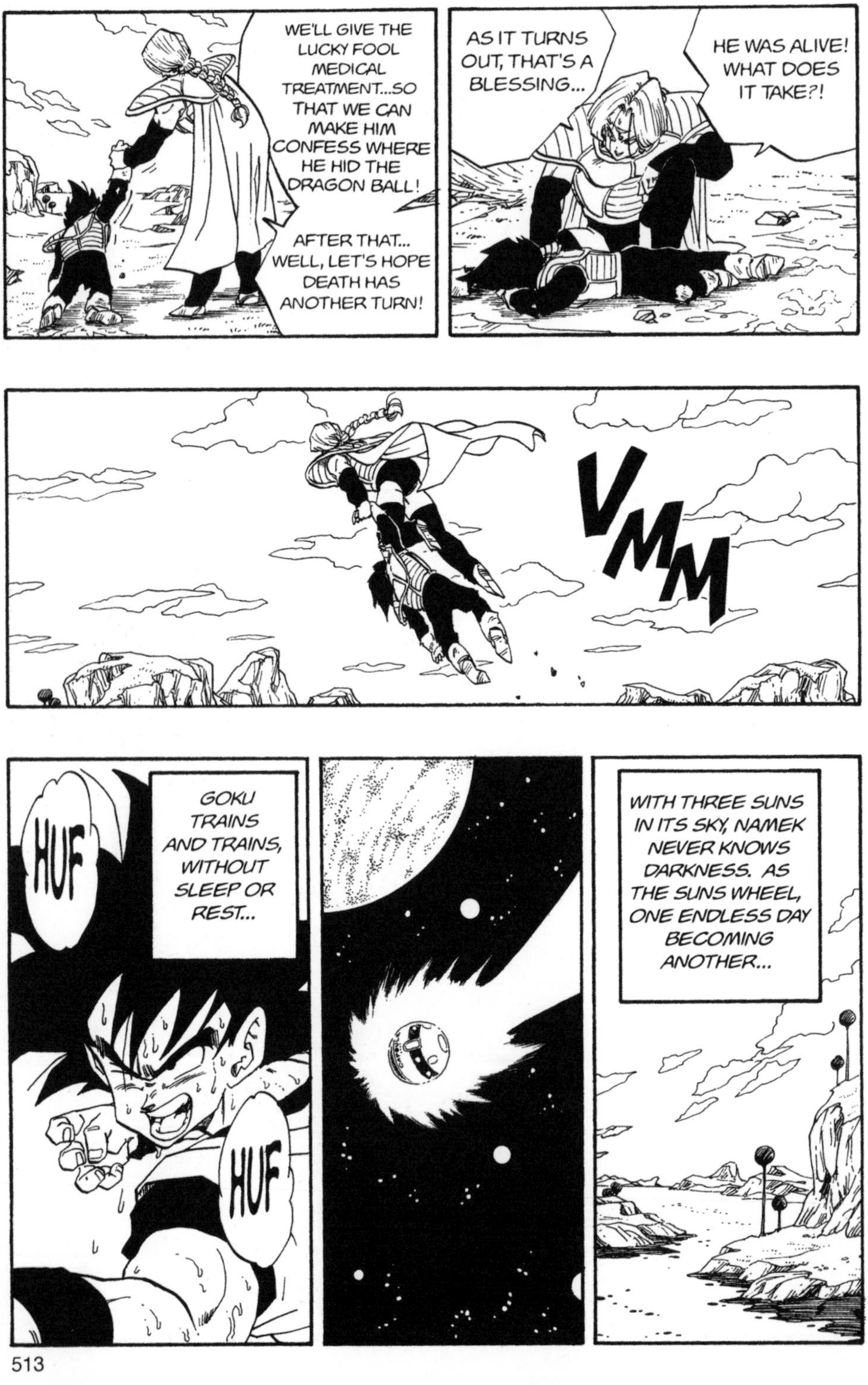
HE WAS ALIVE! WHAT DOES IT TAKE?!
AS IT TURNS OUT, THAT'S A BLESSING...
WE'LL GIVE THE LUCKY FOOL MEDICAL TREATMENT...SO THAT WE CAN MAKE HIM CONFESS WHERE HE HID THE DRAGON BALL!
AFTER THAT... WELL, LET'S HOPE DEATH HAS ANOTHER TURN!
VMM
WITH THREE SUNS IN ITS SKY, NAMEK NEVER KNOWS DARKNESS. AS THE SUNS WHEEL, ONE ENDLESS DAY BECOMING ANOTHER...
GOKU TRAINS AND TRAINS, WITHOUT SLEEP OR REST...
HUF
HUF

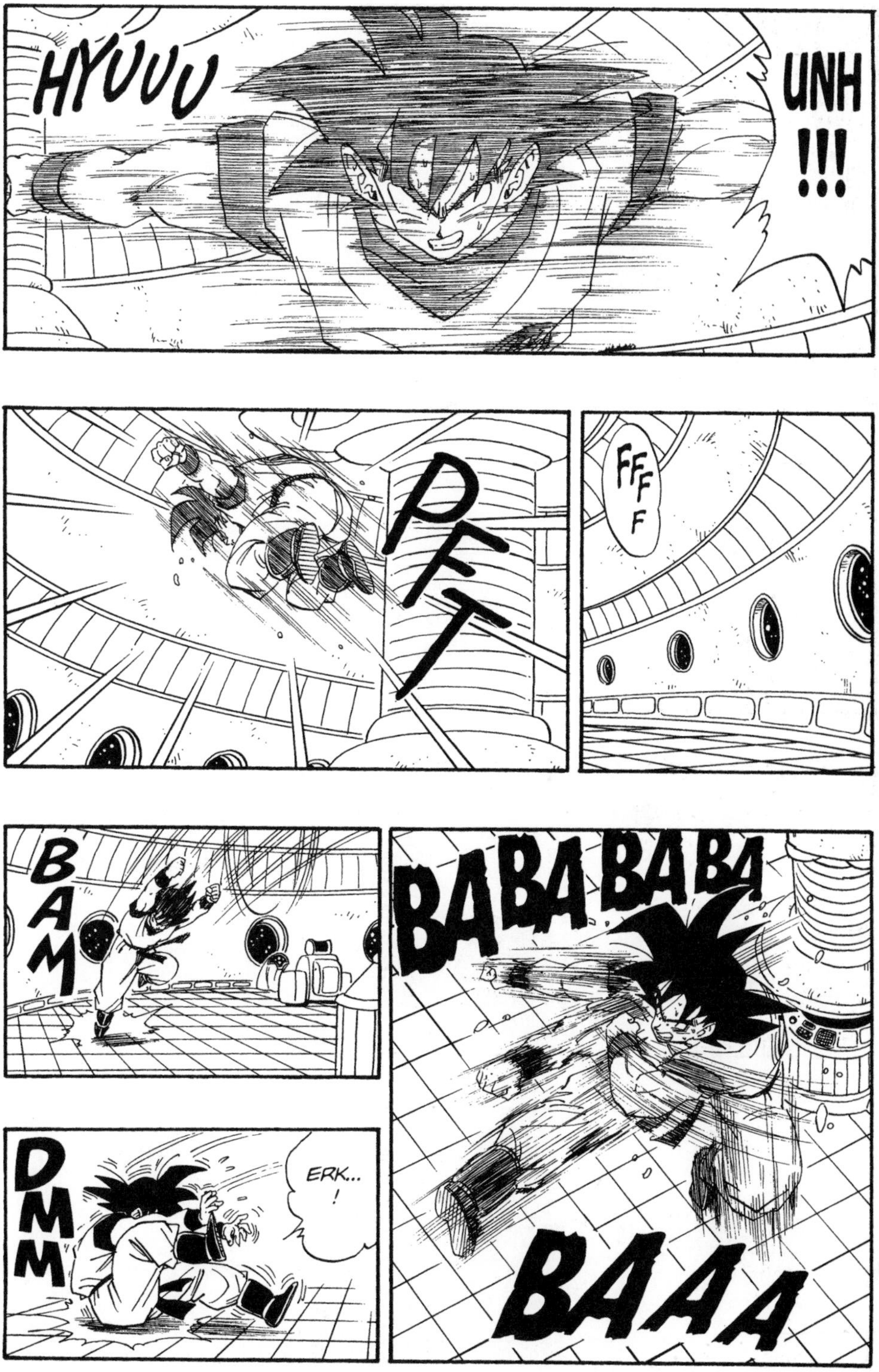
UNH !!!
HYUUU
FFFF
PFT
BABABABA
BAAA
BAM
DMM
ERK... !

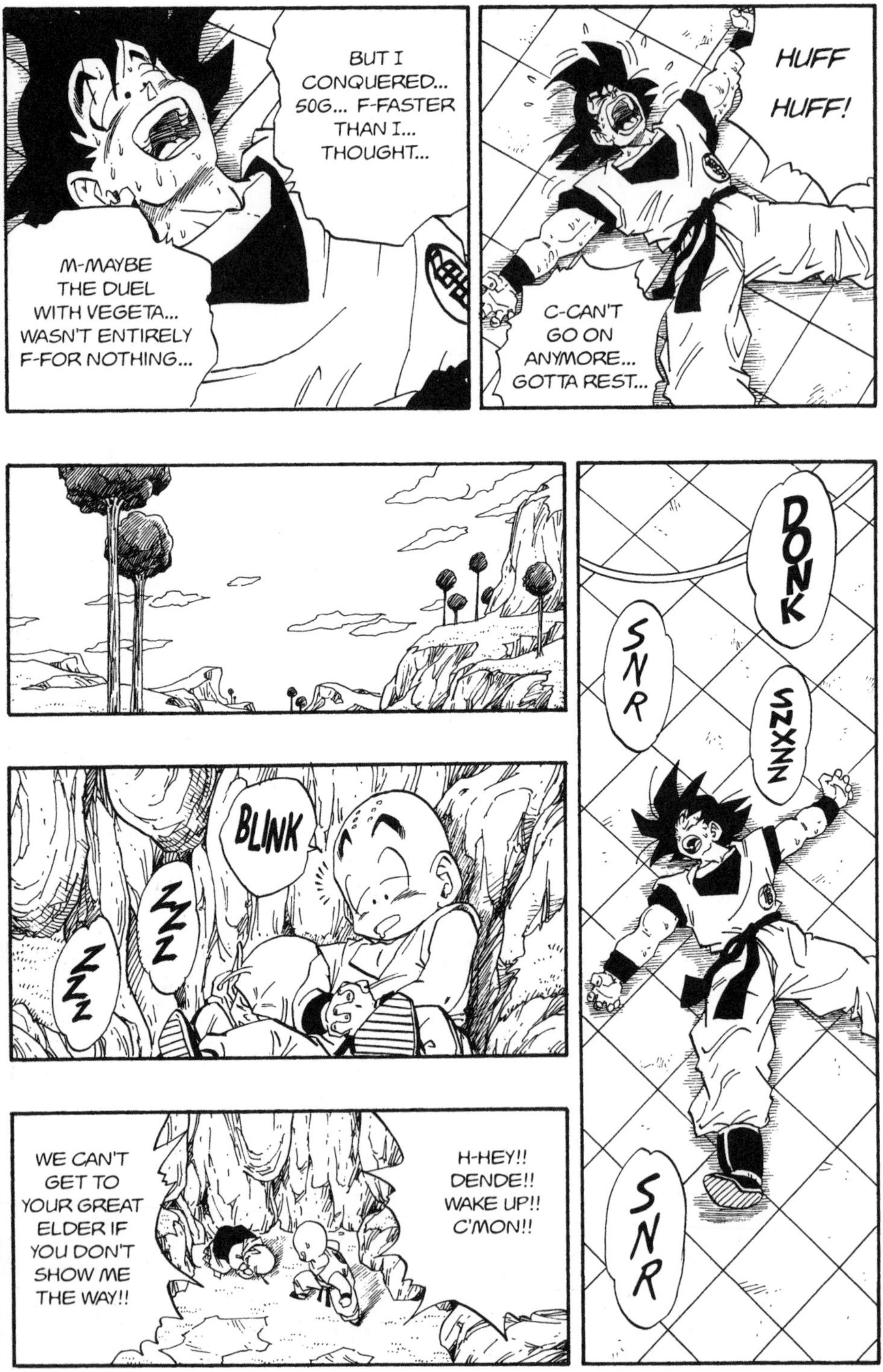
HUFF
HUFF!
C-CAN'T GO ON ANYMORE... GOTTA REST...
BUT I CONQUERED... 50G... F-FASTER THAN I... THOUGHT...
M-MAYBE THE DUEL WITH VEGETA... WASN'T ENTIRELY F-FOR NOTHING...
DONK
SNR
SNXZZ
SNR
BLINK
ZZZ
ZZZ
H-HEY!! DENDE!! WAKE UP!! C'MON!!
WE CAN'T GET TO YOUR GREAT ELDER IF YOU DON'T SHOW ME THE WAY!!

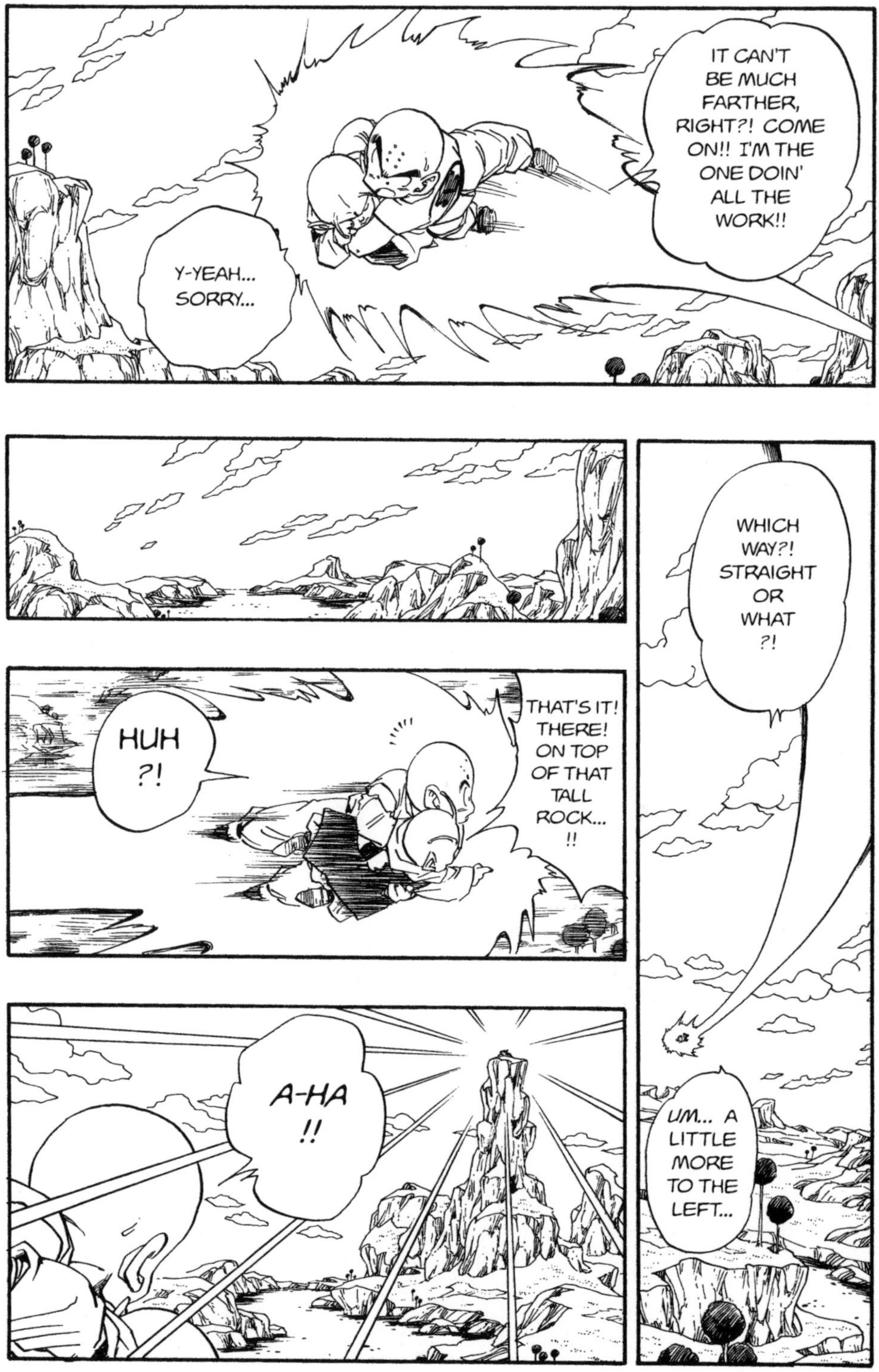
IT CAN'T BE MUCH FARTHER, RIGHT?! COME ON!! I'M THE ONE DOIN' ALL THE WORK!!
Y-YEAH... SORRY...
WHICH WAY?! STRAIGHT OR WHAT ?!
UM... A LITTLE MORE TO THE LEFT...
THAT'S IT! THERE! ON TOP OF THAT TALL ROCK... !!
HUH ?!
A-HA !!

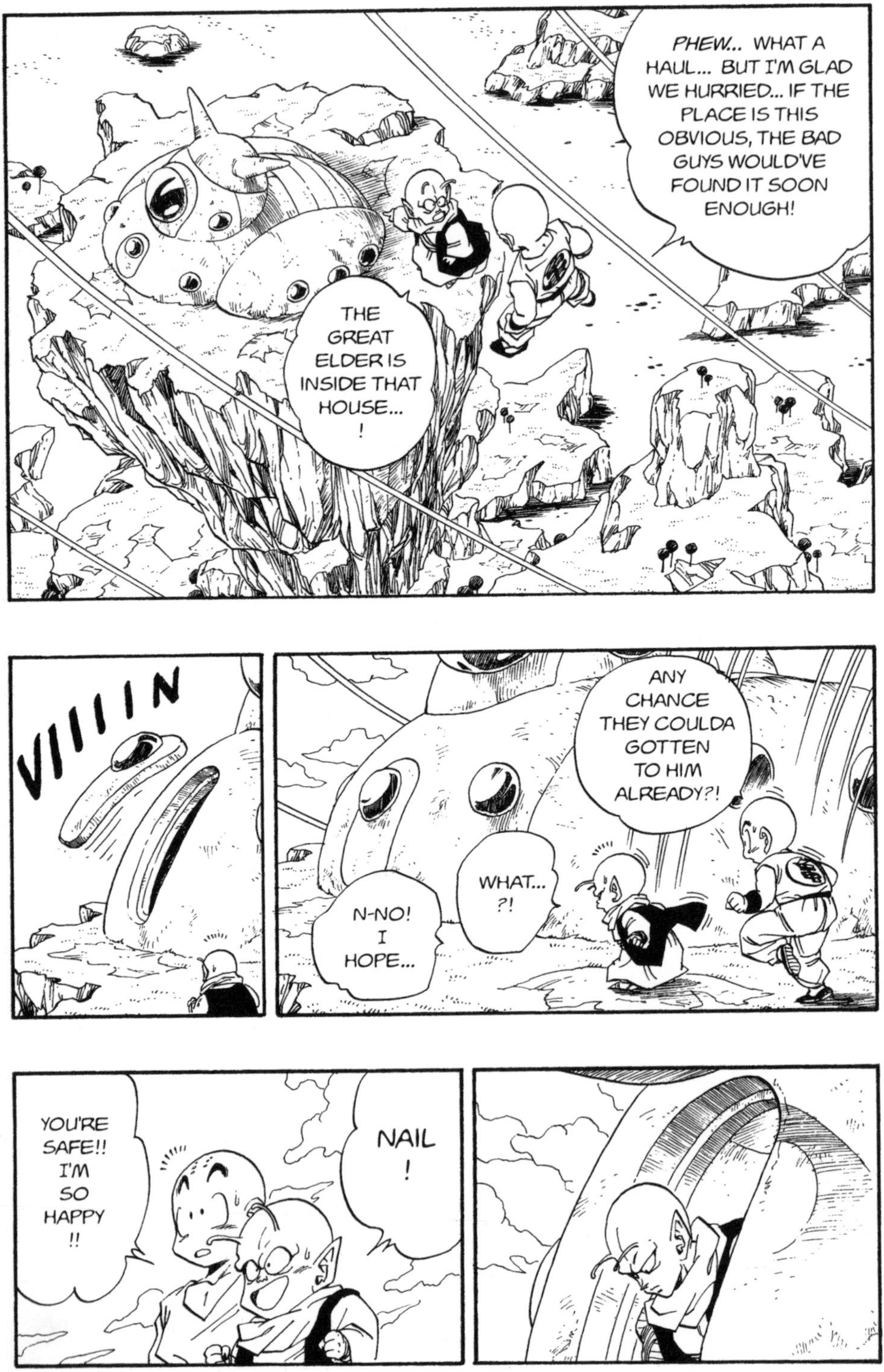
PHEW... WHAT A HAUL... BUT I'M GLAD WE HURRIED... IF THE PLACE IS THIS OBVIOUS, THE BAD GUYS WOULD'VE FOUND IT SOON ENOUGH!
THE GREAT ELDER IS INSIDE THAT HOUSE...!
ANY CHANCE THEY COULDA GOTTEN TO HIM ALREADY?!
WHAT...?!
N-NO! I HOPE...
VIIIIN
NAIL!
YOU'RE SAFE!! I'M SO HAPPY!!

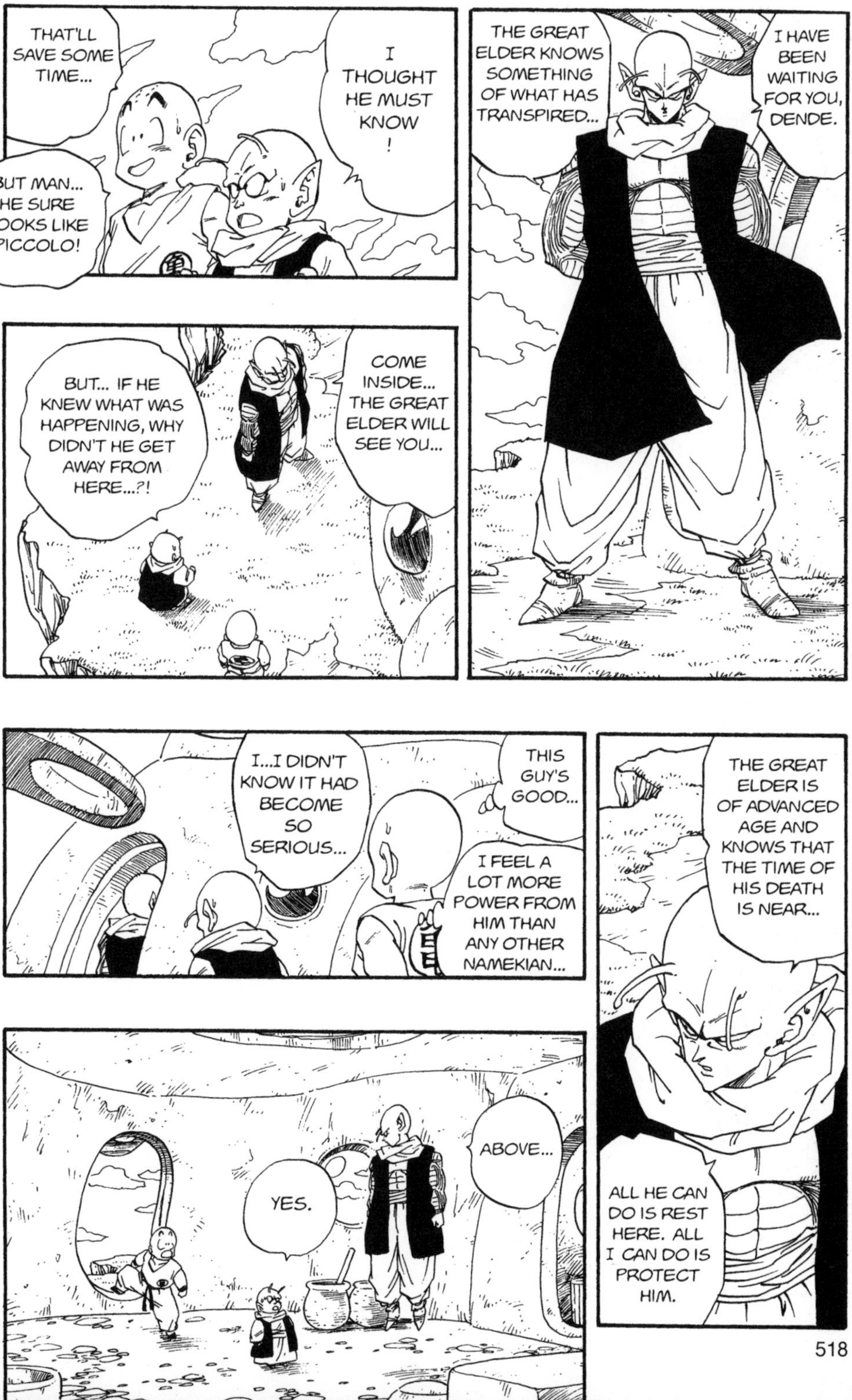
I HAVE BEEN WAITING FOR YOU, DENDE.
THE GREAT ELDER KNOWS SOMETHING OF WHAT HAS TRANSPIRED...
I THOUGHT HE MUST KNOW!
THAT'LL SAVE SOME TIME...
BUT MAN... HE SURE LOOKS LIKE PICCOLO!
COME INSIDE... THE GREAT ELDER WILL SEE YOU...
BUT... IF HE KNEW WHAT WAS HAPPENING, WHY DIDN'T HE GET AWAY FROM HERE...?!
THE GREAT ELDER IS OF ADVANCED AGE AND KNOWS THAT THE TIME OF HIS DEATH IS NEAR...
ALL HE CAN DO IS REST HERE. ALL I CAN DO IS PROTECT HIM.
THIS GUY'S GOOD...
I FEEL A LOT MORE POWER FROM HIM THAN ANY OTHER NAMEKIAN...
I...I DIDN'T KNOW IT HAD BECOME SO SERIOUS...
ABOVE...
YES.

GREAT ELDER, I HAVE BROUGHT DENDE AND A GUEST.
H-HE'S... **HUGE**...
WELCOME. YOU MUST BE FROM EARTH. I WOULD LIKE TO EXPRESS MY GRATITUDE FOR SAVING MY CHILD, DENDE. THANK YOU...
OH, SHOOT, IT WAS...N-N-NOTHIN'!

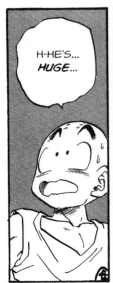

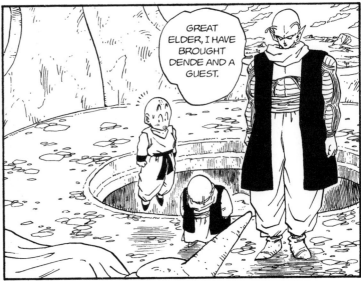

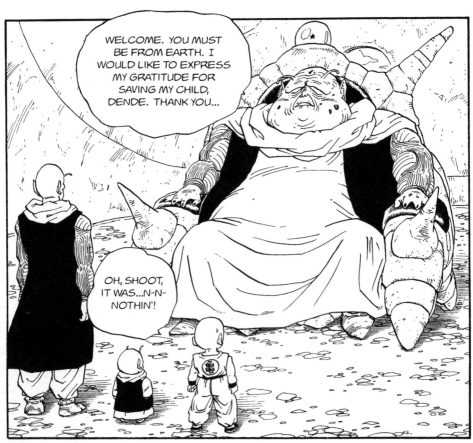

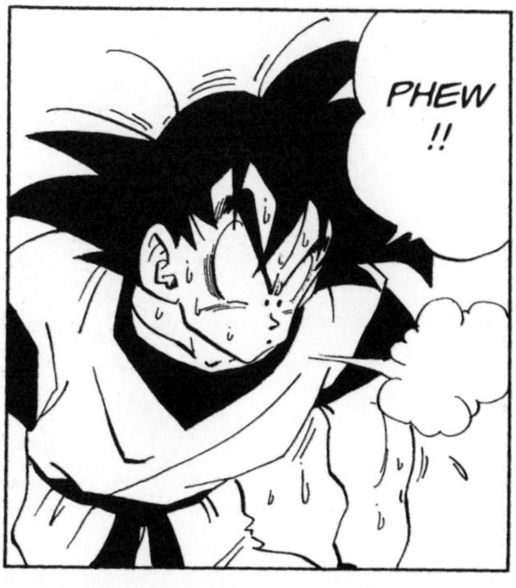
PHEW !!

# ★ TITLE PAGE GALLERY

Following are the title pages for the individual chapters as they appeared during their original serialization in *Weekly Shonen Jump* magazine in Japan from 1988 to 1995.

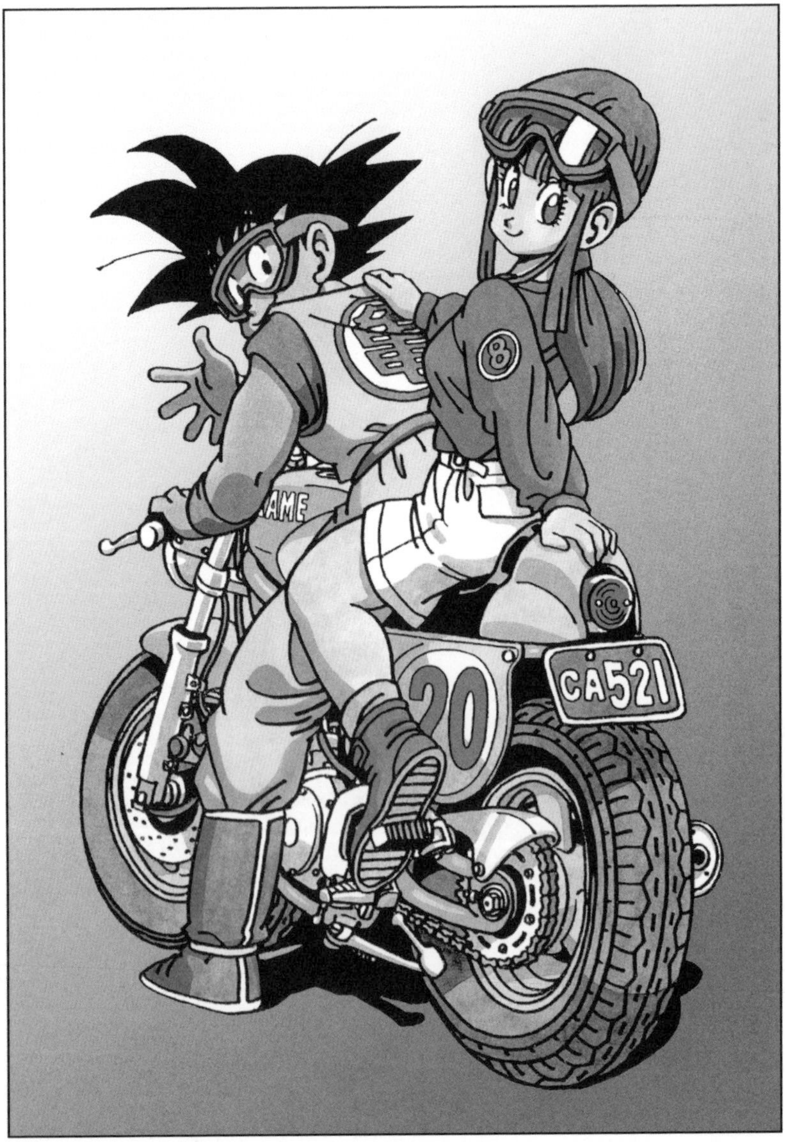

AME
20
CA521

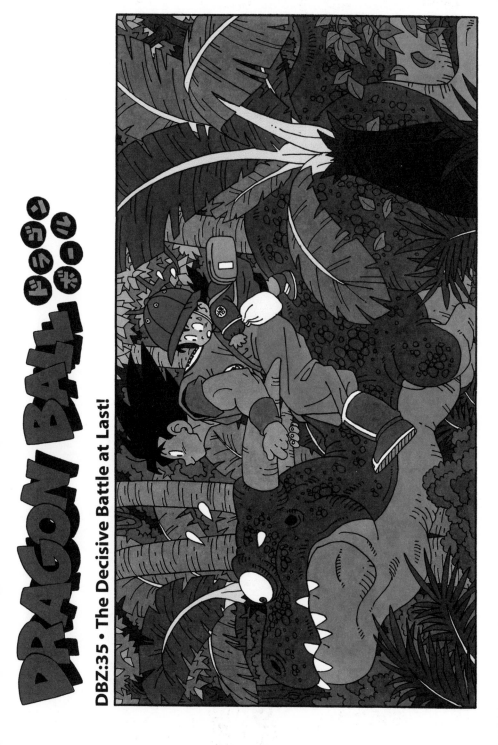

# DRAGON BALL

**DBZ:35 • The Decisive Battle at Last!**

# DBZ:36 • Too Much Power?

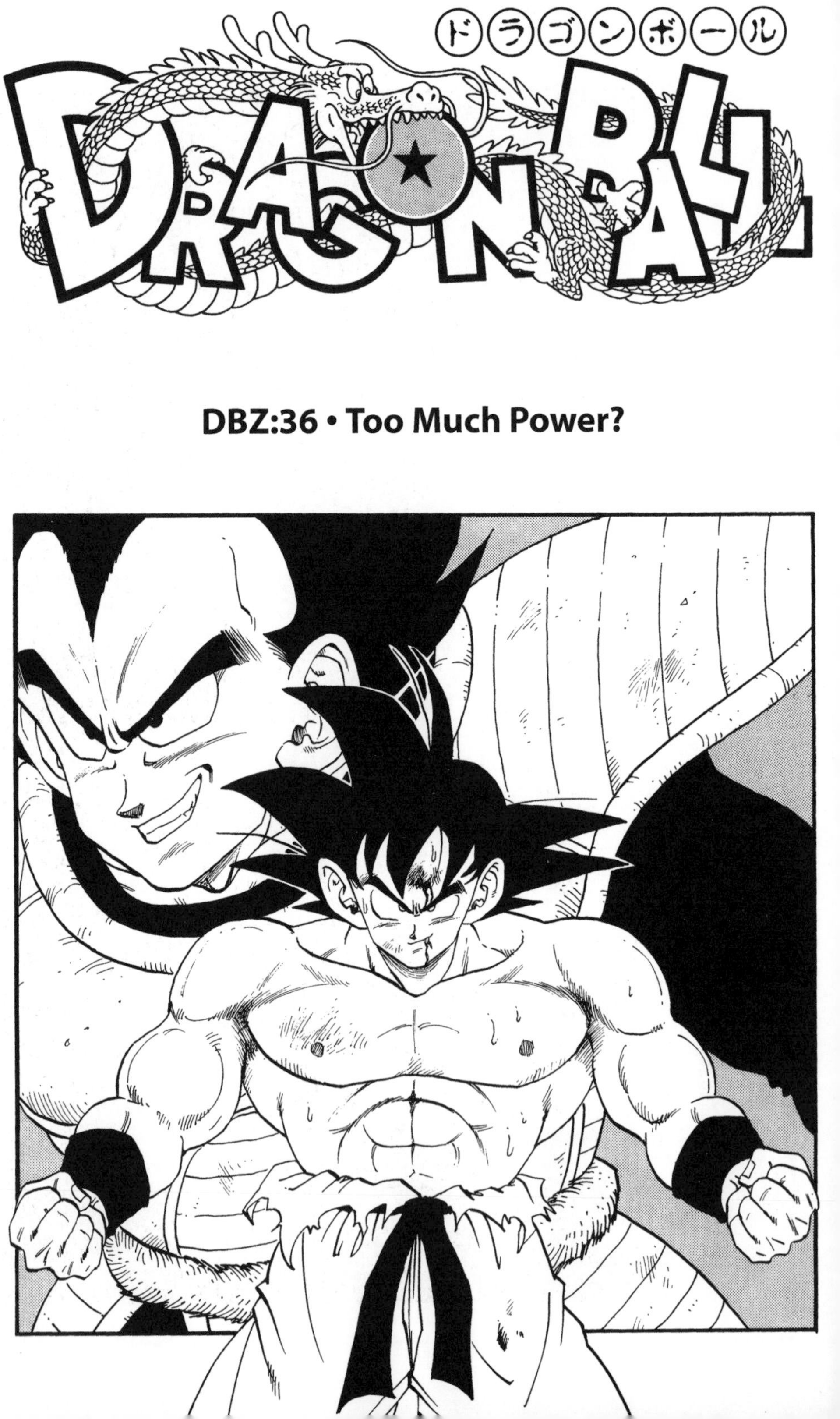

ドラゴンボール

# DRAGON BALL

## DBZ:37 • Battle in the Red Zone!

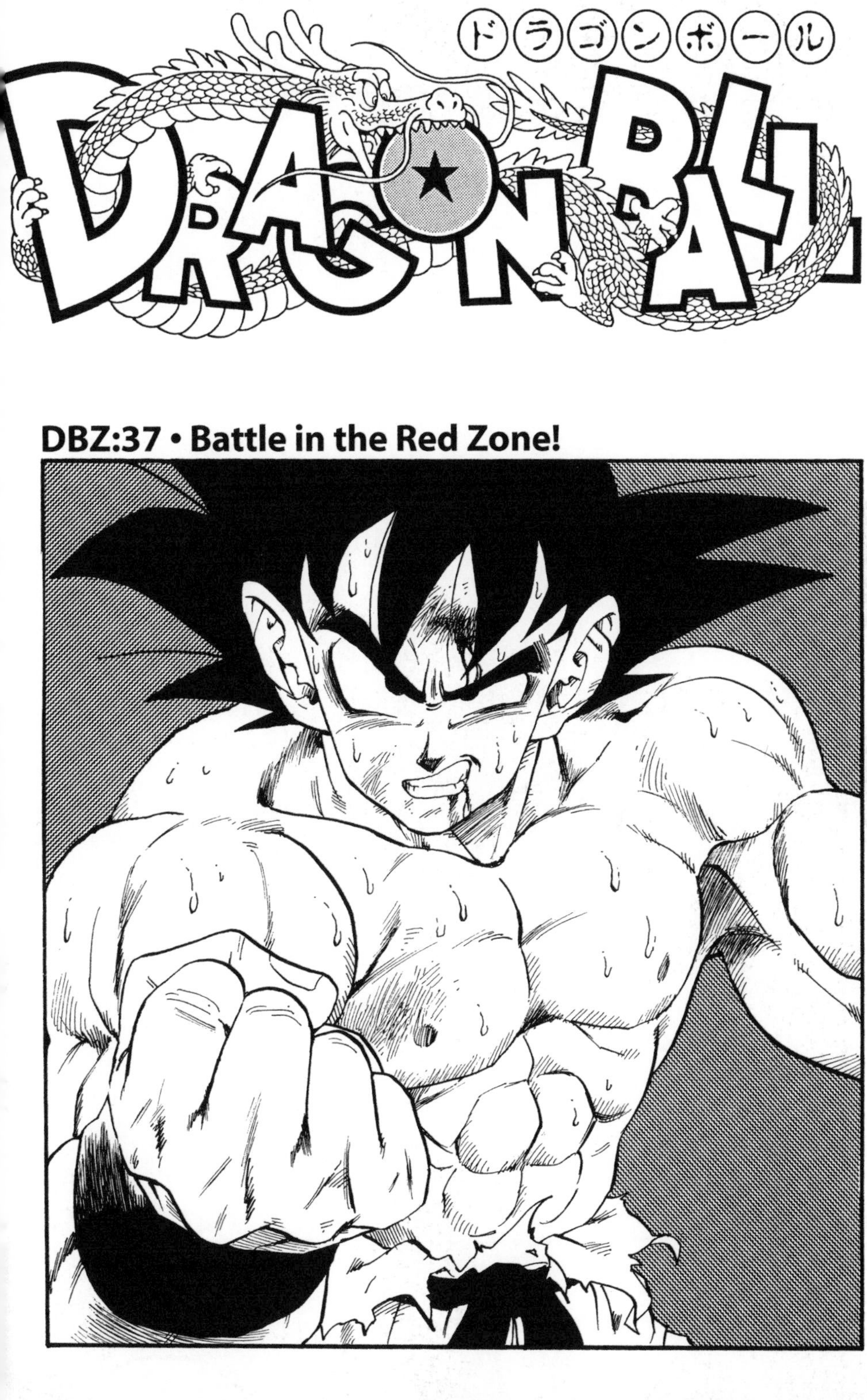

DRAGON BALL

# DBZ:38 • The Moon

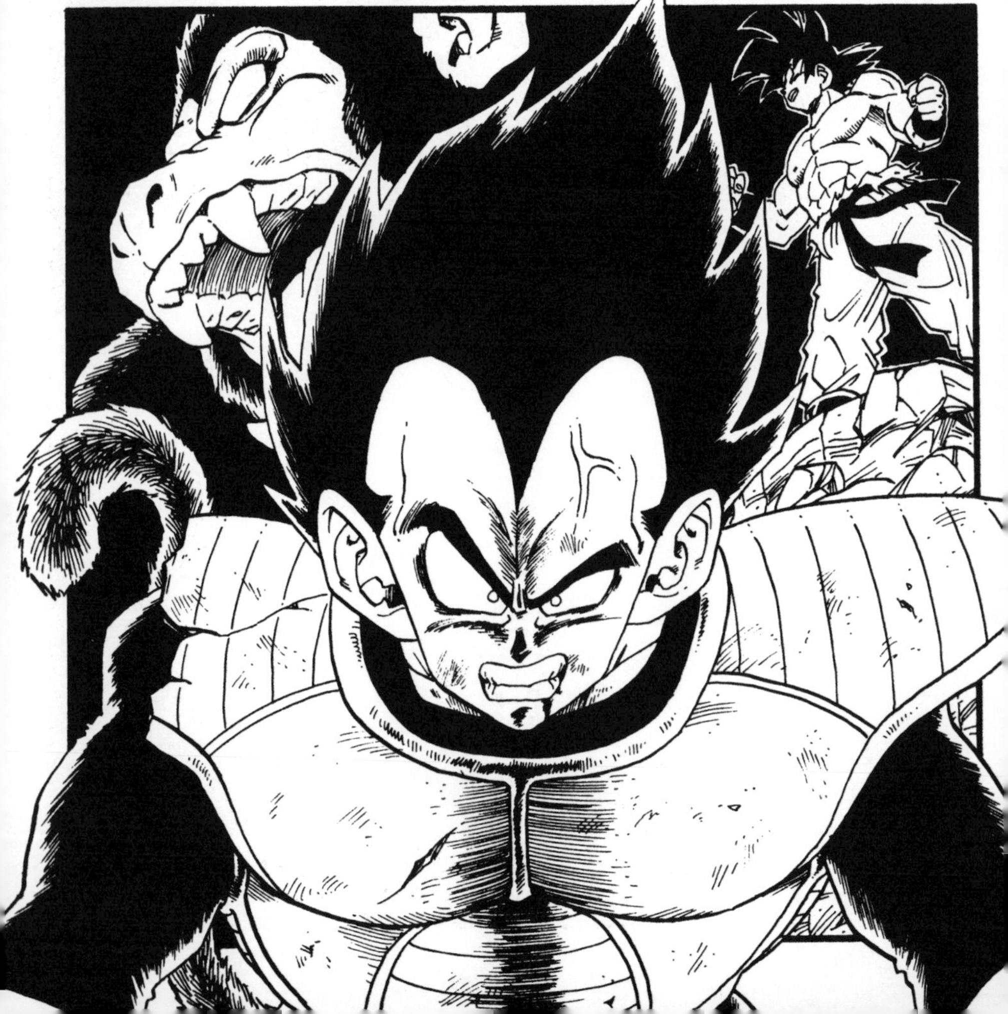

ドラゴンボール

DRAGON BALL

## DBZ:39

## The Energy Sphere

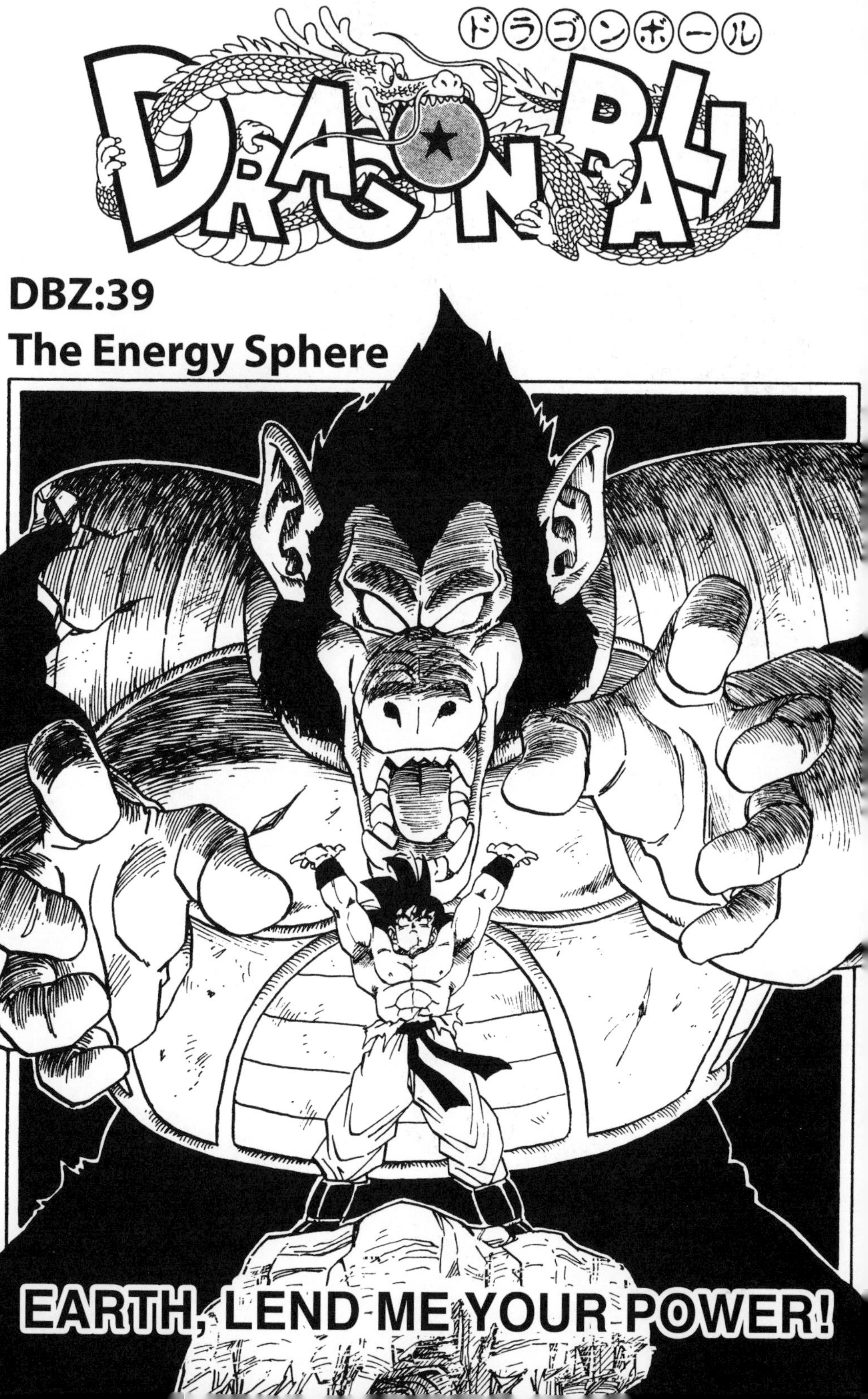
EARTH, LEND ME YOUR POWER!

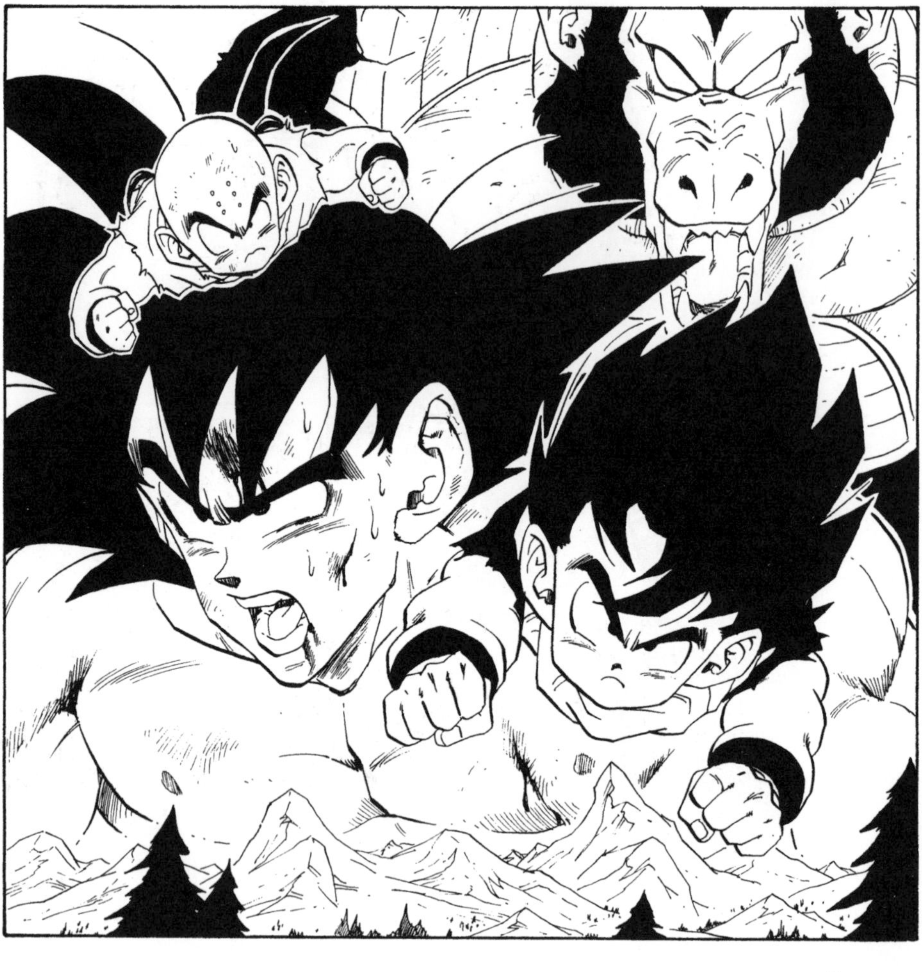

# DRAGON BALL

## DBZ:40 • All That Power...

ドラゴンボール

DRAGON BALL

## DBZ:41 • The Last Heartbeat

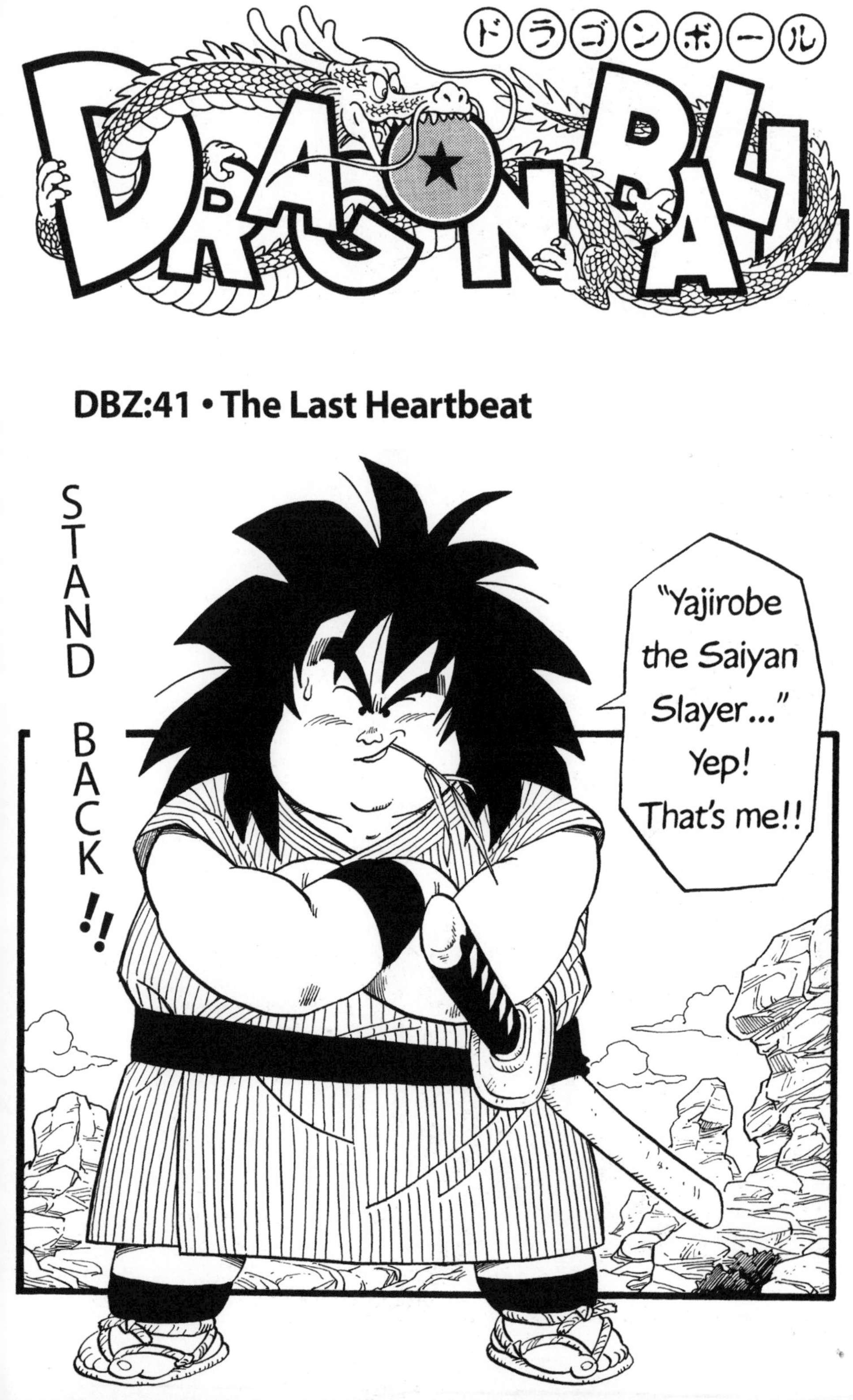
STAND BACK!!
"Yajirobe the Saiyan Slayer..." Yep! That's me!!

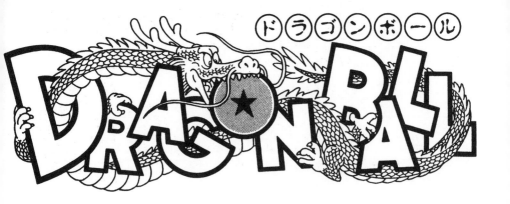

# DBZ:42 • Least Resistance

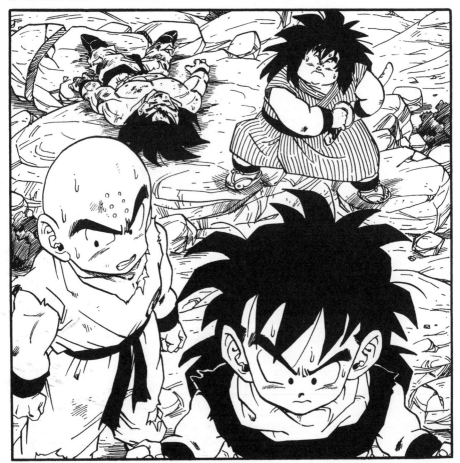

ドラゴンボール

# DBZ:43 • Once More...the Sphere!

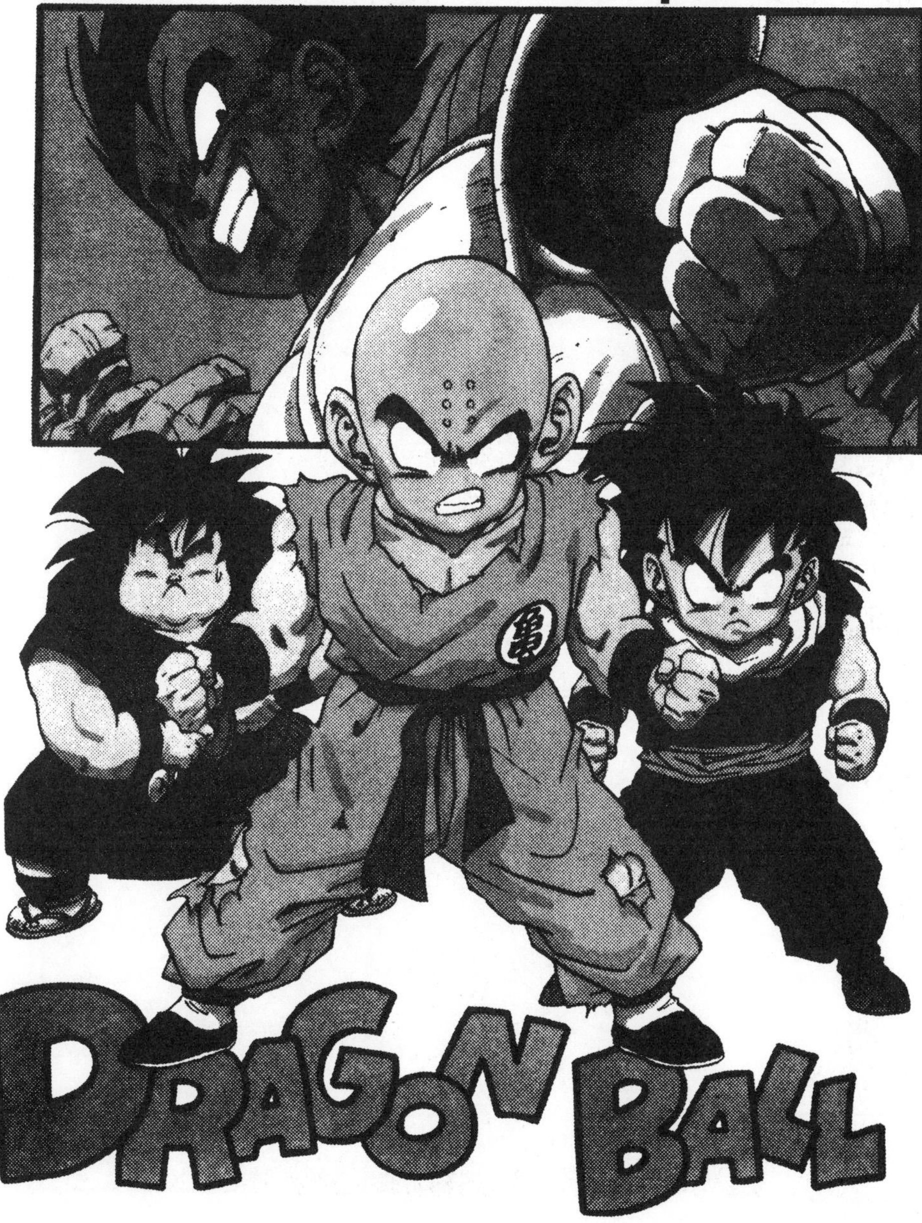
DRAGON BALL

# DRAGON BALL

## DBZ:44 • The Hopes of a Planet

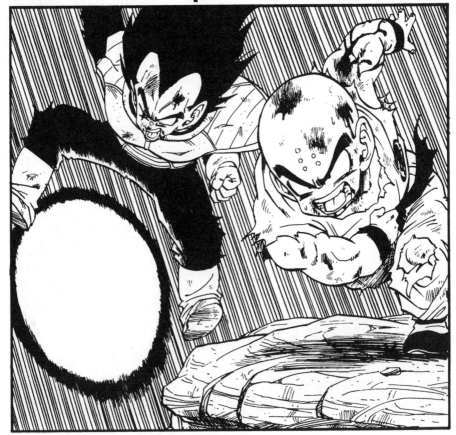

# DRAGON BALL

## DBZ:45 • The Worn-out Warriors

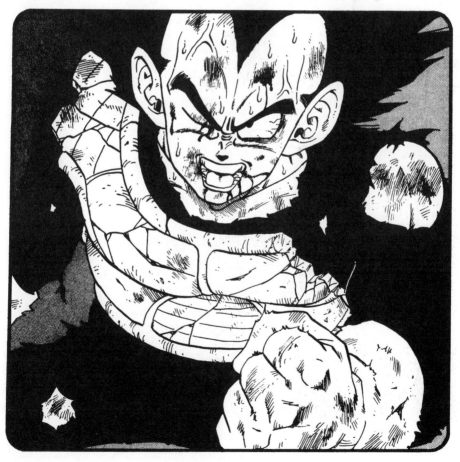

# DRAGON BALL

## DBZ:46 • Monkey in the Moon

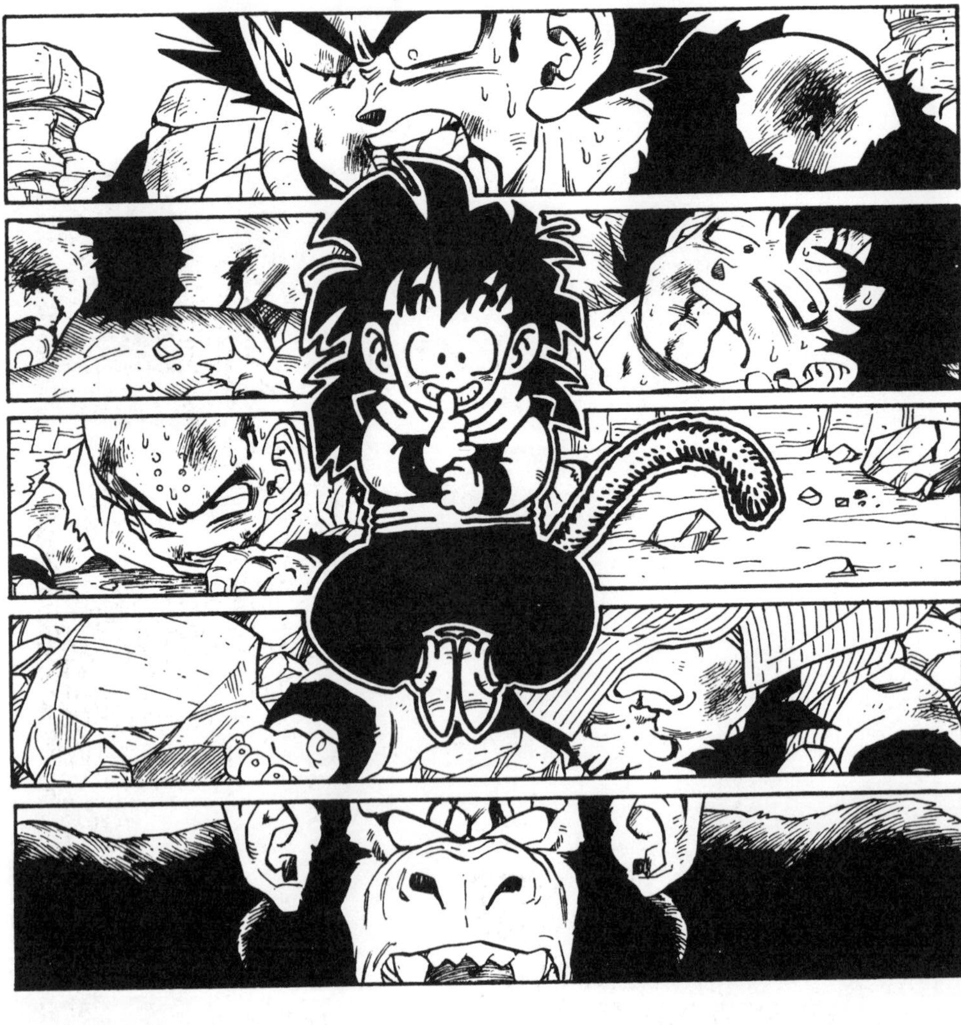

# DRAGON BALL

## DBZ:47

## Goku's Request

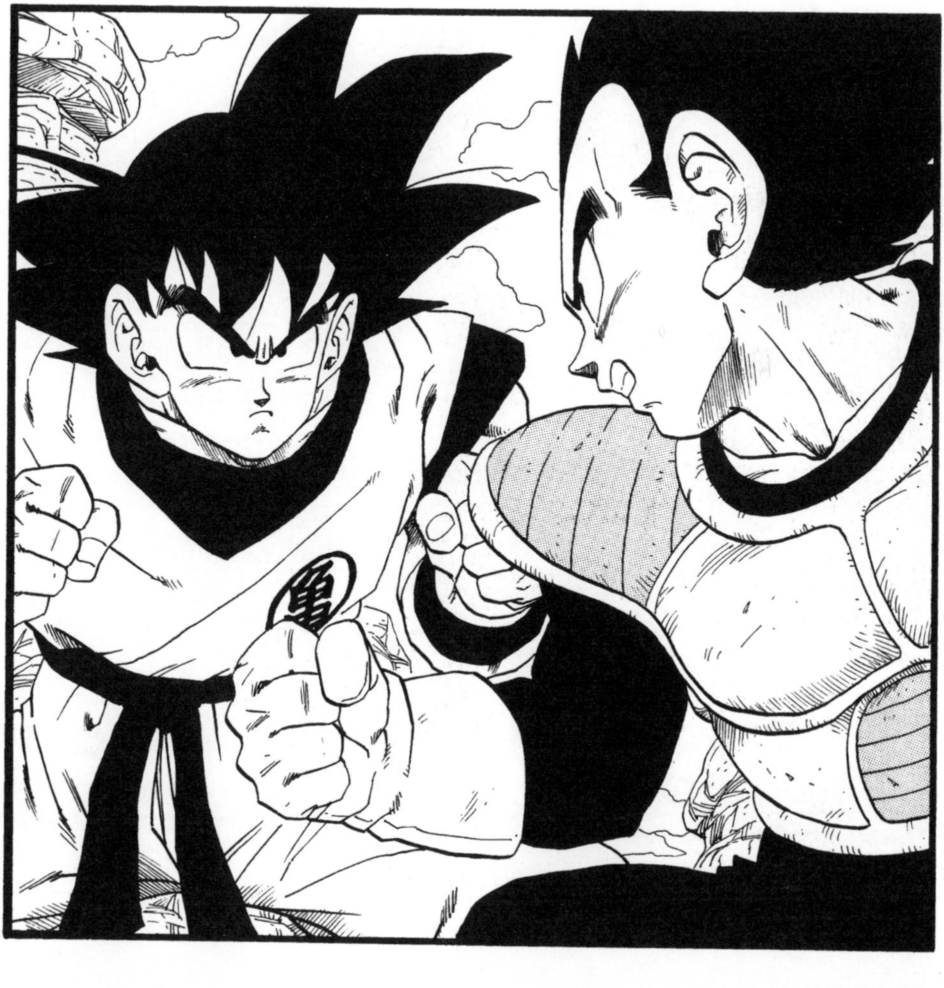
亀

# DBZ:48 • The Bittersweet End

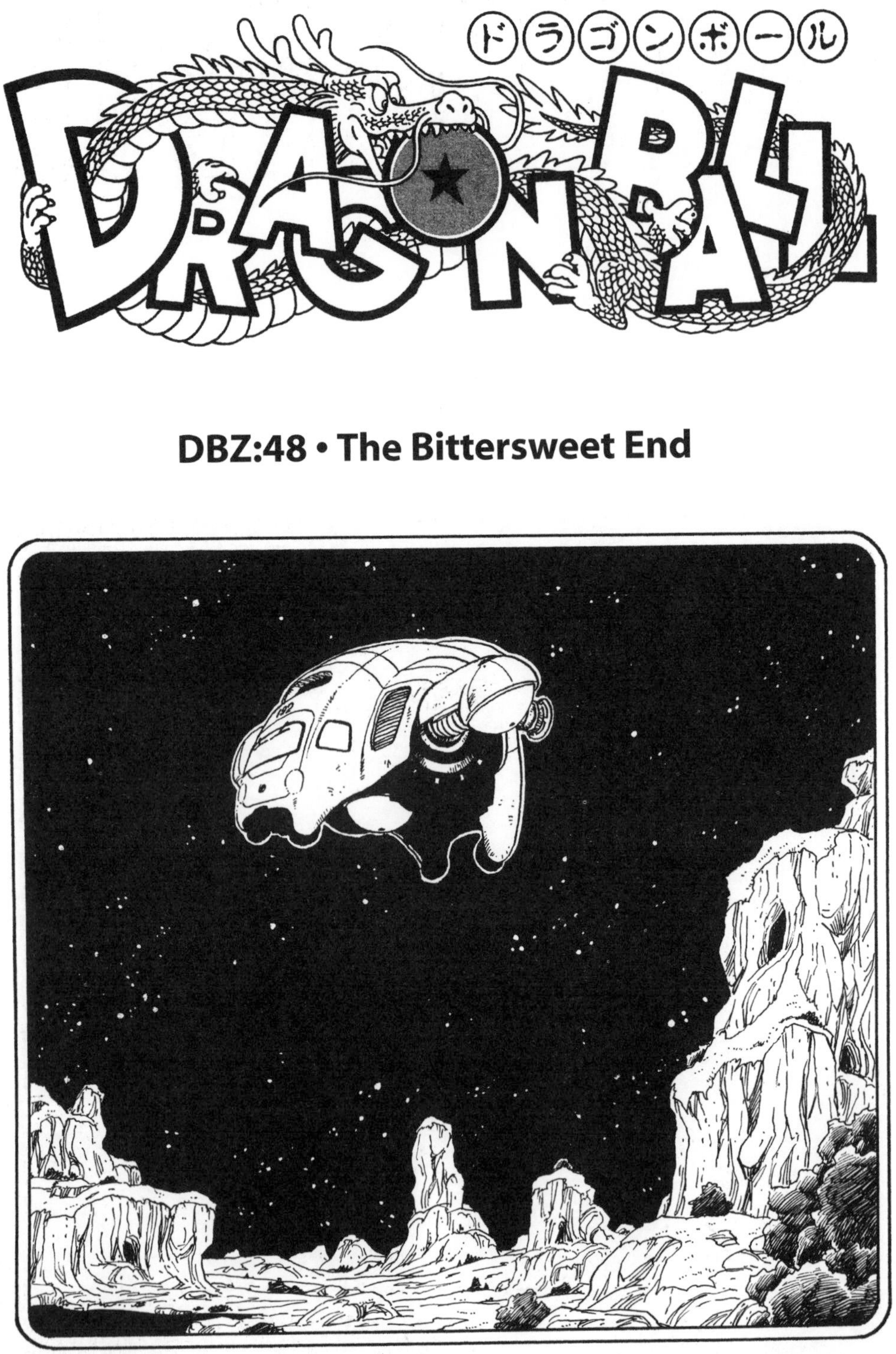

ドラゴンボール

# DRAGON BALL

## DBZ:49 • Destination Namek

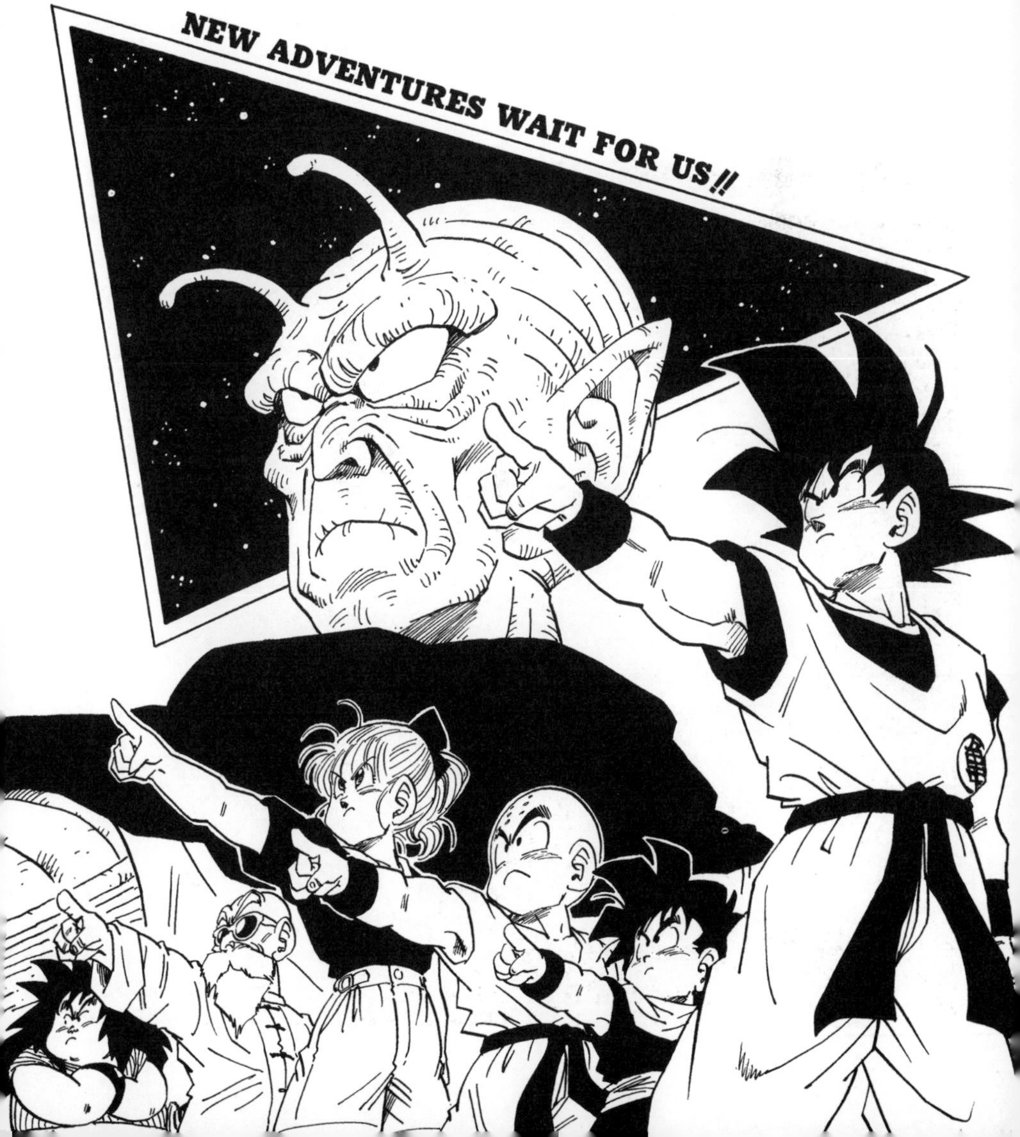
NEW ADVENTURES WAIT FOR US!!

# DRAGON

ドラゴン
ボール

# BALL

## DBZ:50 • The Mysterious Spaceship

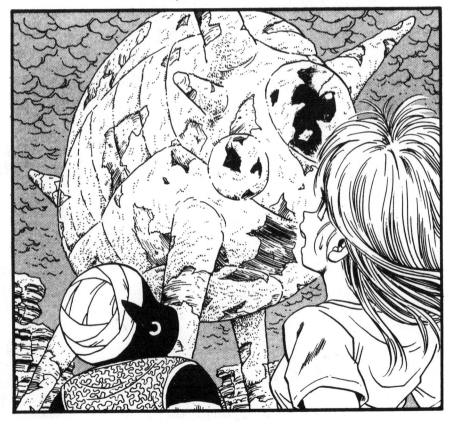

# DRAGON BALL

## DBZ:51 • 3...2...1...Lift Off!

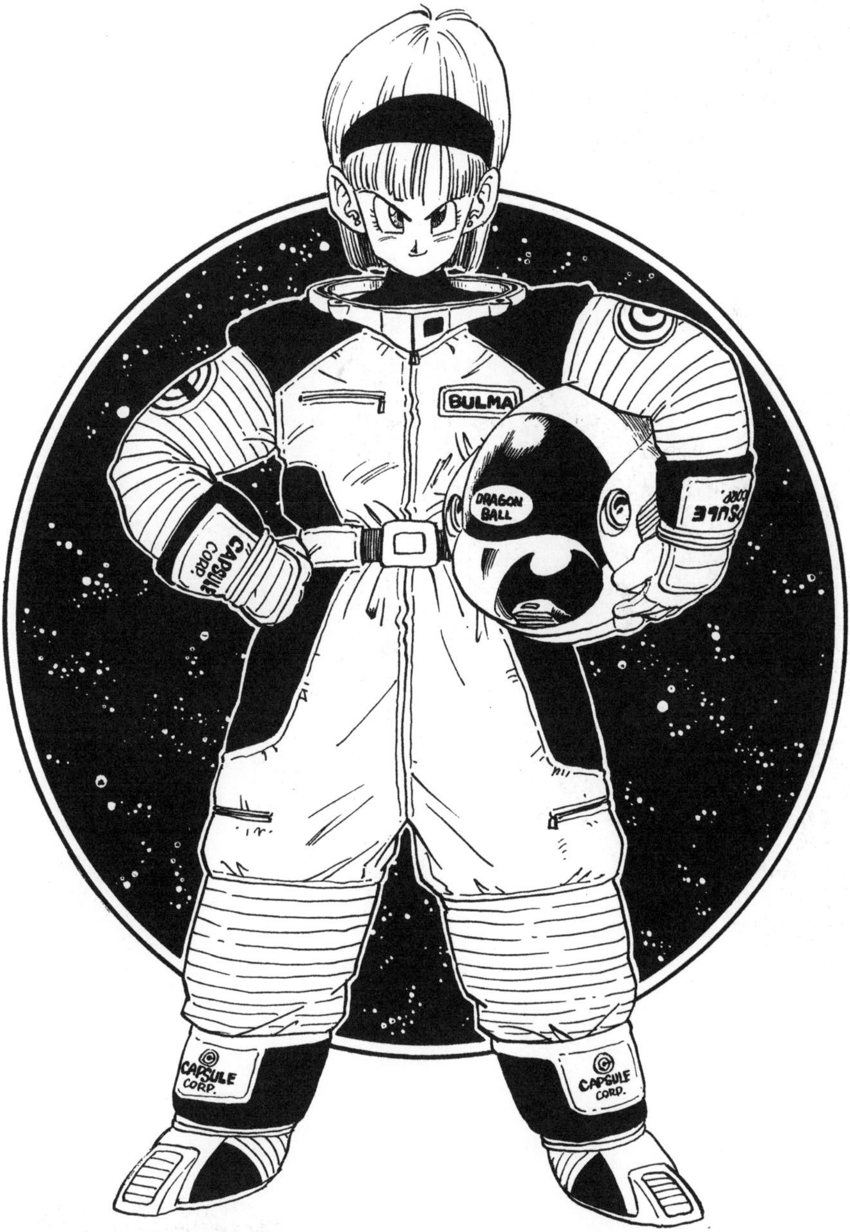
BULMA
DRAGON BALL
CAPSULE CORP.
CAPSULE CORP.
CAPSULE CORP.

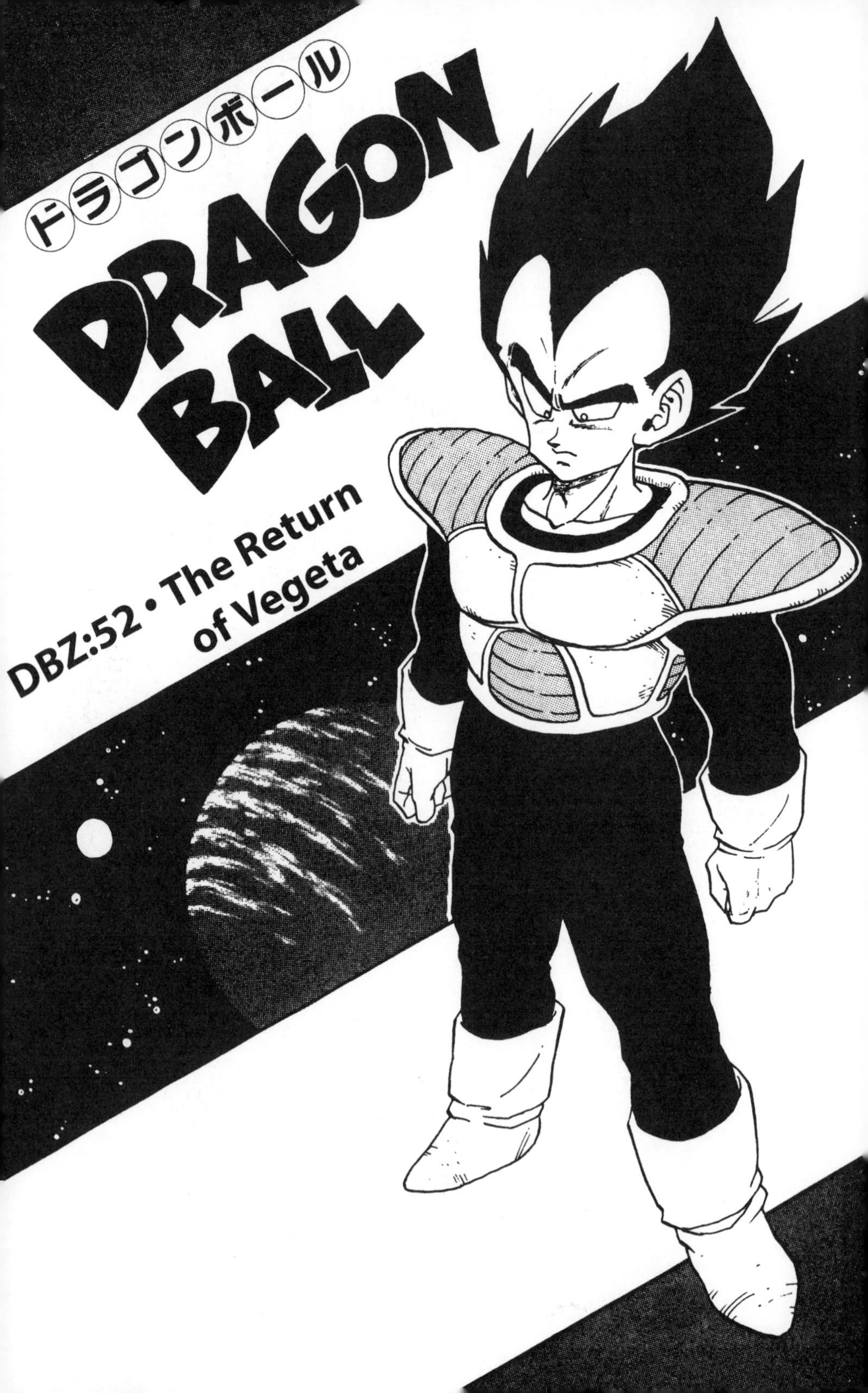
ドラゴンボール
DRAGON BALL
DBZ:52 • The Return of Vegeta

DRAGON BALL

ドラゴンボール

# DBZ:53

## Planet Namek, Cold and Dark

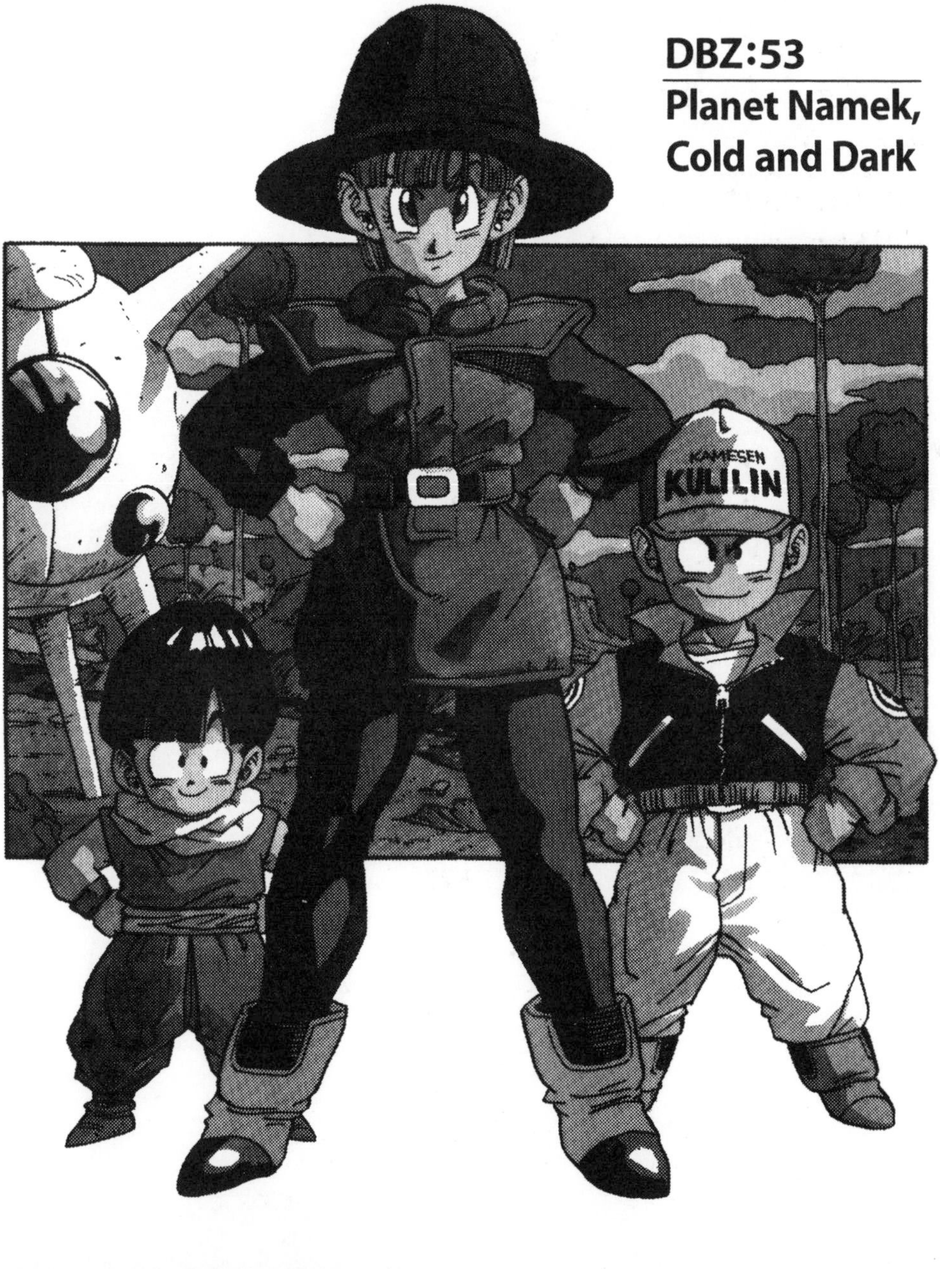
KAMESEN
KULILIN

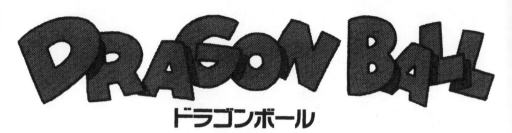

# DBZ:54
## The Mysterious Strangers

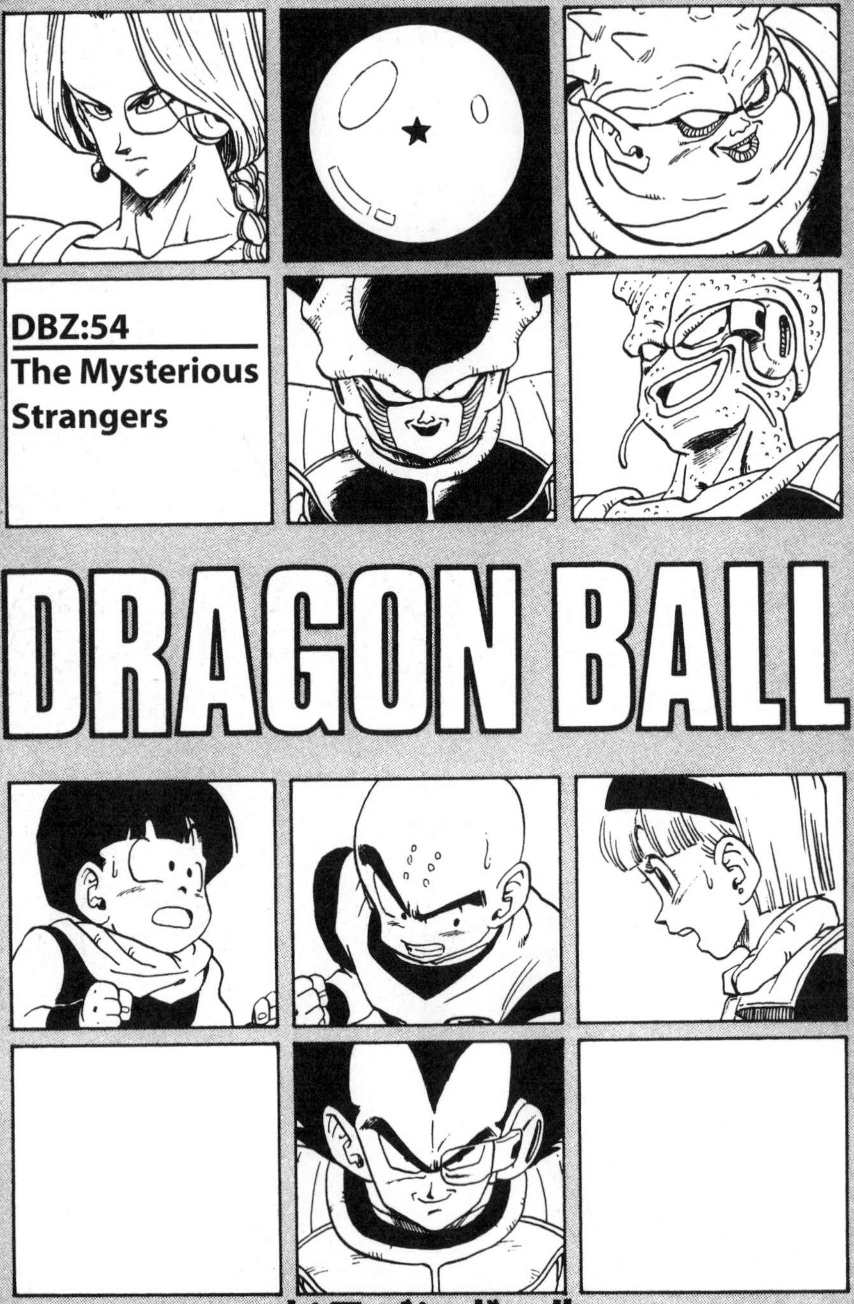
DRAGON BALL
ドラゴンボール

# DRAGON BALL

## DBZ:55 • Vegeta's True Power!

### ☆Who's Who on Planet Namek☆

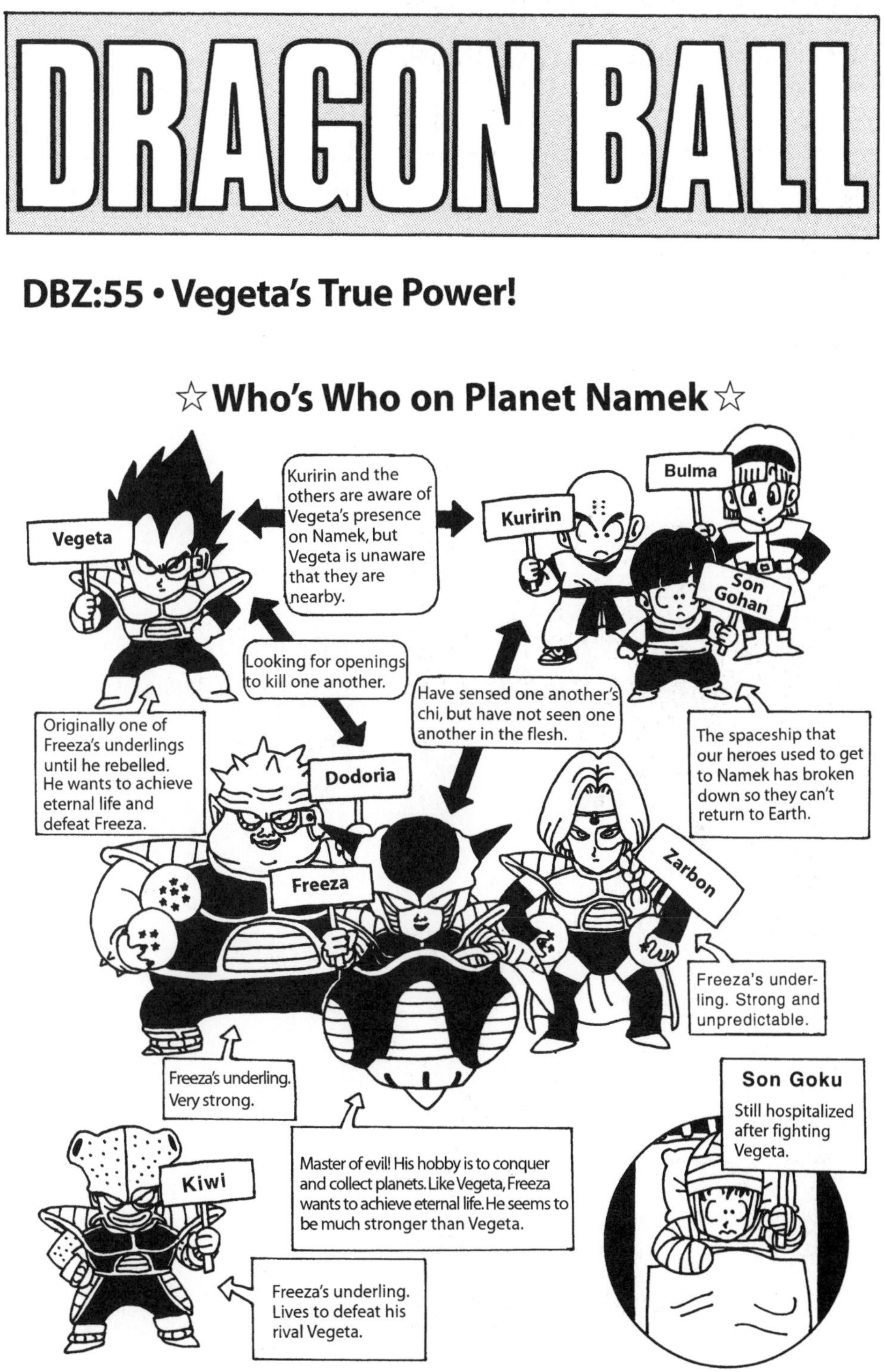

Vegeta
Kuririn and the others are aware of Vegeta's presence on Namek, but Vegeta is unaware that they are nearby.
Kuririn
Bulma
Son Gohan
Looking for openings to kill one another.
Have sensed one another's chi, but have not seen one another in the flesh.
Originally one of Freeza's underlings until he rebelled. He wants to achieve eternal life and defeat Freeza.
The spaceship that our heroes used to get to Namek has broken down so they can't return to Earth.
Dodoria
Freeza
Zarbon
Freeza's underling. Strong and unpredictable.
Freeza's underling. Very strong.
Son Goku
Still hospitalized after fighting Vegeta.
Kiwi
Master of evil! His hobby is to conquer and collect planets. Like Vegeta, Freeza wants to achieve eternal life. He seems to be much stronger than Vegeta.
Freeza's underling. Lives to defeat his rival Vegeta.

# DRAGON BALL

## DBZ:56
## Goku Returns! Again!

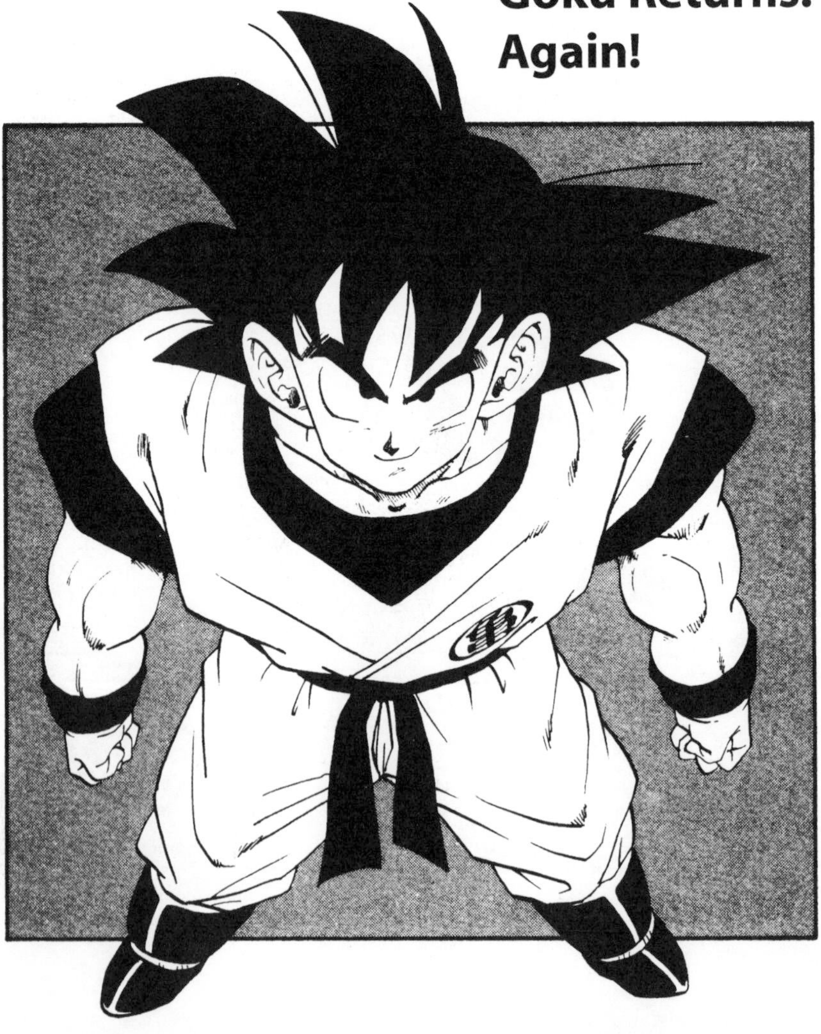

# DRAGON BALL

## DBZ:57 • Son Goku's Spaceship

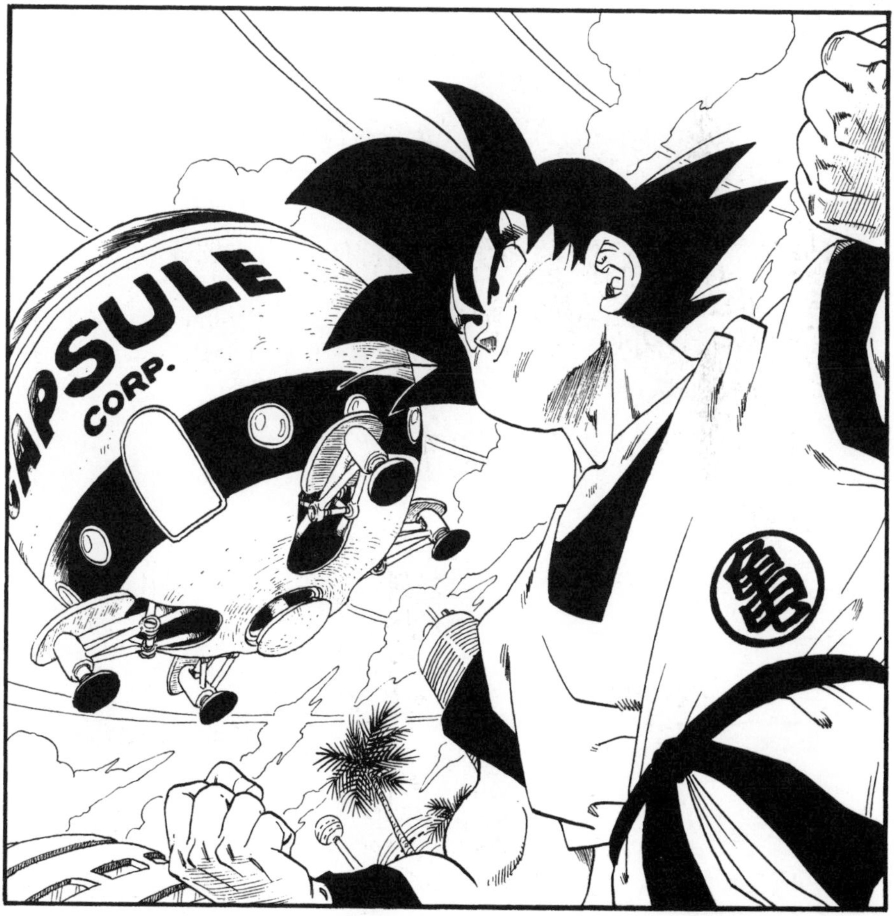

CAPSULE
CORP.

# DRAGON BALL

## DBZ:58 • Namekian Fear

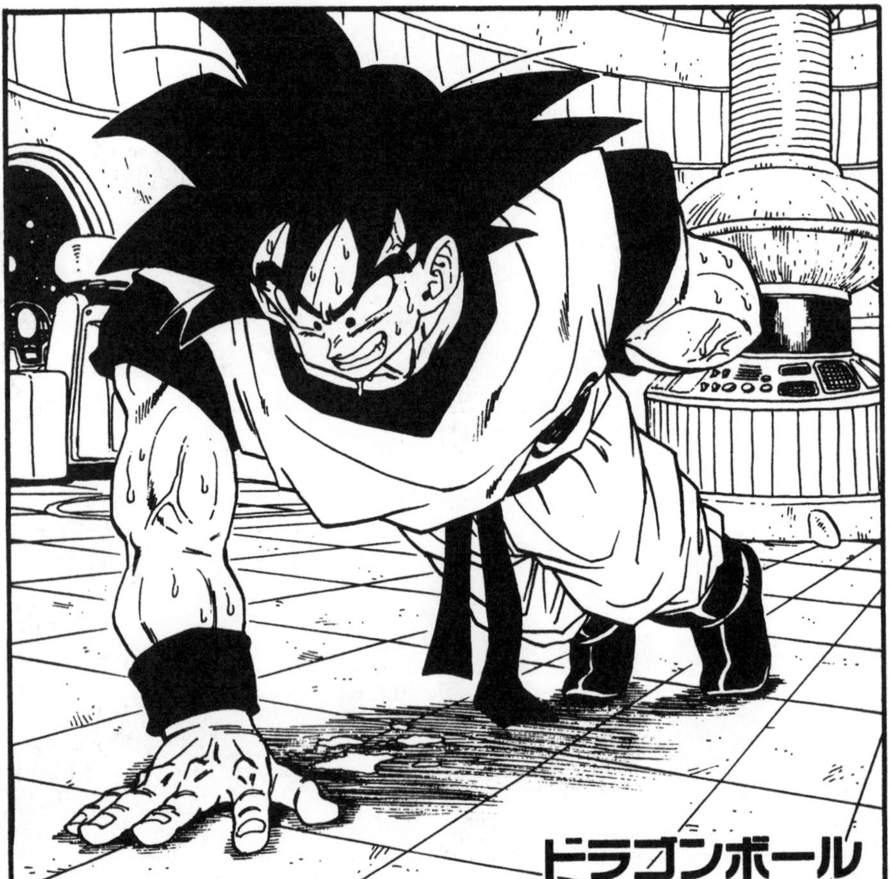
ドラゴンボール

# DRAGON BALL

**DBZ:59 • Showdown!**

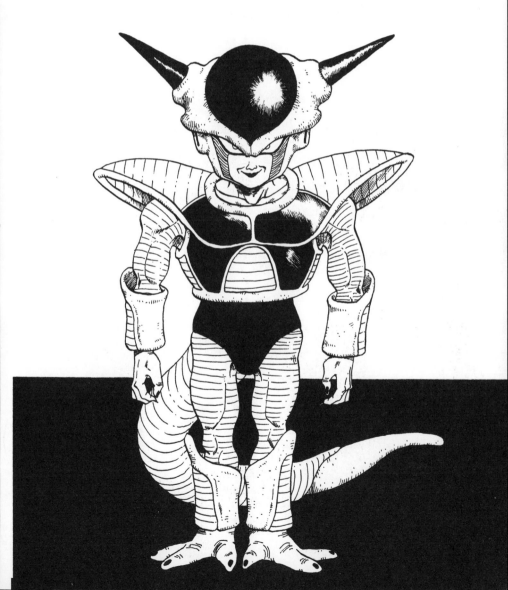

ドラゴンボール

DRAGON BALL

# DBZ:60 • Ten Seconds of Death

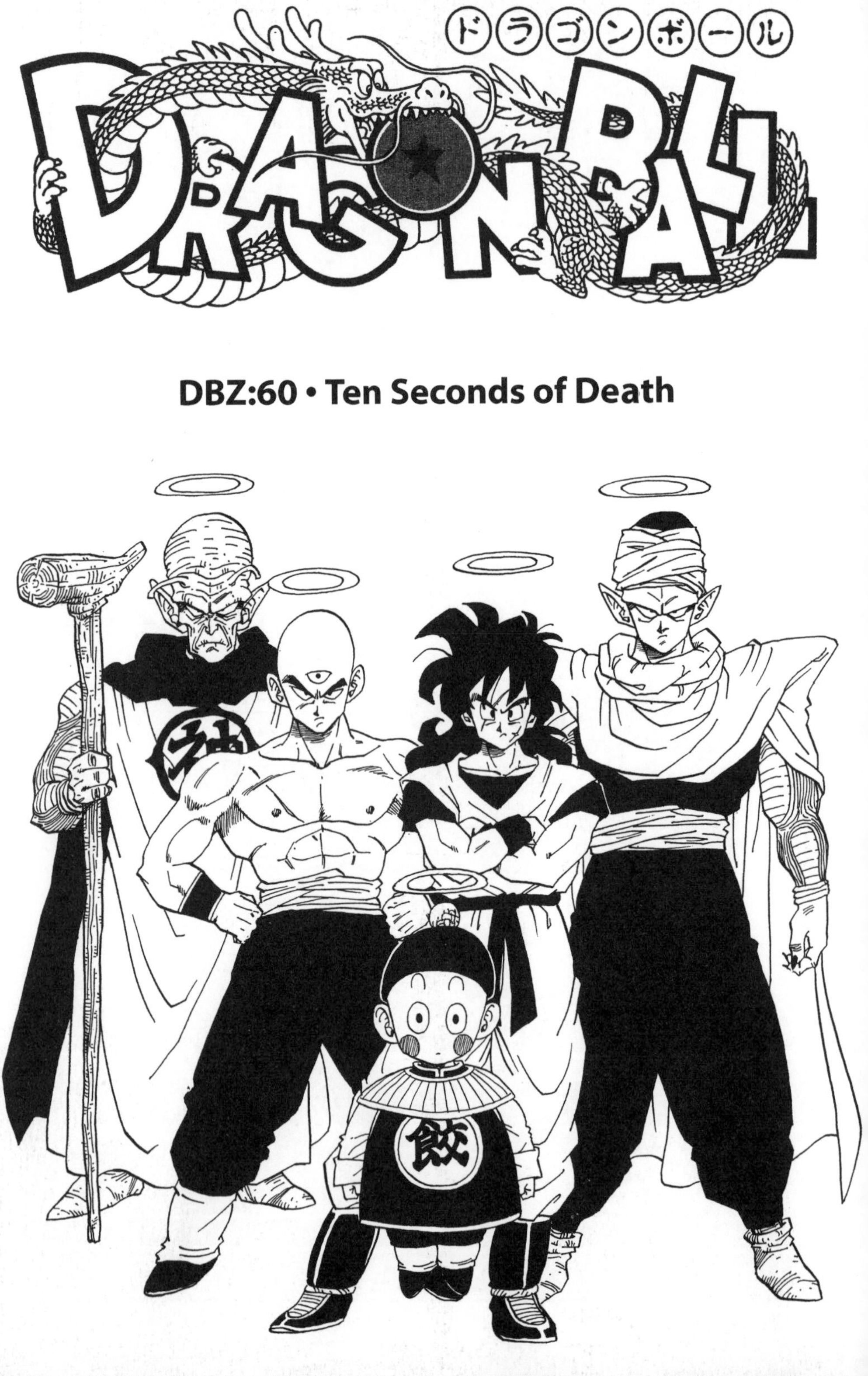

餃

# DRAGON BALL
ドラゴンボール

## DBZ:61 · Son Gohan Snaps!

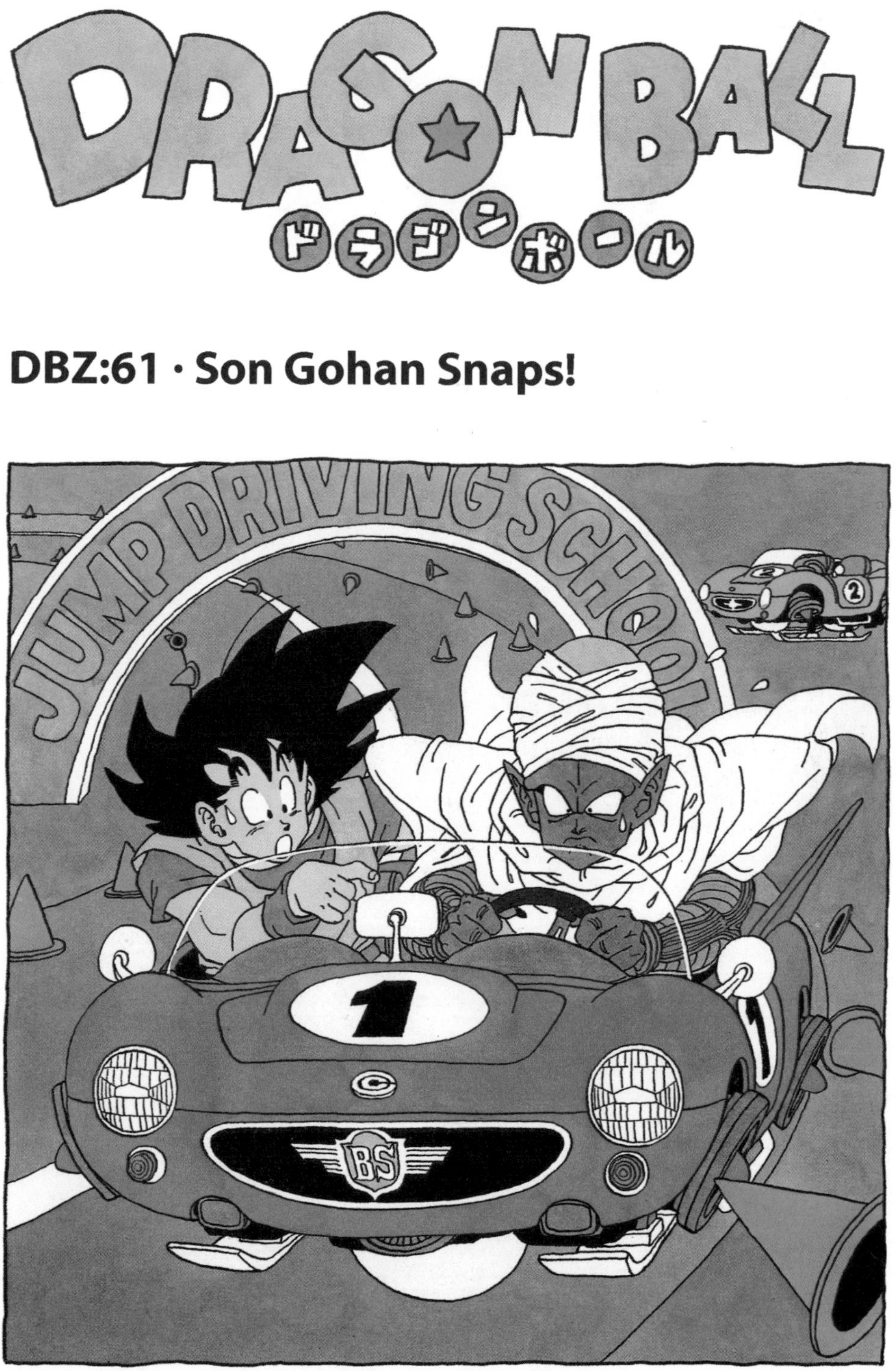
JUMP DRIVING SCHOOL

DRAGON BALL

ドラゴンボール

# DBZ:62 · Death in Flight

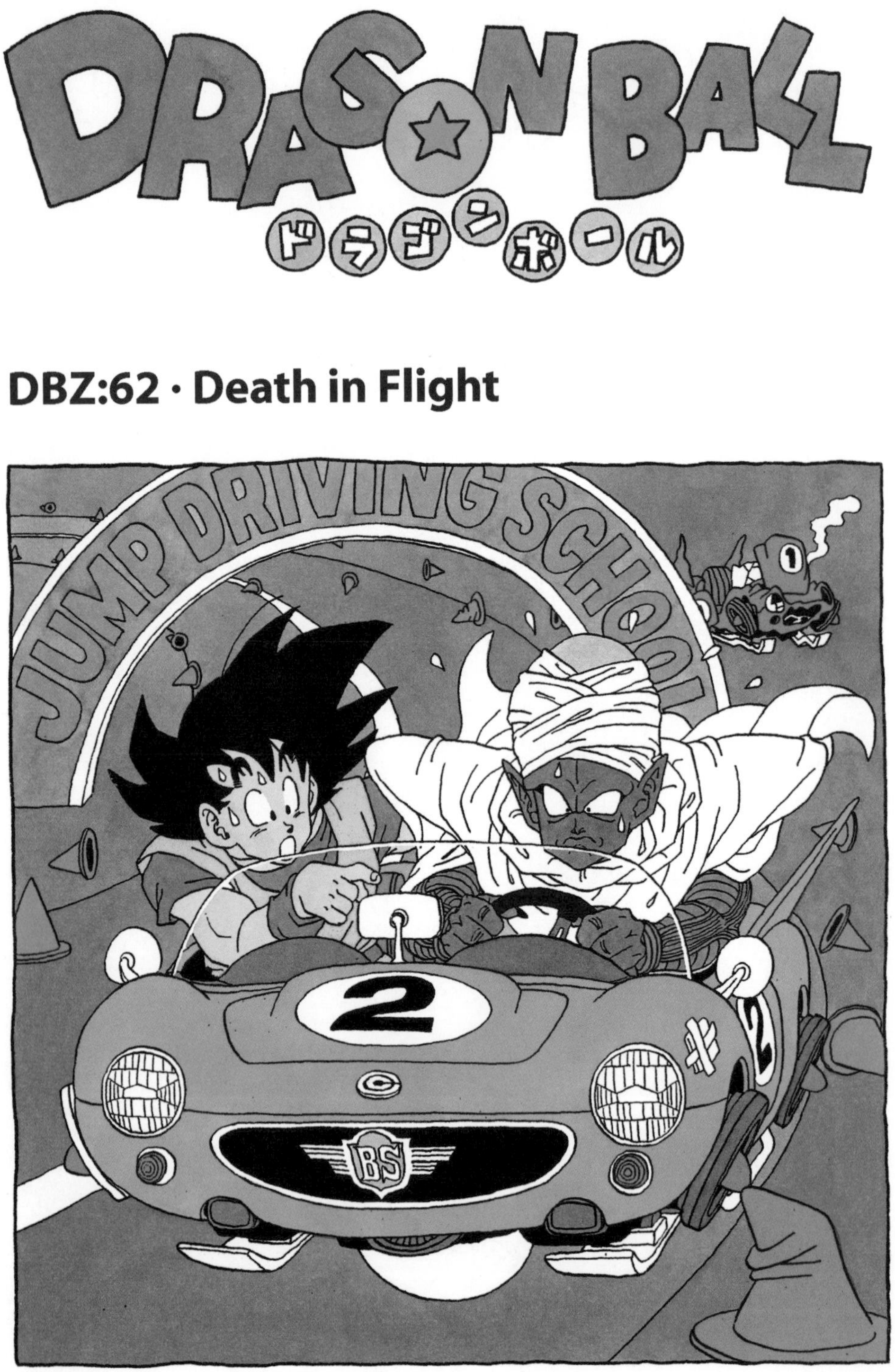
JUMP DRIVING SCHOOL
1
2
2
BS

# DRAGON BALL

ドラゴンボール

## DBZ:63 • Vegeta vs. Dodoria

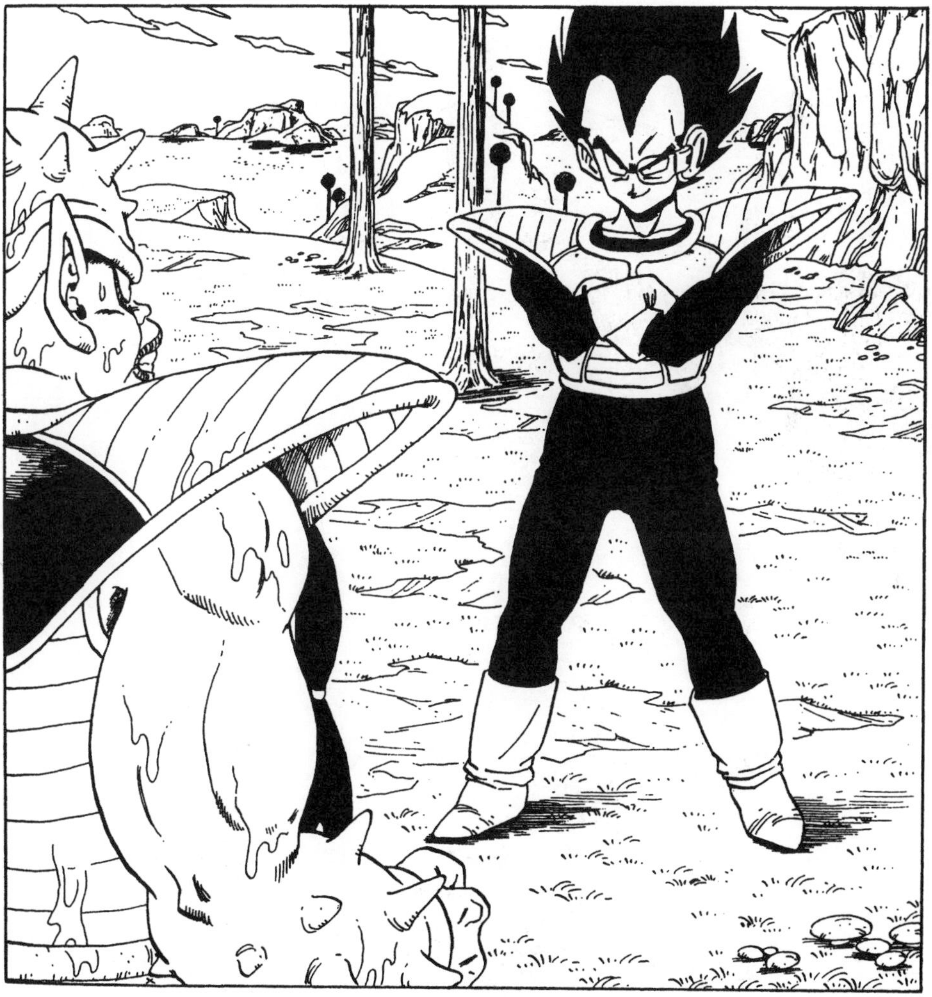

# DRAGON BALL

## DBZ:64 • Hide and Seek

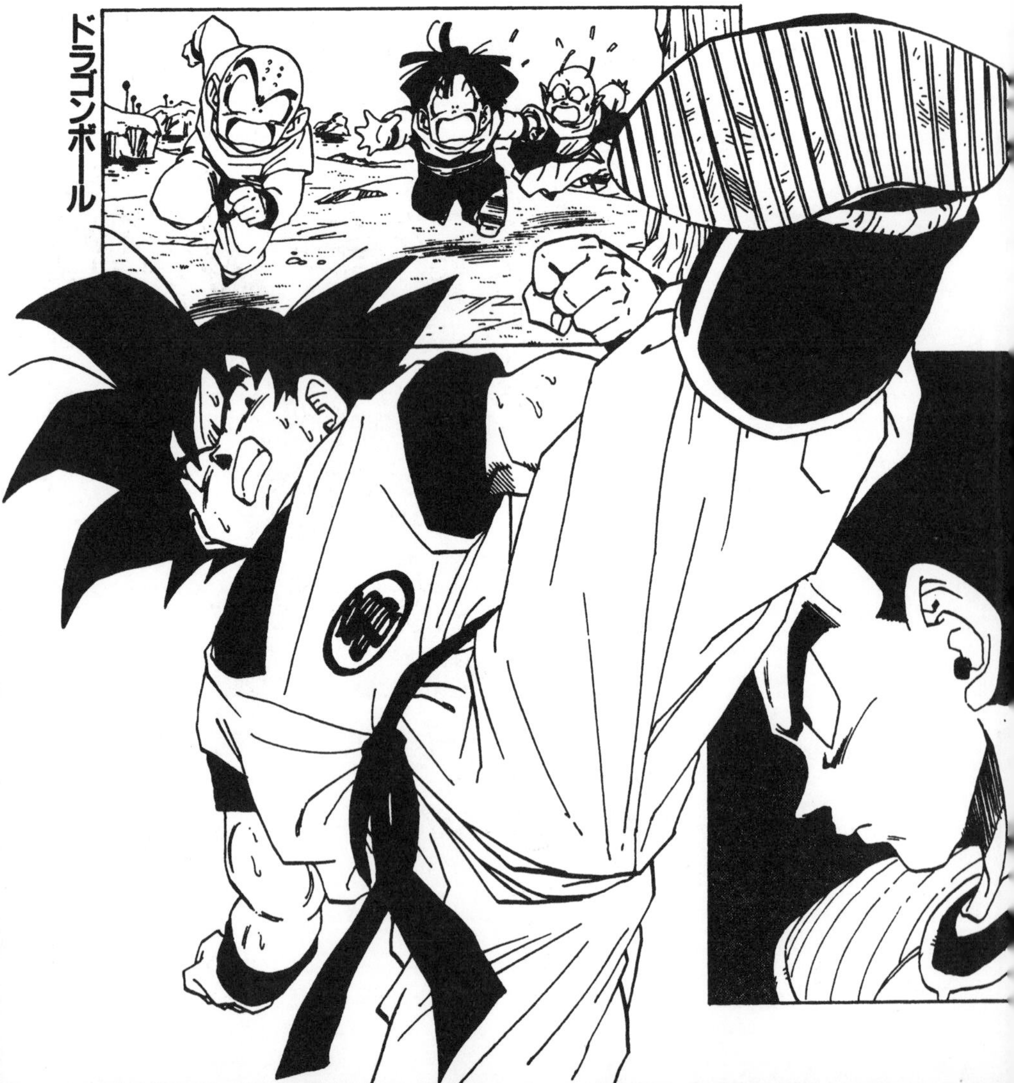
ドラゴンボール

# DRAGON BALL

## DBZ:65 • The Sixth Dragon Ball

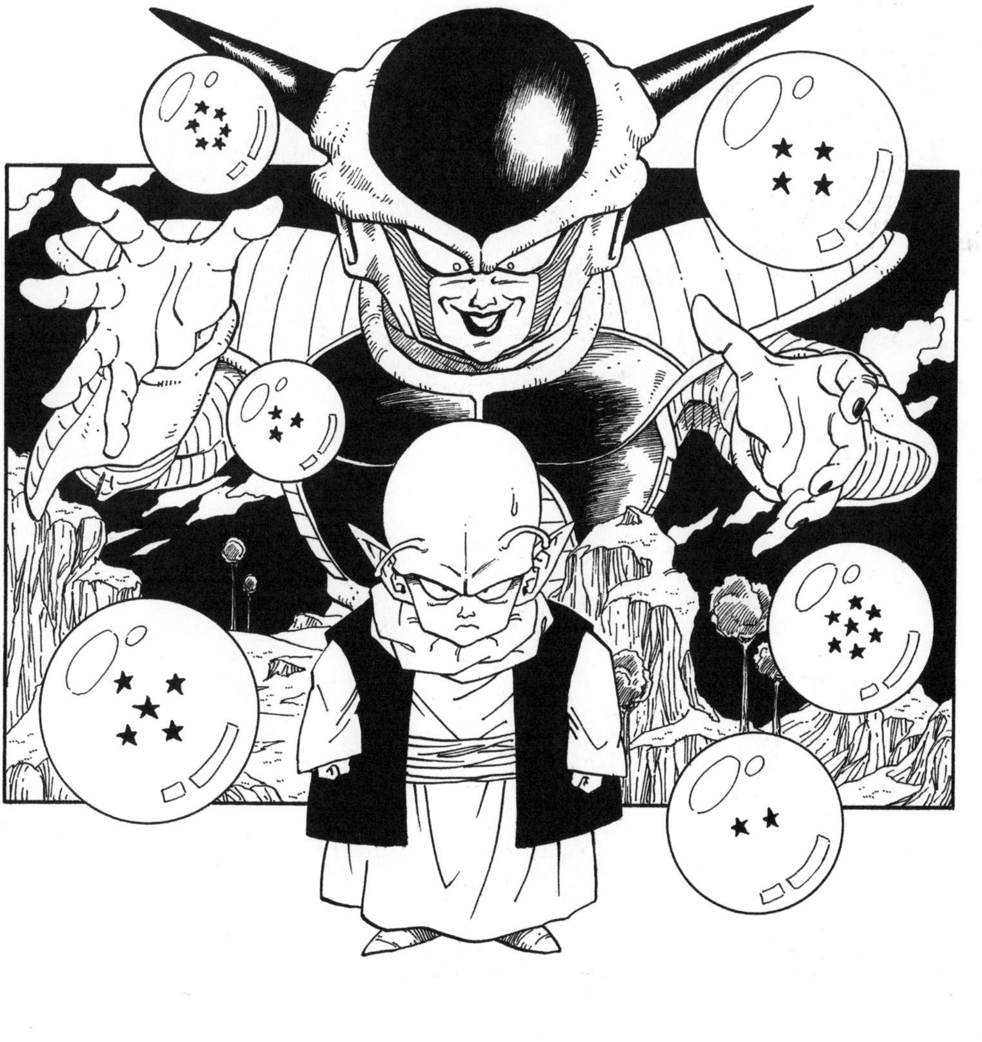

ドラゴンボール

# DRAGON BALL

## DBZ:66 • The Last Dragon Ball

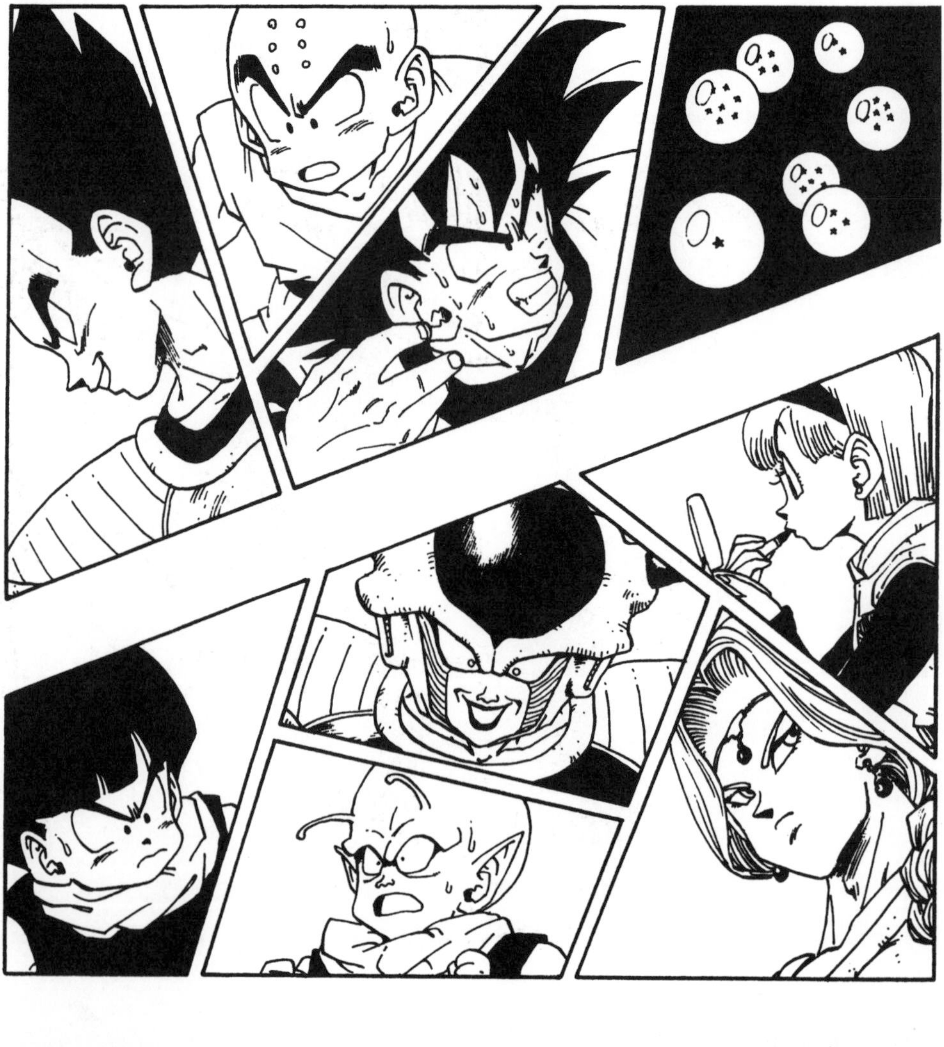

# DRAGON BALL

## DBZ:67 • The Four Dead Heroes

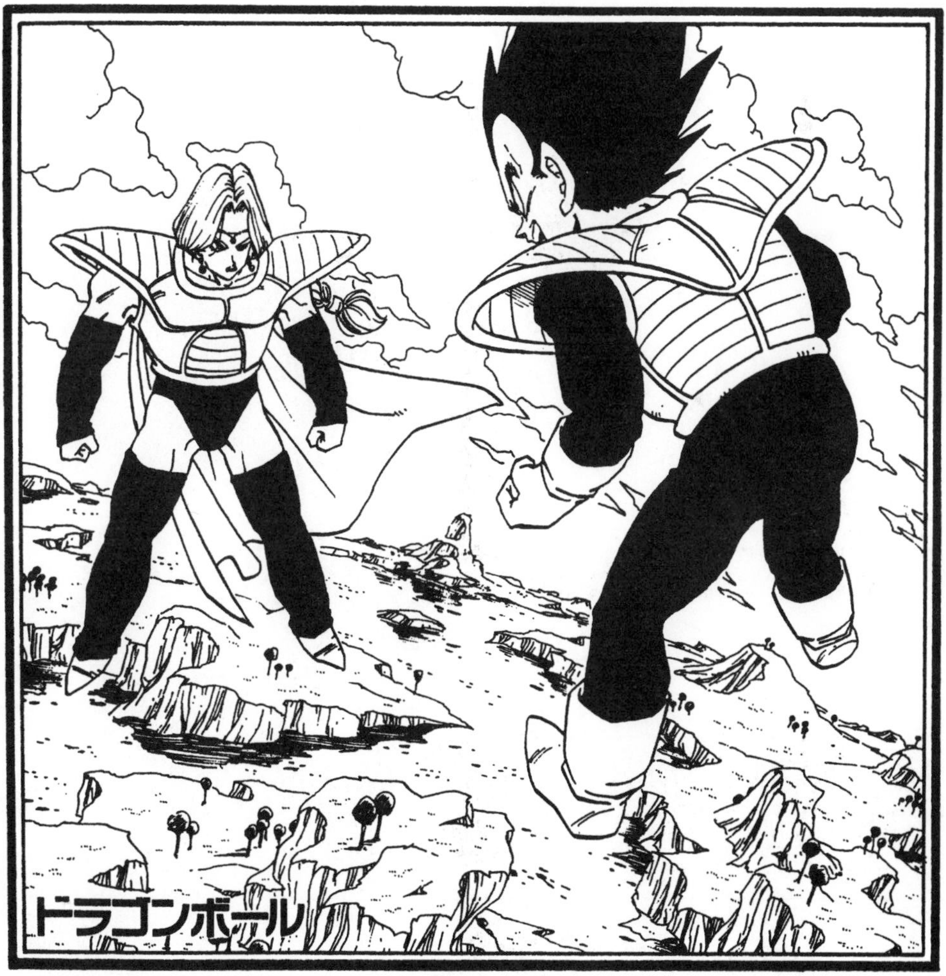
ドラゴンボール

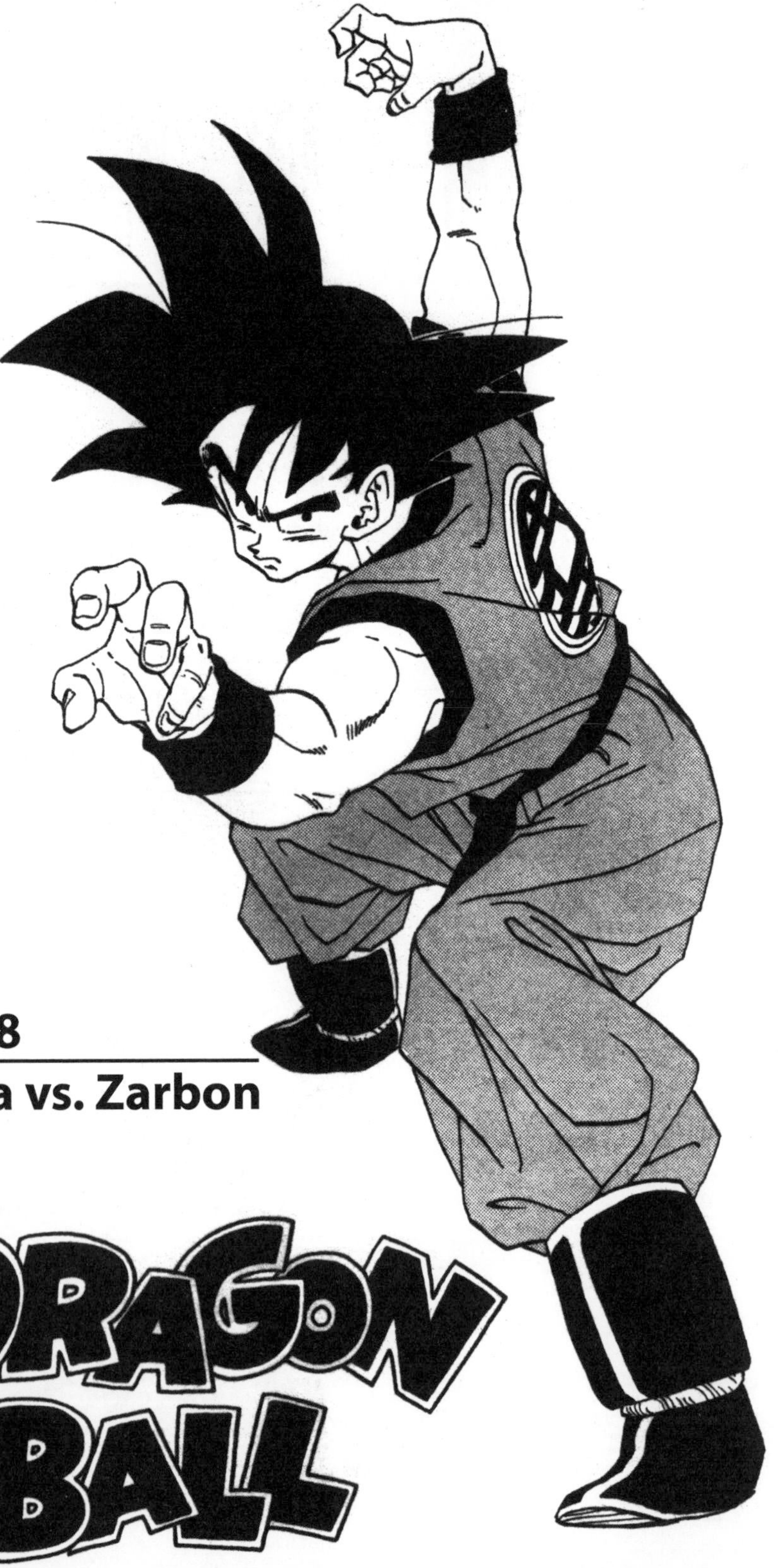

# DBZ:68

## Vegeta vs. Zarbon

DRAGON BALL

# DRAGON BALL

## DBZ:69 • Zarbon's True Power

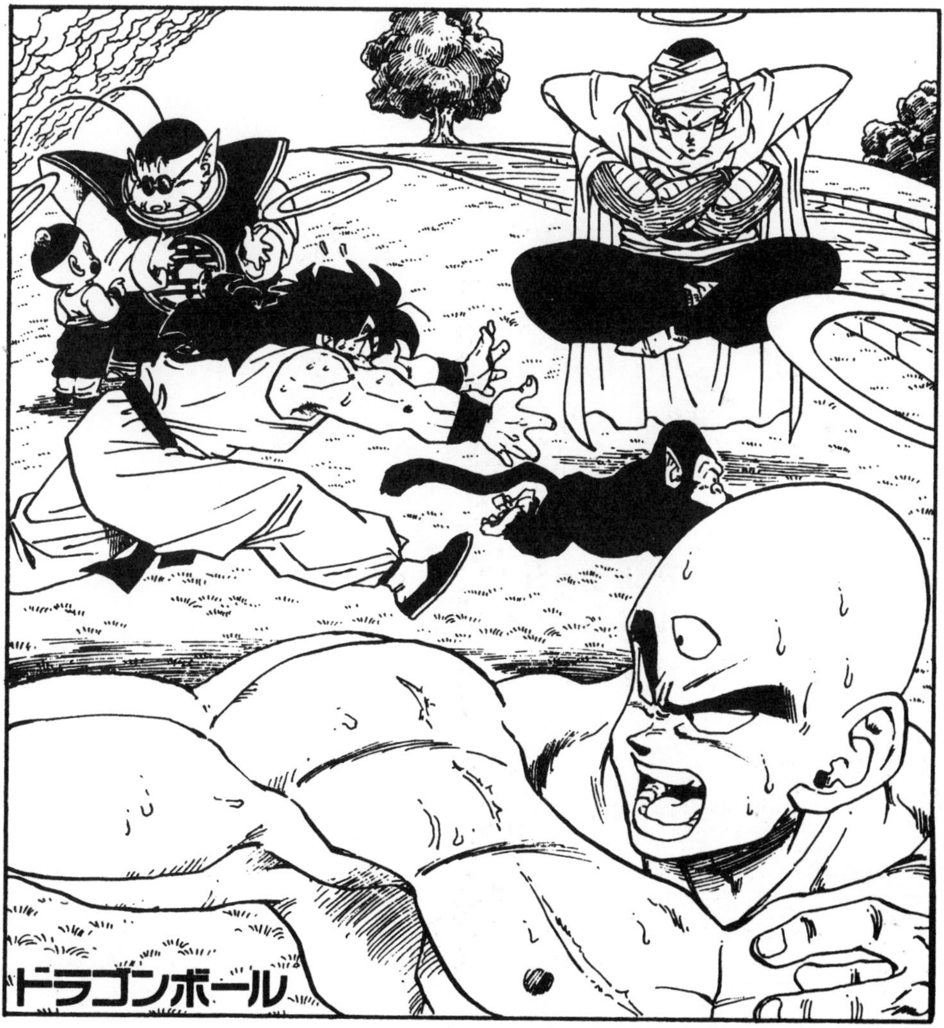
ドラゴンボール

# DRAGON BALL

## DBZ:70 • The Great Elder's House

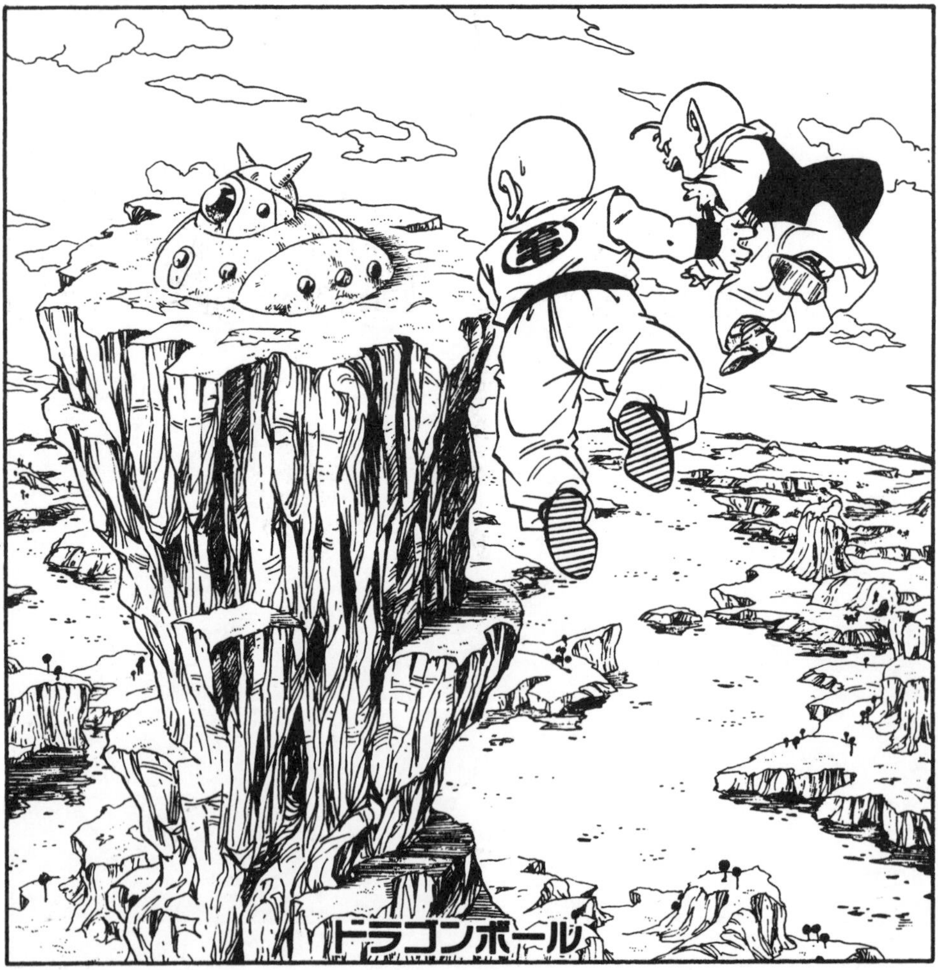
ドラゴンボール

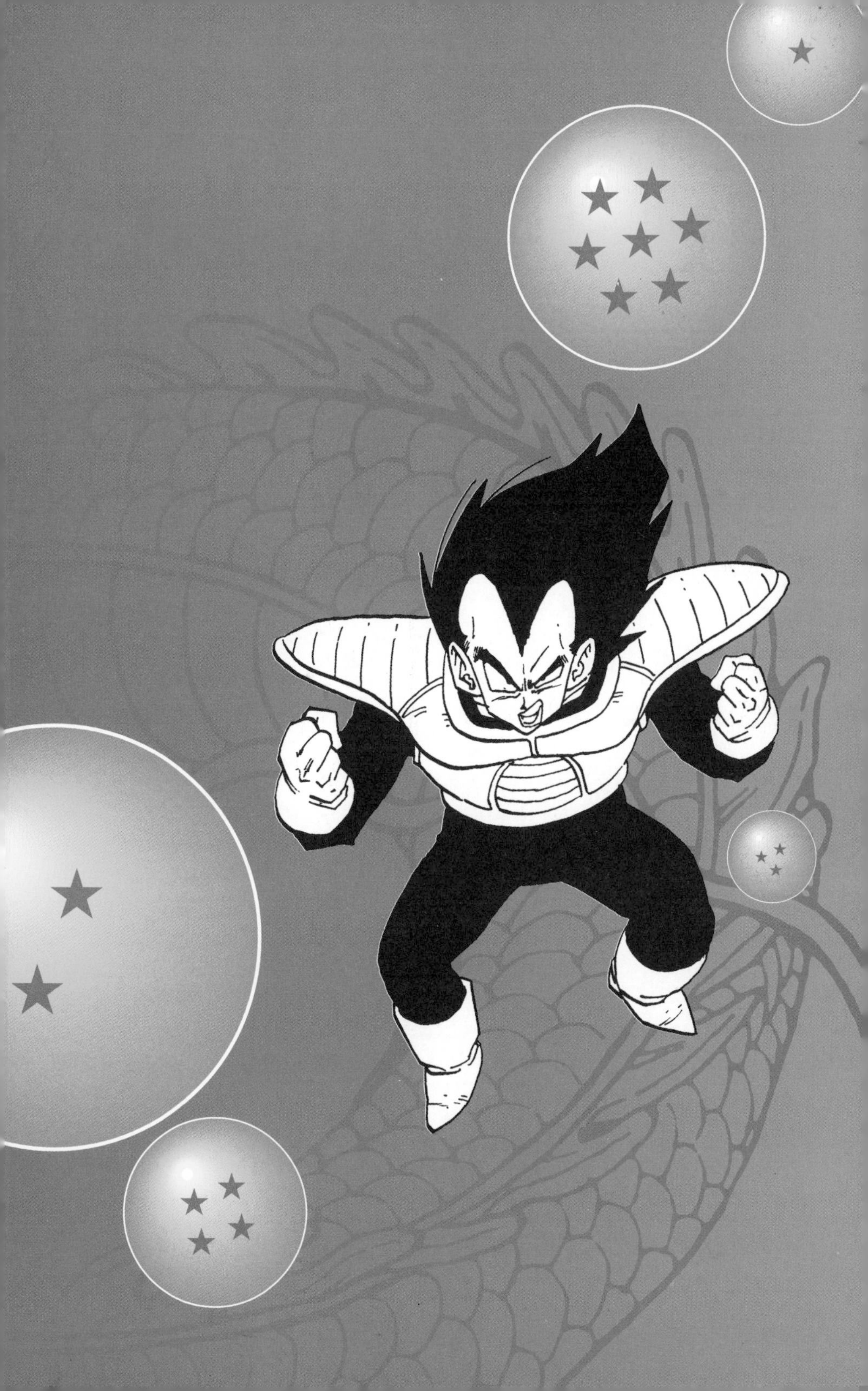

# AUTHOR NOTES

## VOLUME 4

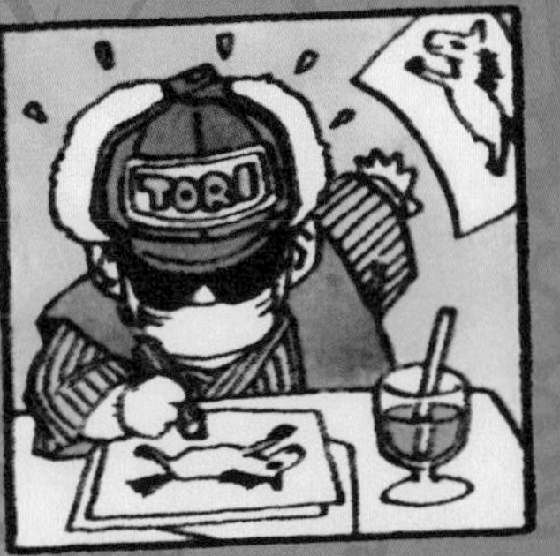
TORI

1990

If I want something I have a habit of drawing it until I get whatever it is or I lose interest in it. When I was a kid I really wanted a horse, so every day I would draw horses. Eventually I gave up on getting a horse, and I just drew monkeys every day. After that I drew bicycles. I kept drawing the things I wanted. As a result, even though I misbehaved, at least I could draw well. That habit eventually developed into my job, and I continue to draw today.

## VOLUME 5

Grrr. The one thing I am truly terrified of happened again. The cavity that I ignored (because I hate going to the dentist) started to get painful. It was the day of my deadline, but the pain was so bad I couldn't even sleep. I couldn't bear it any longer, so I ran to the dentist, only to find out I was too late—the tooth had to be pulled. So then I had to work on my manga while bearing the pain of my just-extracted tooth. It was pretty much my fault, but it was the worst, most awful day I've ever had.

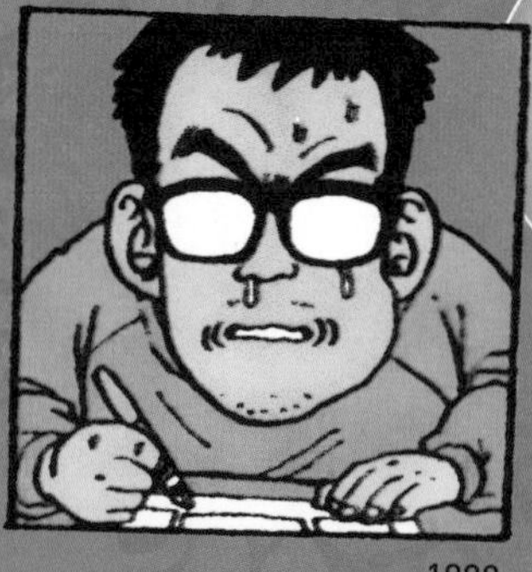

1990

## VOLUME 6

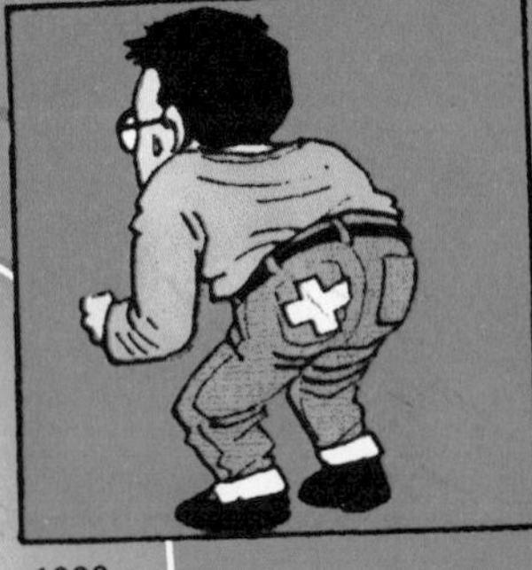

1990

So after the toothache incident, one of the three lumps of fat on my left buttock became inflamed and painful. It was pretty much exactly where I put my weight when I sit down, so I went right away to the hospital to have it surgically removed. The surgery was done without anesthesia, so it hurt so bad I thought I was gonna die! After two weeks, when the wound from the first surgery was healing up, I had the other lumps removed too. So for about one month, I had to work while sitting on my right buttock. Yes indeed, it was torture...

# IN THE NEXT VOLUME



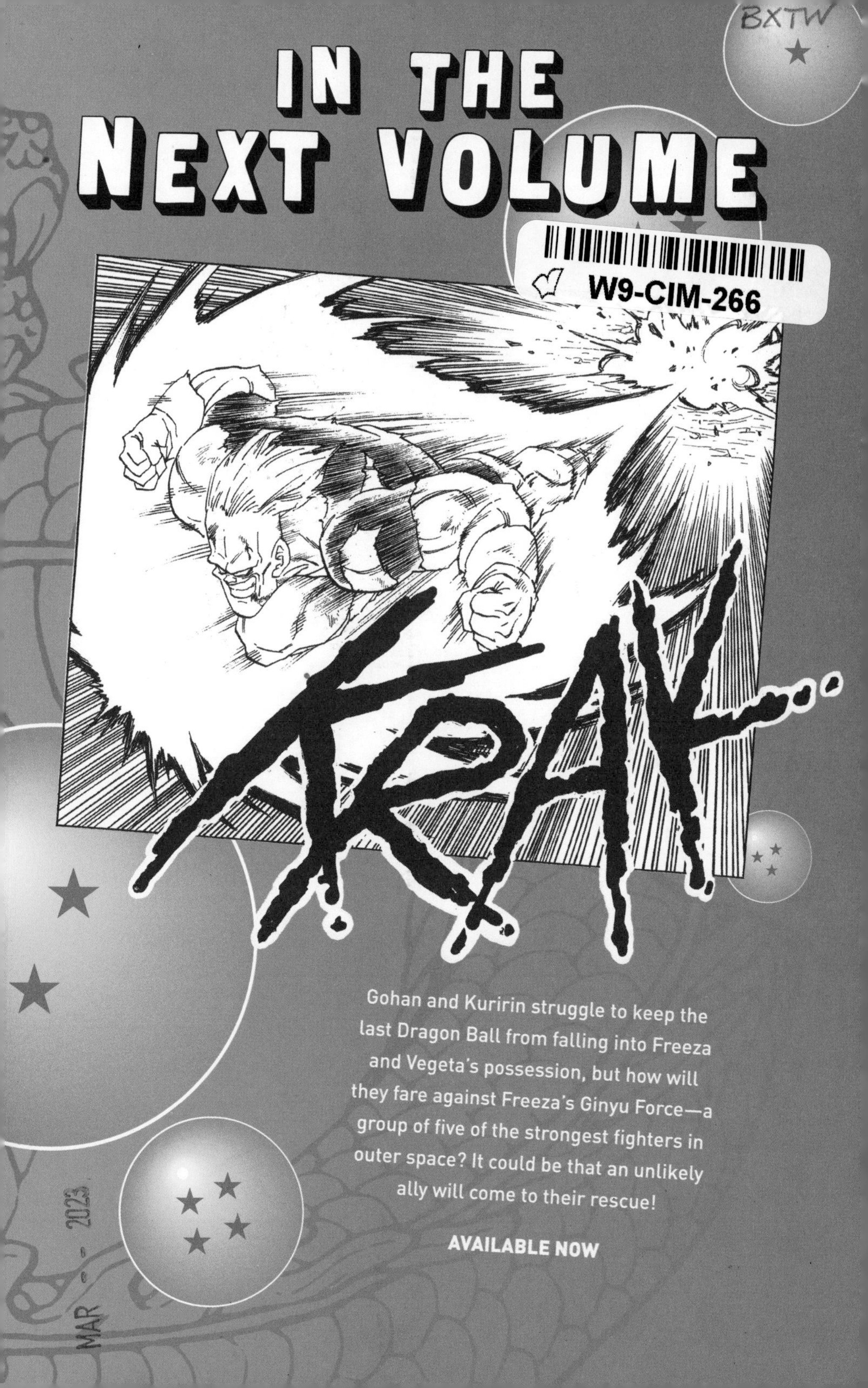
KRAK...

Gohan and Kuririn struggle to keep the last Dragon Ball from falling into Freeza and Vegeta's possession, but how will they fare against Freeza's Ginyu Force—a group of five of the strongest fighters in outer space? It could be that an unlikely ally will come to their rescue!

**AVAILABLE NOW**